D0535717

REMEDIES

CASES, PRACTICAL PROBLEMS AND EXERCISES

Third Edition

■ ■ ■

by

Russell L. Weaver
Professor of Law & Distinguished University Scholar
University of Louisville, Louis D. Brandeis School of Law

David F. Partlett
Asa Griggs Candler Professor of Law
Emory University School of Law

Michael B. Kelly
Professor of Law
University of San Diego School of Law

W. Jonathan Cardi
Professor of Law
Wake Forest University School of Law

AMERICAN CASEBOOK SERIES®

Mat #41292527

444 Cedar Street, Suite 700
St. Paul, MN 55101
1-877-888-1330

Printed in the United States of America

ISBN: 978-0-314-28195-1

To Laurence, Ben and Kate, with love

RLW

To Nan

DFP

To the women who made it possible,
Pam and Eva,
and the young men who make me so proud,
Logan and Preston

MBK

To Juliana and Mia

WJC

PREFACE TO THE THIRD EDITION

In this third edition, our primary objective remained the same: to create a "teacher's book"—a "tool for learning" that is easy to use, that produces rewarding classroom discussion, and that enables students to learn the concepts, doctrines, and analytical tools that underlie remedial analysis. Although Remedies is a topic that lends itself to interesting discussions, we seek to stimulate additional thought and discussion by including problems designed to encourage students to think more deeply about remedial issues and to examine those issues in modern contexts and exercises to introduce practical skills.

A secondary objective is to create a book that presents problems and issues in an integrated way that cuts across substantive boundaries. In first-year courses, students have had the opportunity to examine remedial issues as they relate to discrete doctrinal areas (*e.g.*, contract remedies, tort remedies, property remedies). While this book examines many of these same remedies, the problems and exercises take a comprehensive approach designed to examine the interrelationships between various remedies, and to give students a deeper understanding of the correlation between rights and remedies.

In any book, tradeoffs are necessary. This book makes no attempt to cover comprehensively all available remedies. Students have studied remedies in other courses, and complete coverage is duplicative and time consuming. In addition, the comprehensive approach too often leads to abstraction and superficiality. This book assumes that students have a basic understanding of remedies, and tries to present remedial issues in a more integrated and sophisticated way.

The book is divided into two major sections. The early chapters give students a firm grounding in equity and equitable remedies (*e.g.*, injunctions and special restitutionary remedies), contempt, and the prerogative writs (quo warranto, mandamus and prohibition). While students may have studied these topics in their first year courses, the coverage is often superficial and inadequate. As the semester progresses, students are asked to draw upon this information, as well as upon their prior legal studies, to analyze more difficult (as well as practical) problems. These problems are constructed to cross subject matter boundaries, analyze competing remedial options, and give students a better understanding of the remedial consequences of litigating a case on one theory rather than another.

The authors actively solicit the advice and comments of those who use this book. In addition, the authors are willing to field questions about the cases, problems or exercises. We wish to thank all who assisted us in this project.

RLW, DFP, MBK, WJC

December 2013

SUMMARY OF CONTENTS

TABLE OF CONTENTS

TABLE OF CASES

The principal cases are in bold type.

REMEDIES

CASES, PRACTICAL PROBLEMS AND EXERCISES

Third Edition

CHAPTER 1

OVERVIEW

■ ■ ■

A. INTRODUCTION

Even though many schools teach Remedies as a separate and independent course, usually taught at or near the end of a student's legal education, you have studied remedies in a number of other courses. For example, in Contracts, you studied concepts like specific performance, "benefit of the bargain," and restitution, and you probably examined various equitable defenses (*e.g.*, unclean hands, unconscionability, and estoppel). Likewise, in torts, you examined concepts such as "economic loss" and "non-economic loss," "general" and "special" damages, "pain and suffering" and "medical expenses."

So, why do we have a separate Remedies course? There are a number of reasons. First, although you may have been introduced to many remedial concepts (*e.g.*, equity and conscience), Remedies gives you the chance to consider them in greater depth. The time available in a Contracts course or Torts course does not always permit full exploration of each remedial option. Second, there are many remedies which you may not have studied or may have touched on only tangentially (*i.e.*, preliminary injunctions, temporary restraining orders and permanent injunctive relief). Third, Remedies allows you to see the law in a more integrated way. Established subject boundaries are artificial, and although convenient for classification, they are not responsive to the law in practice or to the remedial policies that transcend substantive areas of the law.

Remedies also allows you to see the relationship between "rights" and "remedies." In many of your first year courses, you were focused on whether plaintiff had a legal right. Is this a tort? Is it a Contract? If so, what are the requirements? One tends to think of a Remedies course as assuming that plaintiff's rights have been violated and to focus on the remedies to which plaintiff is entitled. In fact, as we shall see, how one characterizes the legal right can affect plaintiff's remedial options. For example, a fundamental principle of equity provides that equitable relief is not available except when the plaintiff's legal remedy is inadequate. As a result, during this course, we will frequently find ourselves focusing on plaintiff's "legal" cause of action and the remedies available under that action. Only after we ask, and answer, those questions is it possible to focus more specifically on plaintiff's remedies.

There are many different ways to categorize remedies. Some distinguish between "substitutionary" and "specific remedies." Others distinguish between "legal remedies" and "equitable remedies." Still others distinguish between "damage remedies," "coercive remedies," "declaratory remedies" and "restitutionary remedies." While all of these categorizations are useful, they often overlap and none necessarily excludes other categorization possibilities.

Substitutionary versus Specific Remedies. Some commentators distinguish between so-called "substitutionary remedies" and "specific remedies." "Substitutionary remedies" give plaintiff money in exchange for an otherwise non-compensable loss. For example, suppose that plaintiff loses an arm in an automobile accident. Since a court cannot order defendant to replace the arm, it instead orders defendant to pay plaintiff money to compensate him for lost wages, medical expenses and pain and suffering associated with loss of the arm. By contrast, "specific remedies" give plaintiff the specific item sought. For example, when plaintiff's ex-husband makes off with her family heirloom (*e.g.*, a family Bible), specific relief might come in the form of a court order requiring the ex to return the Bible.

Substitutionary and specific remedies are not mutually exclusive. For example, if defendant breaches a contract to sell personal property, specific performance might be appropriate. (The Uniform Commercial Code provides that specific performance can be ordered when goods are "unique" or in "other appropriate circumstances.") Even though specific performance is ordered, a court might also order substitutionary relief in the form of damages to compensate plaintiff for damages incurred during the period between the breach and the time the goods are finally delivered.

Damage Remedies. Damage remedies can take a variety of forms including nominal, statutory, liquidated or compensatory. Each of these damages is designed to serve different purposes. For example, nominal damages are designed to vindicate plaintiff's rights by making a legal declaration of those rights and providing plaintiff with "nominal" compensation. Compensatory damages are supposed to repay plaintiff for any losses she has suffered, making her whole, in so much as the law is capable of doing so. When plaintiff has lost an arm, compensatory damages are substitutionary and cannot provide an adequate substitute. On the other hand, when plaintiff's automobile has been damaged in an accident, compensatory damages can help him repair the car and make it almost as good as new.

Compensatory damages can vary depending on the case, but generally are designed to compensate plaintiff for a loss. In property cases, for example, a court might award "general" damages involving a calculation of diminution in market value—*e.g.*, the amount by which plaintiff's real estate has decreased in value due to a nuisance. In some cases, the compensatory measure might focus instead on the cost to repair.

Liquidated and statutory damages represent efforts to tell courts how much to award or how to calculate a damage award. Statutory damages are legislative enactments that specify either an amount or a formula (*e.g.*, three times actual damages) for damage recoveries. Liquidated damages represent efforts by parties to a contract to specify either an amount or a formula (*e.g.*, $100 per day) that a court should use in calculating damages.

Coercive Remedies. "Coercive remedies" involve *in personam* orders that are enforceable through the remedy of "contempt of court." "Contempt of court" is an extremely powerful remedy by which a court can impose jail sentences or fines in order to punish a defendant for violating a court order, to coerce defendant to obey the order, or to compensate plaintiff for violation of the order. In this course, we will focus on various types of *in personam* orders including injunctions, specific performance and the so-called prerogative writs (*e.g.*, mandamus, prohibition, quo warranto, habeas corpus).

Declaratory Remedies. Declaratory remedies are commonly available at both the federal level and the state level. The function of declaratory relief is to provide a judicial declaration regarding the rights, obligations, or responsibilities of the parties relating to a particular situation (*e.g.*, a declaration that plaintiff's picketing activities are protected by free speech principles and that an ordinance that purports to restrict those activities is unconstitutional). No money is awarded, no orders are issued; the court simply declares one party's position to be correct under the law.

In providing declaratory relief, the court provides a number of benefits to the parties. First, and foremost, in the example set forth above, if the parties wish to picket and they obtain a legal judgment declaring the statute invalid, the parties can picket without fear of arrest or criminal prosecution. When there is a dispute regarding the meaning of a contract, a declaratory judgment gives the parties a chance to resolve ambiguity early so that neither party is forced to act without full knowledge of his rights and obligations (and thereby incur liability.)

Sometimes, a request for declaratory relief is accompanied by a request for injunctive relief. Even when there is no request for injunctive relief, a declaratory judgment might have the same effect on the parties if they choose to respect and obey it.

Restitutionary Remedies. Restitution is a remedy that is imposed to prevent unjust enrichment. It awards a plaintiff the amount that defendant gained as a result of the wrong, not the amount that the plaintiff lost (as in damages). Restitution includes such remedies as quasi-contract, constructive trust, equitable lien, subrogation, rescission, reformation, accounting for profits, ejectment and replevin. Some of these remedies are specific (*e.g.*, ejectment and replevin give plaintiff specific property to which she is entitled), while others are substitutionary (*i.e.*, quasi-contract gives plaintiff a monetary equivalent for a benefit conferred on defendant).

Legal versus Equitable Remedies. As we shall see, distinctions are also made between so-called "legal remedies" and so-called "equitable remedies." England created two separate and distinct court systems—"law courts" and "equity courts"—that functioned under quite different principles, rules and procedures. Even though most states have merged their law courts and their equity courts into a single unified system, the distinction between "law" and "equity" remains important because remnants of the rules differentiating law and equity continue to apply today. We will examine this topic in greater detail in Chapter 2.

The historical distinction between "legal remedies" and "equitable remedies" led to fundamental differences in the way that those remedies are enforced. Historically, "equitable remedies" have been regarded as *in personam* remedies—involving a direct order to a defendant to engage or refrain from engaging in a particular act—and have been enforced through the remedy of contempt. In other words, if defendant refused to comply with the personal order, defendant might be jailed or fined for the refusal to comply. By contrast, "legal remedies" do not involve *in personam* orders, but rather monetary judgments in favor of one party or the other. Defendant's failure to pay the judgment did not constitute contempt. Plaintiff was forced to enforce the order through the remedies of attachment and execution. In other words, if defendant refused to pay, plaintiff was forced to seize or place liens on defendant's property and eventually sell it in order to satisfy the judgment.

Preliminary versus Permanent Remedies. Distinctions also are made between "preliminary remedies" and "permanent remedies." Preliminary or provisional remedies are interlocutory, issued during the pendency of a suit (*i.e.*, a preliminary or temporary injunction, or a temporary restraining order), and are designed to last only until the end of the suit. Permanent or final remedies (*i.e.*, a permanent injunction or an award of permanent damages) are issued at the end of a suit and are designed to last forever (absent modification or dissolution).

THE PATH AHEAD

As we begin our study, a note about our path and direction is appropriate. The early part of the book is designed to provide students building blocks for dealing with remedial problems. Although most students have some knowledge of equity and equitable remedies,

Chapters Two and Chapter Three are designed to provide you with a more thorough grounding in both equity and the remedy of "contempt." Once this grounding is complete, Chapters four through seven introduce you to the injunctive and declaratory remedies, as well as to restitution, and help you explore how these remedies apply in different contexts. Chapters eight and nine focus more directly on the damage remedy, and give you the opportunity to refresh your recollection on this remedy and to study it in greater depth.

The final chapter is designed to allow you to examine remedies in context, and challenges you to cross jurisdictional boundaries. Especially in the final chapter, you will have the chance to examine remedial problems creatively and apply the many principles that you learned in the prior chapters. The problems raised there ask you to decide which remedy may best serve your client, how best you could lay the groundwork for that remedy, and whether obstacles should divert you to an alternative approach. In short, these chapters ask you to practice law: to take a problem your client presents and work out a strategy that will help solve (or ease) the problem. Very shortly, this is how you will earn your pay. We hope you enjoy the practice.

CHAPTER 2

EQUITY AND EQUITABLE REMEDIES

■ ■ ■

CHAPTER OVERVIEW: In your first year courses, you should have learned something about "equity" and "equitable remedies." For example, in your contracts class, you probably learned that equitable remedies are not available except when the plaintiff's legal remedy is inadequate. Likewise, you might have learned about the defenses of unclean hands, laches and estoppel.

The purpose of this chapter is to provide you with a thorough grounding in equity and equitable principles so that you can apply those principles in modern contexts and under modern procedural and substantive rules. Although the concepts of "equity" and "equitable remedies" are historically based, and historical structures have been abolished or modified in most states in favor of more modern structures, historical concepts continue to be applied by modern courts. In this chapter, we examine the history in an effort to understand how it affects the application of modern rules.

PROBLEM: THE BUILDING LOT CONTROVERSY

Beau Rivage is an exclusive subdivision in one of the nicer sections of this city, and is surrounded by a large wall (erected for security purposes) with a gatehouse at the entrance to the subdivision.

Vacant lots in the subdivision sell for $75,000 and are at least one-half acre in size. All lots are subject to numerous restrictions. Lot owners can only build single family dwellings, the dwellings must be at least 3,500 square feet, must cost at least $200,000, and must be set back from the property line at least 50 feet.

Grace Harlow (a prominent local attorney) purchased a lot in Beau Rivage about a year ago. She chose the lot because it sits on a hill and offers a glorious view of the surrounding city. Grace planned to build a house on the lot, and to begin construction within a year. However, at the time of the purchase, Grace was litigating a major case in a distant state and returned only rarely to check on her Beau Rivage lot.

About the same time that Harlow bought her lot, Herbert Deets (a local factory manager) bought an adjoining lot. Deets began construction immediately on a two story Colonial-style home.

Unfortunately, Deets's builder was confused about the lot lines, and built the home so that it violated not only the 50-foot setback requirement, but extended twenty feet onto Harlow's lot. By the time Harlow returned from her trial, Deets's home was nearly finished.

Harlow was furious when she learned that Deets's home encroached on her lot. Harlow demanded that Deets remove the offending portion of his home from her property. Deets refused to do so, claiming that he would suffer severe economic loss. Indeed, if the offending portion were removed, Deets would have to lop off the kitchen and the family room. Moreover, without those rooms, the house would lose its symmetry and would appear rather strange.

As you work your way through this chapter, you will be asked to think about how this problem should be resolved. Do you have any preliminary thoughts? See if those thoughts change as you go through the chapter.

A. A HISTORICAL PERSPECTIVE

At common law, there existed a dual court system that included "law" courts and "equity" courts (a/k/a "Chancery" courts). Today, most courts have merged "law" and "equity" into a single, unified, court system. However, the merger of law and equity did not eliminate the use of equitable remedies or many of the limitations and conditions applicable to those remedies. In order better to understand how equitable remedies are applied today, it is helpful to know something about the history of equity and the development of equitable remedies.

DAN B. DOBBS, HANDBOOK ON THE LAW OF REMEDIES

(1973).

[The] medieval chancellor was a high minister of the king, more closely analogous to a prime minister than to anything else we are familiar with. He was often a Bishop of the Church. As a kind of prime minister, the Chancellor did the sort of administrative work ministers do—he was an adviser, negotiator, ambassador, propagandist and stand-in for the king.

The other task of the medieval chancellor was more routine. Medieval England was not a highly literate society. Many of the clergy, however, could write, and the Chancellor as a literate man served not only as a "prime minister," but also as head of the royal writing department, supervising literate clerks. Writings from the kings to subjects or officers were drawn up in the chancery. One important kind of writing drawn up in Chancery was the original writ-the document that was used to begin a common law action. Some forms of action were quite common and many of the writs for such actions were drawn by low level clerks and given as a matter of course, each based on some more or less standard forms. Others were a bit more novel and hence controversial—controversial because any new writ was an assertion of power in the king's courts, and any assertion of power in the king's courts took away power from the lords or other local influences.

When the plaintiff came to the chancery for help with an unusual set of facts to which the old writs did not fit, the chancellor sometimes issued a new kind of writ. This might or might not work. The courts could still hold that the writ was improper. None of this writ work by the chancellor and his staff was judicial work. It was not a matter of deciding who was right and who was wrong. If a writ was issued, either as a matter of course or after a special decision by the Chancellor, it did not decide the action; it only gave jurisdiction to the king's courts to do so, and, accordingly, took away jurisdiction of local courts. * * *

The issuance of any new writ tended to expand national power and contract local power. The lords naturally objected to this. In the year 1258, the lords, in the Provisions of Oxford, forbade the chancellor to frame any new writs without the consent of king and council. A generation later, this stringent provision was modified in the Statute of Westminster II (1285) by a rule that allowed new writs to be issued when the facts were *similar* to those for which the old writs were appropriate, that was, writs *in consimili casu*.

[Because of the Provisions of Oxford, by the 1300s the common law courts had only] limited powers: they could grow and develop, but only over long generations. For the special case that did not fit the existing writs and was not similar enough to the old ones, some special aid was required if national justice was to be obtained. [This] was where the chancellor's second role, as an official of high power in the central administration, became important.

The chancellor of the medieval period was a powerful man. He was, first of all, a member of the Council and sat there with other lords of the realm. In addition, the chancellor was often a prelate with the weight of the church behind him. But beyond all this, he was king's right hand man and acted in the king's name on many occasions.

One of the medieval ideals was that the king was the fountain of justice. The ideal of law, with its general rules applied alike to all persons in the realm, was slowly becoming embodied in the common law courts. Where law was not good enough, or strong enough, the plaintiff wanted not law but justice. Law with its generality and evenhandness would do him no good; he needed justice, with its particularity and subjectiveness. These two ideals have never been easy to reconcile, and the medieval

English didn't try very hard to do so; they simply projected the two ideals into two different systems—law and equity.

The king as the fountain of justice would be petitioned by subjects for political favors, that is, for help where law did not reach. For example, a subject might complain to the king that the king himself had done wrong by having the plaintiff's land taken. The plaintiff could not sue the king at law, but he could humbly petition him, which he did. The king referred such petitions to his chancellor for action. The chancellor, in acting on this, probably was not aware of doing any particularly judicial act. He was not an administrator, and he might simply overrule lower echelon officials who had taken the petitioner's land and tell them to restore it.

Another group of these cases did not affect the king. The petitioner sought help because the legal remedy was theoretically workable, but for special reasons ran the risk of grave injustice. These petitions essentially asked for the aid of the king's special power on behalf of some disadvantaged person in a claim against some especially powerful person. When these were referred to the chancellor, his actions were rather more political in nature, since the king's power was used on behalf of one subject and against another. The chancellor was naturally a little cautious about this, and somewhere along the line he developed two habits of considerable importance. One habit was to try to get the facts before he acted. Since he was acting administratively or politically, it did not occur to him to use juries to go through some elaborate feudal wager of law; he wanted the facts, so he got witnesses before him and asked them questions about the petition of the plaintiff, going through each assertion of the petition.

The other habit developed by the chancellor along the way was the habit of giving very pious reasons for his actions. Since he did not act under "law," but apart from it, he must have had both power and propaganda to back him up, and he in fact had both of them. The propaganda-an appeal to justice, conscience, and religion-was essentially religious. The power was essentially royal. The chancellor, so to speak, carried a Bible in a mailed fist.[1]

By the fifteenth century, two separate judicial systems had developed. Professor Dobbs explains:

> Somewhere along the way, the chancellor became not merely an administrative official dispensing political favors, but a judge deciding facts and applying more or less definite principles to those facts. Petitioners, aware that the king would refer their petitions to the chancellor, began to go directly to him. His

1 *See* also 1 Holdsworth, A History of English Law 398 (7th 1956).

procedures became standardized, his substantive principles developed into a vague but more or less coherent body, and he developed devices for enforcing his orders, as well as theories to support his rules.

The chancellor had been gradually doing this sort of thing for a long time. Indeed, the distinction between political action and judicial action was not very clear in medieval England and even the common law courts sometimes entertained bills for special relief, so that on occasion they, too, looked a little like "equity courts." But by the 15th century the chancellor was clearly a judge, recognized as such and acting as such: he was acting regularly in a class of cases where the common law courts or the common law itself seemed inadequate to him, and acting without special authority from the king to hear the particular case.[2]

There were fundamental differences between law courts and equity courts. Equity courts were not bound by the Provisions of Oxford and could hear new forms of action. But, true to their roots, equity courts refused to act except when the common law courts could not provide the plaintiff with an adequate remedy.[3] When the legal remedy was available and adequate, equity would dismiss the case, thereby forcing plaintiff to pursue his legal remedies. Necessarily, equity courts did not apply the same substantive rules as the common law courts.

Equity courts also differed from law courts in regard to the types of judgments that they rendered. A common law court would make an award of monetary damages. Equity acted *in personam*. In other words, rather than making a monetary award, an equity court would issue an order in the name of the king telling the plaintiff to do, or refrain from doing, a specific act. Those who failed to comply could be held in contempt.

True to their religious roots, equity courts were referred to as "courts of conscience," and were supposed to use their powers to bring about "justice" or "equity." As a result, equity judges or chancellors (by this time, equity judges were referred to as "chancellors") could deny relief on equitable or moral grounds. The chancellor could also withhold relief on practical grounds. Over time, as equity courts heard more petitions, they began to develop "rules" or "maxims" governing equitable relief. These "maxims" were generalizations of experience based on the results of prior cases. In other words, the maxims were a loose set of "rules" designed to bring some coherency to the body of decided cases and some consistency to future decisions. The maxims included the following "rules":

---

2 D. Dobbs, Handbook on the Law of Remedies 31 (1973).

3 *Id.* at 401.

1. *He who comes into equity must come with clean hands;*
2. *He who seeks equity must do equity;*
3. *Equity is a court of conscience;*
4. *Equity does not suffer a wrong to go without a remedy;*
5. *Equity abhors a forfeiture;*
6. *Equity regards as done that which ought to have been done;*
7. *Equity delights to do justice and not by halves;*
8. *Equitable relief is not available to one who has an adequate remedy at law;*
9. *Equitable relief is discretionary;*
10. *Equity aids the vigilant, not those who slumber on their rights;*
11. *Equity regards substance rather than form;*
12. *Equity acts in personam;*
13. *Equity is equality;*
14. *Equity follows the law;*
15. *Equity will not aid a volunteer;*
16. *Where the equities are equal, the law will prevail;*
17. *Equity imputes an intent to fulfill an obligation;*
18. *Where the equities are equal, the first in time will prevail.*

Even today, it is not unusual to find judges citing and applying these ancient maxims (much like modern courts use cases as precedent) in deciding whether or not to grant equitable relief.

B. THE DEVELOPMENT OF EQUITY IN THE UNITED STATES

Just as the English common law was transplanted to the United States, equity and equitable principles were transplanted as well. As a result, all thirteen colonies had chancery courts (in one form or another), and these courts continued to function after the Revolution. But, as the nineteenth century progressed, a movement to abolish equity courts emerged.

DAN B. DOBBS, HANDBOOK ON THE LAW OF REMEDIES

(1973).

In the 19th century both England and the American states adopted major procedural reforms. In America the reform began with constitutional amendments and the adoption of Code procedure in the Field Code in New York in 1848 and its spread to other states. [T]he central reform is that the constitutions and codes abolished separate equity or chancery courts and created one form of action, the civil action.

This reform is commonly referred to as the merger of law and equity. Similar provisions for merger can be found in the Federal Rules of Civil Procedure.

Merger has not been uniform throughout the United States. A few states maintain separate equity courts, or separate divisions of a single court, usually with provisions for free transfer of cases between the courts or divisions. Where this is so, special rules or practices may be required, sometimes necessitating two trials. But the judge of a court of general jurisdiction in most states and the judges of the United States District Courts enjoy both the powers of the old chancellors and the powers of the old law judges. Many other states maintain a tier of minor courts of limited jurisdiction such as justice courts or magistrates who are typically not given equity powers. But these limited exceptions come down to saying that, overwhelmingly, the courts of general jurisdiction in America enjoy both law and equity powers.

As Professor Dobbs indicates, only a few states resisted the drive towards merger.[4] Most jurisdictions abolished distinctions between legal and equitable actions. Rule 2 of the Federal Rules of Civil Procedure is illustrative providing that "there shall be one form of action known as the 'civil action.' "

C. EQUITABLE REMEDIES TODAY

Despite merger, courts continue to distinguish between "legal" and "equitable" remedies, and continue to impose historical distinctions on the availability of equitable remedies.

1. STANDARDS FOR THE AVAILABILITY OF EQUITABLE RELIEF

a. Conscience and Equity

As we saw, equity courts developed as "courts of conscience." Today, even though equity courts no longer exist, equitable remedies are only available when "equity" and "conscience" demand them. Courts apply various rules of conscience. They may deny equitable relief to plaintiffs who unduly delay in asserting their rights (even though the statute of

---

[4] *See* TENN. CODE ANN. § 16–11–101 (1980) ("The chancery court has all the powers, privileges, and jurisdiction properly and rightfully incident to a court of equity."); MISS. CONST. Art. 6, § 159 (1972) ("The chancery court shall have full jurisdiction in the following matters and cases, viz.: (a) All matters in equity; (b) Divorce and alimony; (c) Matters testamentary and of administration; (d) Minor's business; (e) Cases of idiocy, lunacy, and persons of unsound mind; (f) All cases of which the said court had jurisdiction under the laws in force when this Constitution is put in operation."); DEL. CODE ANN. tit. 10 § 341 (1974) ("The Court of Chancery shall have jurisdiction to hear and determine all matters and causes in equity.").

limitations has not expired), or who come to court with unclean hands (even though plaintiff's misconduct would not preclude legal relief).

The description of equity as a "court of conscience" was always somewhat misleading. Courts of law had their own "rules of conscience" although they did not necessarily label their rules as such. For example, just as a court of equity might refuse to specifically enforce a contract when the plaintiff's hands are unclean, a court of law might refuse to enforce a contract that violates public policy.

How does a court decide whether a particular result is "unconscionable" or "inequitable?" Equity courts relied on the equitable maxims discussed earlier, as well as the chancellor's own sense of morality or justice. Many modern courts still use the maxims. But are the maxims really designed to bring about justice and equity? Consider them in relation to the building lot controversy (set forth at the beginning of the chapter).

PROBLEM: MORE ON THE BUILDING LOT CONTROVERSY

A problem like this one presents difficult issues for a court. Ms. Harlow's rights have been violated, but what remedy should she receive? A court could order Deets to remove the trespassing portion of the house. Alternatively, it could allow the house to remain intact and force Harlow to accept compensation for her property. Are there other options? What remedy is appropriate in this case?

Is a dispute like this one suitable for judicial resolution? Is there a way to settle the case without the need for litigation? Why might it be in Harlow's interest, as well as Deets's, to settle this dispute amicably? How might that be done?

If the dispute ends up in litigation, do the equitable maxims dictate a particular result? For example:

A. Do they require Mr. Deets to tear down that portion of the house which extends onto Ms. Harlow's property?

B. Do they compel the opposite result: that the encroachment be allowed to stand, and that Ms. Harlow be forced to accept damages (in effect, forcing her to sell a part of her property to Mr. Deets)?

C. Can maxims be found to support both of these positions?

D. Would the maxims support some other result?

As you analyze the maxims, do you have a sense of their function? Are they "rules" which must be applied, and that dictate the outcome of cases? Or, are they more like considerations, similar to the canons of statutory construction which guide courts in resolving problems of statutory interpretation? Professor Karl Llewellyn once argued that the canons of statutory construction are inconsistent with each other, and sought to prove his point by creating two parallel columns of canons. Karl Llewellyn, Remarks on the Theory of Appellate Decision and the Rules or Canons About How Statutes Are to Be Construed, 3 Vand. L. Rev. 395 (1949). Juxtaposed against one row of canons, he placed a second row of inconsistent canons. Included on the list were the following canons:

Thrust		*But Parry*	
1.	*A statute cannot go beyond its text.*	*1.*	*To effectuate its purpose a statute may be implemented beyond its text.*

* * *

7.	*A statute imposing a new penalty or forfeiture, or a new liability or disability, or creating a new right of action will not be construed as having a retroactive effect.*	*7.*	*Remedial statutes are to be construed liberally and if a retroactive interpretation will promote the ends of justice they should receive such construction.*
8.	*Where design has been distinctly stated no place is left for construction.*	*8.*	*Courts have the power to inquire into real—as distinct from ostensible—purpose.*

* * *

25.	*It must be assumed that language has been chosen with due regard to grammatical propriety and is not interchangeable on mere conjecture.*[5]	*25.*	*"And" and "or" may be read interchangeably whenever the change is necessary to give the statute sense and effect.*

Do the equitable maxims suffer from the same problem? On their face, are some maxims inconsistent with others? As applied, do they conflict? If you answered either question in the affirmative, what is the significance of this fact? What does it tell you about the function of the maxims? How does it affect the practice of law?

So, if you are the judge assigned to hear the Deets–Harlow case, how would you resolve it? Would you require Deets to remove the offending portion of the house? Would you, instead, force Harlow to accept damages in lieu of injunctive relief? If so, in what amount? Would you structure relief in some other way? Does it affect your decision that Deets's home violates the

[5] *Id.* at 401–06; *see also* Johnstone, An Evaluation of the Rules of Statutory Construction, 3 U. Kan. L. Rev. 1, 11 (1954).

setback requirements of the subdivision, and therefore he can be sued by any homeowner in the subdivision?

b. Equitable Remedies Are Granted *In Personam*

Another historical distinction that has survived is the rule that "equity acts in personam." When a court renders an "in personam" judgment, it orders the defendant to do, or refrain from doing, some act. A defendant who refuses to comply can be held in contempt and subjected to prison or fine.

By contrast, a law court usually renders a monetary judgment. In other words, it orders a decree stating that defendant owes plaintiff a sum of money. This judgment is not automatically enforcing and defendant cannot be held in contempt for his refusal to pay. On the contrary, plaintiff must bring additional proceedings to try to attach or place liens on defendant's property and thereby to satisfy the judgment.

PROBLEMS

1. *More on the Building Lot Controversy.* Now, let's think a bit more about the encroaching house problem set forth at the beginning of the chapter. If the court enters an injunction against Deets, how would it frame the order? How would a legal order differ? If Harlow had obtained the legal remedy of damages, the court would not order Deets to pay Harlow and would not hold Deets in contempt for his failure to do so. Would the court enter an *in personam* order requiring Deets to pay damages to Harlow, and hold him in contempt of court if he fails or refuses to pay? Or would the court structure the decree in a different way? If so, how?

2. *Enjoining Litigation.* Suppose that plaintiff, a resident of the Commonwealth of Kentucky, seeks injunctive relief precluding defendant from prosecuting a civil action in a nearby state (Tennessee) where suit has been commenced. Suppose that a Kentucky court decides to grant the requested relief. To whom should the order be directed? The Tennessee court? The defendant? Both? Why? Why not?

c. Inadequacy of Legal Remedy/Irreparable Harm

Another equitable maxim that survives today is the principle that equitable relief is not available except when plaintiff's legal remedy is inadequate. This principle is also known as the "irreparable harm" requirement.

CAMPBELL V. SEAMAN

18 Sickels 568 (N.Y. App. 1876).

EARL, J.

Plaintiffs owned about forty acres of land [in] the village of Castleton, on the Hudson river. During the years 1857, 1858 and 1859 they built an expensive dwelling-house, and during those years, and before and since, they improved the land by grading and terracing, building roads and walks, and planting trees and shrubs, both ornamental and useful. The defendant had for some years owned adjoining lands, which he had used as a brick-yard. The brick-yard is southerly of plaintiffs' dwelling-house about 1,320 feet, and southerly of their woods about 567 feet. In burning bricks defendant had made use of anthracite coal. During the burning of a kiln, sulphuric acid gas is generated, which is destructive to some kinds of trees and vines. Gas coming from defendant's kilns had, during the years 1869 and 1870, killed the foliage on plaintiff's white and yellow, pines and Norway spruce, and had, after repeated attacks, killed and destroyed from 100 to 150 valuable pine and spruce trees, and had injured their grape vines and plum trees. Plaintiff's damages from the gas during those years was $500. [This] gas did not continually escape during the burning of a kiln, but only during the last two days, and was carried into and over plaintiff's land only when the wind was from the south.

Every person may exercise exclusive dominion over his own property, and subject it to such uses as will best subserve his private interests. Generally, no other person can say how he shall use or what he shall do with his property. But this general right of property has its exceptions and qualifications. *Sic utere tuo ut alienum non laedas* is an old maxim which has a broad application. It does not mean that one must never use his own so as to do any injury to his neighbor or his property. Such a rule could not be enforced in civilized society. Persons living in organized communities must suffer some damage, annoyance and inconvenience from each other. For these they are compensated by all the advantages of civilized society. If one lives in the city he must expect to suffer the dirt, smoke, noisome odors, noise and confusion incident to city life. *Salvin v. Northbrancepeth Coal Co.* (9 Law R., Ch. Appeals, 705). But every person is bound to make a reasonable use of his property so as to occasion no unnecessary damage or annoyance to his neighbor. If he make an unreasonable, unwarrantable or unlawful use of it, so as to produce material annoyance, inconvenience, discomfort or hurt to his neighbor, he will be guilty of a nuisance to his neighbor. And the law will hold him responsible for the consequent damage. What is reasonable must depend upon the circumstances of each case. A use of property in one locality and under some circumstances may be lawful and reasonable, which, under other circumstances, would be unlawful, unreasonable and a nuisance. To constitute a nuisance, the use must be such as to produce a tangible and appreciable injury to neighboring property, or such as to render its enjoyment specially uncomfortable or inconvenient.

That defendant's brick burning was a nuisance to plaintiffs cannot be doubted. But the claim is made that although the brick burning in this case is a nuisance, a court of equity will not and ought not to restrain it, and the plaintiffs should be left to their remedy at law to recover damages. Injunctions were rarely issued in the case of a nuisance until plaintiff's right had been established at law, and the writ is not matter of right, but of grace. But a suit at law is no longer a necessary preliminary, and the right to an injunction, in a proper case, is just as fixed and certain as the right to any other provisional remedy. The writ can rightfully be demanded to prevent irreparable injury, interminable litigation and a multiplicity of suits, and its refusal in a proper case would be error to be corrected by an appellate tribunal. It is matter of grace in no sense except that it rests in the sound discretion of the court, and that discretion is not an arbitrary one. *Corning v. Troy Iron and Nail Factory,* 40 N. Y., 191. Here the remedy at law was not adequate. The mischief was substantial and irreparable.

The plaintiffs built a costly mansion and had laid out their grounds and planted them with ornamental and useful trees and vines, for their comfort and enjoyment. How can one be compensated in damages for the destruction of his ornamental trees, and the flowers and vines which surrounded his home? How can a jury estimate their value in dollars and cents? The fact that trees and vines are for ornament or luxury entitles them no less to the protection of the law. Every one has the right to surround himself with articles of luxury, and he will be no less protected than one who provides himself only with articles of necessity. The law will protect a flower or a vine as well as an oak. *Cook v. Forbes,* L. R., 5 Eq. Ca., 166. These damages are irreparable too, because the trees and vines cannot be replaced, and the law will not compel a person to take money rather than the objects of beauty and utility which he places around his dwelling to gratify his taste or to promote his comfort and his health.

Here the injunction also prevents a multiplicity of suits. The injury is a recurring one, and every time the poisonous breath from defendant's brick-kiln sweeps over plaintiffs' land they have a cause of action. Unless the nuisance be restrained the litigation would be interminable. The policy of the law favors, and the peace and good order of society are best promoted by the termination of such litigations by a single suit.

The fact that this nuisance is not continual, and that the injury is only occasional, furnishes no answer to the claim for an injunction. The nuisance has occurred often enough within two years to do the plaintiffs large damage. Every time a kiln is burned some injury may be expected, unless the wind should blow the poisonous gas away from plaintiffs' lands. Nuisances causing damage less frequently have been restrained. *Ross v. Butler,* 19 N. J., 294; *Meigs v. Lister,* 23 N. J. Eq. R., 200.

Where the damage to one complaining of a nuisance is small or trifling, and the damage to the one causing the nuisance will be large in case he be restrained, the courts will sometimes deny an injunction. But here the damage to the plaintiffs is large and substantial. It does not appear how much damage the defendant will suffer from the restraint of the injunction. He does not own the only piece of ground where bricks can be made. Material for brick making exists in all parts of our State, and particularly at various points along the Hudson River. An injunction need not therefore destroy defendant's business or interfere materially with the useful and necessary trade of brick making. It does not appear how valuable defendant's land is for a brick-yard, nor how expensive are his erections for brick making. We may infer that they are not expensive and his land may be put to other use just as profitable to him. It does not appear that defendant's damage from an abatement of the nuisance will be as great as plaintiffs' damages from its continuance. Hence this is not a case where an injunction should be denied on account of the serious consequences to the defendant.

Our decision does not improperly embarrass those engaged in the useful trade of brick making. There can be no trouble to find places where brick can be made without damage to persons living in the vicinity. It certainly cannot be necessary to make them in the heart of a village or in the midst of a thickly settled community.

It follows from these views that the judgment should be affirmed.

All concur.

Judgment affirmed.

PROBLEMS

1. *Clearing Timber.* Defendant Camden Lumber Co. has been illegally cutting timber on plaintiff's land. At one point, in the State of West Virginia, standing timber was so plentiful that it was regarded as a nuisance, and damages were regarded as an adequate remedy (so that injunctive relief was inappropriate). As the court stated in *Pardee v. Camden Lumber Co.*, 70 W. Va. 68, 73 S.E. 82 (1911), standing timber was regarded as an "incumbrance and burden upon lands. Having nothing but forests, the chief object or purpose of landowners everywhere was to get rid of the forests, and prepare their lands for agriculture." Suppose that a landowner values the timber on his land, and objects when a timber company wants to cut it down without his permission. If you are the judge assigned to hear the case, would you adhere to the ancient rule and regard monetary damages as an adequate remedy?

2. *Smoke in the Workplace.* By law, an employer has a legal obligation to provide its employees with a "safe and healthy working environment." Plaintiff, a factory employee, began to experience serious respiratory tract discomfort as a result of inhaling tobacco smoke in the workplace, and the discomfort (which included a sore throat, nausea, dizziness, headache, blackouts, loss of memory, difficulty in concentration, aches and pains in joints, sensitivity to noise and light, cold sweat, gagging, choking sensations, and lightheadedness) have become increasingly severe over the years. Plaintiff's doctor has advised him to avoid contact with tobacco smoke whenever possible. When plaintiff complained to defendant (his employer), and provided evidence regarding his medical condition, defendant informed plaintiff that he could either continue to work in the same location with a respirator (which defendant tried, but found was not effective) or move to a job in the computer room where smoking is prohibited. The latter option would entail a pay decrease of about $500 per month, and place plaintiff on a different (lesser) career track. Plaintiff sues seeking injunctive relief requiring his employer to prohibit all smoke in his work area. Defendant responds that plaintiff is not suffering irreparable injury because he can shift to a smokeless area at less salary, and can recover the lost salary in damages. Plaintiff claims that the damages would not be adequate. Is plaintiff suffering irreparable injury? *See Smith v. Western Electric Co.*, 643 S.W.2d 10 (Mo. App. 1983).

FORTNER V. WILSON

202 Okla. 563, 216 P.2d 299 (1950).

HALLEY, JUSTICE.

Plaintiff, R.C. Wilson, sued J.W. Fortner, alleging that he entered into a contract with the defendant, who operated a Chevrolet sales agency, whereby he agreed to purchase and defendant agreed to sell a new Chevrolet car for the list price, plus the usual and ordinary costs of handling, freight and accessories; that the defendant gave plaintiff a written order for the car, bearing the number '44', which showed the order of sequence in which plaintiff would receive the car; that plaintiff deposited $100 to apply on the purchase price; and that the order of sale was signed by both plaintiff and defendant.

In August, 1947, the defendant advised plaintiff by letter that before defendant would deliver the new car, plaintiff would have to deliver a "trade-in" car, for which he could be allowed the sum of $600, with the privilege of re-purchase at $25 per $100 over the trade-in allowance.

Defendant later notified plaintiff that his new car had arrived, but would not be delivered until plaintiff delivered to defendant his secondhand "trade-in" car. Plaintiff alleged that he was able, willing, and ready to receive and pay for the new car and, after seeing it, tendered the full purchase price and demanded delivery, but that the defendant refused to perform his part of the contract.

Plaintiff prayed for a restraining order prohibiting defendant from disposing of the new car, and for judgment requiring defendant to give him title thereto, and, in the alternative, for damages in the sum of $709.51 (sic) and the return of his $100 deposit, with interest, and for $150 attorney's fee. He later filed an amendment to his petition, alleging that to obtain another car he would incur great expense and inconvenience, because new cars were unique commodities at that time, and that he had no other way of receiving a new automobile or to be adequately compensated in an action at law.

Plaintiff filed an election of remedy by which he elected to stand upon his plea for specific performance, and dismissed without prejudice his cause of action for damages.

A careful examination of the evidence discloses that new Chevrolet automobiles were not available on the open market at that time, and could only be obtained at great expense and inconvenience from used-car dealers; but the fact remains that they could be obtained.

The rule which controls in this case is that in the sale of personal property, equity will not force specific performance where plaintiff had an adequate remedy at law. A court of equity will not specifically enforce a contract for the sale of ordinary articles of commerce, which can at all times be bought in the market, such as barroom fixtures, cattle, coal, corn, cotton, logs or lumber, pianos, sauerkraut, whisky, used cars, or an existing business and stock in trade, since the remedy at law for a breach of such contract is regarded as complete and adequate.

Regardless of what our personal views may be as to the business ethics of the defendant in this case, the fact remains that the property being sold was an article which could be obtained, by paying an additional amount of money, in the open market. It was known as a "gray market." This was personal property; there was nothing unique in any way about it which would cause it to come under the exceptions to the rule that specific performance will not be granted as to personal property. We see no reason to depart from the position that we have previously taken, that unless there is something unique in the article sold, or something about it that would prevent money damages from giving full relief, specific performance will not be granted.

NOTE

The common law requirement of irreparable injury survives today, although in somewhat more flexible form. It applies in both contract and non-contract cases. In contracts for the sale of goods, *Fortner's* rule was codified in Uniform Commercial Code, § 2–716: "specific performance may be decreed where the goods are unique or in other proper circumstances." This provision has been interpreted to permit specific performance even though the goods are not unique in the strict sense, but are very scarce or cannot be replaced by alternative sources. *Copylease Corp. of America v. Memorex Corp.*, 408 F.Supp. 758 (S.D.N.Y.1976).

PROBLEMS

1. *More on* Fortner. Suppose that you had been Wilson's attorney in the prior case. You know that Chevrolets are generally regarded as fungible so that the legal remedy constitutes an adequate remedy for breach. Under what circumstances might the legal remedy be inadequate even for a fungible item? In other words, if you represented Wilson, what would you need to show in order to obtain specific performance?

2. *More on the Building Lot Controversy.* The "irreparable harm" requirement might also apply in the Harlow–Deets problem, *supra.* Is Harlow's legal remedy adequate? What would she receive under that remedy? Would that remedy provide adequate compensation for her injury?

3. *Should the Historical Requirement of Inadequacy Be Maintained?* Does it make sense to maintain the historical requirement of inadequacy as a predicate to equitable relief? In *Fortner*, even though Wilson has an adequate legal remedy, why should equitable relief be precluded? He bargained for a particular car, and Fortner agreed to provide it to him. Why should Fortner be allowed to shirk his obligation? Are there modern justifications for continuing to abide by the ancient prohibition against specific performance? Are there any advantages to forcing Wilson to accept an award of damages in lieu of specific performance? What problems might arise if specific performance is given?

MERRILL LYNCH, PIERCE, FENNER & SMITH, INC. V. CALLAHAN

265 F. Supp.2d 440 (2003).

SESSIONS, CHIEF JUDGE.

This case arises out of the defendants' [Cornelius Callahan and John Polanshek] resignation from the Burlington office of Merrill Lynch, Pierce, Fenner & Smith Inc. "Merrill Lynch" where they were employed as financial analysts. Merrill Lynch alleges that after resigning the defendants retained a list of client names and information and used that list to solicit their former clients. Merrill Lynch moved for a temporary restraining order and preliminary injunctive relief prohibiting the defendants from soliciting their former clients or using or disclosing the list of client names and information. It did so based on the fact that Merrill Lynch provided both defendants with significant training as financial analysts. As a condition of their employment with Merrill Lynch, Callahan and Polanshek executed Account Executive Trainee

Agreements. Under these agreements, each promised that in the event of termination of his employment he would not solicit, for one year, any clients he served while at Merrill Lynch or any clients whose names became known to him during that time, within 100 miles of the office in which he was employed. Each also agreed that the names and addresses of Merrill Lynch's clients would remain the property of Merrill Lynch, and would be treated by him as confidential information of Merrill Lynch at all times during his employment and after his termination. In addition, both agreed in writing, on an annual basis, to abide by Merrill Lynch's privacy policy regarding confidentiality of client information which prohibited the sale or rent of clients' personal information and the release of such information without client authorization.

Waltien, a Merrill Lynch employee, admitted that the Company has a policy of hiring experienced financial analysts from other firms. Waltien also testified, based on his 32 years of experience in the financial services industry, that clients value greatly the confidentiality of their personal and financial information. Merrill Lynch has taken numerous steps to protect this confidentiality through the agreements that Callahan and Polanshek signed and through other company policies. He also testified that future revenues from an account are difficult to predict because they are affected by a variety of factors including the stock market and changes in the life of the account-holder. According to Waltien, referrals from current clients are the lifeblood of Merrill Lynch's business and it is difficult to predict the revenue the firm will earn in referrals from any one account. Finally he stated that Callahan and Polanshek's departure with the client list had hurt office morale, had caused employees to be worried that the office might close, and could encourage other employees to take similar offers with competing firms.

To obtain preliminary injunctive relief, Merrill Lynch must show: (a) that it will suffer irreparable harm in the absence of an injunction and (b) either (i) a likelihood of success on the merits or (ii) sufficiently serious questions going to the merits to make them a fair ground for litigation and a balance of hardships tipping decidedly in its favor. *Tom Doherty Assocs., Inc. v. Saban Entm't, Inc.*, 60 F.3d 27, 33 (2d Cir.1995). Merrill Lynch has not met its burden of demonstrating, however, that it will suffer future irreparable harm on these bases. First, it is undisputed that Callahan and Polanshek have already taken the client list and contacted virtually all of their 429 clients twice. In essence, the damage is already done. Second, the Court is not convinced that the financial losses resulting from any client account transfers to Wachovia will be immeasurable. Although many factors affect the future revenue from a client account, a reasonable estimate of the damages can be made based on Merrill Lynch's records of the assets and commissions related to these accounts, similar records created by Wachovia for any accounts that are transferred, and expert testimony. *See Morgan Stanley DW, Inc. v. Frisby,*

163 F.Supp.2d 1371, 1376 (N.D.Ga.2001). The same argument applies to clients who might depart Merrill Lynch based on their loss of trust and confidence related to the disclosure of their names, addresses, and telephone numbers to Wachovia. Merrill Lynch has not demonstrated that the economic loss caused by any such departures is immeasurable, just as it has failed to do so regarding client departures caused by solicitation. It is notable that Callahan and Polanshek have taken only the names, addresses, and phone numbers of their former clients, and not their confidential financial documents, which would be more likely to lead to client distrust.

WHEREFORE, Merrill Lynch's motion for a temporary restraining order and preliminary injunctive relief is DENIED.

NOTE: INADEQUACY & IRREPABILITY

The concept of "inadequacy of the legal remedy" and the "requirement of irreparable injury" are extremely important. As a general rule, harm is irreparable when the legal remedy of damages is inadequate to provide relief. Over the centuries, courts have decreed that the legal remedy is inadequate in various situations: when property is "unique" so that plaintiff cannot readily purchase a substitute; when damages are difficult or impossible to calculate; when defendant is insolvent or it is otherwise impossible to collect a monetary judgment; when plaintiff will be required to bring multiple proceedings to vindicate his rights; and when the plaintiff's injury is of such a nature (*e.g.*, deprivation of civil rights) that the remedy of damages is substitutionary and ineffective.

PROBLEMS

1. *More on* Merrill Lynch. In the prior case, did the court reach the correct decision? On appeal, what is your best argument for overturning the decision?

2. *The Pop Radio Station.* Suppose that plaintiff, who had always wanted to own a radio station, contracts to purchase a local pop radio station from defendant. Because of the limited number of air frequencies, only a small number of license are available in each city, and therefore, only a small number of radio stations can exist in each city. At the moment, no other stations are for sale in the area. Moreover, plaintiff wants this particular station because it is the "market leader" in the pop scene. Suppose that plaintiff sues seeking specific performance. Defendant responds claiming that plaintiff is a business man who desires to buy the station simply to "make money," and therefore money damages would provide an adequate remedy at law. If you are hired to represent plaintiff, what arguments might you make for the proposition that he is entitled to specific performance? How might defendant respond to those arguments? Who should prevail? See *Chamber of Commerce v. Barton*, 195 Ark. 274, 112 S.W.2d 619, 625 (1937).

3. *The Jewelry*. Miller seeks a temporary restraining order prohibiting Schiller from disposing of four pieces of jewelry, including a 5.8 carat diamond engagement ring. The jewelry was purchased by the parties during their amorous relationship, and Schiller seized it when they parted. The evidence suggests that it would be difficult to determine the market value of the jewelry because they are all "unique one of a kind creations." Under the circumstances, can it be said that plaintiff's legal remedy is inadequate? Suppose that Miller bought the jewelry for investment purposes. Does this fact suggest that money would be entirely adequate to compensate him for the loss or retention of this jewelry? If so, is equitable relief inappropriate? Does it matter that plaintiff planned to hold on to the rings for a period of time in the hope that their uniqueness might cause their value to rise? If so, how would damages be measured? *See Schiller v. Miller*, 621 So.2d 481 (Fla.App. 1993).

4. *The Sculpture*. Jacob Simpson, a famous sculptor, agrees to create a "one-of-a-kind" sculpture, for Maynard Knobstead. Later, Simpson received a lavish contract from Endicott Corp. to create sculptures for Endicott's new headquarters building. Because his Endicott contract was so lucrative, Simpson decides to breach his agreement with Knobstead. Suppose that Knobstead comes to you for legal advice. Knobstead would like to force Simpson to specifically perform his obligation. First, think about whether he has an adequate remedy at law. Does he? If so, what is it? If not, would you encourage him to seek specific performance, or to seek some other remedy? Why?

5. *Eliminate the Distinction Between Legal and Equitable Remedies?* Does it make sense to continue to distinguish between equitable remedies and legal remedies? Rhonda Wasserman, in her article, *Equity Transformed: Preliminary Injunctions to Require the Payment of Money*, 70 BULR 623 (1990), has argued that it might be appropriate to extend injunctive relief to new types of cases:

> [When] an individual with no savings or insurance is injured seriously and rendered unable to work, she cannot meet her ordinary living expenses, let alone afford necessary medical care. She needs immediate compensation for her injuries. Yet even if she is likely to prevail on the merits of her claim against the tortfeasor and is in dire need of medical care, and even if the tortfeasor would not suffer undue hardship if ordered to pay some portion of the plaintiff's damages immediately, the personal injury plaintiff must engage in time-consuming and expensive discovery and wait perhaps years until trial before receiving any compensation. If she cannot wait, she will have to settle her claim for less than it is worth. Although a preliminary injunction requiring the defendant to make an interim payment of some portion of the likely damages before trial would spare the plaintiff irreparable harm, courts have not granted such relief in these kinds of cases.

> Three principles of law have inhibited courts from granting such relief: that equity will not "take jurisdiction over a legal claim merely to hurry it along"; that "the temporary loss of income, ultimately to be recovered, does not usually constitute irreparable injury"; and that a court should not grant an equitable remedy to a claimant who has an "adequate" remedy at law.

Do you agree?

d. Equitable Relief Is Discretionary

As at common law, equitable relief remains inherently discretionary. A court may deny equitable relief even though plaintiff's legal remedy is inadequate.

GEORG V. ANIMAL DEFENSE LEAGUE

231 S.W.2d 807 (Tex.Civ.App.1950).

NORVELL, JUSTICE.

Animal Defense League is a corporation organized under the laws of the State of Texas "for the charitable and benevolent purpose of preventing cruelty to animals, to promote humane and kind treatment of them, and to aid and assist by all legal and proper means the enforcement of the laws enacted and that may be enacted by the Legislature of this State for the prevention of cruelty to animals of every kind and nature."

As a part of its activities or functions, the League maintains an animal shelter where stray cats and dogs are cared for until such time as new homes may be found for them. If the animals be diseased or injured beyond hope of recovery they are destroyed and their suffering ended.

The League maintained an animal shelter located on Zercher Road. Because of the growth of the city and the urbanization of the territory surrounding this location, the League's Board of Directors decided to abandon that location and purchased a 25-acre tract north of the city of San Antonio. Although the 25-acre tract is approximately the same distance from the city limits of San Antonio as the Zercher Road location, the surrounding area is not so highly urbanized.

Before the League commenced the construction of its proposed animal shelter upon the Austin Road property, appellants Alvin Georg and others, who own land in the vicinity, brought suit to restrain the League from constructing and operating kennels and shelters upon the property. After due notice and hearing, the court rendered judgment as a matter of law for the Animal Defense League. The case was appealed.

In this case, we have an animal shelter which if constructed may house some 200 dogs. It is a matter of common knowledge that dogs will whine, bark and howl, and that when one of them begins to bark, others will join in. While dogs may be regarded by a substantial portion of our population as wholly unnecessary annoyances, yet man emerged from the pre-historic past with the dog at his side as a servant and companion, and today, even in our great metropolitan cities man lives in the midst of dogs and cats and birds and other creatures. The majority consensus gives the dog a place in modern society. It follows that institutions which contribute to his welfare and protect human beings from the depredations and annoyances of unattached and stray animals must be considered as fostering the common good.

It does not appear that another location could be selected within a reasonable range of the City of San Antonio that would not be subject to objections similar to those raised by the appellants here. If the League is to function at all it must necessarily result in annoyance or discomfort to someone. Furthermore, it is not shown that the site selected is wholly inappropriate when the surrounding vicinity is considered. While there are farms in the area, the district is commercialized. It contains gravel pits, a railroad line, machinery storage yards, a battery factory, motels, liquor stores, gasoline filling stations, barn yards, cow lots, dance halls and beer joints, including one which is perhaps unique in that (according to one witness) it caters exclusively to families and no musical selections other than those from Grand Opera are played upon a phonograph.

All of appellants' houses, except one, are located at least 2800 feet from the proposed location of appellee's buildings. The appellant Kessler has a rent house about 1525 feet from said proposed location which is near the center of the 25-acre tract purchased by the League.

Even though the presence of the proposed animal shelter may result in some annoyance to appellants, their remedy is not by way of injunction but they are relegated to an action for damages. It is not within the jury's province to decide whether the private nuisance which would result from the operation of the proposed animal shelter will be outweighed by the public welfare. This is not a fact issue, but one to be determined by the chancellor in accordance with established equitable rules and principles. Restrictions upon the use of property must necessarily be governed by municipal laws, covenants and sometimes by rules of equity, and not by a jury's opinion as to a proper public policy. We hold that the trial court was correct in rendering judgment for the appellee.

PROBLEM: MORE ON THE BUILDING LOT CONTROVERSY

Now, let's think about how the discretionary nature of equitable relief might apply to the encroaching house problem set forth at the beginning of the chapter. Even if you concluded that Harlow is suffering irreparable injury, that is not compensable in monetary terms, are there discretionary reasons why she should be denied relief? How would you argue the case for

Deets? How might Harlow respond? If you are the judge, how would you rule on this issue?

GROSSMAN V. WEGMAN'S FOOD MARKETS, INC.

43 A.D.2d 813, 350 N.Y.S.2d 484 (Sup.Ct., App.Div.1973).

MEMORANDUM:

Plaintiffs appeal from a judgment dismissing their action to compel defendant by means of specific performance to continue to occupy and operate leased premises as a retail grocery supermarket. Respondent leased the premises consisting of a store in the Big N Shopping Plaza for a term of fifteen years at an annual rental of $48,450 and also agreed to pay a sum equal to 1 per cent of all gross annual sales in excess of $4,845,000. Respondent went into possession of the property in April, 1970. On September 19, 1972 it notified plaintiffs' agent that it intended to vacate the leased premises by October 7, 1972 but it would continue to pay the rent until such time as the premises are re-let. During the time it operated the store, its annual gross sales did not amount to more than $1,292,000. It made no profit and its losses during the two years and seven months that it operated the store amounted to $615,000. The record does not show that there is a reasonable probability that defendant or any other tenant would have gross sales in an amount sufficient to require the payment of percentage rentals. There is evidence, however, that a food store will draw people to a shopping center who will also patronize the other stores and that while the food store is closed the business of the other stores will be diminished. There might well be damage to the other tenants while the food store remains vacant, and, if the vacancy extends over a long period of time, it is possible that a tenant might also vacate its premises with resulting damage to plaintiffs. Of course such possible damage would be avoided if defendant should specifically perform its lease. Such relief should not be granted in this case, however, because courts of equity are reluctant to grant specific performance in situations where such performance would require judicial supervision over a long period of time. "Contracts which require the performance of varied and continuous acts [will] not, as a general rule, be enforced by courts of equity, because the execution of the decree would require such constant superintendence as to make judicial control a matter of extreme difficulty." (*Standard Fashion Co. v. Siegel–Cooper Co.*, 157 N.Y. 60, 66, 51 N.E. 408, 409.) * * *

NOTE: THE DISCRETIONARY NATURE OF EQUITABLE RELIEF

The principle that "equitable relief is discretionary" reflects a number of concerns regarding the wisdom and desirability of granting relief. Consider the following problems in an effort to uncover those concerns.

PROBLEMS

1. *The Shopping Center Lease.* Would it be appropriate for a court to order a shopping center to enter into a lease with a prospective tenant? When the shopping center applied to have its property rezoned, so that it could be used as a shopping center, a favorable outcome was in doubt (the planning commission and the planning staff had already recommended against the application). In an effort to bolster its application, the developer asked plaintiff to provide a letter of support that could be submitted to the planning commission. In exchange, the developer offered to give plaintiff a lease at the new center (if, of course, the application was approved) on terms equal to those given to other major tenants. When the application was approved, defendant refused to give plaintiff a lease. Assume that you are the judge in the case. Would it be appropriate to order the shopping center to comply with the agreement by giving plaintiff a lease at the center? *See Ammerman v. City Stores Company*, 394 F.2d 950, 129 U.S.App.D.C. 325 (D.C. Cir. 1968).

2. *Managing the Contract.* Defendant agreed to furnish the labor, services, materials and equipment necessary to expand and modernize plaintiffs' steel fabricating plant. The parties originally contemplated that defendant would hire sufficient workers to operate two separate shifts. The total price for the work to be performed was $27,500,000, and the area of contract performance extended over a site encompassing sixty acres. Defendant failed to hire sufficient workers to staff two shifts (300 instead of the needed 600), and defendant fell behind on the performance schedule (by two weeks). Is it appropriate for a court to enforce defendant's promise by requiring defendant to hire additional workers and to operate them on two shifts? How might defendant argue that enforcement is inappropriate? How might plaintiffs respond to defendant's argument?

3. *Compelling Admission to the Country Club.* Rambo Royster applies for admission to the Seneca Gardens Country Club (SGCC). SGCC is a private, very exclusive, country club. New members are admitted only with the unanimous consent of all existing members. A number of members have decided to withhold their consent because Rambo is rather nerdish and because he is obsessed with guns. Enraged over the denial of his application, Rambo sues SGCC to compel it to admit him to membership. Is the court likely to grant the request for relief?

D. EQUITABLE DEFENSES

A number of common law equitable defenses are used today to prevent an award of equitable relief. The major defenses are "unclean hands," unconscionability, laches, and estoppel. All of these doctrines are grounded in equitable principles.

1. UNCLEAN HANDS DOCTRINE

The "unclean hands" (or "clean hands") doctrine states that "he who comes to equity must come with clean hands." Equity will deny relief to a plaintiff who comes with "unclean hands."

SALOMON SMITH BARNEY INC. V. VOCKEL

137 F. Supp.2d 599 (E.D. Pa. 2000).

BARTLE, DISTRICT JUDGE.

Salomon Smith Barney Inc. ("Smith Barney") seeks a preliminary injunction against one of its former financial consultants, Stewart M. Vockel, III ("Vockel"). While still employed by Smith Barney and without asking for permission from it or any of his clients, Vockel provided to Paine Webber the account statements for 254 of the 470 accounts he was servicing at Smith Barney. Paine Webber forwarded this material to an outside firm which prepared solicitation packages and mailed them to the account holders. The solicitation package contained a cover letter drafted and signed by Vockel, an account transfer form with each client's Smith Barney account number(s) preprinted on it, and a Paine Webber "new account" form. On the day that the letters were mailed, Vockel submitted his letter of resignation to Smith Barney. He took with him newly printed gain and loss statements for all of the Smith Barney accounts he had serviced and a "household list," which showed the total assets, monthly activity, and gains and losses for each of his Smith Barney accounts. Vockel spent the weekend calling his clients. He told them about his move to Paine Webber and explained that they soon would be receiving solicitation packages that would enable them to transfer their accounts to his new employer.

This was not the first time Vockel had solicited his clients to transfer their accounts to his new place of employment. When he left Merrill Lynch, Pierce, Fenner & Smith, Inc. ("Merrill Lynch"), to go to work for Smith Barney six years earlier, Vockel had been managing accounts worth approximately $23 million. [Smith Barney asked for and received Vockel's Merrill Lynch client account statements, while Vockel was still working at Merrill Lynch. On the day of his resignation from Merrill Lynch, Smith Barney mailed similar solicitation packages to Vockel's clients that] contained an account transfer form and a letter informing clients of his move to Smith Barney. The letter also urged them to transfer their accounts. Vockel used the Smith Barney solicitation letter as a model when he drafted his Paine Webber letter. As a result of Smith Barney's solicitation efforts, approximately 60% of Vockel's accounts were moved to Smith Barney, and another 30% of his accounts resulted from referrals from those clients who had followed him from Merrill Lynch to Smith Barney. When he left Smith Barney, he was managing approximately 470 accounts worth a total of approximately $70 million, and annually these accounts generated over $500,000 in commissions.

During his tenure at Smith Barney, Vockel had access to its computerized database that contained information about the clients he served, including their names, addresses, phone numbers, cash balances, asset values, investment habits, portfolio details, and monthly account activity. Vockel also made use of Smith Barney's investment products, research tools and data, support staff, equipment, and office space.

When he joined Smith Barney, Vockel was told that Merrill Lynch differed from Smith Barney in that Merrill Lynch considered clients "*theirs*" while Smith Barney knew clients were the "*broker's*" and Smith Barney was there to help the broker service his or her clients' accounts. Nonetheless, afterwards, Smith Barney requested and Vockel signed a "Principles Of Employment" agreement with Smith Barney that provided: "[Y]ou must never use (except when necessary in your employment with us) nor disclose with anyone not affiliated with Smith Barney any confidential or unpublished information you obtain as a result of your employment with us. This applies both while you are employed with us and after that employment ends. If you leave our employ, you may not retain or take with you any writing or other record which relates to the above." Vockel also signed an "Employee Acknowledgements" [sic] form wherein he promised:

> I will not publish or otherwise disclose, or use for other than Smith Barney's benefit, either during or after my employment, any unpublished or proprietary or confidential information or secret relating to Smith Barney or its affiliates or any of their businesses or operations, nor will I publish or otherwise disclose proprietary or confidential information of others to which I have had access or obtained knowledge in the course of my employment. If I leave the employ of Smith Barney I will not, without its prior written consent, retain or take with me any writing or other record in any form or nature which relates to any of the foregoing.

Vockel never signed a non-compete agreement.

Even assuming that Smith Barney would otherwise be entitled to a preliminary injunction, Vockel contends that it should be denied because Smith Barney does not come into the court with clean hands. The Supreme Court has declared, "It is one of the fundamental principles upon which equity jurisprudence is founded, that before a complainant can have a standing in court he must first show that not only has he a good and meritorious cause of action, but he must come into court with clean hands." *Keystone Driller Co. v. General Excavator Co.*, 290 U.S. 240, 244 (1933). The Court has cautioned that we must not be made the "abettor of iniquity." *Id.* at 245.

In further explaining the application of the equitable maxim of clean hands, the Supreme Court stated, "The governing principle is that whenever a party who, as actor, seeks to set the judicial machinery in motion and obtain some remedy, has violated conscience, or good faith, or other equitable principle, in his prior conduct, then the doors of the court will be shut against him in limine." *Id.* at 244–45. The rule is not without its limitations. We are not to consider misconduct that has no connection to the case at hand. Rather, any "unconscionable act" of the plaintiff must have "immediate and necessary relation to the equity that he seeks in respect of the matter in litigation." *Id.* at 245.

Plaintiff has painted a picture of Vockel making off with valuable client information in order to woo them surreptitiously and expeditiously to his new employer, one of Smith Barney's arch competitors, and doing so in a manner that made it nearly impossible for Smith Barney to prevent the loss of valuable business. If it does not obtain preliminary relief in this case, argued Smith Barney, clients will be hoodwinked into transferring accounts without realizing what they are doing. According to Smith Barney, competing brokerage firms might be encouraged to lure its brokers away and deprive it of business in which it had invested so many resources to develop.

Unfortunately for Smith Barney, in determining the issue of clean hands, we look solely at the conduct of the plaintiff—the one who seeks the aid of the chancellor—and not the conduct of the defendant. As the Court of Appeals observed in *Monsanto Co. v. Rohm & Haas Co.,* 456 F.2d 592, 598 (3d Cir.1972), "This maxim [of clean hands] is far more than a mere banality. It is a self-imposed ordinance that closes the doors of a court of equity to one tainted with inequitableness or bad faith relative to the matter in which he seeks relief, *however improper may have been the behavior of the defendant.*" (emphasis added).

It is undisputed that in 1994 Smith Barney secretly encouraged and aided Vockel to engage in the same unconscionable behavior of which it now complains. For over five years, Smith Barney has shared in the gains of its unconscionable conduct. At the time it hired Vockel, Smith Barney showed no respect for the confidential nature of Merrill Lynch's client data. It obtained information about Vockel's Merrill Lynch clients and prepared solicitation packages in advance of his departure from Merrill Lynch. It instructed Vockel to resign from Merrill Lynch late on a Friday afternoon and to begin contacting his clients immediately in order to persuade them to transfer their accounts to Smith Barney. It also provided Vockel with a significant signing bonus for joining the firm.

Smith Barney seeks the help of a court of equity to prevent the same conduct by Vockel which it had previously abetted and from which it has handsomely profited. Now it wants the court to prevent the loss of that profit. If what Vockel is doing in 2000 is wrong, it is hard to see why

Vockel's and Smith Barney's conduct in 1994 was not wrong. At the very least, Smith Barney is "tainted with inequitableness or bad faith relative to the matter in which it seeks relief." *Monsanto,* 456 F.2d at 598. The misdeeds of Smith Barney have an "immediate and necessary relation to the equity that it seeks" in this case. *Keystone Driller,* 290 U.S. at 245. While we do not condone the behavior of Vockel, it is the behavior of Smith Barney on which we must focus here. *See Monsanto,* 456 F.2d at 598. Simply put, Smith Barney has not shown that it has come into this court with clean hands. In fact, the opposite has been established. Accordingly, as a court sitting in equity, we will not aid a wrongdoer. We will leave the parties to their monetary and other remedies before the National Association of Securities Dealers.

The motion of Salomon Smith Barney Inc. for a preliminary injunction will be denied.

NOTE: MORE ON ACCOUNT PILFERING

A similar decision was rendered in *Merrill Lynch, Pierce, Fenner & Smith Inc. v. Callahan*, 265 F. Supp.2d 440 (2003). In that case, although Merrill Lynch did not lure Callahan away from a competitor, it did have a practice of recruiting experienced financial analysts from other firms and requiring them to provide their client statements and other client information to Merrill Lynch before and after leaving their old firms. The court applied the clean hands doctrine: "Even if Merrill Lynch had demonstrated irreparable harm, the Court would deny its demand for preliminary injunctive relief under the doctrine of unclean hands. Solicitation of former clients from memory is standard practice both at Merrill Lynch and throughout the financial services industry. By seeking to halt such solicitation, Merrill Lynch seeks to enjoin the same behavior in which it engages as a matter of company policy. Under the doctrine of unclean hands, "he who comes into equity must come with clean hands." "

PROBLEMS

1. *Reconsidering* Salomon Smith Barney. Does the unclean hands preclude Smith Barney from obtaining any relief against Vockel? If not, what remedy might Smith Barney seek and how might that remedy be framed?

2. *Reconsidering* Merrill Lynch. In the *Merrill Lynch* case, referred to in the immediately prior note, can it be argued that the clean hands doctrine should not apply because Merrill Lynch's inequitable conduct is not directly related to its claim against Callahan? In other words, unlike the *Salomon Smith Barney* case, Merrill Lynch did not recruit Callahan away from another firm and encourage him to bring his employee lists with him. Should this distinction matter to the final result?

SHERIDAN V. SHERIDAN

247 N.J.Super. 552, 589 A.2d 1067 (1990).

HERMAN, J.S.C.

This court is asked to decide whether marital property acquired with funds obtained illicitly and not reported for federal and state taxing purposes is subject to equitable distribution. This question appears to be one of first impression.

From an economic perspective the 1977, second marriage for plaintiff, Suzanne E. Sheridan, and defendant, Charles L. Sheridan, was a rags-to-riches affair. According to one family member it was clear to all that "One day we were poor, the next day we were rich." By the time the parties had separated in Sept. 1989, it was back to rags again.

The family's economic rollercoaster ride began in early 1983. Abandoning their Upper Darby, Pa. home to foreclosure and leaving all their furnishings behind, the Sheridans purchased a house in Oak Valley, Deptford Twp., for $57,000. They paid cash which they took from a paper bag at settlement.

From a safety-deposit box, a shoe box, a dog biscuit box and from other hiding places, more cash withdrawals followed. Occasionally, they even withdrew funds from a checking or savings account, those withdrawals being primarily cash. In all, more than $200,000 was spent on various acquisitions & improvements through 1986. Funds were expended for remodeling and decorating, furniture and appliances, a number of vehicles, vacations, jewelry, gifts for family and others and a 6.5 acre vacant parcel of land in Chester Co., Pa. Including private school tuitions, the family budget for the years 1983 through 1987 easily exceeded $25,000 per annum. In total, more than $325,000 was spent during a 5-year period in which plaintiff was a homemaker and defendant's declared income was less than $20,000. Each party readily admitted that their expenses and purchases were covered by "other sources."

Plaintiff testified that defendant, as an oil-delivery truck driver, conspired with his employer to skim large corporate and institutional oil deliveries (billing for more oil than delivered). They would then sell the undelivered, excess oil to third parties. Plaintiff's written records entered into evidence show $42,260 in cash deposited in a dog biscuit box and $70,000 more in a shoe box. Plaintiff also testified that during this period other cash deposits were made in a P.N.B. safety-deposit box from which her husband later withdrew $51,000 towards the N.J. home purchase. She further testified that the defendant continued to work for his employer until the end of 1986, that he continued to derive substantial, unreported cash from this enterprise. Family and friends also testified that defendant stated that he was involved in an oil skimming scheme.

Notwithstanding their testimonial differences, the parties did agree on one point: That no inheritance, gift or income taxes were ever paid or ever declared on any of the above sums.

The court finds that the more than $325,000 spent by the parties between 1983 and 1987 for real estate, personalty & annual living expenses, represented a commingling of untaxed, undeclared cash, a portion of which was a parental gift, but far less than the $180,000 defendant asserts; and that at least $250,000 of the cash shared by the parties was the result of illegal activities; and that it is impossible to trace—or to even identifiably segregate—the funding source of the marital property purchased, initially or now remaining.

Historically, courts of equity have reflected the collective public conscience of what should and should not be done. Equity involves the obedience to dictates of morality and conscience. The morality of which equity speaks is that of society and not the judge's personal view of right and wrong. As the ultimate repository, the gatekeeper of that conscience and morality, equity's forum can never be used to promote or condone crime or clearly defined breaches of public morality.

Likewise, no court, be it equity or law, will enforce or entertain construction of a contract in a manner incompatible with the laws or public policies of the state. Nothing in our law indicates that marriage contracts should be interpreted or construed differently.

When the marriage contract is terminated by death or divorce, public policy as expressed in legislative enactment and amplified by judicial decision, seeks to protect as well those same marriage interests of the surviving or divorcing spouse. However, even the broadest of public policy umbrellas has coverage limits. In the context of this marriage contract, that limit has been reached in this court today.

The Legislature did not intend its judges to be tellers or its courtrooms counting houses for the division of tainted assets purchased with dirty money. The policy of this state is unambiguous in that regard: We do not reward wrongdoers! That policy is administered with equal vigor in civil as well as criminal proceedings.

To allow plaintiff to seek equity's aid in dividing marital assets acquired with illicit funds would substantially demean that policy and sully the judicial process. Courts cannot permit that to be done. Accordingly, this court concludes that a fair and common sense interpretation of the statutory purpose in permitting the division of "legally and beneficially acquired" property bars the equitable division of property obtained with illicit or illegal funds.

Even in the absence of such statutory direction, the result must be the same: equity will follow the common law precept that no one shall be allowed to benefit by his own wrongdoing, nor enrich himself as a result of his own criminal acts. For a court of equity can never be used to promote or condone crime or clearly defined breaches of public morality.

Therefore, subject to the terms of a stay hereinafter imposed, the parties for purposes of equitable distribution being in pari delicto will be left exactly where the court found them at the commencement of this litigation. [It] is every citizen's duty to uphold the law and as part of that duty to report any knowledge she or he may have of a crime committed or to be committed. In order to preserve public confidence in the integrity of the judiciary, a judge must be the ultimate exemplar of that good citizenship. Sworn testimony before [that] a crime has been committed—as in this case—requires the judge to make a prompt report to proper authority. That I have done. * * *

NOTES

1. *The* Highwayman's *Case.* In the *Highwaymen's Case,* perhaps the most famous unclean hands case, two bandits agreed to rob travellers and split the profits. When one of the partners refused to share the profits on the agreed basis, the other sued for an accounting. The Chancellor, after invoking the unclean hands doctrine and dismissing the case, fined plaintiff's solicitors for contempt. *See Everet v. Williams*, Ex. (1725), 9 L.Q.Rev. 197 (1893).

2. *Unclean Hands and Legal Claims.* Some courts apply the unclean hands defense to claims for legal relief. Consider *Makela v. Roach*, 142 Ill.App.3d 827, 492 N.E.2d 191, 96 Ill.Dec. 949 (1986), in which a woman consulted a lawyer about how to conceal assets from her creditors. Her husband's health was failing and she feared large medical bills. The lawyer advised her to transfer assets to her daughter. The lawyer failed to advise her that he held an unsatisfied $4,000 judgment against the daughter. The lawyer executed on the judgment. Afterwards, the daughter and her husband spent the remaining money on their own behalf. The woman then sued the lawyer for malpractice, and the court rejected her claim:

> Where a party voluntarily elects to follow advice intended to extricate herself from a questionable situation, she comes to this court with unclean hands and may not seek relief from her wrongful conduct through a legal malpractice action. We pass no judgment on the advice given by defendant, as our refusal to aid Mabel is a decision based upon her attempt to evade the law. A long and unbroken series of precedents establishes the rule that courts will not aid a fraudfeasor who invokes the court's jurisdiction to profit from his own fraud by recovering damages. The trial court, therefore, did not err in dismissing counts I and II of the amended complaint.

But see Zappa v. Automotive Precision Machinery, Inc., 205 Ga.App. 584, 423 S.E.2d 286 (Ga.App.1992)("[T]he doctrine of clean hands applies only to equitable rights related directly to the cause of action.")

PROBLEMS

1. *Reconsidering the* Highwayman's *Case.* In the *Highwayman's Case,* the court found that the parties were *in pari delicto* and decided to leave them right where it found them. In other words, the court left one robber in possession of a disproportionate share of the stolen proceeds. Was this a wise, just and equitable result? Is there anything else the court could have done that would have been preferable?

2. *Reconsidering the* Sheridan *Case.* Did the Court reach a just result in the *Sheridan* case? Is there anything else that the court could have done besides leaving the parties where it found them? What orders might the court have entered (besides the one that it did enter of making a proper report to authorities)?

3. *Ill-Gotten Gains and Child Support.* In *Sheridan,* the wife was given custody of the couple's thirteen year-old daughter and sought alimony, child support and counsel fees. At the time, neither party had much income. Prior to the divorce, plaintiff had worked but her husband did not. However, plaintiff had marginal job skills and little likelihood of substantial economic advancement. After the separation, defendant went to work but did not earn much. The court held that plaintiff was barred on equitable grounds from obtaining a percentage of the ill-gotten gains. As a result, defendant was left with the assets. Should plaintiff also be barred from obtaining child support from the loot? If you represent the plaintiff, how would you argue that the loot should be considered in determining defendant's child support obligation? If you represent defendant, how would you respond? How would you rule as a court? Should the court consider defendant's total assets, including the stolen money, in awarding child support?

4. *The Political Hack.* Plaintiff described himself as "a political hack employed in a make-work position doing virtually nothing in an unnecessary job." He openly admitted that he did not do any work, that he refused to do any, and that he had no intention of doing any. When a new administration took office, plaintiff was fired for political reasons. Based on *Elrod v. Burns,* 427 U.S. 347, 96 S.Ct. 2673, 49 L.Ed.2d 547 (1976), which held that the First Amendment prohibits a public employer from firing an employee on political grounds, plaintiff sought reinstatement with back pay. Should the court consider plaintiff's job performance in deciding whether to grant an injunction requiring reinstatement? In other words, does plaintiff's job performance, and his attitude towards his job, constitute unclean hands? Is his conduct sufficiently related to the issue before the court? *See Byron v. Clay,* 867 F.2d 1049 (7th Cir.1989).

The unclean hands doctrine has always been subject to exceptions which allow courts to grant relief notwithstanding the presence of "unclean hands." Consider the following case.

SEAGIRT REALTY CORP. V. CHAZANOF

13 N.Y.2d 282, 196 N.E.2d 254, 246 N.Y.S.2d 613 (1963).

BURKE, JUDGE.

This action, brought by plaintiff as the owner of real property, seeks, in effect, to remove a cloud on title. Defendant, the owner of record, conveyed the property to plaintiff in 1950. Plaintiff did not record this deed and it is now lost. The specific relief requested is a decree compelling the execution of a replacement deed. Although these findings of fact warrant the relief requested, the Appellate Division has dismissed the complaint on the theory of "unclean hands" because of a certain transaction concerning the property that occurred prior to that sued on here.

In 1934 Jacob Landau, the sole stockholder and concededly alter ego of plaintiff corporation, caused it to convey the subject property, together with other property, to his son, Alfred Landau, without consideration, and for the purpose of concealing it from his creditors. Alfred agreed to hold the property for his father's benefit. It also appears that Jacob Landau filed a petition in bankruptcy in 1945 in which he swore that he had no interest in real property. In 1950, Alfred, at his father's request, discharged his oral promise of 1934 by conveying the subject property to the defendant Chazanof, the son-in-law of Jacob Landau. This conveyance was also without consideration. The courts below have found that, simultaneously with the conveyance to him, defendant orally promised to convey to plaintiff, and did in fact execute and deliver a deed to plaintiff.

In view of the ground upon which the Appellate Division has reversed, it is important to note that any connection between defendant's promise to convey to plaintiff and the illegality of the conveyance to Alfred Landau in 1934 would be relevant only if plaintiff were suing on that promise. In such a case we would be called upon to apply the rule that the unclean hands doctrine bars only causes of action founded in illegality or immorality. This, in turn, would require an examination into motive and circumstances surrounding the conveyance to defendant, to which his promise to convey to plaintiff was incident.

This case, however, presents no such issue. Plaintiff is not seeking to enforce a contractual duty of defendant against which illegality could be argued, or to enforce an "inequitable" interest in real property, in bar of which unclean hands could be raised (as where the "equity" lay in a promise given in consideration of a fraudulent conveyance). However vulnerable to attack may have been defendant's promise to convey to plaintiff, and we express no opinion on this, that promise has been fully performed. The property has been conveyed to plaintiff, who now holds title, both legal and equitable. Defendant has no interest whatever in the property. It is established by the unanimous assent of authority that a voluntary reconveyance to the fraudulent grantor, even from the immediate fraudulent grantee, is effective as between the parties and is entitled to the protection of the courts in its enjoyment. Such incidental protection of ownership is typified in cases where a reconveyance to a fraudulent grantor subsequently required the assistance of the courts in replacing a lost deed.

It is suggested, nevertheless, that moral considerations of fundamental importance require a different result in this case. The short answer is that equity is not an avenger at large (2 POMEROY, EQUITY JURISPRUDENCE, § 399). Conceding that the relief sought in this case is of equitable origin the maxim must be applied only where the plaintiff has dealt unjustly in the very transaction of which he complains. It must also be remembered, as we are reminded by the late Professor Zechariah Chafee, that moral indignation against the plaintiff must operate, not in a vacuum, but in harmony with other important purposes and functions of the substantive law involved. As he criticized the application of the unclean hands doctrine in a situation similar to that here present, "This ethical attitude seems entirely out of place. What ought to count is the strong social policy in favor of making the land records furnish an accurate map of the ownership of all land in the community. Whatever A's old misdeeds, he is the lawful owner of this lot and the records ought to show this fact. The existing record falsely makes R owner. It may mislead scores of honest citizens people who have strong reasons for wishing to buy the lot, such as creditors of A, creditors of R, or lawyers drawing deeds of adjoining lots who are anxious to insert an accurate description. What is the sense of perpetuating an erroneous land record in order to penalize A for past misdeeds by causing him inconvenience? Better regard his dirty hands as washed during the lapse of twenty years rather than mess up the recording system." (CHAFEE, SOME PROBLEMS OF EQUITY, 21–22 (1950).)

We find this reasoning persuasive. When equitable relief is sought, not to enforce an executory obligation arising out of an illegal transaction, but to protect a status of legal ownership, wrongs done by Jacob Landau to creditors in respect of the property at some time prior to the acquisition of the title now in issue may not now be raised by this defendant to defeat otherwise available relief.

The judgment of the Appellate Division should be reversed and that of the Supreme Court reinstated, without costs.

DESMOND, CHIEF JUDGE (dissenting).

Plaintiff is being awarded a decree which will crown with final success a fraudulent transaction begun by its sole stockholder Jacob Landau in 1934 when he conveyed this same land to his son Alfred Landau, without consideration and in fraud of his creditors. The fraudulent transaction was carried a step further in 1945 when Jacob

Landau took bankruptcy proceedings but swore in the schedules that he had no real property. In 1950 son Alfred conveyed the property to son-in-law defendant Chazanof, again without consideration, and Chazanof simultaneously conveyed the land to Jacob Landau's corporation, plaintiff Seagirt Realty Corporation. The latter deed was never recorded but was lost and plaintiff now asks the court to require the son-in-law to deliver another deed. This a court of equity cannot do.

The judgment should be affirmed, with costs.

SCILEPPI, JUDGE (dissenting).

I cannot agree that the plaintiff is entitled to the relief sought herein. The majority is permitting this plaintiff corporation's president to invoke the aid of the court to bring to a successful conclusion that which he admits was a scheme to defraud his creditors. These conveyances were calculated steps in Landau's design to keep the property concealed from his creditors. It is well-established law that our courts will not grant relief to a plaintiff who does not come into equity with "clean hands." [In addition,] relief will not be granted by our courts to one who stands to profit by his own fraud, and the plaintiff in this action should not be permitted to do so.

It is suggested that equity is not an avenger at large and that it should not invoke the "clean hands" doctrine to separate transactions except where the plaintiff has dealt unjustly in the very transaction of which he complains. There can be little doubt that Landau dealt fraudulently and unjustly with his property. In the circumstances here this fraudulent conduct taints with the same fraud the very transaction of which he complains. To say that the conveyance from the son to the defendant was a separate transaction and, therefore, does not come within the "clean hands" doctrine is to overlook the realities of these family conveyances, all of which were initiated at the direction and for the benefit of Landau. Certainly, if plaintiff here were seeking a reconveyance of the property from the immediate transferee, there is no doubt that the relief would be denied. So, in this case, dealing as we are with an integral and necessary part of the fraudulent scheme, to grant the relief sought would be to "put a premium upon dishonorable conduct."

The judgment should be affirmed, with costs.

PROBLEMS

1. *Reconsidering* Seagirt. The rule applied in *Seagirt*, that the clean hands doctrine only applies when the plaintiff has acted unjustly in the very transaction of which he complains, is widely accepted. *See Pryor v. Pryor*, 263 Ga. 153, 429 S.E.2d 676 (1993). But did the court apply the rule properly in *Seagirt?* Consider *Dixon v. Murphy*, 259 Ga. 643, 385 S.E.2d 408 (1989), which involved similar facts. Dixon had previously declared bankruptcy, and

had failed to disclose her interest in twelve acres of land. Later, Dixon conveyed the land to Chapman who obtained a loan and then transferred the property to Dixon's son, Murphy. Dixon and Murphy assumed Chapman's loan and paid it. By prior agreement, Murphy was then supposed to convey the property back to Dixon. Murphy refused and Dixon sued to have the original deed to Chapman set aside. In *Dixon*, the Georgia Supreme Court concluded that Dixon's suit was barred by the doctrine of unclean hands. Was *Dixon* correctly decided? Is *Dixon's* holding preferable to *Seagirt's*?

2. Seagirt *and the Accuracy of Land Records.* In *Seagirt*, was the court correct in concluding that, if the court left the parties where it found them, the land records would have been inaccurate? In other words, had the court not intervened, who would have held legal title to the property? Who would have held "equitable" title (if a court of equity was unable to give relief)? If plaintiff did not hold either legal or equitable title, then in what respect were the land records inaccurate?

3. Seagirt *and the Protection of Defrauded Creditors.* As a condition of granting relief, could the court have required Seagirt Realty Corporation to pay off the defrauded creditors? Does a court of equity possess such power? Might the court have taken other steps to protect the creditors? If so, what?

4. *The Brothers and the Jointly Held Property.* Two brothers jointly owned real estate. One brother sued the other for partition of the land and for an accounting. The other brother asserted unclean hands noting that the plaintiff brother had embezzled money from a bank account that received income from the property and from which certain expenses of the property were paid. Is the plaintiff's brother's conduct sufficiently related to the subject matter of the litigation so that it is appropriate to apply the clean hands doctrine to the request for partition? Should it also bar the accounting? If the court decides to make the partition and accounting, should it credit the defendant brother for the amount that was embezzled? *See Goldberg v. Goldberg*, 173 A.D.2d 679, 570 N.Y.S.2d 333 (Sup. Ct., App.Div.1991).

5. *The Diocese and Unclean Hands.* A Roman Catholic Diocese attempted to remove trustees who were administering foundation funds (established to provide scholarships to young men and women desirous of becoming nuns or priests) claiming that they had engaged in self-dealing and commingling of funds. The trustees tried to block the Diocese's petition based on the doctrine of unclean hands. In the trial court, the trustees showed that the Diocese had not awarded a single scholarship, and in fact had used the funds for other purposes without regard for the settlor's intent. If you represent the Diocese, how would you try to avoid the clean hands doctrine? What response might the trustees make? Should the court consider the interest of innocent third parties? How should the court rule? *See In re Francis Edward McGillick Foundation*, 406 Pa.Super. 249, 594 A.2d 322 (1991).

6. *Illegal Aliens and Backpay.* A company employed undocumented alien workers, a number of whom signed union authorization cards

prompting a representation election which the union ultimately won. After the election, the employer reported the aliens to the Immigration and Naturalization Service (INS) which immediately deported them from the United States. The NLRB concluded that the firms had engaged in unfair labor practices prohibited by the National Labor Relations Act. The Board ordered the company to cease and desist. In addition, it ordered the company to give the aliens the "conventional remedy of reinstatement with backpay." The Court of Appeals, believing that the workers would not be able to return to work because of their undocumented status, awarded them six months backpay. Should the Board and the court have considered the employees status as illegal aliens in deciding whether to grant relief? If you represent the company, what would you argue on its behalf? What would you argue on behalf of the undocumented workers? *See Sure–Tan, Inc. v. NLRB*, 467 U.S. 883, 104 S.Ct. 2803, 81 L.Ed.2d 732 (1984).

AMERICAN UNIVERSITY V. WOOD

294 Ill. 186, 128 N.E. 330 (1920).

FARMER, J.

Plaintiff, the American University, operates a school of chiropractic medicine that offers courses primarily by correspondence. The school has a student body of approximately 2,500 to 3,000 students. Defendant Wood worked from American from 1913 to 1916 when he was fired. In 1917, defendant the Chicago University of American Sciences was incorporated, with D.E. Wood faculty head, after which numerous communications were sent by him to complainant's students, some of them addressed "to my old students," advising them of the superior facilities of the Chicago University of American Sciences for teaching chiropractic, the plain purpose of which was to secure them as students for the new Chicago University. In some of the communications students were advised to pay no more on their contract of enrollment with complainant; that complainant had violated its contract with them by depriving them of his (Wood's) services throughout their course. He spoke of the stockholders of complainant as "money-grabbing stockholders," and offered to give the students a better course of instruction for less money if they would come with him. Numerous communications were sent out to complainant's students by Wood, addressed "Dear Student," belittling complainant and its instructor in chiropractic, and advising them of the advantages of becoming a student of Wood because of his abilities, and promising to give them good service and satisfaction, or their instruction would not cost them anything. The communications were numerous, some of them lengthy, and the foregoing is but a brief outline of a few of them.

It is contended that the bill cannot be maintained because complainant did not come into a court of equity with clean hands. [T]he proof showed it was conducting its business and enterprise in a fraudulent manner. It was on this ground that the Appellate Court dismissed the bill.

American's advertising was filled with falsities. In some of its advertising it stated the income of some of its graduates was. One of "our graduates" said to have made in cash in the year 1912, $11,077.50, while the proof shows it had no graduates then, and that it had no knowledge of the income of any of its graduates. There can be no doubt the advertising was well calculated to make the impression that the American University was an educational institution with various departments, one of which was the department of chiropractic. The impression the skillful wording of the catalogue would be that the university extension or home study course of that department was for the benefit of those who had not the means or did not wish to incur the expense of attending the university to receive personal instruction, but that such instruction was given to those who desired it. The fact is complainant gave instructions in no other way than by correspondence.

There are many other things, which might be referred to, to show that complainant was practicing fraud and deception in the conduct of its business; but American insists that its business of teaching chiropractic by correspondence is lawful; that its methods of conducting and managing its business are immaterial, so far as defendants are concerned, and should not be considered as a bar to relief from the malicious and unlawful acts of defendants, committed for the purpose of destroying complainant's business; also that "puffing" and "exaggerations" in its advertising do not constitute fraud or unclean hands. There can be no dispute that defendants were conducting a campaign against complainant for the purpose of destroying or injuring its business. The Chicago University was incorporated almost immediately after Wood's discharge by complainant, for the purpose of teaching chiropractic by correspondence. Wood was made its chancellor, and complainant's lists of patrons were used by him and his university in the very vigorous and malicious campaign conducted to injure complainant and themselves profit by complainant's destruction. Nothing in the attitude and conduct of defendants toward complainant commends them to the consideration of a court of equity, and their advertising methods were no less objectionable and misleading than those of complainant. In fact, Dr. Wood, whose picture was on some of the Chicago University publications, and, following his name, LL.B., D.M.T., Opt. D., D.O., M.D., D.C., was as much responsible for the character of complainant's advertising and the method of conducting its business while he was its president as any one else, and has carried similar methods into the conduct of defendants' business.

The maxim that he who comes into a court of equity must come with clean hands was never intended to bar every one guilty of wrongful conduct from relief in a court of equity, and as a general rule it is required that the wrongdoing or fraud of the complainant, to bar him from relief on the ground that he comes with unclean hands, must be connected with the subject of the litigation, and have some relation to the rights of the parties arising out of the transaction. That rule is not applicable to the facts in this record. It is true the fraud and wrongdoing of complainant did not affect the private rights of defendants, and afforded no justification in morals for their seeking to profit by exposing them, but on the ground of the public interest and policy we do not think complainant's grievance is of a character to be redressed in a court of equity. The misrepresentations of complainant in the conduct of its business affected the public, and it would seem a strange thing if a court of conscience should be required to protect a suitor in the commission of a fraud upon the public.

A court of equity is a court of conscience, and will exercise its extraordinary powers only to enforce the requirements of conscience. It is no part of its function to aid a litigant in the promotion of a fraud upon the public. To our minds the principle seems so sound that we think it should be applied here, even if it has not been previously applied. On that ground we think the judgment of the Appellate Court was right, and it is affirmed.

Judgment affirmed.

PROBLEMS

1. *Reconsidering* American University. Does *American University's* holding make sense? What is the practical result of the Court's decision? Before the litigation, both plaintiff and defendant were perpetuating frauds on the public. Does this decision stop either from doing so? On the contrary, are both of them free to continue their fraudulent conduct? What else might the Court have done? Did the Court have the power to order both parties to cease and desist from their fraudulent activities?

2. *The Fig Syrup Case.* Consider *Clinton E. Worden & Co. v. California Fig Syrup Co.*, 187 U.S. 516, 23 S.Ct. 161, 47 L.Ed. 282 (1903), in which defendants sold a product that imitated plaintiffs "with the design and intent of deceiving purchasers and inducing them to buy defendant's preparation instead of the complainant's." However, the evidence revealed that, even though plaintiff's product was marketed as a "fig syrup," it contained "only a very small percentage of fig juice." The laxative ingredient in it was senna. While fig fruit has some laxative properties arising from the seeds and skin, fig syrup is no more a laxative than any other fruit syrup. In fact, it was admitted that the use of figs was found to be deleterious, and their use, as a substantial or material ingredient, was abandoned. Nevertheless, the company marketed its product as "Syrup of Figs. The California Liquid Fruit Remedy, Gentle and Effective." How should a court handle plaintiff's request for injunctive relief?

NOTE: A FINAL WORD ON UNCLEAN HANDS

"Unclean hands" includes all misconduct and wrongdoing that is sufficiently related to the plaintiff's claim. Almost any conduct considered to be unfair, unethical or improper—including, of course, the illegal—can be raised as a bar against equitable relief. Courts can also raise the issue, *sua sponte*. In addition to the nexus ("relatedness") requirement, the misconduct must also be serious enough to justify withholding an equitable remedy which would otherwise be available, and relegating plaintiff instead to her legal remedies.

2. UNCONSCIONABILITY

Since equity developed as a "court of conscience," courts feel free to deny equitable relief on the grounds of conscience.

CAMPBELL SOUP CO. V. WENTZ

172 F.2d 80 (3d Cir.1948).

GOODRICH, CIRCUIT JUDGE.

These are appeals from judgments of the District Court denying equitable relief to the buyer under a contract for the sale of carrots. The transactions which raise the issues may be briefly summarized. On June 21, 1947, Campbell Soup Company (Campbell), a New Jersey corporation, entered into a written contract with George B. Wentz and Harry T. Wentz, who are Pennsylvania farmers, for delivery by the Wentzes to Campbell of all the Chantenay red cored carrots to be grown on fifteen acres of the Wentz farm during the 1947 season. The contract provides, however, for delivery of the carrots at the Campbell plant in Camden, New Jersey. The prices specified in the contract ranged from $23 to $30 per ton according to the time of delivery. The contract price for January, 1948 was $30 a ton.

The Wentzes harvested approximately 100 tons of carrots from the fifteen acres covered by the contract. Early in January, 1948, they told a Campbell representative that they would not deliver their carrots at the contract price. The market price at that time was at least $90 per ton, and Chantenay red cored carrots were virtually unobtainable. The Wentzes then sold approximately 62 tons of their carrots to the defendant Lojeski, a neighboring farmer. Lojeski resold about 58 tons on the open market, approximately half to Campbell and the balance to other purchasers. On January 9, 1948, Campbell, suspecting that Lojeski was selling it "contract carrots," refused to purchase any more, and instituted these suits against the Wentz brothers and Lojeski to enjoin further sale of the contract carrots to others, and to compel specific performance of the contract. The trial court denied equitable relief.

On the question of adequacy of the legal remedy the case is one appropriate for specific performance. At the time of the trial it was "virtually impossible to obtain Chantenay carrots in the open market." This Chantenay carrot is one which the plaintiff uses in large quantities, furnishing the seed to the growers with whom it makes contracts.

We affirm because the contract is too hard a bargain and too one-sided an agreement to entitle the plaintiff to relief in a court of conscience. For each individual grower the agreement is made by filling in names and quantity and price on a printed form furnished by the buyer. This form has quite obviously been drawn by skillful draftsmen with the buyer's interests in mind.

Paragraph 2 provides for the manner of delivery. Carrots are to have their stalks cut off and be in clean sanitary bags or other containers approved by Campbell. This paragraph concludes with a statement that Campbell's determination of conformance with specifications shall be conclusive.

The defendants attack this provision as unconscionable. We do not think that it is, standing by itself. We think that the provision is comparable to the promise to perform to the satisfaction of another and that Campbell would be held liable if it refused carrots which did in fact conform to the specifications.

The next paragraph allows Campbell to refuse carrots in excess of twelve tons to the acre. The next contains a covenant by the grower that he will not sell carrots to anyone else except the carrots rejected by Campbell nor will he permit anyone else to grow carrots on his land. Paragraph 10 provides liquidated damages to the extent of $50 per acre for any breach by the grower. There is no provision for liquidated or any other damages for breach of contract by Campbell.

The provision of the contract which we think is the hardest is paragraph 9, set out in the margin.[11] It will be noted that Campbell is excused from accepting carrots under certain circumstances. But even under such circumstances the grower, while he cannot say Campbell is liable for failure to take the carrots, is not permitted to sell them elsewhere unless Campbell agrees. This is the kind of provision which the late Francis H. Bohlen would call "carrying a good joke too far." What the

[11] "Grower shall not be obligated to deliver any Carrots which he is unable to harvest or deliver, nor shall Campbell be obligated to receive or pay for any Carrots which it is unable to inspect, grade, receive, handle, use or pack at or ship in processed form from its plants in Camden (1) because of any circumstance beyond the control of Grower or Campbell, as the case may be, or (2) because of any labor disturbance, work stoppage, slow-down, or strike involving any of Campbell's employees. Campbell shall not be liable for any delay in receiving Carrots due to any of the above contingencies. During periods when Campbell is unable to receive Grower's Carrots, Grower may with Campbell's written consent, dispose of his Carrots elsewhere. Grower may not, however, sell or otherwise dispose of any Carrots which he is unable to deliver to Campbell."

grower may do with his product under the circumstances set out is not clear. He has covenanted not to store it anywhere except on his own farm and also not to sell to anybody else.

We are not suggesting that the contract is illegal. Nor are we suggesting any excuse for the grower in this case who has deliberately broken an agreement entered into with Campbell. We do think, however, that a party who has offered and succeeded in getting an agreement as tough as this one is, should not come to a chancellor and ask court help in the enforcement of its terms. That equity does not enforce unconscionable bargains is too well established to require elaborate citation.

The judgments will be affirmed.

NOTES

1. *Calculating Damages.* The court denied Campbell equitable relief, but allowed it to recover damages. Ordinarily, there will be little difference between expectation damages and specific performance. Wentz can sell the carrots to another, but must pay the difference between the market price and the contract price to Campbell. U.C.C. § 2–713. If the market price is about $90/ton, that means Wentz collects $90/ton, but must pay Campbell $60/ton, netting $30 per ton—the same amount it would receive if specific performance was ordered. Once incidental and other damages are included, the result might be even worse for Wentz. Here, the liquidated damages clause limited Campbell's recovery to $50 per acre ($750).

2. *The UCC and Unconscionability.* You probably encountered unconscionability when studying contracts. Is it the same doctrine that the court applied here? Consider the provisions of the Uniform Commercial Code (UCC):

> (1) If a court as a matter of law finds the contract or any term of the contract to have been unconscionable at the time it was made the court may refuse to enforce the contract, or it may enforce the remainder of the contract without the unconscionable term, or it may so limit the application of any unconscionable terms as to avoid any unconscionable result.
>
> (2) [If] any term [may] be unconscionable [the] parties shall be afforded a reasonable opportunity to present evidence as to its commercial setting, purpose and effect to aid the court in making the determination. U.C.C. § 2–302 (May 2001 proposed revision).

Unconscionable is not defined, though the comments offer some clarification: "The principle is one of the prevention of oppression and unfair surprise (Cf. Campbell Soup Co. v. Wentz) and not of disturbance of allocation of risks because of superior bargaining power." U.C.C. § 2–302 comment 1.

PROBLEMS

1. *Reconsidering* Campbell Soup. Did the Court in *Campbell* pursue any of the alternative remedies mentioned in the UCC? Would any of the UCC alternatives produce a better result? Is note 1 easier to answer under the UCC?

2. *Evaluating Unconscionability.* Were the terms to which the court objected really unconscionable, either singly or in combination? Consider the following suggestions as to the purpose of each provision:

- Either party can clean the carrots, at some cost (in time, water, equipment). It might be easier to clean them before the dirt dries and will certainly be cheaper to transport them without the extra weight of the dirt. The price can be adjusted in favor of the cleaning party.

- Twelve tons per acre might be the maximum yield, unless the farmer overplants (producing carrots with less nutritional value) or leaves the carrots in the ground too long (producing tougher, less flavorful carrots). Wentz produced less than 7 tons per acre.

- Prohibiting the farmer from planting carrots on other parts of the land eliminates confusion regarding which carrots belonged to Campbell and which belonged to Wentz, as might arise if one field proved more productive than another. Wentz could use the land for other crops.

- Did the liquidated damages clause actually favor Campbell in this case? How much will Campbell collect under it? Remember, it specifies damages per acre, not per ton. Did Wentz need a corresponding liquidated damages clause? What will Wentz lose if Campbell breaches? Will that loss be hard to quantify?

- Did the escape clause give Campbell more power than impracticability would allow under the law? Does a clause that embodies, or even slightly expands, the power to react to unforeseen contingencies offend the conscience? Is the problem that Wentz cannot sell to others without Campbell's permission? If Campbell does not want the carrots, would it withhold permission? Might withholding permission be a breach of good faith?

3. *The Purpose of the UCC Provisions.* If unconscionability was raised as a defense, the parties could present the issue to the judge for her consideration. Is there any indication that the judge gave any consideration to the purpose of these provisions? Might the judge have exercised equitable discretion on this issue without the benefit of briefing?

3. LACHES

A third defense that can be used to defeat an equitable claim is the defense of "laches," which is associated with the maxim: "Equity aids the vigilant." This defense is applied today in many different types of cases, but particularly in tort and contract cases. Broadly defined, laches is any unreasonable delay by the plaintiff in instituting or prosecuting an action under circumstances where the delay causes prejudice to the defendant. *See e.g.*, Restatement Second of Torts § 939 (1977).

CITY OF EUSTIS V. FIRSTER

113 So.2d 260 (Fla.App.1959).

LUCKIE, CHARLES A., ASSOCIATE JUDGE.

The appeal is from a mandatory injunction requiring the City of Eustis, Florida, to remove certain piers, docks, and boathouses owned or maintained by the city.

In Florida the right of an upland owner to an unobstructed view of adjoining waters has been recognized as a riparian right. Thus the question in the present case concerns an encroachment by appellant's pier and boathouses on appellee's riparian right to an unobstructed view over the waters of Lake Eustis and, to a lesser extent, to his riparian right of access to those waters.

The dock and boathouses were built in 1921. These boathouses have been leased from time to time to various individuals, and the city receives the proceeds from such leases. The city has from time to time necessarily expended funds in the maintenance of the structures, there being evidence that approximately $3,000 was expended for general repairs from 1954 through 1956; and appellee testified that in 1954 the city built an additional encroaching boathouse. In addition the lessees of the individual boathouses have been required to maintain them. The record discloses the names of ten lessees of the boathouses, none of whom were made parties to this suit, and further shows that these lessees reside in the cities of Eustis, Mount Dora, and Tavares. Appellee testified that in 1953 or 1954 he saw a notice in the paper advertising that new leases were being made on the boathouses and that the city started making leases to various parties.

The appellee acquired title to his lots on September 7, 1946; and this suit was filed August 27, 1956, approximately ten years after his acquisition of title. The appellee bought his lots sight unseen at a time when the structures now complained of had existed for 25 years. After appellee purchased his lots he became aware that the dock and boathouses encroached to some extent on his riparian right to an unobstructed view and to a lesser degree on his right of access to the lake, and he was aware of these encroachments at the time he built the bulkhead in 1947.

The application of the doctrine of laches depends upon the circumstances of each particular case. It is the doctrine of stale demands. The test of laches is whether there has been a delay which has resulted in the injury, embarrassment, or disadvantage of any person, but particularly the persons against whom relief is sought. In the present case the appellee brought his suit to overthrow rights long since accrued to the appellant and to third persons almost ten years after he became aware of the circumstances. He bought his property sight unseen when slight investigation could have disclosed the encroachments to the appurtenant riparian rights, of which encroachments he now complains. Through long years since appellee acquired his title, the structures have been maintained by the appellant city and city funds expended for repairs and for building an additional boathouse. Third persons not joined herein have acquired rights in individual boathouses, by virtue of leases obtained, with appellee's knowledge, since he acquired title, and also by virtue of their repairs and maintenance of the same. The remedy of a mandatory injunction for removal of encroachments is a drastic one and should be granted only cautiously and sparingly, depending in each controversy upon circumstances peculiar to it. In the present case the injunction requiring removal of the encroachments necessarily infringes upon rights long since accrued to the appellant and is accompanied by great mischief done to the rights of third persons. Under the circumstances the defense of laches is shown and the court should not have granted the mandatory injunction as it did.

Reversed.

PROBLEM: MORE ON THE BUILDING LOT CONTROVERSY

Now, let's think about how the concept of laches might apply to the controversy involving the building lot. Can it be argued that either party was guilty of laches? Should the laches doctrine prevent Harlow from obtaining the requested relief?

NAHN V. SOFFER

824 S.W.2d 442 (Mo.App.1991).

AHRENS, JUDGE.

Respondents Nahns owned 1.26 undeveloped acres near Telegraph Road in St. Louis County. On June 28, 1986, Soffer and respondents entered into a one-year option contract for the sale of the property. On June 10, 1987, Soffer notified respondents he was exercising the option subject to rezoning as provided by the option contract. Nahns' attorney replied that, because the transaction had not been closed by June 28,

1987, the option had expired and Soffer had "no further contractual rights in this matter."

At some point, Soffer assigned his interest in the property to Ten–Eighteen, a "shell corporation" Soffer uses to shelter his identity. Thereafter, on February 16, 1988, Ten–Eighteen entered into an option contract with Shell Oil for the sale of the Nahns' property. Shell Oil filed a petition for rezoning of the property on June 8, 1988.

In a November 28, 1988, letter to Soffer, the Nahns denied Soffer had any legal or equitable interest in the property, and demanded Soffer "record an appropriate affidavit or quit claim deed renouncing any interest in the property." Shell Oil withdrew its petition for rezoning in February, 1989. In a February 2, 1989 letter, Soffer's attorney notified the Nahns that Soffer would close the transaction on March 16, 1989.

On March 24, 1989, the Nahns filed this quiet title action seeking an order declaring them to be "fee simple absolute owners" of the property, and declaring that neither Soffer or Ten–Eighteen "has any right, title or interest" in the property. Soffer and Ten–Eighteen filed a counterclaim for specific performance of the sale contract. In their reply to the counterclaim, the Nahns asserted, inter alia, that appellants' claim was "barred by breach of contract and by laches." The trial court entered judgment in favor of the Nahns on their petition to quiet title, and against Soffer and Ten–Eighteen on the counterclaim for specific performance.

Appellants contend that "Soffer timely exercised his option to purchase the subject property, creating a binding bilateral contract, which he was at all times ready, willing, and able to perform, but the Nahns repudiated Soffer's rights under the option and refused to convey the subject property."

The option contract permitted Soffer to void the "option or the contract arising by reason of the acceptance of this option" if he was "unable to obtain an ordinance or permit from the proper authorities to conduct second party's or his assign's business upon said premises." Soffer presented evidence that the process to obtain approval of a zoning request in St. Louis County can take more than a year. Thus, the Nahns' repudiated the contract when they notified Soffer in July, 1987 that he had no further rights in the contract because he had not closed by June 28, 1987,—the expiration date of the option.

Specific performance "is purely an equitable remedy" which "is invoked primarily that complete justice may be done between the parties, and courts of equity will not decree specific performance where it will result in injustice." *Kopp v. Franks*, 792 S.W.2d 413, 419 (Mo.App.1990). [S]pecific performance "is not a matter of right but is a remedy applied by courts of equity, depending upon the facts in the particular case; and the trial court has judicial discretion within the established doctrines and principles of equity to award or withhold the remedy."

"The invocation of laches requires that a party with the knowledge of facts giving rise to its rights unreasonably delays asserting them for an excessive period of time and the other party suffers legal detriment therefrom." *Scheble v. Missouri Clean Water Comm'n*, 734 S.W.2d 541, 560 (Mo.App.1987). In determining whether the doctrine of laches applies in a particular case, an examination is made of "the length of delay, the reasons therefor, how the delay affected the other party, and the overall fairness in permitting the assertion of the claim."

In the present case, twenty-one months passed from the time Soffer exercised the option to the date scheduled for closing. Contrary to appellants' assertions, the delay was not justified by Nahns' repudiation of the contract and the time required to seek zoning changes. While the Nahns' repudiation excused appellants' further performance under the contract, it did not excuse appellants' delay in asserting a claim for specific performance. Appellants' evidence indicated that in St. Louis County the processing of a zoning petition can take over a year; however, there was no evidence the process requires twenty-one months to complete. Further, the evidence established that a petition to rezone the property was not filed until June 8, 1988—nearly one year after Soffer exercised the option.

From the time the option contract was executed, the property's value increased from $200,000 to between $300,000 and $350,000. Moreover, Soffer failed to pay the real estate taxes on the property for 1986 and all subsequent years as required by the option contract. Appellants argue the Nahns' repudiation excused them from performing that condition. For the purpose of determining the applicability of laches, however, Soffer's failure to pay those taxes, together with the appreciation in the property's value supports a determination that respondents were adversely affected by appellants' unreasonable delay in asserting their claim.

The length of appellants' delay, the lack of justification therefor, and the effect of the delay on respondents, support a determination that it would be unfair to permit appellants to assert their claim for specific performance. The doctrine of laches barred appellants' claim.

Thus, the trial court did not abuse its discretion in denying appellants' counterclaim for specific performance. The evidence established respondents' title to the property is good as against appellants. Therefore, the trial court did not err in quieting title to the property in the Nahns. The trial court's judgment is affirmed.

PROBLEMS

1. *Does the Mere Passage of Time Constitute Laches?* In the 1970s, defendant obtained an easement for the installation of electrical towers, poles and wires across plaintiff Billie McComb's property. In 1987, defendant installed additional, larger, equipment across McComb's property. McCombs complained that the additional installation caused harmful electromagnetic fields (EMFs) to be emitted on the property for the first time thereby imposing new and additional burdens on the plaintiff's servient estate. However, Ms. McComb failed to sue until 1994. Since the installation constituted a "continuing trespass," it was not barred by the statute of limitations. In justification of the delay, McCombs contended that, prior to 1992, there was no scientific proof of the fact that EMFs posed a health risk to people who live in close proximity to an electrical source. In 1992, a scientific study conclusively demonstrated the link. Suppose that defendant fails to present evidence of prejudice from McComb's delay in filing suit. Should the passage of time, by itself, prevent McCombs from obtaining injunctive relief against the second installation? What arguments can be made on McComb's behalf? How might defendant respond to those arguments?

2. *The West Coast Lumber Case.* Plaintiffs and West Coast Lumber Sales, which is not a party to this action, had a contract whereby West Coast would cut plaintiffs' logs at plaintiffs' site for orders pre-sold by West Coast and approved by plaintiffs. In May 1980, West Coast removed 285,000 board feet of lumber from plaintiffs' site without plaintiffs' approval. In September 1980, plaintiffs sued West Coast seeking only money damages for conversion of the lumber. Plaintiffs did not seek replevin, or an injunction to prevent the sale of the lumber, or a constructive trust on the proceeds.

In February 1981, while the litigation between plaintiffs and West Coast was pending, Commercial Credit, defendant in this action, opened a line of credit for West Coast which was secured by inventory and accounts. West Coast's attorney advised defendant of the pending litigation between plaintiffs and West Coast, but the attorney advised defendant that the existence of the litigation did not prevent defendant from making a loan to West Coast so long as plaintiffs were making no claim to the collateral on which defendant was relying in making the loan. In June 1982, plaintiffs won a judgment for $192,011.17 against West Coast for conversion. Shortly thereafter, West Coast filed a petition for bankruptcy.

Under the terms of the accounts receivable contract between West Coast and defendant, all money received by West Coast was turned over to defendant; defendant would then make fresh advances. During the one and one-half years that the contract was in operation, defendant loaned West Coast approximately $2,000,000 more than it received back. Defendant declared West Coast in default in July 1982.

During the pendency of the bankruptcy proceeding, plaintiffs learned that defendant claimed a security interest in all of West Coast's inventory, including the converted lumber and the money generated from the sales of the converted lumber. In March 1983, plaintiffs filed this action asserting a claim against the proceeds West Coast received from the sale of the converted lumber which, plaintiffs asserted, defendant received as part of the revolving credit arrangement with West Coast.

Suppose that you represent defendant. Can you argue that plaintiff's claim is barred by laches? How? If you represent plaintiff, how would you respond to these arguments? *See Mattson v. Commercial Credit Business Loans, Inc.*, 301 Or. 407, 723 P.2d 996 (In Banc, 1986).

STONE V. WILLIAMS

873 F.2d 620 (2d Cir.1989).

CARDAMONE, CIRCUIT JUDGE:

This dispute arises over copyright renewal proceeds for 60 published and copyrighted songs written or performed by country and western singer Hank Williams (Williams, Sr.) who died intestate on January 1, 1953 at the age of 29. During his lifetime the well-known singer and composer wrote such popular hits as "Your Cheatin' Heart" and "Hey Good Lookin." We set forth the facts briefly in chronological order.

Appellant Stone was born on January 6, 1953 in Alabama, five days after Williams, Sr. died. While Ms. Stone's biological mother, Bobbie Jett, was pregnant with her in October of 1952, she and Williams, Sr. executed an agreement under which he acknowledged that he might be the father of appellant, but specifically did not admit paternity. The agreement further provided that Williams, Sr. pay Bobbie Jett for Ms. Stone's support, and placed the infant's custody until age 2 in Lillian Williams Stone, mother of Williams, Sr. Pursuant to its terms, Lillian Stone adopted plaintiff. Until her death in 1955 Mrs. Stone cared for appellant. At that point, [Stone] became a ward of the State of Alabama, and at age three in 1956 a foster child of the Deupree family. The Deuprees adopted her in 1959.

Williams, Sr. had a son, Hank Williams, Jr. The assignment of Hank Williams, Jr.'s copyright interests in his father's music generated litigation in 1967 and 1968 in the Circuit Court of Montgomery County, Alabama. That court appointed a guardian ad litem, attorney Drayton Hamilton, to ascertain any unknown potential heirs to the Williams' estate and to represent their interests. After investigating, Hamilton concluded that the only such person was appellant Stone. Unbeknownst to Ms. Stone, her adoptive family, the Deuprees, had asked Hamilton to leave her out of the 1967 proceedings, because they thought it unlikely that she would win and were worried that their then 14 year-old daughter would be subjected to embarrassing publicity because of her status as the illegitimate child of a famous country western singer. Nonetheless,

Hamilton zealously litigated Ms. Stone's interests, but to no avail. The Alabama court determined that Hank Williams, Jr. was the sole heir of his father, and further held that appellant, as a natural child who had been adopted by another family, had no rights in any proceeds from the Williams, Sr.'s songs or their renewal rights.

In late 1973, shortly before appellant's 21st birthday, Mrs. Deupree told her of the rumors regarding the identity of her natural father, but added that everything had been decided against her. This disclosure was necessary because, upon turning age 21, Ms. Stone was entitled to a small inheritance from Williams, Sr.'s mother, Lillian Stone. The Deuprees were concerned that appellant might encounter reporters while claiming the inheritance and wanted to arm her with knowledge. After picking up the inheritance check (about $3,800) at the Mobile County Courthouse, Ms. Stone went to a library and read a biography on Williams, Sr., entitled Sing a Sad Song, written by Roger Williams. This book mentioned the possibility that Williams, Sr. had fathered an illegitimate daughter, and the author speculated on the child's entitlement to a renewal interest in his songs. Ms. Stone surmised that she might be that daughter.

In the following years, appellant asked the Deuprees about her background and talked to some attorney acquaintances, but did little else to ascertain her connection to Williams. The record, including appellant's deposition, suggests that her feelings about Williams' parentage were ambivalent.

Her attitude crystallized in 1980 when she received a telephone call from her adoptive father, George Deupree. Evidently alluding to his decision not to pursue Ms. Stone's rights in the 1967–68 lawsuits, Deupree told her that he had undergone a change of heart after seeing Hank Williams, Jr. on a television show. Deupree has since died, but appellant related the conversation in her deposition: "I want to ask you if you would like to find out if Hank Williams is your father. He said think about it. And he said I will help you in any way that I can. And he said I think I was wrong in withholding information from you and not discussing it. And I will do everything I can to help you."

Following this call, Ms. Stone stepped up her efforts to learn about her relationship to Williams, Sr. She looked up newspaper articles about him, and sought out his relatives and those of her natural mother, Bobbie Jett, who had also since died. She met with attorney Hamilton, her former guardian ad litem, and discussed with him the 1952 custody and support agreement between Bobbie Jett and Williams, Sr., and obtained the records from the 1967 and 1968 Circuit Court proceedings. But Ms. Stone did not examine those documents until after she met attorney Keith Adkinson (who later became her husband) in 1984.

Appellant filed the original declaratory judgment complaint in this action on September 12, 1985 which contains two claims. The first claim against all the defendants arises under the Copyright Acts of 1909 and 1976 and seeks a number of declarations, including that Ms. Stone is the natural daughter of Williams, Sr., and as such is entitled to a proportionate share of the renewal rights from his songs. The district court dismissed her complaint based on the doctrine of laches and did not reach the other issues.

Historically, laches developed as an equitable defense based on the Latin maxim *vigilantibus non dormientibus aequitas subvenit* (equity aids the vigilant, not those who sleep on their rights). In contrast to a statute of limitations that provides a time bar within which suit must be instituted, laches asks whether the plaintiff in asserting her rights was guilty of unreasonable delay that prejudiced the defendants. *See, e.g., Gardner v. Panama Railroad Co.*, 342 U.S. 29, 31 (1951). The answers to these questions are to be drawn from the equitable circumstances peculiar to each case.

Although laches promotes many of the same goals as a statute of limitations, the doctrine is more flexible and requires an assessment of the facts of each case—it is the reasonableness of the delay rather than the number of years that elapse which is the focus of inquiry. In holding that Ms. Stone unreasonably delayed in bringing this action to have her rights declared, the district court focused on the years 1974–85, beginning with Mrs. Deupree's conversation with appellant regarding the inheritance, and ending with the filing of the complaint that initiated the instant case.

In our view, the delay for the period from 1974 to 1980 may well have been entirely excusable under the circumstances. First, her relationship with the Deuprees is by all indications the paradigm of a successful adoption. Thus, it is not surprising that loyalty and gratitude to Mr. and Mrs. Deupree, whom she considered her real parents, gave her pause at doing anything that might hurt their feelings. For this reason, George Deupree's telephone call to Ms. Stone is significant. Only after he called in 1980 could appellant be sure that investigating her natural parentage would not damage the only family bonds she knew. Second, Ms. Stone's embarrassment at asserting her relationship to Williams, Sr. is also understandable, because his notoriety would have made publicity almost impossible for her to avoid. This is substantiated by the extensive press coverage of the 1967 and 1968 court proceedings.

Third, only in recent years have courts and the general public come to recognize that children born of unmarried parents should not be penalized by being accorded a status for which they are not to blame. In the 1967 and 1968 proceedings, attorney Hamilton argued on Ms. Stone's behalf that discriminating against illegitimate children violated the

Federal Constitution. Unfortunately for appellant, Hamilton was before his time; the case that would remove much of the stigma associated with illegitimacy was then pending before the Supreme Court, but not decided until after appellant's rights had been adjudicated. *See Levy v. Louisiana*, 391 U.S. 68, 72 (1968).

But even though Ms. Stone might arguably be excused for the reasons just stated from filing suit until 1980, there is simply no plausible explanation for delay in filing the instant complaint until September 1985, after five more years had passed. Appellant's filial loyalty is admirable, and one can sympathize with her feelings of embarrassment and trepidation attendant upon widespread personal publicity. But these reasons for delay cannot last forever for purposes of laches. A point arrives when a plaintiff must either assert her rights or lose them. Here Ms. Stone's procrastination and delay, which silently allowed time to slip away, remain as the only reason for her failure to bring suit earlier.

Where plaintiff has not slept on her rights, but has been prevented from asserting them based, for example, on justified ignorance of the facts constituting a cause of action, personal disability, or because of ongoing settlement negotiations, the delay is reasonable and the equitable defense of laches will not bar an action. There is no such reasonable excuse, or any issue of fact presented in the instant case that would permit a jury to excuse appellant's delay for the five years beginning in 1980 and ending in September 1985.

Laches is not imposed as a bar to suit simply because a plaintiff's delay is found unexcused; it must also be determined whether the defendants have been prejudiced as a result of that delay. *See Saratoga Vichy Spring Co.*, 625 F.2d at 1040. Although an evaluation of prejudice is another subject of focus in laches analysis, it is integrally related to the inquiry regarding delay. Where there is no excuse for delay, as here, defendants need show little prejudice; a weak excuse for delay may, on the other hand, suffice to defeat a laches defense if no prejudice has been shown. *See Larios v. Victory Carriers, Inc.*, 316 F.2d 63, 67 (2d Cir.1963). Defendants may be prejudiced in several different ways. One form of prejudice is the decreased ability of the defendants to vindicate themselves that results from the death of witnesses or on account of fading memories or stale evidence. Another type of prejudice operates on the principle that it would be inequitable in light of some change in defendant's position to permit plaintiff's claim to be enforced. Defendants here were prejudiced in both ways.

Some of the key people having knowledge of the events preceding Ms. Stone's birth have died since 1974—George Deupree, Bobbie Jett and Audrey Mae Williams. All of their deaths are not equally [prejudicial]. Bobbie Jett died in 1974, so absence of her testimony cannot be found to prejudice defendants because she would not have been alive to testify even if appellant had filed suit immediately. Nevertheless, the circumstances giving rise to this appeal have already spanned over two decades and the additional five years of Ms. Stone's unexcused delay doubtless would hamper the defense further—appellant's deposition reveals that even her memory has faded significantly in the interim. We conclude that the defendants were prejudiced to some degree by evidence that was lost by death or weakened during the delay. Because the defendants were injured in other ways by the delay, we need not hold that a finding of this kind of prejudice is alone sufficient to support the laches defense.

Prejudice may also be found if, during the period of delay, the circumstances or relationships between the parties have changed so that it would be unfair to let the suit go forward. The defendants have entered into numerous transactions involving Williams, Sr.'s songs. Ms. Stone responds that these transactions need not be unravelled—she could simply share in the profits. But that argument ignores the fact that the transactions were premised on the apparent certainty of the ownership of the songs' renewal rights—attributable to appellant's delay. This procrastination prejudiced defendants by lulling them into a false sense of security that the renewal rights were as they appeared and that she would not contest the 1967 and 1968 court rulings.

We cannot be sure that defendants would have struck the bargains they did had they anticipated the diminution in their profits that Ms. Stone seeks. This result is not altered by whether the defendants made actual expenditures or whether they simply incurred the opportunity costs implicated in foregoing other ventures. As Judge Learned Hand wrote in a copyright case in which the plaintiff delayed for 16 years before filing suit, it would be unfair for a plaintiff "to stand inactive while the proposed infringer spends large sums of money in its exploitation, and to intervene only when his speculation has proved a success. Delay under such circumstances allows the owner to speculate without risk with the other's money; he cannot possibly lose, and he may win." *Haas v. Leo Feist, Inc.*, 234 F. 105, 108 (S.D.N.Y.1916). The change in relationships and circumstances that occurred while Ms. Stone delayed would prejudice the defendants if the case were allowed to proceed at this late date.

Finally, we note that the underlying value of the laches doctrine, as with statutes of limitations, is that of repose. Even assuming that appellant's claims are meritorious, the availability of the laches defense represents a conclusion that the societal interest in a correct decision can be outweighed by the disruption its tardy filing would cause. Thus, courts, parties and witnesses "ought to be relieved of the burden of trying stale claims when a plaintiff has slept on his rights." *See Burnett v. New York Central R.R. Co.*, 380 U.S. 424, 428 (1965).

We hold therefore that Ms. Stone's delay in filing suit until September 1985 was unexcused and has prejudiced defendants. Accordingly, the order of the district court is affirmed.

NOTES

1. *More on* Stone. In a later decision, the court granted Stone's motion for rehearing and vacated its prior laches holding. The court's action was predicated on a prior decision of the Alabama Supreme Court which held, in a related case, that defendants had "intentionally, willfully and fraudulently concealed plaintiff's identity, existence, claim and rights as a natural child of Hank Williams, Sr.," and set aside decrees declaring that Stone was not an heir to Williams's estate. Because of the fraud, the Alabama court concluded that Stone had asserted her rights in a timely manner. The Alabama decision led the Second Circuit, U.S. Court of Appeals, to reconsider its original laches decision:

> "To allow defendants to bar plaintiff from claiming her rights when the availability of the laches defense was obtained by them in such an unworthy manner would not only grant defendants a windfall in this suit to which they are not entitled, but would also encourage a party to deliberately mislead a court. Courts of equity exist to relieve a party from the defense of laches under such circumstances. Plaintiff therefore should have her day in court and an opportunity to have a jury determine the merits of her claim." *See Stone v. Williams*, 891 F.2d 401 (2nd Cir. 1989).

In subsequent litigation, the court construed the Copyright Act of 1976 to hold that Stone was entitled to renewal royalties. The court held that Stone was not barred from establishing her status as a child of Hank Williams, Sr. However, given that the Act contained a three year statute of limitations, she could not recover royalties for periods that were more than three years before she knew or had reason to know that Williams, Sr. was her natural father. The court tolled the statute for the period of time that a fraud was perpetrated on her, but concluded that she was put on notice no later than October 1979 that she might be the child of Williams, Sr., and therefore the three year time bar began to run on that date. As a result, her 1985 suit was limited to the recovery of renewal royalties only as far back as 1982. As for Stone's other cause of action, which alleged that defendants conspired to prevent disclosure concerning her existence and concomitant claim to the estate of Williams, Sr., the court reversed and remanded. *See Stone v. Williams*, 970 F.2d 1043 (2nd Cir. 1992). On remand, the parties reached a negotiated settlement.

2. *Laches and Statutory Limitation Periods.* In *Jarrow Formulas, Inc. v. Nutrition Now, Inc.*, 304 F.3d 829 (9th Cir. 2002), the court made the following observations regarding the laches defense:

> Laches is an equitable time limitation on a party's right to bring suit," resting on the maxim that "one who seeks the help of a

> court of equity must not sleep on his rights." *Piper Aircraft, Corp.,* 741 F.2d at 939 (Posner, J., concurring). A party asserting laches must show that it suffered prejudice as a result of the plaintiff's unreasonable delay in filing suit. *Couveau v. Am. Airlines, Inc.,* 218 F.3d 1078, 1083 (9th Cir.2000). Laches, an equitable defense, is distinct from the statute of limitations, a creature of law. *E.g., Jackson v. Axton,* 25 F.3d 884, 888 (9th Cir.1994). Statutes of limitation generally are limited to actions at law and therefore inapplicable to equitable causes of action. *E.g., Patton v. Bearden,* 8 F.3d 343, 347 (6th Cir.1993). Laches serves as the counterpart to the statute of limitations, barring untimely equitable causes of action. *E.g., Jackson,* 25 F.3d at 888. While laches and the statute of limitations are distinct defenses, a laches determination is made with reference to the limitations period for the analogous action at law. If the plaintiff filed suit within the analogous limitations period, the strong presumption is that laches is inapplicable. *E.g., Shouse v. Pierce County,* 559 F.2d 1142, 1147 (9th Cir.1977). However, if suit is filed outside of the analogous limitations period, courts often have presumed that laches is applicable. *Brown v. Kayler,* 273 F.2d 588, 592 (9th Cir.1959); *Wilson v. Northwest Marine Iron Works,* 212 F.2d 510, 511 (9th Cir.1954).

The United States Supreme Court has granted cert. and heard argument in Petrella v. MGM, Inc. 695 F. 3d 946 (9th Cir. 2012). The case relates to long delayed copyright claims in respect of the acclaimed 1980 movie "Raging Bull." The Court will settle a split in the federal circuit courts on the issue of whether laches may preclude the recovery of copyright proceeds that would fall within the limitation period stipulated in the copyright legislation.

The relationship between statutes of limitations and laches is particularly challenging when the cause of action was not contemplated at the time of the enactment of the statute of limitations. Even for those limitation statutes more recently enacted it is often the case that causes of action and remedies beyond those normally found are not expressly taken into account. The prime example of such an action, we will examine in Chapter 5, is Restitution and Unjust Enrichment. The sources of this law are drawn from law and equity. In particular, a plaintiff may elect to "waive the tort," where a claim based in tort or contract also rests on unjust enrichment. (Comment *e* of §70 Restatement (Third) Restitution and Unjust Enrichment.) The question is whether the applicable limitation period pertaining to the "waived" tort or contract action obtains. Most courts assert that the action in unjust enrichment is separate and not subject to the Statute of Limitations. Where the claim and remedy are equitable in nature, the Statutes of Limitations are usually inapplicable; they are usually enacted with only legal claims and remedies in mind.

Comment *g* of §70 states that, "in contrast to the fixed time limits set by statutes of limitations, equity [when deciding whether the defense of laches is established] makes an individualized inquiry into the situation of the parties, weighing the justification (if any) for the plaintiff's delay and the prejudice (if any) to the defendant as a result. The difficulty associated with laches lies, not in the doctrine itself, but in determining the role it plays in the modern limitations law of a particular jurisdiction." The Restatement is careful then to refer the issue to local jurisdictions but is useful in facilitating the inquiry by reference of applicable principles. The major line of distinction is the characterization of the claim as legal or equitable in origin.

PROBLEM: THE DAY CARE CENTER

In a residential neighborhood, where local covenants prohibit residents from operating home businesses, Milroy is making plans to remodel his house. Initially, Milroy tells neighbors that he intends to remodel in order to "give his family more space." However, before he begins construction, Milroy announces that he and his wife intend to operate a day care center in the new addition. Suppose that the neighbors, anxious to prevent Milroy from operating a day care center at his house, come to you for legal advice. What actions should the neighbors take to avoid application of the laches defense? How would you advise them? *See Peckham v. Milroy*, 104 Wash.App. 887, 17 P.3d 1256 Feb. 15, 2001.

4. ESTOPPEL

Estoppel is a doctrine that can be used both offensively and defensively. The next two cases illustrate these applications.

FEINBERG V. PFEIFFER COMPANY

322 S.W.2d 163 (Mo.App.1959).

DOERNER, COMMISSIONER.

Plaintiff began working for the defendant, a manufacturer of pharmaceuticals, in 1910, when she was but 17 years of age. By 1947 she had attained the position of bookkeeper, office manager, and assistant treasurer of the defendant. On December 27, 1947, at the annual meeting of the defendant's Board of Directors, the Board of Directors adopted the following resolution: "The Assistant Treasurer, Mrs. Anna Sacks Feinberg, has given the corporation many years of long and faithful service. Not only has she served the corporation devotedly, but with exceptional ability and skill. Although all of the officers and directors sincerely hoped and desired that Mrs. Feinberg would continue in her present position for as long as she felt able, nevertheless, in view of the length of service which she has contributed provision should be made to afford her retirement privileges and benefits which should become a firm obligation of the corporation to be available to her whenever she should see fit to retire from active duty. Retirement pay of $200 per month for life was accorded, with the distinct understanding that the retirement plan is merely being adopted at the present time in order to afford Mrs.

Feinberg security for the future and in the hope that her active services will continue with the corporation for many years to come."

Plaintiff did continue to work for the defendant through June 30, 1949, on which date she retired. In accordance with the foregoing resolution, the defendant began paying her the sum of $200 on the first of each month. After Harris's election as President, a new accounting firm employed by the defendant questioned the validity of the payments. Harris testified that both Ernst and Ernst, the accounting firm, and Kalish the company attorney told him there was no need of giving plaintiff the money. Plaintiff was sent a check for $100 on April 1, 1956. Plaintiff declined to accept the reduced amount, and this action followed.

The basic issue is "[whether] plaintiff has proved that she has a right to recover from defendant based upon a legally binding contractual obligation to pay her $200 per month for life." It is defendant's contention, in essence, that the resolution adopted by its Board of Directors was a mere promise to make a gift, and that no contract resulted either thereby, or when plaintiff retired, because there was no consideration given or paid by the plaintiff.

Plaintiff concedes that a promise based upon past services would be without consideration, but contends that there were two other elements which supplied the required element: First, the continuation by plaintiff in the employ of the defendant for the period from December 27, 1947, the date when the resolution was adopted, until the date of her retirement on June 30, 1949. And, second, her change of position, *i.e.*, her retirement, and the abandonment by her of her opportunity to continue in gainful employment, made in reliance on defendant's promise to pay her $200 per month for life.

There is no language in the resolution predicating plaintiff's right to a pension upon her continued employment so there was lacking that mutuality of obligation which is essential to the validity of a contract. As to the second of these contentions we must agree with plaintiff. The consideration sufficient to support a contract may be either a benefit to the promisor or a loss or detriment to the promisee. *Industrial Bank & Trust Co. v. Hesselberg*, Mo., 195 S.W.2d 470.

Section 90 of the Restatement of the Law of Contracts states that: "A promise which the promisor should reasonably expect to induce action or forbearance of a definite and substantial character on the part of the promisee and which does induce such action or forbearance is binding if injustice can be avoided only by enforcement of the promise." This doctrine has been described as that of "promissory estoppel," as distinguished from that of equitable estoppel or estoppel in pais, the reason for the differentiation being stated as follows: "It is generally true that one who has led another to act in reasonable reliance on his representations of fact cannot afterwards in litigation between the two deny the truth of the representations, and some courts have sought to apply this principle to the formation of contracts, where, relying on a gratuitous promise, the promisee has suffered detriment. Such a case does not come within the ordinary definition of estoppel. If there is any representation of an existing fact, it is only that the promisor at the time of making the promise intends to fulfill it. As to such intention there is usually no misrepresentation and if there is, it is not that which has injured the promisee. In other words, he relies on a promise and not on a misstatement of fact; and the term 'promissory' estoppel or something equivalent should be used to make the distinction." Williston on Contracts, Rev. Ed., Sec. 139, Vol. 1.

Was there such an act on the part of plaintiff, in reliance upon the promise contained in the resolution, as will estop the defendant, and therefore create an enforceable contract under the doctrine of promissory estoppel? We think there was. As the trial court correctly decided, such action on plaintiff's part was her retirement from a lucrative position in reliance upon defendant's promise to pay her an annuity or pension.

The Commissioner therefore recommends, for the reasons stated, that the judgment be affirmed.

PER CURIAM.

The foregoing opinion by DOERNER, C., is adopted as the opinion of the court. The judgment is, accordingly, affirmed.

NOTES

1. *The* Ricketts *Case.* A similar holding was rendered in *Ricketts v. Scothorn*, 57 Neb. 51, 77 N.W. 365, 367 (1898):

> The plaintiff was a working girl, holding a position in which she earned a salary of $10 per week. Her grandfather, desiring to put her in a position of independence, gave her a note accompanying it with the remark that his other grandchildren did not work, and that she would not be obliged to work any longer. In effect, he suggested that she might abandon her employment, and rely in the future upon the bounty which he promised. He doubtless desired that she should give up her occupation, but, whether he did or not, it is entirely certain that he contemplated such action on her part as a reasonable and probable consequence of his gift. Having intentionally influenced the plaintiff to alter her position for the worse on the faith of the note being paid when due, it would be grossly inequitable to permit the maker, or his executor, to resist payment on the ground that the promise was given without consideration.

2. *The Relationship between Laches and Estoppel.* Laches applies when plaintiff unreasonably delays in pursuing a claim, and the defendant

reasonably relies on the delay to his detriment. Although an estoppel claim is conceptually different from a laches claim, laches and estoppel share similarities. Estoppel assumes that plaintiff (or defendant depending on whether the estoppel is offensive or defensive) made misrepresentations on which the other party relied.

PROBLEMS

1. *Estoppel and the Statute of Frauds.* Johnson sued for specific performance of a contract to convey real estate to which Johnson was entitled under a buy-sell agreement with closing scheduled for January 2, 2003. On January 2, 2003, defendant asked for a delay. Two months later, Johnson again sought to close the deal and defendant again sought delay. During this period, while Johnson leased the property, he made changes to the property with defendant's knowledge. In particular, he repaired the roof, changed the garage door, and entered into a five-year sublease. When Johnson again requested closure two months later, defendant denied the deal claiming that it was unenforceable under the Statute of Frauds. At no time, prior to defendant's denial, did he indicate that he intended to repudiate the deal. Should defendant be estopped from asserting the statute of frauds defense? Why? *See O'Sullivan v. Bergenty*, 214 Conn. 641, 573 A.2d 729 (1990).

2. *Estoppel and the Neighbor's Garage.* Neighbor A plans to build a garage on his property. Unsure where the property line is located between his property and that of Neighbor B, Neighbor A talks to Neighbor B who shows Neighbor A where he thinks the line is located. Relying on Neighbor B's advice, Neighbor A builds the garage. It turns out that Neighbor B was in error regarding the location of the property. If Neighbor B sues to require removal of that portion of the garage that sits on his property, should Neighbor B be estopped? Was it reasonable to rely on B's advice rather than obtaining a survey?

UNITED STATES V. GEORGIA–PACIFIC CO.

421 F.2d 92 (9th Cir.1970).

GERALD S. LEVIN, DISTRICT JUDGE:

This suit was instituted by the United States Government to secure declaratory relief and specific performance of an agreement entered into in 1934 between the Government and a predecessor in interest of the Georgia–Pacific Corporation. From a judgment in favor of Georgia–Pacific and denying equitable relief to the Government, the Government has taken this appeal.

Coos Bay Lumber Company owned certain timberlands in 1934, consisting of approximately 58,900 acres in Coos and Douglas Counties, Oregon, both within and without the northern exterior boundaries of the Siskiyou National Forest as it existed in 1934. Those timberlands are known as the 'Eden Ridge Tract.'

In 1933 Oregon's economy and lumber industry were in a depressed condition. In the 1930's many timber owners in the Northwest abandoned cutover lands to eliminate further payment of ad valorem taxes. In 1933, the president of Lumber Company proposed to representatives of the Forest Service that the Government extend the boundaries of the Siskiyou National Forest to include all of the Eden Ridge Tract and that Lumber Company would thereafter convey to the Government its forest lands in the Eden Ridge Tract after the forest growth thereon had been harvested. In 1934, a document was executed under seal incorporating the above proposal. The signatories were Lumber Company and the then Acting Regional Forester of the United States Forest Service, Region 6. The boundaries of the Siskiyou National Forest were thereupon extended to include all the lands described in the 1934 Document.

The 1934 Document was recorded on June 10, 1935, in Douglas County, Oregon. By this unambiguous Document, the Lumber Company assumed a continuing duty to convey lands to the Government as they were cut over. As consideration, the Government extended the boundaries of the Siskiyou National Forest, thus giving the Lumber Company additional fire protection. The 1934 Document created a clear binding contract. Congress performed its function of acceptance and at the same time, by changing the boundaries of the Siskiyou National Forest, provided consideration for the contract.

From 1936 through 1941, Lumber Company conveyed to Government a total of 9,356.82 acres of land within the exterior boundaries of the Siskiyou National Forest. Lumber Company conveyed the lands remaining in its ownership in the Eden Ridge Tract to Timber Company, together with other lands, by Deed dated July 10, 1956. Georgia–Pacific acquired title to the lands from Timber Company by Deed dated December 17, 1962.

From 1934 through April 4, 1958, Lumber Company or its successors did not complete cutting and slash disposal on any quarter section or a portion thereof in the Eden Ridge Tract except for lands previously conveyed to Government.

Public Land Order (P.L.O.) 1610, 23 Fed.Reg. 2340, dated April 4, 1958, was issued after the exterior boundaries of the Siskiyou National Forest were extended by the Act of June 13, 1935. This Order retracted the northern boundary of the Forest, excluding lands described in [the] 1934 Document (except for lands previously conveyed) then owned by Georgia–Pacific, and re-establishing the northern boundary as it was before the 1935 extension. The maps of the Forest were changed and the personnel of the Forest Service then began acting as if this was no longer part of the National Forest. For all practical purposes it was not and is not a part of the National Forest.

Over the years the Government made no claim upon Lumber Company or its successors to convey any land under the 1934 Document. No assertion of ownership or other rights in the land was made until 1961. During the same period of time, Government, without interference, allowed Georgia–Pacific to manage this timberland at a very considerable expense, meanwhile adding a great deal of value to it.

The district court found that the 1934 Document was a valid contract, but whose purposes and objectives were frustrated by the retraction of the boundaries of the Siskiyou National Forest in 1958, thereby terminating the duty of Georgia–Pacific to convey any cutover lands pursuant to the 1934 Document. We affirm the decision of the district court but on grounds other than those upon which its decision is based. . . .

Equitable Estoppel

Equitable estoppel is a doctrine adjusting the relative rights of parties based upon consideration of justice and good conscience. *Smale & Robinson, Inc. v. United States*, 123 F.Supp. 457, 463 (S.D.Cal.1954); 3 POMEROY, EQUITY JURISPRUDENCE §§ 801, 802 (5th ed. Symons 1941). Pomeroy has defined equitable estoppel as having the effect of absolutely precluding a party, both at law and equity

> 'from asserting rights which might perhaps have otherwise existed, either of property, of contract, or of remedy as against another person, who has in good faith relied upon such conduct, and has been led thereby to change his position for the worse, and who on his part acquires some corresponding right, either of property, of contract, or of remedy.'

3 Pomeroy § 804, at 189. Equitable estoppel prevents a party from assuming inconsistent positions to the detriment of another party, or, as stated in BIGELOW, LAW OF ESTOPPEL 603 (6th ed. Carter 1913), "He who keeps silent when duty commands him to speak shall not speak when duty commands him to keep silent."

Equitable estoppel is a rule of justice which, in its proper field, prevails over all other rules. An equitable estoppel will be found only where all the elements necessary for its invocation are shown to the court. The test in this circuit was reiterated in *Hampton v. Paramount Pictures Corp.,* 279 F.2d 100, 104 (9th Cir.1960):

> 'Four elements must be present to establish the defense of estoppel: (1) The party to be estopped must know the facts; (2) he must intend that his conduct shall be acted on or must so act that the party asserting the estoppel has a right to believe it is so intended; (3) the latter must be ignorant of the true facts; and (4) he must rely on the former's conduct to his injury.'

Many kinds of activities—or inactivity—on the part of a defendant may permit the defense of equitable estoppel to be asserted against him. Obviously conduct amounting to fraud would suffice to raise an estoppel against a defendant, but it is clear that conduct far short of actual fraud will also suffice.[5] A party's silence, for example, will work an estoppel if, under the circumstances, he has a duty to speak. A common example of this occurs when a plaintiff knowingly permits a defendant to make expenditures or improvements on property the latter believes to be his, but which in fact the plaintiff knows to be the plaintiff's property. [*See*] *Management & Investment Co. v. Zmunt*, 59 F.2d 663, 664 (6th Cir.1932). . . .

In the instant case, the facts show that Government has engaged in just that kind of conduct which would render it liable to the defense of equitable estoppel. First, the Government certainly 'knew the facts' relevant here. The 1934 Document was a binding agreement signed by both Georgia–Pacific and a representative of the Government, the Regional Forester. Congress was aware of this agreement and knowingly 'ratified' it by the passage of the Act of June 13, 1935. Government also knew the facts when another of its representatives, Assistant Secretary of the Interior Sherman, issued P.L.O. 1600, pursuant to a delegation of authority from the President, to effect the retraction of the Siskiyou National Forest northern boundary. Government knew the facts when, by Act of Congress in August, 1958, the exterior boundaries of the Siskiyou National Forest along the Rogue River to the South of the Eden Ridge Tract were extended, but the northern boundary as reduced by P.L.O. 1600 was not disturbed. Finally, Government knew the facts when it permitted Lumber Company and its successor, Georgia–Pacific, to manage and develop the Eden Ridge Tract until 1958 without making any formal demands for conveyance of cutover lands and when, after P.L.O. 1600 was issued in 1958, the personnel of both Government and the Forest Service treated the boundaries of Siskiyou National Forest as though they had in fact been retracted to the pre-1934 status. Government can hardly claim that it was not aware of the expenditures made by Georgia–Pacific on the lands it thought it owned in the period between 1958 and the Government's bringing suit in 1967.

Second, whether or not Government and its representatives 'intended' that Georgia–Pacific act in reliance on Government's actions (and inactions), it is beyond dispute that Georgia–Pacific had a reasonable right to act in reliance thereon. All of Government's actions during the period 1934–1958 were consistent with the belief that Government was not pressing any claims it had under the 1934 Document other than to accept cutover lands as Lumber Company and its

[5] The 'fraud' often said to be required in order to find an equitable estoppel is really only unconscientious or inequitable behavior. 3 Pomeroy § 803, at 185–186.

successors might convey them. And all of Government's actions during the period 1958–1967 were consistent with Georgia–Pacific's belief that P.L.O. 1600 had in fact reduced the boundaries of Siskiyou National Forest to their status existing prior to the execution of the 1934 Document.

Third, Georgia–Pacific was 'ignorant of the true facts', if, as Government claims, the 'true facts' are that it never relinquished any claims it had under the 1934 Document and that P.L.O. 1600 was ineffective to cut off Government's rights because its issuance was not validly authorized. There was no explicit statute, ruling, order or case authority to give Georgia–Pacific any indication whatsoever that P.L.O. 1600 might have been issued pursuant to an improper delegation of authority. Government and its representatives [treated] the Order as binding, changing the pertinent maps and Forest Service routines to coincide with the changes decreed by the Order.

Fourth and finally, Georgia–Pacific did rely on the representations (or lack of same in some instances) to its injury. Georgia–Pacific spent some $350,000, beginning in 1956, in an intensive forest management program. Georgia–Pacific has maintained a 300-mile road system and has reseeded or planted a new crop of trees. In addition, Georgia–Pacific has continued to pay its annual ad valorem taxes to Coos and Douglas Counties and to pay its annual dues for fire protection to the Fire Patrol Association.

The major issue facing this Court is whether the defense of equitable estoppel can be raised against Government. It has been held generally that the Government is not subject to the same rules of property and estoppel as are private suitors. Such governmental immunity from estoppel is an off-shoot of sovereign immunity. Both the doctrine of sovereign immunity and that of governmental immunity from estoppel have been much discussed, criticized and limited in recent years. While the resulting disfavor with sovereign immunity has resulted in legislation limiting the availability of that defense in certain actions against the Government, a corresponding expansion of the availability of estoppel against the Government has occurred rather more slowly.

In the leading case expressing the limitations of equitable estoppel against the Government, *Utah Power & Light Co. v. United States*, 243 U.S. 389, 409 (1916), the United States Supreme Court said:

> 'The United States is neither bound nor estopped by acts of its officers or agents in entering into an arrangement or agreement to do or cause to be done what the law does not sanction or permit. 'A suit by the United States to enforce and maintain its policy respecting lands which it holds in trust for all the people stands upon a different plane in this and some other respects

from the ordinary private suit to regain the title to real property or to remove a cloud from it.'

The growth of government and the concomitant increase in its functions, power and contacts with private parties has made many courts increasingly reluctant to deny the defense of equitable estoppel in appropriate situations. The Government, in its caretaker role for all the public, should not be bound by the unauthorized or unlawful acts of its representatives. On the other hand, it is hardly in the public's interest for the Government to deal dishonestly or in an unconscientious manner. This is especially imperative in a time when few individuals and corporations, if any, can escape numerous dealings with the Government and its agents.

Numerous cases reflect the position that equitable estoppels may be found against the Government in certain situations. Thus the courts have held that an equitable estoppel may be found against the Government (1) if the Government is acting in its proprietary rather than sovereign capacity; and (2) if its representative has been acting within the scope of his authority. The distinction between proprietary (private) and sovereign (governmental) functions is not often an easy or meaningful one to make.

While it is said that the Government can be estopped in its proprietary role, but not in its sovereign role, the authorities are not clear about just what activities are encompassed by each. In its proprietary role, the Government is acting as a private concern would; in its sovereign role, the Government is carrying out its unique governmental functions for the benefit of the whole public.

In the instant case, the Government is suing to enforce a contract between it and a third party, and is thus acting as a private party would. The question here is not that of preserving public lands—since Government never had title to the cutover lands it is now claiming—but only of enforcing a private contract to gain new title to lands.

Government contends that P.L.O. 1600 was never valid to affect its rights because the officer who issued it, Assistant Secretary of the Interior Sherman, was without lawful authority to do so. Although Sherman issued the Order pursuant to a valid delegation of authority within the Executive branch, the question is whether by so doing he was usurping a function reserved to Congress. An examination of the relevant statutes leads us to the conclusion that nothing forbade the executive issuance of P.L.O. 1600.

Even assuming arguendo that P.L.O. 1600 was invalid for lack of authority in the President to issue it, we are faced with subsequent Congressional action which in effect confirmed the April, 1958, boundary change. Congress, with knowledge of the previous boundary reduction, extended the boundaries of the Siskiyou National Forest, without disturbing the newly retracted northern boundaries. Mr. Justice Holmes once wrote, 'Men must turn square corners when they deal with the Government,' but it is clear that the Government is itself becoming more reasonable by permitting those corners to be rounded when reason and logic demand that the Government be held to the same standard of rectilinear rectitude that it demands from its citizens. One commentator has summarized the law in this area by saying that, 'The claim of the government to an immunity from estoppel is in fact a claim to exemption from the requirements of morals and justice.' We agree, and we find that the dictates of both morals and justice indicate that the Government is not entitled to immunity from equitable estoppel in this case.

The court also concluded that the government was guilty of unclean hands because it described the Government's actions as hardly "comporting with the dictates of good faith, fair dealing or conscience." The court also found that considerations of "justice" and "good conscience" also required denial of the requested relief because it would result in "obvious" and "substantial hardship" to Georgia Pacific.

The judgment of the District Court is affirmed.

NOTE: PROMISSORY ESTOPPEL AND EQUITABLE ESTOPPEL

The doctrines of promissory estoppel and equitable estoppel are distinguishable. As noted in the beginning of this section, estoppel may be used either as a sword or a shield. Equitable estoppel (sometimes referred to as estoppel in pais) involves a misstatement of fact, and its primary use is as a defense. An exception is its use as a means of defeating a statute of limitations defense, a use that might be characterized as offensive versus defensive. *See, e.g., Huhtala v. Travelers Ins. Co.*, 257 N.W.2d 640 (1977). Promissory estoppel, however, involves a promise and is most commonly used as a cause of action for damages, as in *Feinberg* above. *See Tiffany Inc. v. W. M. K. Transit Mix, Inc.*, 16 Ariz. App. 415, 419, 493 P.2d 1220, 1224 (1972). In some jurisdictions, however, promissory estoppel may also be used as a defense. For example, in *Peterson Mechanical, Inc. v. Nereson*, 466 N.W.2d 568 (N.D., 1991), the defendant asserted promissory estoppel (in the form of a waiver signed by the plaintiff) to defeat the plaintiff's action for foreclosure on a mechanic's lien.

PROBLEMS

1. *Estoppel and Immigration.* Salgado–Diaz (SD), an undocumented alien who has lived in the United States for many years, and who has a daughter who was born in the U.S., applied for asylum and withholding of deportation. The Immigration and Naturalization Service (INS) immediately sent him a show cause order as to why he should not be deported. While the cases were pending, border patrol agents arrested SD on a San Diego street. SD explained to them that his request for asylum was pending, and the agents asked him to sign a document that he thought enabled the agents to

investigate his pending status. In fact, the document was one authorizing voluntary deportation and SD was deported to Mexico. SD tried to reenter the U.S. using a fake passport. Given that the use of the fake passport, and the fact that SD had left the U.S., the INS moved to terminate the deportation proceedings and to bring exclusion proceedings against SD. Based on the false passport, an immigration judge dismissed the deportation proceeding, and concluded that any claims regarding INS illegality (in regards to the deportation) would have to be litigated in the exclusion proceeding. In the exclusion proceedings, the judge refused to consider the fact that SD had been forcibly removed from the U.S., and that he should be excluded because of his use of the false passport. Can SD invoke equitable estoppel princples in the proceedings? Can he argue that he was placed in the position of seeking to re-enter the United States only because of the allegedly unconstitutional stop and improper removal by border agents, and therefore he should be returned to his pre-arrest status? *See Salgado–Diaz*, 395 F.3d 1158 (9th Cir. 2005).

2. *Tax Abatement and Corporate Promises.* General Motors Corp. operated two auto manufacturing plants in Ypsilanti, Michigan. The Hydra–Matic plant employed approximately 9,000 workers and the Willow Run plant employed more than 4,000. In the 1970s, the township created industrial development districts for the Hydra–Matic plant and Willow Run plants. Because of these districts, the township granted defendant eight tax abatements at Hydra–Matic and three more at Willow Run. In 1984, the township gave defendant a twelve-year fifty percent abatement of personal property taxes on the corporation's $175 million investment for the introduction of a new car. In 1988, defendant was granted a tax abatement related to its production of a new rear-wheel-drive vehicle, the Chevrolet Caprice, at Willow Run. The abatement included a twelve-year fifty percent abatement of personal property taxes on defendant's planned $75 million project.

Before the abatements were given, Willow Run plant manager Harvey Williams stated that "[u]pon completion of this project and favorable market demand, it will allow Willow Run to continue production and maintain continuous employment for our employees." In a prepared statement, Williams stated that, subject to "favorable market demand," General Motors would "continue production and maintain continuous employment" at the Willow Run plant.

On December 18, 1991, defendant announced that it was going to consolidate the work being done at Willow Run and Arlington, Texas, at Arlington. Defendant claims that the consolidation was necessary because of the company's record losses and because its Caprice sales, projected at 330,000 a year, had been running at about 275,000 a year and had slipped below 100,000 by late 1991.

Following the announcement, the city and county sought an injunction prohibiting General Motors Corp. "from transferring the production of its Caprice sedan, and Buick and Cadillac [sic, Chevrolet] station wagons, from the Willow Run plant to any other facility." Plaintiffs argued that General Motors had made a promise to them: if the Township granted the abatement, General Motors would make the Caprice at Willow Run and not transfer that work somewhere else.

If you represent the City of Ypsilanti, how would you argue that General Motors should be "estopped" from transferring jobs away from the Willow Run plant? How would General Motors Corp. respond? Who should prevail?

E. THE RIGHT TO TRIAL BY JURY

Historical distinctions between law and equity are also important because of the right to trial by jury. The Seventh Amendment to the United States Constitution guarantees the right to trial by jury "[i]n suits at common law, where the value in controversy shall exceed twenty dollars." The Seventh Amendment is reinforced by Rule 38 of the Federal Rules of Civil Procedure which provides that: "The right of trial by jury as declared by the Seventh Amendment to the Constitution or as given by a statute of the United States shall be preserved to the parties inviolate." Although the Seventh Amendment only applies to federal proceedings, many state constitutions also guarantee the right to trial by jury.[6]

Commonly referred to as the "historical approach," most state and federal jury trial provisions "preserve" the right to jury trial as it existed at the federal and state level at the time that those provisions were adopted. When the Seventh Amendment was adopted in 1791, equity cases were generally tried to a judge while legal cases were tried to a jury. As a general matter this is still true. Actions that were traditionally tried in equity—for example, a suit for injunction—are tried by a judge, whereas suits traditionally brought at law—an action for breach of contract for damages, for instance—are tried by jury. But the dividing line between law and equity has never been clear-cut with regard to jury trials. Equity courts sometimes exercised "equitable clean-up" jurisdiction, which provided that when legal and equitable issues were combined in the same case and the legal issues were incidental to the equitable issues, the court could resolve ("clean up") both the legal and equitable issues without a jury. On the other hand, equity courts also sometimes empaneled advisory juries. To make matters more difficult, the merger of law and equity courts has given rise to suits that involve both legal and equitable claims.

Neither federal nor state courts have developed a bright-line rule with regard to jury trials. In general, federal courts have developed a pragmatic approach with a preference for juries. State courts have

[6] Section 7 of Kentucky's Constitution is illustrative. It provides that "The ancient mode of trial by jury shall be held sacred, and the right thereof shall remain inviolate, subject to such modifications as may be authorized by this Constitution."

followed a variety of approaches and remain in flux. The following cases illustrate the issues.

DAIRY QUEEN, INC. V. WOOD

369 U.S. 469, 82 S.Ct. 894, 8 L.Ed.2d 44 (1962).

MR. JUSTICE BLACK delivered the opinion of the Court.

The United States District Court for the Eastern District of Pennsylvania granted a motion to strike petitioner's demand for a trial by jury in an action now pending before it on the alternative grounds that either the action was "purely equitable" or, if not purely equitable, whatever legal issues that were raised were "incidental" to equitable issues, and, in either case, no right to trial by jury existed. The petitioner then sought mandamus in the Court of Appeals for the Third Circuit to compel the district judge to vacate this order.

At the outset, we may dispose of one of the grounds upon which the trial court acted in striking the demand for trial by jury—that based upon the view that the right to trial by jury may be lost as to legal issues where those issues are characterized as "incidental" to equitable issues—for our previous decisions make it plain that no such rule may be applied in the federal courts. After the adoption of the Federal Rules, attempts were made indirectly to undercut that right by having federal courts in which cases involving both legal and equitable claims were filed decide the equitable claim first. The result of this procedure in those cases in which it was followed was that any issue common to both the legal and equitable claims was finally determined by the court and the party seeking trial by jury on the legal claim was deprived of that right as to these common issues.

In *Beacon Theatres, Inc. v. Westover*, 359 U.S. 500 (1959), we held that where both legal and equitable issues are presented in a single case, "only under the most imperative circumstances, circumstances which in view of the flexible procedures of the Federal Rules we cannot now anticipate, can the right to a jury trial of legal issues be lost through prior determination of equitable claims." That holding, of course, applies whether the trial judge chooses to characterize the legal issues presented as "incidental" to equitable issues or not.[8] Consequently, in a case such as this where there cannot even be a contention of such "imperative circumstances," *Beacon Theatres* requires that any legal issues for which a trial by jury is timely and properly demanded be submitted to a jury. There being no question of the timeliness or correctness of the demand

[8] "[It] would make no difference if the equitable cause clearly outweighed the legal cause so that the basic issue of the case taken as a whole is equitable. As long as any legal cause is involved the jury rights it creates control. * * * "

involved here, the sole question which we must decide is whether the action now pending before the District Court contains legal issues.

This proceeding arises out of a controversy between petitioner and the owners of the trademark "DAIRY QUEEN" with regard to a written licensing contract made by them in December 1949, under which petitioner agreed to pay some $150,000 for the exclusive right to use that trademark in certain portions of Pennsylvania. The terms of the contract provided for a small initial payment with the remaining payments to be made at the rate of 50% of all amounts received by petitioner on sales and franchises to deal with the trademark and, in order to make certain that the $150,000 payment would be completed within a specified period of time, further provided for minimum annual payments regardless of petitioner's receipts. In August 1960, the respondents wrote petitioner a letter in which they claimed that petitioner had committed "a material breach of that contract" by defaulting on the contract's payment provisions and notified petitioner of the termination of the contract and the cancellation of petitioner's right to use the trademark unless this claimed default was remedied immediately. When petitioner continued to deal with the trademark despite the notice of termination, the respondents brought an action based upon their view that a material breach of contract had occurred.

The complaint prayed for both temporary and permanent relief, including: (1) temporary and permanent injunctions to restrain petitioner from any future use of or dealing in the franchise and the trademark; (2) an accounting to determine the exact amount of money owing by petitioner and a judgment for that amount; and (3) an injunction pending accounting to prevent petitioner from collecting any money from "Dairy Queen" stores in the territory.

Plaintiff contends that the complaint requests a money judgment it presents a claim which is unquestionably legal. We agree. The most natural construction of the respondents' claim for a money judgment would seem to be that it is a claim that they are entitled to recover whatever was owed them under the contract as of the date of its purported termination plus damages for infringement of their trademark since that date. Alternatively, the complaint could be construed to set forth a full claim based upon both of these theories—that is, a claim that the respondents were entitled to recover both the debt due under the contract and damages for trademark infringement for the entire period of the alleged breach including that before the termination of the contract. Or it might possibly be construed to set forth a claim for recovery based completely on either one of these two theories—that is, a claim based solely upon the contract for the entire period both before and after the attempted termination on the theory that the termination, having been ignored, was of no consequence, or a claim based solely upon the charge of infringement on the theory that the contract, having been breached, could not be used as a defense to an infringement action even for the period prior to its termination. We find it unnecessary to resolve this ambiguity in [the] complaint because we think it plain that their claim for a money judgment is a claim wholly legal in its nature however the complaint is construed. As an action on a debt allegedly due under a contract, it would be difficult to conceive of an action of a more traditionally legal character. And as an action for damages based upon a charge of trademark infringement, it would be no less subject to cognizance by a court of law.

Respondents' contention that this money claim is "purely equitable" is based primarily upon the fact that their complaint is cast in terms of an "accounting," rather than in terms of an action for "debt" or "damages." But the constitutional right to trial by jury cannot be made to depend upon the choice of words used in the pleadings. The necessary prerequisite to the right to maintain a suit for an equitable accounting, like all other equitable remedies, is, as we pointed out in *Beacon Theatres*, the absence of an adequate remedy at law. Consequently, in order to maintain such a suit on a cause of action cognizable at law, as this one is, the plaintiff must be able to show that the "accounts between the parties" are of such a "complicated nature" that only a court of equity can satisfactorily unravel them. In view of the powers given to District Courts by Federal Rule of Civil Procedure 53(b) to appoint masters to assist the jury in those exceptional cases where the legal issues are too complicated for the jury adequately to handle alone, the burden of such a showing is considerably increased and it will indeed be a rare case in which it can be met. This is certainly not such a case. A jury, under proper instructions from the court, could readily determine the recovery, if any, to be had here, whether the theory finally settled upon is that of breach of contract, that of trademark infringement, or any combination of the two. The legal remedy cannot be characterized as inadequate merely because the measure of damages may necessitate a look into petitioner's business records.

Nor is the legal claim [rendered] "purely equitable" by the nature of the defenses interposed by petitioner. Petitioner's primary defense to the charge of breach of contract—that is, that the contract was modified by a subsequent oral agreement—presents a purely legal question having nothing whatever to do either with novation [or] reformation, as suggested by respondents. Such a defense goes to the question of just what, under the law, the contract between the respondents and petitioner is and, in an action to collect a debt for breach of a contract between these parties, petitioner has a right to have the jury determine not only whether the contract has been breached and the extent of the damages if any but also just what the contract is.

We conclude therefore that the district judge erred in refusing to grant petitioner's demand for a trial by jury on the factual issues related to the question of whether there has been a breach of contract. Since these issues are common with those upon which respondents' claim to equitable relief is based, the legal claims involved in the action must be determined prior to any final court determination of respondents' equitable claims.[20] The judgment is therefore reversed and the cause remanded for further proceedings consistent with this opinion.

Reversed and remanded.

NOTE: COUNTERCLAIMS AND THE RIGHT TO JURY TRIAL

Even when the plaintiff's claim is purely equitable, a defendant's legal counterclaim is entitled to a jury trial. *See, e.g., Eldredge v. Gourley,* 505 F.2d 769, 770 (3d Cir.1974) (per curiam); *Thermo–Stitch, Inc. v. Chemi–Cord Processing Corp.,* 294 F.2d 486, 488 (5th Cir.1961). This is also generally true in state courts. *See, e.g., Weltzin v. Nail,* 618 N.W.2d 293 (IA 2000).

FELTNER V. COLUMBIA PICTURES TELEVISION, INC.

523 U.S. 340 (1998).

JUSTICE THOMAS delivered the opinion of the Court.

Petitioner C. Elvin Feltner owns Krypton International Corporation, which in 1990 acquired three television stations in the southeastern United States. Respondent Columbia Pictures Television, Inc., had licensed several television series to these stations, including "Who's the Boss," "Silver Spoons," "Hart to Hart," and "T.J. Hooker." After the stations became delinquent in making their royalty payments to Columbia, Krypton and Columbia entered into negotiations to restructure the stations' debt. These discussions were unavailing, and Columbia terminated the stations' license agreements in October 1991. Despite Columbia's termination, the stations continued broadcasting the programs. Columbia sued Feltner, Krypton, the stations, various Krypton subsidiaries, and certain Krypton officers in Federal District Court alleging, *inter alia,* copyright infringement arising from the stations' unauthorized broadcasting of the programs. Columbia sought various forms of relief under the Copyright Act of 1976 (Copyright Act), 17 U.S.C. § 101 *et seq.,* including a permanent injunction, impoundment of all copies of the programs, actual damages or, in the alternative, statutory damages, and costs and attorney's fees. The District Court entered partial summary judgment as to liability for Columbia on its copyright infringement claims.

[20] This does not, of course, interfere with the District Court's power to grant temporary relief pending a final adjudication on the merits. Such temporary relief has already been granted in this case.

Columbia exercised the option afforded by § 504(c) of the Copyright Act to recover "Statutory Damages" in lieu of actual damages. The District Court denied Feltner's request for a jury trial on statutory damages, ruling instead that such issues would be determined at a bench trial. The Court of Appeals for the Ninth Circuit affirmed. We granted certiorari.

The language of § 504(c) does not grant a right to have a jury assess statutory damages. Statutory damages are to be assessed in an amount that "the court considers just." § 504(c)(1). If "the court finds" the infringement was willful or innocent, "the court in its discretion" may, within limits, increase or decrease the amount of statutory damages. § 504(c)(2). These phrases, like the entire statutory provision, make no mention of a right to a jury trial or, for that matter, to juries at all. The word "court" in this context appears to mean judge, not jury. Cf. *F.W. Woolworth Co. v. Contemporary Arts, Inc.,* 344 U.S. 228 (1952). In fact, the other remedies provisions of the Copyright Act use the term "court" in contexts generally thought to confer authority on a judge, rather than a jury. See, *e.g.,* § 502. In contrast, the Copyright Act does not use the term "court" in the subsection addressing awards of actual damages and profits, see § 504(b), which generally are thought to constitute legal relief. See *Dairy Queen, Inc. v. Wood,* 369 U.S. 469 (1962).

Feltner relies on *Lorillard v. Pons,* 434 U.S. 575, 585 (1978), in which we held that the Age Discrimination in Employment Act of 1967 (ADEA), 29 U.S.C. § 621 *et seq.,* provides a statutory right to a jury trial in an action for unpaid wages even though the statute authorizes "the court to grant such legal or equitable relief as may be appropriate," § 626(b). That holding, however, turned on two crucial factors: The ADEA's remedial provisions were expressly to be enforced in accordance with the Fair Labor Standards Act of 1938, as amended, 29 U.S.C. § 101 *et seq.,* which had been uniformly interpreted to provide a right to a jury trial, and the statute used the word "legal," which we found to be a "term of art" used in cases "in which legal relief is available and legal rights are determined" by juries. Section 504(c), in contrast, does not make explicit reference to another statute that has been uniformly interpreted to provide a right to jury trial and does not use the word "legal" or other language denoting legal relief or rights.

The Seventh Amendment provides that "[i]n Suits at common law, where the value in controversy shall exceed twenty dollars, the right of trial by jury shall be preserved." U.S. Const., Amdt. 7. Since Justice Story's time, the Court has understood "Suits at common law" to refer "not merely [to] suits, which the *common* law recognized among its old and settled proceedings, but [to] suits in which *legal* rights were to be ascertained and determined, in contradistinction to those where equitable rights alone were recognized, and equitable remedies were administered."

Parsons v. Bedford, 3 Pet. 433, 447, 7 L.Ed. 732 (1830). The Seventh Amendment thus applies not only to common-law causes of action, but also to "actions brought to enforce statutory rights that are analogous to common-law causes of action ordinarily decided in English law courts in the late 18th century, as opposed to those customarily heard by courts of equity or admiralty." *Granfinanciera, S.A. v. Nordberg,* 492 U.S. 33, 42 (1989). To determine whether a statutory action is more analogous to cases tried in courts of law than to suits tried in courts of equity or admiralty, we examine both the nature of the statutory action and the remedy sought. Unlike many of our recent Seventh Amendment cases, which have involved modern statutory rights unknown to 18th-century England, see, *e.g., Wooddell v. International Brotherhood of Electrical Workers,* 502 U.S. 93 (1991) (Labor Management Relations Act, 1947, and Labor–Management Reporting and Disclosure Act of 1959); *Granfinanciera v. Nordberg, supra* (fraudulent preference under Bankruptcy Act); *Tull v. United States,* 481 U.S. 412 (1987) (civil penalties under Clean Water Act); *Curtis v. Loether, supra* (Title VIII of Civil Rights Act of 1968), in this case there are close analogues to actions seeking statutory damages under § 504(c). Before the adoption of the Seventh Amendment, the common law and statutes in England and this country granted copyright owners causes of action for infringement. More importantly, copyright suits for monetary damages were tried in courts of law, and thus before juries.

By the middle of the 17th century, the common law recognized an author's right to prevent the unauthorized publication of his manuscript. See, *e.g., Stationers Co. v. Patentees,* Carter's Rep. 89, 124 Eng. Rep. 842 (C.P.1666). This protection derived from the principle that the manuscript was the product of intellectual labor and was as much the author's property as the material on which it was written. Actions seeking damages for infringement of common-law copyright, like actions seeking damages for invasions of other property rights, were tried in courts of law in actions on the case. See *Millar v. Taylor, supra,* at 2396–2397, 98 Eng. Rep., at 251. Actions on the case, like other actions at law, were tried before juries. See *McClenachan v. McCarty,* 1 Dall. 375, 378, 1 L.Ed. 183 (1788). In 1710, the first English copyright statute, the Statute of Anne, was enacted to protect published books. 8 Anne ch. 19 (1710). Like the earlier practice with regard to common-law copyright claims for damages, actions seeking damages under the Statute of Anne were tried in courts of law. See *Beckford v. Hood,* 7 T.R. 621, 627, 101 Eng. Rep. 1164, 1167 (K.B.1798) (opinion of Kenyon, C.J.).

The practice of trying copyright damages actions at law before juries was followed in this country, where statutory copyright protections were enacted even before adoption of the Constitution. In 1783, the Continental Congress passed a resolution recommending that the States secure copyright protections for authors. Twelve States (all except

Delaware) responded by enacting copyright statutes, each of which provided a cause of action for damages, and none of which made any reference to equity jurisdiction. At least three of these state statutes expressly stated that damages were to be recovered through actions at law, while four others provided that damages would be recovered in an "action of debt," a prototypical action brought in a court of law before a jury. See F. Maitland, Forms of Action at Common Law 357 (1929). The available evidence suggests that the practice was for copyright actions seeking damages to be tried to a jury. See *Hudson v. Patten,* 1 Root 133, 134 Conn.Super.1789). Three of the state statutes specifically authorized an award of damages from a statutory range, just as § 504(c) does today. There is no reason to suppose that such actions were intended to deviate from the traditional practice: The damages were to be recovered by an "action of debt" which was an action at law, see Maitland 357.

In 1790, Congress passed the first federal copyright statute, the Copyright Act of 1790, which similarly authorized the awarding of damages for copyright infringements. Act of May 31, 1790, ch. 15, §§ 2, 6, 1 Stat. 124, 125. The Copyright Act of 1790 provided that damages for copyright infringement of published works would be "the sum of fifty cents for every sheet which shall be found in the infringer's possession, to be recovered by action of debt in any court of record in the United States, wherein the same is cognizable." § 2. Like the Statute of Anne, the Copyright Act of 1790 provided that half ("one moiety") of such damages were to go to the copyright owner and half to the United States. For infringement of an unpublished manuscript, the statute entitled a copyright owner to "all damages occasioned by such injury, to be recovered by a special action on the case founded upon this act, in any court having cognizance thereof." § 6. There is no evidence that the Copyright Act of 1790 changed the practice of trying copyright actions for damages in courts of law before juries. As we have noted, actions on the case and actions of debt were actions at law for which a jury was required. Moreover, actions to recover damages under the Copyright Act of 1831—which differed from the Copyright Act of 1790 only in the amount (increased to $1 from 50 cents) authorized to be recovered for certain infringing sheets—were consistently tried to juries. See, *e.g., Backus v. Gould,* 7 How. 798, 802, 12 L.Ed. 919 (1849).

Columbia does not dispute this historical [evidence]. Rather, Columbia [contends] that statutory damages are clearly equitable in nature. We are not persuaded. We have recognized the "general rule" that monetary relief is legal, *Teamsters v. Terry, supra,* at 570, and an award of statutory damages may serve purposes traditionally associated with legal relief, such as compensation and punishment. See *Curtis v. Loether,* 415 U.S., at 196; *Tull v. United States,* 481 U.S., at 422. Nor, as we have previously stated, is a monetary remedy rendered equitable simply because it is "not fixed or readily calculable from a fixed formula." *Id.,* at

422, n. 7. And there is historical evidence that cases involving discretionary monetary relief were tried before juries. See, *e.g., Coryell v. Colbaugh,* 1 N.J.L. 77 (1791). Accordingly, we must conclude that the Seventh Amendment provides a right to a jury trial where the copyright owner elects to recover statutory damages.

The right to a jury trial includes the right to have a jury determine the *amount* of statutory damages, if any, awarded to the copyright owner. It has long been recognized that "by the law the jury are judges of the damages." *Lord Townshend v. Hughes,* 2 Mod. 150, 151, 86 Eng. Rep. 994, 994–995 (C.P. 1677). Thus in *Dimick v. Schiedt,* 293 U.S. 474 (1935), the Court stated that "the common law rule as it existed at the time of the adoption of the Constitution" was that "in cases where the amount of damages was uncertain[,] their assessment was a matter so peculiarly within the province of the jury that the Court should not alter it." And there is overwhelming evidence that the consistent practice at common law was for juries to award damages. See, *e.g., Duke of York v. Pilkington,* 2 Show. 246, 89 Eng. Rep. 918 (K.B.1760) (slander action). [This] was the consistent practice in copyright cases. In *Hudson v. Patten,* 1 Root, at 134, for example, a jury awarded a copyright owner £100 under the Connecticut copyright statute, which permitted damages in an amount double the value of the infringed copy. In addition, juries assessed the amount of damages under the Copyright Act of 1831, even though that statute, like the Copyright Act of 1790, fixed damages at a set amount per infringing sheet. See *Backus v. Gould, supra,* at 802.

Relying on *Tull v. United States, supra,* Columbia contends that the Seventh Amendment does not provide a right to a jury determination of the amount of the award. In *Tull,* we held that the Seventh Amendment grants a right to a jury trial on all issues relating to liability for civil penalties under the Clean Water Act, 33 U.S.C. §§ 1251, 1319(d), but then went on to decide that Congress could constitutionally authorize trial judges to assess the amount of the civil penalties. According to Columbia, *Tull* demonstrates that a jury determination of the amount of statutory damages is not necessary "to preserve 'the substance of the common-law right of trial by jury.'" In *Tull,* however, we were presented with no evidence that juries historically had determined the amount of civil penalties to be paid to the Government. Moreover, the awarding of civil penalties to the Government could be viewed as analogous to sentencing in a criminal proceeding. Here, of course, there is no similar analogy, and there is clear and direct historical evidence that juries, both as a general matter and in copyright cases, set the amount of damages awarded to a successful plaintiff. *Tull* is thus inapposite. As a result, if a party so demands, a jury must determine the actual amount of statutory damages under § 504(c) in order "to preserve 'the substance of the common-law right of trial by jury.'"

For the foregoing reasons, we hold that the Seventh Amendment provides a right to a jury trial on all issues pertinent to an award of statutory damages under § 504(c) of the Copyright Act, including the amount itself. The judgment below is reversed, and we remand the case for proceedings consistent with this opinion.

It is so ordered.

JUSTICE SCALIA, concurring in the judgment.

There was more evidence in *Lorillard* than there is in the present case that "court" was being used to include the jury. The text of § 504(c) lacks such clear indications that "court" is being used in its broader sense. But their absence hardly demonstrates that the broader reading is not "fairly possible," *e.g., Tull v. United States,* 481 U.S. 412, 417, n. 3 (1987).

NOTES

1. *The Right to Jury Trial and Statutory Claims.* The historical approach makes it difficult to determine the right to jury trial in actions based on legislation, especially statutory rights and remedies (including administrative remedies) unknown at common law. *Curtis v. Loether,* 415 U.S. 189, 94 S.Ct. 1005, 39 L.Ed.2d 260 (1974), involved section 812 of the Civil Rights Act of 1968 which allowed private plaintiffs to bring civil suits seeking redress for violations of the Civil Rights Act of 1968. The Act authorized the trial court to award various types of relief including damages and injunctive relief. In *Curtis,* the plaintiff sought compensatory and punitive damages, as well as injunctive relief. The Supreme Court overruled the trial court's denial of respondent's demand for a jury trial. The Court held that "[a]lthough the thrust of the Amendment was to preserve the right to jury trial as it existed in 1791, it has long been settled that the right extends beyond the common-law forms of action recognized at that time." The Court rejected petitioner's argument that the Seventh Amendment is inapplicable "to new causes of action created by congressional enactment" noting that the Seventh Amendment applies "to actions enforcing statutory rights, and requires a jury trial upon demand, if the statute creates legal rights and remedies, enforceable in an action for damages in the ordinary courts of law." The Court concluded that § 812 created "legal rights" because it sounded:

> basically in tort—the statute merely defines a new legal duty, and authorizes the courts to compensate a plaintiff for the injury caused by the defendant's wrongful breach. More important, the relief sought here—actual and punitive damages—is the traditional form of relief offered in the courts of law. Title VIII actions seeking only equitable relief will be unaffected, and preliminary injunctive relief remains available without a jury trial even in damages actions.

2. *Expanding the Right to Jury Trial.* Since there is no constitutional right to a non-jury trial, Congress may expand the right to jury trial to cases which would have been judge-tried in 1791. In deciding whether a statute

does, in fact, expand the right to jury trial, courts usually focus on Congress's intent. *Lorillard v. Pons*, 434 U.S. 575, 98 S.Ct. 866, 55 L.Ed.2d 40 (1978). However, there are limits to Congress's power. In *Lehman v. Nakshian*, 453 U.S. 156, 101 S.Ct. 2698, 69 L.Ed.2d 548 (1981), the Court held that a jury trial was not available under the Age Discrimination in Employment Act (ADEA) in a suit against the U.S. government even though the Act authorized suits for "such legal or equitable relief as will effectuate the purposes of this Act." The Court held that "it has long been settled that the Seventh Amendment right to trial by jury does not apply in actions against the Federal Government." "It hardly can be maintained that under the common law in 1791 jury trial was a matter of right for persons asserting claims against the sovereign." "The United States, as sovereign, 'is immune from suit save as it consents to be sued and the terms of its consent to be sued in any court define that court's jurisdiction to entertain the suit.'" *United States v. Mitchell*, 445 U.S. 535, 538, 100 S.Ct. 1349, 1352, 63 L.Ed.2d 607 (1980), *quoting United States v. King*, 395 U.S. 1, 4, 89 S.Ct. 1501, 1502, 23 L.Ed.2d 52 (1969).

ROSS V. BERNHARD

396 U.S. 531, 90 S.Ct. 733, 24 L.Ed.2d 729 (1970).

MR. JUSTICE WHITE delivered the opinion of the Court.

The Seventh Amendment to the Constitution provides that in "[s]uits at common law, where the value in controversy shall exceed twenty dollars, the right of trial by jury shall be preserved." Whether the Amendment guarantees the right to a jury trial in stockholders' derivative actions is the issue now before us.

Petitioners brought this derivative suit in federal court against the directors of their closed-end investment company, the Lehman Corporation and the corporation's brokers, Lehman Brothers. They contended that Lehman Brothers controlled the corporation through an illegally large representation on the corporation's board of directors, in violation of the Investment Company Act of 1940, and used this control to extract excessive brokerage fees from the corporation. The directors of the corporation were accused of converting corporate assets and of "gross abuse of trust, gross misconduct, willful misfeasance, bad faith, (and) gross negligence." Both the individual defendants and Lehman Brothers were accused of breaches of fiduciary duty. It was alleged that the payments to Lehman Brothers constituted waste and spoliation, and that the contract between the corporation and Lehman Brothers had been violated. Petitioners requested that the defendants "account for and pay to the Corporation for their profits and gains and its losses." Petitioners also demanded a jury trial on the corporation's claims.

We reverse the holding of the Court of Appeals that in no event does the right to a jury trial preserved by the Seventh Amendment extend to derivative actions brought by the stockholders of a corporation. We hold that the right to jury trial attaches to those issues in derivative actions as to which the corporation, if it had been suing in its own right, would have been entitled to a jury.

The Seventh Amendment preserves to litigants the right to jury trial in suits at common law—"not merely suits, which the common law recognized among its old and settled proceedings, but suits in which legal rights were to be ascertained and determined, in contradistinction to those where equitable rights alone were recognized, and equitable remedies were administered. In a jury sense, the amendment then may well be construed to embrace all suits, which are not of equity and admiralty jurisdiction, whatever may be the peculiar form which they may assume to settle legal rights." *Parsons v. Bedford, Breedlove & Robeson*, 3 Pet. 433, 447 (1830).

However difficult it may have been to define with precision the line between actions at law dealing with legal rights and suits in equity dealing with equitable matters, some proceedings were unmistakably actions at law triable to a jury. The Seventh Amendment, for example, entitled the parties to a jury trial in actions for damages to a person or property, for libel and slander, for recovery of land, and for conversion of personal property. Just as clearly, a corporation, although an artificial being, was commonly entitled to sue and be sued in the usual forms of action, at least in its own State. Whether the corporation was viewed as an entity separate from its stockholders or as a device permitting its stockholders to carry on their business and to sue and be sued, a corporation's suit to enforce a legal right was an action at common law carrying the right to jury trial at the time the Seventh Amendment was adopted.

The common law refused, however, to permit stockholders to call corporate managers to account in actions at law. The possibilities for abuse, thus presented, were not ignored by corporate officers and directors. Early in the 19th century, equity provided relief both in this country and in England. The remedy made available in equity was the derivative suit, viewed in this country as a suit to enforce a corporate cause of action against officers, directors, and third parties. One precondition for the suit was a valid claim on which the corporation could have sued; another was that the corporation itself had refused to proceed after suitable demand, unless excused by extraordinary conditions. Thus the dual nature of the stockholder's action: first, the plaintiff's right to sue on behalf of the corporation and, second, the merits of the corporation claim itself.

Derivative suits posed no Seventh Amendment problems where the action against the directors and third parties would have been by a bill in equity had the corporation brought the suit. Our concern is with cases based upon a legal claim of the corporation against directors or third parties. Does the trial of such claims at the suit of a stockholder and without a jury violate the Seventh Amendment?

Under *Beacon* and *Dairy Queen*, where equitable and legal claims are joined in the same action, there is a right to jury trial on the legal claims which must not be infringed either by trying the legal issues as incidental to the equitable ones or by a court trial of a common issue existing between the claims. The Seventh Amendment question depends on the nature of the issue to be tried rather than the character of the overall action.[10] We have noted that the derivative suit has dual aspects: first, the stockholder's right to sue on behalf of the corporation, historically an equitable matter; second, the claim of the corporation against directors or third parties on which, if the corporation had sued and the claim presented legal issues, the company could demand a jury trial. As implied by Mr. Justice Holmes in *Fleitmann*, legal claims are not magically converted into equitable issues by their presentation to a court of equity in a derivative suit. The claim pressed by the stockholder against directors or third parties "is not his own but the corporation's." *Koster v. Lumbermens Mut. Cas. Co.*, 330 U.S. 518, 522 (1947). The corporation is a necessary party to the action; without it the case cannot proceed. Although named a defendant, it is the real party in interest, the stockholder being at best the nominal plaintiff. The proceeds of the action belong to the corporation and it is bound by the result of the suit. The heart of the action is the corporate claim. If it presents a legal issue, one entitling the corporation to a jury trial under the Seventh Amendment, the right to a jury is not forfeited merely because the stockholder's right to sue must first be adjudicated as an equitable issue triable to the court. *Beacon* and *Dairy Queen* require no less.

If under older procedures, now discarded, a court of equity could properly try the legal claims of the corporation presented in a derivative suit, it was because irreparable injury was threatened and no remedy at law existed as long as the stockholder was without standing to sue and the corporation itself refused to pursue its own remedies. Indeed, from 1789 until 1938, the judicial code expressly forbade courts of equity from entertaining any suit for which there was an adequate remedy at law. This provision served "to guard the right of trial by jury preserved by the Seventh Amendment and to that end it should be liberally construed." *Schoenthal v. Irving Trust Co.*, 287 U.S. 92, 94 (1932). If, before 1938, the law and had borrowed from equity, as it borrowed other things, the idea

[10] [The] "legal" nature of an issue is determined by considering, first, the pre-merger custom with reference to such questions; second, the remedy sought; and third, the practical abilities and limitations of juries. [The] first, requiring extensive and possibly abstruse historical inquiry, is obviously the most difficult to apply. *See* James, *Right to a Jury Trial in Civil Actions*, 72 YALE L.J. 655 (1963).

that stockholders could litigate for their recalcitrant corporation, the corporate claim, if legal, would undoubtedly have been tried to a jury.

Of course, this did not occur, but the Federal Rules had a similar impact. Actions are no longer brought as actions at law or suits in equity. Under the Rules there is only one action—a "civil action"—in which all claims may be joined and all remedies are available. Purely procedural impediments to the presentation of any issue by any party, based on the difference between law and equity, was destroyed. In a civil action presenting a stockholder's derivative claim, the court after passing upon the plaintiff's right to sue on behalf of the corporation is now able to try the corporate claim for damages with the aid of a jury. Separable claims may be tried separately, or legal and equitable issues may be handled in the same trial. The historical rule preventing a court of law from entertaining a shareholder's suit on behalf of the corporation is obsolete; it is no longer tenable for a district court, administering both law and equity in the same action, to deny legal remedies to a corporation, merely because the corporation's spokesmen are its shareholders rather than its directors. Under the rules, law and equity are procedurally combined; nothing turns now upon the form of the action or the procedural devices by which the parties happen to come before the court. The "expansion of adequate legal remedies provided by the Federal Rules necessarily affects the scope of equity." *Beacon Theatres, Inc. v. Westover*, 359 U.S., at 509.

Thus, for example, before-merger class actions were largely a device of equity, and there was no right to a jury even on issues that might, under other circumstances, have been tried to a jury. Although at least one post-merger court held that the device was not available to try legal issues, it now seems settled in the lower federal courts that class action plaintiffs may obtain a jury trial on any legal issues they present.

Derivative suits have been described as one kind of "true" class action. We are inclined to agree with the description, at least to the extent it recognizes that the derivative suit and the class action were both ways of allowing parties to be heard in equity who could not speak at law. After adoption of the rules there is no longer any procedural obstacle to the assertion of legal rights before juries, however the party may have acquired standing to assert those rights. Given the availability in a derivative action of both legal and equitable remedies, we think the Seventh Amendment preserves to the parties in a stockholder's suit the same right to a jury trial that historically belonged to the corporation and to those against whom the corporation pressed its legal claims.

In the instant case we have no doubt that the corporation's claim is, at least in part, a legal one. The relief sought is money damages. There are allegations in the complaint of a breach of fiduciary duty, but there are also allegations of ordinary breach of contract and gross negligence. The corporation, had it sued on its own behalf, would have been entitled to a jury's determination, at a minimum, of its damages against its broker under the brokerage contract and of its rights against its own directors because of their negligence. Under these circumstances it is unnecessary to decide whether the corporation's other claims are also properly triable to a jury. The decision of the Court of Appeals is reversed.

It is so ordered.

Decision of Court of Appeals reversed.

MR. JUSTICE STEWART, with whom THE CHIEF JUSTICE and MR. JUSTICE HARLAN join, dissenting.

The Court's holding enlarges the right to a jury trial in civil actions brought in the courts of the United States. The Seventh Amendment, by its terms, does not extend, but merely preserves the right to a jury trial "in Suits at common law." Suits in equity, which were historically tried to the court, were therefore unaffected by it. Rule 38, like the Amendment itself, neither restricts nor enlarges the right to jury trial. Since, as the Court concedes, a shareholder's derivative suit could be brought only in equity, it would seem to me to follow by the most elementary logic that in such suits there is no constitutional right to a trial by jury. Today the Court tosses aside history, logic and over 100 years of firm precedent to hold that the plaintiff in a shareholder's derivative suit does indeed have a constitutional right to a trial by jury. This holding has a questionable basis in policy and no basis whatever in the Constitution.

The Court's effort to force the facts of this case into the mold of *Beacon Theatres* and *Dairy Queen* simply does not succeed. Those cases involved a combination of historically separable suits, one in law and one in equity. Their facts fit the pattern of cases where, before the Rules, the equity cases where, before the Rules, the equity court would have disposed of the equitable claim and would then have either retained jurisdiction over the suit, despite the availability of adequate legal remedies, or enjoined a subsequent legal action between the same parties involving the same controversy.

But the present case is not one involving traditionally equitable claims by one party, and traditionally legal claims by the other. Nor is it a suit in which the plaintiff is asserting a combination of legal and equitable claims. A derivative suit has always been conceived of as a single, unitary, equitable cause of action. It is for this reason, and not because of "procedural impediments," that the courts of equity did not transfer derivative suits to the law side. In short, the cause of action is wholly a creature of equity. And whatever else can be said of *Beacon Theatres* and *Dairy Queen*, they did not cast aside altogether the historic division between equity and law.

If history is to be so cavalierly dismissed, the derivative suit can, of course, be artificially broken down into separable elements. But so then can any traditionally equitable cause of action, and the logic of the Court's position would lead to the virtual elimination of all equity jurisdiction. An equitable suit for an injunction, for instance, often involves issues of fact which, if damages had been sought, would have been triable to a jury. Does this mean that in a suit asking only for injunctive relief these factual issues must be tried to the jury, with the judge left to decide only whether, given the jury's findings, an injunction is the appropriate remedy? Certainly the Federal Rules make it possible to try a suit for an injunction in that way, but even more certainly they were not intended to have any such effect. Yet the Court's approach, it seems, would require that if any "legal issue" procedurally could be tried to a jury, it constitutionally must be tried to a jury.

The fact is, of course, that there are, for the most part, no such things as inherently "legal issues" or inherently "equitable issues." There are only factual issues, and, "like chameleons (they) take their color from surrounding circumstances." Thus the Court's "nature of the issue" approach is hardly meaningful.

The Court's decision today can perhaps be explained as a reflection of an unarticulated but apparently overpowering bias in favor of jury trials in civil actions. It certainly cannot be explained in terms of either the Federal Rules or the Constitution.

NOTES

1. *Asserting the Right.* Although the Constitution specifically preserves the right to jury trial, Rule 38 requires litigant to demand a jury trial:

Rule 38. Right to a Jury Trial; Demand

* * *

(b) **Demand.** On any issue triable of right by a jury, a party may demand a jury trial by:

(1) serving the other parties with a written demand—which may be included in a pleading—no later than 14 days after the last pleading directed to the issue is served; and

(2) filing the demand in accordance with Rule 5(d).

(c) **Specifying Issues.** In its demand, a party may specify the issues that it wishes to have tried by a jury; otherwise, it is considered to have demanded a jury trial on all the issues so triable. If the party has demanded a jury trial on only some issues, any other party may—within 14 days after being served with the demand or within a shorter time ordered by the court—serve a demand for a jury trial on any other or all factual issues triable by jury.

> (d) **Waiver; Withdrawal.** A party waives a jury trial unless its demand is properly served and filed. A proper demand may be withdrawn only if the parties consent.
>
> (e) **Admiralty and Maritime Claims.** These rules do not create a right to a jury trial on issues in a claim that is an admiralty or maritime claim under Rule 9(h).

2. *The Right to Jury Trial in Complex Cases.* Many criticize the wisdom of using juries when courts are not constitutionally required to do so, especially in cases deemed too complex for jury resolution. *Compare In re Japanese Electronic Products Antitrust Litigation*, 631 F.2d 1069 (3d Cir.1980), with *In re U.S. Financial Securities Litigation*, 609 F.2d 411 (9th Cir.1979). The third factor of the *Ross* test—"practical ability and limitations of juries"—has given fuel to such arguments. *See, e.g., Markman v. Westview Instruments, Inc.*, 517 U.S. 370, 116 S.Ct. 1384, 134 L.Ed.2d 577 (1996) (holding that "judges, not juries, are better suited to find the acquired meaning of patent terms").

3. *The Right to Jury Trial in State Courts.* State supreme courts have developed a variety of approaches in applying state constitutional jury trial provisions. The court's opinion in *Merritt v. Craig*, 130 Md.App. 350, 746 A.2d 923 (2000), is exemplary:

> Prior to the comprehensive rules change that became effective July 1, 1984, the historical separation of law and equity had been scrupulously maintained in this State. Civil actions were required to be filed as either law or equity actions. With few exceptions jury trials were unavailable in cases filed on the equity side of the court, and equity relief was unavailable in law actions. The concept of equitable "clean-up" allowed a chancellor in equity to decide virtually all issues that legitimately found their way into the equity court, whether by claim, counterclaim, cross-claim, or third-party action, and whether the issues were historically legal or equitable in nature. This situation gave rise to concern that expansion of equity jurisdiction and the concomitant increase in the exercise of "clean-up" powers not only threatened, but in fact had eroded the right to a jury trial guaranteed by Article 23 of the Maryland Declaration of Rights.

In considering the options where legal and equitable claims are presented to a trial court, [the Maryland Supreme] Court observed:

> Now that the merger of law and equity has been accomplished, and parties may join legal and equitable claims in a single civil action to be decided by a court no longer divided into law and equity sides, this Court must determine the impact the rules change shall have upon the availability of trial by jury. A review of the cases decided by courts of other states that have accomplished the merger of law and equity reveals a variety of approaches and philosophies, ranging from a jealous protection of the right of jury trial to a

> preference for the "efficiency" of having a judge determine all issues in any case involving a legitimate equitable claim. A middle ground of cases makes the right to jury trial depend upon whether the issues in the case are predominantly legal or predominantly equitable in nature.
>
> Thus, it was the concern that the authority vested in the equity court under the concept of equitable "clean-up" resulting in an erosion of the right to a jury trial as to legal issues that, in large measure, prompted the merger of law and equity. In *Mattingly v. Mattingly,* 92 Md.App. 248, 255, 607 A.2d 575 (1992), we observed that "both the Supreme Court and the Court of Appeals have directed that when 'the existence of both legal and equitable issues within the same case requires election between the jury and the court as the determiner of common issues, the discretion of the trial court is very narrowly limited and must, wherever possible, be exercised to preserve jury trial.' " Judge Motz, writing for this Court in *Mattingly,* explained:
>
> Thus, as a result of the "merger of law and equity" it is often difficult to determine whether a particular case contains at least some legal claim and so entitles the litigants to a jury trial, or is wholly equitable, and so carries no entitlement to a jury trial. The Court of Appeals has directed that "we turn to the federal case law for guidance in defining the scope of the right to jury trial in Maryland." The Supreme Court has set forth three factors to be considered when examining whether a particular claim gives rise to a jury trial: (1) the customary manner of trying such a cause before the merger of law and equity; (2) the kind of remedy sought by the plaintiff; and (3) the abilities and limitations of a jury in deciding the issue. *Ross v. Bernhard,* 396 U.S. 531, 538, n. 10, 90 S.Ct. 733, 738, n. 10, 24 L.Ed.2d 729 (1970).

Among the chief concerns voiced by state courts in this context is the potential for difficult procedural hurdles when faced with a case involving mixed questions of law and equity. The following case addresses this issue.

In *Ex Parte Thorn,* 788 So.2d 130 (Ala. 2000), the Alabama Supreme Court followed Ross in holding that a piercing the corporate veil case must be tried to a jury. The court also followed Dairy Queen in holding that equitable clean-up could not be applied.

PROBLEMS

1. *Deciding Which Issues Are Subject to Trial by Jury.* Plaintiff brings a breach of contract claim in federal court against defendant seeking damages and specific performance, but does not request a jury trial. Defendant does make a timely request for jury trial. Which of the following issues should be tried to a jury:

(A) Whether a contract exists;

(B) What are its terms?

(C) Has defendant breached the contract?

(D) Is plaintiff entitled to damages?

(E) If so, in what amount?

(F) Is plaintiff also entitled to specific performance?

2. *The Right to Jury Trial and a Claim for Minor Damages.* In the prior problem, suppose that plaintiff again seeks specific performance, but requests only very minor damages (< $100) for the period between the contract breach and the time that specific performance is granted. Given that only minor damages are requested, which of the above issues must be tried to a jury?

3. *More on the Building Lot Controversy.* Now, let's think about one final problem related to the building lot controversy. Suppose that, in response to Grace Deets's law suit, Deets demands a jury trial. Is he entitled to one as to some or all of the issues in the case? Why? Why not?

EXERCISE

Suppose that the National Football League (NFL) has a rule that precludes its members from moving from one area to another absent approval by three-fourths of the league's members. The NFL's Oakland Raiders football team (Raiders) seeks to move from Oakland to the Los Angeles Memorial Coliseum (the Coliseum), and claims that the NFL's rule precludes it from doing so. The Coliseum, which needs the Raiders now that its existing tenant (the Los Angeles Rams) is moving to another site nearby, views the rule as a violation of the antitrust laws.

Suppose that the Coliseum has come to you for legal advice. It would like to sue the NFL and would like to seek a preliminary injunction against the NFL's rule prohibiting the transfer absent approval. How would you go about demonstrating that the Coliseum is suffering irreparable injury from the NFL's transfer rule? Would it matter whether the NFL has yet voted on whether the Raiders can move (or whether it has voted and has decided to deny approval)? Could the Coliseum demonstrate injury by showing that it will lose significant revenue if the approval is not granted? How else might it show irreparable injury? Please write a short memo discussing how the Coliseum might go about establishing irreparable injury under these circumstances. *See Los Angeles Memorial Coliseum Commission v. National Football League*, 634 F.2d 1197 (9th Cir. 1980).

CHAPTER 3

ENFORCEMENT OF EQUITABLE DECREES

■ ■ ■

CHAPTER OVERVIEW: In your first year courses, you probably spent some time examining the differences between legal remedies and equitable remedies, and the different ways in which those remedies are enforced. In other words, you probably learned that legal remedies generally result in an award of monetary damages. By contrast, you learned about the concept of "contempt" and the notion that equitable remedies are enforceable through the contempt power. In this chapter, we plumb these differences in greater depth by examining the different types of contempt, how equitable (contempt) remedies differ from legal remedies, differences in how they are tried, and some modern approaches to remedial enforcement.

PROBLEM: THE MAYBERRY *CASE*

Consider the facts in *Mayberry v. Pennsylvania*, 400 U.S. 455, 91 S.Ct. 499, 27 L.Ed.2d 532 (1971). Petitioner and two codefendants were tried in a state court for rioting in a prison and holding hostages in a penal institution. The Supreme Court characterized petitioner's conduct as "a shock to those raised in the Western tradition that considers a courtroom a hallowed place of quiet dignity as far removed as possible from the emotions of the street." During the trial, they engaged in the following conduct:

> (1) On the first day of the trial [came] the following colloquy:
>
> "Mr. Mayberry: I would like to have a fair trial of this case and like to be granted a fair trial under the Sixth Amendment.
>
> "The Court: You will get a fair trial.
>
> "Mr. Mayberry: It doesn't appear that I am going to get one the way you are overruling all our motions and that, and being like a hatchet man for the State.
>
> "The Court: This side bar is over.
>
> "Mr. Mayberry: Wait a minute, Your Honor.
>
> "The Court: It is over.
>
> "Mr. Mayberry: You dirty son-of-a-bitch."
>
> (2) The second episode took place on the eighth day of the trial. A codefendant was cross-examining a prison guard and the court sustained objections to certain questions:
>
> "Mr. Codispoti: Are you trying to protect the prison authorities, Your Honor? Is that your reason?

"The Court: You are out of order, Mr. Codispoti. I don't want any outbursts like that again. This is a court of justice. You don't know how to ask questions.

"Mr. Mayberry: Possibly Your Honor doesn't know how to rule on them.

"The Court: You keep quiet.

"Mr. Mayberry: You ought to be Gilbert and Sullivan the way you sustain the district attorney every time he objects to the questions.

"The Court: Are you through? When your time comes you can ask questions and not make speeches."

(3) The next charge stemmed from the examination of an inmate about a riot in prison in which petitioner apparently was implicated. There were many questions asked and many objections sustained. At one point the following outburst occurred:

"Mr. Mayberry: Now, I'm going to produce my defense in this case and not be railroaded into any life sentence by any dirty, tyrannical old dog like yourself.

"The Court: You may proceed with your questioning, Mr. Mayberry."

(5) The fifth charge relates to a protest which the defendants made that at the end of each trial day they were denied access to their legal documents—a condition which the trial judge shortly remedied. The following ensued:

"Mr. Mayberry: You're a judge first. What are you working for? The prison authorities, you bum?

"Mr. Livingston: I have a motion pending before Your Honor.

"The Court: I would suggest—

"Mr. Mayberry: Go to hell. I don't give a good God damn what you suggest, you stumbling dog."

Meanwhile one defendant told the judge if he did not get access to his papers at night he'd "blow your head off." Another defendant said he would not sit still and be "kowtowed and be railroaded into a life imprisonment."

(7) The seventh charge grew out of an examination of a codefendant by petitioner. The following outburst took place:

"By Mr. Mayberry:

"Q. No. Don't state a conclusion because Gilbert is going to object and Sullivan will sustain. Give me facts. What leads you to say that?"

Following other exchanges with the court, petitioner said:

"Mr. Mayberry: Now, just what do you call proper? I have asked questions, numerous questions and everyone you said is improper. I have asked questions that my adviser has given me, and I have repeated these questions verbatim as they came out of my adviser's mouth, and you said they are improper. Now just what do you consider proper?

"The Court: I am not here to educate you, Mr. Mayberry.

"Mr. Mayberry: No. I know you are not. But you're not here to railroad me into no life bit, either.

"Mr. Codispoti: To protect the record—

"The Court: Do you have any other questions to ask this witness?

"Mr. Mayberry: You need to have some kind of psychiatric treatment, I think. You're some kind of a nut. I know you're trying to do a good job for that Warden Maroney back there, but let's keep it looking decent anyway, you know. Don't make it so obvious, Your Honor."

As we go through this chapter, you will be asked to think about whether Mayberry's actions constitute contempt. If so, you will be asked to think about how the contempt issues should be handled. Do you have any preliminary thoughts now? See if those ideas change as you go through this chapter.

We have examined the differences between legal judgments and equitable decrees. Equitable remedies are framed as *in personam* decrees which order a defendant to engage in some act (or refrain from engaging in an act). Such decrees are reinforced by the threat of contempt sanctions including fines and jail. Contempt sanctions can also be used to punish other offenses against the dignity of the courts.

Rule 42. Criminal Contempt

(a) Summary Disposition. A criminal contempt may be punished summarily if the judge certifies that the judge saw or heard the conduct constituting the contempt and that it was committed in the actual presence of the court. The order of contempt shall recite the facts and shall be signed by the judge and entered of record.

(b) Disposition Upon Notice and Hearing. A criminal contempt except as provided in subdivision (a) of this rule shall be prosecuted on notice. The notice shall state the time and place of hearing, allowing a reasonable time for the preparation of the defense, and shall state the essential facts constituting the criminal contempt charged and describe it as such. The notice shall be given orally by the judge in open court in the presence of the defendant or, on application of the United States attorney or of an attorney appointed by the court for that purpose, by an order to show cause or an order of arrest. The defendant is entitled to a trial by jury in any case in which an act of Congress so provides. The defendant is entitled to admission to bail as provided in these rules. If the contempt charged involves disrespect to or criticism of a judge, that judge is disqualified from presiding at the trial or hearing except with the defendant's consent. Upon a verdict or finding of guilt the court shall enter an order fixing the punishment.

A. CONTEMPT DEFINED

"Contempt" is broadly defined as an offense against the dignity of a court. Contemptuous conduct can include a refusal to obey a court order, as well as a variety of other actions: filing a spurious will in a probate proceeding; a physical attack on court officials; the lynching of a prisoner by a sheriff who had been ordered to hold the witness pending the outcome of further proceedings. What other conduct constitutes contempt? Consider the following cases.

IN RE LITTLE

404 U.S. 553, 92 S.Ct. 659, 30 L.Ed.2d 708 (1972).

PER CURIAM.

Petitioner was convicted of committing a direct contempt of a judge of the District Court Division of the Forsyth County, North Carolina, General Court of Justice. He was sentenced to 30 days in jail as summary punishment. He sought habeas corpus relief which was denied.

At Petitioner's trial on a charge of carrying a concealed weapon, petitioner filed a written motion for continuance by reason of another trial engagement of his retained counsel. The trial judge denied the motion and proceeded with the trial. Without benefit of counsel petitioner attempted to defend himself. In summation following the close of the evidence petitioner made statements that the court was biased and had prejudged the case and that petitioner was a political prisoner. The trial judge adjudged petitioner in contempt for disrespectful remarks that tended to subvert and prevent justice."

The order also recites, "As the defendant was being removed from the courtroom by deputy sheriff following the contempt adjudication, he spoke out and called the undersigned presiding judge a M___F___." This language in a courtroom is, of course, reprehensible and cannot be tolerated. But this was not relied upon by either the District Court or the Superior Court for the conviction and sentence and the State defends the conviction in this Court without any reference to it. We therefore also lay it aside for the purpose of our decision.

We hold that in the context of this case petitioner's statements in summation did not constitute criminal contempt. The court's denial of the continuance forced petitioner to argue his own cause. He was therefore clearly entitled to as much latitude in conducting his defense as we have held is enjoyed by counsel vigorously espousing a client's cause. There is no indication, and the State does not argue, that petitioner's statements were uttered in a boisterous tone or in any wise actually disrupted the court proceeding. Therefore, "The vehemence of the language used is not alone the measure of the power to punish for contempt. The fires which it kindles must constitute an imminent, not merely a likely, threat to the administration of justice. The danger must not be remote or even probable; it must immediately imperil. The law of contempt is not made for the protection of judges who may be sensitive to the winds of public opinion. Judges are supposed to be men of fortitude, able to thrive in a hardy climate." *Craig v. Harney*, 331 U.S. 367, 376 (1947). "Trial courts must be on guard against confusing offenses to their sensibilities with obstruction to the administration of justice." *Brown v. United States*, 356 U.S. 148, 153 (1958).

The petition for certiorari is granted and the judgment is reversed.

It is so ordered.

NOTE: THE FEDERAL RULES PROVISIONS

The Federal Rules of Criminal Procedure specifically include two types of conduct within the definition of contempt: failure to obey a judicial subpoena "without adequate excuse," Rule 17, F.R.Cr.P., and violation of the obligation of secrecy by a grand juror. Rule 6, F.R.Cr.P.

PROBLEMS

1. *More on the* Mayberry *Case.* Now, let's think a bit more about the *Mayberry* problem set forth at the beginning of this chapter. Should Mayberry's conduct be regarded as "contempt" in light of Little's suggestion that judges are supposed to be people of "fortitude, able to thrive in a hardy climate"? If the judge treats Mayberry's conduct as contempt, does the judge risk punishing Mayberry for offending his sensibilities rather than for obstructing the administration of justice? Would Mayberry's conduct be any less objectionable if it had been done by a lawyer rather than a *pro se* defense? Suppose that Mayberry had been a civil rights leader and a jailhouse lawyer who is known for his efforts to better prison conditions. *See, e.g., Imprisoned Citizens Union v. Shapp*, 451 F. Supp. 893, 894, 898 (E.D. Pa. 1978). Would it be permissible for him (as a lawyer representing a client) to engage in such behavior?

2. *The Fee Dispute.* Petitioner Robert Snyder was appointed by the Federal District Court for the District of North Dakota to represent a defendant under the Criminal Justice Act. After petitioner completed the assignment, he submitted a claim for $1,898.55 for services and expenses. The claim was reduced by the District Court to $1,796.05. After discussing the matter with the Chief Judge's secretary, petitioner wrote a letter to the secretary which stated in part:

> I am appalled by the amount of money which the federal court pays for indigent criminal defense work. The reason that so few attorneys in Bismarck accept this work is for that exact reason. We have, up to this point, still accepted the indigent appointments, because of a duty to our profession, and the fact that nobody else

> will do it. Now, however, not only are we paid an amount of money which does not even cover our overhead, but we have to go through extreme gymnastics even to receive the puny amounts which the federal courts authorize for this work. We have sent you everything we have concerning our representation, and I am not sending you anything else. You can take it or leave it. Further, I am extremely disgusted by the treatment of us by the Eighth Circuit in this case, and you are instructed to remove my name from the list of attorneys who will accept criminal indigent defense work. I have simply had it. "Thank you for your time and attention."

The Chief Judge viewed the letter as "totally disrespectful to the federal courts and to the judicial system" and felt that it evinced a "lack of respect for the legal process and the courts." The Chief Judge questioned whether, "in view of the letter" petitioner was "worthy of practicing law in the federal courts on any matter." He issued an order to show cause why petitioner should not be suspended from practicing in any federal court in the Circuit for a period of one year unless petitioner apologized. After a hearing, the Chief Judge suspended petitioner from practicing law in the federal courts in the Eighth Circuit for six months. The opinion stated that petitioner "contumaciously refused to retract his previous remarks or apologize to the court." It continued:

> "Petitioner's refusal to show continuing respect for the court and his refusal to demonstrate a sincere retraction of his admittedly 'harsh' statements are sufficient to demonstrate to this court that he is not presently fit to practice law in the federal courts. All courts depend on the highest level of integrity and respect not only from the judiciary but from the lawyers who serve in the court as well. Without public display of respect for the judicial branch of government as an institution by lawyers, the law cannot [survive]. Without hesitation we find Snyder's disrespectful statements as to this court's administration of CJA contumacious conduct. We deem this unfortunate. We find that Robert Snyder shall be suspended from the practice of law in the federal courts of the Eighth Circuit for a period of six months; thereafter, Snyder should make application to both this court and the federal district court of North Dakota to be readmitted."

Did the Chief Judge correctly conclude that the lawyer's letter constitutes contempt? What arguments might you make on the lawyer's behalf? How might the judge respond? *See In re Snyder*, 472 U.S. 634, 105 S.Ct. 2874, 86 L.Ed.2d 504 (1985).

3. *The Profane Witness.* In answering a question on cross-examination at his trial for violating a municipal ordinance, petitioner referred to an

alleged assailant as "chicken shit." In consequence he was prosecuted and convicted under an information that charged him with contempt for "his insolent behavior during open court and in the presence of [the judge], to wit: by using the language 'chicken-shit.'" Was a contempt citation appropriate under these circumstances? Would it matter whether the witness used the phrase in reference to the trial judge, instead of his alleged assailant? Would you reach the same conclusion if, prior to the statement, the trial judge had cautioned the witness regarding court etiquette? *See Eaton v. City of Tulsa*, 415 U.S. 697, 94 S.Ct. 1228, 39 L.Ed.2d 693 (1974).

4. *The Attorney's Attack on the Judge.* After granting a temporary injunction, a judge recused himself from a case on the basis that "his impartiality might reasonably be questioned." Following the recusal and the appointment of a second judge, lawyer Louis M. Waller moved to set aside the injunction. In his motion, he referred to the first judge as a "lying incompetent ass-hole" and questioned whether the judge had graduated from the eighth grade. The second judge issued an order to show cause why Waller should not be held in contempt for his references to the first judge. In response, Waller submitted a pleading styled "Memorandum in Defense of the Use of the Term 'As–Hole' (sic) to Draw the Attention of the Public to Corruption in Judicial Office." The second judge held Waller in contempt for his "intemperate language" and for his failure "to maintain the required respect due this court and the regular Judge thereof." The judge fined $499 and sentenced him to thirty days in the county jail. Did the Chief Judge correctly conclude that the lawyer's letter constitutes contempt? What arguments might you make on the lawyer's behalf? How might the judge respond? Does the First Amendment protect such statements?

5. *The Anonymous Hitchhiker.* A man is arrested for hitchhiking in Graves County, Kentucky. The man refused to identify himself to police. At court, the man did not contest the charge, but again refused to identify himself. Exasperated, the judge ordered the man to identify himself on penalty of contempt. The man refused. The judge ordered the man to be confined in the county jail until such time as he revealed his identity. Once a week for the next 29 weeks, the man appeared before the judge and was asked whether he would agree to identify himself. The man steadfastly refused. Each time, the judge ordered the sheriff to return the man to his cell. The judge ordered that the man continue to be held even though the maximum penalty for hitchhiking is 90 days in jail. Can a defendant be held in contempt for failure to reveal his identity? What arguments can be made on behalf of defendant? How might the court respond? Would it matter whether Kentucky law allows a sentencing judge to consider a defendant's record in imposing sentence? Can you argue that the judge exceeded his authority in holding defendant beyond the maximum penalty for hitchhiking?

B. CIVIL V. CRIMINAL

Contempt is divided into "civil contempt" and "criminal contempt." This division has both procedural and remedial consequences.

DAN B. DOBBS, HANDBOOK ON THE LAW OF REMEDIES

(1973).

It is almost always necessary to distinguish between "civil" and "criminal" contempt hearings and sanctions. The kind of trial procedure used in a contempt hearing must correlate with the sanction: if the sanction is "criminal," then the constitutional and procedural rules applied to criminal trials must be observed. A discorrelation between the procedure and the sanction annuls the conviction. In addition, if the contempt is criminal, the maximum punishment will be set by statute or constitutional rules. * * * The term criminal contempt does not refer to the nature of the act of contempt. Although some acts committed in disobeying a court order may violate criminal statutes, almost any knowing act of disobedience of a court order is sufficiently criminal to permit the court to impose criminal sanctions. The question whether the contempt hearing must respect the criminal procedures or not depends, not on the contemnor's act, but on the sanction to be imposed.

---

1. CIVIL AND CRIMINAL CONTEMPT DISTINGUISHED

How does a court distinguish between civil and criminal contempt? Is the distinction based on the nature of the defendant's conduct, or on some other ground?

UNITED STATES V. PROFESSIONAL AIR TRAFFIC CONTROLLERS ORGANIZATION

678 F.2d 1 (1st Cir.1982).

TORRUELLA, DISTRICT JUDGE.

This appeal questions the validity of a finding of ostensibly civil contempt made against appellant Robert Belanger for violating a Preliminary Injunction Order issued by the United States District Court for the District of New Hampshire. Belanger is President of Local 202 of the Professional Air Traffic Controllers Organization (PATCO) headquartered in Nashua, New Hampshire. On August 3, 1981 a nationwide strike was authorized by PATCO against the Federal Aviation

Administration's (FAA) air traffic control activities, which was joined in by Local 202. The District Court [issued] a temporary restraining order prohibiting certain strike-related activities at the FAA's facilities in Nashua. After a preliminary injunction hearing, of which appellant was notified but failed to appear, the District Court issued an order restraining appellant: "Specifically, from having at any given time more than 30 pickets for informational purposes at or near the entrance to the FAA Air Route Traffic Control Center in Nashua, New Hampshire, and having any such pickets any closer to the entrance/exit gates of said Air Route Traffic Control Center than a distance of 40 feet therefrom and from in any way threatening or attempting to threaten any employees of FAA or lawful visitors therein or employees of any other group who have lawful business upon the premises of said Air Traffic Control Center from either entrance or exit to said premises." Appellant was personally served with a copy of the preliminary injunction order on the day it issued.

On September 7, 1981 the first of several incidents took place which led to appellant's contempt citation. On that day a crowd of two to three hundred persons gathered at the entrance to the Center, at about the time of the 2:30 P.M. shift change. Belanger was present and mingled with the crowd, which undisputedly contained more than 30 PATCO members, although less than that number exhibited picket signs at any one time. As working FAA employees appeared on the scene the crowd responded with various strike-related epithets and interfered with exiting vehicles.

On September 19th a similar incident took place, this time with a crowd numbering about 100 persons, 74 of which were identified as known PATCO members. Appellant mingled with the crowd and led sporadic strike-related cheering through a megaphone. Insulting language again emanated from the crowd against those FAA employees who chose to cross the PATCO picket line.

Finally, appellant was present at the Center's entrance on October 4, 1981. On this occasion he and a group of 20 to 25 PATCO members patrolled back and forth within 5 to 7 feet of the Center's gate. Just before he engaged in such action, appellant was warned by a Nashua police officer that such action could lead to his arrest for violation of the injunction. Belanger replied that the police officer should "do what you want to do and I will do what I have to do," and proceeded to act as previously described.

Next day, similar actions were engaged in by two other PATCO members, James Vacca and George Jones, who were subsequently arrested, charged and indicted for criminal contempt. Both indictments were later dismissed without prejudice.

Appellee petitioned the District Court to hold appellant in contempt of the preliminary injunction order for his conduct of October 4. Following a hearing, appellant was found in civil contempt and a fine of $5,000 was imposed upon him, which was stayed pending disposition of this appeal.

Appellant's allegations bring into focus the distinction between civil and criminal contempt and the consequences resulting therefrom. Appellant contends that the District Court's action in imposing a $5,000 fine denotes a punitive purpose, which is impermissible in a civil proceeding. The distinction between civil and criminal contempt requires an inquiry into the purpose served by the contempt proceeding.

The purpose of a criminal contempt proceeding is the vindication of the court's authority by punishment through fine or imprisonment of the contemnor for his past conduct. On the other hand, civil contempt proceedings are for the purpose of coercing compliance with the orders of the court and/or to compensate complainant for losses sustained by defendant's noncompliance. Coercion may be achieved by imprisonment of the contemnor until he purges himself of the contempt, and/or by a prospective, conditional fine. Where compensation is intended, a fine can also be imposed, payable to the complainant, but: "Such fine must of course be based upon evidence of complainant's actual loss, and his right, as a civil litigant, to the compensatory fine is dependent upon the outcome of the basic controversy." *Mine Workers, supra*, 330 U.S. at 304.

The government, while consistently labeling the proceedings as civil, has not asserted that the present fine is compensatory for any proved [loss]. The Assistant U.S. Attorney argued that appellant "should not go unchallenged for what he has done in the past," and recommended a "substantial fine for his behavior in wilfully disobeying." Here it is argued that the fine's purpose was "to ensure future compliance with the order," and "to cure appellant's wilful disobedience," neither, again, being compensatory.

Sanctions for civil contempt must be "wholly remedial," *Nye v. United States*, 313 U.S. 33, 42–43 (1941), *quoting McCrone v. United States*, 307 U.S. 61, 64 (1939). While "remedy" and "cure" are in one sense interchangeable, that is not the present context, even though a fine may, hopefully, have a "curative effect." A definite fine which is neither compensatory, nor conditioned on future violations of the court order is punitive and can be imposed only in criminal contempt proceedings. The present fine was unconditional, and far from being wholly remedial, was wholly punitive; as a civil sanction, it fails entirely. There is no merit in the government's argument that this holding leaves individuals free to disregard court orders until such time as they are found in civil contempt and prospective sanctions are attached. Criminal proceedings remain available to punish contemnors for past violations.

If viewed as a criminal proceeding, the case was not properly conducted. In the first place, no notice describing the contempt as criminal was given. Nor, in deciding, did the court apply a burden of proof beyond a reasonable doubt. Finally, a $5,000 fine on an individual is "serious," and impermissible without a jury trial. While we could perhaps cure this last by reduction of the fine to a nonserious level, because of the other improper procedures it must be vacated entirely. The bare finding of civil contempt may stand.

Remanded for proceedings consistent with this opinion.

No costs.

PROBLEMS

1. *Distinguishing Civil Contempt from Criminal Contempt.* When is a penalty civil rather than criminal? In the *PATCO* case, the court imposed a $5,000 fine. The court concludes that the fine was criminal. Would it ever be appropriate for a court to impose a lump-sum award for civil purposes? Would it have been appropriate in the prior case?

2. *More on the* Mayberry *Case.* Assuming that Mayberry's conduct constitutes contempt, should that contempt be treated as civil or criminal? What are the arguments for treating it as civil contempt? What are the arguments for treating it as criminal contempt?

YATES V. UNITED STATES

355 U.S. 66, 78 S.Ct. 128, 2 L.Ed.2d 95 (1957).

MR. JUSTICE CLARK delivered the opinion of the Court.

This case is one of criminal contempt for refusal to answer questions at trial. Petitioner, admittedly a high executive officer of the Communist Party of California, and 13 codefendants were indicted and convicted of conspiracy to violate the Smith Act. During the trial, petitioner refused on June 30, 1952, to answer 11 questions relating to whether persons other than herself were members of the Communist Party. The District Court held petitioner in contempt of court for each refusal to answer, and imposed 11 concurrent sentences of one year each. This judgment was affirmed by the Court of Appeals. We granted certiorari.

During the afternoon of the first day of her cross-examination, June 26, 1952, she refused to answer four questions about the Communist membership of a nondefendant and of a codefendant who had rested his case. The District Court adjudged her guilty of civil contempt for refusing to answer these questions, and committed her to jail until she should purge herself by answering the questions or until further order of the court. She was confined for the remainder of the trial.

On the third day of petitioner's cross-examination, June 30, 1952, despite instructions from the court to answer, petitioner refused to answer 11 questions which in one way or another called for her to identify nine other persons as Communists. She expressed a willingness to identify others as Communists—and in one instance did so—if such identification would not hurt them.

After conviction and imposition of sentences in the conspiracy case, the court found petitioner guilty of "eleven separate criminal contempts" for her 11 refusals to answer questions on June 30.

The court sentenced petitioner to imprisonment for one year on each of the 11 separate specifications of criminal contempt. The sentences were to run concurrently and were to commence upon her release from custody following execution of the five-year sentence imposed on the conspiracy charge. Upon imposing sentence, the court stated that if petitioner answered the 11 questions then or within 60 days, while he had authority to modify the sentence under Rule 35 of the Federal Rules of Criminal Procedure, he would be inclined to accept her submission to the authority of the court. However, petitioner persisted in her refusal.

Petitioner claims that the sentences were imposed to coerce her into answering the questions instead of to punish her, making the contempts civil rather than criminal and the sentences to a prison term after the close of the trial a violation of Fifth Amendment due process.

While imprisonment cannot be used to coerce evidence after a trial has terminated, it is unquestioned that imprisonment for a definite term may be imposed to punish the contemnor in vindication of the authority of the court. We do not believe that the sentences under review in this case were imposed for the purpose of coercing answers to the 11 questions. Rather, the record clearly shows that the order was made to "vindicate the authority of the court" by punishing petitioner's "defiance" thereof. The sentencing judge did express the hope that petitioner would still "purge herself to the extent that she bows to the authority of the court" by answering the questions either at the time of the sentencing or within 60 days thereafter. In doing so, however, he acted pursuant to the power of the court under Rule 35 of the Federal Rules of Criminal Procedure rather than under any theory of civil contempt. Indeed, in express negation of the latter idea, he stated that should she answer the questions, "[i]t could have no effect upon this proceeding and need not be accepted as a purge, because of the fact that the time has passed for the administration of justice in this case to be affected by it."

Although there was but one contempt, imposition of the civil sentence for the refusals of June 26 is no barrier to criminal punishment for the refusals of June 30. The civil and criminal sentences served distinct purposes, the one coercive, the other punitive and deterrent; that the same act may give rise to these distinct sanctions presents no double jeopardy problem. Clearly, if the civil and criminal sentences could have been imposed simultaneously by the court on June 26, it scarcely can be argued that the court's failure to invoke the criminal sanction until June 30 was fatal to its criminal contempt powers. Indeed, the more salutary procedure would appear to be that a court should first apply coercive remedies in an effort to persuade a party to obey its orders, and only make use of the more drastic criminal sanctions when the disobedience continues. Had the court imposed a civil sentence and found petitioner guilty of criminal contempt on June 26, it could have postponed imposition of a criminal sentence until termination of the principal case. The distinction between that procedure and the one followed here is entirely formal.

Petitioner's understandable reluctance to be an informer, although legally insufficient to explain her refusals to answer, is a factor, as is her apparently courteous demeanor and the fact that her refusals seem to have had no perceptible effect on the outcome of the trial. All of this points up the necessity, we think, of having the trial judge reconsider the sentence in the cool reflection of subsequent events.

NOTES

1. *More on Witness Refusals. Shilitani v. United States*, 384 U.S. 364 (1966), involved witnesses who were charged with contempt for refusing to answer questions before a grand jury. The question was whether petitioners were entitled to an indictment and a jury trial as part of the contempt proceeding. The Court concluded not because, although each was sentenced to two years' imprisonment, the contempt order contained the following proviso: if either answered the questions before his sentence ended, he would be released. The Court characterized the proceeding as civil rather than criminal contempt because the judgments "conditional imprisonment for the obvious purpose of compelling the witnesses to obey the orders to testify," and the petitioners held "the keys of their prison in their own pockets." "If the petitioners [had obeyed the order, they] would not have faced jail. While any imprisonment, of course, has punitive and deterrent effects, it must be viewed as remedial if the court conditions release upon the contemnor's willingness to testify." However, the Court noted that the justification for coercive imprisonment is premised on the individual's ability to comply with the court's order. As a result, once the grand jury is discharged, "a contumacious witness can no longer be confined since he then has no further opportunity to purge himself of contempt."

2. *Child Support Orders and Inability.* Although parents can be charged with contempt for willfully failing to pay their child support obligations, contempt charges can only be levied against a parent who has the ability to pay. Of course, if a parent has the capacity to work, but willfully chooses not to work, and therefore is unable to make the payment, contempt charges might be appropriate. *See Moss v. Superior Court*, 17 Cal.4th 396, 71 Cal.Rptr.2nd, 950 P.2d 59 (1998).

PROBLEMS

1. *More on the Recalcitrant Witness and the Grand Jury.* A preceding note involved a witness who refused to testify in a grand jury proceeding, was held in civil contempt, and jailed. From the note, we learned that the witness cannot be retained in jail after the grand jury term ends. If you are the judge, what can you do to the witness at that point? Also, what happens if a new grand jury term begins and the witness is called to testify before the new grand jury and again refuses?

2. *The Mobster's Refusal.* A witness refused to testify in an ongoing criminal investigation of organized crime even though he had been given testimonial immunity. The judge ordered the witness imprisoned until such time as he agreed to testify. The witness was imprisoned on March 4, 1970. Five years later, he was still in jail having been released only for short periods to obtain medical treatment and for personal reasons. The witness, who is now 73 and in ill-health, remains steadfast in his refusal to testify. Should the imprisonment be terminated on the basis that it has failed as a coercive measure? If you are the prosecutor, how can you argue that the witness should remain in jail? *See Catena v. Seidl*, 68 N.J. 224, 343 A.2d 744 (N.J.1975).

3. *The Grandmother's Refusal.* In Newport, Rhode Island, a judge found that a 77-year-old grandmother had participated in the abduction of her granddaughters in order to avoid a transfer of custody. When the grandmother refused to reveal the whereabouts of the granddaughters, the judge sent her to jail. Eight days later, the judge orders the grandmother brought to court and asks her further questions regarding the whereabouts of the granddaughters. The grandmother insists that she does not know their whereabouts, and therefore cannot comply with the order. If you are the judge assigned to hear the case, how would you handle this problem?

4. *More on Child Support.* Suppose that a father is in default on child support payments, and is claiming an inability to pay as well as an inability to find gainful employment. Who should bear the burden of proof on this issue (the father or the mother)? If the court finds that the father has "willfully" failed to seek gainful employment, can it imprison the father without running afoul of the constitutional prohibition against imprisonment for debt, and without running afoul of the Thirteenth Amendment prohibition against involuntary servitude?

5. *More on* Clinton v. Nagy. This case, that we examined earlier, involved a twelve year-old girl who sued because she was denied the right to play in a municipal football league on the basis of her sex. The city cited physical limitations and the increased danger that football poses to girls' health as the basis for its decision. Suppose that just before the football season began, the court issued a TRO ordering the city not to discriminate against the girl. Now, considering the following possibilities: a) Suppose that on the fourteenth day at 5:00 pm, the defendant violates the TRO and refuses to let the girl suit up for that evening's game, should she seek civil or

criminal contempt sanctions? b) Suppose that the city broadcasts that it plans to violate the TRO on the third day of the order. Does the plaintiff have an action for contempt? If not, how else might the court discourage the city's conduct? c) What if the city actually violates the TRO on the third day of the injunction, should the plaintiff seek civil or criminal contempt sanctions? Might she seek both? What are the potential limitations of seeking criminal contempt sanction in this scenario? d) What if the court has entered a permanent injunction, and the city violates it each Saturday? What contempt sanctions may and should the plaintiff seek?

INTERNATIONAL UNION, UNITED MINE WORKERS OF AMERICA V. BAGWELL

512 U.S. 821 (1994).

JUSTICE BLACKMUN delivered the opinion of the Court.

We are called upon [to] consider the distinction between civil and criminal contempt. Specifically, we address whether contempt fines levied against a union for violations of a labor injunction are coercive civil fines, or are criminal fines that constitutionally could be imposed only through a jury trial. We conclude that the fines are criminal and, accordingly, we reverse.

Petitioners, the International Union, United Mine Workers of America, and United Mine Workers of America, District 28 (collectively, the union), engaged in a protracted labor dispute with the Clinchfield Coal Company and Sea "B" Mining Company (companies) over alleged unfair labor practices. In April 1989, the companies filed suit in the Circuit Court of Russell County, Virginia, to enjoin the union from conducting unlawful strike-related activities. The trial court entered an injunction which prohibited the union and its members from, among other things, obstructing ingress and egress to company facilities, throwing objects at and physically threatening company employees, placing tire-damaging "jackrocks" on roads used by company vehicles, and picketing with more than a specified number of people at designated sites. The court additionally ordered the union to take all steps necessary to ensure compliance with the injunction, to place supervisors at picket sites, and to report all violations to the court. On May 18, 1989, the trial court held a contempt hearing and found that petitioners had committed 72 violations of the injunction. After fining the union $642,000 for its disobedience,[1] the court announced that it would fine the union $100,000 for any future violent breach of the injunction and $20,000 for any future nonviolent infraction, "such as exceeding picket numbers [or] blocking entrances or exits." The court stated that its purpose was to "impose

[1] A portion of these fines was suspended conditioned on the union's future compliance. The court later vacated these fines, concluding that they were " 'criminal in nature.' "

prospective civil fines, the payment of which would only be required if it were shown the defendants disobeyed the Court's orders."

In seven subsequent contempt hearings held between June and December 1989, the court found the union in contempt for more than 400 separate violations of the injunction, many of them violent. Based on the court's stated "intention that these fines are civil and coercive," each contempt hearing was conducted as a civil proceeding before the trial judge, in which the parties conducted discovery, introduced evidence, and called and cross-examined witnesses. The trial court required that contumacious acts be proved beyond a reasonable doubt, but did not afford the union a right to jury trial. The court levied over $64 million in fines against the union, approximately $12 million of which was ordered payable to the companies. Because the union objected to payment of any fines to the companies and in light of the law enforcement burdens posed by the strike, the court ordered that the remaining roughly $52 million in fines be paid to the Commonwealth of Virginia and Russell and Dickenson Counties, "the two counties most heavily affected by the unlawful activity."

While appeals from the contempt orders were pending, the union and the companies settled the underlying labor dispute, agreed to vacate the contempt fines, and jointly moved to dismiss the case. The trial court granted the motion to dismiss, dissolved the injunction, and vacated the $12 million in fines payable to the companies. After reiterating its belief that the remaining $52 million owed to the counties and the Commonwealth were coercive, civil fines, the trial court refused to vacate these fines, concluding they were "payable in effect to the public." The companies withdrew as parties in light of the settlement and declined to seek further enforcement of the outstanding contempt fines. Because the Commonwealth Attorneys of Russell and Dickenson Counties also had asked to be disqualified from the case, the court appointed respondent John L. Bagwell to act as Special Commissioner to collect the unpaid contempt fines on behalf of the counties and the Commonwealth.

The Court of Appeals of Virginia reversed and ordered that the contempt fines be vacated pursuant to the settlement agreement. The court concluded that "civil contempt fines imposed during or as a part of a civil proceeding between private parties are settled when the underlying litigation is settled by the parties and the court is without discretion to refuse to vacate such fines." The Supreme Court of Virginia reversed, holding that Virginia public policy disfavored the idea that coercive, civil contempt sanctions could be settled, "if the dignity of the law and public respect for the judiciary are to be maintained." The court also rejected petitioners' contention that the outstanding fines were criminal and could not be imposed absent a criminal trial. Because the trial court's prospective fine schedule was intended to coerce compliance with the injunction and the union could avoid the fines through obedience, the court reasoned, the fines were civil and coercive and properly imposed in civil proceedings noting that "the Union controlled its own fate." This Court granted certiorari.

"Criminal contempt is a crime in the ordinary sense," *Bloom v. Illinois,* 391 U.S. 194, 201 (1968), and "criminal penalties may not be imposed on someone who has not been afforded the protections that the Constitution requires of such criminal proceedings," *Hicks v. Feiock,* 485 U.S. 624, 632 (1988). In contrast, civil contempt sanctions, or those penalties designed to compel future compliance with a court order, are considered to be coercive and avoidable through obedience, and thus may be imposed in an ordinary civil proceeding upon notice and an opportunity to be heard. Neither a jury trial nor proof beyond a reasonable doubt is required.[2]

Although the procedural contours of the two forms of contempt are well established, the distinguishing characteristics of civil versus criminal contempts are somewhat less clear. In the leading early case addressing this issue in the context of imprisonment, *Gompers v. Bucks Stove & Range Co.,* 221 U.S., at 441, the Court emphasized that whether a contempt is civil or criminal turns on the "character and purpose" of the sanction involved. Thus, a contempt sanction is considered civil if it "is remedial, and for the benefit of the complainant. But if it is for criminal contempt the sentence is punitive, to vindicate the authority of the court."

As *Gompers* recognized, the stated purposes of a contempt sanction alone cannot be determinative. "When a court imposes fines and punishments on a contemnor, it is not only vindicating its legal authority to enter the initial court order, but it also is seeking to give effect to the law's purpose of modifying the contemnor's behavior to conform to the terms required in the order." Most contempt sanctions, like most criminal punishments, to some extent punish a prior offense as well as coerce an offender's future obedience. *Hicks* accordingly held that conclusions about the civil or criminal nature of a contempt sanction are properly drawn, not from "the subjective intent of a State's laws and its courts," but "from an examination of the character of the relief itself."

The paradigmatic coercive, civil contempt sanction, as set forth in *Gompers,* involves confining a contemnor indefinitely until he complies with an affirmative command such as an order "to pay alimony, or to surrender property ordered to be turned over to a receiver, or to make a conveyance." [*Gompers,*] 221 U.S., at 442. Imprisonment for a fixed term

[2] We address only the procedures required for adjudication of indirect contempts, *i.e.,* those occurring out of court. Direct contempts that occur in the court's presence may be immediately adjudged and sanctioned summarily, see, *e.g., Ex parte Terry,* 128 U.S. 289 (1888), and, except for serious criminal contempts in which a jury trial is required, *Bloom v. Illinois,* 391 U.S. 194, 209–210 (1968), the traditional distinction between civil and criminal contempt proceedings does not pertain, cf. *United States v. Wilson,* 421 U.S. 309, 316 (1975).

similarly is coercive when the contemnor is given the option of earlier release if he complies. *Shillitani v. United States,* 384 U.S. 364 (1966). In these circumstances, the contemnor is able to purge the contempt and obtain his release by committing an affirmative act, and thus " 'carries the keys of his prison in his own pocket.' " *Gompers,* 221 U.S., at 442, quoting *In re Nevitt,* 117 F. 448, 451 (CA8 1902). By contrast, a fixed sentence of imprisonment is punitive and criminal if it is imposed retrospectively for a "completed act of disobedience," such that the contemnor cannot avoid or abbreviate the confinement through later compliance. Thus, the *Gompers* Court concluded that a 12-month sentence imposed on Samuel Gompers for violating an anti-boycott injunction was criminal. When a contempt involves the prior conduct of an isolated, prohibited act, the resulting sanction has no coercive effect. "The defendant is furnished no key, and he cannot shorten the term by promising not to repeat the offense."

This dichotomy between coercive and punitive imprisonment has been extended to the fine context. A contempt fine accordingly is considered civil and remedial if it either "coerces the defendant into compliance with the court's order, or compensates the complainant for losses sustained." *United States v. Mine Workers,* 330 U.S. 258, 303–304 (1947). Where a fine is not compensatory, it is civil only if the contemnor is afforded an opportunity to purge. See *Penfield Co. of Cal. v. SEC,* 330 U.S. 585, 590 (1947). Thus, a "flat, unconditional fine" totaling even as little as $50 announced after a finding of contempt is criminal if the contemnor has no subsequent opportunity to reduce or avoid the fine through compliance. *Id.,* at 588.

A close analogy to coercive imprisonment is a per diem fine imposed for each day a contemnor fails to comply with an affirmative court order. Like civil imprisonment, such fines exert a constant coercive pressure, and once the jural command is obeyed, the future, indefinite, daily fines are purged. Less comfortable is the analogy between coercive imprisonment and suspended, determinate fines. In this Court's sole prior decision squarely addressing the judicial power to impose coercive civil contempt fines, *Mine Workers, supra,* it held that fixed fines also may be considered purgable and civil when imposed and suspended pending future compliance. See also *Penfield,* 330 U.S., at 590; *but see Hicks,* 485 U.S., at 639, and n. 11. *Mine Workers* involved a $3,500,000 fine imposed against the union for nationwide post-World War II strike activities. Finding that the determinate fine was both criminal and excessive, the Court reduced the sanction to a flat criminal fine of $700,000. The Court then imposed and suspended the remaining $2,800,000 as a coercive civil fine, conditioned on the union's ability to purge the fine through full, timely compliance with the trial court's order. The Court concluded, in light of this purge clause, that the civil fine operated as "a coercive imposition upon the defendant union to compel obedience with the court's outstanding order."[4]

This Court has not revisited the issue of coercive civil contempt fines addressed in *Mine Workers.* Since that decision, the Court has erected substantial procedural protections in other areas of contempt law, such as criminal contempts, *e.g., Bloom v. Illinois,* 391 U.S. 194 (1968), and summary contempts, *e.g., Taylor v. Hayes,* 418 U.S. 488 (1974); *Codispoti v. Pennsylvania,* 418 U.S. 506 (1974); *Johnson v. Mississippi,* 403 U.S. 212 (1971); *In re Oliver,* 333 U.S. 257 (1948). Lower federal courts and state courts such as the trial court here nevertheless have relied on *Mine Workers* to authorize a relatively unlimited judicial power to impose noncompensatory civil contempt fines.

Underlying the somewhat elusive distinction between civil and criminal contempt fines is what procedural protections are due before any particular contempt penalty may be imposed. Because civil contempt sanctions are viewed as nonpunitive and avoidable, fewer procedural protections for such sanctions have been required. To the extent that such contempts take on a punitive character, however, and are not justified by other considerations central to the contempt power, criminal procedural protections may be in order. The traditional justification for the relative breadth of the contempt power has been necessity: Courts independently must be vested with "power to impose silence, respect, and decorum, in their presence, and submission to their lawful mandates, [and] to preserve themselves and their officers from the approach and insults of pollution." *Anderson v. Dunn,* 6 Wheat. 204, 5 L.Ed. 242 (1821). Courts thus have embraced an inherent contempt authority, see *Gompers,* 221 U.S., at 450; *Ex parte Robinson,* 19 Wall. 505, 510, 22 L.Ed. 205 (1874), as a power "necessary to the exercise of all others," *United States v. Hudson,* 7 Cranch 32, 34, 3 L.Ed. 259 (1812).

But the contempt power also uniquely is " 'liable to abuse.' " *Bloom,* 391 U.S., at 202, quoting *Ex parte Terry,* 128 U.S. 289, 313 (1888). Unlike most areas of law, where a legislature defines both the sanctionable conduct and the penalty to be imposed, civil contempt proceedings leave the offended judge solely responsible for identifying, prosecuting, adjudicating, and sanctioning the contumacious conduct. Contumacy "often strikes at the most vulnerable and human qualities of a judge's temperament," *Bloom,* 391 U.S., at 202, and its fusion of legislative, executive, and judicial powers "summons forth the prospect of 'the most tyrannical licentiousness,' " *Young v. United States ex rel. Vuitton et Fils*

[4] Although the size of the fine was substantial, the conduct required of the union to purge the suspended fine was relatively discrete. According to the Court, purgation consisted of (1) withdrawal of the union's notice terminating the Krug–Lewis labor agreement; (2) notifying the union members of this withdrawal; and (3) withdrawing and notifying the union members of the withdrawal of any other notice questioning the ongoing effectiveness of the Krug–Lewis agreement.

S.A., 481 U.S. 787, 822 (1987) (SCALIA, J., concurring in judgment), quoting *Anderson,* 6 Wheat., at 228. "[In criminal] contempt cases an even more compelling argument can be made [than in ordinary criminal cases] for providing a right to jury trial as a protection against the arbitrary exercise of official power." *Bloom,* 391 U.S., at 202.

In the instant case, neither any party nor any court of the Commonwealth has suggested that the challenged fines are compensatory. At no point did the trial court attempt to calibrate the fines to damages caused by the union's contumacious activities or indicate that the fines were "to compensate the complainant for losses sustained." *Mine Workers,* 330 U.S., at 303–304. The nonparty governments [never] requested any compensation or presented any evidence regarding their [injuries]. The issue [is] whether these fines, despite their noncompensatory character, are coercive civil or criminal sanctions.

Gompers suggests a possible dichotomy "between refusing to do an act commanded,—remedied by imprisonment until the party performs the required act; and doing an act forbidden,—punished by imprisonment for a definite term." The distinction between mandatory and prohibitory orders is easily applied in the classic contempt scenario, where contempt sanctions are used to enforce orders compelling or forbidding a single, discrete act. In such cases, orders commanding an affirmative act simply designate those actions that are capable of being coerced. But the distinction between coercion of affirmative acts and punishment of prohibited conduct is difficult to apply when conduct that can recur is involved, or when an injunction contains both mandatory and prohibitory provisions. Moreover, in borderline cases injunctive provisions containing essentially the same command can be phrased either in mandatory or prohibitory terms. Under a literal application of petitioners' theory, an injunction ordering the union: "Do not strike," would appear to be prohibitory and criminal, while an injunction ordering the union: "Continue working," would be mandatory and civil. In enforcing the present injunction, the trial court imposed fines without regard to the mandatory or prohibitory nature of the clause violated. Even though a parsing of the injunction's various provisions might support the classification of contempts such as rock throwing and placing tire-damaging "jackrocks" on roads as criminal and the refusal to place supervisors at picket sites as civil, the parties have not asked us to review the order in that manner. In a case like this involving an injunction that prescribes a detailed code of conduct, it is more appropriate to identify the character of the entire decree. Cf. *Hicks,* 485 U.S., at 638, n. 10.

We are not persuaded that dispositive significance should be accorded to the fact that the trial court prospectively announced the sanctions it would impose. Had the trial court simply levied the fines after finding the union guilty of contempt, the resulting "determinate and unconditional" fines would be considered "solely and exclusively punitive." Respondents nevertheless contend that the trial court's announcement of a prospective fine schedule allowed the union to "avoid paying the [fines] simply by performing [the] act required by the court's order," *Hicks,* 485 U.S., at 632, and thus transformed these fines into coercive, civil ones. Respondents maintain that the trial court could have imposed a daily civil fine to coerce the union into compliance, and that a prospective fine schedule is indistinguishable from such a sanction.

Respondents' argument highlights the difficulties encountered in parsing coercive civil and criminal contempt fines. The fines imposed here concededly are difficult to distinguish either from determinate, punitive fines or from initially suspended, civil fines. The fact that the trial court announced the fines before the contumacy, rather than after the fact does not in itself justify respondents' conclusion that the fines are civil or meaningfully distinguish these penalties from the ordinary criminal law. Due process traditionally requires that criminal laws provide prior notice both of the conduct to be prohibited and of the sanction to be imposed. The trial court here simply announced the penalty determinate fines of $20,000 or $100,000 per violation—that would be imposed for future contempts. The union's ability to avoid the contempt fines was indistinguishable from the ability of any ordinary citizen to avoid a criminal sanction by conforming his behavior to the law. The fines are not coercive day fines, or even suspended fines, but are more closely analogous to fixed, determinate, retrospective criminal fines which petitioners had no opportunity to purge once imposed. We therefore decline to conclude that the mere fact that the sanctions were announced in advance rendered them coercive and civil as a matter of constitutional law.

Other considerations convince us that the fines challenged here are criminal. The union's sanctionable conduct did not occur in the court's presence or otherwise implicate the court's ability to maintain order and adjudicate the proceedings before it. Nor did the union's contumacy involve simple, affirmative acts, such as the paradigmatic civil contempts examined in *Gompers.* Instead, the court levied contempt fines for widespread, ongoing, out-of-court violations of a complex injunction. In so doing, the court effectively policed petitioners' compliance with an entire code of conduct that the court itself had imposed. The union's contumacy lasted many months and spanned a substantial portion of the State. The fines assessed were serious, totaling over $52 million.[5] Under such

[5] "[P]etty contempt like other petty criminal offenses may be tried without a jury," *Taylor v. Hayes,* 418 U.S. 488, 495 (1974), and the imposition only of serious criminal contempt fines triggers the right to jury trial. *Bloom,* 391 U.S., at 210. The Court to date has not specified what magnitude of contempt fine may constitute a serious criminal sanction, although it has held that a fine of $10,000 imposed on a union was insufficient to trigger the Sixth Amendment right to jury trial. See *Muniz v. Hoffman,* 422 U.S. 454, 477 (1975). We need not answer today the

circumstances, disinterested factfinding and evenhanded adjudication were essential, and petitioners were entitled to a criminal jury trial.

In reaching this conclusion, we recognize that this Court generally has deferred to a legislature's determination whether a sanction is civil or criminal, and that "when a State's proceedings are involved, state law provides strong guidance about whether or not the State is exercising its authority 'in a nonpunitive, noncriminal manner.'" *Hicks,* 485 U.S., at 631, quoting *Allen v. Illinois,* 478 U.S. 364, 368 (1986). We do not deviate from either tradition today. Where a single judge, rather than a legislature, declares a particular sanction to be civil or criminal, such deference is less appropriate. Cf. *Madsen v. Women's Health Center, Inc.,* 512 U.S. 753 (1994). Moreover, [the] label affixed to a contempt ultimately "will not be allowed to defeat the applicable protections of federal constitutional law." *Hicks v. Feiock,* 485 U.S., at 631. We conclude that the serious contempt fines imposed here were criminal and constitutionally could not be imposed absent a jury trial.

Our decision concededly imposes some procedural burdens on courts' ability to sanction widespread, indirect contempts of complex injunctions through noncompensatory fines. Our holding, however, leaves unaltered the longstanding authority of judges to adjudicate direct contempts summarily, and to enter broad compensatory awards for all contempts through civil proceedings. See, *e.g., Sheet Metal Workers v. EEOC,* 478 U.S. 421 (1986). Because the right to trial by jury applies only to serious criminal sanctions, courts still may impose noncompensatory, petty fines for contempts such as the present ones without conducting a jury trial. We also do not disturb a court's ability to levy, albeit through the criminal contempt process, serious fines like those in this case. Ultimately, whatever slight burden our holding may impose on the judicial contempt power cannot be controlling. "We cannot say that the need to [respect] judges and courts is entitled to more consideration than the interest of the individual not be subjected to serious criminal punishment without the benefit of all the procedural protections worked out carefully over the years and deemed fundamental to our system of justice. Genuine respect, which alone can lend true dignity to our judicial establishment, will be engendered, not by the fear of unlimited authority, but by the firm administration of the law through those institutionalized procedures which have been worked out over the centuries." *Bloom,* 391 U.S., at 208. [Where,] as here, "a serious contempt is at issue, considerations of efficiency must give way to the more fundamental interest of ensuring the even-handed exercise of judicial power." *Id.,* at 209.

The judgment of the Supreme Court of Virginia is reversed.

It is so ordered.

---

difficult question where the line between petty and serious contempt fines should be drawn, since a $52 million fine unquestionably is a serious contempt sanction.

JUSTICE SCALIA, concurring.

One court has expressed the difference between criminal and civil contempts as follows: "Punishment in criminal contempt cannot undo or remedy the thing which has been done, but in civil contempt punishment remedies the disobedience." *In re Fox,* 96 F.2d 23, 25 (CA3 1938). Contemporary courts routinely issue complex decrees which involve them in extended disputes and place them in continuing supervisory roles over parties and institutions. See, *e.g., Missouri v. Jenkins,* 495 U.S. 33, 56–58 (1990); *Swann v. Charlotte–Mecklenburg Bd. of Ed.,* 402 U.S. 1, 16 (1971). When an order governs many aspects of a litigant's activities, rather than just a discrete act, determining compliance becomes much more difficult. Credibility issues arise, for which the factfinding protections of the criminal law (including jury trial) become much more important. And when continuing prohibitions or obligations are imposed, the order cannot be complied with (and the contempt "purged") in a single act; it continues to govern the party's behavior, on pain of punishment—not unlike the criminal law. The use of a civil process for contempt sanctions "makes no sense except as a consequence of historical practice." *Weiss v. United States,* 510 U.S. 163, 198 (1994) (SCALIA, J., concurring in part and concurring in judgment). As the scope of injunctions has expanded, they have lost some of the distinctive features that made enforcement through civil process acceptable. It is not that the times, or our perceptions of fairness, have changed (that is in my view no basis for either tightening or relaxing the traditional demands of due process); but rather that the modern judicial order is in its relevant essentials not the same device that in former times could always be enforced by civil contempt. So adjustments will have to be made. We need not draw that line in the present case, and so I am content to join the opinion of the Court.

JUSTICE GINSBURG, with whom THE CHIEF JUSTICE joins, concurring in part and concurring in the judgment.

Civil contempt proceedings, although primarily remedial, also "vindicate the court's authority"; and criminal contempt proceedings, although designed "to vindicate the authority of the law," may bestow "some incidental benefit" upon the complainant, because "such punishment tends to prevent a repetition of the disobedience." Two considerations persuade me that the contempt proceedings in this case should be classified as "criminal" rather than "civil." First, while the fines were "coercive," in the sense that one of their purposes was to encourage union compliance with the injunction, criminal contempt sanctions may also "coerce" in the same sense, for they, too, "[tend] to prevent a repetition of the disobedience." *Gompers,* 221 U.S., at 443[.] Second, the Virginia courts' refusal to vacate the fines, despite the parties' settlement and joint motion, is characteristic of criminal, not civil, proceedings. The Virginia court's references to upholding public authority and maintaining "the dignity of the law" reflect purposes on the criminal contempt side. Moreover, with the private complainant gone from the scene, and an official appointed by the Commonwealth to collect the fines for the Commonwealth's coffers, it is implausible to invoke the justification of benefiting the civil complainant. If the proceedings were indeed civil from the outset, then the court should have granted the parties' motions to vacate the fines.

PROBLEM: MORE ON CIVIL V. CRIMINAL CONTEMPT

After pleading guilty to racketeering, bribery, tax offenses, and money-laundering in connection with their waste-carting business, appellants were sentenced to prison terms. A district court judge granted appellants immunity and ordered them to testify in a pending criminal case regarding the role of others in these crimes. Appellants refused to testify. The district court imposed fines of $4,000 per business day for civil contempt pursuant to 28 U.S.C. § 1826 (1988). Appellants paid the fines from May 14, 1993 until July 9, 1993. On July 12, 1993, the district court increased the fines to $10,000 per day. Appellants appealed claiming that the increased fines were so large as to be punitive rather than coercive, and therefore criminal rather than civil. Are appellants right? Is it possible to argue that the order is civil? *See United States v. Mongelli*, 2 F.3d 29 (2d Cir.1993).

2. CIVIL COMPENSATORY CONTEMPT

In a civil compensatory contempt proceeding, the court may compensate an injured party for damage that results from violation of a court order. What damages are recoverable? Consider the following case.

TIME–SHARE SYSTEMS, INC. V. SCHMIDT

397 N.W.2d 438 (Minn.App.1986).

NIERENGARTEN, JUDGE.

In late 1983 Gary Schmidt began using the services of Time–Share Systems, Inc. to manage the inventory and accounting aspects of his business, known at that time as The Wooden Bird. Services provided by Time–Share included the creation of software programs as well as the purchase or lease of computer equipment. Over the year Time–Share and Schmidt had extensive dealings with each other as the computer system was expanded.

In 1984 the relationship between the two companies began to break down. Schmidt did not feel he was getting the service he expected and paid for. Time–Share made an effort to remedy the situation but was unable to do so to Schmidt's satisfaction. Schmidt terminated the agreement, Time–Share sued for damages and Schmidt counterclaimed. The parties agreed that Schmidt owned the computer equipment and the dispute revolved around the ownership of certain software designated as "Ease" software.

In December of 1985 Time–Share's motion to replevin the "Ease" software was granted and Schmidt was ordered to turn "Ease" over to Time–Share. This order specifically provided that Schmidt must appear in court to show why he was not in contempt if he failed to deliver the property. The property was not delivered and the parties appeared in court on January 24, 1986. Schmidt's attorney indicated that there was a problem in identifying which software belonged to Time–Share and which software belonged to Schmidt. At that time, the court ordered, inter alia, that: 1. Time–Share was to have access to Schmidt's computers for the purpose of obtaining a file save of all the information on the computer. 2. Schmidt "shall not delete any data or programs from the computer" prior to the file save. 3. If any information has been deleted, Schmidt was to provide Time–Share with its most recent file save. Once this was accomplished there would be another hearing to determine what should be deleted from Schmidt's computers.

Between noon and 1:00 p.m. on January 24, 1986, Time–Share's representative arrived at Schmidt's place of business to carry out the court order. He was not given access to the computer until approximately 5:00 p.m., at which time the file save was done.

An examination of the file save and other evidence indicated that data was deleted from the computer on the same day the court order was issued. Schmidt contended that the deletion was by a computer programmer, formerly employed by Time–Share, without Schmidt's knowledge. The programmer is presently employed by Schmidt's company, as an independent contractor, to develop software to replace the unsatisfactory software they bought from Time–Share. The programmer and Time–Share also are engaged in litigation concerning the programmer's program development. Schmidt's employees had notified the programmer by phone of the court ordered file save. The programmer proceeded to delete certain programs which he claimed were his and not Time–Share's.

On April 9, 1986 the court found Schmidt in contempt of court and ordered him to pay Time–Share $3,000 in costs and attorney's fees and $2,500 in damages for violating the court order.

The failure to obey a court order in favor of an opposing party in a civil proceeding constitutes constructive civil contempt which is punishable and enforceable by fine or imprisonment. Under Minn.Stat. § 588.11 (1984): If any actual loss or injury to a party in an action or special proceeding, prejudicial to his right therein, is caused by such contempt, the court or officer, in addition to the fine or imprisonment imposed therefor, may order the person guilty of the contempt to pay the party aggrieved a sum of money sufficient to indemnify him and satisfy his costs and expenses, including a reasonable attorney's fee incurred in the prosecution of such contempt.

The trial court awarded $3,000 to cover the costs and attorney's fees incurred in the prosecution of the contempt. The record supports the reasonableness of this award and we affirm this award. The trial court also awarded $2,500 to indemnify Time–Share for the contemnors' wrongful activities. However, "indemnity must be based on proof of damages actually suffered or it cannot be sustained." *Westgor*, 381 N.W.2d at 880. There is no evidence to show the amount of damages Time–Share suffered as a result of Schmidt's activities. This award cannot be sustained without proof.

NOTES

1. *The Prima Facie Case for Contempt.* In order to prove criminal contempt, the state must prove beyond a reasonable doubt that the defendant willfully disobeyed a court order. *See, e.g., Department of Environmental Protection of the City of New York v. Department of Environmental Conservation of the State of New York,* 70 N.Y.2d 233 (1987). The *prima facie* case for civil contempt varies in its expression. Some courts require the plaintiff to prove by "clear and convincing evidence that 1) a lawful judicial order expressing a clear directive was disobeyed; 2) the contemnor had knowledge of the order; and 3) the contemnor's disobedience prejudices the rights of a party." *McCain v. Dinkins,* 84 N.Y.2d 216 (1994). In other cases, the plaintiff must merely show "(1) the contemnor's obligation to perform an action as required by the decree; and (2) the contemnor's failure to meet the obligation." *Walters v. Walters,* 181 S.W.3d 135, 138 (Mo. App. 2005). Upon plaintiff's satisfaction of this initial showing, courts typically shift the burden to the alleged contemnor to offer evidence that it did comply, or that it was impossible to obey the order. Courts often define this inquiry by asking "whether defendants have been reasonably diligent and energetic in attempting to accomplish what was ordered." *Natural Resources Defense Council, Inc. v. Train,* 510 F.2d 692, 713 (D.C.Cir.1975). In the final analysis, is the standard for civil contempt "reasonableness," with the burden placed on the defendant to prove it? Or is it closer to strict liability, with some narrow potential for exception? How would these expressions of the civil contempt standard have played out in *Time–Share Systems v. Schmidt*?

2. *Appealability of Contempt Sanctions.* Civil contempt sanctions entered against a party during the course of a civil action are not appealable until final judgment. Criminal contempt sanctions may be immediately appealed, however.

VERMONT WOMEN'S HEALTH CENTER V. OPERATION RESCUE

159 Vt. 141, 617 A.2d 411 (1992).

DOOLEY, JUSTICE.

In November 1988, the superior court issued a TRO directed to Operation Rescue, an anti-abortion organization; defendant Michael McHugh; and "all other persons, groups and organizations acting in concert with either Operation Rescue or Michael McHugh." The TRO, which was extended by the court in December 1988 and remains in effect by stipulation of the parties, prohibits the following conduct: 1. Blocking any doorway, entrance, driveway or parking lot at the Vermont Women's Health Center. 2. Entering or attempting to enter the building. 3. Directing bullhorns, shouting, yelling or otherwise verbally directing sounds to the interior of the Vermont Women's Health Center. 4. Physically blocking the entry of any persons to the Vermont Women's Health Center.

On October 24, 1989, a group led by defendant McHugh of more than fifty persons, including the remaining defendants, physically invaded the grounds and building of the health center. They blocked doorways and exits of the building and positioned a ten-wheel truck to block the driveway. Many of them locked themselves to one another in the hallways of the building; they made a great deal of noise singing and chanting. As a result, health services for women scheduled for that day, including cancer-related examinations and other tests, as well as abortions, were cancelled. Two police officers were injured as they attempted to enter the building through doors pulled shut by protesters. The use of mace and tear gas was ultimately required to gain entry and control. Once inside, the chief of police read the face sheet of the injunction, listing the prohibited activities, in a loud and clear voice, in each of the two main wings of the building. Police then arrested defendants and the other protesters for unlawful trespass and removed them from the building.

Plaintiffs subsequently brought a civil contempt action against defendants for violation of the TRO, serving each with copies of the court's order and the motion for contempt. Following evidentiary hearings held December 20, 1989, and January 17, 1990, the court found defendants in contempt, held them liable to plaintiffs for certain fees, costs, and damages, and subjected them to prospective coercive fines to be assessed in the event of future violations of the court's order. This appeal followed.

Defendants challenge the trial court's decision to hold them jointly and severally liable for plaintiffs' damages of $3,738, the cost of service of the TRO and the new injunction imposed by the court in the amount of $5,000, and the award of more than $14,000 in attorneys' fees.

Defendants claim that the court should not have held them jointly and severally liable for plaintiffs' damages, because they did not equally share fault and responsibility for those damages, emphasizing that the point at which each defendant began to be in contempt of court varied, depending upon when each gained actual knowledge of the court order. Generally, those who act in concert to violate a court order are jointly and severally liable for resulting damages. This rule is consistent with the general principle that tortfeasors are jointly and severally liable for compensatory damages. As defendants point out, we have adopted a different rule for punitive damages. The damages at issue here, however, are entirely compensatory. We see no error in imposing joint and several liability.

Defendants' challenge to the award of attorneys' fees is also without merit. Attorneys' fees are ordinarily awarded in contempt actions as part of the compensation due complainants for defendants' actions, which have put the complainants in the position of having to seek the assistance of the courts to enforce a judgment.

Vermont follows the "American Rule" with respect to attorneys' fees, and generally does not award fees absent statutory authority or a contractual obligation.

In this case, defendants knew by its terms that the order applied to them and that they were violating it when they participated with Michael McHugh and Operation Rescue in the entry into the center. Nor do we accept the argument that the fees could not include amounts incurred in connection with plaintiffs' plan to develop an attempt for personal service of the TRO. The court found that defendants participated in an overall scheme to evade service and should be responsible for plaintiffs' expenses in trying to serve them. The award fell within the court's discretion.

Finally, defendants argue that the court erred in imposing prospective coercive fines of $10,000 per day for the first violation of the order and $20,000 per day for further violations. Although purely prospective fines are not favored in Vermont, civil contempt fines may be imposed in an appropriate circumstance either to compensate complainants or as a coercive sanction. When imposed as a coercive sanction, the fine must be purgeable—that is, capable of being avoided by defendants through adherence to the court's order. Further, the situation must be such that "it is easy to gauge the compliance or noncompliance with an order."

Both requirements are met here. The fine will be due only upon a further violation of the injunction by one of the class of persons to which it is directed, with service or actual notice of its provisions. Here the injunction prohibits clearly defined conduct, participation in which can be readily ascertained.

Further, the circumstances present here are extreme and extraordinary. In concluding that prospective fines were needed, the court emphasized the "violent tendencies" of defendants and the magnitude of the harm. It found that defendants' acts were "willful, outrageous, and presented a clear and present danger to the public health and safety." It also found that defendants claimed to act under "higher law" and did not feel bound by the injunction. This latter finding supports the conclusion that some coercive sanction is necessary in this case to deter repetition. We conclude that the imposition of a prospective coercive fine is reasonable in this case. Our disfavor of the use of prospective coercive fines must give way in this narrow and exceptional set of circumstances. No abuse of discretion is shown.

Affirmed.

NOTES

1. *Prospective Sanctions.* One of the fundamental principles of the criminal law is that criminal punishment typically should only apply to prospectively defined criminal acts with predefined standards of punishment. Civil and criminal contempt sanctions depart from these principles because a judge determines whether an act qualifies for sanctions retrospectively, after the act has occurred. Philip A. Hostak, *International Union, United Mine Workers v. Bagwell: A Paradigm Shift in the Distinction Between Civil and Criminal Contempt*, 81 CORNELL L. REV. 181, 194–95 (1995). Despite this discrepancy, the contempt power has been allowed to survive due to tradition and necessity. *Id.* at 197. *See also Int'l Union, United Mine Workers of America v. Bagwell*, 512 U.S. 821, 831–832 (1994).

2. *Fixed v. Flexible Contempt Sanctions.* Contempt sanctions take a variety of forms. In some situations, the sanctions are fixed in that the court imposes a set fine or set jail term. In other situations, the court imposes a flexible fine or sentence that is dependent on the defendant's response (*i.e.*, fines of $2,000 per day for each day of noncompliance). Contempt sanctions can also be imposed for compensatory purposes (to compensate plaintiff for injuries suffered as a result of noncompliance).

PROBLEMS

1. *The Leaky Septic Tank.* The Indian Hills subdivision presently has septic tanks, but is scheduled to receive sewers within the next two years. Nathan Shrewsbury Lord, a local lawyer, owns a leaky septic tank in the subdivision. Neighbors complain that the tank constitutes a health hazard to them. After conducting an investigation, the City declared the tank to be a public nuisance and ordered Lord to repair or replace it. When Lord refused, the City brought a public nuisance action. Assume that you are the judge assigned to hear the case, and that you ordered Lord to repair or replace the tank within two weeks. The time has passed, Lord did not comply, and the

City has moved to hold him in contempt. Assume that you have decided to hold Lord in contempt, what type of sanction should be imposed? Why?

2. *Sex Abuse Allegations and Disclosure.* A plastic surgeon, divorced from her husband, alleged that the father had sexually abused their daughter. Even though the father vigorously denied the charges, the mother refused to permit the father to see the child. When the court ordered her to permit paternal visitation, the mother moved the daughter into hiding and refused to tell the court where the girl was located. Has the mother committed contempt? If so, how should the court handle the contempt?

C. PROCEDURAL REQUIREMENTS

As the foregoing cases reveal, courts try criminal contempt and civil contempt differently. A person charged with criminal contempt is afforded certain constitutional rights, and the charges must be proven beyond a reasonable doubt. Courts also treat direct contempt differently than indirect contempt. Direct contempt applies to conduct that occurs during judicial proceedings in the presence of the court. Indirect contempt of court generally involves the violation of a court order beyond the physical parameters of the courthouse. In this section, we examine some of the procedural requirements that courts impose.

UNITED STATES V. WILSON

421 U.S. 309 (1975).

MR. CHIEF JUSTICE BURGER delivered the opinion of the Court.

We granted certiorari to decide whether a district court may impose summary contempt punishment under Fed.Rules Crim.Proc. 42(a)[1] when a witness who has been granted immunity, refuses on Fifth Amendment grounds to testify. The Court of Appeals held that in such circumstances a judge cannot dispose of the contempt summarily, but must proceed under Rule 42(b),[2] which calls for disposition only after notice and hearing, and 'a reasonable time for the preparation of the defense.'

---

[1] Rule 42(a) provides: "(a) **Summary Disposition.** A criminal contempt may be punished summarily if the judge certifies that he saw or heard the conduct constituting the contempt and that it was committed in the actual presence of the court. The order of contempt shall recite the facts and shall be signed by the judge and entered of record."

[2] Rule 42(b) provides: "(b) **Disposition Upon Notice and Hearing.** A criminal contempt except as provided in subdivision (a) of this rule shall be prosecuted on notice. The notice shall state the time and place of hearing, allowing a reasonable time for the preparation of the defense, and shall state the essential facts constituting the criminal contempt charged and describe it as such. The notice shall be given orally by the judge in open court in the presence of the defendant or, on application of the United States attorney or of an attorney appointed by the court for that purpose, by an order to show cause or an order of arrest. The defendant is entitled to a trial by jury in any case in which an act of Congress so provides. He is entitled to admission to bail as provided in these rules. If the contempt charged involves disrespect to or criticism of a judge, that judge is disqualified from presiding at the trial or hearing except with the defendant's consent. Upon a verdict or finding of guilt the court shall enter an order fixing the punishment."

Respondents Wilson and Bryan, along with Robert Anderson, were charged in separate indictments with separate bank robberies. Respondent Wilson, and Anderson, were charged with armed robbery of a bank in Tuxedo, N.Y. Respondent Bryan, and Anderson, were charged with armed robbery of a bank in Mount Ivy, N.Y. Prior to Anderson's trial both respondents pleaded guilty to charges against them, but neither was immediately given a final sentence. Sentencing of Wilson was deferred, and, pending a pre-sentence report, Bryan was given a provisional 25-year [sentence]. At Anderson's trial for the two robberies, respondents were summoned as witnesses for the prosecution. When questioned, however, each refused to testify, contending that his answers might incriminate him. The judge then granted them immunity, 18 U.S.C. §§ 6002, 6003, and ordered them to answer forthwith. He informed them that as long as they did not lie under oath they could not be prosecuted by reason of any testimony, but that if they continued to refuse to answer he would hold them in contempt. Respondents nevertheless persisted in their refusals, and the judge summarily held them in contempt. Counsel for Wilson, who acted for both respondents, argued for lenient sentences; however, trial counsel made no objection to the summary nature of the contempt citation, nor was any claim made that more time was needed to prepare a defense to the contempt citation.

Both respondents were then sentenced to six months' imprisonment, consecutive to any sentences imposed for the bank robberies. The judge made it clear that he would consider reducing the contempt sentences, or eliminating them completely, if respondents decided to testify. When counsel pointed out that a presentence study was being prepared on Bryan the judge responded: 'I am going to impose the maximum [with] the deliberate intention of revising that sentence to what might be appropriate in light of the very study that is going to be made.' The trial proceeded, but without Bryan's testimony the evidence against Anderson on the Mount Ivy robbery was such that at the end of the Government's case the judge granted Anderson's motion for acquittal. The jury was unable to reach a verdict on the Tuxedo robbery. At a later trial Anderson was convicted of that robbery.

Respondents appealed their contempt convictions. The Court of Appeals rejected the claim that their Fifth Amendment rights would have been violated by compelling them to testify after they had been granted immunity. The Court of Appeals considered itself bound by this Court's decision in *Harris v. United States*, 382 U.S. 162 (1965). [In] the Court of Appeals' view only a disorderly or obstreperous interference with court proceedings provides an occasion for use of the summary contempt power. We granted certiorari [and] reverse.

Respondents' refusals to answer, although not delivered disrespectfully, plainly fall within the express language of Rule 42(a),[6] and constitute contemptuous conduct. Rule 42(a) was never intended to be limited to situations where a witness uses scurrilous language, or threatens or creates overt physical disorder and thereby disrupts a trial. All that is necessary is that the judge certify that he 'saw or heard the conduct constituting the contempt and that it was committed in the actual presence of the court.' These requirements are met here. Indeed, here each refusal was in the context of a face-to-face encounter between the judge and respondents. *See Illinois v. Allen*, 397 U.S. 337 (1970); *Cooke v. United States*, 267 U.S. 517 (1925).

The refusals were contemptuous of judicial authority because they were intentional obstructions[7] of court proceedings that literally disrupted the progress of the trial and hence the orderly administration of justice. Respondents' contumacious silence, after a valid grant of immunity followed by an explicit, unambiguous order to testify, impeded the due course of Anderson's trial perhaps more so than violent conduct in the courtroom. Violent disruptions can be cured swiftly by bodily removing the offender from the courtroom, or by physical restraints, *Illinois v. Allen, supra*; *see Ex parte Terry*, 128 U.S. 289 (1888), and the trial may proceed. But as this case demonstrates, a contumacious refusal to answer not only frustrates the inquiry but can destroy a prosecution. Here it was a prosecution; the same kind of contumacious conduct could, in another setting, destroy a defendant's ability to establish a case.

The face-to-face refusal to comply with the court's order itself constituted an affront to the court, and when that kind of refusal disrupts and frustrates an ongoing proceeding, as it did here, summary contempt must be available to vindicate the authority of the court as well as to provide the recalcitrant witness with some incentive to testify. *In re Chiles*, 22 Wall. 157, 168, 22 L.Ed. 819 (1875). Whether such incentive is

---

[6] Rule 42 applies the contempt power defined in 18 U.S.C. s 401. That statute provides that a federal court has the power to punish by fine or imprisonment, at its discretion, such contempt of its authority as '(m)isbehavior of any person in its presence or so near thereto as to obstruct the administration of justice.' The predecessor of the statute was enacted to limit the broad power granted by the Judiciary Act of 1789, 1 Stat. 73. *Nye v. United States*, 313 U.S. 33, 45 (1941). Courts had indiscriminately used the summary contempt power to punish persons for acts that occurred far from the court's view and which, in truth, could not be considered direct affronts to its dignity, and obstructions of justice. Thus the phrase 'in its presence or so near thereto' was intended to apply a geographical limitation on the power. *Id.*, at 50. Misbehavior actually in the face of the court remained punishable summarily, and this Court made it clear that contemptuous actions 'actually interrupting the court in the conduct of its business,' were summarily punishable just as 'misbehavior in the vicinity of the court disrupting to quiet and order.' *Ibid.*

[7] The trial judge explained to respondents the protection accorded by the grant of immunity and that if they continued in their refusals he would hold them in contempt. He also offered them an opportunity to speak in their own behalf. *Groppi v. Leslie*, 404 U.S. 496, 501 (1972). Moreover, the judge made it clear that he would consider reducing the sentences if respondents did testify. In view of this their continued refusals to testify can only be termed intentional.

necessary in a particular case is a matter the Rule wisely leaves to the discretion of the trial court.[9]

Our conclusion that summary contempt is available under the circumstances here is supported by the fact that Rule 42 has consistently been recognized to be no more than a restatement of the law existing when the Rule was adopted, and the law at that time allowed summary punishment for refusals to testify, *Hale v. Henkel*, 201 U.S. 43 (1906); *Nelson v. United States*, 201 U.S. 92 (1906); *Blair v. United States*, 250 U.S. 273 1919).

The Court of Appeals considered itself bound by language in *Harris* to hold Rule 42(a) inapplicable to the facts here. The crucial difference between the cases, however, is that Harris did not deal with a refusal to testify which obstructed an ongoing trial. In Harris a witness before a grand jury had been granted immunity, and nevertheless refused to answer certain questions. The witness was then brought before a District Judge and asked the same questions again. When he still refused to answer, the court summarily held him in contempt. We held in that case that summary contempt was inappropriate because there was no compelling reason for an immediate remedy. A grand jury ordinarily deals with many inquiries and cases at one time, and it can rather easily suspend action on any one, and turn to another while proceedings under Rule 42(b) are completed. We noted in Harris that "swiftness was not a prerequisite of [justice]." Trial courts, on the contrary, cannot be expected to dart from case to case on their calendars any time a witness who has been granted immunity decides not to answer questions. In a trial, the court, the parties, witnesses, and jurors are assembled in the expectation that it will proceed as scheduled. Here when defense counsel asked for a continuance; he said: 'I think we cannot delay this trial. I cannot delay it. I have many other matters that are equally important to the people concerned in those cases which are following.' Delay under Rule 42(b) may be substantial and all essential participants in the trial may no longer be readily available when a trial reconvenes. In *Harris* this Court recognized these problems in noting that summary punishment may be necessary where a "refusal [is] an open, serious threat to orderly procedure." A refusal to testify during a trial may be such an open, serious threat, and here it plainly constituted a literal "breakdown" in the prosecution's case.

---

9 In *Shillitani v. United States*, 384 U.S. 364, 371 n. 9 (1966), we said: "[T]he trial judge (should) first consider the feasibility of coercing testimony through the imposition of civil contempt. The judge should resort to criminal sanctions only after he determines, for good reason, that the civil remedy would be inappropriate." Here, of course, that admonition carries little weight because at the time they acted contemptuously [respondents] were incarcerated due to their own guilty pleas. Under the circumstances here the threat of immediate confinement for civil contempt would have provided little incentive for them to testify. Nevertheless, the careful trial judge made it clear to respondents that if they relented and obeyed his order he would consider reducing their sentences; and he also explained that he would consider other factors in deciding whether to reduce the sentences.

In an ongoing trial, with the judge, jurors, counsel, and witnesses all waiting, Rule 42(a) provides an appropriate remedial tool to discourage witnesses from contumacious refusals to comply with lawful orders essential to prevent a breakdown of the proceedings. Where time is not of the essence, however, the provisions of Rule 42(b) may be more appropriate to deal with contemptuous conduct. We adhere to the principle that only "[T]he least possible power adequate to the end proposed" should be used in contempt cases. *Anderson v. Dunn*, 6 Wheat. 204, 231, 5 L.Ed. 242 (1821). As with all power, the authority under Rule 42(a) to punish summarily can be abused; the courts of appeals, however, can deal with abuses of discretion without restricting the Rule in contradiction of its express terms, and without unduly limiting the power of the trial judge to act swiftly and firmly to prevent contumacious conduct from disrupting the orderly progress of a criminal trial.

Reversed.

MR. JUSTICE BLACKMUN, with whom MR. JUSTICE REHNQUIST joins, concurring.

I write separately to express my conviction that *Harris*, at the most, now stands for nothing more than the proposition that a witness' refusal to answer grand jury questions is not conduct "in the actual presence of the court," even when the questions are restated by the district judge and the witness persists in his refusal to [answer]. Summary contempt, especially summary criminal contempt, is not a power lightly to be exercised. Nevertheless, summary criminal contempt is a necessary and legitimate part of a court's arsenal of weapons to prevent obstruction, violent or otherwise, of its proceedings.

MR. JUSTICE BRENNAN, with whom MR. JUSTICE DOUGLAS and MR. JUSTICE MARSHALL join, dissenting.

The Court today declines the Government's invitation to overrule *Harris*, and that case clearly compels affirmance of the judgment of the Court of Appeals. Respondents were witnesses at an ongoing trial while the witness in Harris was a grand jury witness, brought before the judge and asked the same questions he had not answered before the grand jury.

NOTES

1. *Commencement of Contempt Proceedings.* A summary contempt proceeding may be initiated by a judge himself. However, for most criminal contempts, the court will usually ask the state prosecutor to initiate and prosecute the proceeding. However, if the prosecutor declines, the court may appoint a private attorney to handle the prosecution, but should not appoint an attorney for an interested party in the litigation. *See Young v. United States ex rel Vuitton et Files S.A.*, 481 U.S. 787, 788–789 (1987). In a civil

contempt situation, the proceeding may be commenced on the judge's own initiative, or by a party's filing of a motion for order to show cause.

2. *Procedural Requirements in Criminal Contempt Cases.* In non-summary proceedings, various procedural protections apply to criminal contempt proceedings. *See* proceedings, *Hicks v. Feiock,* 485 U.S. 624, 632 (1988); *Bloom v. Illinois,* 391 U.S. 194, 201 (1968). Included are protections against double jeopardy, *In re Bradley,* 318 U.S. 50 (1943), right to notice of charges, assistance of counsel, and the right to present a defense, *Cooke v. United States,* 267 U.S. 517, 537 (1925), the privilege against self-incrimination and the right to require that the state prove the contempt beyond a reasonable doubt, *Gompers v. Bucks Stove & Range Co.,* 221 U.S. 418, 444 (1911), the right to a public trial before an unbiased judge, *In re Oliver,* 333 U.S. 257 (1948), the right to a jury trial for "serious" criminal contempts (those involving imprisonment for more than six months), *Bloom,* 391 U.S., at 199. In contrast, civil contempt sanctions, or those penalties designed to compel future compliance with a court order, are considered to be coercive and avoidable through obedience, and thus may be imposed in an ordinary civil proceeding upon notice and an opportunity to be heard. Neither a jury trial nor proof beyond a reasonable doubt is required. *See International Union, United Mine Workers of America v. Bagwell,* 512 U.S. 821, 831–832 (1994); *Young v. United States ex rel Vuitton et Fils S.A.,* 481 U.S. 787, 788–789 (1987)

3. *The Requirement of "Willfulness."* As a general rule, the conduct that gives rise to a criminal contempt proceeding must be "willfull."

4. *Improper Court Filings.* In *Nye v. United States,* 313 U.S. 33 (1941), petitioners sought dismissal of a law suit alleging that plaintiff's son died as a result of ingesting medicine manufactured and sold by petitioners. The plaintiff was both illiterate and feeble in mind. Petitioners used liquor and persuasion to encourage him to dismiss the law suit, and asked their own lawyer to prepare the necessary documents. Although the acts of persuasion took place some distance from the courthouse, the documents were filed with and mailed to the court. Although the Court recognized that there was an "obstruction in the administration of justice," which resulted from the fact of "the long delay and large expense which the reprehensible conduct of petitioners entailed," the Court concluded that the "that in purpose and effect there was an obstruction in the administration of justice did not bring the condemned conduct within the vicinity of the court in any normal meaning of the term. It was not misbehavior in the vicinity of the court disrupting to quiet and order or actually interrupting the court in the conduct of its business." As a result, "If petitioners can be punished for their misconduct, it must be under the Criminal Code where they will be afforded the normal safeguards surrounding criminal prosecutions."

BLOOM V. ILLINOIS

391 U.S. 194, 88 S.Ct. 1477, 20 L.Ed.2d 522 (1968).

MR. JUSTICE WHITE delivered the opinion of the Court.

Article III, § 2, of the Constitution provides that "the Trial of all Crimes, except in Cases of Impeachment, shall be by Jury." The Sixth Amendment states that "[in] all criminal prosecutions, the accused shall enjoy the right to a speedy and public trial, by an impartial [jury]." The Fifth and Fourteenth Amendments forbid both the Federal Government and the States from depriving any person of "life, liberty, or property, without due process of law." Notwithstanding these provisions, this Court has consistently upheld the constitutional power of the state and federal courts to punish any criminal contempt without a jury trial. This Court has construed the Due Process Clause and the otherwise inclusive language of Article III and the Sixth Amendment as permitting summary trials in contempt cases because at common law contempt was tried without a jury and because the power of courts to punish for contempt without the intervention of any other agency was considered essential to the proper and effective functioning of the courts and to the administration of justice.

Our deliberations have convinced us, however, that serious contempts are so nearly like other serious crimes that they are subject to the jury trial provisions of the Constitution, now binding on the States, and that the traditional rule is constitutionally infirm insofar as it permits other than petty contempts to be tried without honoring a demand for a jury trial. We accept the judgment that criminal contempt is a petty offense unless the punishment makes it a serious one; but, in our view, dispensing with the jury in the trial of contempts subjected to severe punishment represents an unacceptable construction of the Constitution, "an unconstitutional assumption of powers by the courts which no lapse of time or respectable array of opinion should make us hesitate to correct." *Black & White Taxicab & Transfer Co. v. Brown & Yellow Taxicab & Transfer Co.*, 276 U.S. 518, 533 (1928) (Holmes, J., dissenting). The Constitution guarantees the right to jury trial in state court prosecutions for contempt just as it does for other crimes.

Criminal contempt is a crime in the ordinary sense; it is a violation of the law, a public wrong which is punishable by fine or imprisonment or both. Criminally contemptuous conduct may violate other provisions of the criminal law; but even when this is not the case convictions for criminal contempt are indistinguishable from ordinary criminal convictions, for their impact on the individual defendant is the same. Indeed, the role of criminal contempt and that of many ordinary criminal laws seem identical—protection of the institutions of our government and enforcement of their mandates.

Given that criminal contempt is a crime in every fundamental respect, the question is whether it is a crime to which the jury trial provisions of the Constitution apply. We hold that it is, primarily because in terms of those considerations which make the right to jury trial fundamental in criminal cases, there is no substantial difference between serious contempts and other serious crimes. Indeed, in contempt cases an even more compelling argument can be made for providing a right to jury trial as a protection against the arbitrary exercise of official power. Contemptuous conduct, though a public wrong, often strikes at the most vulnerable and human qualities of a judge's temperament. Even when the contempt is not a direct insult to the court or the judge, it frequently represents a rejection of judicial authority, or an interference with the judicial process or with the duties of officers of the court.

The court has long recognized the potential for abuse in exercising the summary power to imprison for contempt—it is an "arbitrary" power which is "liable to abuse." *Ex parte Terry*, 128 U.S. 289, 313 (1888). This course of events demonstrates the unwisdom of vesting the judiciary with completely untrammeled power to punish contempt, and makes clear the need for effective safeguards against that power's abuse. Prosecutions for contempt play a significant role in the proper functioning of our judicial system; but despite the important values which the contempt power protects, courts and legislatures have gradually eroded the power of judges to try contempts of their own authority. In modern times, procedures in criminal contempt cases have come to mirror those used in ordinary criminal cases. Our experience teaches that convictions for criminal contempt, not infrequently resulting in extremely serious penalties are indistinguishable from those obtained under ordinary criminal laws. If the right to jury trial is a fundamental matter in other criminal cases, which we think it is, it must also be extended to criminal contempt cases.

Nor are there compelling reasons for a contrary result. As we read the earlier cases [upholding] the power to try contempts without a jury, it was not doubted that the summary power was subject to abuse or that the right to jury trial would be an effective check. Rather, it seems to have been thought that summary power was necessary to preserve the dignity, independence, and effectiveness of the judicial process—"To submit the question of disobedience to another tribunal, be it a jury or another court, would operate to deprive the proceeding of half its efficiency." *In re Debs*, 158 U.S. 564, 595 (1895). We do not agree: when serious punishment for contempt is contemplated, rejecting a demand for jury trial cannot be squared with the Constitution or justified by considerations of efficiency or the desirability of vindicating the authority of the court.

We place little credence in the notion that the independence of the judiciary hangs on the power to try contempts summarily and are not persuaded that the additional time and expense possibly involved in submitting serious contempts to juries will seriously handicap the effective functioning of the courts. The goals of dispatch, economy, and efficiency are important, but they are amply served by preserving the power to commit for civil contempt and by recognizing that many contempts are not serious crimes but petty offenses not within the jury trial provisions of the Constitution. When a serious contempt is at issue, considerations of efficiency must give way to the more fundamental interest of ensuring the even-handed exercise of judicial power.

Some special mention of contempts in the presence of the judge is warranted. Rule 42 (a) of the Federal Rules of Criminal Procedure provides that "a criminal contempt may be punished summarily if the judge certifies that he saw or heard the conduct constituting the contempt and that it was committed in the actual presence of the court." This rule reflects the common-law rule which is widely if not uniformly followed in the States. Although Rule 42 (a) is based in part on the premise that it is not necessary specially to present the facts of a contempt which occurred in the very presence of the judge, it also rests on the need to maintain order and a deliberative atmosphere in the courtroom. The power of a judge to quell disturbance cannot attend upon the impaneling of a jury. There is, therefore, a strong temptation to make exception to the rule we establish today for disorders in the courtroom. We are convinced, however, that no such special rule is needed. It is old law that the guarantees of jury trial found in Article III and the Sixth Amendment do not apply to petty offenses. Only today we have reaffirmed that position. By deciding to treat criminal contempt like other crimes insofar as the right to jury trial is concerned, we similarly place it under the rule that petty crimes need not be tried to a jury.

Petitioner Bloom was held in contempt of court for filing a spurious will for probate. At his trial it was established that the putative testator died on July 6, 1964, and that after that date Pauline Owens, a practical nurse for the decedent, engaged Bloom to draw and execute a will in the decedent's name. The will was dated June 21, 1964. Bloom knew the will was false when he presented it for admission in the Probate Division of the Circuit Court of Cook County. The State's Attorney of that county filed a complaint charging Bloom with contempt of court. At trial petitioner's timely motion for a jury trial was denied. Petitioner was found guilty of criminal contempt and sentenced to imprisonment for 24 months. On direct appeal to the Illinois Supreme Court, his conviction was affirmed. That court held that neither state law nor the Federal Constitution provided a right to jury trial in criminal contempt proceedings.

Petitioner Bloom contends that the conduct for which he was convicted of criminal contempt constituted the crime of forgery under Ill.

Rev. Stat., c. 38, ¶ 17–3. Defendants tried under that statute enjoy a right to jury trial and face a possible sentence of one to 14 years, a fine not to exceed $1,000, or both. Petitioner was not tried under this statute, but rather was convicted of criminal contempt. Under Illinois law no maximum punishment is provided for convictions for criminal contempt. Bloom was sentenced to imprisonment for two years. Criminal contempt is not a crime of the sort that requires the right to jury trial regardless of the penalty involved. When the legislature has not expressed a judgment as to the seriousness of an offense by fixing a maximum penalty which may be imposed, we are to look to the penalty actually imposed as the best evidence of the seriousness of the offense. Under this rule it is clear that Bloom was entitled to the right to trial by jury, and it was constitutional error to deny him that right. Accordingly, we reverse and remand for proceedings not inconsistent with this opinion.

Reversed and remanded.

NOTES

1. *Jury Trials for Contempt Cases Involving Large Fines.* In *United States v. Twentieth Century Fox Film Corp.*, 882 F.2d 656 (2d Cir.1989), the court held that a corporation is entitled to a jury trial in a prosecution for criminal contempt that results in a substantial fine, in that case, $500,000:

> Interpreting the Sixth Amendment to permit a fine of any amount to be imposed on corporations convicted of criminal contempt without a jury trial would show inadequate respect for the Amendment's general preference for a jury trial in criminal cases. Once *Bloom* abandoned the notion that criminal contempts were so special as to be totally exempt from the scope of the jury trial guarantee, the contention that one category of defendants could be punished up to the limit of the Excessive Fines Clause of the Eighth Amendment without a jury trial became untenable.
>
> Once it is determined that the Sixth Amendment guarantees corporate contemnors a jury trial at some level of punishment severity, the issue becomes whether that level is always to be determined relatively by comparing the amount of a fine to the corporation's financial resources, or whether at some absolute dollar amount a fine is so serious as to require a jury trial regardless of the contemnor's financial condition. We believe that, just as there is a six-month threshold that determines when imprisonment is "serious," there must be some dollar threshold applicable to fines. No matter how prosperous a corporation may be, a large fine is a punishment of significance, and at some point the amount of a fine indicates that an offense is serious, no matter how substantial the financial reserves of the contemnor. Furthermore, since the amount of punishment imposed, rather than authorized, determines the availability of a jury for criminal contempts, the absence of a dollar

threshold would create needless trial uncertainty in those cases where a corporation with considerable resources is likely to be fined a substantial sum.

For fines below the $100,000 threshold, it will remain appropriate to consider whether the fine has such a significant financial impact upon a particular organization as to indicate that the punishment is for a serious offense, requiring a jury trial. We need not consider what the appropriate fine threshold would be for individuals charged with criminal contempt.

2. *Commencement of Contempt Proceedings.* A contempt proceeding can be commenced in one of two ways: on the court's own motion, or at the behest of a party. When a party institutes a contempt proceeding, it does so by filing an "order to show cause" why the defendant should be held in contempt. Consider the following show cause order entered in *Galella v. Onassis*, 533 F.Supp. 1076 (S.D.N.Y.1982):

LET THE PLAINTIFF SHOW CAUSE, in the United States District Court, Room 1505, Foley Square, New York, New York, on December 15, 1971 at 10 A.M., or as soon thereafter as counsel can be heard, why an order should not be entered herein pursuant to Civil Rule 14 of the rules of this Court and 18 U.S.C. § 401(3), adjudging the plaintiff in contempt of this Court for having violated and disregarded the terms of said temporary restraining order, ordering that plaintiff purge himself of said contempt by payment to defendant Jacqueline Onassis of the sum of $10,000, together with all the costs of this proceeding, including attorneys fees, and restraining the plaintiff, Ronald E. Galella, his agents, servants, employees and all persons in active concert and participation with him from photographing the defendant, Jacqueline Onassis, or her children, Caroline B. Kennedy and John F. Kennedy, Jr., from keeping the defendant or her children under surveillance or following them, from approaching within a distance of 200 yards of the apartment building at 1040 Fifth Avenue, New York, New York, from knowingly being physically within 100 yards of the persons of defendant Jacqueline Onassis and her infant children, Caroline B. Kennedy and John F. Kennedy, Jr., or any of them, or from communicating or attempting to communicate with any of them in any fashion. It appearing to the Court that plaintiff is about to commit the acts hereinafter specified and that he will do so unless restrained by order of this Court and that immediate and irreparable injury, loss or damage will result to defendant before notice can be given and the plaintiff or his attorney can be heard in opposition to the granting of a temporary restraining order, in that plaintiff, in spite of the temporary restraining order entered herein on October 8, 1971 and extended by order dated October 28, 1971, has renewed conduct and activities causing immediate and irreparable harm to the mental and physical well being of the defendant, Jacqueline Onassis, and her infant children, Caroline B. Kennedy and John F. Kennedy, Jr., and defendant having previously given security approved by the Court in the sum of $10,000, for the payment of such costs and damages as may be incurred or suffered by any party who is found to have been wrongfully enjoined or restrained; it is further ORDERED, that plaintiff, Ronald E. Galella, his agents, servants, employees and all persons in active concert and participation with him be and they hereby are restrained from keeping the defendant or her children under surveillance or following them, from approaching within a distance of 100 yards of the apartment building at 1040 Fifth Avenue, New York, New York, from knowingly being physically within 50 yards of the persons of defendant Jacqueline Onassis and her infant children, Caroline B. Kennedy and John F. Kennedy, Jr., or any of them, or from communicating or attempting to communicate with any of them in any fashion. This order remains in full force and effect until the final resolution of the within application (the parties consenting thereto).

3. *Aggregate Sentences.* What if an alleged contemnor was sentenced to multiple criminal contempt sanctions, which together exceeded six months—is a jury trial required? In *Codispoti v. Pennsylvania,* 418 U.S. 506, 512, 94 S.Ct. 2687, 2691, 41 L.Ed.2d 912 (1974), the absence of a legislative intent about the offense's seriousness, coupled with concerns about judicial bias, led the Court to hold that multiple consecutive (but not concurrent) sentences must be aggregated for the purpose of determining the jury trial right. In *Codispoti*, the contemnor was tried and sentenced in one hearing. What if the criminal sentences are doled out over the course of a trial, with only the final act of contempt and accompanying sentence breaking the aggregate six-month barrier? Although the Court has not ruled explicitly on this question, it has in dictum indicated that the holding in *Codispoti* is limited to cases in which multiple counts of contempt were tried in one proceeding. *See Lewis v. U.S.*, 518 U.S. 322, 331–33 (1996). Might not a judge get around the jury requirement simply by holding multiple proceedings?

4. *The Jury Trial Right in Civil Compensatory Contempt Hearings.* As noted in Chapter 2, the Seventh Amendment of the United States Constitution states that "In Suits at common law, where the value in controversy shall exceed twenty dollars, the right of trial by jury shall be [preserved]" At the time that the Seventh Amendment was adopted, civil compensatory proceedings were not tried to a jury. Moreover, the federal courts and most state courts have rejected such a claim, however, urging that because the person harmed by contemptuous conduct may sue separately, with a jury, for tort damages, a jury is not required in civil compensatory contempt proceedings. A few state courts have interpreted their analogous state constitutional jury mandates as requiring a jury for civil compensatory contempt hearings.

ILLINOIS V. ALLEN

397 U.S. 337, 90 S.Ct. 1057, 25 L.Ed.2d 353 (1970).

MR. JUSTICE BLACK delivered the opinion of the Court.

The Confrontation Clause of the Sixth Amendment to the United States Constitution provides that: "In all criminal prosecutions, the accused shall enjoy the right [to] be confronted with the witnesses against [him]." We have held that the Fourteenth Amendment makes the guarantees of this clause obligatory upon the States. One of the most basic of the rights guaranteed by the Confrontation Clause is the accused's right to be present in the courtroom at every stage of his trial. The question presented in this case is whether an accused can claim the benefit of this constitutional right to remain in the courtroom while at the same time he engages in speech and conduct which is so noisy, disorderly, and disruptive that it is exceedingly difficult or wholly impossible to carry on the trial.

The facts surrounding Allen's expulsion from the courtroom are set out in the Court of Appeals' opinion sustaining Allen's contention: "After his indictment and during the pretrial stage, the petitioner (Allen) refused court-appointed counsel and indicated to the trial court on several occasions that he wished to conduct his own defense. After considerable argument by the petitioner, the trial judge told him, 'I'll let you be your own lawyer, but I'll ask Mr. Kelly (court-appointed counsel) (to) sit in and protect the record for you, insofar as possible.' The trial began on September 9, 1957. After the State's Attorney had accepted the first four jurors following their voir dire examination, the petitioner began examining the first juror and continued at great length. Finally, the trial judge interrupted the petitioner, requesting him to confine his questions solely to matters relating to the prospective juror's qualifications. At that point, the petitioner started to argue with the judge in a most abusive and disrespectful manner. At last, and seemingly in desperation, the judge asked appointed counsel to proceed with the examination of the jurors. The petitioner continued to talk, proclaiming that the appointed attorney was not going to act as his lawyer. He terminated his remarks by saying, 'When I go out for lunchtime, you're (the judge) going to be a corpse here.' At that point he tore the file which his attorney had and threw the papers on the floor. The trial judge thereupon stated to the petitioner, 'One more outbreak of that sort and I'll remove you from the courtroom.' This warning had no effect on the petitioner. He continued to talk back to the judge, saying, 'There's not going to be no trial, either. I'm going to sit here and you're going to talk and you can bring your shackles out and straight jacket and put them on me and tape my mouth, but it will do no good because there's not going to be no trial.' After more abusive remarks by the petitioner, the trial judge ordered the trial to proceed in the petitioner's absence. The petitioner was removed from the courtroom. The voir dire examination then continued and the jury was selected in the absence of the petitioner. 'After a noon recess and before the jury was brought into the courtroom, the petitioner, appearing before the judge, complained about the fairness of the trial and his appointed attorney. He also said he wanted to be present in the court during his trial. In reply, the judge said that the petitioner would be permitted to remain in the courtroom if he 'behaved (himself) and (did) not interfere with the introduction of the case.' The jury was brought in and seated. Counsel for the petitioner then moved to exclude the witnesses from the courtroom. The (petitioner) protested this effort on the part of his attorney, saying: 'There is going to be no proceeding. I'm going to start talking and I'm going to keep on talking all through the trial. There's not going to be no trial like this. I want my sister and my friends here in court to testify for me.' The trial judge thereupon ordered the petitioner removed from the courtroom. After this second removal, Allen remained out of the courtroom during the presentation of the State's case-in-chief, except that he was brought in on several occasions for purposes of identification. During one of these latter appearances, Allen responded to one of the judge's questions with vile and abusive language. After the prosecution's case had been presented, the trial judge reiterated his promise to Allen that he could return to the courtroom whenever he agreed to conduct himself properly. Allen gave some assurances of proper conduct and was permitted to be present through the remainder of the trial, principally his defense, which was conducted by his appointed counsel.

It is essential to the proper administration of criminal justice that dignity, order, and decorum be the hallmarks of all court proceedings in our country. The flagrant disregard in the courtroom of elementary standards of proper conduct should not and cannot be tolerated. We believe trial judges confronted with disruptive, contumacious, stubbornly defiant defendants must be given sufficient discretion to meet the circumstances of each case. No one formula for maintaining the appropriate courtroom atmosphere will be best in all situations. We think there are at least three constitutionally permissible ways for a trial judge to handle an obstreperous defendant like Allen: (1) bind and gag him, thereby keeping him present; (2) cite him for contempt; (3) take him out of the courtroom until he promises to conduct himself properly.

Trying a defendant for a crime while he sits bound and gagged before the judge and jury would to an extent comply with that part of the Sixth Amendment's purposes that accords the defendant an opportunity to confront the witnesses at the trial. But even to contemplate such a technique, much less see it, arouses a feeling that no person should be tried while shackled and gagged except as a last resort. Not only is it possible that the sight of shackles and gags might have a significant effect on the jury's feelings about the defendant, but the use of this technique is itself something of an affront to the very dignity and decorum of judicial proceedings that the judge is seeking to uphold. Moreover, one of the defendant's primary advantages of being present at the trial, his ability to communicate with his counsel, is greatly reduced when the defendant is in a condition of total physical restraint. It is in part because of these inherent disadvantages and limitations in this method of dealing with disorderly defendants that we decline to hold that a defendant cannot under any possible circumstances be deprived of his right to be present at trial. [In] some situations which we need not attempt to foresee, binding and gagging might possibly be the fairest and most reasonable way to handle a defendant who acts as Allen did here.

It is true that citing or threatening to cite a contumacious defendant for criminal contempt might in itself be sufficient to make a defendant stop interrupting a trial. If so, the problem would be solved easily, and the defendant could remain in the courtroom. Of course, if the defendant is determined to prevent any trial, then a court in attempting to try the defendant for contempt is still confronted with the identical dilemma that the Illinois court faced in this case. And criminal contempt has obvious limitations as a sanction when the defendant is charged with a crime so serious that a very severe sentence such as death or life imprisonment is likely to be imposed. In such a case the defendant might not be affected by a mere contempt sentence when he ultimately faces a far more serious sanction. Nevertheless, the contempt remedy should be borne in mind by a judge in the circumstances of this case.

Another aspect of the contempt remedy is the judge's power, when exercised consistently with state and federal law, to imprison an unruly defendant such as Allen for civil contempt and discontinue the trial until such time as the defendant promises to behave himself. This procedure is consistent with the defendant's right to be present at trial, and yet it avoids the serious shortcomings of the use of shackles and gags. It must be recognized, however, that a defendant might conceivably, as a matter of calculated strategy, elect to spend a prolonged period in confinement for contempt in the hope that adverse witnesses might be unavailable after a lapse of time. A court must guard against allowing a defendant to profit from his own wrong in this way.

The trial court decided under the circumstances to remove the defendant from the courtroom and to continue his trial in his absence until and unless he promised to conduct himself in a manner befitting an American courtroom. We find nothing unconstitutional about this procedure. Allen's behavior was clearly of such an extreme and aggravated nature as to justify either his removal from the courtroom or his total physical restraint. Prior to his removal he was repeatedly warned by the trial judge that he would be removed from the courtroom if he persisted in his unruly conduct, [and] the record demonstrates that Allen would not have been at all dissuaded by the trial judge's use of his criminal contempt powers. Allen was constantly informed that he could return to the trial when he would agree to conduct himself in an orderly manner. Under these circumstances we hold that Allen lost his right guaranteed by the Sixth and Fourteenth Amendments to be present throughout his trial.

It is not pleasant to hold that the respondent Allen was properly banished from the court for a part of his own trial. But our courts, palladiums of liberty as they are, cannot be treated disrespectfully with impunity. Nor can the accused be permitted by his disruptive conduct indefinitely to avoid being tried on the charges brought against him. It would degrade our country and our judicial system to permit our courts to be bullied, insulted, and humiliated and their orderly progress thwarted and obstructed by defendants brought before them charged with crimes. As guardians of the public welfare, our state and federal judicial systems strive to administer equal justice to the rich and the poor, the good and the bad, the native and foreign born of every race, nationality, and religion. Being manned by humans, the courts are not perfect and are bound to make some errors. But, if our courts are to remain what the Founders intended, the citadels of justice, their proceedings cannot and must not be infected with the sort of scurrilous, abusive language and conduct paraded before the Illinois trial judge in this case. The record shows that the Illinois judge at all times conducted himself with that dignity, decorum, and patience that befit a judge. Even in holding that the trial judge had erred, the Court of Appeals praised his "commendable patience under severe provocation."

There is nothing whatever in this record to show that the judge did not act completely within his discretion. Deplorable as it is to remove a man from his own trial, even for a short time, we hold that the judge did not commit legal error in doing what he did.

The judgment of the Court of Appeals is reversed.

Reversed.

MR. JUSTICE BRENNAN, concurring.

When a defendant is excluded from his trial, the court should make reasonable efforts to enable him to communicate with his attorney and, if possible, to keep apprised of the progress of his trial.

PROBLEMS

1. *What Would You Have Done?* Suppose that you were the judge in this case, and petitioners engaged in this conduct. What actions would you take?

2. *Contempt and Self-Representation.* In *Mayberry*, defendant was proceeding *pro se* although "standby counsel" had been appointed. Does the

fact of *pro se* representation limit the judge's options for dealing with contemptuous behavior? Why? Are there ways to avoid potential problems?

3. *More on* Mayberry. In the actual case, when the trial ended, the judge held petitioners guilty of criminal contempt. He found that petitioner had committed one or more contempts on 11 of the 21 days of trial and sentenced him to not less than one nor more than two years for each of the 11 contempts or a total of 11 to 22 years. Was it appropriate for the judge to hear the contempts himself?

IN RE YENGO

84 N.J. 111, 417 A.2d 533 (1980).

The opinion of the Court was delivered by POLLOCK, J.

The issue is whether the unexcused absence of an attorney from a trial constitutes contempt in the presence of the court justifying summary disposition under R. 1:10–1. Respondent, John W. Yengo, represented Leo Leone, one of ten defendants in a multiple defendant gambling conspiracy trial. The nature of the case, the number of defendants and their counsel, together with the complexity of the evidence, presented difficult trial problems. The intricate proofs, which included wiretaps or monitored telephone conversations by court-authorized electronic surveillance, made attorney attendance throughout the trial a matter of highest priority. Both court and counsel recognized the special problems inherent in the management of the case. For example, 18, rather than 12, jurors were impaneled. The trial was estimated to last for five weeks. Those difficulties were compounded by an influenza epidemic and a major snowstorm. Because of bad weather, the scheduled trial date was postponed three times.

Anticipating scheduling difficulties among the numerous defense attorneys, the judge stressed the need for regular attendance. She instructed counsel that she would not tolerate tardiness or absence without her prior approval. On February 8, 1978, she pointedly advised counsel: Now you are considered on trial before me. You are to advise all other courts and all other judges that you are on trial before me. If you have any problem with any judge, you let me know. So, don't get involved in any other case or trial. On February 14, the judge again emphasized the importance of punctuality. Yengo was not only aware of the instructions, but on February 22 he requested Judge Loftus to call another judge before whom he had a matter pending.

Testimony began on February 21, and Yengo appeared regularly until March 2. On that date, without previously informing the judge, he failed to appear at trial. Yengo had discussed the matter with the prosecutor, several of the other defense attorneys and his client. In his place, Lawrence Burns, an attorney admitted to practice in 1975, appeared on behalf of Leone. Burns shared office space with Yengo, received cases from him, and described himself as Yengo's associate. Burns arrived late for the trial.

Leone advised the court that he consented to representation by Burns in Yengo's absence. Earlier Leone had consented to representation by Kenneth R. Claudat, another defense attorney, to "protect his interest" until Burns arrived. [The] trial judge acknowledged Burns' authorization to represent Leone, and heard testimony of the State's wiretap monitor witness until lunchtime. Following the initial hour of testimony, Judge Loftus became concerned about the extent of Burns' knowledge of the case. During the lunchtime recess, the judge questioned Burns in her chambers about Yengo's absence. Burns stated he did not know why Yengo had failed to obtain court approval for his absence, why he was absent, or where he had gone.

Burns informed the judge that Yengo had called Burns at 9 o'clock the preceding evening to advise that he was going out of the country. Burns stated further that he had reviewed the file with Yengo for 15 minutes at 11:00 p.m. on that evening and that previously he had spent two days reviewing the file and discussing it with Yengo.

The trial proceeded with Burns acting as counsel for Leone. Judge Loftus tried several times to locate Yengo through calls placed by her secretary to his answering service. Judge Loftus also called Yengo's home and spoke with his daughter, who told the judge that Yengo had gone to Bermuda on a four day vacation and would return on Sunday, March 5. However, the daughter was unable to inform the court where Yengo was staying in Bermuda. The trial court concluded that she had no alternative but to let the trial continue. The other attorneys stated that the testimony that would be adduced during Yengo's absence would not relate to Leone. Although the court expressed concern that an expert witness for the State might testify before Yengo returned, the trial continued uninterrupted through Friday, March 3.

The judge did not issue a citation for contempt on March 2 or March 3, the days on which Yengo was absent. Instead, she sent a telegram to his home ordering and directing him to appear before her at 9:00 a.m. on Monday, March 6, 1978, the next trial date. On that date, Yengo appeared in court. The trial judge cleared the courtroom, except for court personnel and Yengo. He explained that he had been in Bermuda on business for a supermarket. He stated that he did not communicate with the court because he did not know if he would be going to Bermuda until late Wednesday, March 1. He also explained that, as a matter of trial strategy, he had decided not to cross-examine the monitor witness from the State.

The trial judge stated: I called you here this morning and gave you the opportunity to speak because I thought that maybe the information that had come to my attention by the various phone calls I had to make, that you had gone to Bermuda for the weekend, was wrong. I thought maybe there was some kind of explanation for it, but that is not so. There is absolutely no emergent necessity for you to leave this Country and go to Bermuda. Your actions just bespeak nothing but irresponsible professional conduct toward your client and towards this court. She then cited him for contempt in the presence of the court and stated he would be "dealt with further at another time with regard to the disposition of this particular citation."

On April 14, 1978, Yengo appeared before Judge Loftus. She affirmed the determination of contempt and imposed a fine of $500. In her certification on April 21, 1978, the trial court stated: The action of John Yengo, Esq., in going to Bermuda for two court days in the third week of a five-week, complex wiretap gambling conspiracy case with ten defendants and a seventeen-member jury without prior notice and approval of the Court and without leaving word as to where he could be reached, constituted a disruption in the Court proceedings, disobedience of the Court order prohibiting involvement in other proceedings, a lack of respect for the Court, a lack of professional responsibility, as well as conduct prejudicial to the administration of justice. The certification concluded by stating that Yengo was adjudged guilty of contempt in the presence of the court on March 6, 1978.

Where the conduct of an attorney disrupts the orderliness of a trial, the speed with which a court should respond depends on the offensiveness of the lawyer's conduct and the need to assure the continuity and fairness of the proceeding. When the contempt is in the presence of the court, the judge may act summarily without notice or order to show cause. On other occasions, the proceedings shall be on notice and on an order for arrest or an order to show cause. In addition, the matter may not be heard by the judge allegedly offended, except with the consent of the person charged.

The reasons for notice and hearing for a contempt occurring outside the presence of the court "are, first, that there is no need to deal so abruptly with an offense which does not constitute an obstruction within the courtroom itself, and second, that since the court does not know by its own senses all of the facts constituting the offense, there must a trial to adduce them." *In re Contempt of Carton, supra*, 48 N.J. at 22.

That rationale is consistent with a dual test established by the United States Supreme Court to determine the justification for the exercise of summary contempt powers: (1) the act or omission must occur in the presence of the court so that no further evidence need be adduced for the judge to certify to the observation of the contumacious behavior and (2) the act must impact adversely on the authority of the court. *In re Oliver*, 333 U.S. 257 (1948).

Both this Court and the United States Supreme Court have demonstrated sensitivity to the potential for abuse in summary contempt proceedings. The United States Supreme Court has stated that summary contempt powers should be limited to the "least possible power adequate to the end proposed." *Harris v. United States*, 382 U.S. 162, 165 (1965). That limitation has been followed in New Jersey as well as in federal and other state courts.

Since the power to punish directly inevitably diminishes the procedural due process accorded to the alleged contemnor, the power must be permitted only where necessary. If proof of the contempt depends on evidence from persons other than the judge, the better practice is to proceed on order to show cause even where the contempt is in the face of the court. That procedure comports more closely with concepts of procedural due process and eliminates unseemly confrontations between the court and the contemnor.

The critical question is whether an unexcused absence of an attorney should be classified as a direct or indirect contempt for procedural purposes. The essence of a direct contempt, or contempt in the face of the court, is conduct that a judge can determine through his own senses is offensive and that tends to obstruct the administration of justice. Generally a disruptive act in the presence of the court, such as the use of offensive words or conduct, is a direct contempt.

However, an act may be a direct contempt although it is not committed in the presence of the court. Examples include: threatening letter from an attorney to the clerk in chancery; assault on the incorrectly thought to be a witness; letter from father of husband in divorce proceeding to wife and threats to her attorney; sending an abusive letter to the ordinary abusing a judge of the probate court. More recent examples include: letter from recipient of parking ticket to clerk of municipal court containing obscenities and alleging "ugly" methods of collecting money; letter to judge from recipient of traffic ticket alleging he would not receive a fair trial.

An indirect contempt "is an act committed not in the presence of the court, but at some distance therefrom." *In re Bozorth*, 38 N.J.Super. 184, 188–189 (Ch.Div.1955).

By itself, the unexplained absence of an attorney from a courtroom is an enigma. It demands an explanation. Aside from the unlikely event of complete disappearance of an attorney, the absence will be followed, as here, by a subsequent appearance before the court. At that time, the court invariably will ask for an explanation from the attorney. Generally, the absence alone does not constitute contempt. An essential element of the offense is the inadequacy of the explanation.

Federal courts and other state courts have divided on the issue, but the majority view is that an attorney's unexcused absence is not contempt in the actual presence of the court. The rationale is that, although the absence or late arrival of an attorney can be perceived directly by the court, the conclusion that the absence is inexcusable requires reference to facts not immediately within the court's perception.

We conclude that the mere unexplained absence of an attorney is a hybrid. In fashioning the appropriate judicial response, we adhere to our prior declaration that the summary contempt power should be exercised sparingly. However, we recognize also that strict compliance with the requirement of referring absent attorneys to another judge may not be in the interests of the judiciary, attorneys, or the public. Time would be wasted needlessly if, after observing the absence of an attorney, a judge could not ask, "Where were you?" The answer to that question frequently will obviate the need for further proceedings. Preclusion of the inquiry would prevent any dialogue between court and counsel on an issue that might be resolved without complicated proceedings. The characterization of the contempt as direct or indirect should be deferred until after the attorney has an opportunity to explain his absence.

If there is an adequate explanation, the matter should proceed no further. However, if the attorney refuses to explain, the judge may treat the offense as a direct contempt. Both the absence and the refusal are in the presence of the judge, who may determine the matter summarily. Similarly if the attorney offers an insulting, frivolous, or clearly inadequate explanation, both elements of the offense are in the presence of the judge, who may treat the matter as a direct contempt. Of equal importance the refusal to explain or an offensive explanation creates the need in the court to deal immediately with the matter. The need for immediate adjudication and punishment outweighs the procedural safeguards that would ensue from referring the matter to another judge. In both instances, the attorney has a right to a hearing, albeit before the offended judge. The hearing is limited to proof of facts, legal argument, and the right of allocution.

If there is some evidence of the adequacy of the explanation, the judge should characterize the matter as an indirect contempt and proceed by order to show cause returnable before another judge. The semblance of adequacy dilutes the offensiveness of the explanation and diminishes the need for dealing instantly with the offense. If the proffered explanation may require proof of facts occurring outside the presence of the court, the better practice is to proceed before another judge. Furthermore, referral to another judge eliminates the potential for bias, or at least the appearance of bias. The suggested procedure is consistent with our recent observation that, "In matters involving judicial administration, procedures should be free from even the appearance of unfairness." *In re Court Budget and Court Personnel Essex County*, 81 N.J. 494, 497 (1980).

To the extent the inconvenience of the preferred practice unduly encourages some trial judges to hear the matter themselves, the power of the appellate court to make an independent review of the facts and law provides an adequate safeguard for the allegedly contumacious attorney.

The competing interests create a spectrum for selecting the appropriate procedure. The determination of the procedure depends on where the explanation falls on the spectrum. Where the explanation is clearly inadequate, the need to maintain the authority of the court should predominate. The offense should be treated as a direct contempt. Where there is a good faith excuse, although another judge may find it to be inadequate, the predominant consideration should be enhancement of procedural due process for the alleged contemner. The offense should be treated as an indirect contempt. The explanation and the factual background color the characterization of the offense and affect the determination of the appropriate procedure as well as the ultimate outcome.

Whether the hearing proceeds before the same or another judge, there must be proof of criminal intent to establish contempt as a public offense. As former Chief Justice Weintraub wrote, "The act or omission must be accompanied by a mens rea, a willfulness, an indifference to the court's command." *N.J. Dept. of Health v. Roselle, supra*, 34 N.J. at 337. Consequently, the offended judge must prove willfulness by the alleged contemner, who may present rebuttal evidence.

In this case, the explanation was frivolous. Respondent went to Bermuda in the middle of winter. Whether he went for a vacation, as his daughter stated, or for business, as he asserted, the explanation was clearly inadequate. His unexcused absence was particularly egregious when viewed against the background of a multiple defendant criminal gambling conspiracy case and the admonitions of the trial judge.

There is no evidence of intemperate conduct on the part of the trial judge. Rather, Judge Loftus complied strictly with the requirements of R. 1:10–1 et seq. and the procedures outlined in this opinion.

Accordingly the judgment of the Appellate Division is reversed, and the judgment of conviction by the trial court and the $500 fine are reinstated.

PROBLEMS

1. *More on the* Mayberry *Case.* Is there any basis for arguing that Mayberry's conduct constitutes indirect contempt rather than direct contempt? If so, how would you make the argument?

2. *Defining Direct Contempt.* As mentioned earlier, in most instances, misconduct in a courtroom is treated as a direct contempt. Suppose that, during a hearing, a judge orders a defendant to leave the courtroom and not to return without counsel. When applicant fails to leave the courtroom immediately, the bailiff is ordered to escort her out. Defendant went peacefully with the bailiff until they reached the doorway of the courtroom. At that point, applicant hit a court official. The bailiff then moved to restrain applicant and a general disturbance erupted in which several people were involved. Is it appropriate to treat the applicant's conduct (in causing the altercation) as a direct contempt if the judge did not witness the beginning of the altercation? What arguments might the applicant make? What responses can be made to those arguments? *See Ex parte Daniels*, 722 S.W.2d 707 (Tex.Cr.App., En Banc, 1987).

3. *The Jurors and the Circular.* Suppose that a capital murder case is on trial. Each of the prospective jurors was individually examined out of the presence of the other prospective jurors. Those prospective jurors who were waiting to be examined were directed to remain in the corridor immediately adjacent to the court room. After four jurors were selected and empaneled, defendant distributed the following circular in and around the courthouse and upon the public streets of the city where the trial was being held:

"C. C. C. News"

June 27, 1959

"Vol. #5 #20 Odessa, Texas. For weeks the C. C. C. News has tried to bring you the facts, about your County Officials, now holding office, and the facts have been brought to you the people. They have been presented to you honestly and fearlessly, for many weeks, this publication has tried to tell the people that (Ringmaster) Davis is in complete control of your Commissioners Court, the last week, this was proven beyond any shadow of doubt. Because while the (Ringmaster) was wallering [sic] around in the Ocean Water of California on the taxpayers money, he apparently issued orders for two Commissioners to leave town, and this they did. And two Commissioners did leave town, and this is verified by the Odessa American in Sunday and Monday's issues of this week, and I quote in part, 'Nurman Maney and Ted Roby were out of town,' in other words a quorum of the Commissioners Court were not present. And why was this done, because the (Ringmaster) has already intimated, that he and the other two members of the Big Three were going to appoint the next County Attorney. And the one that they want is the Law Pardner [sic] of Warren Burnett. Mr. Burnett boasts that he already has the District Attorney's office and the District Judge under his heel and now he wants the County Attorney's office under his heel. And certainly this must be true, watch the murder trial which is going on in the District Court this week, and who is the Defense Lawyer Mr. Warren Burnett, at a purported price of Twenty Five Thousand Dollars to defend this man, which is legal and fine, but, Mr. Burnett should have to go into Court without any apparent Fix, in other words, this publication is not criticizing his Fee but, certainly we would criticize the method in which he boasts, to get these cases, in other words his boasting that he and Judge McCollum used to be Law Pardners [sic]."

The judge was convinced that, under the circumstances, the circulation of the publication in the courthouse among the prospective jurors had interfered with the trial of the case to the point that a fair trial could not be had in the murder case nor a jury selected from among the prospective jurors. The four jurors who had been selected were dismissed and the trial of the murder case was postponed.

The judge then charged relator with contempt on the basis that the circular constituted " 'an imminent serious threat to the ability of [the] Court in securing jurors to give fair consideration to the case' and because he considered the publication at the time and when 'viewed in the light and under the circumstances then existing to be a clear, present, and apparent danger to the administration of justice.' " This conclusion was based primarily upon the fact, as stated by Mr. Burnett in his testimony, that the publication "conveyed and calculated and intended to convey, and falsely represented, charging the Court with partiality and charged that the Presiding Judge and District Attorney were corrupt, and influenced in favor of [Burnett] in the Shirley murder case."

Should relator's conduct be considered as "in the presence of the court?" Does the circular constitute protected speech under the first amendment? *See Ex parte Aldridge*, 169 Tex.Crim. 395, 334 S.W.2d 161 (Tex.Cr.App.1959).

4. *More on the Distinction between Direct and Indirect Contempt.* An attorney for a party in a divorce case told his client that he could obtain a favorable decision from the court for a price. Assuming that the statement was made at the attorney's office, rather than in court, does the statement involve direct contempt or indirect contempt? *See Van Sweringen v. Van Sweringen*, 22 N.J. 440, 126 A.2d 334 (1956).

D. THE DUTY TO OBEY: COLLATERAL CHALLENGES

A court order can be directly challenged by appealing the order to a higher court. Is it also possible to challenge the order collaterally? Suppose that you are practicing law, and an injunction is issued against your client. You believe that the issuing court lacked jurisdiction over your client. You also believe that the decree contains unconstitutional terms. Your client wants to know whether it is required to obey the injunction or whether, given the flaws in the decree, it may be violated. What would you tell your client? Consider the following cases.

UNITED STATES V. UNITED MINE WORKERS OF AMERICA

330 U.S. 258, 67 S.Ct. 677, 91 L.Ed. 884 (1947).

MR. CHIEF JUSTICE VINSON delivered the opinion of the Court.

In 1946, the United States was in possession of, and operating, the major portion of the country's bituminous coal mines.[1] On November 13th, the UMW notified Secretary Krug that it was going to terminate the Krug–Lewis Agreement effective at 12:00 o'clock P.M., Midnight, Wednesday, November 20, 1946. The United States obtained a restraining order against the UMW and John L. Lewis prohibiting the strike. When the union went on strike anyway, the United States then sought an order to show cause why defendants should not be held in contempt.

Defendants filed a motion to discharge that challenged the jurisdiction of the court, and raised the grave question of whether the Norris–LaGuardia Act prohibited the granting of the temporary restraining order at the instance of the United States. The court overruled the motion and held that its power to issue the restraining order in this case was not affected by either the Norris–LaGuardia Act or the Clayton Act. The court found that defendants had encouraged the miners to interfere by a strike with the operation of the mines and with the performance of governmental functions, and had interfered with the jurisdiction of the court. Both defendants were found guilty beyond reasonable doubt of both criminal and civil contempt. The court fined defendant Lewis $10,000, and the defendant union $3,500,000. On the same day a preliminary injunction, effective until a final determination of the case, was issued in terms similar to those of the restraining order. Defendants' first and principal contention is that the restraining order and preliminary injunction were issued in violation of the Clayton and Norris–LaGuardia Acts. We have come to a contrary decision.

Although we have held that the Norris–LaGuardia Act did not render injunctive relief beyond the jurisdiction of the District Court, there are alternative grounds which support the power of the District Court to punish violations of its orders as criminal contempt.

The temporary restraining order was served on November 18. This was roughly two and one-half days before the strike was to begin. The defendants filed no motion to vacate the order. Rather, they ignored it, and allowed a nationwide coal strike to become an accomplished fact.

In the case before us, the District Court had the power to preserve existing conditions while it was determining its own authority to grant injunctive relief. The defendants, in making their private determination

[1] The United States had taken possession of the mines [after the President determined] that labor disturbances were interrupting the production of bituminous coal necessary for the operation of the national economy during the transition from war to peace.

of the law, acted at their peril. Their disobedience is punishable as criminal contempt.

Although a different result would follow were the question of jurisdiction frivolous and not substantial, such contention would be idle here. The applicability of the Norris–LaGuardia Act to the United States in a case such as this had not previously received judicial consideration, and both the language of the Act and its legislative history indicated the substantial nature of the problem with which the District Court was faced.

We find impressive authority for the proposition that an order issued by a court with jurisdiction over the subject matter and person must be obeyed by the parties until it is reversed by orderly and proper proceedings. This is true without regard even for the constitutionality of the Act under which the order is issued. Violations of an order are punishable as criminal contempt even though the order is set aside on appeal, or though the basic action has become moot.

We insist upon the same duty of obedience where, as here, the subject matter of the suit, as well as the parties, was properly before the court; where the elements of federal jurisdiction were clearly shown; and where the authority of the court of first instance to issue an order ancillary to the main suit depended upon a statute, the scope and applicability of which were subject to substantial doubt. The District Court on November 29 affirmatively decided that the Norris–LaGuardia Act was of no force in this case and that injunctive relief was therefore authorized. Orders outstanding or issued after that date were to be obeyed until they expired or were set aside by appropriate proceedings, appellate or otherwise. Convictions for criminal contempt intervening before that time may stand.

It does not follow, of course, that simply because a defendant may be punished for criminal contempt for disobedience of an order later set aside on appeal, that the plaintiff in the action may profit by way of a fine imposed in a simultaneous proceeding for civil contempt based upon a violation of the same order. The right to remedial relief falls with an injunction which events prove was erroneously issued, [and] a fortiori when the injunction or restraining order was beyond the jurisdiction of the court. [If] the Norris–LaGuardia Act were applicable in this case, the conviction for civil contempt would be reversed in its entirety.

Assuming, then, that the Norris–LaGuardia Act applied to this case and prohibited injunctive relief at the request of the United States, we would set aside the preliminary injunction of December 4 and the judgment for civil contempt; but we would, subject to any infirmities in the contempt proceedings or in the fines imposed, affirm the judgments for criminal contempt as validly punishing violations of an order then outstanding and unreversed.

Rule 42 (b) of the Rules of Criminal Procedure requires criminal contempt to be prosecuted on notice stating the essential facts constituting the contempt charged. In this respect, there was compliance with the rule here. Notice was given by a rule to show cause served upon defendants together with the Government's petition and supporting affidavit. The petition itself charged a violation of the outstanding restraining order, and the affidavit alleged in detail a failure to withdraw the notice of November 15, the cessation of work in the mines, and the consequent interference with governmental functions and the jurisdiction of the court. The defendants were fairly and completely apprised of the events and conduct constituting the contempt charged. Moreover, defendants were quite aware that a criminal contempt was charged. In their motion to discharge and vacate the rule to show cause, the contempt charged was referred to as criminal. And in argument on the motion the defendants stated and were expressly informed that a criminal contempt was to be tried.

It is urged that the amount of the fine of $10,000 imposed on the defendant Lewis and of the fine of $3,500,000 imposed on the defendant Union were arbitrary, excessive, and in no way related to the evidence adduced at the hearing.

Sentences for criminal contempt are punitive in their nature and are imposed for the purpose of vindicating the authority of the court. interests of orderly government demand that respect and compliance be given to orders issued by courts possessed of jurisdiction of persons and subject matter. One who defies the public authority and willfully refuses his obedience, does so at his peril. In imposing a fine for criminal contempt, the trial judge may properly take into consideration the extent of the willful and deliberate defiance of the court's order, the seriousness of the consequences of the contumacious behavior, the necessity of effectively terminating the defendant's defiance as required by the public interest, and the importance of deterring such acts in the future. Because of the nature of these standards, great reliance must be placed upon the discretion of the trial judge.

The trial court properly found the defendants guilty of criminal contempt. Such contempt had continued for 15 days from the issuance of the restraining order until the finding of guilty. Its willfulness had not been qualified by any concurrent attempt on defendants' part to challenge the order by motion to vacate or other appropriate procedures. Immediately following the finding of guilty, defendant Lewis stated openly in court that defendants would adhere to their policy of defiance. This policy, as the evidence showed, was the germ center of an economic paralysis which was rapidly extending itself from the bituminous coal mines into practically every other major industry of the United States. It was an attempt to repudiate and override the instrument of lawful government in the very situation in which governmental action was indispensable.

The trial court also properly found the defendants guilty of civil contempt. Judicial sanctions in civil contempt proceedings may, in a proper case, be employed for either or both of two purposes; to coerce the defendant into compliance with the court's order, and to compensate the complainant for losses sustained. Where compensation is intended, a fine is imposed, payable to the complainant. Such fine must of course be based upon evidence of complainant's actual loss, and his right, as a civil litigant, to the compensatory fine is dependent upon the outcome of the basic controversy. But where the purpose is to make the defendant comply, the court's discretion is otherwise exercised. It must then consider the character and magnitude of the harm threatened by continued contumacy, and the probable effectiveness of any suggested sanction in bringing about the result desired.

A court which has returned a conviction for contempt must, in fixing the amount of a fine to be imposed as a punishment or as a means of securing future compliance, consider the amount of defendant's financial resources and the consequent seriousness of the burden to that particular defendant.

In the light of these principles, we think the record clearly warrants a fine of $10,000 against defendant Lewis for criminal contempt. A majority of the Court, however, does not think that it warrants the unconditional imposition of a fine of $3,500,000 against the defendant union. If the court below had assessed a fine of $700,000 against the defendant union, this, under the circumstances, would not be excessive as punishment for the criminal contempt theretofore committed; and [in] order to coerce the defendant union into a future compliance with the court's order, it would have been effective to make the other $2,800,000 of the fine conditional on the defendant's failure to purge itself within a reasonable time. Accordingly, the judgment against the defendant union is held to be excessive. It will be modified so as to require the defendant union to pay a fine of $700,000, and further, to pay an additional fine of $2,800,000 unless the defendant union, within five days after the issuance of the mandate herein, shows that it has fully complied with the temporary restraining order issued November 18, 1946, and the preliminary injunction issued December 4, 1946. The defendant union can effect full compliance only by withdrawing unconditionally the notice given by it [to] J.A. Krug, Secretary of the Interior, terminating the Krug–Lewis agreement, [and] by notifying, at the same time, its members of such withdrawal.

We realize the serious proportions of the fines here imposed upon the defendant union. But [the] course taken by the union carried with it such a serious threat to orderly constitutional government, and to the economic and social welfare of the nation, that a fine of substantial size is required in order to emphasize the gravity of the offense of which the union was found guilty. The defendant Lewis, it is true, was the aggressive leader in the studied and deliberate non-compliance with the order of the District Court; but he stated in open court prior to imposition of the fines that "the representatives of the United Mine Workers determined that the so-called Krug–Lewis agreement was breached," and that it was the union's "representatives" who "notified the Secretary of the Interior that the contract was terminated as of November 20th." And certainly it was the members of the defendant union who executed the nationwide strike. Loyalty in responding to the orders of their leader may, in some minds, minimize the gravity of the miners' conduct; but we cannot ignore the effect of their action upon the rights of other citizens, or the effect of their action upon our system of government. The gains, social and economic, which the miners and other citizens have realized in the past, are ultimately due to the fact that they enjoy the rights of free men under our system of government. Upon the maintenance of that system depends all future progress to which they may justly aspire. In our complex society, there is a great variety of limited loyalties, but the overriding loyalty of all is to our country and to the institutions under which a particular interest may be pursued.

Defendants may have sincerely believed that the restraining order was ineffective and would finally be vacated. The restraining order sought to preserve conditions until the cause could be determined, and obedience by the defendants would have secured this result. They had full opportunity to comply, but they deliberately refused obedience and determined for themselves the validity of the order. When the rule to show cause was issued, defendants stated that their position remained unchanged. Their conduct showed a total lack of respect for the judicial process. Punishment in this case is for that which the defendants had done prior to imposition of the judgment in the District Court, coupled with a coercive imposition upon the defendant union to compel obedience with the court's outstanding order.

So ordered.

MR. JUSTICE FRANKFURTER, concurring in the judgment.

The Founders knew that Law alone saves a society from being rent by internecine strife or ruled by mere brute power however disguised. "Civilization involves subjection of force to reason, and the agency of this subjection is law." No one, no matter how exalted his public office or how righteous his private motive, can be judge in his own case. That is what courts are for. And no type of controversy is more peculiarly fit for judicial determination than a controversy that calls into question the power of a court to decide. Controversies over "jurisdiction" are apt to raise difficult technical problems. They usually involve judicial presuppositions, textual doubts, confused legislative history, and like factors hardly fit for final determination by the self-interest of a party. [Only] when a court is so obviously traveling outside its orbit as to be merely usurping judicial forms and facilities, may an order issued by a court be disobeyed and treated as though it were a letter to a newspaper.

To be sure, an obvious limitation upon a court cannot be circumvented by a frivolous inquiry into the existence of a power that has unquestionably been withheld. Thus, the explicit withdrawal from federal district courts of the power to issue injunctions in an ordinary labor dispute between a private employer and his employees cannot be defeated, and an existing right to strike thereby impaired, by pretending to entertain a suit for such an injunction in order to decide whether the court has jurisdiction. In such a case, a judge would not be acting as a court. He would be a pretender to, not a wielder of, judicial power.

That is not this case. It required extended arguments, lengthy briefs, study and reflection preliminary to adequate discussion in conference, before final conclusions could be reached regarding the proper interpretation of the legislation controlling this case. A majority of my brethren find that neither the Norris–LaGuardia Act nor the War Labor Disputes Act limited the power of the district court to issue the orders under review. I have come to the contrary view. But to suggest that the right to determine so complicated and novel an issue could not be brought within the cognizance of the district court, and eventually of this Court, is to deny the place of the judiciary in our scheme of government. And if the district court had power to decide whether this case was properly before it, it could make appropriate orders so as to afford the necessary time for fair consideration and decision while existing conditions were preserved. To say that the authority of the court may be flouted during the time necessary to decide is to reject the requirements of the judicial process.

MR. JUSTICE MURPHY, dissenting.

As a general proposition, individuals cannot be allowed to be the judges of the validity of court orders issued against them. But the problem raised by the violation of the restraining order in this case must be viewed against the background and language of the Norris–LaGuardia Act. This Act specifically prohibits the issuance of restraining orders except in situations not here involved. There is no exception in favor of a restraining order where there is some serious doubt about the court's jurisdiction; indeed, the prohibition against restraining orders would be futile were such an exception recognized for the minds of lawyers and judges are boundless in their abilities to raise serious jurisdictional objections. And so Congress has flatly forbidden the issuance of all restraining orders under this Act. It follows that when such an order is issued despite this clear prohibition, no man can be held in contempt thereof, however unwise his action may be as a matter of policy. When he violates the void order, 28 U.S.C. § 385, 28 U.S.C.A. § 385, comes into operation, forbidding punishment for contempt except where there has been disobedience of a "lawful writ, process, order, rule, decree, or command" of a court. It has been said that the actions of the defendants threatened orderly constitutional government and the economic and social stability of the nation. Whatever may be the validity of those statements, we lack any power to ignore the plain mandates of Congress and to impose vindictive fines upon the defendants.

MR. JUSTICE RUTLEDGE, dissenting.

No man or group is above the law. Nor is any beyond its protection. These truths apply equally to the Government. When its power is exerted against the citizen or another in the nation's courts, those tribunals stand not as partisans, but as independent and impartial arbiters to see that the balance between power and right is held even. In discharging that high function the courts themselves, like the parties, are subject to the law's majestic limitations. We are not free to decide this case, or any, otherwise than as in conscience we are enabled to see what the law commands.

The Norris LaGuardia Act expressly provides the remedies for its enforcement. Beyond seizure of plants, mines and facilities for temporary governmental operation, they are exclusively criminal in character. They do not include injunctive or other equitable relief. Nor was the omission unintentional or due to oversight. It was specific and deliberate.

Since the order was jurisdictionally invalid when issued, by virtue of the War Labor Disputes Act and its adoption of the Norris–LaGuardia Act's policy, it follows that the violation gave no sufficient cause for sustaining the conviction for contempt. *Ex parte Fisk, supra.* Lewis and the United Mine Workers necessarily took the risk that the order would be found valid on review and, in that event, that punishment for contempt would apply. They did not take the risk that it would apply in any event, even if the order should be found void as beyond the jurisdiction of the Court to enter.

Not only was the penalty against the union excessive, as the Court holds. Vice infected both "fines" more deeply. As the proceeding itself is said to have been both civil and criminal, so are the two "fines." Each was imposed in a single lump sum, with no allocation of specific portions as among civil damages, civil coercion and criminal punishment. The Government concedes that some part of each "fine" was laid for each purpose. But the trial court did not state, and the Government has refused to speculate, how much was imposed in either instance for each of those distinct remedial functions.

The law has fixed standards for each remedy, and they are neither identical nor congealable. They are, for damages in civil contempt, the amount of injury proven and no more, for coercion, what may be required to bring obedience and not more, whether by way of imprisonment or fine; for punishment, what is not cruel and unusual or, in the case of a fine, excessive within the Eighth Amendment's prohibition. And for determining excessiveness of criminal fines there are analogies from legislative action which in my opinion are controlling.

NOTES

1. *Defenses Applicable in Contempt Proceedings.* Several defenses can be raised in a contempt proceeding: defendants can claim that they were not bound by the decree; that they did not receive notice of its requirements; or that it was impossible to comply with the decree.

2. *Contempt and the Failed Pager.* In *United States v. Mottweiler*, 82 F.3d 769 (7th Cir.1996), a district judge held two attorneys in criminal contempt for failing to return to court promptly after a jury returned its verdict. Because of their absence, the judge sealed the verdict and reassembled the jurors the next morning, disrupting their lives (the district was so large, and the distances traveled so long, that many jurors missed an entire day's work). The attorneys were ordered to pay the jurors' costs ($1,400.). Based on testimony that the attorneys failed to return to the court because a defective pager failed to alert them, the Seventh Circuit reversed the conviction:

> Mottweiler may have been negligent. Batteries wear down, so caution might have led an attorney to test the pager before leaving the courthouse rather than afterward, as Mottweiler did. Portable electronic devices break, so prudence might have induced an attorney to test the pager again after the playground exercise. Nonetheless, negligence does not support a criminal conviction under § 401.
>
> Negligent failure to be present when the jury returns could support a civil order requiring counsel to reimburse one's adversary, and the judicial system, for the expenses to which that delict leads. [Still,] the district judge did not find that Mottweiler acted negligently. If the court believes that such a conclusion may be warranted, it can issue an order requiring Mottweiler and O'Daniel to show cause why they should not be required to reimburse the Treasury for the outlays their late arrival occasioned.

PROBLEMS

1. *Lack of Jurisdiction.* In the prior case, the Court rejects the idea that the Clayton and Norris–LaGuardia acts precluded the trial court from exercising jurisdiction over the case. However, suppose that those acts did, in fact, deprive the trial court of jurisdiction. Suppose that the trial court, unsure of whether it had jurisdiction over the case, issued a TRO to give itself time to decide the jurisdictional issue. If you represent the defendants (who

have been enjoined), do you advise them that they must comply with the order, or can you advise them that they can ignore it with impunity? Would it matter whether the asserted basis for the jurisdictional claim could be regarded as "frivolous?"

2. *The Invalid Order.* In the prior problem, suppose that the trial court erroneously determines that it has jurisdiction over the case. If defendant violates the TRO following the erroneous determination, may defendant be held in contempt? Is the contempt civil or criminal or both? Can civil contempt remedies be imposed?

WALKER V. CITY OF BIRMINGHAM

388 U.S. 307, 87 S.Ct. 1824, 18 L.Ed.2d 1210 (1967).

MR. JUSTICE STEWART delivered the opinion of the Court.

On Wednesday, April 10, 1963, officials of Birmingham, Alabama, filed a bill of complaint in a state circuit court asking for injunctive relief against 139 individuals and two organizations who planned sit-in demonstrations, parades and picketing. "It was alleged that this conduct was 'calculated to provoke breaches of the peace,' 'threaten(ed) the safety, peace and tranquility of the City,' and placed an undue burden and strain upon the manpower of the Police Department." The circuit judge granted a temporary injunction as prayed in the bill, enjoining the petitioners from, among other things, participating in or encouraging mass street parades or mass processions without a permit as required by a Birmingham ordinance.

Five of the eight petitioners were served with copies of the writ early the next morning. Several hours later four of them held a press conference. There a statement was distributed, declaring their intention to disobey the injunction because it was "raw tyranny under the guise of maintaining law and order." At this press conference one of the petitioners stated: "That they had respect for the Federal Courts, or Federal Injunctions, but in the past the State Courts had favored local law enforcement, and if the police couldn't handle it, the mob would."

That night a meeting took place at which one of the petitioners announced that "injunction or no injunction we are going to march tomorrow." The next afternoon, Good Friday, a large crowd gathered in the vicinity of Sixteenth Street and Sixth Avenue North in Birmingham. A group of about 50 or 60 proceeded to parade along the sidewalk while a crowd of 1,000 to 1,500 onlookers stood by, "clapping, and hollering, and whooping." Some of the crowd followed the marchers and spilled out into the street. At least three of the petitioners participated in this march.

Meetings sponsored by some of the petitioners were held that night and the following night, where calls for volunteers to "walk" and go to jail were made. On Easter Sunday, April 14, a crowd of between 1,500 and

2,000 people congregated in the midafternoon in the vicinity of Seventh Avenue and Eleventh Street North in Birmingham. One of the petitioners was seen organizing members of the crowd in formation. A group of about 50, headed by three other petitioners, started down the sidewalk two abreast. At least one other petitioner was among the marchers. Some 300 or 400 people from among the onlookers followed in a crowd that occupied the entire width of the street and overflowed onto the sidewalks. Violence occurred. Members of the crowd threw rocks that injured a newspaperman and damaged a police motorcycle.

The next day the city officials who had requested the injunction applied to the state circuit court for an order to show cause why the petitioners should not be held in contempt for violating it. At the ensuing hearing the petitioners sought to attack the constitutionality of the injunction on the ground that it was vague and overbroad, and restrained free speech. They also sought to attack the Birmingham parade ordinance upon similar grounds, and upon the further ground that the ordinance had previously been administered in an arbitrary and discriminatory manner.

The circuit judge refused to consider any of these contentions, pointing out that there had been neither a motion to dissolve the injunction, nor an effort to comply with it by applying for a permit from the city commission before engaging in the Good Friday and Easter Sunday parades. Consequently, the court held that the only issues before it were whether it had jurisdiction to issue the temporary injunction, and whether thereafter the petitioners had knowingly violated it. Upon these issues the court found against the petitioners, and imposed upon each of them a sentence of five days in jail and a $50 fine, in accord with an Alabama statute.

We are asked to say that the Constitution compelled Alabama to allow the petitioners to violate this injunction, to organize and engage in these mass street parades and demonstrations, without any previous effort on their part to have the injunction dissolved or modified, or any attempt to secure a parade permit in accordance with its terms. We cannot accept the petitioners' contentions in the circumstances of this case.

The state court that issued the injunction had, as a court of equity, jurisdiction over the petitioners and over the subject matter of the controversy. And this is not a case where the injunction was transparently invalid or had only a frivolous pretense to validity. We have consistently recognized the strong interest of state and local governments in regulating the use of their streets and other public places. When protest takes the form of mass demonstrations, parades, or picketing on public streets and sidewalks, the free passage of traffic and the prevention of public disorder and violence become important objects of legitimate state concern.

The generality of the language contained in the Birmingham parade ordinance upon which the injunction was based would unquestionably raise substantial constitutional issues concerning some of its provisions. The petitioners, however, did not even attempt to apply to the Alabama courts for an authoritative construction of the ordinance. Had they done so, those courts might have given the licensing authority granted in the ordinance a narrow and precise scope. It could not be assumed that this ordinance was void on its face.

The breadth and vagueness of the injunction itself would also unquestionably be subject to substantial constitutional question. But the way to raise that question was to apply to the Alabama courts to have the injunction modified or dissolved. The injunction in all events clearly prohibited mass parading without a permit, and the evidence shows that the petitioners fully understood that prohibition when they violated it.

Petitioners claim that they were free to disobey the injunction because the parade ordinance on which it was based had been administered in the past in an arbitrary and discriminatory fashion. They sought to introduce evidence that, a few days before the injunction issued, requests for permits to picket had been made to a member of the city commission. One request had been rudely rebuffed, and this same official had later made clear that he was without power to grant the permit alone, since the issuance of such permits was the responsibility of the entire city commission. Assuming the truth of this proffered evidence, it does not follow that the parade ordinance was void on its face. The petitioners did not apply for a permit either to the commission itself or to any commissioner after the injunction issued. Had they done so, and had the permit been refused, it is clear that their claim of arbitrary or discriminatory administration of the ordinance would have been considered by the state circuit court upon a motion to dissolve the injunction.

This case would arise in quite a different constitutional posture if the petitioners, before disobeying the injunction, had challenged it in the Alabama courts, and had been met with delay or frustration of their constitutional claims. But there is no showing that such would have been the fate of a timely motion to modify or dissolve the injunction. There was an interim of two days between the issuance of the injunction and the Good Friday march. The petitioners give absolutely no explanation of why they did not make some application to the state court during that period. The injunction had issued ex parte; if the court had been presented with the petitioners' contentions, it might well have dissolved or at least modified its order in some respects. If it had not done so, Alabama procedure would have provided for an expedited process of appellate review. It cannot be presumed that the Alabama courts would have ignored the petitioners' constitutional claims. Indeed, these contentions were accepted in another case by an Alabama appellate court that struck down on direct review the conviction under this very ordinance of one of these same petitioners.

We do not deal here with a situation where a state court has followed a regular past practice of entertaining claims in a given procedural mode, and without notice has abandoned that practice to the detriment of a litigant who finds his claim foreclosed by a novel procedural bar. This is not a case where a procedural requirement has been sprung upon an unwary litigant when prior practice did not give him fair notice of its existence.

These precedents clearly put the petitioners on notice that they could not by-pass orderly judicial review of the injunction before disobeying it. Any claim that they were entrapped or misled is wholly unfounded, a conclusion confirmed by evidence in the record showing that when the petitioners deliberately violated the injunction they expected to go to jail.

The rule of law that Alabama followed in this case reflects a belief that in the fair administration of justice no man can be judge in his own case, however exalted his station, however righteous his motives, and irrespective of his race, color, politics, or religion. This Court cannot hold that the petitioners were constitutionally free to ignore all the procedures of the law and carry their battle to the streets. One may sympathize with the petitioners' impatient commitment to their cause. But respect for judicial process is a small price to pay for the civilizing hand of law, which alone can give abiding meaning to constitutional freedom.

Affirmed.

MR. CHIEF JUSTICE WARREN, whom MR. JUSTICE BRENNAN and MR. JUSTICE FORTAS join, dissenting.

Petitioners are Negro ministers who sought to express their concern about racial discrimination in Birmingham, Alabama, by holding peaceful protest demonstrations in that city on Good Friday and Easter Sunday 1963. For obvious reasons, it was important for the significance of the demonstrations that they be held on those particular dates. A representative of petitioners' organization went to the City Hall and asked "to see the person or persons in charge to issue permits, permits for parading, picketing, and demonstrating." She was directed to Public Safety Commissioner Connor, who denied her request for a permit in terms that left no doubt that petitioners were not going to be issued a permit under any circumstances. 'He said, 'No you will not get a permit in Birmingham, Alabama to picket. I will picket you over to the City Jail,' and he repeated that twice.' A second, telegraphic request was also summarily denied, in a telegram signed by "Eugene 'Bull' Connor," with the added information that permits could be issued only by the full City Commission, a three-man body consisting of Commissioner Connor and two others.[1] According to petitioners' offer of proof, the truth of which is assumed for purposes of this case, parade permits had uniformly been issued for all other groups by the city clerk on the request of the traffic bureau of the police department, which was under Commissioner Connor's direction. The requirement that the approval of the full Commission be obtained was applied only to this one group.

Understandably convinced that the City of Birmingham was not going to authorize their demonstrations under any circumstances, petitioners proceeded with their plans despite Commissioner Connor's orders. The Circuit Court issued the injunction in the form requested, and in effect ordered petitioners and all other persons having notice of the order to refrain for an unlimited time from carrying on any demonstrations without a permit. A permit, of course, was clearly unobtainable; the city would not have sought this injunction if it had any intention of issuing one.

Petitioners were served with copies of the injunction at various times on Thursday and on Good Friday. Unable to believe that such a blatant and broadly drawn prior restraint on their First Amendment rights could be valid, they announced their intention to defy it and went ahead with the planned peaceful demonstrations on Easter weekend. On the following Monday, when they promptly filed a motion to dissolve the injunction, the court found them in contempt, holding that they had waived all their First Amendment rights by disobeying the court order.

These facts lend no support to the court's charges that petitioners were presuming to act as judges in their own case, or that they had a disregard for the judicial process. They did not flee the jurisdiction or refuse to appear in the Alabama courts. Having violated the injunction, they promptly submitted themselves to the courts to test the constitutionality of the injunction and the ordinance it parroted. They were in essentially the same position as persons who challenge the constitutionality of a statute by violating it, and then defend the ensuing criminal prosecution on constitutional grounds. It has never been thought that violation of a statute indicated such a disrespect for the legislature that the violator always must be punished even if the statute was unconstitutional. On the contrary, some cases have required that persons seeking to challenge the constitutionality of a statute first violate it to

[1] The United States Commission on Civil Rights found continuing abuse of civil rights protesters by the Birmingham police, including use of dogs, clubs, and firehoses. Commissioner Eugene "Bull" Connor, a self-proclaimed white supremacist made no secret of his personal attitude toward the rights of Negroes and the decisions of this Court. He vowed that racial integration would never come to Birmingham, and wore a button inscribed "Never" to advertise that vow. Yet the Court indulges in speculation that these civil rights protesters might have obtained a permit from this city and this man had they made enough repeated applications.

establish their standing to sue. Indeed, it shows no disrespect for law to violate a statute on the ground that it is unconstitutional and then to submit one's case to the courts with the willingness to accept the penalty if the statute is held to be valid.

The injunction is patently unconstitutional on its face. Our decisions have consistently held that picketing and parading are means of expression protected by the First Amendment, and that the right to picket or parade may not be subjected to the unfettered discretion of local officials. Although a city may regulate the manner of use of its streets and sidewalks in the interest of keeping them open for the movement of traffic, it may not allow local officials unbridled discretion to decide who shall be allowed to parade or picket and who shall not. When local officials are given totally unfettered discretion to decide whether a proposed demonstration is consistent with "public welfare, peace, safety, health, decency, good order, morals or convenience," as they were in this case, they are invited to act as censors over the views that may be presented to the public. The unconstitutionality of the ordinance is compounded, of course, when there is convincing evidence that the officials have in fact used their power to deny permits to organizations whose views they dislike. The record in this case hardly suggests that Commissioner Connor and the other city officials were motivated in prohibiting civil rights picketing only by their overwhelming concern for particular traffic problems. Petitioners were given to understand that under no circumstances would they be permitted to demonstrate in Birmingham, not that a demonstration would be approved if a time and place were selected that would minimize the traffic difficulties. The only circumstance that the court can find to justify anything other than a per curiam reversal is that Commissioner Connor had the foresight to have the unconstitutional ordinance included in an ex parte injunction issued without notice or hearing or any showing that it was impossible to have notice or a hearing, forbidding the world at large (insofar as it knew of the order) to conduct demonstrations in Birmingham without the consent of the city officials. This injunction was such potent magic that it transformed the command of an unconstitutional statute into an impregnable barrier, challengeable only in what likely would have been protracted legal proceedings and entirely superior in the meantime even to the United States Constitution.

I do not believe that giving this Court's seal of approval to such a gross misuse of the judicial process is likely to lead to greater respect for the law any more than it is likely to lead to greater protection for First Amendment freedoms. The *ex parte* temporary injunction has a long and odious history in this country, and its susceptibility to misuse is all too apparent from the facts of the case.

MR. JUSTICE DOUGLAS, with whom THE CHIEF JUSTICE, MR. JUSTICE BRENNAN, and MR. JUSTICE FORTAS concur, dissenting.

The right to defy an unconstitutional statute is basic in our scheme. Even when an ordinance requires a permit to make a speech, to deliver a sermon, to picket, to parade, or to assemble, it need not be honored when it is invalid on its face. By like reason, where a permit has been arbitrarily denied one need not pursue the long and expensive route to this Court to obtain a remedy. The reason is the same in both cases. For if a person must pursue his judicial remedy before he may speak, parade, or assemble, the occasion when protest is desired or needed will have become history and any later speech, parade, or assembly will be futile or pointless. In the present case the collision between this state court decree and the First Amendment is so obvious that no hearing is needed to determine the issue. The "constitutional freedom" of which the Court speaks can be won only if judges honor the Constitution.

MR. JUSTICE BRENNAN, with whom THE CHIEF JUSTICE, MR. JUSTICE DOUGLAS, and MR. JUSTICE FORTAS join, dissenting.

In the present case we are confronted with a collision between Alabama's interest in requiring adherence to orders of its courts and the constitutional prohibition against abridgment of freedom of speech, more particularly "the right of the people peaceably to assemble," and the right "to petition the Government for a redress of grievances." Special considerations have time and again been deemed by us to attend protection of these freedoms in the face of state interests the vindication of which results in prior restraints upon their exercise, or their regulation in a vague or overbroad manner, or in a way which gives unbridled discretion to limit their exercise to an individual or group of individuals. To give these freedoms the necessary "breathing space to survive," the Court has modified traditional rules of standing and prematurity. We have molded both substantive rights and procedural remedies in the face of varied conflicting interests to conform to our overriding duty to insulate all individuals from the "chilling effect" upon exercise of First Amendment freedoms generated by vagueness, overbreadth and unbridled discretion to limit their exercise.

Were it not for the ex parte injunction, petitioners could have paraded first and challenged the permit ordinance later. But because of the ex parte stamp of a judicial officer on a copy of the invalid ordinance they barred not only from challenging the permit ordinance, but also the potentially more stifling yet unconsidered restraints embodied in the injunction itself.

The suggestion that petitioners be muffled pending outcome of dissolution proceedings without any measurable time limits is particularly inappropriate in the setting of this case. Critical to the plain exercise of the right of protest was the timing of that exercise. First, the marches were part of a program to arouse community support for petitioners' assault on segregation there. A cessation of these activities, even for a short period, might deal a crippling blow to petitioners' efforts. Second, in dramatization of their cause, petitioners, all ministers, chose April 12, Good Friday, and April 14, Easter Sunday, for their protests hoping to gain the attention to their cause which such timing might attract. Petitioners received notice of the order April 11. The ability to exercise protected protest at a time when such exercise would be effective must be as protected as the beliefs themselves. It is a flagrant denial of constitutional guarantees to balance away this principle in the name of "respect for judicial process." To preach "respect" in this context is to deny the right to speak at all.

NOTE: MORE ON THE WALKER *CASE*

For an interesting discussion of the history of the *Walker* litigation, *see* David Benjamin Oppenheimer, *Martin Luther King, Walker v. City of Birmingham, and the Letter from Birmingham Jail*, 26 U.C. Davis L. Rev. 791 (1993); Martin Luther King, *Letter from Birmingham Jail*, 26 U.C. Davis L. Rev. 835 (1993).

PROBLEMS

1. Walker *and the Times.* Bear in mind that the *Walker* case arose during the 1960s in Alabama. The Court suggests that one remedy for the protestors was to apply to the Alabama courts to have the injunction dissolved, or to apply for a parade permit under the ordinance. Is it realistic to think that the courts of that time would have responded, or that the local officials would have issued a parade permit? If not, why should the protestors be required to engage in this futile effort?

2. *Frivolousness and Transparent Invalidity.* The Court suggests that the protestors might have been allowed to violate the injunction if there had been only a "frivolous pretense to validity" or if the injunction were "transparently invalid." After reading the *Walker* case, are you clear about what constitutes "frivolous pretense" or "transparent invalidity?" When would you advise a client that it is free to violate an injunction? Would vagueness or substantial overbreadth provide an adequate basis?

3. *More on Advising the Protestors.* So, given the holding in *Walker*, suppose that you were asked to advise the protestors. An injunction has been issued against them (on the same terms as the injunction issued in the actual case), and the planned protest is only two days. How would you advise the protestors to proceed? If your advised course of action ends up being unsuccessful, should the protestors go ahead with their march or refrain?

4. *Invalid Ordinance.* If this case had involved simply a decision to violate Birmingham's parade ordinance, rather than an injunction, might the result have been different? Might the protestors have been entitled to violate

an invalid parade ordinance without first applying for a permit? In other words, are statutes treated differently than injunctions? If so, why?

5. *Advising Your Client.* In *Shuttlesworth v. City of Birmingham*, 394 U.S. 147, 89 S.Ct. 935, 22 L.Ed.2d 162 (1969), the Court struck down the ordinance at issue in *Walker*. Since the *Walker* injunction imposed a broader prior restraint than the ordinance, the injunction was also unconstitutional. Nonetheless, because of the collateral bar rule, the court still imposed criminal contempt sanctions on defendants for their defiance of the (unconstitutional) injunction. Since the collateral bar rule does not apply to civil contempt, a civil sanction would fail if the injunction were invalidated on appeal.

This distinction, between criminal contempt and civil contempt, is recognized in most jurisdictions. California is one exception. In *In re Berry*, 68 Cal.2d 137, 65 Cal.Rptr. 273, 436 P.2d 273 (1968), defendants deliberately disobeyed an ex parte TRO prohibiting a threatened strike by the Social Worker's Union. In a writ of habeas corpus (a collateral attack), defendants successfully challenged the constitutionality of the TRO. The California Supreme Court invalidated the TRO and vacated the criminal contempt sanctions: "In California [the] rule followed is considerably more consistent with the exercise of First Amendment Freedoms than that adopted in [Alabama]." For lawyers in jurisdictions that follow the *Walker* rule, when is it prudent to advise a client that an injunction is so unconstitutional that it can be defied with impunity? What about in California?

6. *The "Void–Voidable" Distinction.* There is an exception to the collateral bar rule for "transparently invalid" or "void" orders on the one hand, and "merely invalid" or "voidable," on the other. There is no duty to obey a transparently invalid or void decree. Accordingly, criminal contempt sanctions for deliberate violation of such a decree cannot stand. As you read the next case, consider this: in advising clients whether to print the story or seek emergency judicial review, how can one determine, in advance, in which category the order will be held to fall? Do you think that the *Walker* rule is preferable to the *Berry* rule, or vice-versa?

IN RE PROVIDENCE JOURNAL COMPANY

820 F.2d 1342 (1st Cir.1986).

WISDOM, CIRCUIT JUDGE.

This appeal presents an apparent conflict between two fundamental legal principles: the hallowed First Amendment principle that the press shall not be subjected to prior restraints; the other, the sine qua non of orderly government, that, until modified or vacated, a court order must be obeyed.

FACTS

From 1962 to 1965, the Federal Bureau of Investigation conducted electronic surveillance of Raymond L.S. Patriarca, reputedly a prominent figure in organized crime. The FBI conducted this surveillance without a warrant in violation of his Fourth Amendment rights. The FBI later destroyed all tape recordings relating to this surveillance but retained the logs and memoranda compiled from the recordings. In 1976, the Journal requested the logs and memoranda from the FBI under the Freedom of Information Act ("FOIA"). The FBI refused this request on the ground that disclosure would be an unwarranted invasion of personal privacy. The Journal then brought suit in the Federal District Court for the District of Rhode Island to compel disclosure. On appeal, we ruled that the FBI was within its discretion when it refused the Journal's request.

In the spring of 1985, after the death of Raymond L.S. Patriarca, the Journal renewed its FOIA request to the FBI for the logs and memoranda. The FBI assented to this request and furnished the materials not only to the Journal, but also to WJAR Television Ten and other news media. On November 8, 1985, Raymond J. Patriarca, Raymond L.S. Patriarca's son, filed a summons and complaint against the FBI, WJAR, and the Journal. The action was based on the FOIA, Title III of the Omnibus Crime Control and Safe Streets Act of 1968 ("Title III"), and the Fourth Amendment. The complaint alleged that the FBI had wrongfully released the logs and memoranda to the Journal and WJAR. At the same time Patriarca filed the complaint, he filed a Motion for Temporary Injunctive or Injunctive Relief seeking an order "enjoining the named defendants from disseminating or publishing the logs and memoranda."

On November 12, 1985, [the] court entered a temporary restraining order barring publication of the logs and memoranda by the Journal and WJAR.

On November 14, 1985, the day after the district court issued the order, and while that order was still in effect, the Journal published an article on the deceased Patriarca that included information taken from the logs and memoranda. The son filed a motion to judge the Journal in contempt. When he declined to prosecute the criminal contempt motion, the district court invoked Fed.R.Crim.P. 42(b) and appointed a special prosecutor. Following a hearing, the district court found the Journal guilty of criminal contempt. Subsequent to a sentencing hearing, the court imposed an 18-month jail term on Hauser, which was suspended, ordered Hauser to perform 200 hours of public service, and fined the Journal $100,000. The Journal appealed.

DISCUSSION

This appeal propounds a question that admits of no easy answer. Each party stands on what each regards as an unassailable legal principle. The special prosecutor relies on the bedrock principle that court orders, even those that are later ruled unconstitutional, must be complied with until amended or vacated. This principle is often referred to as the "collateral bar" rule. The Journal relies on the bedrock principle that prior restraints against speech are prohibited by the First Amendment. In this opinion we endeavor to avoid deciding which principle should take precedence by reaching a result consistent with both principles.

Of all the constitutional imperatives protecting a free press under the First Amendment, the most significant is the restriction against prior restraint upon publication. Prohibiting the publication of a news story or an editorial is the essence of censorship. The power to censor is the power to regulate the marketplace of ideas, to impoverish both the quantity and quality of debate, and to restrict the free flow of criticism against the government at all levels. It is plain now as it was to the framers of the Constitution and Bill of Rights that the power of censorship is, in the absence of the strictest constraints, too great to be wielded by any individual or group of individuals.

If a publisher is to print a libelous, defamatory, or injurious story, an appropriate remedy, though not always totally effective, lies not in an injunction against that publication but in a damages or criminal action after publication. Although the threat of damages or criminal action may chill speech, a prior restraint "freezes" speech before the audience has the opportunity to hear the message. Additionally, a court asked to issue a prior restraint must judge the challenged speech in the abstract. And, as was true in the instant case, a court may issue a prior restraint in the form of a temporary restraining order or preliminary injunction without a full hearing; a judgment for damages or a criminal sanction may be imposed only after a full hearing with all the attendant procedural protections.

Equally well-established is the requirement of any civilized government that a party subject to a court order must abide by its terms or face criminal contempt. As a general rule, a party may not violate an order and raise the issue of its unconstitutionality collaterally as a defense in the criminal contempt proceeding. Rather, the appropriate method to challenge a court order is to petition to have the order vacated or amended.

In *Walker v. City of Birmingham*, the Supreme Court upheld contempt citations against Dr. Martin Luther King, Jr. and other civil rights protestors enjoined from parading without a permit. * * *

At first glance, *Walker* would appear to control the instant case. *Walker* declares that the contemnors are collaterally barred from challenging the constitutionality of the order forming the basis of the contempt citation. The *Walker* Court was, however, careful to point out that the order issued by the Alabama court was not "transparently invalid." The Court specifically noted that "this is not a case where the injunction was transparently invalid or had only a frivolous pretense to validity." The unmistakable import of this language is that a transparently invalid order cannot form the basis for a contempt citation.

Court orders are not sacrosanct. An order entered by a court clearly without jurisdiction over the contemnors or the subject matter is not protected by the collateral bar rule. Were this not the case, a court could wield power over parties or matters obviously not within its authority—a concept inconsistent with the notion that the judiciary may exercise only those powers entrusted to it by law.

The same principle supports an exception to the collateral bar rule for transparently invalid court orders. Requiring a party subject to such an order to obey or face contempt would give the courts powers far in excess of any authorized by the Constitution or Congress. Recognizing an exception to the collateral bar rule for transparently invalid orders does not violate the principle that "no man can be judge in his own case" anymore than does recognizing such an exception for jurisdictional defects. The key to both exceptions is the notion that although a court order—even an arguably incorrect court order—demands respect, so does the right of the citizen to be free of clearly improper exercises of judicial authority.

Although an exception to the collateral bar rule is appropriate for transparently void orders, it is inappropriate for arguably proper orders. This distinction is necessary both to protect the authority of the courts when they address close questions and to create a strong incentive for parties to follow the orderly process of law. No such protection or incentive is needed when the order is transparently invalid because in that instance the court is acting so far in excess of its authority that it has no right to expect compliance and no interest is protected by requiring compliance.

The line between a transparently invalid order and one that is merely invalid is, of course, not always distinct. As a general rule, if the court reviewing the order finds the order to have had any pretence to validity at the time it was issued, the reviewing court should enforce the collateral bar rule. Such a heavy presumption in favor of validity is necessary to protect the rightful power of the courts. Nonetheless, there are instances where an order will be so patently unconstitutional that it will be excepted from the collateral bar rule. We now turn to consider whether the order issued by the district court on November 13, 1985, was, as the Journal contends, transparently invalid.

As noted, the principal purpose of the First Amendment's guaranty is to prevent prior restraints. The Supreme Court has declared: "Any prior restraint on expression comes to this Court with a 'heavy presumption' against its constitutional validity." When, as here, the prior restraint impinges upon the right of the press to communicate news and involves expression in the form of pure speech—speech not connected with any conduct—the presumption of unconstitutionality is virtually insurmountable.

The distinction between pure speech and speech involving conduct clearly distinguishes the order at issue in *Walker* from the order at issue in the instant case.

A different result, or at a minimum a different analysis, would have been required had the Walker order restrained pure speech.

In its nearly two centuries of existence, the Supreme Court has never upheld a prior restraint on pure speech. In *New York Times Co. v. United States*, the *Pentagon Papers* case, the Court held that the New York Times and other newspapers could not be restrained even during wartime from publishing documents that had been classified top secret and obtained without authorization. Notwithstanding that the source who had provided the documents had obtained them possibly as a result of criminal conduct and notwithstanding the government's contention that publication would gravely and irreparably jeopardize national security, the Court refused to uphold the restraint. In his concurring opinion, Justice Stewart stated that a prior restraint upon publication was improper absent proof that publication "will surely result in direct, immediate, and irreparable damage to our Nation or its people."

The only interest implicated by the Journal's publication is Patriarca's right to privacy. That publication would prove embarrassing or infringe Patriarca's privacy rights is, however, an insufficient basis for issuing a prior restraint. Rather, Patriarca's sole remedy was a subsequent action for damages, an alternative that he did not pursue.

An additional point to note is that the prior restraint was issued prior to a full and fair hearing with all the attendant procedural protections. A prior restraint issued in these circumstances faces an even heavier presumption of invalidity, and the transparent unconstitutionality of the order is made even more patent by the absence of such a hearing.

The special prosecutor argues, however, that the order was to last only a short period and merely preserved the status quo while allowing the court a full opportunity to assess the issues. We are sympathetic with the district court on this score. This matter came before the district court on an emergency basis. The court was forced to drop its other duties and immediately address this issue. Counsel for the Journal had received the papers less than 24 hours before they presented their arguments to the district court. Based on counsel's hastily prepared authority and without the opportunity for cool reflection, the district court was forced to make a decision. The court's natural instinct was to delay the matter temporarily so that a careful, thoughtful answer could be crafted. This approach is proper in most instances, and indeed to follow any other course of action would often be irresponsible. But, absent the most compelling circumstances, when that approach results in a prior restraint on pure speech by the press it is not allowed.

It must be said, it is misleading in the context of daily newspaper publishing to argue that a temporary restraining order merely preserves the status quo. The status quo of daily newspapers is to publish news promptly that editors decide to publish. A restraining order disturbs the status quo and impinges on the exercise of editorial discretion. News is a constantly changing and dynamic quantity. Today's news will often be tomorrow's history. This is especially true in the case of news concerning an imminent event such as an election. A restraining order lasting only hours can effectively prevent publication of news that will have an impact on that event and on those that the event affects.

Although there is no question that the Patriarca story was not news concerning an imminent event, extraneous factors required its reasonably prompt publication. The Journal had promised its readers that the Patriarca story would be forthcoming. Moreover, other media not subject to the court order had the same logs and memoranda. Were they to disseminate this information while the Journal remained silent, some readers of the Journal might lose confidence in that paper's editorial competence.

As the Supreme Court recognized in *Elrod v. Burns*, "[t]he loss of First Amendment Freedoms, for even minimal periods of time, unquestionably constitutes irreparable injury." The heavy presumption of unconstitutionality against a prior restraint "is not reduced by the temporary nature of [the] restraint." In the Pentagon Papers case, Justice Brennan noted in his concurrence that "every restraint in this case, whatever its form, has violated the First Amendment—and not less so because that restraint was justified as necessary to afford the courts an opportunity to examine the claim more thoroughly."

CONCLUSION

We conclude that the district court's order of November 13, 1985, was transparently invalid. The order constituted a presumptively unconstitutional prior restraint on pure speech by the press. The burden necessary to sustain such an order is tremendously heavy and was not met in this case. The only potential danger posed by the restrained speech was to an individual's privacy right. That right can be adequately protected by a subsequent damages action. Moreover, the district court failed to find with certainty that the restraint would accomplish its goal and that no less restrictive alternatives were available. Indeed, it is clear that the court could not have found that the order would necessarily be effective.

Because the order was transparently invalid, the appellants should have been allowed to challenge its constitutionality at the contempt proceedings. A fortiori, the order cannot serve as the basis for a contempt citation. The order of the district court finding the Providence Journal Company and its executive editor, Charles M. Hauser, in criminal contempt is therefore reversed.

NOTE: OTHER ENFORCEMENT METHODS

In addition to contempt sanctions, there are other methods of enforcing equitable decrees. These other options are discussed in later chapters. *See* Rule 70, FRCP.

EXERCISE: CHILD SUPPORT ENFORCEMENT

James and Joanna Willis divorced seven years ago after twenty years of marriage. The marriage produced four children (currently ranging in age from 12 to 19). The divorce decree required James to pay Joanna maintenance for a period of two years. It also required him to pay $1,200 per month to Joanna for the support of his children, and to provide each child with the sum of $4,000 per year for four years of college.

Four years ago, James remarried. He has two children by his second wife (currently ages one and two). Until a year ago, James was employed at a local manufacturing plant where he made approximately $30,000 per year (regular pay plus overtime). On his income James struggled to support his new family and make his child support payments. Somehow, he managed to do both. When the plant closed due to outsourcing, James was unable to meet all his obligations. As a result, his car was repossessed. James continued making his child support payments. James eventually found another job, but it paid him only $18,000 a year including overtime.

The present controversy arose when James refused to meet his obligations under the divorce decree. James claimed that his economic situation precluded him from doing so. At the time, he was making rent payments of $300 per month. Because his new job did not include health insurance, James bought his own insurance at a cost of $350 per month. By the time he paid living expenses for his new family, James had little left. Accordingly, James refused to contribute towards his oldest daughter's college education, and began sending his ex-wife only $500 per month. James claimed that he was "unable" to pay more.

EXERCISE INSTRUCTIONS

Your instructor will assign you to represent either James or Joanna. If you are assigned to represent Joanna, draft the documents necessary to have James held in contempt for his failure to comply with the divorce decree. If you are assigned to represent James, respond to Joanna's pleadings as appropriate. Both parties should comply with the Rules of Court set forth at the end of the next chapter.

CHAPTER 4

INJUNCTIONS

■ ■ ■

CHAPTER OVERVIEW: You might have examined the topic of injunctions in your first year course in civil procedure, and you may have also seen injunctions in various contexts in your contracts, property and torts courses. However, your exposure to this remedy was probably more limited or passing in nature.

In this chapter, we examine the injunctive remedy in some depth. We began by distinguishing between the various types of injunctions, and we focus in particular on the requirements for preliminary injunctive relief. In addition, we examine how some of the principles that we examined earlier—in particular, the distinction between legal and equitable remedies and the ways in which those remedies are enforced—apply in the injunction context. We also examine so-called "structural injunctions," and issues relating to how the injunctive remedy has been applied in various substantive contexts.

PROBLEM: THE DIAMOND DERBY CELEBRITY GALA

The Kentucky Derby is always run on the first Saturday in May. It is preceded by the Kentucky Derby Festival which includes The Great Steamboat Race, a hot-air balloon race, and various other events. Private individuals also hold their own parties. Some of the parties are events designed to raise money for charity. Derby Eve is the most popular party night with events attended by celebrities from all over the world.

For several years, a private group has held the "Diamond Derby Celebrity Gala" at a private residence in an upscale residential area. The Gala routinely attracts the rich and famous. The party always has a theme which is brought to life through props, local actors in costume, and music. One year, the theme was "Babes in Toyland." The lawn was transformed into "Toyland." Child actors and actresses were present dressed as stuffed animals, toy soldiers and ballerinas. Tickets for the Gala cost $300 each. Proceeds went to a local charity.

Tom and Bernice Jackson live next door to the Gala and are not happy about the annual event. On several occasions, the Jacksons have called the police complaining about noise levels. Recently, the Jacksons filed suit claiming that the Gala interrupts the "peace and contentment" of the neighborhood. The suit claims that the Gala creates "deafening noise." In addition, it attracts gawkers and onlookers hoping to get a glimpse of the celebrities at the party. The suit also complains that the party flows across the back yard (where a band performs) and down the long sloping front yard where costumed children sing and dance enacting the party theme. The suit claims that gawkers and party-goers trample and litter their yard.

Gala organizers respond that, "[p]articularly on Derby Eve, [this] community is replete with people hosting parties and enjoying themselves." As a result, the neighbors should be more "accommodating." In the view of the sponsors, "this case is essentially a dispute between neighbors; this is simply not a federal case."

It is now February. Derby Eve is a little more than two months away. The Jacksons have filed a legal action, and plan to seek a preliminary injunction against the Gala.

As we go through this chapter, we will ask you to think about how this problem should be resolved. Should injunctive relief issue? If so, how should it be framed? Do you have any preliminary thoughts on these issues? See if your ideas change as you go through the chapter.

A. NATURE AND PURPOSE OF INJUNCTIVE RELIEF

The injunction is perhaps the most powerful judicial remedy, and is used to order defendants to engage in, or to refrain from engaging in, an act (or acts). Some injunctions are mandatory while others are prohibitory: an injunction which compels an act is referred to as mandatory, while one which forbids an act is a prohibitory injunction.

Injunctions can be used to accomplish many different objectives: preventative injunctions protect against continuing or threatened harm; reparative injunctions require defendant to restore plaintiff to his/her rights; and structural injunctions apply to organizations (*e.g.*, a prison or school system) and are designed to bring it into compliance with legal requirements (*i.e.*, if a prison is holding prisoners in violation of the Eighth Amendment to the United States Constitution (which prohibits "cruel and unusual punishment"), a court might order reforms designed to make the punishment constitutionally acceptable). *See* Owen M. Fiss, The Civil Rights Injunction (1978). In a given case, the court might issue injunctions designed to achieve more than one of these objectives (*i.e.*, preventative and reparative).

Historically, injunctions have been used to enjoin both private and public conduct, especially in nuisance and trespass cases. The following cases are illustrative:

- Suit to prevent operation of cattle feedlot as a nuisance. *See Carpenter v. Double R Cattle Co., Inc.*, 108 Idaho 602, 701 P.2d 222 (1985).
- Suit to prevent radio-controlled model airplane club from interfering with the use and enjoyment of nearby residences. *See Kaiser v. Western R/C Flyers, Inc.*, 239 Neb. 624, 477 N.W.2d 557 (1991).
- Suit to prevent construction of house in violation of building restrictions. *See Hohman v. Bartel*, 125 Or.App. 306, 865 P.2d 1301 (1993).
- Injunction requiring removal of trespassing wall. *See Seid v. Ross*, 120 Or.App. 564, 853 P.2d 308 (1993).
- Action to enjoin public nuisance. *See Union County v. Hoffman*, 512 N.W.2d 168 (S.D.1994).
- Injunction requiring removal of junk tires prohibited by local zoning ordinances. *See Saurer v. Board of Zoning Appeals*, 629 N.E.2d 893 (Ind.App.1994).
- Suit to prevent owner of dirt track from creating excessive levels of dust. *See Decatur Auto Auction, Inc. v. Macon County Farm Bureau, Inc.*, 255 Ill.App.3d 679, 194 Ill.Dec. 487, 627 N.E.2d 1129 (1993).
- Injunction to prohibit rock concerts with loud music and large crowds. *See McQuade v. Tucson Tiller Apartments, Ltd.*, 25 Ariz.App. 312, 543 P.2d 150 (1975).
- Injunction seeking removal of a spite fence. *See Sundowner, Inc. v. King*, 95 Idaho 367, 509 P.2d 785 (1973).
- Suit to prevent construction of animal shelter designed to house 200 animals. *Georg v. Animal Defense League*, 231 S.W.2d 807 (Tex.Civ.App.1950).

Injunctive relief has also been sought in suits against federal, state or local governments. The following cases are illustrative:

- Suit by abortion clinics to enjoin Pennsylvania's Abortion Control Act as unconstitutional. *Planned Parenthood of Southeastern Pennsylvania v. Casey*, 510 U.S. 1309, 114 S.Ct. 909, 127 L.Ed.2d 352 (1994).
- Suit to enjoin erection of a Ten Commandments in the rotunda of the Alabama Supreme Court. *See Capital Square Review and Advisory Board v. Pinette*, 510 U.S. 1307, 114 S.Ct. 626, 126 L.Ed.2d 636 (1993).

- Suit to prevent government from maintaining records pertaining to plaintiff. *United States v. Meinhold*, 510 U.S. 939, 114 S.Ct. 374, 126 L.Ed.2d 324 (1993).
- Suit to prevent U.S. Immigration and Naturalization Service from deporting Haitian refugees. *Sale v. Haitian Centers Council, Inc.*, 509 U.S. 155, 113 S.Ct. 2549, 125 L.Ed.2d 128 (1993).
- Suit to enjoin city ordinance giving preferential treatment to minority-owned businesses in the awarding of city contracts. *Northeastern Florida Chapter of the Associated General Contractors of America v. City of Jacksonville*, 508 U.S. 656, 113 S.Ct. 2297, 124 L.Ed.2d 586 (1993).
- Suit challenging electoral districts. *Growe v. Emison*, 507 U.S. 25, 113 S.Ct. 1075, 122 L.Ed.2d 388 (1993).
- Suit by religious organization against restrictions on distributing literature and soliciting funds in airport terminal. *International Society for Krishna Consciousness, Inc. v. Lee*, 505 U.S. 672, 112 S.Ct. 2701, 120 L.Ed.2d 541 (1992).
- Suit by student and her father to prevent prayer in graduation ceremonies at public school. *Lee v. Daniel Weisman*, 505 U.S. 577, 112 S.Ct. 2649, 120 L.Ed.2d 467 (1992).
- Suit by athlete to prevent athletic federations from interfering with his ability to compete in the Olympic trials. *Reynolds v. International Amateur Athletic Federation*, 505 U.S. 1301, 112 S.Ct. 2512, 120 L.Ed.2d 861 (1992).

B. STANDARDS FOR ISSUANCE OF INJUNCTIVE RELIEF

As equitable remedies, injunctions are subject to the ordinary rules governing equitable relief (*e.g.*, inadequacy of legal remedies & equitable discretion), but they are also subject to their own special rules. There are different types of injunctions and each has its own function. Some injunctions are permanent in nature: they are issued after a determination of the merits of a lawsuit and are designed to apply prospectively and permanently unless modified or dissolved. Other injunctions are temporary in nature, including the temporary restraining order (TRO) and the preliminary injunction (a/k/a temporary injunction). A preliminary injunction is issued at the beginning of litigation and is designed to prevent irreparable harm from occurring during the pendency of a suit (*i.e.*, before the merits can be decided). A TRO can sometimes be issued *ex parte* and is designed to maintain the status quo only until a hearing can be held on whether to grant a preliminary injunction.

1. REQUIREMENTS FOR PROVISIONAL RELIEF

Preliminary injunctions and TROs are subject to specific requirements imposed by rule and case law. In order to obtain either of these types of injunctions, a plaintiff must show that immediate and irreparable injury will result absent the injunction. When a preliminary injunction is sought, plaintiff must show that this injury will occur during the pendency of the lawsuit. When a TRO is sought, plaintiff must show that it will occur before a hearing can be heard on whether to grant a preliminary injunction.

Rule 65 (F.R.Civ.P.). Injunctions and Restraining Orders

(a) Preliminary Injunction.

(1) *Notice.* The court may issue a preliminary injunction only on notice to the adverse party.

(2) *Consolidating the Hearing with the Trial on the Merits.* Before or after the hearing on a motion for a preliminary injunction, the court may advance the trial on the merits and consolidate it with the hearing. Even when consolidation is not ordered, evidence that is received on the motion and that would be admissible at trial becomes part of the trial record and need not be repeated at trial. But the court must preserve any party's right to a jury trial.

(b) Temporary Restraining Order.

(1) *Issuing Without Notice.* The court may issue a temporary restraining order without written or oral notice to the adverse party or its attorney only if:

(A) specific facts in an affidavit or a verified complaint clearly show that immediate and irreparable injury, loss, or damage will result to the movant before the adverse party can be heard in opposition; and

(B) the movant's attorney certifies in writing any efforts made to give notice and the reasons why it should not be required.

(2) *Contents; Expiration.* Every temporary restraining order issued without notice must state the date and hour it was issued; describe the injury and state why it is irreparable; state why the order was issued without notice; and be promptly filed in the clerk's office and entered in the record. The order expires at the time after entry—not to exceed 14 days—that the court sets, unless before that time the court, for good cause extends it for a

like period or the adverse party consents to a longer extension. The reasons for an extension must be entered in the record.

(3) *Expediting the Preliminary–Injunction Hearing.* If the order is issued without notice, the motion for a preliminary injunction must be set for hearing at the earliest possible time, taking precedence over all other matters except hearings on older matters of the same character. At the hearing, the party who obtained the order must proceed with the motion,; if the party does not, the court must dissolve the order.

(4) *Motion to Dissolve.* On 2 days' notice to the party who obtained the order without notice—or on shorter notice set by the court—the adverse party may appear and move to dissolve or modify the order. The court must then hear and decide the motion as promptly as justice requires.

HUGHES V. CRISTOFANE

486 F.Supp. 541 (D.Md.1980).

HERBERT F. MURRAY, DISTRICT JUDGE. The plaintiffs are the owners and major shareholders of the Three Captains House of Seafood Restaurant in Bladensburg, Maryland; the defendants are the mayor and town councilmen of Bladensburg. The plaintiffs, whose restaurant has until recently provided entertainment in the form of "topless" dancing, seek a temporary restraining order enjoining enforcement of a recently-enacted Bladensburg town ordinance which prohibits such entertainment in establishments that serve alcoholic beverages or food. After hearing oral [argument, and] having considered the applicable law, the court has concluded that the restraining order should issue.

Under the ordinance, any person who engages in any of the proscribed conduct, or suffers the conduct to be engaged in on licensed premises, is subject to a fine or imprisonment or both, and to possible revocation of his or her entertainment license. The plaintiffs contend that the ordinance is overbroad, and that it deprives them of their rights under the first and fourteenth amendments to the Federal Constitution and 42 U.S.C. § 1983.

In order to obtain relief by a temporary restraining order under Rule 65 of the Federal Rules, the plaintiffs must show:

(1) that unless the restraining order issues, they will suffer irreparable harm;

(2) that the hardship they will suffer absent the order outweighs any hardship the defendants would suffer if the order were to issue;

(3) that they are likely to succeed on the merits of their claims;

(4) that the issuance of the order will cause no substantial harm to the public; and

(5) that they have no adequate remedy at law.

See Blackwelder Furniture Co., Etc. v. Seilig Mfg. Co., 550 F.2d 189 (4th Cir.1977). The plaintiffs have satisfied each of the prerequisites.

If a restraining order did not issue, the owners of the Three Captains Restaurant would suffer irreparable harm both to their financial interests and to their interest in the free exercise of constitutional rights. According to the affidavit of plaintiff Bernard Hughes, filed with the court on February 20, 1980, the gross income of his restaurant was "generally" over $1000 and rarely less than $800 per day before he clothed his dancers on February 14th in order to comply with Ordinance 3–80. Since he has complied, the business has averaged $700 a day. Because Mr. Hughes requires at least $750 to $800 gross income per day to meet expenses, he has been operating at a loss since the topless dancing ceased. He anticipates that his business may fail if the dancers must continue to comply with the ordinance. Other courts have found that loss of revenue, when specifically described, constitutes irreparable harm, and this court believes Mr. Hughes has made an adequate showing under that standard.

More importantly, the plaintiffs have made an adequate showing that if enforcement of the ordinance is not enjoined, the law might operate to infringe the first and fourteenth amendment freedoms not only of the plaintiffs, but also of other proprietors and entertainers subject to the law's requirements. Such a showing satisfies not only the irreparable harm requirement, but also the likelihood-of-success requirement.

[The] weight of authority in the federal courts is that nude dancing which cannot be characterized as obscene is a form of expression entitled to some protection under the first amendment. The plaintiffs have also made an adequate showing that Ordinance 3–80 may be unconstitutionally overbroad, and may violate principles of equal protection. The law purports to prohibit topless dancing in all business establishments serving liquor or food. [D]efendants have made no showing that first amendment activity can be constitutionally curtailed merely because food is served on the premises. Furthermore, the language of the ordinance on its face may sweep in activity which is clearly entitled to first amendment protection, such as a performance of the play "Equus" at a legitimate dinner theater. As for the equal protection problems, the defendants have not satisfactorily explained why there is even a rational basis for, much less a compelling state interest in discriminating between an establishment that offers food and nude entertainment, and an establishment that offers such entertainment with only soft drinks or no refreshment at all. Although the court voices no opinion about the ultimate outcome of the case, the constitutional issues raised are substantial enough to justify affording the plaintiffs temporary relief.

Given the plaintiffs' substantial showing of threatened irreparable harm, it is not difficult to conclude that the balance of hardships tips in the plaintiffs' favor. If the temporary restraining order should issue, the only resulting hardship to the defendants will be a return to the status quo before the ordinance took effect. Because the defendants have not shown that the status quo injured anything other than their moral sensibilities, the court feels that the importance of the plaintiffs' constitutional rights outweighs the defendants' interests.[1] For the same reasons, the court finds that enjoining the enforcement of Ordinance 3–80 will not substantially harm the public interest.

The plaintiffs have also satisfied the court that they have no adequate remedy at law. If the status quo is not preserved, the passage of time required to litigate the plaintiffs' claims will work the irreparable injury the plaintiffs have described.

The plaintiffs have thus met all the prerequisites for obtaining a temporary restraining order. The court is mindful that the remedy is an extraordinary one, but is persuaded that the case presents the urgency and special circumstances that make extraordinary relief necessary.

Accordingly, the Town of Bladensburg and its agents will be temporarily enjoined from enforcing Ordinance 3–80, and the court will issue a separate order to that effect. However, nothing in this opinion or in the order should be deemed to affect any state proceedings stemming from enforcement of the ordinance prior to today's date.

ORDER

For the reasons set forth in the Memorandum Opinion dated this 22nd day of February, 1980, it is this same date, by the United States District Court for the District of Maryland,

ORDERED:

(1) that the plaintiffs' request for a temporary restraining order be, and the same hereby is, Granted;

(2) that effective immediately, defendants Mayor and Councilmen of the Town of Bladensburg and their agents be, and the same hereby are Restrained from enforcing Ordinance 3–80 of the Town of Bladensburg for a period of ten days from the date of this Order;

---

1 The court does not mean to imply that the town's moral concerns are frivolous, but only that they are not of constitutional dimension.

(3) that plaintiffs give security by filing forthwith with the Clerk of this Court a bond in the sum of $500.00 for the payment of such costs and damages as may be incurred or suffered by defendants if found to be wrongfully enjoined or restrained;

(4) that this matter be heard on plaintiffs' request for preliminary injunction at 4:30 p.m. on Monday, March 3, 1980.

NOTES

1. *The Prohibitory–Mandatory Distinction.* The distinction between prohibitory and mandatory injunctions has important consequences. In many jurisdictions, temporary restraining orders (TROs) can only be prohibitory and not mandatory. Consider, for example, Kentucky Rule of Civil Procedure 65.01: "A restraining order shall only restrict the doing of an act. An injunction may restrict or mandatorily direct the doing of an act."

The distinction between mandatory and prohibitory injunctions is based on substance rather than form. Thus, even though a TRO is stated in prohibitory form (*e.g.*, defendant is prohibited from permitting a wall to remain on plaintiff's property), it may in fact be mandatory (by requiring the removal of the wall).

2. *Impact of the Mandatory–Prohibitory Distinction.* Compared to prohibitory injunctions, mandatory preliminary injunctions are generally disfavored. *See Ferry–Morse Seed Co. v. Food Corn, Inc.*, 729 F.2d 589 (8th Cir. 1984). For example, if defendant seeks to build a wall on land that both plaintiff and defendant claim to own, a court might be inclined to issue a prohibitory preliminary injunction (precluding the building of the wall) until the parties' rights can be determined. However, in doing so, the court is simply preserving the status quo pending the outcome of the case. By contrast, if plaintiff seeks a preliminary order requiring defendant to tear down a wall between his property and a neighbor's party, a court might be disinclined to grant the order on a preliminary basis. Once the wall is torn down, it would require substantial expense and effort to rebuild it, and such an order should (generally) not issue until the parties' rights have been finally determined.

Courts might issue preliminary mandatory injunctions in a couple of instances. One is when the defendant has violated a preliminary injunction. For example, suppose that a court enters a preliminary injunction ordering defendant not to tear down a wall between plaintiff's property and defendant's property. In violation of the injunction, defendant tears down the wall. The court might require defendant to rebuild the wall notwithstanding the fact that litigation has not been finally resolved. The second situation when a mandatory preliminary injunction might be appropriate is when the status quo is a state of action. For example, in *Ferry–Morse Seed Co. v. Food Corn, Inc., supra*, plaintiff sought a preliminary injunction requiring defendant to turn over seed corn under a prior agreement which gave defendant an exclusive license agreement to sell the corn. Because defendant had breached a pre-existing agreement, and there were no alternative sources, the court ordered defendant to deliver six thousand bags of corn: "[While] the granting of preliminary injunctions is not favored unless the right to such relief is clearly established, where the status quo is a condition not of rest, but of action, and the condition of rest (in this case the refusal to deliver the seed corn) will cause irreparable harm, a mandatory preliminary injunction is proper. *Canal Authority v. Callaway,* 489 F.2d 567, 576 (5th Cir.1974). We view this as a case where mandatory relief could properly be found to be necessary to prevent irreparable harm to [plaintiff]. Ferry–Morse had been marketing the Food Corn seed just as it had the year before. It was this status quo that was destroyed by the action of Food Corn, and we cannot conclude that the district court abused its discretion in restoring the earlier relationship by requiring that Food Corn turn over the seed corn."

PROBLEMS

1. *Deciding* Hughes *Today.* In *Barnes v. Glen Theatre, Inc.*, 501 U.S. 560 (1991), the United States Supreme Court held that Indiana could require dancers to wear "pasties" and a "G-string." The state did so under a statute that prohibited nudity in public and that was not targeted specifically at nude dancing. The Court treated the law as a reasonable time, place and manner restriction under the *O'Brien* test. In reaching its decision, the Court concluded that "nude dancing of the kind sought to be performed here is expressive conduct within the outer perimeters of the First Amendment, though we view it as only marginally so." Given the holding in *Barnes*, would *Hughes* be decided differently today? In other words, is the likelihood of success diminished to the point that injunctive relief becomes less appropriate?

2. Hughes *and the Propriety of a TRO.* Was it appropriate for the court to enter a temporary restraining order in this case? Is there evidence suggesting that plaintiff would suffer severe and irreparable injury prior to the time that a hearing could be held on whether a preliminary injunction should issue?

3. *More on the Diamond Derby Gala.* Assume that you are the judge assigned to hear the case. Is this case an appropriate one for granting preliminary injunctive relief? Do the Jacksons meet the requirements for temporary relief? Why? Why not?

4. *The Terminated Hockey Club.* The Central Hockey League, Inc. (CHL) decides to terminate the Flying Cross Check. L.L.C.'s ("FCC") franchise, and end its season effective immediately for violations of league rules. FCC seeks injunctive relief preventing the CHL, from terminating the franchise, as well as from cancelling previously scheduled games or preventing the Scarecrows from participating in the playoffs. Since there are only two games remaining in the regular season, a TRO would effectively allow the Scarecrows to finish the season and enter the playoffs. FCC claims that it will suffer injury if it is not allowed to finish the season because it will lose goodwill with its fans, thereby impacting the value of its franchise, and

will also lose money from gate receipts. FCC claims that the community as a whole will suffer injury because there is excitement about the Scarecrows making the playoffs, and possibly winning the CHL championship. Finally, FCC claims that it has signed contracts with its coach and players, and would have no way to pay them absent game gate receipts. By contrast, the CHL claims that it will suffer injury if the injunction is issued because it will be morally obligated to reimburse other CHL teams for costs incurred ($30,000 to $40,000) in altering their schedules, including lost revenue and additional travel expenses. Regarding the merits, FCC claims that the CHL wrongfully terminated its franchise. The CHL argues that the FCC failed to enforce and comply with CHL rules and regulations by not enforcing its rules and regulations on team salary caps, and that it thereby gained an unfair advantage over other teams. Suppose that you are the judge assigned to hear the case. Should you grant a TRO in the FCC's favor? *See Flying Cross Check, L.L.C. v. Central Hockey League, Inc.*, 153 F. Supp.2d 1253 (D. Kan. 2001).

5. *The Corruption Charges.* A local newspaper plans to publish a four part series accusing the mayor of your city of corruption and abuse of office and has already published the first installment. The local mayor is extremely angry about the first publication. He believes that the article was inadequately researched, failed to comply with even minimal investigative reporting standards, and has caused him serious reputational injury. The mayor has come to you for advice, and is prepared to present proof showing that the first article contained "grave inaccuracies" In addition, the mayor believes that the article is injurious to him and to the public interest because it misinforms the public. It is now Friday, and the newspaper plans to publish the second installment in the series on Sunday. Can the mayor obtain a TRO preventing the Sunday publication on grounds that the series is malicious and defamatory and will cause him irreparable injury? If you represent the newspaper, how would you respond?

6. *The Star Running Back.* Last season, a star college running back led his team to a national championship. He was suspended by the school for the upcoming football season for "serious violations of team rules." Rather than sit out, the player decided to leave school and enter the National Football League (NFL). However, he was prevented from doing so by an NFL rule that made players ineligible until they had been out of high school for three years. At the time, the player was only a sophomore in college, had only been out of high school for a year, and therefore was not eligible for the draft for two years. The player filed a law suit, challenging the NFL rule as anti-competitive, and seeking injunctive temporary relief requiring the NFL to conduct a special draft for him so that he could play in the NFL during the upcoming season. Assuming that the player has a good chance of success on the merits, in terms of being able to show that the NFL's rule is anti-competitive, is he likely to obtain the requested injunctive relief? The player claims that he will suffer irreparable injury by being forced to sit out for a year because his football skills will get "rusty" and his reputation will diminish from lack of public exposure. In addition, he claims that his morale will suffer from being forced to watch from the sidelines for a season. The

NFL defends the rule on the theory that underclassmen need time to mature (both physically and mentally) before entering the physically demanding NFL environment. If you are the judge assigned to hear the case, would you grant the player's request for preliminary injunctive relief?

WINTER V. NATURAL RESOURCES DEFENSE COUNCIL, INC.

555 U.S. 7 (2008).

CHIEF JUSTICE ROBERTS delivered the opinion of the Court.

"To be prepared for war is one of the most effectual means of preserving peace." 1 Messages and Papers of the Presidents 57 (J. Richardson comp. 1897). So said George Washington in his first Annual Address to Congress, 218 years ago. One of the most important ways the Navy prepares for war is through integrated training exercises at sea.

The Navy deploys its forces in "strike groups," which are groups of surface ships, submarines, and aircraft centered around either an aircraft carrier or an amphibious assault ship. Seamless coordination among strike-group assets is critical. Before deploying a strike group, the Navy requires extensive integrated training in analysis and prioritization of threats, execution of military missions, and maintenance of force protection. Antisubmarine warfare is currently the Pacific Fleet's top war-fighting priority. Modern diesel-electric submarines pose a significant threat to Navy vessels because they can operate almost silently, making them extremely difficult to detect and track. Potential adversaries of the United States possess at least 300 of these submarines. [The] most effective technology for identifying submerged diesel-electric submarines [is] active sonar, which involves emitting pulses of sound underwater and then receiving the acoustic waves that echo off the target. Active sonar is a particularly useful tool because it provides both the bearing and the distance of target submarines; it is also sensitive enough to allow the Navy to track enemy submarines that are quieter than the surrounding marine environment. This case concerns the Navy's use of "mid-frequency active" (MFA) sonar, which transmits sound waves at frequencies between 1 kHz and 10 kHz.

Not surprisingly, MFA sonar is a complex technology, and sonar operators must undergo extensive training to become proficient in its use. Sonar reception can be affected by countless different factors, including the time of day, water density, salinity, currents, weather conditions, and the contours of the sea floor. When working as part of a strike group, sonar operators must be able to coordinate with other Navy ships and planes while avoiding interference. The Navy conducts regular training exercises under realistic conditions to ensure that sonar operators are thoroughly skilled in its use in a variety of situations.

The waters off the coast of southern California (SOCAL) are an ideal location for conducting integrated training exercises, as this is the only area on the west coast that is relatively close to land, air, and sea bases, as well as amphibious landing areas. At issue in this case are the Composite Training Unit Exercises and the Joint Tactical Force Exercises, in which individual naval units (ships, submarines, and aircraft) train together as members of a strike group. A strike group cannot be certified for deployment until it has successfully completed the integrated training exercises, including a demonstration of its ability to operate under simulated hostile conditions. In light of the threat posed by enemy submarines, all strike groups must demonstrate proficiency in antisubmarine warfare. Accordingly, the SOCAL exercises include extensive training in detecting, tracking, and neutralizing enemy submarines. The use of MFA sonar during these exercises is "mission-critical," given that MFA sonar is the only proven method of identifying submerged diesel-electric submarines operating on battery power.

Sharing the waters in the SOCAL operating area are at least 37 species of marine mammals, including dolphins, whales, and sea lions. The parties strongly dispute the extent to which the Navy's training activities will harm those animals or disrupt their behavioral patterns. The Navy emphasizes that it has used MFA sonar during training exercises in SOCAL for 40 years, without a single documented sonar-related injury to any marine mammal. The Navy asserts that, at most, MFA sonar may cause temporary hearing loss or brief disruptions of marine mammals' behavioral patterns.

The plaintiffs are the Natural Resources Defense Council, Inc., Jean–Michael Cousteau (an environmental enthusiast and filmmaker), and several other groups devoted to the protection of marine mammals and ocean habitats. They contend that MFA sonar can cause much more serious injuries to marine mammals than the Navy acknowledges, including permanent hearing loss, decompression sickness, and major behavioral disruptions. According to the plaintiffs, several mass strandings of marine mammals (outside of SOCAL) have been "associated" with the use of active sonar. They argue that certain species of marine mammals—such as beaked whales—are uniquely susceptible to injury from active sonar; these injuries would not necessarily be detected by the Navy, given that beaked whales are "very deep divers" that spend little time at the surface.

The Marine Mammal Protection Act of 1972 (MMPA), 86 Stat. 1027, generally prohibits any individual from "taking" a marine mammal, defined as harassing, hunting, capturing, or killing it. The Secretary of Defense may "exempt any action or category of actions" from the MMPA if such actions are "necessary for national defense." In January 2007, the Deputy Secretary of Defense—acting for the Secretary—granted the Navy a 2-year exemption from the MMPA for the training exercises at issue in this case. The exemption was conditioned on the Navy adopting several mitigation procedures, including: (1) training lookouts and officers to watch for marine mammals; (2) requiring at least five lookouts with binoculars on each vessel to watch for anomalies on the water surface (including marine mammals); (3) requiring aircraft and sonar operators to report detected marine mammals in the vicinity of the training exercises; (4) requiring reduction of active sonar transmission levels by 6 dB if a marine mammal is detected within 1,000 yards of the bow of the vessel, or by 10 dB if detected within 500 yards; (5) requiring complete shutdown of active sonar transmission if a marine mammal is detected within 200 yards of the vessel; (6) requiring active sonar to be operated at the "lowest practicable level"; and (7) adopting coordination and reporting procedures. The National Environmental Policy Act of 1969 (NEPA), 83 Stat. 852, requires federal agencies "to the fullest extent possible" to prepare an environmental impact statement (EIS) for "[every] major Federal [action] significantly affecting the quality of the human environment." An agency is not required to prepare a full EIS if it determines—based on a shorter environmental assessment (EA)—that the proposed action will not have a significant impact on the environment.

In February 2007, the Navy issued an EA concluding that the 14 SOCAL training exercises scheduled through January 2009 would not have a significant impact on the environment. The EA divided potential injury to marine mammals into two categories: Level A harassment, defined as the potential destruction or loss of biological tissue (*i.e.*, physical injury), and Level B harassment, defined as temporary injury or disruption of behavioral patterns such as migration, feeding, surfacing, and breeding. The Navy's computer models predicted that the SOCAL training exercises would cause only eight Level A harassments of common dolphins each year, and that even these injuries could be avoided through the Navy's voluntary mitigation measures, given that dolphins travel in large pods easily located by Navy lookouts. The EA also predicted 274 Level B harassments of beaked whales per year, none of which would result in permanent injury. Beaked whales spend little time at the surface, so the precise effect of active sonar on these mammals is unclear. Erring on the side of caution, the Navy classified all projected harassments of beaked whales as Level A. In light of its conclusion that the SOCAL training exercises would not have a significant impact on the environment, the Navy determined that it was unnecessary to prepare a full EIS.

Shortly after the Navy released its EA, the plaintiffs sued the Navy, seeking declaratory and injunctive relief on the grounds that the Navy's SOCAL training exercises violated NEPA, the Endangered Species Act of 1973(ESA), and the Coastal Zone Management Act of 1972 (CZMA). The

District Court granted plaintiffs' motion for a preliminary injunction and prohibited the Navy from using MFA sonar during its remaining training exercises. The Court of Appeals agreed with the District Court that preliminary injunctive relief was appropriate. The Navy then sought relief from the Executive Branch. The President, pursuant to 16 U.S.C. § 1456(c)(1)(B), granted the Navy an exemption from the CZMA. Section 1456(c)(1)(B) permits such exemptions if the activity in question is "in the paramount interest of the United States." The President determined that continuation of the exercises as limited by the Navy was "essential to national security." He concluded that compliance with the District Court's injunction would "undermine the Navy's ability to conduct realistic training exercises that are necessary to ensure the combat effectiveness of strike groups." Simultaneously, the Council on Environmental Quality (CEQ) authorized the Navy to implement "alternative arrangements" to NEPA compliance in light of "emergency circumstances." The CEQ determined that alternative arrangements were appropriate because the District Court's injunction "creates a significant and unreasonable risk that Strike Groups will not be able to train and be certified as fully mission capable." Under the alternative arrangements, the Navy would be permitted to conduct its training exercises under the mitigation procedures adopted in conjunction with the exemption from the MMPA. The CEQ also imposed additional notice, research, and reporting requirements. The Navy then moved to vacate the District Court's injunction with respect to the 2,200-yard shutdown zone and the restrictions on training in surface ducting conditions. The District Court refused [and] the Court of Appeals affirmed. We granted certiorari and now reverse and vacate the injunction.

A plaintiff seeking a preliminary injunction must establish that he is likely to succeed on the merits, that he is likely to suffer irreparable harm in the absence of preliminary relief, that the balance of equities tips in his favor, and that an injunction is in the public interest. See *Munaf v. Geren,* 553 U.S. 674 (2008); *Amoco Production Co. v. Gambell,* 480 U.S. 531 (1987); *Weinberger v. Romero–Barcelo,* 456 U.S. 305 (1982). The Navy argues that plaintiffs' likelihood of success is low because the CEQ reasonably concluded that "emergency circumstances" justified alternative arrangements to NEPA compliance. The District Court and the Ninth Circuit held that when a plaintiff demonstrates a strong likelihood of prevailing on the merits, a preliminary injunction may be entered based only on a "possibility" of irreparable harm. The Navy contends that plaintiffs' alleged injuries are too speculative to give rise to irreparable injury, given that ever since the Navy's training program began 40 years ago, there has been no documented case of sonar-related injury to marine mammals in SOCAL. And even if MFA sonar does cause a limited number of injuries to individual *marine mammals,* plaintiffs have failed to offer evidence of species-level harm that would adversely affect *their* scientific, recreational, and ecological interests. We agree that the "possibility" standard is too lenient. Plaintiffs seeking preliminary relief must demonstrate that irreparable injury is *likely* in the absence of an injunction. *Los Angeles v. Lyons,* 461 U.S. 95 (1983); *Granny Goose Foods, Inc. v. Teamsters,* 415 U.S. 423 (1974); *O'Shea v. Littleton,* 414 U.S. 488, 502 (1974). Issuing a preliminary injunction based only on a possibility of irreparable harm is inconsistent with our characterization of injunctive relief as an extraordinary remedy that may only be awarded upon a clear showing that the plaintiff is entitled to such relief. *Mazurek v. Armstrong,* 520 U.S. 968 (1997) (*per curiam*).

This is not a case in which the defendant is conducting a new type of activity with completely unknown effects on the environment. [NEPA] imposes only procedural requirements to "ensure that the agency, in reaching its decision, will have available, and will carefully consider, detailed information concerning significant environmental impacts." Part of the harm NEPA attempts to prevent in requiring an EIS is that, without one, there may be little if any information about prospective environmental harms and potential mitigating measures. Here, the plaintiffs are seeking to enjoin—or substantially restrict—training exercises that have been taking place for the last 40 years. And the latest series of exercises were not approved until after the defendant took a "hard look at environmental consequences," as evidenced by the issuance of a detailed, 293-page EA. Even if plaintiffs have shown irreparable injury from the Navy's training exercises, any such injury is outweighed by the public interest and the Navy's interest in effective, realistic training of its sailors. A proper consideration of these factors alone requires denial of the requested injunctive relief. For the same reason, we do not address the lower courts' holding that plaintiffs have also established a likelihood of success on the merits.

A preliminary injunction is an extraordinary remedy never awarded as of right. *Munaf,* 553 U.S., at 689–690. [C]ourts "must balance the competing claims of injury and must consider the effect on each party of the granting or withholding of the requested relief." *Amoco Production Co.,* 480 U.S., at 542. "In exercising their sound discretion, courts of equity should pay particular regard for the public consequences in employing the extraordinary remedy of injunction." *Romero-Barcelo,* 456 U.S., at 312. In this case, the District Court and the Ninth Circuit significantly understated the burden the preliminary injunction would impose on the Navy's ability to conduct realistic training exercises, and the injunction's consequent adverse impact on the public interest in national defense. This case involves "complex, subtle, and professional decisions as to the composition, training, equipping, and control of a military force," which are "essentially professional military judgments." *Gilligan v. Morgan,* 413 U.S. 1, 10 (1973). We "give great deference to the professional judgment of military authorities concerning the relative importance of a particular military interest." *Goldman v. Weinberger,* 475 U.S. 503, 507 (1986). "Neither this Court nor most federal judges begin the day with briefings that may describe new and serious threats to our Nation and its people." *Boumediene v. Bush,* 553 U.S. 723, 797 (2008).

Here, the record contains declarations from some of the Navy's most senior officers, all of whom underscored the threat posed by enemy submarines and the need for extensive sonar training to counter this threat. Several Navy officers emphasized that realistic training cannot be accomplished under the two challenged restrictions imposed by the District Court—the 2,200-yard shutdown zone and the requirement that the Navy power down its sonar systems during significant surface ducting conditions. These interests must be weighed against the possible harm to ecological, scientific, and recreational interests. Plaintiffs have submitted declarations asserting that they take whale watching trips, observe marine mammals underwater, conduct scientific research on marine mammals, and photograph these animals in their natural habitats. Plaintiffs contend that the Navy's use of MFA sonar will injure marine mammals or alter their behavioral patterns, impairing plaintiffs' ability to study and observe the animals.

We conclude that the balance of equities and consideration of the overall public interest in this case tip strongly in favor of the Navy. For the plaintiffs, the most serious possible injury would be harm to an unknown number of the marine mammals that they study and observe. In contrast, forcing the Navy to deploy an inadequately trained antisubmarine force jeopardizes the safety of the fleet. Active sonar is the only reliable technology for detecting and tracking enemy diesel-electric submarines, and the President—the Commander in Chief—has determined that training with active sonar is "essential to national security." The public interest in conducting training exercises with active sonar under realistic conditions plainly outweighs the interests advanced by the plaintiffs. Of course, military interests do not always trump other considerations, and we have not held that they do. In this case, however, the proper determination of where the public interest lies does not strike us as a close question.

We do not address the underlying merits of plaintiffs' claims. [The] factors examined above—the balance of equities and consideration of the public interest—are pertinent in assessing the propriety of any injunctive relief, preliminary or permanent. See *Amoco Production Co.,* 480 U.S., at 546, n. 12. Given that the ultimate legal claim is that the Navy must prepare an EIS, not that it must cease sonar training, there is no basis for enjoining such training in a manner credibly alleged to pose a serious threat to national security. This is particularly true in light of the fact that the training has been going on for 40 years with no documented episode of harm to a marine mammal. A court concluding that the Navy is required to prepare an EIS has many remedial tools at its disposal, including declaratory relief or an injunction tailored to the preparation of an EIS rather than the Navy's training. In the meantime, we see no basis for jeopardizing national security, as the present injunction does.

President Theodore Roosevelt explained that "the only way in which a navy can ever be made efficient is by practice at sea, under all the conditions which would have to be met if war existed." [P]laintiffs' ecological, scientific, and recreational interests in marine mammals [are] plainly outweighed by the Navy's need to conduct realistic training exercises to ensure that it is able to neutralize the threat posed by enemy submarines. The District Court abused its discretion by imposing a 2,200-yard shutdown zone and by requiring the Navy to power down its MFA sonar during significant surface ducting conditions. The judgment of the Court of Appeals is reversed, and the preliminary injunction is vacated to the extent it has been challenged by the Navy.

It is so ordered.

JUSTICE BREYER, with whom JUSTICE STEVENS joins as to Part I, concurring in part and dissenting in part.

I

The record lacks adequate support for an injunction imposing the controverted requirements. The evidence of need is weak or uncertain. The Navy has filed multiple affidavits from Navy officials explaining in detail the seriousness of the harm that the delay associated with completion of this EIS (approximately one year) would create in respect to the Navy's ability to maintain an adequate national defense and the District Court did not explain *why* it rejected the Navy's affidavits.

II

The Navy's past use of mitigation conditions makes clear that the Navy can effectively train under *some* mitigation conditions.

JUSTICE GINSBURG, with whom JUSTICE SOUTER joins, dissenting.

I would hold that, in imposing manageable measures to mitigate harm until completion of the EIS, the District Court conscientiously balanced the equities and did not abuse its discretion.

NOTE: MORE ON THE STANDARDS FOR PRELIMINARY INJUNCTIVE RELIEF

In *Citigroup Global Markets, Inc. v. VCG Special Opportunities Master*, 598 F.3d 30 (2nd Cir. 2010), which was decided after *Winter*, the court addressed the question of whether a plaintiff who seeks preliminary injunctive relief can prevail without showing a "likelihood of success" on the merits. The court decided that *Winter* did not preempt the "sufficiently serious questions" standard, noting that requiring "in every case a showing that ultimate success on the merits is more likely than not "is unacceptable as a general rule," noting that the "very purpose of an injunction is to give temporary relief based on a preliminary estimate of the strength of plaintiff's suit, prior to the resolution at trial of the factual disputes and difficulties presented by the case." The court rejected the idea that recent U.S. Supreme Court cases (like *Winter*) had altered the standard for relief: "While *Winter* rejected the Ninth Circuit's conceptually separate "possibility of irreparable harm" standard, it expressly withheld any consideration of the merits of the parties' underlying claims."

The court noted three situations when it would apply the higher standard: 1) when the moving party seeks to stay government action taken in the public interest pursuant to a statutory or regulatory scheme, the court should not apply the "serious questions" standard and should require a showing of a likelihood of success on the merits; 2) a " 'substantial likelihood' standard may also be required when the requested injunction would provide the plaintiff with all the relief that is sought and could not be undone by a judgment favorable to defendants on the merits at trial"; 3) a mandatory preliminary injunction that commands some positive act, as opposed to a prohibitory injunction seeking only to maintain the status quo, should issue only upon a 'clear showing' that the moving party is entitled to the relief requested, or where 'extreme' or 'very serious' damage will result from a denial of preliminary relief."

CLINTON V. NAGY

411 F.Supp. 1396 (N.D., Ohio, 1974).

LAMBROS, DISTRICT JUDGE.

Plaintiff, Brenda Clinton seeks to enjoin defendants from depriving her of equal recreational opportunities because of her sex and a declaratory judgment that the policies, customs, and practices of the defendants are in violation of the Constitution and laws of the United States. The Court granted plaintiff's motion for the temporary restraining order.

Plaintiff's daughter is a twelve year old female who wanted to play for the 97th Street Bulldogs football team. The team is licensed by the City as part of the Cleveland Browns Muny Football Association. Mrs. Clinton signed the Medical Service Agreement required of all Muny league players, and has otherwise met all of the requirements of the Cleveland Browns Muny Football Association. On September 28, 1974, and on several subsequent Saturday afternoons, plaintiff was suited and ready to play but was informed by defendant Hall that she would not be permitted to play because she was a female. Mrs. Clinton then signed a waiver, not required of males who participated in the Association's program, absolving the City and its agents from liability for any injuries which plaintiff might receive. Mrs. Clinton signed after receiving a representation that, if the special waiver was signed, plaintiff would be able to play football with the team. Nevertheless, Mrs. Clinton was notified that Brenda could not play because that 'was the law.'

At the hearing on the temporary restraining order, defendants argued that the City's rules and regulations which govern the playing of sports specifically exclude females from participating in contact sports and that such exclusion is lawful because it bears a rational relationship to a legitimate state purpose of providing for the safety and welfare of females. The sole issue before this Court at the hearing on the motion for a temporary restraining order was whether plaintiff had shown a substantial likelihood of success on the merits of her claim that the defendants should be enjoined from enforcing the City's regulations which exclude females from the opportunity to qualify for participation in Muny league football, a contact sport, because such regulations do not bear a reasonable relationship to any legitimate state purpose. Defendants urged that the exclusion of females from contact sports was necessary for their safety and welfare and asserted that its medical experts would establish that the rule is rationally related to that purpose. Defendants contended that their experts would testify that even at age ten, eleven, or twelve, boys are beginning to develop speed and greater physical stamina at a faster pace than are girls of those ages. The testimony was based upon the alleged naturally heavier musculature and generally greater speed of males between the ages of eight to twelve.

The present action did not seek to enjoin defendants from refusing to allow all females to play football. This action was brought by one named-plaintiff who alleges that she has a right to pursue the opportunity to qualify to play football with the Muny leagues. Defendants did not assert that Miss Clinton does not meet the standards required of the other members of the 97th Street Bulldogs, except that she is a female. Nor did it appear that defendants planned to offer testimony that physical trauma will have more of an impact on girls than boys or that girls are always more susceptible to disease as a result of physical trauma.

The plaintiff has cited several recent cases in which courts have struck down school regulations which bar females from participating in school athletics solely on the basis of their sex. In *Morris v. Michigan State Board of Education*, 472 F.2d 1207 (1973), the Sixth Circuit [stated] that where a regulation is based upon a classification by sex, that 'classification is subject to scrutiny under the Equal Protection Clause of the Fourteenth Amendment to ascertain whether there is a rational relationship to a valid state purpose'

In evaluating the plaintiff's motion for the issuance of a temporary restraining order herein the Court concludes that plaintiff has shown a substantial likelihood of success of the merits of her claim that defendants have precluded her from participating in the Muny League football games because she is a female, and solely because she is a female. Defendants have offered no evidence that Miss Clinton does not possess the qualifications and physical ability required of male members to participate in the league's games. The defendants offered no argument or factual basis that Miss Brenda Clinton is more susceptible to injury than are the other 'Bulldogs.' Every qualified member of the Muny league teams receives equipment that includes shoulder pads, face guards, helmets and mouth pieces. The Court is satisfied [that] those safeguards that are deemed adequate to protect the male members of the team will be similarly adequate protection for Brenda Clinton.

Defendants argued, however, that she made no showing that she would suffer irreparable harm if she were not permitted to play with [the team. Of course, females have not engaged in traditionally male sports, and as a result, in many instances females lack the requisite training to qualify for membership on all-male teams, particularly those teams established for the playing of contact sports. Perhaps those who find merit in the more traditional male-female roles may have great difficulty in understanding how a young girl will suffer irreparable harm if she is precluded from engaging in the rough and sometimes even brutal contest of football. Many adults, no doubt, may feel that young girls will in fact suffer great harm, both physically and socially, if they are permitted to participate in 'boys' games. However, football is by its very nature a physically dangerous game, and the threat of injuries to young boys has alarmed many parents in the community for years.

Nevertheless, organized contact sports such as football continue to be played, and those individuals who encourage young men to participate in these sports seem to do so with a sincere belief that although the game is potentially dangerous, the rewards which will be reaped from participation in the game offset the potential dangers. Organized contact sports have generally been thought of as an opportunity and means for a young boy to develop strength of character, leadership qualities and to provide competitive situations through which he will better learn to cope with the demands of the future. Yet, although these are presumably qualities to which we desire all of the young to aspire, the opportunity to qualify to engage in sports activities through which such qualities may be developed has been granted to one class of the young and summarily denied to the other.

It is necessary that we begin to focus on the individual rather than thinking in broad generalities, which have oftentimes resulted in the imposition of irrational barriers, against one class or another. The issue before this Court is whether one young person, Brenda Clinton, who apparently qualifies to play with the 97th Street Bulldogs in every respect except for her sex, should be given the opportunity to participate in the game of football and to develop strength and character in that way in which she, with her mother's approval, believes will be the most valuable to her. The Court concluded that to deprive a qualified twelve year old girl of an opportunity to engage in that activity would cause her to suffer irreparable harm, particularly in light of the fact that there are only two remaining games this season.

The motion for the temporary restraining order is granted. Accordingly, the defendants, their agents, employees, and all persons having actual knowledge of this order are hereby enjoined from prohibiting plaintiff Brenda Clinton from participating as a member of the 97th Street Bulldogs in its football games solely because of her sex.

IT IS SO ORDERED.

PROBLEMS

1. *More on* Clinton. Suppose that Brenda shows up for the final two football games, and Coach Thomas tells her that he intends to play her. However, both games are tightly contested, and Coach Thomas decides that the team's best interest is served by playing others. As a result, Brenda does not get to play. In addition to Brenda, some boys do not get into the game either. Should Coach Thomas be held in contempt of court?

2. *The Ramsey Mansion.* Suppose that John Newhouse Ramsey IV ("Ramsey IV") holds a life interest in a Nineteenth Century mansion, and that his son holds the remainder interest (given to him by Ramsey IV on the occasion of the son's marriage). When Ramsey IV becomes upset with his son, he begins stripping the mansion of lead windows, expensive antique fixtures, and other expensive items. The son sues seeking injunctive relief to prevent Ramsey IV from further wasting the mansion. Assuming that the law prohibits the holder of a life interest from "wasting" the property, and assuming that the stripping constitutes waste, is the son entitled to a temporary injunction against Ramsey IV prohibiting further waste? Should the court also grant the son temporary injunctive relief requiring Ramsey IV to repair and replace those items that have been stripped from the house? Would such an injunction be mandatory or prohibitory?

3. *The PGA and U-Shaped Irons.* The PGA Tour Inc. (PGA) adopts a rule that prohibits the use of golf irons with U-shape grooves (as opposed to the traditional V-shape grooves) in PGA events. The PGA does so because of a concern that U-shape irons significantly affect the way a golf ball spins and thereby changes the nature of the game. PGA players who like to use U-shaped irons claim that the rule precludes them from using their preferred equipment, as well as that they have less comfort with and confidence in V-shape irons, and thereby makes it more difficult for them to compete and to earn a living. The rule is also challenged by manufacturers of U-shape irons who claim that the new rule dampens sales of their irons and thereby subjects them to economic injury. The manufacturers claim that amateur golfers like to use the same irons that professional golfers use, and that the prohibition on the use of U-shape irons in professional events means that

amateur golfers are less likely to use the irons as well. Both the golfers and the manufacturers claim that the rule was not adopted in accord with PGA bylaws. The PGA responds that its bylaws were followed, and that injunctive relief would undercut the PGA's status as professional golf's rulesmaker, and thereby diminish its authority. Assume that you are the judge assigned to hear the case. Should you grant preliminary injunctive relief? What factor(s) would affect your decision? *See Gilder v. PGA Tour, Inc.*, 727 F.Supp. 1333 (D.Az.1989).

4. *Mandatory Injunctions Requiring the Payment of Money.* Suppose that plaintiffs sue claiming that a drug manufacturer's product has subjected their children to the risk of developing cancer. Although the children have not manifested any symptoms, plaintiffs claim that early detection of the illness is essential to a positive long-term prognosis. Attorneys seek an injunction requiring defendant to pay $200,000 into a fund that would pay for preventive diagnostic testing. The manufacturers respond that only a few individuals have developed cancer while taking the drug, and that there is no definitive link between the drug and the cancers. Is it appropriate for the court to enter such an order? *See Friends for All Children, Inc. v. Lockheed Aircraft Corp.*, 746 F.2d 816 (D.C.Cir.1984).

5. *More on Mandatory Injunctions Requiring the Payment of Money.* In the prior problem, would your analysis be different if the Food & Drug Administration (FDA) had found a link between the drug and cancer, and had ordered the manufacturers to remove the drug from the market?

WASHINGTON CAPITOLS BASKETBALL CLUB, INC. V. BARRY

304 F.Supp. 1193 (N.D.Cal.1969).

LEVIN, DISTRICT JUDGE.

On June 19, 1967, Richard F. Barry III ("Barry") granted to Charles E. Boone and S.D. Davidson an option to acquire his services as a professional basketball player for the 1967–68 season, and received an assignment for the transfer of a certain undivided interest in the Oakland franchise of the American Basketball Association ("ABA"). Pursuant to the option Barry signed an ABA Uniform Player Contract with Oaks, the owner and operator of the ABA franchise for Oakland, California, of a professional basketball team under the name of Oaks. Barry also signed an amendment to the aforesaid ABA contract, dated October 31, 1967, which provides that the term of the employment of Barry by Oaks is for three years commencing on October 2, 1968.

This agreement, as amended, provides "for a salary of $75,000.00 per year plus an amount equal to the lesser of (a) Five (5%) per cent of all gross gate receipts received by the Club per year in excess of the sum of $60,000.00 plus Player's compensation, or (b) $15,000.00." The agreement also provides [that the Club shall have the right to assign the contract to any other professional basketball club in the Association and the Player

Agrees to accept such assignment. On August 28, 1969, Washington agreed to purchase all of Oaks property and assets. Washington paid $750,000 extra for the purchase of Barry's contract.]

On August 29, 1969, Barry entered into a contract to play professional basketball with defendant San Francisco Warriors, a limited partnership, organized and existing under the laws of the State of California, the owner of a professional basketball team franchise of the National Basketball Association ("NBA") for a term of five years commencing October 2, 1969, and terminating October 1, 1974.

Plaintiff seeks a preliminary injunction to enjoin Barry from playing professional basketball with any team other than plaintiff "for so long as Barry remains in default under his contract with plaintiff."

The grant or refusal of injunctive relief is a matter of equitable jurisdiction. A Court of Equity will grant the relief when it determines it essential to restrain an act contrary to equity and good conscience.

The purpose of the preliminary injunction is to maintain the status quo between the litigants pending final determination of the case. In order for plaintiff to succeed in its motion for a preliminary injunction, it is fundamental that it show at least first, a reasonable probability of success in the main action and second, that irreparable damage would result from a denial of the motion.

The status quo is the last, peaceable, uncontested status between the parties which preceded the present controversy. The parties have differed in their interpretation of the meaning of the status quo in this case. It seems exceedingly clear that the status quo of the parties to the action was that peaceable state of affairs existing when Barry was under contract to Oaks and, prior to his injury, playing professional basketball for that team during the 1968–69 season. Although it is manifest that Barry cannot now play basketball for Oaks, their assets having been sold to Washington, the assignment of Barry's contract to Washington makes his obligations to them the closest to the status quo that can be attained. Permitting Barry to play with Warriors, which Barry indicated he would do if the preliminary injunction were not granted, would not be preserving any semblance of the situation as it existed just prior to the commencement of the present litigation.

It is uncertain whether plaintiff will prevail at the trial on the merits; however, it is clear that plaintiff need not prove its case with absolute certainty prior to the trial in order to succeed in its motion for a preliminary injunction. In the *Hamilton Watch case, supra* 206 F.2d at 740, the Court noted that "[it] will ordinarily be enough that the plaintiff has raised questions going to the merits so serious, substantial, difficult and doubtful, as to make them a fair ground for litigation and thus for more deliberate investigation." Moreover, "The burden (of showing probable success) is less where the balance of hardships tips decidedly toward the party requesting the temporary relief." *Checker Motors Corporation v. Chrysler Corporation*, 405 F.2d 319, 323 (2d Cir.1969), *cert. den.*, 394 U.S. 999 (1969).

Defendants have not shown that the contract between Oaks and Barry, which was assigned by Oaks to Washington, is itself unconscionable, unenforceable or otherwise void. It is under this contract that Washington seeks to assert its rights to Barry's services and the protection of this Court from violation of those rights. The precedents for granting injunctive relief against "star" athletes "jumping" their contracts—and certainly defendants do not deny that Barry is a unique, a "star" athlete—are numerous. *Houston Oilers, Inc. v. Neely*, 361 F.2d 36 (10th Cir.1966), *cert. den.* 385 U.S. 840, *reh. den.*, 385 U.S. 942 (1966); *Winnipeg Rugby Football Club v. Freeman*, 140 F.Supp. 365 (N.D.Ohio 1955).

Plaintiff must also make a showing of irreparable injury in order to be awarded injunctive relief. Although Rule 65 of the Federal Rules of Civil Procedure does not by its terms so state, it is well settled in equity jurisprudence that such a showing of injury must be made in order to support the granting of a preliminary injunction. BARRON AND HOLTZOFF, FEDERAL PRACTICE AND PROCEDURE 1433, p. 490.

Irreparable injury is that which cannot be compensated by the award of money damages; it is injury which is certain and great. Such injury exists when an athletic team is denied the services of an irreplaceable athlete. Barry is just such an irreplaceable athlete. He was the leading collegiate basketball scorer in the United States during the 1964–65 season and was voted Rookie of the Year during his first season of professional basketball in 1965–66 while playing with the Warriors. He was the leading scorer in the NBA during the 1966–67 season and was voted Most Valuable Player in the 1967 National Association All Star Basketball Game. Finally, while playing for Oaks during the 1968–69 season, he was the team's and ABA's leading scorer until an injury forced him to cease play. It is apparent today that with such a surfeit of fine basketball players in the United States graduating annually from collegiate ranks, the mere signing of a player to a professional basketball contract is substantial evidence of his outstanding qualities. When, like Barry, a player has proven his superior ability under the rigorous conditions of professional basketball, it is clear that money alone cannot replace his loss.

Barry claims that an undesirable situation would be created if he were forced to play for a party with whom he is now in litigation and with whose arrangements he is dissatisfied. The simple answer is that in granting a preliminary injunction this Court is not forcing Barry to play for Washington. He is free to "sit it out" if he so desires, the course of action which Barry took in 1967–68.

Barry alludes to his goodly personal and financial interests in the San Francisco Bay Area, all of which he claims would be jeopardized by a move to the Washington, D.C. area. Again, the answer is that Barry need do nothing, if he so desires, while this preliminary injunction is in effect. Every famous athlete may suffer some damage to his local business and personal interests or other inconvenience when the assignment of his contract requires him to relocate in another city; but nothing is more commonplace in the history of organized professional sports in America than such moves, through trades and otherwise. Even were Barry to go to Washington, we see nothing preventing him from developing similar business interests and opportunities flowing from his unique basketball skills, if he desires to utilize them.

No matter which side prevails on the merits in this controversy, it is indisputable that the other side may suffer substantial harm. This element of relative harm is one of the matters that this Court has considered in reaching its decision. "In determining whether to grant a preliminary injunction it is proper for a court to 'weigh the equities' and 'balance the hardships.' " *Clairol Incorporated v. Gillette Company*, 270 F.Supp. 371, 381 (E.D.N.Y.1967), *aff'd* 389 F.2d 264 (2d Cir.1968).

Although the consequences of this determination may result in the departure of Barry from the San Francisco Bay Area to his claimed detriment, equitable considerations constrain this Court to sign this day the proposed findings of fact, conclusions of law, and order granting to plaintiff a preliminary injunction.

PROBLEMS

1. *Are the Capitols Entitled to Affirmative Specific Performance?* In the *Barry* case, should the court have enforced Barry's agreement to play basketball (as opposed to just the negative covenant not to play for someone else)? What factors might influence the court to grant or deny affirmative specific performance?

2. *More on the* Barry *Case.* If a court has valid reasons for denying the Washington Capitols Basketball Club affirmative specific performance, do those same considerations suggest that the Capitols should be denied negative specific performance (an order precluding Barry from playing for someone else) as well? Why? Why not?

3. *The Expelled Student.* Sheila West, a student at Glenview Hills University (GHU), is accused of academic dishonesty (cheating) on an organic chemistry examination. GHU's academic dean holds a hearing at which she finds that West engaged in cheating, and concludes that West should receive a failing grade in the course and should be suspended for two semesters. West sues claiming that GHU failed to comply with the University's

disciplinary guidelines (set forth in the student handbook) because it did not provide her with a hearing before her peers. West seeks a TRO prohibiting GHU from enforcing the suspension pending the outcome of the matter. West claims that an immediate suspension would cause her irreparable injury by forcing her to miss a semester (or two) of classes, and thereby delaying her graduation date even if she ultimately prevails in the case. GHU claims that it must retain the right to suspend cheaters. Otherwise, it will have no way to force students to act honestly. If you are the judge assigned to hear the case, how would you rule on the request for injunctive relief? *See Melvin v. Union College*, 195 A.D.2d 447, 600 N.Y.S.2d 141 (1993).

4. *More on the Expelled Student.* Would you reach a different result in the prior problem if, instead of being expelled for academic dishonesty, GHU had expelled West because it found that she was mentally unstable, had threatened other students, and therefore was a danger to other students? Would it matter that GHU appears to have violated its own guidelines by having the case tried by an academic dean rather than by West's peers?

5. *Free Meals for Indigents.* Defendant Episcopal Community Services of Arizona (ECS) opened the St. Martin's Center in Tucson. The Center's sole purpose was to provide one free meal a day to indigent persons. Plaintiff Armory Park Neighborhood Association (APNA), a non-profit corporation organized for the purpose of "improving, maintaining and insuring the quality of the neighborhood," sought a preliminary injunction prohibiting ECS from operating its free food distribution program. APNA claimed that ECS's program constituted a public and private nuisance by attracting transient persons to the neighborhood. The area is primarily residential with only a few small businesses. When the Center began operating, many transients entered the area to come to the Center. Although the Center is only open from 5:00 to 6:00 p.m., patrons begin lining up around 3:00 p.m. and often linger in the neighborhood long after finishing their meals. The Center rents an adjacent fenced lot for a waiting area and organized neighborhood cleaning projects, but these efforts have proven inadequate to prevent transients from trespassing onto residents' yards, sometimes urinating, defecating, drinking and littering on the residents' property. A few have broken into storage areas and unoccupied homes, and some have asked residents for handouts. The number of arrests in the area has increased dramatically. Many residents are frightened or annoyed by the transients. What arguments might the residents make on behalf of a request for preliminary injunctive relief against the Center? How might the Center respond? If you were the judge to this case, how would you rule? *See Armory Park Neighborhood Ass'n v. Episcopal Community Services in Arizona*, 148 Ariz. 1, 712 P.2d 914 (In Banc, 1985).

6. *The No Smoking Ban.* The City of Louisville, Kentucky, decides to impose a no smoking ban in all indoor public places (*e.g.*, restaurants and bars). In passing the ban, the City relies heavily on evidence suggesting that second hand smoke has a significant negative impact on those who do not smoke. Particularly impacted are those who work in restaurants and bars

who are continually (and, sometimes, involuntarily) subjected to smoke. On the day that the ordinance is scheduled to take effect, a coalition of restaurant and bar owners ("RBO") files suit seeking temporary injunctive relief to prevent the ban from taking effect. RBO fears that the ban will prompt smoking patrons to stay away from their establishments resulting in devastating economic losses. The basis for RBO's suit is its claim that the ban deprives smokers of equal protection, and deprives bar owners of their property (their businesses) without providing just compensation. Suppose that you work for the trial court judge that has been assigned to hear the case. How do you evaluate the case, and how would you advise the judge about whether to grant injunctive relief on behalf of the RBO?

7. *The Dismissed Director*. In 1999, Mr. Benjamin Chavis was removed as Director of the National Association for the Advancement of Colored People (NAACP). Chavis claimed that his removal was inconsistent with the NAACP's bylaws, as well as with various civil rights laws. Chavis sued seeking reinstatement to the Director's position. Even if Mr. Chavis's claims are correct, is a trial court likely to grant temporary injunctive relief requiring Mr. Chavis's reinstatement? Why? Why not?

AMERICAN HOSPITAL SUPPLY CORPORATION V. HOSPITAL PRODUCTS LTD.

780 F.2d 589 (7th Cir.1986).

POSNER, CIRCUIT JUDGE.

A supplier terminated a distributor, who sued for breach of contract and got a preliminary injunction. The supplier, Hospital Products, a small firm now undergoing reorganization in bankruptcy, is one of the world's two principal manufacturers of "reusable surgical stapling systems for internal surgical procedures." The terminated distributor, American Hospital Supply Corporation, the world's largest distributor of medical and surgical supplies, in 1982 became the exclusive distributor in the United States of Hospital Products' surgical stapling systems. The contract of distribution was for three years initially, but provided that it would be renewed automatically for successive one-year periods (to a limit of ten years) unless American Hospital Supply notified Hospital Products at least 90 days before the three years were up (or any successive one-year period for which the contract had been renewed) that it wanted to terminate the contract; and this meant, by June 3, 1985.

On that day Hospital Products hand-delivered a letter to American Hospital Supply demanding to know whether it intended to renew the contract and reminding it that if it failed to respond by the end of the day this would mean that the contract had been renewed. American Hospital Supply responded the same day in a letter which pointed out that since it wasn't terminating, the contract was, indeed, renewed. But on the next day Hospital Products announced that it was going to treat the contract as having been terminated, and on June 7 it sent a telegram to American Hospital Supply's dealers informing them that effective June 3 American Hospital Supply was "no longer the authorized distributor of [Hospital Products'] stapling products."

American Hospital Supply [sued Hospital Products for] breach of contract and moved for a preliminary injunction, which was granted on July 8 after an evidentiary hearing. The injunction forbids Hospital Products to take any action in derogation of American Hospital Supply's contract rights so long as the injunction is in force (*i.e.*, pending the outcome of the trial). It also requires Hospital Products to notify American Hospital Supply's dealers that American Hospital Supply is still Hospital Products' authorized distributor, and this has been done. Hospital Products counterclaimed, alleging breach of contract, fraud, and unfair competition.

A district judge asked to decide whether to grant or deny a preliminary injunction must choose the course of action that will minimize the costs of being mistaken. Because he is forced to act on an incomplete record, the danger of a mistake is substantial. And a mistake can be costly. If the judge grants the preliminary injunction to a plaintiff who it later turns out is not entitled to any judicial relief—whose legal rights have not been violated—the judge commits a mistake whose gravity is measured by the irreparable harm, if any, that the injunction causes to the defendant while it is in effect. If the judge denies the preliminary injunction to a plaintiff who it later turns out is entitled to judicial relief, the judge commits a mistake whose gravity is measured by the irreparable harm, if any, that the denial of the preliminary injunction does to the plaintiff.

These mistakes can be compared, and the one likely to be less costly can be selected, with the help of a simple formula: grant the preliminary injunction if but only if $P \times H_p > (1 - P) \times H_d$,[1] or, in words, only if the harm to the plaintiff if the injunction is denied, multiplied by the probability that the denial would be an error (that the plaintiff, in other words, will win at trial), exceeds the harm to the defendant if the injunction is granted, multiplied by the probability that granting the injunction would be an error. That probability is simply one minus the probability that the plaintiff will win at trial; for if the plaintiff has, say, a 40 percent chance of winning, the defendant must have a 60 percent chance of winning (1.00 – .40 = .60). The left-hand side of the formula is simply the probability of an erroneous denial weighted by the cost of denial to the plaintiff, and the right-hand side simply the probability of an erroneous grant weighted by the cost of grant to the defendant.

---

[1] Author's note: P stands for probability and H stands for irreparability, with subscripts to show which party's harm is referenced.

This formula, a procedural counterpart to Judge Learned Hand's famous negligence formula, is not offered as a new legal standard; it is intended not to force analysis into a quantitative straitjacket but to assist analysis by presenting succinctly the factors that the court must consider in making its decision and by articulating the relationship among the factors. It is actually just a distillation of the familiar four (sometimes five) factor test that courts use in deciding whether to grant a preliminary injunction. The court asks whether the plaintiff will be irreparably harmed if the preliminary injunction is denied (sometimes also whether the plaintiff has an adequate remedy at law), whether the harm to the plaintiff if the preliminary injunction is denied will exceed the harm to the defendant if it is granted, whether the plaintiff is reasonably likely to prevail at trial, and whether the public interest will be affected by granting or denying the injunction (*i.e.*, whether third parties will be harmed—and these harms can then be added to H_p or H_d as the case may be). The court undertakes these inquiries to help it figure out whether granting the injunction would be the error-minimizing course of action, which depends on the probability that the plaintiff is in the right and on the costs to the plaintiff, the defendant, or others of granting or denying the injunction. The formula is new; the analysis it capsulizes is standard.

The formula does not depend on the legal basis of the plaintiff's claim, whether it is antitrust law or trademark law or, as here, the common law of contract, although the nature of the right asserted by the plaintiff may affect the weighting of the harms. So may the nature of the permanent remedy to which the plaintiff would be entitled if he prevailed at trial. For example, prevailing parties in breach of contract cases normally are not awarded specific performance, that is, a mandatory injunction to perform. Since many breaches of contract are involuntary, implying that performance would be very costly, routinely ordering specific performance would create situations where the defendant was forced to bargain desperately to buy his way out of the injunction. The high bargaining costs that would result are a deadweight cost of equitable relief. To the extent that those costs attend a preliminary injunction, they are of course relevant to the decision whether to issue such an injunction. But the formula takes account of this; the case we have described would be one where the harm to the defendant from granting the injunction would be very great. Thus the fact that a plaintiff might have no hope of getting specific performance ordered at the conclusion of the trial need not prevent him from obtaining a preliminary injunction. The premise of the preliminary injunction is that the remedy available at the end of trial will not make the plaintiff whole; and, in a sense, the more limited that remedy, the stronger the argument for a preliminary injunction—provided the remedy is not limited for reasons that would make a preliminary injunction equally inappropriate.

We have now to apply these precepts, and we begin with the balance of harms. Although American Hospital Supply was able to replace Hospital Products' line of surgical stapling systems in the interval between the mailgram of June 7 and the entry of the preliminary injunction a month later, the mailgram, unless retracted as ordered by the injunction, might have impaired American Hospital Supply's goodwill, a factor emphasized in other cases where terminated dealers sought preliminary injunctions. The suddenness of the termination and the urgent mode of announcement might have made the dealers think that American Hospital Supply must have engaged in unethical or unreasonable conduct. We do not put much weight on this point, however. It is speculative, and any harm may have been cured by the retraction, in which event the harm could not support the rest of the injunction.

But in addition, on June 7 American Hospital Supply was holding a large unsold inventory of Hospital Products' surgical stapling systems. To help Hospital Products overcome serious financial problems, American Hospital Supply had advanced it millions of dollars—part in loans, part by buying more of the product than it needed and keeping the excess in inventory. The mailgram jeopardized its investment because dealers might be reluctant to buy Hospital Products' goods from American Hospital Supply, not wanting to become enmeshed in a legal dispute between it and its supplier or perhaps even fearing that there might be some defect in the particular items being sold by American Hospital Supply. True, its investment would probably not be totally wiped out. American Hospital Supply might be able to sell the product to its dealers immediately at a sharp mark-down or with extra warranties or with promises of indemnity; or if it waited till it prevailed on the merits against Hospital Products, at no mark-down, in which event its loss would be just the interest and storage costs of keeping the product in inventory longer than expected. (If it didn't prevail, its losses would not be recoverable anyway.) No effort was made to quantify the loss to American Hospital Supply caused by the alleged breach of contract. But in the nature of things reliable estimation may have been infeasible; and since the estimates of the size of the unsold inventory range from $10 million to almost $30 million, probably the threatened loss was substantial.

What made the loss irreparable was not only or mainly the difficulty that American Hospital Supply might encounter down the road in quantifying its loss, although this difficulty has been stressed in other cases where a distributor sought a preliminary injunction in part to protect goodwill, it was Hospital Products' insolvency, which was apparent when the district judge granted the preliminary injunction, even though the firm had not yet declared bankruptcy. The victim of a breach of contract, certainly one committed before the contract breaker declares bankruptcy, is just another general creditor, and it is well known that general creditors fare poorly in most bankruptcy proceedings. This is true whether the proceeding ends in liquidation or in reorganization, though as a matter of fact most bankruptcies that start in reorganization nonetheless end in liquidation. Maybe, as Hospital Products argues, if only it could get the injunction lifted it would soon recover its solvency, even to the point of being able to pay any damages that American Hospital Supply is awarded in the trial of this case. But if Hospital Products really believes that, it ought to have gone to the district judge and asked him to dissolve the injunction, and it did not—an omission that makes us profoundly skeptical of Hospital Products' claim that the grant of the injunction precipitated its declaration of bankruptcy.

Although a defendant's insolvency is a standard ground for concluding that a plaintiff's harm if the preliminary injunction is denied will not be cured by an award of damages at the end of the trial, to use the defendant's insolvency as a reason for granting the plaintiff an injunction now rather than making him wait for damages till the end of the trial may seem to give the plaintiff a preference in the distribution of the defendant's assets and thus impose harms on third parties, the defendant's other creditors. The responsibility for assessing those harms, however, has been placed in the bankruptcy court rather than the court asked to grant a preliminary injunction.

We conclude that there was a threat of irreparable harm to the plaintiff; and although the dollar amount of that harm is not known with any precision and we hesitate to call it great, it seems substantial. We must next consider the irreparable harm to the defendant from the injunction. The district judge found there would be none, because American Hospital Supply—which has billions of dollars in sales and earns substantial profits—will be good for any money judgment that Hospital Products may obtain on its counterclaim. This ground is not entirely satisfactory. There is a difference between the damages caused Hospital Products by the breach of contract or other (alleged) misconduct committed by American Hospital Supply before this suit began, damages which we may assume American Hospital Supply is good for, and damages caused Hospital Products by the preliminary injunction—that is, by an order fastening Hospital Products to American Hospital Supply for another year. Those are not the damages that Hospital Products seeks to recover on its counterclaim, and while there may be considerable overlap between the injunction damages and the counterclaim damages, we cannot say that the overlap is complete.

But we may not overlook the bond that a plaintiff who obtains a preliminary injunction is required to post (see Fed.R.Civ.P. 65(c)) and that this plaintiff did post, in an amount, $5 million, whose adequacy Hospital Products does not challenge. Again it can be argued that damages may be hard to prove. The injunction bond merely puts a ceiling on damages—they must still be proved. But the irreparability that comes from the difficulty of proving damages is not of the same order as that which comes from the uncollectibility of a damage judgment. The award of damages in a case where injury is difficult to measure is as likely to overcompensate as to undercompensate the injured party. When a court speaks of damages as being "irreparable" because they are difficult to measure it can mean only that confining the injured party to a remedy of damages creates a risk he may not like (because he is risk averse—the disposition that leads people to buy insurance), even though the upside risk is as large as the downside risk. That is, the plaintiff is as likely to do better than he expects as he is to do worse, but he would lose more utility by losing big than he would gain utility by winning equally big. So there is a harm, but probably not a big one.But what of the fact that an award of damages on the injunction bond, even if it made Hospital Products' creditors whole (and it might not), might not come in time to save the company itself? Many reorganizations in bankruptcy end in liquidation, and Hospital Products' reorganization may end there too, before the case is tried on the merits and therefore before the injunction bond can be enforced; and even if the company is successfully reorganized, the shareholders may be wiped out, and all the stock come into the hands of creditors. But the full financial losses to Hospital Products' shareholders from the bankruptcy are not the correct measure of the harm from granting the injunction. Bankruptcy is not, not intentionally anyway, a device for reducing wealth, but a device for distributing the impact of a business failure over various claimants to the bankrupt's assets. The costs that bankruptcy imposes, as distinct from the costs that the underlying failure imposes, are therefore merely the costs of administering the bankruptcy proceeding. Nevertheless these costs are not negligible. Although the expenses of administration are paid to someone—to lawyers, accountants, etc.—they are paid for time that would have value elsewhere; and that value is a deadweight loss from bankruptcy, as it cannot be recovered by a payment of damages to the bankrupt estate. A preliminary injunction that will or may precipitate a firm into bankruptcy is therefore a source of costs which ought to be considered in deciding whether to grant such an injunction.

A related and often more significant type of cost, but one whose implications for legal policy are more ambiguous, is the cost of the business failure itself. If the firm's assets would be worth less on the auction block than as part of a going concern, this might seem a powerful argument against granting a preliminary injunction that increased the risk of failure. It is not a complete answer to point out that the creditors will get the benefit of any injunction damages awarded the bankrupt; those damages may not offset the loss of going-concern value. But since business failure provides social as well as private benefits—provides, indeed, the essential discipline of the capitalist system—it seems questionable to give firms that conduct their affairs in an unduly risky or careless manner an advantage in litigation. A more mundane point is that Hospital Products should have asked for a bigger injunction bond if it thought the injunction might play the role of the proverbial nail for want of which the kingdom was lost.

It is enough that the effect of a preliminary injunction in precipitating insolvency is a factor arguing against the grant of the injunction (how strongly we shall not have to decide). Reflection on this overlooked point might conceivably persuade the district judge to grant a motion to dissolve the preliminary injunction, should such a motion be made, as it can be at any time. But it does not persuade us that the preliminary injunction was in error. It does not even persuade us that the district judge erred in concluding that the balance of harms inclined in favor of granting the preliminary injunction. Keep in mind that when the district judge acted, Hospital Products had not yet declared bankruptcy. The judge thought the injunction bond might tide the company over the crisis; he also pointed out (and this has great relevance to the issue of American Hospital Supply's chances of winning the case on the merits, of which more presently) that American Hospital Supply had loaned millions of dollars to Hospital Products to prevent the latter from going broke.

We attach no legal significance to the difference in the size of the parties. Although American Hospital Supply is a giant and Hospital Products a pygmy, we cannot think what legal difference that makes. We have taken an oath to do justice to rich and poor alike—and one can't tell merely from the relative size of two corporations what the relative wealth of their shareholders is. Relative size is relevant where one party, being small and weak, faces bankruptcy if the preliminary injunction is granted or denied; for bankruptcy imposes social costs, as we have [seen].

It could be argued that the relative size of the companies, viewed separately from the issue of bankruptcy costs, strengthens the case for the preliminary injunction. American Hospital Supply might suffer an irrecoverable loss of many millions of dollars if the injunction is denied it; Hospital Products' small size puts a cap on its loss of $5 million if the injunction bond was computed correctly. Even if there were no clear basis for differentiating between the irreparable harms to American Hospital Supply from denying and to Hospital Products from granting a preliminary injunction, in which event those harms would have to be treated as equal, Hospital Products' appeal would fail. If the harms to the plaintiff and the defendant of denying and granting the injunction, respectively, are equal, the injunction must be granted if the plaintiff has a better than 50 percent chance of winning the case, for then P in our preliminary-injunction formula must exceed $1 - P$, and therefore $P \times H_p$ must exceed $(1 - P) \times H_d$ from the assumption that $H_p = H_d$.

The district judge was persuaded that Hospital Products, not American Hospital Supply, had broken the contract, implying a very high P. He undoubtedly was correct if the contract was renewed on June 3 and in force the next day when Hospital Products announced that the contract was terminated. But we must consider as did he whether American Hospital Supply repudiated the contract before this announcement. That would make this a case of anticipatory breach of contract—American Hospital Supply indicates that it will not perform its obligations under the renewed contract, Hospital Products therefore treats the contract as terminated. Hospital Products points to a letter from American Hospital Supply which threatens to end financial assistance to Hospital Products and call its loans unless Hospital Products agrees to modify the contract in American Hospital Supply's favor. American Hospital Supply responds with much show of reason that it had advanced millions of dollars to Hospital Products beyond anything that it was contractually obligated to do, and therefore had every right to condition the making of new loans or the extension of existing ones on contract concessions. Hospital Products says that no loans were due and what the letter referred to as financial assistance was a euphemism for money due on goods sold and delivered—to which another round of replies asserts that if no loans were due, Hospital Products had nothing to worry about and that American Hospital Supply actually had bought far more surgical stapling products from Hospital Products than it needed or was contractually obligated to buy, so that what looked like payment on the contract really was financial assistance.

As nearly as we can determine, the able and experienced district judge who resolved the uncertainty in American Hospital Supply's favor was on solid ground in doing so.

AFFIRMED.

SWYGERT, SENIOR CIRCUIT JUDGE, dissenting.

[The] majority describes its formula as a procedural counterpart to Judge Hand's negligence formula first appearing in *United States v. Carroll Towing*, 159 F.2d 169, 173 (2d Cir.1947). *Carroll Towing* was an admiralty case in which a shipowner's duty to provide against injuries resulting from the breaking of a vessel's moorings was expressed in algebraic terms. In Hand's formula the liability of the shipowner depends on whether $B < PL$, where P is the probability that the ship will break away; where L is the gravity of the resulting injury if she does; and where B is the burden of adequate precautions. Various attempts have been made to apply the Hand formula, or some derivation of it, to areas other than negligence. My quarrel is not with *Carroll Towing* but rather with the majority's attempt today to create its equitable analogue. A quantitative approach may be an appropriate and useful heuristic device in determining negligence in tort cases, but it has limited value in determining whether a preliminary injunction should issue. Proceedings in equity and cases sounding in tort demand entirely different responses of a district judge. The judgment of the district judge in a tort case must be definite; the judgment of the district judge in an injunction proceeding cannot, by its very nature, be as definite. The judgment of a district judge in an injunction proceeding must be flexible and discretionary—within the bounds of the now settled four-prong test.

I question the necessity and the wisdom of the court's adoption of a mathematical formula as the governing law of preliminary injunctions. The majority claims that its formula is merely a distillation of the traditional four-prong test. But if nothing is added to the substantive law, why bother? The standard four-prong test for determining whether a preliminary injunction should issue has survived for so many years because it has proven to be a workable summation of the myriad factors a district court must consider in deciding whether to grant an injunction. The test [may] not exhibit the "precision" the majority seems to demand, but such "precision" is antithetical to the underlying principles of injunctive relief. Equity, as the majority concedes, involves the assessment of factors that cannot be quantified. A district court faced with the task of deciding whether to issue a preliminary injunction must to some extent, the majority concedes, rely on the "feel" of the case. The majority's formula will not assist the district courts in their assessment of this aspect of the decision to grant a preliminary injunction. The traditional element of discretion residing in the decision of a trial court to grant a preliminary injunction has been all but eliminated by today's decision.

Ironically, the majority never attempts to assign a numerical value to the variables of its own formula. We are never told how to measure P or H_p or H_d. I believe, and the majority appears to concede, that a numerical value could never be assigned to these variables. Who can say, for instance, what exactly the probability is that the granting of the injunction was an error? How then will the majority's formula ease in a meaningful way the responsibilities of the district courts? Judges asked to issue a preliminary injunction must, in large part, rely on their own judgment, not on mathematical quanta.

We must, of course, be mindful not to vest too much imprecision in the preliminary injunction standard, for law implies a system of known and generally applicable rules. The existing four-prong test, however, represents the historical balance struck by the courts between the rigidity of law and the flexibility of equity.

The majority disavows any effort to force the district courts into a "quantitative straitjacket," but I suspect that today's decision may lead to just that. District judges operate under enormous pressure to be decisive and precise. Much rides on their smallest decisions. Like a Homeric Siren the majority's formula offers a seductive but deceptive security. Moreover, the majority's formula invites members of the Bar to dust off their calculators and dress their arguments in quantitative clothing. The resulting spectacle will perhaps be entertaining, but I do not envy the task we have given [the lower courts].

NOTE: ANTICIPATED NUISANCES

As a general rule, courts are reluctant to enjoin an "anticipated nuisance." In other words, they are reluctant to enjoin an alleged nuisance that has not yet come into existence, and is not yet causing injury. Courts will enjoin anticipated nuisances when the challenged activity cannot be conducted without creating a nuisance. For example, a number of courts have held that a mortuary in a residential neighborhood is a "nuisance per se." *See Jack v. Torrant*, 136 Conn. 414, 71 A.2d 705 (1950). Mortuaries can cause morbid feelings regardless of how they are operated, and some states find them to be objectionable under these circumstances. On the other hand, if it is possible to conduct the activity without creating a nuisance, courts will usually wait to see whether the activity is conducted in such a way as to create a nuisance (a so-called "nuisance in fact"). Occasionally, courts will intervene against a nuisance in fact when the evidence of anticipated injury is overwhelming. *See Brainard v. Town of West Hartford*, 140 Conn. 631, 103 A.2d 135 (1954).

PROBLEMS

1. *The Hazardous Waste Incinerator.* Jacob Weber is a homeowner who lives in Kansas City, Missouri. Diversified Scientific Services (DSS), has decided to build a hazardous waste incinerator on property across the street from the Weber residence. Weber fears that the incinerator will spew out hazardous waste, thereby creating a public and private nuisance, and interfering with the health and welfare of himself and his family (a wife and three children). Weber relies on EPA studies discussing the potential harms of hazardous waste incinerators, and suggesting strong adverse health effects. DSS disagrees noting that the incinerator is being built in compliance with all federal and state regulations, and it claims that Weber's claims of injury are speculative. How should the court resolve these competing claims? If it is "possible" to operate the incinerator without creating a nuisance, is it appropriate for the court to issue the injunction before the incinerator is finished and operating? But, if the court allows the incinerator to be built, is there any chance that it would enjoin its operation? Would it matter whether the area was zoned residential so that the operation of an incinerator is illegal? *See Pace v. Diversified Scientific Services, Inc.*, 1993 WL 573 (Tenn.App.); *R & D Trucking Co., Inc. v. Carter*, 592 So.2d 1040 (Ala.1992).

2. *The SGA Election.* Seneca University (SU), a large state university, has a very active student government association (SGA). SU imposes a mandatory student activity fee of $150 per semester on all students that is used to support SGA activities (social and sports events, as well as speakers)

and student organizations. Historically, SGA offices have been dominated by members of SU' fraternities and sororities ("Greeks"). Fed-up with Greek domination of SGA offices, a coalition of minority groups decides to run its own slate of candidates (SGA elections are always held in late April. Officers are installed in early May and hold office until the following spring). Although the minority coalition actively campaigns for its candidates, those candidates a defeated in a close election in which they garnered 48% of the vote. Coalition members feel that they were denied victory by irregularities in the election process (double voting by some SGA members). It is now early May, and the victorious Greek candidates are about to be installed in office. Coalition members seek a declaration that the recent election was fraudulently conducted, and would like to have SU order new elections. Suppose that Coalition members hire you to represent them. How would you advise them to proceed (*i.e.*, should they sue, negotiate, etc.)? Suppose that Coalition members want to seek temporary injunctive relief preventing the installation of new officers. Is a court likely to give them an injunction under these circumstances? Would it be better to request other, or different, relief?

3. *The Ban on Robo Calls.* Kentucky's legislature is convinced that some politicians unfairly and improperly make "robo calls" (phone calls by computers) in support of their re-election efforts. The legislature believes that robo calls significantly interfere with the quality of life because such calls often come at inopportune times (*e.g.*, dinner time), as well as because some residential phone customers receive five or more telemarketing calls per evening. As a result, the legislature decides to pass anti-robo legislation that prohibits politicians from using computers to make phone calls on their behalf. The law is immediately challenged by a Louisville politician (who pays for lots of robo calls), as well as by a coalition of robo call corporations. Robo call companies claim that the law will destroy their businesses, and the politician claims that the law will infringe his First Amendment rights. Kentucky's Attorney General (AG) attempts to defend the law by arguing that the Commonwealth has a compelling governmental interest in protecting residences against intrusive phone calls. In addition, the AG claims that the law does not prohibit politicians from campaigning, and does not even prohibit them from calling their constituents. It simply prohibits them from making pitches through robo calls. The statute is scheduled to take effect in two days, and the politicians and robo phone companies are seeking an injunction preventing it from taking effect. Given the standards for preliminary injunctive relief, should the injunction issue?

2. HEARING REQUIREMENT

In order to obtain either a TRO or a preliminary injunction, plaintiffs must satisfy several procedural requirements. In general, judicial orders should only be issued after a contested hearing. The TRO is unique because it can be granted *ex parte*. As a general rule, the due process clause requires that all affected individuals be given notice of an injunction hearing and an opportunity to participate therein. When a

TRO is sought, there is not always time for a contested hearing. Plaintiff may suffer serious and irreparable injury before notice can be given and a hearing can be held.

Rule 65 of the Federal Rules of Civil Procedure responds to this problem by allowing courts to issue *ex parte* TROs, but creates a strong presumption in favor of contested hearings. However, Rule 65(a)(1) prohibits courts from issuing *ex parte* preliminary injunctions. Many state procedural provisions contain comparable provisions.

IN RE VUITTON ET FILS S.A.

606 F.2d 1 (2d Cir.1979).

PER CURIAM:

Vuitton et Fils S.A. ("Vuitton") seeks a writ of mandamus direct[ing] the United States District Court for the Southern District of New York to issue Ex parte a temporary restraining order. In our judgment, we are justified in asserting mandamus jurisdiction in this peculiar case, and we direct the district judge to issue an appropriate Ex parte order under Fed.R.Civ.P. 65.

Vuitton is a French company engaged in the sale and distribution of expensive leather goods, including a wide variety of luggage, handbags, wallets and jewelry cases, all under a trademark registered with the United States Patent Office in 1932. This trademark, a distinctive arrangement of initials and designs, has been extensively advertised over the years. Vuitton has commenced 84 actions nationwide and 53 actions in this Circuit charging trademark infringement and unfair competition. This present dispute originated in one of these actions.

On January 16, 1979, Vuitton filed a complaint in the district court seeking preliminary and permanent injunctions against the defendants, Dame Belt & Bag Co., Inc. and an individual named Morty Edelstein, and requesting damages. The gist of the complaint was that the defendants had infringed Vuitton's trademark and engaged in unfair competition by offering for sale luggage and handbags identical in appearance to those merchandised by Vuitton. Accompanying the complaint was an affidavit by Vuitton's attorney explaining why service of process had not been effected and requesting that an Ex parte temporary restraining order be issued against the defendants under Fed.R.Civ.P. 65(b). Vuitton explains its need for an Ex parte order in the following terms:

> Vuitton's experience, based upon the 84 actions it has brought and the hundreds of other investigations it has made has led to the conclusion that there exist various closely-knit distribution networks for counterfeit Vuitton products. In other words, there does not exist but one or two manufacturers of counterfeit merchandise, but rather many more, but a few of

which have been identified to date. Vuitton's experience in several of the earliest filed cases also taught it that once one member of this community of counterfeiters learned that he had been identified by Vuitton and was about to be enjoined from continuing his illegal enterprise, he would immediately transfer his inventory to another counterfeit seller, whose identity would be unknown to Vuitton. In most Vuitton cases defendants maintain few, if any, records. The now too familiar refrain from a "caught counterfeiter" is "I bought only a few pieces from a man I never saw before and whom I have never seen again. All my business was in cash. I do not know how to locate the man from whom I bought and I cannot remember the identity of the persons to whom I sold." If after Vuitton has identified a counterfeiter with an inventory of fake merchandise, that counterfeiter is permitted to dispose of that merchandise with relative impunity after he learns of the imminence of litigation but before he is enjoined from doing so, Vuitton's trademark enforcement program will be stymied and the community of counterfeiters will be permitted to continue to play its "shell game" at great expense and damage to Vuitton.

A hearing on this application was held the next day [before] Judge Brieant. Counsel for Vuitton explained: "All we seek this Court to do but for a few hours is to maintain the status quo, namely the defendants' inventory of counterfeit Vuitton merchandise." Vuitton also explained that, if notice of the pending litigation was required, "by the time this Court entered an order, most if not all of the merchandise would have been removed from the premises." Because Vuitton was capable of giving the defendants in this action notice, however, a matter readily conceded by Vuitton, the district court declined to grant the request. That decision is, of course, not appealable. The district court denied certification of the question presented by this case under 28 U.S.C. § 1292(b), and this petition followed. For the reasons that follow, we instruct the district court to grant an appropriate Ex parte Temporary restraining order pursuant to Fed.R.Civ.P. 65(b), narrow enough and of brief enough duration to protect the interests of the defendants, the precise terms of which shall be determined by the district court.

Rule 65(b) provides in relevant part as follows: A temporary restraining order may be granted without written or oral notice to the adverse party or his attorney only if (1) it clearly appears from specific facts shown by affidavit or by the verified complaint that immediate and irreparable injury, loss, or damage will result to the applicant before the adverse party or his attorney can be heard in opposition, and (2) the applicant's attorney certifies to the court in writing the efforts, if any, which have been made to give the notice and the reasons supporting his claim that notice should not be required. As explained by the Supreme

Court in *Granny Goose Foods, Inc. v. Teamsters*, 415 U.S. 423, 438–39 (1974), "the stringent restrictions imposed [on] the availability of Ex parte temporary restraining orders reflect the fact that our entire jurisprudence runs counter to the notion of court action taken before reasonable notice and an opportunity to be heard has been granted both sides of a dispute. Ex parte temporary restraining orders are no doubt necessary in certain circumstances, [but] under federal law they should be restricted to serving their underlying purpose of preserving the status quo and preventing irreparable harm just so long as is necessary to hold a hearing, and no longer."

Although this Court has "frowned upon temporary restraining orders issued without even telephoned notice," *Emery Air Freight Corp. v. Local 295, supra*, 449 F.2d at 591, there are occasions when such orders are to be countenanced. In our judgment, this case is just such an occasion. [Assuming] that all of the other requirements of Rule 65 are met, the rule by its very terms allows for the issuance of an Ex parte temporary restraining order when (1) the failure to issue it would result in "immediate and irreparable injury, loss, or damage" and (2) the applicant sufficiently demonstrates the reason that notice "should not be required." In a trademark infringement case such as this, a substantial likelihood of confusion constitutes, in and of itself, irreparable injury sufficient to satisfy the requirements of Rule 65(b) (1). Here, we believe that such a likelihood of product confusion exists. The allegedly counterfeit Vuitton merchandise is virtually identical to the genuine items. Indeed, the very purpose of the individuals marketing the cheaper items is to confuse the buying public into believing it is buying the true article.

We also believe that Vuitton has demonstrated sufficiently why notice should not be required in a case such as this one. If notice is required, that notice all too often appears to serve only to render fruitless further prosecution of the action. This is precisely contrary to the normal and intended role of "notice," and it is surely not what the authors of the rule either anticipated or intended.

Accordingly, we hold that, when a proper showing is made, such as was made in this case, and when the rule is otherwise complied with, a plaintiff is entitled to have issued an Ex parte temporary restraining order. Such an order should be narrow in scope and brief in its duration. The petition is granted.

PROBLEMS

1. *Labor Strife.* You are a federal judge, and an employer seeks *ex parte* injunctive relief to prevent its employees from picketing near its plant. The complaint alleges that picketers are blocking the entrance to the plant, threatening those that attempt to enter the plant, preventing entry to the plant by automobile, and ignoring demands to cease and desist. Based on the

complaint, do you have an adequate basis for issuing an *ex parte* TRO? What else would you require plaintiff to show to obtain *ex parte* relief? *See Bettendorf–Stanford Bakery Equipment Co. v. International Union*, 49 Ill.App.3d 20, 6 Ill.Dec. 920, 363 N.E.2d 867 (1977).

2. *The Reno Air Show.* Reno Air operates the National Championship Air Races, an annual air show at the Reno Airport in Nevada. The show, which features airplanes that race around pylons for cash prizes and stunt aircraft that perform acrobatic maneuvers, attracts 80,000 to 90,000 people per year and generates millions of dollars of revenue. Reno Air uses a logo featuring a checkered pylon with two airplanes circling it to identify the event and merchandise promoting the event. Reno Air is the registered owner of two federal trademarks regarding the logo. Through special licensing agreements, Reno Air permits vendors situated inside the gates of the show to sell merchandise bearing the trademarks. For many years, McCord has sold merchandise, including t-shirts, caps and mugs, depicting the term "Reno Air Races" and artwork containing images of at least one airplane and a pylon, from booths located just outside of the gates of the air races. Reno Air has filed a complaint alleging McCord's infringement of the federally registered "pylon logo" mark and the "Reno Air Races" mark. Reno Air also filed an ex parte application for a TRO pursuant to Rule 65(b), stating that notice to McCord was unnecessary because "of the immediate and irreparable harm that will occur if the restraining order is not immediately issued [because] of the significant risk that [McCord] may leave the Reno Airport area and destroy or conceal [his] infringing merchandise once [he] receive[s] notice of the lawsuit." Suppose that you are the judge assigned to the case. Has Reno Air made a sufficient showing of need to bring itself within the *Vuitton* exception to the notice requirement? Can you accept counsel's assertions of risk (that McCord will conceal or destroy the infringing merchandise) without additional proof? *See Reno Air Racing Association, Inc. v. McCord*, 452 F.3d 1126 (9th Cir. 2006).

3. *More on the Diamond Derby Gala.* Now, let's think about the concept of an *ex parte* injunction as applied to the Diamond Derby Gala problem, and assume that you are the judge assigned to hear the case. Is this an appropriate case for granting *ex parte* relief? What arguments could be made on behalf of the Jacksons in favor of *ex parte* relief? If you are the judge, how should you rule?

AMERICAN CAN COMPANY V. MANSUKHANI

742 F.2d 314 (7th Cir.1984).

CUDAHY, CIRCUIT JUDGE.

Plaintiff, a manufacturer and seller of commercial ink jets, sought preliminary injunctive relief preventing defendant from misappropriating its trade secrets. Plaintiff alleged that defendant violated a confidentiality agreement by taking with him copies of patent applications, ink formulas and other documents when he left his old job. The district court also found that Mansukhani had contacted several former customers and had sold jet inks to them for substantially lower prices. Mansukhani had had access to information needed to formulate inks suitable for those customers' specific needs, and the inks Mansukhani had sold were precisely identical to the "400 Series" inks he had helped to develop for plaintiff. Applying Wisconsin trade secret law, the court found that the formulas for the 400 Series inks were trade secrets and that defendants had misappropriated those secrets. The court entered a permanent injunction on June 18, 1982.

On July 25, 1983, plaintiff presented a second *ex parte* motion. In the motion, plaintiff sought an *ex parte* temporary restraining order which (1) would enjoin defendants from selling jet inks of any type to any of plaintiff's customers and (2) would permit plaintiff's employees (in the company of United States Marshals) to enter defendants' premises for the purpose of seizing ink samples and various documents.

On July 25, 1983, the district court held an *ex parte* hearing on plaintiff's motion for the temporary restraining order. The next morning, the district court signed the *ex parte* order which enjoined defendants from selling jet inks of any type, including defendants' SK–2914 and SK–2916 jet inks, to any of plaintiff's customers, previously serviced by Mansukhani when he was employed by plaintiff or its predecessors. That portion of the order was in effect for ten days. The court also ordered United States Marshals to accompany plaintiff's employees to the defendants' plant and to seize ink samples and documents which plaintiff's employees would identify. The temporary restraining order directed the marshals to keep the materials pending a further order from the court. In addition, the order set a hearing date of August 5 with respect to plaintiff's request for a preliminary injunction. After the court issued the *ex parte* order, plaintiff's employees and United States Marshals went to defendants' plant, served defendants with the temporary restraining order and took the samples pursuant to the order. Also that same day, plaintiff notified all of its commercial jet ink customers that the defendants were subject to the temporary restraining order.

We conclude that the district court abused its discretion by ordering *ex parte* relief when there was no valid reason for proceeding *ex parte* and by disregarding the strict procedural requirements of Fed.R.Civ.P. 65(b) for the issuance of such *ex parte* orders. The circumstances in which an *ex parte* order should be granted are extremely limited. The "stringent restrictions" imposed on the availability of *ex parte* temporary restraining orders reflect the fact that our entire jurisprudence runs counter to the notion of court action taken before reasonable notice and an opportunity to be heard has been granted both sides of a dispute. *ex parte* temporary restraining orders are no doubt necessary in certain circumstances, but under federal law they should be restricted to serving their underlying purpose of preserving the status quo and preventing irreparable harm just so long as is necessary to hold a hearing, and no longer.

Ex parte temporary restraining orders are most familiar to courts where notice to the adversary party is impossible either because the identity of the adverse party is unknown or because a known party cannot be located in time for a hearing. Here the identities of the defendants and their attorneys were known to plaintiff and to the district court well before the issuance of the temporary restraining order. Also, time was not a pressing factor, for the court did not issue the order until six days after the plaintiff first made its *ex parte* application. During that period, neither the plaintiff nor the court made any effort to notify defendants of the proceedings.

Plaintiff agrees that notice could have been given to the defendants, but it argues that this case falls within a very narrow band of cases in which *ex parte* orders are proper because notice to the defendant would render fruitless the further prosecution of the action. American Can argues that it "entertained the same fears as Vuitton" because notice of its *ex parte* request "would have immediately caused appellants to alter the inks in their factory and secrete the pertinent documents. In addition, notice would have permitted defendants to dispose of inks. Notice, in effect, would have frustrated the very purpose of the action, namely, to ascertain the existence of infringing goods." Because an *ex parte* order is proper only when there is no reasonable alternative, we must examine each of the operative terms of the restraining order to determine whether this asserted risk justified the *ex parte* actions.

The first operative portion of the *ex parte* order enjoined defendants for ten days "from the continued sale of jet inks of any type [to] any of plaintiff's customers, previously serviced by Mansukhani when he was employed by plaintiff or its predecessors." There is no plausible reason for issuing this portion of the order *ex parte*. Even if we were to conclude that American Can had shown sufficient reason under Vuitton to permit the *ex parte* order for the preservation of ink samples and documents, that reason has utterly no application to the portion of the order which, for practical purposes, closed defendants' business for ten days. As the Supreme Court explained in [*Granny Goose Foods, Inc. v. Brotherhood of Teamsters & Auto Truck Drivers Local No. 70 of Alameda County,* 415 U.S. 423, 438–39 (1974)], *ex parte* temporary restraining orders "should be restricted to serving their underlying purpose of preserving the status quo and preventing irreparable harm just so long as is necessary to hold a hearing, and no longer." This order was not thus restricted, and it should not have been issued.

The second portion of the *ex parte* order authorized plaintiff's employees, with the assistance of the United States Marshals, to enter defendants' premises, take samples of jet inks and obtain for copying "all documents relating to defendants' sales of jet inks including sales to plaintiff's customers, defendants' production documents used to prepare the inks and Mansukhani's correspondence with customers of plaintiff." We agree that *ex parte* orders of very limited scope and brief duration may be justified in order to preserve evidence where the applicant shows that notice would result in destruction of evidence. The problem is whether American Can made a sufficient showing of the need for proceeding *ex parte*.

Where there are no practical obstacles to giving notice to the adverse party, an *ex parte* order is justified only if there is no less drastic means for protecting the plaintiff's interests. In this case, it would have been possible for the court to issue an order *ex parte* telling defendants to be prepared to show cause in an immediate hearing why an order permitting such sampling and disclosure of documents should not have been entered. Such an order could have instructed defendants not to disturb their inventory or to secrete documents pending the hearing, and an order of that scope would not have raised the concerns we have here about the *ex parte* proceedings. To show that a less drastic order would not have been sufficient to protect its interests, plaintiff must show, in effect, that the defendants would have disregarded a clear and direct order from the court to preserve the inks and documents for a few hours until a hearing could have been held.

American Can supported its assertion that the defendants would hide or destroy documents and falsify ink samples by saying that the defendants had failed to produce [any] formula, ink sample or document in response to plaintiff's discovery requests and subpoenas. Plaintiff also pointed out that Mansukhani had had a number of plaintiff's confidential documents in his possession at the time of the court's permanent injunction. Mansukhani turned those documents over to plaintiff in compliance with the court's order. We conclude that the record does not support a presumption that the defendants would have deliberately disregarded a direct court order to preserve inks and documents for a few hours. The record reveals numerous discovery disputes, but there is nothing unusual about such disputes in a trade secret case where both sides seek highly confidential information. Both sides have sought technical data, financial information and customer lists from one another, and nothing suggests that defendants did not comply with the court's orders. There is simply no basis for inferring that a party who resists in good faith the opponent's discovery requests will also deliberately disobey the court's discovery orders.

American Can also claims that defendants were shown to have been willing to disregard court orders because the inks they were selling were in violation of the terms of the court's permanent injunction. However, an *ex parte* allegation of contempt, upon which the *ex parte* order was based, is far different from a court's conclusion that its order has been violated. In addition, the scope of the permanent injunction was not entirely clear, and we do not think the plaintiff or the court could infer from the defendants' actions a willingness to disobey clear, specific and direct court orders.

NOTES

1. *Appealing Injunctive Orders.* At the federal level, an order "granting, continuing, modifying, refusing or dissolving" an injunction can be immediately appealed. 28 U.S.C. § 1291(a)(1). In general, and subject to some exceptions, TROs do not fall within the scope of § 1291 and are therefore not appealable. *See Sampson v. Murray*, 415 U.S. 61, 94 S.Ct. 937, 39 L.Ed.2d 166 (1974).

2. *Termination of the Management Contract.* In *G & J Parking Co. v. City of Chicago*, 168 Ill.App.3d 382, 522 N.E.2d 774, 119 Ill.Dec. 112 (1988), plaintiff sought a TRO prohibiting the City of Chicago from terminating its contract for the management of six city owned parking lots. The TRO was granted after an *ex parte* hearing. The court held that the TRO was improperly granted:

> The granting of injunctive relief without notice is an extraordinary remedy and is appropriate only under the most extreme and urgent circumstances. Applying these principles, we believe that the complaint did not contain sufficient factual allegations of immediate and irreparable harm to alleviate the need for notice. Although the complaint states that if the injunctive relief is not granted plaintiff will suffer irreparable injury and damages, the pleadings fail to indicate how the plaintiff would be irreparably injured by notifying the defendants of the hearing. Nothing appears in the record to indicate why at least a minimum of notice such as a telephone call could not have been afforded to the defendants. Consequently, we find that the TRO was improperly entered.

PROBLEM: THE CABLE DECODER

Plaintiff, Illinois X, LLC, alleges that defendant distributes devices that de-scramble or decode cable television services, and thereby enable parties to view programs without paying for them. Plaintiff seeks an *ex parte* temporary restraining order that would authorize plaintiff's agents, with the assistance of federal marshals, to enter defendant's home to seize his business records and any decoders on the premises and freezing defendant's assets.

The evidence reveals that defendant's website offered to sell devices that decode cable television programs. Defendant, who operates a business out of his home, and is a leading seller of non-addressable decoders (devices that cannot be tracked by a cable company), and bulletproof decoders (devices that are immune to electronic security countermeasures). The sale of such decoders is illegal if the seller intends that they be used to intercept cable television signals without authorization from the cable company.

When he discovered defendant's website, plaintiff, using an alias, ordered a decoder from defendant. Shortly thereafter, a package arrived C.O.D. at plaintiff's headquarters in Chicago. Several days later, defendant endorsed the money order and sent plaintiff the decoder. The decoder enabled plaintiff to view all of its scrambled premium and pay-per-view channels.

In support of its motion for an *ex parte* TRO, plaintiff claims that it would suffer irreparable harm if defendant received notice of the suit before the requested relief was ordered. In particular, plaintiff claims that if it notifies defendant of the suit before executing a seizure, defendant will secrete or destroy his business records, transfer any decoders that he possesses to others and hide his illicit profits. Plaintiff states that this would make it more difficult to prove the full extent of the relief to which it is entitled.

Plaintiff therefore requests orders: (1) restraining defendant from advertising and selling decoders; (2) restraining him from secreting or destroying evidence such as business records and from transferring to others any decoders that he possesses; (3) freezing his assets; (4) authorizing plaintiff, with the assistance of federal marshals, to enter defendant's home, by force if necessary, and seize the business records and decoders found there; (5) requiring defendant to immediately disclose any other location where his business records and decoders may be found; and (6) granting expedited discovery.

If you are the judge assigned to hear the case, which of these requests would you grant? Would an order not to destroy evidence and to retain records of any sales of decoders made between the date of this order and the date of the hearing be sufficient? Would it matter that other sellers of decoders had violated court orders or destroyed evidence? Likewise, would it matter that defendant differs from other decoder sellers because he uses his real name and address in conducting his business, and that he is also different because he sells numerous other apparently legal products? Moreover, even if evidence is destroyed, does plaintiff have sufficient evidence to prosecute its case? Would it matter that federal statutes provide for damages of up to $60,000 per violation? *See Comcast of Illinois* X, LLC v. Till, 293 F. Supp.2d 936 (E.D. Wis., 2003).

MARQUETTE V. MARQUETTE

686 P.2d 990 (Okla. App. 1984).

REYNOLDS, JUDGE:

Jeff L. Marquette appeals trial court's orders of October 13, 1982, and November 19, 1982, restraining him from abusing, injuring, threatening or harassing his ex-wife, Julie M. Marquette. The trial court entered both orders under the Protection from Domestic Abuse Act, 22 O.S.Supp. 1983 § 60 *et seq.*

Appellant and Appellee were divorced on September 10, 1982. Appellee was given custody of the parties' two young sons. On October 13, 1982, Appellee filed a petition for protective order. She gave the following reasons for requesting the protective order:

> continued harassment & assault following the divorce granted Sept. 10, 1982. Throws children's clothes, shoes, toys, & children at me. Verbal threats are made to me in front of the children. I am afraid of being harmed as I have in the past. And afraid of emotional damage these scenes are doing to my children.

Appellee requested the court to enter an emergency *ex parte* order. The court granted her request, and set a show cause hearing on November 1, 1982. The *ex parte* order prohibited Appellant from abusing, injuring, visiting, communicating with, or threatening Appellee. It also instructed Appellant not to abuse or injure the minor children. After the hearing was delayed a couple of times, the court held a trial and entered a mutual protective order.

Domestic violence has wide-ranging ramifications and can certainly be characterized as an issue of broad public interest. Further, under the *ex parte* order of October 13, 1982, Appellant was effectively denied his parental visitation since he could not communicate with his ex-wife, the custodial parent. In the absence of any legislative history, it is reasonable to assume the passage of the Act is a result of increased public awareness regarding the serious nature of domestic violence. The Legislature has attempted to remedy this problem by providing immediate, as well as long-range, protection for the victims of domestic abuse.

Appellant alleges denial of due process under the October 13 *ex parte* order. The due process guarantee is intended to protect an individual against arbitrary acts of the government. Appellant was effectively denied his right to visit his children from October 13 until November 3. This occurred because he could not communicate with his ex-wife, the custodial parent.

This interference with Appellant's visitation rights is significant. Appellant alleges this right has been violated without procedural due process. We do not take the interference with parental visitation lightly, but we note that such interference can only occur for a total of ten days prior to the deprived parent receiving a full hearing. This infringement must be balanced against the government's interest in issuing the order and the risk of erroneous deprivation under existing procedures.[23]

---

[23] *Mathews v. Eldridge,* 424 U.S. 319 (1976).

The State's interest in providing this protection to the victims of domestic abuse is apparent. The legislation promotes the health, safety and general welfare of its citizens. Domestic violence has become a problem of considerable magnitude.

The consequences of allowing battering to continue can be serious. Experts believe that domestic violence is likely to escalate in cyclical fashion, at times resulting in the woman's death. Women caught in the cycle of abuse may, in the process of defending themselves, kill their assailant. Children exposed to such patterns of violence not only may suffer immediate emotional distress, but also may reproduce their parents' behavior patterns as adults.

Temporary restraining orders issued without notice have survived constitutional attack. *See, e.g. United States v. Spilotro,* 680 F.2d 612 (9th Cir.1982); *State v. B Bar Enterprises, Inc.,* 133 Ariz. 99, 649 P.2d 978 (Ariz.1982). The Act provides the following procedures prior to issuance of the *ex parte* order. An *ex parte* order is not issued unless good cause is shown by petitioner at a hearing held by the court. Only then may the court issue such order as is necessary to protect the victim from immediate and present danger of domestic abuse. Under the 1983 version of the Act, a hearing must be held within ten days after the petition is filed regardless of whether an *ex parte* order has been issued. Although there is always some chance of erroneous deprivation, the trial court will have opportunity to judge the credibility of the petitioner prior to issuing the order. The court may be able to see first hand the evidence of domestic violence.

If a plaintiff requests an emergency *ex parte* order pursuant to Section 60.2 of this title, the court shall hold an *ex parte* hearing on the same day the petition is filed. The court may, for good cause shown at the hearing, issue any emergency *ex parte* order that it finds necessary to protect the victim from immediate and present danger of domestic abuse.

Carefully considering all the above factors, we find the procedural safeguards employed under the Act prior to the issuance of an *ex parte* order, coupled with the state's interest in securing immediate protection for abused victims, of sufficient weight to meet Appellant's due process challenge.

We hold the trial court properly exercised its authority under the Act.

AFFIRMED.

3. PERSONS BOUND

Because injunctions are *in personam* orders, they typically do not bind people or entities not party to the litigation. Nonetheless, courts have traditionally recognized six categories of nonparties that may be bound by injunction: (1) agents of the enjoined party; (2) aiders and abettors of the enjoined party; (3) persons cognizant of the decree; (4) successors in interest of the enjoined party; (5) those coming into contact with a particular res, and (6) members of the same class in a class action suit. Richard A Bales & Ryan A. Allison, *Enjoining Nonparties*, 26 Am. J. Trial Advoc. 79, 80 (2002). Federal Rule of Civil Procedure 65(d) provides that injunctions and TROs bind "only the following who receive actual notice of it by personal service or otherwise: (A) the parties; (B) the parties' officers, agents, servants, employees, and attorneys; and (C) other persons who are in active concert or participation with anyone described in Rule 65(d)."

PLANNED PARENTHOOD GOLDEN GATE V. GARIBALDI

107 Cal.App.4th 345, 132 Cal.Rptr.2d 46 (2003).

HAERLE, J.

In 1995 Planned Parenthood Association of San Mateo County obtained a permanent injunction limiting demonstration activity outside its clinic in San Mateo. In February 2001, Planned Parenthood Golden Gate (PPGG) filed the instant action seeking a declaration that the 1995 injunction applies to appellants, Rossi Foti and Jeannette and Louie Garibaldi.

The 1995 injunction was sought and granted to remedy problems caused by demonstration activities at Planned Parenthood's clinic in San Mateo which commenced in 1988 and continued even after Planned Parenthood obtained temporary federal injunctive relief.[2]

The 1995 injunction was entered against two named defendants, Operation Rescue of California (ORC) and Robert Cochran (Cochran). According to its terms, the 1995 injunction applies to: "Defendants and their agents, employees, representatives and all persons acting in concert or participation with them, or either of them, and all persons with actual notice of this judgment."

The 1995 injunction restricts demonstration activities at the San Mateo clinic. The provisions pertaining to the San Mateo clinic restrain

---

[2] During this period, the defendants organized and coordinated regular protests at the clinic. Those protests included "several 'very large blockades' of more than 100 protestors that resulted in the clinic's temporary closure. Typically, 'rows of people blocked all the doors' to the clinic. On at least one occasion police arrested protestors inside the clinic. Patients found the protests threatening, and some did not come into the clinic for appointments. Noise from the protests could be heard in the patient waiting room, which abuts the sidewalk. The protests caused the clinic to shift its entrance doors and to hire and train staff for an 'escort program' to bring patients through the protestors." Patients were angered, upset and frightened by these protestors who tried to prevent people from driving into the clinic parking lot and demonstrated so loudly they could be heard inside the clinic. There was evidence that the patients' heightened stress levels complicated their medical procedures. Some required additional counseling or medication. Others canceled or delayed appointments in order to avoid protestors. The evidence showed that delaying an abortion procedure increased the likelihood patients would experience complications.

and enjoin individuals subject to the 1995 injunction from directly or indirectly: (1) "Entering or blocking or obstructing the free and direct passage of any other person into or out of" the clinic; (2) "Demonstrating, picketing, distributing literature, or counseling" on clinic property "or within fifteen (15) feet of such private property"; (3) "Entering or blocking or obstructing the ingress or egress of any vehicle to or from any parking area" in front of or behind the clinic; (4) "Obstructing or impeding the movement of any person" who is moving between a vehicle and the clinic or using a walkway leading to the clinic; (5) "Shouting, screaming or otherwise producing loud noises which can be heard" in the clinic; (6) "Physically touching threatening to physically touch, or shouting" at people entering or exiting the clinic.

On February 16, 2001, PPGG filed a complaint for declaratory relief against Foti and the Garibaldis. PPGG alleged that defendants were served with the 1995 injunction but "continue to demonstrate, picket and distribute literature on and within fifteen feet of the San Mateo Clinic property and also enter and obstruct the free and direct passage of people into and out of the Clinic." PPGG also alleged, on information and belief, that defendants act in concert and participation with ORC when conducting their demonstration activities. PPGG sought a declaration that "defendants are bound by the 1995 Injunction and must therefore comply with its terms or face contempt."

On May 8, 2001, the Garibaldis filed motions to strike PPGG's complaint pursuant to the anti-SLAPP Strategic Lawsuits Against Public Participation statute, Code of Civil Procedure section 425.16. The Garibaldis argued the complaint lacks merit and was "brought solely for the purpose of interfering with the valid exercise of their constitutional rights to freedom of speech." The court denied the Garibaldis' motions to strike.

On January 18, 2002, PPGG filed a motion for summary judgment. It argued that Foti and the Garibaldis are subject to the 1995 injunction as a matter of law because undisputed facts show that they act in concert with each other and in concert or participation with ORC and Cochran in conducting their demonstration activities at the San Mateo clinic. PPGG also argued that the 1995 injunction applies to all persons with actual notice of it and that undisputed facts establish that Foti and the Garibaldis have notice of the 1995 injunction. On March 4, 2002, a hearing on the summary judgment motion was held before the Honorable Joseph Bergeron. On March 5, the court filed an order granting PPGG's motion for summary judgment. Judgment was entered on March 22, 2002.

"An injunction is obviously a personal decree. It operates on the person of the defendant by commanding him to do or desist from certain action." Indeed it may "deprive the enjoined parties of rights others enjoy precisely because the enjoined parties have abused those rights in the past." Thus, it is well established that "injunctions are not effective against the world at large." On the other hand, the law recognizes that enjoined parties "may not nullify an injunctive decree by carrying out prohibited acts with or through nonparties to the original proceeding." Thus, an injunction can properly run to classes of persons with or through whom the enjoined party may act. However, "a theory of disobedience of the injunction cannot be predicated on the act of a person not in any way included in its terms or acting in concert with the enjoined party and in support of his claims."

These legal principles establish that the actual notice provision in the 1995 injunction is not enforceable. "Personal jurisdiction and notice are not enough to subject a person to the restraint of an injunction. The *order* must be directed against that person, either by naming that person as an individual or by designating a class of persons to which that person belongs. If the person charged with violation was neither named in the injunction individually or as a member of a class, nor as aiding or abetting a person so included, he cannot be brought within the prohibition merely by being served with a copy of the writ."

PPGG contends the "actual notice provision is an indispensable tool to effectuate the court's power to grant equitable relief among all parties affected by the intense emotions surrounding the abortion debate." In fact, the actual notice provision is inconsistent with the very nature and purpose of injunctive relief because it purports to extend a remedy beyond the context of the specific dispute which justifies that remedy. "An injunction, by its very nature, applies only to a particular group (or individuals) and regulates the activities, and perhaps the speech, of that group. It does so, however, because of the group's past actions in the context of a specific dispute between real parties. The parties seeking the injunction assert a violation of their rights; the court hearing the action is charged with fashioning a remedy for a specific deprivation, not with the drafting of a statute addressed to the general public."

The intensity of the "abortion debate" does not somehow entitle PPGG to broader relief than parties seeking equitable relief in other contexts. If anything, the opposite is true. "As a general matter, protestors enjoy full constitutional protection for the expression and communication of their views concerning the public issue of abortion. This is particularly true when these protected activities occur on the public streets and sidewalks, traditionally viewed as the quintessential public forum. An injunction curtailing protected expression will be upheld only if the challenged provisions of the injunction burden no more speech than necessary to serve a significant government interest." The actual notice provision cannot satisfy this requirement; because it purports to enjoin all demonstrators in addition to the enjoined parties, the restriction is overbroad on its face.

PPGG argues that, without the actual notice provision, one anti-choice protestor can simply be replaced with another and avoid the reach of the injunction. But anti-choice protestors are not fungible. A " 'mutuality of purpose' is not enough" to bind non-parties to an injunction restricting demonstration activity at an abortion clinic; "it must be their actual relationship to an enjoined party, and not their convictions about abortion, that make them contemners." If we permit PPGG to utilize an actual notice provision to obtain injunctive relief against all anti-abortion protestors, the injunction would be content-based and virtually impossible to justify under current First Amendment jurisprudence.[5]

PPGG's legitimate concern that an enjoined party might attempt to undermine the effect of an injunction by enlisting the aid of a nonparty can be adequately addressed by a provision extending the reach of the injunction to agents, employees and those who act in concert with an enjoined party. The 1995 injunction contains such a provision. That in concert provision ensures that "a nonparty to an injunction is subject to the contempt power of the court when, with knowledge of the injunction, the nonparty violates its terms with or for those who are restrained."

PPGG's final contention is that this court should enforce the actual notice provision because it effectuates one of the basic policies underlying injunctive relief—to prevent a multiplicity of judicial proceedings. This policy is not effectuated by the actual notice provision which purports to bind a nonparty to a judgment. Absent evidence that Foti and the Garibaldis act together with or on behalf of parties enjoined by the 1995 injunction, the controversy between these appellants and PPGG does not involve the same parties, subject matter, or facts which supported the judgment pursuant to which the 1995 injunction was entered.

For all of these reasons, we hold the actual notice provision does not bind Foti and the Garibaldis to the 1995 injunction. Actual notice of an injunction is a requirement but cannot be an independent ground upon which to apply an injunction to a nonparty. Therefore, the 1995 injunction applies to the defendants against whom it was entered (ORC and Cochran) and their agents, employees, representatives and all persons acting in concert or participation with them, or either of them who have actual notice of the judgment.

---

[5] These same considerations undermine PPGG's argument that appellants can be subject to the 1995 injunction as members of the class that was intended to be restrained. PPGG misconstrues the language of the actual notice provision as applying to a class consisting of all anti-abortion protestors with notice. Such a provision, had it been included in the 1995 injunction, would have been constitutionally invalid.

NOTE

1. *A Parallel Approach*. Applying similar reasoning, the court in *Roe v. Operation Rescue*, 54 F.3d 133 (3d Cir. 1995), held that the trial court had abused its discretion in failing to hold nonparty abortion clinic protesters in contempt for violating an injunction. The court found compelling evidence that the nonparties did not act independently, but were acting as "agents of" or "in concert with" the parties subject to the injunction.

PROBLEMS

1. *Reconsidering* Planned Parenthood. In the prior case, suppose that you had been hired to represent Planned Parenthood. What type of evidence might you develop that would be sufficient to find defendants subject to the injunction?

2. *The Earl and the Duchess.* Why shouldn't an injunction bind the entire world? In *Lord Wellesley v. Earl of Mornington* Ch., 1848 50 Eng.Rep. 786, Lord Wellesley obtained an injunction prohibiting the Earl of Mornington and his agents from cutting timber on the Lord's property. The case involved an attempt to hold Batley, the Earl's agent and manager, in contempt. Suppose that Duchess Zurk lives on the other side of the Earl's property. The Duchess and the Earl also have a boundary dispute regarding the same tract of land. Can the *Lord Wellesley* case be fairly construed as adjudicating the Duchess's claims against the Earl? Does the Duchess have the right to have her claims separately adjudicated?

3. *Binding Duchess Zurk.* What would the Earl of Mornington be required to show in order to bind Duchess Zurk by the original decree?

4. *Must Each Potential Infringer Be Individually Sued?* Must courts separately adjudicate every claimant's rights? Suppose that an abortion clinic seeks and obtains an injunction against a pro-life group prohibiting them from picketing within 50 feet of the clinic and also prohibiting them from approaching women entering the clinic. After the injunction issues, the group moves it picketing outside the 50 foot limit. However, other anti-abortion protestors (who belong to another pro-life group) picket within 50 feet of the clinic and approach women entering the clinic. Assuming that the second group of protestors had knowledge of the injunction against the first group, can the second group be held in contempt? Alternatively, must the clinic seek and obtain a new injunction against each subsequent group of protestors? Consider the following two cases, as well as *Madsen v. Women's Health Center, Inc., infra* at 285.

5. *More on the Need to Sue Individual Infringers.* In the immediately prior problem involving the anti-abortion protestors, would it matter that the new group of protestors were members of a different anti-abortion group that used quite different tactics? Would such facts make the court less willing to apply the original decree to the protestors?

6. *Patent Infringement.* Plaintiff sued John Staff for infringement of his patent. Even though the original suit also named John's brother (Joseph) as a defendant, he was dismissed after testifying that he was not involved in the business. An injunction was issued enjoining John, "his agents, employees, associates and confederates," from infringing, or "aiding or abetting or in any way contributing to the infringement," and a writ in the same terms was served upon the counsel for both defendants. At the time of the suit Joseph was a salesman for John, but later, having left his employ, he set up in business for himself, and was proved to have infringed the patent. The plaintiff sought to punish Joseph for contempt, asserting that he was bound by the decree, and that his new business was a violation of the writ. Can Joseph be held in contempt? If you represent the plaintiff, what types of evidence might help you hold him in contempt? How might you obtain that evidence? *See Alemite Mfg. Corp. v. Staff*, 42 F.2d 832 (2d Cir.1930).

STATE UNIVERSITY OF NEW YORK V. DENTON

35 A.D.2d 176, 316 N.Y.S.2d 297 (Sup.Ct.1970).

FRANK DEL VECCHIO, JUSTICE PRESIDING:

Appellants, 45 members of the faculty of the State University of New York at Buffalo, appeal from a judgment adjudging them guilty of criminal contempt for violating a preliminary injunction. The 30-day jail sentence has been stayed pending determination of the appeal.

In the course of student disturbances and disorders on the University campus in late February 1970 the administration requested the aid of the Buffalo city police. A sizable number of police moved onto the campus where clashes with students ensued. Members of the University administration were barred from campus offices and a basketball game was disrupted by students demanding the removal of the police officers. The State concedes that the appellants, as distinguished from the students, "were not party to the violent and disruptive actions leading to the injunction."

In an attempt to prevent further acts of violence, the University, by order to show cause, commenced an action against 13 named students and John Doe and Jane Doe for a permanent injunction. The order to show cause, which was coupled with a temporary restraining order, required the named students to show cause why a temporary injunction restraining certain conduct on the campus should not issue. On March 5, the return day of the show cause order, no appearance was made on behalf of the students, and an order was made enjoining the students "and all other persons receiving notice of this preliminary injunction, whether acting individually or in concert" (1) from acting within or adjacent to plaintiff's buildings in such unlawful manner as to disrupt or interfere with plaintiff's lawful and normal operations or unlawfully to interfere with ingress to or egress from such properties or otherwise to disrupt the lawful educational function of the university, and (2) from employing unlawful force or violence or the unlawful threat of force and violence against persons or property.

The preliminary injunction was served by posting copies at various locations on the campus. On March 11 the Faculty Senate passed a resolution urging the acting president of the institution to order the withdrawal of the police from the campus, but he took no such action.

The judgment we are reviewing found appellants faculty members guilty of willfully violating the provisions of the preliminary injunction of March 5 in that, acting individually and in concert with each other and in concert with others with notice of the preliminary injunction, they entered the office of the president of the University located on the campus and unlawfully refused to leave the office when asked to do so. Appellants were not among the named defendants in the injunction action, were not parties to the application for the temporary injunction and were never personally served with the order.

The threshold question is whether appellants were bound by the order of March 5, which was addressed to the named student defendants and "all persons having knowledge" of the order, and whether accordingly appellants may be found guilty of criminal contempt for its violation. Well settled principles of law require a negative answer. The rules respecting preliminary injunctions were laid down in the landmark case of *Rigas v. Livingston*, 178 N.Y. 20, 70 N.E. 107. There, speaking of the statutory authority for the issuance of such injunctions, the Court of Appeals said: "The Code authorizes an injunction against the defendant only, not the whole world. So far as the order purported to restrain all other persons having knowledge of the injunction, this provision was inoperative to enlarge its effect. It is true that persons not parties to the action may be bound by an injunction if they have knowledge of it, provided they are servants or agents of the defendants, or act in collusion or combination with them. But the underlying principle, on which is founded the court's power to punish for the violation of its mandate persons not parties to the action, is that the parties so punished were acting either as the agents or servants of the defendants, or in combination or collusion with them or in assertion of their rights or claims. Persons who are not connected in any way with the parties to the action, are not restrained by the order of the court." *Alemite Mfg. Corp. v. Staff*, 2 Cir., 42 F.2d 832.

Measured by these criteria, the appellants were not made subject to the preliminary injunction by the language "all persons receiving notice of this preliminary injunction." The record is devoid of any proof that the students violated the injunction and the evidence is legally insufficient to establish that the faculty members either were agents of or acted in collusion with them. The injunction was specifically aimed at the conduct of the students. The faculty members were not parties to the disruptive actions which led to the injunction nor were they charged with acting in concert with or as agents of the students. Consequently, even if they had knowledge of its provisions, they could not be held in contempt for their independent action in disobeying the injunction.

Plaintiff offered proof that after the faculty members entered the president's office one of the group handed to a University staff member a paper which stated that the group would remain until the police were removed from the campus and that they were in sympathy with the general purposes of the strike. The mere fact that an actor may be sympathetic to the desires of one properly bound by an injunction, or that by his conduct the former accomplishes what the party enjoined wants accomplished, is not sufficient to establish beyond a reasonable doubt that the conduct was carried out in combination or collusion with the named enjoinee. We conclude therefore that appellants were not bound by the injunction and that the application to punish appellants for contempt of court arising out of a violation of the order of March 5 should have been denied. Judgment unanimously reversed on the law and facts and proceeding dismissed, without costs.

PROBLEM: MORE ON THE DIAMOND DERBY GALA

Assuming that you have decided to grant an injunction against the Diamond Derby Gala. Who should that injunction apply to? The organizers? Attendees? Gawkers? Can you extend the injunction to all of the above?

DALTON V. MEISTER

84 Wis.2d 303, 267 N.W.2d 326 (1978).

CALLOW, JUSTICE.

On December 29, 1969, LeRoy Dalton obtained a judgment in the amount of $151,749.98 against Howard Meister in a defamation action. Almost one year later, on September 24, 1970, Mr. Dalton obtained an order to show cause in the defamation action why Mr. Meister should not be ordered to turn over to the sheriff certain shares of UTI stock.

The affidavit in support of the order to show cause alleged that an order enjoining Mr. Meister to turn over the stock is authorized by sec. 408.317(2), Stats., a provision of the Uniform Commercial Code governing the attachment and levies upon investment securities; that executions upon the judgment have been returned unsatisfied; that a substantial number of the shares registered to Mr. Meister have since been transferred to a third party; and that, unless the court orders the UTI stock turned over to the sheriff immediately, Mr. Meister will attempt to dispose of the remainder of the stock to frustrate Mr. Dalton's recovery on the judgment.

At the hearing on the order to show cause, Dalton and Meister were represented, but UTI was not. Counsel for Mr. Dalton estimated the value of this stock in excess of $300,000. For reasons which it did not explain, the trial court concluded that it did not have power to direct the delivery of the shares of stock to the sheriff. Instead, the court enjoined Mr. Meister from transferring the stock, and upon Mr. Dalton's request, it also enjoined UTI from transferring title to this stock on its stock books. The injunction was dated September 30, 1970, and was to remain in effect until further action by the court. The injunction decree was served on UTI.

On November 12, 1971, approximately fourteen months after the issuance of the injunction against UTI, UTI registered transfer of the shares of stock covered by the injunction to the American City Bank and Trust Company. On March 14, 1974, Mr. Dalton obtained an order to show cause why UTI should not be held in contempt for violating the injunction. UTI responded by filing a Notice of Special Appearance challenging the jurisdiction of the court to find it in contempt.

At the hearing on the contempt motion, Kenneth Baird, senior vice president of UTI, testified that on November 12, 1971, transfer of 26,747 shares of UTI stock was registered on the transfer books and a new certificate issued to the American City Bank and Trust Company. Mr. Baird testified that this transfer was made pursuant to a foreclosure agreement on June 20, 1971, between the American City Bank, the Continental Bank, UTI, and Mr. Meister and his family.[1] Mr. Dalton was given no notice of the agreement despite the fact that it purported to transfer the shares of stock covered by the injunction. Mr. Baird admitted that at the time Mr. Meister's shares of UTI stock were transferred on the stock books he was aware of the injunction, though he was never personally served with a copy of it; but because he believed the injunction was jurisdictionally defective and because he feared that UTI would be liable to American City Bank if it did not register transfer of the stock, he decided to transfer the stock in disregard of the injunction.

The trial court concluded that it had the power to enjoin UTI from transferring the stock on its stock transfer books even though UTI was never made a party to the injunction proceedings. Accordingly, the court found UTI in contempt of court for transferring the stock in disregard of the injunction. UTI has brought this appeal.

Where a security cannot be readily levied upon by ordinary legal process, a judgment creditor who seeks to reach a security registered to the judgment debtor may also obtain the assistance of the court "by

[1] Counsel for UTI explained that UTI believed that the shares transferred to American City Bank had been used as collateral to secure the multimillion dollar loans that American City made to Meister in August, 1969, before the Dalton judgment was entered and that American City's interest in the stock was superior to Dalton's.

injunction or otherwise." Sec. 408.317(2), Stats. Thus Mr. Dalton can enjoin the transfer by UTI of Mr. Meister's stock in order to protect his ability to execute on the judgment until the sheriff can take physical possession of the stock. The issue here is whether, in view of the failure to make UTI a party to the injunction proceedings, the injunction obtained pursuant to the code is binding on UTI.

Injunctions operate *in personam* and will not issue against one who is beyond the court's jurisdiction. It is undisputed that UTI was not a party to the defamation action, was not served with a copy of the order to show cause for the injunction, and had no opportunity to be heard at any time with regard to whether it should be enjoined from transferring the stock. The injunction was thus issued without obtaining personal jurisdiction over UTI.

There are some circumstances under which nonparties who have actual notice of the injunction have been held in contempt for violating it whether they are named in the decree or not. At common law a decree of injunction not only bound parties defendant but also those identified with them in interest, in privity with them, represented by them, or subject to their control. The common law rule has been expanded to bind persons in active concert or participation with a party to the decree. In addition, an injunction may bind nonparties who succeed in interest to property which is subject to litigation. However, it is uniformly agreed that a court may not punish by contempt persons who violate an injunction by independent conduct and whose rights have not been adjudicated.

The question of whether a nonparty is sufficiently identified in interest with a party to the decree or is acting in concert or aiding and abetting a party to the decree is a question of fact to be determined by the court. Though the court relied on cases in which such findings were made, the court made no such findings here. Instead, the court held that it had "inherent power" to enjoin UTI. The only cases which contain language that support the trial court's conclusion that it had "inherent power" to find UTI in contempt are this court's opinion in *Upper Lakes Shipping, Ltd. v. Seafarers' International Union of Canada, supra*, and the federal case of *United States v. Hall*, 472 F.2d 261 (5th Cir. 1972).

In the federal case *United States v. Hall, supra*, the federal court entered an order requiring a school board to balance the racial composition of two high schools and retained jurisdiction to enter further orders in the cause. At an *ex parte* session, the plaintiff in the desegregation suit obtained an injunction forbidding anyone with notice of the injunction from entering the grounds of the schools marked for desegregation. One Eric Hall willfully violated the order, though he was not a party to the injunction proceedings and was not named in the decree. Nonetheless, the court in *Hall* held that he was properly held in contempt because his conduct interfered with the court's power to make a binding adjudication between the parties properly before it.

Hall observed that the district court had retained jurisdiction to enter further necessary orders and that Hall's disruptive conduct would not only jeopardize the effect of the court's judgment already entered but would also undercut its power to enter binding desegregation orders in the future. The court also observed that, since school desegregation orders excite strong community passions and are typically vulnerable to attack by an indefinable class of persons who are neither parties nor acting at the instigation of parties, broad contempt powers may be necessary to protect the court's ability to design appropriate remedies and to make their remedies effective. The court in *Hall* noted that, since the violation of the injunction took place within four days of the issuance of the injunction itself, the court's injunction operated, in effect, like a temporary restraining order. The court accordingly concluded that: "the district court had the inherent power to protect its ability to render a binding judgment between the original parties to the (desegregation) litigation by issuing an interim *ex parte* order against an undefinable class of persons" and that "willful violation of that order by one having notice of it constitutes criminal contempt."

Hall is the only case in which a nonparty has been held in contempt for violating an injunction based solely on the inherent power of a court to preserve its ability to render a final judgment. The particular circumstances of that case, which were crucial to the court's reasoning, are not present here. While in *Hall* the contemner's violation of the order subverted the court's order requiring the plaintiff to desegregate the schools and frustrated the judicial process itself, here UTI's violation of the injunction not to transfer the stock had no effect upon the rights and duties adjudicated in the underlying defamation action. It merely affected the plaintiff's power to realize on his judgment by executing upon some of the property of the defendant. In *Hall* the court was faced with the possibility that its desegregation order would be frustrated by the conduct of an indefinable class of community members and that it would be impossible to sue for an injunction against each one. But in this case UTI is the only issuer of the stock. Mr. Dalton's failure to make UTI a party was not the result of difficulty in predicting who might violate the injunction against the transfer of the stock but was the result of a decision at the hearing that restraining UTI would implement the type of relief that Mr. Dalton sought. Finally, in *Hall* the injunction, though permanent in form, was characterized as essentially an interim order, analogous to a temporary restraining order. In this case the injunction was in existence for over a year before it was violated. It did not operate as a temporary restraining order to preserve the status quo pending a resolution of the controversy involving the party restrained but rather as a permanent injunction against UTI's power to transfer the stock. We see substantial differences between this case and the *Hall* case. We note the hesitation of other federal courts to apply *Hall* to circumstances other than the desegregation context, and therefore we do not consider it to be applicable here.

Although we believe that the trial court erroneously concluded that it had the inherent power to hold UTI in contempt, on the record before us, we believe that contempt may be proper. At the hearing it was shown that, after the injunction was served upon UTI but without notice to Mr. Dalton, UTI, Mr. Meister, and American City Bank and Trust Company agreed to a transfer of the stock which was the subject of the injunction. As we have previously pointed out, a nonparty may be held in contempt for violating an injunction if he is in privity with a party or subject to his control if he is acting in concert with a party, or if he aids and abets a party in violating the injunction.

Though we cannot affirm the trial court's finding of contempt on the legal basis of inherent power, we believe that Mr. Dalton is entitled to a factual determination of whether UTI's transfer of the stock pursuant to this agreement was contemptuous under any of the theories enumerated above. We, therefore, set aside the order of contempt and remand the cause for further proceedings on whether UTI should be held in contempt.

Order reversed and cause remanded for proceedings not inconsistent with this opinion.

NOTES

1. *Issuance of Stays.* In *Securities and Exchange Commission v. Wencke*, 622 F.2d 1363 (9th Cir.1980), a trial court appointed a receiver to take control of property in a securities fraud case, and issued a stay prohibiting "all investors, creditors, and other persons" from "commencing, prosecuting, continuing or enforcing any suit" against the receivership entities, except by leave of the court. The court then sought to apply its order to nonparties "without prior notice to them." The stay was upheld on appeal:

> The power of the district court to issue a stay, effective against all persons, of all proceedings against the receivership entities rests as much on its control over the property placed in receivership as on its jurisdiction over the parties to the securities fraud action. The district court took control over the properties in question when it imposed the receivership and appointed Gould as receiver to manage those properties. The blanket stay was found by the district court necessary to achieve the purposes of the receivership. We conclude the district court had the power to enter the order.
>
> A receiver appointed by a court in the wake of a securities fraud scheme may encounter difficulties sorting out the financial status of the defrauded entity or entities. There may be a genuine danger that some litigation against receivership entities amounts to

little more than a continuation of the original fraudulent scheme. Similarly, the securities fraud may have left the finances of the receivership entities so obscure or complex that the receiver is hampered in conducting litigation. Moreover, the expense involved in defending the many lawsuits which often are filed against an entity in the wake of a securities fraud scheme may be overwhelming unless some are temporarily deferred. A stay of proceeding against receivership entities except by leave of the court may be an appropriate response to the above concerns, and the district court did not abuse its discretion in this case by entering the blanket stay.

2. *Substitution of Parties.* If the parties to a controversy change, Rule 25, F.R.Civ.P., allows for the substitution of parties. It provides:

Rule 25. Substitution of Parties

* * *

(d) *Public Officers; Death or Separation From Office.*

An action does not abate when a public officer who is a party in an official capacity dies, resigns, or otherwise ceases to hold office while the action is pending. The officer's successor is automatically substituted as a party. Later proceedings should be in the substituted party's name, but any misnomer not affecting the parties' substantial rights must be disregarded. The court may order substitution at any time, but the absence of such an order does not affect the substitution.

See Amos v. Board of School Directors, 408 F.Supp. 765 (E.D.Wis.1976) (case involving succeeding board members. Court held that order was enforceable against the present board members and the present superintendent of schools, "and the Court will order that further proceedings in this case be conducted in their names."); *United States v. Board of Education*, 331 F.Supp. 466 (N.D.Ga.1971) (desegregation suit against the board's individual members and the superintendent of schools in which the court ordered the substitution of successors in office).

3. *Joinder of Parties.* Rule 25 is supplemented by Rule 19 which provides for the substitution or joinder of parties:

Rule 19. Required Joinder of Parties

(a) Persons to be Joined if Feasible. A person who is subject to service of process and whose joinder will not deprive the court of subject-matter jurisdiction must be joined as a party if:

(A) in that person's absence, the court cannot accord complete relief among existing parties; * * *.

PROBLEMS

1. *Successors in Public Office*. A federal court orders a school board to desegregate all public schools. The board resigns and is replaced by a new board. Does the original decree bind the subsequent board? Would it matter that the board members were replaced in an election? What does Rule 25 provide?

2. *More on Successors in Office*. In the prior problem, assume that the decree applied to both the board and various private individuals including the President of PAI (Parents Against Integration). In regard to the private parties, the order prohibits them from interfering with desegregation efforts. If the President of PAI resigns and is replaced by a new President, does the original decree bind the new President? If not, what must the plaintiffs do to make sure that the new President is bound?

GOLDEN STATE BOTTLING CO., INC. V. NLRB

414 U.S. 168, 94 S.Ct. 414, 38 L.Ed.2d 388 (1973).

MR. JUSTICE BRENNAN delivered the opinion of the Court.

Petitioners are Golden State Bottling Co., Inc. (Golden State), and All American Beverages, Inc. (All American). All American bought Golden State's soft drink bottling and distribution business after the National Labor Relations Board had ordered Golden State, "its officers, agents, successors, and assigns" to reinstate with backpay a driver-salesman, Kenneth L. Baker, whose discharge by Golden State was found by the Board to have been an unfair labor practice. In a subsequent back-pay specification proceeding to which both Golden State and All American were parties, the Board found that All American continued after the acquisition to carry on the business without interruption or substantial changes in method of operation, employee complement, or supervisory personnel. In that circumstance, although All American was a bona fide purchaser of the business, unconnected with Golden State, the Board found that All American, having acquired the business with knowledge of the outstanding Board order, was a "successor" for purposes of the National Labor Relations Act and liable for the reinstatement of Baker with backpay under the principles announced in *Perma Vinyl Corp.*, 164 N.L.R.B. 968 (1967). The Board therefore ordered that All American reinstate Baker and that Golden State and All American jointly or severally pay Baker a specified sum of net backpay. The Court of Appeals enforced the order. We granted certiorari. We affirm.

We must consider whether the issuance of a reinstatement and backpay order against a bona fide successor exceeds the Board's remedial powers under § 10(c) of the Act, 29 U.S.C. § 160(c). We agree that the Board's remedial powers under § 10(c) include broad discretion to fashion and issue the order before us as relief adequate to achieve the ends, and effectuate the policies, of the Act. Early on, this Court recognized that § 10(c) does not limit the Board's remedial powers to the actual perpetrator of an unfair labor practice and thereby prevent the Board from issuing orders binding a successor who did not himself commit the unlawful act. A Board order that, as in this case, runs to the "officers, agents, successors, and assigns" of an offending employer, may be applied, not only to a new employer who is "merely a disguised continuance of the old employer," but also "in appropriate circumstances to those to whom the business may have been transferred, whether as a means of evading the judgment or for other reasons." *Regal Knitwear Co. v. NLRB*, 324 U.S. 9, 14 (1945). If the words "person named in the complaint has engaged in any such unfair labor practice" in § 10(c) do not restrict Board authority to prevent orders running to the offending employer's successors and assigns who have acquired the business as a means of evading the Board order, we do not see how those words may be read to bar the Board from issuing reinstatement and backpay orders against bona fide successors when the Board has properly found such orders to be necessary to protect the public interest in effectuating the policies of the Act. The Board's orders run to the evader and the bona fide purchaser, not because the act of evasion or the bona fide purchase is an unfair labor practice, but because the Board is obligated to effectuate the policies of the Act.

It is argued that Fed.Rule Civ.Proc. 65(d) is a bar to judicial enforcement of a Board order requiring that a bona fide successor reinstate with backpay an employee illegally discharged by its predecessor. We disagree. Rule 65(d) provides that injunctions and restraining orders shall be "binding only upon the parties to the action, their officers, agents, servants, employees, and attorneys, and upon those persons in active concert or participation with them who receive actual notice of the order by personal service or otherwise." Rule 65(d) "is derived from the common-law doctrine that a decree of injunction not only binds the parties defendant but also those identified with them in interest, in 'privity' with them, represented by them or subject to their control." *Regal Knitwear*, 324 U.S., at 14. Persons acquiring an interest in property that is a subject of litigation are bound by, or entitled to the benefit of, a subsequent judgment, despite a lack of knowledge. RESTATEMENT OF JUDGMENTS § 89, and comment c (1942). This principle has not been limited to *in rem* or *quasi in rem* proceedings. We apply that principle here in order to effectuate the public policies of the Act. We hold that a bona fide purchaser, acquiring, with knowledge that the wrong remains unremedied, the employing enterprise which was the locus of the unfair labor practice, may be considered in privity with its predecessor for purposes of Rule 65(d).

Our holding in no way contravenes the policy underlying Rule 65(d), of not having "order(s) or injunction(s) so broad as to make punishable the conduct of persons who act independently and whose rights have not been adjudged according to law." *Regal Knitwear*, 324 U.S., at 13. The tie between the offending employer and the bona fide purchaser of the business, supplied by a Board finding of a continuing business enterprise, establishes the requisite relationship of dependence. Moreover, there will be no adjudication of liability against a bona fide successor "without affording it a full opportunity at a hearing, after adequate notice, to present evidence on the question of whether it is a successor which is responsible for remedying a predecessor's unfair labor practices. The successor will also be entitled, of course, to be heard against the enforcement of any order issued against it." 164 N.L.R.B., at 969.

In this case, All American has no complaint that it was denied due notice and a fair hearing. It was made a party to the supplemental backpay specification proceeding, given notice of the hearing, and afforded full opportunity, with the assistance of counsel, to contest the question of its successorship for purposes of the Act and its knowledge of the pendency of the unfair labor practice litigation at the time of purchase.

We now turn to the question whether the Board properly exercised its discretion in issuing the order against All American. The Board's decisional process has involved striking a balance between the conflicting legitimate interests of the bona fide successor, the public, and the affected employee. What we said of the Board's decisional process in another context is pertinent here: "The ultimate problem is the balancing of the conflicting legitimate interests. The function of striking that balance to effectuate national labor policy is often a difficult and delicate responsibility, which the Congress committed primarily to the National Labor Relations Board, subject to limited judicial review." *NLRB v. Truck Drivers Local Union 449 International Brotherhood of Teamsters*, 353 U.S. 87, 96 (1957).

The Board's decisions emphasize protection for the victimized employee. The Board found support for this policy in *John Wiley & Sons, Inc. v. Livingston*, 376 U.S. 543, 549 (1964): 'Employees ordinarily do not take part in negotiations leading to a change in corporate ownership. The negotiations will ordinarily not concern the well-being of the employees, whose advantage or disadvantage, potentially great, will inevitably be incidental to the main considerations. The objectives of national labor policy, reflected in established principles of federal law, require that the rightful prerogative of owners independently to rearrange their businesses and even eliminate themselves as employers be balanced by some protection to the employees from a sudden change in the employment relationship.'

When a new employer, such as All American, has acquired substantial assets of its predecessor and continued, without interruption or substantial change, the predecessor's business operations, those employees who have been retained will understandably view their job situations as essentially unaltered. Under these circumstances, the employees may well perceive the successor's failure to remedy the predecessor employer's unfair labor practices arising out of an unlawful discharge as a continuation of the predecessor's labor policies. To the extent that the employees' legitimate expectation is that the unfair labor practices will be remedied, a successor's failure to do so may result in labor unrest as the employees engage in collective activity to force remedial action. Similarly, if the employees identify the new employer's labor policies with those of the predecessor but do not take collective action, the successor may benefit from the unfair labor practices due to a continuing deterrent effect on union activities. Moreover, the Board's experience may reasonably lead it to believe that employers intent on suppressing union activity may select for discharge those employees most actively engaged in union affairs, so that a failure to reinstate may result in a leadership vacuum in the bargaining unit.

Avoidance of labor strife, prevention of a deterrent effect on the exercise of rights guaranteed employees by § 7 of the Act, 29 U.S.C. § 157, and protection for the victimized employee—all important policies subserved by the National Labor Relations Act—are achieved at a relatively minimal cost to the bona fide successor. Since the successor must have notice before liability can be imposed, 'his potential liability for remedying the unfair labor practices is a matter which can be reflected in the price he pays for the business, or he may secure an indemnity clause in the sales contract which will indemnify him for liability arising from the seller's unfair labor practices.' Perma Vinyl Corp., 164 N.L.R.B., at 969. If the reinstated employee does not effectively perform, he may, of course, be discharged for cause.

Affirmed.

NOTE: PURCHASERS OF COMPANIES SUBJECT TO INJUNCTIVE DECREES

In *Golden State*, the Court qualified its holding in the following way: "A purchasing company cannot be obligated to carry out under § 10(c) every outstanding and unsatisfied order of the Board. For example, because the purchaser is not obligated by the Act to hire any of the predecessor's employees, the purchaser, if it does not hire any or a majority of those employees, will not be bound by an outstanding order to bargain issued by the Board against the predecessor or by any order tied to the continuance of the bargaining agent in the unit involved."

4. NOTICE REQUIREMENT

Although the Constitution and various federal statutes generally require that an injunction proceeding be conducted only with notice to opposing parties (and after service of the summons and complaint), TROs can be issued *ex parte*. As a result, some interested parties may not be present (or represented) at the hearing. Thus, they may not know that an injunction has been issued. As a general rule, *ex parte* hearings might be regarded as violative of statutory and constitutional provisions requiring notice to opposing parties (of the filing of suit, and service of the summons and complaint) and an opportunity to appear and defend. Fed. R. Civ. P. 65(d) responds to this problem by providing that a TRO or preliminary injunction is binding only on those "who receive actual notice of the order by personal service or otherwise."[2]

But how specific must the notice be? Actual service on the defendant is clearly sufficient. In *Hsu v. United States*, 392 A.2d 972, 976 (D.C.App.1978), plaintiff's attorney saw defendant in the courthouse (defendant was there on another matter), and told him of the TRO hearing that was about to take place. Defendant failed to appear at the hearing. After obtaining the order, plaintiff's attorney sought out defendant and personally served the order on him. The attorney took a city housing inspector along to serve as a witness.[3] Suppose that plaintiff had used a less direct means of service. Would the notice still be sufficient?

THE CAPE MAY & SCHELLINGER'S LANDING R.R. CO. V. JOHNSON

35 N.J.Eq. Rep. 422 (Ch., 1882).

VAN FLEET, V.C. The defendants are before the court on a charge of contempt. On the 20th day of June, 1881, an order was made directing the city council of the city of Cape May to desist and refrain from passing a certain ordinance, and also to show cause, at a subsequent day, why an injunction should not issue restraining the same act. The order was granted at Newark about midday on the day of its date. The council, it was understood, were to meet on the evening of the same day for the purpose of doing the act which the order was intended to restrain. The distance between the point where the order was made and the point where the defendants were to meet, rendered an actual service of the order impossible before the next day. Notice of the fact that an order had

---

2 Under Kentucky Rule 65.03(5), "A restraining order becomes effective and binding on the party to be restrained at the time of service or when he is informed of the order, whichever is earlier." Under Kentucky Rule 65.04(4), somewhat different rules apply to temporary injunctions: "A temporary injunction becomes effective and binding on the party enjoined when the order is entered."

3 In *Hsu*, defendant later denied in court, under oath, that he was served with the order. The *Hsu* case involved a perjury charge that grew out of defendant's statements.

been made prohibiting the passage of the ordinance was sent to the president of the council by telegraph, which he received before the council convened on the evening of the 20th, and afterwards read to the council in open meeting. A special messenger, sent by the complainants, gave the council the same notice while they were in session on the evening of the 20th. The council the next day (June 21st) passed the ordinance.

The facts just stated are undisputed. They show that the defendants are guilty. The regularity, validity or correctness of the order contemned cannot be examined on this proceeding. While an order of a court remains in force it must be obeyed. Even if it was improvidently granted or irregularly obtained, it must nevertheless be respected until it is annulled by the proper authority.

The notice that the defendants had of the order, at the time they violated the command, was, according to the authorities, entirely sufficient. Where the charge is that the defendant has willfully contemned the authority of the court, all that need be shown is that he knew of the existence of the order at the time he violated it. Lord Eldon held that if a defendant is in court when an injunction is granted, he has sufficient notice of it to make it his duty to respect it. He also held that if the defendant is not in court when an order for an injunction is made, but is informed that such an order has been made, by a person who was in court when the order was made, he has sufficient notice of the injunction to render him liable to punishment for its breach. *Vansandau v. Rose, 2 Jac. & Walk. 264.*

Notice given by telegraph has recently been adjudged in England to be sufficient. The solicitor of the party obtaining the injunction, immediately after it was granted, notified the defendant, by telegram, that an injunction had been granted. The defendant disregarded the notice, and proceeded to do what the notice informed him he had been commanded not to do. The defendant was brought before the court on a charge of contempt, and Bacon, V.C., held that the telegram constituted sufficient notice, and adjudged the defendant guilty of contempt. *In re Bryant*, L.R. (4 Ch. Div.) 98.

Notice, to be sufficient, need possess but two requisites—first, it must proceed from a source entitled to credit; and second, it must inform the defendant clearly and plainly from what act he must abstain. The notice in the case under consideration possessed both requisites. It was sent by the counsel who obtained the order, and it not only informed the defendants what act the order prohibited, but warned them, if they disregarded the order, their disobedience would be a contempt of the authority of the court. There is nothing in the conduct of the defendants indicating that they had the least doubt concerning the authenticity of the notice or the truth of its contents. They made no inquiry respecting its authenticity or its truth, but say that they consulted counsel whether or not they could safely disregard it, and were advised that they could. This advice, to say the least of it, was both injudicious and dangerous. It affords the defendants neither justification nor palliation. They must be adjudged guilty of contempt.

While the fact that the order contemned was improvidently or erroneously made, neither justifies nor excuses the defendants, it is a matter which it is proper the court should consider in awarding punishment. Each of the six defendants must pay to the clerk, for the use of the state, a fine of $10, and they must also jointly pay the taxed costs of this proceeding.

PROBLEMS

1. *Service of the Court Order.* Suppose that, in the *Cape May* case, one of the defendants was actually served with a copy of the court order which specifically informed him of the prohibited acts. However, defendant did not believe that it was a court order because it did not contain a fancy seal and an accompanying red ribbon. Did defendant receive sufficient notice of the injunction? Does defendant's error mean that he did not receive notice from a source "entitled to credit?"

2. *Notifying the Striking Teachers.* When a court issues an order involving a large number of defendants, the court may have difficulty providing actual notice to all of them. For example, suppose that a teacher's union decides to go on strike, and so many teachers are absent (hundreds of them) that the school board closes all schools. In an effort to reopen the schools, the board seeks and obtains an injunction against the union and the teachers requiring the teachers to return to work. The order is signed at noon on a Wednesday afternoon.

In an effort to inform its membership, the Union calls a members meeting for that very evening. The local sheriff attends the meeting and personally serves 66 teachers with a copy of the order. In addition, he makes a list of 213 teachers who answered the roll call at the meeting. Once the roll is called, the sheriff uses a microphone to read a copy of the restraining order to the assembled teachers. Since some teachers were not personally served, and were not present at the meeting, the local newspaper ran a front page article discussing the court's decision and the injunctive order. Nevertheless, some 75 teachers fail to report for work and fail to call in sick.

The school board seeks and obtains a show cause order against the absent teachers. Which of the following teachers can be held in contempt under the order? a) A teacher who was personally served with a copy of the injunctive order, but failed to read it; b) A teacher who was present at the meeting, although not served with a copy of the order, who heard the announcement regarding the order; c) A teacher who was present at the meeting, although not served with a copy of the order, who failed to hear the announcement of the order (because she was in the bathroom); d) A teacher who did not attend the meeting, was not served with a copy of the order, but did see the newspaper article; e) A teacher who did not attend the meeting, was not served with a copy of the order, and failed to see the newspaper article. *See Joint School District No. 1 v. Wisconsin Rapids Education Ass'n*, 70 Wis.2d 292, 234 N.W.2d 289 (1975).

MIDLAND STEEL PRODUCTS CO. V. INTERNATIONAL UNION, UNITED AUTOMOBILE, AEROSPACE AND AGRICULTURAL IMPLEMENT WORKERS OF AMERICA, LOCAL 486

61 Ohio St.3d 121, 573 N.E.2d 98 (1991).

MOYER, CHIEF JUSTICE.

[An injunction prohibited picketing outside Midland Steel Product Co's plant, and specifically mentioned certain union members. Union members, not named in the injunction, were charged with violating the order.]

The parties agree that the appellants, except for Tate, were bound by the TRO only if they, as persons in active concert, received "actual notice of the order whether by personal service or otherwise." They disagree about the meaning of the phrase "actual notice of the order." Midland Steel contends that "actual notice of the order" requires only that the person have general knowledge that an order has been issued, rather than specific knowledge regarding the terms of the order. We reject this contention. A court's order is an "order" only to the extent of its terms. To know an order, one must know its terms. Criminal contempt must be proven beyond a reasonable doubt. We therefore must determine whether the trial court could reasonably conclude beyond a reasonable doubt that the appellants had actual notice of those TRO terms that they were convicted of violating. Although the evidence is not overwhelming, we conclude that the evidence was sufficient under this standard of review.

It is well-established that the state of mind of an accused may be proven by circumstantial evidence. In particular, "proof of the elements of criminal contempt may be established by circumstantial evidence." *Walker v. City of Birmingham* (1967), 388 U.S. 307, 312 fn. 4. The trial court reasonably could have concluded that the appellants were aware of the terms of the TRO. The evidence showed that a number of the appellants' associates had their attention drawn directly to the TRO by way of attempted personal service or posting. Fifteen to twenty copies of the TRO were distributed shortly after its issuance, and the TRO was delivered to the union hall. Local president McGhee clearly was aware of the terms of the TRO, and was present when six of the appellants, and possibly a seventh, committed their acts of misconduct. A newspaper provided another source by which union members' attention could have been drawn to the TRO.

Despite the existence of these numerous possible sources of information regarding the TRO, the appellants contend that the evidence showed that they at most knew of the limit of two pickets per entrance. Four of the appellants, Tate, Orbas, Gregg, and Monahan, testified to that effect. Appellants contend that their compliance with the two-picket limit showed only that they knew of that limit, not the other limits in the TRO. These arguments are not persuasive. In light of the availability and probable notoriety of the TRO among picketers because of publicity and posting, the trial court reasonably could have rejected the appellants' contention that the union leadership had successfully shielded them from knowledge of the TRO terms. In combination with the other circumstances in this case, the appellants' knowledge of the two-picket limit, as demonstrated by their compliance with that limit, raises an inference that they knew of the other limits in the TRO.

Finally, we note the particular evidence concerning Tate, Orbas, Vano, and Monahan. Tate testified that he was responsible for assigning persons to picket duty and overseeing the conduct of the strike. Vano testified that he performed similar assignment duties as a strike "coordinator." The trial court could have inferred from this evidence that they had special access in those positions to knowledge regarding the TRO. Furthermore, both Orbas and Monahan admitted that they had performed picket duty prior to their misconduct. Their performance of picket duty raised an inference that they had seen the copies of the TRO that were posted at the facility's entrances. In light of the foregoing evidence, we find the evidence sufficient to support the criminal contempt convictions of each of the appellants.

WRIGHT, JUSTICE, CONCURRING.

Individual service of process on all striking workers of restraining orders would be next to impossible and far less effective than posting the orders at picket sites and at union halls. A striking employee can avoid service of process for weeks, thereby clothing the striker with ignorance of the restraining order and immunity therefrom under the dissent's rationale. Service by certified mail may be refused, personal service may be avoided, and service by ordinary mail may easily be disclaimed under the dissent's beyond-a-reasonable-doubt standard for actual notice of restraining order contents. The posting of restraining orders at picket sites and at union halls coupled with personal service on union leaders makes defendants' disclaimer of notice look rather incredible.

DOUGLAS, JUSTICE, DISSENTING.

The majority makes quantum leaps of assumption in order to arrive at its desired result. In doing so, the majority ignores the facts of record, the Civil Rules and the case law of this court. Against this "evidence" we have the sworn testimony of the defendants that, at most, they were aware that there was some court order and that the order limited pickets to two per entrance—a section of the order, incidentally, that defendants were not charged with or convicted of violating. The majority still finds that the criminal contempt of the defendants was "proven beyond a reasonable doubt." The record is clear as to the volatility and confusion surrounding the strike. This is not unlike most work stoppages that are being hotly contested—especially when an attempt is being made to break a strike with replacement workers. To assume that each person on the picket line knows the terms of an order, absent, of course, a general announcement either at the picket line or at a union meeting attended by those persons charged with violation, is to ignore reality. Without the majority's presumption upon presumption, there is no showing that beyond a reasonable doubt, the defendants herein had the notice of the order as required by Civ.R. 65(D).

ALICE ROBIE RESNICK, JUSTICE, dissenting.

Persons who do not receive actual notice cannot be bound by an injunction or restraining order. In order to give actual notice of the contents of a TRO, something more has to be done than simply posting copies thereof on the building entrances and placing a number of copies in circulation. We must be able to say with substantial certainty that they all had an opportunity to receive a copy of the TRO and acquaint themselves with it. Actual notice can never be presumed or inferred from the facts. It must be clearly established by the evidence that each individual involved actually had an opportunity to be served or otherwise be informed of the contents of the TRO. Actual notice was not given to the contemnors in this case and therefore the judgment of the court of appeals should be reversed.

NOTE: MORE ON MIDLAND

In *Midland*, defendant Tate was named as a party, but claimed that he could not be held in contempt because he had not been served at the time he violated the court's order. The court disagreed. Justice Douglas dissented: "Tate was a named party. Therefore, Tate could not be bound by an order he had never received unless, of course, we make another one of the giant leaps of faith of the majority and assume he must have known about the order because others in the vicinity had heard about it. We move very quickly from the sublime to the ridiculous."

PROBLEM: MORE ON THE DIAMOND DERBY GALA

Assume that the judge has granted an injunction against the Diamond Derby Gala, and that you are the plaintiff's attorney. How would you go about providing legally binding notice to the parties? Would you provide notice to anyone else? How? Why?

VERMONT WOMEN'S HEALTH CENTER V. OPERATION RESCUE

159 Vt. 141, 617 A.2d 411 (1992).

DOOLEY, JUSTICE.

On October 24, 1989, a group of more than fifty persons, including the remaining defendants, physically invaded the grounds and building of the health center. They blocked doorways and exits of the building and positioned a ten-wheel truck to block the driveway. Many of them locked themselves to one another in the hallways of the building; they made a great deal of noise singing and chanting. As a result, health services for women scheduled for that day, including cancer-related examinations and other tests, as well as abortions, were cancelled. Two police officers were injured as they attempted to enter the building through doors pulled shut by protesters. The use of mace and tear gas was ultimately required to gain entry and control. Once inside, the chief of police read the face sheet of the injunction, listing the prohibited activities, in a loud and clear voice, in each of the two main wings of the building. Police then arrested defendants and the other protesters for unlawful trespass and removed them from the building.

Plaintiffs subsequently brought a civil contempt action against defendants for violation of the TRO, serving each with copies of the court's order and the motion for contempt. Following evidentiary hearings, the court found defendants in contempt, held them liable to plaintiffs for certain fees, costs, and damages, and subjected them to prospective coercive fines to be assessed in the event of future violations of the court's order. This appeal followed.

Defendants argue that the court's findings were erroneous. V.R.C.P. 65(d) sets forth the elements necessary for enforcement of an injunction against persons unnamed in the order. Plaintiffs must show that defendants acted in concert or participation with named parties, that the order was specific and unambiguous, and that they violated the order with actual knowledge of its mandate. All defendants have stipulated that they acted in concert and participation with defendants McHugh and Operation Rescue in an effort to stop abortion procedures that they believed were to take place that day. The clarity of the court's order is undisputed. Defendants claim that except for McHugh they lacked actual notice of the TRO on that day. Certain of the defendants further argue that their actions did not amount to a violation of the TRO's provisions.

There was no direct evidence that a number of the defendants had personal knowledge of the injunction prior to their arrest, and many testified that they were unaware of the existence of the order until after they had been arrested and no longer had an opportunity to comply. The trial court determined that the circumstantial evidence put on by plaintiffs on the issue of notice was more credible than the claims and denials made by defendants.

In addition to Michael McHugh, defendant Mary Alexander admitted in her testimony to having known of the order prior to her participation in the protest. As for the other defendants, all but four—Kathryn Trudell, Richard Trudell, Ann Kenney and Jennifer Rock—were present in a part of the building in which the police chief read the order aloud. If those who were present for the reading did not hear and understand the injunction, it was because they sang and chanted in an attempt to drown out the officer's voice. In addition, each of these defendants was handed a copy of the injunction and offered a chance to leave before being arrested. When they refused to take the copy of the injunction, a copy was placed on their person.

Kathryn Trudell was on the porch during the readings and could not hear them. She testified that she had been in court for contempt proceedings earlier in 1989 against defendant McHugh and others for a prior violation of the same injunction. The court found that her assertion that she did not understand the nature of those proceedings and remained unaware of the order was not credible.

The remaining defendants did not attend earlier court proceedings enforcing the court's order and were not present in the parts of the building where the chief read the injunction. Police witnesses testified, however, that all of the defendants were told, after the locks had been removed and defendants were free to move about, that their trespassing was in violation of a court order and that they could leave without being arrested. In addition, police placed a copy of the injunction on the person or nearby each of these defendants when they refused to take it.

Courts in other jurisdictions have held that actual notice can be found based on the kind of evidence that was presented here. We concur with the court that it could consider the actions of defendants in attempting to drown out the reading of the injunction. Such conduct is probative that they were already aware of the content of the order and were trying to prevent the formality of notice. We do not accept that the concerted actions to defeat notice can be effective for that purpose. There was substantial, credible evidence to support the trial court's findings that each defendant knew of the terms of the order. At a minimum, the findings are supported by testimony that police officers informed each protester, prior to making an arrest, that the protester was violating a court order and could leave without being arrested and placed a copy of the order on or near each protester.

5. BOND REQUIREMENT

At both the federal level and the state level, one who obtains a preliminary injunction or a TRO must usually post security to protect the defendant against loss. Rule 65(c) of the Federal Rules of Civil Procedure provides as follows:

> "(c) **Security.** The court may issue a preliminary injunction or a temporary restraining order only if the movant gives security in an amount that the court considers proper to pay the costs and damages sustained by any party found to have been wrongfully enjoined or restrained. The United States, its officers, and its agencies are not required to give security."

NINTENDO OF AMERICA, INC. V. LEWIS GALOOB TOYS, INC.

16 F.3d 1032 (9th Cir. 1994).

DAVID R. THOMPSON, CIRCUIT JUDGE:

Nintendo of America, Inc. appeals execution of a $15 million bond in favor of Lewis Galoob Toys, Inc. Nintendo posted the bond as security for a preliminary injunction against Galoob in a copyright infringement action Nintendo later lost. The district court awarded Galoob the entire amount of the bond after finding the injunction caused Galoob at least $15 million in damages. We affirm.

We review *de novo* a district court's decision to execute a bond. *Matek v. Murat,* 862 F.2d 720, 733 (9th Cir.1988). An allegation that a district court ignored legal procedure raises a question of law we also review *de novo. Anderson v. United States,* 966 F.2d 487, 489 (9th Cir.1992). A district court's computation of damages is a finding we review under the clearly erroneous standard. *Stephens v. City of Vista,* 994 F.2d 650, 655 (9th Cir.1993).

The first issue is whether Galoob was wrongfully enjoined. We conclude it was. We then consider what standard we should apply to ascertain whether the district court erred in determining that Galoob was entitled to damages. Finally, we consider whether the district court erred in computing the amount of damages. Rule 65(c) of the Federal Rules of Civil Procedure provides: No restraining order or preliminary injunction shall issue except upon the giving of security by the applicant, in such sum as the court deems proper, for the payment of such costs and damages as may be incurred or suffered by any party who is found to have been wrongfully enjoined or restrained. Fed.R.Civ.P. 65(c).[3] A party has been wrongfully enjoined within the meaning of Rule 65(c) when it turns out the party enjoined had the right all along to do what it was

[3] Because this case involves a preliminary injunction rather than a temporary restraining order, we use the term "wrongfully enjoined" rather than "wrongfully restrained."

enjoined from doing.[4] *See Blumenthal v. Merrill Lynch, Pierce, Fenner & Smith, Inc.*, 910 F.2d 1049, 1054 (2d Cir.1990).

Here, Nintendo obtained a preliminary injunction enjoining Galoob from selling the Game Genie. As it turned out, Galoob prevailed in the underlying litigation. The district court held Galoob could sell the Game Genie and vacated the preliminary injunction. We affirmed. Thus, Galoob was wrongfully enjoined. Is Galoob entitled to have the bond executed in its favor? Although there seems to be some variance in how other circuits respond to this question, we join what appears to be the majority and hold there is a rebuttable presumption that a wrongfully enjoined party is entitled to have the bond executed and recover provable damages up to the amount of the bond. *See, e.g., National Kidney Patients Ass'n v. Sullivan,* 958 F.2d 1127 (D.C.Cir.1992), *cert. denied,* 506 U.S. 1049 (1993).

We believe this rule is sound. By adhering to this standard, the party enjoined will usually recover damages, thus discouraging parties from requesting injunctions based on tenuous legal grounds. *See Coyne–Delaney Co. v. Capital Dev. Bd.,* 717 F.2d 385 (7th Cir.1983). Furthermore, a presumption that damages will be awarded from the bond assures district court judges that defendants will receive compensation for their damages in cases where it is later determined a party was wrongfully enjoined. Moreover, demands on judicial resources may be relieved to some extent, because a defendant who can recover damages against a preliminary injunction bond will be less likely to file a separate malicious prosecution action. Finally, this standard provides an equitable means by which courts can decline to impose damages on the rare party who has lost a case on the merits but nevertheless should not suffer the execution of the preliminary injunction bond.

Nintendo argues it rebutted this presumption. Nintendo points out it acted in good faith in bringing its copyright infringement lawsuit, Galoob failed to assert defenses to the preliminary injunction it could have asserted at the preliminary injunction hearing, public policy favors the issuance of injunctions in intellectual property infringement suits, and to award Galoob $15 million imposes a punitive sanction against Nintendo. We reject Nintendo's good faith argument. Good faith in the maintenance of litigation is the standard expected of all litigants. That a party lives up to this standard simply means the party did what it ought to have done. On the other hand, if a party obtains a preliminary injunction in bad faith, that party "flunks the good faith test and the presumption in favor of enforcement of the bond congeals virtually into a rock." *National Kidney,* 958 F.2d at 1135.

---

[4] Rule 65(c) speaks in terms of a party who has been "wrongfully enjoined," rather than an injunction as having been "wrongfully issued." Fed.R.Civ.P. 65(c). A court that complies with the applicable law in issuing a preliminary injunction does not "wrongfully" issue it.

Nintend argues that Galoob failed to assert all of its defenses at the time. The essence of this argument is that Galoob took advantage of Nintendo by initially making its case appear to be worse than it really was, thus lulling Nintendo into obtaining the preliminary injunction. The implication is that Galoob cunningly got the court to raise the amount of the bond on two successive occasions, finally pushing it up to $15 million, while concealing the hole cards it intended to play at the time of trial. Nintendo argues it would be inequitable to permit Galoob to recover damages when it pursued such wily litigation tactics.

There is no indication that Galoob sandbagged Nintendo into prevailing on its application for the preliminary injunction, knowing all the while that it could have defeated that application. All that appears is that Galoob had additional defenses it asserted at the time of trial, defenses it had not asserted at the preliminary injunction hearing. While it is true Galoob persuaded the court on two successive occasions to increase the amount of the bond, thus raising the stakes of the game, it is also true that Nintendo called these raises by putting up additional amounts of the bond. We conclude Galoob's litigation conduct does not preclude it from recovering on the bond.

Nintendo's public policy argument is premised on its assertion that public policy favors the issuance of injunctions in intellectual property infringement lawsuits. This assertion is correct only when a *permanent* injunction is sought once infringement has been established. *See, e.g., Universal City Studios, Inc. v. Sony Corp. of Am.*, 659 F.2d 963, 976 (9th Cir.1981), *rev'd on other grounds*, 464 U.S. 417 (1984). Public policy does not advocate the liberal issuance of *preliminary* injunctions in copyright infringement actions.

The damage award was not punitive, but compensatory. Every dollar the court awarded to Galoob compensated it for the injury it had suffered because of the injunction. *Cf. Coyne–Delaney*, 717 F.2d at 392.

We next consider whether the district court erred in determining that Galoob suffered at least $15 million in damages by reason of the issuance of the injunction. Nintendo argues the court failed to require Galoob to meet any burden of proof in establishing its damages. The record belies this contention. In its order directing entry of partial judgment, the district court stated, "Galoob has proved by a preponderance of the evidence that it sustained actual injury as a result of the wrongful issuance of the preliminary injunction." The court explicitly named the standard it applied to Galoob and explicitly stated Galoob met that burden.

Nintendo argues that Galoob failed to prove with reasonable certainty that it suffered any damage. *See Palmer v. Connecticut Ry. & Lighting Co.*, 311 U.S. 544, 561 (1941). According to Nintendo, Galoob was not damaged by the injunction because the injunction only delayed

Game Genie sales, it did not prevent them permanently. That is, although NES owners who wanted to purchase the Game Genie in 1990 could not do so because of the injunction, they most likely waited a year until the injunction was lifted, and then bought the product anyway. This argument is premised on speculation, and "defies common sense." Galoob established with reasonable certainty that it was damaged by the issuance of the injunction.

Did the district court err in computing the amount of damages Galoob suffered? "The district court's computation of damages is insulated from review unless clearly erroneous." *Laborers Clean–Up Contract Admin. Trust Fund v. Uriarte Clean–Up Serv., Inc.,* 736 F.2d 516, 520 n. 2 (1984). Throughout its calculation of damages, the district court chose figures favoring Nintendo. The court assumed the Game Genie would sell only as well as the Nintendo Advantage, even though the Advantage was, in its opinion, "not as versatile or long-lasting a peripheral" as the Game Genie. When the court checked the accuracy of its estimate of lost sales, using the Canadian multiplier method, it chose a figure of 190,000 Canadian sales, which was "at the conservative end of the level," and used a multiplier of eleven, which was far below the multiplier of thirty-eight that the Advantage enjoyed. The court also adopted Galoob's highest estimate of its anticipated 1992 sales. It then deducted this high-end estimate, together with Galoob's actual 1991 sales, from the total sales it determined Galoob would have made "but for" the issuance of the injunction. In sum, in determining the number of lost sales, the district court repeatedly used the most conservative ends of available ranges. While it is true that Galoob did not likely lose *exactly* 1.6 million sales of the Game Genie, it is reasonably certain it lost at least that amount. The district court's method of calculating the number of lost sales was not erroneous.

With regard to the court's finding that Galoob's profit margin for the Game Genie was 27.6 percent, the court began with the "rational and reliable" estimate of Galoob's economist that the profit margin was 42.74 percent, considered the evidence and contentions of the parties and reduced that figure to 27.6 percent. It did not clearly err in making this finding.

Galoob was wrongfully enjoined from selling the Game Genie. As a result, it was presumptively entitled to recover damages. Nintendo did not rebut this presumption. Galoob proved with reasonable certainty it was damaged by the injunction. The district court did not err in finding Galoob's damages exceeded the $15 million amount of the bond. Galoob was entitled to have the full amount of the bond executed in its favor.

AFFIRMED.

COYNE–DELANY CO., INC. V. CAPITAL DEVELOPMENT BOARD

717 F.2d 385 (7th Cir.1983).

POSNER, CIRCUIT JUDGE.

The State of Illinois's Capital Development Board let a contract for replacement of plumbing fixtures in a prison cellhouse, and Coyne–Delany Co. was awarded a subcontract to install flush valves. The valves were installed, but malfunctioned. When Coyne–Delany shipped redesigned valves which also malfunctioned, the prison authorities asked the Capital Development Board to designate another valve subcontractor. The Board received new bids. Two days before the bids were to be unsealed, Coyne–Delany obtained a temporary restraining order preventing the Board from opening the bids.

The state asked that Coyne–Delany be ordered to post a $50,000 bond, pointing out that the temporary restraining order was preventing it from proceeding with the entire project and that indefinite delay could be extremely costly. But the judge required a bond of only $5,000.

Coyne–Delany's civil rights suit against the Capital Development Board was based on case law which suggested that the state had violated Coyne–Delaney's property rights. After the trial judge granted the preliminary injunction, we held that a bidder has no property right in being allowed to bid on a public contract and that Coyne–Delany therefore had no claim against the Board under the Fourteenth Amendment.

The Board moved the district court to award the Board damages of $56,000 for the wrongfully issued preliminary injunction and statutory costs of $523. Judge Bua refused to award either costs or damages.

The Board must have lost much more than $5,000 on the difference in the bids alone. And it may well have incurred other costs from the delay of the project by a year.

The language of Rule 65(c) does not tell the court in so many words to order the applicant to pay the wrongfully enjoined party's damages. But it is told to require a bond or equivalent security in order to ensure that the plaintiff will be able to pay all or at least some of the damages that the defendant incurs from the preliminary injunction if it turns out to have been wrongfully issued. The draftsmen must have intended that when such damages were incurred the plaintiff or his surety would normally be required to pay the damages, at least up to the limit of the bond. Plaintiffs dismiss Rule 65(c)'s requirement of a bond or other security by pointing out that the district court can require a bond of nominal amount in appropriate cases, for example if the plaintiff is indigent. But it is one thing to say that the requirement of a bond can be waived when there is a good reason for doing so and another to say that where a substantial bond is clearly required by the equities of the case the district court nevertheless has carte blanche to excuse the plaintiff from paying any damages on the bond.

Most cases hold that a prevailing defendant is entitled to damages on the injunction bond unless there is a good reason for not requiring the plaintiff to pay in the particular case. We agree with the majority approach. Not only is it implied by the text of Rule 65(c) but it makes the law more predictable and discourages the seeking of preliminary injunctions on flimsy (though not necessarily frivolous) grounds.

It is not a sufficient reason for denying costs or damages on an injunction bond that the suit had as in this case been brought in good faith. That would be sufficient only if the presumption were against rather than in favor of awarding costs and damages on the bond to the prevailing party, as it would be if the issue were attorney's fees under the American rule, which in the absence of bad faith leaves each party to bear his own attorney's fees. The award of damages on the bond is not punitive but compensatory.

A good reason for not awarding such damages would be that the defendant had failed to mitigate damages. We find no such failure in this case. A good reason for awarding damages in this case was that the bond covered only a small fraction of the defendant's damages. The Board asked for and should have been granted a much larger bond; and when the heavy damages that the Board had predicted in asking for the larger bond materialized, it had a strong equitable claim to recover its damages up to the limit of the bond. The plaintiff is not a poor person but a substantial corporation that will not be crushed by having to pay $5,523 in damages and costs. It is difficult to understand the judge's refusal to award any damages, or the trivial amount of costs, conceded to be reasonable in amount, asked by the defendant.

In deciding whether to withhold costs or injunction damages, not only is the district court to be guided by the implicit presumption in Rules 54(d) and 65(c) in favor of awarding them, but the ingredients of a proper decision are objective factors—such as the resources of the parties, the defendant's efforts or lack thereof to mitigate his damages, and the outcome of the underlying suit—accessible to the judgment of a reviewing court. In the spectrum of decisions embraced by the overly broad and unfortunately named "abuse of discretion" standard, the decision to deny costs and injunction damages is near the end that merges into the standard of simple error used in reviewing decisions of questions of law.

We are not prepared to hold that the Board is entitled as a matter of law to its costs and to its injunction damages up to the limit of the bond. We do not believe that a change in the law is always a good ground for denying costs and injunction damages to a prevailing party, but it is a legitimate consideration. In any event, a remand is necessary to allow Judge Bua to consider and weigh all the relevant factors.

It remains to consider whether on remand the Board should be allowed to seek injunction damages above the limit of the bond. The surety cannot be required to pay more than the face amount of the bond, but it is a separate question whether the plaintiff can be. The Ninth Circuit has held that the bond is the limit of the damages the defendant can obtain for a wrongful injunction, even from the plaintiff, provided the plaintiff was acting in good faith, which is not questioned here. (Another exception might be where the plaintiff was seeking restitution rather than damages.) The Supreme Court has held that "a party injured by the issuance of an injunction later determined to be erroneous has no action for damages in the absence of a bond." *W.R. Grace & Co. v. Local Union 759, United Rubber Workers*, 461 U.S. 757, 770 n. 14 (1983). Although there was a bond in the present case, it states unequivocally: "The obligation of this bond is limited to $5,000.00." In asking for more, the Board is necessarily relying not on the bond but on some principle of equity that *Grace* says does not exist.

Rightly or wrongly, American common law, state and federal, does not attempt to make the winner of a lawsuit whole by making the loser reimburse the winner's full legal expenses, even when the winner is the defendant, who unlike a prevailing plaintiff does not have the consolation of a damage recovery. In noninjunctive suits, except those brought (or defended) in bad faith, the winner can recover only his statutory costs, invariably but a small fraction of his expenses of suit. It would be incongruous if a prevailing defendant could obtain the full, and potentially the staggering, consequential damages caused by a preliminary injunction. The preliminary injunction in this case halted work on a major construction project for a year; it could easily have been two or three years, and the expenses imposed on the defendant not $56,000 but $560,000. It might be a very great boon to the legal system of this country to discourage injunction suits by putting plaintiffs at such risk, but we do not see how such an approach can be squared with the general attitude toward litigation implied by the American rule on attorney's fees. Although that rule may soon have to be curtailed to cope with the flood of litigation in the state and federal courts today, we are not authorized to curtail it.

A right to injunction damages potentially unlimited in amount would be in one sense a more extreme remedy against a losing litigant than allowing the winner to have his attorney's fees reimbursed. Not only would the amounts involved be much greater in some cases, but the burden of the rule would fall entirely on plaintiffs. Of course, having to post a bond is also a deterrent just to plaintiffs. But if the plaintiff's damages are limited to the amount of the bond, at least he knows just what his exposure is when the bond is set by the district court. It is not unlimited. If the bond is too high he can drop the suit.

A defendant's inability to obtain damages in excess of the bond unless the plaintiff was acting in bad faith can have unfortunate results, which are well illustrated by this case where the district court required too small a bond. But a defendant dissatisfied with the amount of bond set by the district court can, on appeal from the preliminary injunction, ask the court of appeals to increase the bond which the defendant here did not do. A defendant who wanted the court of appeals to increase the bond would have to ask for accelerated consideration of his request in order to mitigate his damages and thus reduce the plaintiff's exposure.

Since Coyne–Delany is conceded to have brought this suit in good faith, the Board is not entitled to any damages above the $5,000 fixed in the bond. * * *

NOTES

1. *Is the Bond Requirement Mandatory?* Under the Federal Rules of Civil Procedure, the requirement of a bond is mandatory. In general, the court must hold findings and determine the appropriate amount of security to be required. *See Hill v. Xyquad, Inc.*, 939 F.2d 627, 632 (8th Cir. 1991) ("Although we allow the district court much discretion in setting bond, we will reverse its order if it abuses that discretion due to some improper purpose, or otherwise fails to require an adequate bond or to make the necessary findings in support of its determinations."). However, courts have discretion regarding the amount of the bond. For example, in *Nicole Davis v. Mineta*, 302 F.3d 1104, 1126 (10th Cir. 2002), a case in which plaintiff sought to enjoin construction of a public highway, the court held that: "when a party is seeking to vindicate the public interest, a minimal bond amount should be considered." *See also Friends of the Earth, Inc. v. Brinegar*, 518 F.2d 322 (9th Cir.1975). In some instances, when the plaintiff is indigent, and the public interest is implicated by the case, courts have refused to require any bond at all. *See Moltan Company v. Eagle–Picher Industries, Inc.*, 55 F.3d 1171 (6th Cir. 1995) ("the rule in our circuit has long been that the district court possesses discretion over whether to require the posting of security."); *Borough of Palmyra, Board of Education v. F.C.*, 2 F. Supp.2d 637 (D. N.J. 1998).

2. *Recovering Damages for a Wrongfully Issued Injunction.* The general rule is that, in the absence of a bond, there can be no recovery for damages sustained from the wrongful issuance of a preliminary injunction, aside from suit for malicious prosecution or unjust enrichment. In addition, even when a bond is posted, ordinarily a party's liability is limited by the terms of the bond or the order of the court that required the posting. *See Buddy Systems, Inc. v. Exer–Genie, Inc.*, 545 F.2d 1164 (9th Cir. 1976). However, when a low injunction bond is imposed *ex parte*, and the trial court wrongfully rejects defendant's request for an evidentiary hearing on the size

of the bond, the court might permit a wrongfully enjoined party to recover more than the amount of the bond. *See SeaEscape, Ltd., Inc. v. Maximum Marketing Exposure, Inc.*, 568 So.2d 952 (Fla. App. 1990). In addition, liability might be imposed when a statute provides for it, or by other source (*e.g.*, under Rule 11 of the Fed. R. Civ. P.), and when plaintiff has sought and obtained an exemption from the bond requirement.

PROBLEM: THE SCHOOL BOARD AND THE PARENTS

Parents sue a school board under Section 504 of the Rehabilitation Act, 29 U.S.C. § 794. The parents claim that their child suffers from Attention Deficit Hyperactivity Disorder (ADHD), that the school district cannot adequate respond to his needs, and therefore the student's parent's argue that the board should be required to pay the tuition and transportation costs for the child's attendance at private school. Suppose that you are the judge, and you decided to issue a preliminary injunction requiring the board to pay the costs. You believe that the parents have a high likelihood of success on the merits. How large of a bond should be required? Suppose that the annual tuition and transportation costs would run $25,000. Should the court require a $25,000 bond? Suppose that the parents are of relatively limited means and cannot afford to post a bond. Can the bond requirement be waived altogether? Is that fair to the board? *See Borough of Palmyra, Board of Education v. F.C.*, 2 F. Supp.2d 637 (D.N.J. 1998).

SMITH V. CORONADO FOOTHILLS ESTATES HOMEOWNERS ASS'N, INC.

117 Ariz. 171, 571 P.2d 668 (In Banc, 1977).

CAMERON, CHIEF JUSTICE.

We granted this petition for review to answer only one question: May the recovery of damages for wrongful injunction exceed the amount of the bond given pursuant to Rule 65(e), Arizona Rules of Civil Procedure?

Appellee, Coronado Foothills Estates Homeowners Association (Association), filed a complaint for permanent injunction on 4 June 1974, against Mrs. Beulah Smith, appellant, claiming it would be irreparably damaged if Mrs. Smith was allowed to continue building her home contrary to deed restrictions. The Association, without notice to Mrs. Smith, obtained a temporary restraining order on the day the complaint was filed prohibiting Mrs. Smith from further construction of her residence alleged to be in violation of deed restrictions. The court set the amount of bond as $10. Mrs. Smith was served with the temporary restraining order on 10 June 1974. The temporary restraining order was dissolved by the trial court on 13 June 1974 after Mrs. Smith was heard on the matter pursuant to the order to show cause. On 28 June 1974, the trial court determined a preliminary injunction could not issue.

The trial court and the Court of Appeals determined that under Rule 65(e), Arizona Rules of Civil Procedure, Mrs. Smith's recovery was limited to the $10 cash bond. We do not agree.

In the instant case, we are concerned with a bond issued with a temporary restraining order obtained ex parte. A bond is usually required at this stage in order to indemnify the party enjoined for damages incurred as a result of an improperly granted restraining order obtained without an opportunity by the party to be heard.

Rule 65(e) of the Arizona Rules of Civil Procedure, 16 A.R.S., provides: "Security. No restraining order or preliminary injunction shall issue except upon the giving of security by the applicant, in such sum as the court deems proper, for the payment of such costs and damages as may be incurred or suffered by any party who is found to have been wrongfully enjoined or restrained. No such security shall be required of the State or of an officer or agency thereof."

This rule is almost identical to Federal Rule of Civil Procedure, Rule 65(c). The federal courts as well as an overwhelming majority of the state courts hold that recovery for wrongful injunction is limited to the amount of the bond unless malicious prosecution is shown. "The philosophy of the matter is that an error in granting an injunction is an error of the court, for which there is no recovery in damages unless the same is sufficiently intentional as to be the basis of a suit for malicious prosecution, otherwise the damage is damnum absque injuria." *United Motors Service, Inc. v. Tropic–Aire, Inc.*, 57 F.2d 479, 483 (8th Cir.1932). * * *

The majority view ignores the procedures usually involved in obtaining a temporary restraining order at the commencement of a lawsuit. The application is usually made ex parte and the court has no opportunity to hear from the person being enjoined or restrained. If the attorney for the plaintiff believes, as he usually does, that his cause is just and that there are few or no equities on the side of the person being sued, he can feel justified in suggesting to the court that only a nominal bond is necessary. To give a party what, in actual practice, amounts to the right to limit the amount of damages that may be recovered against him is too great a temptation even to the most fair minded. Having caused the injury in the first place, we see no injustice in allowing a recovery for actual damages against the party who asked for and obtained the wrongful issuance of the injunction. "The amount of the bond in such cases is usually little more than an estimate by the court based upon matters of opinion or ex parte statements, and, where it proves to be wholly inadequate to cover the injured party's actual damages, we see no good reason why the party causing the damage should not be held responsible for it. This rule, of course, would not apply to the sureties on the injunction bond. Their liability is limited to the amount fixed in the bond." *Miller Surfacing Co. v. Bridgers*, 269 S.W. 838, 840 (Tex.Civ.App.1924).

In the instant case the $10 cash bond was patently insufficient to provide the security "for the payment of such costs and damages as may be incurred or suffered by any party who is found to have been wrongfully enjoined or restrained." Arizona Rules of Civil Procedure, 65(e), 16 A.R.S. Therefore, we hold that the Association is liable beyond the amount of the bond for damages incurred or suffered as the result of the wrongful temporary restraining order.

The judgment of the trial court is reversed and the matter remanded for proceedings not inconsistent with this opinion. The opinion of the Court of Appeals is vacated.

CONTINUUM CO., INC. V. INCEPTS, INC.

873 F.2d 801 (5th Cir.1989).

ALVIN B. RUBIN, CIRCUIT JUDGE:

The issue is whether a district court order increasing the amount of a bond to be provided for an interlocutory injunction previously issued and dissolving the injunction for failure to post the increased bond should be stayed pending appeal of the order.

The Continuum Company, Inc. sued Incepts, Inc., and others in Texas state court for alleged appropriations of trade secrets, breaches of contract, and breaches of confidential relationships, contending that Incepts had wrongfully used Continuum's computer-software system. In addition to other relief, Continuum sought an injunction to prevent Incepts' use of the software. After an eleven-week hearing, the Texas court issued a temporary injunction against Incepts, granting most of the relief Continuum had sought on the condition that Continuum post a $200,000 bond for any damages Incepts might suffer if it proved the injunction to have been wrongfully issued. The court also set an expedited trial date.

Nine months later Incepts filed a motion in federal district court to dissolve the injunction or, alternatively, to increase the bond from $200,000 to $5,000,000. The district court entered an order continuing the injunction in force on the condition that the bond be increased to $2,000,000. On April 11, Continuum appealed this order and sought a stay of that part of the order increasing the bond pending the appeal. We granted a stay pending further orders of the court. * * *

Fed.R.Civ.Proc. 65(c) provides that a bond must be posted before a federal court may issue an interlocutory injunction and that the enjoined defendant may recover on the bond if a court later determines that it was "wrongfully enjoined." This bond requirement serves two functions: (1) it assures the enjoined party that it may readily collect damages from the funds posted or the surety provided in the event that it was wrongfully enjoined, without further litigation and without regard to the possible insolvency of the assured, and (2) it provides the plaintiff with notice of the maximum extent of its potential liability, since the amount of the bond "is the limit of the damages the defendant can obtain for a wrongful injunction, provided the plaintiff was acting in good faith." The bond can thus be viewed as a contract in which the court and plaintiff "agree" to the bond amount as the "price" of a wrongful injunction.

While a district court's failure to require the posting of a bond or other security constitutes grounds for reversal of the injunction, some courts have waived the security requirement when they have found that the plaintiff was financially responsible or was very likely to succeed on the merits. Courts that have waived the bond requirement have apparently assumed that, should the plaintiff later lose on the merits, the defendant may recover the damages inflicted by the injunction. That assumption was rendered doubtful, however, by the Supreme Court's declaration in *W.R. Grace & Co. v. Local Union 759* that "a party injured by the issuance of an injunction later determined to be erroneous has no action for damages in the absence of a bond."

Courts that have waived the bond requirement have done so without determining whether the plaintiff should be excused from liability even if it had wrongfully obtained the injunction. If the plaintiff's claim subsequently proved to be nonmeritorious, the court would be compelled either to follow the rule that restricts liability to the bond amount and thus unjustly deny the defendant compensation, or to compensate the defendant, thus defeating the reasonable expectations of the plaintiff under Rule 65(c).

In this case, the district court increased the already substantial bond of $200,000 to ensure that Incepts would be compensated for any additional damages that it might suffer in the time before trial. When the appeal is heard on the merits, it appears that there is a substantial likelihood that Continuum may obtain an order continuing the injunction in effect and reducing the amount of the bond, for Incepts proffered little more than conclusory evidence to support its contention that the bond should be increased. In contrast, Continuum has presented evidence that its annual profit is $2.5 million, indicating that it would be able to satisfy any judgment for damages that might be obtained against it as a result of a wrongful issuance of the injunction, but that providing a bond in the amount of $2,000,000 would impose great hardship on it and, as a practical matter, might well render the injunction infeasible or useless.

Because Incepts might suffer damages in excess of $200,000 if the injunction were eventually held to have been wrongfully issued, it should be shielded against that contingency if protection can be provided without imposing undue hardship on Continuum. We, therefore, stay, pending decision of the appeal to this court, the order of the district court modifying the amount of the bond, contingent upon Continuum continuing its bond of $200,000 in full force and, in addition, filing an undertaking with this court that the amount of the bond will not limit the amount of damages for which it might be liable, should it be liable for any, as a result of a wrongful issuance of the injunction.

The STAY of the district court's order dissolving the injunction and increasing the amount of the bond is CONTINUED in effect pending further orders of this court.

NOTE: MORE ON BOND RECOVERIES

Even though a temporary restraining order is vacated, courts have discretion to deny recovery on the bond. In *Kansas ex rel. Stephan v. Adams*, 705 F.2d 1267 (10th Cir.1983), plaintiff obtained a temporary restraining order requiring defendants to continue operating passenger trains on certain routes. After Congress enacted a law authorizing the discontinuation of passenger service on the routes in question, the temporary injunction was vacated. Thereafter, defendants sought to recoup the costs incurred in operating trains subject to the TRO. The trial court denied the request, and the Tenth Circuit affirmed: "The decision whether to award damages, and the extent thereof, is in the discretion of the district court and is based upon considerations of equity and justice. A court, in considering the matter of damages, must exercise its equity power and must effect justice between the parties, avoiding an inequitable result. The end result is that a defendant who is wrongfully enjoined will not always be made whole by recovery of damages. In our judgment the trial court did not abuse its discretion by holding that costs and expenses were not to be awarded. The record discloses that the plaintiffs raised valid environmental concerns. Moreover, the restraining order was vacated not because the concerns on the part of plaintiffs-appellees were unfounded. It was the intervention of Congress that brought about the change."

PROBLEMS

1. *More on the Diamond Derby Gala.* Assume that you are the judge assigned to hear the case, and you have decided to issue an injunction against the Diamond Derby Gala. How large of a bond should be required?

2. *The Ex-Employee.* Webb Printing has a custom publishing division which creates, designs, prints and distributes custom magazines for companies across the United States. Webb hired Neal Fosshage, who had 27 years of experience in marketing, as an account executive. Fosshage solicited business and assisted Webb's clients in developing marketing strategies. Fosshage was the primary contact between Webb and four of its clients that produced $1.7 million of Webb's annual $3.8 million in custom publishing

revenue. As part of the hire, Webb required Fosshage to sign an agreement not to compete for at least 18 months after he left Webb's employ.

When Webb terminated Fosshage's employment, because of his aggressive style, Fosshage started his own custom publishing corporation and solicited Webb's clients who cancelled their contracts. Webb brought this action seeking injunctive relief and damages based on Fosshage's noncompetition agreement. Webb claims that it has lost forty-five percent of its revenue, suffered damage to its business reputation, and suffered indeterminable future loss. The trial court granted the temporary restraining order (for 10 days) prohibiting Fosshage until further order from soliciting any of Webb's customers. What amount of bond should be imposed? *See Webb Publishing Co. v. Fosshage*, 426 N.W.2d 445 (Minn.App.1988).

3. *More on* Hughes v. Cristofane. In *Hughes v. Cristofane*, *supra* at 174, the court entered the following order: "(3) that plaintiffs give security by filing forthwith with the Clerk of this Court a bond in the sum of $500.00 for the payment of such costs and damages as may be incurred or suffered by defendants if found to be wrongfully enjoined or restrained." Was the $500 bond adequate? If your answer is "no," how much bond should have been required?

4. Hughes*: Take Three.* Suppose that the City of Bladensburg had tried to enjoin Hughes from having topless dancing at his bar. Would a $500 bond have been adequate? What amount would be appropriate?

5. *The Bond in* Vuitton. In the *Vuitton* case that we examined earlier with reference to the notice requirement, we saw that the Court issued an *ex parte* TRO permitting the seizure of defendant's merchandise. How large of a bond should be required in such a case? How will (should) the fact that the TRO is issued *ex parte* affect the amount of the bond?

6. *The Washington Capitols' Case.* In *Washington Capitols Basketball Club, Inc. v. Barry*, *supra* at 191, the court ordered the basketball club to post a $100,000 bond. Was this bond sufficient? Why was it so much higher than the bond required in *Hughes*?

7. *Posting Bond in the* Melvin *Case.* The amount of the bond will vary from case to case. Consider the *Melvin* case, *supra,* in which a student sought an order readmitting her to school. How much bond should be required in a case like that?

C. PERMANENT INJUNCTIONS

EBAY INC. V. MERCEXCHANGE, L.L.C.

547 U.S. 388, 126 S.Ct. 1837, 164 L.Ed.2d 641 (2006).

JUSTICE THOMAS delivered the opinion of the Court.

Ordinarily, a federal court considering whether to award permanent injunctive relief to a prevailing plaintiff applies the four-factor test historically employed by courts of equity. Petitioners eBay Inc. and Half.com, Inc., argue that this traditional test applies to disputes arising under the Patent Act. We agree and, accordingly, vacate the judgment of the Court of Appeals.

Petitioner eBay operates a popular Internet Web site that allows private sellers to list goods they wish to sell, either through an auction or at a fixed price. Petitioner Half.com, now a wholly owned subsidiary of eBay, operates a similar Web site. Respondent MercExchange, L.L.C., holds a number of patents, including a business method patent for an electronic market designed to facilitate the sale of goods between private individuals by establishing a central authority to promote trust among participants. MercExchange sought to license its patent to eBay and Half.com, as it had previously done with other companies, but the parties failed to reach an agreement. MercExchange subsequently filed a patent infringement suit against eBay and Half.com in the United States District Court for the Eastern District of Virginia. A jury found that MercExchange's patent was valid, that eBay and Half.com had infringed that patent, and that an award of damages was appropriate.

Following the jury verdict, the District Court denied MercExchange's motion for permanent injunctive relief. The Court of Appeals for the Federal Circuit reversed, applying its "general rule that courts will issue permanent injunctions against patent infringement absent exceptional circumstances." We granted certiorari to determine the appropriateness of this general rule.

According to well-established principles of equity, a plaintiff seeking a permanent injunction must satisfy a four-factor test before a court may grant such relief. A plaintiff must demonstrate: (1) that it has suffered an irreparable injury; (2) that remedies available at law, such as monetary damages, are inadequate to compensate for that injury; (3) that, considering the balance of hardships between the plaintiff and defendant, a remedy in equity is warranted; and (4) that the public interest would not be disserved by a permanent injunction. See, *e.g., Weinberger v. Romero–Barcelo,* 456 U.S. 305 (1982); *Amoco Production Co. v. Gambell,* 480 U.S. 531 (1987). The decision to grant or deny permanent injunctive relief is an act of equitable discretion by the district court, reviewable on appeal for abuse of discretion. See, *e.g., Romero–Barcelo,* 456 U.S., at 320.

These familiar principles apply with equal force to disputes arising under the Patent Act. As this Court has long recognized, "a major departure from the long tradition of equity practice should not be lightly implied." *Ibid.* Nothing in the Patent Act indicates that Congress intended such a departure. To the contrary, the Patent Act expressly provides that injunctions "may" issue "in accordance with the principles of equity." 35 U.S.C. § 283.[2]

To be sure, the Patent Act also declares that "patents shall have the attributes of personal property," including "the right to exclude others from making, using, offering for sale, or selling the invention," § 154(a)(1). According to the Court of Appeals, this statutory right to exclude alone justifies its general rule in favor of permanent injunctive relief. But the creation of a right is distinct from the provision of remedies for violations of that right. Indeed, the Patent Act itself indicates that patents shall have the attributes of personal property "subject to the provisions of this title," including, presumably, the provision that injunctive relief "may" issue only "in accordance with the principles of equity," § 283.

This approach is consistent with our treatment of injunctions under the Copyright Act. Like a patent owner, a copyright holder possesses "the right to exclude others from using his property." *Fox Film Corp. v. Doyal,* 286 U.S. 123, 127. Like the Patent Act, the Copyright Act provides that courts "may" grant injunctive relief "on such terms as it may deem reasonable to prevent or restrain infringement of a copyright." 17 U.S.C. § 502(a). This Court has consistently rejected invitations to replace traditional equitable considerations with a rule that an injunction automatically follows a determination that a copyright has been infringed. See, *e.g., New York Times Co. v. Tasini,* 533 U.S. 483 (2001).

Neither the District Court nor the Court of Appeals below fairly applied these traditional equitable principles in deciding respondent's motion for a permanent injunction. Although the District Court recited the traditional four-factor test, it appeared to adopt certain expansive principles suggesting that injunctive relief could not issue in a broad swath of cases. Most notably, it concluded that a "plaintiff's willingness to license its patents" and "its lack of commercial activity in practicing the patents" would be sufficient to establish that the patent holder would not suffer irreparable harm if an injunction did not issue. But traditional equitable principles do not permit such broad classifications. For example, some patent holders, such as university researchers or self-made inventors, might reasonably prefer to license their patents, rather than undertake efforts to secure the financing necessary to bring their works to market themselves. Such patent holders may be able to satisfy the traditional four-factor test, and we see no basis for categorically denying them the opportunity to do so. To the extent that the District Court adopted such a categorical rule, then, its analysis cannot be squared with the principles of equity adopted by Congress.

---

2 Section 283 provides that "[t]he several courts having jurisdiction of cases under this title may grant injunctions in accordance with the principles of equity to prevent the violation of any right secured by patent, on such terms as the court deems reasonable."

In reversing the District Court, the Court of Appeals departed in the opposite direction from the four-factor test. The court articulated a "general rule," unique to patent disputes, "that a permanent injunction will issue once infringement and validity have been adjudged." The court further indicated that injunctions should be denied only in the "unusual" case, under "exceptional circumstances" and " 'in rare instances to protect the public interest.' " Just as the District Court erred in its categorical denial of injunctive relief, the Court of Appeals erred in its categorical grant of such relief. Cf. *Roche Products v. Bolar Pharmaceutical Co.,* 733 F.2d 858, 865 (C.A.Fed.1984).

Because we conclude that neither court below correctly applied the traditional four-factor framework that governs the award of injunctive relief, we vacate the judgment of the Court of Appeals, so that the District Court may apply that framework in the first instance. We hold only that the decision whether to grant or deny injunctive relief rests within the equitable discretion of the district courts, and that such discretion must be exercised consistent with traditional principles of equity, in patent disputes no less than in other cases governed by such standards.

Accordingly, we vacate the judgment of the Court of Appeals, and remand for further proceedings consistent with this opinion.

It is so ordered.

CHIEF JUSTICE ROBERTS, with whom JUSTICE SCALIA and JUSTICE GINSBURG join, concurring.

I agree with the Court's holding that "the decision whether to grant or deny injunctive relief rests within the equitable discretion of the district courts, and that such discretion must be exercised consistent with traditional principles of equity, in patent disputes no less than in other cases governed by such standards," and I join the opinion of the Court. From at least the early 19th century, courts have granted injunctive relief upon a finding of infringement in the vast majority of patent cases. This "long tradition of equity practice" is not surprising, given the difficulty of protecting a right to *exclude* through monetary remedies that allow an infringer to *use* an invention against the patentee's wishes—a difficulty that often implicates the first two factors of the traditional four-factor test. This historical practice, as the Court holds, does not *entitle* a patentee to a permanent injunction or justify a *general rule* that such injunctions should issue. At the same time, there is a difference between exercising equitable discretion pursuant to the established four-factor test and writing on an entirely clean slate.

JUSTICE KENNEDY, with whom JUSTICE STEVENS, JUSTICE SOUTER, and JUSTICE BREYER join, concurring.

The Court is correct to hold that courts should apply the well-established, four-factor test—without resort to categorical rules—in deciding whether to grant injunctive relief in patent cases. To the extent earlier cases establish a pattern of granting an injunction against patent infringers almost as a matter of course, this pattern simply illustrates the result of the four-factor test in the contexts then prevalent.

In cases now arising trial courts should bear in mind that in many instances the nature of the patent being enforced and the economic function of the patent holder present considerations quite unlike earlier cases. An industry has developed in which firms use patents not as a basis for producing and selling goods but, instead, primarily for obtaining licensing fees. See FTC, To Promote Innovation: The Proper Balance of Competition and Patent Law and Policy, Ch. 3, pp. 38–39 (Oct.2003). For these firms, an injunction, and the potentially serious sanctions arising from its violation, can be employed as a bargaining tool to charge exorbitant fees to companies that seek to buy licenses to practice the patent. When the patented invention is but a small component of the product the companies seek to produce and the threat of an injunction is employed simply for undue leverage in negotiations, legal damages may well be sufficient to compensate for the infringement and an injunction may not serve the public interest. In addition injunctive relief may have different consequences for the burgeoning number of patents over business methods, which were not of much economic and legal significance in earlier times. The potential vagueness and suspect validity of some of these patents may affect the calculus under the four-factor tests of the cases before them. With these observations, I join the opinion of the Court.

PROBLEMS

1. *Applying the Test.* On remand, assuming that you represent Merc–Exchange, L.L.C., how would you argue that injunctive relief is appropriate? What kinds of evidence might help you establish the need for injunctive relief? Now, assuming that you represent eBay Inc. and Half.com, Inc., how would you respond to these arguments? What types of evidence might help establish these arguments?

2. *The Overgrown Trees.* Defendant planted ten elm trees on his own property close to the line between his and plaintiff's property. Over the years, the trees grew very large and the tree trunks now encroach on plaintiff's property by fourteen inches. The land adjacent to the trees on plaintiff's side is vacant and is used primarily for growing alfalfa or other field crops. The evidence suggests that plaintiff's actions in providing water and nutrients to crops located on her land have caused the trees to grow toward her property and that defendant negligently maintained the elm trees, allowing the roots and branches to damage the crops on plaintiff's property and rendering the land near the trees less productive. Removing the portion of the trees that are on plaintiff's land would cause them to die. However, the roots can be

trenched and the branches can be trimmed. The total for all of these actions, including damage to plaintiff's property, would cost $420.80 per year.

Plaintiff would prefer to force defendant to cut down and remove all the trees which encroach on the boundary line. Defendant objects noting that, to cut out any portion of the trunk of the trees would have a substantial detrimental effect on the remainder of the tree. In addition, defendant argues that the trees are attractive and enhance the value of defendant's property, and that the trees are not interfering with any residence or physical structure on the property of plaintiff, or causing any damage or harm thereto.

If you are hired to represent plaintiff, how would you argue that he is entitled to permanent injunctive relief? Now, assuming that you are instead hired to represent defendant, how would you respond to those arguments? Could plaintiff have exercised self-help? Why do you think plaintiff sought injunctive relief rather than choosing to exercise this option? *See Garcia v. Sanchez*, 108 N.M. 388, 772 P.2d 1311 (1989).

WALGREEN COMPANY V. SARA CREEK PROPERTY COMPANY, B.V.

966 F.2d 273 (7th Cir. 1992).

POSNER, CIRCUIT JUDGE.

This appeal from the grant of a permanent injunction raises fundamental issues concerning the propriety of injunctive relief. The essential facts are simple. Walgreen has operated a pharmacy in the Southgate Mall in Milwaukee since its opening in 1951. Its current lease, carrying a 30-year, 6-month term, contains a clause in which the landlord, Sara Creek, promises not to lease space in the mall to anyone else who wants to operate a pharmacy or a store containing a pharmacy. Such an exclusivity clause, common in shopping-center leases, is occasionally challenged on antitrust grounds, but that is an issue for another day. In 1990, fearful that its largest tenant—the "anchor tenant"—having gone broke was about to close its store, Sara Creek informed Walgreen that it intended to buy out the anchor tenant and install a discount store operated by Phar–Mor Corporation, a "deep discount" chain, rather than, like Walgreen, just a "discount" chain. Phar–Mor's store would occupy 100,000 square feet, of which 12,000 would be occupied by a pharmacy the same size as Walgreen's. The entrances to the two stores would be within a couple of hundred feet of each other.

Walgreen filed this diversity suit for breach of contract against Sara Creek and Phar–Mor and asked for an injunction against Sara Creek's letting the anchor premises to Phar–Mor. After a hearing, the judge found a breach of Walgreen's lease and entered a permanent injunction against Sara Creek's letting the anchor tenant premises to Phar–Mor until the expiration of Walgreen's lease. He did this over defendants' objection that

Walgreen had failed to show that its remedy at law—damages—for the breach of the exclusivity clause was inadequate. Sara Creek put on an expert witness who testified that Walgreen's damages could be readily estimated, and Walgreen countered with evidence from its employees that its damages would be very difficult to compute, among other reasons because they included intangibles such as loss of goodwill.

Sara Creek reminds us that damages are the norm in breach of contract as in other cases. Many breaches, it points out, are "efficient" in the sense that they allow resources to be moved into a more valuable use. *Patton v. Mid–Continent Systems, Inc.,* 841 F.2d 742 (7th Cir.1988). Perhaps this is one—the value of Phar–Mor's occupancy of the anchor premises may exceed the cost to Walgreen of facing increased competition. If so, society will be better off if Walgreen is paid its damages, equal to that cost, and Phar–Mor is allowed to move in rather than being kept out by an injunction. That is why injunctions are not granted as a matter of course, but only when the plaintiff's damages remedy is inadequate. *Northern Indiana Public Service Co. v. Carbon County Coal Co.,* 799 F.2d 265 (7th Cir.1986). The projection of business losses due to increased competition is a routine exercise in calculation. Damages representing either the present value of lost future profits or (what should be the equivalent, *Carusos v. Briarcliff, Inc.,* 76 Ga.App. 346, 45 S.E.2d 802 (1947)) the diminution in the value of the leasehold have either been awarded or deemed the proper remedy in a number of reported cases for breach of an exclusivity clause in a shopping-center lease. *Coach House of Ward Parkway, Inc. v. Ward Parkway Shops, Inc.,* 471 S.W.2d 464 (Mo.1971); *Krikorian v. Dailey,* 171 Va. 16, 197 S.E. 442 (1938). Why, Sara Creek asks, should they not be adequate here?

Sara Creek makes a beguiling argument that contains much truth, but we do not think it should carry the day. If damages have been awarded in some cases of breach of an exclusivity clause in a shopping-center lease, injunctions have been issued in others. *Handy Andy Home Improvement Centers, Inc. v. American National Bank & Trust Co.,* 177 Ill.App.3d 647, 126 Ill.Dec. 852, 532 N.E.2d 537 (1988). The choice between remedies requires a balancing of the costs and benefits of the alternatives. *Hecht Co. v. Bowles,* 321 U.S. 321 (1944); *Yakus v. United States,* 321 U.S. 414. 834 (1944). The task of striking the balance is for the trial judge, subject to deferential appellate review in recognition of its particularistic, judgmental, fact-bound character. As we said in an appeal from a grant of a preliminary injunction—but the point is applicable to review of a permanent injunction as well—"The question for us appellate judges is whether the district judge exceeded the bounds of permissible choice in the circumstances, not what we would have done if we had been in his shoes." *Roland Machinery Co. v. Dresser Industries, Inc.,* 749 F.2d 380, 390 (7th Cir.1984).

The plaintiff who seeks an injunction has the burden of persuasion—damages are the norm, so the plaintiff must show why his case is abnormal. But when the issue is whether to grant a permanent injunction, not whether to grant a temporary one, the burden is to show that damages are inadequate, not that the denial of the injunction will work irreparable harm. "Irreparable" in the injunction context means not rectifiable by the entry of a final judgment. *Diginet, Inc. v. Western Union ATS, Inc.,* 958 F.2d 1388, 1393 (7th Cir.1992). It has nothing to do with whether to grant a permanent injunction, which, in the usual case anyway, *is* the final judgment. The use of "irreparable harm" or "irreparable injury" as synonyms for inadequate remedy at law is a confusing usage. It should be avoided.

The benefits of substituting an injunction for damages are twofold. First, it shifts the burden of determining the cost of the defendant's conduct from the court to the parties. If it is true that Walgreen's damages are smaller than the gain to Sara Creek from allowing a second pharmacy into the shopping mall, then there must be a price for dissolving the injunction that will make both parties better off. Thus, the effect of upholding the injunction would be to substitute for the costly processes of forensic fact determination the less costly processes of private negotiation. Second, a premise of our free-market system, and the lesson of experience here and abroad as well, is that prices and costs are more accurately determined by the market than by government. A battle of experts is a less reliable method of determining the actual cost to Walgreen of facing new competition than negotiations between Walgreen and Sara Creek over the price at which Walgreen would feel adequately compensated for having to face that competition.

That is the benefit side of injunctive relief but there is a cost side as well. Many injunctions require continuing supervision by the court, and that is costly. *Roland Machinery Co. v. Dresser Industries, Inc., supra,* 749 F.2d at 391–92. A request for specific performance (a form of mandatory injunction) of a franchise agreement was refused on this ground in *North American Financial Group, Ltd. v. S.M.R. Enterprises, Inc.,* 583 F.Supp. 691 (N.D.Ill.1984). Some injunctions are problematic because they impose costs on third parties. *Shondel v. McDermott,* 775 F.2d 859 (7th Cir.1985). A more subtle cost of injunctive relief arises from the situation that economists call "bilateral monopoly," in which two parties can deal only with each other: the situation that an injunction creates. *Goldstick v. I.C.M. Realty,* 788 F.2d 456 (7th Cir.1986). The sole seller of widgets selling to the sole buyer of that product would be an example. But so will be the situation confronting Walgreen and Sara Creek if the injunction is upheld. Walgreen can "sell" its injunctive right only to Sara Creek, and Sara Creek can "buy" Walgreen's surrender of its right to enjoin the leasing of the anchor tenant's space to Phar–Mor only from Walgreen. The lack of alternatives in bilateral monopoly creates a bargaining range, and the costs of negotiating to a point within that range may be high. Suppose the cost to Walgreen of facing the competition of Phar–Mor at the Southgate Mall would be $1 million, and the benefit to Sara Creek of leasing to Phar–Mor would be $2 million. Then at any price between those figures for a waiver of Walgreen's injunctive right both parties would be better off, and we expect parties to bargain around a judicial assignment of legal rights if the assignment is inefficient. R.H. Coase, "The Problem of Social Cost," 3 *J. Law & Econ.* 1 (1960). But each of the parties would like to engross as much of the bargaining range as possible—Walgreen to press the price toward $2 million, Sara Creek to depress it toward $1 million. With so much at stake, both parties will have an incentive to devote substantial resources of time and money to the negotiation process. The process may even break down, if one or both parties want to create for future use a reputation as a hard bargainer; and if it does break down, the injunction will have brought about an inefficient result. All these are in one form or another costs of the injunctive process that can be avoided by substituting damages.

The costs and benefits of the damages remedy are the mirror of those of the injunctive remedy. The damages remedy avoids the cost of continuing supervision and third-party effects, and the cost of bilateral monopoly as well. It imposes costs of its own, however, in the form of diminished accuracy in the determination of value, on the one hand, and of the parties' expenditures on preparing and presenting evidence of damages, and the time of the court in evaluating the evidence, on the other.

The weighing up of all these costs and benefits is the analytical procedure that is or at least should be employed by a judge asked to enter a permanent injunction, with the understanding that if the balance is even the injunction should be withheld. The judge is not required to explicate every detail of the analysis and he did not do so here, but as long we are satisfied that his approach is broadly consistent with a proper analysis we shall affirm; and we are satisfied here. The determination of Walgreen's damages would have been costly in forensic resources and inescapably inaccurate. *Roland Machinery Co. v. Dresser Industries, Inc., supra,* 749 F.2d at 386. The lease had ten years to run. So Walgreen would have had to project its sales revenues and costs over the next ten years, and then project the impact on those figures of Phar–Mor's competition, and then discount that impact to present value. All but the last step would have been fraught with uncertainty.

It is difficult to forecast the profitability of a retail store over a decade, let alone to assess the impact of a particular competitor on that profitability over that period. Of course one can hire an expert to make such predictions, Glen A. Stankee, "Econometric Forecasting of Lost

Profits: Using High Technology to Compute Commercial Damages," 61 *Fla.B.J.* 83 (1987), and if injunctive relief is infeasible the expert's testimony may provide a tolerable basis for an award of damages. Damages have been awarded for the breach of an exclusivity clause in a shopping-center lease because it is better to give a wronged person a crude remedy than none at all. It is the same theory on which damages are awarded for a disfiguring injury. No one thinks such injuries readily monetizable, *City of Panama,* 101 U.S. 453 (1880). Sara Creek presented evidence of what happened (very little) to Walgreen when Phar–Mor moved into other shopping malls in which Walgreen has a pharmacy, and it was on the right track in putting in comparative evidence. But there was a serious question whether the other malls were actually comparable to the Southgate Mall, so we cannot conclude, in the face of the district judge's contrary conclusion, that the existence of comparative evidence dissolved the difficulties of computing damages in this case. Sara Creek complains that the judge refused to compel Walgreen to produce all the data that Sara Creek needed to demonstrate the feasibility of forecasting Walgreen's damages. Walgreen resisted, on grounds of the confidentiality of the data and the cost of producing the massive data that Sara Creek sought. Those are legitimate grounds; and the cost (broadly conceived) they expose of pretrial discovery, in turn presaging complexity at trial, is itself a cost of the damages remedy that injunctive relief saves.

Damages are not always costly to compute, or difficult to compute accurately. In the standard case of a seller's breach of a contract for the sale of goods where the buyer covers by purchasing the same product in the market, damages are readily calculable by subtracting the contract price from the market price and multiplying by the quantity specified in the contract. But this is not such a case and here damages would be a costly and inaccurate remedy; and on the other side of the balance some of the costs of an injunction are absent and the cost that is present seems low. The injunction here, like one enforcing a covenant not to compete (standardly enforced by injunction), is a simple negative injunction—Sara Creek is not to lease space in the Southgate Mall to Phar–Mor during the term of Walgreen's lease—and the costs of judicial supervision and enforcement should be negligible. There is no contention that the injunction will harm an *unrepresented* third party. It may harm Phar–Mor but that harm will be reflected in Sara Creek's offer to Walgreen to dissolve the injunction. (Anyway Phar–Mor *is* a party.) The injunction may also, it is true, harm potential customers of Phar–Mor—people who would prefer to shop at a deep-discount store than an ordinary discount store—but their preferences, too, are registered indirectly. The more business Phar–Mor would have, the more rent it will be willing to pay Sara Creek, and therefore the more Sara Creek will be willing to pay Walgreen to dissolve the injunction.

The only substantial cost of the injunction in this case is that it may set off a round of negotiations between the parties. In some cases, illustrated by *Boomer v. Atlantic Cement Co.,* 26 N.Y.2d 219, 309 N.Y.S.2d 312, 257 N.E.2d 870 (1970), this consideration alone would be enough to warrant the denial of injunctive relief. There is nothing so dramatic here. Sara Creek does not argue that it will have to close the mall if enjoined from leasing to Phar–Mor. Phar–Mor is not the only potential anchor tenant. *Liza Danielle, Inc. v. Jamko, Inc.,* 408 So.2d 735 (Fla.App.1982), on which Sara Creek relies, presented the converse case where the grant of the injunction would have forced an existing tenant to close its store. The size of the bargaining range was also a factor in the denial of injunctive relief in *Gitlitz v. Plankinton Building Properties, Inc.,* 228 Wis. 334, 280 N.W. 415 (1938).

To summarize, the judge did not exceed the bounds of reasonable judgment in concluding that the costs (including forgone benefits) of the damages remedy would exceed the costs (including forgone benefits) of an injunction. We need not consider whether exclusivity clauses in shopping-center leases should be considered presumptively enforceable by injunctions. Although we have described the choice between legal and equitable remedies as one for case-by-case determination, the courts have sometimes picked out categories of case in which injunctive relief is made the norm. The best-known example is specific performance of contracts for the sale of real property. *Anderson v. Onsager,* 155 Wis.2d 504, 455 N.W.2d 885 (1990). The rule that specific performance will be ordered in such cases as a matter of course is a generalization of the considerations discussed above. Because of the absence of a fully liquid market in real property and the frequent presence of subjective values (many a homeowner, for example, would not sell his house for its market value), the calculation of damages is difficult; and since an order of specific performance to convey a piece of property does not create a continuing relation between the parties, the costs of supervision and enforcement if specific performance is ordered are slight. The exclusivity clause in Walgreen's lease relates to real estate, but we hesitate to suggest that every contract involving real estate should be enforceable as a matter of course by injunctions. Suppose Sara Creek had covenanted to keep the entrance to Walgreen's store free of ice and snow, and breached the covenant. An injunction would require continuing supervision, and it would be easy enough if the injunction were denied for Walgreen to hire its own ice and snow remover and charge the cost to Sara Creek. On the other hand, injunctions to enforce exclusivity clauses are quite likely to be justifiable by just the considerations present here—damages are difficult to estimate with any accuracy and the injunction is a one-shot remedy requiring no continuing judicial involvement. So there is an argument for making injunctive relief presumptively appropriate in such cases, but we need not decide in this case how strong an argument.

AFFIRMED.

WEINBERGER V. ROMERO–BARCELO

456 U.S. 305, 102 S.Ct. 1798, 72 L.Ed.2d 91 (1982).

JUSTICE WHITE delivered the opinion of the Court.

The issue is whether the Federal Water Pollution Control Act (FWPCA or Act), 86 Stat. 816, as amended, 33 U.S.C. § 1251 *et seq.* (1976 ed. and Supp. IV), requires a district court to enjoin immediately all discharges of pollutants that do not comply with the Act's permit requirements or whether the district court retains discretion to order other relief to achieve compliance. The Court of Appeals for the First Circuit held that the Act withdrew the courts' equitable discretion. *Romero–Barcelo v. Brown, 643 F.2d 835 (1981).* We reverse.

For many years, the Navy has used Vieques Island, a small island off the Puerto Rico coast, for weapons training. Currently all Atlantic Fleet vessels assigned to the Mediterranean Sea and the Indian Ocean are required to complete their training at Vieques because it permits a full range of exercises under conditions similar to combat. During air-to-ground training, however, pilots sometimes miss land-based targets, and ordnance falls into the sea. That is, accidental bombings of the navigable waters and, occasionally, intentional bombings of water targets occur. The District Court found that these discharges have not harmed the quality of the water.

In 1978, respondents, who include the Governor of Puerto Rico and residents of the island, sued to enjoin the Navy's operations on the island. Their complaint alleged violations of numerous federal environmental statutes and various other Acts. After an extensive hearing, the District Court found that the Navy had violated the Act by discharging ordnance into the waters surrounding the island without first obtaining a permit from the Environmental Protection Agency (EPA).

Recognizing that violations of the Act "must be cured," the District Court ordered the Navy to apply for an NPDES National Pollutant Discharge Elimination System permit. It refused, however, to enjoin Navy operations pending consideration of the permit application. It explained that the Navy's "technical violations" were not causing any "appreciable harm" to the environment. Moreover, because of the importance of the island as a training center, "the granting of the injunctive relief sought would cause grievous, and perhaps irreparable harm, not only to Defendant Navy, but to the general welfare of this Nation." The District Court concluded that an injunction was not necessary to ensure suitably prompt compliance by the Navy. It emphasized an equity court's traditionally broad discretion in deciding appropriate relief. * * *

The Court of Appeals vacated the order and remanded with instructions to order the Navy to cease the violation until it obtained a permit. Relying on *TVA v. Hill*, 437 U.S. 153 (1978), which held that an imminent violation of the Endangered Species Act required injunctive relief, the court concluded that the District Court erred in undertaking a traditional balancing of the parties' competing interests. "Whether or not the Navy's activities in fact harm the coastal waters, it has an absolute statutory obligation to stop any discharges of pollutants until the permit procedure has been followed and the Administrator of the Environmental Protection Agency, upon review of the evidence, has granted a permit." The court suggested that if the order would interfere significantly with military preparedness, the Navy should request that the President grant it an exemption from the requirements in the interest of national security.

Because this case posed an important question regarding the power of the federal courts to grant or withhold equitable relief for violations of the FWPCA, we granted certiorari. We now reverse.

In exercising their sound discretion, courts of equity should pay particular regard for the public consequences in employing the extraordinary remedy of injunction. *Railroad Comm'n v. Pullman Co.*, 312 U.S. 496, 500 (1941). Thus, the Court has noted that "the award of an interlocutory injunction by courts of equity has never been regarded as strictly a matter of right, even though irreparable injury may otherwise result to the plaintiff," and that "where an injunction is asked which will adversely affect a public interest for whose impairment, even temporarily, an injunction bond cannot compensate, the court may in the public interest withhold relief until a final determination of the rights of the parties, though the postponement may be burdensome to the plaintiff." The grant of jurisdiction to ensure compliance with a statute hardly suggests an absolute duty to do so under any and all circumstances, and a federal judge sitting as chancellor is not mechanically obligated to grant an injunction for every violation of law.

These commonplace considerations applicable to cases in which injunctions are sought in the federal courts reflect a "practice with a background of several hundred years of history," a practice of which Congress is assuredly well aware. Of course, Congress may intervene and guide or control the exercise of the courts' discretion, but we do not lightly assume that Congress has intended to depart from established principles. As the Court said in *Porter v. Warner Holding Co.*, 328 U.S. 395, 398 (1946): "Moreover, the comprehensiveness of this equitable jurisdiction is not to be denied or limited in the absence of a clear and valid legislative command. Unless a statute in so many words, or by a necessary and inescapable inference, restricts the court's jurisdiction in equity, the full scope of that jurisdiction is to be recognized and applied. 'The great principles of equity, securing complete justice, should not be yielded to light inferences, or doubtful construction.' "

In *TVA v. Hill*, we held that Congress had foreclosed the exercise of the usual discretion possessed by a court of equity. There, we thought that "one would be hard pressed to find a statutory provision whose terms were any plainer" than that before us. The statute involved, the Endangered Species Act, 87 Stat. 884, 16 U.S.C. § 1531 *et seq.*, which required the District Court to enjoin completion of the Tellico Dam in order to preserve the snail darter, a species of perch. The purpose and language of the statute, not the bare fact of a statutory violation, compelled that conclusion. Section 7 of the Act, 16 U.S.C. § 1536, requires federal agencies to "insure that actions authorized, funded, or carried out by them do not jeopardize the continued existence of any endangered species or result in the destruction or modification of habitat of such species which is determined to be critical." The statute thus contains a flat ban on the destruction of critical habitats. It was conceded in *Hill* that completion of the dam would eliminate an endangered species by destroying its critical habitat. Refusal to enjoin the action would have ignored the "explicit provisions of the Endangered Species Act." Congress, it appeared to us, had chosen the snail darter over the dam. The purpose and language of the statute limited the remedies available to the District Court; only an injunction could vindicate the objectives of the Act.

That is not the case here. An injunction is not the only means of ensuring compliance. The FWPCA itself, for example, provides for fines and criminal penalties. 33 U.S.C. §§ 1319(c) and (d). Respondents suggest that failure to enjoin the Navy will undermine the integrity of the permit process by allowing the statutory violation to continue. The integrity of the Nation's waters, however, not the permit process, is the purpose of the FWPCA.

This purpose is to be achieved by compliance with the Act, including compliance with the permit requirements. Here, however, the discharge of ordnance had not polluted the waters, and, although the District Court declined to enjoin the discharges, it neither ignored the statutory violation nor undercut the purpose and function of the permit system. The court ordered the Navy to apply for a permit. It temporarily, not permanently, allowed the Navy to continue its activities without a permit.

Other aspects of the statutory scheme also suggest that Congress did not intend to deny courts the discretion to rely on remedies other than an immediate prohibitory injunction. Although the ultimate objective of the FWPCA is to eliminate all discharges of pollutants into the navigable waters by 1985, the statute sets forth a scheme of phased compliance. It called for the achievement of the "best practicable control technology currently available" by July 1, 1977, and the "best available technology economically achievable" by July 1, 1983. 33 U.S.C. § 1311(b). This scheme of phased compliance further suggests that this is a statute in which Congress envisioned, rather than curtailed, the exercise of discretion.

Both the Court of Appeals and respondents attach particular weight to the provision of the FWPCA permitting the President to exempt federal facilities from compliance with the permit requirements. 33 U.S.C. § 1323(a) (1976 ed., Supp. IV). They suggest that this provision indicates congressional intent to limit the court's discretion. According to respondents, the exemption provision evidences Congress' determination that only paramount national interests justify failure to comply and that only the President should make this judgment. We read the FWPCA as permitting the exercise of a court's equitable discretion, whether the source of pollution is a private party or a federal agency, to order relief that will achieve compliance with the Act. The exemption serves a different and complementary purpose, that of permitting noncompliance by federal agencies in extraordinary circumstances. * * *

Should the Navy receive a permit here, there would be no need to invoke the machinery of the Presidential exemption. If not, this course remains open. The exemption provision would enable the President, believing paramount national interests so require, to authorize discharges which the District Court has enjoined. Reading the statute to permit the exercise of a court's equitable discretion in no way eliminates the role of the exemption provision in the statutory scheme.

The exercise of equitable discretion, which must include the ability to deny as well as grant injunctive relief, can fully protect the range of public interests at issue at this stage in the proceedings. The District Court did not face a situation in which a permit would very likely not issue, and the requirements and objective of the statute could therefore not be vindicated if discharges were permitted to continue. Should it become clear that no permit will be issued and that compliance with the FWPCA will not be forthcoming, the statutory scheme and purpose would require the court to reconsider the balance it has struck.

Because Congress, in enacting the FWPCA, has not foreclosed the exercise of equitable discretion, the proper standard for appellate review is whether the District Court abused its discretion in denying an immediate cessation order while the Navy applied for a permit. We reverse and remand to the Court of Appeals for proceedings consistent with this opinion.

It is so ordered.

JUSTICE STEVENS, dissenting.

I am convinced that Congress has circumscribed the district courts' discretion on the question of remedy so narrowly that a general rule of immediate cessation must be applied in all but a narrow category of cases. The Court cites no precedent for its holding that an ongoing deliberate violation of a federal statute should be treated like any garden-variety private nuisance action in which the chancellor has the widest discretion in fashioning relief. The Court distinguishes *TVA v. Hill*, 437 U.S. 153, on the ground that the Endangered Species Act contained a "flat ban" on the destruction of critical habitats. The decision in *TVA v. Hill* did not depend on any peculiar or unique statutory language. Nor did it rest on any special interest in snail darters. The decision reflected a profound respect for the law and the proper allocation of lawmaking responsibilities in our Government. There we refused to sit as a committee of review. Today the Court authorizes freethinking federal judges to do just that. Instead of requiring adherence to carefully integrated statutory procedures that assign to nonjudicial decisionmakers the responsibilities for evaluating potential harm to our water supply as well as potential harm to our national security, the Court unnecessarily and casually substitutes the chancellor's clumsy foot for the rule of law.

PROBLEM: MORE ON WEINBERGER

Following *Weinberger*, suppose that Congress decides to amend the FWPCA to limit judicial discretion to apply traditional equitable principles. What language must Congress use to achieve its objective?

D. FRAMING THE INJUNCTION

Whether a court issues a preliminary injunction or a permanent injunction, the court must be concerned about how the order is worded or "framed." Fed. R. Civ. P. 65(d) imposes limits on the form, scope and content of injunctions: "**(d) Contents and Scope of Every Injunction and Restraining Order.** (1) *Contents.* Every order granting an injunction and every restraining order must: (A) state the reasons why it issued; (B) state its terms specifically; and (C) describe in reasonable detail—and not by referring to the complaint or other document—the act or acts restrained or required."

MURRAY V. LAWSON

136 N.J. 32, 642 A.2d 338 (1994).

CLIFFORD, J.

In Boffard v. Barnes, the Appellate Division upheld a Chancery Division restriction forbidding defendants, anti-abortion protestors, from picketing within the immediate vicinity of plaintiffs' residence. Dr. Daryl Boffard is a New Jersey-licensed obstetrician and gynecologist. He practices with an Irvington medical group that offers obstetrical and gynecological care, including abortion services. Defendants, anti-abortion protestors, had been picketing the Irvington clinic for two years before they picketed the Boffard residence. Dr. Boffard lives in a house in Short Hills with his wife, plaintiff Virginia Boffard, and three young children. The Boffard residence is on a quiet cul-de-sac containing only one other house, and the street is so narrow that only one car at a time may traverse it. Because the Boffards do not have a backyard, their children play in the front yard of the house and on an adjoining lot.

On September 8, 1990, approximately twenty picketers gathered in front of the Boffard residence. The picketers carried placards saying, among other things, "Dr. Daryl Boffard Kills Babies" and "God Says Thou Shalt Not Kill." Other signs had pictures; one showed a mutilated full-term baby, and another showed bloody fetal parts with the caption "This is an abortion." When Mrs. Boffard approached the demonstrators, they refused to move. One demonstrator said to her, "Your husband is a murderer." Another demonstrator gave a teenage neighbor a bible and told her, "The doctor who lives there is a murderer."

The Boffard injunction prohibits defendants "from gathering, parading, patrolling for the purpose of demonstrating or picketing within the immediate vicinity of plaintiffs' residence." Because we conclude that the Chancery Division could have more precisely defined the spatial scope of its ban, we remand to that court.

Injunctions are supposed to "be specific in terms; and describe in reasonable detail the act or acts sought to be restrained." R. 4:52–4. The description "within the immediate vicinity of" contained in the Boffard injunction is neither specific nor reasonably detailed. Although defendants do not argue that the restriction is unconstitutionally vague, we are sure that neither the parties nor the police can determine with any certainty how close to plaintiffs' residence "within the immediate vicinity of" can legitimately take one. We could limit that language to preclude picketing "before or about the residence or dwelling of" plaintiffs—a restriction that the Supreme Court upheld in *Frisby, supra,* 487 U.S. at 482, by interpreting it to "prohibit only picketing focused on, and taking place in front of, a particular residence." But "within the immediate vicinity of" seems to prohibit more than picketing only "in front of" plaintiffs' residence. "Vicinity" means "a surrounding area or district: locality, neighborhood," Webster's Third New International Dictionary, 2550 (1971), and "immediate" means "characterized by contiguity: existing without intervening space or substance: being near or at hand: not far apart or distant." *Id.* at 1129.

Because "within the immediate vicinity of" does not describe sufficiently the area in which the injunction's prohibition applies, we remand to the Chancery Division to set forth more precisely the scope of the ban. When imposing the "within the immediate vicinity of" restriction, the Chancery Division may have had a particular area in mind. If so, the court could easily clarify that restriction. We recognize, however, that if it is to impose a more specific restriction, the Chancery Division may have to make additional findings. We are mindful as well that the Chancery Division has great flexibility in defining the scope of the ban; the court could, for example, preclude picketing on plaintiffs' street, or could prohibit that activity within a specific number of feet from, within sight distance of, or in front of plaintiffs's residence. We leave that determination to the Chancery Division.

NOTES

1. *Vagueness Issues.* As the *Murray* case suggests, defendants can sometimes defeat an injunction based on a claim that an injunction is too vague. Recall that this challenge must be made on direct appeal. As *Walker v. City of Birmingham* and *In re Providence Journal Co.*, discussed in the last chapter, suggest, a collateral challenge based on a vagueness argument will not be permitted. Only where the injunction is so vague that it is "transparently invalid or had only a frivolous pretense to validity" might it be collaterally attacked—a rare occurrence, indeed.

2. *More on Vagueness Issues.* Courts rarely conclude that an injunction is so vague as to be invalid and unenforceable except in situations when greater precision is required (*e.g.*, the injunction implicates First Amendment interests). In most cases, the court concludes that, even if an injunction did suffer from some vagueness, it was sufficiently precise so that defendants knew that their conduct was prohibited. Illustrative is *People v. Evans*, 165 Ill.App.3d 942, 117 Ill.Dec. 513, 520 N.E.2d 864 (1988), in which plaintiff was prohibited "from providing mortgages or any other financing" of whatever kind in the State of Illinois. The order also required Evans to notify, in writing, all consumers who had pending loan applications that defendants were so restrained. Thereafter, she cashed a mortgage check and provided mortgage information. The trial court held her in contempt. The order was upheld on appeal: "We cannot agree that the TRO was vague, unclear, or susceptible to more than one interpretation. It was not necessary that the order specify every act leading up to the actual acquisition of the mortgage. Obtaining financing for the purchase of real estate is a process and we agree with the trial court that cashing the check and making phone calls regarding the closing of the deal were acts in furtherance of providing a mortgage or other financing. Therefore these acts were properly construed as acts of contempt. We do not agree that the TRO was too vague and unclear to specifically give Evans notice as to what conduct was prohibited. Based on the evidence in the record, we find that the State proved beyond a reasonable doubt that Evans willfully committed acts in violation of the TRO and for this reason the finding of contempt must be affirmed."

PROBLEMS

1. *The* Murray *Order and Specificity.* In the *Murray* case, how could the Court have made the order specific enough? What language would the court have been forced to use?

2. *Enjoining Picketers.* In *Bettendorf–Stanford Bakery Equipment Co. v. International Union*, 49 Ill.App.3d 20, 6 Ill.Dec. 920, 363 N.E.2d 867 (1977), an employer sought injunctive relief preventing its employees from picketing near its plant. The complaint alleged that picketers were blocking the entrance to the plant, threatening those that attempted to enter the plant, preventing entry to the plant by automobile, and ignoring demands to cease and desist. Assume that the requirements for preliminary injunctive relief have been satisfied, and that the court has decided to enter the injunction. How should it be framed? Would it be appropriate for the court to enter a TRO enjoining defendants from "interfering with and restraining the movement of traffic upon Plaintiff's premises, and from committing any other illegal or unlawful acts of intimidation or acts unrelated to the purposes for which picketing or demonstrations might be conducted." Or is greater specificity required? How could this order be made more specific?

3. *The Stalker.* Robin Matlock seeks injunctive relief against Jon Weets, a man who she dated for a short period (4–5 weeks) before she terminated the relationship. Following the break-up, Jon had difficulty accepting the idea that Robin did not want to see him, and he began following and watching her. He continued to call her and began leaving presents on her front door step. She asked him to stop. He then began sending her cards and letters and jogging by Robin's house on a daily basis. On Valentine's Day, Jon entered Robin's house uninvited, with gifts, laid them on the kitchen table, and left. Robin's mother, who lived with Robin, was startled and frightened by his entering the house. Afterwards. Jon began appearing at various places on Robin's way to and from work, and her lunch hour, suggesting a thorough knowledge of the details of her schedule. On weekends, Jon would pass Matlock's house often beginning at 6:30 a.m., and continuing four to six times before noon. Sometimes Jon followed Robin's car or passed her car at a high rate of speed. These acts made Robin feel fearful and threatened. When Robin saw Jon, she often observed him staring at her. Robin felt threatened by his staring. At one point, Weets sent Matlock some birthday cards, another letter, and a tape. Matlock opened the package because the handwriting had been disguised so she did not realize it was from Jon. In this letter he stated:

> I know I am nothing more than an unpleasant, vague, and faded memory of a mistake in your life. Now I am just completing the cycle for me. You know that everything that happened or didn't happen between us is absolute poetic justice where I am concerned. Rude, crude, and socially unacceptable former saloon keepers, former civil servants, and former ex-cons sometimes referred to as Hollywood Hayden never die, they just disappear into a magical, mystical, and sometimes inebriated haze as the spirit that ignored age finds itself trapped in the beginnings of twilight time. I deeply miss all the time we never spent together and all the things we never did and all the laughter and happiness we never shared.

After receiving this letter, Robin began feeling greater anxiety and fear for her safety. She spoke with a police officer, the county attorney and a friend about the situation. Although all three spoke with Jon, and even though he told all three that he was through with Robin, the conduct continued. The county attorney told Robin about his concern that Jon would show up at her doorstep and try to commit suicide in front of her because he had attempted a similar act in the past. Is injunctive relief appropriate in a case like this? If so, how should the order be framed? *See Matlock v. Weets*, 531 N.W.2d 118 (1995).

RENO AIR RACING ASSOCIATION, INC. V. MCCORD

452 F.3d 1126 (9th Cir. 2006).

MCKEOWN, CIRCUIT JUDGE.

Since 1964, Reno Air has operated the National Championship Air Races, an annual air show at the Reno/Stead Airport in Nevada. The show features airplanes that race around pylons for cash prizes and stunt aircraft that perform acrobatic maneuvers. Approximately 80,000 to 90,000 people attend the event which generates millions of dollars of revenue. Reno Air extensively advertises and promotes the event through a variety of print and electronic media, referring to it both as "Reno Air Races" and "National Championship Air Races."

Reno Air has used a logo featuring a checkered pylon with two airplanes circling it ("pylon logo") to identify the event and merchandise promoting the event. Reno Air is the registered owner of two federal trademarks for the "pylon logo;" the marks are identical, although one is a trademark and the other a service mark. The marks have been registered with the United States Patent and Trademark Office since 1985 and have acquired incontestable status. The trademark registrations are in four classes that include entertainment services, printed materials, cloth patches, caps and t-shirts. Through special licensing agreements, Reno Air permits vendors situated inside the gates of the show to sell merchandise bearing the trademarks.

McCord owns Western Sales Distributing Company, a sole proprietorship. Between 1999 and 2002, McCord sold merchandise, including t-shirts, caps and mugs, depicting the term "Reno Air Races" and artwork containing images of at least one airplane and a pylon, from booths located just outside of the gates of the air races. In 2000, McCord received a letter and telephone call from Reno Air's attorney, who objected to McCord's sale of merchandise at the air races. The following year, a representative from Reno Air advised McCord that his sale of such merchandise violated Reno Air's rights. On September 13, 2002, Reno Air filed a complaint in the District of Nevada, alleging McCord's infringement of the federally registered "pylon logo" mark in violation of 15 U.S.C. § 1114(1)(a) and infringement of the unregistered "Reno Air

Races" mark in violation of 15 U.S.C. § 1125(a). That same day, Reno Air also filed an ex parte application for a TRO pursuant to Rule 65(b) and a motion for a preliminary injunction. The district court granted the application after a telephonic hearing, and issued an *ex parte* TRO that prohibited McCord from engaging in the following activities:

> (1) making, manufacturing, using, distributing, shipping, licensing, selling, developing, displaying, delivering, advertising and/or otherwise marketing or disposing of any goods, packaging or any other items which bear the trademarks set forth in Exhibit F to Mr. Houghton's declaration, or any confusingly similar variations thereof;
>
> (2) disposing of, destroying, moving, relocating or transferring any and all goods and other items bearing the trademarks set forth in Exhibit F to Mr. Houghton's declaration, or any confusingly similar variations thereof;
>
> (3) disposing of, destroying, moving, relocating or transferring any means for making products having the trademarks set forth in Exhibit F to Mr. Houghton's declaration, or any confusingly similar variations thereof;
>
> (4) disposing of, destroying, moving, relocating or transferring any documents pertaining to the creation, development of items bearing the trademarks set forth in Exhibit F to Mr. Houghton's declaration, or any marks confusingly similar thereto.

"Exhibit F," to which the TRO referred extensively, contained a picture of a t-shirt design sold by McCord that depicted a stylized image of two airplanes and a checkered pylon, with the words "Reno Air Races" underneath.

Reno Air served McCord with the TRO late in the afternoon on September 13, 2002, the Friday of the air races weekend. McCord was outside the gates of the show when he was served and was packing up for the day. He did not read the TRO until later that evening and over the weekend had difficulty locating an attorney with whom he could consult about the meaning of the injunction. Even after the weekend, finding an attorney in the Reno area who did had not have a conflict of interest as a result of a prior relationship with Reno Air was not easy. As of Saturday, September 14, 2002, McCord stopped selling t-shirts containing the exact design pictured in Exhibit F. McCord continued to sell merchandise containing the term "Reno Air Races" and depicting a pylon and airplanes until the end of the air show on Sunday, September 15, 2002. In April 2003, Reno Air filed a motion for contempt and claimed that McCord violated the TRO. A two-day bench trial was held in February 2004. The district court entered a final judgment in April 2004.

The district court found that McCord infringed "Reno Air Races" and the "pylon logo," which were protectable marks under the Lanham Act. The district court awarded Reno Air $6,727 in damages arising from the sale of infringing merchandise and permanently enjoined McCord from "making, manufacturing, or distributing any goods, packaging or any other items which bear the Marks, or any confusingly similar variations thereof." The district court also found McCord in civil contempt for continuing to sell infringing merchandise after being served with the TRO on September 13, 2002. The district court imposed contempt sanctions in an amount equal to Reno Air's reasonable attorneys' fees and costs in connection with the TRO and contempt motion.

"We review for abuse of discretion the district court's civil contempt order, including the decision to impose sanctions." *Hook v. Arizona Dep't of Corrections,* 107 F.3d 1397, 1403 (9th Cir.1997). "We will not reverse unless we have a definite and firm conviction that the district court committed a clear error of judgment after weighing the relevant factors." *In re Dual–Deck Video Cassette Recorder Antitrust Litig.,* 10 F.3d 693, 695 (9th Cir.1993).

"Civil contempt in this context consists of a party's disobedience to a specific and definite court order by failure to take all reasonable steps within the party's power to comply." *Id.* The contempt " 'need not be willful,' " *id.* (quoting *In re Crystal Palace Gambling Hall, Inc.,* 817 F.2d 1361, 1365 (9th Cir.1987)); however, a person should not be held in contempt if his action "appears to be based on a good faith and reasonable interpretation of the court's order." *Id.*

The TRO was deficient for lack of specificity. Rule 65(d) requires that any injunction or restraining order be "specific in terms" and describe "in reasonable detail, and not by reference to the complaint or other document, the act or acts sought to be restrained." Fed.R.Civ.P. 65(d). "If an injunction does not clearly describe prohibited or required conduct, it is not enforceable by contempt." *Gates v. Shinn,* 98 F.3d 463, 468 (9th Cir.1996). As the Supreme Court explained in *Int'l Longshoremen's Ass'n. v. Philadelphia Marine Trade Ass'n,* 389 U.S. 64 (1967): The judicial contempt power is a potent weapon. When it is founded upon a decree too vague to be understood, it can be a deadly one. Congress responded to that danger by requiring that a federal court frame its orders so that those who must obey them will know what the court intends to require and what it means to forbid. Thus, we look to the language of the TRO to determine if it provided McCord with fair and well-defined notice of the prohibited conduct. Here, the TRO fell short.

The TRO enjoined McCord from making, distributing or disposing of "items which bear the trademarks set forth in Exhibit F to Mr. Houghton's declaration, or any confusingly similar variations thereof." McCord suggests that the TRO's reference to an outside document—

Exhibit F—automatically violated Rule 65(d). Although a number of our sister circuits read the "no reference" requirement strictly, we have permitted incorporation by reference in certain limited scenarios, for example, where the referenced document is "physically attached to the order itself." *State of California v. Campbell,* 138 F.3d 772, 783 (9th Cir.1998); *Henry Hope X–Ray Prods., Inc. v. Marron Carrel, Inc.,* 674 F.2d 1336 (9th Cir.1982).

Here, the district court noted that Exhibit F was "made a part of the TRO and provided to McCord at the time that the order was served on him." Thus, while ordinarily the TRO should not incorporate by reference another document, the attached Exhibit F does not, in and of itself, invalidate the contempt finding. However, incorporation by reference should be the rare exception rather than the rule, and district courts should be particularly cautious where the injunctive order is issued at the outset of litigation, before the receiving party has acquired a context for understanding the referenced document and the subject matter of the dispute. The language of Rule 65 is exacting and we underscore that the narrow exceptions do not merit expansion, and certainly not in this case.

More problematic in this case is the fact that neither the TRO nor Exhibit F clearly identified and described the "trademarks" at issue. The operative language of the TRO did not reference the trademark registrations and curiously did not describe the marks themselves.[7] Exhibit F simply contained a copy of a t-shirt design sold by McCord. The t-shirt included the terms "Reno Air Races," "Reno, Nevada," "USA," "2002," and a picture of two airplanes positioned to the left of a checkered pylon. Looking at this t-shirt design, one is hard pressed to know what trademarks are referenced in the order, whether the "trademarks" invoked in the TRO referred to the t-shirt, the design as a whole, the phrase "Reno Air Races," all of the words depicted, the checkered pylon, one or more airplanes, the pylon plus one or more airplanes, or some other combination.

In addition to the unexplained "trademarks," McCord points to the ambiguity of the phrase "confusingly similar variations thereof." If a reader of the TRO were left in the dark about what trademarks were covered, then surely bootstrapping the order to include "confusingly similar variations thereof" would leave the reader's head spinning with more confusion. "Variations of what?" Because the underlying order failed to identify the trademarks with sufficient specificity, the order was hardly enforceable as to the "variations thereof" language.

---

[7] Although the paragraph relating to the show cause order referred generally to "the 'pylon logo' or 'Reno Air Races' trademarks," it did not reference the registrations, photographs or clarifying information that described the actual trademarks at issue. The operative paragraphs of the TRO did not even reach this level of identification.

Ultimately, there are no magic words that automatically run afoul of Rule 65(d), and the inquiry is context-specific. "The fair notice requirement of Rule 65(d) must be applied 'in the light of the circumstances surrounding the order's entry.'" *Common Cause v. Nuclear Reg. Comm'n,* 674 F.2d 921, 927 (D.C.Cir.1982) (quoting *United States v. Christie Indus., Inc.,* 465 F.2d 1000, 1002 (3d Cir.1971)). This case not only points out the pitfall of incorporating documents by reference in a TRO but also the hazard of failing to identify with particularity the enjoined conduct in conjunction with specific identification and description of the trademarks. The recipient of a TRO, which usually takes effect immediately, should not be left guessing as to what conduct is enjoined. The benchmark for clarity and fair notice is not lawyers and judges, who are schooled in the nuances of trademark law. The "specific terms" and "reasonable detail" mandated by Rule 65(d) should be understood by the lay person, who is the target of the injunction. This is a circumstance, among many in the legal field, that cries out for "plain English."

Here, the TRO was issued the same day the action commenced, and the parties had no prior litigation history. Although they had engaged in limited communications, Reno Air could not even find the letter it purportedly sent to McCord. Given this backdrop and the failure of the TRO (and Exhibit F) to clearly identify the trademarks at issue, the TRO's prohibition—*i.e.* enjoining infringement of "the trademarks set forth in Exhibit F or any confusingly similar variations thereof"—would certainly have left a lay person scratching his head in confusion. The TRO failed to meet even the most minimal fair notice requirement.

As the TRO was improperly issued *ex parte* and failed to describe the prohibited conduct with specificity, the order cannot serve as the foundation for a finding of civil contempt. We vacate and reverse the part of the district court's order finding McCord in contempt for violating the TRO and imposing contempt sanctions.

PROBLEM: REFINING THE INJUNCTION

How could Reno Air have framed the injunction in order to provide the necessary clarity and specificity?

KILGROW V. KILGROW

268 Ala. 475, 107 So.2d 885 (1958).

GOODWYN, JUSTICE.

A father (Jack Kilgrow) and mother (Christine), husband and wife who were living together as a family unit but who were of different religious faiths, disagreed about where their seven year-old daughter should attend school. Although the parties had entered into an antenuptial agreement providing that the girl would go to a parochial school, the mother enrolled her in a public school and insisted on taking her there. The husband sought permanent injunctive relief precluding the mother from "interfering or attempting to interfere and prevent the said Margaret Kilgrow from continuing her education at Loretta School."

Following a hearing, husband was awarded a decree that provided as follows:

> "that it is for the best interest of the minor child involved in these proceedings that she remain in the school where the father has placed her and that the mother refrain from interfering with the schooling of said minor child. It is, therefore,
>
> "Ordered, adjudged and decreed by the court
>
> "1) that it is for the best welfare of the child, Margaret Kilgrow, that she continue her studies where her father has placed her, in Loretta School.
>
> "2) That Mrs. Christine B. Kilgrow be and she is hereby enjoined and restrained from interfering with the schooling of the said child at Loretta School, and that said child continue her schooling there until and unless this order be changed in proper proceedings."

The decisive question presented is whether a court of equity has inherent jurisdiction to resolve a family dispute between parents as to the school their minor child should attend. In other words, should the jurisdiction of a court of equity extend to the settlement of a difference of opinion between parents as to what is best for their minor child when the parents and child are all living together as a family group?

This appears to be a case of first impression. In fact, no case has been cited to us, nor have we found any, which has dealt with the precise problem before us.

There can be no doubt that if this were a proceeding to determine the child's custody the equity court would have jurisdiction for that purpose. *Ex parte White*, 245 Ala. 212, 214, 16 So.2d 500. But that is not the situation before us. There is no issue as to the child's custody. Here, the injunctive process is employed at the instance of the father to restrain the mother, who continues to live with the father as a member of the family group and who also has natural custodial rights over her minor child.

If we should hold that equity has jurisdiction in this case such holding will open wide the gates for settlement in equity of all sorts and varieties of intimate family disputes concerning the upbringing of children. The absence of cases dealing with the question indicates a reluctance of the courts to assume jurisdiction in disputes arising out of the intimate family circle. It does not take much imagination to envision the extent to which explosive differences of opinion between parents as to the proper upbringing of their children could be brought into court for attempted solution.

In none of our cases has the court intervened to settle a controversy between unseparated parents as to some matter incident to the well-being of the child, where there was no question presented as to which parent should have custody. In all of our cases the real question has been which parent should properly be awarded custody. Never has the court put itself in the place of the parents and interposed its judgment as to the course which otherwise amicable parents should pursue in discharging their parental duty. Here, the sole difference between the parties is which school the child should attend. And, that difference seems not to have affected the conjugal attitude of the parents one to the other.

The inherent jurisdiction of courts of equity over infants is a matter of necessity, coming into exercise only where there has been a failure of that natural power and obligation which is the province of parenthood. It is a jurisdiction assumed by the courts only when it is forfeited by a natural custodian incident to a broken home or neglect, or as a result of a natural custodian's incapacity, unfitness or death. It is only for compelling reason that a parent is deprived of the custody of his or her child. The court only interferes as between parents to the extent of awarding custody to the one or the other, with the welfare of the child in mind. And it is in awarding custody that the court invokes the principle that the welfare of the child is the controlling consideration. We do not think a court of equity should undertake to settle a dispute between parents as to what is best for their minor child when there is no question concerning the child's custody.

It would be anomalous to hold that a court of equity may sit in constant supervision over a household and see that either parent's will and determination in the upbringing of a child is obeyed, even though the parents' dispute might involve what is best for the child. Every difference of opinion between parents concerning their child's upbringing necessarily involves the question of the child's best interest.

What was said in *Knighton v. Knighton*, 252 Ala. 520, 525, 41 So.2d 172, 175, is equally pertinent here: "It intrigues the imagination to contemplate the lengths to which such a power once attempted may be carried, and the difficulty to be encountered in the enforcement of such a decree. Considerations of policy and expediency forbid a resort to injunctive relief in such a case."

It may well be suggested that a court of equity ought to interfere to prevent such a direful consequence as divorce or separation, rather than await the disruption of the marital relationship. Our answer to this is that intervention, rather than preventing or healing a disruption, would quite likely serve as the spark to a smoldering fire. A mandatory court decree supporting the position of one parent against the other would hardly be a composing situation for the unsuccessful parent to be confronted with daily. One spouse could scarcely be expected to entertain a tender, affectionate regard for the other spouse who brings him or her under restraint. The judicial mind and conscience is repelled by the thought of disruption of the sacred marital relationship, and usually voices the hope that the breach may somehow be healed by mutual understanding between the parents themselves.

The prenuptial agreement as to the child's religious education has no bearing on the question of the trial court's jurisdiction in this case. The bill does not even attempt to make that agreement a basis for relief.

The decree appealed from is due to be reversed and one rendered here dismissing the petition. It is so ordered.

Reversed and rendered.

All the Justices concur.

PROBLEMS

1. *Order Requiring That Children Be Reared in the Catholic Religion.* Consider *Lynch v. Uhlenhopp,* 248 Iowa 68, 78 N.W.2d 491 (1956), in which a divorced mother and father agreed that the mother would have custody of the children and that the father would provide child support, but that the children would be "reared in the Roman Catholic religion." The agreement was incorporated into a final divorce decree and resulted in a court order. Although the father was Catholic, the mother was not. The evidence revealed that the mother never took the children to the Catholic church, and sometimes took them to a Protestant church. The father sometimes took the children to the Catholic church. Can the father have the mother held in contempt for failing to "rear" the children in the Catholic faith? If the agreement is enforceable, what would the mother have to do to avoid contempt? Regularly take the children to the Catholic church? Would she also be required to instruct them in the doctrine of the church, and to observe Catholic rituals at home? Would she be precluded from taking them to Protestant churches?

2. *Framing the Order.* In *Lynch,* regardless of whether you concluded that the original decree was enforceable, please think about whether there was a preferable way to frame it. What language would you use?

3. *Representing the Mother in Challenging the Order.* Now, suppose that you represent the mother. How would you challenge the language you drafted?

PEGGY LAWTON KITCHENS, INC. V. HOGAN

403 Mass. 732, 532 N.E.2d 54 (1989).

O'CONNOR, JUSTICE.

Peggy Lawton Kitchens, Inc. (Kitchens), manufactures and sells chocolate chip cookies. In November, 1981, Kitchens brought an action against the defendants in this case (Hogans) alleging that the Hogans had stolen a secret chocolate chip cookie recipe from Kitchens and were manufacturing and selling cookies using that formula. No damages were awarded as a result of that action, but the Hogans were permanently enjoined from "making, baking and selling chocolate chip cookies which use or utilize Kitchens's formula."

Approximately one year after Lawton Drayer Wolf (Wolf), one of the founders of Kitchens, had begun producing chocolate chip cookies, he developed "a distinctive twist" by incorporating walnut shavings, also called "chaff, nut meal, nut dust, and nut crunch," into the cookie mix. After that, "sales took off immediately. The nut meal did to the cookies what butter does to popcorn, or salt to a pretzel. It really made the flavor sing."

The judge made findings with respect to the ingredients and proportions thereof used by Kitchens and by the Hogans, which we need not repeat. He found that many of the ingredients used by Kitchens and the Hogans are common to most commercially made chocolate chip cookies, but no commercial cookie manufacturer, except Kitchens, uses nut meal. He found that "it is the nut meal which gives Peggy Lawton Chocolate Chip Cookies their unique and distinctive flavor."

Following the injunction, the Hogans did not use nut meal in their chocolate chip cookies, and they added four ounces of vanilla per batch of approximately 1,100 cookies. Kitchens did not use vanilla in its cookies. "As a result of this substitution, Hogan's cookies which previously had a nutty taste similar to Peggy Lawton, thereafter developed a distinctive vanilla flavor." The judge also determined that the Hogans altered their formula in other ways that affected their chocolate chip cookies' texture and taste.

Kitchens challenges as "clearly erroneous" the judge's factual conclusion that "Hogie Bear does not make, bake and sell chocolate chip cookies which use or utilize the Peggy Lawton formula." Kitchens also challenges the judge's conclusion that Kitchens had not established the Hogans' contempt of the injunction against their "making, baking and selling chocolate chip cookies, which use or utilize Kitchens' formula."

The principal thrust of Kitchens' argument is that its chocolate chip cookie formula, which includes not only specific ingredients but also the proportions in which those ingredients are used, has been adjudicated a trade secret, and that, therefore, others rightfully may neither manufacture nor sell competing products derived from it. Kitchens argues that the evidence at trial inescapably showed that the Hogans "used" Kitchens' formula even though, as the judge found, they modified it in numerous ways. The contention is that, despite the modifications, the Hogans did not produce an "independent product," but rather produced the "substantial equivalent" of Kitchens' product—a product substantially derived from Kitchens' formula. It is precisely that conduct, Kitchens says, that the injunction against "using or utilizing" its formula was designed to prevent.

Kitchens presents sound arguments. Nevertheless, we must focus primarily on the language of the injunction. Trade secret law, and the conduct which under that law may be the basis of liability to pay damages is not controlling. "To constitute civil contempt as is alleged here, there must be a clear and undoubted disobedience of a clear and unequivocal command." *Manchester v. Department of Envtl. Quality Eng'g*, 381 Mass. 208, 212, 409 N.E.2d 176 (1980). The Appeals Court's statement that "the injunction forbids only use of Kitchens' precise formula," would seem to suggest that the injunction goes no further than to command the Hogans not to produce cookies containing the exact same ingredients in the exact same proportions as Kitchens' cookies. Whether the command does indeed go further and, if so, how much further it goes, is not clear. While perhaps the injunction reasonably could be construed as forbidding the Hogans to manufacture, bake, and sell chocolate chip cookies made from a formula "substantially derived" from Kitchens' formula, the injunction does not "clearly and unequivocally" do so. Furthermore, even if the injunction had expressly prohibited the Hogans from producing cookies according to a formula "substantially derived" from Kitchens' formula, those terms are too imprecise to justify, let alone require, a finding of contempt in the circumstances of this case. Therefore, we affirm the decision of the judge in the Superior Court dismissing the plaintiff's contempt petition.

So ordered.

PROBLEMS

1. *Framing the* Peggy Lawton Kitchens *Order.* In the *Peggy Lawton Kitchens* case, would it have been possible to frame an injunction that would have precluded plaintiffs from doing what they did? How should the injunction have been framed? For example, could the court have prohibited defendants from baking and selling chocolate chip cookies? Alternatively, could the court have prohibited defendants from making chocolate chip cookies using a recipe that was substantially similar to the one used by plaintiff? Would such an injunction be appropriate? Is some difficulty created by the fact that most chocolate chip cookie recipes are essentially similar?

2. *More on the Diamond Derby Gala.* Assume that you are the judge in this case, and you have decided to issue an injunction. How should the order be framed? Should you enter an order precluding the organizers from holding the Gala at all? Should you issue a more limited order?

MADSEN V. WOMEN'S HEALTH CENTER, INC.

512 U.S. 753, 114 S.Ct. 2516, 129 L.Ed.2d 593 (1994).

CHIEF JUSTICE REHNQUIST delivered the opinion of the Court.

Petitioners challenge the constitutionality of an injunction entered by a Florida state court which prohibits antiabortion protestors from demonstrating in certain places and in various ways outside of a health clinic that performs abortions. We hold that the establishment of a 36-foot buffer zone on a public street from which demonstrators are excluded passes muster under the First Amendment, but that several other provisions of the injunction do not.

Respondents operate abortion clinics throughout central Florida. Petitioners and other groups and individuals are engaged in activities near the site of one such clinic in Melbourne, Florida. They picketed and demonstrated where the public street gives access to the clinic. In September 1992, a Florida state court permanently enjoined petitioners from blocking or interfering with public access to the clinic, and from physically abusing persons entering or leaving the clinic. Six months later, respondents sought to broaden the injunction, complaining that access to the clinic was still impeded by petitioners' activities and that such activities had also discouraged some potential patients from entering the clinic, and had deleterious physical effects on others. The trial court thereupon issued a broader injunction, which is challenged here. * * *

We begin by addressing petitioners' contention that the state court's order, because it is an injunction that restricts only the speech of antiabortion protesters, is necessarily content or viewpoint based. Accordingly, they argue, we should examine the entire injunction under the strictest standard of scrutiny. We disagree. To accept petitioners' claim would be to classify virtually every injunction as content or viewpoint based. An injunction, by its very nature, applies only to a particular group (or individuals) and regulates the activities, and perhaps the speech, of that group. It does so, however, because of the group's past actions in the context of a specific dispute between real parties. The parties seeking the injunction assert a violation of their rights; the court hearing the action is charged with fashioning a remedy for a specific deprivation, not with the drafting of a statute addressed to the general public.

The fact that the injunction in the present case did not prohibit activities of those demonstrating in favor of abortion is justly attributable to the lack of any similar demonstrations by those in favor of abortion, and of any consequent request that their demonstrations be regulated by injunction. There is no suggestion in this record that Florida law would not equally restrain similar conduct directed at a target having nothing to do with abortion; none of the restrictions imposed by the court were directed at the contents of petitioner's message.

Our principal inquiry in determining content neutrality is whether the government has adopted a regulation of speech "without reference to the content of the regulated speech." *Ward v. Rock Against Racism*, 491 U.S. 781, 791 (1989); *R.A.V. v. St. Paul*, 112 S.Ct. 2538, 2553 (1992) ("The government may not regulate speech based on hostility—or favoritism—towards the underlying message expressed"). We thus look to the government's purpose as the threshold consideration. Here, the state court imposed restrictions on petitioners incidental to their antiabortion message because they repeatedly violated the court's original order. That petitioners all share the same viewpoint regarding abortion does not in itself demonstrate that some invidious content- or viewpoint-based purpose motivated the issuance of the order. It suggests only that those in the group whose conduct violated the court's order happen to share the same opinion regarding abortions being performed at the clinic. In short, the fact that the injunction covered people with a particular viewpoint does not itself render the injunction content or viewpoint based. Accordingly, the injunction issued in this case does not demand a level of heightened scrutiny.

If this were a content-neutral, generally applicable statute, instead of an injunctive order, its constitutionality would be assessed under the standard set forth in *Ward v. Rock Against Racism, supra*, 491 U.S., at 791, and similar cases. Given that the forum around the clinic is a traditional public forum, we would determine whether the time, place, and manner regulations were "narrowly tailored to serve a significant governmental interest." *Ward, supra*, 491 U.S., at 791.

There are obvious differences, however, between an injunction and a generally applicable ordinance. Ordinances represent a legislative choice regarding the promotion of particular societal interests. Injunctions, by contrast, are remedies imposed for violations (or threatened violations) of a legislative or judicial decree. Injunctions also carry greater risks of censorship and discriminatory application than do general ordinances.

We believe that these differences require a somewhat more stringent application of general First Amendment principles in this context. In past cases evaluating injunctions restricting speech, we have relied upon such general principles while also seeking to ensure that the injunction was no broader than necessary to achieve its desired goals. Our close attention to the fit between the objectives of an injunction and the restrictions it imposes on speech is consistent with the general rule, quite apart from First Amendment considerations, "that injunctive relief should be no more burdensome to the defendants than necessary to provide complete relief to the plaintiffs." *Califano v. Yamasaki*, 442 U.S. 682, 702 (1979). When evaluating a content-neutral injunction, we think that our standard time, place, and manner analysis is not sufficiently rigorous. We must ask instead whether the challenged provisions of the injunction burden no more speech than necessary to serve a significant government interest. * * *

We begin with the 36-foot buffer zone. The state court prohibited petitioners from "congregating, picketing, patrolling, demonstrating or entering" any portion of the public right-of-way or private property within 36 feet of the property line of the clinic as a way of ensuring access to the clinic. This speech-free buffer zone requires that petitioners move to the other side of Dixie Way and away from the driveway of the clinic, where the state court found that they repeatedly had interfered with the free access of patients and staff. The buffer zone also applies to private property to the north and west of the clinic property. We examine each portion of the buffer zone separately.

We have noted a distinction between the type of focused picketing banned from the buffer zone and the type of generally disseminated communication that cannot be completely banned in public places, such as handbilling and solicitation. Here the picketing is directed primarily at patients and staff of the clinic.

The 36-foot buffer zone protecting the entrances to the clinic and the parking lot is a means of protecting unfettered ingress to and egress from the clinic, and ensuring that petitioners do not block traffic on Dixie Way. The state court seems to have had few other options to protect access given the narrow confines around the clinic. Dixie Way is only 21 feet wide in the area of the clinic. The state court was convinced that allowing the petitioners to remain on the clinic's sidewalk and driveway was not a viable option in view of the failure of the first injunction to protect access. And allowing the petitioners to stand in the middle of Dixie Way would obviously block vehicular traffic.

The need for a complete buffer zone near the clinic entrances and driveway may be debatable, but some deference must be given to the state court's familiarity with the facts and the background of the dispute between the parties even under our heightened review. Moreover, one of petitioners' witnesses conceded that the buffer zone was narrow enough to place petitioners at a distance of no greater than 10 to 12 feet from cars approaching and leaving the clinic. Protesters standing across the narrow street from the clinic can still be seen and heard from the clinic parking lots. We also bear in mind the fact that the state court originally issued a much narrower injunction, providing no buffer zone, and that this order did not succeed in protecting access to the clinic. The failure of the first order to accomplish its purpose may be taken into consideration in evaluating the constitutionality of the broader order. On balance, we hold that the 36-foot buffer zone around the clinic entrances and driveway burdens no more speech than necessary to accomplish the governmental interest at stake.

The inclusion of private property on the back and side of the clinic in the 36-foot buffer zone raises different concerns. The accepted purpose of the buffer zone is to protect access to the clinic and to facilitate the orderly flow of traffic on Dixie Way. Patients and staff wishing to reach the clinic do not have to cross the private property abutting the clinic property on the north and west, and nothing in the record indicates that petitioners' activities on the private property have obstructed access to the clinic. Nor was evidence presented that protestors located on the private property blocked vehicular traffic on Dixie Way. Absent evidence that petitioners standing on the private property have obstructed access to the clinic, blocked vehicular traffic, or otherwise unlawfully interfered with the clinic's operation, this portion of the buffer zone fails to serve the significant government interests relied on by the Florida Supreme Court. We hold that on the record before us the 36-foot buffer zone as applied to the private property to the north and west of the clinic burdens more speech than necessary to protect access to the clinic.

In response to high noise levels outside the clinic, the state court restrained the petitioners from "singing, chanting, whistling, shouting, yelling, use of bullhorns, auto horns, sound amplification equipment or other sounds or images observable to or within earshot of the patients inside the clinic" during the hours of 7:30 a.m. through noon on Mondays through Saturdays. We must take account of the place to which the regulations apply in determining whether these restrictions burden more speech than necessary. We have upheld similar noise restrictions in the past, and as we noted in upholding a local noise ordinance around public schools, "the nature of a place, 'the pattern of its normal activities, dictate the kinds of regulations that are reasonable.'" *Grayned v. City of Rockford*, 408 U.S. 104, 116 (1972). Noise control is particularly important around hospitals and medical facilities during surgery and recovery periods. We hold that the limited noise restrictions imposed by the state court order burden no more speech than necessary to ensure the health and well-being of the patients at the clinic. The First Amendment does not demand that patients at a medical facility undertake Herculean efforts to escape the cacophony of political protests.

The same, however, cannot be said for the "images observable" provision of the state court's order. Clearly, threats to patients or their families, however communicated, are proscribable under the First Amendment. But rather than prohibiting the display of signs that could be interpreted as threats or veiled threats, the state court issued a blanket ban on all "images observable." This broad prohibition on all "images observable" burdens more speech than necessary to achieve the purpose of limiting threats to clinic patients or their families. Similarly, if the blanket ban on "images observable" was intended to reduce the level of anxiety and hypertension suffered by the patients inside the clinic, it would still fail. The only plausible reason a patient would be bothered by "images observable" inside the clinic would be if the patient found the expression contained in such images disagreeable. But it is much easier for the clinic to pull its curtains than for a patient to stop up her ears, and no more is required to avoid seeing placards through the windows of the clinic. This provision of the injunction violates the First Amendment.

The state court ordered that petitioners refrain from physically approaching any person seeking services of the clinic "unless such person indicates a desire to communicate" in an area within 300 feet of the clinic. The state court was attempting to prevent clinic patients and staff from being "stalked" or "shadowed" by the petitioners as they approached the clinic. But it is difficult, indeed, to justify a prohibition on all uninvited approaches of persons seeking the services of the clinic, regardless of how peaceful the contact may be, without burdening more speech than necessary to prevent intimidation and to ensure access to the clinic. Absent evidence that the protesters' speech is independently proscribable (*i.e.*, "fighting words" or threats), or is so infused with violence as to be indistinguishable from a threat of physical harm, this provision cannot stand. "As a general matter, we have indicated that in public debate our own citizens must tolerate insulting, and even outrageous, speech in order to provide adequate breathing space to the freedoms protected by the First Amendment." *Boos v. Barry*, 485 U.S., at 322. The "consent" requirement alone invalidates this provision; it burdens more speech than is necessary to prevent intimidation and to ensure access to the clinic.

The final substantive regulation challenged by petitioners relates to a prohibition against picketing, demonstrating, or using sound amplification equipment within 300 feet of the residences of clinic staff. The prohibition also covers impeding access to streets that provide the sole access to streets on which those residences are located. The same analysis applies to the use of sound amplification equipment here as that discussed above: the government may simply demand that petitioners turn down the volume if the protests overwhelm the neighborhood.

As for the picketing, our prior decision upholding a law banning targeted residential picketing remarked on the unique nature of the home, as "the last citadel of the tired, the weary, and the sick." *Frisby*, 487 U.S., at 484. We stated that "the State's interest in protecting the well-being, tranquility, and privacy of the home is certainly of the highest order in a free and civilized society."

But the 300-foot zone around the residences in this case is much larger than the zone provided for in the ordinance which we approved in *Frisby*. The ordinance at issue there made it "unlawful for any person to engage in picketing before or about the residence or dwelling of any individual." The prohibition was limited to "focused picketing taking place solely in front of a particular residence." By contrast, the 300-foot zone would ban "general marching through residential neighborhoods, or even walking a route in front of an entire block of houses." The record before us does not contain sufficient justification for this broad a ban on picketing; it appears that a limitation on the time, duration of picketing, and number of pickets outside a smaller zone could have accomplished the desired result.

Accordingly, the judgment of the Florida Supreme Court is

Affirmed in part, and reversed in part.

JUSTICE STEVENS, concurring in part and dissenting in part.

As the Court notes, legislation is imposed on an entire community, regardless of individual culpability. By contrast, injunctions apply solely to an individual or a limited group of individuals who, by engaging in illegal conduct, have been judicially deprived of some liberty—the normal consequence of illegal activity. Given this distinction, a statute prohibiting demonstrations within 36 feet of an abortion clinic would probably violate the First Amendment, but an injunction directed at a limited group of persons who have engaged in unlawful conduct in a similar zone might well be constitutional.

The standard governing injunctions has two obvious dimensions. On the one hand, the injunction should be no more burdensome than necessary to provide complete relief. In a First Amendment context, as in any other, the propriety of the remedy depends almost entirely on the character of the violation and the likelihood of its recurrence. For this reason, standards fashioned to determine the constitutionality of statutes should not be used to evaluate injunctions. On the other hand, even when an injunction impinges on constitutional rights, more than "a simple proscription against the precise conduct previously pursued" may be required; the remedy must include appropriate restraints on "future activities both to avoid a recurrence of the violation and to eliminate its consequences." *National Society of Professional Engineers v. United States*, 435 U.S. 679, 697–698 (1978). Moreover, "the judicial remedy for a proven violation of law will often include commands that the law does not impose on the community at large." *Teachers v. Hudson*, 475 U.S. 292, 309–310, n. 22 (1986). As such, repeated violations may justify sanctions that might be invalid if applied to a first offender or if enacted by the legislature.

In this case, the trial judge heard three days of testimony and found that petitioners not only had engaged in tortious conduct, but also had repeatedly violated an earlier injunction. The injunction is thus twice removed from a legislative proscription applicable to the general public and should be judged by a standard that gives appropriate deference to the judge's unique familiarity with the facts. * * *

JUSTICE SCALIA, with whom JUSTICE KENNEDY and JUSTICE THOMAS join, concurring in the judgment in part and dissenting in part.

A restriction upon speech imposed by injunction (whether nominally content based or nominally content neutral) is at least as deserving of strict scrutiny as a statutory, content-based restriction. That is so for several reasons: The danger of content-based statutory restrictions upon speech is that they may be designed and used precisely to suppress the ideas in question rather than to achieve any other proper governmental aim. But that same danger exists with injunctions. Although a speech-restricting injunction may not attack content as content (in the present case, as I shall discuss, even that is not true), it lends itself just as readily to the targeted suppression of particular ideas. When a judge, on the motion of an employer, enjoins picketing at the site of a labor dispute, he enjoins (and he knows he is enjoining) the expression of pro-union views. Such targeting of one or the other side of an ideological dispute cannot readily be achieved in speech-restricting general legislation except by making content the basis of the restriction; it is achieved in speech-restricting injunctions almost invariably. The proceedings before us here illustrate well enough what I mean. The injunction was sought against a single-issue advocacy group by persons and organizations with a business or social interest in suppressing that group's point of view.

The second reason speech-restricting injunctions are at least as deserving of strict scrutiny is obvious enough: they are the product of individual judges rather than of legislatures—and often of judges who have been chagrined by prior disobedience of their orders. The right to free speech should not lightly be placed within the control of a single man or woman. And the third reason is that the injunction is a much more powerful weapon than a statute, and so should be subjected to greater safeguards. Normally, when injunctions are enforced through contempt proceedings, only the defense of factual innocence is available. The collateral bar rule of *Walker v. Birmingham*, 388 U.S. 307 (1967), eliminates the defense that the injunction itself was unconstitutional. Thus, persons subject to a speech-restricting injunction who have not the money or not the time to lodge an immediate appeal face a Hobson's choice: they must remain silent, since if they speak their First Amendment rights are no defense in subsequent contempt proceedings. This is good reason to require the strictest standard for issuance of such orders.

The Court seeks to minimize the similarity between speech-restricting injunctions and content-based statutory proscriptions by observing that the fact that "petitioners all share the same viewpoint regarding abortion does not in itself demonstrate that some invidious content- or viewpoint-based purpose motivated the issuance of the order," but rather "suggests only that those in the group whose conduct violated the court's order happen to share the same opinion regarding abortions." *Simon & Schuster v. New York Crime Victims Bd.*, 112 S.Ct. 501, 509 (1991) (*quoting Minneapolis Star & Tribune Co. v. Minnesota Comm'r of Revenue*, 460 U.S. 575, 592 (1983)). The vice of content-based legislation—what renders it deserving of the high standard of strict scrutiny—is not that it is always used for invidious, thought-control purposes, but that it lends itself to use for those purposes. And, because of the unavoidable "targeting" discussed above, precisely the same is true of the speech-restricting injunction.

Finally, though I believe speech-restricting injunctions are dangerous enough to warrant strict scrutiny even when they are not technically content based, the injunction in the present case was content based (indeed, viewpoint based) to boot. The Court claims that it was directed, not at those who spoke certain things (anti-abortion sentiments), but at those who did certain things (violated the earlier injunction). If that were true, then the injunction's residual coverage of "all persons acting in concert or participation with the named individuals and organizations, or on their behalf" would not include those who merely entertained the same beliefs and wished to express the same views as the named defendants. All those who wish to express the same views as the named defendants are deemed to be "acting in concert or participation." * * *

An injunction against speech is the very prototype of the greatest threat to First Amendment values, the prior restraint. We have said that a "prior restraint on expression comes to this Court with a 'heavy presumption' against its constitutional validity," and have repeatedly struck down speech-restricting injunctions. * * *

I now turn to the Court's application of the second part of its test: whether the provisions of the injunction "burden no more speech than necessary" to serve the significant interest protected. This test seems to me amply and obviously satisfied with regard to the noise restriction that the Court approves: it is only such noise as would reach the patients in the abortion clinic that is forbidden—and not even at all times, but only during certain fixed hours and "during surgical procedures and recovery periods." With regard to the 36-foot speech-free zone, however, it seems to me just as obvious that the test which the Court sets for itself has not been met.

Assuming a "significant state interest" of the sort cognizable for injunction purposes (*i.e.*, one protected by a law that has been or is threatened to be violated) in both (1) keeping pedestrians off the paved portion of Dixie Way, and (2) enabling cars to cross the public sidewalk at the clinic's driveways without having to slow down or come to even a "momentary" stop, there are surely a number of ways to protect those interests short of banishing the entire protest demonstration from the 36-foot zone. For starters, the Court could have (for the first time) ordered the demonstrators to stay out of the street (the original injunction did not remotely require that). It could have limited the number of demonstrators permitted on the clinic side of Dixie Way. And it could have forbidden the pickets to walk on the driveways. The Court's only response to these options is that "the state court was convinced that they would not work in view of the failure of the first injunction to protect access." * * *

PROBLEMS

1. *Enjoining Alienation of Affection.* Plaintiff and her husband are successful partners in the practice of medicine. About two years ago, the plaintiff and her husband hired defendant as a laboratory technician. Defendant began a steady course of conduct toward plaintiff's husband designed to alienate his affection. Although plaintiff fired defendant, defendant continued to pursue plaintiff's husband. Plaintiffs maintained a complete telephone service, including an emergency number, in connection with their medical practice. After repeated phone calls from defendant, plaintiffs were forced to discontinue the service. Plaintiff claims that defendant's conduct has made her irritable and nervous and made it difficult for plaintiff to maintain the consortium, affection, society and services of her husband. Is plaintiff entitled to injunctive relief? Would it be appropriate for the court to enter the following injunction: "Defendant is prohibited from telephoning plaintiff, or plaintiff's husband, and from seeing, visiting, writing or talking to the plaintiff or the plaintiff's husband until the further order of the court." Should it matter that the suit is brought by the wife rather than by the husband? If an injunction is appropriates, how should the order be framed? *See Lyon v. Izen*, 131 Ill.App.2d 594, 268 N.E.2d 436 (1971).

2. *The Errant Golf Balls.* Since 1965, John and Miriam Fenton have lived next to the ninth hole of Quaboag Country Club's (QCC) golf course. Almost from the start, the Fentons encountered serious problems from errant golf balls that caused property damage, including broken windows, and threatened life and limb. The Fentons sued and obtained a monetary judgment of $5,387 against QCC, as well as an order to abate the interference. The Club tried to protect the Fentons home by erecting a 24 foot fence along the Fenton's property line, but the fence did not work. Over the next two months, approximately 600 golf balls landed in their yard (about 10 a day). Suppose that you are the trial judge in the case. The Fentons seek an order providing them with further protection against the barrage of golf balls. In light of prior orders, how should that order be framed? If you represent the Fentons, what terms might you argue for? If you represent QCC, how might you respond?

3. *Ordering the Parties to Mediation?* In the case between QCC and the Fentons, would it have been appropriate for the judge to order the parties to mediation? Suppose that the judge had told the parties that it intended to issue an injunction in the case, but told them that it would not enter one

broad enough to enjoin use of the golf course. Would it then be appropriate for the judge to order the parties to mediation to see if they could find their own solution? Would it be appropriate or desirable for the court to enter such an order as opposed to simply imposing its own order? What advantages or disadvantages might result from ordering the parties to mediate?

4. *Framing the Armory Park Neighborhood Injunction.* Recall the *Armory Park Neighborhood* case, *supra*, in which neighbors complained that a food kitchen (which provided one hot meal a day to indigents) constituted a public and private nuisance by attracting transient persons to the neighborhood. The area was primarily residential with only a few small businesses. When the food kitchen began, many transients crossed the area daily on their way to and from the kitchen. Although the kitchen is only open from 5:00 to 6:00 p.m., patrons line up well before this hour and often linger in the neighborhood long after finishing their meal. Although the kitchen rented an adjacent fenced lot for a waiting area, and organized neighborhood cleaning projects, transients frequently trespass onto residents' yards, sometimes urinating, defecating, drinking and littering on the residents' property. A few have broken into storage areas and unoccupied homes, and some have asked residents for handouts. Arrests in the area have increased dramatically. Many residents are frightened or annoyed by the transients and have altered their lifestyles to avoid them. Assuming that the court grants the injunction, how should it be framed? *See Armory Park Neighborhood Ass'n v. Episcopal Community Services in Arizona*, 148 Ariz. 1, 712 P.2d 914 (In Banc, 1985).

5. *More on Ordering the Parties to Mediation.* In the *Armory Park Neighborhood* case, as with the QCC case, would it be desirable or advantageous to order the parties to mediation (on threat of the court imposing a solution if they fail), or would it be preferable for the court simply to impose a solution on them?

6. *The Shale Mine Pit.* In an effort to raise money to pay debts, Evangel Church wants to mine shale on a lot adjacent to church property. Neighbors, upset that the mining will interfere with the use and enjoyment of their property, form a group called "Stop the Pits." The group holds news conferences and protests outside the church. Some group members picket the church holding signs which read "Put the pastor out to pasture" and "Evangel's God is money." In addition, group members yell at church members on their way to church, and try to force anti-mining literature on them. The church seeks a preliminary injunction prohibiting "Stop the Pits" members from protesting near the church. Is a court likely to grant the injunction? If so, how should the injunction be framed?

E. EXPERIMENTAL AND CONDITIONAL INJUNCTIONS

Since injunctions are equitable decrees and their grant or denial is inherently discretionary, courts are free to shape their orders as required by the circumstances. Thus, the mere fact that plaintiff is suffering injury does not mean that he will receive the injunctive relief desired.

Although courts are willing to grant relief, they try to enter decrees that accommodate the parties' interests. In other words, courts are moved by the equities (including disproportionate economic consequences, the public interest, and other factors) to mold their decrees by entering partial injunctions (a/k/a, "experimental injunctions") designed to provide relief to the plaintiff, but allowing defendant to continue her conduct as much as possible. In other instances, courts enter conditional injunctions (a/k/a compensated injunctions). *See* Jeff L. Lewin, *Compensated Injunctions and the Evolution of Nuisance Law,* 71 IOWA L. REV. 775 (1986); Calabresi & Melamed, *Property Rules, Liability Rules, and Inalienability: One View of the Cathedral,* 85 HARV. L. REV. 1089 (1972). The following cases are illustrative.

BOOMER V. ATLANTIC CEMENT COMPANY

26 N.Y.2d 219, 257 N.E.2d 870, 309 N.Y.S.2d 312 (1970).

BERGAN, JUDGE.

Defendant operates a large cement plant near Albany. These are actions for injunction and damages by neighboring land owners alleging injury to property from dirt, smoke and vibration emanating from the plant. A nuisance has been found after trial, temporary damages have been allowed; but an injunction has been denied.

The public concern with air pollution arising from many sources in industry and in transportation is currently accorded ever wider recognition accompanied by a growing sense of responsibility in State and Federal Governments to control it. Cement plants are obvious sources of air pollution in the neighborhoods where they operate.

But there is now before the court private litigation in which individual property owners have sought specific relief from a single plant operation. The threshold question raised on this appeal is whether the court should resolve the litigation between the parties now before it as equitably as seems possible; or whether, seeking promotion of the general public welfare, it should channel private litigation into broad public objectives.

A court performs its essential function when it decides the rights of parties before it. Its decision of private controversies may sometimes greatly affect public issues. Large questions of law are often resolved by the manner in which private litigation is decided. But this is normally an incident to the court's main function to settle controversy. It is a rare exercise of judicial power to use a decision in private litigation as a purposeful mechanism to achieve direct public objectives greatly beyond the rights and interests before the court.

Effective control of air pollution is a problem presently far from solution even with the full public and financial powers of government. In large measure adequate technical procedures are yet to be developed and some that appear possible may be economically impracticable.

It seems apparent that the amelioration of air pollution will depend on technical research in great depth; on a carefully balanced consideration of the economic impact of close regulation; and of the actual effect on public health. It is likely to require massive public expenditure and to demand more than any local community can accomplish and to depend on regional and interstate controls.

A court should not try to do this on its own as a by-product of private litigation and it seems manifest that the judicial establishment is neither equipped in the limited nature of any judgment it can pronounce nor prepared to lay down and implement an effective policy for the elimination of air pollution. This is a direct responsibility for government and should not thus be undertaken as an incident to solving a dispute between property owners and a single cement plant—one of many—in the Hudson River valley.

The cement making operations of defendant have been found by the court of Special Term to have damaged the nearby properties of plaintiffs in these two actions. That court found that defendant maintained a nuisance. The total damage to plaintiffs' properties is, however, relatively small in comparison with the value of defendant's operation and with the consequences of the injunction which plaintiffs seek.

The ground for the denial of injunction, notwithstanding the finding both that there is a nuisance and that plaintiffs have been damaged substantially, is the large disparity in economic consequences of the nuisance and of the injunction. This theory cannot, however, be sustained without overruling a doctrine which has been consistently reaffirmed in several leading cases in this court and which has never been disavowed here, namely that where a nuisance has been found and where there has been any substantial damage shown by the party complaining an injunction will be granted. The rule in New York has been that such a nuisance will be enjoined although marked disparity be shown in economic consequence between the effect of the injunction and the effect of the nuisance. *Whalen v. Union Bag & Paper Co.*, 208 N.Y. 1, 101 N.E. 805. Whenever the damage resulting from a nuisance is found not "unsubstantial," viz., $100 a year, injunction would follow.

Although the court at Special Term and the Appellate Division held that injunction should be denied, it was found that plaintiffs had been damaged in various specific amounts up to the time of the trial and damages to the respective plaintiffs were awarded for those amounts. The effect of this was, injunction having been denied, plaintiffs could maintain successive actions at law for damages thereafter as further damage was incurred. The court at Special Term also found the amount of permanent damage attributable to each plaintiff, for the guidance of the parties in the event both sides stipulated to the payment and acceptance of such permanent damage as a settlement of all the controversies among the parties. The total of permanent damages to all plaintiffs thus found was $185,000. This basis of adjustment has not resulted in any stipulation by the parties.

This result at Special Term and at the Appellate Division is a departure from a rule that has become settled; but to follow the rule literally would be to close down the plant at once. This court is fully agreed to avoid that immediately drastic remedy; the difference in view is how best to avoid it.*

One alternative is to grant the injunction but postpone its effect to a specified future date to give opportunity for technical advances to permit defendant to eliminate the nuisance; another is to grant the injunction conditioned on the payment of permanent damages to plaintiffs which would compensate them for the total economic loss to their property present and future caused by defendant's operations. For reasons which will be developed the court chooses the latter alternative.

If the injunction were to be granted unless within a short period—*e.g.*, 18 months—the nuisance be abated by improved methods, there would be no assurance that any significant technical improvement would occur.

The parties could settle this private litigation at any time if defendant paid enough money and the imminent threat of closing the plant would build up the pressure on defendant. If there were no improved techniques found, there would inevitably be applications to the court for extensions of time to perform on showing of good faith efforts to find such techniques.

Moreover, techniques to eliminate dust and other annoying by-products of cement making are unlikely to be developed by any research the defendant can undertake within any short period, but will depend on the total resources of the cement industry nationwide and throughout the world. The problem is universal wherever cement is made.

For obvious reasons the rate of the research is beyond control of defendant. If at the end of 18 months the whole industry has not found a technical solution a court would be hard put to close down this one cement plant if due regard be given to equitable principles.

On the other hand, to grant the injunction unless defendant pays plaintiffs such permanent damages as may be fixed by the court seems to

* Respondent's investment in the plant is in excess of $45,000,000. There are over 300 people employed there.

do justice between the contending parties. All of the attributions of economic loss to the properties on which plaintiffs' complaints are based will have been redressed.

The nuisance complained of by these plaintiffs may have other public or private consequences, but these particular parties are the only ones who have sought remedies and the judgment proposed will fully redress them. The limitation of relief granted is a limitation only within the four corners of these actions and does not foreclose public health or other public agencies from seeking proper relief in a proper court.

It seems reasonable to think that the risk of being required to pay permanent damages to injured property owners by cement plant owners would itself be a reasonable effective spur to research for improved techniques to minimize nuisance.

The power of the court to condition on equitable grounds the continuance of an injunction on the payment of permanent damages seems undoubted.

The theory of damage is the "servitude on land" of plaintiffs imposed by defendant's nuisance. This judgment, by allowance of permanent damages imposing a servitude on land, would preclude future recovery by plaintiffs or their grantees. This understanding should be placed beyond debate by a provision of the judgment that the payment by defendant and the acceptance by plaintiffs of permanent damages found by the court shall be in compensation for a servitude on the land.

The orders should be reversed, without costs, and the cases remitted to Supreme Court, Albany County to grant an injunction which shall be vacated upon payment by defendant of such amounts of permanent damage to the respective plaintiffs as shall for this purpose be determined by the court.

JASEN, JUDGE (dissenting).

It has long been the rule in this State that a nuisance which results in substantial continuing damage to neighbors must be enjoined. To now change the rule to permit the cement company to continue polluting the air indefinitely upon the payment of permanent damages is, in my opinion, compounding the magnitude of a very serious problem in our State and Nation today.

In recognition of this problem, the Legislature of this State has enacted the Air Pollution Control Act declaring that it is the State policy to require the use of all available and reasonable methods to prevent and control air pollution.

The harmful nature and widespread occurrence of air pollution have been extensively documented. Congressional hearings have revealed that air pollution causes substantial property damage, as well as being a contributing factor to a rising incidence of lung cancer, emphysema, bronchitis and asthma.

The specific problem faced here is known as particulate contamination because of the fine dust particles emanating from defendant's cement plant. Cement production has recently been identified as a significant source of particulate contamination in the Hudson Valley. This type of pollution, wherein very small particles escape and stay in the atmosphere, has been denominated as the type of air pollution which produces the greatest hazard to human health. We have thus a nuisance which not only is damaging to the plaintiffs, but also is decidedly harmful to the general public.

I see grave dangers in overruling our long-established rule of granting an injunction where a nuisance results in substantial continuing damage. In permitting the injunction to become inoperative upon the payment of permanent damages, the majority is, in effect, licensing a continuing wrong. It is the same as saying to the cement company, you may continue to do harm to your neighbors so long as you pay a fee for it. Furthermore, once such permanent damages are assessed and paid, the incentive to alleviate the wrong would be eliminated, thereby continuing air pollution of an area without abatement.

This kind of inverse condemnation may not be invoked by a private person or corporation for private gain or advantage. Inverse condemnation should only be permitted when the public is primarily served in the taking or impairment of property. The promotion of the interests of the polluting cement company has, in my opinion, no public use or benefit.

Nor is it constitutionally permissible to impose servitude on land, without consent of the owner, by payment of permanent damages where the continuing impairment of the land is for a private use. This is made clear by the State Constitution (art. I, § 7, subd. (a)) which provides that "private property shall not be taken for *Public use* without just compensation." It is, of course, significant that the section makes no mention of taking for a *Private use.*

In sum, then, by constitutional mandate as well as by judicial pronouncement, the permanent impairment of private property for private purposes is not authorized in the absence of clearly demonstrated public benefit and use.

I would enjoin the defendant cement company from continuing the discharge of dust particles upon its neighbors' properties unless, within 18 months, the cement company abated this nuisance.[7] I am aware that

[7] The issuance of an injunction to become effective in the future is not an entirely new concept. For instance, in *Schwarzenbach v. Oneonta Light & Power Co.*, 207 N.Y. 671, 100 N.E. 1134, an injunction against the maintenance of a dam spilling water on plaintiff's property was issued to become effective one year hence.

the trial court found that the most modern dust control devices available have been installed in defendant's plant, but, I submit, this does not mean that *better* and more effective dust control devices could not be developed within the time allowed to abate the pollution. I believe it is incumbent upon the defendant to develop such devices, since the cement company, at the time the plant commenced production (1962), was well aware of the plaintiffs' presence in the area, as well as the probable consequences of its contemplated operation. Yet, it still chose to build and operate the plant at this site.

In a day when there is a growing concern for clean air, a highly developed industry should not expect acquiescence by the courts, but should, instead, plan its operations to eliminate contamination of our air and damage to its neighbors.

Accordingly, the orders of the Appellate Division, insofar as they denied the injunction, should be reversed, and the actions remitted to Supreme Court, Albany County to grant an injunction to take effect 18 months hence, unless the nuisance is abated by improved techniques prior to said date. * * *

QUESTIONS AND PROBLEMS

1. *More on the* Boomer *Decision.* Would the result in *Boomer* have been different if the cement company had been operating in violation of federal and state pollution laws? Would that fact have altered the court's conception of the "public interest" and the "balancing of the equities?" How? Why?

2. *Alternative Ways to Frame the Injunction.* Was it appropriate for the court to grant an injunction that could be lifted on the payment of damages? Would it have been preferable for the court to enter a binding injunction, but try to frame it in such a way as to accommodate both party's interests? Could the court have ordered changes that would have affected the way the plant operated and limited the nuisance? What steps might it have ordered defendant to take?

3. *Entering an Experimental Injunction.* Would it have been preferable for the court to enter an "experimental" injunction? In other words, would it have been more desirable for the court to order to order defendant to take ameliorative action, and then to revisit the situation a few months later to see how things are working out (and, perhaps, enter a modified order)?

4. *More on the Diamond Derby Gala.* If you are the judge, and if you decide to issue an injunction, would this be an appropriate case for entry of a conditional injunction or an experimental injunction? If so, why? How should the order be framed?

SPUR INDUSTRIES, INC. V. DEL E. WEBB DEVELOPMENT CO.

108 Ariz. 178, 494 P.2d 700 (In Banc, 1972).

CAMERON, VICE CHIEF JUSTICE.

From a judgment permanently enjoining the defendant, Spur Industries, Inc., from operating a cattle feedlot near the plaintiff Del E. Webb Development Company's Sun City, Spur appeals. Webb cross-appeals. It is necessary to answer only two questions. They are: 1. Where the operation of a business, such as a cattle feedlot is lawful in the first instance, but becomes a nuisance by reason of a nearby residential area, may the feedlot operation be enjoined in an action brought by the developer of the residential area? 2. Assuming that the nuisance may be enjoined, may the developer of a completely new town or urban area in a previously agricultural area be required to indemnify the operator of the feedlot who must move or cease operation because of the presence of the residential area created by the developer?

The area in question is located in Maricopa County, Arizona, some 14 to 15 miles west of the urban area of Phoenix. Farming started in this area about 1911. In 1929, with the completion of the Carl Pleasant Dam, gravity flow water became available to the property located to the west of the Agua Fria River, though land to the east remained dependent upon well water for irrigation. By 1950, the only urban areas in the vicinity were the agriculturally related communities of Peoria, El Mirage, and Surprise located along Grand Avenue. Along 111th Avenue, approximately one mile south of Grand Avenue and 1 1/2 miles north of Olive Avenue, the community of Youngtown was commenced in 1954. Youngtown is a retirement community appealing primarily to senior citizens.

In 1956, Spur's predecessors in interest developed feed-lots, about 1/2 mile south of Olive Avenue, in an area between the confluence of the usually dry Agua Fria and New Rivers. The area is well suited for cattle feeding and in 1959, there were 25 cattle feeding pens or dairy operations within a 7 mile radius of the location developed by Spur's predecessors. In 1959, the Northside Hay Mill was feeding between 6,000 and 7,000 head of cattle and Welborn approximately 1,500 head on a combined area of 35 acres.

In May of 1959, Del Webb began to plan the development of an urban area to be known as Sun City. For this purpose, the Marinette and the Santa Fe Ranches, some 20,000 acres of farmland, were purchased for $15,000,000 or $750.00 per acre. This price was considerably less than the price of land located near the urban area of Phoenix, and along with the success of Youngtown was a factor influencing the decision to purchase the property in question.

By September 1959, Del Webb had started construction of a golf course south of Grand Avenue and Spur's predecessors had started to level ground for more feedlot area. In 1960, Spur purchased the property in question and began a rebuilding and expansion program extending both to the north and south of the original facilities. By 1962, Spur's expansion program was completed and had expanded from approximately 35 acres to 114 acres.

Accompanied by an extensive advertising campaign, homes were first offered by Del Webb in January 1960 and the first unit to be completed was south of Grand Avenue and approximately 2 1/2 miles north of Spur. By 2 May 1960, there were 450 to 500 houses completed or under construction. At this time, Del Webb did not consider odors from the Spur feed pens a problem and Del Webb continued to develop in a southerly direction, until sales resistance became so great that the parcels were difficult if not impossible to sell. * * *

By December 1967, Del Webb's property had extended south to Olive Avenue and Spur was within 500 feet of Olive Avenue to the north. Del Webb filed its original complaint alleging that in excess of 1,300 lots in the southwest portion were unfit for development for sale as residential lots because of the operation of the Spur feedlot.

Del Webb's suit complained that the Spur feeding operation was a public nuisance because of the flies and the odor which were drifting or being blown by the prevailing south to north wind over the southern portion of Sun City. At the time of the suit, Spur was feeding between 20,000 and 30,000 head of cattle, and the facts amply support the finding of the trial court that the feed pens had become a nuisance to the people who resided in the southern part of Del Webb's development. The testimony indicated that cattle in a commercial feedlot will produce 35 to 40 pounds of wet manure per day, per head, or over a million pounds of wet manure per day for 30,000 head of cattle, and that despite the admittedly good feedlot management and good housekeeping practices by Spur, the resulting odor and flies produced an annoying if not unhealthy situation as far as the senior citizens of southern Sun City were concerned. There is no doubt that some of the citizens of Sun City were unable to enjoy the outdoor living which Del Webb had advertised and that Del Webb was faced with sales resistance from prospective purchasers as well as strong and persistent complaints from the people who had purchased homes in that area.

In one of the special actions before this court, Spur agreed to, and did, shut down its operation without prejudice to a determination of the matter on appeal. On appeal the many questions raised were extensively briefed. Neither the citizens of Sun City nor Youngtown are represented in this lawsuit and the suit is solely between Del E. Webb Development Company and Spur Industries, Inc.

MAY SPUR BE ENJOINED?

The difference between a private nuisance and a public nuisance is generally one of degree. A private nuisance is one affecting a single individual or a definite small number of persons in the enjoyment of private rights not common to the public, while a public nuisance is one affecting the rights enjoyed by citizens as a part of the public. To constitute a public nuisance, the nuisance must affect a considerable number of people or an entire community or neighborhood.

Where the injury is slight, the remedy for minor inconveniences lies in an action for damages rather than in one for an injunction. Moreover, some courts have held, in the "balancing of conveniences" cases, that damages may be the sole remedy. Thus, it would appear from the admittedly incomplete record as developed in the trial court, that, at most, residents of Youngtown would be entitled to damages rather than injunctive relief.

We have no difficulty, however, in agreeing with the trial court that Spur's operation was an enjoinable public nuisance as far as the people in the southern portion of Del Webb's Sun City were concerned.

§ 36–601, subsec. A reads as follows:

> "Public nuisances dangerous to public health A. The following conditions are specifically declared public nuisances dangerous to the public health: 1. Any condition or place in populous areas which constitutes a breeding place for flies, rodents, mosquitoes and other insects which are capable of carrying and transmitting disease-causing organisms to any person or persons."

By this statute, before an otherwise lawful (and necessary) business may be declared a public nuisance, there must be a "populous" area in which people are injured: "It hardly admits a doubt that, in determining the question as to whether a lawful occupation is so conducted as to constitute a nuisance as a matter of fact, the locality and surroundings are of the first importance. A business which is not per se a public nuisance may become such by being carried on at a place where the health, comfort, or convenience of a populous neighborhood is affected. What might amount to a serious nuisance in one locality by reason of the density of the population, or character of the neighborhood affected, may in another place and under different surroundings be deemed proper and unobjectionable." *MacDonald v. Perry*, 32 Ariz. 39, 49–50, 255 P. 494, 497 (1927).

It is clear that as to the citizens of Sun City, the operation of Spur's feedlot was both a public and a private nuisance. They could have successfully maintained an action to abate the nuisance. Del Webb, having shown a special injury in the loss of sales, had a standing to bring suit to enjoin the nuisance. The judgment of the trial court permanently enjoining the operation of the feedlot is affirmed.

MUST DEL WEBB INDEMNIFY SPUR?

A suit to enjoin a nuisance sounds in equity and the courts have long recognized a special responsibility to the public when acting as a court of equity:

§ 104. Where public interest is involved. "Courts of equity may, and frequently do, go much further both to give and withhold relief in furtherance of the public interest than they are accustomed to go when only private interests are involved. Accordingly, the granting or withholding of relief may properly be dependent upon considerations of public interest." § 27 Am.Jur.2d, Equity, page 626.

In addition to protecting the public interest, however, courts of equity are concerned with protecting the operator of a lawfully, albeit noxious, business from the result of a knowing and willful encroachment by others near his business.

In the so-called "coming to the nuisance" cases, the courts have held that the residential landowner may not have relief if he knowingly came into a neighborhood reserved for industrial or agricultural endeavors and has been damaged thereby: "Plaintiffs chose to live in an area uncontrolled by zoning laws or restrictive covenants and remote from urban development. In such an area plaintiffs cannot complain that legitimate agricultural pursuits are being carried on in the vicinity, nor can plaintiffs, having chosen to build in an agricultural area, complain that the agricultural pursuits carried on in the area depreciate the value of their homes. The area being primarily agricultural, and opinion reflecting the value of such property must take this factor into account. The standards affecting the value of residence property in an urban setting, subject to zoning controls and controlled planning techniques, cannot be the standards by which agricultural properties are judged." People employed in a city who build their homes in suburban areas of the county beyond the limits of a city and zoning regulations do so for a reason. Some do so to avoid the high taxation rate imposed by cities, or to avoid special assessments for street, sewer and water projects. They usually build on improved or hard surface highways, which have been built either at state or county expense and thereby avoid special assessments for these improvements. It may be that they desire to get away from the congestion of traffic, smoke, noise, foul air and the many other annoyances of city life. But with all these advantages in going beyond the area which is zoned and restricted to protect them in their homes, they must be prepared to take the disadvantages." *Dill v. Excel Packing Company*, 183 Kan. 513, 525, 526, 331 P.2d 539, 548, 549 (1958).

And: "a party cannot justly call upon the law to make that place suitable for his residence which was not so when he selected it." *Gilbert v. Showerman*, 23 Mich. 448, 455, 2 Brown 158 (1871). Were Webb the only party injured, we would feel justified in holding that the doctrine of "coming to the nuisance" would have been a bar to the relief asked by Webb, and, on the other hand, had Spur located the feedlot near the outskirts of a city and had the city grown toward the feedlot, Spur would have to suffer the cost of abating the nuisance as to those people locating within the growth pattern of the expanding city: "The case affords, perhaps, an example where a business established at a place remote from population is gradually surrounded and becomes part of a populous center, so that a business which formerly was not an interference with the rights of others has become so by the encroachment of the population." *City of Ft. Smith v. Western Hide & Fur Co.*, 153 Ark. 99, 103, 239 S.W. 724, 726 (1922).

We agree, however, with the Massachusetts court that: "The law of nuisance affords no rigid rule to be applied in all instances. It is elastic. It undertakes to require only that which is fair and reasonable under all the circumstances. In a commonwealth like this, which depends for its material prosperity so largely on the continued growth and enlargement of manufacturing of diverse varieties, 'extreme rights' cannot be enforced." *Stevens v. Rockport Granite Co.*, 216 Mass. 486, 488, 104 N.E. 371, 373 (1914).

There was no indication in the instant case at the time Spur and its predecessors located in western Maricopa County that a new city would spring up, full-blown, alongside the feeding operation and that the developer of that city would ask the court to order Spur to move because of the new city. Spur is required to move not because of any wrongdoing on the part of Spur, but because of a proper and legitimate regard of the courts for the rights and interests of the public.

Del Webb, on the other hand, is entitled to the relief prayed for (a permanent injunction), not because Webb is blameless, but because of the damage to the people who have been encouraged to purchase homes in Sun City. It does not equitably or legally follow, however, that Webb, being entitled to the injunction, is then free of any liability to Spur if Webb has in fact been the cause of the damage Spur has sustained. It does not seem harsh to require a developer, who has taken advantage of the lesser land values in a rural area as well as the availability of large tracts of land on which to build and develop a new town or city in the area, to indemnify those who are forced to leave as a result.

Having brought people to the nuisance to the foreseeable detriment of Spur, Webb must indemnify Spur for a reasonable amount of the cost of moving or shutting down. It should be noted that this relief to Spur is limited to a case wherein a developer has, with foreseeability, brought into a previously agricultural or industrial area the population which makes necessary the granting of an injunction against a lawful business and for which the business has no adequate relief.

It is therefore the decision of this court that the matter be remanded to the trial court for a hearing upon the damages sustained by the defendant Spur as a reasonable and direct result of the granting of the permanent injunction. Since the result of the appeal may appear novel and both sides have obtained a measure of relief, it is ordered that each side will bear its own costs.

Affirmed in part, reversed in part, and remanded for further proceedings consistent with this opinion.

QUESTIONS AND PROBLEMS

1. *Requiring Indemnification for Moving Costs.* Does the court's holding in this case (giving the injunction but requiring Del Webb to pay Spur Industries moving costs) make sense? Because of the Del Webb development, isn't it likely that Spur Industries property has increased significantly in value? If Spur Industries sells its property and moves to a very rural area, isn't it likely that Spur Industries will sell high and buy low? In other words, in deciding whether to require Del Webb to pay, should the court consider the fact that Del Webb's development may have enriched Spur Industries by making its property more valuable?

2. *Coming to the Nuisance.* One of the problems raised by this case is whether one who comes to a nuisance is entitled to complain about the nuisance and to seek equitable relief. This is an issue that you saw before (although not directly raised) in the QCC problem (involving individuals who bought a home next to a golf course and then complained about golf balls raining down on their home). Obviously, the *Del Webb* court concludes that "coming to the nuisance" is not a defense. Does this holding make sense? Should the fact that the feedlot located in the area prior to the Del Webb development mean that the new homeowners should be required to put up with the feedlot smells indefinitely?

3. *The Cricket Pitch and the Complaining Neighbor.* As you think about the "coming to the nuisance" defense, consider the facts of *Miller v. Jackson* 1977 1 Q.B. 966. In an English village, there was a cricket ground that had been in use for more than 70 years. The ground, which was well kept with a club house and seats for fans, was used for matches on Saturdays and Sundays. A developer purchased vacant land next to the cricket field and constructed homes. Plaintiff, who purchased one of the homes, became upset when cricket balls land in his garden and seeks injunctive relief to prevent the playing of cricket on the grounds. Should coming to the nuisance be a defense in a case like *Miller*? If the court decides to grant relief, can it do so short of ordering the cricketeers to stop playing on the pitch? If so, how might it frame the order? In other words, what should it order the cricket club to do or to refrain from doing?

F. DECREES AFFECTING THIRD PARTIES

In some instances, a court may find it necessary to enjoin third parties in order to grant complete relief to a plaintiff. When is it appropriate to award relief against third parties? Consider the following cases.

HILLS V. GAUTREAUX

425 U.S. 284, 96 S.Ct. 1538, 47 L.Ed.2d 792 (1976).

MR. JUSTICE STEWART delivered the opinion of the Court.

The United States Department of Housing and Urban Development (HUD) violated the Fifth Amendment and the Civil Rights Act of 1964 in connection with the selection of sites for public housing in the city of Chicago. The issue before us is whether the remedial order of the federal trial court may extend beyond Chicago's territorial boundaries.

The complaint alleged that CHA Chicago Housing Authority deliberately selected the sites to "avoid the placement of Negro families in white neighborhoods" in violation of federal statutes and the Fourteenth Amendment. In a companion suit against HUD the respondents claimed that it had "assisted in the carrying on and continues to assist in the carrying on of a racially discriminatory public housing system within the City of Chicago" by providing financial assistance and other support for CHA's discriminatory housing projects.

In February 1969, the court entered summary judgment against CHA on the ground that it had violated the respondents' constitutional rights by selecting public housing sites and assigning tenants on the basis of race. In order to prohibit future violations and to remedy the effects of past unconstitutional practices, the court directed CHA to build its next 700 family units in predominantly white areas of Chicago and thereafter to locate at least 75% of its new family public housing in predominantly white areas inside Chicago or in Cook County. In addition, CHA was ordered to modify its tenant-assignment and site-selection procedures and to use its best efforts to increase the supply of dwelling units as rapidly as possible in conformity with the judgment.

The District Court then granted HUD's motion to dismiss the complaint for lack of jurisdiction and failure to state a claim. After the Court of Appeals reversed, the trial court consolidated the CHA and HUD cases and ordered the parties to formulate "a comprehensive plan to remedy the past effects of unconstitutional site selection procedures." The court denied the respondents' motion to consider metropolitan area relief because "the wrongs were committed within the limits of Chicago and solely against residents of the City" and there were no allegations that

"CHA and HUD discriminated or fostered racial discrimination in the suburbs."

On appeal, the Court of Appeals for the Seventh Circuit reversed and remanded the case for "the adoption of a comprehensive metropolitan area plan that will not only disestablish the segregated public housing system in the City of Chicago but will increase the supply of dwelling units as rapidly as possible." * * *

In *Milliken v. Bradley,* 418 U.S. 717, this Court considered the proper scope of a federal court's equity decree in the context of a school desegregation case. The respondents in that case had brought an action alleging that the Detroit public school system was segregated on the basis of race as the result of official conduct. Although there had been neither proof of unconstitutional actions on the part of neighboring school districts nor a demonstration that the Detroit violations had produced significant segregative effects in those districts, the court established a desegregation panel and ordered it to prepare a remedial plan consolidating the Detroit school system and 53 independent suburban school districts. The Court of Appeals for the Sixth Circuit affirmed. This Court reversed the Court of Appeals, holding that the multidistrict remedy contemplated by the desegregation order was an erroneous exercise of the equitable authority of the federal courts.

Although the *Milliken* opinion discussed the many practical problems that would be encountered in the consolidation of numerous school districts by judicial decree, the Court's decision rejecting the metropolitan area desegregation order was actually based on fundamental limitations on the remedial powers of the federal courts to restructure the operation of local and state governmental entities. That power is not plenary. It "may be exercised 'only on the basis of a constitutional violation.'" 418 U.S., at 738, quoting *Swann v. Charlotte–Mecklenburg Board of Education*, 402 U.S. 1, 16. Once a constitutional violation is found, a federal court is required to tailor "the scope of the remedy" to fit "the nature and extent of the constitutional violation." In *Milliken*, there was no finding of unconstitutional action on the part of the suburban school officials and no demonstration that the violations committed in the operation of the Detroit school system had had any significant segregative effects in the suburbs. The desegregation order in *Milliken* requiring the consolidation of local school districts in the Detroit metropolitan area thus constituted direct federal judicial interference with local governmental entities without the necessary predicate of a constitutional violation by those entities or of the identification within them of any significant segregative effects resulting from the Detroit school officials' unconstitutional conduct. Under these circumstances, the Court held that the interdistrict decree was impermissible because it was not commensurate with the constitutional violation to be repaired.

Since the *Milliken* decision was based on basic limitations on the exercise of the equity power of the federal courts and not on a balancing of particular considerations presented by school desegregation cases, it is apparent that the Court of Appeals erred in finding *Milliken* inapplicable on that ground to this public housing case. * * *

The question presented in this case concerns only the authority of the District Court to order HUD to take remedial action outside the city limits of Chicago. We reject the contention that, since HUD's constitutional and statutory violations were committed in Chicago, *Milliken* precludes an order against HUD that will affect its conduct in the greater metropolitan area. Our prior decisions counsel that in the event of a constitutional violation "all reasonable methods be available to formulate an effective remedy," and that every effort should be made by a federal court to employ those methods "to achieve the greatest possible degree of (relief), taking into account the practicalities of the situation." *Davis v. School Comm'rs of Mobile County*, 402 U.S. 33, 37. * * *

Nothing in the *Milliken* decision suggests a *per se* rule that federal courts lack authority to order parties found to have violated the Constitution to undertake remedial efforts beyond the municipal boundaries of the city where the violation occurred. The District Court's proposed remedy in *Milliken* was impermissible because of the limits on the federal judicial power to interfere with the operation of state political entities that were not implicated in unconstitutional conduct. Here, unlike the desegregation remedy found erroneous in *Milliken*, a judicial order directing relief beyond the boundary lines of Chicago will not necessarily entail coercion of uninvolved governmental units, because both CHA and HUD have the authority to operate outside the Chicago city limits.

In this case, it is entirely appropriate and consistent with *Milliken* to order CHA and HUD to attempt to create housing alternatives for the respondents in the Chicago suburbs. Here the wrong committed by HUD confined the respondents to segregated public housing. The relevant geographic area for purposes of the respondents' housing options is the Chicago housing market, not the Chicago city limits. An order against HUD and CHA regulating their conduct in the greater metropolitan area will do no more than take into account HUD's expert determination of the area relevant to the respondents' housing opportunities and will thus be wholly commensurate with the "nature and extent of the constitutional violation." To foreclose such relief solely because HUD's constitutional violation took place within the city limits of Chicago would transform *Milliken's* principled limitation on the exercise of federal judicial authority into an arbitrary and mechanical shield for those found to have engaged in unconstitutional conduct.

The more substantial question under *Milliken* is whether an order against HUD affecting its conduct beyond Chicago's boundaries would impermissibly interfere with local governments and suburban housing authorities that have not been implicated in HUD's unconstitutional conduct. A remedial plan designed to insure that HUD will utilize its funding and administrative powers in a manner consistent with affording relief to the respondents need not abrogate the role of local governmental units in the federal housing-assistance programs. Under the major housing programs in existence at the time the District Court entered its remedial order pertaining to HUD, local housing authorities and municipal governments had to make application for funds or approve the use of funds in the locality before HUD could make housing assistance money available. An order directed solely to HUD would not force unwilling localities to apply for assistance under these programs but would merely reinforce the regulations guiding HUD's determination of which of the locally authorized projects to assist with federal funds.

In sum, there is no basis for the petitioner's claim that court-ordered metropolitan area relief in this case would be impermissible as a matter of law under the *Milliken* decision. In contrast to the desegregation order in that case, a metropolitan area relief order directed to HUD would not consolidate or in any way restructure local governmental units. The remedial decree would neither force suburban governments to submit public housing proposals to HUD nor displace the rights and powers accorded local government entities under federal or state housing statutes or existing land-use laws. The order would have the same effect on the suburban governments as a discretionary decision by HUD to use its statutory powers to provide the respondents with alternatives to the racially segregated Chicago public housing system created by CHA and HUD.

Since we conclude that a metropolitan area remedy in this case is not impermissible as a matter of law, we affirm the judgment of the Court of Appeals remanding the case to the District Court "for additional evidence and for further consideration of the issue of metropolitan area relief." Our determination that the District Court has the authority to direct HUD to engage in remedial efforts in the metropolitan area outside the city limits of Chicago should not be interpreted as requiring a metropolitan area order. The nature and scope of the remedial decree to be entered on remand is a matter for the District Court in the exercise of its equitable discretion, after affording the parties an opportunity to present their views.

The judgment of the Court of Appeals remanding this case to the District Court is affirmed, but further proceedings in the District Court are to be consistent with this opinion.

It is so ordered.

Affirmed.

GENERAL BUILDING CONTRACTORS ASSOCIATION, INC. v. PENNSYLVANIA

458 U.S. 375, 102 S.Ct. 3141, 73 L.Ed.2d 835 (1982).

JUSTICE REHNQUIST delivered the opinion of the Court.

The hiring hall system that is the focus of this litigation originated in a collective-bargaining agreement negotiated in 1961 by Local 542 and four construction trade associations in the Philadelphia area, three of whom are petitioners in this Court. The agreement was concluded only after a 10-week strike prompted by the resistance of the trade associations to the Union's demand for an exclusive hiring hall. Under the terms of the agreement, the Union was to maintain lists of operating engineers, or would-be engineers, classified according to the extent of their recent construction experience. Signatory employers were contractually obligated to hire operating engineers only from among those referred by the Union from its current lists. Workers affiliated with the Union were barred from seeking work with those employers except through Union referrals. Thus, the collective-bargaining agreement effectively channeled all employment opportunities through the hiring hall. Since 1961 this requirement has been a constant feature of contracts negotiated with Local 542 by the trade associations, as well as of contracts signed with the Union by employers who were not represented by one of those associations in collective bargaining.

Among the means of gaining access to the Union's referral lists is an apprenticeship program established in 1965 by Local 542 and the trade associations. The program, which involves classroom and field training, is administered by the Joint Apprenticeship and Training Committee (JATC), a body of trustees half of whom are appointed by the Union and half by the trade associations. While enrolled in the program, apprentices are referred by the Union for unskilled construction work. Graduates of the program become journeymen operating engineers and are referred for heavy equipment jobs.

This action was filed in 1971 by the Commonwealth of Pennsylvania and 12 black plaintiffs representing a proposed class of minority group members residing within the jurisdiction of Local 542. The complaint charged that the Union and the JATC had violated numerous state and federal laws prohibiting employment discrimination. The complaint alleged that these defendants had engaged in a pattern and practice of racial discrimination, by systematically denying access to the Union's referral lists, and by arbitrarily skewing referrals in favor of white workers, limiting most minority workers who did gain access to the hiring hall to jobs of short hours and low pay. The contractor employers and trade associations were also named as defendants, although the complaint did not allege a Title VII cause of action against them.

The District Court found that the hiring hall system established by collective bargaining was neutral on its face. Indeed, after May 1, 1971, the contracts contained a provision expressly prohibiting employment discrimination on the basis of race, religion, color, or national origin. But the court found that Local 542, in administering the system, "practiced a pattern of intentional discrimination and that union practices in the overall operation of a hiring hall for operating engineers created substantial racial disparities." The court made similar findings regarding the JATC's administration of the job-training program. On the basis of these findings, the District Court held that Local 542 and the JATC had violated Title VII, both because they intentionally discriminated and because they enforced practices that resulted in a disparate racial impact. The court also interpreted 42 U.S.C. § 1981 to permit imposition of liability "on roughly the same basis as a Title VII claim," and therefore concluded that the Union and the JATC had also violated § 1981.

The court found that the plaintiffs had failed to prove "that the associations or contractors viewed simply as a class were actually aware of the union discrimination," and had failed to show "intent to discriminate by the employers as a class." Nevertheless, the court held the employers and the associations liable under § 1981 for the purpose of imposing an injunctive remedy "as a result of their contractual relationship to and use of a hiring hall system which in practice effectuated intentional discrimination, whether or not the employers and associations knew or should have known of the Union's conduct." * * *

The District Court held that petitioners had violated 42 U.S.C. § 1981 notwithstanding its finding that, as a class, petitioners did not intentionally discriminate against minority workers and neither knew nor had reason to know of the Union's discriminatory practices. We conclude that § 1981, like the Equal Protection Clause, can be violated only by purposeful discrimination. * * *

Respondents urge several independent bases for the issuance of an injunction against the petitioners and the allocation to them of a portion of the costs of the remedial decree. Respondents first assert that the court had inherent equitable power to allocate remedial costs among all the named defendants. They also rely on the All Writs Act, 28 U.S.C. § 1651(a), as an independent basis for the injunctive portions of the District Court's order running against petitioners. We shall deal with these contentions in turn.

The District Court in an opinion issued after judgment set forth the basis for its holding that "defendants held injunctively liable solely under a theory of vicarious responsibility are nevertheless liable for 'a share' of the costs under Rule 54(d)." *Pennsylvania v. Local 542, Int'l Union of Operating Engineers*, 507 F.Supp. 1146, 1152 (1980). The District Court framed the inquiry before it as whether a party held vicariously liable to an injunction, but not for damages, might nonetheless have a proportionate share of the costs assessed against it. While this may have been an entirely appropriate frame of reference for the District Court, following its holding that petitioners were vicariously liable and therefore subject to an injunction, it is obviously not the proper frame of reference for our discussion. We have concluded that petitioners were not properly subject to an injunction on any of the theories set forth by the District Court. The issue before us, therefore, is whether a party not subject to liability for violating the law may nonetheless be assessed a proportionate share of the costs of implementing a decree to assure nondiscriminatory practices on the part of another party which was properly enjoined.

We find respondent's arguments based on the traditional equitable authority of courts to be unpersuasive. We read our earlier decisions as recognizing "fundamental limitations on the remedial powers of the federal courts." Those powers could be exercised only on the basis of a violation of the law and could extend no farther than required by the nature and the extent of that violation. This principle, we held, was not one limited to school desegregation cases, but was instead "premised on a controlling principle governing the permissible scope of federal judicial power, a principle not limited to a school desegregation context."

We think that the principle enunciated in these cases, transposed to the instant factual situation, offers no support for the imposition of injunctive relief against a party found not to have violated any substantive right of respondents. This is not to say that defendants in the position of petitioners might not, upon an appropriate evidentiary showing, be retained in the lawsuit and even subjected to such minor and ancillary provisions of an injunctive order as the District Court might find necessary to grant complete relief to respondents from the discrimination they suffered at the hands of the Union. But that sort of minor and ancillary relief is not the same, and cannot be the same, as that awarded against a party found to have infringed the statutory rights of persons in the position of respondents.

The order of the District Court, insofar as it runs against petitioners, cannot be regarded as "minor" or "ancillary" in any proper sense of those terms. First, it imposes considerable burdens on the employers and associations. It directs the employers to meet detailed "minority utilization goals" in their hiring, keyed to the number of hours worked. If they are unable to do so through referrals from Local 542, they are required to hire minority operating engineers who are not affiliated with the Union. *Ibid.* If the goals are still not satisfied, the employers must recruit and hire unskilled minority workers from the community and provide on-the-job training. The employers are also obligated to make quarterly reports detailing the extent of their compliance with these directives. Finally, the District Court imposed on the employers and the associations a share of the financial cost incidental to enforcement of the remedial decree as a whole. According to petitioners, the expense of the decree in the first year of its 5-year life exceeded $200,000.

Absent a supportable finding of liability, we see no basis for requiring the employers or the associations to aid either in paying for the cost of the remedial program as a whole or in establishing and administering the training program. Nor is the imposition of minority hiring quotas directly upon petitioners the sort of remedy that may be imposed without regard to a finding of liability. If the Union and the JATC comply with the decree by training and referring minority workers, we see no reason to assume, absent supporting evidence, that the employers will not hire the minority workers referred pursuant to the collective-bargaining agreement, and employ them at wages and hours commensurate with those of nonminority workers. If experience proves otherwise, the District Court will then have more than sufficient grounds for including the employers within the scope of the remedial decree.

To the extent that the remedy properly imposed upon the Union and the JATC requires any adjustment in the collective-bargaining contract between petitioners and the Union, it is entirely appropriate for the District Court to fashion its injunctive remedy to so provide, and to have that remedy run against petitioners as well as the Union and the JATC. But the injunctive decree entered by the District Court as presently drawn treats petitioners as if they had been properly found liable for the Union's discrimination. A decree containing such provisions, we hold, is beyond the traditional equitable limitations upon the authority of a federal court to formulate such decrees.

Nor does the All Writs Act, 28 U.S.C. § 1651(a), support the extensive liability imposed upon petitioners by the District Court. The District Court did not rely upon this Act, and we think it completely wide of the mark in justifying the relief granted by the District Court. That Act was most recently considered by this Court in United States v. New York Telephone Co., 434 U.S. 159 (1977), where we said: "This Court has repeatedly recognized the power of a federal court to issue such commands under the All Writs Act as may be necessary or appropriate to effectuate and prevent the frustration of orders it has previously issued in its exercise of jurisdiction otherwise obtained." On the record before the District Court the petitioners could not properly be held liable to any sort of injunctive relief based on their own conduct.

Thus insofar as respondents' arguments for the imposition of remedial obligations upon petitioners rests upon the assumption that petitioners were properly found liable for the violation of respondents' rights to be free from discrimination, that assumption can no longer stand in view of the conclusions previously set forth in this opinion. Insofar as respondents' assertions are based on some authority of the District Court to impose the sort of obligations which it did upon petitioners even though petitioners could not be held liable on the record before the District Court, we hold that such obligations can be imposed neither under traditional equitable authority of the District Court nor under the All Writs Act.

The judgment of the Court of Appeals is reversed, and the case is remanded for proceedings consistent with this opinion.

It is so ordered.

JUSTICE O'CONNOR, with whom JUSTICE BLACKMUN joins, concurring.

I agree with the Court's holding that "a party not subject to liability for violating the law may not be assessed a proportionate share of the costs of implementing a decree to assure nondiscriminatory practices on the part of another party which was properly enjoined."[2] I also agree with the Court's ancillary holding that the District Court may not require quarterly reports from the employers detailing their compliance with the court's ill-founded injunction. Of course, since the employers are not liable for general injunctive relief, such reports are unnecessary. It is conceivable that quarterly reports providing employment statistics necessary for the court to ascertain whether its injunctive decree is being properly implemented could be ordered under the court's equitable powers to effectuate its decree.

JUSTICE MARSHALL, with whom JUSTICE BRENNAN joins, dissenting.

I cannot agree that the petitioner contracting associations should be immunized, even from injunctive liability, for the intentional discrimination practiced by the union hall to which they delegated a major portion of their hiring decisions. The contracting associations attempt to hide behind the veil of ignorance, shifting their responsibility under § 1981 to the very entity which they chose to assist them in making hiring decisions. By immunizing the employer from the injunctive relief necessary to remedy the intentional discrimination practiced by those through whom the employer makes its hiring decisions, the Court removes the person most necessary to accord full relief—the entity with whom the aggrieved persons will ultimately make a contract. * * *

[2] In the present cases, the District Court ordered the three employer associations to pay 10% of the costs of remedial relief, and the employer, Glasgow, to pay 5%. Because the cost of relief to date has been approximately $200,000, the petitioners' share of the cost has been $70,000.

G. APPEALS OF INJUNCTION RULINGS

When dealing with appeals related to temporary restraining orders and preliminary injunctions, a number of issues may arise. These include questions of jurisdiction as well as the time-sensitive nature of the issues being appealed.

1. JURISDICTION OVER APPEALS

Permanent injunction rulings are "final decisions" and are therefore appealable as are other final resolutions of suits. By contrast, temporary restraining orders and preliminary injunctions are "interlocutory orders," and interlocutory orders are not ordinarily appealable. Nevertheless, Congress and most states have provided for appeals of preliminary injunction rulings because the duration of a preliminary injunction is often considerable and it can have serious effects. In the federal system, 28 U.S.C. § 1292(a) provides that the "courts of appeals shall have jurisdiction of appeals from: (1) Interlocutory orders granting, continuing, modifying, refusing or dissolving injunctions, or refusing to dissolve or modify injunctions, except where a direct review may be had in the Supreme Court."

Unlike permanent and preliminary injunctions, temporary restraining orders are of short duration and are often issued *ex parte* and without an adversarial hearing. For these reasons, federal and most state courts have held that TRO rulings are not generally appealable. Courts have recognized exceptions to this general rule, however. The following case illustrates the most common exception, that an appeal may be heard when the TRO has "ripened" into a preliminary injunction.

NUTRASWEET CO. V. VIT–MAR ENTERPRISES, INC.

112 F.3d 689 (3d Cir. 1997).

STAPLETON, CIRCUIT JUDGE:

In this grey market case, the district court entered a "temporary restraining order" that had remained in effect for seventy-seven days as of the time of the filing of appellant's notice of appeal. We conclude that we have jurisdiction to review that "temporary restraining order," and we will remand to the district court with instructions to vacate it.

Nutrasweet sold certain shipments of its sweetener Equal to Vitmar Enterprises and the Shiba Group at a 50%–75% discount based on the condition that the buyer would only distribute the product outside the United States. The bill of lading for the shipments contained a provision stating, "THESE COMMODITIES ARE LICENSED BY THE UNITED STATES FOR THE FINAL DESTINATION UKRAINE OR YAKUTSK REGION, RUSSIA. ANY DIVERSIONS ARE AGAINST THE LAW."

While the current record is unclear as to exactly what transpired after the shipment was sold to the Shiba Group, defendant/appellant Tekstilschik, a business entity organized under the laws of the Russian Federation, claims to have acquired one of the shipments in Russia from another Russian company in a barter transaction. Tekstilschik further claims that its decision to have it shipped to the United States was made without knowledge of the marketing restriction imposed by Nutrasweet. Tekstilschik allegedly hired Romano Fashions ("Romano") as its agent for the purpose of bringing the shipment to the United States and processing it through Customs.[1] While the shipment was being processed by the Customs Office, Nutrasweet learned of the shipment's whereabouts and filed the present action to keep Romano from introducing it into the U.S. market. Nutrasweet also learned that the six prior shipments that had been sold for foreign export and distribution only had already been reintroduced into the United States successfully.

Nutrasweet filed its suit on May 14, 1996, and made an emergency application for a temporary restraining order on the same day. Nutrasweet and Romano appeared before the district court when that application was presented. At 5:00 p.m. that day, the district court granted a restraining order. The order enjoined the named defendants and "John Does X, Y & Z, being any other persons or entities participating in the domestic import, sale or transport of the subject shipment" from taking possession of or otherwise dealing with the "NutraSweet Pre–Entry Product." The court's order set a hearing on an application for a preliminary injunction for May 22, 1996, and authorized expedited depositions. On May 29, 1996, the hearing had not been held, however, and the district court entered an order resetting it for June 10, 1996. That date, in turn, passed without a hearing on a preliminary injunction having been held and the temporary restraining order remained in effect on June 18, 1996, when Tekstilschik entered a "special appearance for the sole purpose of contesting the temporary restraints."

On Tekstilschik's application, the court issued an order to show cause why the temporary restraining order should not be dissolved, returnable June 27, 1996. In connection with the June 27th hearing, Tekstilschik submitted an affidavit of Marina Martinova, one of its officers. The affidavit describes how Tekstilschik allegedly acquired the Equal in Russia in good faith and how it had arranged with Romano to oversee its importation into the United States for a commission of 2–1/2%. In May of

[1] Romano Fashions is owned by Manoj and Nimisha Parekh, also named as defendants in this action. Apparently, the Parekhs own the Shiba Group, Vit–Mar Enterprises and numerous other entities. It is Nutrasweet's position that the Parekhs are involved in a profitable scam whereby they purchase shipments of Equal under the guise of these companies at the discounted price by misrepresenting to Nutrasweet that the shipment will be exported and sold in a foreign market. After purchasing the product at a substantial discount, Nutrasweet alleges that the Parekhs fraudulently distribute it in the U.S. via the different companies, disrupting Nutrasweet's domestic market.

1996, Ms. Martinova was advised in Russia by a named defendant other than Romano that the Nutrasweet had been seized by a court in the United States. It was allegedly from the papers subsequently obtained from this suit that Tekstilschik first learned of Nutrasweet's marketing restrictions.

The district court decided to deny Tekstilschik's motion to dissolve the temporary restraining order because Tekstilschik had failed to demonstrate "standing" to challenge the restraining order. At the close of the hearing, counsel for Nutrasweet suggested that the court enter a preliminary injunction. The court declined to do so in the absence of a unanimous agreement of counsel, however, noting that no preliminary injunction record had been developed and observing: "If I am going to grant a preliminary injunction, I have got to make specific findings of fact." On July 15th, the district court entered an order denying Tekstilschik's application to dissolve the temporary restraining order as to it.

On July 18, 1996, before a hearing on a preliminary injunction had been held, the district court granted an application of defendants other than Tekstilschik that all proceedings be stayed pending completion of a criminal investigation of several of the defendants. On July 30, 1996, Tekstilschik filed this appeal. Its notice of appeal states that it seeks to challenge (1) the temporary restraining order, (2) the order denying its motion to dissolve that order, and (3) the order staying all proceedings.

As a general proposition, orders granting or denying temporary restraining orders are unappealable. However, orders granting or denying preliminary injunctions are immediately appealable pursuant to 28 U.S.C. § 1292(a)(1). Section 1292(a)(1) states that "the courts of appeals shall have jurisdiction of appeals from interlocutory orders of the district courts of the United States granting, continuing, modifying, refusing or dissolving, or refusing to dissolve or modify injunctions, except where a direct review may be had in the Supreme Court." The rationale for distinguishing between a temporary restraining order and a preliminary injunction is that temporary restraining orders are of short duration and terminate with a ruling on the preliminary injunction, making an immediate appeal unnecessary to protect the rights of the parties.

Tekstilschik claims that we have appellate jurisdiction pursuant to 28 U.S.C. § 1292(a)(1). Nutrasweet's position, on the other hand, is that we lack jurisdiction because the district court has done nothing more than enter a temporary restraining order.

Rule 65(b) of the Federal Rules of Civil Procedure directs that a temporary restraining order issued without notice to the adverse party shall expire by its own terms no later than 10 days after its entry, unless, for good cause shown, it is extended for a like period or unless the party against whom it is entered consents to an extension. The time limitations imposed by this rule thus apply, when read literally, only to temporary restraining orders issued without notice. According to Nutrasweet, the rule is inapplicable here because Tekstilschik allegedly received notice of the TRO application, as a matter of law, when its agent Romano received such notice. While it is not clear to us that Romano was Tekstilschik's agent for purposes of this litigation, or that notice to Romano in the United States on the day of the application should be imputed to Tekstilschik in Russia, we may assume for present purposes that the temporary restraining order was entered with notice to Tekstilschik.

A temporary restraining order can inflict substantial injury on a defendant whether or not it had an opportunity to oppose its entry. In recognition of this fact, courts have held that temporary restraining orders, even when entered with notice, cannot be continued indefinitely without observance of the safeguards required for entry of a preliminary injunction and that temporary restraining orders of indefinite duration, whether or not issued with notice, are subject to appellate review. The most prevalent view is that a temporary restraining order, even if issued with notice, cannot be continued beyond the periods prescribed in Fed.R.Civ.P. 65(b) without being treated as the equivalent of a preliminary injunction and thus subject to appellate review.

In *Sampson v. Murray,* 415 U.S. 61 (1974), the district court had entered a temporary restraining order restraining the government from carrying out a decision to discharge the plaintiff and had set a hearing on the application for a preliminary injunction for the following week. In connection with the application for a preliminary injunction, the district court wished to hear the testimony of the official who made the discharge decision. When the government refused to produce this witness, the district court ordered the temporary restraining order continued indefinitely, stating that the plaintiff would suffer irreparable injury without a continuation. The restraining order remained in effect at the time the government filed its notice of appeal.

The Supreme Court held that the temporary restraining order should be treated as a preliminary injunction, noting that an adversary hearing had been held. The Court observed:

> The Court of Appeals has held that a temporary restraining order continued beyond the time permissible under Rule 65 must be treated as a preliminary injunction, and must conform to the standards applicable to preliminary injunctions. We believe that this analysis is correct and comports with general principles imposing strict limitations on the scope of temporary restraining orders. A district court, if it were able to shield its orders from appellate review merely by designating them as temporary restraining orders, rather than as preliminary injunctions, would have virtually unlimited authority over the parties in an

> injunctive proceeding. In this case, where an adversary hearing has been held, and the court's basis for issuing the order strongly challenged, classification of the potentially unlimited order as a temporary restraining order seems particularly unjustified.

In our opinion the restraining order now in effect must be treated as a temporary injunction, issued without the consent of the defendant, in the face of his motion to dissolve it, and contrary to the provisions of Rule 52(a). It is clear that an appeal lies from a temporary injunction. *Deckert v. Independence Shares Corporation,* 311 U.S. 282 (1940). The appeal at bar therefore may not be dismissed and the order restraining the defendant must be reversed.

On July 15, 1996, the district court's temporary restraining order in this case had been in effect for sixty-two days, and the district court had been aware for twenty-seven days that Tekstilschik did not consent to its continuing existence. The district court's order of July 15th continued that "temporary" restraint indefinitely. Under these circumstances, we hold that we have jurisdiction under 28 U.S.C. § 1292(a) to review the district court's order of July 15, 1996, denying the motion to vacate and continuing the "temporary restraining order" over Tekstilschik's objection. The district court's July 15th order denying the motion to vacate and thus continuing the temporary restraining order must be vacated because it had the same effect as a preliminary injunction, but was entered without the development of a preliminary injunction record and findings of fact by the court. The district court is, of course, not precluded from entering a preliminary injunction applicable to Tekstilschik if that injunction is entered with the safeguards required by law.

NOTES AND QUESTIONS

1. *Other Considerations.* In addition to considering whether the TRO has ripened into a preliminary injunction, courts also consider a number of other factors in deciding whether to grant appeal of a TRO ruling. If the TRO disturbs the status quo between the parties, courts are more likely to grant appeal, and vice-versa. An appeal of a mandatory injunction is more likely to be heard than an appeal of a prohibitory injunction. Finally, as hinted in *Nutrasweet,* TROs entered after a full, adversarial hearing are more readily appealed than TROs issued after a truncated hearing—for the practical reason that the appellate court needs some record to review.

2. *TRO Appealable as "Permanent Injunction."* Courts will also grant appeal of a TRO when its effect is that of a permanent injunction, that is when it grants all the relief sought by the winning party. *See, e.g., Romer v. Green Point Savings Bank,* 27 F.3d 12 (2d Cir. 1994) (granting appeal of a TRO that would have prevented defendant company from going forward with its conversion plan within the time period allowed by law, dealing the

defendant an irreversible blow and effectively handing plaintiffs final victory in the litigation).

3. *Standard of Review.* In reviewing a trial court's injunction decision, appellate courts apply an abuse of discretion standard. *See, e.g.*, *Haggblom v. City of Dillingham*, 191 P.3d 991 (Alaska 2008).

4. *Modification of TROs and Preliminary Injunctions.* Either party may move the trial court to dissolve or modify an injunction. With respect to TROs and preliminary injunctions, the standard for such decisions is the same as the court applied when issuing the injunction. *See, e.g.*, *Sierra Club v. United States Army Corps of Engineers*, 732 F.2d 253 (2d Cir. 1984). The standard for modification or dissolution of a permanent injunction is discussed in Section H, *infra* at 327.

PROBLEMS

1. *The Second Floor Addition.* Bert had begun to implement his longstanding plans to add a second-floor apartment to his one-story ranch-style house. Building had commenced and would likely finish within the month. Bert's neighbor, Ernie, believed that the addition violated covenants attached to Bert's land and that it constituted a nuisance, blocking Ernie's view of the panoramic Bigbird Mountains. Ernie sued Bert and requested a temporary restraining order. The court denied Ernie's request for a TRO and scheduled a preliminary injunction hearing for thirty days following entry of the order. Assuming that federal rules apply, should the appellate court hear Ernie's appeal?

2. *A TRO for Twenty Days.* What if the trial court instead issued a TRO for a term of 20 days. Should the appellate court hear Bert's appeal?

2. PRE-APPEAL RELIEF

If a party appeals an injunction or the denial of an injunction (whether permanent, preliminary, or TRO), the party may also seek pre-appeal relief. Such relief may take one of two forms. If the party has appealed the issuance of an injunction, pre-appeal relief would constitute a stay of the injunction pending appeal. If the party has appealed the denial of an injunction, pre-appeal relief would take the form of an injunction pending appeal of the denial.

In the federal system, the process of pre-appeal relief is governed by Rule 62(c) of the Federal Rules of Civil Procedure and Rule 8 of the Federal Rules of Appellate Procedure. Rule 62(c) provides that once a court has granted appeal of an injunction ruling, "the court may suspend, modify, restore, or grant an injunction on terms for bond or other terms that secure the opposing party's rights."

RULE 8. STAY OR INJUNCTION PENDING APPEAL

(a) Motion for Stay.

(1) Initial Motion in the District Court. A party must ordinarily move first in the district court for the following relief:

(A) a stay of the judgment or order of a district court pending appeal;

(B) approval of a supersedeas bond; or

(C) an order suspending, modifying, restoring, or granting an injunction while an appeal is pending.

(2) Motion in the Court of Appeals; Conditions on Relief. A motion for the relief mentioned in Rule 8(a)(1) may be made to the court of appeals or to one of its judges.

(A) The motion must:

(i) show that moving first in the district court would be impracticable; or

(ii) state that, a motion having been made, the district court denied the motion or failed to afford the relief requested and state any reasons given by the district court for its action.

(B) The motion must also include:

(i) the reasons for granting the relief requested and the facts relied on;

(ii) originals or copies of affidavits or other sworn statements supporting facts subject to dispute; and

(iii) relevant parts of the record.

(C) The moving party must give reasonable notice of the motion to all parties.

(D) A motion under this Rule 8(a)(2) must be filed with the circuit clerk and normally will be considered by a panel of the court. But in an exceptional case in which time requirements make that procedure impracticable, the motion may be made to and considered by a single judge.

(E) The court may condition relief on a party's filing a bond or other appropriate security in the district court.

(b) Proceeding Against a Surety. If a party gives security in the form of a bond or stipulation or other undertaking with one or more sureties, each surety submits to the jurisdiction of the district court and irrevocably appoints the district clerk as the surety's agent on whom any papers affecting the surety's liability on the bond or undertaking may be served. On motion, a surety's

> liability may be enforced in the district court without the necessity of an independent action. The motion and any notice that the district court prescribes may be served on the district clerk, who must promptly mail a copy to each surety whose address is known.

Federal courts have interpreted Rules 8 and 62(c), to mandate that a party first seek pre-appeal relief in the trial court, unless to do so would be "impracticable." The decision of the trial court regarding the stay may then be appealed to a "motions panel." Or, if it is impracticable to request relief from the trial courts, then the appellant may seek pre-appeal relief from the motions panel directly. The motions panel typically consists of three appellate court judges, although in emergency situations it might be staffed by only one judge. The motions panel will sometimes convene within hours, and certainly within days, of the requested review.

In considering pre-appeal relief, the district court and the motions panel should "preserve the case for appeal." This task is sometimes interpreted as being synonymous with "preserving the status quo," but it also might mean simply to ensure that the appeal of the injunction decision does not become moot. Although the legal standard governing pre-appeal relief is similar to the standard governing injunctions, the procedural posture of the decision influences courts' analysis of the test. Consideration of the "likelihood of success" prong in the context of pre-appeal relief, for example, concerns the likelihood of the appellant's success in appealing the injunction decision, not the plaintiff's eventual likelihood of success in the litigation. The relevant measure of "irreparable harm" is the harm to be suffered by the appellant pending appeal should the pre-appeal relief not issue. The following motions panel decision discusses the application of the injunction standard in the context of a request for pre-appeal relief.

One who believes that an *ex parte* TRO was improperly granted can seek relief from the court that issued the order, as governed by Rule 65(b) of the Federal Rules of Civil Procedure. Under F.R.Civ.P. 65(b):

> On 2 days notice to the party who obtained the temporary restraining order without notice or on such shorter notice as the court may prescribe, the adverse party may appear and move its dissolution or modification and in that event the court shall proceed to hear and determine such motion as expeditiously as the ends of justice require.

WASHINGTON METROPOLITAN AREA TRANSIT COMMISSION v. HOLIDAY TOURS, INC.

559 F.2d 841 (D.C.Cir.1977).

LEVENTHAL, CIRCUIT JUDGE:

The District Court granted the Washington Metropolitan Area Transit Commission a permanent injunction restraining Holiday Tours from operating a motor coach sightseeing service without a certificate of public convenience and necessity. Then, on motion of Holiday Tours, the District Court stayed its injunction pending appeal. We deny the Commission's motion to vacate the District Court's stay, and in doing so find it necessary to refine the discussion in *Virginia Petroleum Jobbers Association v. FPC*, 104 U.S.App.D.C. 106, 259 F.2d 921 (1958).

In that case, we articulated the following criteria regarding stays: (1) Has the petitioner made a strong showing that it is likely to prevail on the merits of its appeal? Without such a substantial indication of probable success, there would be no justification for the court's intrusion into the ordinary processes of administration and judicial review. (2) Has the petitioner shown that without such relief, it will be irreparably injured? (3) Would the issuance of a stay substantially harm other parties interested in the proceedings? (4) Where lies the public interest?

The final three factors enumerated above clearly favored the District Court's grant of a stay. The harm to Holiday Tours in the absence of a stay would be its destruction in its current form as a provider of bus tours. In contrast to this irreparable harm, there is little indication that a stay pending appeal will result in substantial harm to either appellee Commission or to other tour bus operators. As to harm to the public interest, this is not a case where the Commission has ruled that the service performed by appellant is contrary to the public interest. Indeed for all that the record discloses, appellant might obtain a certificate, perhaps not precisely for the operation it prefers, if it made application. The interest of the Commission and of the riding public is largely the same as that of the general public in having legal questions decided on the merits, as correctly and expeditiously as possible. But the question is whether there is a further interest, that precludes maintaining the status quo while the merits are being decided on appeal.

In this context, Holiday Tours was undoubtedly not entitled to a stay on a showing "that it is likely to prevail on the merits of its appeal." Implicit in the Commission's argument against the stay is the view, commonly shared by litigants interpreting *Virginia Petroleum Jobbers*, that a stay is never appropriate unless the movant can show that success on appeal is "probable." Adherents of this view maintain that a lesser showing, of, say, a chance of prevailing that is only fifty percent or less is insufficient even though the "balance of equities," as determined by a consideration of the other three factors, clearly favors a stay.

Although this approach adopts a linguistically permissible interpretation of *Virginia Petroleum Jobbers*, it is mandated only if one assumes that the Court was using language in an exceedingly precise, technical sense. In light of the unnecessarily harsh results sometimes engendered by this approach, we decline to entertain this assumption. Instead, we hold that under *Virginia Petroleum Jobbers* a court, when confronted with a case in which the other three factors strongly favor interim relief may exercise its discretion to grant a stay if the movant has made a substantial case on the merits. The court is not required to find that ultimate success by the movant is a mathematical probability, and indeed, as in this case, may grant a stay even though its own approach may be contrary to movant's view of the merits. The necessary "level" or "degree" of possibility of success will vary according to the court's assessment of the other factors. This approach is reflected in *Virginia Petroleum Jobbers* where the court wrote: But injury held insufficient to justify a stay in one case may well be sufficient to justify it in another, where the applicant has demonstrated a higher probability of success on the merits. The view that a 50% plus probability is required by that opinion, although frequently encountered, is thus contrary to both the language and spirit of that opinion.

To justify a temporary injunction it is not necessary that the plaintiff's right to a final decision, after a trial, be absolutely certain, wholly without doubt; if the other elements are present (*i.e.*, the balance of hardships tips decidedly toward plaintiff), it will ordinarily be enough that the plaintiff has raised questions going to the merits so serious, substantial, difficult and doubtful, as to make them a fair ground for litigation and thus for more deliberative investigation. One moving for a preliminary injunction assumes the burden of demonstrating either a combination of probable success and the possibility of irreparable injury or that serious questions are raised and the balance of hardships tips sharply in his favor.

We believe that this approach is entirely consistent with the purpose of granting interim injunctive relief, whether by preliminary injunction or by stay pending appeal. Generally, such relief is preventative, or protective; it seeks to maintain the status quo pending a final determination of the merits of the suit. An order maintaining the status quo is appropriate when a serious legal question is presented, when little if any harm will befall other interested persons or the public and when denial of the order would inflict irreparable injury on the movant. There is substantial equity, and need for judicial protection, whether or not movant has shown a mathematical probability of success.

Another weakness of adherence to a strict "probability" requirement is that it leads to an exaggeratedly refined analysis of the merits at an early stage in the litigation. If, to use Judge Frank's phrase, there exists "a fair ground for litigation and thus for more deliberative investigation," a court should not be required at an early stage to draw the fine line between a mathematical probability and a substantial possibility of success. The endeavor may be necessary in some circumstances when interim relief would cause substantial harm to another party or person, or when the balance of equities may come to require a more careful heft of the merits. However, it is not required in all cases.

The doctrine thus stated is congruent with Rules 8 and 18 of the Federal Rules of Appellate Procedure, which state that motions for stay "must ordinarily be made in the first instance" to the district court or agency which issued the challenged order. Prior recourse to the initial decisionmaker would hardly be required as a general matter if it could properly grant interim relief only on a prediction that it has rendered an erroneous decision. What is fairly contemplated is that tribunals may properly stay their own orders when they have ruled on an admittedly difficult legal question and when the equities of the case suggest that the status quo should be maintained.

Applying this standard to the instant motion, we cannot say that the District Court abused its discretion in staying its permanent injunction. Although a more searching inquiry into the merits might compel the tentative conclusion that Holiday Tours is less likely than not to prevail on the merits, we have satisfied ourselves that the case is a difficult one warranting plenary review. In light of the balance of equities in this case, that suffices to sustain the stay.

The Commission's motion to vacate the District Court's order staying its permanent injunction is denied.

So ordered.

NOTE: STATE COURTS

States have adopted a variety or procedures regarding pre-appeal relief—some institute automatic stays pending appeal; others enter stays or not depending on whether the relief requested is mandatory or prohibitory; still others follow procedures similar to the federal courts.

PROBLEM: GIRLS AND THE MUNICIPAL FOOTBALL LEAGUE

Peggy Sue is twelve years old and wants to play in the Pleasantville municipal football league. Her would-be coach is sympathetic and would like to let her play, but the municipality has a rule prohibiting girls from playing in the league. Peggy Sue seeks an injunction against Pleasantville and the league ordering them to allow her to play. Three days before the season begins, she files her complaint and moves the court for a TRO. The parties have a full hearing on the matter, and the court grants the injunction. 1) Should the trial court require Peggy Sue to post a security bond? 2) Suppose that Pleasantville appeals the TRO. Should the appellate court grant review of the trial court's decision? Which court will decide the question of appealability? Does the answer depend on whether Pleasantville requests a stay of the TRO? 3) Suppose that the trial court denies the defendant's request for a stay and that Pleasantville does not seek review from a motions panel. Suppose also that the appellate court will not be able to convene a merits panel (the panel that will decide the "merits" of the appeal) until the ninth day of the TRO. Why as a matter of trial strategy might Pleasantville continue to seek review of the TRO from the merits panel? 4) If the appellate court hears Pleasantville's appeal and overturns the TRO, what happens next? May Peggy Sue seek a preliminary injunction? 5) In light of the advancing season, the trial court expedites the trial on the merits of Peggy Sue's claim. At the conclusion of trial, the court enters a permanent injunction. What should Pleasantville do next? What likely results?"

H. MODIFICATION OF PERMANENT INJUNCTIONS

Even though "permanent" injunctions are issued at the conclusion of a lawsuit and are designed to last indefinitely, and in that sense "permanently," they can be modified or dissolved under appropriate circumstances. Rule 60b, F.R. Civ. Pro., provides that "on motion and just terms, the court may relieve a party or its legal representative from a final judgment, order, or proceeding for the following reasons: (5) the judgment has been satisfied, released or discharged; it is based on an earlier judgment that has been reversed or vacated; or applying it prospectively is no longer equitable; or (6) any other reason that justifies relief."

AGOSTINI V. FELTON

521 U.S. 203, 117 S.Ct. 1997, 138 L.Ed.2d 391 (1997).

JUSTICE O'CONNOR delivered the opinion of the Court.

In *Aguilar v. Felton*, 473 U.S. 402 (1985), this Court held that the Establishment Clause barred the city of New York from sending public school teachers into parochial schools to provide remedial education to disadvantaged children. On remand, the trial court entered a permanent injunction reflecting our ruling. Twelve years later, petitioners seek relief from its operation. Petitioners maintain that *Aguilar* cannot be squared with our intervening Establishment Clause jurisprudence and ask that we explicitly recognize that *Aguilar* is no longer good law.

Congress enacted Title I of the Elementary and Secondary Education Act of 1965 to "provide full educational opportunity to every child regardless of economic background." Toward that end, Title I channels federal funds, through the States, to "local educational agencies" (LEA's). The LEA's spend funds to provide remedial education, guidance, and job counseling to eligible students. An eligible student is one (i) who resides within the attendance boundaries of a public school located in a low-income area, and (ii) who is failing, or is at risk of failing, the State's student performance standards. Title I funds must be made available to *all* eligible children, regardless of whether they attend public schools, and the services provided to children attending private schools must be "equitable in comparison to services and other benefits for public school children."

Title I services may be provided only to those private school students eligible for aid, and cannot be used to provide services on a "school-wide" basis. In addition, the LEA must retain complete control over Title I funds; retain title to all materials used to provide Title I services; and provide those services through public employees or other persons independent of the private school and any religious institution. The Title I services themselves must be "secular, neutral, and nonideological," and must "supplement, and in no case supplant, the level of services" already provided by the private school.

Petitioner Board of Education of the City of New York (Board), an LEA, first applied for Title I funds in 1966. Approximately 10% of the total number of students eligible for Title I services are private school students. Recognizing that more than 90% of the private schools within the Board's jurisdiction are sectarian, the Board initially arranged to transport children to public schools for after-school Title I instruction. Attendance was poor, teachers and children were tired, and parents were concerned for the safety of their children. The Board then moved the instruction onto private school campuses during school hours. Only public employees could serve as Title I instructors and counselors. Assignments to private schools were made on a voluntary basis and without regard to the religious affiliation of the employee or the wishes of the private school. A majority of Title I teachers worked in nonpublic schools with religious affiliations different from their own.

Title I employees were told that (i) they were employees of the Board and accountable only to their public school supervisors; (ii) they had exclusive responsibility for selecting students for the Title I program and could teach only those children who met the eligibility criteria for Title I; (iii) their materials and equipment would be used only in the Title I program; (iv) they could not engage in team-teaching or other cooperative instructional activities with private school teachers; and (v) they could not introduce any religious matter into their teaching or become involved in any way with the religious activities of the private schools. All religious symbols were to be removed from classrooms used for Title I services.

Title I teachers could consult with a student's regular classroom teacher to assess the student's particular needs and progress, but were required to limit those consultations to mutual professional concerns regarding the student's education. To ensure compliance, a publicly employed field supervisor was to make at least one unannounced visit to each teacher's classroom every month.

Six federal taxpayers sued the Board seeking declaratory and injunctive relief. The District Court granted summary judgment for the Board, but the court of appeals reversed. In a 5–4 decision, this Court affirmed on the ground that the Board's Title I program necessitated an "excessive entanglement of church and state in the administration of Title I benefits." On remand, the District Court permanently enjoined the Board "from using public funds for any plan or program under Title I to the extent that it requires, authorizes or permits public school teachers and guidance counselors to provide teaching and counseling services on the premises of sectarian schools."

The Board then modified its Title I program to revert to its prior practice of providing instruction at public school sites, at leased sites, and in mobile instructional units (essentially vans converted into classrooms) parked near the sectarian school. The Board also offered computer-aided instruction, which could be provided "on premises" because it did not require public employees to be physically present on the premises of a religious school.

The additional costs of complying with *Aguilar's* mandate are significant. Since the 1986–1987 school year, the Board has spent over $100 million providing computer-aided instruction, leasing sites and mobile instructional units, and transporting students to those sites. These "*Aguilar* costs" reduce the amount of money an LEA has available for remedial education, and LEA's have reduced the number of students who receive Title I benefits.

Petitioners filed motions seeking relief from the permanent injunction because the "decisional law had changed." Specifically, petitioners pointed to the statements of five Justices in *Board of Ed. of Kiryas Joel Village School Dist. v. Grumet*, 512 U.S. 687 (1994), calling for the overruling of *Aguilar*. The District Court denied the motion. We granted certiorari and now reverse.

The question we must answer is a simple one: Are petitioners entitled to relief from the District Court's permanent injunction under Rule 60(b)? Rule 60(b)(5), the subsection under which petitioners proceeded below, states:

> On motion and upon such terms as are just, the court may relieve a party from a final judgment or order when it is no

longer equitable that the judgment should have prospective application.

In *Rufo v. Inmates of Suffolk County Jail,* 112 S.Ct., at 760, we held that it is appropriate to grant a Rule 60(b)(5) motion when the party seeking relief from an injunction or consent decree can show "a significant change either in factual conditions or in law." A court may recognize subsequent changes in either statutory or decisional law. See *Railway Employees v. Wright,* 364 U.S. 642 (1961).

Petitioners point to three changes in the factual and legal landscape that they believe justify their claim for relief under Rule 60(b)(5). They first contend that the exorbitant costs of complying with the District Court's injunction constitute a significant factual development warranting modification of the injunction. Petitioners also argue that there have been two significant legal developments since *Aguilar* was decided: a majority of Justices have expressed their views that *Aguilar* should be reconsidered or overruled, and *Aguilar* has in any event been undermined by subsequent Establishment Clause decisions, including *Witters v. Washington Dept. of Servs. for Blind,* 474 U.S. 481 (1986), *Zobrest v. Catalina Foothills School Dist.,* 509 U.S. 1 (1993), and *Rosenberger v. Rector and Visitors of Univ. of Va.,* 515 U.S. 819 (1995).

Respondents counter that, because the costs of providing Title I services off site were known at the time *Aguilar* was decided, and because the relevant case law has not changed, the District Court did not err in denying petitioners' motions. Obviously, if neither the law supporting our original decision in this litigation nor the facts have changed, there would be no need to decide the propriety of a Rule 60(b)(5) motion. Accordingly, we turn to the threshold issue whether the factual or legal landscape has changed since we decided *Aguilar.*

We agree with respondents that petitioners have failed to establish the significant change in factual conditions required by *Rufo.* Both petitioners and this Court were, at the time *Aguilar* was decided, aware that additional costs would be incurred if Title I services could not be provided in parochial school classrooms. That these predictions of additional costs turned out to be accurate does not constitute a change in factual conditions warranting relief under Rule 60(b)(5).

We also agree with respondents that the statements made by five Justices in *Kiryas Joel* do not, in themselves, furnish a basis for concluding that our Establishment Clause jurisprudence has changed. In *Kiryas Joel,* we considered the constitutionality of a New York law that carved out a public school district to coincide with the boundaries of the village of Kiryas Joel, which was an enclave of the Satmar Hasidic sect. Before the new district was created, Satmar children wishing to receive special educational services under the Individuals with Disabilities Education Act (IDEA), 20 U.S.C. § 1400 *et seq.,* could receive those services at public schools located outside the village. Because Satmar parents rarely permitted their children to attend those schools, New York created a new public school district within the boundaries of the village so that Satmar children could stay within the village but receive IDEA services on public school premises from publicly employed instructors. In the course of our opinion, we observed that New York had created the special school district in response to our decision in *Aguilar,* which had required New York to cease providing IDEA services to Satmar children on the premises of their private religious schools. Five Justices joined opinions calling for reconsideration of *Aguilar.* But the question of *Aguilar*'s propriety was not before us. The views of five Justices that the case should be reconsidered or overruled cannot be said to have effected a change in Establishment Clause law.

In light of these conclusions, petitioners' ability to satisfy the prerequisites of Rule 60(b)(5) hinges on whether our later Establishment Clause cases have so undermined *Aguilar* that it is no longer good law.

In order to evaluate whether *Aguilar* has been eroded, it is necessary to understand the rationale upon which *Aguilar*, as well as its companion case, *School Dist. of Grand Rapids v. Ball*, 473 U.S. 373 (1985), rested. In *Ball*, the Court evaluated two programs implemented by the School District of Grand Rapids, Michigan. The Shared Time program provided remedial and "enrichment" classes, at public expense, to students attending nonpublic schools. The classes were taught during regular school hours by publicly employed teachers, using materials purchased with public funds, on the premises of nonpublic schools. The Shared Time courses were in subjects designed to supplement the "core curriculum" of the nonpublic schools. Of the 41 nonpublic schools eligible for the program, 40 were " 'pervasively sectarian.' "

The Court applied the so-called *Lemon* test. The Court's conclusion that the Shared Time program in *Ball* had the impermissible effect of advancing religion rested on three assumptions: (i) any public employee who works on the premises of a religious school is presumed to inculcate religion in her work; (ii) the presence of public employees on private school premises creates a symbolic union between church and state; and (iii) any and all public aid that directly aids the educational function of religious schools impermissibly finances religious indoctrination, even if the aid reaches such schools as a consequence of private decisionmaking. Additionally, in *Aguilar* there was a fourth assumption: that New York City's Title I program necessitated an excessive government entanglement with religion because public employees who teach on the premises of religious schools must be closely monitored to ensure that they do not inculcate religion.

Our more recent cases have undermined the assumptions upon which *Ball* and *Aguilar* relied. We continue to ask whether the government acted with the purpose of advancing or inhibiting religion. Likewise, we continue to explore whether the aid has the "effect" of advancing or inhibiting religion. What has changed is our understanding of the criteria used to assess whether aid to religion has an impermissible effect.

Cases subsequent to *Aguilar* have modified the approach we use to assess indoctrination. First, we abandoned the presumption that the placement of public employees on parochial school grounds inevitably results in the impermissible effect of state-sponsored indoctrination or constitutes a symbolic union between government and religion. In *Zobrest v. Catalina Foothills School Dist.*, 509 U.S. 1 (1993), we examined whether the IDEA, 20 U.S.C. § 1400 et seq., was constitutional as applied to a deaf student who sought to bring his state-employed sign-language interpreter with him to his Roman Catholic high school. We held that this was permissible and refused to presume that a publicly employed interpreter would be pressured by the pervasively sectarian surroundings to inculcate religion. We assumed that the interpreter would dutifully discharge her responsibilities as a public employee and comply with the ethical guidelines of her profession by accurately translating what was said.

Second, we departed from the rule that all government aid that directly aids the educational function of religious schools is invalid. In *Witters v. Washington Dept. of Servs. for Blind*, 474 U.S. 481 (1986), we held that the Establishment Clause did not bar a State from issuing a vocational tuition grant to a blind person who wished to use the grant to attend a Christian college and become a pastor, missionary, or youth director. Even though the grant recipient would use the money to obtain religious education, the tuition grants were " 'made available generally without regard to the sectarian-nonsectarian, or public-nonpublic nature of the institution benefited.' " The grants were disbursed directly to students, who then used the money to pay for tuition at the educational institution of their choice. Any money that ultimately went to religious institutions did so "only as a result of the genuinely independent and private choices of" individuals. The same logic applied in *Zobrest*, where we allowed the State to provide an interpreter, even though she would be a mouthpiece for religious instruction, because the IDEA's neutral eligibility criteria ensured that the interpreter's presence in a sectarian school was a "result of the private decision of individual parents" and "could not be attributed to state decisionmaking."

Under current law, the Shared Time program in *Ball* and New York City's Title I program in *Aguilar* will not be deemed to have the effect of advancing religion through indoctrination. Each of the premises upon which we relied in *Ball* to reach a contrary conclusion is no longer valid. First, there is no reason to presume that, simply because she enters a parochial school classroom, a full-time public employee will depart from her assigned duties and instructions and embark on religious indoctrination. *Zobrest* also repudiates *Ball's* assumption that the presence of Title I teachers in parochial school classrooms will, without more, create the impression of a "symbolic union" between church and state.

Nor under current law can we conclude that a program placing full-time public employees on parochial campuses to provide Title I instruction would impermissibly finance religious indoctrination. The provision of instructional services under Title I is indistinguishable from the provision of sign-language interpreters under the IDEA. As in *Zobrest*, Title I services are by law supplemental to the regular curricula. These services do not, therefore, "relieve sectarian schools of costs they otherwise would have borne in educating their students."

We are also not persuaded that Title I services supplant the remedial instruction and guidance counseling already provided in New York City's sectarian schools. We are unwilling to speculate that all sectarian schools provide remedial instruction and guidance counseling.

What is most fatal to the argument that New York City's Title I program directly subsidizes religion is that it applies with equal force when those services are provided off-campus, and *Aguilar* implied that providing the services off-campus is entirely consistent with the Establishment Clause. A financial incentive to undertake religious indoctrination is not present where the aid is allocated on the basis of neutral, secular criteria that neither favor nor disfavor religion, and is made available to both religious and secular beneficiaries on a nondiscriminatory basis.

Applying this reasoning to New York City's Title I program, it is clear that Title I services are allocated on the basis of criteria that neither favor nor disfavor religion. The services are available to all children who meet the Act's eligibility requirements, no matter what their religious beliefs or where they go to school. The Board's program does not, therefore, give aid recipients any incentive to modify their religious beliefs or practices in order to obtain those services.

We turn now to *Aguilar's* conclusion that New York City's Title I program resulted in an excessive entanglement between church and state. The finding of "excessive" entanglement in *Aguilar* rested on three grounds: (i) the program would require "pervasive monitoring by public authorities" to ensure that Title I employees did not inculcate religion; (ii) the program required "administrative cooperation" between the Board and parochial schools; and (iii) the program might increase the dangers of "political divisiveness." Under our current understanding of the Establishment Clause, the last two considerations are insufficient by themselves to create an "excessive" entanglement. They are present no matter where Title I services are offered. Further, the assumption underlying the first consideration has been undermined. We no longer presume that public employees will inculcate religion simply because they happen to be in a sectarian environment. Since we have abandoned the assumption that properly instructed public employees will fail to discharge their duties faithfully, we must also discard the assumption that pervasive monitoring of Title I teachers is required. There is no suggestion that unannounced monthly visits of public supervisors are insufficient to prevent or to detect inculcation of religion by public employees.

To summarize, New York City's Title I program does not run afoul of any of three primary criteria we currently use to evaluate whether government aid has the effect of advancing religion: it does not result in governmental indoctrination; define its recipients by reference to religion; or create an excessive entanglement. We therefore hold that a federally funded program providing supplemental, remedial instruction to disadvantaged children on a neutral basis is not invalid under the Establishment Clause when such instruction is given on the premises of sectarian schools by government employees pursuant to a program containing safeguards such as those present here. The same considerations that justify this holding require us to conclude that this carefully constrained program also cannot reasonably be viewed as an endorsement of religion. Accordingly, we must acknowledge that *Aguilar*, as well as the portion of *Ball* addressing Grand Rapids' Shared Time program, are no longer good law.

Our Establishment Clause jurisprudence has changed significantly since we decided *Ball* and *Aguilar*. We therefore overrule *Ball* and *Aguilar* to the extent those decisions are inconsistent with our current understanding of the Establishment Clause. We reverse the Court of Appeals and remand to the District Court with instructions to vacate its order.

It is so ordered.

JUSTICE SOUTER, with whom JUSTICE STEVENS and JUSTICE GINSBURG join, and with whom JUSTICE BREYER joins as to Part II, dissenting.

Aguilar was a correct and sensible decision. The State is forbidden to subsidize religion directly and is just as surely forbidden to act in any way that could reasonably be viewed as religious endorsement. These principles were violated by the programs at issue in *Aguilar* and *Ball*, as a consequence of several significant features common to both Title I and the Grand Rapids Shared Time program: each provided classes on the premises of the religious schools; while their services were termed "supplemental," the programs and their instructors necessarily assumed responsibility for teaching subjects that the religious schools would otherwise have been obligated to provide, the public employees carrying out the programs had broad responsibilities involving the exercise of considerable discretion, while the programs offered aid to nonpublic school students generally, participation by religious school students in each program was extensive, and, finally, aid under Title I and Shared Time flowed directly to the schools in the form of classes and programs.

NOTES

1. *Modifications Based on a Change in the Law.* In *Railway Labor Executives' Ass'n v. Metro–North Commuter R.R. Co.*, 759 F.Supp. 1019 (S.D.N.Y.1990), Metro–North sought to modify an injunction based on a change of law. The court granted the modification, noting that plaintiff's "contention that this court's earlier ruling is res judicata is incorrect." Even assuming that an injunction has the effect of a "final judgment on the merits," Rule 60(b)(5), F.R.Civ.P., "explicitly authorizes the court on motion to relieve such a judgment of its prospective effect": "the court may relieve a party from a final judgment, order, or proceeding" if "it is no longer equitable that the judgment should have prospective application." The court went on to hold that a "subsequent change in decisional law is an appropriate basis for dissolving a continuing injunction. *Toussaint v. McCarthy*, 801 F.2d 1080 (9th Cir.1986)." In general, " 'when a change in the law authorizes what had previously been forbidden, it is abuse of discretion for a court to refuse to modify an injunction founded on the superseded law.' " *Toussaint, supra*, 801 F.2d at 1090 (*quoting American Horse Protection Ass'n v. Watt*, 694 F.2d 1310, 1316 (D.C.Cir.1982)). Changes in controlling decisional law have undermined the basis of the injunction.

2. *Consent Decrees.* Federal courts have ruled that Rule 60(b) applies equally to consent decrees. *See Rufo v. Inmates of Suffolk County Jail*, 502 U.S. 367 (1992). Although many state courts concur, some states do not allow modification of consent decrees in deference to the parties right to contract. *See, e.g., Cecil Township v. Klements*, 821 A.2d 670 (Pa. Commw. Ct 2003).

3. *Significant Change.* The significant change in facts or law standard does not apply when a court considers whether to modify a TRO or preliminary injunction. Rather, the applicable standard is simply the same standard the court used to issue the injunction. *Weight Watchers International, Inc. v. Luigino's, Inc.*, 423 F.3d 137 (2nd Cir. 2005).

PROBLEMS

1. *Injunctive Decrees as "Vested Rights"?* When a court enters a permanent injunction, does the injunction give plaintiff a "vested" property right in the relief that was granted? *See Ladner v. Siegel*, 298 Pa. 487, 148 A. 699 (1930)

2. *The Bridge Injunction.* In *Penna. v. Wheeling & Belmont Bridge Co.*, 59 U.S. 421 (1855), a company was enjoined from building a bridge across a navigable river. After the injunction was entered, Congress passed an act

expressly permitting the bridge. Would it be permissible for the court to lift the injunction?

3. *The Parking Garage.* Siegel wanted to build a 400 car garage on his property. The trial court enjoined construction of the garage on the basis that the area was almost exclusively residential, and that the ventilating system designed to remove gasses and odors and the other effects from the use proposed would not give the desired protection to the neighborhood. Suppose that the surrounding area changes from residential to mostly commercial, and that Siegel modifies his plans to provide proper ventilation. Is it appropriate for the trial court to consider a request to lift the injunction? *See Ladner v. Siegel*, 298 Pa. 487, 148 A. 699 (1930).

4. *The Labor Picketing.* A court entered an injunction prohibiting a labor union from picketing plaintiffs' two establishments. The picketing was enjoined on two grounds: (1) that it was attended by violence, and (2) that its object was to coerce plaintiffs into forcing their employees to join the union. Ten years later, when the union wanted to picket "solely for organizational purposes, that is, to persuade non-union employees of an establishment to join the union," the union moved to dissolve the injunction. Is dissolution appropriate? *See Pappas v. Local Joint Executive Board of Philadelphia*, 374 Pa. 34, 96 A.2d 915 (1953).

5. *Conditions at the County Jail.* A class of persons detained at the county jail sued the county, alleging conditions there were unconstitutional. The city denied any violation of the constitution. To settle the litigation, the parties entered a consent decree. The decree ordered the county to build a new jail meeting specified conditions (such as cell size) and to house only one detainee per cell. After the jail was built, the county sought a modification allowing it to house more than one detainee per cell. The motion pointed out that, after the consent decree was entered, the Supreme Court had ruled that shared cells did not violate the Constitution in and of themselves. Should the court grant modification? What other facts would you need to know? What arguments would you make?

6. *More on Conditions at the County Jail.* In problem 5, suppose that instead of a consent decree, the parties had entered a settlement agreement and the court had dismissed the case. After the Supreme Court decision, the county breached the settlement agreement by housing two detainees per cell. Plaintiffs sued seeking specific performance of the agreement. If defendant asks the court to modify the agreement, should the court grant the modification.

7. *The Divorce Decree.* Would the answers be different if the case involved money? In a divorce case, the spouses agree that one will pay the other spousal support in the amount of $1,000 a month until the payee dies or remarries. Is the agreement modifiable (either up if the payee's needs increase or down if the payor's income decreases) if it is embodied in a consent decree? What if the settlement agreement leads to dismissal instead

of a consent decree? Can you draft a consent decree to protect your client from involuntary modification?

BOARD OF EDUCATION V. DOWELL

498 U.S. 237, 111 S.Ct. 630, 112 L.Ed.2d 715 (1991).

CHIEF JUSTICE REHNQUIST delivered the opinion of the Court.

Petitioner Board of Education of Oklahoma City sought dissolution of a decree entered by the District Court imposing a school desegregation plan. The District Court granted relief over the objection of respondents Robert L. Dowell, et al., black students and their parents. The Court of Appeals for the Tenth Circuit reversed, holding that the Board would be entitled to such relief only upon " 'nothing less than a clear showing of grievous wrong evoked by new and unforeseen conditions.' " We hold that the Court of Appeals' test is more stringent than is required either by our cases dealing with injunctions or by the Equal Protection Clause of the Fourteenth Amendment.

This school desegregation litigation began almost 30 years ago. In 1961, respondents, black students and their parents, sued petitioners, the Board of Education of Oklahoma City (Board), to end de jure segregation in the public schools. In 1963, the District Court found that Oklahoma City had intentionally segregated both schools and housing in the past, and that Oklahoma City was operating a "dual" school system—one that was intentionally segregated by race. In 1965, the District Court found that the School Board's attempt to desegregate by using neighborhood zoning failed to remedy past segregation because residential segregation resulted in one-race schools. Residential segregation had once been state imposed, and it lingered due to discrimination by some realtors and financial institutions. The District Court found that school segregation had caused some housing segregation. In 1972, finding that previous efforts had not been successful at eliminating state imposed segregation, the District Court ordered the Board to adopt the "Finger Plan," under which kindergartners would be assigned to neighborhood schools unless their parents opted otherwise; children in grades 1–4 would attend formerly all white schools, and thus black children would be bused to those schools; children in grade five would attend formerly all black schools, and thus white children would be bused to those schools; students in the upper grades would be bused to various areas in order to maintain integrated schools; and in integrated neighborhoods there would be stand-alone schools for all grades.

In 1977, after complying with the desegregation decree for five years, the Board made a "Motion to Close Case." The District Court held in its "Order Terminating Case": "The Court has concluded that the Finger Plan worked and that substantial compliance with the constitutional requirements has been achieved. * * *

In 1984, the School Board faced demographic changes that led to greater burdens on young black children. As more and more neighborhoods became integrated, more stand-alone schools were established, and young black students had to be bused further from their inner-city homes to outlying white areas. In an effort to alleviate this burden and to increase parental involvement, the Board adopted the Student Reassignment Plan (SRP), which relied on neighborhood assignments for students in grades K–4 beginning in the 1985–1986 school year. Busing continued for students in grades 5–12. Any student could transfer from a school where he or she was in the majority to a school where he or she would be in the minority. Faculty and staff integration was retained, and an "equity officer" was appointed.

In 1985, respondents filed a "Motion to Reopen the Case," contending that the School District had not achieved "unitary" status and that the SRP was a return to segregation. Under the SRP, 11 of 64 elementary schools would be greater than 90% black, 22 would be greater than 90% white plus other minorities, and 31 would be racially mixed. * * *

The District Court found that demographic changes made the Finger Plan unworkable, that the Board had done nothing for 25 years to promote residential segregation, and that the school district had bused students for more than a decade in good-faith compliance with the court's orders. The District Court found that present residential segregation was the result of private decisionmaking and economics, and that it was too attenuated to be a vestige of former school segregation. It also found that the district had maintained its unitary status, and that the neighborhood assignment plan was not designed with discriminatory intent. The court concluded that the previous injunctive decree should be vacated and the school district returned to local control. The Court of Appeals reversed.

The Court of Appeals reversed, relying upon language from this Court's decision in *United States v. Swift and Co.*, for the proposition that a desegregation decree could not be lifted or modified absent a showing of "grievous wrong evoked by new and unforeseen conditions." It also held that "compliance alone cannot become the basis for modifying or dissolving an injunction," *relying on United States v. W.T. Grant Co.*, 345 U.S. 629 (1953). We hold that its reliance was mistaken.

United States v. United Shoe Machinery Corp., 391 U.S. 244 (1968), explained that the language used in *Swift* must be read in the context of the continuing danger of unlawful restraints on trade which the Court had found still existed. "*Swift* teaches a decree may be changed upon an appropriate showing, and it holds that it may not be changed if the purposes of the litigation as incorporated in the decree have not been fully achieved." In the present case, a finding by the District Court that the Oklahoma City School District was being operated in compliance with the commands of the Equal Protection Clause of the Fourteenth Amendment, and that it was unlikely that the school board would return to its former ways, would be a finding that the purposes of the desegregation litigation had been fully achieved. No additional showing of "grievous wrong evoked by new and unforeseen conditions" is required of the school board.

In *Milliken v. Bradley* (*Milliken II*), 433 U.S. 267 (1977), we said: "Federal-court decrees must directly address and relate to the constitutional violation itself. Because of this inherent limitation upon federal judicial authority, federal-court decrees exceed appropriate limits if they are aimed at eliminating a condition that does not violate the Constitution or does not flow from such a violation." From the very first, federal supervision of local school systems was intended as a temporary measure to remedy past discrimination. *Brown* considered the "complexities arising from the transition to a system of public education freed of racial discrimination" in holding that the implementation of desegregation was to proceed "with all deliberate speed." *Green* also spoke of the "transition to a unitary, nonracial system of public education."

Considerations based on the allocation of powers within our federal system, we think, support our view that quoted language from *Swift* does not provide the proper standard to apply to injunctions entered in school desegregation cases. Such decrees, unlike the one in *Swift*, are not intended to operate in perpetuity. Local control over the education of children allows citizens to participate in decisionmaking, and allows innovation so that school programs can fit local needs. The legal justification for displacement of local authority by an injunctive decree in a school desegregation case is a violation of the Constitution by the local authorities. Dissolving a desegregation decree after the local authorities have operated in compliance with it for a reasonable period of time properly recognizes that "necessary concern for the important values of local control of public school systems dictates that a federal court's regulatory control of such systems not extend beyond the time required to remedy the effects of past intentional discrimination."

A district court need not accept at face value the profession of a school board which has intentionally discriminated that it will cease to do so in the future. But in deciding whether to modify or dissolve a desegregation decree, a school board's compliance with previous court orders is obviously relevant. In this case the original finding of de jure segregation was entered in 1961, the injunctive decree from which the Board seeks relief was entered in 1972, and the Board complied with the decree in good faith until 1985. Not only do the personnel of school boards change over time, but the same passage of time enables the District Court to observe the good faith of the school board in complying with the decree. The test espoused by the Court of Appeals would condemn a school district, once governed by a board which intentionally discriminated, to judicial tutelage for the indefinite future. Neither the principles governing the entry and dissolution of injunctive decrees, nor the commands of the Equal Protection Clause of the Fourteenth Amendment, require any such Draconian result.

Petitioners urge that we reinstate the decision of the District Court terminating the injunction, but we think that the preferable course is to remand the case to that court so that it may decide, in accordance with this opinion, whether the Board made a sufficient showing of constitutional compliance as of 1985, when the SRP was adopted, to allow the injunction to be dissolved. The District Court should address itself to whether the Board had complied in good faith with the desegregation decree since it was entered, and whether the vestiges of past discrimination had been eliminated to the extent practicable.

In considering whether the vestiges of de jure segregation had been eliminated as far as practicable, the District Court should look not only at student assignments, but "to every facet of school operations—faculty, staff, transportation, extra-curricular activities and facilities." *Green*, 391 U.S., at 435. After the District Court decides whether the Board was entitled to have the decree terminated, it should proceed to decide respondent's challenge to the SRP. A school district which has been released from an injunction imposing a desegregation plan no longer requires court authorization for the promulgation of policies and rules regulating matters such as assignment of students and the like, but it of course remains subject to the mandate of the Equal Protection Clause of the Fourteenth Amendment. If the Board was entitled to have the decree terminated as of 1985, the District Court should then evaluate the Board's decision to implement the SRP under appropriate equal protection principles. *See Washington v. Davis*, 426 U.S. 229 (1976).

The judgment of the Court of Appeals is reversed, and the case is remanded to the District Court for further proceedings consistent with this opinion.

It is so ordered.

JUSTICE MARSHALL, with whom JUSTICE BLACKMUN and JUSTICE STEVENS join, dissenting.

The practical question now before us is whether, 13 years after the injunction was imposed, the same School Board should have been allowed to return many of its elementary schools to their former one-race status. The majority today suggests that 13 years of desegregation was enough. The Court remands the case for further evaluation of whether the purposes of the injunctive decree were achieved sufficient to justify the decree's dissolution. However, the inquiry it commends to the District Court fails to recognize explicitly the threatened reemergence of one-race schools as a relevant "vestige" of de jure segregation.

In my view, the standard for dissolution of a school desegregation decree must reflect the central aim of our school desegregation precedents. In *Brown v. Board of Education*, 347 U.S. 483 (1954) (*Brown I*), a unanimous Court declared that racially "separate educational facilities are inherently unequal." This holding rested on the Court's recognition that state-sponsored segregation conveys a message of "inferiority as to the status of Afro-American school children in the community that may affect their hearts and minds in a way unlikely ever to be undone." Remedying this evil and preventing its recurrence were the motivations animating our requirement that formerly de jure segregated school districts take all feasible steps to eliminate racially identifiable schools.

I believe a desegregation decree cannot be lifted so long as conditions likely to inflict the stigmatic injury condemned in *Brown I* persist and there remain feasible methods of eliminating such conditions. Because the record here shows, and the Court of Appeals found, that feasible steps could be taken to avoid one-race schools, it is clear that the purposes of the decree have not yet been achieved and the Court of Appeals' reinstatement of the decree should be affirmed. I therefore dissent.

NOTES

1. *The* Freeman *Case.* In *Freeman v. Pitts*, 503 U.S. 467 (1992), the Court extended *Dowell.* The DeKalb County School System (DCCS), Dekalb County, Georgia, maintained a racially segregated school system until 1969 when it came under the supervision and control of a federal court. In 1986, petitioners filed a motion for final dismissal. The District Court concluded that DCSS had not achieved unitary status in all respects but had done so in student attendance and three other categories. In its order the District Court relinquished remedial control as to those aspects of the system in which unitary status had been achieved, and retained supervisory authority only for those aspects of the school system in which the district was not in full compliance. The Court of Appeals for the Eleventh Circuit reversed, holding that a district court should retain full remedial authority over a school system until it achieves unitary status in six categories at the same time for several years. The United States Supreme Court reversed "holding that a district court is permitted to withdraw judicial supervision with respect to discrete categories in which the school district has achieved compliance with a court-ordered desegregation plan." The Court explained:

> A federal court in a school desegregation case has the discretion to order an incremental or partial withdrawal of its supervision and control. This discretion derives both from the constitutional authority which justified its intervention in the first instance and its ultimate objectives in formulating the decree. The authority of the court is invoked at the outset to remedy particular constitutional violations. In construing the remedial authority of the

district courts, we have been guided by the principles that "judicial powers may be exercised only on the basis of a constitutional violation," and that "the nature of the violation determines the scope of the remedy." *Swann*, 402 U.S., at 16. A remedy is justifiable only insofar as it advances the ultimate objective of alleviating the initial constitutional violation.

Partial relinquishment of judicial control, where justified by the facts of the case, can be an important and significant step in fulfilling the district court's duty to return the operations and control of schools to local authorities. In *Dowell*, we emphasized that federal judicial supervision of local school systems was intended as a "temporary measure." Although this temporary measure has lasted decades, the ultimate objective has not changed—to return school districts to the control of local authorities.

Just as a court has the obligation at the outset of a desegregation decree to structure a plan so that all available resources of the court are directed to comprehensive supervision of its decree, so too must a court provide an orderly means for withdrawing from control when it is shown that the school district has attained the requisite degree of compliance. A transition phase in which control is relinquished in a gradual way is an appropriate means to this end.

Upon a finding that a school system subject to a court-supervised desegregation plan is in compliance in some but not all areas, the court in appropriate cases may return control to the school system in those areas where compliance has been achieved, limiting further judicial supervision to operations that are not yet in full compliance with the court decree. In particular, the district court may determine that it will not order further remedies in the area of student assignments where racial imbalance is not traceable, in a proximate way, to constitutional violations.

2. *Modifying Consent Decrees.* In *Railway Employees v. Wright*, 364 U.S. 642 (1961), a railroad and its unions were sued for violating the Railway Labor Act, 45 U.S.C. § 151 et seq., which banned discrimination against nonunion employees, and the parties entered a consent decree that prohibited such discrimination. Later, the Railway Labor Act was amended to allow union shops, and the union sought a modification of the decree. Although the amendment did not require but purposely permitted union shops, this Court held that the union was entitled to the modification because the parties had recognized correctly that what the consent decree prohibited was illegal under the Railway Act as it then read and because a "court must be free to continue to further the objectives of the Act when its provisions are amended."

I. INJUNCTIONS AGAINST CRIMINAL ACTIVITY

In general, courts have been reluctant to enjoin the commission of future crimes. As a result, if Al Capone were still alive and robbing banks, courts would be loath to enjoin him from committing future bank robberies. Various justifications have been offered for this reluctance including the fact that courts are reluctant to enter futile decrees, and that the criminal laws are "sufficiently effective in deterring similar conduct of these parties, thereby affording plaintiff an adequate legal remedy" *City of Chicago v. Stern*, 96 Ill.App.3d 264, 51 Ill.Dec. 752, 421 N.E.2d 260 (1981). But there are other reasons as well. In *Amalgamated Clothing & Textile Workers Int'l Union v. Earle Industries, Inc.*, 318 Ark. 524, 886 S.W.2d 594 (1994), Justice Dudley, dissenting, offered the following explanation:

> Four potential harms are always present when a case involves an injunction against criminal offenses. First, there is a potential harm in the possible conflict with the constitutional guarantee of the right to trial by jury. Equity does not afford a jury trial, and the absence of that protection is a substantial factor to be weighed against chancery assuming jurisdiction. Second, the proof necessary for a conviction in a criminal court is constitutionally designed to require a high standard of proof, proof beyond a reasonable doubt. The proof necessary to sustain a civil action for contempt is lesser, a preponderance of the evidence. Third, a court of equity can issue a show cause order and the person cited must show why he should not be held in contempt. In a criminal proceeding the accused cannot be compelled to give evidence against himself. As a result, when a court of equity enjoins the commission of a crime, the person enjoined might be cited for contempt in a court of equity and stands to lose these three constitutional guarantees. Fourth, the person enjoined will suffer some stigma or embarrassment comparable to that suffered by being labeled a habitual offender because, before a court of equity assumes jurisdiction, there must be proof that the person enjoined committed acts of violence with such systematic persistence as to warrant a finding that they would be continued unless restrained.

Are there other concerns? In *State v. Western Union Tel. Co.*, 336 Mich. 84, 57 N.W.2d 537 (1953), the state obtained injunctive relief prohibiting defendant from accepting money bet on horse races, and then sought discovery regarding defendant's actions. The appellate court was concerned that discovery might violate defendant's privilege against self-incrimination.

STATE v. H. SAMUELS COMPANY, INC.

60 Wis.2d 631, 211 N.W.2d 417 (1973).

HALLOWS, CHIEF JUSTICE.

The issue is whether the repeated violation of a city ordinance constitutes a public nuisance which ought to be enjoined. H. Samuels Company, Inc., has operated a salvage business in block 137 in the city of Portage since the early 1900's. In 1948 the junk business was expanded to include the salvaging of metals from automobiles and other machinery. Cranes were used after 1949, a guillotine shears after 1966, and a hammer mill about 1971. At one time Samuels operated around the clock, but at the time of trial the operation at night had been reduced. In the processing of scrap metal, Samuels utilized railroad cars, trucks, heavy duty cranes, guillotine shears, oscillators, conveyor belts, air tools, hammer mill, and metal-sorting equipment. Prior to 1966, block 137 was zoned commercial and light industry, but in 1966 the zoning was changed to heavy industrial. Block 137 is the only block so zoned in the developed portion of Portage. The areas immediately adjacent to block 137 are zoned either residential, single-family homes or commercial and light industry.

The defendant has a license to operate a junk yard. In its operation, the defendant unloads scrap metal from railroad cars with a magnetized crane and drops the metal into a steel guillotine shears which snaps the metal and drops it onto an oscillating conveyor belt, which in turn drops it on a pile or to a sorting house. Other operations involve a two-ton magnet lifting a car engine to the height of four feet and dropping it onto a large piece of steel wedged into the ground. Air tools are used to dismantle the engines and the hammer mill is used to hammer metal into pieces in a large drum and to drop them on a conveyor belt where they are washed and sorted. The alleged nuisance consists of the air noise and ground vibrations created by the operation.

The city of Portage has an ordinance prescribing maximum permissible noise and vibration levels. The state contended the Samuels company has repeatedly violated this ordinance and will continue to do so to the injury of the public. At the trial the state of Wisconsin attempted to prove the alleged nuisance by the testimony of two expert witnesses who monitored the noise and by the testimony of neighborhood homeowners of the disruption of their life patterns. The homeowners testified to their loss of sleep, domestic discord, added expense in remodeling their homes, suspension of home remodeling, moving from the neighborhood, rattling of windows, loss of hobbies such as working out of doors, loss of use of porches and yards for relaxation, shaking of pictures and furniture, shaking of beds and rattling of dishes. The two experts testified their tests showed that at various times the sounds caused by the operation exceeded the maximum permissible decibel levels and sound frequencies established by the city ordinance of Portage. They also testified that the vibrations emanating from the salvage yard exceeded permissible displacement values prescribed by the ordinance for areas zoned heavy industrial.

The trial court was impressed by the reasoning in the concurring opinion in *State ex rel. Abbott v. House of Vision* (1951), 47 N.W.2d 321, to the effect that before an injunction will issue when a statute has been violated an effort must first be made to prosecute for the violation of the statute, as this remedy is presumably adequate.

True, a court of equity will not enjoin a crime because it is a crime, *i.e.*, to enforce the criminal law, but the fact the acts complained of cause damage and also constitute a crime does not bar injunctive relief. The criminality of the act neither gives nor ousts the jurisdiction of equity. In such cases, equity grants relief, not because the acts are in violation of the statute, but because they constitute in fact a nuisance.

This view must be distinguished from the doctrine that the repeated violation of a criminal statute constitutes per se a public nuisance. This doctrine justifies the issuance of an injunction not to enforce the criminal statute but to enjoin illegal conduct which, because of its repetition, constitutes a nuisance. Under this doctrine, a violation or a threatened violation of the statute does not constitute a nuisance. The violations of the statute must take place and be repeated to the extent their repetition effects such public rights as will constitute a nuisance.

The modern concept of injunctional relief is to use it when it is a superior or more effective remedy. This concept is illustrated by the many statutory provisions using an injunction to enforce sanctions and regulations in the commercial world. In *State v. J. C. Penney Company* (1970), 179 N.W.2d 641, this court enjoined repeated violations of a usury statute on the ground that the open, notorious, and flagrant violation of valid laws enacted for the benefit of the people of this state constituted a public nuisance. The court took judicial notice of the wide-spread use of the revolving-charge accounts and the large number of Wisconsin citizens affected by these practices, and thus concluded the violations were a public nuisance which ought to be enjoined.

It would seem this court is now committed to the proposition that the repeated violation of criminal statutes constitutes per se a public nuisance. But whether such nuisance should be enjoined depends upon the amount of damages caused thereby and upon the application of the doctrine of the balancing of equities or comparative injury in which the relative harm which would be alleviated by the granting of the injunction is considered in balance with the harm to the defendant if the injunction is granted. If the public is injured in its civil or property rights or privileges or in respect to public health to any degree, that is sufficient to constitute a public nuisance; the degree of harm goes to whether or not the nuisance should be enjoined. The abatement of a nuisance by an in rem action is to be distinguished as those cases generally involve a statutory declaration of what conduct constitutes a public nuisance and a statutory authorization for abatement against the property.

We need not decide whether defendant's operations in this case amount to a criminal-law nuisance because we think the repeated violations of the city ordinance constituted as a matter of law a public nuisance. It does not follow necessarily that the public nuisance resulting from the repeated violation of a statute or ordinance will be enjoined; this depends upon the degree of harm. In this case it may well be the amount of harm caused by the repeated violations during the normal working hours of the day is insufficient to call forth an injunction, but the same degree of violation impairing the public's right to the enjoyment of their homes after normal working hours causes a greater injury and ought to be enjoined. If we were to consider this case in relation to establishing a criminal-law nuisance, it might well be an operation less than that allowed by the ordinance would constitute a public nuisance which should be enjoined. However, the briefs ask for an injunction to limit the operation to what is permitted by the ordinance between 5:00 o'clock p.m. and 7:00 o'clock a.m.

Judgment is reversed, with directions to enter a judgment enjoining the operation of the defendant from violating the city ordinance as to noise and ground vibration during the hours of 5:00 o'clock p.m. and 7:00 o'clock a.m. each day of the week.

PROBLEMS

1. *Enjoining the Mortuary.* In *Samuels*, although the court is willing to grant the injunction, it suggests that traditional equitable principles will govern its decision to grant or withhold equitable relief. Among those principles are considerations of the "public interest" and a "balancing of the equities." Suppose that defendant plans to open a mortuary in an area zoned exclusively for residential development. Neighbors sue to prevent the construction and operation of the mortuary. Will the existence of the zoning law affect the court's decision regarding whether to issue an injunction? Would the law affect the court's conception of the "public interest" and the "balancing of the equities?"

2. *Limiting Noise Levels.* Is the *Samuels* case distinguishable from the mortuary case by virtue of the fact that the City of Portage's ordinance did not prohibit the company's operations altogether, but simply prescribed maximum permissible noise levels? How, if at all, does this distinction affect the court's view regarding the equities and the public interest? Should it affect how the court shapes its decree? Was the decree entered in the *Samuels* case permissible and appropriate?

3. *Enjoining Gambling Operations.* Defendants operated a gambling establishment and saloon, called the "Sycamore Café," in Louisville,

Kentucky. The property is owned by Roscoe, Luther and J.W. Goose who held restaurant and soft drink licenses, and recently held a liquor license. The establishment was raided numerous times by the police who found evidence of bet taking, as well as various forms of gambling with cards, dice and other devices. In addition, the police had arrested the Goose brothers a number of times for "suffering gaming on the premises, gambling, disorderly conduct, malicious assault and other offenses." In response to some of the charges, the Goose brothers paid small fines. After numerous criminal prosecutions, the Commonwealth of Kentucky sought injunctive relief against the Goose brothers prohibiting them from conducting gambling operations at the Sycamore Café. Is it appropriate for the court to grant the injunction? *See Goose v. Commonwealth*, 305 Ky. 644, 205 S.W.2d 326 (App.1947).

4. *Enjoining the Brothel.* Defendant maintained a brothel named the "Crystal Pistol" in Houston, Texas. The City of Houston sought to enjoin the activity claiming that prostitutes were permitted to reside on the premises for the purpose of plying their vocation, and that the premises were actually and habitually used by prostitutes for the purpose of prostitution. Is it appropriate for a court to enjoin the brothel as a public nuisance? *See Benton v. City of Houston*, 605 S.W.2d 679 (Tex.Civ.App.1980).

5. *Enjoining the Unlicensed Practice of Medicine.* Jonathon Quack, who is not licensed to practice medicine, has been operating a medical office in Prospect, Kentucky, for more than a year. At the office, he purports to diagnose medical ailments and do minor surgery. If Kentucky's Attorney General seeks injunctive relief prohibiting "Dr." Quack from the unauthorized practice of medicine, would it be appropriate for a court to grant the injunction?

6. *Re-Evaluating the Maxim Against Enjoining the Commission of Crime.* Now that you have examined the *Samuels* case, what is left of the traditional rule that "equity will not enjoin the commission of crimes?" Suppose that, in Louisville, Kentucky, one man has committed 30+ bank robberies over the last two years. The police have been unable to identify the man, much less to catch him. Would it be appropriate for a court to enjoin further bank robberies as a "public nuisance?" If not, how do you distinguish the bank robber from the activities enjoined in *Samuels*?

7. *The Trespassing Neighbor.* Wanda Willis owns a farm in rural Henry County, Kentucky, which is conveniently located to a major interstate highway. On the other side of Willis's farm is Harriett Ewell's farm. Because of the way the local roads are situated, Ewell must drive ten miles to reach the interstate. For many years, Willis and Ewell were best friends and Willis allowed Ewell to use a road on the backside of her property to quickly reach the interstate. Recently, Willis and Ewell had an argument and Willis ordered Ewell not to drive across her property any more. Ewell continues to do so. What remedies are available to Willis? If you were hired to represent Willis, how would you advise her to proceed?

J. INJUNCTIONS AGAINST LITIGATION

In some instances, courts are asked to enjoin litigation pending in other courts. In the early common law, when separate courts of law and equity existed, courts of equity frequently enjoined litigation in the law courts in order to protect their jurisdiction. For example, A agrees to buy 10 bushels of wheat from B at $10 per bushel, but the contract incorrectly lists the price as $100 per bushel. In a law court, B sues A for $100 per bushel. If the law court does not rectify the mistake through reformation, as it would not have done at one time, then the legal action would have proceeded to judgment on the terms of the contract as written. An equity court might reform the contract to the agreed-upon price. While the equity court was considering the case, it might enjoin B from proceeding with the legal action pending conclusion of the equitable action. If reformation was granted, the legal action would proceed based on the reformed contract. Following the merger of law and equity, a single court can hear B's contract claim and A's reformation claim at the same time, giving relief as appropriate. Thus, the need for injunctive relief has disappeared (in states where law and equity have merged).

Modern courts are also asked to enjoin pending litigation, but in somewhat different contexts including: 1) requests to state courts to enjoin litigation in other state courts; 2) requests to state courts to enjoin litigation in federal courts; & 3) requests to federal courts to enjoin litigation in state courts.

1. STATE COURT INJUNCTIONS AGAINST STATE LITIGATION

Assuming that a state court can obtain personal jurisdiction over the parties, a state court may have the power to enjoin litigation in other states. The court does so by ordering the parties not to proceed with the foreign litigation. However, merely because a state has the power to enjoin litigation does not mean that it should exercise that power. As the following case demonstrates, there may be persuasive reasons why courts should refuse to enjoin foreign litigation.

JAMES V. GRAND TRUNK WESTERN RAILROAD COMPANY

14 Ill.2d 356, 152 N.E.2d 858 (1958).

BRISTOW, JUSTICE.

Plaintiff, Lois M. Kahl, as administratrix of her deceased husband's estate, instituted suit against defendant, Grand Trunk Western Railroad Company, on February 16, 1956, in an Illinois court, under the Michigan Wrongful Death Act, for the death of her husband on February 16, 1955, allegedly through the negligence of the defendant railroad. Defendant obtained, without notice to plaintiff, a temporary injunction in Cass

County, Michigan, where plaintiff resided, restraining plaintiff from prosecuting her Illinois action. Plaintiff thereupon filed a supplemental complaint in the Illinois court, alleging that she could not obtain a fair trial in Cass County, Michigan; that such Michigan suit was instituted by defendant to prevent plaintiff from obtaining a fair trial in the Illinois courts and to force her into an unjust settlement of her cause of action, and would result in irreparable injury.

On the basis of these allegations, plaintiff moved for a temporary injunction enjoining the enforcement of the Michigan injunction. On August 9, 1956, the trial court denied plaintiff's motion. The Appellate Court affirmed.

Plaintiff did not appeal from the Michigan injunction when it was learned that the appeal bond would not have the effect of staying the proceedings. Thereafter, plaintiff was arrested pursuant to a body attachment a writ issued by the court directing authorities to bring a person who has been found in civil contempt before the court issued by the Michigan court on the application of defendant's counsel, O'Connor, and was advised that she would be imprisoned for contempt unless she complied with the injunction. Although she wrote to her Illinois attorney discharging him and directing him to withdraw her case from the Illinois courts, she subsequently advised him that the letter did not express her true desires, but had been coerced by threat of imprisonment by defendant's counsel.

A second injunction suit was instituted by defendant in Michigan. Plaintiff did not appear and was defaulted, and an order was entered enjoining her from further prosecuting her Illinois action and directing her to withdraw it.

Thereafter, on September 6, 1957, upon a showing that defendant's attorney was insisting that plaintiff sign a stipulation to dismiss her Illinois proceedings, a Justice of this court entered an order restraining the defendant from taking further action against plaintiff on the two Michigan injunction suits, "or in any other suit filed in said Court of Cass County, Michigan, or in any other Court, until the Supreme Court of Illinois has acted upon the Petition for Leave to Appeal." On September 20, 1957, this court denied defendant's motion to vacate that restraining order, allowed the petition for leave to appeal, and entered a similar injunction restraining defendant until this court disposed of the case.

Defendant argues that this court will not, by counterinjunction, aid a citizen of another State to violate an injunction against prosecuting an action in Illinois; that the counterinjunction cannot be justified to protect the prior injunction of the Illinois court, since the Michigan injunction was in personam only; and that such counterinjunction would compel a party to give up vested rights and would violate the full-faith-and-credit and due process clauses of the Federal constitution.

The precise issues of the operative effect of an out-of-State injunction on pending litigation, and the propriety of the issuance of a counterinjunction involved herein, have never been adjudicated by this court. It is uncontroverted that the Illinois trial court had proper jurisdiction of the parties, and that it was bound under the full-faith-and-credit clause of the Federal constitution to recognize the Wrongful Death Act of Michigan, and could not refuse to entertain plaintiff's action on the ground that it was based on the wrongful death statute of a sister State. Moreover, it is the undisputed policy of this State to keep its courts open to residents and nonresidents alike.

Where, however, suits by nonresidents have no connection whatever with this jurisdiction, and the selection of this forum is purely vexatious, this court has held that the doctrine of forum non conveniens may be invoked to dismiss such cases. In the instant case, however, no defense of forum non conveniens was interposed by defendant. Instead, it sought to remove the case from the Illinois court by enjoining plaintiff in the State of her residence from prosecuting the Illinois action.

With reference to the Michigan injunction, while we quite agree with defendant's repeated assertion that a court of equity has power to restrain persons within its jurisdiction from instituting or proceeding with foreign actions, we note that the exercise of such power by equity courts has been deemed a matter of great delicacy, invoked with great restraint to avoid distressing conflicts and reciprocal interference with jurisdiction.

Illinois has consistently followed the course of refusing to restrain the prosecution of a prior instituted action pending in a sister State unless a clear equity is presented requiring the interposition of the court to prevent a manifest wrong and injustice; and neither a difference of remedy afforded by the domicile and the forum nor mere inconvenience and expense of defending will constitute grounds for such an injunction. That course is based on the policy that after suits are commenced in one State, it is inconsistent with inter-State harmony if their prosecution be controlled by the courts of another State.

Conversely, where other States have enjoined litigants from proceeding with a previously instituted Illinois action, this jurisdiction has followed the overwhelming judicial opinion that neither the full-faith-and-credit clause nor rules of comity require compulsory recognition of such injunctions so as to abate or preclude the disposition of the pending case. RESTATEMENT, CONFLICT OF LAWS, sec. 450, p. 534.

In the instant case the Michigan injunction was apparently issued pursuant to the policy of the State embodied in a Michigan statute restricting venue in suits against railroads to the county in which plaintiff resides, if the railroad lines traverse that county. Similar statutes confining transitory actions to the State of plaintiff's residence have been held unconstitutional. * * *

In the light of this reasoning, we cannot escape the observation that if statutes prohibiting or circumscribing the export of causes of action may not be given extraterritorial effect, it is hard to see why an equity decree should be entitled to any greater recognition. A court should be subject to the same limitations.

Therefore, it is evident that legal consistency, as well as the weight of authority, do not require us to recognize the Michigan injunction, and we may retain jurisdiction and proceed with plaintiff's wrongful death action. Such a course, however, is not practicable in the instant case, unless plaintiff, who is subject to imprisonment and other coercive tactics if she fails to dismiss her Illinois action, is protected by enjoining defendant from enforcing the Michigan injunction by contempt proceedings. A plaintiff cannot be expected or required to risk imprisonment so that the court may retain jurisdiction of a cause.

This brings us to the ultimate issue in this case: whether the court which first acquires jurisdiction of the parties and of the merits of the cause can issue a counterinjunction restraining a party before it from enforcing an out-of-State injunction which requires the dismissal of the local cause and ousts the forum of jurisdiction.

There is no quarrel with the basic principle that a court has a duty, as well as power, to protect its jurisdiction over a controversy in order to decree complete and final justice between the parties and may issue an injunction for that purpose, restraining proceedings in other courts.

Defendant claims that there is no reason to invoke this principle in the instant case since the Michigan injunction in no way interferes with the jurisdiction of this court, but merely affects the litigants. In support thereof defendant cites the equitable maxim, "equity acts in personam," invoked since the days of Coke and Bacon to obviate open conflicts between law and equity courts, and the general principle that courts of equity have the power to prevent those amenable to their own process from instituting or carrying on suits in other States which will result in injury or fraud.

We cannot close our eyes to the fact that the intended effect of the Michigan injunction, though directed at the parties and not at this court, is to prevent the Illinois court from adjudicating a cause of action of which it had proper jurisdiction. If the litigants are coerced to dismiss the Illinois action, it is our rightfully acquired jurisdiction that is thereby destroyed. Therefore, the Michigan injunction was in everything but form an order restraining the Illinois court and determining the cases it may properly try.

The Illinois court should be entitled to the same respect for its jurisdiction that it accords the courts of other States, and in the absence of such respect, should be able to protect its jurisdiction from unjustifiable interference by the courts of other States. It is one thing for Illinois to have a policy against enjoining pending litigation on the merits in other States, in the absence of cogent equitable grounds, but it is quite another to stand by impotently and see a litigant, in a case of which the Illinois court has prior jurisdiction of the merits, forced by an out-of-State injunction to dismiss that legitimate cause of action for no reason other than that defendant would prefer to defend the lawsuit elsewhere. Reluctance to be an interloper is not synonymous with abdication.

In the instant case, furthermore, this court would not only be deprived of jurisdiction, but would be required to remain oblivious of defendant's coercive tactics of having plaintiff removed as administratrix of her husband's estate as punishment for proceeding with her Illinois action, and superseded by an administrator who was not only friendly to defendant, but who selected counsel to prosecute the estate's claim against defendant, subject to defendant's approval and direction. Neither the Federal constitution, nor comity requires such abdication.

The Illinois court is not so barren of authority, nor so calcified in its reasoning, as to cower behind the equitable maxim that "equity acts in personam," and to parrot, as defendant urges, that it is only the litigants and not the jurisdiction of this court that is being interfered with by the Michigan injunction. We are entitled to recognize that their coercion destroys our jurisdiction, and unless we can protect the litigant from such coercion, it is idle to say that we can protect our jurisdiction.

If Illinois were not the appropriate forum to try this, or any other transitory action, the defense of forum non conveniens could be interposed, and, if meritorious, the Illinois court would dismiss the case. However, this court need not, and will not, countenance having its right to try cases, of which it has proper jurisdiction, determined by the courts of other States, through their injunctive process. We are not only free to disregard such out-of-State injunctions, and to adjudicate the merits of the pending action, but we can protect our jurisdiction from such usurpation by the issuance of a counterinjunction restraining the enforcement of the out-of-State injunction.

It was therefore error for the trial court to dismiss plaintiff's supplemental complaint and her motion for a counterinjunction.

Reversed and remanded, with directions.

SCHAEFER, JUSTICE (dissenting).

I agree with the majority that the Michigan injunction is not entitled to full faith and credit. But the question in this case goes a step beyond the issue as to full faith and credit. What is here sought is a counterinjunction to restrain the railroad from enforcing the injunction entered by the Michigan court. The difficulties that attend the kind of injunction that the Michigan court entered were stated long ago by Chancellor Walworth: "If this court should sustain an injunction bill to restrain proceedings previously commenced in a sister state, the court of that state might retaliate upon the complainant, who was defendant in the suit there; and, by process of attachment, might compel him to relinquish the suit subsequently commenced here. By this course of proceeding, the courts of different states would indirectly be brought into collision with each other in regard to jurisdiction; and the rights of suitors might be lost sight of in a useless struggle for what might be considered the legitimate powers and rights of courts." *Mead v. Merritt and Peck*, N.Y.Chan.1831, 2 Paige 402. What was there said with respect to an initial injunction applies with added force to a counterinjunction. Just as the first injunction sired the second, so the second might sire a third. The ultimate end is not foreseeable.

The place to stop this unseemly kind of judicial disorder is where it begins. The peculiar preference of one State for a particular venue in a single class of cases does not, it seems to me, afford a basis for indirect interference with litigation pending in another jurisdiction. The salutary power of a court of equity to restrain the prosecution of inequitable actions in a foreign court originated and developed upon more substantial considerations. But we are not called upon to review the propriety of the Michigan injunction. Plaintiff did not seek to review it in the Michigan courts. While venue statutes are usually permissive, Michigan's special provision with respect to actions against railroads appears to require that such actions be brought only in a particular county. The Michigan court applied its statute to a Michigan administrator. Illinois has no connection whatever with the occurrences out of which the administrator's claim arose. The policy of Illinois with respect to the maintenance of foreign wrongful death actions was expressed in section 2 of the Injuries Act which prohibited them. While it is true that this prohibition is no longer effective, the policy that it expressed is also of significance in determining whether or not a counterinjunction should have been issued.

I think that the trial court and the Appellate Court were right, and so I would affirm.

NOTE: "FRAUD, GROSS WRONG OR OPPRESSION"

Courts have held that injunctions against foreign litigation can be justified by a need to protect the defendant against "fraud, gross wrong or oppression." *See Tabor & Co. v. McNall*, 30 Ill.App.3d 593, 333 N.E.2d 562 (1975).

PROBLEMS

1. *Enjoining the Illinois Court?* In the prior case, who did the Michigan court enjoin? Would it have been appropriate for the Michigan court to directly enjoin the Illinois court? Why? Why not?

2. *The Propriety of the Michigan Injunction.* Should the Michigan court have entered the injunction in the first instance? In Chapter Two, we saw that a court of equity will deny relief to a plaintiff who has an adequate remedy at law. Did the Michigan plaintiff have an adequate remedy at law in the Illinois courts? If so, what was it?

TIDIK V. RITSEMA

938 F.Supp. 416 (E.D. Mich. 1996).

GADOLA, DISTRICT JUDGE.

The facts underlying the plaintiff's complaint are fairly straightforward. The plaintiff was the plaintiff in a divorce action in Wayne County Circuit Court against defendant Lisa Tidik. Defendant Judge Kaufman presided at that trial and issued a final Judgment of Divorce on September 28, 1995. As part of the divorce decree, Judge Kaufman included a provision requiring that the plaintiff post a bond with each motion filed with the court as security against costs or sanctions potentially awardable under Michigan Court Rule 2.114(E). This was due to plaintiff's filing of numerous motions during the course of his divorce proceedings.

The plaintiff alleges that he has a constitutional right to visit his children, and that that right has been consistently violated by all the defendants. The complaint alleges that all defendants are involved in a complex conspiracy to violate his rights to visit his children. However, the plaintiff's lengthy complaint fails to reveal any specific examples supporting the conspiracy allegation, or that any constitutional rights were violated. The plaintiff accuses defendants Judge Kaufman and Court Clerk Lynn Watson of refusing to docket or hear his motions, and of holding hearings without the plaintiff's presence. Defendant Paul Longton allegedly violated the plaintiff's rights by drafting the motion provision for defendant Kaufman's signature. Finally, regarding Wayne County Friend of the Court officials, defendants Gerhard Ritsema, David March, David Manville and John Lemire, the plaintiff alleges these individuals, as non-judicial authorities, conducted proceedings and drafted orders violating his constitutional right to visit his children. The plaintiff claims these constitutional violations continue to this very day.

The record indicates that the plaintiff filed a claim of appeal with the Michigan Court of Appeals. The record further indicates that the plaintiff has filed several motions with the Michigan Court of Appeals, including a motion seeking disqualification of Judge Kaufman which was denied.

As indicated previously, defendant Kaufman has filed a motion to enjoin the plaintiff from filing any further actions relating to his 1995 divorce proceeding.[2] His request for injunctive relief is premised on Rule 11 which imposes an affirmative duty upon any individual who signs a pleading, motion or other paper filed in federal court to conduct a reasonable inquiry into the issues presented in that filing to assure that the document is well grounded in fact, the positions taken are warranted by existing law or as good faith arguments for the extension or modification of existing law, and the document is not filed for an improper purpose, such as harassment. Fed.R.Civ.P. 11. To determine whether Rule 11 has been violated, the court must assess whether the individual's conduct was objectively reasonable under the circumstances. *Business Guides v. Chromatic Communications Enterprises, Inc.,* 498 U.S. 533, 554 (1991).

Sanctions pursuant to Rule 11 serve the dual purpose of deterring frivolous lawsuits and compensating those parties forced to defend such suits. The case law interpreting and the amendments to Rule 11 make clear that the primary purpose of the Rule is to deter baseless filings and curb abuses of the judicial system, not to reward parties who are victimized by litigation. *Cooter & Gell v. Hartmarx Corp.,* 496 U.S. 384 (1990). The Rule also provides that any sanctions imposed should be no more severe than is necessary to deter these abuses. *See* Fed.R.Civ.P. 11(c)(2). In fashioning an appropriate sanction, the court may consider past conduct of the individual responsible for violating Rule 11.

Rule 11 gives the court wide discretion in selecting an appropriate remedy, including the authority to issue directives of a nonmonetary nature. Fed.R.Civ.P. 11(c)(2). In determining whether to impose a sanction restricting a litigant's future access to the courts, courts in the Eastern District have adopted a five-factor test which considers:

(1) The litigant's history of litigation and in particular whether it entails vexatious, harassing or duplicative lawsuits;

(2) The litigant's motive in pursuing the litigation, *e.g.* does the litigant have an objective good faith expectation of prevailing?

(3) Whether the litigant is represented by counsel.

(4) Whether the litigant has caused needless expense to other parties or has posed an unnecessary burden on the courts and their personnel; and

(5) Whether other sanctions would be adequate to protect the courts and the other parties. Ultimately, the question the court must answer is whether a litigant who has a history of vexatious

---

[2] Defendants Ritsema, Lynn Watson, Lemire, March and Manville have joined in this motion. Because this is the plaintiff's first action filed against these defendants this court does not find that injunctive relief is warranted at this time [as] to [these] defendants. . . .

litigation is likely to continue to abuse the judicial process and harass other parties.

Kersh v. Borden Chemical, 689 F.Supp. 1442, 1450 (E.D.Mich.1988).

Where the history of vexatious litigation is particularly odious, the traditional standards for injunctive relief do not apply and the court may impose injunctive sanctions without a request by an offended party. Moreover, courts have recognized that injunctive sanctions may be appropriate, even where the litigant has not been involved in multiple actions, where that litigation has been unusually protracted or burdensome, and the losing party simply refuses to bound by the outcome. *Michigan v. City of Allen Park,* 573 F.Supp. 1481 (E.D.Mich.1983). The injunction must, however, be sufficiently tailored to the vice so as not to infringe upon the litigator's right of access to the courts.

This court finds that the previous conduct of the plaintiff clearly satisfies the standards for injunctive relief as to defendant Kaufman. This is the plaintiff's second action against defendant Kaufman in this court. The first complaint was dismissed by this court in December of 1995 based on the defendant's absolute immunity from suit. That dismissal stated unambiguously that defendant Kaufman was not subject to suit for any claims based upon acts taken in his capacity as the judge presiding over the plaintiff's divorce action. By filing a second complaint alleging virtually identical claims against Judge Kaufman, the plaintiff has exhibited a stubborn and unjustifiable defiance of this court's prior ruling. The plaintiff's present complaint against Judge Kaufman clearly has no chance of success. The plaintiff's present complaint is duplicative, vexatious, has caused defendant Kaufman to incur needless expenses, and has burdened this court system with litigation solely intended to intimidate and harass the named defendants. The plaintiff's lack of good faith in pursuing this second action against Judge Kaufman is precisely the type of conduct that Rule 11 was intended to deter. Accordingly, defendant Kaufman's motion for injunctive relief will be granted.

PROBLEMS

1. *Enjoining Vexatious Litigants.* Petitioner filed for divorce in Rhode Island. Respondent, who at that time resided in Rhode Island, entered an appearance. The Rhode Island court ordered respondent to pay $300 child support every two weeks. Respondent failed to meet his obligations and was held in contempt. The arrearages reached $2,246 and respondent was held in contempt three times. The court continued the case for 3 months to allow respondent to attempt to purge his contempt. Respondent moved to Maryland and instituted new divorce proceedings there. Petitioner sought an injunction restraining respondent from proceeding with the Maryland action. Should the

trial court grant the injunction? *See Brown v. Brown*, 120 R.I. 340, 387 A.2d 1051 (1978).

2. *More on Enjoining Vexatious Litigants.* Defendant instituted six pro se law suits in federal court charging violations of his constitutional rights. Many of the suits were filed against judges who had entered rulings against him. Also sued were opposing attorneys and law firms and other participants in the suits. Defendant had also filed no less than six cases in Colorado state courts. The trial court concluded that "all of the cases reflect a history of frivolous complaints and abusive litigation tactics intended to harass and intimidate opposing parties, opposing attorneys and court officers." The State of Colorado and others filed a complaint, seeking protection from defendant's "unmeritorious and abusive" pro se civil actions. Mr. Fleming filed his answer, which contained counterclaims alleging violations of constitutional rights secured by 42 U.S.C. §§ 1983 and 1985. Is it appropriate for a court to issue an injunction in this situation? What arguments can you make in favor of issuing the injunction? How might defendant respond?

3. *Framing the Decree.* If the court decides to enter an injunction in the *Fleming* case, how should the order be framed?

VANNECK V. VANNECK

49 N.Y.2d 602, 404 N.E.2d 1278, 427 N.Y.S.2d 735 (App.1980).

COOKE, CHIEF JUDGE.

John and Isabelle Vanneck were married in New York in 1965 and lived together with their three children in this State until December, 1978. On the 19th of that month, during the children's winter school recess, Isabelle Vanneck took the children to the family's home in North Stamford, Connecticut, and decided to remain. Alleging the irretrievable breakdown of the marriage, Isabelle, defendant here, commenced an action in Connecticut on December 30, 1978 by personal service upon plaintiff in that State, seeking dissolution of the marriage, alimony and custody of the children. Two weeks later, on January 13, 1979, plaintiff commenced this New York action for divorce on the ground of cruelty or, in the alternative, for separation on the ground of abandonment. He too sought custody of the parties' three children.

Plaintiff moved in the New York court to enjoin defendant from prosecuting the divorce action in Connecticut, contending that defendant's move was undertaken to establish divorce jurisdiction in that State to enable her to exploit its equitable distribution laws. Plaintiff also sought temporary custody of the children, urging that daily transportation to New York schools was not in the children's best interest. In opposition, defendant asserted the bona fides of her residence in Connecticut, as well as that of the children, and, in support of her custody of the children, that they had been enrolled in Connecticut schools for the spring 1979 term.

In light of the custody issue present in both the New York and Connecticut actions, Special Term put aside consideration of the traditional criteria for restraining prosecution of a foreign divorce action and applied article 5–A of the Domestic Relations Law, which codifies the Uniform Child Custody Jurisdiction Act (UCCJA) (L.1978, Ch. 493, eff. Sept. 1, 1978). Considering such factors as the family's residence in New York of long duration, the children's attendance at schools here, and the secondary nature of the Connecticut home prior to the separation, the court concluded that New York had a substantial interest in the family unit. The court further determined that irrespective of defendant's contacts, residence or domicile in Connecticut, New York bore the closest connection to the children and the family and provided access to evidence concerning the children's care, protection, training and personal relationships. The court therefore granted the injunction against prosecuting the Connecticut action pending a final determination of the New York action for divorce and other relief. The intermediate court of appeals reversed and the matter came before the New York Court of Appeals.

Traditionally, an injunction against prosecution of a foreign divorce would be granted when the rights of a resident spouse were threatened. The grant of such relief involves the exercise of discretion after consideration of such factors as the bona fides of the domicile established in the other State, the motivation for commencing an action there and the substantiality of contacts with that forum. When the parties to a divorce proceeding seek as ancillary relief a child custody determination, however, the UCCJA is applicable. A separate inquiry, with proper weight accorded to the provisions of the act, is required for determining whether the custody phase of the litigation may proceed in the foreign court. To assure that the best interests of the child and salutary provisions of the act are not subordinated to the parents' interest in obtaining the best terms of the divorce, the court should determine whether to enjoin prosecution of the divorce only after the inquiry concerning the custody issues has been undertaken. Of course, the decision whether to exercise custody jurisdiction is a factor in determining the propriety of injunctive relief against the divorce phase, and the weight to be accorded this factor may vary depending on the circumstances of the particular case. The preliminary decision concerning New York's exercise of jurisdiction over the custody issues, however, must have as its foundation the proper application of the UCCJA.

The UCCJA represents a considered effort to give stability to child custody decrees, minimize jurisdictional competition between sister States, promote co-operation and communication between the courts of different States, all to the end of resolving custody disputes in the best interests of the child. The act offers a standard for determining in the first instance whether the necessary predicate for jurisdiction exists.

Custody may be determined in the child's "home state," defined as "the state in which the child at the time of the commencement of the custody proceeding, has resided with his parents, a parent, or a person acting as parent, for at least six consecutive months," or in the State that had been the child's home State within six months before commencement of the proceeding where the child is absent from the State through removal by a person claiming custody and a parent lives in the State. A jurisdictional predicate also exists in New York when "it is in the best interest of the child that a court of this state assume jurisdiction because (i) the child and his parents, or the child and at least one contestant, have a significant connection with this state, and (ii) there is within the jurisdiction of the court substantial evidence concerning the child's present or future care, protection, training, and personal relationships."

The inquiry is not completed merely by a determination that a jurisdictional predicate exists in the forum State, for then the court must determine whether to exercise its jurisdiction. There, too, the act guides the determination, commanding the court to consider whether it is an inconvenient forum or whether the conduct of the parties militates against an exercise of jurisdiction. Notwithstanding that this State has jurisdiction, a court "shall not exercise its jurisdiction under this article if at the time of filing the petition a proceeding concerning the custody of the child was pending in a court of another state exercising jurisdiction substantially in conformity with this article." Once a court of this State learns of the pendency of another proceeding, the court "shall stay (its own) proceeding and communicate with the court in which the other proceeding is pending to the end that the issue may be litigated in the more appropriate forum and that information be exchanged in accordance with sections seventy-five-s through seventy-five-v of this article" (Domestic Relations Law, § 75–g, subd. 3).

The express statutory command of section 75–g was all but ignored by Special Term. Given the pendency of the Connecticut action, the question with which the court should have been concerned was not whether New York had jurisdiction to determine the custody dispute, nor whether New York was the most appropriate forum. Rather, at that stage of the proceeding, the focus of inquiry should have been whether Connecticut was "exercising jurisdiction substantially in conformity" with article 5–A.

The instant case calls into play the jurisdictional predicate of section 75–d (subd. 1, par. (b)), which provides that a State may exercise jurisdiction when it serves the best interests of the child because there is a significant connection to the forum and there is available substantial evidence concerning the child's present or future welfare. Particularly relevant to the jurisdictional determination is whether the forum in which the litigation is to proceed has "optimum access to relevant evidence" (Prefatory Note of Commissioners on Uniform State Laws, 9 ULA (Master Ed.), § 3, p. 124). Maximum rather than minimum contacts with the State are required. The general language of this subdivision permits a flexible approach to various fact patterns. This imprecision, however, must not destroy the legislative design "to limit jurisdiction rather than to proliferate it."

We need not decide whether the pendency of a proceeding in a forum totally lacking a jurisdictional predicate would mandate that a New York court suspend its action for purposes of communicating with the other court. But, at least where the claim of sister State jurisdiction is colorable, a New York court must heed the statutory command to defer adjudicating the dispute and communicate with the foreign court. Such a claim exists here, as defendant has alleged that she and the children have significant ties to Connecticut developed prior to the commencement of the proceeding there.

Thus, defendant's assertions here, at least as a threshold matter, support an exercise of jurisdiction by the Connecticut court, and required Special Term to open channels of communication with the Connecticut court before enjoining prosecution of the action there. The New York court's unilateral decision to exercise jurisdiction and prevent Connecticut's exercise of jurisdiction is contrary to the avowed purposes of the legislation adopted by both States. Rather than promote co-operation between courts, it fosters the very jurisdictional competition sought to be avoided.

The Appellate Division therefore properly determined that the injunction against prosecuting the action in Connecticut was inappropriate. The Appellate Division, in the exercise of discretion, could have enjoined only the divorce phase of the litigation, for, as noted above, that question is separate from the question whether jurisdiction exists to entertain a custody dispute. Indeed, plaintiff argues that such relief is proper here, pointing to defendant's recent search for a New York residence and continuing contacts with this State and asserting that defendant's decision to remain in Connecticut and her commencement of the action there represents forum shopping for a more favorable disposition. While such discretionary relief might be appropriate to protect the rights of a resident spouse in some circumstances, there was no abuse of discretion in the Appellate Division's failure to bifurcate the proceeding given defendant's assertion of a bona fide domicile in Connecticut, the family's previous contacts with that State, and the pendency of the custody issues there. Finally, we have examined plaintiff's remaining contentions and find them to be without merit.

Accordingly, the order of the Appellate Division should be affirmed, with costs.

PROBLEMS

1. *Desirability of the UCCJA.* Does the Uniform Child Custody Jurisdiction Act provide a preferable method for addressing jurisdictional issues?

2. *The Mississippi Tobacco Case.* Up until this point, we have been thinking about the injunctive issues from a policy standpoint. In other words, our focus has been on how courts should or should not handle (or have handled) injunctions in this context. Now, let us think about the same issues from the standpoint of a practicing lawyer and an actual case.

When the State of Mississippi sued Brown & Williamson Tobacco Corp. (and other tobacco companies) to recover money it had spent treating poor people for tobacco-related illnesses, it subpoenaed former B & W executive Jeffrey Wigand to testify in Mississippi. Wigand had previously been B & W's Vice President for Research. By the time that the subpoena issued, Wigand had left B & W and was teaching high school. However, Wigand had given an interview to CBS's "60 Minutes" regarding B & W. Although CBS decided not to air the story on the advice of its attorneys, it was widely believed that the interview was damaging to B & W's case. In subpoenaing Wigand, Mississippi hoped that he would provide information about the alteration or falsification of documents relating to the carcinogenic effects of tobacco, the illegal shipment of tobacco seeds overseas, and whether B & W had killed efforts to develop a safer cigarette.

When he worked for B & W, Wigand signed an agreement not to testify about his B & W activities without first conferring with B & W. The agreement was designed to protect B & W trade secrets and confidential information. One week prior to the deposition, Wigand had not conferred with B & W. Wigand lives in Louisville, Kentucky, where B & W is headquartered. Suppose that you represent B & W. What is the best way to protect B & W's interests? What remedy might you seek against Wigand? Where should it be sought?

2. STATE COURT INJUNCTIONS AGAINST FEDERAL LITIGATION

Do different considerations apply when a state court tries to enjoin federal court litigation?

DONOVAN V. CITY OF DALLAS

377 U.S. 408, 84 S.Ct. 1579, 12 L.Ed.2d 409 (1964).

MR. JUSTICE BLACK delivered the opinion of the Court.

The question presented here is whether a state court can validly enjoin a person from prosecuting an action in personam in a district or appellate court of the United States which has jurisdiction both of the parties and of the subject matter.

The City of Dallas, Texas, owns Love Field, a municipal airport. In 1961, 46 Dallas citizens who owned or had interests in property near the airport filed a class suit in a Texas court to restrain the city from building an additional runway and from issuing and selling municipal bonds for that purpose. The complaint alleged many damages that would occur to the plaintiffs if the runway should be built and charged that issuance of the bonds would be illegal for any number of reasons. The case was tried, summary judgment was given for the city, the Texas Court of Civil Appeals affirmed, the Supreme Court of Texas denied review, and we denied certiorari. Later 120 Dallas citizens, including 27 of the plaintiffs in the earlier action, filed another action in the United States District Court for the Northern District of Texas seeking similar relief. A number of new defendants were named in addition to the City of Dallas, all the defendants being charged with taking part in plans to construct the runway and to issue and sell bonds in violation of state and federal laws. The complaint sought an injunction against construction of the runway, issuance of bonds, payment on bonds already issued, and circulation of false information about the bond issue, as well as a declaration that all the bonds were illegal and void. None of the bonds would be approved, and therefore under Texas law none could be issued, so long as there was pending litigation challenging their validity. The city filed a motion to dismiss and an answer to the complaint in the federal court. But at the same time the city applied to the Texas Court of Civil Appeals for a writ of prohibition to bar all the plaintiffs in the case in the United States District Court from prosecuting their case there. The Texas Court of Civil Appeals denied relief, holding that it was without power to enjoin litigants from prosecuting an action in a federal court and that the defense of res judicata on which the city relied could be raised and adjudicated in the United States District Court. On petition for mandamus the Supreme Court of Texas took a different view, however, held it the duty of the Court of Civil Appeals to prohibit the litigants from further prosecuting the United States District Court case, and stated that a writ of mandamus would issue should the Court of Civil Appeals fail to perform this duty. The Court of Civil Appeals promptly issued a writ prohibiting all the plaintiffs in the United States District Court case from any further prosecution of that case and enjoined them "individually and as a class from filing or instituting any further litigation, law suits or actions in any court, the purpose of which is to contest the validity of the airport revenue bonds or from in any manner interfering with the proposed bonds." The United States District Court in an unreported opinion dismissed the case pending there. Counsel Donovan, who is one of the petitioners here, filed an appeal from that dismissal in the United States Court of Appeals for the Fifth Circuit. The Texas Court of Civil Appeals thereupon cited Donovan and the other United States District Court claimants for contempt and convicted 87 of them on a finding that they had violated its "valid order." Donovan was sentenced to serve 20 days in jail, and the other 86 were fined $200 each, an aggregate of $17,200. These penalties were imposed upon each contemner for having either (1) joined as a party plaintiff in the United States District Court case; (2) failed to request and contested the dismissal of that case; (3) taken exceptions to the dismissal preparatory to appealing to the Court of Appeals; or (4) filed a separate action in the Federal District Court seeking to enjoin the Supreme Court of Texas from interfering with the original federal-court suit. After the fines had been paid and he had served his jail sentence, counsel Donovan appeared in the District Court on behalf of himself and all those who had been fined and moved to dismiss the appeal to the United States Court of Appeals. His motion stated that it was made under duress and that unless the motion was made "the Attorney for Defendant City of Dallas and the Chief Judge of the Court of Civil Appeals have threatened these Appellants and their Attorney with further prosecution for contempt resulting in additional fines and imprisonment." The United States District Court then dismissed the appeal.

We think the Texas Court of Civil Appeals was right in its first holding that it was without power to enjoin these litigants from prosecuting their federal-court action, and we therefore reverse the State Supreme Court's judgment upsetting that of the Court of Appeals. We vacate the later contempt judgment of the Court of Civil Appeals, which rested on the mistaken belief that the writ prohibiting litigation by the federal plaintiffs was "valid."

Early in the history of our country a general rule was established that state and federal courts would not interfere with or try to restrain each other's proceedings. That rule has continued substantially unchanged to this time. An exception has been made in cases where a court has custody of property, that is, proceedings in rem or quasi in rem. In such cases this Court has said that the state or federal court having custody of such property has exclusive jurisdiction to proceed. It may be that a full hearing in an appropriate court would justify a finding that the state-court judgment in favor of Dallas in the first suit barred the issues raised in the second suit, a question as to which we express no opinion. But plaintiffs in the second suit chose to file that case in the federal court. They had a right to do this, a right which is theirs by reason of congressional enactments passed pursuant to congressional policy. And whether or not a plea of res judicata in the second suit would be good is a question for the federal court to decide. While Congress has seen fit to authorize courts of the United States to restrain state-court proceedings in some special circumstances, it has in no way relaxed the old and well-established judicially declared rule that state courts are completely without power to restrain federal-court proceedings in in personam actions like the one here. And it does not matter that the prohibition here was addressed to the parties rather than to the federal court itself. * * *

Petitioners being properly in the federal court had a right granted by Congress to have the court decide the issues they presented, and to appeal to the Court of Appeals from the District Court's dismissal. They have been punished both for prosecuting their federal-court case and for appealing it. They dismissed their appeal because of threats to punish them more if they did not do so. The legal effect of such a coerced dismissal on their appeal is not now before us, but the propriety of a state court's punishment of a federal-court litigant for pursuing his right to federal-court remedies is. That right was granted by Congress and cannot be taken away by the State. The Texas courts were without power to take away this federal right by contempt proceedings or otherwise.

It is argued here, however, that the Court of Civil Appeals' judgment of contempt should nevertheless be upheld on the premise that it was petitioners' duty to obey the restraining order whether that order was valid or invalid. Whether the Texas court would have punished petitioners for contempt had it known that the restraining order petitioners violated was invalid, we do not know. Since that question was neither considered nor decided by the Texas court, we leave it for consideration by that court on remand. We express no opinion on that question at this time.

The judgment of the Texas Supreme Court is reversed, the judgment of the Texas Court of Civil Appeals is vacated, and the case is remanded to the Court of Civil Appeals for further proceedings not inconsistent with this opinion.

It is so ordered.

MR. JUSTICE HARLAN, whom MR. JUSTICE CLARK and MR. JUSTICE STEWART join, dissenting.

Given the Texas Supreme Court's finding, amply supported by the record and in no way challenged by this Court, that this controversy "has reached the point of vexatious and harassing litigation," I consider both the state injunction and the ensuing contempt adjudication to have been perfectly proper.

This Court, in 1941, expressly recognized the power of a state court to do precisely what the Texas court did here. In *Baltimore & Ohio R. Co. v. Kepner*, 314 U.S. 44, the Court, although denying the state court's power to issue an injunction in that case, said: "The real contention of petitioner is that despite the admitted venue respondent is acting in a vexatious and inequitable manner in maintaining the federal court suit in a distant jurisdiction when a convenient and suitable forum is at respondent's doorstep. Under such circumstances petitioner asserts power, abstractly speaking, in the Ohio court to prevent a resident under its jurisdiction from doing inequity. Such power does exist." Mr. Justice Frankfurter, dissenting on other grounds, observed that the opinion of the

Court did not "give new currency to the discredited notion that there is a general lack of power in the state courts to enjoin proceedings in federal courts." In light of the foregoing, there was no impropriety in the issuance of the state court's injunction in the present case.

QUESTIONS: ADEQUATE FEDERAL COURT REMEDIES?

Did the federal courts plaintiffs have an adequate remedy available to them in federal court? If so, what was it? Should they have been required to avail themselves of this remedy?

NOTES: THE PREROGATIVE WRITS

Donovan involves the so-called "prerogative writs"—although the court uses them in an unusual way.

Dobbs, Handbook of the Law of Remedies 111–12

A final group of writs included the prerogative writs, or extraordinary remedies. In this group the writ was in itself a coercive order, even though it issued out of the law rather than equity court.

The main writs in this group were the writ of *habeas corpus*, the writ of *prohibition*, and the writ of *mandamus*.

The habeas writ issued to compel the person to whom it was directed to produce the body of a named person—that is, to free him from imprisonment. The proceeding to obtain this writ is a civil action at law. In earlier times the writ of habeas corpus was directed mainly at official restraints, for example, imprisonment under a sentence of the court. The writ usually issued only when the court lacked jurisdiction or exceeded its jurisdiction in sentencing the prisoner. * * *

The writ of prohibition was likewise a coercive order, and like the early habeas writ, it was directed to an official. Prohibition was directed to a judge, and it ordered him to cease trial of a case or to cease certain actions in it. Obviously, the writ was issued only by a superior court. Its purpose was to limit the lower courts to their proper jurisdiction. It was seldom needed, since an act beyond the court's jurisdiction ordinarily can be attacked on appeal. However, the prohibition writ operates today to facilitate early review of serious actions by a trial judge.

The writ of mandamus is broader than either habeas or prohibition. It orders a person, usually some official of the executive branch of the government, or the judge of a lower court, to carry out some affirmative action. But, unlike the injunction, mandamus is used only to compel a specific kind of behavior—compliance with a ministerial duty of an office. It does not issue to compel action that is discretionary. It is sometimes used today to compel some affirmative action by a trial judge, and, like prohibition, it may serve to effect an early review of some serious ruling in the case that does not meet the rules for appealability.

These coercive orders at law all resemble injunctions and operate much like injunctions. With the merger of law and equity, and with the adoption of "one form of action," perhaps these coercive orders can be thought of as merely special forms of an injunction.

3. FEDERAL COURT INJUNCTIONS AGAINST STATE LITIGATION

Federal court injunctions against state court proceedings present quite different problems.

MITCHUM V. FOSTER

407 U.S. 225, 92 S.Ct. 2151, 32 L.Ed.2d 705 (1972).

MR. JUSTICE STEWART delivered the opinion of the Court.

The federal anti-injunction statute provides that a federal court "may not grant an injunction to stay proceedings in a State court except as expressly authorized by Act of Congress, or where necessary in aid of its jurisdiction, or to protect or effectuate its judgments." An Act of Congress, 42 U.S.C. § 1983, expressly authorizes a "suit in equity" to redress "the deprivation," under color of state law, "of any rights, privileges, or immunities secured by the Constitution" The question before us is whether this "Act of Congress" comes within the "expressly authorized" exception of the anti-injunction statute so as to permit a federal court in a § 1983 suit to grant an injunction to stay a proceeding pending in a state court. * * *

The prosecuting attorney of Bay County, Florida, brought a proceeding in a Florida court to close down the appellant's bookstore as a public nuisance under the claimed authority of Florida law. The state court entered a preliminary order prohibiting continued operation of the bookstore. After further inconclusive proceedings in the state courts, the appellant filed a complaint in the United States District Court for the Northern District of Florida, alleging that the actions of the state judicial and law enforcement officials were depriving him of rights protected by the First and Fourteenth Amendments. Relying upon 42 U.S.C. § 1983, he asked for injunctive and declaratory relief against the state court proceedings, on the ground that Florida laws were being unconstitutionally applied by the state court so as to cause him great and irreparable harm. A single federal district judge issued temporary restraining orders, and a three-judge court was convened pursuant to 28 U.S.C. §§ 2281 and 2284. After a hearing, the three-judge court dissolved the temporary restraining orders and refused to enjoin the state court proceeding, holding that the "injunctive relief sought here as to the proceedings pending in the Florida courts does not come under any of the exceptions set forth in Section 2283. It is not expressly authorized by Act of Congress, it is not necessary in the aid of this court's jurisdiction and it is not sought in order to protect or effectuate any judgment of this court." * * *

In denying injunctive relief, the District Court relied on this Court's decision in *Atlantic Coast Line R. Co. v. Brotherhood of Locomotive Engineers*, 398 U.S. 281. The *Atlantic Coast Line* case did not deal with the "expressly authorized" exception of the anti-injunction statute, but the Court's opinion in that case does bring into sharp focus the critical importance of the question now before us. For in that case we expressly rejected the view that the anti-injunction statute merely states a flexible doctrine of comity, and made clear that the statute imposes an absolute ban upon the issuance of a federal injunction against a pending state court proceeding, in the absence of one of the recognized exceptions. * * *

It follows, in the present context, that if 42 U.S.C. § 1983 is not within the "expressly authorized" exception of the anti-injunction statute, then a federal equity court is wholly without power to grant any relief in a § 1983 suit seeking to stay a state court proceeding. The anti-injunction law absolutely prohibits all federal equitable intervention in a pending state court proceeding, whether civil or criminal, and regardless of how extraordinary the particular circumstances may be.

The anti-injunction statute goes back almost to the beginnings of our history as a Nation. In 1793, Congress enacted a law providing that no "writ of injunction be granted (by any federal court) to stay proceedings in any court of a state" Act of March 2, 1793, 1 Stat. 335. The precise origins of the legislation are shrouded in obscurity, but the consistent understanding has been that its basic purpose is to prevent "needless friction between state and federal courts." *Oklahoma Packing Co. v. Oklahoma Gas & Elec. Co.*, 309 U.S. 4, 9. * * *

Despite the seemingly uncompromising language of the anti-injunction statute prior to 1948, the Court soon recognized that exceptions must be made to its blanket prohibition if the import and purpose of other Acts of Congress were to be given their intended scope. So it was that, in addition to the bankruptcy law exception that Congress explicitly recognized in 1874, the Court through the years found that federal courts were empowered to enjoin state court proceedings, despite the anti-injunction statute, in carrying out the will of Congress under at least six other federal laws. These covered a broad spectrum of congressional action: (1) legislation providing for removal of litigation from state to federal courts, (2) legislation limiting the liability of ship-owners, (3) legislation providing for federal interpleader actions, (4) legislation conferring federal jurisdiction over farm mortgages, (5) legislation governing federal habeas corpus proceedings, and (6) legislation providing for control of prices.

In addition to the exceptions to the anti-injunction statute found to be embodied in these various Acts of Congress, the Court recognized other "implied" exceptions to the blanket prohibition of the anti-injunction statute. One was an "in rem" exception, allowing a federal court to enjoin a state court proceeding in order to protect its jurisdiction of a res over which it had first acquired jurisdiction. Another was a "relitigation" exception, permitting a federal court to enjoin relitigation in a state court of issues already decided in federal litigation. Still a third exception, more recently developed permits a federal injunction of state court proceedings when the plaintiff in the federal court is the United States itself, or a federal agency asserting "superior federal interests."

In *Toucey v. New York Life Ins. Co.*, 314 U.S. 118, the Court in 1941 issued an opinion casting considerable doubt upon the approach to the anti-injunction statute reflected in its previous decisions. The Court's opinion expressly disavowed the "relitigation" exception to the statute, and emphasized generally the importance of recognizing the statute's basic directive "of 'hands off' by the federal courts in the use of the injunction to stay litigation in a state court." The congressional response to *Toucey* was the enactment in 1948 of the anti-injunction statute in its present form in 28 U.S.C. § 2283, which, as the Reviser's Note makes evident, served not only to overrule the specific holding of *Toucey*, but to restore "the basic law as generally understood and interpreted prior to the *Toucey* decision."

We proceed, then, upon the understanding that in determining whether § 1983 comes within the "expressly authorized" exception of the anti-injunction statute, the criteria to be applied are those reflected in the Court's decisions prior to *Toucey*. A review of those decisions makes reasonably clear what the relevant criteria are. In the first place, it is evident that, in order to qualify under the "expressly authorized" exception of the anti-injunction statute, a federal law need not contain an express reference to that statute. Indeed, none of the previously recognized statutory exceptions contains any such reference. Secondly, a federal law need not expressly authorize an injunction of a state court proceeding in order to qualify as an exception. Three of the six previously recognized statutory exceptions contain no such authorization. Thirdly, it is clear that, in order to qualify as an "expressly authorized" exception to the anti-injunction statute, an Act of Congress must have created a specific and uniquely federal right or remedy, enforceable in a federal court of equity, that could be frustrated if the federal court were not empowered to enjoin a state court proceeding. This is not to say that in order to come within the exception an Act of Congress must, on its face and in every one of its provisions, be totally incompatible with the prohibition of the anti-injunction statute. The test, rather, is whether an Act of Congress, clearly creating a federal right or remedy enforceable in a federal court of equity, could be given its intended scope only by the stay of a state court proceeding.

With these criteria in view, we turn to consideration of 42 U.S.C. § 1983. Section 1983 was originally § 1 of the Civil Rights Act of 1871. It was "modeled" on § 2 of the Civil Rights Act of 1866, and was enacted for the express purpose of "enforcing the Provisions of the Fourteenth Amendment." The predecessor of § 1983 was thus an important part of the basic alteration in our federal system wrought in the Reconstruction era through federal legislation and constitutional amendment. As a result of the new structure of law that emerged in the post-Civil War era—and especially of the Fourteenth Amendment, which was its centerpiece—the role of the Federal Government as a guarantor of basic federal rights against state power was clearly established. Section 1983 opened the federal courts to private citizens, offering a uniquely federal remedy against incursions under the claimed authority of state law upon rights secured by the Constitution and laws of the Nation.

It is clear from the legislative debates surrounding passage of § 1983's predecessor that the Act was intended to enforce the provisions of the Fourteenth Amendment "against State action whether that action be executive, legislative, or judicial." *Ex parte Virginia*, 100 U.S. 339. Proponents of the legislation noted that state courts were being used to harass and injure individuals, either because the state courts were powerless to stop deprivations or were in league with those who were bent upon abrogation of federally protected rights.

This legislative history makes evident that Congress clearly conceived that it was altering the relationship between the States and the Nation with respect to the protection of federally created rights; it was concerned that state instrumentalities could not protect those rights; it realized that state officers might, in fact, be antipathetic to the vindication of those rights; and it believed that these failings extended to the state courts.

Section 1983 was thus a product of a vast transformation from the concepts of federalism that had prevailed in the late 18th century when the anti-injunction statute was enacted. The very purpose of § 1983 was to interpose the federal courts between the States and the people, as guardians of the people's federal rights—to protect the people from unconstitutional action under color of state law, "whether that action be executive, legislative, or judicial." *Ex parte Virginia*, 100 U.S., at 346. In carrying out that purpose, Congress plainly authorized the federal courts to issue injunctions in § 1983 actions, by expressly authorizing a "suit in equity" as one of the means of redress. And this Court long ago recognized that federal injunctive relief against a state court proceeding can in some circumstances be essential to prevent great, immediate, and irreparable loss of a person's constitutional rights. For these reasons we conclude that, under the criteria established in our previous decisions construing the anti-injunction statute, § 1983 is an Act of Congress that falls within the "expressly authorized" exception of that law.

In so concluding, we do not question or qualify in any way the principles of equity, comity, and federalism that must restrain a federal court when asked to enjoin a state court proceeding. These principles, in the context of state criminal prosecutions, were canvassed at length in *Younger v. Harris* and its companion cases. They are principles that have been emphasized by this Court many times in the past. Today we decide only that the District Court in this case was in error in holding that, because of the anti-injunction statute, it was absolutely without power in this § 1983 action to enjoin a proceeding pending in a state court under any circumstances whatsoever.

The judgment is reversed and the case is remanded to the District Court for further proceedings consistent with this opinion. It is so ordered.

Reversed and remanded.

MR. CHIEF JUSTICE BURGER, with whom MR. JUSTICE WHITE and MR. JUSTICE BLACKMUN join, concurring.

The Court's opinion does nothing to "question or qualify in any way the principles of equity, comity, and federalism that must restrain a federal court when asked to enjoin a state court proceeding." * * *

YOUNGER V. HARRIS

401 U.S. 37, 91 S.Ct. 746, 27 L.Ed.2d 669 (1971).

MR. JUSTICE BLACK delivered the opinion of the Court. Appellee, John Harris, Jr., was indicted in a California state court, charged with violation of the California Criminal Syndicalism Act. He then filed a complaint in the Federal District Court, asking that court to enjoin the appellant, Younger, the District Attorney of Los Angeles County, from prosecuting him, and alleging that the prosecution and even the presence of the Act inhibited him in the exercise of his rights of free speech and press, rights guaranteed him by the First and Fourteenth Amendments. Appellees Jim Dan and Diane Hirsch intervened as plaintiffs in the suit, claiming that the prosecution of Harris would inhibit them as members of the Progressive Labor Party from peacefully advocating the program of their party, which was to replace capitalism with socialism and to abolish the profit system of production in this country. Appellee Farrell Broslawsky, an instructor in history at Los Angeles Valley College, also intervened claiming that the prosecution of Harris made him uncertain as to whether he could teach about the doctrines of Karl Marx or read from the Communist Manifesto as part of his classwork. All claimed that unless the United States court restrained the state prosecution of Harris each would suffer immediate and irreparable injury. A three-judge

Federal District Court concluded that the State's Criminal Syndicalism Act was void for vagueness and overbreadth and restrained the District Attorney from "further prosecution of the currently pending action against plaintiff Harris for alleged violation of the Act."

The case is before us on appeal. The brief for the State of California argues that issuance of the injunction was a violation of a longstanding judicial policy and of 28 U.S.C. § 2283, which provides: "A court of the United States may not grant an injunction to stay proceedings in a State court except as expressly authorized by Act of Congress, or where necessary in aid of its jurisdiction, or to protect or effectuate its judgments." We have concluded that the judgment of the District Court, enjoining appellant Younger from prosecuting under these California statutes, must be reversed as a violation of the national policy forbidding federal courts to stay or enjoin pending state court proceedings except under special circumstances. We express no view about the circumstances under which federal courts may act when there is no prosecution pending in state courts at the time the federal proceeding is begun.

Appellee Harris has been indicted, and was actually being prosecuted by California for a violation of its Criminal Syndicalism Act at the time this suit was filed. He thus has an acute, live controversy with the State and its prosecutor. But none of the other parties plaintiff in the District Court, Dan, Hirsch, or Broslawsky, has such a controversy. None has been indicted, arrested, or even threatened by the prosecutor. If these three had alleged that they would be prosecuted for the conduct they planned to engage in, and if the District Court had found this allegation to be true—either on the admission of the State's district attorney or on any other evidence—then a genuine controversy might be said to exist. But here appellees Dan, Hirsch, and Broslawsky do not claim that they have ever been threatened with prosecution, that a prosecution is likely, or even that a prosecution is remotely possible. They claim the right to bring this suit solely because, in the language of their complaint, they "feel inhibited." We do not think this allegation even if true, is sufficient to bring the equitable jurisdiction of the federal courts into play to enjoin a pending state prosecution. A federal lawsuit to stop a prosecution in a state court is a serious matter. And persons having no fears of state prosecution except those that are imaginary or speculative, are not to be accepted as appropriate plaintiffs in such cases. * * *

Since the beginning of this country's history Congress has, subject to few exceptions, manifested a desire to permit state courts to try state cases free from interference by federal courts. In 1793 an Act unconditionally provided: "Nor shall a writ of injunction be granted to stay proceedings in any court of a state." 1 Stat. 335, c. 22, § 5. A comparison of the 1793 Act with 28 U.S.C. § 2283, its present-day successor, graphically illustrates how few and minor have been the exceptions granted from the flat, prohibitory language of the old Act. During all this lapse of years from 1793 to 1970 the statutory exceptions to the 1793 congressional enactment have been only three; (1) "except as expressly authorized by Act of Congress"; (2) "where necessary in aid of its jurisdiction"; and (3) "to protect or effectuate its judgments." In addition, a judicial exception to the longstanding policy evidenced by the statute has been made where a person about to be prosecuted in a state court can show that he will, if the proceeding in the state court is not enjoined, suffer irreparable damages.

The precise reasons for this longstanding public policy against federal court interference with state court proceedings have never been specifically identified but the primary sources of the policy are plain. One is the basic doctrine of equity jurisprudence that courts of equity should not act, and particularly should not act to restrain a criminal prosecution, when the moving party has an adequate remedy at law and will not suffer irreparable injury if denied equitable relief. The doctrine may originally have grown out of circumstances peculiar to the English judicial system and not applicable in this country, but its fundamental purpose of restraining equity jurisdiction within narrow limits is equally important under our Constitution, in order to prevent erosion of the role of the jury and avoid a duplication of legal proceedings and legal sanctions where a single suit would be adequate to protect the rights asserted. This underlying reason for restraining courts of equity from interfering with criminal prosecutions is reinforced by an even more vital consideration, the notion of "comity," that is, a proper respect for state functions, a recognition of the fact that the entire country is made up of a Union of separate state governments, and a continuance of the belief that the National Government will fare best if the States and their institutions are left free to perform their separate functions in their separate ways. This, perhaps for lack of a better and clearer way to describe it, is referred to by many as "Our Federalism," and one familiar with the profound debates that ushered our Federal Constitution into existence is bound to respect those who remain loyal to the ideals and dreams of "Our Federalism." The concept does not mean blind deference to "States' Rights" any more than it means centralization of control over every important issue in our National Government and its courts. The Framers rejected both these courses. What the concept does represent is a system in which there is sensitivity to the legitimate interests of both State and National Governments, and in which the National Government, anxious though it may be to vindicate and protect federal rights and federal interests, always endeavors to do so in ways that will not unduly interfere with the legitimate activities of the States. It should never be forgotten that this slogan, "Our Federalism," born in the early struggling days of our Union of States, occupies a highly important place in our Nation's history and its future. The normal thing to do when federal courts are asked to enjoin pending proceedings in state courts is not to issue such injunctions. * * *

In all of these cases the Court stressed the importance of showing irreparable injury, the traditional prerequisite to obtaining an injunction. In addition, however, the Court also made clear that in view of the fundamental policy against federal interference with state criminal prosecutions, even irreparable injury is insufficient unless it is "both great and immediate." Certain types of injury, in particular, the cost, anxiety, and inconvenience of having to defend against a single criminal prosecution, could not by themselves be considered "irreparable" in the special legal sense of that term. Instead, the threat to the plaintiff's federally protected rights must be one that cannot be eliminated by his defense against a single criminal prosecution. Thus, in the *Buck* case, *supra*, 313 U.S., at 400, we stressed: "Federal injunctions against state criminal statutes, either in their entirety or with respect to their separate and distinct prohibitions, are not to be granted as a matter of course, even if such statutes are unconstitutional. 'No citizen or member of the community is immune from prosecution, in good faith, for his alleged criminal acts. The imminence of such a prosecution even though alleged to be unauthorized and hence unlawful is not alone ground for relief in equity which exerts its extraordinary powers only to prevent irreparable injury to the plaintiff who seeks its aid.' " * * *

This is where the law stood when the Court decided *Dombrowski v. Pfister*, 380 U.S. 479 (1965), and held that an injunction against the enforcement of certain state criminal statutes could properly issue under the circumstances presented in that case. [4] In *Dombrowski*, unlike many of the earlier cases denying injunctions, the complaint made substantial allegations that:

> "the threats to enforce the statutes against appellants are not made with any expectation of securing valid convictions, but rather are part of a plan to employ arrests, seizures, and threats

[4] Neither the cases dealing with standing to raise claims of vagueness or overbreadth, nor the loyalty oath cases, changed the basic principles governing the propriety of injunctions against state criminal prosecutions. In the standing cases we allowed attacks on overly broad or vague statutes in the absence of any showing that the defendant's conduct could not be regulated by some properly drawn statute. But in each of these cases the statute was not merely vague or overly broad "on its face"; the statute was held to be vague or overly broad as construed and applied to a particular defendant in a particular case. If the statute had been too vague as written but sufficiently narrow as applied, prosecutions and convictions under it would ordinarily have been permissible.

In *Baggett* and similar cases we enjoined state officials from discharging employees who failed to take certain loyalty oaths. We held that the States were without power to exact the promises involved, with their vague and uncertain content concerning advocacy and political association, as a condition of employment. Apart from the fact that any plaintiff discharged for exercising his constitutional right to refuse to take the oath would have had no adequate remedy at law, the relief sought was of course the kind that raises no special problem—an injunction against allegedly unconstitutional state action (discharging the employees) that is not part of a criminal prosecution.

of prosecution under color of the statutes to harass appellants and discourage them and their supporters from asserting and attempting to vindicate the constitutional rights of Negro citizens of Louisiana."

The appellants in *Dombrowski* had offered to prove that their offices had been raided and all their files and records seized pursuant to search and arrest warrants that were later summarily vacated by a state judge for lack of probable cause. They also offered to prove that despite the state court order quashing the warrants and suppressing the evidence seized, the prosecutor was continuing to threaten to initiate new prosecutions of appellants under the same statutes, was holding public hearings at which photostatic copies of the illegally seized documents were being used, and was threatening to use other copies of the illegally seized documents to obtain grand jury indictments against the appellants on charges of violating the same statutes. These circumstances, as viewed by the Court sufficiently establish the kind of irreparable injury, above and beyond that associated with the defense of a single prosecution brought in good faith, that had always been considered sufficient to justify federal intervention. Indeed, after quoting the Court's statement in *Douglas* concerning the very restricted circumstances under which an injunction could be justified, the Court in *Dombrowski* went on to say: "But the allegations in this complaint depict a situation in which defense of the State's criminal prosecution will not assure adequate vindication of constitutional rights. They suggest that a substantial loss of or impairment of freedoms of expression will occur if appellants must await the state court's disposition and ultimate review in this Court of any adverse determination. These allegations, if true, clearly show irreparable injury." And the Court made clear that even under these circumstances the District Court issuing the injunction would have continuing power to lift it at any time and remit the plaintiffs to the state courts if circumstances warranted. * * *

It is against the background of these principles that we must judge the propriety of an injunction under the circumstances of the present case. Here a proceeding was already pending in the state court, affording Harris an opportunity to raise his constitutional claims. There is no suggestion that this single prosecution against Harris is brought in bad faith or is only one of a series of repeated prosecutions to which he will be subjected. In other words, the injury that Harris faces is solely "that incidental to every criminal proceeding brought lawfully and in good faith," and therefore under the settled doctrine we have already described he is not entitled to equitable relief "even if such statutes are unconstitutional."

The District Court, however, thought that the *Dombrowski* decision substantially broadened the availability of injunctions against state criminal prosecutions and that under that decision the federal courts may give equitable relief, without regard to any showing of bad faith or harassment, whenever a state statute is found "on its face" to be vague or overly broad, in violation of the First Amendment. We recognize that there are some statements in the *Dombrowski* opinion that would seem to support this argument. But, as we have already seen, such statements were unnecessary to the decision of that case, because the Court found that the plaintiffs had alleged a basis for equitable relief under the long-established standards. In addition, we do not regard the reasons adduced to support this position as sufficient to justify such a substantial departure from the established doctrines regarding the availability of injunctive relief. It is undoubtedly true, as the Court stated in *Dombrowski*, that "a criminal prosecution under a statute regulating expression usually involves imponderables and contingencies that themselves may inhibit the full exercise of First Amendment freedoms." But this sort of "chilling effect," as the Court called it, should not by itself justify federal intervention. In the first place, the chilling effect cannot be satisfactorily eliminated by federal injunctive relief. In *Dombrowski* itself the Court stated that the injunction to be issued there could be lifted if the State obtained an "acceptable limiting construction" from the state courts. The Court then made clear that once this was done, prosecutions could then be brought for conduct occurring before the narrowing construction was made, and proper convictions could stand so long as the defendants were not deprived of fair warning. The kind of relief granted in *Dombrowski* thus does not effectively eliminate uncertainty as to the coverage of the state statute and leaves most citizens with virtually the same doubts as before regarding the danger that their conduct might eventually be subjected to criminal sanctions. The chilling effect can, of course, be eliminated by an injunction that would prohibit any prosecution whatever for conduct occurring prior to a satisfactory rewriting of the statute. But the States would then be stripped of all power to prosecute even the socially dangerous and constitutionally unprotected conduct that had been covered by the statute, until a new statute could be passed by the state legislature and approved by the federal courts in potentially lengthy trial and appellate proceedings. Thus, in *Dombrowski* itself the Court carefully reaffirmed the principle that even in the direct prosecution in the State's own courts, a valid narrowing construction can be applied to conduct occurring prior to the date when the narrowing construction was made, in the absence of fair warning problems.

Moreover, the existence of a "chilling effect," even in the area of First Amendment rights, has never been considered a sufficient basis, in and of itself, for prohibiting state action. Where a statute does not directly abridge free speech, but—while regulating a subject within the State's power—tends to have the incidental effect of inhibiting First Amendment rights, it is well settled that the statute can be upheld if the effect on speech is minor in relation to the need for control of the conduct and the lack of alternative means for doing so. Just as the incidental "chilling effect" of such statutes does not automatically render them unconstitutional, so the chilling effect that admittedly can result from the very existence of certain laws on the statute books does not in itself justify prohibiting the State from carrying out the important and necessary task of enforcing these laws against socially harmful conduct that the State believes in good faith to be punishable under its laws and the Constitution.

Beyond all this is another, more basic consideration. Procedures for testing the constitutionality of a statute "on its face" in the manner apparently contemplated by *Dombrowski*, and for then enjoining all action to enforce the statute until the State can obtain court approval for a modified version, are fundamentally at odds with the function of the federal courts in our constitutional plan. The power and duty of the judiciary to declare laws unconstitutional is in the final analysis derived from its responsibility for resolving concrete disputes brought before the courts for decision; a statute apparently governing a dispute cannot be applied by judges, consistently with their obligations under the Supremacy Clause, when such an application of the statute would conflict with the Constitution. But this vital responsibility, broad as it is, does not amount to an unlimited power to survey the statute books and pass judgment on laws before the courts are called upon to enforce them. Ever since the Constitutional Convention rejected a proposal for having members of the Supreme Court render advice concerning pending legislation it has been clear that, even when suits of this kind involve a "case or controversy" sufficient to satisfy the requirements of Article III of the Constitution, the task of analyzing a proposed statute, pinpointing its deficiencies, and requiring correction of these deficiencies before the statute is put into effect, is rarely if ever an appropriate task for the judiciary. The combination of the relative remoteness of the controversy, the impact on the legislative process of the relief sought, and above all the speculative and amorphous nature of the required line-by-line analysis of detailed statutes ordinarily results in a kind of case that is wholly unsatisfactory for deciding constitutional questions, whichever way they might be decided. In light of this fundamental conception of the Framers as to the proper place of the federal courts in the governmental processes of passing and enforcing laws, it can seldom be appropriate for these courts to exercise any such power of prior approval or veto over the legislative process.

For these reasons, fundamental not only to our federal system but also to the basic functions of the Judicial Branch of the National Government under our Constitution, we hold that the *Dombrowski* decision should not be regarded as having upset the settled doctrines that have always confined very narrowly the availability of injunctive relief against state criminal prosecutions. We do not think that opinion stands for the proposition that a federal court can properly enjoin enforcement of a statute solely on the basis of a showing that the statute "on its face" abridges First Amendment rights. There may, of course, be extraordinary circumstances in which the necessary irreparable injury can be shown even in the absence of the usual prerequisites of bad faith and harassment. For example, as long ago as the *Buck* case, *supra*, we indicated: "It is of course conceivable that a statute might be flagrantly and patently violative of express constitutional prohibitions in every clause, sentence and paragraph, and in whatever manner and against whomever an effort might be made to apply it." Other unusual situations calling for federal intervention might also arise, but there is no point in our attempting now to specify what they might be. It is sufficient for purposes of the present case to hold, as we do, that the possible unconstitutionality of a statute "on its face" does not in itself justify an injunction against good-faith attempts to enforce it, and that appellee Harris has failed to make any showing of bad faith, harassment, or any other unusual circumstance that would call for equitable relief. Because our holding rests on the absence of the factors necessary under equitable principles to justify federal intervention, we have no occasion to consider whether 28 U.S.C. § 2283, which prohibits an injunction against state court proceedings "except as expressly authorized by Act of Congress" would in and of itself be controlling under the circumstances of this case.

The judgment of the District Court is reversed, and the case is remanded for further proceedings not inconsistent with this opinion.

Reversed.

MR. JUSTICE DOUGLAS, dissenting.

The fact that we are in a period of history when enormous extrajudicial sanctions are imposed on those who assert their First Amendment rights in unpopular causes emphasizes the wisdom of *Dombrowski*. There we recognized that in times of repression, when interests with powerful spokesmen generate symbolic pogroms against nonconformists, the federal judiciary, charged by Congress with special vigilance for protection of civil rights, has special responsibilities to prevent an erosion of the individual's constitutional rights.

The special circumstances when federal intervention in a state criminal proceeding is permissible are not restricted to bad faith on the part of state officials or the threat of multiple prosecutions. They also exist where for any reason the state statute being enforced is unconstitutional on its face. As Mr. Justice Butler, writing for the Court, said in *Terrace v. Thompson*, 263 U.S. 197, 214; "Equity jurisdiction will be exercised to enjoin the threatened enforcement of a state law which contravenes the federal Constitution wherever it is essential in order effectually to protect property rights and the rights of persons against injuries otherwise irremediable; and in such a case a person, who as an officer of the state is clothed with the duty of enforcing its laws and who threatens and is about to commence proceedings, either civil or criminal, to enforce such a law against parties affected, may be enjoined from such action by a Federal court of equity." Our *Dombrowski* decision was only another facet of the same problem.

In *Younger*, "criminal syndicalism" is defined so broadly as to jeopardize "teaching" that socialism is preferable to free enterprise. Harris's "crime" was distributing leaflets advocating change in industrial ownership through political action. If the "advocacy" which Harris used was an attempt at persuasion through the use of bullets, bombs, and arson, we would have a different case. But Harris is charged only with distributing leaflets advocating political action toward his objective. He tried unsuccessfully to have the state court dismiss the indictment on constitutional grounds. He resorted to the state appellate court for writs of prohibition to prevent the trial, but to no avail. He went to the federal court as a matter of last resort in an effort to keep this unconstitutional trial from being saddled on him.

The eternal temptation, of course, has been to arrest the speaker rather than to correct the conditions about which he complains. I see no reason why these appellees should be made to walk the treacherous ground of these statutes. They, like other citizens, need the umbrella of the First Amendment as they study, analyze, discuss, and debate the troubles of these days. When criminal prosecutions can be leveled against them because they express unpopular views, the society of the dialogue is in danger.

PROBLEMS

1. *Does* Younger *Apply to Threatened Prosecutions?* While petitioner was distributing handbills (protesting American involvement in Bosnia) on a shopping center sidewalk, center employees asked him to stop handbilling and leave. When petitioner declined the request, the center called the police who told petitioner that he would be arrested unless he stopped handbilling. At that point, petitioner left to avoid arrest. Petitioner and a companion returned to the shopping center several days later and again began handbilling. The police were called and once again demanded that petitioner stop handbilling or face arrest. Petitioner left to avoid arrest. Although Petitioner desired to return to the shopping center to distribute handbills, he did not do so for fear that he, too, would be arrested. Does *Younger* preclude petitioner from obtaining injunctive relief against a threatened prosecution? What arguments can be made on Petitioner's behalf? How might the state respond? *See Steffel v. Thompson*, 415 U.S. 452 (1974).

2. *More on* Younger *and Threatened Prosecutions.* In the immediately prior problem, would it make any difference that petitioner's friend, who was

with him when he was told to leave or face arrest, stayed and was arrested? If a criminal action is pending against the friend, should petitioner be denied relief?

3. *Does* Younger *Apply to Requests for Declaratory Relief?* Appellants, who were indicted in a New York state court on charges of criminal anarchy, wish to challenge the anarchy law in federal court on void for vagueness grounds. Fearing that *Younger* will bar a claim for injunctive relief, appellants seek only declaratory relief to the effect that the law is void for vagueness. Under *Younger*, is federal declaratory relief permissible during the pendency of a state criminal prosecution? How might the State argue that *Younger* bars the federal action? How might appellants respond? *See Samuels v. Mackell*, 401 U.S. 66 (1971).

4. *Does a Subsequent Prosecution Require Dismissal of a Pending Federal Proceeding?* Plaintiff owns and operates The Pussycat adult theater. The police seize four copies of one of plaintiff's films, and charge two of plaintiff's employees under a state obscenity statute. No charges are filed against plaintiff. Two weeks later, plaintiff files a federal action seeking declaratory and injunctive relief regarding the seizure of the films. Shortly before a federal court hearing on the request for injunctive relief, local prosecutors (who are also defendants in the federal suit) amend the state criminal complaint to name plaintiff as a criminal defendant and move to dismiss the federal suit under *Younger*. Suppose that you are the judge in the federal suit. Now that plaintiff is a defendant in a state proceeding, can you still consider the request for declaratory and injunctive relief? How might local officials argue that the case should be dismissed? How might plaintiff respond to those arguments? *See Hicks v. Miranda*, 422 U.S. 332 (1975).

5. *Enjoining Prosecution.* Greg and Karen Trucke are the parents of two school-age children who are home schooled, but neither of them is a certified teacher. The children also receive instruction one day each week for three or four hours from a certified teacher. State law requires parents to have their children taught by a certified teacher for at least 120 days during the school year. In response to a letter from the school district, the Truckes stated that they would not provide the board with information regarding the schooling of their children. The School Board then passed the following resolution: "Based on the fact that Greg and Karen Trucke refused to supply any information concerning the home schooling of their children, the Board has cause to believe that the children may not be receiving instruction by a certified teacher as required by state law and the regulations of the Department of Education. The Superintendent is directed to refer the matter to the County Attorney for his opinion and determination of appropriate action in this matter."

Six days later, the Truckes seek injunctive relief prohibiting the County Attorney and the school board from prosecuting them for violating state educational laws. The Truckes claim that those laws are void for vagueness, and that the School Board cannot be impartial because the Board's funding is based on the number of pupils who attend public schools. Does *Younger* prevent the trial court from entertaining the case? How might the County Attorney and school board argue that *Younger* applies? How might the Truckes respond? *See Trucke v. Erlemeier*, 657 F.Supp. 1382 (N.D.Iowa 1987).

6. *More on the Diamond Derby Gala.* Suppose that a state court issues an injunction precluding the organizers from holding the Gala this year. Some of the charities that benefit from the Diamond Derby Gala believe that they will suffer irreparable injury (loss of funds critical to their mission) from the injunction. As a result, they seek federal court relief enjoining the Jacksons from proceeding with the state court litigation. Should the injunction issue? Why? Why not?

K. STRUCTURAL INJUNCTIONS

Many injunction cases involve relatively discrete matters between private litigants. Some involve broad challenges to the operation of a school district or prison system. In these latter cases, litigants sometimes ask a court to enter a "structural injunction" directed at governmental officials. These structural injunctions are designed to eliminate past violations and regulate the way a school, prison, or police department functions in the future. Is it appropriate for federal courts to issue "structural injunctions" against state officials?

MISSOURI V. JENKINS

515 U.S. 70, 115 S.Ct. 2038, 132 L.Ed.2d 63 (1995).

CHIEF JUSTICE REHNQUIST delivered the opinion of the Court.

In 1977, the Kansas City Missouri School District (KCMSD) the school board, and the children of two school board members brought suit against the State and other defendants. Plaintiffs alleged that the State, the surrounding suburban school districts (SSD's), and various federal agencies had caused and perpetuated a system of racial segregation in the schools of the Kansas City metropolitan area. The District Court realigned the KCMSD as a nominal defendant and certified as a class, present and future KCMSD students. The KCMSD brought a cross-claim against the State for its failure to eliminate the vestiges of its prior dual school system.

The District Court dismissed the case against the federal defendants and the SSD's, but determined that the State and the KCMSD were liable for an intradistrict violation, *i.e.*, they had operated a segregated school system within the KCMSD. The District Court determined that prior to 1954 "Missouri mandated segregated schools for black and white children." Furthermore, the KCMSD and the State had failed in their affirmative obligations to eliminate the vestiges of the State's dual school system within the KCMSD.

In 1985, the District Court issued its first remedial order and established as its goal the "elimination of all vestiges of state imposed segregation." The District Court determined that "segregation had caused a system wide reduction in student achievement in the schools of the KCMSD." The District Court made no particularized findings regarding the extent that student achievement had been reduced or what portion of that reduction was attributable to segregation. * * *

The District Court, pursuant to plans submitted by the KCMSD and the State, ordered a wide range of quality education programs for all students attending the KCMSD. First, the District Court ordered that the KCMSD be restored to an AAA classification, the highest classification awarded by the State Board of Education. Second, it ordered that the number of students per class be reduced so that the student-to-teacher ratio was below the level required for AAA standing. The District Court justified its reduction in class size as "an essential part of any plan to remedy the vestiges of segregation in the KCMSD. Reducing class size will serve to remedy the vestiges of past segregation by increasing individual attention and instruction, as well as increasing the potential for desegregative educational experiences for KCMSD students by maintaining and attracting non-minority enrollment." The District Court also ordered programs to expand educational opportunities for all KCMSD students: full-day kindergarten; expanded summer school; before- and after-school tutoring; and an early childhood development program. Finally, the District Court implemented a state-funded "effective schools" program that consisted of substantial yearly cash grants to each of the schools within the KCMSD.

The KCMSD was awarded an AAA rating in the 1987–1988 school year, and there is no dispute that since that time it has " 'maintained and greatly exceeded AAA requirements.' " The total cost for these quality education programs has exceeded $220 million.

The District Court also set out to desegregate the KCMSD but believed that "to accomplish desegregation within the boundary lines of a school district whose enrollment remains 68.3% black is a difficult task." Because it had found no interdistrict violation, the District Court could not order mandatory interdistrict redistribution of students between the KCMSD and the surrounding SSD's. The District Court refused to order additional mandatory student reassignments because they would "increase the instability of the KCMSD and reduce the potential for desegregation." * * *

In November 1986, the District Court approved a comprehensive magnet school and capital improvements plan and held the State and the KCMSD jointly and severally liable for its funding. Under the District Court's plan, every senior high school, every middle school, and one-half of the elementary schools were converted into magnet schools. The

District Court adopted the magnet-school program to "provide a greater educational opportunity to all KCMSD students," and because it believed "that the proposed magnet plan was so attractive that it would draw non-minority students from the private schools who have abandoned or avoided the KCMSD, and draw in additional non-minority students from the suburbs." The District Court felt that "the long-term benefit of all KCMSD students of a greater educational opportunity in an integrated environment is worthy of such an investment." Since its inception, the magnet school program has operated at a cost, including magnet transportation, in excess of $448 million. * * *

In June 1985, the District Court ordered substantial capital improvements to combat the deterioration of the KCMSD's facilities. In formulating its capital-improvements plan, the District Court dismissed as "irrelevant" the "State's argument that the present condition of the facilities was not traceable to unlawful segregation." Instead, the District Court focused on its responsibility to "remedy the vestiges of segregation" and to "implement a desegregation plan which would maintain and attract non-minority members." The initial phase of the capital improvements plan cost $37 million. The District Court also required the KCMSD to present further capital improvements proposals "in order to bring its facilities to a point comparable with the facilities in neighboring suburban school districts." In November 1986, the District Court approved further capital improvements in order to remove the vestiges of racial segregation and "to attract non-minority students back to the KCMSD."

In September 1987, the District Court adopted, for the most part, KCMSD's long-range capital improvements plan at a cost in excess of $187 million. The plan called for the renovation of approximately 55 schools, the closure of 18 facilities, and the construction of 17 new schools. The District Court rejected what it referred to as the " 'patch and repair' approach proposed by the State" because it "would not achieve suburban comparability or the visual attractiveness sought by the Court as it would result in floor coverings with unsightly sections of mismatched carpeting and tile, and individual walls possessing different shades of paint." The District Court reasoned that "if the KCMSD schools underwent the limited renovation proposed by the State, the schools would continue to be unattractive and substandard, and would certainly serve as a deterrent to parents considering enrolling their children in KCMSD schools." As of 1990, the District Court had ordered $260 million in capital improvements. Since then, the total cost of capital improvements ordered has soared to over $540 million.

As part of its desegregation plan, the District Court has ordered salary assistance to the KCMSD. In 1987, the District Court initially ordered salary assistance only for teachers within the KCMSD. Since that time, however, the District Court has ordered salary assistance to all but three of the approximately 5,000 KCMSD employees. The total cost of this component of the desegregation remedy since 1987 is over $200 million.

The District Court's desegregation plan has been described as the most ambitious and expensive remedial program in the history of school desegregation. The annual cost per pupil at the KCMSD far exceeds that of the neighboring SSD's or of any school district in Missouri. Nevertheless, the KCMSD, which has pursued a "friendly adversary" relationship with the plaintiffs, has continued to propose ever more expensive programs. As a result, the desegregation costs have escalated and now are approaching an annual cost of $200 million. These massive expenditures have financed

> "high schools in which every classroom will have air conditioning, an alarm system, and 15 microcomputers; a 2,000-square-foot planetarium; green houses and vivariums; a 25-acre farm with an air-conditioned meeting room for 104 people; a Model United Nations wired for language translation; broadcast capable radio and television studios with an editing and animation lab; a temperature controlled art gallery; movie editing and screening rooms; a 3,500-square-foot dust-free diesel mechanics room; 1,875-square-foot elementary school animal rooms for use in a zoo project; swimming pools; and numerous other facilities."

Not surprisingly, the cost of this remedial plan has "far exceeded KCMSD's budget, or for that matter, its authority to tax." The State, through the operation of joint-and-several liability, has borne the brunt of these costs. The District Court candidly has acknowledged that it has "allowed the District planners to dream" and "provided the mechanism for those dreams to be realized." In short, the District Court "has gone to great lengths to provide KCMSD with facilities and opportunities not available anywhere else in the country."

The State has challenged the District Court's requirement that it fund salary increases for KCMSD instructional and noninstructional staff. The State claimed that funding for salaries was beyond the scope of the District Court's remedial authority. Second, the State has challenged the District Court's order requiring it to continue to fund the remedial quality education programs for the 1992–1993 school year. The State contended that under *Freeman v. Pitts*, 503 U.S. 467 (1992), it had achieved partial unitary status with respect to the quality education programs already in place. As a result, the State argued that the District Court should have relieved it of responsibility for funding those programs.

Almost 25 years ago, in *Swann v. Charlotte–Mecklenburg Bd. of Ed.*, 402 U.S. 1 (1971), we dealt with the authority of a district court to fashion remedies for a school district that had been segregated in law in violation of the Equal Protection Clause of the Fourteenth Amendment. Although recognizing the discretion that must necessarily adhere in a district court in fashioning a remedy, we also recognized the limits on such remedial power.

Three years later, in *Milliken I, supra*, we held that a District Court had exceeded its authority in fashioning interdistrict relief where the surrounding school districts had not themselves been guilty of any constitutional violation. We said that a desegregation remedy "is necessarily designed, as all remedies are, to restore the victims of discriminatory conduct to the position they would have occupied in the absence of such conduct." "Without an interdistrict violation and interdistrict effect, there is no constitutional wrong calling for an interdistrict remedy." * * *

Three years later, in *Milliken v. Bradley*, 433 U.S. 267 (1977) (*Milliken II*), we articulated a three-part framework derived from our prior cases to guide district courts in the exercise of their remedial authority.

> "In the first place, like other equitable remedies, the nature of the desegregation remedy is to be determined by the nature and scope of the constitutional violation. The remedy must therefore be related to 'the condition alleged to offend the Constitution.' Second, the decree must indeed be remedial in nature, that is, it must be designed as nearly as possible 'to restore the victims of discriminatory conduct to the position they would have occupied in the absence of such conduct.' Third, the federal courts in devising a remedy must take into account the interests of state and local authorities in managing their own affairs, consistent with the Constitution."

We added that the "principle that the nature and scope of the remedy are to be determined by the violation means simply that federal-court decrees must directly address and relate to the constitutional violation itself."

Because "federal supervision of local school systems was intended as a temporary measure to remedy past discrimination," we also have considered the showing that must be made by a school district operating under a desegregation order for complete or partial relief from that order. In *Freeman*, we stated that

> "among the factors which must inform the sound discretion of the court in ordering partial withdrawal are the following: 1 whether there has been full and satisfactory compliance with the decree in those aspects of the system where supervision is to be withdrawn; 2 whether retention of judicial control is necessary or practicable to achieve compliance with the decree in other facets of the school system; and 3 whether the school district has

> demonstrated, to the public and to the parents and students of the once disfavored race, its good-faith commitment to the whole of the courts' decree and to those provisions of the law and the Constitution that were the predicate for judicial intervention in the first instance."

The ultimate inquiry is "whether the constitutional violator has complied in good faith with the desegregation decree since it was entered, and whether the vestiges of past discrimination have been eliminated to the extent practicable."

Proper analysis of the District Court's orders challenged here, then, must rest upon their serving as proper means to the end of restoring the victims of discriminatory conduct to the position they would have occupied in the absence of that conduct and their eventual restoration of "state and local authorities to the control of a school system that is operating in compliance with the Constitution." We turn to that analysis.

The proper response by the District Court should have been to eliminate to the extent practicable the vestiges of prior de jure segregation within the KCMSD: a system-wide reduction in student achievement and the existence of 25 racially identifiable schools with a population of over 90% black students.

The District Court and Court of Appeals, however, have felt that because the KCMSD's enrollment remained 68.3% black, a purely intradistrict remedy would be insufficient. Instead of seeking to remove the racial identity of the various schools within the KCMSD, the District Court has set out on a program to create a school district that was equal to or superior to the surrounding SSD's. Its remedy has focused on "desegregative attractiveness," coupled with "suburban comparability."

The purpose of desegregative attractiveness has been not only to remedy the system-wide reduction in student achievement, but also to attract nonminority students not presently enrolled in the KCMSD. This remedy has included an elaborate program of capital improvements, course enrichment, and extracurricular enhancement not simply in the formerly identifiable black schools, but in schools throughout the district. The District Court's remedial orders have converted every senior high school, every middle school, and one-half of the elementary schools in the KCMSD into "magnet" schools. The District Court's remedial order has all but made the KCMSD itself into a magnet district.

We previously have approved of intradistrict desegregation remedies involving magnet schools. Magnet schools have the advantage of encouraging voluntary movement of students within a school district in a pattern that aids desegregation on a voluntary basis, without requiring extensive busing and redrawing of district boundary lines. * * *

The District Court's remedial plan, however, is not designed solely to redistribute the students within the KCMSD in order to eliminate racially identifiable schools within the KCMSD. Instead, its purpose is to attract nonminority students from outside the KCMSD schools. But this interdistrict goal is beyond the scope of the intradistrict violation identified by the District Court. In effect, the District Court has devised a remedy to accomplish indirectly what it admittedly lacks the remedial authority to mandate directly: the interdistrict transfer of students.

Respondents argue that the District Court's reliance upon desegregative attractiveness is justified in light of the District Court's statement that segregation has "led to white flight from the KCMSD to suburban districts." The lower courts' "findings" as to "white flight" are both inconsistent internally, and inconsistent with the typical supposition, bolstered here by the record evidence, that "white flight" may result from desegregation, not *de jure* segregation. * * *

In *Freeman*, we stated that "the vestiges of segregation that are the concern of the law in a school case may be subtle and intangible but nonetheless they must be so real that they have a causal link to the de jure violation being remedied." The record here does not support the District Court's reliance on "white flight" as a justification for a permissible expansion of its intradistrict remedial authority through its pursuit of desegregative attractiveness.

The District Court's pursuit of "desegregative attractiveness" cannot be reconciled with our cases placing limitations on a district court's remedial authority. It is certainly theoretically possible that the greater the expenditure per pupil within the KCMSD, the more likely it is that some unknowable number of nonminority students not presently attending schools in the KCMSD will choose to enroll in those schools. Under this reasoning, however, every increased expenditure, whether it be for teachers, noninstructional employees, books, or buildings, will make the KCMSD in some way more attractive, and thereby perhaps induce nonminority students to enroll in its schools. But this rationale is not susceptible to any objective limitation.

Nor are there limits to the duration of the District Court's involvement. The expenditures per pupil in the KCMSD currently far exceed those in the neighboring SSD's. Sixteen years after this litigation began, the District Court recognized that the KCMSD has yet to offer a viable method of financing the "wonderful school system being built." Each additional program ordered by the District Court—and financed by the State—to increase the "desegregative attractiveness" of the school district makes the KCMSD more and more dependent on additional funding from the State; in turn, the greater the KCMSD's dependence on state funding, the greater its reliance on continued supervision by the District Court. But our cases recognize that local autonomy of school districts is a vital national tradition, and that a district court must strive to restore state and local authorities to the control of a school system operating in compliance with the Constitution.

The District Court's order requiring the State to continue to fund the quality education programs because student achievement levels were still "at or below national norms at many grade levels" cannot be sustained. The State does not seek from this Court a declaration of partial unitary status with respect to the quality education programs. It challenges the requirement of indefinite funding of a quality education program until national norms are met, based on the assumption that while a mandate for significant educational improvement, both in teaching and in facilities, may have been justified originally, its indefinite extension is not.

Our review in this respect is needlessly complicated because the District Court made no findings in its order approving continued funding of the quality education programs. The basic task of the District Court is to decide whether the reduction in achievement by minority students attributable to prior de jure segregation has been remedied to the extent practicable. Under our precedents, the State and the KCMSD are "entitled to a rather precise statement of their obligations under a desegregation decree." Although the District Court has determined that "segregation has caused a system wide reduction in achievement in the schools of the KCMSD," it never has identified the incremental effect that segregation has had on minority student achievement or the specific goals of the quality education programs.

In reconsidering this order, the District Court should apply our three-part test from *Freeman v. Pitts*. The District Court should consider that the State's role with respect to the quality education programs has been limited to the funding, not the implementation, of those programs. As all the parties agree that improved achievement on test scores is not necessarily required for the State to achieve partial unitary status as to the quality education programs, the District Court should sharply limit, if not dispense with, its reliance on this factor. Just as demographic changes independent of de jure segregation will affect the racial composition of student assignments, so too will numerous external factors beyond the control of the KCMSD and the State affect minority student achievement. So long as these external factors are not the result of segregation, they do not figure in the remedial calculus. Insistence upon academic goals unrelated to the effects of legal segregation unwarrantably postpones the day when the KCMSD will be able to operate on its own.

The District Court also should consider that many goals of its quality education plan already have been attained: the KCMSD now is equipped with "facilities and opportunities not available anywhere else in the country." KCMSD schools received an AAA rating eight years ago, and the present remedial programs have been in place for seven years. It may be that in education, just as it may be in economics, a "rising tide lifts all boats," but the remedial quality education program should be tailored to remedy the injuries suffered by the victims of prior de jure segregation. Minority students in kindergarten through grade 7 in the KCMSD always have attended AAA-rated schools; minority students in the KCMSD that previously attended schools rated below AAA have since received remedial education programs for a period of up to seven years.

On remand, the District Court must bear in mind that its end purpose is not only "to remedy the violation" to the extent practicable, but also "to restore state and local authorities to the control of a school system that is operating in compliance with the Constitution."

The judgment of the Court of Appeals is reversed.

It is so ordered.

JUSTICE O'CONNOR, concurring.

What the District Court did in this case, and how it transgressed the constitutional bounds of its remedial powers, is to make desegregative attractiveness the underlying goal of its remedy for the specific purpose of reversing the trend of white flight. However troubling that trend may be, remedying it is within the District Court's authority only if it is "directly caused by the constitutional violation." The District Court admitted that the segregative effects of KCMSD's constitutional violation did not transcend its geographical boundaries. In light of that finding, the District Court cannot order remedies seeking to rectify regional demographic trends that go beyond the nature and scope of the constitutional violation. We have recognized the ample authority legislatures possess to combat racial injustice. The necessary restrictions on our jurisdiction and authority contained in Article III of the Constitution limit the judiciary's institutional capacity to prescribe palliatives for societal ills. The unfortunate fact of racial imbalance and bias in our society, however pervasive or invidious, does not admit of judicial intervention absent a constitutional violation.

JUSTICE THOMAS, concurring.

Instead of focusing on remedying the harm done to those black schoolchildren injured by segregation, the District Court sought to convert KCMSD into a "magnet district" that would reverse the "white flight" caused by desegregation. District Courts must not confuse the consequences of de jure segregation with the results of larger social forces or of private decisions. As state-enforced segregation recedes farther into the past, it is more likely that "these kinds of continuous and massive demographic shifts" will be the real source of racial imbalance or of poor educational performance in a school district.

The District Court here ordered massive expenditures by local and state authorities, without congressional or executive authorization and without any indication that such measures would attract whites back to KCMSD or raise KCMSD test scores. The time has come for us to put the genie back in the bottle.

Resistance to *Brown I* produced little desegregation. Our impatience with the pace of desegregation and with the lack of a good-faith effort on the part of school boards led us to approve extraordinary remedial measures. But such powers should have been temporary and used only to overcome the widespread resistance to the dictates of the Constitution. The judicial overreaching we see today perhaps is the price we now pay for our approval of such extraordinary remedies in the past.

Our prior decision in this litigation suggested that we would approve the continued use of these expansive powers even when the need for their exercise had disappeared. The District Court in this case ordered an increase in local property taxes in order to fund its capital improvements plan. Although we held that principles of comity barred the District Court from imposing the tax increase itself (except as a last resort), we also concluded that the Court could order KCMSD to raise taxes, and could enjoin the state laws preventing KCMSD from doing so.

Two clear restraints on the use of the equity power—federalism and the separation of powers—derive from the very form of our Government. Federal courts should pause before using their inherent equitable powers to intrude into the proper sphere of the States. Education is primarily a concern of local authorities. In this case, not only did the district court exercise the legislative power to tax, it also engaged in budgeting, staffing, and educational decisions, in judgments about the location and aesthetic quality of the schools, and in administrative oversight and monitoring. These functions involve a legislative or executive, rather than a judicial, power. When federal judges undertake such local, day-to-day tasks, they detract from the independence and dignity of the federal courts and intrude into areas in which they have little expertise.

In the absence of special circumstances, the remedy for de jure segregation ordinarily should not include educational programs for students who were not in school (or were even alive) during the period of segregation. Although I do not doubt that all KCMSD students benefit from many of the initiatives ordered by the court, it is for democratically accountable state and local officials to decide whether they are to be made available to those who were never harmed by segregation. This Court should never approve a State's efforts to deny students, because of their race, an equal opportunity for an education. But the federal courts also should avoid using racial equality as a pretext for solving social problems that do not violate the Constitution. * * *

JUSTICE SOUTER, with whom JUSTICE STEVENS, JUSTICE GINSBURG, and JUSTICE BREYER join, dissenting.

There is no dispute that before the District Court's remedial plan was placed into effect the schools in the unreformed segregated system were physically a shambles. The cost of turning this shambles into habitable schools was enormous. Property tax-paying parents of white children, seeing the handwriting on the wall in 1985, could well have decided that the inevitable cost of clean-up would produce an intolerable tax rate and could have moved to escape it. The District Court's remedial orders had not yet been put in place. Was the white flight caused by segregation or desegregation? The distinction has no significance. * * *

JUSTICE GINSBURG, dissenting.

The Court stresses that the present remedial programs have been in place for seven years. But compared to more than two centuries of firmly entrenched official discrimination, the experience with the desegregation remedies ordered by the District Court has been evanescent. The Court declares illegitimate the goal of attracting nonminority students to the KCMSD, and thus stops KCMSD's efforts to integrate. Given the deep, inglorious history of segregation in Missouri, to curtail desegregation at this time and in this manner is an action at once too swift and too soon.

NOTES

1. *Articles on Structural Injunctions.* There are a number of articles discussing structural injunctions, *see, e.g.*, Fletcher, *The Discretionary Constitution: Institutional Remedies and Judicial Legitimacy*, 91 Yale L.J. 635 (1982); Frug, *The Judicial Power of the Purse*, 126 U. Pa. L. Rev. 715 (1978); Nagel, *Separation of Powers and the Scope of Federal Equitable Remedies*, 30 Stan. L. Rev. 661 (1978); Chayes, *The Role of the Judge in Public Law Litigation*, 89 Harv. L. Rev. 1281 (1976).

2. *Modification of Structural Injunctions.* In *Rufo v. Inmates of the Suffolk County Jail*, 502 U.S. 367 (1992), the Court refined and relaxed the "changed circumstances" standard for modification of structural injunctions, emphasizing the need for flexibility: changed factual conditions make compliance substantially more onerous; unforeseen obstacles render the decree unworkable; enforcement would be detrimental to the public interest; or changed law legalizes the conduct previously enjoined or makes one or more of the obligations placed on defendant impermissible. Although *Rufo* involved a consent decree, its flexible approach and more relaxed standard for modification of structural injunctions in all likelihood extends to litigated cases as well.

RIZZO V. GOODE

423 U.S. 362, 96 S.Ct. 598, 46 L.Ed.2d 561 (1976).

MR. JUSTICE REHNQUIST delivered the opinion of the Court.

The central thrust of respondents' efforts in the two trials was to lay a foundation for equitable intervention, in one degree or another, because of an assertedly pervasive pattern of illegal and unconstitutional mistreatment by police officers. This mistreatment was said to have been directed against minority citizens in particular and against all Philadelphia residents in general. The principal petitioners here the Mayor, the City Managing Director, and the Police Commissioner were charged with conduct ranging from express authorization or encouragement of this mistreatment to failure to act in a manner so as to assure that it would not recur in the future.

Hearing some 250 witnesses during 21 days of hearings, the District Court was faced with a staggering amount of evidence; each of the 40-odd incidents might alone have been the piece de resistance of a short, separate trial. The District Court carefully and conscientiously resolved often sharply conflicting testimony, and made detailed findings of fact with respect to eight of the incidents presented by the Goode respondents and with respect to 28 of those presented by COPPAR.

The District Court found that the evidence did not establish the existence of any policy on the part of the named petitioners to violate the legal and constitutional rights of the plaintiff classes, but it did find that evidence of departmental procedure indicated a tendency to discourage the filing of civilian complaints and to minimize the consequences of police misconduct. It found that as to the larger plaintiff class, the residents of Philadelphia, only a small percentage of policemen commit violations of their legal and constitutional rights, but that the frequency with which such violations occur is such that "they cannot be dismissed as rare, isolated instances." * * *

The District Court directed petitioners to draft, for the court's approval, "a comprehensive program for dealing adequately with civilian complaints," to be formulated along the following "guidelines" suggested by the court: "(1) Appropriate revision of police manuals and rules of procedure spelling out in some detail, in simple language, the 'dos and don'ts' of permissible conduct in dealing with civilians (for example, manifestations of racial bias, derogatory remarks, offensive language, etc.; unnecessary damage to property and other unreasonable conduct in executing search warrants; limitations on pursuit of persons charged only with summary offenses; recording and processing civilian complaints, etc.). (2) Revision of procedures for processing complaints against police, including a ready availability of forms for use by civilians in lodging complaints against police officers; (b) a screening procedure for eliminating frivolous complaints; (c) prompt and adequate investigation of complaints; (d) adjudication of nonfrivolous complaints by an impartial individual or body, insulated so far as practicable from chain of command pressures, with a fair opportunity afforded the complainant to present his complaint, and to the police officer to present his defense; and (3) prompt notification to the concerned parties, informing them of the outcome." While noting that the "guidelines" were consistent with "generally recognized minimum standards" and imposed "no substantial burdens" on the police department, the District Court emphasized that respondents had no constitutional *right* to improved police procedures for handling civilian complaints. But given that violations of constitutional rights of citizens occur in "unacceptably" high numbers, and are likely to continue to occur, the court-mandated revision was a "necessary first step" in attempting to prevent future abuses. The Court of Appeals affirmed.

The District Court's findings disclose a central paradox which permeates that court's legal conclusions. Individual police officers not named as parties to the action were found to have violated the constitutional rights of particular individuals, only a few of whom were parties plaintiff. There was no affirmative link between the occurrence of the various incidents of police misconduct and the adoption of any plan or policy by petitioners express or otherwise showing their authorization or approval of such misconduct. The sole causal connection found between petitioners and the individual respondents was that in the absence of a change in police disciplinary procedures, the incidents were likely to continue to occur, not with respect to them, but as to the members of the classes they represented. In sum, the genesis of this lawsuit is a heated dispute between individual citizens and certain policemen has evolved into an attempt by the federal judiciary to resolve a "controversy" between the entire citizenry of Philadelphia and the petitioning elected and appointed officials over what steps might "appear to have the potential for prevention of future police misconduct."

We entertain serious doubts whether the facts establish the requisite Art. III case or controversy between the individually named respondents and petitioners. In *O'Shea v. Littleton*, 414 U.S. 488 (1974), the individual respondents, plaintiffs in the District Court, alleged that petitioners, a county magistrate and judge, had embarked on a continuing, intentional practice of racially discriminatory bond setting, sentencing, and assessing of jury fees. No specific instances involving the individual respondents were set forth in the prayer for injunctive relief against the judicial officers. Even though respondents' counsel stated that some of the named respondents had in fact "suffered from the alleged unconstitutional practices," the Court concluded that "past exposure to illegal conduct does not in itself show a present case or controversy regarding injunctive relief, however, if unaccompanied by any continuing, present adverse effects." The Court further recognized that while "past wrongs are evidence bearing on whether there is a real and immediate threat of repeated injury," the attempt to anticipate under what circumstances the respondents there would be made to appear in the future before petitioners "takes us into the area of speculation and conjecture." These observations apply here with even more force, for the individual respondents' claim to "real and immediate" injury rests not upon what the named petitioners might do to them in the future such as set a bond on the basis of race but upon what one of a small, unnamed minority of policemen might do to them in the future because of that unknown policeman's perception of departmental disciplinary procedures. This hypothesis is even more attenuated than those allegations of future injury found insufficient in *O'Shea* to warrant invocation of federal jurisdiction. Thus, insofar as the individual respondents were concerned, we think they lacked the requisite "personal stake in the outcome," *i.e.*, the order overhauling police disciplinary procedures.

Unlike *O'Shea*, this case did not arise on the pleadings. The District Court, having certified the plaintiff classes, bridged the gap between the facts shown at trial and the classwide relief sought with an unprecedented theory of § 1983 liability. It held that the classes' § 1983 actions for equitable relief against petitioners were made out on a showing of an "unacceptably high" number of those incidents of constitutional dimension, some 20 in all, occurring at large in a city of three million inhabitants, with 7,500 policemen.

The theory of liability underlying the District Court's opinion is that even without a showing of direct responsibility for the actions of a small percentage of the police force, petitioners' failure to act in the face of a statistical pattern is indistinguishable from active conduct. Respondents posit a constitutional "duty" on the part of petitioners (and a corresponding "right" of the citizens of Philadelphia) to "eliminate" future police misconduct; a "default" of that affirmative duty being shown by the statistical pattern, the District Court is empowered to act in petitioners' stead and take whatever preventive measures are necessary, within its discretion, to secure the "right" at issue. Such reasoning, however, blurs accepted usages and meanings in the English language in a way which would be quite inconsistent with the words Congress chose in § 1983. We have never subscribed to these amorphous propositions, and we decline to do so now.

Respondents claim that the theory of liability embodied in the District Court's opinion is supported by desegregation cases such as *Swann v. Charlotte–Mecklenburg Board of Education*, 402 U.S. 1 (1971). But *Swann* simply reaffirmed the body of law originally enunciated in *Brown v. Board of Education*, 347 U.S. 483 (1954). Once a right and a violation have been shown, the scope of a district court's equitable powers to remedy past wrongs is broad, for breadth and flexibility are inherent in equitable remedies.

Respondents, in their effort to bring themselves within the language of *Swann*, ignore a critical factual distinction between their case and the desegregation cases decided by this Court. In the latter, segregation imposed by law had been implemented by state authorities for varying periods of time, whereas in the instant case the District Court found that the responsible authorities had played no affirmative part in depriving any members of the two respondent classes of any constitutional rights. Those against whom injunctive relief was directed in cases such as *Swann* and *Brown* were not administrators and school board members who had in their employ a small number of individuals, which latter on their own deprived black students of their constitutional rights to a unitary school system. They were administrators and school board members who were found by their own conduct in the administration of the school system to have denied those rights. Here, the District Court found that none of the petitioners had deprived the respondent classes of any rights secured under the Constitution. This case presented no occasion for the District Court to grant equitable relief against petitioners.

Respondents also assert that given the citizenry's "right" to be protected from unconstitutional exercises of police power, and the "need for protection from such abuses," respondents have a right to mandatory equitable relief in some form when those in supervisory positions do not institute steps to reduce the incidence of unconstitutional police misconduct. The scope of federal equity power, it is proposed, should be extended to the fashioning of prophylactic procedures for a state agency designed to minimize this kind of misconduct on the part of a handful of its employees. However, not only is this novel claim quite at odds with the settled rule that in federal equity cases "the nature of the violation determines the scope of the remedy," but important considerations of federalism are additional factors weighing against it. Where, as here, the exercise of authority by state officials is attacked, federal courts must be constantly mindful of the "special delicacy of the adjustment to be preserved between federal equitable power and State administration of its own law."

Even in an action between private individuals, it has long been held that an injunction is "to be used sparingly, and only in a clear and plain case." When a plaintiff seeks to enjoin the activity of a government agency, even within a unitary court system, his case must contend with "the well-established rule that the Government has traditionally been granted the widest latitude in the 'dispatch of its own internal affairs.'" The District Court's injunctive order here, significantly revising the internal procedures of the Philadelphia police department, was indisputably a sharp limitation on the department's "latitude in the 'dispatch of its own internal affairs.' "

When the frame of reference moves from a unitary court system, governed by the principles just stated, to a system of federal courts representing the Nation, subsisting side by side with 50 state judicial, legislative, and executive branches, appropriate consideration must be given to principles of federalism in determining the availability and scope of equitable relief.

Even where the prayer for injunctive relief does not seek to enjoin the state criminal proceedings themselves, we have held that the principles of equity nonetheless militate heavily against the grant of an injunction except in the most extraordinary circumstances. In *O'Shea v. Littleton, supra*, we held that "a major continuing intrusion of the equitable power of the federal courts into the daily conduct of state criminal proceedings is in sharp conflict with the principles of equitable restraint which this Court has recognized in the decisions previously noted." And the same principles of federalism may prevent the injunction by a federal court of a state civil proceeding once begun.

Thus the principles of federalism which play such an important part in governing the relationship between federal courts and state governments, though initially expounded and perhaps entitled to their greatest weight in cases where it was sought to enjoin a criminal prosecution in progress, have not been limited either to that situation or indeed to a criminal proceeding itself. We think these principles likewise have applicability where injunctive relief is sought, not against the judicial branch of the state government, but against those in charge of an executive branch of an agency of state or local governments such as petitioners here. Indeed, in the recent case of *Mayor v. Educational Equality League*, 415 U.S. 605 (1974), in which private individuals sought injunctive relief against the Mayor of Philadelphia, we expressly noted the existence of such considerations, saying: "There are also delicate issues of federal-state relationships underlying this case."

Contrary to the District Court's flat pronouncement that a federal court's legal power to "supervise the functioning of the police department is firmly established," it is the foregoing cases and principles that must govern consideration of the type of injunctive relief granted here. When it injected itself by injunctive decree into the internal disciplinary affairs of this state agency, the District Court departed from these precepts.

For the foregoing reasons the judgment of the Court of Appeals which affirmed the decree of the District Court is

Reversed.

MR. JUSTICE BLACKMUN with whom MR. JUSTICE BRENNAN and MR. JUSTICE MARSHALL join, dissenting.

Federal-court intervention in the daily operation of a large city's police department is undesirable and to be avoided if at all possible. What the Court did here was to engage in a careful and conscientious resolution of often sharply conflicting testimony and to make detailed findings of fact that attack the problem that is the subject of the respondents' complaint. The remedy was one evolved with the defendant officials' assent, reluctant though that assent may have been, and it was one that the police department concededly could live with. No one disputes the apparent efficacy of the relief or the fact that it effectuated a betterment in the system and should serve to lessen the number of instances of deprival of constitutional rights of members of the respondent classes.

The District Court here, with detailed, careful, and sympathetic findings, ascertained the existence of violations of citizens' constitutional rights, of a pattern of that type of activity, of its likely continuance and recurrence, and of an official indifference as to doing anything about it. There must be federal relief available against persistent deprival of federal constitutional rights. Small as the ratio of incidents to arrests may be, the District Court nevertheless found a pattern of operation, even if no policy, and one sufficiently significant that the violations "cannot be dismissed as rare, isolated instances." One properly may wonder how many more instances actually existed but were unproved because of the pressure of time upon the trial court, or because of reluctant witnesses, or because of inherent fear to question constituted authority in any degree, or because of a despairing belief, unfounded though it may be, that nothing can be done about it anyway and that it is not worth the effort. It is clear that an official may be enjoined from consciously permitting his subordinates, in the course of their duties, to violate the constitutional rights of persons with whom they deal.

NOTE: POLICE CHOKEHOLDS

In *City of Los Angeles v. Lyons*, 461 U.S. 95 (1983), plaintiff challenged a Los Angeles Police Department practice of subduing certain persons arrested by means of a chokehold. In a 5–4 decision, the Court denied injunctive relief on the ground that Lyons could not show a substantial threat that it was likely to happen to him again.

PROBLEMS: N.Y.C. AND RACIAL PROFILING

1. *Is Relief Mandated/Permitted? Floyd v. The City of New York*, 2013 WL 4046209 (S.D.N.Y. 2013), dealt with racial profiling in N.Y.C. The evidence shows that the NYPD had made 4.4 million stops over an eight year period, and that over 80% of these stops had involved blacks or Hispanics. A group of blacks and Hispanics file suit, claiming that their constitutional rights had been violated during stops and frisks, and that they had been targeted because of their race. They also allege that the City has *a policy* or *custom* of violating the Constitution by making unlawful stops and

conducting unlawful frisks, and that it has acted with "deliberate indifference" to the rights of citizens. Suppose that you are the judge, and you believe that the NYPD had a policy of encouraging stops, and that it failed to provide sufficient training to police officers in order to ensure constitutional action. Plaintiffs do not seek to ban all stop and frisks, but do demand that such stops comply with constitutional mandates. In particular, they demand that stops be based only a showing of a "reasonable suspicion" of criminal activity, and that all stops be conducted in a racially neutral manner. After *Rizzo*, is it appropriate for the trial court to consider this case as a class action on behalf of those seeking damages for violations of their constitutional rights?

2. *How Should the Decree Be Framed?* In *Floyd v. City of New York*, 2013 WL 4046217 (S.D.N.Y. 2013), after agreeing with the plaintiffs, the judge decided to issue an injunction against the NYPD. Which of the following provisions should the injunctive order contain? 1) the appointment of a master to oversee the reform process who will develop, in consultation with the parties, reforms of the NYPD's policies and training regarding stop and frisk issues; 2) a requirement that police officers record (with specificity) stop and frisk activity in memo books, otherwise known as activity logs, which must include a separate explanation of why each pat-down, frisk, or search was performed; 3) the development of an improved system for monitoring, supervision, and discipline of police officers; 4) the use of body-worn cameras as part of a pilot project (paid for by the NYPD) to allow the monitoring of all stops, and the adoption of procedures for the preservation of stop recordings, and review of those recordings by supervisors and, as appropriate, more senior managers; 5) the imposition of an obligation to work with the various stakeholders to give them an opportunity to "be heard in the reform process." The court is thinking about defining the term "stakeholders" broadly to include members of the communities where stops most often take place, including representatives of religious, advocacy, and grassroots organizations, NYPD personnel and representatives of police organizations, the District Attorneys' offices, representatives of groups concerned with public schooling, public housing, and other local institutions, local elected officials and community leaders, representatives of the parties, such as the Mayor's office, the NYPD, and the lawyers in this case, and the non-parties that submitted briefs, the Civil Rights Division of the DOJ, Communities United for Police Reform, and the Black, Latino, and Asian Caucus of the New York City Council. 6) a requirement that the NYPD work with a facilitator to develop additional reforms to supplement those already ordered. After *Rizzo*, does the trial court have the authority to appoint the master and require the NYPD to implement these changes? *See Floyd v. City of New York*, 2013 WL 4046217 (S.D.N.Y. 2013).

HUTTO V. FINNEY

437 U.S. 678, 98 S.Ct. 2565, 57 L.Ed.2d 522 (1978).

MR. JUSTICE STEVENS delivered the opinion of the Court.

This litigation is a sequel to two earlier cases holding that conditions in the Arkansas prison system violated the Eighth and Fourteenth Amendments. The routine conditions that the ordinary Arkansas convict had to endure were characterized by the District Court as "a dark and evil world completely alien to the free world." That characterization was amply supported by the evidence. The punishments for misconduct not serious enough to result in punitive isolation were cruel, unusual, and unpredictable. It is the discipline known as "punitive isolation" that is most relevant for present purposes.

Confinement in punitive isolation was for an indeterminate period of time. An average of 4, and sometimes as many as 10 or 11, prisoners were crowded into windowless 8'x10' cells containing no furniture other than a source of water and a toilet that could only be flushed from outside the cell. At night the prisoners were given mattresses to spread on the floor. Although some prisoners suffered from infectious diseases such as hepatitis and venereal disease, mattresses were removed and jumbled together each morning, then returned to the cells at random in the evening. Prisoners in isolation received fewer than 1,000 calories a day; their meals consisted primarily of 4-inch squares of "grue," a substance created by mashing meat, potatoes, oleo, syrup, vegetables, eggs, and seasoning into a paste and baking the mixture in a pan.

After finding the conditions of confinement unconstitutional, the District Court did not immediately impose a detailed remedy of its own. Instead, it directed the Department of Correction to "make a substantial start" on improving conditions and to file reports on its progress. When the Department's progress proved unsatisfactory, the District Court found some improvements, but concluded that prison conditions remained unconstitutional. Again the court offered prison administrators an opportunity to devise a plan of their own for remedying the constitutional violations, but this time the court issued guidelines, identifying four areas of change that would cure the worst evils: improving conditions in the isolation cells, increasing inmate safety, eliminating the barracks sleeping arrangements, and putting an end to the trusty system. The Department was ordered to move as rapidly as funds became available.

After this order was affirmed on appeal, more hearings were held in 1972 and 1973 to review the Department's progress. Finding substantial improvements, the District Court concluded that continuing supervision was no longer necessary. The court held, however, that its prior decrees would remain in effect and noted that sanctions, as well as an award of costs and attorney's fees, would be imposed if violations occurred.

The Court of Appeals reversed the District Court's decision to withdraw its supervisory jurisdiction, and the District Court held a fourth set of hearings. It found that, in some respects, conditions had seriously deteriorated since 1973, when the court had withdrawn its supervisory jurisdiction. Cummins Farm, which the court had condemned as overcrowded in 1970 because it housed 1,000 inmates, now had a population of about 1,500. The situation in the punitive isolation cells was particularly disturbing. There were twice as many prisoners as beds in some cells. And because inmates in punitive isolation are often violently antisocial, overcrowding led to persecution of the weaker prisoners. The "grue" diet was still in use, and practically all inmates were losing weight on it. The cells had been vandalized to a "very substantial" extent. Because of their inadequate numbers, guards assigned to the punitive isolation cells frequently resorted to physical violence, using nightsticks and Mace in their efforts to maintain order. Prisoners were sometimes left in isolation for months, their release depending on "their attitudes as appraised by prison personnel."

The court concluded that the constitutional violations identified earlier had not been cured. It entered an order that placed limits on the number of men that could be confined in one cell, required that each have a bunk, discontinued the "grue" diet, and set 30 days as the maximum isolation sentence. The District Court gave detailed consideration to the matter of fees and expenses, made an express finding that petitioners had acted in bad faith, and awarded counsel "a fee of $20,000.00 to be paid out of Department of Correction funds." The Court of Appeals affirmed and assessed an additional $2,500 to cover fees and expenses on appeal.

The Eighth Amendment's ban on inflicting cruel and unusual punishments, made applicable to the States by the Fourteenth Amendment, "proscribes more than physically barbarous punishments." *Estelle v. Gamble*, 429 U.S. 97, 102. It prohibits penalties that are grossly disproportionate to the offense, as well as those that transgress today's " 'broad and idealistic concepts of dignity, civilized standards, humanity, and decency.' " *Estelle v. Gamble, supra*, at 102, *quoting Jackson v. Bishop*, 404 F.2d 571, 579 (C.A.8 1968). Confinement in a prison or in an isolation cell is a form of punishment subject to scrutiny under Eighth Amendment standards. Petitioners do not challenge this proposition; nor do they disagree with the District Court's original conclusion that conditions in Arkansas' prisons, including its punitive isolation cells, constituted cruel and unusual punishment. Rather, petitioners single out that portion of the District Court's most recent order that forbids the Department to sentence inmates to more than 30 days in punitive isolation. Petitioners assume that the District Court held that indeterminate sentences to punitive isolation always constitute cruel and unusual punishment. This assumption misreads the District Court's holding.

Read in its entirety, the District Court's opinion makes it abundantly clear that the length of isolation sentences was not considered in a vacuum. In the court's words, punitive isolation "is not necessarily unconstitutional, but it may be, depending on the duration of the confinement and the conditions thereof." It is perfectly obvious that every decision to remove a particular inmate from the general prison population for an indeterminate period could not be characterized as cruel and unusual. If new conditions of confinement are not materially different from those affecting other prisoners, a transfer for the duration of a prisoner's sentence might be completely unobjectionable and well within the authority of the prison administrator. It is equally plain, however, that the length of confinement cannot be ignored in deciding whether the confinement meets constitutional standards. A filthy, overcrowded cell and a diet of "grue" might be tolerable for a few days and intolerably cruel for weeks or months.

The question before the trial court was whether past constitutional violations had been remedied. The court was entitled to consider the severity of those violations in assessing the constitutionality of conditions in the isolation cells. The court took note of the inmates' diet, the continued overcrowding, the rampant violence, the vandalized cells, and the "lack of professionalism and good judgment on the part of maximum security personnel." The length of time each inmate spent in isolation was simply one consideration among many. We find no error in the court's conclusion that, taken as a whole, conditions in the isolation cells continued to violate the prohibition against cruel and unusual punishment.

In fashioning a remedy, the District Court had ample authority to go beyond earlier orders and to address each element contributing to the violation. The District Court had given the Department repeated opportunities to remedy the cruel and unusual conditions in the isolation cells. If petitioners had fully complied with the court's earlier orders, the present time limit might well have been unnecessary. But taking the long and unhappy history of the litigation into account, the court was justified in entering a comprehensive order to insure against the risk of inadequate compliance.

The order is supported by the interdependence of the conditions producing the violation. The vandalized cells and the atmosphere of violence were attributable, in part, to overcrowding and to deep-seated enmities growing out of months of constant daily friction. The 30-day limit will help to correct these conditions. Moreover, the limit presents little danger of interference with prison administration, for the Commissioner of Correction himself stated that prisoners should not ordinarily be held in punitive isolation for more than 14 days. Finally, the exercise of discretion in this case is entitled to special deference because of the trial judge's years of experience with the problem at hand and his recognition of the limits on a federal court's authority in a case of this kind. Like the Court of Appeals, we find no error in the inclusion of a 30-day limitation on sentences to punitive isolation as a part of the District Court's comprehensive remedy.

The judgment of the Court of Appeals is accordingly affirmed.

It is so ordered.

MR. JUSTICE REHNQUIST, dissenting.

No person of ordinary feeling could fail to be moved by the Court's recitation of the conditions formerly prevailing in the Arkansas prison system. Yet I fear that the Court has allowed itself to be moved beyond the well-established bounds limiting the exercise of remedial authority by the federal district courts. The remedy must, first, be related to 'the condition alleged to offend the Constitution.' Second, the decree must indeed be remedial in nature, that is, it must be designed as nearly as possible 'to restore the victims of discriminatory conduct to the position they would have occupied in the absence of such conduct.' Third, the federal courts in devising a remedy must take into account the interests of state and local authorities in managing their own affairs, consistent with the Constitution.

The Court's affirmance of this decree fails adequately to take into account the third consideration cited in *Milliken II*: "the interests of state and local authorities in managing their own affairs, consistent with the Constitution." The prohibition against extended punitive isolation, a practice which has not been shown to be inconsistent with the Constitution, can only be defended because of the difficulty of policing the District Court's explicit injunction against the overcrowding and inadequate diet which have been found to be violative of the Constitution. But even if such an expansion of remedial authority could be justified in a case where the defendants had been repeatedly contumacious, this is not such a case. The District Court's dissatisfaction with petitioners' performance under its earlier direction to "make a substantial start," on alleviating unconstitutional conditions cannot support an inference that petitioners are prepared to defy the specific orders now laid down by the District Court and not challenged by the petitioners. A proper respect for "the interests of state and local authorities in managing their own affairs," requires the opposite conclusion. * * *

NOTES

1. *Attorneys Fees.* As a general rule, in the United States, each side must pay its own attorneys fees. However, various federal statutes override this rule and allow litigants to recover their attorneys fees in litigation with the government. *See, e.g.*, Voting Rights Act of 1965, 42 U.S.C. § 1973(e);

Freedom of Information Act, 5 U.S.C. § 552(a)(4)(B); Civil Rights Attorneys Fees Awards Act, 42 U.S.C. § 1988 (which allows recovery by a "prevailing party" to recover "a reasonable attorney's fee (and experts fees) as part of the costs"); Equal Access to Justice Act (EAJA), 28 U.S.C. § 2412(d)(2)(B) (provides that attorneys fees (and expert fees) can be recovered by plaintiffs with a net worth of $2 million or less, as well as by businesses, tax-exempt charitable organizations, or other organizations that qualify as "small entities." Recovery can be denied if the government's position was "substantially justified" or if "special circumstances make an award unjust." The award need not bear any relationship to the amount of compensatory damages awarded).

2. *Contempt against Governmental Officials.* In *Spallone v. United States*, 493 U.S. 265, 110 S.Ct. 625, 107 L.Ed.2d 644 (1990), a district court judge held petitioners, four Yonkers city councilmembers, in contempt for refusing to vote in favor of legislation implementing a consent decree earlier approved by the city. The Supreme Court held that the court abused its discretion:

> The portion of the District Court's order of July 26 imposing contempt sanctions against petitioners if they failed to vote in favor of the court-proposed ordinance was an abuse of discretion under traditional equitable principles. Sanctions directed against the city for failure to take actions such as those required by the consent decree coerce the city legislators and, of course, restrict the freedom of those legislators to act in accordance with their current view of the city's best interests. But we believe there are significant differences between the two types of fines. The imposition of sanctions on individual legislators is designed to cause them to vote, not with a view to the interest of their constituents or of the city, but with a view solely to their own personal interests. Even though an individual legislator took the extreme position—or felt that his constituents took the extreme position—that even a huge fine against the city was preferable to enacting the Affordable Housing Ordinance, monetary sanctions against him individually would motivate him to vote to enact the ordinance simply because he did not want to be out of pocket financially. Such fines thus encourage legislators, in effect, to declare that they favor an ordinance not in order to avoid bankrupting the city for which they legislate, but in order to avoid bankrupting themselves.
>
> This sort of individual sanction effects a much greater perversion of the normal legislative process than does the imposition of sanctions on the city for the failure of these same legislators to enact an ordinance. In that case, the legislator is only encouraged to vote in favor of an ordinance that he would not otherwise favor by reason of the adverse sanctions imposed on the city. A councilman who felt that his constituents would rather have the city enact the Affordable Housing Ordinance than pay a

"bankrupting fine" would be motivated to vote in favor of such an ordinance because the sanctions were a threat to the fiscal solvency of the city for whose welfare he was in part responsible. This is the sort of calculus in which legislators engage regularly. The District Court should have proceeded with contempt sanctions first against the city alone in order to secure compliance with the remedial order. Only if that approach failed to produce compliance within a reasonable time should the question of imposing contempt sanctions against petitioners even have been considered. "This limitation accords with the doctrine that a court must exercise 'the least possible power adequate to the end proposed.'" *Anderson v. Dunn*, 6 Wheat. 204, 231 (1821).

PROBLEM: MANDATING LEGISLATIVE REAPPORTIONMENT

Baker v. Carr, 369 U.S. 186 (1962), involved a challenge to the Tennessee Legislature's failure to reapportion its legislative districts. The Tennessee Constitution provided that an enumeration of the voters and an apportionment of the Representatives in the General Assembly should take place every ten years. Reapportionment took place in each decade from 1871 to 1901. After 1901, "all proposals in both Houses of the General Assembly for reapportionment failed to pass" even though Tennessee experienced "substantial growth and redistribution of her population." "In 1901 the population was 2,020,616, of whom 487,380 were eligible to vote. The 1960 Federal Census reports the State's population at 3,567,089, of whom 2,092,891 are eligible to vote." "It appears from the record that 37% of the voters of Tennessee elect 20 of the 33 Senators while 40% of the voters elect 60 of the 99 members of the House." "There is a wide disparity of voting strength between the large and small counties. Some samples are: Moore County has a total representation of two with a population (2,340) of only one-eleventh of Rutherford County (25,316) with the same representation; Decatur County (5,563) has the same representation as Carter (23,303) though the latter has four times the population; likewise, Loudon County (13,264), Houston (3,084), and Anderson County (33,990) have the same representation, *i.e.*, 1.25 each." The suit was brought by citizens of underrepresented counties against Tennessee's Secretary of State, Attorney General, Coordinator of Elections, and members of the State Board of Elections. The suit was brought under the equal protection clause and 42 U.S.C. § 1983 and 1988. "The appellants claim that no General Assembly constituted according to the 1901 Act will submit reapportionment proposals either to the people or to a Constitutional Convention."

In *Baker*, the Court recognized that the plaintiffs are entitled to challenge Tennessee's apportionment on equal protection grounds. Assuming that plaintiffs ultimately prevail, what relief is available to them? In other words, how should a reviewing court frame its injunction? In analyzing this issue, consider the *Baker* plaintiffs' request for relief:

a declaratory judgment striking down the existing reapportionment Act, an injunction restraining defendants from any acts necessary to the holding of elections until such time as the legislature is reapportioned 'according to the Constitution of the State of Tennessee,' and an order directing defendants to declare the next primary and general elections for members of the Tennessee Legislature on an at large basis—the thirty-three senatorial candidates and the ninety-nine representative candidates receiving the highest number of votes to be declared elected. Consider also the plaintiffs' amended request for relief which asked for a remand to the District Court with directions to provide 'the necessary spur to legislative action.' If this proves insufficient, appellants will ask the 'additional spur' of an injunction prohibiting elections under the 1901 Act, or a declaration of the Act's unconstitutionality, or both. Finally, all other means failing, the District Court is invited by the plaintiffs, greatly daring, to order an election at large or redistrict the State itself or through a master.

L. EXTRA-TERRITORIAL DECREES

1. DECREES AFFECTING LAND

DESCHENES V. TALLMAN

248 N.Y. 33, 161 N.E. 321 (App.1928).

CARDOZO, C. J.

Plaintiffs sold the land to the defendant Francis Tallman in April, 1925. A predecessor in title was Miller & Lockwell, Limited, a Canadian corporation. By a decree of the courts of the province of Quebec, made in 1911, the corporation was adjudged insolvent, and its property, real and personal, was ordered to be sold by two liquidators duly appointed according to the laws of the province. The liquidators conveyed the land to the plaintiffs, who thereafter sold to Tallman with covenant of seizin. The land is located in the city of New York. The defendants insist that title does not pass under a deed by foreign liquidators.

A second and confirmatory deed, made in December, 1926, is also the subject of attack. After the sale to Tallman, the plaintiffs procured the execution of a quitclaim deed by the Canadian corporation. This deed, made by the corporation to the defendant Francis Tallman, contains a recital that it is given "in confirmation of a deed" made by the liquidators. Defendants insist that the later deed, being made under compulsion, adds nothing to the first one and leaves the title where it was.

The answer demands judgment for the cancellation of the purchase-money mortgage, the return of the cash payment, and reimbursement for the value of subsequent improvements. We think the counterclaim must fail.

There is no need to determine what effect would be given to the liquidators' deed considered by itself. If they were chancery receivers, or receivers or assignees in insolvency or bankruptcy, their deed would be a nullity. They would not gain a title to land within this state by force of their appointment in a foreign jurisdiction, and, not having it themselves, could not transmit it to another. If they were the universal successors of the corporation, the representatives in dissolution proceedings of its personality and powers, a different consequence would follow. The character and purpose of the proceedings in the courts of Canada are exhibited too imperfectly to enable us to judge with certainty of the origin and measure of the liquidators' powers. We leave the question open till decision becomes necessary.

If the deed by the liquidators be assumed to be inoperative, there was none the less a conveyance of title upon delivery by the corporation of a confirmatory deed of grant. A judgment of a foreign court will not avail, of its own force, to transfer the title to land located in this state. It will not avail though a conveyance be executed by the sheriff or a master or other agent of the court in fulfillment of its mandate. "The court not having jurisdiction of the res cannot affect it by its decree nor by a deed made by a master in accordance with the decree." But the rule is different where the conveyance is executed by the owner, though he act under compulsion. The conveyance, and not the judgment, is then the source of title. As to this the law has been undoubted since *Penn v. Lord Baltimore* (1 Ves. Sr. 444). The distinction is between a judgment directed against the res itself, and one directed against the person of the owner, who acts upon the res. His deed transmits the title irrespective of the pressure exerted on his will.

A different question would be here if we were required to determine whether the title would prevail against the remedies of creditors. A title acquired in foreign insolvency proceedings is subordinated to local creditors with executions or attachments against the goods and chattels of a debtor. We do not know from the answer whether any such claims exist. Very likely they have been extinguished, for fifteen years have elapsed between the appointment of the liquidators and the service of the counterclaim. In the view of the pleader, title has so failed that the transaction in all its parts must be undone from the beginning. More must be shown, to justify that upheaval, than the threat of a potential lien.

The order of the Appellate Division and that of the Special Term should be reversed and judgment ordered in favor of the plaintiffs for the relief demanded in the complaint * * *.

NOTE: CONVEYING TITLE TO LAND IN A FOREIGN JURISDICTION

The principle articulated in *Deschenes*—that a court cannot convey title to land located in a foreign jurisdiction—is well established. In *Fall v. Eastin*, 215 U.S. 1 (1909), a court in Washington state appointed a commissioner who purported to convey land in Nebraska. The Court concluded that the conveyance was invalid noting "the doctrine that the court, not having jurisdiction of the res, cannot affect it by its decree, nor by a deed made by a master in accordance with the decree, is firmly established." But the Court went on to note that: "A court of equity, having authority to act upon the person, may indirectly act upon real estate in another state, through the instrumentality of this authority over the person."

PROBLEM: THE ITALIAN LAND PURCHASE

Plaintiff, who lived in Forio, Ischia, Italy, paid defendant the sum of $3,000 to consummate the purchase of real estate in Forio. Defendant, who lived in the United States, promised to track down the owner (who lived in Rhode Island in the United States) and make the purchase. Defendant did make the purchase, using plaintiff's money, but recorded the deed in his own name. Plaintiff sued in Rhode Island, seeking to compel a transfer of the property, and effected service of process. Afterwards, defendant returned to Italy where plaintiff still lives. Does the Rhode Island court have the power to order defendant to convey the property in question "by deed in form appropriate for recording in Italy?" *See Matarese v. Calise*, 111 R.I. 551, 305 A.2d 112 (1973).

BURNLEY V. STEVENSON

24 Ohio St. 474 (1873).

MCILVAINE, J.

In recognition of military services, General Charles Scott was awarded 1,666 2/3 acres of land in Ohio. Scott hired John Evans, a surveyor, to "locate, survey, and obtain patents" on the land. In consideration for Evan's services, Scott agreed to convey to Evans "one-fifth of all the lands so located, surveyed and patented."

Soon after the patents were issued, Scott died without having conveyed the land. Evans filed a chancery suit in the Circuit Court of Fayette County, Kentucky, against Scott's heirs and legal representatives (defendants) seeking to compel specific performance of the contract. (*i.e.*, to force a conveyance of the lands to which he was entitled under the agreement) Evans obtained jurisdiction over defendants, and eventually won a judgment directing them to convey the lands to him. The judgment also provided that, if defendants failed to make the conveyance, one Robert Scott, a master commissioner of the court, should do so. When defendants failed to convey, Scott executed and delivered a fee simple deed to Evans. Scott's heirs sued in Ohio and the trial court rendered judgment for defendant.

The main proposition submitted in this case is, whether, under and by virtue of the decree of the Circuit Court of Kentucky and the master's deed made in pursuance thereof, or of either of them, such an estate or right was vested in John Evans as entitles the defendant, who has succeeded to all the rights of Evans, to the possession of the lands in controversy, as against the plaintiffs, whose claim of title is derived from the parties against whom the decree was rendered.

It appears that the Circuit Court of Kentucky which pronounced the decree, was a court of general equity jurisdiction; that some of the defendants in the cause were properly served with the process of the court, and that all others voluntarily appeared and submitted themselves to its jurisdiction, and that the subject-matter of the bill on which the decree was rendered, was the enforcement of a trust and the specific performance of a contract to convey lands situate in the State of Ohio.

That courts exercising chancery powers in one state have jurisdiction to enforce a trust, and to compel the specific performance of a contract in relation to lands situate in another state, after having obtained jurisdiction of the persons of those upon whom the obligation rests, is a doctrine fully settled by numerous decisions.

It does not follow, however, that a court having power to compel the parties before it to convey lands situated in another state, may make its own decree to operate as such conveyance. Indeed, it is well settled that the decree of such court can not operate to transfer title to lands situate in a foreign jurisdiction. And this, for the reason that a judgment or decree in rem can not operate beyond the limits of the jurisdiction or state wherein it is rendered. And if a decree in such case can not effect the transfer of the title to such lands, it is clear that a deed executed by a master, under the direction of the court, can have no greater effect. The master's deed to Evans must therefore be regarded as a nullity.

The next inquiry then is as to the force and effect of the decree rendered by the Circuit Court directing the heirs of Gen. Scott to convey the land in Ohio to Evans. This decree was in personam, and bound the consciences of those against whom it was rendered. In it, the contract of their ancestor to make the conveyance was merged. The fact that the title which had descended to them was held by them in trust for Evans, was thus established by the decree of a court of competent jurisdiction. Such decree is record evidence of that fact, and also of the fact that it became and was their duty to convey the legal title to him. The performance of that duty might have been enforced against them in that court by attachment as for contempt; and the fact that the conveyance was not made in pursuance of the order, does not affect the validity of the decree in so far as it determined the equitable rights of the parties in the land in controversy. In our judgment, the parties, and those holding under them with notice, are still bound thereby.

Under our code of practice, equitable as well as legal defenses may be set up in an action for the recovery of land. The defendant in the court below set up this decree of the Circuit Court of Kentucky as a defense to the plaintiffs' action. That it did not constitute a good defense at law may be admitted, but we think, in equity, it was a sufficient defense.

The constitution of the United States declares that full faith and credit shall be given in each state to the records and judicial proceedings of every other state, and provides that Congress may prescribe the mode of proving such records and proceedings, and the effect thereof. By an act of May 26, 1790, Congress declared that the "records and judicial proceedings of the state courts," when properly authenticated, "shall have the same faith and credit given to them in every court within the United States, as they have, by law or usage, in the courts of the state from whence they are or shall be taken." When, therefore, a decree rendered by a court in a sister state, having jurisdiction of the parties and of the subject-matter, is offered as evidence, or pleaded as the foundation of a right, in any action in the courts of this state, it is entitled to the same force and effect which it had in the state where it was pronounced. That this decree had the effect in Kentucky of determining the equities of the parties to the land in this state, we have already shown; hence the courts of this state must accord to it the same effect. True, the courts of this state can not enforce the performance of that decree, by compelling the conveyance through its process of attachment; but when pleaded in our courts as a cause of action, or as a ground of defense, it must be regarded as conclusive of all the rights and equities which were adjudicated and settled therein, unless it be impeached for fraud.

Motion overruled.

THE SALTON SEA CASES

172 Fed. 792 (9th Cir.1909).

MORROW, CIRCUIT JUDGE.

Appellee diverted water from the Colorado River into irrigation canals for farming purposes. The water spilled over onto appellant's lands which were used for mining, gathering, and refining salt. Appellant's lands were below sea level. The water created a lake more than 20 miles in length and several miles in width. Initially, the lake destroyed tons of appellant's salt and submerged its railroad. Eventually, the lake expanded and destroyed appellant's plant, sheds, mill and machinery. Appellant sought injunctive relief precluding appellee from diverting water "unless suitable headgates were provided to control the water, so that the flow would not be in excess of the amount used for irrigation purposes."

Defendant admitted many of the complaint's allegations, but alleged that the waters referred to were diverted from the Colorado river in Mexico by a corporation organized under the laws of the republic of Mexico, known as La Sociedad de Yrrigacion y Terrenos de la Baja California (Sociedad Anonima), which corporation owned all canals leading from the Colorado river in Mexico to the town of Calexico, Cal.; and denied that it diverted any water from the Colorado river which flowed into either the Alamo or New river or upon any of complainant's land.

A decree was entered by the court in favor of the complainant perpetually restraining and enjoining the defendant from diverting from the Colorado river any of the waters thereof in excess of the substantial needs of the people dependent upon the canal described in complainant's bill of complaint for water supply for domestic and irrigation uses and purposes, and such other lawful purposes as the same might be applied to; that the water so diverted, whatever might be the amount, should be so controlled and used that the same should not flow upon the lands of the complainant described in the bill of complaint; that the defendant regulate the flow of any water that might be diverted by it so that there should be no waste water flowing therefrom as the result of such diversion upon or over the lands of complainant; that defendant should be restrained from turning out of its canals any waste water at any point whence the same would naturally flow upon or over the lands of complainant or into the lake covering the Salton Sink, and thereby substantially increase the amount of water therein, or prevent the decrease thereof by any causes. It was further adjudged that the complainant had been damaged in the sum of $456,746.23 by reason of the commission of the acts mentioned in the bill of complaint by defendant, that complainant was entitled to recover compensation therefor; and it was ordered, adjudged, and decreed that complainant should have and recover from the defendant the said sum of $456,746.23, together with costs and disbursements. The defendant has brought the case here on appeal.

It is objected that the court had no jurisdiction to compel the defendants to construct headgates in the republic of Mexico for the reason that the defendant would not have been permitted by the laws of Mexico to construct such headgates until the plans for such structures had been approved by the proper engineering authority of Mexico. The answer to this objection is the fact shown by the evidence that the only site for controlling headgates on the river below what is known as the Laguna dam, above Yuma, is at Hanlon's Heading, in California. This point was originally selected for that purpose and the title to the land for such headworks was acquired by the California Development Company. "This site," said Mr. Meserve, in his statement attached to the President's message, "also controls what might be called or termed the gateway for the carrying of waters into Mexico, and through Mexico again into the United States." This statement is fully confirmed by the evidence we find in the record. The decree does not compel the defendant to construct headgates in Mexico. * * *

It is further objected that the court had no jurisdiction to decree an injunction in effect abating a nuisance caused by the construction of intakes in the republic of Mexico, and it is claimed that there is a rule supporting this objection to the effect that a court of equity can never compel a defendant to do anything which is not capable of being physically done within the territorial jurisdiction of the court. This rule undoubtedly obtains where the property injured is itself outside the jurisdiction of the court, which was the case in *Northern Indiana R. Co. v. Michigan Cent. R. Co.*, 56 U.S. 233. In that case the action was brought in the United States Circuit Court for the District of Michigan. Relief was prayed for an injury threatened or done to complainant's real estate in Indiana, and to its franchise which was inseparably connected with the realty in that state. The Supreme Court held that the Circuit Court in Michigan was without jurisdiction to protect property in Indiana. * * *

In the case of *Gilbert v. Moline Water Power & Manufacturing Co.*, 19 Iowa, 319, it was held that an Iowa court could not restrain a defendant from maintaining a dam across a portion of the channel of the Mississippi river between points in the state of Illinois whereby plaintiff's land in Iowa was overflowed. It does not appear that the overflow of plaintiff's land was because of any negligence on the part of the defendant in erecting or maintaining the dam. It had been maintained for many years, was supposed to have been placed where it was by consent of the state of Illinois, and was a legal structure in that state serving a legitimate and useful purpose. The controversy in the case was over the question of the concurrent jurisdiction of the states of Illinois and Iowa over the Mississippi river in such a case. The jurisdiction was denied. It would seem, however, from the facts stated that the remedy was an action at law for damages in a court of competent jurisdiction. We do not think that the law of such a case is applicable here.

The injury charged in the present case was an injury to property within the jurisdiction of the court, and the party charged with the commission of the injury was also within the jurisdiction of the court. The cause of the injury was not serving a useful purpose for any one, and the relief asked for was that the party causing the injury might be enjoined from continuing to injure complainant's property within the jurisdiction of the court. Why may not a court restrain a party over whom it has jurisdiction from injuring property within its jurisdiction? How does it affect the question of jurisdiction or venue to say that the party on whom the court must act may find it necessary to do things outside the jurisdiction of the court in order to comply with the order of the court? May this not often happen, and would it not happen oftener, if it were determined that such an excuse was sufficient to defeat the jurisdiction of the court? * * *

The court had jurisdiction in the present case to protect property within its jurisdiction, and to restrain the defendant from diverting the waters of the Colorado river to the damage of such property, notwithstanding the defendant may find it necessary in complying with the decree of the court to perform acts beyond the jurisdiction of the court.

The decree of the Circuit Court is affirmed.

NOTES

1. *Comity Principles.* Although courts need not give Full Faith and Credit to foreign injunctive decrees, they often do so as a matter of comity and statutes sometimes require comity (as in Vanneck). State court equitable decrees, ordering a defendant (over whom the court has valid jurisdiction) to convey land in a foreign state are routinely recognized and enforced by courts where the land is located.

2. *Requiring Actions in a Foreign Country.* Note that, in the *Salton Sea* case, the court did not require the defendant to do anything specific in Mexico. Instead, it prohibited defendant from diverting water in any way that injured plaintiff's property in California—leaving it up to the defendant to figure out how to comply.

PROBLEMS

1. *The Irish Sweepstakes.* McNulty, who won the Irish Sweepstakes, collected 50,000 Irish pounds ($128,410) which he deposited in a secret bank account on the Island of Jersey, which is located between the United Kingdom and France. When McNulty failed to pay taxes on the winnings, he was charged with, and ultimately convicted of, tax evasion, and ordered to pay back taxes, interest and penalties in the amount of $67,791. Since McNulty has no other assets to pay the award, the government seeks an order requiring McNulty to transfer his funds from Jersey to the United States. You are a law clerk to the judge assigned to hear the case (McNulty has been properly served so that the court has personal jurisdiction over him). Does the judge have the power to order McNulty to send the assets in his Jersey bank account to the United States? The judge is familiar with the equitable maxim which states that courts should not issue futile decrees. What does the maxim mean? Does it apply in this case? *See United States v. McNulty*, 446 F.Supp. 90 (N.D. Cal. 1978).

2. *Foreign Decrees and Public Policy. McElreath v. McElreath*, 162 Tex. 190, 345 S.W.2d 722 (1961), involved the following facts: "This is a suit

to enforce an Oklahoma equitable decree ordering James Dorsey McElreath to convey lands in Texas to Evelyn Ann McElreath. Both courts below refused the relief prayed for. The decree was entered in a divorce suit between the parties both of whom were residents of Oklahoma and Oklahoma was their matrimonial domicile. The order is valid and enforceable in Oklahoma and has been affirmed by the court of last resort in that State. However, after the decree was entered, but before the Oklahoma court could enforce its order, McElreath crossed the Red River and now asserts sanctuary in Texas." Suppose that the Texas land was separate, rather than marital, property. Also suppose that, under Texas law, separate property cannot be awarded to the other spouse. If the wife tries to enforce the Oklahoma decree in a Texas court, may the Texas court refuse enforcement on the grounds of public policy?

2. DECREES AFFECTING PERSONAL PROPERTY

MADDEN V. ROSSETER

114 Misc. 416, 187 N.Y.S. 462 (Sup.Ct.1921).

FORD, J.

Plaintiff is a resident of New York and the defendant of California. Each owns a half interest in the thoroughbred stallion Friar Rock, which the plaintiff now values at $250,000. In fact, the defendant paid the plaintiff $30,000 for a half interest in the horse more than 2½ years ago.

Under the written agreement of sale, dated June 29, 1918, the defendant was to have possession and use of Friar Rock in California during the seasons of 1919 and 1920; the plaintiff to have him for use in Kentucky during the seasons of 1921 and 1922; 'thereafter on new arrangements mutually satisfactory.' The season of 1921 is now open or opening, and plaintiff by the agreement is entitled in his turn to possess and use the stallion, but defendant flatly refuses to abide by his agreement, unless the plaintiff enters into a new agreement which is unsatisfactory to him.

The defendant has utterly no right to insist upon any conditions of any kind for returning the horse to plaintiff, except those expressed in the agreement of sale, and those require his shipment forthwith to the plaintiff's stock farm in Kentucky. Indeed, he has already been kept by the defendant so far beyond the reasonable time of shipment as to substantially prejudice the plaintiff's rights. The horse should have been sent in August or September of 1920, in order to get the stallion acclimated and fit for the season of 1921.

Personal service of the summons upon the defendant has been made in this state, and he has duly appeared by his attorneys. The plaintiff now asks for a mandatory injunction requiring the defendant to ship Friar Rock to Kentucky as provided in the agreement, and enjoining other disposition of him; also for a receiver of the stallion, with power to proceed to California and to take appropriate steps there or elsewhere, including the invoking of the aid of the courts of that or any other state, or of the federal courts, to gain possession of the animal and ship him to the plaintiff's stock farm in Kentucky.

Plaintiff's application for relief is quite novel, but so is the situation in which he finds himself. Already his rights have been prejudiced, and further irreparable damage is threatening him. There must be a remedy, and I do not believe this court is powerless to give it to him. The relief prayed for seems to be the most practicable and appropriate which is available to him. The courts of sister states may be relied upon to aid in serving the ends of justice whenever our own process falls short of effectiveness.

The motion will be granted, and the amount of the receiver's bond will be fixed upon the settlement of the order.

PROBLEMS

1. Madden *and Jurisdictional Issues.* If you had been plaintiff's attorney, would you have filed this case in New York or in California? Do you agree with the court that "the courts of sister states may be relied upon to aid in serving the ends of justice" if the court's own "process falls short of effectiveness"? Is your conclusion affected by the actual outcome in *Madden*? In a later opinion, the court summarized the outcome as follows: "the receiver carried out the order with tact and diplomacy, avoiding any litigation or ancillary receivership in California. He delivered the horse to plaintiff on May 23, 1921, in good condition." The court awarded the receiver a fee of $5,000 plus $500 attorneys fees. Defendant was required to pay the fees. *Madden v. Rosseter*, 117 Misc. 244, 192 N.Y.S. 113 (Sup.Ct.1921).

2. *The New York Receiver in California.* Suppose that the New York receiver had gone to California to retrieve the horse, and defendant had refused to turn it over to him. What should the receiver have done then? Could the receiver have had defendant held in contempt in the New York proceeding (for interfering with a receiver in the performance of his duties)? What else might the receiver have done?

3. *The Nude Boxer.* In *Ali v. Playgirl, Inc.*, 447 F.Supp. 723 (S.D.N.Y.1978), plaintiff, Muhammad Ali, the former heavyweight boxing champion of the world, sought injunctive relief against the alleged unauthorized printing, publication and distribution of an objectionable portrait of Ali in the February, 1978 issue of Playgirl Magazine ("Playgirl"). "The portrait depicted a nude black man seated in the corner of a boxing ring and is claimed to be unmistakably recognizable as Ali." The requested injunction would have directed Playgirl, Inc. "to cease distribution and dissemination of the February, 1978 issue of Playgirl Magazine, to withdraw that issue from circulation and recover possession of all copies presently offered for sale, and to surrender to plaintiff any printing plates or devices

used to reproduce the portrait complained of." The court has announced its intention to grant an injunction. However, Playgirl has unilaterally offered to withdraw the magazine from publication—except in England. Playgirl argues that a New York court should not restrain acts to be performed in a foreign country. Assuming that the court has personal jurisdiction over Playgirl, are there arguments for not enjoining Playgirl from committing acts in England? How might Ali respond to these arguments?

M. NATIONAL SECURITY

NEW YORK TIMES COMPANY V. UNITED STATES

403 U.S. 713, 91 S.Ct. 2140, 29 L.Ed.2d 822 (1971).

PER CURIAM.

We granted certiorari in these cases in which the United States seeks to enjoin the New York Times and the Washington Post from publishing the contents of a classified study entitled "History of U.S. Decision-Making Process on Viet Nam Policy." The Pentagon Papers

"Any system of prior restraints of expression comes to this Court bearing a heavy presumption against its constitutional validity." *Bantam Books, Inc. v. Sullivan*, 372 U.S. 58, 70 (1963). The Government "thus carries a heavy burden of showing justification for the imposition of such a restraint." *Organization for a Better Austin v. Keefe*, 402 U.S. 415, 419 (1971). The District Court for the Southern District of New York in the New York Times case, and the District Court for the District of Columbia and the Court of Appeals for the District of Columbia Circuit in the Washington Post case held that the Government had not met that burden. We agree.

The judgment of the Court of Appeals for the District of Columbia Circuit is therefore affirmed. The order of the Court of Appeals for the Second Circuit is reversed, and the case is remanded with directions to enter a judgment affirming the judgment of the District Court for the Southern District of New York. The stays entered June 25, 1971, by the Court are vacated. The judgments shall issue forthwith.

So ordered.

MR. JUSTICE BLACK, with whom MR. JUSTICE DOUGLAS joins, concurring.

The Government's case against the Washington Post should have been dismissed and the injunction against the New York Times should have been vacated without oral argument when the cases were first presented to this Court. Every moment's continuance of the injunctions against these newspapers amounts to a flagrant, indefensible, and continuing violation of the First Amendment. * * *

Madison and the other Framers of the First Amendment, able men that they were, wrote in language they earnestly believed could never be misunderstood: "Congress shall make no law abridging the freedom of the press." Both the history and language of the First Amendment support the view that the press must be left free to publish news, whatever the source, without censorship, injunctions, or prior restraints.

The press was to serve the governed, not the governors. The Government's power to censor the press was abolished so that the press would remain forever free to censure the Government. The press was protected so that it could bare the secrets of government and inform the people. Only a free and unrestrained press can effectively expose deception in government. And paramount among the responsibilities of a free press is the duty to prevent any part of the government from deceiving the people and sending them off to distant lands to die of foreign fevers and foreign shot and shell. Far from deserving condemnation for their courageous reporting, the New York Times, the Washington Post, and other newspapers should be commended for serving the purpose that the Founding Fathers saw so clearly. In revealing the workings of government that led to the Vietnam war, the newspapers nobly did precisely that which the Founders hoped and trusted they would do.

To find that the President has "inherent power" to halt the publication of news by resort to the courts would wipe out the First Amendment and destroy the fundamental liberty and security of the very people the Government hopes to make "secure." No one can read the history of the adoption of the First Amendment without being convinced beyond any doubt that it was injunctions like those sought here that Madison and his collaborators intended to outlaw in this Nation for all time.

The word "security" is a broad, vague generality whose contours should not be invoked to abrogate the fundamental law embodied in the First Amendment. The guarding of military and diplomatic secrets at the expense of informed representative government provides no real security for our Republic. The Framers of the First Amendment, fully aware of both the need to defend a new nation and the abuses of the English and Colonial Governments, sought to give this new society strength and security by providing that freedom of speech, press, religion, and assembly should not be abridged. * * *

MR. JUSTICE DOUGLAS, with whom MR. JUSTICE BLACK joins, concurring.

The First Amendment leaves, in my view, no room for governmental restraint on the press. There is, moreover, no statute barring the publication by the press of the material which the Times and the Post seek to use. * * *

As we stated in *Organization for a Better Austin v. Keefe*, 402 U.S. 415, 419 "any prior restraint on expression comes to this Court with a 'heavy presumption' against its constitutional validity."

The Government says that it has inherent powers to go into court and obtain an injunction to protect the national interest, which in this case is alleged to be national security. *Near v. Minnesota ex rel. Olson*, 283 U.S. 697, repudiated that expansive doctrine in no uncertain terms.

The dominant purpose of the First Amendment was to prohibit the widespread practice of governmental suppression of embarrassing information. It is common knowledge that the First Amendment was adopted against the widespread use of the common law of seditious libel to punish the dissemination of material that is embarrassing to the powers-that-be. The present cases will, I think, go down in history as the most dramatic illustration of that principle. A debate of large proportions goes on in the Nation over our posture in Vietnam. That debate antedated the disclosure of the contents of the present documents. The latter are highly relevant to the debate in progress.

Secrecy in government is fundamentally anti-democratic, perpetuating bureaucratic errors. Open debate and discussion of public issues are vital to our national health. On public questions there should be "uninhibited, robust, and wide-open" debate.

I would affirm the judgment of the Court of Appeals in the Post case, vacate the stay of the Court of Appeals in the Times case and direct that it affirm the District Court. The stays in these cases that have been in effect for more than a week constitute a flouting of the principles of the First Amendment as interpreted in *Near v. Minnesota ex rel. Olson*.

MR. JUSTICE BRENNAN, concurring.

The error that has pervaded these cases from the outset was the granting of any injunctive relief whatsoever, interim or otherwise. The entire thrust of the Government's claim throughout these cases has been that publication of the material sought to be enjoined "could," or "might," or "may" prejudice the national interest in various ways. But the First Amendment tolerates absolutely no prior judicial restraints of the press predicated upon surmise or conjecture that untoward consequences may result. Our cases have indicated that there is a single, extremely narrow class of cases in which the First Amendment's ban on prior judicial restraint may be overridden. Our cases have thus far indicated that such cases may arise only when the Nation "is at war," *Schenck v. United States*, 249 U.S. 47, 52 (1919), during which times "no one would question but that a government might prevent actual obstruction to its recruiting service or the publication of the sailing dates of transports or the number and location of troops." *Near v. Minnesota ex rel. Olson*, 283 U.S. 697, 716 (1931). Even if the present world situation were assumed to be tantamount to a time of war, or if the power of presently available armaments would justify even in peacetime the suppression of information that would set in motion a nuclear holocaust, in neither of these actions has the Government presented or even alleged that publication of items from or based upon the material at issue would cause the happening of an event of that nature. Only governmental allegation and proof that publication must inevitably, directly, and immediately cause the occurrence of an event kindred to imperiling the safety of a transport already at sea can support even the issuance of an interim restraining order. In no event may mere conclusions be sufficient. And therefore, every restraint issued in this case, whatever its form, has violated the First Amendment—and not less so because that restraint was justified as necessary to afford the courts an opportunity to examine the claim more thoroughly. Unless and until the Government has clearly made out its case, the First Amendment commands that no injunction may issue.

MR. JUSTICE STEWART, with whom MR. JUSTICE WHITE joins, concurring.

In the absence of the governmental checks and balances present in other areas of our national life, the only effective restraint upon executive policy and power in the areas of national defense and international affairs may lie in an enlightened citizenry—in an informed and critical public opinion which alone can here protect the values of democratic government. For this reason, it is perhaps here that a press that is alert, aware, and free most vitally serves the basic purpose of the First Amendment. For without an informed and free press there cannot be an enlightened people.

It is elementary that the successful conduct of international diplomacy and the maintenance of an effective national defense require both confidentiality and secrecy. Other nations can hardly deal with this Nation in an atmosphere of mutual trust unless they can be assured that their confidences will be kept. Within our own executive departments, the development of considered and intelligent international policies would be impossible if those charged with their formulation could not communicate with each other freely, frankly, and in confidence. In the area of basic national defense the frequent need for absolute secrecy is, of course, self-evident.

There can be but one answer to this dilemma. The responsibility must be where the power is. If the Constitution gives the Executive a large degree of unshared power in the conduct of foreign affairs and the maintenance of our national defense, then under the Constitution the Executive must have the largely unshared duty to determine and preserve the degree of internal security necessary to exercise that power successfully. It is an awesome responsibility, requiring judgment and wisdom of a high order. I should suppose that moral, political, and practical considerations would dictate that a very first principle of that wisdom would be an insistence upon avoiding secrecy for its own sake. For when everything is classified, then nothing is classified, and the system becomes one to be disregarded by the cynical or the careless, and to be manipulated by those intent on self-protection or self-promotion. I should suppose, in short, that the hallmark of a truly effective internal security system would be the maximum possible disclosure, recognizing that secrecy can best be preserved only when credibility is truly maintained. But be that as it may, it is clear to me that it is the constitutional duty of the Executive—as a matter of sovereign prerogative and not as a matter of law as the courts know law—through the promulgation and enforcement of executive regulations, to protect the confidentiality necessary to carry out its responsibilities in the fields of international relations and national defense.

This is not to say that Congress and the courts have no role to play. Undoubtedly Congress has the power to enact specific and appropriate criminal laws to protect government property and preserve government secrets. But in the cases before us we are asked neither to construe specific regulations nor to apply specific laws. We are asked, quite simply, to prevent the publication by two newspapers of material that the Executive Branch insists should not, in the national interest, be published. I am convinced that the Executive is correct with respect to some of the documents involved. But I cannot say that disclosure of any of them will surely result in direct, immediate, and irreparable damage to our Nation or its people. That being so, there can under the First Amendment be but one judicial resolution of the issues before us. I join the judgments of the Court.

MR. JUSTICE WHITE, with whom MR. JUSTICE STEWART joins, concurring.

I concur in today's judgments, but only because of the concededly extraordinary protection against prior restraints enjoyed by the press under our constitutional system. I do not say that in no circumstances would the First Amendment permit an injunction against publishing information about government plans or operations. Nor, after examining the materials the Government characterizes as the most sensitive and destructive, can I deny that revelation of these documents will do substantial damage to public interests. Indeed, I am confident that their disclosure will have that result. But I nevertheless agree that the United States has not satisfied the very heavy burden that it must meet to warrant an injunction against publication in these cases, at least in the absence of express and appropriately limited congressional authorization for prior restraints in circumstances such as these.

The Government's position is simply stated: The responsibility of the Executive for the conduct of the foreign affairs and for the security of the Nation is so basic that the President is entitled to an injunction against publication of a newspaper story whenever he can convince a court that the information to be revealed threatens "grave and irreparable" injury to the public interest; and the injunction should issue whether or not the material to be published is classified, whether or not publication would be lawful under relevant criminal statutes enacted by Congress, and regardless of the circumstances by which the newspaper came into possession of the information.

At least in the absence of legislation by Congress, based on its own investigations and findings, I am quite unable to agree that the inherent powers of the Executive and the courts reach so far as to authorize remedies having such sweeping potential for inhibiting publications by the press. Much of the difficulty inheres in the "grave and irreparable danger" standard suggested by the United States. If the United States were to have judgment under such a standard in these cases, our decision would be of little guidance to other courts in other cases, for the material at issue here would not be available from the Court's opinion or from public records, nor would it be published by the press. Indeed, even today where we hold that the United States has not met its burden, the material remains sealed in court records and it is properly not discussed in today's opinions. Moreover, because the material poses substantial dangers to national interests and because of the hazards of criminal sanctions, a responsible press may choose never to publish the more sensitive materials. To sustain the Government in these cases would start the courts down a long and hazardous road that I am not willing to travel, at least without congressional guidance and direction.

Terminating the ban on publication of the relatively few sensitive documents the Government now seeks to suppress does not mean that the law either requires or invites newspapers or others to publish them or that they will be immune from criminal action if they do. That the Government mistakenly chose to proceed by injunction does not mean that it could not successfully proceed in another way. Congress has not authorized the injunctive remedy against threatened publication. It has apparently been satisfied to rely on criminal sanctions and their deterrent effect on the responsible as well as the irresponsible press. * * *

MR. JUSTICE MARSHALL, concurring.

Congress has on several occasions given extensive consideration to the problem of protecting the military and strategic secrets of the United States. This consideration has resulted in the enactment of statutes making it a crime to receive, disclose, communicate, withhold, and publish certain documents, photographs, instruments, appliances, and information. Congress has provided penalties ranging from a $10,000 fine to death for violating the various statutes. In order for this Court to issue an injunction it would require a showing that such an injunction would enhance the already existing power of the Government to act. It is a traditional axiom of equity that a court of equity will not do a useless thing just as it is a traditional axiom that equity will not enjoin the commission of a crime. Here there has been no attempt to make such a showing. * * *

MR. CHIEF JUSTICE BURGER, dissenting.

The Times has had unauthorized possession of the documents for three to four months, during which it has had its expert analysts studying them, presumably digesting them and preparing the material for publication. During all of this time, the Times, presumably in its capacity as trustee of the public's "right to know," has held up publication for purposes it considered proper and thus public knowledge was delayed. No doubt this was for a good reason; the analysis of 7,000 pages of complex material drawn from a vastly greater volume of material would inevitably take time and the writing of good news stories takes time. But why should the United States Government, from whom this information was illegally acquired by someone, along with all the counsel, trial judges, and appellate judges be placed under needless pressure? After these months of deferral, the alleged "right to know" has somehow and suddenly become a right that must be vindicated instanter.

Would it have been unreasonable, since the newspaper could anticipate the Government's objections to release of secret material, to give the Government an opportunity to review the entire collection and determine whether agreement could be reached on publication? Stolen or not, if security was not in fact jeopardized, much of the material could no doubt have been declassified, since it spans a period ending in 1968. With such an approach the newspapers and Government might well have narrowed the area of disagreement as to what was and was not publishable, leaving the remainder to be resolved in orderly litigation, if necessary. To me it is hardly believable that a newspaper long regarded as a great institution in American life would fail to perform one of the basic and simple duties of every citizen with respect to the discovery or possession of stolen property or secret government documents. That duty, I had thought—perhaps naively—was to report forthwith, to responsible public officers. * * *

The consequence of all this melancholy series of events is that we literally do not know what we are acting on. We have been forced to deal with litigation concerning rights of great magnitude without an adequate record, and surely without time for adequate treatment either in the prior proceedings or in this Court. Counsel were frequently unable to respond to questions on factual points. Not surprisingly they pointed out that they had been working literally "around the clock" and simply were unable to review the documents that give rise to these cases and were not familiar with them. This Court is in no better posture. We all crave speedier judicial processes but when judges are pressured as in these cases the result is a parody of the judicial function.

MR. JUSTICE HARLAN, with whom THE CHIEF JUSTICE and MR. JUSTICE BLACKMUN join, dissenting.

Both the Court of Appeals for the Second Circuit and the Court of Appeals for the District of Columbia Circuit rendered judgment on June 23. The New York Times' petition for certiorari, its motion for accelerated consideration thereof, and its application for interim relief were filed in this Court on June 24 at about 11 a.m. The application of the United States for interim relief in the Post case was also filed here on June 24 at about 7:15 p.m. This Court's order setting a hearing before us on June 26 at 11 a.m., a course which I joined only to avoid the possibility of even more peremptory action by the Court, was issued less than 24 hours before. The record in the Post case was filed with the Clerk shortly before 1 p.m. on June 25; the record in the Times case did not arrive until 7 or 8 o'clock that same night. The briefs of the parties were received less than two hours before argument on June 26.

These are difficult questions of fact, of law, and of judgment; the potential consequences of erroneous decision are enormous. The time which has been available to us, to the lower courts,* and to the parties has been wholly inadequate for giving these cases the kind of consideration they deserve. Forced as I am to reach the merits of these cases, I dissent from the opinion and judgments of the Court. * * *

In my judgment the judiciary may not properly redetermine for itself the probable impact of disclosure on the national security. "The very nature of executive decisions as to foreign policy is political, not judicial. Such decisions are wholly confided by our Constitution to the political departments of the government, Executive and Legislative. They are delicate, complex, and involve large elements of prophecy. They are and should be undertaken only by those directly responsible to the people whose welfare they advance or imperil. They are decisions of a kind for which the Judiciary has neither aptitude, facilities nor responsibility and have long been held to belong in the domain of political power not subject to judicial intrusion or inquiry." *Chicago & Southern Air Lines, Inc. v. Waterman Steamship Corp.*, 333 U.S. 103, 111 (1948) (Jackson J.).

---

* The hearing in the Post case before Judge Gesell began at 8 a.m. on June 21, and his decision was rendered, under the hammer of a deadline imposed by the Court of Appeals, shortly before 5 p.m. on the same day. The hearing in the Times case before Judge Gurfein was held on June 18 and his decision was rendered on June 19. The Government's appeals in the two cases were heard by the Courts of Appeals for the District of Columbia and Second Circuits, each court sitting en banc, on June 22. Each court rendered its decision on the following afternoon.

Even if there is some room for the judiciary to override the executive determination, it is plain that the scope of review must be exceedingly narrow. I can see no indication in the opinions of either the District Court or the Court of Appeals in the Post litigation that the conclusions of the Executive were given even the deference owing to an administrative agency, much less that owing to a co-equal branch of the Government operating within the field of its constitutional prerogative.

Accordingly, I would vacate and remand. Before the commencement of such further proceedings, due opportunity should be afforded the Government for procuring from the Secretary of State or the Secretary of Defense or both an expression of their views on the issue of national security. I cannot believe that the doctrine prohibiting prior restraints reaches to the point of preventing courts from maintaining the status quo long enough to act responsibly in matters of such national importance as those involved here.

MR. JUSTICE BLACKMUN, dissenting.

The First Amendment is only one part of an entire Constitution. Article II of the great document vests in the Executive Branch primary power over the conduct of foreign affairs and places in that branch the responsibility for the Nation's safety. Each provision of the Constitution is important, and I cannot subscribe to a doctrine of unlimited absolutism for the First Amendment at the cost of downgrading other provisions. What is needed here is a weighing, upon properly developed standards, of the broad right of the press to print and of the very narrow right of the Government to prevent. Such standards are not yet developed. I therefore would remand these cases to be developed expeditiously, of course, but on a schedule permitting the orderly presentation of evidence from both sides, with the use of discovery, if necessary, as authorized by the rules, and with the preparation of briefs, oral argument, and court opinions of a quality better than has been seen to this point. * * *

PROBLEMS

1. *The Progressive Case.* In *United States v. Progressive, Inc.*, 467 F.Supp. 990 (W.D.Wis.1979), the U.S. government sought to enjoin the Progressive, Inc., from publishing an article entitled "The H–Bomb Secret: How We Got It, Why We're Telling It." The article provides information on how to build a hydrogen bomb. The government sought injunctive relief under 42 U.S.C. §§ 2274(b) and 2280 which authorizes relief against one who would disclose restricted data "with reason to believe such data will be utilized to injure the United States or to secure an advantage to any foreign nation." The magazine responds that it wants to publish the article to demonstrate laxness in the government's security system.

The government believes that much of the article's information is not in the public domain, and some of the information has never before been published. However, the magazine claims that the article is based on publicly available information. While disagreeing, the government contends that, whether or not the information is publicly available, others could not replicate the author's feat—the preparation of an article on the technical processes of thermonuclear weapons. The government emphasizes that the article is dangerous because it exposes concepts never heretofore disclosed in conjunction with one another. The government fears that the article could help a medium sized nation build the H-bomb.

Suppose that you are the judge assigned to hear this case. After *New York Times Co. v. United States*, is it appropriate for you to enjoin the Progressive, Inc. from publishing this article? Is this case distinguishable from that one? Can you give any injunctive relief, even preliminary relief, to allow you to consider the issue more deliberately?

2. *The* Snepp *Case.* In *Snepp v. United States*, 444 U.S. 507, 100 S.Ct. 763, 62 L.Ed.2d 704 (1980), while working for the Central Intelligence Agency (CIA), Snepp agreed not to disclose classified information without the agency's consent. In addition, Snepp agreed to submit all writings about the agency for prepublication review. After leaving the agency, Snepp violated the agreement when he wrote a book about CIA activities in South Vietnam and published it without submitting the book to the Agency for prepublication review. Suppose that you are an attorney at the CIA. Your boss, the Director, wants to know what remedies are available against Snepp. What are the advantages and disadvantages of the various alternatives? How would you advise the Director to proceed?

EXERCISES

Okay, now that you understand how the injunctive remedy works, are you ready to apply that remedy in the context of written work? Consider the following exercises.

EXERCISE #1: THE ROCK QUARRY

Carter Rock and Stone Co. (Carter) has operated a rock quarry at the same location since 1912. Carter does a brisk business employing 45 people and recording annual sales in excess of $1 million.

Carter's extraction techniques involve explosives and large machinery, both of which create dust, noise and vibration. For the first 70+ years of Carter's existence, no one complained about Carter's method of operation. In 1912, the quarry was more than ten miles from the nearest city. The land around the quarry was farmland, and the noise, etc., did not bother the farmers.

During the last several decades, the land around the quarry has changed. The city expanded outward towards the quarry, and its limits now come within two miles of the quarry. About ten years ago, a local developer bought most of the surrounding land and started building upscale homes.

Since then, he has built some 50 homes. 200 people now live within a two-mile radius of Carter's quarry. The developer plans to build more homes.

From the beginning, relations between the new homeowners and Carter were poor. Some of the homeowners believe that Carter's blasting has damaged their homes. Two of them claim severe damage (cracks in their foundations). Almost all of the homeowners complain about the dust and the noise. They also complain about dump trucks which leave Carter carrying rock. A few homeowners, who have allergies or asthma, believe that the dust makes them ill.

Recently, the homeowners hired a lawyer to represent them. They demanded that Carter alter its operations to eliminate the noise, dust and vibrations. Carter refused. Carter claims that it cannot operate without using explosives and creating dust. As a result, if it complies with the homeowners' request, it would have to shut down.

After Carter's refusal to alter its operations, the homeowner's filed suit. They seek injunctive relief prohibiting Carter from using explosives or creating dust.

INSTRUCTIONS FOR EXERCISE #1

You will be assigned to one of two groups. If you are assigned to group #1, you will represent the homeowners. Draft a motion for a preliminary injunction on their behalf. If you are assigned to group #2, you will represent the rock quarry. Draft a memorandum in opposition to the homeowners' motion. Both groups should comply with the Rules of Court (set forth at the end of the chapter).

EXERCISE #2: THE "WHITE SUPREMACIST" RALLY

Johnson is the President of a white supremacist organization called the National States Rights Party (NSRP). Three days ago, the NSRP held a public outside the courthouse in the town of Princess Anne, Maryland. The authorities did not attempt to interfere with the rally. However, because of the tense atmosphere surrounding the rally, about 60 state policemen were brought to the area. Petitioners' speeches, amplified by a public address system so that they could be heard for several blocks, were aggressively and militantly racist. Their target was primarily blacks and, secondarily, Jews, and petitioners engaged in deliberately derogatory, insulting, and threatening language, scarcely disguised by protestations of peaceful purposes. Listeners might well have construed their words as both a provocation to the blacks in the crowd and an incitement to the whites. The rally continued for something more than an hour. In the course of the proceedings it was announced that the rally would be resumed the following night at 8:00 p.m.

Your professor will assign you to represent either one side (the city or the National States Rights Party), or to write the opinion of the court. Follow the instructions below.

1. *Representing the City.* Suppose that you represent Princess Anne, and you want to prevent the rally from going forward. You believe that the NSRP's proposed rally would be detrimental to the health, welfare and morals of society, as well as that it may result in violence. Please write a motion for temporary restraining order seeking injunctive relief against the rally. Comply with the Rules of Court.

2. *Representing the NSRP.* Suppose that you represent the NSRP, and you believe that you have the right to go ahead with the rally. Assume that the city has sought a temporary restraining order on the grounds set forth in the immediately prior paragraph. Your client seeks to oppose the TRO. Write a brief opposing it. Comply with the Rules of Court.

3. *Deciding the Case.* Now, suppose that you are the judge assigned to hear the case. Write an opinion deciding whether to grant the TRO.

EXERCISE #3: THE AIRPORT EXPANSION

Two years ago, the Louisville Regional Airport Authority (LRAA) dramatically expanded Louisville's Standiford Field airport. As part of its expansion plan, the LRAA condemned several nearby neighborhoods taking the land to build three new runways. These new runways gave Standiford Field the capacity to handle twice as much air traffic as before.

Once the expansion project was complete, airplane traffic at Standiford Field significantly increased. Several new airlines began flying out of Louisville. Two of the airlines offered inexpensive fares that attracted many passengers. Also, a national parcel service expanded its Louisville operations. The parcel service, an overnight delivery service, made numerous flights during the middle of the night.

LRAA officials, as well as City and County officials, were thrilled with the expansion's economic impact. In addition to the expansion's direct impact (new jobs created by the airlines and the parcel service), there was indirect impact which trickled through the entire community (jobs in hotels, car rental agencies, etc.).

The airport's expansion was not welcomed by everyone. Some nearby residential areas had always experienced noise disturbances from Standiford Field's operations. After the expansion, the situation worsened. Moreover, some residential areas that had previously been unaffected by noise disturbances were now disturbed by new runways which created new traffic patterns. Noise disturbances in these areas became common.

Before the expansion, most of the noise disturbance was confined to daylight hours. Afterwards, because the parcel service operated at night, the noise disturbance was constant. Some neighbors complained that they were unable to sleep, or that they were unable to sleep well because of the constant flow of airplanes.

Over a period of months, a group, Citizens Against Airport Noise (CAAN), pressured LRAA to abate the noise. When LRAA refused to do so, citing the adverse economic effects that would result, CAAN filed suit. CANN sought injunctive relief.

After a hearing, the judge asked the parties to submit proposed orders, along with briefs (not to exceed five pages) explaining why they think that their proposed order should be adopted. Your professor will assign you to represent either CAAN or LRAA. Prepare the proposed order and brief on behalf of your client.

Rules of Court

This Court has adopted this state's Rules of Civil Procedure, as well as the rules set forth below. To the extent that there is an inconsistency between these rules and this state's civil rules, these rules control.

Rule 1. Motion Practice

(a) Motions. All motions shall state precisely the relief requested. Except for routine motions, such as for extensions of time, each motion shall be accompanied by a supporting memorandum which complies with the provisions of this rule. The supporting memorandum shall not exceed ten (10) pages. Failure to comply will be grounds for denying the motion.

(b) Time for Filing Responses and Replies.

> ***(1) Opposing Memorandum.*** An opposing memorandum must be filed within seven (7) days from the date of service of the motion which may be extended for no more than thirty (30) additional days by written stipulation filed with the Court unless the stipulation would extend the time beyond a deadline established by the Court. The opposing memorandum shall not be longer than ten (10) pages. Failure to file an opposing memorandum may be grounds for granting the motion.
>
> ***(2) Reply Memorandum.*** A reply memorandum may be filed within three (3) days from the date of service of the opposing memorandum. A reply memorandum shall be limited to matters newly raised in the opposing memorandum, and shall not exceed five (5) pages in length.

(c) Copies of Orders. No motion, supporting memorandum, or memorandum in opposition shall be accepted for filing unless accompanied by a proposed order granting the requested relief or denying the motion, as the case may be.

(d) Hearings on Motions. A party may request a hearing on a motion by filing a request for oral argument which explains why argument may assist the court in ruling on the motion.

Rule 2. Briefs, Pleadings and Memoranda; Proof of Service

(a) Name of Counsel. All briefs, pleadings and memoranda filed with the Court shall include the student exam number (or name, as appropriate) of each attorney of record for the party filing them.

(b) Paper Size and Binding. 8½′ x 11″ paper stock shall be used for briefs, pleadings and memoranda filed with the Court. All pleadings shall be side-bound.

(c) Citation Form. All briefs, pleadings and memoranda shall use a generally accepted manner of citation.

(d) Copies of Memoranda and Cases. Parties shall file the original of all memoranda with the Clerk.

(e) Service. All briefs, pleadings, memoranda and orders filed with the Court shall be served on all other parties to the litigation.

(f) Manner of Service. Whenever a party is required or permitted to serve pleadings upon a party represented by an attorney, the party shall personally deliver a copy to the attorney or place a copy in the attorney's law school mail box.

(g) Proof of Service. All briefs, pleadings and memoranda filed with the Court shall have proof of service by written certification of counsel, except in an instance for which another method of proof of service is prescribed in this state's R. Civ. P. In the case of an ex parte proceeding, proof may be by written certification of service or by affidavit of the person making the service. Proof of service shall state the date and manner of service.

CHAPTER 5

RESTITUTION

■ ■ ■

CHAPTER OVERVIEW: You will know the term "restitution" from elsewhere in your studies. In Contracts you will have examined "quantum meruit" in respect of implied contracts. In Torts you will have examined cases where unjust enrichment has played a part in imposing tort liability. It is likely however that you have not systematically examined the law that draws on both legal and equitable legal concepts. The law of restitution and unjust enrichment has not received separate treatment in most law school curricular. This is likely to change with the revivification of the law in the publication of RESTATEMENT (THIRD) OF RESTITUTION AND UNJUST ENRICHMENT, *Andrew Kull,* Reporter, St. Paul: American Law Institute Publishers, 2011. Volume One. pp. 1, 670. Volume Two. pp. 3, 745. (herein referred to as *The Restatement (Third) of Restitution and Unjust Enrichment*

This chapter is designed to provide you with a thorough grounding in restitution and restitutionary remedies. It begins by examining the underlying principles of restitution, the circumstances under which recovery of unjustified benefits might be allowed, defenses to restitution, and how courts measure the enrichment. It then examines the concept of tracing, and the special restitutionary devices (*e.g.*, constructive trusts, equitable liens and subrogation) that are variously employed in effecting a plaintiff's restitutionary recovery.

PROBLEM: THE STOLEN STEERS

Hill and Stewart (H & S) stole 10 of plaintiff's steers which had a fair market value of $850. H & S delivered the steers to Lamb (an aider and abetter in the theft) who shipped the steers, along with 15 head of his own cattle, to market. The 25 head brought $1,600. Subsequently, Lamb invested the $1,600 in 49 head of yearling steers which were shipped to Lamb's ranch.

The evidence revealed that, prior to the theft, Lamb's bank account had a balance of $100. After the sale, he deposited the $1,600 check that he received for the sale. Lamb withdrew $600 from the account which he applied towards the purchase of the 49 steers. He paid the remainder of the purchase price from other funds. Lamb frittered away the remaining $1,100 in the bank account.

As you work your way through this chapter, you will be asked to think about how this problem should be resolved. Please consider how restitutionary principles apply to such a situation. Do you have any preliminary thoughts? See if your ideas change as you work your way through the chapter.

A. GENERAL PRINCIPLES

The doctrinal core of restitution is deceivingly simple: "A person who is unjustly enriched at the expense of another is subject to liability in restitution." The Restatement (Third) of Restitution & Unjust Enrichment § 1. In other words, the purpose of restitution is simply to give the plaintiff a remedy when a defendant obtains unjust benefits at the plaintiff's expense. Despite the simplicity, restitutionary remedies can be extremely powerful and flexible.

Quasi-contract is perhaps the best known aspect of restitution. In *Moses v. MacFerlan*, 2 Burr. 1005, 97 Eng.Rep. 676 (King's Bench 1760), Chapman Jacob issued four promissory notes to Moses. Moses endorsed the notes to MacFerlan in order to allow MacFerlan to proceed directly against Jacob. MacFerlan expressly agreed that he would not hold Moses liable on the endorsements. In breach of his agreement, MacFerlan sued Moses on the notes and obtained a judgment in what might be called the modern analogue to small claims court. Because of the limited "subject matter" jurisdiction of that court, Moses was not allowed to interpose the agreement as a defense.

Moses then sued MacFerlan for a refund, and the King's Bench held in Moses's favor. Lord Mansfield, writing for a unanimous court, stated that "t]he ground of this action is not, 'that the judgment was wrong:' but, 'that, (for a reason which the now plaintiff could not avail himself of against that judgment,) the defendant ought not in justice to keep the money.'" Lord Mansfield concluded that "the defendant [MacFerlan], upon the circumstances of the case, is obliged by the ties of natural justice and equity to refund the money."

Lord Mansfield broadly states the principle, and its context in breach of promise led to the fiction, created by judges of less capacity than the famous judge, that the recovery was a species of implied promise. The modern law is not trammeled by the fiction and the basis of the law lies in the wider right of restitution based on unjust enrichment.

BEACON HOMES, INC. V. HOLT

266 N.C. 467, 146 S.E.2d 434 (1966).

LAKE, JUSTICE.

[T]he complaint alleges that Mary Holt Richardson, mother of the defendant, contracted with the plaintiff for the construction by it of the house upon the lots in question, giving the plaintiff a warranty that she, Mary Holt Richardson, owned the land, in reliance upon which warranty the plaintiff, in good faith, constructed the house upon the land, improving its value by $3,300; that the defendant, who was and is the owner of the land, claimed ownership thereof and of the house after the construction was complete; the plaintiff thereupon offered to remove the building and restore the lots to their original condition but the defendant has refused to permit the plaintiff to do so; the defendant has assumed dominion over the house and has rented it to a tenant from whom she has collected rent; that the plaintiff has not been paid for the construction of the house and the defendant has been unjustly enriched to the extent of the improvement, in value, of her land.

Taking these allegations to be true, as we must upon a demurrer, they state a cause of action in favor of the plaintiff against the defendant for unjust enrichment. This right of action is not the same as the common law right, or the right under the statute, General Statutes, Chap. I, Art. 30, to claim for betterments when one, in possession of land under color of title, constructs permanent improvements thereon and is thereafter sued in ejectment by the true owner. That right was and is a defensive right. It accrues when an owner of the land seeks and obtains the aid of the court to enforce his right to possession. It applies only where the improvement was constructed by one who was in possession of the land under color of title and who, in good faith and reasonably, believed he had good title to the land.

In *Rhyne v. Sheppard*, 32 S.E.2d 316, the plaintiff having acquired title to two lots in a real estate development, in good faith built a house on two other lots, believing them to be the lots described in his deed. He sued the true owner of the lots for the value of the improvement. [T]his Court, through Barnhill, J., later C.J., [stated]: "[The] recipient of a benefit voluntarily bestowed without solicitation or inducement is not liable for their value. But he cannot retain a benefit which knowingly he has permitted another to confer upon him by mistake."

In the present case, the complaint does not allege facts sufficient to show an estoppel of the defendant by silently standing by and permitting the construction with knowledge of it. [Defendant] owed no duty to the plaintiff to maintain a watch upon her lot to see that no unauthorized person built a house upon it. Therefore, the allegation that she "knew or should have known" that it was being built is not sufficient to charge her with actual knowledge thereof.

Neither can the complaint be sustained on the theory that by exercising dominion over the house and renting it to tenants the defendant ratified the contract made by her mother with the plaintiff. There can be no ratification unless the person making the contract professed to do so on behalf of the person claiming or claimed to be the principal. * * *

We are thus brought to the question of whether the plaintiff can maintain this action solely on the ground of unjust enrichment of the defendant through a bona fide mistake of fact by the plaintiff, which mistake is not induced by the conduct of the defendant.

The plaintiff did not construct the house believing itself to be the owner of the land. It did so believing the person with whom it contracted was the owner. The plaintiff could certainly have brought suit upon its contract against the defendant's mother with whom it made its contract. That right it has not lost by virtue of the defendant's ownership of the land. * * *

The plaintiff does not seek in this action to hold the defendant liable for the payment of the contract price of the house, nor does it seek to recover from her its expenses in the construction. The right of a landowner to remove from his premises a structure placed thereon by a trespasser, innocently or otherwise, and to sue the trespasser for damages, including the cost of such removal, is not involved in this action. The question is, can the owner of a lot upon which a house has been built by another, who acted in good faith under a mistake of fact, believing he had a right to build it there, keep the house, refuse to permit the builder to remove it so as to restore the property to its former condition, enjoy the enhancement of the value of the property and pay nothing for the house? For the owner to do so is as contrary to equity and good conscience as it would be if the builder had believed itself to be the owner of the land.

[It] is as contrary to equity and good conscience for one to retain a house, which he has received as the result of a bona fide and reasonable mistake of fact as it is for him to retain money so received. We, therefore, hold that where through a reasonable mistake of fact one builds a house upon the land of another, the landowner, electing to retain the house upon his property, must pay therefor the amount by which the value of his property has been so increased. Consequently, the complaint states a cause of action and the demurrer ore tenus is overruled.

NOTES

1. *Restitution's Roots.* Scholars debate the proper foundations of restitution. Often "restitution" is used to describe a remedy resulting from a number of causes of action including liability for wrongs causing harm but also to non-wrongs, that is liability that arises because of unjust enrichment or claims to vindicate property rights. Otherwise restitution may be said to rest on the universal foundation of unjust enrichment. Restitution for wrongs then forms part of the law of unjust enrichment.

The jurisprudential uncertainties stem from the mists of history. Under the old common law forms of action, a plaintiff may seek a remedy grounded on the type of benefit received by the defendant. Thus the count of "indebitatus assumpsit" included actions for "money had and received," "quantum meruit," and "quantum valebant." The plain language correspondence is restitution of money, and restitution of fair value of services and goods. Moreover, a hodge-podge of other remedies could be unearthed, for example, wayleaves, mesne profits, reasonable royalties and damages assessed on the basis of a user principle. The old forms of action, arcane as they were, did not require revelation of the reason for restitution. When a reason was proffered it was framed sometimes as an implied contract. This as we saw, was a fiction convenient for courts but obstructive for the development of the law. The Equity courts exercising their jurisdiction in ameliorating the strictures of the common law that limited its remedial powers added, in its in personam exercise of power, remedies of constructive trust, equitable lien, and subrogation. Importantly these equitable remedies grant powerful proprietary rights against others that are critical in a world in which a personal right to a money award may be nugatory.

2. *Defining Unjust Enrichment and Restitution.* The term "unjust enrichment" has become the term of art. The *Restatement (Third) of Restitution and Unjust Enrichment* accepts the nomenclature although the Comments to § 1 suggest that the term "unjustified enrichment" may be more helpful. At the same time, the term "restitution" has proven to be misleading. The First Restatement adopted the term because unjust enrichment leads in most circumstances to the avoidance of a transfer or to an obligation on the part of the transferee to pay for what has been transferred. However, that is not always the case: Profits may be disgorged and benefits wrongfully obtained given up in excess of the plaintiff's loss. See § 51. To complicate matters restitution may be based on no unjust enrichment of the defendant. For example, if a transfer has been induced by misrepresentation, the transferor is entitled to rescission and restitution even if the transferee, having paid market value, was not enriched. See § 13.

3. *The Defaulting Lessee.* In *Siskron v. Temel–Peck Enterprises, Inc,* 26 N.C.App. 387, 216 S.E.2d 441 (1975), a lessee promised to "keep and maintain the improvements, equipment, fixtures and furnishings in good repair," and to "make all necessary and appropriate repairs and replacements to the premises." When the lessee contracted for repairs, and then refused to pay the contractor, the contractor sued the lessor for unjust enrichment. The court rejected the claim: "the general rule of equity applies and the defendant [lessor], having had no suitable opportunity to accept or decline the benefits, could not be held liable in restitution for the benefits conferred."

PROBLEMS

1. *Variations on the* Beacon Homes *Case.* Suppose that we alter the facts of the *Beacon Homes* case a bit. In which of the following situations has

defendant been unjustly enriched by plaintiff's construction of a house on her land:

A) *The Wildlife Sanctuary.* Defendant had no advance notice of the fact that plaintiff intended to build the house on her property, and was not in collusion with her mother. In fact, defendant desired to use the property to create a wildlife sanctuary. When defendant learned that the house had been built, she immediately demanded that plaintiff tear it down and return the land to its natural state. When plaintiff refused to do so, defendant spent her own money to have the house torn down and the land restored. When plaintiff sues seeking restitution for the cost of building the house, defendant counterclaims seeking restitution of the money she spent to destroy the house and restore the land. Who should prevail?

B) *The Ultra Modern Design.* Again, defendant had no advance notice of the fact that plaintiff intended to build the house on her property, and was not in collusion with her mother. In fact, defendant wanted to build a house on the property, and had always dreamed of building a center hall Colonial. The house that plaintiff built was ultra-modern and defendant hated it. Defendant demanded that the house be removed, but plaintiff refused and demanded payment. Defendant then paid to have the house removed and the land restored, intending all along to build the house of her dreams. When plaintiff sues seeking restitution for the cost of building the house, defendant counterclaims seeking restitution of the money she spent to destroy the house and restore the land. Who should prevail?

C) *The Empty House.* Again, defendant had no advance notice of the fact that plaintiff was going to build the house on her property, and again defendant was not in collusion with her mother. Moreover, once again, defendant does not like the style of house and would have preferred to leave the land in an unimproved condition. As a result, defendant does not move into the house, does not rent it out, and instead simply leaves it vacant. Plaintiff demands that defendant pay for the house, but defendant refuses. Was defendant unjustly enriched? Would your view be different if, a year later, defendant sold the land touting the house as an asset?

2. *The Lost Tickets.* Will Deveroe bought a season ticket for New York Rangers Hockey Club home games played at Madison Square Garden. At the time of the purchase, Deveroe signed an invoice stating that, upon receipt, "risk of loss or theft of said tickets shall pass to [Deveroe] and that the [Garden] shall not be obligated to admit subscriber to events unless tickets delivered hereunder are presented at such time."

Deveroe lost his tickets, and the Garden agreed to sell him a second set of tickets allowing Deveroe to sit in his normal seat. The agreement required the Garden to refund the second payment if Deveroe found his lost tickets.

The agreement required Deveroe to vacate the seat if someone possessing plaintiff's original tickets tried to claim the seat.

A) *Seeking Restitution for the Extra Payment.* After receiving the second set of ticket, Deveroe sued the Garden for restitution claiming that the exaction of two payments for the same seat unjustly enriched the Garden. What arguments can you make on Deveroe's behalf that the Garden was "unjustly enriched?" How might the Garden respond to those arguments? Who should win? *See Sloame v. Madison Square Garden Center, Inc.*, 56 A.D.2d 92, 391 N.Y.S.2d 576 (Sup.Ct.1977).

B) *Deveroe and the Thief.* Suppose that Deveroe pays for the new set of tickets, and goes to the next game. When he arrives, he finds someone (Billings) sitting in his seat. Since the very next seat is open, Deveroe sits there and engages Billings in conversation. He eventually learns that Billings stole his tickets and sues him for restitution. Can Deveroe obtain restitution from Billings?

C) *Deveroe and the BFP.* In the prior paragraph, suppose that Deveroe does not find Billings sitting in his seats, but instead finds a man named Stenger. In talking to Stenger, Deveroe learns that Stenger purchased the tickets from a scalper outside of Madison Square Garden. Stenger paid a price that was above face value. Stenger knew nothing about how the seller came by the tickets. On the theory that the tickets are his, rather than Stenger's, Deveroe sues Stenger for restitution of the value of the tickets. Can Deveroe recover?

3. *The Lost Luggage.* Ann Perry decided to see the U.S. by bus. Ann stopped at Eustis Springs, a small town in New Mexico, for a short visit. When Ann reboarded the bus, she unintentionally left her luggage behind. The proprietor of the bus stop found the luggage and placed it in storage. Several weeks later, Ann returned to claim the luggage. The proprietor demanded that Ann pay him a storage fee before he would release the luggage. Ann sued to regain possession of the luggage, and the proprietor counterclaimed for restitution (to recoup the storage fees).

Is the proprietor entitled to restitution? What arguments can you make on his behalf? What arguments can you make on Ann's behalf? Who should win?

4. *The Flea Market "Find."* While Molly Weaver was browsing through a $1.99 "cosmetic" jewelry bin at a flea market, she found a real diamond worth thousands of dollars. Molly immediately purchased the diamond from a clerk who thought that it was glass. Afterwards, Molly sold the diamond for $7,000 to a jeweler.

If you represent the owner of the jewelry stall from which Molly purchased the diamond, how can you argue that she was "unjustly enriched?" What response might you make on Molly's behalf? How should this matter be resolved?

5. *More on the Flea Market "Find."* Would you reach the same result if Molly had purchased a picture at a flea market? The seller thought that it was worthless. Molly, who was very knowledgeable about art, realized that it was very valuable. Molly purchased it for $5, and later resold it for $25,000.

STEWART V. WRIGHT

147 Fed. 321 (8th Cir.1906).

HOOK, CIRCUIT JUDGE.

[For] some years there existed in Webb City, Mo., an organization styled an athletic club, the ostensible purpose of which was the promotion of athletic sports and pastimes. It was really an organized band of swindlers, some of whom masqueraded as wealthy miners, and so notorious did they become that they were commonly known in the community as the "Buckfoot gang," and their continued operations became an intolerable public scandal. The only branch of their operations with which we are concerned is the fake foot racing, so called. Their plan was to entice men of means to Webb City, and deprive them of their money by various pretexts and devices in connection with foot races, the result of which was always secretly prearranged. Complaints and protests from the victims were sometimes met by threats, with a show of force. Their operations covered a wide territory, extending from Iowa to Texas, and they had a regular staff of decoys in the field. The victims were selected with great care, and various stories were told to induce them to go to Webb City. Their vanity and sympathy were sometimes played upon, and always their cupidity and desire for ill-gotten gain. Some of them were falsely assured at the outset that they were not expected to hazard their own money upon the races, but were told that it would be well for them to take along letters of credit or drafts, to impress the others at Webb City with their responsibility and financial standing. Sometimes the scheme outlined to the intended victims was that they assist in doing an act of justice to a foot racer of great merit who had been unfairly treated in the past, and who intended to match himself with one backed by the club, whom he could easily defeat. Sometimes the victim was induced to bet upon what he was led to believe was a certain and assured result of a foot race. In other instances he was to be a stakeholder, and in still others, as in the case at bar, he was, upon a promise of a percentage of the winnings, to handle and bet the money secretly furnished him by Boatright, who was to act as stakeholder, and pretended that he did not wish it known that he was doing the betting. But, however the scheme varied in its details, the ultimate purpose always in view was to beguile the victim to bring money or to arrange that drafts be honored by his home bank; to get actual possession of his money by some pretext or another when at Webb City, and in doing so to place him in such a position that to complain or make trouble for them he would have to admit his own moral obliquity. They seemed to be vaguely aware of the maxim "in pari delicto," and prepared to use it as a shield of defense. To induce a victim to bring letters of credit or drafts, or to arrange for the honoring of drafts by his home bank, it was represented that the advent of a stranger upon the scene, possessed, apparently, of considerable means, was essential to the consummation of the scheme. By slow, cautious, and progressive approach, and with the wiles employed by confidence men, they generally succeeded in securing the trust of the victim, and he was induced to go to Webb City with one or more of the decoys. In some instances, as in the case at bar, they were met outside the city by Boatright, who would hand the victim several thousand dollars in currency to wager upon a race, the result of which was alleged to be not in doubt. One of the numerous conspirators would then accompany the victim to the defendant bank to see that the money was safely deposited there, and it would be suggested to him that he exhibit to the bank officials, the Stewarts, proof of his own financial resources. He would then be conducted or directed across the street to a saloon, where the subject of foot racing would be casually mentioned, and where he would be introduced to Boatright as though they had met for the first time. The members of the band would quickly gather, and they would then adjourn to a room above the saloon, represented to be the headquarters of the club. A foot race would be arranged, the betting would grow fast and furious, and large sums of money would apparently be wagered. The victim would bet the money which had been given him by Boatright, and the latter would from time to time secretly pass him sums taken from the stakes or money which had already been wagered, and the victim would in turn wager them upon the result of the proposed race. Then someone with a quarrelsome and truculent manner would claim that he had made a bet which had not been recorded, and would demand a count of the money in the hands of Boatright in order to prove his assertion. Boatright, who is said to have been a consummate actor, would appear to be in great distress, and in fear of the vengeance of the others should they discover that he had abstracted money from the stakes and handed it to the stranger to be wagered. The victim would then be induced by Boatright's pleading to make drafts upon his own bank, which would be cashed at the defendant bank, and the money would be placed, as he supposed temporarily, in the hands of Boatright, to relieve the latter from his embarrassment. When this was done the disturbance would cease, and, if there was no chance to secure more money from the victim, the betting would be closed, the money would be quickly placed in a satchel, and deposited in a place safe from the reach of the victim—sometimes in the defendant bank. The crowd would then adjourn to the place where the pretended foot race was to be run, and the man who the victim thought would win the race would fall down or otherwise fail in his pretended endeavor. It would then be claimed that the victim had wagered his money on the race, and if he evinced a disposition to make trouble revolvers would be drawn, and he would be cowed into submission. This was but one of the various methods employed to rob the victims of their money. The details of the scheme were frequently changed to suit the exigencies of the particular case, but the result was always the same. No stranger ever won anything, and none ever escaped without being defrauded. In some cases their money was given up under circumstances almost amounting to duress. We need not further particularize the facts in Wright's case, except to say that, while protesting that he was being robbed and demanding the return of his money, he was nevertheless induced to hold one end of the string at the pretended foot race.

[After Wright lost $5,100 on a race, he sued for restitution. Defendants claimed] that Wright should be denied relief because of the maxim "*In pari delicto potior est conditio defendentis.*" It was an essential part of the scheme to defraud that the victim should be led on by degrees to place himself in such a position that he would be prevented from having recourse to the courts. And this defense, so contrived in advance, is now produced for recognition, and it is said that, the plaintiff being equally culpable with the conspirators, a court of justice should therefore leave him where it finds him. It must be admitted that when Wright left his home for Webb City he thought he was going to participate in an unlawful scheme to defraud others. But, after all, it amounted to nothing more than a mere belief on his part. That he was betting upon a foot race at Webb City was but a fragment of his imagination. In reality there was no betting and no foot race, and it was not intended that there should be. It was all a pretense and a sham. He was merely a puppet, who was acting the will of the conspirators to his own undoing. The real design behind the scenes was one in which Wright did not participate except as the victim. If he was particeps criminis, it was to an offense against himself. Boatright and his associates sought Wright in his home, awakened in him a desire for wrongful gain that might otherwise have remained dormant, inspired in his mind an unfounded idea that he was going to secure it, and then by fraud and false pretenses deprived him of his money. We are unable to agree with counsel that the victim was in equal wrong with those who despoiled him merely because, at their instance, and as a result of their wiles, he entertained a purpose which it was never intended he should consummate. To hold otherwise would be to accord too much weight to the unsubstantial, and to enable those whose active occupation was swindling to successfully avail themselves of the false position in which, as part of their predetermined scheme, they succeeded in placing others they intended to defraud. Courts of justice should not thus reward criminal ingenuity. This is not a case in which, two persons having conspired to rob an innocent third, one of the two robs the other. The pretended miners, who were members of the counterfeit athletic club, and against whose wealth Boatright falsely assumed to direct his designs, were in fact his criminal accomplices. They were confidence men, not miners. They, as well as the defendants, played their part in the scheme to defraud, the whole machinery of which was employed, not against themselves, but against their victim.

We are also of the opinion that, viewing the conduct of Wright in its most reprehensible light, nevertheless the interest and welfare of the public would be better subserved by causing the loss to fall upon those who aided and assisted in criminal practices followed as an occupation than by the punishment of the individual victim. It would be doubtful wisdom to extend encouragement to organizations of confidence men, who prey upon the public, by allowing them the use of the rule "in pari delicto" as a shield of defense, when a part of the scheme they employ is to place those they seek and then defraud in the position they rely on.

[The] judgment of the Circuit Court is affirmed.

SANBORN, CIRCUIT JUDGE (dissenting).

The plaintiff agreed with Boatright that for 20 per cent of their winnings he would wager Boatright's money on a fake foot race, which Boatright agreed to make certain to result in their favor, so that they could thereby defraud the miners who bet against them out of their money. The plaintiff wagered large sums of money which he knew Boatright fraudulently furnished to him from the stakes and some of his own money in the performance of this corrupt agreement. Boatright broke his contract, and fixed the race against him. The plaintiff made and performed his part of his illegal contract to defraud others. He participated in the betting for this purpose. His intent and his acts were no less criminal and fatal to his case because they proved abortive.

The result of the opinion of the majority is that the plaintiff may recover because the gambling was fraudulent, because while the plaintiff was performing his agreement to cheat others by the fraudulent device of inducing them to bet upon the fake foot race they were engaged in a like endeavor to defraud him by the same device; an endeavor in which they succeeded while he failed. It is that one who is defrauded in gaming while he is engaged in an endeavor to defraud others thereby may recover the losses he sustains. The argument is that the plaintiff was induced by fraud to make his corrupt agreement, and to perform his part of it by betting upon a fraudulent race, and that he was not gaming because the result was certain. But the same argument holds good in every case of foul play, because in every such case the losing gambler is induced to bet upon a sure thing by the fraudulent representation that the play will be fair. If this argument be sound, and if the conclusion in this case illustrates the true rule, every gambler may recover in the courts the losses he sustains upon fixed races, marked cards, or foul plays upon the ground that in such cases there is no uncertainty in the result, while in cases in which the races and plays are fair he is remediless; and henceforth the courts must, as Judge Sherwood said in *Kitchen v.*

Greenabaum, 61 Mo. 115, "sit as the arbiters of the gaming table and the umpires of the prize ring," for they must hear the evidence upon and determine the issue in every losing gambler's case, whether the race or play was foul or fair, and give judgment for or against him accordingly. A rule and practice of this nature runs counter to my views of the law, to those of more eminent judges who have preceded me, and to the established rule that no cause of action lies for fraud which induces, or damage which results from, a contract or transaction which involves the moral turpitude of the plaintiff, or his violation of a general law of public policy.

NOTES

1. *Abbe v. Marr*, 14 Cal. 210, 212 (1859), a case discussed in *Stewart*, involved essentially similar facts:

> [The] members of a gang swindlers, by false representations and promises that they had arranged to fix a horse race so that the plaintiffs' horse would surely win, induced them to bet their horses, cows, wood, and money on this race, and then they so fixed the race that the plaintiffs lost. They brought an action directly against the members of the gang to recover back their property.

In *Abbe*, the court refused to hear the case:

> No court of justice can listen to such a case. When the plaintiff asserts his own turpitude in this way he sends his case out of court. If in attempting, by way of reprisal or otherwise, to swindle another becomes the victim of his own arts, it may become a question in morals or in honor which party is more culpable. Courts of law entertain no discussion on the subject, but terminate the controversy by shutting their doors in the face of the intruder.

Is *Abbe's* holding preferable to *Stewart's*? Is *Stewart's* holding—that defendants are more culpable than plaintiff—defensible? Is it appropriate for a "court of conscience" to consider the relative culpability of two parties, both of whom were trying to cheat the other?

2. a. How far is the undue influence of one over the other relevant?

b. The *Restatement (Third) Restitution and Unjust Enrichment* § 32 deals with illegality.

> A person who renders performance under an agreement that is illegal or otherwise unenforceable for reasons of public policy may obtain restitution from the recipient in accordance with the following rules:
>
> (1) Restitution will be allowed, whether or not necessary to prevent unjust enrichment, if restitution is required by the policy of the underlying prohibition.

(2) Restitution will also be allowed, as necessary to prevent unjust enrichment, if the allowance of restitution will not defeat or frustrate the policy of the underlying prohibition. There is no unjust enrichment if the claimant receives the counterperformance specified by the parties' unenforceable agreement.

(3) Restitution will be denied, notwithstanding the enrichment of the defendant at the claimant's expense, if a claim under subsection (2) is foreclosed by the claimant's inequitable conduct (§ 63).

The policies of the law in granting restitution to uphold interparty justice and the public policy to condemn the transaction are in play. Restitution is available to prevent unjust enrichment if the claim does not defeat the underlying transaction.

The following will resonate with you. An email invites you participate in a scheme to defraud the government of Nigeria. You agree to join the venture and send the $25,000 to the person at the other end of the email. The sum will be used to bribe Nigerian bank officials. Can you claim restitution against the emailer? See Adler v. Federal Republic of Nigeria, 219 F.3d 869 (9th Cir. 2000).

PROBLEM: THE CROPS

Norton, the owner of a farm, conveyed it to a bank and then leased the property back from the bank on a year lease. In October of the following year, just as the lease was about to expire, Norton filed for bankruptcy and listed the farm as an asset. Based on the bankruptcy proceeding, Norton refused to surrender or vacate the premises.

In March of the next year, the bankruptcy referee dismissed the lease from the bankruptcy proceedings. The bank immediately brought an action to evict Norton from the land. Norton appealed the referee's determination and obtained a TRO preventing the bank from evicting him. Norton then proceeded with spring planting investing large amounts of his own time plus $135.25 worth of seed.

In May, the appellate court affirmed the referee's ruling and vacated the TRO. The bank then succeeded in evicting Norton. It harvested and sold the crop. Norton sues the bank on an "unjust enrichment" theory to recover the value of the crops.

If you were hired to represent Norton, how would you argue that he is entitled to restitution? How might the bank respond? How should the court rule? *See Mehl v. Norton*, 201 Minn. 203, 275 N.W. 843 (1937).

ST. MARY'S MEDICAL CENTER, INC. V. UNITED FARM BUREAU FAMILY LIFE INSURANCE COMPANY

624 N.E.2d 939 (Ind. App. 1993).

NAJAM, JUDGE.

St. Mary's Medical Center, Inc., ("St. Mary's") appeals from [a] judgment granting restitution to United Farm Bureau Family Life Insurance Co. ("Farm Bureau") for a medical insurance payment that Farm Bureau made to St. Mary's under a mistake of fact. Elizabeth Munford assigned her Farm Bureau health insurance benefits to St. Mary's. After paying the claim, Farm Bureau discovered that Munford was no longer an insured and requested return of the payment. St. Mary's refused, Farm Bureau filed suit and the trial court granted restitution. . . .

[It] is generally recognized in the law of restitution that if one party pays money to another party under a mistake of fact that a contract or other obligation required such payment, the payor is entitled to restitution. *See Restatement of Restitution* § 18 (1937). Restitution in such cases is grounded in the equitable principle that one who has paid money to another who is not entitled to have it should not suffer unconscionable loss nor unjustly enrich the other. *See id.* at § 1. Unjust enrichment is typically regarded as a prerequisite to restitution. *Id.; National Benefit Administrators v. MMHRC* (S.D.Miss.1990), 748 F.Supp. 459, 465.

In a number of cases applying these general principles, an insurer has sought restitution for payment made under a mistake of fact that the terms of a health or hospitalization insurance contract required such payment. The general rule in such cases is that the insurer is entitled to restitution from the payee, even though the insurer's mistake was due to its own lack of care. However, the rule has been subject to limitation and exception under the following circumstances: where the payee has so changed his position that it would be inequitable to require him to make restitution; where at the time payment was made, there was some doubt as to the existence of the fact from which the obligation of the insurer arose; and where the payee is an innocent third party creditor of the insured who neither had notice of the insurer's mistake nor made any misrepresentations to induce the payment. *Monroe Financial Corp. v. DiSilvestro* (1988), Ind.App., 529 N.E.2d 379, 384, *trans. denied; Barker v. Federated Life Ins. Co.* (1965), 111 Ga.App. 171, 173, 141 S.E.2d 206, 207.

[The] innocent third party creditor exception [derives] from the fact that there has been no unjust enrichment of the innocent third party creditor. *National Benefit Administrators,* 748 F.Supp. at 465. The creditor is not unjustly enriched because the creditor is actually owed the money it receives and has exchanged value for the right to receive the money. *Id.* On this theory, St. Mary's contends that it gave value to

Munford in the form of medical services, that it was entitled to receive payment for such services and, therefore, was not unjustly enriched. In addition, St. Mary's contends that it made no misrepresentations and acted in good faith without knowledge of Farm Bureau's mistake. Thus, St. Mary's asserts that it is an innocent third party creditor of Munford and should not be required to make restitution to Farm Bureau.

[The] decision in *Good Samaritan Hospital* was based on the rationale of Section 14(1) of the Restatement of Restitution, which provides that:

> "A creditor of another or one having a lien on another's property who has received from a third person any benefit in discharge of the debt or lien, is under no duty to make restitution therefor, although the discharge was given by mistake of the transferor as to his interests or duties, if the transferee made no misrepresentations and did not have notice of the transferor's mistake."

The court likened the hospital to a bona fide purchaser for value, stating that it was not required to show a change of position in reliance and to its detriment. *Id.* Thus, the court determined that the hospital did not have to fall within the change of position exception to avoid making restitution to the insurer.

Further, the court noted the health insurance industry's "widespread use of assignments of policy benefits to hospitals by patients," stating that:

> "To subject a hospital to possible refund liability if the insurer later discovers a mistaken overpayment, lasting until all such claims are barred by the statute of limitations, would be to place an undue burden of contingent liability on such institutions. [By] this ruling, we place the burden for determining the limits of policy liability squarely upon the only party (as between the insurer and the assignee hospital) in a position to know the policy provisions and its liability under that contract of insurance. Someone must suffer the loss, and as between plaintiff insurer and defendant hospital, the party making the mistake should bear that loss."

Id. at 495–96. . . .

Farm Bureau contends that if we adopt [the innocent third party] exception it will result in disparate treatment of insurance companies, place insurers under a substantial burden and exclude them from the protection of the doctrine of restitution. Farm Bureau also asserts that requiring the hospital to make restitution would not place an undue burden upon it. . . .

[St. Mary's] is an innocent third party creditor of Munford, as it was not unjustly enriched by Farm Bureau's mistake, had no notice of the mistake, and did not induce the mistake through misrepresentation. . . .

Reversed with instructions.

NOTE ON BENEFITS CONFERRED

The First Restatement used the "familiar epithets" of "volunteer" and "officious intermeddler" to define those circumstances in which a benefit conferred could be retained. The terms were not helpful. The problematic area is that of "voluntary" payment. If A pays money to B without coercion, mistake or request, A or a person for whom the payment is made cannot claim restitution. A contractor paying to remedy the shoddy work of a subcontractor should be able to recover the payment from the subcontractor in most cases. (§ 24 cmt. d). If payment is made voluntarily in the face of uncertainty as to the payor's obligation to pay to pay it is unrecoverable. An example is a settlement of a claim that always in uncertain. Those monies cannot be clawed back on latter clarification. This is not a mistake that invalidates the transfer. The general rule is stated in § 22 of the *Restatement (Third) of Restitution and Unjust Enrichment*.

> (1) A person who performs another's duty to a third person or to the public is entitled to restitution from the other as necessary to prevent unjust enrichment, if the circumstances justify the decision to intervene without request.
>
> (2) Unrequested intervention may be justified in the following circumstances:
>
> > (a) the claimant may be justified in paying another's money debt if there is no prejudice to the obligor in substituting a liability in restitution for the original obligation;
> >
> > (b) the claimant may be justified in performing another's duty to furnish necessaries to a third person, to avoid imminent harm to the interests of the third person; and
> >
> > (c) the claimant may be justified in performing another's duty to the public, if performance is urgently required for the protection of public health, safety, or general welfare.
>
> (3) There is no unjust enrichment and no claim in restitution by the rule of this section except insofar as the claimant's intervention has relieved the defendant of an otherwise enforceable obligation.

The case of Western Coach below illustrates the application of a payment made that will found a restitution claim.

PROBLEMS

1. *Restitution from the Insured.* In the prior case, assume that the insurance company decides to seek restitution from Munford, the insured on

whose behalf the payment was made. Even though the insurer cannot recover from St. Mary's Medical Center, can it recover from Munford?

2. *Mitigating Losses.* Two years after purchasing a mobile home from Western Coach Corporation (Western), Mr. & Mrs. Roscoe sold the home to Chambers who agreed to assume all responsibility on the loan (although the Roscoes remained liable to Western). Western repossessed the home after Chambers defaulted, and found that the home had been vandalized, stripped of its furnishings and otherwise damaged. After taking possession, Western towed the mobile home to its sales lot, where it repaired and refurbished the home in order to obtain a better price. After proper notice, Western sold the home at a public sale and the proceeds were applied to the balance owing on the purchase contract. Western then instituted this action against the Roscoes to recover the sums it claims to have expended to refurbish the home. *See Western Coach Corporation v. Roscoe*, 133 Ariz. 147, 154, 650 P.2d 449, 456 (In Banc, 1982) (holding that plaintiff had an interest in seeing that security for debt was preserved and was therefore not 'officious meddler' precluded from recovery of sums paid for . . . costs of repairing and refurbishing [the trailer] under theory of unjust enrichment).

3. *The Drifting Boat Rescue.* Suppose that an unmanned houseboat breaks loose from its mooring on the Ohio River near Louisville, Kentucky. If left to drift down river, it is likely that the boat will be destroyed (*e.g.*, by running into a bridge pier or crashing into the river locks). JAC Towing Co., which is in the business of providing river tug and salvage services, rescues the boat from certain destruction. Is JAC entitled to restitution from the boat's owner for the recovery operation?

4. *The Wheat Field.* Plaintiff Jackson owned a wheat stubble field in which defendant Bartholomew stored a stack of wheat. When he put the wheat in the field, defendant promised to remove it in time for plaintiff to prepare the ground for the fall crop. When the time for planting arrived, plaintiff sent a message to defendant requesting immediate removal of the wheat so that plaintiff could burn the field the next morning. Defendant was absent so the message was delivered to his family. Defendant's sons replied that they would remove the wheat by 10:00am the next morning.

By 10:00am, the wheat had not been removed. Plaintiff set fire to the stubble in a remote part of the field. The fire spread rapidly and threatened to burn the unmoved stack of wheat. In order to save the wheat, plaintiff decided to move it himself. Plaintiff sued defendant for the work and labor involved in its removal. Should plaintiff be allowed to recover? What arguments can be made on his behalf? How might defendant respond? *See Bartholomew v. Jackson*, 20 Johns. 28, 11 Am.Dec. 237 (N.Y.Sup.1822).

5. *The Elderly Woman and the Priest.* Martine Merl Payne accumulated approximately $1 million through inheritance, investment and work. Few people were aware of her wealth since she lived like a pauper. Late in life, Payne became enamored with a young Catholic priest, the pastor of her neighborhood church. She bought him a car and a pickup truck, paid

$1,000 for his trip to Rome, and gave him furniture and diamonds that had been in the family for four generations. After her death, Payne's family discovered that her will left her entire estate to the local Catholic diocese.

Suppose that you are a lawyer, and you have been approached by Payne's relatives who want to challenge the will. They believe that the young priest unduly influenced Payne. You have decided to investigate the case in contemplation of suit. What facts would be helpful to the relative's case? How would you investigate the facts?

B. DEFENSES TO RESTITUTION

Defenses may be stated explicitly. Under the *Restatement (Third) of Restitution and Unjust Enrichment* they are set forth in Chapter 8. They include defenses commonly found in equity, *e.g.* unclean hands and bona fide purchasers. The most developed defense in restitution is change of position § 65. If receipt of a benefit has led a recipient without notice to change position in such manner that an obligation to make restitution of the original benefit would be inequitable to the recipient, the recipient's liability in restitution is to that extent reduced.

The defendant may submit that the benefit has led a recipient to change her position making restitution inequitable. The recipient must have been without notice. The allocation of loss turns on the comparison of fault of the recipient and claimant. Where the recipient has innocently changed his position even though the claimant too is innocent, the equities shift to deny restitution. Usually the defense is found in mistaken payments. An agent paying over innocently may claim benefit of the defense. The change of position must cause a loss as a consequence of obtaining the benefit. The general hardship suffered by the recipient/defendant does not count. Edelman and Bant state in *Unjust Enrichment in Australia* (Melbourne: Oxford UP, 2006) at 322 that one operative rationale for the defence of change of position is the legitimate interest in the security of the receipt. This can be derived from the Australian case of David *Securities Pty Ltd v Commonwealth Bank of Australia* [1992] HCA 175 CLR 353 at 385. Few judicial expositions of the need for certainty in payment systems could have been better expressed than by Andrews J writing for a unanimous New York Court of Appeals in 1879 in *Stephens v Board of Education of Brooklyn*: 79 NY 183 at 186–188.

"It is absolutely necessary for practical business transactions that the payee of money in due course of business shall not be put upon inquiry at his peril as to the title of the payor. Money has no ear-mark. The purchaser of a chattel or a chose in action may, by inquiry, in most cases, ascertain the right of the person from whom he takes the title. But it is generally impracticable to trace the source from which the possessor of money has derived it. It would introduce great confusion into commercial dealings if the creditor who receives money in payment of a debt is subject to the risk of accounting therefor to a third person who may be able to show that the debtor obtained it from him by felony or fraud. The law wisely, from considerations of public policy and convenience, and to give security and certainty to business transactions, adjudges that the possession of money vests the title in the holder as to third persons dealing with him and receiving it in due course of business and in good faith upon a valid consideration. If the consideration is good as between the parties, it is good as to all the world."

C. MEASURING THE ENRICHMENT

FRAMBACH V. DUNIHUE

419 So.2d 1115 (Fla.App.1982).

FRAND D. UPCHURCH, JR., JUDGE.

[The] history of this case is an amazing account of human relationships. Why people who for many years had demonstrated an incredible ability to solve their disputes would ultimately end up in litigation is mystifying.

Dunihue was a widower with seven children to raise ranging in age from three to eleven. The Frambachs lived nearby with their four children. Contact between the parties started when Mrs. Frambach, a devoted churchwoman, asked if she could take the Dunihue children to church. She later became a babysitter and took care of the Dunihue children sometimes at their home and sometimes at hers for which she was paid $25 per week.

This arrangement continued for a few months. In September, 1960, the Frambachs and the Dunihues waited out a hurricane in the Frambachs' home. The Frambachs' house was small (a bedroom, living room and kitchen, 600 square feet in all) and had no inside plumbing. As fate would have it, the relationships which developed as the storm howled proved so interesting and the two families so congenial that the Frambachs and Dunihues decided to see if the two families could live together.

Dunihue set out to enlarge the house. A bedroom and bath were added and various improvements made. As the years passed, Mrs. Frambach had another child and for a time, until the Dunihue children began to move out, fifteen people (three adults and twelve children) lived in the house. Mrs. Frambach ran the household, did the cooking, and saw that the children cleaned, helped with the washing, and did such chores as were required and within their capabilities.

Both Dunihue and the Frambachs were employed. Dunihue on several occasions obtained employment for Mr. Frambach and their earnings were not substantially different, although Dunihue had the larger income. The Frambachs and Dunihue each had a bank account into which they deposited their respective earnings. Mrs. Frambach wrote checks on both accounts and decided in large measure which account would be used to pay a particular bill. Dunihue's characterization of the arrangement was probably the most appropriate, that it was just one family and whatever money was available was used wherever it was most needed. Very often the three shopped together for clothes, furniture, and automobiles.

Improvements in the home continued to be made. Dunihue's contributions to these improvements undoubtedly were the most valuable although everyone assisted. At the time of this litigation, the value of the home had appreciated to approximately $65,000. The court received considerable testimony of Dunihue's contributions to the improvements, but very little evidence was adduced as to the value of the services received by Dunihue and his family.

This arrangement lasted for nineteen years until the last of the Dunihue children were grown and gone. The relationship was suddenly terminated when Mrs. Frambach called Dunihue at work and told him to come get his things and get out. He was given thirty minutes to comply. The reason for the sudden end to the friendship was not clear.

After being ejected from the Frambachs' home, Dunihue brought suit to impose an equitable lien on the property. Dunihue claimed that the Frambachs had promised him a place to live for the rest of his life in exchange for his work. He further alleged that he had relied on this promise and that the Frambachs will be unjustly enriched at his expense if he is not compensated for his work. The Frambachs denied that they had made any such promise to Dunihue claiming that without the improvements it would have been impossible to house that many people.

The trial court determined that the two families had operated as a single family. While emphasizing that he was not making such an inference, the judge opined that the association of the parties was almost as close as though there had been a single wife and two husbands. The court then found that the pooling of assets and commingling of everything into a common pot was to assure Dunihue that he would have a home as long as he lived and that it would award Dunihue an equitable lien in the home. Regarding the amount of the lien, the court stated the following: They did start out with a thousand-dollar equity. But in effect because of the way they treated everything through the years, they really are just as though this was a divorce. And we are dividing up the property between a wife that had two husbands, so to speak. That's why I think the only fair thing to do is to make them tenants in common right down the middle. So that's my judgment.

As a general rule, a court of equity may give restitution to a plaintiff and prevent the unjust enrichment of a defendant by imposing a constructive trust or by imposing an equitable lien upon the property in favor of the plaintiff. However, where the plaintiff makes improvements upon the land of another under circumstances which entitle him to restitution, he is entitled only to an equitable lien upon the land and he cannot charge the owner of the land as constructive trustee and compel the owner to transfer the land to him. RESTATEMENT OF RESTITUTION § 161, Comment a. Neither a constructive trust nor a resulting trust arises in favor of a person who pays no part of the purchase price even though he pays for improvements on the property. 5 SCOTT, THE LAW OF TRUSTS, §§ 455.7,472 (3d ed. 1967). The person does not become, in whole or in part, a beneficial owner of the property although he may be entitled to reimbursement.

In the present case, the court, in effect, determined that the Frambachs held an undivided one-half interest in the property in trust for Dunihue. However, there was no evidence of a promise or agreement to deed a portion of the Frambachs' property to Dunihue in return for the improvements. Nor has Dunihue alleged that he actually paid a part of the purchase price. In these circumstances, Dunihue was not entitled to have a constructive trust imposed on the property. We therefore reverse the award to Dunihue of a tenancy in common and remand the cause for further consideration.

Upon remand, the trial court should determine the value of the respective contributions of Dunihue and the Frambachs. This can be accomplished by calculating the fair market value of the improvements attributable to Dunihue and the fair market value of the services rendered by the Frambachs to him during the nineteen years the parties lived together. In the alternative, the court could determine the cost to Dunihue for his labor, services and material in making the improvements as compared to the cost to the Frambachs of providing services to Dunihue. We suspect that, under either measure, the contributions of the parties will be equal. However, if the court finds that Dunihue's contributions exceed the value of the benefits received by him from the Frambachs, an equitable lien in this amount should be imposed to prevent the unjust enrichment of the Frambachs.

REVERSED and REMANDED.

PROBLEMS

1. *Restitution and the Insurance Proceeds.* Reichert owned the Bakersfield Inn which was destroyed by fire. Reichert contracted with Herb Deets to remove debris from the property for the sum of $18,900. Deets performed his part of the bargain, but Reichert went bankrupt and was unable to pay.

Throughout the cleanup, Grace Harlow held a deed of trust on the property. After the bankruptcy, Harlow executed on the deed and took the property. Deets did not have a mechanics' lien on the property. Moreover, even if Deets had perfected a lien, it would have been discharged when Harlow foreclosed her deed of trust.

Deets sought restitution from Harlow for the value of the labor he expended in cleaning up the property. Deets claimed that Harlow benefited from the labor by receiving the property in improved condition. The facts show that Harlow filed a notice of default against the property a mere four days after Deets and Reichert signed their contract. Deets did not learn of the notice until much later.

Harlow argued that there was no direct relationship between she and Deets with regard to either the work performed on the property after the fire or in relation to the fire insurance policies, and that the contract for debris removal was between Deets and Reichert. Harlow did not induce Deets, directly or indirectly, to enter into the contract. Harlow claimed that he was unaware of Deets' work until after the job was finished.

What arguments might Deets use to establish an "unjust enrichment" claim? How might Harlow respond to these arguments? If there is "unjust enrichment," how should it be measured? *See Kossian v. American National Ins. Co.*, 254 Cal.App.2d 647, 62 Cal.Rptr. 225 (1967).

2. *More on the Insurance Proceeds.* Would you answer to the problem be different if you knew that Harlow maintained an insurance policy on the Inn? Following the fire, Harlow recovered on the policy. Part of the recovery was for the cleanup and removal of debris done by Deets.

If you would let Deets recover, how much should he recover? Suppose that Harlow submitted an insurance claim for $160,000, $18,000 of which was for cleanup and removal. The insurer rejected Harlow's claim, and ultimately compromised by paying $135,000, an unspecified part of which was supposed to cover debris clean up and removal?

PYEATTE V. PYEATTE

135 Ariz. 346, 661 P.2d 196 (1983).

CORCORAN, JUDGE.

This is an appeal by the husband from an award of $23,000 in favor of the wife as ordered in a decree of dissolution. . . . The husband, H. Charles Pyeatte (appellant), and the wife, Margrethe May Pyeatte (appellee), were married [in] 1972. At the time of the marriage both had received bachelors degrees. Appellee was coordinator of the surgical technical program at Pima College. Appellant was one of her students. In early 1974, the parties had discussions and reached an agreement concerning postgraduate education for both of them.

Appellee testified that they agreed she would put him through three years of law school without his having to work, and when he finished, he would put [her] through for [her] masters degree without [her] having to work. [There was no contingency expressed or implied that this would not be carried out or enforced in the event of a divorce.] Appellant attended law school in Tucson, Arizona, from 1974 until his graduation. He was admitted to the State Bar shortly thereafter.

During appellant's first two years of law school appellee supported herself and appellant on the salary she earned at Pima College. During the last year, appellee lost her job, whereupon savings were used to support the couple. Although each spouse contributed to the savings, a significant amount was furnished by appellee.

After appellant's admission to the Bar, the couple moved to Prescott, Arizona, where appellant was employed by a law firm. Both parties realized that appellant's salary would not be sufficient to support the marriage and pay for appellee's education for a masters degree simultaneously. Appellee then agreed to defer her plans for a year or two until her husband got started in his legal career. In the meantime, she obtained part-time employment as a teacher.

In April, 1978, appellant told appellee that he no longer wanted to be married to her.... At the time of [dissolution], there was little community property and no dispute as to division of any community or separate property. Spousal maintenance was neither sought by nor granted to appellee....

Although the terms and requirements of an enforceable contract need not be stated in minute detail, it is fundamental that, in order to be binding, an agreement must be definite and certain so that the liability of the parties may be exactly fixed.... [I]t is readily apparent that a sufficient mutual understanding regarding critical provisions of their agreement did not exist. For example, no agreement was made regarding the time when appellee would attend graduate school[, or] the cost of the program to which appellee would be entitled under this agreement.... [Nevertheless, appelllee] argues that appellant's education, which she subsidized and which he obtained through the exhaustion of community assets constitutes a benefit for which he must, in equity, make restitution....

Restitution is available to a party to an agreement where he performs services for the other believing that there is a binding contract.... *Restatement of Restitution* § 40(b) at 155 (1937). In order to be granted restitution, appellee must demonstrate that appellant received a benefit, that by receipt of that benefit he was unjustly enriched at her expense, and that the circumstances were such that in good conscience appellant should make compensation. *John A. Artukovich & Sons v.*

Reliance Truck Co., 126 Ariz. 246, 614 P.2d 327 (1980); *Restatement of Restitution* § 1 at 13 (1937). . . .

A benefit may be any type of advantage, including that which saves the recipient from any loss or expense. *See Artukovich, supra.* Appellee's support of appellant during his period of schooling clearly constituted a benefit to appellant. Absent appellee's support, appellant may not have attended law school, may have been forced to prolong his education because of intermittent periods of gainful employment, or may have gone deeply into debt. Relieved of the necessity of supporting himself, he was able to devote full time and attention to his education.

The mere fact that one party confers a benefit on another, however, is not of itself sufficient to require the other to make restitution. Retention of the benefit must be unjust.

Historically, restitution for the value of services rendered has been available upon either an implied-in-fact contract or upon quasi-contractual grounds. 1 Williston, *Contracts* § 3 and 3A at 10–15 (3d ed. 1957). [A] quasi-contract is not a contract at all, but a duty imposed in equity upon a party to repay another to prevent his own unjust enrichment. The intention of the parties to bind themselves contractually in such a case is irrelevant. 1 Williston, *Contracts* § 3A at 12–15 (3d ed. 1957). . . . While a quasi-contractual obligation may be imposed without regard to the intent of the parties, such an obligation will be imposed only if the circumstances are such that it would be unjust to allow retention of the benefit without compensating the one who conferred it. *See* Williston, *supra.* One circumstance under which a duty to compensate will be imposed is when there was an expectation of payment or compensation for services at the time they were rendered. *Osborn v. Boeing Airplane Co.*, 309 F.2d at 102.

Although we found that the spousal agreement failed to meet the requirements of an enforceable contract, the agreement still has importance in considering appellee's claim for unjust enrichment because it both evidences appellee's expectation of compensation and the circumstances which make it unjust to allow appellant to retain the benefits of her extraordinary efforts.

We next address the question of whether restitution on the basis of unjust enrichment is appropriate in the context of the marital relationship. . . . Where both spouses perform the usual and incidental activities of the marital relationship, upon dissolution there can be no restitution for performance of these activities. Where, however, the facts demonstrate an agreement between the spouses and an extraordinary or unilateral effort by one spouse which inures solely to the benefit of the other by the time of dissolution, the remedy of restitution is appropriate. . . .

A number of jurisdictions have addressed the issue of restitution in the context of the marital relationship. The cases which have dealt with the issue involve two factual patterns: (1) The first group consists of those cases in which the couples had accumulated substantial marital assets over a period of time from which assets the wife received large awards of property, maintenance and child support. The courts have refused to apply the theory of restitution on the basis of unjust enrichment in each of these cases. (2) The second group consists of those cases in which the parties are divorced soon after the student spouse receives his degree or license and there is little or no marital property from which to order any award to the working spouse.

In the first group the courts have consistently refused to find a property interest in the husband's education, degree, license or earning capacity or to order restitution in favor of the wife.... Because the property award itself is largely the product of the education, degree, license or earning capacity in which the wife sought a monetary interest, the courts hold that the wife realized her investment in the husband's education by having received the benefits of his increased earning capacity during marriage and by receipt of an award of property upon its dissolution. *Lucas v. Lucas*, 27 Cal.3d 808, 166 Cal.Rptr. 853, 614 P.2d 285 (1980)....

The second group presents the more difficult problem of the working spouse claiming entitlement to an equitable recovery where there is little or no marital property to divide and therefore the conventional remedies of property division or spousal maintenance are unavailable. [In this context,] restitution to the working spouse is appropriate to prevent the unjust enrichment of the student spouse. *See Inman v. Inman,* 578 S.W.2d 266 (Ky.1979); *DeLa Rosa v. DeLa Rosa,* 309 N.W.2d 755 (Minn.1981).... The record shows that the appellee conferred benefits on appellant-financial subsidization of appellant's legal education-with the agreement and expectation that she would be compensated therefor by his reciprocal efforts after his graduation and admission to the Bar. Appellant has left the marriage with the only valuable asset acquired during the marriage-his legal education and qualification to practice law. It would be inequitable to allow appellant to retain this benefit without making restitution to appellee....

The award to appellee should be limited to the financial contribution by appellee for appellant's living expenses and direct educational expenses. *See DeLa Rosa v. DeLa Rosa,* 309 N.W.2d 755.... Under the agreement between the parties, the anticipated benefit to appellee may involve a monetary benefit in a lesser amount than the benefit conferred by appellee on appellant. In that event, the award to appellee should be limited to the amount of the anticipated benefit to appellee. Appellee should not recover more than the benefit of her bargain. *Restatement of Restitution,* § 107, Comment b, at 449 (1937). . . .

The relief granted to appellee is equitable in nature. . . . The fact that this case presents a novel resolution of a difficult issue, without precedent, will not prevent this court from ordering relief in an amount and manner appropriate to the circumstances. . . . It is the distinguishing feature of equity jurisdiction that it will apply settled rules to unusual conditions and mold its decrees so as to do equity between the parties. . . . Since the benefit bestowed upon appellant by appellee was periodic in nature and dependent on her income, we find no abuse of the equity power of the court in awarding appellee periodic payments, especially where she can use them periodically to pursue her own education. [W]e do not mean to promulgate a rule that will uniformly govern all awards in subsequent cases of that nature. Each will, by virtue of the equitable nature of the claim, require relief tailored to the facts and circumstances of the individuals. *DeLa Rosa v. DeLa Rosa,* 309 N.W.2d at 759, n. 11. . . .

The portion of the judgment in the amount of $23,000 is reversed and remanded for proceedings in accordance with this opinion.

PROBLEMS

1. *More on Spousal Support.* Contrast the holding in *Pyeatte* with the holding in *Kuder v. Schroeder*, 110 N.C.App. 355, 430 S.E.2d 271 (1993). In that case, the husband agreed to allow the wife to be a stay-at-home wife and mother in exchange for her agreement to pay for his education. As in *Pyeatte*, after the husband obtained his law degree, he decided to divorce his wife. In rejecting the wife's claim, the court stated that: "[W]e are sympathetic to [the wife's] apparent dilemma, and certainly would not condone defendant's apparent knavish ingratitude, but we do not find support in the law of this State for such a claim and therefore hold that the trial court correctly dismissed plaintiff's claims. . . . Under the law of this State, there is a personal duty of each spouse to support the other, a duty arising from the marital relationship, and carrying with it the corollary right to support from the other spouse. So long as the coverture endures, this duty of support may not be abrogated or modified by the agreement of the parties to a marriage." Which decision is preferable—*Pyeatte* or *Kuder*?

2. *One Final Spousal Support Scenario.* A father and his son operated a bar for many years. Although they started out as co-owners of the business, the father later transferred his interest in the business to his son in exchange for a guarantee of support during his lifetime, but with the agreement that the father would assist the son in operating the business. The father's wife (the son's stepmother) did not know about the transfer until after her husband's death. Nearly every day for six years until the father's death, the wife (plaintiff) accompanied her husband to the place of business around eight or nine in the morning, remained there until about one in the afternoon, and returned later in the evening. Plaintiff prepared breakfast for her

husband after arriving at the tavern and also prepared certain other meals at the tavern for him and for defendant as well. She at times also performed such services as cleaning, and scrubbing, tending bar, and furnishing some meals for guests or patrons. Plaintiff received no pay from defendant for these services. However, when she learned that the son owned all of the business, she sought restitution. Is plaintiff entitled to restitution for the services performed? *See Dusenka v. Dusenka*, 221 Minn. 234, 21 N.W.2d 528 (1946).

BRON V. WEINTRAUB

42 N.J. 87, 199 A.2d 625 (1964).

WEINTRAUB, C.J.

In 1935 the Township of Woodbridge sold certain vacant lands for unpaid taxes and itself was the buyer at the sale. In 1940 it foreclosed the tax sale certificates in the former Court of Chancery. That proceeding ran against Danwil Developers, Inc., as owner. However, in 1929 that company had conveyed to El–Ka Holding Co., Inc., which in turn conveyed to Harry Weintraub in 1931. Weintraub apparently was the secretary of both corporations. He died intestate in 1933, survived by two sisters who lived in California. The searcher did not pick up the conveyances just mentioned and hence the 1940 foreclosure suit ran only against Danwil Developers, Inc., as we have said.

In 1952 Woodbridge conveyed the lands to a developer who erected homes and sold them for $10,000 to $11,000 each. Ten such parcels are here involved. In 1959 one of the homes was resold and a search in that connection revealed the failure to bar the Weintraub interests. The township was asked to foreclose those interests, and it started a suit to that end. N.J.S.A. 54:5–86.1 et seq. Judgment was entered fixing November 13, 1959 as the date by which the unknown heirs of Weintraub had to redeem or be barred. At the eleventh hour Hudson Trading Corporation and Frank Altomare redeemed on the basis of deeds obtained from the Weintraub heirs (the deeds ran to Hudson which in turn conveyed a quarter interest to Altomare).

The present actions ensued, the householders seeking to quiet title and Hudson and Altomare demanding possession and mesne profits. Hudson and Altomare conceded the householders were equitably entitled to remove the improvements or to buy the land at its value unaffected by the improvements. The trial court entered a judgment under which the householders would have to pay for the land the sum of $19,551.11, found to be its value as of the time of the deeds to Hudson and Altomare, plus mesne profits of $2,856.91. Hudson had paid the Weintraub heirs but $400. The Appellate Division affirmed and we granted certification.

The householders urge that Hudson and Altomare be declared constructive trustees and be required to convey title upon payment of the $400 they gave the Weintraub heirs. * * *

We need consider only the [proposition] that Hudson and Altomare should receive no more than what they paid the Weintraub heirs, since we are satisfied the householders are entitled to prevail upon it.

Here ten homes were purchased in the Bona fide belief that title was good. The defect in the 1940 foreclosure was discovered in 1959, some 28 years after the original owners of the vacant land had last paid a penny of taxes. The municipality started a second suit to perfect the title, and in that action it was necessary to advertise as against the Weintraub heirs. In that way Hudson learned of an opportunity to make some money out of the predicament of these householders.

Hudson located Weintraub's sisters in California. Exactly when we do not know but on November 7, only six days before the date fixed for redemption, one Herbert Harvey wrote to them. His letter opened with a statement that it related to "lots in Middlesex County, New Jersey, in which, according to the record, the late Harry Weintraub had an interest." That the interest was ownership in fee was not disclosed. The letter correctly said the property was sold for taxes in 1935 and a foreclosure action was brought in 1940, but added only that the foreclosure action was deemed "possibly defective." It continued that "you might claim an interest" and we are writing to inquire whether you "will furnish a voluntary release of your possible claim" for a "courtesy consideration" of $50 "for the release." It adds that "The required instrument, in the form of a quit claim deed, is enclosed." We interpolate that trial counsel for Hudson and Altomare placed on the record: "It is Mr. Harvey's practice to take quit-claim deeds. I say that all the deeds he gets, 90 percent are quit-claim deeds. He knows by law a quit-claim deed is just as good as any other kind of deed." Mr. Harvey was well informed in that regard, but we assume, as no doubt he did, that the recipient of his letter would likely think only of some claim to be released to the existing holder of title in fee. Indeed the letter said the deed "will have the effect of releasing any claim which you have or may have in the land therein described." Finally the letter noted that "this instrument will serve its purpose only if it reaches us without delay—actually no later than November 13, which seems practically return mail." Appreciation was promised for "your cooperation" and the letter closed "With thanks for your courtesy in the matter."

This letter was palpably deceptive. It was deceptive as to the nature of the outstanding interest. It was deceptive as to identity of the parties on whose behalf it was written. In the latter respect, if no more appeared, it would permit an inference that Harvey led the Weintraub heirs to believe he was acting for the householders, and upon such a finding a constructive trust could be imposed in their favor. The cause, however, was not tried on the theory of fraud, and since we are told there were further communications with the Weintraub heirs not spread on the record, we should not decide the case on that basis. Nonetheless we refer to the fraudulent nature of this communication as a sample of the kind of thing to be expected if we hold that strangers may exploit these situations.

[We] are dealing with tax titles. Contrary to early hostility to such titles, the policy today is to support them, thereby to aid municipalities in raising revenue.

Everybody knows that taxes must be paid. True, there may be instances in which the individual concerned is unaware of his property interest, but such cases are rare. Usually the owner omits to pay knowing the end result will be a tax sale. It is therefore understandable that the Legislature found it fair to bar the right to redeem by a strict foreclosure, *i.e.*, by a judgment that payment be made by a fixed date, in default of which the right to redeem shall end, rather than by a sale as in the case of the foreclosure of a mortgage. The point we stress is that, whereas with respect to the initial sale for taxes, the statute intends to attract third parties to the opportunity to acquire the property and provides for public notice to that end, there is no like policy to invite the public to participate with respect to the foreclosure of the right to redeem.

Hence the foreclosure process concerns only the holder of the tax sale certificate and the holders of existing interests in the property. Hudson learned of this situation, not because it was the policy of the law to advertise to solicit its interest, but because of the fortuitous circumstance that the foreclosing municipality had not located the Weintraub heirs. If they had been found, they could have been served without the need for publication. In short, our rules of court called for this public notice solely to reach the holders of existing interests, but Hudson read a communication intended for another and sought to turn that information to its own gain, thereby depriving the householders of a chance to work out their misfortunes with the holders of the outstanding interests upon a basis presumably no more onerous that the basis upon which Hudson acquired those interests.

In attacking the legality of Hudson's activity, the householders appeal to public policy, the ultimate source of justice. Public policy, the ultimate source of justice. Public policy has been described but never quite defined. [In] substance, it may be said to be the community common sense and common conscience, extended and applied throughout the state to matters of public morals, public health, public safety, public welfare, and the like. It is that general and well-settled public opinion relating to man's plain, palpable duty to his fellow men, having due regard to all the circumstances of each particular relation and situation. Sometimes such public policy is declared by Constitution; sometimes by statute; sometimes by judicial decision. More often, however, it abides only in the customs and conventions of the people—in their clear consciousness and conviction of what is inherently just and right between and inherently just and right between man and man. * * *

[With] respect to the factual pattern before us, no one disputes the right of the holders of existing interests to convey them to third persons if they wish. What is challenged is the legality of the intrusion into the scene by third persons who seek only to further their own interests rather than the interests already on hand. [The] burden upon individuals situated as are the householders in this case is evident enough. These manifest hurts should not be tolerated unless it can be said that some other legitimate interest or advantage is served. We find none. We see no social value or contribution in the activities of Hudson. On the contrary, decent men must sense only revulsion in this traffic in the misfortunes of others.

[We] have no doubt the common conscience condemns the conduct of Hudson and Altomare as an undue interference with the rights of the householders. Hudson and Altomare having acquired the outstanding title under "circumstances which render it unconscientious for the holder of the legal title to retain and enjoy the beneficial interests, equity impresses a constructive trust on the property thus acquired in favor of the one who is truly and equitably entitled to the same." 4 POMEROY, EQUITY JURISPRUDENCE (5th ed. 1941) § 1053, p. 119. The householders are equitably entitled to the property upon the payment of the sum of $400 plus simple interest from the date of the payment to the Weintraub heirs.

The judgments are therefore reversed and the matters remanded to the trial court with directions to enter judgments in harmony with this opinion.

PROBLEMS

1. *More on the Stolen Steers.* Now, let's think a bit more about the stolen steer case presented at the beginning of the chapter. Since the bulls were stolen, no one doubts that Hill and Stewart were unjustly enriched. The more difficult question is how to measure the enrichment. How should it be measured?

2. *The Idea and the Soap Company.* Plaintiff alleged that she sent Proctor and Gamble Corp. (P & G) a written offer to sell a new kind of laundry soap. She alleged that this idea was in specific and concrete form and included a specific name for the product as well as advertising phrases and promotion suggestions. P & G advised her that her ideas were not original. On the contrary, those ideas had previously been considered and rejected by P & G, and rejected in favor of a different approach.

Plaintiff further alleged that on or before May 1, 1953, P & G utilized her ideas, including the name, formula and other suggestions. Plaintiff claimed that P & G's actions constituted an unlawful appropriation of her ideas in which she had a property right.

If plaintiff can prove her allegations, was Proctor & Gamble unjustly enriched? In what amount?

IACOMINI V. LIBERTY MUTUAL INSURANCE COMPANY

127 N.H. 73, 497 A.2d 854 (1985).

DOUGLAS, JUSTICE.

[On] August 10, 1983, the plaintiff, Richard Iacomini, d/b/a Motor Craft of Raymond, contracted with one Theodore Zadlo for the towing, storage, and repair of a 1977 Mercedes Benz 450–SL. Mr. Zadlo represented himself to be the owner of the car and presented the plaintiff with a New Hampshire registration certificate for the car bearing Zadlo's name. In fact, the car did not belong to Mr. Zadlo but had been stolen in 1981 from a car lot in New Jersey. The defendant, Liberty Mutual Insurance Company, had earlier fulfilled its policy obligations by reimbursing the owner of the stolen car $22,000. It thereby had gained title to the vehicle.

Extensive damage was done to the car after its theft, and Zadlo brought the car to Mr. Iacomini for the purpose of repairing this damage. The plaintiff kept the car at his garage, where he disassembled it in order to give a repair estimate. He apparently never fully reassembled it. Mr. Zadlo periodically returned to the plaintiff's garage to check the status of the repair work.

In October 1983, the Raymond Police Department notified the plaintiff that the Mercedes was a stolen car and also notified Liberty Mutual of the location of the car. Mr. Iacomini at that point moved the vehicle from the lot to the inside of his garage where it remained for the next several months. Liberty Mutual contacted the plaintiff soon after it learned of the vehicle's location to arrange its pick-up. The plaintiff refused to relinquish the car until he had been reimbursed for repair and storage fees.

On December 12, 1983, Liberty Mutual instituted a replevin [action]. [T]he Court (Korbey, J.) found that the plaintiff (defendant in that action) did not have a valid statutory lien since the vehicle was brought to the plaintiff by one other than the owner. The court then ordered Mr. Iacomini to make the vehicle available forthwith to Liberty Mutual with the proviso that Liberty Mutual retain the vehicle in its possession and ownership for a period of at least ninety days in order to allow Mr. Iacomini the opportunity to file an action against Liberty Mutual relating to repairs.

The plaintiff petitioned for an ex parte attachment on April 16, 1984, claiming approximately $10,000, most of which was for storage fees. On or about July 3, 1984, the same court entered judgment in Liberty Mutual's favor finding that "the plaintiff was not authorized or instructed by the legal or equitable owner of the automobile to perform any repair work on the vehicle." On either the day before, or the day of, the hearing, July 3, 1984, the plaintiff filed a Motion to Specify Claim to include an action for unjust enrichment. [T]he court denied the motion. It also denied the plaintiff's requests for findings that the value of the car had been enhanced by the plaintiff and that denial of the plaintiff's claim would result in unjust enrichment. This appeal followed.

The law generally recognizes three types of liens: statutory, common law, and equitable.

Although the facts of this case do not establish either a statutory or a common law lien [because such liens can only be created with the consent of the owner], the plaintiff may be entitled to restitution under principles of equity. An equitable lien may be imposed to prevent unjust enrichment in an owner whose property was improved, for the increased value of the property. "In the absence of a contractual agreement, a trial court may require an individual to make restitution for unjust enrichment if he has received a benefit which would be unconscionable to retain." *Petrie–Clemons v. Butterfield*, 441 A.2d 1167, 1171 (1982). The trial court must determine whether the facts and equities of a particular case warrant such a remedy.

[We] here note that "when a court assesses damages in an unjust enrichment case, the focus is not upon the cost to the plaintiff, but rather it is upon the value of what was actually received by the defendants." *R. Zoppo, Inc. v. City of Manchester*, 453 A.2d 1311, 1314 (N.H.1982). In this case, the damages would thus be the difference between the value of the vehicle before and after the plaintiff worked on it, regardless of its worth when stolen.

Reversed and remanded.

All concurred.

NOTES

1. *The Restatement.* Consider the Restatement of Restitution, Comment to § 1, at 13:

> *d.* Ordinarily the benefit to the one and the loss to the other are coextensive, and the result of the remedies given under the rules stated in the Restatement of this subject is to compel the one to surrender the benefit which he has received and thereby to make restitution to the other for the loss which he has suffered. * * *

2. *Remedial Measures.* In contrast to damages, which are usually measured by plaintiff's loss, restitution can be measured by defendant's gain. The issue that frequently arises, however, is how to measure or value the benefit to the defendant. There are many alternatives. The appropriate choice will depend in large part upon the facts of the case, and on the nature of the benefit conferred (*i.e.*, money, property, profits, services, etc.), the nature or degree of defendant's wrongdoing, and the substantive policies underlying the claim or defense.

PROBLEMS

1. *More on* Beacon Homes. Reconsider the *Beacon Homes* case, *supra* at 430, in which plaintiff built a house on defendant's lot at the request of defendant's mother's. Since the house was built without defendant's consent or knowledge, she refused to pay for it and also refused to let plaintiff remove it. The court concluded that defendant was unjustly enriched. How should the enrichment be measured? Suppose that it cost plaintiff $25,000 to build the house, but the house increased the value of defendant's lot by $35,000. Should plaintiff recover $25,000 or $35,000? Should the "unjust enrichment" be measured in some other way? Suppose that defendant rented the house for $500 a month.

2. *Environmental Contamination.* In the *Beacon Homes* case, what if plaintiff had constructed the house under an agreement with defendant to buy the land. However, plaintiff later found out that defendant had defrauded him (the land suffered from environmental contamination), and plaintiff obtained rescission of the contract after the house had been built. Given these facts, would you measure plaintiff's recovery differently than in the prior problem? What arguments can you make on behalf of plaintiff? How might defendant respond?

3. *The Stolen Trees.* George Johnson stole 3 mahogany trees from James Mail's property. The trees were worth $15,000. Johnson milled the trees into lumber, and used the lumber as studs in a new house that he is building. Since the studs could not be seen, Johnson could have used much cheaper lumber (that would have been equally sturdy and effective) in place of the mahogany. This other wood could have been purchased for $4,000. Mail seeks restitution from Johnson. How much can he recover—$4,000 or $15,000?

4. *Good Faith Mistake.* Would it have made any difference if, instead of stealing the trees, Johnson had taken them mistakenly (he cut them down thinking that the trees were on his own property, and later found out that they were on Mail's property)?

5. *The Mistaken Delivery.* Debbie King owned a lumber yard, and Kathy Regan ordered lumber for use as studs. Ordinarily, such wood would cost $4,000. King mistakenly shipped Regan mahogany wood (worth $15,000). Regan did not notice the mistake, and used the mahogany for studs.

King demanded payment of $15,000. Regan refused to pay claiming that King is only entitled to $4,000. Who is right?

6. *The Sculptor and the Stolen Rock.* A starving sculptor stole a large rock from plaintiff's land. The rock had very little value ($5). The sculptor labored over the rock for years eventually creating a masterpiece (the equivalent of Rodin's Thinker) worth $3 million. How much can the rock's owner recover from the sculptor? Can the owner repossess the rock?

7. *The Stolen Ring.* Janice Washington stole a diamond ring from Bruce Willett that was worth $10,000. Shortly after the theft, the bottom fell out of the diamond market, and the value of the ring plummeted to $1,000. Willett sued Washington for restitution claiming that he was entitled to $10,000. Washington claimed that the ring should be valued at $1,000. Who is right?

8. *The Purchaser of the Stolen Ring.* Suppose that Washington had bought the ring from Alexander Dumas for $8,000 believing that Dumas owned the ring. Later, Washington found out that Dumas had stolen the ring from Bruce Willett. Would Willett be entitled to restitution? If so, how much should he recover?

9. *The Jilted Author.* Professor Younger agrees to write a property casebook for South Publishing Co. Professor Younger dutifully prepares the book, but South refuses to accept it. South believes that Professor Younger produced an excellent book. However, the casebook market has changed (publishers are now producing electronic casebooks rather than hard copy books), and South no longer wishes to publish the book. Is Professor Younger entitled to restitution? If so, how much can he recover?

D. SPECIAL RESTITUTIONARY REMEDIES

The equitable side of restitution includes a number of special restitutionary devices including the constructive trust, equitable lien and subrogation. Because each of these devices is powerful and flexible, they can provide a plaintiff with unique advantages in providing proprietary rights.

1. THE CONSTRUCTIVE TRUST

SIEGER V. SIEGER

162 Minn. 322, 202 N.W. 742 (1925).

WILSON, C.J.

Plaintiff sues his divorced wife. Prior to the divorce he, being unable to read or write, intrusted his wife with the purchase of the real estate involved and on which they were then living. He relied upon her, and reposed absolute confidence in her, and believed that she would guard his interests, and that the legal title to the property would be taken in his name as grantee, but, contrary thereto, and in violation of the trust imposed, she wrongfully and without his knowledge or consent procured a deed with her name as grantee, and caused the same to be recorded. Plaintiff did not learn of this until sixteen months later, when he demanded a conveyance to him. She refused.

Plaintiff has been an industrious and frugal man and the defendant a hard-working and provident woman. Except for $525 received by the wife from her mother's estate, the property owned by the parties was largely the product of plaintiff's labor. When this property was acquired for $3,400 the sum of $2,000 received from the sale of other property and belonging to plaintiff was used, and the balance of the purchase price was paid principally out of funds belonging to defendant. The property is now worth $5,000.

The court found that plaintiff was the owner of an undivided two-fifths of the property, and that defendant held the title to such interest in trust for plaintiff.

[The] conduct of defendant as found by the court shows that she obtained the title to this property in bad faith, and in taking advantage of a fiduciary relation. She did this in such an unconscientious manner that she should not in equity and good conscience be permitted to keep it. Under such circumstances equity will impress a constructive trust upon it in favor of the husband. Such trusts are those which arise purely by construction in equity and are independent of any actual or presumed intention of the parties. They are known as trusts ex maleficio or ex delicto. They sound in fraud.

There is some confusion between resulting and constructive trusts. In the former there is always the element, although it is an implied one, of an intention to create a trust. The latter arises by operation of law, without any reference to any actual or supposed intention of creating a trust, and frequently directly contrary to such intention. In fact, just as in the case at bar, the grantee in the deed holds title in hostility to the world, but equity in its benevolence forces a trust upon her conscience and compels her to respond to that which is right. It is put against one not assenting.

[We] think the rule should be, both as to constructive trusts and resulting trusts, that a trust exists pro tanto the amount of the funds used when the amount thereof is definite or constitutes an aliquot part of the whole consideration. Substance and not form is the important element in equity. The owner of the money that pays for the property should be the owner of the property. Such is the foundation for a resulting trust, and equity should be no less considerate of one whose property has been misappropriated for an investment than for one who intended that the beneficial interest is not to go with the legal title.

[Under] the facts in this case we hold, first, that there was a violation of a trust within the meaning of the statute; and, secondly, that it is not necessary for the *cestui que trust* to pay all the consideration, but it is sufficient if he pays a definite or aliquot part thereof, and then he is entitled to a trust pro tanto. Constructive trusts are created by equity for the purposes of protecting those who are wronged. Equity cannot look with favor upon the suggestion that the wrongdoer may use 2 percent of his own money and 98 percent of money belonging to another, and by virtue of this mixture avoid a trust. This would ignore the reason for the trust, namely, the protection of the party wronged.

Affirmed.

NOTES: THE RESTATEMENT

§ 55 *Restatement (Third) of Restitution and Unjust Enrichment defines Constructive Trust as follows:*

> (1) If a defendant is unjustly enriched by the acquisition of title to identifiable property at the expense of the claimant or in violation of the claimant's rights, the defendant may be declared a constructive trustee, for the benefit of the claimant, of the property in question and its traceable product.
>
> (2) The obligation of a constructive trustee is to surrender the constructive trust property to the clamant, on such conditions as the court may direct.

The constructive trust is the quintessential equitable remedy. The holder of the legal title may not in good conscience hold the beneficial interest. When Justice Cardozo gave the law its definitive statement in *Beatty v. Guggenheim Exploration Co.,* 225 N.Y.380, 122 N.E. 378 (1919) the rules were familiar to lawyers of the day. The elements in the transaction are: i) unjust enrichment of the defendant; ii) defendant's acquisition of identifiable property; iii); at the expense of the claimant or in violation of the claimant's rights. The constructive trust does not depend, as does the express trust on a fiduciary or confidential relationship. The terminology of "trust" is used to convey the conclusion that the constructive trust shares with the express trust the notion that the legal titleholder is subject to the equitable interest of the claimant. The use of constructive trust as remedy can be useful in the two party context where the claimant is intent on establishing title over specific property because it has increased in value for example. Even more potent is its use in the) three party context where the property is claimed in priority in a bankruptcy. See § 60 *Restatement (Third) of Restitution and Unjust Enrichment*

PROBLEMS

1. *The Dairy Farmer and the Younger Woman.* Upon the death of his wife of 32 years, plaintiff, a 56-year-old dairy farmer whose education did not

go beyond the eighth grade, developed a very close relationship with defendant, a school teacher and a woman 16 years his junior. Defendant assisted plaintiff in disposing of his wife's belongings, performed certain domestic tasks for him such as ironing his shirts and was a frequent companion of the plaintiff. Plaintiff came to depend upon defendant's companionship and, eventually, declared his love for her, proposing marriage to her. Notwithstanding her refusal of his proposal of marriage, defendant continued her association with plaintiff and permitted him to shower her with many gifts, fanning his hope that he could induce defendant to alter her decision concerning his marriage proposal. Defendant was given access to plaintiff's bank account, from which it is not denied that she withdrew substantial amounts of money. Eventually, plaintiff made a will naming defendant as his sole beneficiary and executed a deed naming her a joint owner of his farm. The record reveals that numerous alterations in the way of modernization were made to plaintiff's farmhouse in alleged furtherance of domestic plans made by plaintiff and defendant.

In September, 1971, while the renovations were still in progress, plaintiff transferred his remaining joint interest to defendant. At the time of the conveyance, a farm liability policy was issued to plaintiff naming defendant and her daughter as additional insureds. Furthermore, the insurance agent was requested by plaintiff, in the presence of defendant, to change the policy to read "J. Rodney Sharp, life tenant. Jean C. Kosmalski, owner." In February, 1973, the liaison between the parties was abruptly severed as defendant ordered plaintiff to move out of his home and vacate the farm. Defendant took possession of the home, the farm and all the equipment thereon, leaving plaintiff with assets of $300.

Should a constructive trust be imposed in favor of plaintiff? Should it matter that "plaintiff knowingly and voluntarily conveyed his property without agreement or condition of any kind, express or implied, and with full knowledge of their legal effect?" Should it matter that there is no confidential or fiduciary relationship? *See Sharp v. Kosmalski*, 40 N.Y.2d 119, 386 N.Y.S.2d 72, 351 N.E.2d 721 (Ct.App.1976). Contrast with this case *Moak v. Raynor*, 28 App. Div. 3d 900, 814 N.Y.S2d 289 (2006) where the court stressed the flexibility of the constructive trust. This comports with the modern ideas of it as a strong and malleable remedy for specific restitution.

2. *The Niece and the House.* Plaintiff Amelia Nockelun is the maternal aunt of the defendant Constance Sawicki. The plaintiff, who was 86 years old at the time of the trial in June 1992, had no children and her only living relatives were the defendant and the defendant's mother, who is the plaintiff's sister. The testimony of the plaintiff shows that in 1975, she prepared a will leaving all her estate, including the property in question, to the defendant. She gave the will to the defendant for safekeeping. Subsequently, the defendant approached her and stated that should the plaintiff have to enter a nursing home, social services and creditors would attach the plaintiff's house for the payment of debts. Defendant asked plaintiff to convey the house to her to ensure that the house passed to her.

Defendant promised to help plaintiff with the bills pertaining to the house and to reconvey the house to the plaintiff should she so desire at a future date.

In 1991, the plaintiff sought to obtain a home equity loan to enable her to make repairs to the house and also to pay several debts she owed. The bank required that she obtain legal title to the house before she could get the loan.

Defendant refused to reconvey the house to the plaintiff. Defendant admitted that during the 15 years the deed was in her name, she did not help the plaintiff with the payment of taxes on the property or with any other bills pertaining to the property, with the exception of $200 to assist the plaintiff in repairing the roof.

Can plaintiff force defendant to hold the property in constructive trust for her? Should a court of equity help plaintiff given her original motive? What arguments might plaintiff make? How might defendant respond?

FLETCHER V. NEMITZ

186 So.2d 232 (Miss.1966).

GILLESPIE, PRESIDING JUSTICE.

[This] dispute [is] between Mrs. Nemitz and Mrs. Fletcher concerning [an] oral agreement entered into in Ohio prior to 1948. Mrs. Nemitz testified that Mrs. Fletcher agreed that if Mr. and Mrs. Nemitz and the children would move to Cleveland, Mississippi, Mrs. Fletcher would borrow funds and construct a building for use as a flower shop and set up Mr. and Mrs. Nemitz in the flower business, and that Mrs. Fletcher would deed the flower shop property to Mrs. Nemitz when the loan was repaid. Mrs. Fletcher denied that she agreed to deed the property to Mrs. Nemitz, her contention being that she was trying to get the Nemitz family out of undesirable living conditions in Cleveland, Ohio, and [that] there was a fine opportunity for a flower shop business.

[The chancellor found that] there was an agreement between the parties prior to the move of the Nemitz family to Mississippi [that] if the Complainant and her husband would move back to Mississippi, and would repay the funds necessary for construction of a flower shop on the property of Defendant, [the] Defendant would convey that property in fee simple to [Complainant]. [As a result, the chancellor entered the following decree:] it is my opinion that the requirements for finding a constructive trust have been [met].

[Mrs.] Fletcher [contends] that even if the chancellor's findings of fact are correct, a constructive trust did not arise therefrom. Mrs. Fletcher bases her argument mainly on the ground that the oral contract involved in this case is unenforceable under the statute of frauds unless a trust shall arise or result, by implication of law '[out] of a conveyance of [land]', as provided in the last sentence of Mississippi Code Annotated section 269, and there was no conveyance in this case out of which a constructive trust could arise. We pretermit consideration of this interesting question, and base our decision on the absence of fraud or other unconscionable conduct on the part of Mrs. Fletcher and the fact that she was not unjustly enriched, irrespective of whether a constructive trust must arise out of a conveyance.

In *Saulsberry v. Saulsberry*, 78 So.2d 758, 760 (1955), this Court stated the general rule as to when and under what circumstances a constructive trust will arise, using the following language: A constructive trust is one that arises by operation of law against one who, by fraud, actual or constructive, by duress or abuse of confidence, by commission of wrong, or by any form of unconscionable conduct, artifice, concealment, or questionable means, or who in any way against equity and good conscience, either has obtained or holds the legal right to property which he ought not, in equity and good conscience, to hold and enjoy. A constructive trust is an appropriate remedy against unjust enrichment. The mere failure to perform an agreement does not raise a constructive trust, but a breach of an agreement or promise may, in connection with other circumstances, give rise to such a trust. A distinction exists between the breach of a promise not fraudulently made and the breach of a promise made with no intention of performing it. [In] the case before the Court we fail to find any fraud, actual or constructive, or other unconscionable conduct on the part of Mrs. Fletcher. There is no evidence of any abuse of the confidential relationship said to exist between Mrs. Fletcher and Mrs. Nemitz. Unjust enrichment is an essential fact in nearly every case where a constructive trust is raised. Mrs. Fletcher was not enriched. If a constructive trust is raised and the flower shop property is given to Mrs. Nemitz, Mrs. Fletcher will experience a total loss of the following: (1) the lot of land where the flower shop is located, (2) the $6,800 she voluntarily put into the flower shop business, (3) nearly five years of work in the flower shop for which she received nothing, and (4) all sums paid out for ad valorem taxes on the flower shop property from 1948 to 1964. If Mrs. Nemitz's claim of a constructive trust is rejected, Mrs. Fletcher still will have lost items (2) and (3). On the other hand, a reversal of the decree and denial of Mrs. Nemitz's claim of a constructive trust will not result in a loss to Mrs. Nemitz of the amount paid on the flower shop construction loan, as that item will be adjudged to constitute a lien on the premises subject to being offset by the fair rental value of the flower shop property, as hereinafter provided. The fact that the Nemitz family left Ohio, and Mr. Nemitz quit his job, is not a determinative factor. Such collateral personal decisions attend most business decisions. It may be a fact that Mrs. Fletcher meddled in her daughter's affairs, but under the evidence in this case it cannot be said that Mrs. Fletcher was guilty of any fraud or unconscionable conduct in connection with Mr. Nemitz quitting his job in Ohio. There is no proof that Mrs. Fletcher did anything more than spend a great deal of time and money, foolishly perhaps, in an effort to put her daughter and her son-in-law in the flower business in Cleveland, Mississippi, and it is not shown that the welfare of the Nemitz family was worsened by the move to Mississippi.

We hold, as a matter of law, that the facts and circumstances shown by the evidence, when viewed in the light most favorable to Mrs. Nemitz, were insufficient to raise a constructive trust. The decree is reversed insofar as it established a trust on the flower shop property in favor of Mrs. Nemitz.

We hold that the oral promise of Mrs. Fletcher to convey the flower shop property to Mrs. Nemitz is unenforceable under the statute of frauds. Miss. Code Ann. § 264 (1956).

Mrs. Fletcher concedes that if there was an oral promise to convey, Mrs. Nemitz has an equitable lien on the flower shop property to secure the sums paid on the construction loan which the trial court held to be purchase money payments. We further hold that there should be an adjustment of the mutual accounts of the parties and that Mrs. Nemitz should be charged with a reasonable rental for the use and occupation of the premises. [There] is no fraud on the part of either party in the case before the Court, and there is no valid reason why the Court should not adjust the mutual accounts equitably so as to restore the status quo as near as it reasonably can. On remand, Mrs. Nemitz should be credited with all sums paid to the bank in liquidation of Mrs. Fletcher's notes executed for the purpose of borrowing funds for construction of the flower shop, plus any sums paid out by Mrs. Nemitz for any improvements that Mrs. Fletcher should have made if the relation of landlord and tenant had existed, also all sums paid out by Mrs. Nemitz for fire and extended coverage insurance on the flower shop building. Mrs. Fletcher should be allowed credit against the sums allowed Mrs. Nemitz for the reasonable value of the use and occupation of the flower shop property. It is not intended to limit the factors to be considered by the chancellor in adjusting the mutual accounts of the parties if it should develop that there are other items not considered by this Court.

The decree is reversed, and judgment is entered in this Court adjudging that the facts did not give rise to a constructive trust, and the case is remanded for adjustment of the mutual accounts between the parties.

Reversed and remanded.

PROBLEM: MORE ON THE STOLEN STEERS

Now, let's think a bit more about the stolen steer problem presented at the beginning of this chapter. Could constructive trust principles be applied to a situation like this one? If so, how should they be applied?

2. EQUITABLE LIEN

An equitable lien is similar to a constructive trust, but, instead of requiring defendant to hold the property in trust, the court imposes a lien against property as security for plaintiff's interest. The *Restatement (Third) of Restitution and Unjust Enrichment* § 56 states it as follows:

> (1) If a defendant is unjustly enriched by a transaction in which
>
> > (a) the claimant's assets or services are applied to enhance or preserve the value of particular property to which the defendant has legal title, or more generally
> >
> > (b) the connection between unjust enrichment and the defendant's ownership of particular property makes it equitable that the claimant have recourse to that property for the satisfaction of the defendant's liability in restitution,
>
> the claimant may be granted an equitable lien on the property in question.
>
> (2) An equitable lien secures the obligation of the defendant to pay the claimant the amount of the defendant's unjust enrichment as separately determined. Foreclosure of an equitable lien is subject to such conditions as the court may direct.
>
> (3) A claimant who would be entitled to ownership of particular property via constructive trust (§ 55) may elect to obtain an equitable lien on the property instead.
>
> (4) The remedy of equitable lien is also a means to restrict the claimant's recovery, in cases where restitution via personal liability or constructive trust would exceed limits set by § 50 or § 61

LEYDEN V. CITICORP INDUSTRIAL BANK

782 P.2d 6 (Colo., En Banc, 1989).

JUSTICE ERICKSON delivered the Opinion of the Court.

[The] facts are not in dispute. In 1980, petitioner and Tommy Howe were divorced. The decree of dissolution was entered on August 20, 1980, in the dissolution court. In a contested property settlement hearing, the dissolution court found that the marital residence, located at 41 South

Eagle Circle, Aurora, Arapahoe County (the property), was held in joint tenancy by petitioner, Tommy Howe, and Tommy Howe's mother, Lois [Howe].

[T]he court ordered petitioner to quitclaim her one-third undivided interest in the property to Tommy Howe and his mother. Tommy Howe was ordered to contemporaneously execute a promissory note in the principal value of $10,000, with interest as provided in the order, and that was to become due upon the terms set forth in the decree.

[After the transfer,] petitioner filed the dissolution decree (but apparently not the promissory note), in the records of Arapahoe County, where the property was located.

Subsequently, Citicorp extended a loan to Tommy Howe, his new wife Blanche, and Lois Howe (the Howes). In exchange, the Howes executed a promissory note in the principal amount of $19,600.77 to Citicorp, secured by a deed of trust on the property. The deed of trust was recorded on September 20, 1982.

[A]fter the deed of trust was recorded, the Howes filed for bankruptcy, and the debt evidenced by the promissory note to petitioner was discharged. The Howes disclaimed any interest they had in the property, and Citicorp, after obtaining relief from the automatic stay in the bankruptcy court, foreclosed on the property and obtained a public trustee's deed.

After the discharge in bankruptcy, the petitioner filed a complaint in the district court on February 7, 1984, asking for a declaratory judgment that the recorded dissolution decree created either a judicial or equitable lien on the property, praying for foreclosure of the lien, and requesting attorney fees as provided in the promissory note. On the same day, petitioner filed a lis pendens on the property in Arapahoe County. While the declaratory action was pending, Citicorp transferred the property by deed to the Evanses on March 28, 1985.

[The] two questions that must be answered are [whether] an equitable lien arose under the circumstances of this case and, [if] it did, whether the petitioner may enforce the lien against Citicorp and the Evanses.

[It] has not been argued in this court that an equitable lien arose here because of a written contract. If a lien exists, therefore, it must be of the second type, that is, it must arise by virtue of the relations of the parties and the circumstances of this case. The discretion of a court of equity in declaring that an equitable lien exists is not unbounded, however, since the purpose of the lien is to prevent unjust enrichment. As the court in *Caldwell* [*v. Armstrong*, 342 F.2d 485, 490 (10th Cir.1965)] stated:

> An equitable lien is a creature of equity, is based on the equitable doctrine of unjust enrichment, and is the right to have a fund or specific property applied to the payment of a particular debt. Such a lien may be declared by a court of equity out of general considerations of right and justice as applied to the relationship of the parties.

Caldwell, 342 F.2d at 490. The law has long recognized that, under some circumstances, legal remedies are inadequate to protect the interests of the parties. An equitable lien that is imposed by a court of equity to prevent unjust enrichment is a special form of constructive trust.[8]

The court of appeals apparently believed that the sole factor to consider in a case where an equitable lien is alleged to arise out of a judicial decree is whether the judge issuing the judgment or decree consciously intended that a lien be created. Although the intention of the dissolution court is relevant, it is not the only consideration.

If an equitable lien were not imposed here, Tommy Howe would be unjustly enriched. He would have obtained the petitioner's one-third share in the marital home (valued at $10,000 in 1980 by the dissolution court) without any cost to him. After the divorce, Tommy received the benefits of a loan secured by encumbering the property, but he has paid the petitioner nothing, and has secured a discharge in bankruptcy of the debt evidenced by the promissory note to petitioner. In addition, the promissory note executed by Tommy Howe obviously dealt with or was related to specific real property, 4 S. SYMONS, POMEROY'S EQUITY JURISPRUDENCE, *supra*, § 1234 at 695. The execution of the promissory note was tied to the petitioner's relinquishment of her interest in the property, and repayment of the note was conditioned in part on events involving disposition of the property. Under these circumstances, the district court did not err in concluding that an equitable lien should be imposed on the property. Our conclusion is consistent with that reached by other courts in similar circumstances.

[T]he issue remains whether the lien may be enforced against Citicorp and the Evanses, since there was no evidence that they would be unjustly enriched. An equitable lien is "good as against all persons who acquired an interest with knowledge or notice of plaintiff's [equitable] lien, but it would not be good as against one who acquired an interest without such knowledge or notice." *Valley State Bank v. Dean*, 47 P.2d at

[8] The relationship between an equitable lien and a constructive trust [is] that where the constructive trust gives a complete title to the plaintiff, the equitable lien only gives him a security interest in the property, which he can then use to satisfy a money claim. Thus an equitable lien may be "foreclosed," by selling the property that has been subjected to the lien and by applying the proceeds to payment of the plaintiff's claim. This results in only a money payment to the plaintiff and obviously does not carry with it the advantages of recovering specific property. On the other hand, it operates like the constructive trust in affording a preference over other creditors and in utilizing the rules for following property into its product.

927. If property which is subject to an equitable lien is transferred to a third person who has notice of the equitable lien or who does not give value, the equitable lien can be enforced against the property in the hands of the third person. On the other hand, an equitable lien, like other equitable interests, is cut off if the property is transferred to a bona fide purchaser. RESTATEMENT OF RESTITUTION § 161 comment d (1937). Thus, if a transferee who pays value for the property is on notice of the equitable lien, the transferee takes the property subject to the lien. "Notice," in the context of an equitable lien or constructive trust, is notice of the facts giving rise to the lien or constructive trust, and "a person has notice of facts giving rise to a constructive trust if he knows the facts or should know them." *Id.* at § 174. In particular, [a] person has notice of facts giving rise to a constructive trust [or equitable lien] not only when he knows them, but also when he should know them; that is when he knows facts which would lead a reasonably intelligent and diligent person to inquire whether there are circumstances which would give rise to a constructive trust, and if such inquiry when pursued with reasonable intelligence and diligence would give him knowledge or reason to know of such circumstances. We agree with the district court that both Citicorp and the Evanses were on at least constructive notice of the facts and circumstances giving rise to the equitable lien when they obtained their interest in the property. When Citicorp extended the loan to the Howes, the decree of dissolution was recorded and in the chain of title of the property. Citicorp has not argued that it lacked actual knowledge of the contents of the decree.

Similarly, when the property was transferred to the Evanses, the decree was in the chain of title. In addition, when the Evanses took the property, there was a lis pendens on file that would lead a reasonable person to inquire regarding its source. The reason for the filing of the lis pendens was this very lawsuit, in which the petitioner was claiming an equitable lien.

Contrary to the contention of the respondents, recognition of an equitable lien under these circumstances would not defeat the purposes of the recording acts. The concept of constructive notice is explicitly recognized in section 38–35–109(1); 16A C.R.S. (1982 & 1988 Supp.). Accordingly, we conclude that the district court properly held that the petitioner's equitable lien was enforceable against both Citicorp and the [Evanses].

NOTES

Measurement of the unjust enrichment is a central element: the equitable lien secures the defendant's obligation to make a money payment and the quantum of that must be established under the rules of §§ 49–53. The claimant also must establish a nexus between the transaction giving rise to the liability in unjust enrichment and the property in which the claimant seeks the equitable lien. As you will see the claimant may chose in many cases between an equitable lien and a constructive trust.

PROBLEM: THE DAUGHTER AND THE DEFAULTING PARENTS

Mary Middlebrooks loaned $25,000 to her parents, W.L. and Elvira Lonas. Later, she sued them for restitution, claiming that her parents fraudulently obtained the loan not intending to repay it. Middlebrooks sought to impose a constructive trust on the $50,000 home which her parents partially paid for with the $25,000 loaned to them. Is a constructive trust or an equitable lien more appropriate in this case? *See Middlebrooks v. Lonas*, 246 Ga. 720, 272 S.E.2d 687 (1980). Are both remedies appropriate? What would be the advantage of one over the other?

JONES V. SACRAMENTO SAVINGS AND LOAN ASSOCIATION

248 Cal.App.2d 522, 56 Cal.Rptr. 741 (1967).

FRIEDMAN, ASSOCIATE JUSTICE.

[A developer purchased 13 lots in Yuba County, California. He bought the lots with borrowed money for which he gave notes and purchase money trust deeds.] The deeds secured purchase money loans of $806.45 per lot. All were recorded August 21, 1959. All contained subordination provisions, the effect of which is now in dispute. Yuba County Title Company was designated as trustee.

Somewhat over a year later the owners took out construction loans aggregating $143,900 and approximating $11,000 to $12,000 a lot. The owners gave Sacramento Savings instalment notes with principal and interest payable at the rate of $86 per month. These notes included a due-on-sale clause, giving the holder an option to accelerate maturity upon any sale by the borrower.

Before making the construction loans Sacramento Savings issued escrow instructions to Yuba County Title Company, stating: 'Please secure subordination.' The title company refused to issue insurance covering the Sacramento Savings trust deeds unless it received additional subordination agreements from the trustee of the purchase money trust deeds. Sacramento Savings then withdrew the escrow from Yuba County Title Company and another title company became the escrow depositary. Sacramento Savings then made the construction loans and its deeds of trust were recorded. No subordination agreements were executed, other than those contained in the purchase money trust deeds.

Homes were built on the 13 lots. Both the purchase money loans and the construction loans became delinquent. Jones bought up the defaulted purchase money notes and commenced the sale of individual parcels. The parties have effectually stipulated that Jones' proceedings complied with

[California law]. At sales held in August and September 1961, Jones bid in three of the lots. At trustee's sales held in February and April 1962 he bid in three more lots.

In the meantime Sacramento Savings' trustee commenced sale proceedings under the construction money trust deeds. In November 1961 it caused notices of default to be recorded against 11 of the lots. In May 1962 Sacramento Savings bid in these 11 lots at a sale held by its own trustee. Six of these were the lots which had already been sold to Jones at sales held by his own trustee. The other five had not yet been foreclosed by Jones, and as to these the sales to Sacramento Savings preceded the sales to Jones under the purchase money trust deeds. The remaining two lots were the subject of sales to Jones in April 1962 and to Sacramento Savings in November 1962. Not only did the timing of the various trustee's sales overlap; so did recordation of notices of default and notices of sale. Neither party chose to bid at any of the other's sales. Neither chose to exercise a junior lienor's right to reinstate the senior loan after the latter had become delinquent. Each, apparently, relied upon the assumption that its own trust deeds had superiority.

[There] is no claim that any of the trustees' sales produced bids exceeding the secured debt. The sales to Jones in enforcement of the senior liens wiped out the junior liens of Sacramento Savings. In those cases where Jones' trustee was the first to give notices and hold sales, the subsequent sales conveyed no title to Sacramento Savings and succeeded only in clouding Jones' title. Where Sacramento Savings' trustee was the first to give notices and hold sales, Sacramento Savings purchased title subordinate to the senior liens of the purchase money trust deeds. It is immaterial that in some cases the junior lienholder was the first to give notice and hold sales.

Sacramento Savings charges Jones with unclean hands. It points out that equity's denial of relief extends not only to outright fraud, but to any kind of unconscionable conduct on a plaintiff's part. The evidence indicates that Jones bought up the purchase money notes (of the face amount of $806.45 each) at a discount, knowing that the value of the lots securing them had been enhanced by the construction of homes financed by Sacramento Savings. Presumably Jones was also aware that he was buying deeds of trust burdened by subordination provisions.

There is nothing unconscionable in such conduct. Neither party lacked notice of any step taken by the other. Whatever of value Jones might gain is attributable: (a) to the disingenuous draftsmanship of Sacramento Savings, which sought subordination of the purchase money liens by supplying the form but not the substance of long-term financing; (b) to Jones' willingness to gamble on continued superiority of the purchase money liens; (c) to Sacramento Savings' expenditure of construction money in the face of recorded purchase money liens and its misplaced reliance on the subordinating effect of its own loan papers; (d) to Sacramento Savings' unwillingness to reinstate the defaulted purchase money loans or to bid in at the ensuing sales. Jones did nothing to prevent these latter steps. Had Sacramento Savings chosen to take either action, it could have protected its own large investment in these lots and limited Jones' profit to the difference between the unpaid purchase money notes and the discounted price paid for them by Jones.

Nevertheless, Sacramento Savings seeks an equitable lien premised upon the doctrine of unjust enrichment, pointing out that a decree for the plaintiff will present him with the financial benefit of expensive improvements constructed with its money. It assigns trial court error in the denial of its motion to amend pleadings and in the rejection of its request for findings permitting imposition of such a lien. * * *

We have concluded that Sacramento Savings is entitled to an equitable lien on the properties in Jones' hands. Nonconflicting evidence demonstrates and this court finds that both the then owner and the lender intended that the construction loan be secured by first liens; that the savings and loan association advanced construction funds of $143,900 in reliance, however erroneous, on expected first liens; that the loan funds were actually applied to the construction of improvements having a value far exceeding that of the land; that Jones, buyer of liens on the land, was aware of the improvements financed by the lending institution when he bought these liens. Since he paid a discounted price for the purchase money notes, his investment is but a fraction of the value of the improved properties. He would be unjustly enriched were he permitted to hold or sell the properties without making restitution for the improvements built at the expense of the savings and loan association.

A general doctrine of equity permits imposition of an equitable lien where the claimant's expenditure has benefited another's property under circumstances entitling the claimant to restitution. A specific application of the doctrine occurs when a lender advances money which benefits the land of another in mistaken reliance upon an imperfect mortgage or lien upon that land. The present circumstances fit both the general doctrine and the specific rule with nicety.

It is necessary that the lien claimant's money be spent upon the expected security of the property against which the lien is sought. The evidence permits no question but that such reliance existed here.

A quiet title suit aimed at terminating claims upon real estate is in one sense a strict foreclosure. Equitable principles apply in a quiet title action and, in the absence of a breach of duty, the court may protect against. There is a distinction between a constructive trust arising from the property owner's wrongdoing and an equitable lien imposed to prevent his unjust enrichment. The former may call for sale of the property and distribution of its proceeds. Equity imposes a lien here not to vindicate a wrong but to prevent unjust enrichment. The objective may be accomplished by a decree impressing the lien but without demanding an immediate sale. Equitable liens in favor of Sacramento Savings should be paid off at such times and under such circumstances as will avoid undue hardship on Jones. The record on appeal does not disclose whether any of the homes has been marketed. Framing of an appropriate decree to protect the parties' respective interests should await further inquiry and consideration by the trial court.

The circumstances do not call for an award of interest as part of the lien, either before or after judgment. The lien is not created to enforce an express or quasi contractual obligation, but will originate in the decree of equity. Thus, neither the interest rate fixed by the promissory notes nor interest under Civil Code, section 3287 is payable. * * *

[The] judgment is reversed and the cause remanded with directions to enter judgment and to take such other proceedings not inconsistent with this opinion as may be necessary or appropriate.

PROBLEM: MORE ON THE STOLEN STEERS

Now, let's think a bit more about the stolen steer problem presented at the beginning of this chapter. Could equitable lien trust principles be applied to a situation like this one? If so, how should they be applied? What, precisely, would plaintiff seek?

ROLFE V. VARLEY

860 P.2d 1152 (Wyo.1993).

CARDINE, JUSTICE.

[Appellant], Harley Rolfe (Harley), moved to Jackson, Wyoming in 1976, where he purchased the Western Motel. Before moving to Jackson, Harley worked in sales and marketing for several large communications corporations. Harley has a masters degree in business administration, with a concentration in marketing.

In 1979, Harley married appellant, Pauline Rolfe. [When] Harley and Pauline married, they each owned real estate in Jackson. Harley held title to the Western Motel complex which included eight lots. Pauline owned four properties, also located in Jackson, which were leased to local business professionals.

Since purchasing the Western Motel, Harley had wanted to develop it into a resort complex. [Previously,] Harley had contact with three other groups or individuals concerning the potential development of his Western Motel property. One of those individuals, Gary Smith (Smith), an attorney from Kentucky, acted as an intermediary between Harley and potential investors in the proposed resort project. These individual investors would advance Harley money, in anticipation of forming a business relationship with Harley for the development of the Western Motel. Harley used the money advanced by these potential investors to service the growing debt he and Pauline had accrued on their properties.

Then along came appellee John Varley. He is from Chicago and has a masters degree in business administration. He worked as a mortgage banker and then became self-employed, managing his own properties in the Chicago area. Varley first contacted Harley and Pauline in 1983 when he stayed at the Western Motel during a ski vacation in Jackson. Harley and Varley met again in Jackson in 1985, and in 1987 they engaged in their first serious discussions about developing the Western Motel property. After their meeting in 1987, Harley and Varley corresponded by mail and phone. These meetings and contacts culminated in the drafting and signing of a document titled, Agreement, on April 6, 1987.

During negotiations for the Agreement, Smith was also present. Smith and Harley drafted the Agreement using Harley's typewriter. The document was drawn as an agreement between the Rolfes (Harley and Pauline) and Varley. The Agreement provided that the Rolfes and Varley would enter into another agreement forming a partnership within thirty days of the execution of the Agreement. The Agreement stated that the future partnership must include the following "rights and obligations of the parties": (1) Harley must contribute the Western Motel property to the partnership, and (2) Varley must "provide the means to satisfy all current and existing debts and obligations encumbering or relating to the [Western Motel] property." The Agreement also stated that Varley, "for the benefit of the partnership and proposed development, shall use his best effort to purchase six [6] lots" and that Varley will pay Harley and Pauline $10,000.00 for expenses already accrued. In addition, the Agreement described the possibility of a "wrap-mortgage" if Varley satisfied either part or all of the Western Motel debts; this section of the Agreement, however, was very ambiguous. The Rolfes and Varley never entered into the contemplated partnership agreement.

After the Agreement was signed, Harley and Varley vigorously pursued their dream of creating a resort complex on the Western Motel property. Using Varley's money, the parties hired a builder, an architect and several different consultants to assist in the development efforts. Originally, in 1987, the parties contemplated a $7,000,000.00 project; however, after several changes on advice from the consultants, the proposed cost of the project grew to an estimated cost of $30,000,000.00 in 1988. At this point, the project was in jeopardy, and the parties attempted to downsize the project to make it workable.

Over the two-year period, beginning in April of 1987 with the $10,000.00 described in the Agreement and ending in 1989 when the joint effort to develop collapsed, Varley advanced Harley and Pauline

$397,316.45 for the payment of their debts on the Western Motel. During October 1989, after the $30,000,000.00 figure appeared and after attempts to downsize the project, Varley discontinued paying the Western Motel debts. Throughout this period of debt service by Varley, he made several demands from the Rolfes for a personal note and mortgage as security for the debt payments. The Rolfes, however, refused to execute a note and mortgage.

The debt, which the Rolfes had accrued on the Western Motel, was over $500,000.00. Several of these loans were secured, not only by the Western Motel property, but also by Pauline's property. When Varley signed the Agreement, it was his understanding that the payments he made for the Western Motel debt were to be secured by the same collateral as was securing the underlying debts.

In addition to the money Varley expended for servicing the Western Motel debt, he also spent $347,556.85 towards trying to develop the resort complex. These funds were payments made to the builder, the architect and the host of consultants the parties hired.

Finally, in September 1990, Varley filed this suit in district court. [T]he district court awarded judgment to Varley for his two years of Western Motel debt payment and for his expenditures in pursuit of the resort development. In addition, the district court granted Varley interest on those damages, an equitable lien on all of Harley's and Pauline's property, and terminated whatever formal relationship existed between the Rolfes and Varley.

[The] first three arguments raised by the Rolfes involve the same issue, whether the court erred in granting Varley an equitable lien against the properties of Pauline and Harley. * * *

The equitable lien has been described generally as a right, not recognized at law, which a court of equity recognizes and enforces as distinct from strictly legal rights, to have a fund or specific property, or the proceeds, applied in full or in part to the payment of a particular debt or demand. Equitable liens arise in two ways, either by a contract or by implication. An equitable lien created expressly by contract occurs where a contract states that certain property will act as security but for some reason or another it fails to create a lien enforceable at law and thus the court enforces it in equity. Where there is no contract, equitable liens are implied by courts to avoid unjust enrichment.

Equitable liens are related to several other equity concepts. They are imposed to prevent unjust enrichment where the unjust enrichment might result from the "receipt of particular property." An equitable lien is said to be a "special, and limited, form of the constructive trust" and closely related to subrogation because each is a remedy used to prevent unjust enrichment or fraud, and to allow restitution.

[The] district court did not err in imposing an equitable lien on both Pauline's and Harley's properties. Both Pauline and Harley signed the Agreement and accepted Varley's payments, thus they are obligated to Varley for his payments towards the Western Motel debt. Varley's payments went toward debts for which both Pauline and Harley were personally liable and which were secured by the Western Motel property. In addition, at least one of the debts was secured by Pauline's four properties. Thus, their obligation to Varley attaches to a recognizable res. The record demonstrates that the parties intended Pauline's and Harley's property to serve as security because the Agreement described a "wrap-mortgage" and because Varley testified that he understood that he would get a wrap-mortgage. Therefore, [the] district court ruled in accordance with law when it imposed an equitable lien on Pauline's and Harley's property for the debt payments made by Varley.

There is further support for imposing an equitable lien. It is generally held that an equitable lien exists where one party has paid another party's liabilities or debts owed upon certain, identifiable property. The general rule is: Where debts or claims against property are paid in good faith by another on the express or implied request of the owner of the property, the one so paying is entitled to an equitable lien on the property for his reimbursement. However, a person is not entitled to such lien if he voluntarily pays the debts of another without such other's [request]. In addition, where money advances are made by one party to another "under an agreement or circumstances showing that it was the intention of the parties to pledge [certain] property as security for the advancements," equitable liens have been imposed.

We agree that Pauline was properly found to be jointly and severally liable for the debt to Varley. Although the Rolfes testified to the contrary, it is clear from the Agreement and through the Rolfes' course of business, that Pauline was involved in the development process. First, she signed the Agreement which named her as one of the parties who was to enter into the partnership. Second, Pauline endorsed most of the checks made out by Varley to the Rolfes for Western Motel debt payments, and Pauline's testimony demonstrated that her finances and property management were heavily co-mingled with Harley's. Third, there is evidence, in a brochure created for potential investors, that Pauline was to be an integral part of the development. The brochure stated: "the principal(s) of the Managing General Partner will be Harley F. Rolfe and Pauline ___. Rolfe, his [wife]."

[The] Agreement and the testimony of the parties clearly demonstrates that Harley and Pauline requested Varley to pay their Western Motel debts and that Varley did pay those debts for a period of two years. Both Pauline's and Harley's properties were pledged as security for the underlying debts, and they both were personally liable;

hence, both of their properties benefitted from Varley's payments. The district court, therefore, did not err in imposing an equitable lien on the Rolfes' property. * * *

PROBLEMS

1. *The Stolen Tantalum.* Doing business through Fairmont Metals Company, Abney purchased scrap metal known as tantalum from Barreda at a price approximately ten percent of the true market value and then sold the tantalum to Powell. Abney purchased the tantalum with full knowledge that Barreda, a warehouse employee of Union Carbide Corporation, acquired the tantalum by stealing it from Union Carbide's warehouse. Abney subsequently was indicted and found guilty of transporting the stolen tantalum from Texas to Illinois, the principal office of Powell. Upon discovery of the scheme, Powell sued Abney, claiming a breach of an implied warranty of good title and seeking damages caused by the breach. The district court rendered judgment in favor of Powell for $115,965.04, and as it was able to trace only $27,000 of that amount into specific property—the Abney homestead—the district court imposed an equitable lien on the Abney homestead to the extent of $27,000. Shortly after the entry of judgment, Abney sought to discharge the equitable lien by paying the amount of the lien plus interest. Abney's objective was to maintain his homestead exemption and prevent a forced sale of the property. Powell refused to accept the payment contending that it would be an injustice to discharge the equitable lien and in effect allow Abney the right to designate whether his payment should be applied first to discharge the equitable lien or to the balance of the judgment. Should the lien be discharged? *See Powell, Inc. v. Abney*, 669 F.2d 348 (5th Cir.1982).

2. *Partitioning Improved Joint Property.* Plaintiff and defendants jointly owned a piece of real property. Plaintiff sued for partition and defendants agreed to purchase plaintiff's interest. The court found that both the plaintiffs and defendants had improved the property, but that the plaintiffs' improvements had increased the value of the real property by $7,500 more than the defendants' improvements. Defendants argue that when both parties in a partition action occupy the premises, any increases in overall value resulting from improvements by those parties should not be considered. Defendants point out that the improvements were made over 20 years ago to plaintiffs' apartment and were solely used and enjoyed by plaintiffs. Plaintiff argues that it is appropriate to consider the overall increase in the value of the real property resulting from those improvements and credit the parties accordingly. Plaintiffs argue that, otherwise, defendants would receive a windfall. Should "unjust enrichment" principles allow plaintiff to establish an equitable lien against the property for the value of the improvements? *See Donnelly v. Capodici*, 227 N.J.Super. 310, 547 A.2d 329 (Ch.Div.1987).

3. *The Personal Injury Settlement.* Husband and wife were in the process of getting divorced when plaintiff suffered severe personal injuries in an automobile accident. After the accident, the man was unable to work and

eventually received a sizeable settlement for his injuries. The couple had one child, and the man had been ordered to pay the family debts and to make child support payments of $100 per month. When the man received his settlement, he was behind on both payments. Would it be appropriate for the divorce court to impose an equitable lien on the settlement to assure payment of the family debts and the child support? What arguments might be made on behalf of the man against the lien? How might the woman respond to these arguments? *See In re Bull*, 48 Or.App. 565, 617 P.2d 317 (1980).

3. SPECIAL ADVANTAGES OF CONSTRUCTIVE TRUSTS AND EQUITABLE LIENS

Both the constructive trust and equitable lien offer plaintiffs special advantages over other remedies. The two most important advantages are that both devices allow plaintiffs to "trace" their property into other forms, and give plaintiffs priority over other creditors.

a. Tracing

G & M MOTOR COMPANY V. THOMPSON

567 P.2d 80 (Okla.1977).

BERRY, JUSTICE.

[M]ay a trial court impress a constructive trust upon proceeds of life insurance policies where a portion of the premiums were paid with wrongfully obtained funds? We hold sound reason and interest of justice require an affirmative answer.

The facts, for the purpose of deciding this question, are simple. A. Wayne Thompson was an accountant for G & M Motor Company (motor company) from January 1, 1968, until his death on August 2, 1970. During this period decedent embezzled $78,856.45 from motor company; a portion of which was used to pay premiums on various insurance policies insuring the life of decedent. The trial court impressed a constructive trust upon various items of real and personal property and a portion of the insurance proceeds in possession of decedent's surviving wife, Shirley Thompson, and child.

[The] proper basis for impressing a constructive trust is to prevent unjust enrichment. RESTATEMENT OF RESTITUTION § 160, Comment c (1937). The Restatement of Restitution foresaw that a wrongdoer may exchange misappropriated property for other property; thus, § 202 provides: "Where a person wrongfully disposes of property of another knowing that the disposition is wrongful and acquires in exchange other property, the other is entitled [to] enforce [a] constructive trust of the property so acquired." The drafters explained § 202 as follows: "Where a person by the consciously wrongful disposition of the property of another acquires other property, the person whose property is so used [is] entitled [to] the property so acquired. If the property so acquired is or becomes more valuable than the property used in acquiring it, the profit thus made by the wrongdoer cannot be retained by him; the person whose property was used in making the profit is entitled to it. The result, it is true, is that the claimant obtains more than the amount of which he was deprived, more than restitution for his loss; he is put in a better position than that in which he would have been if no wrong had been done to him. Nevertheless, since the profit is made from his property, it is just that he should have the profit rather than that the wrongdoer should keep it. It is true that if there had been a loss instead of a profit, the wrongdoer would have had to bear the loss, since the wrongdoer would be personally liable to the claimant for the value of the claimant's property wrongfully used by the wrongdoer. If, however, the wrongdoer were permitted to keep the profit, there would be an incentive to wrongdoing, which is removed if he is compelled to surrender the profit. The rule which compels the wrongdoer to bear any losses and to surrender any profits operates as a deterrent upon the wrongful disposition of the property of others. Accordingly, the person whose property is wrongfully used in acquiring other property can by a proceeding in equity reach the other property and compel the wrongdoer to convey it to him. The wrongdoer holds the property so acquired upon a constructive trust for the claimant." Thus, it is not necessary for a plaintiff to have suffered any loss or suffer a loss as great as the benefit of defendant.

Where the wrongdoer mingles wrongfully and rightfully acquired funds, owner of wrongfully acquired funds is entitled to share proportionately in acquired property to the extent of his involuntary contribution. This principle is specifically applicable to life insurance proceeds where a portion of the premiums were paid with wrongfully acquired money. *Id.* § 210, Comment a. The drafters said: "[Just] as the claimant is entitled to enforce a constructive trust upon property which is wholly the product of his property, so he is entitled to enforce a constructive trust upon property which is the product in part of his own property and in part of the property of the wrongdoer. The difference is that where the property is the product of his property only in part, he is not entitled by enforcing a constructive trust to recover the whole of the property, but only a share in such proportion as the value of his property bore to the value of the mingled fund." More particularly, § 210, Comment d, Illustration 5 addressed the instant matter. Illustration 5 provides: "A insures his life for $10,000 and pays the premiums half with money wrongfully taken from B and half with money of his own. A dies. B is entitled to half of the proceeds of the [policy]." The record indicates trial court determined extent of premiums paid with wrongfully acquired funds and impressed a constructive trust upon proceeds consistent with Illustration 5.

Having carefully considered the matter, we adopt the Restatement view. However, Motor Company has sought no more than the embezzled monies, interest and costs. Further, the surviving wife is an innocent beneficiary. Therefore, we cannot say trial court's judgment is against the clear weight of evidence. We hold Motor Company is entitled to a pro rata share of insurance proceeds, but not to exceed the total amount of embezzled monies, interest and costs.

Appellee granted certiorari. Appellant denied certiorari. Court of Appeals opinion vacated in part. Judgment of trial court affirmed.

PROBLEMS

1. *The Embezzlement and the Insurance Policy.* In *G & M Motor Co.*, plaintiff was given a lien equal to the amount that had been embezzled from it. The case does not give you any information regarding the face value of the policy. Suppose that the proceeds amounted to $300,000, and that 50% of the proceeds had come from embezzled funds. How much could G & M recover? $78,856.45? $150,000.00? If you represented plaintiff, how would you argue for the higher amount? If you represented defendant, how would you argue for the lower amount?

2. *More on the Embezzlement and the Insurance Policy.* Would your answer be different if all the premiums had been paid with embezzled funds?

IN RE ALLEN

724 P.2d 651 (Colo., En Banc, 1986).

LOHR, JUSTICE. [Roger Allen] and Pamela Allen obtained a decree dissolving their marriage on February 7, 1980. Incorporated into the decree was a stipulation for permanent orders containing the Allens' agreement as to property division, child support, and maintenance. The stipulation provided, among other things, that before March 1, 1980, Pamela would receive from Roger cash payments totaling $93,200. In addition, she was to receive a promissory note from Roger in the amount of $75,000 secured by a deed of trust on the Allens' home (the family home). The note and $75,000 of the cash represented one-half of the equity that had accumulated in the family home as of the time of the dissolution. The remainder of the cash payments represented the value of a fur coat and a Jaguar automobile surrendered by Pamela to Roger. The stipulation further provided that upon receipt of the cash, the promissory note, and the deed of trust, Pamela would convey her interest in the family home to Roger.

In January and February 1980, Roger made the cash payments and gave a secured note to Pamela as provided for in the stipulation. Roger obtained $3,200 of the cash through a loan from a friend. He obtained the remaining $90,000 through a loan from Arapahoe Bank & Trust, secured by a second deed of trust on the family home. On the same day that she received the $90,000, Pamela invested $88,413.02 in a house on Driver Lane in Littleton (Driver Lane residence). She sold the Driver Lane residence on July 9, 1980, and received $89,593.74 as proceeds of the sale. She immediately transferred $75,000 of that money to a bank in Florida. Soon after, Pamela purchased an interest in a home in Florida, spending almost $44,000 to buy the interest and to redecorate the home. Within several months of the purchase, she expended the remaining proceeds of approximately $45,000 that she had received from the sale of the Driver Lane residence.

Meanwhile, in late March 1980, Roger Allen's employer, UMC, discovered that Roger had embezzled $589,823.24 from UMC during 1979 and 1980. In his position as vice-president of UMC in charge of construction lending, Roger was able to write checks on some UMC accounts without obtaining the approval of any other UMC employee. Because Roger wrote the checks primarily on accounts for two projects of which he was in charge, the embezzlement went undetected for more than a year. The trial court found that $190,000 of UMC's money was used to pay for construction of the family home, approximately $40,000 was used to buy furnishings for the home, $13,000 was used to purchase the Jaguar automobile, and $3,200 went to repay the loan that Roger had received from his friend.

Criminal charges were filed against Roger, and UMC also brought a civil action to recover the stolen moneys from Roger. Roger entered into a settlement agreement with UMC pursuant to which he conveyed the family home to UMC. He also filed a post-judgment motion in the dissolution of marriage action, requesting that the trial court set aside the stipulated permanent orders that had been incorporated into the decree of dissolution. In his motion, Roger stated that his financial condition would change substantially as a result of the legal proceedings surrounding the embezzlement, rendering unconscionable the enforcement of the permanent orders. UMC filed a motion to intervene in the dissolution action, and the trial court granted that motion. In its complaint in intervention, UMC asked that the permanent orders be set aside because they were based on a fraudulent misrepresentation of marital assets to the court and because they divided property that belonged to UMC. It further asserted, among other things, that UMC was entitled to a constructive trust and an equitable lien on the Driver Lane residence[1] and to a constructive trust on the promissory note and on the deed of trust on the family home securing that note.

---

[1] UMC apparently was unaware of the sale of the Driver Lane residence when the complaint in intervention was filed. Later, without amending the pleadings, UMC sought a constructive trust on the proceeds of that sale.

[The] trial court recognized that fraud on the court necessitates the reopening of a judgment, but refused to set aside the property division on the grounds that Roger, the fraudulent party, should not be allowed to benefit from his fraud by utilizing the property distributed to Pamela to reduce the restitution obligations imposed on him in other civil and criminal proceedings. The trial court's resolution of the issue, however, ignores the position of UMC as a party to this action. From UMC's perspective, Roger is an adverse party who perpetrated a fraud upon the trial court. The trial court and the parties to the dissolution arrived at the property disposition without regard to any rights or interests that UMC might have had in the property. UMC is entitled to have the judgment set aside regardless of whether Roger also benefits from such an action.

[UMC] can reach certain property in Pamela Allen's possession through the court's equitable powers to impose an equitable lien or a constructive trust on that property. In its complaint in intervention, UMC requested a constructive trust as to the $75,000 promissory note and the deed of trust that secures that note, and a constructive trust and an equitable lien on the Driver Lane property to the extent of funds invested in that property that were obtained by borrowing against the family home. At trial, UMC contended that it also was entitled to the difference between the amount of funds Pamela received from the sale of the Driver Lane residence and the amount she invested in the Florida residence. We hold that UMC is entitled to either an equitable lien, a constructive trust, or both, on certain property held by Pamela. On remand, the trial court can fashion an appropriate remedy after making necessary factual findings as to the circumstances under which Pamela acquired the property and the present interests of Pamela, UMC, and other parties in that property.

[When] imposed to prevent unjust enrichment, an equitable lien is a special and limited form of a constructive trust. RESTATEMENT OF RESTITUTION § 161. Whereas the beneficiary of a constructive trust receives title to the trust property, a plaintiff who receives an equitable lien obtains merely a security interest in the property held by the defendant and can use that interest to satisfy a money claim against the defendant. 5 SCOTT, THE LAW OF TRUSTS, § 463 at 3425. An equitable lien is the proper remedy "where part of the property or part of the fund belongs in good conscience to the defendant, or at any rate belongs to someone other than the plaintiff." DOBBS, HANDBOOK ON THE LAW OF REMEDIES, § 4.3 at 249–50. An equitable lien also may be the preferable remedy in a case in which the defendant has used the plaintiff's property to purchase other property and the other property has decreased in value. In such a case, in proper circumstances the plaintiff can have an equitable lien on the later-acquired property and a money judgment against the defendant for any deficiency between the value of the plaintiff's property and the value of the later-acquired property. 5 Scott, The Law of Trusts, § 463 at 3425.

Neither an equitable lien nor a constructive trust is available against a bona fide purchaser for value. RESTATEMENT OF RESTITUTION § 172. Pamela Allen contends that she is a bona fide purchaser for value. She argues that she gave significant value for the property pursuant to the settlement agreement since by entering into the agreement, she surrendered further claims to property division, maintenance, child support and attorney's fees. The trial court agreed with Pamela's contention that she gave value, noted that she had no knowledge of UMC's claimed interests in the Allens' marital property, and concluded that she was a bona fide purchaser for value. The court of appeals neither affirmed nor rejected this conclusion.

We hold that even though Pamela Allen took property without knowledge of UMC's interests, she is not a bona fide purchaser because she did not give value for the property she received in the dissolution proceeding. Although agreeing to accept a specified amount of property, maintenance, and child support may be adequate consideration to support a property settlement agreement, it does not constitute "value" sufficient to make Pamela a bona fide purchaser for the purpose of defending against UMC's equitable claims. The focus in a case like the present one should not be on a strict definition of value, but instead should be on whether the person claiming bona fide purchaser status has been unjustly enriched. It is uncontroverted that Roger Allen embezzled money from UMC, used that money to invest in the family home and other property, and then subjected that property to division as marital property. The property was never truly a marital asset and should never have been subject to the Allens' property division negotiations. To allow Pamela Allen to gain legal and equitable title to the products of Roger's embezzlement simply by entering into a property settlement would be to enrich her unjustly at the expense of UMC.

Furthermore, many courts have refused to recognize bona fide purchaser status in the spouses of persons who have misappropriated property. Most of these courts base their refusal on a determination that the spouse has not given value for the misappropriated property, but rather has gained an interest in the property simply by virtue of being married to the person who misappropriated the property. One court has stated that "[m]arriage itself has been considered value, so as to make the wife a bona fide purchaser, only where the marriage is in consideration of the transfer of the property." *Hirsch v. Travelers Insurance Co.*, 341 A.2d at 694. There is no reason to enhance a spouse's interest in misappropriated property merely because the spouse subsequently decides to dissolve the marriage.

As a person who acquired title to property without notice that another party had equitable ownership of the property, but who did not pay value, Pamela Allen is not a bona fide purchaser for value. 5 SCOTT, THE LAW OF TRUSTS, § 510 at 3595. She is instead an innocent donee or a gratuitous transferee. A constructive trust or an equitable lien can be imposed on the product of wrongfully obtained property even when that product has been transferred to an innocent donee, since the equitable interests that attached to the product before it was transferred are not cut off by the transfer, RESTATEMENT OF RESTITUTION § 168. However, an innocent donee is liable only to the extent to which she is unjustly enriched at the time when she acquires notice of the equitable ownership of the other party. Moreover, the donee may be entitled to reimbursement for improvements she makes or value she contributes to the product of the wrongfully obtained property.

Thus, because Pamela Allen is only an innocent donee, not a bona fide purchaser, UMC is entitled to an equitable lien, a constructive trust or both on those products of the embezzled money that are now in Pamela's hands. The precise remedy will have to be fashioned by the trial court on remand. UMC must have the opportunity to trace its property (the embezzled funds) into the products of that property that are now in Pamela's possession. It also must decide whether it wants to request a constructive trust or an equitable lien on that product. The trial court will have to determine whether other parties, including Pamela Allen, have ownership interests in some or all of that product—for example, the Florida house—since an equitable lien, and not a constructive trust, would be the appropriate means of recognizing UMC's interest in such circumstances. In addition, Pamela is entitled to assert claims for reimbursement for improvements or contributions she may have made to whatever property is subject to trust or lien.

The judgment of the court of appeals is affirmed.

PROBLEMS

1. *The Misappropriation and the House Purchase.* A woman misappropriated $2,500 from a trust fund, and used it, along with $2,500 of her own money, to make a down payment on a $40,000 house. The woman paid $400 a month on the house for a year, $350 of which was for interest and the remainder was for principal. At the end of the year, the woman sold the house for $55,000 and placed the money in a bank account.

If the trust beneficiaries sue the woman, what remedies are available to them and in what amount? Should the woman be given credit for improvements to the home? Should the court consider that she deducted home mortgage interest on her income tax return? *See Sears v. Grover*, 116 N.J.Eq. 111, 172 A. 525 (1934).

2. *The Termite Infestation.* Diana and Donald Coppinger sold their home to Diane McKay for $152,000. The Coppingers, due to prior inspections, were on notice that the foundations of the home were infested with termites. After the sale, McKay discovered termites in the interior walls in the living room, bathroom, and hallway, and additional cracks in the foundation through which termites were travelling in large numbers. Meanwhile, the Coppingers had used the proceeds from the sale to purchase another residence. Can Mckay impose a constructive trust on the Coppinger's new home? *See Coppinger v. Superior Court of Orange County*, 134 Cal.App.3d 883, 185 Cal.Rptr. 24 (1982).

3. *The* Myers *Case.* Consider the facts in *Myers v. Matusek*, 98 Fla. 1126, 125 So. 360 (1929):

> [On] May 28, 1926, Dr. Bleil wrote Mr. Carter, the trust officer of the Palm Beach Bank & Trust Company, that he had $25,000 that he would not need until the following October, and asked 'if Mr. Clayton's Mortgage Company had any guaranteed notes that would come due around that date' and which he (Bleil) could buy. On June 4, 1926, the trust officer replied, saying that Mr. Clayton stated that he did not have any notes in his mortgage company that would mature in the neighborhood of that date and for that reason he (Clayton) could not use the money; but he added: 'We have some securities in the Trust Department that will yield 7% to you. You could send the money down in the nature of a trust deposit, subject to call and to be withdrawn October 1st, we would turn over to this account securities to that amount, and pay you 7% interest on the money at the time you requested the return of said money to you, this interest to be paid from the date of the receipt of the money by us until you called it in.'
>
> On June 9th, Dr. Bleil wrote the trust officer as follows: 'I am enclosing check for $25,000.00 to be used as a trust deposit, subject to call, on which your Trust Department will pay me 7% from the time you receive this money until I withdraw it. I believe this is in accordance with the proposition you made to me. Kindly let me know if this is correct and oblige,' etc. [The bank received the money and made an appropriate entry on its books].
>
> [Based on the letter and the entry on the bank's books, the court concluded that plaintiff had accepted] the proposition made in the trust officer's letter of June 4th, and that the interest-bearing deposit so made constituted a special deposit to be secured by the setting aside of sufficient securities, in the nature of collateral, to secure the deposit. [T]he Palm Beach bank mingled the funds thus received with its general funds, the cash assets, of the bank, in its commercial department. On June 28, 1926, fourteen days after acknowledging receipt of the check, the bank closed its doors, and it was taken over by the comptroller, who appointed Orel J. Myers as receiver, which appointment was confirmed by the court and all the

> assets, books, and affairs of the bank were turned over to such receiver. The bank did not list this $25,000 among its liabilities, and the trust officer testified that this money was not loaned to the bank or treated as a loan by the bank. No note or passbook, or other evidence of debt, was ever issued by the bank to Dr. Bleil.
>
> On October 9, 1926, Dr. Bleil filed with the receiver his claim for the sum of $25,000, asking that said sum of money be returned to him or that the same be made a preferred claim against the assets of said bank. This claim was rejected by the receiver as a preferred claim but was allowed by him to remain on file in his office as a general claim against the bank. * * *
>
> [The facts also revealed that, when the] check was received by the bank, it was sent to one of its several correspondent banks with which it kept a deposit, namely, the Atlantic National Bank of Jacksonville, where it was deposited, on June 12th, to the credit of the Palm Beach Bank & Trust Company. The Palm Beach bank received credit for the check on that date; in effect, it 'cashed' the check. It was paid on June 16th through the New York clearing house by the New York bank on which it was drawn. The Palm Beach bank had on deposit with the Atlantic National in excess of $40,000 from June 12th to June 14th. This deposit was reduced to $19,124.72 on June 16th. However, on the following day, June 17th, additional deposits were made, increasing the total deposits to the credit of the Palm Beach bank on that day to $97,649.03. On June 18th this amount had risen still further to $142,263.51. With the exception of two days from that time on until the Palm Beach bank closed its doors, it had on deposit daily with the Atlantic National Bank sums in excess of $80,000; on June 22d its deposits with said Jacksonville bank were upwards of $143,000; and on June 28th, the day the Palm Beach bank closed, it has on deposit with the Atlantic National something over $140,000, which came into the hands of the receiver of the Palm Beach bank.

Is plaintiff entitled to preferred status? If so, in what amount?

4. *The Worthless Notes.* Bierschwale sold an apartment complex to Herbert Oakes in return for fifty-nine promissory notes payable to Oakes. The notes were executed by three different people: James H. Shoffner, William E. Goyen, Jr., and Louis R. Davis.

Oakes conveyed the apartment complex to his wholly owned corporation, United Properties, Inc., and it in turn sold the apartment complex to Eugene J. Goldman, a bona fide purchaser. Oakes received from Goldman $40,000 in cash plus twenty-four notes (the "Goldman notes"). Twenty-three of the notes were for $4,000 and the twenty-fourth was for $1,879.10.

When Bierschwale learned that the Shoffner, Goyen and Davis notes were worthless, he immediately filed an action to rescind the sale. He also sought to impress a constructive trust on the proceeds of the Goldman sale. Is a constructive trust appropriate? *See Meadows v. Bierschwale*, 516 S.W.2d 125 (Tex.1974).

MATTSON V. COMMERCIAL CREDIT BUSINESS LOANS, INC.

301 Or. 407, 723 P.2d 996 (En Banc, 1986).

CAMPBELL, JUSTICE. This case involves conversion of lumber and the payment to defendant of the proceeds from the converted lumber. Plaintiffs, owners of the converted lumber, sought recovery of the proceeds from the sale of the lumber from the defendant creditor of the converter based on two claims for relief. The first was labeled money had and received, pursuant to which plaintiffs requested actual and punitive damages. The second, which was labeled unjust enrichment, requested a constructive trust.

Plaintiffs and West Coast Lumber Sales, which is not a party to this action, had a contract whereby West Coast would cut plaintiffs' logs at plaintiffs' site for orders pre-sold by West Coast and approved by plaintiffs. In May 1980, West Coast removed 285,000 board feet of lumber from plaintiffs' site without plaintiffs' approval. In September 1980, plaintiffs sued West Coast seeking only money damages for conversion of the lumber. Plaintiffs did not seek replevin, or an injunction to prevent the sale of the lumber, or a constructive trust on the proceeds.

In February 1981, while the litigation between plaintiffs and West Coast was pending, Commercial Credit, defendant in this action, opened a line of credit for West Coast which was secured by inventory and accounts. West Coast's attorney advised defendant of the pending litigation between plaintiffs and West Coast, but the attorney advised defendant that the existence of the litigation did not prevent defendant from making a loan to West Coast so long as plaintiffs were making no claim to the collateral on which defendant was relying in making the loan. In June 1982, plaintiffs won a judgment for $192,011.17 against West Coast for conversion. Shortly thereafter, West Coast filed a petition for bankruptcy.

Under the terms of the accounts receivable contract between West Coast and defendant, all money received by West Coast was turned over to defendant; defendant would then make fresh advances. During the one and one-half years that the contract was in operation, defendant loaned West Coast approximately $2,000,000 more than it received back. Defendant declared West Coast in default in July 1982.

During the pendency of the bankruptcy proceeding, plaintiffs learned that defendant claimed a security interest in all of West Coast's inventory, including the converted lumber and the money generated from the sales of the converted lumber. In March 1983, plaintiffs filed this action asserting a claim against the proceeds West Coast received from the sale of the converted lumber which, plaintiffs asserted, defendant received as part of the revolving credit arrangement with West Coast.

Defendant moved for summary judgment and the trial court granted the motion. The Court of Appeals affirmed without opinion. We reverse and remand.

[The trial court may have] granted summary judgment on the basis that, even in the absence of a valid security interest, plaintiffs could not recover proceeds from the sale of the converted property from third parties. Plaintiffs assert that they are entitled to recover identifiable proceeds based on the theories of tracing rights and unjust enrichment.

[T]racing doctrine operates against innocent transferees who receive no legal title and transferees who are not bona fide purchasers and receive legal but not equitable title. If either type of transferee exchanges the acquired property for other property, or receives income from the acquired property, tracing may apply. *See* RESTATEMENT OF RESTITUTION §§ 204, 205 (1937).

Defendant argues that the tracing of proceeds of converted goods in the hands of third party transferees should not be permitted because "the parties liable would increase like an inverted pyramid ever upward and outward" making such tracing commercially impracticable. Defendant asserts that under plaintiffs' theory if West Coast had used the proceeds from the sale of the converted lumber to pay its employees, its employees would be liable to plaintiffs. Similarly, each lumber company that bought plaintiffs' lumber presumably later resold it and used those proceeds to pay its bills. Defendant argues that under plaintiffs' theory the creditors of subsequent converters who are paid with those proceeds are also liable.

Defendant's commercial impracticability argument ignores the reality that tracing of proceeds into the hands of third, fourth, fifth, etc. party transferees is permitted under the Uniform Commercial Code. ORS 79.3060(2) indicates that tracing proceeds into the hands of remote transferees is considered commercially practicable. ORS 79.3060(2) provides: "(2) Except where ORS 79.1010 to 79.5070 otherwise provide, a security interest continues in collateral notwithstanding sale, exchange or other disposition thereof unless the disposition was authorized by the secured party in the security agreement or otherwise, and also continues in any identifiable proceeds including collections received by the debtor."

Tracing proceeds into the hands of third party transferees is routinely sanctioned in a variety of UCC contexts. *See, e.g., In Re Guaranteed Muffler Supply Co., Inc.*, 1 B.R. 324, 27 UCC Rep. 1217 (Bankr.N.D.Ga.1979) (permitting secured creditor to trace proceeds from sale of debtor's inventory and accounts into hands of third-party transferee).

Defendant's argument also ignores the fact that a bona fide purchaser would cut off plaintiffs' tracing rights. Section 208(1) of the Restatement on Restitution provides: "(1) Where a person wrongfully disposes of property of another knowing that the disposition is wrongful and in exchange therefore other property is transferred to a third person, the other can enforce a constructive trust or an equitable lien upon the property, unless the third person is a bona fide purchaser."

The creditors or employees of the companies that bought the lumber are analogous to purchasers in that they are exchanging their services for money. If they "purchased" in good faith without knowledge that the money they received was proceeds from stolen property, they would be like bona fide purchasers and thus would also cut off plaintiffs' tracing rights.

Whether defendant is a bona fide purchaser cutting off plaintiffs' tracing rights is a question of material fact which precludes summary judgment. An innocent purchaser is one who has no reasonable grounds to suspect that the person from whom he buys an article did not have good title. As this court noted long ago, whether one is a purchaser in good faith is an issue of fact that must be determined from many circumstances, including actual and constructive notice and suspicious circumstances. The facts surrounding the transaction, including any unusual or peculiar business methods of the vendor that were known to the purchaser, may properly be submitted to the jury to be considered on the ultimate question of good or bad faith.

[West Coast] applied to defendant in January 1981, for a line of credit. As part of this application West Coast provided a letter from West Coast's attorney stating that plaintiffs had filed an action for willful conversion of Douglas Fir lumber against West Coast. Thus defendant knew of plaintiffs' claim for conversion against West Coast. Accordingly, defendant was on notice that if plaintiffs prevailed on their claim, some portion of the payments on account which defendant received might represent proceeds from the sale of stolen property. Defendant admits that it received notice that the action was pending, but notes that it had received an explanatory letter from West Coast's attorney and it felt that the existence of the litigation for money damages did not prevent it from making a loan so long as no claim was being asserted to the collateral upon which it was relying.

The fact that defendant knew of the pending litigation is undisputed. However, reasonable persons could draw different inferences and conclusions from this undisputed fact regarding whether defendant had acted in good faith and was thus a bona fide purchaser cutting off plaintiffs' tracing rights.

In addition, plaintiffs' right to recover under a tracing theory is limited by their ability to trace the proceeds from the converted lumber. If they cannot trace the proceeds to defendant then they cannot recover under this theory. Plaintiffs submitted evidentiary materials to the trial court describing how such tracing could be established. Defendant claims that the proceeds from the sale of the converted lumber have long since passed through its hands to undetermined third parties. Plaintiffs' ability to identify and trace proceeds from the sale of the converted lumber is evidentiary, a matter of proof. It is not an appropriate basis for summary judgment.

[Defendant] also argued that where one of two parties must bear the loss caused by a third party's wrongdoing (here, West Coast), the loss should fall on the party with knowledge and in the better position to avoid the loss by policing the wrongdoer's conduct. Defendant claims that plaintiffs could have avoided the loss by asserting either a request for claim and delivery, for an injunction to prevent the sale of the lumber, for a constructive trust on the proceeds, for an equitable lien, or for replevin.

Plaintiffs agree that when there is a dispute between two essentially innocent parties the one who was in the best position to prevent the loss should bear it. Plaintiffs argue that defendant was in the best position to prevent the loss. Plaintiffs assert that they had no ability to control the actions of West Coast. Conversely, according to plaintiffs, defendant voluntarily entered into its financing arrangement knowing of plaintiffs' claims for conversion and was on notice that if plaintiffs prevailed on their claim, some portion of the payments on account which defendant received would represent proceeds from the sale of stolen property. Thus plaintiffs assert that the burden of loss must fall on defendant because it was in a position to investigate the validity of plaintiffs' conversion claims, to police West Coast's conduct, and to avoid the ultimate loss.

In this case, both plaintiffs and defendant will suffer because of West Coast's conversion and subsequent activities. Plaintiffs have lost lumber valued at $192,011.17. Defendant lost approximately $2,000,000 which it had loaned West Coast on a revolving credit basis. Although defendant lost more money than did plaintiffs, that does not indicate that defendant has not been unjustly enriched; defendant may have lost $192,011.17 less than it would have otherwise. As plaintiffs argue, defendant is not entitled to keep plaintiffs' property to make its loss less painful.

Defendant has been enriched by West Coast's actions if defendant received proceeds from the sale of the converted lumber in which it had no security interest and if it was in the best position to prevent the loss.[6] Whether defendant or plaintiffs were in the best position to prevent the

[6] If the proceeds cannot be traced because defendant has expended the money, there is nothing upon which a constructive trust could be imposed. However, plaintiffs may still be entitled to a money judgment if defendant was unjustly enriched. See Johnson v. Steen, 281 Or. 361, 372, 575 P.2d 141 (1978).

loss is a question of fact. Summary judgment on this basis would be inappropriate.

[In] light of these genuine issues of material fact, the grant of summary judgment to defendant was error. The decision of the Court of Appeals is reversed. The case is remanded to the trial court for further proceedings.

PROBLEMS

1. *More on the Stolen Steers.* Now, let's think a bit more about the stolen steer problem presented at the beginning of the chapter. Could tracing principles be invoked in a case like this? If so, how might they be applied. *See Lamb v. Rooney*, 72 Neb. 322, 100 N.W. 410 (1904).

2. *The Embezzled Money.* W.B. Barnes embezzled $5,815.03 from his employer, Brodie Bros. Inc., over a five year period before his death. Barnes frittered away approximately $2,000, and used the remaining money to purchase a home. The total cost of the house was $10,000. Barnes paid $2,000 down (this money was not embezzled), and made $2,500 in payments before he began embezzling.

After the embezzlement, Barnes commingled embezzled funds with other funds (legitimately earned) in a bank account and made the remaining payments on the house from this account.

After Barnes' death, the embezzlement was discovered. Brodie Bros. made a claim against Barnes' estate, but the claim was rejected. Brodie Bros. then sued the estate and Barnes's widow for restitution.

The trial court held that the real estate should be sold (its fair market value is $10,000). From the proceeds of the sale, Brodie should be paid $3,815.03, and Barnes' widow shall be entitled to the remainder of the sale proceeds.

Did the trial court reach the right result? What remedies should Brodie Bros. have received, and in what amounts? *See Brodie v. Barnes*, 56 Cal.App.2d 315, 132 P.2d 595 (1942).

3. *More on Embezzlement.* Suppose that a corporation's (P corporation) President embezzled $170,000 to buy bonds, and then transferred the bonds to two other corporations (D corporations) which he controlled. D corporations used these bonds to develop and perfect inventions and patents. Should the corporation be able to trace the embezzled money into the inventions and patents? *See Flannery v. Flannery Bolt Co.*, 108 F.2d 531 (3d Cir.1939).

4. *The Fraudulent Loans.* Poindexter defrauded a bank into loaning him money on two occasions. The first loan was for $2,123 and the second was for $1,019.67. Poindexter, who did not own any cows, represented that he owned 150 and that he needed the loans to feed and care for the cows. In fact, Poindexter used the money to pay the premiums on insurance policies payable to his wife. Poindexter was insolvent at the time.

After Poindexter's death, the bank discovered the fraud. Poindexter's wife collected $50,000 under the policies. Over the years, Poindexter had paid $3,208.80 of his own money in premiums on the policies. Poindexter diverted $186 of the bank's money for this purpose as well. At the time of the diversion, Poindexter was insolvent and not otherwise able to pay the required premiums. Absent the premium, the policies would have lapsed.

Should the bank be allowed to impose a constructive trust or equitable lien on the insurance proceeds? If so, in what amount? $186? $3,139.67? $50,000? *See Exchange State Bank v. Poindexter*, 137 Kan. 101, 19 P.2d 705 (1933); *Thum v. Wolstenholme*, 21 Utah 446, 61 P. 537 (1900).

b. Priority Over Other Creditors

IN RE RADKE

5 Kan.App.2d 407, 619 P.2d 520 (1980).

ABBOTT, JUDGE: This action involves the appeals of Keith Cook and Icer Addis, two creditors of Dwaine F. Radke and Barbara Radke, from a judgment denying their claimed priorities in the distribution of assets in the Radkes' voluntary receivership action. We will refer to Dwaine F. Radke and Barbara Radke as the Radkes, and to Dwaine F. Radke's mother either as his mother or as Mary Hazel Radke.

The claims of Cook and Addis are separate and unrelated, but both of them claim priority to monies produced by the sale of land identified as the Beltz land. Cook and Addis were held to be general creditors. All other creditors are general creditors and none is a party to this appeal.

The sale of the Doebbling land produced net proceeds of $27,626.70. The judgment liens of Rickel, Inc., and Anspaugh amounted to $20,557.23. The sale of the Beltz land produced $13,495.74. Those sums were further reduced by court costs and fees totaling $5,091.50 that was ordered paid 67 percent from the Doebbling proceeds and 33 percent from Beltz funds. After the judgment liens of Rickel, Inc., and Anspaugh are satisfied, the remaining $18,841.58 is to be distributed to the remaining general creditors proportionately, to the total of their claims in the amount of $148,354.85.

Addis claims priority on the Beltz proceeds, which presently amount to a net of $11,798.57 after fees and expenses to date are deducted. * * *

The basis of Addis's claim is that on January 13, 1976, the Radkes entered into a contract to sell the Beltz and Doebbling lands to Addis. On that same day, Addis paid $37,000 on the purchase price, as follows:

> (a) $17,000 to the First State Bank of Ness City, Kansas, the amount of an overdue payment that Addis was to assume on an existing contract of purchase between Dwaine Radke's mother and a third party.

(b) $20,000 to the Radkes' attorney as the down payment, which was disbursed to the Radkes and their attorney.

The Radkes had represented that they were in possession of the Beltz tract by virtue of an assignment of a contract of sale from Dwaine's mother, Mary Hazel Radke. Addis subsequently learned the Radkes were in possession of the Beltz land as a tenant of Dwaine's mother; he then disaffirmed the Radke–Addis contract for misrepresentation on April 29, 1976. The Beltz land was assigned to the receiver on January 8, 1977, by Mary Hazel Radke and sold by the receiver for the sums noted above. The record does not indicate that the Radkes ever had any interest in the Beltz land and Mary Hazel Radke assigned the land to the receiver without any apparent legal compulsion to do so. As a practical matter, she was paid for her equity, and the only funds derived from the Beltz land sale came from Addis's $17,000 payment. Addis is a creditor for $37,000 and claims first priority on the sum of $11,798.57 remaining from the sale of the Beltz land.

Addis claims priority on the Beltz land sale proceeds as a defrauded purchaser whose payment, made in good faith before discovery of the misrepresentation, enhanced the net recovery by virtue of the $17,000 payment on the contract of purchase, and he is entitled to recover that sum from the proceeds of the sale. Addis acknowledges that only $11,798.57 remains in the Beltz "pot" and that the remainder of his $37,000 payment would fall into the general creditor category.

[On] April 29, 1976, Addis disaffirmed the Radke–Addis contract of sale, and that disaffirmance has never been contested. In May 1976, the Radkes contracted to sell the Doebbling land to Kent Davidson. The creditors subsequently agreed to the completion of the sale provided the net proceeds would be distributed among the Radkes' creditors as determined by the court.

[Having] determined that Cook is a general creditor, and recognizing that the two judgment lien holders will be paid from the Doebbling land sale proceeds, we turn to Addis's claim of unjust enrichment as to the proceeds from the sale of the Beltz land.

Addis claims he has a right to the remaining proceeds from the sale of the Beltz land in the amount of $11,798.57, less any additional fees and expenses the district court might allow on remand. It is his position that the receiver received at least $17,000 more for the Beltz land than would have been obtained without the $17,000 Addis paid, and the trial court's finding to this effect is unchallenged. As a result, Addis contends Mary Hazel Radke, and ultimately the creditors of the Radkes, would be unjustly enriched in the amount of $11,798.57 if he is not allowed priority on that sum. We agree. As noted in *United States Fidelity & Guaranty Co. v. Marshall*, 4 Kan.App.2d 9, 10, 601 P.2d 1169 (1979), restitution and unjust enrichment are similar terms and their substance "lies in a promise, implied by law, that one will restore to the person entitled thereto that which in equity and good conscience belongs to him." None of the parties disputes the fact that Addis is the source of the $11,798.57, nor do they dispute the fact that he paid that sum pursuant to a contract of purchase under the mistaken belief that the contract was valid and that he had assumed the responsibility of making the overdue $17,000 payment. The fact that the Radkes were not the title holders of record and that an earlier investigation of the actual facts would have led to discovery of the fact the Radkes had no assignment to the underlying contract of purchase does not defeat Addis's claim. Restatement of the Law of Restitution § 59 (1936), states: "A person who has conferred a benefit upon another by mistake is not precluded from maintaining an action for restitution by the fact that the mistake was due to his lack of care," for the reason that unless the lack of care resulted in harm to an interested party, it should not be penalized. In this case, Mary Hazel Radke was not harmed; in fact she benefited from the contract being brought current. The record title holder benefited by receiving payment on the contract. The general creditors are not harmed. In fact, they may have benefited by the difference between Addis's payment and the amount left after the payment of fees and expenses, a substantial part of which would have otherwise been charged against the Doebbling land sale proceeds, thus reducing the amount available to the general creditors. *See also* RESTATEMENT OF THE LAW OF RESTITUTION § 17c (1936). At the time Addis had to make his decision, he was acting in good faith under a mistake of fact and cannot be considered to have made a voluntary payment so as to be classified as an intermeddler into the affairs of others. He did not knowingly confer an unsolicited benefit on another, an action which usually bars restitution.

Equity has long allowed a person who pays money to another under the mistaken belief a valid contract exists to recover that money when the contract is subsequently canceled for fraud or mistake and the rights of innocent parties have not intervened. RESTATEMENT OF THE LAW OF RESTITUTION §§ 17, 28 (1936); IV Palmer, Law of Restitution § 22.1 (1978). Equity permits the tracing of assets and the impression of a trust or equitable lien on them without the showing that a money judgment against the party who precipitated the fraud would be uncollectible. I Palmer, Law of Restitution § 3.14(a)(1978). In any event, the record in this case convincingly shows the Radkes to be insolvent.

Kansas allows funds to be traced in equity cases and the owner to reclaim them when they can be identified. "It matters not how much it may have changed, either in form or character, it still belongs to the owner, and if it, or its fruits or substitute, can be found among the assets of the trustee, the amount of the fund may be taken out of such assets, providing no superior rights of innocent third parties have intervened." *Bank v. Bank*, 64 P. 634 (1901). In *Steele et al. v. State Bank et al.*, 227 p.

352 (1924), a person defrauded in a land sale was allowed a preferred claim over general creditors of a bank against land transferred to the bank as a result of fraud.

We hold that the trial court erred in denying Addis's claim of priority to the funds remaining from the sale of the Beltz land. As to the remainder of Addis's claim, he is a general creditor. In view of our holding, it will be necessary for the trial court to redetermine the percentages due the general creditors.

Affirmed in part, reversed in part and remanded with directions.

PROBLEM: MORE ON THE STOLEN STEERS

Now, let's think a bit more about the stolen steer problem at the beginning of the chapter. In a case like this, would it be appropriate to give plaintiff priority over other creditors? Why? Why not?

CUNNINGHAM V. BROWN

265 U.S. 1, 44 S.Ct. 424, 68 L.Ed. 873 (1924).

MR. CHIEF JUSTICE TAFT delivered the opinion of the Court.

These were six suits in equity brought by the trustees in bankruptcy of Charles Ponzi to recover of the defendants sums paid them by the bankrupt within four months prior to the filing of the petition in bankruptcy on the ground that they were unlawful preferences. The facts and defenses are the same in all the cases, except that, in that of Benjamin Brown, there was an additional defense that he was a minor when the transactions occurred. We have brought the cases into this court by writ of certiorari.

The litigation grows out of the remarkable criminal financial career of Charles Ponzi. In December, 1919, with a capital of $150, he began the business of borrowing money on his promissory notes. He did not profess to receive money for investment for account of the lender. He borrowed the money on his credit only. He spread the false tale that on his own account he was engaged in buying international postal coupons in foreign countries and selling them in other countries at 100 percent profit, and that this was made possible by the excessive differences in the rates of exchange following the war. He was willing, he said, to give others the opportunity to share with him this profit. By a written promise in 90 days to pay them $150 for every $100 loaned, he induced thousands to lend him. He stimulated their avidity by paying his 90-day notes in full at the end of 45 days, and by circulating the notice that he would pay any unmatured note presented in less than 45 days at 100 percent of the loan. Within eight months he took in $9,582,000, for which he issued his notes for $14,374,000. He paid his agents a commission of 10 percent. With the 50 per cent. promised to lenders, every loan paid in full with the profit would cost him 60 per cent. He was always insolvent, and became daily more so, the more his business succeeded. He made no investments of any kind, so that all the money he had at any time was solely the result of loans by his dupes.

[By] July 1st, Ponzi was taking in about $1,000,000 a week. Because of an investigation by public authority, Ponzi ceased selling notes on July 26th, but offered and continued to pay all unmatured notes for the amount originally paid in, and all matured notes which had run 45 days, in full. The report of the investigation caused a run on Ponzi's Boston office by investors seeking payment, and this developed into a wild scramble when, August 2d, a Boston newspaper, most widely circulated, declared Ponzi to be hopelessly insolvent, with a full description of the situation, written by one of his recent employees. To meet this emergency, Ponzi concentrated all his available money from other banks in Boston and New England in the Hanover Trust Company, a banking concern in Boston, which had been his chief depository. There was no evidence of any general attempt by holders of unmatured notes to secure payment prior to the run which set in after the investigation July 26th.

The money of the defendants was paid by them between July 20th and July 24th and was deposited in the Hanover Trust Company. At the opening of business July 19th, the balance of Ponzi's deposit accounts at the Hanover Trust Company was $334,000. At the close of business July 24th it was $871,000. This sum was exhausted by withdrawals of July 26th of $572,000, of July 27th of $228,000, and of July 28th of $905,000, or a total of more than $1,765,000. In spite of this, the account continued to show a credit balance, because new deposits from other banks were made by Ponzi. It was finally ended by an overdraft on August 9th of $331,000. The petition in bankruptcy was then filed. The total withdrawals from July 19th to August 10th were $6,692,000. The claims which have been filed against the bankrupt estate are for the money lent, and not for the 150 per cent. promised.

Both courts held that the defendants had rescinded their contracts of loan for fraud and that they were entitled to a return of their money; that other dupes of Ponzi who filed claims in bankruptcy must be held not to have rescinded, but to have remained creditors, so that what the latter had paid in was the property of Ponzi; that the presumption was that a wrongdoing trustee first withdrew his own money from a fund mingled with that of his *cestui que trustent*, and therefore that the respective deposits of the defendants were still in the bank and available for return to them in rescission; and that payments to them of these amounts were not preferences, but merely the return of their own money.

[In] the first place, we do not agree that the action of the defendants constituted a rescission for fraud and a restoration of the money lent on that ground. As early as April, his secretary testifies that Ponzi adopted the practice of permitting any who did not wish to leave his money for 45 days to receive it back in full without interest, and this was announced from time to time. [Certainly] Ponzi was not returning their money on any admission of fraud. The lenders merely took advantage of his agreement to pay his unmatured notes at par of the actual loan. Such notes were paid under his agreement exactly as his notes which were matured were paid at par and 50 per cent. The real transaction between him and those who were seeking him is shown by the fact that there were 500 to whom he gave checks in compliance with his promise, and who were defeated merely because there were no more funds.

The District Court found that, when these defendants were paid on and after August 2d, they had reason to believe that Ponzi was insolvent. [On] the morning of August 2d, when news of Ponzi's insolvency was broadly announced, there was a scramble and a race. The neighborhood of the Hanover Bank was crowded with people trying to get their money, and for eight days they struggled. Why? Because they feared that they would be left only with claims against an insolvent debtor. In other words, they were seeking a preference by their diligence. Thus they came into the teeth of the Bankruptcy Act, and their preferences in payment are avoided by it.

But, even if we assume that the payment of these unmatured notes was not according to the contract with Ponzi, and that what the defendants here did was a rescission for fraud, we do not find them in any better case. They had one of two remedies to make them whole. They could have followed the money wherever they could trace it and have asserted possession of it on the ground that there was a resulting trust in their favor, or they could have established a lien for what was due them in any particular fund of which he had made it a part. These things they could do without violating any statutory rule against preference in bankruptcy, because they then would have been endeavoring to get their own money, and not money in the estate of the bankrupt. But to succeed they must trace the money, and therein they have failed. It is clear that all the money deposited by these defendants was withdrawn from deposit some days before they applied for and received payment of their unmatured notes. It is true that by the payment into the account of money coming from other banks and directly from other dupes the bank account as such was prevented from being exhausted; but it is impossible to trace into the Hanover deposit of Ponzi after August 1st, from which defendants' checks were paid, the money which they paid him into that account before July 26th. There was, therefore, no money coming from them upon which a constructive trust, or an equitable lien could be fastened.

Lord Chancellor Eldon, in *Clayton's Case*, [1816] Ch. 1 Merivale, 572, held that, in a fund in which were mingled the moneys of several defrauded claimants insufficient to satisfy them all, the first withdrawals were to be charged against the first deposits, and the claimants were entitled to be paid in the inverse order in which their moneys went into the account. Ponzi's withdrawals from his account with the Hanover Trust Company on July 26, 27, and 28 were made before defendants had indicated any purpose to rescind. Ponzi then had a defeasible title to the money he had received from them, and could legally withdraw it. By the end of July 28th he had done so, and had exhausted all that was traceable to their deposits. The rule in Clayton's Case has no application.

The courts below relied on the rule established by the English Court of Appeals in *Knatchbull v. Hallett*, L.R. 13 Ch. D. 696, in which it was decided by Sir George Jessel, Master of the Rolls, and one of his colleagues, that, where a fund was composed partly of a defrauded claimant's money and partly of that of the wrongdoer, it would be presumed that in the fluctuations of the fund it was the wrongdoer's purpose to draw out the money he could legally and honestly use rather than that of the claimant, and that the claimant might identify what remained as his res, and assert his right to it by way of an equitable lien on the whole fund, or a proper pro rata share of it. To make the rule applicable here, we must infer that in the deposit and withdrawal of more than $3,000,000 between the deposits of the defendants prior to July 28th, and the payment of their checks after August 2d, Ponzi kept the money of defendants on deposit intact and paid out only his subsequent deposits. Considering the fact that all this money was the result of fraud upon all his dupes, it would be running the fiction of *Knatchbull v. Hallett* into the ground to apply it here. The rule is useful to work out equity between a wrongdoer and a victim; but, when the fund with which the wrongdoer is dealing is wholly made up of the fruits of the frauds perpetrated against a myriad of victims, the case is different. To say that, as between equally innocent victims, the wrongdoer, having defeasible title to the whole fund, must be presumed to have distinguished in advance between the money of those who were about to rescind and those who were not, would be carrying the fiction to a fantastic conclusion.

After August 2d the victims of Ponzi were not to be divided into two classes, those who rescinded for fraud and those who were relying on his contract to pay them. They were all of one class, actuated by the same purpose to save themselves from the effect of Ponzi's insolvency. Whether they sought to rescind, or sought to get their money as by the terms of the contract, they were, in their inability to identify their payments, creditors, and nothing more. It is a case the circumstances of which call strongly for the principle that equality is equity, and this is the spirit of the bankrupt law. Those who were successful in the race of diligence violated not only its spirit, but its letter, and secured an unlawful preference.

[The] decrees are reversed.

NOTES

1. *The Madoff Affair.* Charles Ponzi's scheme was replicated, albeit on a bit grander scale, by Bernard Madoff who ran a fraudulent securities business. Madoff's "clients" thought that they Madoff was investing their money with his firm. In fact, Madoff was simply running a Ponzi scheme. After the nature of Madoff's business was revealed, there was a mad scramble for assets.

2. *The Restatement and Co-Mingled Money.* Consider *Restatement (Third) Restitution and Unjust Enrichment*: § 59:

> (1) If property of the claimant is deposited in a common account or otherwise commingled with other property so that it is no longer separately identifiable, the traceable product of the claimant's property may be identified in
>
> (a) the balance of the commingled fund or a portion thereof, or
>
> (b) property acquired with withdrawals from the commingled fund, or a portion thereof, or
>
> (c) a combination of the foregoing, in accordance with the further rules stated in this section.
>
> (2) If property of the claimant has been commingled by a recipient who is a conscious wrongdoer or a defaulting fiduciary (§ 51) or equally at fault in dealing with the claimant's property (§ 52):
>
> (a) Withdrawals that yield a traceable product and withdrawals that are dissipated are marshaled so far as possible in favor of the claimant.
>
> (b) Subsequent contributions by the recipient do not restore property previously misappropriated from the claimant, unless the recipient affirmatively intends such application.
>
> (c) After one or more withdrawals from a commingled fund, the portion of the remainder that may be identified as the traceable product of the claimant's property may not exceed the fund's lowest intermediate balance.
>
> (3) If property of the claimant has been commingled by an innocent recipient (§ 50), the claimant's property may be traced into the remaining balance of the commingled fund and any product thereof in the manner permitted by § 59(2), but restitution from property so identified may not exceed the amount for which the recipient is liable by the rules of §§ 50 and 53.
>
> (4) If a fund contains the property of multiple restitution claimants (such as the victims of successive fraud by the recipient):

(a) Each claimant's interest in the fund and any product thereof is determined by the proportion that such claimant's contributions bear to the balance of the fund upon each contribution and withdrawal, but only if the accounting necessary to this calculation can be established without using the presumptions or marshaling rules of § 59(2).

(b) If the evidence does not permit the court to distinguish the interests of multiple restitution claimants by reference to actual transactions, such claimants recover ratably from the fund and any product thereof in proportion to their respective losses.

(5) The balance from time to time of a commingled fund may be determined by whatever method of accounting is practicable and appropriate to the circumstances of a particular case.

c. Circumvention of Debtor Exemptions

PALM BEACH SAVINGS & LOAN ASSOCIATION, F.S.A. V. FISHBEIN

619 So.2d 267 (Fla.1993).

GRIMES, JUSTICE.

[In] October of 1984, Lawrence Fishbein acquired a house in Palm Beach. He took title in his own name, assumed an existing mortgage on the house, and also executed a purchase money mortgage. The following year, Mr. Fishbein, joined by his wife Deborah, executed another mortgage on the house in which the existence of the prior mortgages was acknowledged. Mr. and Mrs. Fishbein lived in the house for several years.

In March of 1988, Mr. Fishbein borrowed $1,200,000 from Palm Beach Savings & Loan Association (bank) and secured the debt with a mortgage on the house. Despite its knowledge that Mr. and Mrs. Fishbein were then engaged in dissolution proceedings, the bank permitted Mr. Fishbein to obtain his wife's signature on the mortgage without requiring her to sign the document in the bank's presence. Unknown to either Mrs. Fishbein or the bank, Mr. Fishbein forged his wife's signature to the mortgage. Approximately $930,000 of the loan proceeds was applied directly to the payment of the three existing mortgages and taxes on the property. The remaining sum was used by Mr. Fishbein for other purposes.

In August of 1988, Mr. and Mrs. Fishbein entered into a property settlement agreement which provided that Mr. Fishbein would buy his wife a $275,000 home and pay her $225,000 and that she would give up any interest in the Palm Beach house. As collateral for his promises, Mr. Fishbein gave his wife's attorney a quitclaim deed conveying the Palm

Beach house to Mr. and Mrs. Fishbein. He represented that the house was free and clear of liens except those claimed by his mother and sister. Mrs. Fishbein then moved out of the Palm Beach house, and the parties were divorced. However, Mr. Fishbein failed to buy Mrs. Fishbein a new house or to pay her the promised money. In the meantime, the mortgage on the Palm Beach house went into default, and the bank commenced foreclosure proceedings. Mrs. Fishbein moved back into the Palm Beach house, and Mr. Fishbein was incarcerated. Finally, the judge in the dissolution proceeding set aside the property settlement agreement for fraud in the procurement and awarded Mrs. Fishbein the Palm Beach house nunc pro tunc.

In the foreclosure proceeding, the bank and Mrs. Fishbein stipulated that her only interest in the Palm Beach house at the time of the bank's loan was a homestead interest. Following the trial, the judge ruled that Mrs. Fishbein had not abandoned her homestead interest in the house and that the mortgage could not be foreclosed against the house. However, the judge permitted the bank to have an equitable lien on the house to the extent that its funds were used to satisfy the preexisting mortgages and taxes. The judge stayed any foreclosure sale on the equitable lien for six months to permit Mrs. Fishbein to try to make a private sale of the house.

[Article X, section 4] of our constitution provides in pertinent part: (a) There shall be exempt from forced sale under process of any court, and no judgment, decree or execution shall be a lien thereon, except for the payment of taxes and assessments thereon, obligations contracted for the purchase, improvement or repair thereof, or obligations contracted for house, field or other labor performed on the realty, the following property owned by a natural person: (1) a [homestead]. In light of this provision and the fact that Mrs. Fishbein never signed the mortgage, the bank does not assert in this Court that its mortgage may be foreclosed against the Palm Beach house. The bank argues, however, that because its loan proceeds were used to satisfy the prior liens, it stands in the shoes of the prior lienors under the doctrine of equitable subrogation. Thus, the bank argues that it has the same rights to enforce a lien against the homestead property as the prior lienholders. Mrs. Fishbein argues that the bank's equitable position cannot be sustained because its claim does not fall within the language of the exceptions in article X, section 4.

In the seminal case of *Jones v. Carpenter*, 106 So. 127, 130 (1925), this Court permitted the trustee of a bankrupt bread company to have an equitable lien against the house of the company's former president which had been improved by funds embezzled from the company. While explaining the nature of equitable liens, the Court cited *Capen v. Garrison*, 92 S.W. 368 (1906), for the proposition that the doctrine of equitable liens followed the doctrine of subrogation and that they "are applied only in cases where the law fails to give relief and justice would suffer without them." Jones, 90 Fla. at 413, 106 So. at 129. In rejecting the defense that the lien could not be imposed on a homestead, we observed that: [W]hile this court has repeatedly held that organic and statutory provisions relating to homestead exemptions should be liberally construed in the interest of the family home, they should not be applied so as to make them an instrument of fraud or imposition upon [creditors].

[Thus,] it is apparent that where equity demands it this Court has not hesitated to permit equitable liens to be imposed on homesteads beyond the literal language of article X, section 4. However, the court below was not so concerned with the constitutional language as it was with its belief that an equitable lien could not be imposed because Mrs. Fishbein was not a party to the fraud. Yet, there was no fraud involved in [prior cases]. In those cases, the equitable liens were imposed to prevent unjust enrichment. Moreover, in both cases the homestead interest of the spouse of the party whose conduct led to the unjust enrichment was also subject to the equitable lien.

[Plaintiff] should have an equitable lien on the property to the extent that its loan proceeds were used to pay the preexisting mortgage which had attached the homestead and the unpaid taxes. While Palm Beach Savings could have been more prudent in handling the closing and such prudence may have avoided the fraud, I do not believe that any such negligence should be a bar to an equitable lien. Palm Beach Savings' mistake, if any, was one of neglect not one of active misfeasance. Additionally, the signature which they relied upon was supported by the attestation of two witnesses and the seal of a notary. Lastly, the homestead would have been liable for these preexisting mortgages and taxes if the Palm Beach Savings' loan had not been procured. Thus, if an equitable lien attaches, Mrs. Fishbein stands in no worse position than she stood in prior to the fraudulent mortgage.

There is competent and substantial evidence to support the finding that Mrs. Fishbein stands in no worse position than she stood before the execution of the mortgage. When the bank made its loan, one of the prior mortgages was already overdue. Mr. Fishbein testified that by that time he had no other assets which could be used to pay off the preexisting liens, and Mrs. Fishbein testified that she had no funds with which to pay them. Of course, Mrs. Fishbein should not be made to suffer because the bank was not more careful in ensuring that her signature on the mortgage was genuine. This is why the bank can make no claim against the property for the $270,000 not used to benefit the homestead. On the other hand, Mrs. Fishbein is not entitled to a $930,000 windfall. The homestead exemption is intended to be a shield, not a sword.

We quash the decision below to the extent that it denies the bank the equitable lien imposed by the trial judge and remand with directions to affirm the trial court's judgment.

It is so ordered.

SHAW, JUSTICE, dissenting.

The Florida constitution clearly sets forth the homestead exemption and its three exceptions, which this Court has consistently held must be strictly construed. The majority opinion rewrites the Constitution to embrace a fourth exception, *i.e.*, claims that it perceives to be within the "spirit of the exception." I am disinclined to have the Court impose an equitable lien on homestead in clear violation of the constitution.

d. Subrogation

WILSON V. TODD

217 Ind. 183, 26 N.E.2d 1003 (1940).

SHAKE, CHIEF JUSTICE.

[D]uring the year 1930 the appellee Roy W. Todd perpetrated an actionable fraud upon the appellant, Charles Wilson, by means of which more than $12,000 in money was extorted from said appellant. The money so obtained was deposited by said Roy W. Todd to his account in a bank. Thereafter, he used $774.38 thereof to pay and discharge a mortgage held by one Henry N. Wilson on a 33-acre tract of land. The further sum of $3,548.16 was withdrawn from said bank by said appellee and applied to the payment of a mortgage held by the Fletcher Joint Stock Land Bank on a 160-acre farm. Title to both pieces of real estate was held by the appellees, who are husband and wife, as tenants by the entireties, and they were both personally liable for the payment of the debts secured by said mortgages. On September 21, 1934, the appellant obtained a tort judgment against Roy W. Todd for the sum of $12,000, for the money that had been obtained by [fraud]. This judgment has never been satisfied. The appellee Ruth A. Todd had no knowledge of the fraudulent acts of her husband at the time said acts were [committed]. The complaint was drawn upon the theory of subrogation. The prayer was that the satisfaction of the [mortgage] liens be set aside and vacated; that there be an adjudication that said liens stand for appellant's use and benefit; and that said mortgages be foreclosed, said real estate sold, and the proceeds applied on the appellant's claim. On the facts found the trial court pronounced conclusions of law to the effect that the law was with the appellant on the issues joined as to his right of subrogation to the mortgage on the 33-acre tract of land, which was discharged by the payment of $774.38; that the law was with the appellee Ruth A. Todd as to the appellant's right of subrogation with respect to the mortgage on the

160-acre farm, which was discharged by the payment of $3,548.16; and that the appellant was entitled to recover from the appellee Roy W. Todd the sum of $12,000, less any amount recovered from the foreclosure of the mortgage on the 33-acre tract of land. * * *

[A]ppellees contend that the conclusion denying subrogation to the mortgage on the 160-acre farm was proper because the findings and the evidence failed to disclose certain essential facts, namely: (1) Knowledge on the part of Ruth A. Todd of the fraud practiced by her husband or of the judgment rendered against him therefor; (2) that the mortgage debts were paid with money belonging to the appellant; (3) that in discharging the mortgage liens Roy W. Todd acted for Ruth A. Todd; and (4) that demand was made on Ruth A. Todd prior to the bringing of this action.

Subrogation is the substitution of another person in the place of a creditor, so that the person in whose favor it is exercised succeeds to the right of the creditor in relation to the debt. So, one whose property is applied by others to the satisfaction of a debt or incumbrance is subrogated to the rights of the creditor or incumbrancer; and subrogation may also be allowed where funds to which one is equitably entitled have been applied to the payment of the debts of another, in which case the former is subrogated to the position of the latter. If it be conceded that the appellant Ruth A. Todd had no knowledge of the fraud perpetrated by her husband, by means of which he obtained the funds out of which he discharged the mortgage debts, and that in paying said debts the husband acted for himself and not as her agent, we do not think this would preclude appellant's right to recover. After being charged with full knowledge of the facts, Ruth A. Todd failed to disavow the acts of her husband, retained the benefits thereof, and resisted the appellant's efforts to obtain redress. She thereby ratified all that had been done by her husband and placed herself in a position to be estopped from denying knowledge of the transaction and the authority of her husband to act for her. And if there was no ratification or no estoppel, we do not think the contention of the appellee Ruth A. Todd could be sustained. According to her own theory she occupies the position of a third party so far as the relation of her husband and the appellant is concerned. She parted with nothing, and will suffer no disadvantages on account of the appellant being subrogated to the rights of the mortgagees.

It cannot be seriously contended that the mortgage debts were not discharged with money that belonged to the appellant. The funds that were fraudulently taken from him were directly traced into the bank account of Roy W. Todd and paid to the mortgagees by checks drawn by him on said account. The court's special findings set out in detail the means by which this was accomplished. There was no such commingling of funds as would require a holding that they could not be identified or followed.

Inasmuch as the transaction by which the appellant was deprived of his money and the appellees obtained the benefit thereof was tainted with fraud, no demand for restitution before suit was necessary. The situation may be distinguished from one where the party proceeded against has done no actionable wrong and a demand is necessary to render him liable or put him in the wrong.

[The] judgment is reversed, with directions to the trial court to restate its third and fourth conclusions of law in conformity with this opinion, and to enter judgment in favor of the appellant.

BANTON V. HACKNEY

557 So.2d 807 (Ala.1989).

PER CURIAM.

[We] set out the lengthy opinion of the trial court so that the factual and legal complexities of this case will be more clearly understood:

"[The] claims asserted by Hackney in this case are the result of his purchase from Banton and Long of all of the outstanding shares of capital stock of Banton, Inc., which in turn owned all of the outstanding stock of its subsidiary, Banton Industries, Inc. For purposes of this order, the two corporations will hereinafter be referred to as Banton, Inc.

"In his complaint, Hackney says that he was induced to agree to buy the shares of stock of Banton, Inc., and that he did buy such shares in reliance on the materially false representations made to him by Banton and Long with respect to the financial condition of Banton, Inc., and the results of its operations. Hackney alleges in his complaint that he paid to Banton and Long the sum of $1,100,000 in cash and also executed guarantees of approximately $5,000,000 of Banton's debt in connection with such purchase. * * *

"The sale was closed on February 2, 1988. At the closing, Banton received $683,980.59 and Long received $16,019.41. On February 10, 1988, Banton went to AmSouth Bank and, on the strength of Hackney's personal guarantee, borrowed $400,000. Banton represented to AmSouth that he wanted the proceeds for "an investment." Banton told AmSouth that he expected to repay the loan with the proceeds of Hackney's promissory note to be executed following the balance sheet audit as of the closing date."

"Banton did not invest the money as he had represented to Hackney and AmSouth. He paid off mortgages of $404,569.95 (a mortgage on his residence) and $153,387.68 (a mortgage on his condominium). The sum of $350,000 was also deposited by Banton in an account in a Florida bank in the name of his wife, Susan A. Banton. * * *

"Hackney has sought in this case to have a constructive trust imposed over the money and also the real estate purchased by Banton with the cash proceeds received by him from Hackney as a result of the sale of the common stock of Banton, Inc. The evidence presented by Hackney indicated that Banton received cash in the amount of $683,908.59 at the closing of the sale of the common stock of Banton, Inc., on February 2, 1988. He deposited the entire amount received from Hackney evidenced by checks signed by Hackney into a newly opened account of Colonial Bank (the "Colonial account").

"Banton then signed the following checks drawn on the Colonial account:

"(1) A $42,718.45 check dated February 3, 1988, payable to Sam Sumner, the business broker;

"(2) A $14,498.15 check dated February 4, 1988, payable to Banton's mother; and

"(3) An $8,118.40 check also dated February 4, 1988, payable to Banton's mother.

"On February 10, 1988, Banton went to AmSouth Bank and, on the strength of Hackney's personal guarantee, borrowed $400,000. Banton also deposited the proceeds of the AmSouth loan in the Colonial account later that day.

"On February 10, 1988, Banton withdrew $404,569.95 from the Colonial account and paid in full the indebtedness secured by a mortgage on his home. He wrote another check drawn against the Colonial account in the amount of $153,387.68 to pay in full the indebtedness secured by a mortgage on his condominium.

"On February 22, 1988, the sum of $350,000 was withdrawn from the Colonial account and deposited in the name of Banton's wife, Susan Banton, in a Florida bank. No consideration was paid to Banton for the transfer of the $350,000 to Susan Banton.

"The proceeds of the stock sale have therefore been traced to: (1) satisfaction of the $404,569.95 mortgage on Banton's residence; (2) the $350,000 certificate of deposit in the name of Susan Banton; and (3) the satisfaction of the $153,387.68 mortgage on the condominium.

"Susan Banton, the wife of James Banton, is also named as a defendant in this action. * * *

"In the present case before this court, Banton and Long intentionally misrepresented the financial condition of Banton, Inc., and the results of its business operations in material respects, and thereby fraudulently obtained $1,100,000 from Hackney. Hackney has also provided conclusive evidence tracing the following amounts paid by Banton: $350,000 certificate of deposit purchased in the name of Susan Banton; $404,569.95

paid in satisfaction of a mortgage on his residence; and $153,387.68 paid in satisfaction of a mortgage on a condominium owned by Banton and his wife, Susan Banton, located in Okaloosa County, Florida. Hackney is therefore legally entitled to impose a constructive trust on all such sums as representing the proceeds of the amount paid by him to Banton in connection with the purchase of the common stock of Banton, Inc., such purchase which he is now entitled to rescind.

"In accordance with this opinion, it is hereby ordered by this court as follows:

1. Judgment is hereby rendered in favor of T. Morris Hackney against James F. Banton and Jane J. Long on the claims asserted by Morris Hackney under § 8–6–19(a)(2), Alabama Code 1975. It is hereby declared by the court that the purchase of the stock of Banton, Inc., made by Morris Hackney is hereby rescinded.

2. Judgment is hereby rendered in favor of T. Morris Hackney against James F. Banton in the amount of $1,083,980.50 plus interest at the rate of six percent per annum from February 2, 1988, representing the proceeds paid by T. Morris Hackney to James F. Banton in connection with the purchase of the stock of Banton, Inc. Judgment is hereby rendered in favor of T. Morris Hackney against Jane J. Long in the amount of $16,019.41 plus interest at the rate of six percent per annum from February 2, 1988, representing the proceeds paid by T. Morris Hackney to Jane J. Long in connection with the purchase of the common stock of Banton, Inc. These judgments are pro tanto judgments and represent only part of the damages sustained by T. Morris Hackney. T. Morris Hackney reserves the right to make claim for the additional damages he has sustained in connection with and as a result of the transaction involving the purchase of stock of Banton, Inc.

3. As stated in this opinion, T. Morris Hackney guaranteed a loan made by AmSouth Bank to James F. Banton, and AmSouth Bank has obtained a judgment against both James F. Banton and T. Morris Hackney. That judgment has been partially paid or satisfied by the payment of the monies ordered paid to the Register of this Court from the $350,000 certificate of deposit formerly held by a Florida bank. The judgment in favor of T. Morris Hackney against James F. Banton will therefore be partially reduced or satisfied to the extent of such payment.

Upon satisfaction of the above judgments in full by the defendants James F. Banton and Jane J. Long, the Register is directed to deliver the outstanding capital stock of Banton, Inc. (which Hackney has tendered to the Register) to James F. Banton and Jane J. Long, who now own such subject to their obligations set forth in this order to repay Hackney.

4. Judgment is hereby rendered declaring that T. Morris Hackney is entitled to impose a constructive trust on the residence of James F.

Banton at 2748 Abingdon Road, Birmingham, Alabama. It is hereby declared that Hackney is subrogated to the right of the mortgagees whose mortgages were satisfied with the proceeds of the stock sale in the same manner and to the same extent as if such mortgages had been assigned by the mortgagees to T. Morris Hackney by virtue of the satisfaction of said mortgages with funds fraudulently obtained from T. Morris Hackney. An equitable lien on the following described real estate in the amount of $404,569.95 plus interest from February 2, 1988, at the rate prescribed in the note secured by the mortgage and on the same terms and conditions as the mortgage is hereby declared. * * *

5. T. Morris Hackney is also subrogated to the rights of the mortgagee holding the mortgage on the condominium owned by James F. Banton and his wife Susan A. Banton, located in Okaloosa County, Florida. An equitable lien on the following-described real estate is hereby declared in the amount of $153,387.68 plus interest from February 2, 1988, at the rate prescribed in the note secured by that mortgage and on the same terms and conditions stated in that mortgage. * * *

6. James F. Banton and Susan A. Banton are hereby enjoined and ordered not to transfer, encumber or sell their interest in the residence at 2849 Abingdon Road, Mountain Brook, Alabama, or their interest in the condominium located at 3071 Shoreline Towers Condominium in Destin, Florida, except as follows:

James F. Banton and Susan A. Banton may execute mortgages or conveyances on said properties which are expressly and unambiguously subject to and inferior to Hackney's interest therein in the amount of $404,569.95 plus interest on the Abingdon Road property and in the amount of $153,387.68 plus interest on the condominium. . . .

8. All remaining issues (including the remaining claims for damages asserted by T. Morris Hackney) are hereby set for trial . . . ."

T. Morris Hackney is also subrogated to the rights of the mortgagee holding the mortgage on the condominium owned by James F. Banton and his wife Susan A. Banton, located in Okaloosa County, Florida.

NOTES

1. *The Restatement and Subrogation.* Consider Restatement (Third) of Restitutional Unjust Enrichment § 57:

> (1) If the defendant is unjustly enriched by a transaction in which property of the claimant is used to discharge an obligation of the defendant or a lien on the defendant's property, the claimant may obtain restitution
>
> > (a) by succeeding to the rights of the oblige or lienor against the defendant or the defendant's property as though such discharge had not occurred, and

(b) by succeeding to the collateral rights of the defendant in the transaction concerned.

(2) Recovery via subrogation may not exceed reimbursement to the claimant.

(3) The remedy of subrogation may be qualified or withheld when necessary to avoid an inequitable result in the circumstances of a particular case.

2. *Subrogation and Tracing.* Subrogation is another equitable restitutionary remedy in which tracing can be used to give the plaintiff the benefit of a secured interest and/or a preferred position. However, one who tries to subrogate is subject to all defenses the defendant might have raised against the discharged creditor.

EXERCISE: RESTITUTION FROM THE DEFAULTING COACH?

Jeremy Royster ("Rambo Royster") Jones became the University of Louisville's (U of L) head football coach ten years ago and promised to place the program on a "collision course with the national championship." Over the next 10 years, Rambo slowly built the U of L program. During that period, Rambo lost slightly more games than he won, but the team won two bowl games and steadily improved. Rambo built sufficient community support so that U of L developed plans to build a new football stadium.

Yesterday, Rambo resigned to become the head football coach at Seneca University (SU). SU officials approached Rambo at a coaches' conference and asked whether he was interested in the SU job. Rambo initially said "no," but later changed his mind. In a whirlwind recruitment process, Rambo flew to the Seneca campus and accepted the job.

When he signed with SU, Rambo was obligated to U of L by a long-term contract. The contract ran for five more seasons. Under the contract's terms, Rambo was to be paid $300,000 per year in salary and fringe benefits. Under the SU contract, Rambo is to be paid $520,000 in salary and fringe benefits.

You work for a law firm that represents U of L. Immediately after Rambo "resigned," U of L called you for an assessment of its remedial options. U of L would prefer to retain Rambo as its head football coach. If that isn't possible, U of L would like to know about other remedial options. Please analyze those options taking into account all important considerations, both legal and practical.

In your answer take account of § 39 *Restatement (Third) of Restitution and Unjust Enrichment* that reads as follows:

(1) If a deliberate breach of contract results in profit to the defaulting promisor and the available damage remedy affords inadequate protection to the promisee's contractual entitlement, the promise has a claim to restitution of the profit realized by the promisor as a result of the breach. Restitution by the rule of this section is an alternative to a remedy in damages.

(2) A case in which damages afford inadequate protection to the promisee's contractual entitlement is ordinarily one in which damages will not permit the promise to acquire a full equivalent to the promised performance in a substitute transaction.

(3) Breach of contract is profitable when it results in gains to the defendant (net of potential liability in damages) greater than the defendant would have realized from performance of the contract. Profits from breach include saved expenditure and consequential gains that the defendant would not have realized but for the breach, as measured by the rules that apply in other cases of disgorgement (§ 51(5)).

An aside on § 39:

The Damages chapter explores fully the usual conditions attending the recovery of damages for breach of contract. Oliver Wendell Holmes famously wrote that an aggrieved party in contract had the expectation of damages in lieu of performance. This led to the theory of efficient breach whereby if performance is more costly than breach, economic rationality calls for breach proved the breaching party covered the contractual expectations of the other. Damages however may be an inadequate remedy when breaches are of a kind that would unjustly enrich the breaching party. Thus if the relationship is one in which beyond contract the breaching party owes fiduciary obligations or a relation of trust and confidence, the remedy may be a disgorgement of profits garnered by the breach. § 43. Thus a company director who allows his duty and interest to conflict in taking a corporate opportunity must disgorge profits derived from the breach. A constructive trust may be awarded over the profits. Moreover, the inadequacy of damages may justify the equitable remedies of injunction or specific performance. *See Patton v. Mid–Continent Systems, Inc.*, 841 F.2d 742 (7th Cir. 1988).

Under this section a claimant may recover profits resulting from the breach even if they exceed the provable loss to the claimant from the defendant's defaulted performance. The Restatement provision is a bold statement that is prefigured in much academic writing and in decisions of overseas courts but is not strongly present in the United States. The element of unjust enrichment arises from the opportunistic breach that leaves a party vulnerable where she is limited to ordinary expectation damages. She will be left short of her full entitlement under the contract. Accordingly the promisor is unjustly enriched. The remedy also reinforces the contractual position of the vulnerable party guarding against conscious advantage taking. It is akin to tort protection and faces parties to the contract with reasons to adhere to the contract. If the promisor wishes to negotiate to avoid contractual performance she will take account of the remedy of disgorgement that would be available to the promise

Limit your discussion to ten, double-spaced, typed pages.

CHAPTER 6

DECLARATORY JUDGMENTS

■ ■ ■

CHAPTER OVERVIEW: The declaratory judgment remedy is one that you may have studied in your first year civil procedure course. While you may have examined the prerequisites for declaratory relief in that course, here you will have the opportunity to examine how that remedy is applied in different subject matter contexts.

PROBLEM: THE PORNOGRAPHY PEDDLER

Lust magazine has established a niche as one of the nation's leading publishers of sexually explicit albeit nonobscene periodicals. A special governmental commission, set up to determine whether a causal link exists between pornography and antisocial behavior, held extensive public hearings. At one of those sessions, a representative of Modern Morality testified that the nation's leading grocery chain (Eatalot) also was the foremost distributor of *Lust*. Following discussion, the commission sent a copy of the testimony to Eatalot's president along with a letter inviting a response. The letter indicated the commission's sense that the company should have an opportunity to respond before an official report named the grocery chain as a primary distributor. It further noted that the commission had linked *Lust* with abuse of women and children and planned to publish that finding. The letter closed with the warning that a failure to respond would be understood as an indication that Eatalot admitted to Modern Morality's assertion. *Lust's* publisher has a source on the commission who leaked information indicating that it had no real intention to identify distributors and had not even established a cause and effect relationship between its style of pornography and abuse.

As you work your way through this chapter, you will be asked to think about whether Lust is entitled to declaratory relief. If so, how should the order be framed?

A. GENERALLY

The declaratory judgment is a procedural innovation that has been both analogized to and distinguished from legal and equitable remedies. As a statutorily created remedy of twentieth century origins, declaratory judgments are without a pure equity pedigree. Considerations of an equitable nature are sometimes referenced, however, in determining whether to enter declaratory relief. *E.g., Spivey v. Barry*, 665 F.2d 1222, 1235 (D.C.Cir.1981) ("[i]ssuing a declaratory judgment is an act of equitable discretion" to be avoided when it "would not achieve any useful objective"). The basic purpose of declaratory judgment is to determine rights, obligations or status. Unlike other litigative methods, such as an action for damages or an injunction, a declaratory judgment does not operate coercively. Its primary utility is in eliminating uncertainty. To a significant extent, therefore, declaratory proceedings may be understood as an exercise in preventive justice.

Although not formally established in the United States until this century, the declaratory judgment has notable antecedents. Equitable remedies such as bills *quia timet*, bills of peace, bills to remove cloud from titles, rescission and even injunctions historically have functioned to provide certainty and security in legal relations. The availability of such relief is conditioned upon an actual breach of duty or wrongdoing, however, that is accounted for by means of a coercive judgment. A significant attraction of declaratory judgments is their capacity to resolve disputes without the need to repudiate obligations or abrogate rights. They thus represent a departure from common law norms allowing no adjudication of duties or expectations absent an alleged violation thereof.

Provisions for declaratory judgments began to appear in the American legal system during the early part of the last century. Statutes providing for declaratory judgments initially were enacted in 1919 in Florida, Michigan and Wisconsin. Since then, provisions for declaratory judgments have become pervasive and largely standardized among the states. The Uniform Declaratory Judgments Act (UDJA) now adopted verbatim or substantially in 41 states was proposed in 1922, and the Federal Declaratory Judgment Act (FDJA) was enacted in 1934. Prefacing the actual advent of declaratory judgment acts were influential academic commentaries stressing the logic and historical support for such relief. Especially significant was the work of Professor Edwin M. Borchard, who helped draft both the UDJA and FDJA.

THE DECLARATORY JUDGMENT—A NEEDED PROCEDURAL REFORM

28 Yale L.J. 1, 105 (1918).

[A] study of modern social and industrial conditions emphasizes the conviction that the social equilibrium is disturbed not only by a violation of private rights, privileges, powers and immunities but by the placing of these individual advantages in grave doubt and uncertainty. If the status of children as legitimate or illegitimate or of persons as married or unmarried is uncertain, not only the individual but the State has an interest in having the uncertainty settled by an authoritative determination. If the title to property is uncertain, the State, as well as the individuals concerned, has an interest in removing the uncertainty, and within certain limitations courts of equity entertain jurisdiction to remove clouds from title. If the meaning of a contract is in doubt, it must be broken in order to obtain an authoritative construction of it, with expensive litigation to boot. Similarly, apart from the trustee's bill for advice, a hostile attack must generally precede the adjudication of conflicting claims under a will. To determine these questions, which are illustrations merely, our law now requires an elaborate procedure involving delay, uncertainty and considerable expense, when all that is desired is an authoritative determination of a simple issue of fact or of law. Parties are compelled to indulge in legal hostilities whether they want to or not in order that their legal relations may be cleared of doubt or uncertainty. That the law has not been oblivious to the necessity of certainty and security in legal relations is evidenced in the fact that certain agreements in order to obtain judicial recognition must be reduced to writing or must be recorded. It is also evidenced in the employment of such equitable remedies as bills *quia timet*, bills of peace and bills to remove cloud from title, bills for the rescission and cancellation of written instruments, in the action to perpetuate testimony and in the bill of injunction. While the general purposes of these equitable remedies is to create security, remove uncertainty and prevent litigation, many of the remedies are cumbersome and their grant is dependent upon very technical conditions precedent. * * *

At the outset it will be well to circumscribe the concept of "declaratory judgment." [We] would confine that term to those judgments which merely declare the existence of a jural relation, *i.e.*, some right, privilege, power, or immunity in the plaintiff or some duty, no-right, liability or disability in the defendant. They do not presuppose a wrong already done, a breach of duty. They cannot be executed, as they order nothing to be done. They do not constitute operative facts creating new legal relations of a secondary or remedial character; they purport merely to declare preexisting relations and create no secondary or remedial ones. Their distinctive characteristic lies in the fact that they constitute merely an authentic confirmation of already existing relations.

While the purpose of the declaratory judgment [is] not to enable people to "sleep o'nights," such a judgment will be rendered in the exercise of the court's discretion when it will serve some practical purpose; for example, when it will guide parties to a contract as to their future conduct under it, and "with a view rather to avoid litigation than in aid of it." Aside from its employment in cases in which the preventive equitable remedies above mentioned are inapplicable, thus giving relief in a new class of cases, it has by is simplicity and effectiveness served largely to replace those equitable remedies where they were formerly employed; and furthermore, appreciation in practice of the fact that an amicable remedy is often more desirable than and fully as useful as a non-amicable means of adjusting disputes, has persuaded litigants frequently to employ the declaratory action instead of the coercive executory action. * * *

The close analogy between the declaratory judgment and arbitration will already have become apparent. In countries authorizing the declaratory judgment, the law now furnishes parties with official "arbitrators" whose function it is to declare the legal relations existing between the parties and the law endows their decision with binding force. * * *

The affirmative declaratory judgment finds its origin in the Roman law. In the Roman law of procedure, as in our won, the action at law led to an executory judgment, *condemnatio*. But it often proved necessary to decide in a preliminary way certain questions of law or of fact which the parties themselves, by agreement, or the magistrate or *praetor*, at the request of one of the parties, might submit to the *judex* for decision. This decision was merely a declaration of the *judex* in response to the question submitted. Instead of commanding the performance of some act, his decision constituted merely the affirmation of an existing state of facts or of law. Being merely incidental or preliminary to an ordinary executory action, it was known as a *prae-judicium*. It ended in a *pronuntiatio*, not in a *condemnatio*. In the period of the *legis actiones* this *pronuntiatio* was obtained by means of the *sponiso*, so far as the question was not taken up in the *legis actio* itself. In the formulary procedure the form of submission was greatly simplified. In the *intentio* the formula stated the specific question of law or fact which had to be determined; it was much like the regular formula for the trial of an action, except that the *condemnatio* was omitted.

This procedure proved so useful that it was ultimately extended to independent actions where no executory judgment (*condemnatio*) was required or desired. The actions then received the same *actiones praejudiciales*, the dignity of *actiones* having therefore been denied them. In application they were limited to certain classes of cases, principally questions of status and of certain property rights and relations incidental to status, such as the amount of a wife's dowry which had to be returned to her on the termination of the marriage, and less frequently, questions of the validity of legal instruments. These actions, which were personal actions *in rem*, are grouped by Windscheid as including questions of *status libertatis, civitatis, familiae*. The questions, among others, more frequently submitted to determination related to the status of and property in slaves; declarations of liberty; questions of the power of the master, and of the father over his children; questions of legitimacy and of family relationships; the validity or invalidity of a will (*querela inofficiosi testamenti*) and of other legal instruments.

It is interesting to observe that in the development of the declaratory judgment during the Middle Ages and after the "reception" of Roman law in continental Europe in 1495, questions of status, of property rights connected therewith, and of the validity or invalidity of wills and other legal instruments, constitute the principal subjects of declaratory actions. At the present time, however, instead of being confined to a limited number of subjects with individual forms, the declaratory action is almost unlimited as to subjects and has a general form sufficiently wide to accommodate any specific questions.

After the "reception" of the Roman law in central Europe both forms of declaratory action, the positive and the negative, were recognized, and down to the end of the nineteenth century the codes of civil procedure of numerous states provided for the *praejudiciales* actions and for the *provocatios*. * * *

The purpose of the declaratory action is the security desired by the plaintiff against the uncertainty of his rights and other jural relations due to their being questioned by the defendant or to the assertion of conflicting claims, or merely to the existence of records ostensibly to the advantage of the defendant which of themselves place in uncertainty the plaintiff's legal position. There need be no threat to violate the plaintiff's rights, etc.; the mere proof of those operative facts which either of themselves, or in the hands of the defendant, endanger the security of the plaintiff's rights, etc., suffices. It is for the court to determine whether the dispute, danger of uncertainty was of such a nature, either by reason of its source or its extent, as to justify the making of the declaration asked. Some danger to the plaintiff's rights, etc., must exist, and as may be inferred, the danger or threat of attack must move either from the defendant or from records within his control or by which he is ostensibly benefited. * * *

As a measure of preventive justice, the declaratory judgment probably has its greatest efficacy. It is designed to enable parties to ascertain and establish their legal relations, so as to conduct themselves accordingly, and thus to avoid the necessity of future litigation. * * *

The purpose for which a declaration is desired is one of the considerations entering into the exercise of the court's discretion in rendering a declaratory judgment. The equitable nature of the relief is evidence in the fact that the court may inquire into the purpose for which the declaration is asked, and must be convinced that its judgment will serve a practical end in quieting or stabilizing uncertain or disputed jural relations either as to present obligations or prospectively. Thus, if the purpose of the action is merely to get a court's opinion on a hypothetical question which is not disputed or which requires no determination in order to settle uncertain relations or conflicting claims, no declaration will be made. * * *

Declarations of disability of the defendant, while often combined with declarations of immunity of the plaintiff, are nevertheless emphasized as the principal jural relation in issue when the validity of a state act is contested. Thus, declarations have been sought that particular acts of governmental authorities were *ultra vires* (*i.e.*, that the authority had no power to create any new legal relations by executing them), *e.g.*, the repudiation of an agreement by the postmaster general, the issuance of certain forms by the internal revenue officers, the requisitioning of certain services and profits of the plaintiffs, the expropriation of certain land, the manner of cancelling certain mining leases by the governor, the method of imposing taxes by local authorities, and the manner of rejecting votes against the acts of private persons acting under private acts, charters or agreements. * * *

Declaratory judgments operate as *res judicata* and bind the parties and their privies within the same limitations as attach to other final judgments. Their forces as judgments *in rem* in cases of status and title to property is fortified by the power of the court, in England, at least, to bring before it any person who may be interested in the matter in issue. They cannot, of course, be executed, a feature which constitutes their principal difference from executory judgments. In the case of those judgements which declare a duty, a new action must be founded on them to convert them into judgments on which execution can issue. But this point is more academic than practical, for it rarely proves necessary to resort to this measure; and in fact, when some executory relief is desired in England, the demand for it is generally incorporated with the request for the declaration. Often, indeed, the negative form of declaratory judgment of privilege or immunity cannot be followed by any form of coercive relief at all, the mere declaration that the defendant has no claim against the plaintiff satisfying all the plaintiff's requirements. Should the defendant, nevertheless, subsequently bring an action, he would be met the plea of *res judicata.* The old judgment can only be reopened or impeached in the same manner and under the same conditions as any final executory judgment.

Declaratory judgments are provided for in all but a few states pursuant to the UDJA. Key elements of the UDJA include:

§ 1. Scope

> Courts of record within their respective jurisdictions shall have power to declare rights, status, and other legal relations whether or not further relief is or could be claimed. No action or proceeding shall be open to objection on the ground that a declaratory judgment or decree is prayed for. The declaration may be either affirmative or negative in form and effect; and

such declarations shall have the force and effect of a final judgment or decree.

§ 2. Power to Construe, etc.

Any person interested under a deed, will, written contract or other writings constituting a contract, or whose rights, status or other legal relations are affected by a statute, municipal ordinance, contract or franchise, may have determined any question of construction or validity arising under the instrument, statute, ordinance, contract, or franchise and obtain a declaration of rights, status or other legal relations thereunder.

§ 3. Before Breach

A contract may be construed either before or after there has been a breach thereof.

§ 4. Executor, etc.

Any person interested as or through an executor, administrator, trustee, guardian or other fiduciary, creditor, devisee, legatee, heir, next of kin, or cestui que trust, in the administration of a trust, or of the estate of a decedent, an infant, lunatic, or insolvent, may have a declaration of rights or legal relations in respect thereto:

(a) To ascertain any class of creditors, devisees, legatees, heirs, next of kin or others; or

(b) To direct the executors, administrators, or trustees to do or abstain from doing any particular act in their fiduciary capacity; or

(c) To determine any question arising in the administration of the estate or trust, including questions of construction of wills and other writings.

§ 5. Enumeration Not Exclusive

The enumeration in Sections 2, 3, and 4 does not limit or restrict the exercise of the general powers conferred in Section 1, in any proceeding where declaratory relief sought, in which a judgment or decree will terminate the controversy or remove an uncertainty.

§ 6. Discretionary

The court may refuse to render or enter a declaratory judgment or decree where such judgment or decree, if rendered or entered, would not terminate the uncertainty or controversy giving rise to the proceeding.

§ 7. Review

All orders, judgments and decrees under this act may be reviewed as other orders, judgments and decrees.

§ 8. Supplemental Relief

Further relief based on a declaratory judgment or decree may be granted whenever necessary or proper. The application therefor shall be by petition to a court having jurisdiction to grant the relief. If the application be deemed sufficient, the court shall, on reasonable notice, require any adverse party whose rights have been adjudicated by the declaratory judgment or decree, to show cause why further relief should not be granted forthwith.

§ 9. Jury Trial

When a proceeding under this Act involves the determination of an issue of fact, such issue may be tried and determined in the same manner as issues of fact are tried and determined in other civil actions in the court in which the proceeding is pending.

* * *

§ 11. Parties

When declaratory relief is sought, all persons shall be made parties who have or claim any interest which would be affected by the declaration, and no declaration shall prejudice the rights of persons not parties to the proceeding. In any proceeding which involves the validity of a municipal ordinance or franchise, such municipality shall be made a party, and shall be entitled to be heard, and if the statute, ordinance or franchise is alleged to be unconstitutional, the Attorney–General of the State shall also be served with a copy of the proceeding and be entitled to be heard.

§ 12. Construction

This act is declared to be remedial; its purpose is to settle and to afford relief from uncertainty and insecurity with respect to rights, status and other legal relations; and is to be liberally construed and administered. * * *

The UDJA, although framed a decade prior to the FDJA, was amended to provide for interpretation that not only promotes uniformity among the states but "harmonize(s) as far as possible, with federal laws and regulations on the subject of declaratory judgments and decrees." UDJA,

Sec. 15. Given that imperative, the balance of this chapter will focus primarily upon the federal act and its interpretation.

The FDJA achieves much the same purpose as the UDJA albeit in more concise terms.

FEDERAL DECLARATORY JUDGMENT ACT

28 U.S.C. §§ 2201–02.

§ 2201. Creation of remedy

(a) In a case of actual controversy within its jurisdiction, except with respect to Federal taxes other than actions brought under section 7418 of the Internal Revenue Code of 1986, a proceeding under section 505 or 1146 of title 11, or in any civil action involving an antidumping or countervailing duty proceeding regarding a class or kind of merchandise of a free trade area country (as defined in section 516(f)(10) of the Tariff Act of 1930), as determined by the administering authority, any court of the United States, upon the filing of an appropriate pleading, may declare the rights and other legal relations of any interested party seeking such declaration, whether or not further relief is or could be sought. Any such declaration shall have the force and effect of a final judgment or decree and shall be reviewable as such.

(b) For limitations on actions brought with respect to drug patents see section 505 or 512 of the Federal Food Drug, and Cosmetic Act.

§ 2202. Further relief

Further necessary or proper relief based on a declaratory judgment or decree may be granted, after reasonable notice and hearing, against any adverse party whose rights have been determined by such judgment.

Procedure for federal declaratory judgments is governed by Rule 57 of the Federal Rules of Civil Procedure, which has four significant aspects. Pursuant to Rule 57, "procedure for obtaining a declaratory judgment" is governed generally by the federal rules. Notwithstanding any similarities to equitable proceedings, "the right to trial by jury may be demanded" in accordance with Rules 38 and 39 and "another adequate remedy does not" necessarily preclude a declaratory judgment. Finally, consistent with the interests of preventive justice, courts "may order a speedy hearing of an action for a declaratory judgment and may advance it on their calendar."

Although accounted for by federal rule, the actual right to a jury trial in a declaratory judgment proceeding requires attention to additional factors. The right in a given proceeding generally is dependent upon whether, at the time the Seventh Amendment was ratified, the relevant issue would have been resolved by a court of law or equity. It is essential, therefore, to determine the nature of the underlying claim and calculate whether it historically arose in a legal or equitable context. Declaratory relief may be provided within the ambit of a legal or equitable proceeding and does not independently determine the availability of a jury trial.

B. CASE OR CONTROVERSY

By its terms, the FDJA operates only in "a case of actual controversy." 28 U.S.C. § 2201. Such a prerequisite reaffirms the pertinence of Article III, Section 2 of the United States Constitution which limits the federal judicial power to "Cases" and "Controversies." Given such constitutional and statutory imperatives, it is evident that the FDJA creates no exemption to requirements of standing, subprinciples of mootness and ripeness and the prohibition against collusive actions or advisory opinions. Insofar as declaratory judgments have an essentially informational or "advisory" function, it is not surprising that they tend to attract challenges on justiciability grounds. A constitutional command against advisory opinions initially was enunciated in *Muskrat v. United States*, 219 U.S. 346, 362, 31 S.Ct. 250, 256, 55 L.Ed. 246 (1911), when the Supreme Court held that the federal judiciary only was allowed to enter judgments that could be executed. Citing to *Muskrat* several years before enactment of the FDJA, the Court refused to review a state court's declaratory judgment because "[t]o grant that relief is beyond the power conferred upon the federal judiciary." *Willing v. Chicago Auditorium Assn.*, 277 U.S. 274, 289, 48 S.Ct. 507, 509, 72 L.Ed. 880 (1928). Despite such ominous indications, the FDJA soon after its adoption survived a "controversy" challenge.

AETNA LIFE INSURANCE CO. V. HAWORTH

300 U.S. 227, 57 S.Ct. 461, 81 L.Ed. 617 (1937).

MR. CHIEF JUSTICE HUGHES delivered the opinion of the Court.

The question presented is whether the District Court had jurisdiction of this suit under the Federal Declaratory Judgment Act.

[P]laintiff's complaint [was] dismissed by the District Court upon the ground that it did not set forth a "controversy" in the constitutional sense and hence did not come within the legitimate scope of the statute. The decree of dismissal was affirmed by the Circuit Court of Appeals. We granted certiorari.

From the complaint it appears that plaintiff is an insurance company which had issued to the defendant, Edwin P. Haworth, five policies of insurance upon his life, the defendant Cora M. Haworth being named as beneficiary. The complaint set forth the terms of the policies. They contained various provisions which for the present purpose it is unnecessary fully to particularize. It is sufficient to observe that they all provided for certain benefits in the event that the insured became totally and permanently disabled. * * *

The complaint asks for a decree that the four policies be declared to be null and void by reason of lapse for nonpayment of premiums and that the obligation upon the remaining policy be held to consist solely in the duty to pay the sum of $45 upon the death of the insured, and for such further relief as the exigencies of the case may require.

[The] Constitution limits the exercise of the judicial power to "cases" and "controversies." "The term 'controversies,' if distinguishable at all from 'cases,' is so in that it is less comprehensive than the latter, and includes only suits of a civil nature." The Declaratory Judgment Act of 1934, in its limitation to "cases of actual controversy," manifestly has regard to the constitutional provision and is operative only in respect to controversies which are such in the constitutional sense. The word "actual" is one of emphasis rather than of definition. Thus the operation of the Declaratory Judgment Act is procedural only. In providing remedies and defining procedure in relation to cases and controversies in the constitutional sense the Congress is acting within its delegated power over the jurisdiction of the federal courts which the Congress is authorized to establish. Exercising this control of practice and procedure the Congress is not confined to traditional forms or traditional remedies. The judiciary clause of the Constitution "did not crystallize into changeless form the procedure of 1789 as the only possible means for presenting a case or controversy otherwise cognizable by the federal courts." In dealing with methods within its sphere of remedial action the Congress may create and improve as well as abolish or restrict. The Declaratory Judgment Act must be deemed to fall within this ambit of congressional power, so far as it authorizes relief which is consonant with the exercise of the judicial function in the determination of controversies to which under the Constitution the judicial power extends.

A "controversy" in this sense must be one that is appropriate for judicial determination. A justiciable controversy is thus distinguished from a difference or dispute of a hypothetical or abstract character; from one that is academic or moot. The controversy must be definite and concrete, touching the legal relations of parties having adverse legal interests. It must be a real and substantial controversy admitting of specific relief through a decree of a conclusive character, as distinguished from an opinion advising what the law would be upon a hypothetical state of facts. Where there is such a concrete case admitting of an immediate and definitive determination of the legal rights of the parties in an adversary proceeding upon the facts alleged, the judicial function may be appropriately exercised although the adjudication of the rights of the litigants may not require the award of process or the payment of damages. And as it is not essential to the exercise of the judicial power that an injunction be sought, allegations that irreparable injury is threatened are not required.

With these principles governing the application of the Declaratory Judgment Act, we turn to the nature of the controversy, the relation and interests of the parties, and the relief sought in the instant case.

[There] is here a dispute between parties who face each other in an adversary proceeding. The dispute relates to legal rights and obligations arising from the contracts of insurance. The dispute is definite and concrete, not hypothetical or abstract. Prior to this suit, the parties had taken adverse positions with respect to their existing obligations. Their contentions concerned the disability benefits which were to be payable upon prescribed conditions. On the one side, the insured claimed that he had become totally and permanently disabled and hence was relieved of the obligation to continue the payment of premiums and was entitled to the stipulated disability benefits and to the continuance of the policies in force. The insured presented this claim formally, as required by the policies. It was a claim of a present, specific right. On the other side, the company made an equally definite claim that the alleged basic fact did not exist, that the insured was not totally and permanently disabled and had not been relieved of the duty to continue the payment of premiums, that in consequence the policies had lapsed, and that the company was thus freed from its obligation either to pay disability benefits or to continue the insurance in force. Such a dispute is manifestly susceptible of judicial determination. It calls, not for an advisory opinion upon a hypothetical basis, but for an adjudication of present right upon established facts.

[Our] conclusion is that the complaint presented a controversy to which the judicial power extends and that authority to hear and determine it has been conferred upon the District Court by the Declaratory Judgment Act. * * *

Although upholding the FDJA, the Court's opinion did not draw a bright line between declaratory judgments and advisory opinions. Because both the allowable and proscribed methodologies have significant similarities, with respect to providing information and evaluation, the distinction appears to be a function of degree. As the Court subsequently noted, in *Maryland Casualty Co. v. Pacific Coal and Oil Co.*, terms such as "definite and concrete" and "real and substantial controversy" must be assessed in the particular factual context to determine whether "sufficient immediacy and reality" exist.

The difference between an abstract question and a "controversy" contemplated by the Declaratory Judgment Act is necessarily one of degree, and it would be difficult, if it would be possible, to fashion a precise test for determining in every case whether there is such a controversy. Basically, the question in each case is whether the facts alleged, under all the circumstances, show that there is a substantial controversy, between parties having adverse legal interests, of sufficient immediacy and reality to warrant the issuance of a declaratory judgment. It is immaterial that frequently, in the declaratory judgment suit, the positions of the parties in the conventional suit are reversed; the inquiry is the same in either case.[1]

Determinations of "immediacy and reality" run across a spectrum from easy to hard cases. When a purported liability creating act already has occurred, such as an alleged patent infringement, the condition of an actual controversy is readily satisfied. Instead of awaiting action by the patent holder, the other party may seek a determination of nonliability. Less clear may be circumstances in which a real controversy is contingent. In a prosecutorial or civil enforcement setting, relevant factors may include whether the plaintiff has been arrested or cited or commenced upon a collision course with the law.

UNITED PUBLIC WORKERS OF AMERICA V. MITCHELL

330 U.S. 75, 67 S.Ct. 556, 91 L.Ed. 754 (1947).

[Certain employees of the executive branch of the Federal Government and a union of such employees sued to enjoin the members of the Civil Service Commission from enforcing the provision [of] the Hatch Act, [which] forbids such employees to take "any active part in political management or in political campaigns" and for a declaratory judgment holding the Act unconstitutional.]

MR. JUSTICE REED delivered the opinion of the Court.

The Hatch Act, enacted in 1940, declares unlawful certain specified political activities of federal employees. Section 9 forbids officers and employees in the executive branch of the Federal Government, with exceptions, from taking "any active part in political management or in political campaigns." * * *

The present appellants sought an injunction before a statutory three-judge district court of the District of Columbia against appellees, members of the United States Civil Service Commission, to prohibit them

---

1 Maryland Casualty Co. v. Pacific Coal and Oil Co., 312 U.S. 270, 273 (1941).

from enforcing against appellants the provisions of the second sentence of § 9 (a) of the Hatch Act for the reason that the sentence is repugnant to the Constitution of the United States. A declaratory judgment of the unconstitutionality of the sentence was also sought. The sentence referred to reads, "No officer or employee in the executive branch of the Federal Government [shall] take any active part in political management or in political campaigns."

Various individual employees of the federal executive civil service and the United Public Workers of America, a labor union with these and other executive employees as members, as a representative of all its members, joined in the suit. It is alleged that the individuals desire to engage in acts of political management and in political campaigns. * * *

None of the appellants, except George P. Poole, has violated the provisions of the Hatch Act. They wish to act contrary to its provisions and those of § 1 of the Civil Service Rules and desire a declaration of the legally permissible limits of regulation. Defendants moved to dismiss the complaint for lack of a justiciable case or controversy. The District Court determined that each of these individual appellants had an interest in their claimed privilege of engaging in political activities, sufficient to give them a right to maintain this [suit]. The District Court further determined that the questioned provision of the Hatch Act was valid and that the complaint therefore failed to state a cause of action. It accordingly dismissed the complaint and granted summary judgment to defendants.

[As] is well known, the federal courts established pursuant to Article III of the Constitution do not render advisory opinions. For adjudication of constitutional issues, "concrete legal issues, presented in actual cases, not abstractions," are requisite. This is as true of declaratory judgments as any other field. These appellants seem clearly to seek advisory opinions upon broad claims of rights protected by the First, Fifth, and Tenth Amendments to the generality of citizens, [but] the facts of their personal interest in their civil rights, of the general threat of possible interference with those rights by the Civil Service Commission under its rules, if specified things are done by appellants, does not make a justiciable case or controversy. Appellants want to engage in "political management and political campaigns," to persuade others to follow appellants' views by discussion, speeches, articles and other acts reasonably designed to secure the selection of appellants' political choices. Such generality of objection is really an attack on the political expediency of the Hatch Act, not the presentation of legal issues. It is beyond the competence of courts to render such a decision.

The power of courts, and ultimately of this Court, to pass upon the constitutionality of acts of Congress arises only when the interests of litigants require the use of this judicial authority for their protection against actual interference. A hypothetical threat is not enough. We can only speculate as to the kinds of political activity the appellants desire to engage in or as to the contents of their proposed public statements or the circumstances of their publication. It would not accord with judicial responsibility to adjudge, in a matter involving constitutionality, between the freedom of the individual and the requirements of public order except when definite rights appear upon the one side and definite prejudicial interferences upon the other.

The Constitution allots the nation's judicial power to the federal courts. Unless these courts respect the limits of that unique authority, they intrude upon powers vested in the legislative or executive branches. Judicial adherence to the doctrine of the separation of powers preserves the courts for the decision of issues, between litigants, capable of effective determination. Judicial exposition upon political proposals is permissible only when necessary to decide definite issues between litigants. When the courts act continually within these constitutionally imposed boundaries of their power, their ability to perform their function as a balance for the people's protection against abuse of power by other branches of government remains unimpaired. Should the courts seek to expand their power so as to bring under their jurisdiction ill-defined controversies over constitutional issues, they would become the organ of political theories. Such abuse of judicial power would properly meet rebuke and restriction from other branches. By these mutual checks and balances by and between the branches of government, democracy undertakes to preserve the liberties of the people from excessive concentrations of authority. No threat of interference by the Commission with rights of these appellants appears beyond that implied by the existence of the law and the regulations. We should not take judicial cognizance of the situation presented on the part of the appellants considered in this subdivision of the opinion. These reasons lead us to conclude that the determination of the trial court, that the individual appellants, other than Poole, could maintain this action, was erroneous.

The appellant Poole does present by the complaint and affidavit matters appropriate for judicial determination. The affidavits filed by appellees confirm that Poole has been charged by the Commission with political activity and a proposed order for his removal from his position adopted subject to his right under Commission procedure to reply to the charges and to present further evidence in refutation. We proceed to consider the controversy over constitutional power at issue between Poole and the Commission as defined by the charge and preliminary finding upon one side and the admissions of Poole's affidavit upon the other. Our determination is limited to those facts. This proceeding so limited meets the requirements of defined rights and a definite threat to interfere with a possessor of the menaced rights by a penalty for an act done in violation of the claimed restraint.

Because we conclude hereinafter that the prohibition of § 9 of the Hatch Act and Civil Service Rule 1, are valid, it is unnecessary to consider, as this is a declaratory judgment action, whether or not this appellant sufficiently alleges that an irreparable injury to him would result from his removal from his position. Nor need we inquire whether or not a court of equity would enforce by injunction any judgment declaring rights. Since Poole admits that he violated the rule against political activity and that removal from office is therefore mandatory under the act, there is no question as to the exhaustion of administrative remedies. The act provides no administrative or statutory review for the order of the Civil Service Commission. As no prior proceeding, offering an effective remedy or otherwise, is pending in the courts, there is no problem of judicial discretion as to whether to take cognizance of this case. Under such circumstances, we see no reason why a declaratory judgment action, even though constitutional issues are involved, does not lie.

Section 15 of the Hatch Act, defines an active part in political management or political campaigns as the same activities that the United States Civil Service Commission has determined to be prohibited to classified civil service employees by the provisions of the Civil Service Rules when § 15 took effect July 19, 1940. The activities of Mr. Poole, as ward executive committeeman and a worker at the polls, obviously fall within the prohibitions of § 9 of the Hatch Act against taking an active part in political management and political campaigns. They are also covered by the prior determinations of the Commission. * * *

MR. JUSTICE DOUGLAS, dissenting in part.

I disagree with the Court on two of the four matters decided.

[There] are twelve individual appellants here asking for an adjudication of their rights. The Court passes on the claim of only one of them, Poole. It declines to pass on the claims of the other eleven on the ground that they do not present justiciable cases or controversies. With this conclusion I cannot agree.

It is clear that the declaratory judgment procedure is available in the federal courts only in cases involving actual controversies and may not be used to obtain an advisory opinion in a controversy not yet arisen. The requirement of an "actual controversy," which is written into the statute and has its roots in the Constitution, seems to me to be fully met here.

What these appellants propose to do is plain enough. If they do what they propose to do, it is clear that they will be discharged from their positions. * * *

Their proposed conduct is sufficiently specific to show plainly that it will violate the Act. The policy of the Commission and the mandate of the Act leave no lingering doubt as to the consequences.

On a discharge these employees would lose their jobs, their seniority, and other civil service benefits. They could, of course, sue in the Court of Claims. But the remedy there is a money judgment, not a restoration to the office formerly held. Of course, there might be other remedies available in these situations to determine their rights to the offices from which they are discharged. But to require these employees first to suffer the hardship of a discharge is not only to make them incur a penalty; it makes inadequate, if not wholly illusory, any legal remedy which they may have. Men who must sacrifice their means of livelihood in order to test their rights to their jobs must either pursue prolonged and expensive litigation as unemployed persons or pull up their roots, change their life careers, and seek employment in other fields. At least to the average person in the lower income groups the burden of taking that course is irreparable injury, no matter how exact the required showing.

The declaratory judgment procedure may not, of course, be used as a substitute for other equitable remedies to defeat a legislative policy, or to circumvent the necessity of exhausting administrative remedies. But it fills a need and serves a high function previously "performed rather clumsily by our equitable proceedings and inadequately by the law courts."

The declaratory judgment procedure is designed "to declare rights and other legal relations of any interested party [whether] or not further relief is or could be prayed." The fact that equity would not restrain a wrongful removal of an officeholder but would leave the complainant to his legal remedies, is, therefore, immaterial. A judgment which, without more, adjudicates the status of a person is permissible under the Declaratory Judgment Act. The "declaration of a status was perhaps the earliest exercise of this procedure." The right to hold an office or public position against such threats is a common example of its use. Declaratory relief is the singular remedy available here to preserve the status quo while the constitutional rights of these appellants to make these utterances and to engage in these activities are determined. The threat against them is real not fanciful, immediate not remote. The case is therefore an actual not a hypothetical one. And the present case seems to me to be a good example of a situation where uncertainty, peril, and insecurity result from imminent and immediate threats to asserted rights.

PROBLEMS

1. *First Amendment Follies.* The Governor of the State of Secrecy has issued an order directing all executive agencies to establish new rules for public and media access to government documents. The order has been entered in the context of a controversy over the governor's refusal to disclose records concerning the nature and scope of his travel and entertainment expenses. Because the order urges more restrictive terms of access, the state's

leading newspaper, the *Daily Doormat*, has sued in federal court to have it declared violative of the First Amendment and to enjoin the governor from enforcing it. A week later, it brought a similar action in state court alleging that the order crossed the state constitution. The state court entered a temporary restraining order pending a final ruling. The federal court meanwhile declared the order unconstitutional and permanently enjoined its enforcement. What issues might arise on appellate review with respect to the declaratory judgment? Is there a case or controversy? Did the plaintiff have standing to commence the action? What jurisdictional requirements must be satisfied? Should declaratory relief be conditioned upon the inadequacy of other remedies? Does an adequate alternative remedy exist? What implications do the imperatives of federalism have? What discretion does the court have to grant or deny relief? Once the district court makes a decision, what standard should govern appellate review? *See El Dia, Inc. v. Hernandez Colon*, 963 F.2d 488 (1st Cir.1992).

2. *More on the Pornography Peddler*. Are the requirements for declaratory relief present in a case like this?

COMMUNITY FOR CREATIVE NON-VIOLENCE V. HESS

745 F.2d 697 (D.C.Cir.1984).

SPOTTSWOOD W. ROBINSON, CHIEF JUDGE.

Appellants instituted this litigation to vindicate their position that a practice pursued by certain judges of the Superior Court of the District of Columbia violated the Free Exercise Clause of the First Amendment. Appellants sought a judgment declaring that the practice was unlawful, and an injunction against conduct conforming to it. The District Court dismissed their suit on the ground that the case had become moot. Our review of the record leads us to conclude that, whether or not the controversy between appellants and the judges had so abated as to require dismissal, it has become so attenuated as to call for an exercise of discretionary judicial authority to forego a decision on appellant's constitutional claim.

The individual appellants subscribe to religious tenets forbidding them to exhibit respect for any worldly entity. They thus assert that they are precluded from rising when a judge enters or exits the courtroom. These appellants also are members of the Community for Creative Non-Violence (CCNV), the activities of which require members to attend court frequently as parties or observers. Members thus often find their religious beliefs in conflict with the ancient custom of standing when the courtroom session opens, recesses or adjourns.

In the recent past, CCNV members have encountered this difficulty in the Superior Court of the District of Columbia. One judge of that court jailed a member who refused to take part in the rising ceremony; two other judges threatened non-rising members with arrest and incarceration; another judge had a non-rising member removed from the courtroom; and still another directed non-rising members to remain outside the courtroom until court convened. These practices, it is contended, transgress the Free Exercise Clause.

It is clear enough, however, that none of the involved judges was then aware that the religious scruples of those so treated were at odds with rising. After a remand of this case on an earlier appeal, the judges through affidavits and a status report, informed the District Court that they would not have acted as they did had they known the reason for the refusals to rise. The judges suggested, as a means of avoiding future confrontations, that CCNV members attending court and claiming a First Amendment right to remain seated during the rising ritual notify the judges to that effect through court personnel prior to opening of the session. Though expressly reserving the right to confirm an attendee's sincerity, the judges indicated that once they are satisfied that non-rising is religiously motivated, they will accommodate the attendee's beliefs, presumably by allowing him to remain seated throughout opening and closing ceremonies. On the strength of this assurance, the District Court dismissed the action as one no longer presenting a live controversy.

[In] determining whether it should dismiss a case which is not technically moot, but in which the defendant voluntarily has discontinued the challenged activity, the court should consider whether there remains "some cognizable danger of recurrent violation, something more than the mere possibility which serves to keep the case alive." The court should take into account "the bona fides of the expressed intent to comply, the effectiveness of the discontinuance and, in some cases, the character of the past violations." These factors, so vital in suits for injunction, are equally important in declaratory judgment actions, as this one eventually became. As the Supreme Court has said, "sound discretion withholds [a declaratory judgment] where it appears that a challenged 'continuing practice' is, at the moment adjudication is sought, undergoing significant modifications so that its ultimate form cannot be confidently predicted." That is precisely the situation before us.

While the Superior Court judges joined herein have not completely and absolutely discarded their former practices, and thus perhaps have not actually mooted this case, they clearly have modified their behavior significantly since suit was brought. And appellants' counsel, at oral argument, informed us that appellants have no religious, and hence, no constitutional, objection to providing advance notice of their intended presence in the judges' courtrooms. We therefore think the likelihood of recurrent confrontations between appellants and the judges is much too small to warrant decision of the issue tendered on this appeal.

However the treatment accorded CCNV members in the past might fare constitutionally, the judges have volunteered to reconcile their needs for respect and order in the courtroom with members' religious dictates. For the moment at least, any estimate of the fact or nature of future difficulty would be hazardous. That, combined with members' willingness to make known their expected court attendances, leads us to exercise our discretion to stop short of resolution of the pre-existing constitutional dispute.

[W]e [are] guided by Supreme Court decisions to the conclusion that the events that had transpired after institution of the suit had caused it to "become so attenuated and remote as to warrant dismissal [pursuant] to the court's discretionary authority to grant or withhold declaratory relief." Similarly, we find the controversy tendered here so "attenuated" and "remote" as to call for an exercise of our discretion in the same direction. * * *

C. JURISDICTION

Equally fatal to declaratory judgments as the lack of a justiciable controversy is the absence of personal or subject matter jurisdiction. As noted by the Court in the *Aetna Life Insurance* case, 300 U.S. at 240, the FDJA is strictly "procedural" and thus provides no independent jurisdictional basis. Actions for declaratory judgments must satisfy the same requirements for diversity or federal question jurisdiction that generally govern access to federal courts. In a diversity proceeding, jurisdictional analysis largely is unaffected by a request for declaratory relief. Such is not the case for federal questions, insofar as jurisdiction is conditioned upon the well-pleaded complaint rule. Pursuant to that requirement, a federal question must be evident on the face of a well-pleaded complaint. Stressing that the Federal Declaratory Judgment Act is procedural only in operation, the Supreme Court has determined that a request for declaratory relief does not alter the requirement that a federal question must be stated, rather than anticipated by, the plaintiff.

SKELLY OIL CO. V. PHILLIPS PETROLEUM CO.

339 U.S. 667, 70 S.Ct. 876, 94 L.Ed. 1194 (1950).

MR. JUSTICE FRANKFURTER delivered the opinion of the Court.

In 1945, Michigan–Wisconsin Pipe Line Company sought from the Federal Power Commission a certificate of public convenience and necessity, required by [for] the construction and operation of a pipe line to carry natural gas from Texas to Michigan and Wisconsin. A prerequisite for such a certificate is adequate reserves of gas. To obtain these reserves Michigan–Wisconsin entered into an agreement with Phillips Petroleum Company [whereby] the latter undertook to make available gas from the Hugoton Gas Field, sprawling over Kansas, Oklahoma and Texas, which it produced or purchased from others. Phillips had contracted with petitioners, Skelly Oil Company, Stanolind Oil and Gas Company, and Magnolia Petroleum Company, to purchase gas produced by them in the Hugoton Field for resale to Michigan–Wisconsin. Each contract provided that "in the event Michigan–Wisconsin Pipe Line Company shall fail to secure from the Federal Power Commission on or before [October 1, 1946] a certificate of public convenience and necessity for the construction and operation of its pipe line, Seller [a petitioner] shall have the right to terminate this contract by written notice to Buyer [Phillips] delivered to Buyer at any time after December 1, 1946, but before the issuance of such certificate." The legal significance of this provision is at the core of this litigation.

The Federal Power Commission, in response to the application of Michigan–Wisconsin, on November 30, 1946, ordered that "A certificate of public convenience and necessity be and it is hereby issued to applicant [Michigan–Wisconsin], upon the terms and conditions of this order." * * *

News of the Commission's action was released on November 30, 1946, but the actual content of the order was not made public until December 2, 1946. Petitioners severally, on December 2, 1946, gave notice to Phillips of termination of their contracts on the ground that Michigan–Wisconsin had not received a certificate of public convenience and necessity. Thereupon Michigan–Wisconsin and Phillips brought suit against petitioners in the District Court for the Northern District of Oklahoma. Alleging that a certificate of public convenience and necessity, "within the meaning of said Natural Gas Act and said contracts" had been issued prior to petitioners' attempt at termination of the contracts, they invoked the Federal Declaratory Judgment Act for a declaration that the contracts were still "in effect and binding upon the parties thereto." [The] case [went] to the merits, and the District Court decreed that the contracts between Phillips and petitioners had not been "effectively terminated and that each of such contracts remain [sic] in full force and effect." The Court of Appeals for the Tenth Circuit affirmed, and we brought the case here, because it raises in sharp form the question whether a suit like this "arises under the Constitution, laws or treaties of the United States," 28 U.S.C. § 1331, so as to enable District Courts to give declaratory relief under the Declaratory Judgment Act.

"The operation of the Declaratory Judgment Act is procedural only." Congress enlarged the range of remedies available in the federal courts but did not extend their jurisdiction. When concerned as we are with the power of the inferior federal courts to entertain litigation within the restricted area to which the Constitution and Acts of Congress confine them, "jurisdiction" means the kinds of issues which give right of entrance to federal courts. Jurisdiction in this sense was not altered by the Declaratory Judgment Act. Prior to that Act, a federal court would entertain a suit on a contract only if the plaintiff asked for an immediately enforceable remedy like money damages or an injunction, but such relief could only be given if the requisites of jurisdiction, in the sense of a federal right or diversity, provided foundation for resort to the federal courts. The Declaratory Judgment Act allowed relief to be given by way of recognizing the plaintiff's right even though no immediate enforcement of it was asked. But the requirements of jurisdiction—the limited subject matters which alone Congress had authorized the District Courts to adjudicate—were not impliedly repealed or modified.

If Phillips sought damages from petitioners or specific performance of their contracts, it could not bring suit in a United States District Court on the theory that it was asserting a federal right. And for the simple reason that such a suit would "arise" under the State law governing the contracts. Whatever federal claim Phillips may be able to urge would in any event be injected into the case only in anticipation of a defense to be asserted by petitioners. "Not every question of federal law emerging in a suit is proof that a federal law is the basis of the suit." [I]t has been settled doctrine that where a suit is brought in the federal courts "upon the sole ground that the determination of the suit depends upon some question of a Federal nature, it must appear, at the outset, from the declaration or the bill of the party suing, that the suit is of that character." But "a suggestion of one party, that the other will or may set up a claim under the Constitution or laws of the United States, does not make the suit one arising under that Constitution or those laws." The plaintiff's claim itself must present a federal question "unaided by anything alleged in anticipation of avoidance of defenses which it is thought the defendant may interpose."

[To] be observant of these restrictions is not to indulge in formalism or sterile technicality. It would turn into the federal courts a vast current of litigation indubitably arising under State law, in the sense that the right to be vindicated was State-created, if a suit for a declaration of rights could be brought into the federal courts merely because an anticipated defense derived from federal law. Not only would this unduly swell the volume of litigation in the District Courts but it would also embarrass those courts—and this Court on potential review—in that matters of local law may often be involved, and the District Courts may either have to decide doubtful questions of State law or hold cases pending disposition of such State issues by State courts. To sanction suits for declaratory relief as within the jurisdiction of the District Courts merely because, as in this case, artful pleading anticipates a defense based on federal law would contravene the whole trend of jurisdictional legislation by Congress, disregard the effective functioning of the federal judicial system and distort the limited procedural purpose of the Declaratory Judgment Act. Since the matter in controversy as to which Phillips asked for a declaratory judgment is not one that "arises under the [laws] of the United States" and since as to Skelly and Stanolind jurisdiction cannot be sustained on the score of diversity of citizenship, the proceedings against them should have been dismissed.

D. STANDARDS OF REVIEW

1. AVAILABILITY OF REMEDY

Unlike injunctions, declaratory judgments generally are not conditioned upon the inadequacy of remedial alternatives. By its terms, F.R.Civ.P. 57 specifies that "another adequate remedy does not preclude a judgment for declaratory relief in cases where it is appropriate." Prior to statutory creation of the declaratory judgment remedy, comparable relief at best was approximated by injunctive orders or other means of recourse. An action for rescission in a contract dispute, for instance, essentially seeks declaratory relief. Availability of the remedy, however, is conditioned upon demonstrating inadequate remedies of law. Because it is not inherently the recourse of last resort, commentators have stressed that declaratory judgments are not "an extraordinary remedy" but "should be considered a simple, ordinary auxiliary remedy [to] be asked for and given whenever it will remove uncertainty in the rights of a litigant or settle a controversy existing or incipient." Charles Alan Wright and Arthur R. Miller, Federal Practice and Procedure § 2758, at 620–21 (*quoting* Clark, Code Pleading § 53, at 336 (1947)).

Standards governing the availability of declaratory judgments, although relaxed in contrast with those conditioning equitable relief, are not indiscriminate. Although inadequacy of other remedies is not a prerequisite for a declaratory judgment, courts properly exercise their discretion in denying such relief if convinced that it would be less effective than another methodology or is unnecessary.

Efficacy of remedial alternatives also may be a relevant consideration when an issue is the subject of an action in another forum. To the extent that a declaratory judgment is sought on claims paralleling an action in another tribunal—judicial or administrative—denial of such relief may be apt. In the exercise of its discretion, however, a court may enter a declaratory judgment notwithstanding a parallel action if satisfied that its forum provides greater efficiency, expertise, convenience or resolution.

To the extent that a pending action is in state court, a federal judge's decision with respect to entering declaratory relief may need to factor principles of federalism. In deference to the nation's bifurcated system of governance and independent sovereigns, the federal judiciary is obligated to avoid undue intrusions into state court proceedings. By itself the FDJA does not provide an independent basis for removal of actions from state to federal court or to bring state claims into a federal forum. When jurisdictional requirements and statutory objectives are satisfied, however, the federal interest may prevail even to the extent of superseding a pending state action.

PROVIDENT TRADESMENS BANK & TRUST CO. V. PATTERSON

390 U.S. 102, 88 S.Ct. 733, 19 L.Ed.2d 936 (1968).

MR. JUSTICE HARLAN delivered the opinion of the Court.

This controversy, involving in its present posture the dismissal of a declaratory judgment action for nonjoinder of an "indispensable" party, began nearly 10 years ago with a traffic accident. An automobile owned by Edward Dutcher, who was not present when the accident occurred, was being driven by Donald Cionci, to whom Dutcher had given the keys. John Lynch and John Harris were passengers. The automobile crossed the median strip of the highway and collided with a truck being driven by Thomas Smith. Cionci, Lynch, and Smith were killed and Harris was severely injured.

Three tort actions were brought. Provident Tradesmens Bank, the administrator of the estate of passenger Lynch and petitioner here, sued the estate of the driver, Cionci, in a diversity action. Smith's administratrix, and Harris in person, each brought a state-court action against the estate of Cionci, Dutcher the owner, and the estate of Lynch. These Smith and Harris actions, for unknown reasons, have never gone to trial and are still pending. The Lynch action against Cionci's estate was settled for $50,000, which the estate of Cionci, being penniless, has never paid.

Dutcher, the owner of the automobile and a defendant in the as yet untried tort actions, had an automobile liability insurance policy with Lumbermens Mutual Casualty Company, a respondent here. That policy had an upper limit of $100,000 for all claims arising out of a single accident. This fund was potentially subject to two different sorts of claims by the tort plaintiffs. First, Dutcher himself might be held vicariously liable as Cionci's "principal"; the likelihood of such a judgment against Dutcher is a matter of considerable doubt and dispute. Second, the policy by its terms covered the direct liability of any person driving Dutcher's car with Dutcher's "permission."

The insurance company had declined, after notice, to defend in the tort action brought by Lynch's estate against the estate of Cionci, believing that Cionci had not had permission and hence was not covered by the policy. The facts allegedly were that Dutcher had entrusted his car to Cionci, but that Cionci had made a detour from the errand for which Dutcher allowed his car to be taken. The estate of Lynch, armed with its $50,000 liquidated claim against the estate of Cionci, brought the present diversity action for a declaration that Cionci's use of the car had been "with permission" of Dutcher. The only named defendants were the company and the estate of Cionci. The other two tort plaintiffs were joined as plaintiffs. Dutcher, a resident of the State of Pennsylvania as were all the plaintiffs, was not joined either as plaintiff or defendant. The failure to join him was not adverted to at the trial level.

The major question of law contested at trial was a state-law question. The District Court had ruled that, as a matter of the applicable (Pennsylvania) law, the driver of an automobile is presumed to have the permission of the owner. Hence, unless contrary evidence could be introduced, the tort plaintiffs, now declaratory judgment plaintiffs, would be entitled to a directed verdict against the insurance company. The only possible contrary evidence was testimony by Dutcher as to restrictions he had imposed on Cionci's use of the automobile. The two estate plaintiffs claimed, however, that under the Pennsylvania "Dead Man Rule" Dutcher was incompetent to testify on this matter as against them. The District Court upheld this claim. It ruled that under Pennsylvania law Dutcher was incompetent to testify against an estate if he had an "adverse" interest to that of the estate. It found such adversity in Dutcher's potential need to call upon the insurance fund to pay judgments against himself, and his consequent interest in not having part or all of the fund used to pay judgments against Cionci. The District Court, therefore, directed verdicts in favor of the two estates. Dutcher was, however, allowed to testify as against the live plaintiff, Harris. The jury, nonetheless, found that Cionci had had permission, and hence awarded a verdict to Harris also.

[A]t the time the present declaratory judgment action came to trial two tort actions were pending in the state courts. In one, the estate of the deceased truck driver, Smith, was suing the estate of Cionci, as tortfeasor, plus Dutcher, on the theory that Cionci was doing an errand for him at the time of the accident, plus Lynch's estate, on the theory that Lynch had been in "control" of Cionci. Harris, the injured passenger, was suing the same three defendants on the same theories in a separate action. The Court of Appeals concluded that since these actions "presented the mooted question as to the coverage of the policy," the issue presented in the present proceeding, the District Court should have declined jurisdiction in order to allow the state courts to settle this question of state law.

We believe the Court of Appeals decided this question incorrectly. While we reaffirm our prior holding that a federal district court should, in the exercise of discretion, decline to exercise diversity jurisdiction over a declaratory judgment action raising issues of state law when those same issues are being presented contemporaneously to state courts, we do not find that to be the case here.

This issue, [was] not raised at trial. While we do not now declare that a court of appeals may never on its own motion compel dismissal of an action as an unwarranted intrusion upon state adjudication of state law, we do conclude that, this being a discretionary matter, the existence of a verdict reached after a prolonged trial in which the defendants did not invoke the pending state actions should be taken into consideration in deciding whether dismissal is the wiser course.

It can hardly be said that Lynch's administrator, the plaintiff and petitioner in this case, would have had a satisfactory opportunity to litigate the issue of Cionci's permission in the state actions. The Court of Appeals said that "all the persons involved in the accident were parties" to the state-court actions. If the implication is that the state actions could have resulted in judgments in favor of Lynch's estate and against the insurance company on the issue of Cionci's permission, this implication is not correct. The insurance company was not a party to the tort actions, and was not defending Cionci's estate. Lynch's estate was a party only in the sense that Lynch's personal representative (a different person from Lynch's administrator, the plaintiff in this case) was made a defendant in tort. Furthermore, the Smith and Harris actions against Cionci had nothing to do with the issue of insurance coverage: had Smith or Harris won a judgment against Cionci's estate, they would have had to bring a further action against the insurance company; this further action could well have been brought in a federal court. In short, the net result of dismissal here would presumably have been a diversity action identical with this one, except that Lynch's estate would have been compelled to wait upon the convenience of plaintiffs over whom it had no control, and would have been dependent upon a victory by those plaintiffs in a suit in which it was a defendant.

The issues that were before the state courts in the tort actions were not the same as the issues presented by this case. To be sure, a critical question of fact in both cases was what Dutcher said to Cionci when he gave him the keys. But in the state-court actions the ultimate question was whether Cionci was acting as Dutcher's agent, thus making Dutcher personally liable for Cionci's tort. In this case the question was simply whether Cionci had "permission," thus bringing Cionci's own liability within the coverage of the insurance policy. Resolution of the "agency" issue in the state court would have had no bearing on the "permission" issue even if that resolution were binding on Lynch's estate. Furthermore, although the state court would have had to rule (and still will have to do so, if the cases are ever tried) whether or not Dutcher may testify against the estates under the Dead Man Rule, this question is also a different one in the state and federal cases. In the state cases, Dutcher was a defendant, and the question would be whether he could testify in defense against his own liability. In the present case the question was rather whether he could testify, as a nonparty, on the coverage of his insurance policy.

We think it clear that the judgment below cannot stand.

Declaratory judgments generally are inappropriate when a particular method of resolving an issue is statutorily prescribed. That rule may give way, however, against the weight of exigent circumstances especially when a profound public interest is at stake.

KATZENBACH V. MCCLUNG

379 U.S. 294, 85 S.Ct. 377, 13 L.Ed.2d 290 (1964).

MR. JUSTICE CLARK delivered the opinion of the Court.

This case was argued with *Heart of Atlanta Motel v. United States*, decided this date, in which we upheld the constitutional validity of Title II of the Civil Rights Act of 1964 against an attack by hotels, motels, and like establishments. This complaint for injunctive relief against appellants attacks the constitutionality of the Act as applied to a restaurant. The case was heard by a three-judge United States District Court and an injunction was issued restraining appellants from enforcing the Act against the restaurant. On direct appeal, we noted probable jurisdiction. We now reverse the judgment.

1. The Motion to Dismiss.

The appellants moved in the District Court to dismiss the complaint for want of equity jurisdiction and that claim is pressed here. The grounds are that the Act authorizes only preventive relief; that there has been no threat of enforcement against the appellees and that they have alleged no irreparable injury. It is true that ordinarily equity will not interfere in such cases. However, we may and do consider this complaint as an application for a declaratory judgment under 28 U.S. C. §§ 2201 and 2202. In this case, of course, direct appeal to this Court would still lie under 28 U.S. C. § 1252. But even though Rule 57 of the Federal Rules of Civil Procedure permits declaratory relief although another adequate remedy exists, it should not be granted where a special statutory proceeding has been provided. See Notes on Rule 57 of Advisory Committee on Rules, 28 U.S.C. App.5178. Title II provides for such a statutory proceeding for the determination of rights and duties arising thereunder, and courts should, therefore, ordinarily refrain from exercising their jurisdiction in such cases.

The present case, however, is in a unique position. The interference with governmental action has occurred and the constitutional question is before us in the companion case of *Heart of Atlanta Motel* as well as in this case. It is important that a decision on the constitutionality of the Act as applied in these cases be announced as quickly as possible. For these reasons, we have concluded, with the above caveat, that the denial of discretionary declaratory relief is not required here.

[Insofar] as a state criminal action is pending, the interests of federalism ordinarily disfavor federal declaratory relief. With respect to pending state tax collection proceedings, the Supreme Court has held "that those considerations which have led federal courts of equity to refuse to enjoin the collection of state taxes, except in exceptional cases, require a like restraint in the use of the declaratory judgment procedure." Similar analysis, referenced to traditional conditions for equitable discretion, governs requests for declaratory relief when state prosecutions are pending. Citing to its tax cases, the Court in *Samuels v. Mackell* reaffirmed that "[a]lthough the declaratory judgment sought by the plaintiffs was a statutory remedy rather than a traditional form of equitable relief, . . . a suit for declaratory judgment was nevertheless 'essentially an equitable cause of action,' and 'was analogous to the equity jurisdiction in suits *quia timet* or for a decree quieting title.' " At least to the extent that a state criminal action has commenced before the federal suit, therefore, the record must demonstrate "irreparable injury" for a declaratory judgment to be rendered. Typically, such harm is not established "in the absence of the usual prerequisites of bad faith and harassment." As the *Samuels* Court noted

> [I]n both situations deeply rooted and long-settled principles of equity have narrowly restricted the scope for federal intervention, and ordinarily a declaratory judgment will result in precisely the same interference with and disruption of state proceedings that the long-standing policy limiting injunctions was designed to avoid. This is true for at least two reasons. In the first place, the Declaratory Judgment Act provides that after a declaratory judgment is issued the district court may enforce it by granting "further necessary or proper relief," and therefore a declaratory judgment issued while state proceedings are pending might serve as the basis for a subsequent injunction against those proceedings to "protect or effectuate" the declaratory judgment, and thus result in a clearly improper interference with the state proceedings. Secondly, even if the declaratory judgment is not used as a basis for actually issuing an injunction, the declaratory relief alone has virtually the same practical impact as a formal injunction would. * * *

We therefore hold that, in cases where the state criminal prosecution was begun prior to the federal suit, the same equitable principles relevant to the propriety of an injunction must be taken into consideration by federal district courts in determining whether to issue a declaratory judgment, and that where an injunction would be impermissible under these principles, declaratory relief should ordinarily be denied as well.

We do not mean to suggest that a declaratory judgment should never be issued in cases of this type if it has been concluded that injunctive relief would be improper. There may be unusual circumstances in which an injunction might be withheld because, despite a plaintiff's strong claim for relief under the established standards, the injunctive remedy seemed particularly intrusive or offensive; in such a situation, a declaratory judgment might be appropriate and might not be contrary to the basic equitable doctrines governing the availability of relief. Ordinarily, however, the practical effect of the two forms of relief will be virtually identical, and the basic policy against federal interference with pending state criminal prosecutions will be frustrated as much by a declaratory judgment as it would be by an injunction.[2]

[At] least with respect to declaratory judgments, the calculus with respect to their availability differs when a state action is possible but not actually pending. Under such circumstances, a showing of irreparable harm is impossible to establish. Principles of federalism that would preclude the powerful methodology of injunctive relief, however, may be less of an impediment when the milder method of declaratory relief is sought.

Although a federal court possesses the power to stay a declaratory judgment action, grounds for such an action have been subject to debate. In *Wilton v. Seven Falls Co.*, the Supreme Court resolved a conflict among circuits with respect to operative standards.

WILTON V. SEVEN FALLS CO.

515 U.S. 277, 115 S.Ct. 2137, 132 L.Ed.2d 214 (1995).

JUSTICE O'CONNOR delivered the opinion of the Court.

This case asks whether the discretionary standard set forth in *Brillhart v. Excess Ins. Co. of America,* or the "exceptional circumstances" test developed in *Colorado River Water Conservation Dist. v. United States,* and *Moses H. Cone Memorial Hospital v. Mercury Constr. Corp.*, governs a district court's decision to stay a declaratory judgment action during the pendency of parallel state court proceedings. * * *

In early 1992, a dispute between respondents (the Hill Group) and other parties over the ownership and operation of oil and gas properties in Winkler County, Texas, appeared likely to culminate in litigation. The Hill Group asked petitioners (London Underwriters) to provide them with

---

[2] *Samuels*, 401 U.S. at 72–73.

coverage under several commercial liability insurance policies. London Underwriters refused to defend or indemnify the Hill Group in a letter dated July 31, 1992. In September 1992, after a 3-week trial, a Winkler County jury entered a verdict in excess of $100 million against the Hill Group on various state law claims.

The Hill Group gave London Underwriters notice of the verdict in late November 1992. On December 9, 1992, London Underwriters filed suit in the United States District Court for the Southern District of [Texas]. London Underwriters sought a declaration under the Declaratory Judgment Act, 28 U.S.C. § 2201(a), that their policies did not cover the Hill Group's liability for the Winkler County judgment. After negotiations with the Hill Group's counsel, London Underwriters voluntarily dismissed the action on January 22, 1993. London Underwriters did so, however, upon the express condition that the Hill Group give London Underwriters two weeks' notice if they decided to bring suit on the policy.

On February 23, 1993, the Hill Group notified London Underwriters of their intention to file such a suit in Travis County, Texas. London Underwriters refiled their declaratory judgment action in the Southern District of Texas on February 24, 1993. As promised, the Hill Group initiated an action against London Underwriters on March 26, 1993 in state court in Travis County. The Hill Group's codefendants in the Winkler County litigation joined in this suit and asserted claims against certain Texas insurers, thus rendering the parties nondiverse and the suit nonremovable.

On the same day that the Hill Group filed their Travis County action, they moved to dismiss or, in the alternative, to stay London Underwriters' federal declaratory judgment action. After receiving submissions from the parties on the issue, the District Court entered a stay on June 30, 1993. The District Court observed that the state lawsuit pending in Travis County encompassed the same coverage issues raised in the declaratory judgment action and determined that a stay was warranted in order to avoid piecemeal litigation and to bar London Underwriters' attempts at forum shopping. London Underwriters filed a timely appeal.

The United States Court of Appeals for the Fifth Circuit affirmed in an unpublished opinion filed on July 29, 1994. Noting that under Circuit precedent, "[a] district court has broad discretion to grant (or decline to grant) declaratory judgment," the Court of Appeals did not require application of the test articulated in *Colorado River*, and *Moses H. Cone*, under which district courts must point to "exceptional circumstances" to justify staying or dismissing federal proceedings. Citing the interests in avoiding duplicative proceedings and forum shopping, the Court of Appeals reviewed the District Court's decision for abuse of discretion, and found none.

We granted certiorari to resolve circuit conflicts concerning the standard governing a district court's decision to stay a declaratory judgment action in favor of parallel state litigation. * * *

Over 50 years ago, in *Brillhart v. Excess Ins. Co.*, this Court addressed circumstances virtually identical to those present in the case before us today. An insurer, anticipating a coercive suit, sought a declaration in federal court of nonliability on an insurance policy. The District Court dismissed the action in favor of pending state garnishment proceedings, to which the insurer had been added as a defendant.

[The] question for a district court presented with a suit under the Declaratory Judgment Act, the Court found, is "whether the questions in controversy between the parties to the federal suit, and which are not foreclosed under the applicable substantive law, can better be settled in the proceeding pending in the state court."

Brillhart makes clear that district courts possess discretion in determining whether and when to entertain an action under the Declaratory Judgment Act, even when the suit otherwise satisfies subject matter jurisdictional prerequisites. Although *Brillhart* did not set out an exclusive list of factors governing the district court's exercise of this discretion, it did provide some useful guidance in that regard. The Court indicated, for example, that in deciding whether to enter a stay, a district court should examine "the scope of the pending state court proceeding and the nature of defenses open there." This inquiry, in turn, entails consideration of "whether the claims of all parties in interest can satisfactorily be adjudicated in that proceeding, whether necessary parties have been joined, whether such parties are amenable to process in that proceeding, etc." Other cases, the Court noted, might shed light on additional factors governing a district court's decision to stay or to dismiss a declaratory judgment action at the outset. But *Brillhart* indicated that, at least where another suit involving the same parties and presenting opportunity for ventilation of the same state law issues is pending in state court, a district court might be indulging in "[g]ratuitous interference," if it permitted the federal declaratory action to proceed.

Brillhart, without more, clearly supports the District Court's decision in this case. (That the court here stayed, rather than dismissed, the action is of little moment in this regard, because the state court's decision will bind the parties under principles of res judicata.) Nonetheless, London Underwriters argue, and several Courts of Appeals have agreed, that intervening case law has supplanted *Brillhart's* notions of broad discretion with a test under which district courts may stay or dismiss actions properly within their jurisdiction only in "exceptional circumstances." In London Underwriters' view, recent cases have established that a district court must point to a compelling reason—which, they say, is lacking here—in order to stay a declaratory judgment action in favor of pending state proceedings. To evaluate this argument, it is necessary to examine three cases handed down several decades after *Brillhart.*

In *Colorado River Water Conservation Dist. v. United States*, the Government brought an action in Federal District Court under 28 U.S.C. § 1345 seeking a declaration of its water rights, the appointment of a water master, and an order enjoining all uses and diversions of water by other [parties]. Without discussing *Brillhart,* the Court began with the premise that federal courts have a "virtually unflagging obligation" to exercise the jurisdiction conferred on them by Congress. The Court determined, however, that a district court could nonetheless abstain from the assumption of jurisdiction over a suit in "exceptional" circumstances, and it found such exceptional circumstances on the facts of the case. Specifically, the Court deemed dispositive a clear federal policy against piecemeal adjudication of water rights; the existence of an elaborate state scheme for resolution of such claims; the absence of any proceedings in the District Court, other than the filing of the complaint, prior to the motion to dismiss; the extensive nature of the suit; the 300-mile distance between the District Court and the situs of the water district at issue; and the prior participation of the Federal Government in related state proceedings.

Two years after *Colorado River* we decided *Will v. Calvert Fire Ins. Co.,* 437 U.S. 655 (1978), in which a plurality of the Court stated that, while " 'the pendency of an action in the state court is no bar to proceedings concerning the same matter in the Federal court having jurisdiction,' 'a district court is under no compulsion to exercise that jurisdiction,' " 437 U.S. at 662, *quoting Brillhart. Will* concerned an action seeking damages for an alleged violation of federal securities laws brought in federal court during the dependency of related state proceedings. Although the case arose outside the declaratory judgment context, the plurality invoked *Brillhart* as the appropriate authority. *Colorado River,* according to the plurality, "in no way undermine[d] the conclusion of *Brillhart* that the decision whether to defer to the concurrent jurisdiction of a state court is, in the last analysis, a matter committed to the district court's discretion." *Will, supra*, 437 U.S., at 664. Justice Blackmun, concurring in the judgment, criticized the plurality for not recognizing that Colorado River had undercut the "sweeping language" of *Brillhart.* 437 U.S., at 667. Four Justices in dissent urged that the *Colorado River* "exceptional circumstances" test supplied the governing standard.

The plurality's suggestion in *Will* that *Brillhart* might have application beyond the context of declaratory judgments was rejected by the Court in *Moses H. Cone Memorial Hospital v. Mercury Constr. Corp.*, 460 U.S. 1 (1983). In *Moses H. Cone*, the Court established that the

Colorado River "exceptional circumstances" test, rather than the more permissive *Brillhart* analysis, governs a district court's decision to stay a suit to compel arbitration under § 4 of the Arbitration Act in favor of pending state litigation. Noting that the combination of Justice Blackmun and the four dissenting Justices in *Will* had made five to require application of *Colorado River*, the Court rejected the argument that *Will* had worked any substantive changes in the law. " 'Abdication of the obligation to decide cases,' " the Court reasoned, " 'can be justified [only] in the exceptional circumstance where the order to the parties to repair to the State court would clearly serve an important countervailing interest.' " As it had in *Colorado River*, the Court articulated non-exclusive factors relevant to the existence of such exceptional circumstances, including the assumption by either court of jurisdiction over a res, the relative convenience of the fora, avoidance of piecemeal litigation, the order in which jurisdiction was obtained by the concurrent fora, whether and to what extent federal law provides the rules of decision on the merits, and the adequacy of state proceedings. Evaluating each of these factors, the Court concluded that the District Court's stay of federal proceedings was, under the circumstances, inappropriate.

Relying on these post-*Brillhart* developments, London Underwriters contend that the *Brillhart* regime, under which district courts have substantial latitude in deciding whether to stay or to dismiss a declaratory judgment suit in light of pending state proceedings (and need not point to "exceptional circumstances" to justify their actions), is an outmoded relic of another era. We disagree. Neither *Colorado River,* which upheld the dismissal of federal proceedings, nor *Moses H. Cone*, which did not, dealt with actions brought under the Declaratory Judgment Act. Distinct features of the Declaratory Judgment Act, we believe, justify a standard vesting district courts with greater discretion in declaratory judgment actions than that permitted under the "exceptional circumstances" test of *Colorado River* and *Moses H. Cone.* No subsequent case, in our view, has called into question the application of the *Brillhart* standard to the *Brillhart* facts.

Since its inception, the Declaratory Judgment Act has been understood to confer on federal courts unique and substantial discretion in deciding whether to declare the rights of litigants. On its face, the statute provides that a court "may declare the rights and other legal relations of any interested party seeking such declaration," 28 U.S.C. § 2201(a). The statute's textual commitment to discretion, and the breadth of leeway we have always understood it to suggest, distinguish the declaratory judgment context from other areas of the law in which concepts of discretion surface. We have repeatedly characterized the Declaratory Judgment Act as "an enabling Act, which confers a discretion on the courts rather than an absolute right upon the litigant." When all is said and done, we have concluded, "the propriety of declaratory relief in a particular case will depend upon a circumspect sense of its fitness informed by the teachings and experience concerning the functions and extent of federal judicial power." * * *

2. JUDICIAL DISCRETION

Notwithstanding prerequisites that are less demanding, at least when measured against those for equitable relief, entry of a declaratory judgment remains a function of judicial discretion. The UDJA explicitly authorizes courts to refuse "a declaratory judgment or decree when such judgment or decree would not terminate the uncertainty or controversy giving rise to the proceeding." UDJA, Sec. 6. Case law at both the federal and state level establishes that such considerations are not exclusive. Other factors may include the availability of more effective relief, existence of another action that will resolve the issue more comprehensively, tactical maneuvering calculated to harass, delay or achieve res judicata, procedural fencing, an inadequately developed record and demands of federalism. Reinforcing or competing against such considerations may be the public interest.

NATIONAL WILDLIFE FEDERATION V. UNITED STATES

626 F.2d 917 (D.C.Cir.1980).

MCGOWAN, CIRCUIT JUDGE:

This appeal is from the District Court's dismissal of a suit requesting declaratory relief and mandamus against the President of the United States and the Director of the Office of Management and Budget. At issue is the adequacy *vel non* of certain disclosures and explanations accompanying the President's proposed fiscal 1979 budget in light of section 8(b) of the Forest and Rangeland Renewable Resources Planning Act, 16 U.S.C. § 1606(b)(1976). For the reasons set forth below, we think the District Court properly declined to provide the relief sought. We therefore affirm.

I

The Statutory Framework

The Forest and Rangeland Renewable Resources Planning Act of 1974, requires the President and the administration to develop what is, in effect, a master plan for the management and use of forests and rangelands. The master plan is highly multifarious. Its components include a "Renewable Resource Assessment," a "Renewable Resource Program," a system of "annual reports," a presidential "Statement of Policy," and various presidential "budget statements." * * *

D. *The "Statement of Policy"*

[T]he President is required to submit a "Statement of Policy" to Congress "to be used in framing budget requests by that Administration for Forest Service activities." The Statement of Policy must accompany each revision of the Assessment and the Program. The Statement of Policy apparently is intended to reflect the administration's future plans for Forest Service programs and activities in light of the Assessment and the Program. Either House of Congress may disapprove the Statement of Policy within 90 days of its issuance. Congress also may modify the statement by conventional legislation.

E. *The Budget Statements*

The final document required by the Act is designed to tie together the numerous reports and studies described above. Each year the President is required to submit, with the Forest Service budget request, a statement "express[ing] in qualitative and quantitative terms the extent to which the programs and policies projected under the budget meet the policies approved by the Congress." Should the proposed budget fail to meet these policies, the Act states that the President "shall specifically set forth the reason or reasons for requesting the Congress to approve the lesser programs or policies presented" (the Statement of Reasons).

II

The Response of the Executive Branch to the Act

* * *

A. *The Fiscal 1979 Budget Process*

President Carter submitted the proposed fiscal 1979 budget to Congress on January 20, 1978. The President proposed a $1.8 billion budget for the Forest Service. A budget that included all the money envisioned by the Program would have totalled about $2.4 billion. The budget report noted, correctly, that "the proposed budget for the Forest Service is considerably less than that suggested by the reports prepared pursuant to the Resources Planning Act." The Forest Service the same day transmitted to Congress a document entitled *Explanatory Notes*, which stated, in pertinent part:

> The President's goal is to balance the Federal budget by 1981 and to hold Federal employment to minimum levels. To meet this goal, decisions must be made now which identify programs which are not of the highest priority and which propose the necessary action to reduce and/or eliminate these programs. The Forest Service operates a large and aggressive program including the Young Adult Conservation Corps and Job Corps programs, and will accomplish the highest priority work within these capabilities and fiscal policy. The fiscal year 1979 budget

reflects this effort, and while the budget is somewhat less than fiscal year 1978, it is considerably more than fiscal year 1977.

House and Senate appropriations subcommittees held hearings on the proposed Forest Service budget during March and April, 1978. At the hearings, subcommittee members asked for, and obtained, figures disclosing the differences between the budget requests and the amounts needed fully to achieve the goals of the Program. Various legislators criticized the proposed budget as excessively penurious in light of the Program's recommendations. At no time during the hearings, however, did a legislator or witness assert that the President had failed to comply with [the Act] in any respect.

The National Wildlife Federation on April 28, 1978, sent a letter to President Carter. The letter argued, *inter alia*, that he had not complied with [the Act]. The letter asked the President promptly to supply an adequate Statement of Reasons for recommending lesser Forest Service funding. The President apparently neither replied to the letter nor offered any further explanation of the proposed budget.

The House passed the Forest Service appropriations bill on June 21, 1978. The Senate passed a similar bill on August 9, 1978. Each chamber approved the conference report. The President signed the hill October 17, 1978.

The cyclical budget process began again in January, 1979, with the President's submission of a proposed budget for fiscal 1980. The proposed budget included a new Statement of Reasons required by the Act.

B. The Lawsuit

[A]ppellant filed this suit asking for mandamus and declaratory relief. It asserted, first, that the President had failed to comply with the requirement that the budget request "express in qualitative and quantitative terms the extent to which the programs and policies projected under the budget" fall short of the plans established by the Statement of Policy accepted by Congress. Second, the suit alleged that the President had failed adequately to set forth the "reason or reasons for requesting the Congress to approve the lesser programs or policies." The essence of appellant's contention on this count is that although a reason was given for proposing a *total* budget of lesser magnitude than that envisioned by the Program, no reasons were given for favoring certain components of the Forest Service budget over others.

III

* * *

C. *The Public Interest in Offering Discretionary Relief*

Among the factors to be considered in deciding whether to grant declaratory relief in a particular case is the public interest *vel non* in resolving the controversy. Similarly, the exercise of discretion to issue a writ of mandamus also must be guided by the court's perception of the public interest.

Sometimes the great public importance of an issue militates in favor of its prompt resolution. *See Duke Power Co. v. Carolina Environmental Study Group, Inc.*, (Rehnquist, J., concurring) & (Stevens, J., concurring)(contending that the majority ignored powerful jurisdictional and justiciability arguments because it thought it important to consider on the merits the constitutionality of the Price–Anderson Act's liability limitations for nuclear accidents). At other times, however, the public interest dictates that courts exercise restraint in passing upon crucial issues. *See, e.g., Public Affairs Associates, Inc. v. Rickover*. We think such restraint is necessary where, as here, appellants ask us to intervene in wrangling over the federal budget and budget procedures. Such matters are the archetype of those best resolved through bargaining and accommodation between the legislative and executive branches. We are reluctant to afford discretionary relief when to do so would intrude on the responsibilities including the shared responsibilities of the coordinate branches.

[Our] decision is grounded in the discretionary power we possess to withhold mandamus or a declaratory judgment. Exercising that discretionary power is appropriate here for several reasons in addition to the serious justiciability questions already noted.

First, no legislator complained that the President's informational submissions violated the Act. The funding levels proposed by the budget received much scrutiny and much criticism during the congressional hearings. Some legislators expressed dismay that the *overall budget* was only about 71% of that envisioned by the Program. Legislators also attacked proposed funding reductions for even the most obscure *individual programs*. But no legislator at any time complained that the President had violated the Act by supplying inadequate *information*. No complaint was forthcoming even after the National Wildlife Federation sent to all the appropriations committee members a copy of its letter to President Carter.

The absence of congressional complaints is highly relevant, we think, in light of the Act's purpose. Congress in 1974 was frustrated by President Nixon's impoundment of appropriated funds. The Renewable Resources Planning Act to some extent reflected these sentiments. The Act was designed to help legislators understand when, and to what extent, budget requests were inadequate to fulfill policies approved by Congress. In light of the Act's purpose, one would expect that legislators dissatisfied with the President's submissions would have made their dissatisfaction known. Appellant concedes that not one legislator did so.

Second, appellant also concedes that no witness at the appropriations hearings—not even appellant's own witness—complained that the President's submission was inadequate, or that debate was handicapped by the inadequacy of the presidential statement.

Third, we are hesitant to venture to rule on the President's compliance with the Act because this issue may never arise again. As the District Court recognized, passage of time under the Act may produce a greater accommodation of appellant's view of the statutory requirements and the President's response to them. Indeed, this already may have occurred. The President's Statement of Reasons accompanying the proposed 1980 budget is more elaborate than that accompanying the 1979 budget. Moreover, the Assessment, Program, and Statement of Policy all have been newly revised during the pendency of this appeal, or are in the process of being revised. This controversy never will recur unless future budget statements diverge from the plans envisioned by the updated versions of these documents. That it is wholly speculative that this dispute will arise again militates against awarding discretionary relief.

We think for all these reasons that it would be improvident, on the record before us, to afford mandamus or a declaratory judgment. We therefore ground our affirmance of the District Court's decision on the discretionary power federal courts possess to withhold such relief. Accordingly, we do not assess the adequacy of the President's submissions under the Act.

NOTES: DISCRETION TO GRANT DECLARATORY RELIEF

Although declaratory relief is committed to a court's sound discretion, the Supreme Court has noted that such judgment is not absolute. In *Public Affairs Associates, Inc. v. Rickover*, 369 U.S. 111, 112, 82 S.Ct. 580, 7 L.Ed.2d 604 (1962), the Court thus noted that a trial judge "cannot decline to entertain such an action as a matter of whim or personal disinclination." Regardless of grounds, a court's refusal to enter a declaratory judgment is appealable. However, responding to arguments that discretion to entertain declaratory judgments was "vested [in] the entire judicial system," and thus appellate courts might grant or deny declaratory relief *de novo*, the Court in *Wilton v. Seven Falls Co.* concluded that it is "more consistent with the [Federal Declaratory Judgment Act] to vest district courts with discretion in the first instance because facts bearing on the declaratory judgment remedy, and the fitness of the case for resolution," are peculiarly within their grasp.[16]

[16] *Wilton v. Seven Falls Co.*, 515 U.S. 277, 278, 115 S.Ct. 2137, 2138, 132 L.Ed.2d 214 (1995).

E. DECLARATORY JUDGMENTS IN CONTEXT

1. WRITTEN INSTRUMENTS

Declaratory relief may be a particularly useful means for resolving doubt and controversy over the operation of contracts, wills, trust agreements and other written instruments. To the extent that legal issues are in dispute, a declaratory judgment enables parties to minimize risks to transactions, expectations and relations that would be created by breach, repudiation or an action with coercive consequences. A declaratory judgment does this by allowing parties to a written instrument to obtain an authoritative legal interpretation resolving incipient or full-fledged controversies over such issues as document validity, scope and coverage, waiver and appurtenant rights and obligations.

The UDJA explicitly notes the availability of declaratory judgments for persons "interested under a deed, will, written contract, or other writing constituting a contract, or whose rights, status, or other legal relations are affected by a constitutional provision, statute, [or] rule." UDJA, Sec. 2. By separate provision, it specifies that "[a] contract may be construed by a declaratory judgment either before or after there has been a breach thereof." Id., Sec. 3. Although the FDJA does not textually delineate or suggest specific subject matter, history and interpretation define an ambit at least coextensive with the UDJA—which itself specifies that any enumeration with respect to its coverage "does not limit or restrict the exercise of the general powers" to enter declaratory judgments. Id., Sec. 5.

FEDERAL KEMPER INSURANCE COMPANY V. RAUSCHER

807 F.2d 345 (3d Cir.1986).

GARTH, CIRCUIT JUDGE:

This case arose out of a tragic automobile accident involving both the appellants, Linda and Robert Griffith, and the insured, Richard Rauscher. The accident occurred [while] Rauscher was driving a Volkswagen Rabbit owned by his girlfriend's mother. The Griffiths were passengers in the car, and both incurred injuries. Ms. Griffith, who suffered substantial brain damages as a result of a traumatic brain stem lesion, is now permanently disabled.

The automobile involved in the accident was insured by the Government Employees Insurance Company (GEICO) for a maximum of $50,000. Rauscher was insured by the appellee, Federal Kemper Insurance Company, under a commercial liability policy with a limit of $100,000. Rauscher's policy only covered Rauscher's commercial vehicle, a pick-up truck, or any "temporary substitute auto." The policy defined "temporary substitute auto" as "any auto you do not own while used as a temporary substitute for a covered auto which is out of normal use because of its breakdown, repair, servicing, loss or destruction." The automobile involved in the accident did not fall within the policy's definition of "temporary substitute auto," because at the time of the accident Rauscher's pick-up truck was not "out of normal use." Apparently unaware of the policy's lack of coverage, Rauscher reported the accident to Kemper.

The Griffiths sued Rauscher for damages in February 1983 in the Philadelphia Court of Common Pleas. Kemper refused, on the ground of noncoverage, Rauscher's request for a defense. This case is still pending.

Kemper desired a determination of the extent of its obligation to Rauscher and brought this declaratory judgment action against Rauscher and the Griffiths. Kemper sought a declaration that the automobile Rauscher was operating at the time of the accident was not a "covered" auto within the meaning of the policy and that therefore [the] accident was not within the coverage of the policy.

Not surprisingly, presentation of the relevant facts underlying the coverage dispute has been impeded by the default judgment against Rauscher and the simultaneous judgment against the Griffiths. Certain facts, however, can be gleaned from the affidavits presented on motion for reconsideration.

Apparently, Rauscher's previous policy, which had been written by Prudential Insurance Company, covered Rauscher when he drove vehicles other than his pick-up truck. * * *

[Rauscher's insurance broker, a licensed agent for Kemper,] testified in his deposition that he told Rauscher that there was no difference between the coverage provided by the Prudential policy he previously held and that provided by the Federal Kemper policy. Rauscher chose the Federal Kemper policy and paid the first premium at Trone's office on January 27, 1981.

Rauscher testified on deposition that he believed that he was covered to the same extent by the Federal Kemper policy as he was by his previous policies. He stated that: "Because every other insurance policy I have ever had I was covered driving someone else's vehicle. And I assumed it would be the same with Kemper." In addition, Mr. Rauscher testified that when he made his first premium [payment], he was told that a copy of the insurance policy would soon be sent to him. He also testified that he was unsure whether he had received a copy of the insurance policy by the time of the accident, three and one half weeks after the payment of his first premium.

Kemper filed its complaint for a declaratory [judgment]. It sought to have the district court construe the terms of the policy and declare that the automobile operated by Rauscher at the time of the accident was not a "covered auto" within the meaning of the policy, and that therefore the insurance company was not obligated to provide a defense or indemnity for Rauscher in the pending state action.

The Griffiths [answered], asserting, among other things, that Kemper's policy should be construed to provide coverage for the accident. Rauscher failed to answer and on November 29, 1985, Kemper thereupon moved for default judgment against Rauscher. The district court, holding that the Griffiths' rights were purely derivative of Rauscher's rights, entered judgment against the Griffiths, after default judgment had been entered against Rauscher.

The Griffiths filed a motion for reconsideration arguing that equitable grounds existed for the reformation of the Kemper policy to provide coverage for the February 1981 accident. The "equitable grounds" put forward were the facts surrounding Trone's representation to Rauscher that the Kemper commercial policy provided the same coverage as his previous policy.

The district court denied the [motion]. In its consideration of the issue of the Griffiths' standing to participate as sole defendants in the case, the court stated that their motion for reconsideration presented "no grounds for relief," and that the Griffiths had "no standing to seek reformation of the Kemper policy." After dismissing the Griffiths' claim of standing, and therefore acknowledging the court's lack of jurisdiction over the matter, the district court went on to discuss the merits of the insurance policy claim and concluded that the Griffiths' claim for reformation had no merit.

[It] is settled law that, as a procedural remedy, the federal rules respecting declaratory judgment actions, apply in diversity cases. While state law must determine the substantive rights and duties of the parties to the insurance contract, the question of justiciability is a federal issue to be determined only by federal law. "Thus a federal court decides for itself whether a party has standing to raise a particular issue, or that a particular matter is justiciable or that it is not." If it were otherwise, then when state law exhibited more leniency in its definition of "case or controversy," the federal courts would be improperly exercising federal jurisdiction over a diversity action.

[The] Seventh Circuit case of *Hawkeye–Security Insurance Co. v. Schulte*, is strikingly similar to the one at hand. Following an automobile accident involving a DeSoto owned by the insured Schulte and a vehicle driven by Ginley, the Hawkeye–Security Insurance Company brought a declaratory judgment action against the insured party, Schulte; his son, the driver; and Ginley, the injured party. Hawkeye–Security sought a declaration that its policy did not cover the insured's son, the driver at the time of the accident.

Schulte and his son failed to answer the complaint and default judgment was entered against them. In its consideration of Hawkeye–Security's motion for a default judgment, the district court concluded that Ginley was only a "nominal party" to the suit and that he was not entitled to relief in the suit because he was not a party to the insurance contract. The district court then directed that Ginley be dismissed. As in our case, the injured party "was precluded from litigating the issue raised by his answer to the complaint," because the district court "determined the merits of the complaint on the default of the other two defendants contrary to [the injured party's] contentions."

The Seventh Circuit, *citing Maryland Casualty [Co. v. Pacific Coal & Oil Co.]*, stated that it would be anomalous to hold that while an actual controversy existed between an insurance company and an injured party, an injured party could be denied the right to actually participate in the controversy. As the court stated: "Appellee [the insurance company] voluntarily brought the appellant [the injured party] into this litigation as a party defendant." As a proper party to the action, Ginley, "should be heard to assert any proper defense raised by his answer to the complaint." The court of appeals therefore held that the district court erred in dismissing the injured party Ginley from the declaratory judgment action brought by Hawkeye–Security.

The principles announced in these cases lead inevitably to the conclusion that a "case or controversy" exists between Kemper and the Griffiths, and that therefore the Griffiths have standing to defend the declaratory judgment action despite the absence of Rauscher, the actual insured.

[It] is clear that under the authority of these cases an actual controversy, within both the meaning of the Federal Declaratory Judgment Act and the Constitution, exists between Kemper and the Griffiths. * * *

Although it is not necessary to our analysis or our conclusion, we note that our decision is supported by the fact that the Griffiths are indispensable parties to this type of declaratory judgment action and, under Pennsylvania No–Fault Law, are capable of bringing a direct action against Kemper. Indeed, because it has been held that a "case or controversy" exists between the insurance company and the injured parties in the instant procedural posture, it would be error to hold that the default of the insured could foreclose the rights of injured parties.

Concluding that the injured party has an independent, and not a derivative right, to be heard, is not only jurisprudentially sound, but is also realistic: "Certainly from a pragmatic viewpoint, it is quite true that in many of the liability insurance cases, the most real dispute is between the injured third party and the insurance company, not between the injured and an oftentimes impecunious insured." In terms of fairness, the injured party should be able to present its case upon the ultimate issues, even if the insured does not choose to participate.

This equitable consideration is especially persuasive in view of the fact that the insurance company in this case initiated the action and brought the Griffiths into federal court. As a result it would be anomalous to hold that the Griffiths should not be given an opportunity to establish their case against Kemper because of a default which they could not prevent. We are satisfied therefore that the Griffiths had standing and that their rights are independent and not derivative of Rauscher's.

PROBLEM: WILL THE INSURANCE COVER US?

On a stormy evening, Fred Firestone was taking his companion home from their first date. As he stopped at a red light, Firestone turned to his companion, gazed in her eyes, leaned over and kissed her. As their lips touched, Firestone felt a powerful jolt throughout his body. Looking up, he realized that his foot had slipped from the brake pedal to the accelerator causing him to slam into the vehicle that had stopped just ahead. The accident resulted in significant damage to the rear-ended car and injuries to its occupants. The injured parties, Marvin and Marva Mabree, filed a negligence action against Firestone whose insurance company (Nostate Auto and Life) denied his request to defend him. Nostate's refusal is based upon the fact that the policy covers only vehicles that the insured owns, and Firestone was driving a rented car. Firestone maintains that, in purchasing a policy from Nostate, he instructed the company's agent to provide exactly the same coverage that he had with his former insuror. He asserts that the representative assured him the policies were identical with respect to their terms and scope. Seeking a formal judgment of nonliability under the policy, Nostate brought an action for declaratory relief against Firestone and the Mabrees. The Mabrees answered in a timely fashion, but Firestone never responded to the complaint. A default judgment thus was entered against him. Nostate now maintains that any rights that the Mabrees purport, being derivative of Firestone's, have been extinguished by the judgment against him. Is there a case or controversy between Nostate and the Mabrees? What affect does the declaratory judgment against Firestone have on the Mabrees' claim against Nostate? Does it matter that declaratory relief was the function of a default judgment? Are the Mabrees indispensable parties? Could they sue Nostate independently?

2. INTELLECTUAL PROPERTY

Declaratory relief is a significant remedy for owners of patents, copyrights and trademarks and may be at least as valuable to alleged infringers thereof. Without a competitor's ability to obtain a declaratory judgment, patent holders in particular might exercise undue market leverage. By merely threatening an infringement action, a patent owner could discourage competition by or effectively extort a settlement from otherwise remediless individuals or entities. Such circumstances defined reality prior to the legislated advent of declaratory judgments.

TREEMOND CO. V. SCHERING CORPORATION

122 F.2d 702 (3d Cir.1941).

CLARK, CIRCUIT JUDGE.

Some District Courts seem to have found difficulty in freeing themselves from the strait-jacket of the "adversary" conception. They exhibit a tendency toward a narrow and technical interpretation of an Act intended to be construed in accordance with its broad and wise purpose. The case at bar is, we think, a typical instance. The defendant-patentee, a manufacturer, informed the customers of the plaintiff-appellant, an importer and vendor of a certain chemical known as "Estradiol" that it alone had the right to manufacture that chemical. It also had the following advertisement published in a trade journal:

> "To Purchasers of Estradiol Notice By Schering Corporation United States Letters Patent No. 2,096,744 for Hydrogenation Products of Follicle Hormones and Method of Producing Same, has been issued to us. Notice is hereby given to manufacturers and importers that our patent covers the product known as Estradiol.

Estradiol is also known as dihydroxyestrin, dihydrofolliculin or dihydrotheelin. Our patent also covers the process of making the same.

All uses of this material, without our consent, including medicinal, pharmaceutical and cosmetic, are a violation of our giths (grants) under this patent.

We are giving this notice to the trade so that there may be no misunderstanding or doubt as to the exclusiveness of our rights in the United States to the product Estradiol (also known as dihydroxyestrin, dihydrofolliculin or dihydrotheelin).

Schering Corporation Bloomfield—New Jersey"

Plaintiff-appellant thereupon brought suit for a judgment declaring the defendant's patent invalid and/or not infringed and for an injunction for unfair competition. The learned District Judge dismissed the complaint for the reasons that (1) since the plaintiff alleged that it was not infringing defendant's patent, no actual controversy existed; (2) the plaintiff did not allege that it had been given notice of the claimed infringement, and (3) the notice in the trade publication was made in good faith and therefore could not give rise to a cause of action.

Such a construction of the Federal Declaratory Judgment Act would, in our opinion, destroy its entire usefulness in patent litigation. Before the passage of that Act patentees received greater protection from the law than was warranted by their patent monopoly. Competitors desiring to introduce an article somewhat similar to one already patented met with much difficulty. The patentee could, without bringing suit, publicly claim an infringement and threaten to sue the manufacturer or anyone who dealt with the product in issue. Unless the patentee's actions were of such a character that he might he shackled with the sanctions of the law of unfair competition, he had his alleged infringer at his mercy. Although the competitor's business was gravely injured, he was remediless and in order to survive, he might be forced to make a settlement with a patentee whose claim of infringement was absolutely unfounded. Prior to the New Federal Rules of Civil procedure, the patentee might even bolster his charges by bringing an action for infringement and publicly advertising the fact to the trade. Then after postponing trial as long as possible, he could move for a dismissal without prejudice an repeat the process.

[There] can be no doubt that an "actual controversy" does not exist until the patentee makes some claim that his patent is being infringed. The claim need not be formally asserted; nor should it be necessary that notice be give directly to the plaintiff. [Although] defendant's notice in a trade journal was craftily phrased, it does threaten purchasers with suits for contributory infringement if they purchased plaintiff's product. Indeed the only purpose of this notice can be to make such a threat and thereby intimidate would-be purchasers into buying its own product rather than the plaintiff's. It was unnecessary if defendant really intended to enjoin the infringement. Notice to infringers that a patent exists is not a condition precedent to a subsequent action to obtain an injunction in an infringement action. If the courts were to impose a requirement that direct notice by a patentee to an alleged infringer was necessary before a declaratory judgment action might he maintained, the Federal Declaratory Judgment Act would be in effect repealed so far as patent actions were concerned. Once again patentees might threaten a manufacturer's customers with suit and the manufacturer would be helpless until such time when he was directly notified. * * *

PROBLEM: PATENT PERILS

Patchwork, Inc. manufactures and distributes a tonic, marketed under the trade name Evalast, that when applied to gray hair permanently restores the original color. The company published a notice in a trade journal to the following effect:

> Patchwork, Inc. hereby gives notice to all manufacturers that our patent covers the product known as Evalast and the process for making it. Any use without Patchwork's consent infringes our patent. This notice is provided to eliminate any uncertainty regarding our rights.

Prior to publication of the notice, Cutnpaste, Inc. was prepared to market and distribute a competing product. Cutnpaste believes that Patchwork's patent is invalid and, alternatively, its product would not infringe any rights. As a start-up company with limited resources, however, it cannot afford the risk of a significant damages award in the event found liable for patent infringement. If Cutnpaste withholds its product from the market, however, it risks early insolvency. Does Cutnpaste have any options other than to take the chance of marketing the product and hoping that Patchwork does not sue? What if any claims might it assert? Would there be an actual controversy and basis for standing? Is there a ripeness problem? How should any relief be framed?

3. CONSTITUTIONAL CLAIMS

Although not statutorily prohibited, federal courts have been reluctant to resolve constitutional controversies by means of declaratory judgments. In many instances, such relief has been denied on grounds the need for it was "remote or speculative." *E.g., Eccles v. Peoples Bank of Lakewood Village, California*, 333 U.S. 426, 432, 68 S.Ct. 641, 644, 92 L.Ed. 784 (1948). Especially to the extent that a declaratory judgment may be sought in a context short of a full-blown trial, the Supreme Court has stressed that "[c]aution is appropriate against the subtle tendency to decide public issues free from the safeguards of critical scrutiny of the facts, through the use of a declaratory summary judgment." *Id.* at 434. Such reticence is driven by the judiciary's generally professed inclination to avoid constitutional controversies whenever possible. *See Kremens v. Bartley*, 431 U.S. 119, 133–34, 97 S.Ct. 1709, 1717, 52 L.Ed.2d 184 (1977); *Ashwander v. Tennessee Valley Authority*, 297 U.S. 288, 341, 56 S.Ct. 466, 480, 80 L.Ed. 688 (1936) (Brandeis, J., concurring).

Like many other general rules, the proscription against unnecessary resolution of constitutional issues is not infrequently honored by breach rather than observance. Responding to Justice Frankfurter's observation that courts "do not review issues, especially constitutional issues, until they have to," one commentator notes that "one is tempted to add, until they want to badly enough." Laurence H. Tribe, American Constitutional Law, 2D ED., Sec. 3–8, at 72 (1988).

PENTHOUSE INTERNATIONAL, LTD. V. MEESE

939 F.2d 1011 (D.C.Cir.1991).

SILBERMAN, CIRCUIT JUDGE

Concerned with what he perceived as a serious problem of pornography in American society, President Reagan requested that the Attorney General establish a commission to study the matter and advise the Department of Justice as to appropriate remedies. The Attorney General, accordingly, created the Commission on Pornography in 1985, pursuant to the Federal Advisory Committee Act (FACA), "to determine the nature, extent, and impact on society of pornography in the United States, and to make specific recommendations to the Attorney General concerning more effective ways in which the spread of pornography could be contained, consistent with constitutional guarantees." The Commission took testimony from some 200 witnesses at a series of six public hearings around the country. * * *

One of the witnesses, Reverend Donald Wildmon, Executive Director of the National Federation of Decency, accused a number of well-known corporations of distributing pornography. Reverend Wildmon submitted a written statement entitled "Pornography in the Family Marketplace," setting forth his views about the role of corporations that were "household names" in selling pornographic films, television, and magazines. He asserted that the 7–Eleven national chain of convenience stores was "the leading retailer[ ]" of *Penthouse* and *Playboy*, which he termed "porn magazines," and predicted that the withdrawal of this major sales outlet would financially "cripple" both magazines. After discussion whether to include Reverend Wildmon's testimony in the report, the Commission decided to send a letter to the corporations named by Reverend Wildmon, asking for a response to the accusation. The letter, dated February 11, 1986, which was sent to 23 corporations, included a copy of Reverend Wildmon's testimony, but failed to identify him as its author. The letter stated:

> Authorized Representative:
>
> The Attorney General's Commission on Pornography has held six hearings across the United States during the past seven months on issues related to pornography. During the hearing in Los Angeles, in October 1985, the Commission received testimony alleging that your company is involved in the sale or distribution of pornography. The Commission has determined that it would be appropriate to allow your company an opportunity to respond to the allegations prior to drafting its final report section on identified distributors.
>
> You will find a copy of the relevant testimony enclosed herewith. Please review the allegations and advise the Commission on or before March 3, 1986, if you disagree with the statements enclosed. Failure to respond will necessarily be accepted as an indication of no objection. * * *

The response varied. Time Inc. called the "accusations" "outrageous" and chastised the Commission for relying on "uncorroborated, gratuitous statements" from unidentified sources in what it characterized as a "slipshod and misguided effort." Southland Corporation, owner of the 7–Eleven chain, on the other hand, wrote that since the corporation had decided to stop selling adult magazines in light of the public concern about the effects of pornography it "urge[d] that any references to Southland or 7–Eleven be deleted from [the Commission's] final report."

Southland's decision, Penthouse alleges, was influenced by a telephone call from one of the members of the Commission to the General Counsel and Vice President of Southland, [allegedly to the affect] that the Commission believed that *Playboy* and similar magazines were linked to child abuse and the Commission intended to publish this finding in its report. Southland, which had been leading a national campaign to fight child abuse, believed that if the Commission published those views on the connection between magazines sold by Southland and child abuse, the resulting publicity would be embarrassing to Southland, whether or not there was in fact such a link. Penthouse alleges that the Commission member's information was false in two respects—the Commission had found no causal connection between *Playboy* or other such magazines and child abuse, and it had no intention of discussing any such link in its report. Penthouse also claims that the Commission member deliberately spread these allegedly false allegations to Southland with the intention of inducing the company to withdraw as a distributor of *Penthouse*.

Playboy Enterprises, Inc. and Penthouse sought a preliminary injunction against publication of any "blacklist" of corporations which distributed their respective publications and an order withdrawing the Commission's letter, as well as other relief, including a statement from the Commission that it did *not* view their magazines as obscene. The district court granted preliminary relief. The court determined that Playboy had shown that it was likely to prevail on the merits in establishing that the Commission's actions amounted to an informal scheme of government censorship constituting a prior administrative restraint. The court therefore granted a preliminary injunction, requiring the Commission to send a follow-up letter to the named corporations, withdrawing the first letter and stating that no reply to it would be necessary as the Commission had already decided that no corporations would be named in the final report. The Commission complied. The court refused, however, to be drawn further into the dispute—by considering whether or not the publications were obscene or pornographic or preventing the Commission from doing so—and therefore refused further injunctive relief.

The two publications persisted in their claims for permanent injunctive and declaratory relief, as well as with a *Bivens* claim for damages. Defendants at that point moved for summary judgment asserting the claims for equitable relief were moot and that the damages claim was barred by the doctrine of good faith or qualified immunity because the Commission's action did not violate any clearly-established First Amendment right. Plaintiffs contended that defendants' conduct is unconstitutional under the principle established in *Bantam Books, Inc. v.*

Sullivan, 372 U.S. 58 (1963). The district court granted summary judgment to defendants on all grounds. Penthouse alone appeals the judgment.

Appellant, of course, wishes a determination from the judiciary that the government's conduct was unlawful. Such an opinion, appellant believes, will enable it to persuade retailers who have discontinued selling *Penthouse* to change their minds, and prevent a similar effort in the future which might threaten appellant's circulation. Appellant's primary claim, designed to gain such a determination, is its *Bivens* claim for damages. It is asserted that the Commission sought to prevent ("chill") the distribution of constitutionally protected speech and thereby violated appellant's First Amendment rights. The government has no right to prohibit adult pornography that does not qualify as obscenity, and, in any event, the government may not impose a prior restraint on the distribution even of arguably obscene materials.

[Appellant,] employing a number of forceful verbs and adjectives, would have us extend *Bantam Books*. It is argued that the Commission's action "chilled," "intimidated," "condemned," and "censored" distribution of *Penthouse*; the very fact that the 7–Eleven chain discontinued sales of *Penthouse* proves that the Commission's actions abridged appellant's First Amendment rights. That argument seems to us to stretch too far. We do not see why government officials may not vigorously criticize a publication for any reason they wish. As part of the duties of their office, these officials surely must be expected to be free to speak out to criticize practices, even in a condemnatory fashion, that they might not have the statutory or even constitutional authority to regulate. If the First Amendment were thought to be violated any time a private citizen's speech or writings were criticized by a government official, those officials might be virtually immobilized.

[At] least when the government threatens no sanction—criminal or otherwise—we very much doubt that the government's criticism or effort to embarrass the distributor threatens anyone's First Amendment rights. "[W]e know of no case in which the first amendment has been held to be implicated by governmental action consisting of no more than governmental criticism of the speech's content."

In any event, it is unnecessary to decide whether a government official's appeal to a distributor not to sell a particular publication, backed by no more than a "threat" by the official to characterize the publications with a strong pejorative, could, under any circumstances, violate the First Amendment. [In] sum, appellees are entitled to immunity from suit for damages for a constitutional tort because "government officials performing discretionary functions, generally are shielded from liability for civil damages insofar as their conduct does not violate clearly established statutory or constitutional rights of which a reasonable person would have known."

[Nor] do we believe that the truth or falsity of the statements included in the Commissioner's alleged phone call to Southland's general counsel is a basis for a constitutional tort. One of the purported assertions—that pornography causes child abuse—is not the kind of statement that appears susceptible to a true/false evaluation, and the second—that the Commission would make such a link in its report—appears to be only a prediction. In any event, we very much doubt that a constitutional line could or should be drawn between "true" government speech that impacts on the publications or speech of private citizens and "false" government speech of that character.

Appellant also contends that the members of the Commission are not entitled to immunity because the letter suggesting that the Commission might publish a list of distributors in its final report was outside their legitimate investigative mandate. We think this argument without merit. The Commission's charter, which defined the scope of the Commission's inquiry, called for the Commission to make "an examination of the means of production and distribution of pornographic materials" and "the recommendation of possible roles and initiatives that the Department of Justice and agencies of local, State, and Federal government could pursue in controlling, consistent with constitutional guarantees, the production and distribution of pornography." Given this charter, it could hardly be said that a letter inquiring (however clumsily) into the distribution of pornography is " 'manifestly or palpably beyond the authority [of the Commission].' "

Although Penthouse does not appeal the district court's holding that its claim for a permanent injunction is moot because Penthouse cannot show that it will ever "again be subject to the alleged illegality," it nevertheless renews its request for a declaratory judgment. Article III case or controversy requirements apply as forcefully, of course, to relief sought under the Declaratory Judgment Act as to any other form of relief. The question for us, then, is whether at the time relief is sought " 'the facts alleged, under all the circumstances, show that there is a substantial controversy, between parties having adverse legal interests, *of sufficient immediacy and reality to warrant the issuance of a declaratory judgment.*' "

The district court's issuance of a temporary injunction sufficiently responded to the injury for which Penthouse sought equitable relief in its original complaint to raise a real question whether any dispute still remains for the court to adjudicate. When a litigant has already received relief for the injury complained of, no live controversy remains. To be sure, the district court's preliminary injunction issued only on behalf of Playboy International Enterprises, and did not specifically refer to

Penthouse because Penthouse chose to seek discovery and therefore refused consolidation with Playboy's suit. Penthouse, nevertheless, obtained the equitable relief it was seeking—the letter to which it objected was withdrawn and the Commission's final report was published without listing the distributors of appellant's magazine as "distributors of pornography."

(A) case is moot only when "(1) it can be said with assurance that 'there is no reasonable expectation [that] the alleged violation will recur [and] (2) interim relief or events have completely and irrevocably eradicated the effects of the alleged violation.'" Since the Commission's dissolution ensures that the violation will not recur, Penthouse rests its argument against mootness on the second part of the test. It asserts that it continues to suffer "considerable reputational and financial injury," because distributors who dropped its magazine in response to the Commission's letter are still refusing to carry the magazine, despite the retraction of the letter by the Commission. Penthouse argues that a declaratory judgment that the Commission's action violated Penthouse's First Amendment rights will mitigate this continuing harmful effect by "help[ing to] allay the concerns of distributors who fear that association with plaintiff's publication may subject them to governmental condemnation or possibly even prosecution."

We are skeptical whether this claimed continuing injury is adequate to keep the controversy alive. In all the cases in which this court, (in line with Supreme Court precedent), has found that the effects of an alleged injury were not eradicated, some tangible, concrete effect, traceable to the injury, and curable by the relief demanded, clearly remained. [The] continuing harm of which Penthouse complains appears to fall short of this type of showing. Penthouse claims that distributors are fearful of prosecution for carrying the magazine. While a controversy is not moot so long as a real danger of prosecution remains, a mere speculative or remote chance of legal action will not suffice.

Nor is the claim that distributors fear future government condemnation less speculative. Even if we assume that the Commission's letter was intended to show its disapproval of distributors of pornography (including distributors of *Penthouse* magazine), Penthouse offers no evidence that *any* governmental body continues to wage a campaign to discourage its distributors. So there is no ongoing threat that can account for the distributors' alleged fear of government disapproval. As to the argument that the distributors' fear is a continuing effect of the Commission's original action, Penthouse offers no reason why, if the retraction of the letter and the demise of the Commission itself failed to persuade distributors to return once again to the Penthouse fold, a declaratory judgment would be likely to do so. Appellant has not shown, therefore, that even were it to prevail on the merits, the declaratory relief which it now seeks would actually redress the reputational and business injuries from which it claims to be suffering. It seems highly speculative that any action short of requiring the distributors to carry *Penthouse* would give appellant relief.

Even assuming that there is some trace of a continuing injury sufficient to satisfy Article III, we still must determine whether declaratory relief would be appropriate as an exercise of the court's discretionary, equitable powers. Where it is so unlikely that the court's grant of declaratory judgment will actually relieve the injury, the doctrine of prudential mootness—a facet of equity—comes into play. This concept is concerned, not with the court's power under Article III to provide relief, but with the court's discretion in exercising that power. Declaratory relief, like other forms of equitable relief, is discretionary. The Declaratory Judgment Act states only that a court "*may* declare the rights and other legal relations of any interested party seeking such declaration." Where it is uncertain that declaratory relief will benefit the party alleging injury, the court will normally refrain from exercising its equitable powers. This is especially true where the court can avoid the premature adjudication of constitutional issues. Here we are faced with a constitutional issue of first impression—the scope of the government's right to speak where the government's speech discourages the constitutionally-protected speech of private citizens. The Supreme Court has signalled its reluctance to decide this very question, while pointing to the troubling implications of limiting the government's free speech rights. We should wait to decide this issue until it is squarely presented. We therefore affirm the district court's denial of Penthouse's request for a declaratory judgment.

For an example of a decision setting aside the traditional aversion toward declaratory judgments when constitutional issues are at stake, *see Powell v. McCormack*, 395 U.S. 486 (1969).

PROBLEM: MORE ON THE PORNOGRAPHY PEDDLER

Now, let's think a bit more about the Pornography Peddler problem at the beginning of the chapter. Does *Lust* have any constitutional claims and remedies? Is the government's action the functional equivalent of a prior restraint? If so, should the strong presumption against any system of prior restraint offset the general disinclination of courts to avoid resolution of constitutional issues through declaratory proceedings? Does the government have the freedom to express itself as the commission did in its letter to Eatalot's president? Should issues of such constitutional significance be resolved pursuant to a declaratory judgment? When should a court deviate from its general predisposition to avoid constitutional issues?

F. THE EFFECT OF DECLARATORY JUDGMENTS

Declaratory judgments, like any final judgment entered by a court, bind the parties. Although the doctrines of res judicata and collateral estoppel thus apply, their range may be narrower if an action is dismissed pursuant to a determination that it is not apt for declaratory relief. Such a dismissal will be binding for purposes of barring relitigation calculated to obtain a declaratory judgment. Although a declaration of rights, obligations or status effectively may resolve a controversy, both the UDJA and FDJA provide for further relief to the extent "necessary or proper." Declaration that a zoning ordinance is unconstitutional, for instance, might obligate a court to determine the reasonable uses for affected property so that it is not left in an unzoned status. Both the UDJA and FDJA provide for "further" relief when "necessary and proper." UDJA, Sec. 8; FDJA, 28 U.S.C. § 2202. Both federal and state case law establishes that a request for declaratory relief does not preclude other remedies, essential to a full resolution of the controversy, even if coercive in nature. *See, e.g., Powell v. McCormack*, 395 U.S. 486, 489, 89 S.Ct. 1944, 1947, 23 L.Ed.2d 491 (1969); *Berry v. Daigle*, 322 A.2d 320, 325 (Me.1974).

CHAPTER 7

DAMAGE REMEDIES

■ ■ ■

CHAPTER OVERVIEW: Damages are one form of monetary relief, based on the harm the successful plaintiff suffered. Chapter 5 covered Restitution, monetary relief based on one party's unjust gain. Earlier chapters on Injunctions explain why courts rarely order one party to pay a sum of money to another. Damages seek to compensate parties for the harm they already have suffered.

This chapter details the various types of damages that an aggrieved party may seek and how the law determines the amount of compensation a party may recover. The chapter is organized by the kinds of losses that a party might suffer, rather than causes of action because, to a large extent, damage rules apply across boundaries. An employee who loses income will find the law measures that loss in much the same way whether the loss resulted from a tort (wrongful discharge or personal injury), breach of contract, or breach of a statute.

With some exceptions, the doctrines governing damages seek to keep recoveries as close as feasible to the actual loss suffered by the aggrieved party. When recovery exceeds the loss, theories justifying compensation lose their force. For instance, the recovery begins to resemble a fine or punishment, remedies typically seen only in cases of extreme recklessness or intentional wrongdoing. The chapter seeks to work through the key damage issues in detail, building on the basic understanding you gained in first year courses such as contracts and torts. Many units begin by reviewing the lessons those courses may already have taught, laying the groundwork for a more detailed discussion of how damages might be calculated.

Before we begin our exploration of damages with the Casey's Inhaler opening problem, it is helpful to get a quick lay of the land and introduce some terminology. Damages may be awarded as four general types: compensatory (with a special sub-category of attorney's fees), punitive, nominal, and statutory (or presumed). Each category of damages serves a distinct purpose. Statutory damages are typically assigned because actual compensatory damages are difficult to determine or because there is particular reason to be concerned about adequately deterring the relevant wrongful behavior (hence, the occasional statutory assignment of double or treble damages). The purpose of nominal damages is two-fold: (1) to give representational significance to a wrongdoing for which no actual, measurable harm was done, and (2) to serve as a basis for the attachment of punitive damages (and sometimes attorneys' fees), where compensatory damages are unavailable. Punitive damages are to punish, but also to deter particularly odious and, to the defendant, otherwise rewarding behavior. Finally, compensatory damages are meant to return a plaintiff to the position she would have occupied had she not been wronged. This category might be seen to include attorneys' fees, which were also occasioned by the defendant's wrongdoing.

Compensatory damages may be subdivided into four subcategories: general damages, special (or consequential) damages, and incidental damages, and pre and post-judgment interest. In a breach of contract setting, general damages are those which are the natural and probable consequence of the breach—that is, they give the party what was promised in the contract. Special damages in the contracts arena do not directly flow from the breach and are recoverable only upon a showing that they were (1) not too speculative and (2) foreseeable by the parties at the time the contract was made. These distinctions will be addressed in more detail later in this Chapter.

In torts cases, by contrast, general damages are nonpecuniary damages—for example, pain and suffering, loss of consortium, emotional distress, and loss of enjoyment of life. Special damages are pecuniary damages—typically lost wages and medical expenses, but including any out-of-pocket expenses resulting from a tort.

In either contract or tort actions, incidental damages are costs incurred in mitigation. For example, in a breach of contract action, a plaintiff's costs in finding a replacement supplier would constitute incidental damages.

With these terms and basic principles in mind, consider the following hypothetical.

OPENING PROBLEM: CASEY'S INHALER

In August 2013, Casey consulted Dr. Park, who diagnosed a congenital pulmonary disorder that impaired Casey's breathing. Dr. Park prescribed an inhaler to treat the symptoms; the condition could not be cured. On August 14, 2013, Casey filled the prescription at Blue Wall, a pharmacy chain. The pharmacist, Sean Fein, misread the prescription, selling Casey the wrong inhaler. Refills were based on the original item sold, perpetuating the error. The prescribed drug costs $100 per inhaler; the drug supplied costs only $50 per inhaler. Of this, Casey paid $30 each month. Casey's health insurer paid less ($20 rather than $70) because of the error.

Casey's breathing did not improve and affected his job performance. Some days Casey was unable to work at all. Casey earned an average of $1000 per week when able to work five days. From August through March, Casey averaged four days of work each week. Casey's condition deteriorated during the winter months. Breathing problems not only led to more frequent absences, but also impaired Casey's leisure activities (basketball, skiing) and household activities (playing with the children, bathing them, etc.). Casey began to feel chest pain and needed frequent rests. On March 12, 2014, Casey was fired for excessive absences. Casey survived on unemployment payments ($700 a week) and savings. The pain continued and got worse, even though Casey largely remained at home during this period. Casey made minimal efforts to seek a substitute job, as required by the state unemployment office, but felt unable to work full time because of the continuing trouble breathing.

Supervisory jobs that involved less physical labor were available at that time; Casey probably could have performed that work despite the breathing problem. People with less experience than Casey sometimes obtained these jobs, though there were dozens of applicants for each position. Supervisory positions averaged $1,200 per week.

At Casey's physical on August 6, 2014, Dr. Park discovered the pharmacy's error. Using the correct inhaler, the pain disappeared and the difficulty breathing diminished. Casey soon felt better than before his first visit to Dr. Park, well enough to resume work. Despite employers reluctant to take on an employee with a history of absenteeism and no recent employment, Casey was able to obtain spot jobs, averaging $500 a week. Resuming work ended Casey's unemployment benefits. Because savings were exhausted, Casey used credit cards to pay essential expenses. On October 16, 2014, Casey started a full time job at $1000 per week. This allowed Casey to stop using credit cards for ordinary household expenses, but did not eliminate the $3,000 balance built up during this period. Interest through October 16, 2014, totaled $60; until paid, an additional $10/week in interest will accrue. The credit limit on the card is $3,000, so no further charges are possible. Casey has no cushion if the new job does not work out.

Depending on how subsequent events play out, Casey might raise any of four different causes of action:

1. A tort action for the pharmacy's negligence;
2. A contract action for the pharmacy's breach by delivering nonconforming goods;
3. A malpractice action against an attorney who failed to file the tort action before the one-year statute of limitations barred the action. (Assume the contract action was barred by res judicata because the attorney did not include it in the original complaint.)
4. A malpractice action against an attorney who negligently failed to recognize and file the contract cause of action before the four-year statute of limitations barred the action (but who correctly advised Casey that the tort action already was barred by the one-year statute of limitations at the time Casey consulted the attorney).

A. GENERAL DAMAGE PRINCIPLES

1. THE BASIC MEASURE OF DAMAGES

DEALERS HOBBY, INC. V. MARIE ANN LINN REALTY CO.

255 N.W.2d 131 (Iowa 1977).

MOORE, CHIEF JUSTICE. Plaintiff tenant brought this action for breach of lease agreement to recover damages after partial collapse of leased warehouse building roof. From trial court order dismissing its petition as it related to damages for breach of warranty, plaintiff has appealed. We affirm.

On June 10, 1959 defendant Marie Ann Linn Realty Company leased a warehouse . . . consisting of 20,000 square feet, to plaintiff Dealers Hobby, Inc. for storage purposes. The commercial lease . . . was to . . . continue for a term of 15 years at the monthly rate of $1,166.66. Included in its terms was the following clause:

> SIXTH: That the landlord shall at his own expense maintain in good repair the roof and exterior structure, except as to damage caused by the negligence of the tenants, its agents, employees, invitees or guests. Tenant shall make no alterations or changes of the interior or exterior without first receiving permission from the landlord in writing.

On April 30, 1973 after a heavy rain, a small portion of the roof collapsed and as a result damage was caused to some of plaintiff's property stored in the building although only 1000 square feet of the warehouse was rendered unusable by the leakage. An inspection on May 3, 1973 by Des Moines city officials disclosed that the building did not comply with the city building code in several particulars and an "Official Notice of Unsafe Building" was issued by the City's Building Inspection Department. Neither party was aware of any defects in the building prior to the collapse.

Despite the incident, plaintiff continued to use a vast majority of the warehouse for storage during the 18-day period in which the premises were being repaired. When this work was completed the parties renewed the lease and plaintiff continued its occupancy.

In October 1973 plaintiff tenant initiated this action against Marie Ann Linn Realty Company. Plaintiff sought recovery for damages caused to its merchandise and inventory stored in the building together with incidental damages which totaled $16,037.94. . . . Additionally in paragraph 8 it sought to recover $193,082.23 which sum allegedly represented the difference between the fair rental value of the premises as warranted and the fair rental value of the premises as they actually existed for the entire duration of the lease prior to the collapse.

Defendants . . . filed a motion for partial summary judgment seeking dismissal of that portion of plaintiff's petition which sought damages under paragraph 8 for retroactive diminution of the fair rental value of the premises based on the implied and express warranty theories. . . . Trial court sustained the motion. . . .

Prior to trial defendants landlord, contractor and architect paid plaintiff all the paragraph 7 itemized damages, an agreed amount of $16,921.41. [P]laintiff did not waive any right to appeal the ruling sustaining the summary judgment motion. . . .

Plaintiff appeals ... challenging the earlier interlocutory ruling dismissing its claim for retroactive diminution of the fair rental value of the warehouse premises.

[T]he decisive issue is one of damages. Determination of the other issues is therefore unnecessary.

To determine the appropriate measure of recovery here it is necessary to turn to the general law of damages. It is axiomatic that the principle underlying allowance of damages is that of compensation, the ultimate purpose being to place the injured party in as favorable a position as though no wrong had been committed. . . . Stated otherwise, the plaintiff's damages are limited to its actual loss. . . . Of course, mere difficulty in ascertaining the amount of damages does not alone constitute a cause for denial of recovery. . . .

The usual measure of damages for breach of a lessor's agreement to make repairs or improvements is measured by the difference between the fair rental value of the premises if they had been as warranted and the fair rental value of the premises as they were during occupancy. . . . Additionally a tenant may recover other consequential damages including compensation for injury to his merchandise or business. . . . "The rule to be applied is very largely to be determined from the circumstances." . . .

In applying these rules to the case at hand we bear in mind the admonition cited in *DeWaay v. Muhr*, 160 N.W.2d 454, 458 (Iowa 1968) from 25 C.J.S. Damages § 74, pages 849, 850 (1966 vol.):

> " * * *. Specific rules are subordinate to the general rule that compensatory damages are designed to put the injured party in as good a position as he would have had if performance had been rendered as promised; a given formula is improvidently invoked if it defeats a commonsense solution."

It is manifest in consideration of these principles in light of the facts herein presented that no breach of the express covenant of repair occurred until April 30, 1973 when a portion of the roof collapsed at the warehouse premises. Prior to this time neither party had any knowledge of any defects in the structure. Prior to this time plaintiff suffered no harm whatsoever and to allow recovery for a retroactive diminution of the rental value for almost 14 years is in contravention of the aforementioned basic tenets of damages. Peril proceeding [sic] injury, of which plaintiff is ignorant, is not a proper element of damages. . . .

We believe after careful examination of the pleadings that paragraph 7 of plaintiff's petition which detailed its actual losses fully stated the full amount of recovery it was entitled to.

In *Darnall v. Day*, 240 Iowa 665, 672, 37 N.W.2d 277, 281 [Iowa 1949], we stated the ordinary measure of damages. However, as stated previously we have never applied a rule in order to give a plaintiff more than to which it is entitled. . . .

In *Int'l Harv. Co. v. C., M. & St. P. Ry. Co.*, 186 Iowa 86, 104, 172 N.W. 471, 478, 479, we state: "No rule of the law of damages permits the injured party to receive more than he has lost."

Here those portions of plaintiff's petition wherein it sought to recover its actual loss from April 30, 1973 were properly unaffected by trial court's order. These included damages alleged in paragraph 7 to merchandise and inventory, and incidental expenses covering such items as alternate rental expenses and cleanup work occasioned by the water damage. Under these circumstances where the specific elements of plaintiff's loss were plead in a manner different from *Darnall* but consistent with the overall theory of compensation inherent in our law of damages, we find plaintiff's arguments that the proper measure of damages was removed from the case are without merit. Therefore the trial court's judgment must be affirmed.

NOTES AND PROBLEMS

1. *Fundamental Rule.* The court identifies the basic measure of damages: the amount of money necessary to place the successful plaintiff, as closely as possible, in the position it would have occupied if the wrong had not been committed. This entire chapter explores that principle. The doctrines studied reflect ways that courts implement that basic measure—or, in a few cases, ways in which courts deviate from that principle.

2. *Other Causes of Action.* Would the result differ in tort? Suppose defendant's negligence caused a crane at a nearby construction site to fall over and damage the warehouse roof—with identical injury to the plaintiff's property when rain fell before repairs could be made. Would plaintiff's damages be any different? What if the case were a bailment—if defendant agreed to hold plaintiff's goods and stored them in the warehouse, where they were damaged?

3. *Alternative Measure of Damages.* The court relied on the basic measure to limit damages. Plaintiff asked for damages using a common formula: the value of the premises if they had been as promised (no construction defects) minus the value they had as received, plus incidental and consequential damages. *Cf.* UCC § 2–714(2) (sales of goods). Iowa awarded that measure in other cases. *Mease v. Fox*, 200 N.W.2d 791 (Iowa 1972). Here, the consequential damages (to the items stored in the warehouse) were conceded, but the lost value of the leasehold contested.

4. *Casey's Inhaler.* Casey's loss of employment is a consequential loss, like the damage to the goods stored in the warehouse. Casey also received a product worth less than the product Casey offered to buy. Should Casey recover the difference between the value of the promised inhaler ($100) and the value of the inhaler received ($50)? Or perhaps the full $100, if the wrong

inhaler had no value whatsoever to Casey? Is the value of the promised inhaler anything more than the value of preventing the health effects of living without proper treatment for the condition? Would Casey ever have received proper treatment without paying for it?

5. *Defect without Consequential Loss.* The lease includes an implied warranty that the space complies with the building codes. Defendant breached that promise; the building was defective from the outset.

a. If no goods are damaged, can plaintiff recover any damages for the substandard quality of the premises it received? Is it being overcharged given the defects?

b. Is plaintiff's calculation persuasive? In seeking a retroactive diminution of the fair rental value of the premises in the amount of $193,082.23, Plaintiff essentially demands a refund of the entire rent for the 14 years it occupied the premises. The formula would support that amount if the value warranted equaled the rent, but the value actually received was zero.

c. If plaintiff's claim was excessive, was rejecting the measure entirely the best way to limit recovery?

6. *Damages without Injury.* Chris, a consumer, alleges that a pharmaceutical manufacturer withheld information concerning the side-effects of a particular medication. Chris was not afflicted with the side-effect. But Chris brings a consumer class action suit alleging violation of state consumer fraud laws and breach of warranty. Chris requests as damages the difference between the value of the medication as warranted and the value as received. Is a drug with no side effects worth more than one with a side effect? Should consumers who did not suffer the side effect recover damages on this basis?

In your first year studies, you may have learned two different ways to implement the basic measure of damages. Many contracts classes discuss the expectation interest and the reliance interest. The expectation interest seeks to place the plaintiff in the position she would have occupied if the contract had been performed—that is, if a breach had not been committed. This is the general rule with one substitution: the wrong has been specified as the breach. The reliance interest seeks to place the plaintiff in the position she would have occupied if the contract had not been made—that is, if the duty had never existed. This version substitutes the making of the contract for the wrong. Lon L. Fuller & William R. Perdue, Jr., *The Reliance Interest in Contract Damages*, 46 YALE L.J. 52, 373 (1936–1937). Courts usually prefer the expectation interest. The reliance interest is an exception, used when the expectation interest is unavailable for technical reasons (such as uncertainty) or when policy reasons will not justify full expectation.

BASILIKO V. PARGO CORPORATION

532 A.2d 1346 (D.C.1987).

NEWMAN, ASSOCIATE JUDGE

This controversy arises from a series of unconsummated real estate transactions involving 3411 Holmead Place, Northwest. The property, securing a note held by Montgomery Federal Savings & Loan Association, was scheduled for a Trustee's sale by virtue of a power of sale in the deed of trust on May 1, 1979. The day before the sale, however, on April 30, five minutes before the bank closed for the day, the borrower made a payment curing the delinquency. This payment, while immediately credited to the borrower's account by computer, apparently did not come to the attention of substitute trustees Arnold L. Karp and James A. Early, Jr. before the sale took place on the following day.

George Basiliko entered the successful bid on the property at the auction held on May 1, offering a price of $28,000 and securing his purchase with a $1000 deposit. Two days later, on May 3, 1979, Basiliko entered into a resale contract with Pargo Corporation in which Pargo agreed to pay $35,100 for the Holmead Place property. Basiliko expressly conditioned this sale on his "obtaining good title at [the] foreclosure sale." Pargo, in turn, contracted on May 7, 1979, to sell the same property for $44,000 to Morgan O'Neill Builders.

On May 29, the date scheduled for settlement on the foreclosure sale, trustees Karp and Early refused to convey the property to Basiliko because they had been without authority to hold the sale. When Basiliko subsequently failed to deliver the property to Pargo Corporation, Pargo sued Basiliko, along with Montgomery Federal, Karp and Early. Basiliko cross-claimed against the other defendants. Following trial, Judge Doyle issued an Opinion and Order dismissing on the merits both Pargo's complaint and Basiliko's cross-claim. The dismissal of the cross-claim is the subject of this appeal.

[Judge] Doyle took the view that the purchaser at a void foreclosure sale, "relieved as he is of paying the purchase price [also] loses any right to sue the trustees [for] breach of contract to recover in damages the benefit of his bargain."[2] We disagree.

The long-settled rule in this jurisdiction is that a seller who breaches an executory contract for the sale of real property is liable to the would-be purchaser for compensatory damages measured by the difference between the sales contract price and the fair market value of the property at the time that the property should have been conveyed. The District of Columbia thus follows the "American rule," which allows the frustrated

---

[2] The trial court thus would have limited Basiliko's recovery to the return of his deposit, which it understood to have been already tendered by the cross-defendants.

purchaser of real property, like any other victim of a breach of contract, the benefit of the bargain he has negotiated.

This "benefit of the bargain" formula, the standard contract damage remedy, should not be confused with an award of special or consequential damages compensating a disappointed buyer for the value of a *resale* contract with a third party (for example, in this case, the contract between Basiliko and Pargo Corporation). Our jurisdiction has squarely rejected the availability of damages for the lost profit of anticipated resale.

The trial court's decision would, in effect, apply the "English rule" of *Flureau v. Thornhill,* 2 W.Bl. 1078, 96 Eng.Rep. 635 (C.P.1776), to this case, allowing the disappointed purchaser merely the return of his deposit plus interest and expenses, thereby restoring him to the position he occupied prior to negotiating the contract rather than compensating him for the expectation that has been breached. We can find no justification in law or policy for such exceptional treatment in the case of a foreclosure sale.

A principal reason given for the development of the *Flureau* rule in England was the absence there of an adequate system for assuring certainty of title. Under such circumstances, the law recognized the unfairness of imposing the risk of this uncertainty on the seller alone. By contrast, in the United States, where recording systems developed, many jurisdictions, including the District of Columbia, have favored a rule treating breach of an executory contract for sale of real property just as breach of any other sales contract.

The rationale offered for the English rule suggests why its application would be especially inappropriate to the facts of this case. In the District of Columbia, a purchaser of real estate is entitled to damages for the benefit of his bargain, regardless of the reasons for the seller's breach, including a defect in title that the buyer might have been able to discover before sale. For the District to impose a harsher rule against the purchaser when the cause of the seller's breach involves a matter within the seller's exclusive control, and not detectable by the buyer, would be to turn the logic of *Flureau* on its head. Indeed, even in those jurisdictions following the *Flureau* rule, damages have sometimes been awarded when the seller had been mistaken about his authority to sell land belonging to another or about his ability to obtain title between the date of sale and the date of conveyance or fails to convey "for reasons within his control.

In this case, the contractual breach was occasioned by a circumstance—the erroneous foreclosure of the loan—that was within the sole knowledge and control of the seller/lender Montgomery Federal and its agents, trustees Karp and Early. Under such circumstances, it would be especially unfair for the buyer to be required to bear the risk of this mistake. . . .

[T]he contention that it would be bad policy to award benefit of the bargain damages to a disappointed purchaser at a foreclosure sale because such an award would amount to a "windfall" to such a buyer is also without merit. It may be true that prices at foreclosure sales classically surface somewhere below fair market value. This fact, however, is an argument for—rather than against—the award of benefit of the bargain damages in this case. By awarding contract damages to Basiliko, we assure all future bidders at foreclosure sales that their expectation will be compensated if the seller breaches for reasons such as those that occurred in this case. By compensating foreclosure buyers—just as buyers generally—for this risk, we enhance the public policy of maintaining the adequacy of foreclosure sale prices and reinforce the legal duty of trustees to garner a reasonable price for mortgagor and mortgagee.

Accordingly, we are unpersuaded of any reason to deviate in this case from our settled rule that a seller who breaches an executory contract for the sale of real property is liable to the frustrated purchaser in contract damages measured by the difference between the sales price of that contract (here, the price contracted for by Basiliko at the foreclosure sale) and the fair market value of the property at the time the property should have been conveyed. On remand, the trial court must determine what that fair market value would have been, guided by the principle that fair market value is "the price that an owner willing but not compelled to sell ought to receive from one willing but not compelled to buy." In making this assessment, the trial court may consider as evidence the price at which Basiliko had agreed to resell the property to Pargo Corporation. A resale contract provides sufficient evidence of fair market value on which to base an award of damages for breach of the initial sales contract. *[S]ee also Rogers v. Lion Transfer & Storage Co.,* 120 U.S.App.D.C. 186, 187, 345 F.2d 80, 81 (1965).

We remand for entry of judgment in favor of Basiliko on his cross-claim against Montgomery Federal, Karp, and Early, and for a determination of the amount of damages.

NOTES AND PROBLEMS

1. *Fundamental Rule.* The result flows from the general rule. If the seller had performed, then the buyer would have possession of the land. Although the court here cannot put buyer into possession, it can put him in the same net financial position by awarding him the value of the land. However, since in order to obtain the land buyer would have had to pay the full price, the contract price must be subtracted from the recovery. (We might say the unpaid portion of the contract price should be subtracted. Instead, rules often start by refunding any down payment then subtracting the full contract price.) An offset for benefits of the breach—often expenses saved—occurs in many cases. We study it explicitly in section C.2. below.

The same rule applies to sales of goods. UCC § 2–713. For goods, however, buyer has an additional option: she can make a reasonable purchase of substitute goods and collect the difference between cover price (the cost of the substitute goods) and contract price. UCC § 2–712. Would that approach work for sales of land? Would services be any different?

2. *Covering Land or Services.* Consider the following variations on the case:

a. If Basiliko, after breach, purchased another similar property for $36,000, should defendant pay $8,000 as damages?

b. Terry hired Hank the Handyman to install a light switch in her home for $50. Hank breached. Terry hired Ernie the Electrician to do the same job for $150. How much may Terry recover from Hank? Would it matter if Ernie were another handyman?

3. *Other Causes of Action.* Basiliko involves a breach of contract. Would the process be any different if a tort were involved? Consider the following examples:

a. Silas owns an island. Negligent blasting on a nearby island causes Silas' island to sink into the sea. How should Silas' recovery be calculated? Would your answer differ if Silas had a right to buy the island, but had not yet paid for it?

b. Owen O'Phile collects wine. A disgruntled former employee broke into the collection and destroyed several bottles. How should Owen's recovery be calculated?

4. *Seller's Recovery.* The same rules apply when seller seeks recovery from buyer. Seller gets the difference between the contract price promised and the market value of the land (or goods). UCC § 2–708. If seller actually resells the property to another, the difference between the contract price and the actual price at resale may be used—again, assuming the transaction was reasonable. UCC § 2–706. Do the problems noted when buyers cover with substitute land apply when sellers resell for a substitute price?

5. *Exceptions to Expectation.* Expectation interest is the general rule for contract damages in Britain and America. The British (and some states) make an exception when defendant is unable to deliver good title to land. The exception emerged before recording statutes made it easier to discover (or overcome) defects in title. Innocent breach by a party that thought it owned the land but actually did not were more common. The *Flureau* rule applies the reliance interest, limiting recovery to a refund plus any expenses incurred (such as a title search) in pursuance of the transaction, plus interest on these amounts. The reliance interest is recognized as an alternative measure of damages for contract. RESTATEMENT (SECOND) OF CONTRACTS § 349. Does this recovery put the plaintiff in the position she would have occupied if the wrong had not occurred?

The exception is quite limited. It protects a party who mistakenly believed he had good title at the time he entered the contract to sell the land.

It will not protect a party who knew her title was bad. It will not protect a seller who could convey good title but chose not to do so. Nor will it protect a seller whose inability to convey good title results from his own contrivance—such as conveying the land to another in order to create an inability to convey it to the buyer. While most states seem to prefer the rule stated in *Basiliko*, some of the largest states (CA, MI, NY, PA, TX, VA) cling to the exception at least under these limited circumstances.

CHATLOS SYSTEMS, INC. V. NATIONAL CASH REGISTER CORP.

670 F.2d 1304 (3d Cir.1982).

PER CURIAM.

[Plaintiff-appellee] Chatlos Systems, Inc., initiated this action in the Superior Court of New Jersey, alleging, inter alia, breach of warranty regarding an NCR 399/656 computer system it had acquired from defendant National Cash Register Corp. Following a non-jury trial, the district court determined that defendant was liable for breach of warranty and awarded $57,152.76 damages for breach of warranty and consequential damages in the amount of $63,558.16. Defendant appealed and this court affirmed the district court's findings of liability, set aside the award of consequential damages, and remanded for a recalculation of damages for breach of warranty. On remand, applying the "benefit of the bargain" formula of N.J. Stat. Ann. § 12A:2–714(2) (Uniform Commercial Code § 2–714(2)), the district court determined the damages to be $201,826.50, to which it added an award of prejudgment interest. [The district court found the fair market value of the system as warranted to be $207,826.50; from this it subtracted its determination of the value of the goods delivered, $6,000.] Defendant now appeals from these damage determinations, contending that the district court erred in failing to recognize the $46,020 contract price of the delivered NCR computer system as the fair market value of the goods as warranted, and that the award of damages is without support in the evidence presented. Appellant also contests the award of prejudgment interest.

Waiving the opportunity to submit additional evidence as to value on the remand, appellant chose to rely on the record of the original trial and submitted no expert testimony on the market value of a computer which would have performed the functions NCR had warranted. Notwithstanding our previous holding that contract price was not necessarily the same as market value, appellant faults the district judge for rejecting its contention that the contract price for the NCR 399/656 was the only competent record evidence of the value of the system as warranted. The district court relied instead on the testimony of plaintiff-appellee's expert, Dick Brandon, who, without estimating the value of an NCR model 399/656, presented his estimate of the value of a computer system that would perform all of the functions that the NCR 399/656 had been warranted to perform. Brandon did not limit his estimate to equipment of any one manufacturer; he testified regarding manufacturers who could have made systems that would perform the functions that appellant had warranted the NCR 399/656 could perform. He acknowledged that the systems about which he testified were not in the same price range as the NCR 399/656. Appellant likens this testimony to substituting a Rolls Royce for a Ford, and concludes that the district court's recomputed damage award was therefore clearly contrary to the evidence of fair market value—which in NCR's view is the contract price itself.

Appellee did not order, nor was it promised, merely a specific NCR computer model, but an NCR computer system with specified capabilities. The correct measure of damages, under N.J. STAT. ANN. § 12A:2–714(2), is the difference between the fair market value of the goods accepted and the value they would have had if they had been as warranted. Award of that sum is not confined to instances where there has been an increase in value between date of ordering and date of delivery. It may also include the benefit of a contract price which, for whatever reason quoted, was particularly favorable for the customer. Evidence of the contract price may be relevant to the issue of fair market value, but it is not controlling. *Mulvaney v. Tri State Truck & Auto Body, Inc.*, 70 Wis.2d 760, 767, 235 N.W.2d 460, 465 (1975). Appellant limited its fair market value analysis to the contract price of the computer model it actually delivered. Appellee developed evidence of the worth of a computer with the capabilities promised by NCR, and the trial court properly credited the evidence.

Appellee was aided, moreover, by the testimony of Frank Hicks, NCR's programmer, who said that he told his company's officials that the "current software was not sufficient in order to deliver the program that the customer (Chatlos) required. They would have to be rewritten or a different system would have to be given to the customer." Hicks recommended that Chatlos be given an NCR 8200 but was told, "that will not be done." Gerald Greenstein, another NCR witness, admitted that the 8200 series was two levels above the 399 in sophistication and price. This testimony supported Brandon's statement that the price of the hardware needed to perform Chatlos' requirements would be in the $100,000 to $150,000 range.

Essentially, then, the trial judge was confronted with the conflicting value estimates submitted by the parties. Chatlos' expert's estimates were corroborated to some extent by NCR's supporters. NCR, on the other hand, chose to rely on contract price. Credibility determinations had to be made by the district judge. Although we might have come to a different conclusion on the value of the equipment as warranted had we been sitting as trial judges, we are not free to make our own credibility and factual findings. We may reverse the district court only if its factual determinations were clearly erroneous.

Upon reviewing the evidence of record, therefore, we conclude that the computation of damages for breach of warranty was not clearly erroneous. We hold also that the district court acted within its discretion in awarding pre-judgment interest.

The judgment of the district court will be affirmed.

ROSENN, CIRCUIT JUDGE, dissenting.

[There] are a number of major flaws in the plaintiff's attempt to prove damages in excess of the contract price. I commence with an analysis of plaintiff's basic theory. Chatlos presented its case under a theory that although, as a sophisticated purchaser, it bargained for several months before arriving at a decision on the computer system it required and the price of $46,020, it is entitled, because of the breach of warranty, to damages predicated on a considerably more expensive system. Stated another way, even if it bargained for a cheap system, *i.e.*, one whose low cost reflects its inferior quality, because that system did not perform as bargained for, it is now entitled to damages measured by the value of a system which, although capable of performing the identical functions as the NCR 399, is of far superior quality and accordingly more expensive.

The statutory measure of damages for breach of warranty specifically provides that the measure is the difference at the time and place of acceptance between the value "of the goods accepted" and the "value they would have had if they had been as warranted." The focus of the statute is upon "the goods accepted"—not other hypothetical goods which may perform equivalent functions. "Moreover, the value to be considered is the reasonable market value of the goods delivered, not the value of the goods to a particular purchaser or for a particular purpose." *KLPR TV, Inc. v. Visual Electronics Corp.*, 465 F.2d 1382, 1387 (8th Cir.1972). The court, however, arrived at value on the basis of a hypothetical construction of a system as of December 1978 by the plaintiff's expert, Brandon. The court reached its value by working backward from Brandon's figures, adjusting for inflation.

[A] review of Brandon's testimony reveals its legal inadequacy for establishing the market value of the system Chatlos purchased from NCR. Brandon never testified to the fair market value which the NCR 399 system would have had had it met the warranty at the time of acceptance. He was not even asked the question. . . .

It is undisputed that in September 1976 there were vendors of computer equipment of the same general size as the NCR 399/656 with disc in the price range of $35,000 to $40,000 capable of providing the same programs as those required by Chatlos, including IBM, Phillips, and

Burroughs. They were the very companies who competed for the sale of the computer in 1974 in the same price range. On the other hand, Chatlos' requirements could also be satisfied by computers available at "three levels higher in price and sophistication than the 399 disc." Each level higher would mean more sophistication, greater capabilities, and more memory. Greenstein, NCR's expert, testified without contradiction that equipment of Burroughs, IBM, and other vendors in the price range of $100,000 to $150,000, capable of performing Chatlos' requirements, was not comparable to the 399 because it was three levels higher. Such equipment was more comparable to the NCR 8400 series.

[The] purpose of the N.J.S.A. 12A:2–714 is to put the buyer in the same position he would have been in if there had been no breach. *See* Uniform Commercial Code 1–106(1). The remedies for a breach of warranty were intended to compensate the buyer for his loss; they were not intended to give the purchaser a windfall or treasure trove. The buyer may not receive more than it bargained for; it may not obtain the value of a superior computer system which it did not purchase even though such a system can perform all of the functions the inferior system was designed to serve. Thus, in *Meyers v. Antone*, 227 A.2d 56 (D.C.App.1967), the court held that where the buyers contracted for a properly functioning used oil heating system which proved defective, they were free to substitute a gas system (which they did), change over to forced air heating, or even experiment with a solar heating plant. "They could not, however, recover the cost of such systems. They contracted for a used oil system that would function properly, and can neither receive more than they bargained for nor be put in a better position than they would have been had the contract been fully performed."

[Because] Brandon's testimony does not support Chatlos' grossly extravagant claim of the fair market value of the NCR 399 at the time of its acceptance, the only evidence of the market value at the time is the price negotiated by the parties for the NCR computer system as warranted. There are many cases in which the goods will be irreparable or not replaceable and therefore the costs of repair or replacement can not serve as a yardstick of the buyer's [damages]. When fair market value cannot be easily determined [the] purchase price may turn out to be strong evidence of the value of the goods as warranted. J. WHITE & R. SUMMERS, UNIFORM COMMERCIAL CODE § 10–2, at 380 (2d ed. 1980). . . .

Thus, where there is no proof that market value of the goods differs from the contract price, the contract price will govern, and in this case that amounts to $46,020. Chatlos has retained the system hardware and the district court fixed its present value in the open market at $6,000. The court properly deducted this sum from the damages awarded.

PROBLEMS

1. *Calculating Lost Value.* The court had to determine the value of a machine that did not exist: a 399/656 that would perform as warranted. No market transactions exist to verify the value of an imaginary good. How should the court assign a value to it? Is NCR correct that the value as warranted should be the price? That would allow Chatlos a discount for the shortcomings. Or is Chatlos entitled to the cost of a machine that will perform as promised, even though such a machine will do many things that NCR did not promise to provide? If others are buying 399/656's for $46,020, is that the value as received?

2. *Casey's Inhaler.* What is the value of the right inhaler? The pharmacy's asking price of $100 probably is pretty close to what other pharmacy's would ask and receive. Is that the value as warranted? Or does value as warranted include the benefits the inhaler would have for Casey? Is the wrong inhaler worthless? It doesn't treat Casey's condition. But it has a value of $50 on the market. Is there any basis for ignoring that value in calculating Casey's loss? Would the same argument apply to *Chatlos*?

3. *Reliance Interest.* Should the court have resorted to the reliance interest? How much would that allow Chatlos to recover? Do we need to know what Chatlos would have done instead of buying the NCR 399/656? Is that less imaginary? Will reliance include the money spent trying to make the machine work? Should that be called consequential reliance and denied like other consequential losses? If not, might reliance damages exceed expectation damages? Should the remedy exceed expectation?

4. *Another Alternative.* In *Dealers Hobby*, the court rejected this measure of damages and limited the plaintiff to consequential losses. Is that an apt solution here?

LIBERTY NATIONAL LIFE INSURANCE COMPANY V. SANDERS

792 So.2d 1069 (Ala.2000).

JOHNSTONE, JUSTICE.

[In] 1993, Sanders decided that she needed life insurance to insure her own life and the life of her son David Ogle, a disabled adult. [R]ecalling her past experience with Liberty National, Sanders telephoned the local Liberty National office and asked to speak with a salesman about purchasing a life insurance policy. [In February, Liberty] National sent insurance agents Tim McLain and Keith Mahone to Sanders's mobile home. At that time Sanders purchased a Liberty National life insurance policy insuring her own life. The policy had a face amount of $10,000 and had a monthly premium amount of $54.22.

[In March 1993, Sanders tried to purchase a $10,000 policy "like the one insuring her own life" to insure Ogle's life. Sanders informed Mahone that Ogle was a schizophrenic and a smoker. Malone completed the application for Ogle's policy and tendered it and the premium to Liberty National, which rejected the application because Mahone quoted the wrong premium amount. Liberty National cancelled Ogle's policy and returned the premium to Sanders.]

In April 1993, Sanders asked Mahone to complete another application for a life insurance policy to insure Ogle. Sanders again brought Ogle home to meet with Mahone, and again told Mahone that Ogle was a schizophrenic and a smoker. She told Mahone that she wanted the policy because she would not have the money to bury Ogle unless she had insurance. Mahone asked Ogle the questions on the application for life insurance. One of the questions was whether the applicant suffered from a "brain disease." Ogle responded, "Yes." On April 19, 1993, Mahone completed, and Ogle signed, the application for insurance on Ogle's life. The next day, April 20, 1993, Sanders paid the monthly premium of $192 to Mahone. Sanders testified that on April 20, 1993, Mahone

> assured [her that] the policy was effective when I gave him the money. Mr. Russell H. Hurst was present when I gave the money to Mr. Mahone and was aware of his accepting the money and declaring the policy was effective upon receipt of the money. Mr. Mahone did not give me a receipt for the money, but took it, with Mr. Hurst present assuring me the policy was effective immediately.

On April 23, 1993, Liberty National issued Sanders a policy insuring the life of Ogle, but Sanders never received the policy. On April 24, 1993, Ogle died of natural causes. . . .

Liberty National mailed Sanders a check in the amount of $193.30, comprising the one premium Sanders had paid plus 10% interest on that premium. Sanders did not accept the check and did obtain counsel, who sent a Mahone [sic] letter inquiring when Sanders could expect payment of the full $10,000. [Liberty] National sent Sanders's counsel a letter stating it had paid Sanders the full amount owed under the policy. . . .

The application stated that, if the applicant answered "yes" to the question whether he suffered from a "brain disease," as Ogle answered, then he was eligible only for a "Modified Benefit Limited Payment Life Plan (ALX)." Moreover, Ogle's weight disqualified him for the type of policy that insured the plaintiff's own life and allowed him only a " 'Modified Benefit Limited Payment Life Plan' (ALX)." The application did not state, but the "ALX policy" which Sanders never received did state, [that] the policy would *not* pay the full face-value benefit of $10,000 if the applicant died of natural causes before the expiration of those first three years, but would pay only the sum of premiums then paid plus ten percent. . . . [The policy would pay $10,000 for accidental death during the first three years and for any cause of death after the first three years.]

Sanders testified that Mahone never told her about the three-year waiting period. She testified that he "assured [her] the policy was effective when I gave him the money" and that, after she paid the premium, he assured her "the policy was effective immediately." While Sanders's testimony to this effect is disputed, the jury resolved the conflict in favor of Sanders. She testified further that, had she known of the three-year waiting period, she would not have bought the policy. [The jury awarded $10,000 in compensatory damages and $135,000 in punitive damages.]

A.1. The Difference Between Represented Value and True Value

Liberty National and Mahone specifically argue that Sanders failed to prove any actual damage inasmuch as Sanders testified that she would not have purchased the policy if she had known of the three-year waiting period. A fraud victim's proof of reliance, however, hardly negates the victim's proof of damages.

This Court has held:

> [T]here is [a] well-settled rule pertaining to the measure of damages resulting from fraudulent conduct or representations, to the effect that *such damages will be fixed by an amount which would place the defrauded person in the position he would occupy if the representations had been true.*

Fogleman v. National Surety Co., 222 Ala. 265, 268, 132 So. 317 (1931) (emphasis added).

The evidence viewed in the light most favorable to Sanders establishes that, although Mahone represented the policy to be worth $10,000.00 for the death of Ogle regardless of when or how he died, in reality the policy, as it would have been received by Sanders, was worth only the paid premium plus ten percent. The evidence is undisputed that Liberty National did not tender $10,000 to Sanders and that Sanders did not accept the $193.30 tendered to her by Liberty National.

The law of fraud measures Sanders's actual damages as the almost-$10,000 difference between the value of the policy as represented and the value in reality. Therefore, the evidence supported an award for that difference plus the $193.30 tendered and refused. Indeed, the jury did award Sanders compensatory damages in precisely that sum, $10,000, which placed Sanders in the monetary position she would have occupied if Mahone's representations about the life insurance policy had been true. Sanders's statement that she would not have purchased the policy if she had known of the three-year waiting period proved the reliance elements of her fraud and suppression claims and did not negate her proof of actual damage. Sanders's proof of mental anguish is further support for the $10,000 compensatory award, already entirely supported by the economic proof.

A.2. Lost Opportunity

Although Liberty National and Mahone assert that Sanders did not prove "lost opportunity" to support compensatory damages and that therefore Sanders did not prove any damage to support a compensatory award, a fraud victim need not prove all types of damage which could result from the fraud, so long as she does prove damage according to some legally recognized theory, as Sanders did. Moreover, while Sanders did not rely on "lost opportunity" as her theory of recovery of compensatory damages, the record does contain evidence that the defendants' misrepresentations and suppressions cost Sanders an opportunity to obtain at least $2,500 in immediate coverage for her son.

The president of Liberty National, Anthony L. McWhorter, testified that both Liberty National and United American Insurance Company are owned by Torchmark. He stated that Liberty National agents are licensed to sell United American life insurance policies. In 1993, United American had a "stair-step" life insurance policy comparable to Liberty National's ALX policy. The United American "stair-step" policy paid $2,500 for a death from natural causes in the first year and paid $5,000 for a death from natural causes in the second year.

McWhorter testified that, although the State of Alabama licenses Liberty National agents to sell United American life insurance policies, Liberty National does not permit its agents to sell United American life insurance policies. He testified also that Liberty National studies the "products" of other insurance companies in order for Liberty National to design its own "products." McWhorter testified that he would not be surprised to learn that other companies sold a better "product," without a three-year waiting period, than Liberty National's ALX policy.

Thus, the evidence tends to prove an opportunity for Sanders to have purchased a policy with substantial coverage without the three-year waiting period from another insurance company, if Mahone had been truthful about the waiting period. This evidence of lost opportunity, together with Sanders's evidence of mental anguish supports the jury's award of $10,000 in compensatory damages on theories of damages independent of her primary theory that she was entitled to recover the value of the policy as represented. . . .

NOTES AND PROBLEMS

1. *Naming Rules.* In misrepresentation cases, expectation and reliance have different names. The benefit-of-the-bargain rule seeks to put plaintiff in the position she would have occupied if the statement had been true—here, if the policy on Ogle was just like the one on Sanders. The out-of-pocket rule seeks to put plaintiff in the position she would have occupied if a true statement had been made—here, if Mahone revealed the phase-in period, probably meaning Sanders would not have bought the policy. Is there any

difference between suing for breach of warranty and suing for misrepresentation under the benefit-of-the-bargain rule?

2. *Applying the Basic Measure.* Is the result in *Liberty National* consistent with the general remedial rule? Where would the plaintiff have been if the wrong had not been committed? What is the wrong: making the false statement or providing coverage that did not comply with the false statement? What would Sanders have done if told the truth? How much would she recover under the general remedial rule? Does this depend on what other insurers would offer? What if no insurer available to Sanders would offer immediate coverage of Ogle (whether for weight, smoking, brain disease, or any other reason)? Does that make the result here as imaginary as *Chatlos*?

3. *Different Causes of Action.* Should Chatlos and Sanders be treated differently? Does one victim deserve an expectation recovery and the other a reliance recovery? Which one deserves which? Is there any difference in the kind of statement that the defendants made? In the reliance that resulted? *See* Michael B. Kelly, *The Phantom Reliance Interest in Tort Damages*, 38 SAN DIEGO L. REV. 169 (2001). Could Chatlos have sought recovery for misrepresentation instead of breach of warranty? Why did Chatlos sue for breach of warranty instead? Should a court apply a misrepresentation theory, even though Chatlos requested relief on a different theory?

---

2. PROPERTY DAMAGE

TERRA–PRODUCTS V. KRAFT GEN. FOODS, INC.

653 N.E.2d 89 (Ind.App.1995).

NAJAM, JUDGE

Terra–Products, Inc. ("Terra") is an Indiana corporation that produces and sells liquid handling products for industry and agriculture. From the 1960's until June of 1992, Terra conducted business on a tract of land known as "Terra Site." Between 1957 and 1969, P.R. Mallory, Inc. owned property adjacent to Terra Site, known as "Mallory Site," where Mallory operated a battery manufacturing facility. The batteries contained polychlorinated biphenyls ("PCBs"). In 1969, the Mallory facility was destroyed by fire and was never rebuilt. Sometime after 1969, P.R. Mallory was purchased by Kraft and renamed Duracell International, Inc. Terra purchased Mallory Site from Kraft in 1975. In June of 1986, the Indiana Department of Environmental Management ("IDEM") and the United States Environmental Protection Agency ("EPA") determined there was PCB contamination at Mallory Site which violated state and federal regulations. The EPA issued an administrative order to both Terra and Kraft, as Potentially Responsible Parties under the Comprehensive Environmental Response Compensation and Liability

Act ("CERCLA"), and required them to implement a cleanup plan. Thereafter, Kraft agreed to be responsible for the cleanup and to pay for the entire cost of remediation.

In 1988, Kraft's contractor discovered that Terra Site was also contaminated by the migration of PCBs from Mallory Site. Kraft subsequently agreed to perform and pay for the cleanup of Terra Site as well. In June of 1992, Terra sold both Terra Site and Mallory Site at public auction.

Terra then filed this action against Kraft and sought damages for loss of value to its real property in the amount of $830,000.00. Terra claimed damages based on an appraised value of $1.1 million for both sites, assuming no contamination, minus the auction sale price of $270,000.00. Terra also claimed additional damages of more than $3 million, plus the cost of a two-week shutdown when, according to its complaint, Terra was required to move its business to a new location because of the contamination. Kraft filed a counterclaim against Terra and alleged unjust enrichment of approximately $12.5 million, half of the $25 million Kraft paid for the cleanup. Kraft completed the cleanup of both sites in August of 1993.

Both parties filed motions for summary judgment, and the trial court granted Kraft's motion on all counts of Terra's complaint. The court also entered summary judgment for Terra on Kraft's counterclaim for unjust enrichment, finding that the entry of judgment for Kraft rendered its counterclaim moot.

Discussion and Decision

Measure of Damages

In this case of first impression in Indiana, we are asked to consider the proper measure of damages for injury to land contaminated by PCBs. Under Indiana law, the measure of damages in a case of injury to real property depends first upon a determination of whether the injury is "permanent" or "temporary." Permanent injury to unimproved land occurs where "the cost of restoration exceeds the market value [prior] to injury." If the injury is permanent, the measure of damages is limited to the difference between the fair market value of the property before and after the injury, based on the rationale that "economic waste" results when restoration costs exceed the economic benefit. For a temporary injury the proper measure of damages is the cost of restoration.

It is undisputed that the cost to remediate Terra Site far exceeded the value of the land itself. Applying the common law distinction between permanent and temporary damage to these facts, the damage to Terra Site would be considered permanent and the measure of damages would be the difference between the value of the property before and after the remediation. That is the measure of damages advocated by Terra on appeal.

Kraft argues and the trial court determined that remediation repaired Terra Site and, thus, that the PCB contamination was temporary damage. The court agreed with Kraft that Terra could not "seek to recover damages allowed for permanent injury and also to keep the rewards allowed under temporary injury that have already been performed."

The trial court's judgment was based on its determination that "under recent case law and through statements of the EPA and Indiana legislature, PCB contamination has been treated as a temporary injury despite the high cost of repair." The court relied on the federal district court decision in *In Re Paoli R.R. Yard PCB Litigation* (E.D.Pa.1992), 811 F.Supp. 1071, and on Indiana statutes and regulations, and reasoned that those authorities were "contrary to the common law policy of avoiding repair at costs which greatly exceed the value of the land." The trial court concluded that "the current policy of the State of Indiana as well as the United States [preempts] the common law doctrine for assessing the appropriate damages to real property and requires PCB contamination to be considered a temporary injury."

We agree with the trial court that in light of the often exorbitant costs of remediation, the traditional common law economic waste analysis is inadequate when measuring damages to land from environmental contamination. Land subject to hazardous waste or PCB contamination is required to be remediated virtually without regard to cost. PCB contamination, therefore, will generally be considered a temporary injury capable of being remediated or "repaired."

Nevertheless, the traditional distinction between temporary and permanent injury to real property is ill-suited for determining damages in the context of environmental contamination. In *In re Paoli R.R. Yard Litigation* (3rd Cir.1994), 35 F.3d 717, the court reversed the determination that the plaintiffs were not entitled to damages for diminution in value because PCB contamination of their property was "temporary and remediable." Although the plaintiffs may not have presented evidence of permanent "physical" damage, they did present expert evidence that the PCB contamination had not been completely remediated and that "the stigma of living on property which once contained significant amounts of PCBs" constituted "permanent, irremediable damage to [property]."

The Third Circuit determined it was not necessary, under Pennsylvania law, "that an injury to land [be] physical for it to be considered permanent." The Court observed that the term "permanent injury" was meant to apply whenever repair costs would be an inappropriate measure of damages. "An appropriate measure of damages is generally defined as what is necessary to compensate fully the plaintiff." The court concluded:

> This approach is normally consistent with the view that, when physical damage is temporary, only repair costs are recoverable, because in a perfectly functioning market, fully repaired property will return to its former value. Thus, an award of repair costs will be fully [compensatory]. Hence, normally, it is only when property cannot be repaired that courts must award damages for diminution in value in order to fully compensate plaintiffs. However, the market sometimes fails and repair costs are not fully compensatory. In such cases, [plaintiffs] should be compensated for their remaining loss. Absent such an approach, plaintiffs are permanently deprived of significant value without any compensation.

The law of damages in Indiana is consistent with the Third Circuit's interpretation of Pennsylvania law. As in Pennsylvania, the aim in awarding damages in Indiana is to fairly and adequately compensate an injured party for his loss. In discussing the appropriate measure of damages which will fully compensate the plaintiff for an item of personal property that is damaged but not destroyed, this court has stated:

> the fundamental measure of damages is the reduction in fair market value caused by the negligence of the tortfeasor. . . . The reduction in fair market value may be proved by a combination of evidence of the cost of repair and evidence of the fair market value before the causative event and the fair market value after repair, where repair will not restore [the] property to its fair market value before the causative event.

We see no reason why [this] combination or hybrid theory of recovery, which utilizes both the cost of repair and any reduction in the property's value after repair, should not also apply to environmental damage to real property. If the plaintiff can demonstrate that repairs to real property fail to restore the land to its former value, recovery of damages for the property's reduction in value is the only measure of damages which will fully compensate the landowner for his loss.

The fundamental measure of Terra's damages is any reduction in the fair market value of Terra Site caused by Kraft. If as Terra contends the value of Terra Site after remediation was less than its value before discovery of PCB contamination, the property was permanently damaged. Thus, Terra would be entitled to compensation for any "remaining loss" in the property's fair market value after remediation in that, under such circumstances, remediation would be inadequate to compensate Terra fully for its loss.

We cannot agree with Kraft's argument that its remediation of Terra Site necessarily relieved it of any further liability to Terra for common law damages. CERCLA serves two essential purposes: (1) to provide a swift and effective response to hazardous waste sites and (2) to place the cost of that response on those responsible for creating or maintaining the hazardous condition. CERCLA is not intended to exclude other remedies available to an injured landowner but explicitly provides that "nothing in this chapter shall affect or modify in any way the obligations or liabilities of any persons under other Federal or State law, including common law, with respect to the releases of hazardous substances or other pollutants or [contaminants]." Restoration under CERCLA is not, as a matter of law, Terra's exclusive remedy for damage to its land.

Nevertheless, Terra has not met its burden of designating evidence which would tend to establish that Kraft's remediation did "not restore the value [of Terra Site] to its fair market value before the causative event. Terra established the auction sale price of Terra Site, but the sale occurred before remediation. Even if the auction price was a reliable measure of its post-remediation value, there is also no evidence of Terra Site's fair market value before PCB contamination was discovered. The $1.1 million appraisal included both Terra Site and Mallory Site. Terra's only remaining viable claim concerns Terra Site, and it cannot be inferred from the combined appraisal that Terra has incurred a loss in Terra Site's fair market value.

There is no evidence in the record to establish the value of the land before and after remediation and, thus, no evidence of any permanent damage to Terra Site. The trial court did not err when it granted summary judgment for Kraft.

The judgment of the trial court is affirmed.

NOTES AND QUESTIONS

1. *Repair vs. Lost Value.* When plaintiff's property is damaged but not destroyed, either of two roads might put plaintiff in the position she would have occupied but for the wrong: (a) a court could award plaintiff the cost of restoring the property to its original condition and value (cost of repair); or (b) a court could award plaintiff the difference in value between the uninjured property and the injured property (diminution in value). Cost of repair gives plaintiff the thing she had before: the property in good condition. Diminution in value gives plaintiff the same net worth that he had before: the full value of the property. In theory, the two measures will be very close. If a house was worth $300,000 before a tort and could be restored to that value for repairs that would cost $20,000, how much is it worth without repairs? No one would pay more than $280,000 for it; would you expect to pay much less in a market with more than one bidder? Does it make sense to say any property is worth $250,000 if, by investing $20,000, you would have property worth $300,000?

2. *Contracts.* The same problem can arise in contract cases. Sometimes performance, though delivered, is not as valuable as promised. If so, buyer might be able to reject the performance and seek restitution or cover with substitute goods. If buyer elects to keep the performance, she is entitled to compensation. If goods can be repaired, the cost of repair might be recoverable. Alternatively, buyer might recover the difference in value between the performance as promised (or as warranted) and the performance as delivered. UCC § 2–714. That is similar to diminution in value, the difference between the value you should have and the value you do have. Is a similar remedy needed for sellers? Should buyers be allowed to recover the cost to repair the performance?

3. *Terminology.* Courts use various terms to describe why one remedy might be preferred. While *Terra–Products* distinguishes between temporary injury (cost of repair) and permanent injury (diminution in value), some courts refer to damaged or destroyed property. Neither formulation is entirely accurate; each treats property as permanently injured (or destroyed) when the cost of repairs is excessive, even if repairs would restore it to full value. Why? Would a reasonable person spend $4,000 to repair a car if the car would be worth only $2,000 more after the repairs? If not, why should plaintiff be allowed to spend $4,000 of defendant's money on ill-advised repairs? Why, then, does the court permit recovery of repair costs in *Terra–Products*? Does the statute deviate from the general rule of damages or implement it?

4. *Probing the Rule.* The court states that an injury is permanent when "the cost of restoration exceeds the market value [prior] to injury." Is that the right approach? Or should we compare the cost of repairs with the amount of increase in the market value of the property if repairs are completed? The problems below seek to frame this question in concrete settings.

Would it make more sense to choose the remedy that fits the facts of the case, rather than arguing about whether an injury was permanent or temporary? This approach might focus on the reasonableness of repairs instead of the permanence of the injury. That echoes the avoidable consequences doctrine (mitigation of damages), which we will study shortly. In some cases, repairs might be reasonable even if they cost a little more than the actual loss in value. Can you explain why and identify examples where this might be appropriate? Is that why the court uses a value before the injury standard instead of a value added by repairs standard? Should repairs be favored even more strongly? What about allowing the cost of repair unless it is disproportionate to the diminution in the value of the property?

5. *Unrestored Value.* The court acknowledged that cost of repair may not provide adequate compensation in some cases of property damage—particularly where repairs leave the property less valuable than it was before the injury. In those cases, plaintiff needs to recover both the cost of repair (assuming repairs increase the value of the property by more than they cost)

plus any remaining diminution in value. Anything less leaves her in a worse position than before the wrong.

6. *Personal Injuries*. When a person suffers physical injury, medical costs are the cost of repair. Would any circumstances justify the conclusion that the medical costs were unreasonable and therefore not recoverable? Patients (or their surrogates, acting in the patients' best interests) sometimes refuse additional care, suggesting that in some cases, the value of care does not exceed the cost—at least when one includes the human cost of treatment, not just the price of treatment. Could a court ever make that judgment, effectively denying damages for medical costs? Or should a tortfeasor always pay for the medical costs, even if those costs exceed the benefits. Would the alternative measure ever be less? But the difference between life uninjured and life with the untreated injuries poses no conceptual difficulties. It is routinely applied to any injury that cannot be treated—some spinal cord injuries, for example—or where a plaintiff reasonably chooses to forego treatment. If the life expectancy (before injury) was short, the disability of the untreated injury modest, and the cost of treatment high, might a court conclude that medical costs are not recoverable?

PROBLEMS

1. *Expensive Repairs*. Donna Driver (D) injured Pat Plaintiff's (P) car. The car was worth $8,000 immediately before the accident. Immediately after the accident, the car was worth $500 as scrap or spare parts. The car could be restored to its prior condition—with a value of $8,000—for a cost of $10,000.

2. *Modest Repairs*. Same problem, but the value after the accident is $6,000 and the cost of full repair is only $3,000. Would your answer be the same if the vehicle were a freighter and the numbers had four more zeros on the end ($80 million, $60 million, and $30 million)?

3. *Appreciating Asset*. Donna Driver (D) injured Pat Plaintiff's (P) antique collectible car. The car was worth $80,000 immediately before the accident. Immediately after the accident, the car was worth $1,000 as scrap or spare parts. The car could be restored to its prior condition, but the work will take two years and cost $90,000. Because the car is rare, it is likely to be worth $100,000 when repairs are complete.

4. *Damaged over Time*. D improperly stored P's antique car and mice chewed the upholstery and water rusted the metal. The value before the improper storage was $80,000; the value today is $1,000, repairs would cost $90,000, but the car would be worth $100,000 if it were repaired.

5. *Value Not Restored*. Donna Driver (D) injured Pat Plaintiff's (P) car. The car was worth $8,000 immediately before the accident. Immediately after the accident, the car was worth $500 as scrap or spare parts. The car could be repaired to its former working condition for $5,000. If repaired, the car would be worth only $6,000—not because time has passed, but because cars that have been extensively damaged are worth less than cars (of identical quality)

that have not been extensively damaged. If the car had never been injured, it would still be worth $8,000.

6. *Even Less Value Restored.* Donna Driver (D) injured Pat Plaintiff's (P) car. The car was worth $8,000 immediately before the accident. Immediately after the accident, the car was worth $500 as scrap or spare parts. The car could be repaired to its former working condition for $5,000. If repaired, the car would be worth only $4,000—not because time has passed, but because cars that have been extensively damaged are worth less than cars (of identical quality) that have not been extensively damaged. If the car had never been injured, it would still be worth $8,000.

7. *Real Estate.* Bobby Builder, in order to construct a landfill, excavated a deep hole. Bobby negligently failed to shore up the sides of the hole, causing adjacent land to shift toward the hole. The cost to repair the land will be $60,000. The land was vacant with a pretort value of only $5,000. Would it matter that the owner believes that the land will appreciate as the city grows?

8. *Externalities.* In problem 7, what if the damage to the land put other property at risk? Suppose the shifting land threatens to damage sewer pipes running under the vacant lot. What if continued shifting would threaten a highway on the other side of the vacant lot?

The preceding cases assume that market value can be calculated with relative ease. That is often the case when similar goods are sold in the market regularly. Real estate, of course, poses an additional problem because each parcel is unique. Appraisers use actual sales of similar parcels and adjust for differences between them when estimating market value. Actual sales of similar property are not the only technique for determining value.

O'BRIEN BROS. V. THE HELEN B. MORAN

160 F.2d 502 (1947).

[In December 1942, a Navy tug hit and sank a barge owned by libellant O'Brien Bros. The United States admitted liability for 80% of the loss, but appealed the judgment that the loss exceeded $61,000 (making its share about $49,000).]

The United States introduced evidence to the effect that the value of the barge at the time of the collision was $15,000 to $16,000. The libellant showed what the repairs had cost and what hire it received for its barge. While the net of $101.85 per day, and an apparent likelihood of prolonged use, were some evidence of a greater value than $16,000, the United States introduced evidence that a similar barge could have been built new for $33,000 and that upon such an assumed cost there should be allowed a depreciation of $17,800 in order to obtain a proper valuation of a barge that was twelve years old at the time of the collision. The actual cost of the barge according to books of the libellant was $44,653, and the depreciation taken on the books was $28,212, leaving a book value of $16,441. Yet the Commissioner and the District Judge allowed $7,732.21 for expenses of raising the wreck, $37,014.99 for repairs, $6,230.23 for repairs still to be made, $3,423.91 for miscellaneous items of damage, and $6,620.25 for demurrage [loss of use]. . . .

[The court allowed the cost to raise the barge as a necessary expense in order to determine whether repairs were reasonable. Repairs in excess of the value of the barge could not be recovered. The value of the barge, however, proved a vexing question. The Commissioner found that no similar barges were available on the open market. Having failed to prove the value of the barge, defendant had failed to prove that repairs were unreasonable.]

[The court assigned the burden to prove value to the libellant and remanded to allow additional evidence.] The libellant should have met this evidence by showing not merely that the worth was greater but what it actually was. This might have been founded upon (a) a capitalization of earning capacity, (b) the cost of a barge of a similar type in the open market, (c) the cost of constructing a new barge if that was feasible. In each case—*i.e.*, of (a), (b) and (c)—there should be a deduction of proper depreciation due to the age and deterioration of the vessel involved in the collision.

[If any of these techniques produced a value less than $37,000, then the value, not the repair cost, was the measure of damages. The court also held that demurrage was unavailable if the repair cost exceeded value, following the rule that demurrage was available for damaged property pending repairs, but not for destroyed property pending replacement.]

NOTES AND PROBLEMS

1. *Alternative Methods.* The court notes three ways to assess the value of property: the market value of similar property (other 12-year-old barges in like condition); replacement cost less depreciation (the price of new property, minus the percentage of the original property already used up); and capitalization of earnings (an estimate of the current value of an item based on how much income it will produce over time). In theory, the values will be very close. When they are not, a little scrutiny might reveal either that one measure or another was miscalculated or that one measure or another doesn't fit the facts and circumstances of the case.

2. *Market Value.* Does it make any sense to say that a barge could not be obtained on the market? If offered enough money, wouldn't someone who owned a 12-year-old barge decide to sell it? Does it matter that no one was actively seeking a buyer? Is the problem one of timing: the most recent sales

establish the market value in the past, not necessarily the market value today? How would you respond to that position?

3. *Depreciation.* Replacement cost less depreciation starts with the price of a new barge, then deducts a percentage to account for the portion of the original barge already used up. The figures in this case imply that new barges have a useful life of 22 years ($17,800 is about 12/22 of $33,000). If the figures are right, why did O'Brien Bros. spend $37,000 to repair a 12-year-old barge when for $33,000 (partially paid by the Navy) they could have had a new barge?

4. *Capitalization of Earnings.* Appraisers estimate the current value of an item by estimating how much income it will produce over time. Presumably, someone will pay an amount (of capital) today in exchange for the income stream (earnings) the asset will produce. When buying rental property (apartment or office buildings, shopping malls) prospective owners care little about intrinsic value; they look to the amount of rent it will produce each year, deduct the annual costs (taxes, maintenance, insurance, personnel) to produce that income, and discount to present value. The same can be done with a barge. Suppose net income was $50 a day ($101.85 may omit some expenses), and the barge can be rented 300 days a year (no Sundays plus 13 days for maintenance), and had 10 useful years remaining. That totals $150,000 ($15,000 a year for the next 10 years). No one would pay that much for the barge. Investing $150,000 in a savings account, even at 2%, would produce more after 10 years than paying $150,000 for the barge. The barge carries risks: the income stream might be less than projected; the barge might sink sooner (without someone else's fault); or the war might end, reducing demand for barges (or increasing supply as shipyards making warships start making peacetime vessels). We must discount the income to account for risk and other investment opportunities. The chart below shows one calculation. You need to know how to do this. Before you hire an accounting expert—perhaps before you decide whether to take a case—you may need some estimate of damages. Take a deep breath and follow along.

The column for income contains the estimated annual net earnings. For this example, we assumed a 6% discount rate. The rate needs to be about equal with other investments of equal risk. Savings accounts are safer, junk bonds are riskier, and 6% seems about right for the 1940s. Multiply each year's income by 1 divided by 1 plus the interest rate chosen, to the power of the year. You don't need to do that calculation; you can read it from a chart of discount rates or let your spreadsheet program calculate it. The result gives you the amount of money you would need to invest today at the interest rate chosen in order to withdraw $15,000 in the year specified. If you invested $10,574.41 today at 6%, you could withdraw $15,000 after 6 years. Since the owner will get $15,000 in each year, we need to add the present value of each row to get the total value of a barge with 10 useful years left.

Year	Income		Discount		Present Value
1	$15,000	×	0.94339623 (or 1/1.06)	=	$ 14,150.94
2	$15,000	×	0.88999644 (or $1/1.06^{2}$)	=	$ 13,349.95
3	$15,000	×	0.83961928 (or $1/1.06^{3}$)	=	$ 12,594.29
4	$15,000	×	0.79209366 (or $1/1.06^{4}$)	=	$ 11,881.40
5	$15,000	×	9.74725817 (or $1/1.06^{5}$)	=	$ 11,208.87
6	$15,000	×	0.70496054 (or $1/1.06^{6}$)	=	$ 10,574.41
7	$15,000	×	0.66505711 (or $1/1.06^{7}$)	=	$ 9,975.86
8	$15,000	×	0.62741237 (or $1/1.06^{8}$)	=	$ 9,411.19
9	$15,000	×	0.59189846 (or $1/1.06^{9}$)	=	$ 8,878.48
10	$15,000	×	0.55839478 (or $1/1.06^{10}$)	=	$ 8,375.92
			Total		$110,401.31

In other words, a buyer satisfied with a 6% expected return would pay up to $110,401.31 for this barge—assuming the income and expenses are realistic. Nothing here suggests the repairs exceeded the value.

Your turn. If the venture were a little riskier than assumed, investors might demand a 7% return. If so, how much would the barge be worth on the assumptions stated here?

5. *Disparity*. Why do these techniques produce such dramatic differences in the value of the barge? Which should be preferred? The court says that the lowest value produced by any method should be used. Could you persuade a court to adopt a different measure in this case?

3. APPLYING MARKET MEASURES

Pecuniary losses are objective, at least to some extent. Evidence of actual market transactions provides some estimate of the size of the loss. Some pecuniary losses can be proven with precision. If we want to figure out how much Kraft spent on repairs, we can total the bills. Other market measures are less certain. If someone damages your car, how much will it cost to rent a substitute vehicle? There probably are several rental companies in each of several nearby locations offering similar car models (but perhaps none offering precisely this age, make, and model), at several different rates (daily, weekly, monthly), at several different discounts, with the rates changing over time. These variations make *the* market value illusory, consisting of a range of transactions, not a single amount. From those real transactions, courts (often aided by experts) must pick a number and call it the market price or fair market value.

Market price is an abstract, an estimate, an average of real market transactions. As a result, testimony concerning market values differs, even among appraisers using the same data in a relatively stable market, like housing prices. Predictions of future wages introduce additional wrinkles, requiring guesses concerning how long plaintiff will work, how much wages will increase over the coming years, how much overtime plaintiff might work, and a host of other factors that cannot be known with absolute certainty. Before we move on, some attention to how market measures are used seems apt.

SEMENZA V. BOWMAN

268 Mont. 118, 885 P.2d 451 (1994).

TRIEWEILER, JUSTICE.

[Defendants] Ronald Bowman and Eric Johnson operated L & R Spraying Service [L & R] as a partnership. Semenza owns and farms land near Helmville (Helmville farm) and near Utica (Utica farm). Plaintiff Faye Fitzgerald owns a farm near Stanford (Stanford farm), which Semenza custom farmed. In the spring of 1987, Semenza seeded approximately 260 acres of his Helmville farm, about 180 acres of his Utica farm, and roughly 521 acres of Fitzgerald's Stanford farm, with Klages barley. Semenza asked L & R to spray those crops, and they did. L & R used a mixture of Banvel II and Low Vol 6 (LV6) which was an "off label" mixture not authorized for use on spring barley. In May 1987, L & R sprayed this mixture on Semenza's and Fitzgerald's barley and spring wheat crops. In July 1987, Fitzgerald noticed that her barley crop was damaged. Semenza discovered similar problems with his barley crop. . . .

The court found that L & R's spraying caused the crop damage, and that Fitzgerald was damaged in the amount of $47,737.28, based on calculations done by her expert, Neal Fehringer. The basis for that amount was the court's finding that she should have been able to sell all of her barley as malt barley at $3.69/bushel and would have harvested at least 13,194 more bushels. In addition, the court found that Semenza had to rent equipment for $3,000 to screen out "thins" to ensure the maximum amount of Fitzgerald's barley was suited for malt, and added that amount to her damage award.

Fehringer also testified, and the District Court found, that based on crop reduction at both of his locations, Semenza sustained damages in the total amount of $55,073.02. The District Court also found that L & R knew that Semenza's damages were at least the amount set forth above, and awarded Semenza and Fitzgerald prejudgment interest to accrue from September 15, 1989. . . .

Issue 3

Did the District Court err in its calculation of Semenza's and Fitzgerald's damages?

Montana law provides that the measure of damages in a crop loss claim is the net value of the crops lost; in other words, the amount the crops are sold for, less the expenses incurred to harvest and market them. At issue in this case is whether the value of crops lost should be measured by the price at which the crops were sold, or the market price on the date that they were harvested. The former value was $3.69 per bushel, the latter was $2.40.

L & R claims that based on decisions from other jurisdictions, we should hold that the $2.40 value at the time of harvest must be used to calculate damages. *See Decatur County Ag–Services, Inc. v. Young* (Ind.1981), 426 N.E.2d 644. However, § 27–1–317, MCA, provides that damages shall compensate for all the detriment proximately caused, whether or not it could have been anticipated. In addition, § 27–1–302, MCA, requires that damages be reasonable. We have previously stated that compensatory damages to property are designed to return the damaged party to the same, or nearly the same, position enjoyed before the property is damaged.

In this case, testimony indicated that it was a common practice to delay selling crops for weeks or months to enable farmers to achieve a higher price for their crop. Testimony also indicated that pursuant to another common farming practice, Semenza and Fitzgerald, at the time of harvest, took out United States Government loans for the value of the crop, and then sought to sell the crop at a later date because of the glut in the barley market on the date of harvest. Semenza and Fitzgerald follow this practice whether or not their crop is damaged. Because this is their common practice, and was not done to enhance their damages, they are entitled to recognize the amount they would ordinarily recognize on the date of sale. This ensures Semenza and Fitzgerald are put in the position they would have attained and are compensated for all detriment that was proximately caused by L & R's negligent acts.

We conclude, based on the evidence presented to the District Court, and Montana's statutory law of damages, that the District Court's finding regarding plaintiffs' damages was supported by substantial evidence, it was not clearly erroneous, and it was not contrary to the laws of this State. . . .

The judgment of the District Court is affirmed.

NOTES AND QUESTIONS

1. *Diminished Value of Land.* If fire damaged a building, one could appraise the value of the land with the undamaged building and subtract the

appraised value of the land with the damaged building. Would that work for crops, too? Crops can't be repaired, but the land can be appraised. The difference between the value immediately before and after the spraying is likely to represent reduced value of the crops. (It might also include concerns for future crops, if the chemicals might have effects beyond this crop. Should that be included, if proven?)

2. *Timing.* Once courts start to value the crops instead of the land, they must choose between three plausible dates: the date of the injury, the date of harvest, and the date of sale. The court here did not consider the date of the injury, the closest to the normal rule. Why not choose that date?

3. *Moral Hazard.* The court rejected the date of harvest in favor of the date plaintiff actually sold the surviving portion of the crop. Assuming plaintiff would have sold the entire crop at one time, this gives plaintiff the benefit of the extra bushels at the price it really would have obtained. But on similar facts (plaintiff held the surviving crop until the Spring, a practice he regularly followed), the Indiana Supreme Court reversed a trial court's award of damages based on the date of sale. *Decatur County Ag–Services, Inc. v. Young*, 426 N.E.2d 644 (Ind.1981). Consider the court's reasoning.

> To the extent that Plaintiff elected not to sell his harvest at the time it was first marketable, he was speculating that its market value would be greater at some subsequent date. The risk inherent in such speculation is not chargeable to the defendant. The lost beans could have been replaced from the market place at the time of harvest. Whatever this market value was at that time was the gross loss and, in this case, the extent of Plaintiff's damages.

426 N.E.2d at 647. Confronted with that reasoning, could you persuade your state to follow Montana instead of Indiana?

4. *Securities.* When an insider trades on information not yet made public, the sellers (whoever they are) have been defrauded. Rescission based on fraudulent inducement often satisfies the plaintiff. If restitution is not available, how should damages be calculated?

PROBLEMS

1. *Falling Market.* In *Semenza*, suppose the price had fallen from $2.40 after harvest. Plaintiffs held onto their crop for awhile, hoping the price would recover, then finally sold it for $1.80 a bushel. At 28,000 bushels between them, how much should they recover: $67,200 ($2.40/bu), $50,400 ($1.80/bu), or some other amount?

2. *Futures Markets.* Farmer Jo hired Ace to dust the soybean crop. Ace negligently destroyed the crop. But for the wrong, Jo would have harvested 1000 bushels in October. The price of October soybeans (in the futures market) on the date of spraying was $2 per bushel. In October, the price was $2.40 per bushel. February soybeans sold for $2.25 per bushel on the date of

spraying and $2.50 per bushel at harvest in October. In February, soybeans sold for $3.69 per bushel. How much should Jo recover?

3. *No Crop Planted.* Farmer Jo hired NRich to chemically improve the soil on the farm. NRich negligently added the wrong chemicals, which made the land useless for one year. The mistake was discovered before Jo planted the soybean crop. The price of soybeans on the date of the wrong, proposed harvest, and following February are the same as in problem 2.

4. *Insider Selling.* On July 1, Terry bought 1000 shares of SpecCo for $30 a share. That same day, Chris, an officer of SpecCo, sold 100,000 shares of the company's stock for $30 a share. Chris knew that on July 5, SpecCo would revise its earnings estimate downward, causing the price of the stock to plummet. On July 5, the price immediately fell to $18 a share. On July 12, the price stabilized at about $13 a share. In an action for stock fraud, how much can Terry recover? Would your answer be different if Terry held on to the stock until September 1, when the price was $20 a share, and then sold it? If the price was only $5 a share when she sold on September 1? *Dura Pharmaceuticals, Inc. v. Broudo*, 544 U.S. 336, 125 S. Ct. 1627, 161 L. Ed. 2d 577 (2005).

5. *Delayed Decline.* In problem 4, suppose the purchase and sale occurred on May 1, but Chris already knew the bad news. If the stock rose to $40 a share on July 3, then fell to $13 a share following the announcement, how much could Terry recover?

6. *Insider Buying.* On July 1, Leslie sold 1000 shares of Spec Co. for $30 a share. That same day, Sean, an officer of SpecCo, bought 100,000 shares of the company's stock for $30 a share. Sean knew that on July 5, SpecCo would announce a new discovery that would cause the price of the stock to skyrocket. On July 5, the price immediately rose to $42 a share. On July 12, the price stabilized at about $50 a share. In an action for stock fraud, how much can Leslie recover? Would your answer be different if Leslie bought 1000 shares of SpecCo on September 1, when the price was $60 a share? If the price was only $40 a share when she bought on September 1?

7. *Delayed Increase.* In problem 6, suppose the purchase and sale occurred on May 1, but Sean already knew the good news. If the price fell to $25 a share on July 3, then rose to $50 after the announcement, how much could Leslie recover?

UNITED TRUCK RENTAL EQUIPMENT LEASING, INC. V. KLEENCO CORP.

84 Hawai'i 86, 929 P.2d 99 (Ct.App.1996).

ACOBA, JUDGE.

[Kleenco, a commercial cleaning service, rented a truck from United. The truck was stolen when a Kleenco employee left the keys in the ignition of the unattended and unlocked truck.] Kleenco contends that the court erred in awarding United $7,500 because the award was based on the retail market value of the truck rather than "on the wholesale or 'bulk' market" value. United purchased the truck at the wholesale price of $6,419.93 plus tax. Consequently, Kleenco reasons, the $7,500 award placed United in a better position than it would have been in had there been no breach of contract. Accordingly, Kleenco does not appear to challenge the fair market value aspect of the award but rather the market, retail or wholesale, used by United's expert in arriving at his opinion.[11]

[In] awarding damages, the court adopted the amount at which Duane Lee (Lee), United's "expert in the area of vehicle appraisal and vehicle evaluation," valued the truck. Lee testified that $7,500 is the "actual cash value"[12] of the lost truck and is based on the average dealer estimate of a "like kind vehicle." Specifically, Lee spoke with three local dealers, Windward Toyota, Kaimuki Toyota, and Toyota City. Lee testified that he gave each dealer such information as the "year, make, model, condition, equipment, [and] mileage," of the lost vehicle and he asked each dealer for the selling price of such a vehicle on the open market on the date of the loss. The "local market" and the "Kelly bluebook" price of the vehicle were also considered in arriving at his opinion. On cross-examination, Lee stated that his valuation was based upon the retail market value and not wholesale market value of the vehicle.

"Whether the retail or wholesale price will govern when calculating damages depends on the replacement market available to the injured party." 4 J. Nates et al., *Damages in Tort Actions* § 37.01[1][b], at 18 (1994). Thus, a consumer, who usually is limited to purchasing an item at retail prices, is entitled to recover the retail market value for the loss of that item. Contrastingly, when a retailer's stock-in-trade is damaged, the retailer is entitled to recover the wholesale market value of the stock because that value represents the retailer's actual replacement cost. *See e.g.* Chevron Chem. Co. v. Streett Indus., 534 F.Supp. 801 (E.D.Mo.1982); D. Dobbs, *Remedies* § 5.10, at 377 (1973). "The theory underlying this rule is that if the owner of lost or destroyed property is a retailer . . . the goods may be replaced at their wholesale value and subsequently sold at retail just as the original goods would have sold." Because a retailer purchases goods at wholesale and then sells the goods at retail, awarding a retailer the retail market value of damaged or lost goods would be tantamount to giving the retailer his or her profits without the retailer having to incur the expense of selling the goods.

---

[11] Fair market value is defined as "[t]he amount at which property would change hands between a willing buyer and a willing seller, neither being under any compulsion to buy or sell and both having reasonable knowledge of the relevant facts."

[12] Actual cash value is considered synonymous with fair market value. Lee's estimate did not include the four per cent excise tax or a three dollar certificate fee that would be charged in an actual purchase.

Because United was a rental company it was not strictly a consumer or a retailer. In this case, the stolen truck was part of United's fleet of rental vehicles. Conceivably, United could purchase a replacement either in the retail or the wholesale market. If United made purchases on a regular basis as a typical retailer, then the truck's value should be based on the retail market value. However, according to the testimony of Martin Yasuda (Yasuda), United's President, the truck had been one of ten trucks purchased in bulk from one seller, and it would "probably cost [United] too much to buy another one." Also, according to Victoria Yasuda, United's bookkeeper (the Bookkeeper), United always purchased its vehicles in bulk to enable it to purchase the vehicles at "wholesale" prices. . . . There was no evidence that a single vehicle replacement could be purchased by United at the wholesale price. Hence, the evidence supports the conclusion that unless United was buying in "bulk," the wholesale market was not available to it.

As a result, the market price which would accurately or as precisely as possible compensate United for its stolen truck, under these circumstances, was the retail market price. *See* Richards, 880 P.2d at 1238–39 ("All of the different measures for damages to personal property are merely guides to common sense, and the question in each case is ultimately a question of fully compensating the injured party. Thus, the various measures should be adjusted as required to meet the goal of compensation. It follows then that no mechanical rule can be applied with exactitude in the assessment of property damage and each case must rest on its own facts and circumstances as supported by the proof in the record.")

The trial court's award was consistent with the proof of market value submitted by United and did not, under the evidence, amount to a windfall profit to United. The evidence presented by United was adequate to establish the replacement cost or value of the truck. In this context, the trial court's acceptance of United's expert opinion was reasonable. Therefore, we hold that the trial court correctly adopted the retail market value as the appropriate standard for measuring the replacement cost of a single truck to United.

Kleenco also challenges the trial court's award of loss of use damages. . . . [T]he trial court "den[ied] the request for lost profits" and awarded United $550.00 for "[l]oss of vehicle use," the $550.00 representing "one month of rental."

On appeal, Kleenco contends that "[t]he trial court erred in awarding United 'lost volume' damages although United failed to present any evidence of the net profits it would have made from one month's rental." Kleenco argues that "damages for business lost volume are limited to loss of *net profit,*" and therefore, a "party seeking lost volume damages must prove what those net profits are." Although Kleenco uses the term "lost volume damages," Kleenco is really arguing the law of lost profits.

> Lost profits damages and loss of use damages are not synonymous.
>
> Loss of profits [are] measured by the amount of profit that a plaintiff could prove would have been generated had the plaintiff not been deprived of the use of the property, less the amount of profit actually generated during the deprivation. Loss of use, on the other hand, is the loss of an incident of ownership—the right to use.

While loss of use damages are normally awarded to a party deprived of a vehicle during the period of repair, traditionally, recovery could not be had for loss of a vehicle's use during the period required to replace it. However, a "growing number of state and federal courts have abandoned the traditional approach and have awarded damages for loss of use in cases of total destruction."

The abandonment of the distinction between loss occurring from repairable vehicles and totally destroyed vehicles is based upon the realization "that the economic loss to the owner who is deprived of a vehicle because it has been totally demolished is the same as the loss to the owner who is deprived of a vehicle during the period required for repair." We agree with this reasoning and, therefore, adopt the rule that damages for loss of use may be recovered when a vehicle is totally destroyed. Because a vehicle is a complete loss if stolen, a stolen vehicle should be treated in the same way as a completely destroyed vehicle for purposes of loss of use damages.

However, recovery for loss of use damages must be limited to a period of time reasonably necessary for securing a replacement. Here, United indicated it could not afford to purchase a replacement. But, a plaintiff's recovery should not be premised on his or her actual ability to purchase a replacement.

The rationale supporting this proposition is that regardless of whether the plaintiff furnishes the funds to hire a substitute vehicle, he or she still suffers an injury while deprived of the vehicle and should be awarded damages for the inconvenience.[21]

There are several mutually exclusive means of measuring damages for loss of use. They are: "(1) the rental value or the amount that could have been realized by renting out the property; (2) the reasonable cost of

---

[21] Neither party contends that one month was an unreasonable amount of time upon which to base an award of damages for loss of use. By the time of trial, United still had not replaced the truck. Thus, United was deprived of the use of the truck from January 1988 through June 1991, approximately forty-one months. Under these facts, we believe loss of use damages based upon one month was well within reason.

renting a substitute; or (3) the ordinary profits that could have been made from the use of the property."

United did not rent a substitute. Therefore, option number two is inapplicable. The third option is usually only used to determine loss of use damages when a rental substitute is not available or when the kind of property damaged is not the type that is normally rented. United did not present any evidence that a rental substitute was unavailable, and clearly the truck does not qualify as the type of property which is not normally rented. Consequently, option number three is also inapplicable.

Thus, the appropriate means of measuring damages for loss of use is rental value. In cases where the owner of damaged property is in the business of hiring the property out, courts recognize that the rental value also reflects gross profits and hence must be adjusted accordingly. Therefore, whatever the owner has saved in overhead or other costs while the property is being repaired must be deducted from an award for loss of use damages. We believe this rationale applies equally to a case of total loss.

Here, the court awarded loss of use damages based upon the amount that would have been received from renting out the truck for one month, without any deductions. At trial, Yasuda testified that the truck was rented out at a daily rate of $35, a weekly rate of $175, and a monthly rate of $550.

When the court heard Kleenco's motion to alter or amend the judgment, it stated:

> [Kleenco's counsel] has a point in that there are certain amount of expenses that should be deducted from the 5–50[sic]. This amount seems to be rather minuscule. The best this Court can estimate is approximately a dollar a day, or perhaps $30 at best. Viewing, however, that this is a fairly new vehicle, the court does not believe that there was very much, if any, maintenance expense.

Consequently, although the court acknowledged that the $550 award based on rental value should reflect appropriate deductions, it made none to the award.

The rental value awarded as the measure of loss of use damages should have been reduced by the amount that United saved in overhead or other associated costs while not in possession of the truck. Because United presented no evidence of these costs, the trial court erred in calculating loss of use damages at $550.

Accordingly, although United proved loss of the use of its truck, United is only entitled to nominal loss of use damages because it failed to prove the associated costs which should have been deducted from the rental amount awarded.

For the foregoing reasons, we affirm the October 15, 1991 judgment except for that part awarding damages for loss of use. As to such damages, we remand for entry of judgment awarding nominal damages.

PROBLEMS

1. *Retail or Wholesale?* The case arose under the rental contract, though a bailment theory probably would produce the same result. Sales contracts under the UCC pose the same issue. If seller fails to deliver the goods, buyer can recover cover price minus contract price (if she does buy a substitute) or market price minus contract price (if she does not). *See* UCC §§ 2–712,–713. A buyer who covers in the retail market may confront arguments that cover was not "in good faith" or "reasonable," as required by the UCC.

2. *Market and Loss of Use.* Suppose United rented a similar truck from one of its competitors while seeking a replacement—option 2 on the court's list. Would the court award that amount (presumably about $550)? Or would the court find it unreasonable to rent in the retail market instead of leasing from a dealer? Does it matter that dealers require longer lease terms, usually at least two years, while the court only allowed one month as the reasonable time to replace the truck? Is leasing actually a way to replace the truck, not a component of loss of use at all?

3. *Cover Price or Market Price?* If United has bought a fleet of 10 trucks between the theft and the trial, would one of those have been a substitute for the stolen truck? If so, should the court have awarded the cost of that truck instead of the $7,500 retail value? Does your answer depend on whether the new truck cost more or less than $7,500?

4. *Market Location.* Suppose United purchased a substitute truck in the retail market of a nearby city, instead of buying locally. Would the cover price of that transaction apply? Even if the local dealer testifies that it would have sold United a truck for less? Does it matter why United dealt with the nearby competitor? What reasons would be persuasive? Would the argument work the other way: if United purchased locally, but the price was better in the neighboring town, should the court use the market price in the neighboring town instead of the cover price? The UCC looks to the place for tender (or arrival, if goods arrive before they are rejected). UCC § 2–713(2). "Place" is not clearly defined, leaving room to argue whether the neighborhood, the city, the county, the region, or the state is proper. The UCC provides some flexibility:

> If evidence of a price prevailing at the times or places described in this Article is not readily available the price prevailing . . . at any other place which in commercial judgment or under usage of trade would serve as a reasonable substitute for the [place] described may

> be used, making any proper allowance for the cost of transporting the goods to or from such other place.

UCC § 2–723. Does this imply that recourse to nearby markets is not permitted, despite commercial judgment or usage of trade, when a local market price is readily available?

5. *Product Market. Texaco v. Pennzoil Co.*, 729 S.W.2d 768 (Tex.App.1987), illustrates how the choice of market can make a huge difference in damage awards. In 1984, Texaco persuaded Getty Oil's shareholders to abandon negotiations with Pennzoil and instead sell 3/7 of Getty stock to Texaco. Pennzoil sued Texaco for interference with contract. Texaco paid $10 a share more for the stock than Pennzoil had offered; thus, the stock's market value exceeded the price Pennzoil would have paid by at least that much, and perhaps more if Texaco's offer was a bargain. The court, however, computed damages without regard to the market value of the stock. Owning 3/7 of the stock entitled Pennzoil to 3/7 of Getty's proven reserves (oil still in the ground) if Getty could not be reorganized—a serious possibility. Pennzoil's expert testified that it would cost Pennzoil about $10.87 per barrel to find that much oil by exploration, much more than the $3.40 per barrel they would pay for the stock. Texaco presented no testimony concerning damages. The jury accepted Pennzoil's calculation, awarding $7.53 billion as damages.

Did the court assess market value in the right market (or, stated another way, of the right product)? Pennzoil bought in the market for stock, but intended to obtain oil and to sell in the market for oil. Should a court use that market to calculate the value of what Pennzoil purchased? (If so, should it consider only the cost to find substitute oil or the profit on the oil?) Or should the court have limited Pennzoil to the value of the stock instead of the value of the oil? Did Pennzoil get a great discount on oil reserves by buying stock from Getty instead of buying oil rights from unknown owners of not-yet-discovered reserves? If this deal was so great, why weren't others competing in the market? Texaco was, but bid little more than Pennzoil ($125 a share vs. $115 a share, or $3.69 a barrel vs. $3.40 a barrel). During negotiations, Pennzoil refused to pay $120 a share. If the profit margin on oil was as large as indicated, why didn't someone bid $230 a share ($6.80 a barrel, for a profit exceeding $4 billion)? Did Pennzoil, Texaco, and other potential bidders know something the expert didn't? The price of oil collapsed shortly after the deal.

The claim here involved tortious interference with contract. Would damages be calculated any differently if Pennzoil sued Getty's shareholders for breach of contract? Should the law permit the choice of which claim to plead (or which defendant to sue) to make a difference in the amount of recovery?

4. LOSSES BEYOND VALUE

Repairing or replacing the thing lost will not always put plaintiff in the position she would have occupied if the wrong had not occurred.

Sometimes depriving a party of his rights or property causes losses beyond the value of the thing itself. When that happens, the basic rule has clear implications. To put the party in the position she would have occupied if the wrong had not occurred, courts must allow recovery of the additional losses as well. The following cases introduce the subject of consequential damages. Most of the complex issues regarding consequential damages arise from doctrines limiting their recovery when they should have been avoided, could not have been foreseen, or cannot be established with reasonable certainty. Those issues will be addressed in detail later, though they cannot be entirely ignored here. Still, the focus here remains on the basic rule for damage recovery.

FUKIDA V. HON/HAWAII SERVICE AND REPAIR

97 Hawai'i 38, 33 P.3d 204 (2001).

LEVINSON, J.

In May 1996, Fukida sought to have his vehicle repaired by an automotive repair shop operated by the defendants. According to Fukida, after an employee of the shop informed him that his vehicle did not pass the safety check because of "transmission problems," he authorized the shop to install a rebuilt transmission, which he was told would cost approximately $2,100 to $2,250. However, at the time he authorized the work, he informed the employee (1) that he wanted, prior to installation of the transmission, to review the receipt for the rebuilt transmission in order to ensure that a rebuilt transmission, rather than a used one, was actually being installed in his vehicle and (2) that he wished to be advised as to when they were "ready to go" so that he could inspect the transmission to be installed.

Thereafter, an employee of the shop informed Fukida that his vehicle was ready to be picked up. When he arrived at the shop, he was further informed that the total amount due for the installation of the rebuilt transmission was $2,478.95; Fukida refused to pay the bill because the shop had not contacted him prior to installing the transmission as he had requested. The repair shop then informed Fukida that it would retain his vehicle until he paid for the repair work and, subsequently, began billing Fukida for the amount it believed was due for the installation, as well as for accrued storage fees calculated at $20.00 per day.

Fukida filed a complaint, in which he sought the return of his vehicle, special damages for the cost of renting an automobile while the repair shop retained his vehicle, and attorney's fees and costs. The defendants filed a counterclaim against Fukida, seeking the cost of repairing the vehicle, as well as storage fees in the amount of $2,260.00 (calculated at $20.00 per day) and any additional storage fees that accrued until Fukida paid for the repair work. [T]he district court, after a bench trial, [held] that the lien on Fukida's vehicle was unlawful. [I]nsofar as the shop had not complied with Fukida's requests upon which his authorization for the installation of a rebuilt transmission was predicated, the shop could not lawfully impose a lien upon the vehicle.

Consequently, the district court dismissed the defendants' counterclaim, ruled that the installed transmission must remain in the vehicle, and ordered the defendants to return Fukida's vehicle to him. The district court also awarded Fukida "loss of use" damages for the period of time during which the shop had wrongfully retained possession of his vehicle [June 2, 1996 to August 29, 1998], calculated at $10.00 per day, in the total amount of $6,970.00. [The Intermediate Court of Appeals (ICA) reversed the award of damages for loss of use. The Supreme Court reversed and remanded.]

On remand, the ICA held that the district court's award of "loss of use" damages was excessive; consequently, it vacated the district court's award and remanded the matter . . . so as to award "loss of use" damages "that are capped by the value of [the vehicle] at the time it was placed under lien." Fukida filed an application for a writ of certiorari, which we once again granted. . . .

The only analysis contained in the ICA's opinion on this point was the following:

As noted in 66 Am. Jur. 2d Replevin § 122, at 910 (1973):

> In determining the value of the use [of a chattel in a replevin action], care should be taken not to permit the fixing of an amount out of all proportion to the value of the thing itself; otherwise, the result is not compensation for use, but punishment for a wrong, in a case where exemplary damages, as such, would not be allowed. So, where damages allowed for the detention of property for less than a year were more than twice the value of the property, it was held that the damages were grossly excessive.

[T]he ICA correctly held that Fukida was not required to establish that he actually rented a replacement vehicle during the time his own vehicle was retained by the defendants. [I]n light of Fukida's testimony that a comparable vehicle rented at approximately $32.00 per day, the district court's determination that he should be compensated at the rate of $10.00 per day in "loss of use" damages was neither unreasonable nor unsupported by the evidence. We affirm this aspect of the ICA's opinion. See, *e.g.*, Cress v. Scott, 117 N.M. 3, 868 P.2d 648, 650–51 (1994) (holding, inter alia, that "loss-of-use damages may be measured by the reasonable rental value of a substitute vehicle, even in the absence of actual rental").

Nonetheless, the ICA further held as follows:

> [D]amages for loss of use of property should not exceed the value of the property. [T]he Kelley Blue Book retail value for a 1986 Honda Civic with similar features ... would approximate $4,900.00, an amount more than $2,000.00 less than the total loss-of-use damages awarded to Fukida by the district court. Fukida's Civic might be appraised, depending on its condition, at less than the Kelley Blue Book value. [C]omparable Civics were being sold on the marketplace for $1,800.00.
>
> The district court did not enter any finding as to the value of Fukida's Civic at the time it was placed under lien. Since the award of loss-of-use damages cannot exceed the value of Fukida's Civic at the time the lien was placed on the Civic, the district court must determine the Civic's value on remand.

[T]he rule that the ICA adopted is somewhat antiquated. In *Anderson*, a 1957 decision and the sole authority—other than an article appearing in American Jurisprudence 2d (1973)—upon which the ICA relied, the Kansas Supreme Court indeed observed that,

> where property attached to [land] ... is damaged or destroyed, the owner is entitled to damages, which may not exceed the value of the property, for his [or her] loss of use or for loss of rental up to the time when, with ordinary diligence, it could have been restored, whether in fact it was restored or not.

... Because the case did not address the question whether the jury's award of "loss of use" damages was excessive for having exceeded the value of the home, Anderson is silent—except for the isolated clause in the passage quoted *supra*—with regard to the issue that Fukida raises.

More recent jurisprudence reflects an evolution of the "black-letter" principle.... For example, in *Mondragon v. Austin*, 954 S.W.2d 191 (Tex.Ct.App.1997),[11] the court noted that, "a person whose car has been totally destroyed may recover only the value of the car, while a person whose car is repairable may also recover the loss of use of the car." The court noted that the distinction is drawn

> because courts assume that a person does not suffer loss of use damages when a car is a total loss. Courts assume that the car can be replaced immediately. In contrast, we assume a partially damaged car, while repairable, cannot be repaired immediately. Consequently, a person whose car is only partially damaged

[11] In *Mondragon*, the plaintiff lost the use of his vehicle because the defendant collided with it while "driving drunk and backwards down the road." The plaintiff's vehicle could not be driven and, because the plaintiff was of limited financial means and had no collision insurance, he remained unable to obtain an estimate for repairing the vehicle for over a year following the accident. In the meantime, the plaintiff was obliged to make monthly payments on the vehicle, send additional money to his daughter (for whom the vehicle was purchased) for transportation at college, and travel six hundred miles each way to transport her back and forth on holidays.

> suffers damage in addition to loss in value of the car. The person also suffers loss of use of the car, a value not necessarily correlative to the value of the car.

Believing that the "the assumption made in partial damage cases is more realistic than that made in total destruction cases," the *Mondragon* court expressed its view that the "better policy might be to reconsider permitting loss of use damages in total destruction cases."

The Iowa Supreme Court has, in fact, done just that. Acknowledging that the historical rule was that "loss of use" damages were unavailable in cases involving complete destruction but were available in cases involving reparable damage, the Iowa Supreme Court held that it does not, in a great number of instances, permit full compensation to the plaintiff. *See Long v. McAllister*, 319 N.W.2d 256, 258–61 (Iowa 1982).

> Loss of use damages will be incurred as readily when a vehicle is totally destroyed or when it cannot be restored by repair to its prior condition as when the vehicle can be restored by repair. Just as loss of use damages are necessary for full compensation when the vehicle can be restored to its prior condition, they are warranted when the vehicle is destroyed or cannot be so restored. No logical basis exists for cutting them off when the total reaches the vehicle's market value before the injury. . . .
>
> When an automobile is damaged through the negligence of another, compensation for the temporary loss of use is directed at plaintiff's economic loss, the amount of money plaintiff had to pay for rental of a car. This is an injury different in kind from property damage, the amount of money necessary to repair or replace the damaged vehicle. A plaintiff in a total destruction case deprived of his [or her] reasonable loss-of-use expenses has simply not been made whole. The same reasoning is applicable in a repair situation.

The foregoing logic loses none of its vitality in the context before us here, where no damage has been done the vehicle, but, nonetheless, Fukida has been deprived of its use for over two years by the tortious conduct of the defendants.

We agree with the Iowa Supreme Court's analysis in *Long*. In our view, permitting a plaintiff to recover "loss of use" damages in any case involving a tortious deprivation of the use of property comports with the very purpose of allowing recovery of such damages: "to provide reasonable compensation for inconvenience or monetary loss suffered during the time required for repair of damaged property." A person whose vehicle is completely destroyed suffers an indistinguishable inconvenience, during the reasonable period of time necessary to obtain a replacement vehicle, from that borne by a person, whose vehicle is only partially damaged, while he or she awaits the completion of repairs. Fukida, insofar as he was deprived of the use of his vehicle as a result of the defendants' tortious retention of possession of it, has no less suffered a comparable inconvenience. As such, we perceive no plausible rationale for adopting a rule distinguishing between these sundry scenarios, much less a rule such as the ICA has approved, by which the amount of recovery for such inconvenience is arbitrarily capped by the vehicle's value, a factor that bears no relation to the inconvenience that the loss of use of one's vehicle causes. . . .

[W]e hold that, where a person is deprived of the use of his or her property due to the tortious conduct of another, he or she may recover "loss of use" damages. Of course, such damages are, as a general matter, limited to the period of time reasonably necessary to obtain a replacement, to effect repairs, or [to recover possession of] the property. The totality of the circumstances should be evaluated to determine the reasonableness of the period of time that the plaintiff claims he or she was deprived of the property, including whether the plaintiff reasonably could have mitigated the damages in some manner; however, the value of the property, in and of itself, is not determinative in assessing "loss of use" damages.

We reverse the ICA's opinion to the extent that it held that Fukida's "loss of use" damages may not exceed the value of his vehicle. We affirm the ICA's opinion in all other respects.

PROBLEMS

1. *Fundamental Rule.* Did the court put Fukida in the position he would have occupied if no wrong had occurred? That question has two components, only one of which receives attention on appeal. The court first returned Fukida's car to him. Did that ruling comport with the general rule? If you represented defendant, do any tactics remain open to prevent overcompensating Fukida?

2. *Rental Cost.* The court also awarded damages for "loss of use." That is tort terminology; in contract, the loss would be called "consequential." If the court limited its order to replevin, returning the car to Fukida, would that be consistent with the general rule? If Fukida had rented a car at a reasonable rate (say, $32 a day, times 697 days, totaling $22,304), would anything less satisfy the rule? The car was worth no more than $4,900. If Fukida consulted you before renting a substitute, would you advise him to rent under these circumstances?

Would it matter if the vehicle was not a family car, but a business vehicle, such as a delivery van or a barge? How would loss of use be measured in that case?

3. *Incidental Losses.* There is a third component of the loss: the cost of making substitute arrangements. It might take Fukida a little time, some

phone calls, and a cab ride to rent a substitute car. That cost, too, would not have been incurred if the defendant had not committed the wrong. The UCC refers to these as incidental losses. UCC §§ 2–710,–715(1) (for seller and buyer, respectively). In other contexts, they might be called the costs to minimize the loss. Did the court neglect them because they were modest or nonexistent? Or did Fukida's attorney overlook this component of damages? Incidental damages can be large enough to fight over.

4. *Unintended Consequences.* Treating loss of use differently can distort decisions about whether or not to repair property. Reconsider *O'Brien Bros., supra* at 595. If repaired, the government would be liable for over $6,000 in demurrage (the admiralty term for loss of use). But if declared a total loss, libellant could not collect demurrage. Building a new barge might have taken longer than repairs to the old one, increasing the uncompensated loss libellant would bear. Even if the government was right that a new barge would cost only $33,000, the losses incurred immediately while waiting for replacement might outweigh the benefit 10 years down the road when the barge need not be replaced as soon. Does this show that repair was reasonable? Or were repairs a strategic decision to recover losses to which libellant was not entitled?

5. *Losses without Renting.* Fukida did not rent a car. Does that mean he suffered no losses? What would you ask Fukida in an effort to identify any losses?

6. *Other Causes of Action.* What if the case involved a breach of contract—say, Fukida was buying a used Civic, paid the price, but the seller failed to deliver until two years later. Assume the basic remedy would still require replevin or specific performance. *See* UCC § 2–716. Would the loss of use be calculated any differently? If specific performance would not be required, would loss of use be denied?

7. *Real Property.* If defendant occupied and retained Fukida's home (or a rental property), could a court make Fukida whole without awarding the fair rental value of that property? Even if that exceeded the cost to purchase a substitute property?

8. *Personal Injury.* What if Fukida were injured in a traffic accident. Is there any difference between the cost of repairing the car and the cost of repairing Fukida's body (measured by medical expenses, in most cases)? Is there any difference between the loss of use of the car and the loss of use of Fukida's body (measured by lost wages, in most cases)?

9. *Casey's Inhaler.* Suppose Casey recovers all costs connected to purchasing the wrong inhaler. Casey's body was repaired relatively quickly and even improved beyond his condition before using the inhaler. Is that enough to compensate Casey for the loss suffered?

SEMENZA V. BOWMAN

268 Mont. 118, 885 P.2d 451 (1994).

TRIEWEILER, JUSTICE.

[The facts of this case begin on page 599.]

Issue 4

Did the District Court err when it awarded Semenza and Fitzgerald prejudgment interest?

[L & R] challenges the District Court's Conclusion No. 6 which awarded Semenza and Fitzgerald prejudgment interest at ten percent per annum from August 16, 1989, the date of a letter from plaintiffs' counsel to L & R's insurance company, which conveyed the amount of Semenza's initial damage calculation. On January 7, 1994, the District Court amended its order to provide that interest would accrue from September 15, 1989, instead of August 16, a date 30 days after the written notice as required by § 27–1–210, MCA.

L & R asserts that the District Court erred because its prejudgment interest award was not based on an amount that plaintiffs were able to establish as a sum certain at a specific date before trial. L & R cites cases interpreting § 27–1–211, MCA, for this proposition. However, the District Court's interest award was based on §§ 27–1–210 and–212, MCA.

Section 27–1–212, MCA, provides that "[i]n an action for the breach of an obligation not arising from contract and in every case of oppression, fraud, or malice, interest may be given, in the discretion of the jury." [T]his section also applies in cases where the judge is the fact finder. Section 27–1–212, MCA, is derived from a California statute, and we followed the California Supreme Court's conclusion that their analogous section did not require liquidated damages. Accordingly, if § 27–1–212, MCA, applies, the judge has discretion to award prejudgment interest whether or not a plaintiff can reduce his or her claim to a sum certain prior to judgment. There is no showing by L & R that the District Court abused its discretion by its award of prejudgment interest under the facts in this case. Therefore, we conclude that the District Court did not err by its award of prejudgment interest pursuant to § 27–1–212, MCA. . . .

NOTES

1. *Rationale.* Interest constitutes damages for the loss of use of money. Just as Fukida, deprived of his car, needed to rent one, Semenza and Fitzgerald, deprived of money they should have received upon the sale of the crop, arguably needed to rent (that is, borrow) some. Interest is the rental fee on money. Interest is available even if the plaintiff did not borrow money—again, just as Fukida recovered loss of use even though he did not rent a substitute car.

2. *Doctrinal Limitations.* The preceding paragraph is perfectly good theory, but the interest rules often deviate from the theory. Part of the problem lies in a deep-rooted Anglo–Saxon distaste for interest charges, perhaps dating from medieval anti-Semitism. Legal doctrines often place limitations on the availability of interest. For instance:

a. Courts often deny prejudgment interest when the claim is not liquidated—that is, ascertainable as a specific amount of money. Thus, defendant in *Semenza* opposed interest because plaintiffs could not "establish [the amount of their claim] as a sum certain at a specific date before trial."

b. Courts sometimes say consequential damages are not available for the nonpayment of money. When these same courts award interest, they treat it as something other than consequential damages. Indeed, interest calculations frequently are performed by the court rather than the jury.

c. Courts sometimes treat prejudgment interest as discretionary rather than required in order to make the plaintiff whole. Focus can shift to litigation misconduct or other concerns. See, *e.g.*, *DiLieto v. County Obstetrics & Gynecology Group*, 74 A.3d 1212 (Conn. 2013) (treating postjudgment interest as discretionary).

d. Courts tend to award simple interest rather than compound interest.

e. Courts or statutes sometimes specify rates that differ from market rates.

The first few problems that follow walk through some of the intricacies of rulings on interest.

3. *Significance.* Interest can be enormous. In *Hughes Communications Galaxy, Inc. v. United States*, 271 F.3d 1060 (Fed. Cir. 2001), the court awarded Hughes over $102 million on a contract claim, but denied prejudgment interest. (Sovereign immunity protects the government from prejudgment interest without an express waiver in a statute or contract. *United States v. Alcea Band of Tillamooks*, 341 U.S. 48, 71 S. Ct. 552, 95 L. Ed. 738 (1951).) Hughes tried to make a takings claim, which would have allowed interest. Interest would have run from 1994 at the latest, perhaps as early as 1986. Even at 2%, the millions start adding up. Hughes' damages were based on the cover price minus contract price—money it actually spent, not some gain it never received. Has it been placed in the position it would have occupied but for the breach?

4. *Exceptions.* Denying consequential damages for nonpayment of money may not leave plaintiff in the position she would have occupied but for the wrong. The last few problems below suggest situations where exceptions either have been or could be recognized. They also hint at some of the difficulties exceptions might face. Can you build arguments for or against these exceptions?

PROBLEMS

1. *Judgment Interest and Prejudgment Interest.* Bobby agreed to pay Sean $100,000 for a herd of cattle. Sean delivered the cattle. Payment was due on July 1, 2007, but Bobby never paid. Sean sued Bobby for breach of contract on July 1, 2008. On July 1, 2010, a court entered judgment for Sean in the amount of $100,000. On July 1, 2012, Bobby finally paid Sean the $100,000.

a. Is interest due for the period from July 1, 2010, until July 1, 2012?

b. Should the judgment have included interest from July 1, 2008, until July 1, 2010? Or should interest have started on July 1, 2007?

c. Suppose the price was $1,000 per head of cattle. Bobby disputes the number of cattle delivered. The court ultimately concluded that 100 head were delivered, making $100,000 the correct price. Would these facts change your answer to a. or b?

d. If the judgment had included prejudgment interest, would postjudgment interest be due on the prejudgment interest? Does this question unnecessarily complicate the issue? Should we just award interest on $100,000 from July 1, 2007, until July 1, 2012, without differentiating the periods before and after judgment?

e. If Bobby paid for the cattle, but Sean did not deliver them, for which periods (if any) should Bobby get interest? If your answer is different, what justifies the difference?

2. *Interest as an Incentive.* When did the court in *Semenza* start the interest running? Was this the right date? Does the date suggest anything about the way the court viewed the interest award?

3. *Interest in Personal Injury Cases.* On July 1, 2011, while driving negligently, Deane struck and injured Pat. Pat sued, claiming the following components of damages: (a) $10,000 for an ambulance and emergency treatment on July 1, 2011; (b) $25,000 for surgery on October 1, 2011; (c) $6,000 for medications between July 1, 2011, and the date of judgment (July 1, 2014); (d) $150,000 in lost wages for the period from July 1, 2011, until July 1, 2013, when Deane returned to work; (e) $500,000 in pain and suffering from July 1, 2011, until the date of judgment; (f) $50,000, the present value of expected future medical expenses; and (g) $1 million, the present value of expected future pain and suffering. From what date should interest be available on these claims? If Deane had been liable for punitive damages, should interest be applied to them?

4. *Casey's Inhaler.* Should Casey recover interest? On what amounts? At what rate?

5. *Choosing an Interest Rate.* At what interest rate should interest be awarded? The rate at which plaintiff could have earned interest if she had invested the money in a safe source (say, Treasury Bills)? If plaintiff can

show how he would have invested the money if it had been received on time, should the return on that investment be used instead? Or should we focus on the rate plaintiff would have had to pay to borrow the money from a bank? What if plaintiff could not borrow money from a bank, but had to resort to a higher-interest lender in order to secure substitute funds? Does it matter whether plaintiff did borrow money? Does it matter whether plaintiff could have held out without the money (the way Fukida held out without the car)?

6. *Breach of Investment Loans.* Lender promises Borrower a mortgage on a particular parcel of real estate at a specified interest rate. Lender breaches the promise. Borrower, despite diligent effort, cannot find a substitute mortgage in time to close the sale. Thus, the parcel is sold to another. Is the difference between the interest rate Lender would have collected and the market interest rate sufficient to put Borrower in the position he would have occupied if the promise had been performed? *See Ma v. Community Bank*, 686 F.2d 459 (7th Cir.1982).

7. *Breach of Other Loans.* Would your analysis of problem 5 be different if the loan were a home equity loan for unspecified purposes? Would an unsecured loan be any different?

8. *Breach Causing Foreclosure.* Company fires Employee in breach of contract. Employee, despite diligent efforts, cannot find a new job for a full year. In the meantime, Employee is unable to maintain payments on her mortgage. The bank forecloses and sells the property at a bona fide sale, but the price did not exceed the amount due to the bank. Are lost wages sufficient to place Employee in the position she would have occupied but for the wrong? Would it matter if the discharge were a tort instead of breach of contract?

9. *Breach Affecting Investments.* Would your analysis of problem 8 be different if Employee managed to make payments on the mortgage, but had to forego investments in her IRA? What if she simply stopped visiting casinos or racetracks? *See Meinrath v. Singer Co.* 87 F.R.D. 422 (S.D.N.Y.1980).

10. *Breach of an Insurance Policy.* Driver negligently injured Pedestrian. Pedestrian agreed to settle her claim against Driver for $100,000, the limit of Driver's insurance policy. Insurer refused the offer, choosing to litigate the claim. At trial, a jury awarded Pedestrian a judgment against Driver of $1 million. Assuming Insurer's failure to settle the claim was a breach of contract, should Driver's recovery be limited to $100,000 plus interest? What if Driver's claim is treated as a tort?

MISSISSIPPI CHEMICAL CORP. V. DRESSER–RAND CO.

287 F.3d 359 (5th Cir.2002).

E. GRADY JOLLY, CIRCUIT JUDGE:

MCC produces ammonia at its fertilizer plant in Yazoo City, Mississippi. For the most part, the ammonia is used as an input in fertilizer—a small amount is sold on the market or stored in inventory for future use. The production of ammonia involves the compression of gas in a compressor train. Each train consists of, among other things, a low case and a high case compressor.

In 1989, in an effort to increase its ammonia production, MCC bought a specially designed compressor train from Dresser. The sales contract for the train contained an express warranty guaranteeing that the train would be free from defects and comport with certain technical specifications. As an exclusive remedy for the breach of this warranty, Dresser offered to correct promptly any defect at its own expense.

In April 1990, the high case compressor broke. MCC notified Dresser of the problem and shipped the high case compressor to New Orleans for repair. Dresser supplied a redesigned compressor and assured MCC that this new compressor would cure all the defects in the train.

In December 1992, however, MCC began to experience excessive vibrations in the low case compressor. In May 1993, these vibrations became sufficiently severe to require a reduction in the speed of the compressor train. This reduction resulted in a loss of ammonia production.

In September 1993, Dresser identified a fracture in a component [an impeller] of the low case compressor as the cause of the vibration problem and recommended a modification of that component. In December 1993 and again in November–December 1996, similar vibration problems were identified in the other components of the low case compressor [impellers]. In December 1996, Dresser advised MCC that similar repairs would have to be made to the impeller components of the high case compressor.

In March 1997, MCC filed suit for breach of the express warranty, breach of the implied warranties of merchantability and fitness for a particular purpose, and negligent design.

The case proceeded to trial. [The] jury found that Dresser had breached (1) the implied warranty of merchantability; (2) the implied warranty of fitness for a particular purpose; and (3) the express warranty. The jury based its breach of the express warranty finding on a conclusion that the exclusive "repair and replacement" remedy had failed its essential purpose. The jury awarded MCC $4,422,876.92 in damages for the profits lost during the three different periods when the compressor train was malfunctioning.

* * *

[MCC] put on evidence of the damages resulting from the lost production of ammonia during the three different periods when the compressor train was malfunctioning. [D]uring each of these three periods the compressor train continued to produce ammonia, albeit at a diminished rate.

MCC's damage calculation—which was accepted in whole by the jury—consisted of a three-step process: First, MCC computed the profit per unit of ammonia during each of the three malfunctioning periods.[10] Second, it estimated the quantity of ammonia lost in each malfunctioning period because of the reduction in the speed of the compressor train. Finally, it multiplied the profit per unit by the number of units lost to come up with the total amount of damages (*i.e.*, lost profits) caused by the malfunctioning compressor train.

Dresser lodges two objections to this damage calculation. First, it suggests that because MCC dipped into other sources of ammonia (*e.g.*, its existing inventory, its production from its Donaldsonville plant, and the open market [collectively, "inventory"]) to make up for the lost production from the malfunctioning compressor train, its damages should be limited to the replacement cost of these substitute sources. Dresser refers to these substitute sources in UCC parlance as "cover," and contends that it is entitled to judgment as a matter of law because MCC offered no evidence concerning the value of this "cover." * * *

"[T]he point of an award of damages, whether it is for breach of contract or for a tort, is, so far as possible, to put the victim where he would have been had the breach or tort not taken place." *Chronister Oil Co. v. Unocal Refining and Marketing (Union Oil Co. of California),* 34 F.3d 462, 464 (7th Cir.1994) (Posner, C.J.). This general principle serves as the focal point of the appropriate measure of damages as we work our way through applicable provisions of the Mississippi UCC.

In the event of a breach of warranty, a buyer may seek direct, incidental, and consequential damages. MISS. CODE ANN. § 75–2–714. Here, the jury was only instructed on—and presumably only awarded—consequential damages. We therefore restrict our attention to consequential damages and do not consider any direct damages caused by the breach of the express warranty.

Under the Mississippi UCC, "consequential damages" include:

---

10 MCC did this by first subtracting from the gross sales of ammonia (*i.e.*, market price x quantity of ammonia) the cost of delivery and other discounts. MCC then divided this figure by the total quantity of ammonia sold—this yielded the so-called "net-back" price of the ammonia. From this net-back price, MCC subtracted the per unit costs of electricity, natural gas, and the other variable inputs used in the production of ammonia.

Dresser contends that this lost profit calculation is incorrect because MCC used the market price to compute the profit per unit even though the majority of MCC's ammonia production was, in fact, used as inputs into other products (e.g., fertilizer). We do not find this argument persuasive.

The market price is a reasonably good proxy for the lost ammonia's value as an input. To be sure, we can think of no better proxy. After all, if the ammonia's value to MCC as an input was less than the market value, one assumes that MCC would have sold all of the ammonia it manufactured on the open market, which it did not.

Therefore, throughout the rest of our analysis of the damage issue, we ignore the fact that much of the ammonia production lost because of the malfunctioning compressor train was destined for use as an input.

(a) Any loss resulting from general or particular requirements and needs of which the seller at the time of contracting had reason to know and which could not reasonably be prevented by cover or otherwise; and

(b) Injury to person or property proximately resulting from any breach of warranty.

MISS. CODE ANN. § 75–2–715(2). Under Mississippi law, lost profits are recoverable as consequential damages if three requirements are met: (1) the seller had reason to know at the time of contracting that if he breached the contract, the buyer would be deprived of those profits—*i.e.*, the lost profits were foreseeable; (2) the lost profits are reasonably ascertainable; and (3) the lost profits could not have been reasonably prevented.

The first requirement, foreseeability, requires that the breaching party, at the time of contracting, have reason to know that such "lost profits" were possible. Foreseeability is to a large extent a notice requirement that requires buyers—at the time of contracting—to disclose the potential extent of their damages or forfeit the right to claim such damages upon breach. Such notice is critical because it ensures that the "contracted for" price reflects the entire scope of the risk (*i.e.*, the potential liability for breach) that the seller has agreed to bear. *See* RICHARD A. POSNER, ECONOMIC ANALYSIS OF LAW 141 (5th ed. 1998).

Whether damages are reasonably foreseeable is a finding of fact within the province of the jury. Here, the jury heard evidence that: (1) Dresser knew if the compressor train malfunctioned the ammonia plant would have to be shut-down; (2) Dresser knew that ammonia was necessary for the production of MCC products; and (3) in the past Dresser's predecessors in interest had made—and serviced—compressor trains for MCC. From this evidence, a reasonable jury could draw the conclusion that the lost profits from the lost production of ammonia were "reasonably foreseeable."[13]

---

[13] Dresser also argues that it could not have foreseen that the ammonia plant would ever produce more than 1400 tpd (tons of ammonia per day). Dresser bases this argument on the initial design contract in which MCC requested a compressor train that would allow the ammonia plant to produce up to 1400 tpd.

Dresser further contends that because MCC's damage calculation was based on expected production rates of 1402 tpd for the first claim period, 1531 tpd for the second claim period, and 1521 tpd for the third claim period, the jury could not have adopted—as a matter of law—MCC's damage calculation.

The jury heard evidence that the compressors in the compressor train were designed to run at 10,800 rpm (revolutions per minute). During the malfunctioning periods, the jury heard evidence that the compressors ran at a slower rpm. The jury also heard evidence that when the train functioned normally, that is, the compressors functioned at the designed 10,800 rpm, the plant produced more than 1400 tpd. Based on this evidence, a reasonable jury could have concluded that Dresser should have foreseen that malfunctioning compressors would run at lower rpm's, resulting in a reduction in ammonia production. This is the only conclusion with respect to foreseeability that the jury had to reach to adopt MCC's damage calculation.

We now turn to the "cover" requirement necessary for the recovery of "lost profits." As noted above, Dresser argues that MCC's damages should be limited to the value of the substitute ammonia it secured to replace the diminished production by the compressor train. Under Section 715(2) consequential damages are restricted to those damages "which could not be prevented by cover or otherwise." MISS. CODE ANN. § 75–2–715. This "cover" requirement imposes on the buyer a duty to mitigate his damages. When dealing with lost profits, this duty means that a buyer "cannot recover for losses he reasonably could have prevented."

Dresser cites a number of cases for the proposition that because MCC covered by securing alternative ammonia, its damages are limited to the cost of *that* cover. This argument does not reflect the law in Mississippi for the recovery of lost profits. To reiterate, the applicable law provides that the buyer can only recover for the lost profits he "could not have prevented by cover or otherwise." MISS. CODE ANN. § 75–2–715(2)(a). If the buyer chooses not to cover, (*i.e.*, mitigate his damages) and cover would have prevented the lost profits, the buyer cannot recover for lost profits. *See H & W Indus., Inc. v. Occidental Chemical Corp.,* 911 F.2d 1118, 1123 n. 9 (5th Cir.1990) ("Failure to cover does not deprive the buyer of all remedies but he may not recover consequential damages."); *Dura–Wood Treating Co. v. Century Forest Indus., Inc.,* 675 F.2d 745, 755 (5th Cir.) ("The so-called loss of potential profits could have reasonably been prevented by a different form of cover or otherwise. In the absence of such preventive measures, the district court's award of consequential damages . . . is not authorized[.]"), *cert. denied,* 459 U.S. 865 (1982). In short, this "duty to mitigate" restriction on the award of lost profits has nothing to do with the actual cost of the cover.

To recognize that "cover," as argued by Dresser, is not mitigation of lost profits in this case, one must understand that the substitute sources of ammonia—that is, ammonia from inventory—represented a profit opportunity for MCC. It makes no ultimate difference whether the jury measured the damages as it did here or as Dresser argues the jury should have measured the damages—*i.e.*, by computing the value of the ammonia units procured from MCC's own inventory. The ammonia was completely fungible. Because MCC had to make up for the lost ammonia production by dipping into its own inventory, it had fewer total units of ammonia. The jury heard evidence about the fewer number of units. It also heard evidence concerning the value (in terms of profits) of each of these units. The jury multiplied these two terms together to come up with the amount of lost profits. This award places MCC in the same position as it would have been but for the breach of warranty—that is, if MCC had not had to dip into its own inventory. As noted earlier, this is the precise point of a contract damage award.

Accordingly, the damage award was not—under de novo review of the legal issues involved—incorrect. Moreover, [a] reasonable jury, drawing all inferences in favor of MCC, could have determined the amount of damages as awarded in this case. [T]he district court did not err by denying Dresser's motions for remittitur, a new trial, or judgment as matter of law based on an alleged misguided damage calculation.

AFFIRMED.

NOTES

1. *Cover.* Literally, cover would involve buying a new compressor train, not buying substitute ammonia. Suppose MCC chose that route: it returned the machine, recovered the price, bought a new one, and sued for the additional cost (cover price minus contract price). Would that be enough to put MCC in the position it would have occupied if the machine had worked properly in the first place? Should it have kept the machine and sought the difference between the value of the machine as warranted and the value as delivered? UCC § 2–714. Would that have put it in the position it would have occupied if the machine had worked properly?

2. *Defining "Consequential."* The court approaches consequential damages by way of elimination. It explores three possible reasons to reject them (foreseeability, certainty, and avoidability) and, finding none apply, awards them. That approach follows from the UCC definition, which does not really explain how to tell which damages are consequential, but limits their recovery to cases where they are foreseeable and unavoidable. Typically, consequential damages involve the way a party intended to use the thing of which he was wrongfully deprived, as opposed to the value of (or damage to) the thing itself. One could easily call the consequential damages here loss of use.

3. *Lingering Hostility.* This section may give you the impression that consequential damages are a natural part of damage recoveries. However strong that position may be, the law continues to show some animosity toward consequential damages. The UCC rejects consequential damages unless expressly allowed. UCC § 1–305 (formerly § 1–106). The limitations noted in the case can pose serious obstacles to recovery of consequential damages in practice even when allowed in theory. Many contracts, like this one, contain provisions seeking to eliminate liability for consequential damages. We explore these problems in more detail later. For now, be aware that consequential damages occupy tenuous ground.

4. *Casey's Inhaler.* Is Casey's inhaler similar to the machine in this case? With it, Casey's productivity would have increased. Without it, Casey suffered a loss of productivity. Should a court include Casey's reduced productivity in the recovery? How should it be calculated? Typically, courts do not use the same terminology when addressing injuries to the person. But the same components are present. Conceptually, loss of use of a human body is no different from loss of use of a machine. Physical injuries may keep an

individual from using his or her body in productive ways. Lost income is the most obvious compensation for loss of use due to physical injuries. Other uses—leisure activities, family duties, etc.—also can figure into damage awards.

PROBLEMS

1. *Farm Equipment.* Farmer purchased a combine from Dealer for $150,000. The machine did not perform as promised, taking twice as much time to harvest crops, despite Dealer's efforts to repair the machine. Because the harvest season is limited, Farmer had to hire someone to harvest some of his crops one year. The next year, Farmer managed to harvest his own crops, but was unable to accept jobs harvesting others' crops because the combine was too slow. Farmer estimates that he lost $90,000 in profit for these two years. Farmer returned the machine, having paid only $30,000 of the contract price. How much can Farmer recover for breach of warranty? *See Parker Tractor & Implement Company, Inc. v. Johnson*, 819 So.2d 1234 (Miss.2002) (en banc).

2. *Lumbermill Equipment.* Miller purchased sawmill machinery from Company. The machinery never operated as promised, despite Company's efforts to repair the machinery. After nine months, Miller's customers stopped buying, forcing Miller out of business. The machinery was repossessed by the bank and sold at auction for less than the amount of the loan, leaving Miller owing $200,000. If the machinery had worked properly, Miller would have earned $350,000 in profits during the nine months the company was operating. How much can Miller recover for breach of warranty? *See Bobb Forest Prods. v. Morbark Indus.*, 151 Ohio App.3d 63, 783 N.E.2d 560 (2002).

B. LIMITS OF MARKET MEASURES

1. SUBJECTIVE VALUE AND OTHER ALTERNATIVES TO MARKET MEASURES

The injuries discussed so far are largely pecuniary. For all the imprecision of market price, at least there is a market to which the trier of fact can look for some verification that the requested amount is plausible. For some losses, however, market measures provide little or no guidance in assessing the victim's losses. In these situations, the court may decide to measure the loss by the market value—the value it would have to others—despite the inaccuracy this injects into the award. But there is room to urge alternatives that might come closer to achieving our compensatory goals. Direct consideration of subjective value is one approach.

MIESKE V. BARTELL DRUG CO.

92 Wash.2d 40, 593 P.2d 1308 (1979).

BRACHTENBACH, J.

[P]laintiffs delivered already developed movie film to a retail store for the sole purpose of having the film spliced onto larger reels. The film was lost or destroyed by the retailer's processing agent. A jury verdict of $7,500 was returned against the retailer and the agent-processor. Those defendants appeal. We affirm.

[O]ver a period of years the plaintiffs had taken movie films of their family activities. The films started with the plaintiffs' wedding and honeymoon and continued through vacations in Mexico, Hawaii and other places, Christmas gatherings, birthdays, Little League participation by their son, family pets, building of their home and irreplaceable pictures of members of their family, such as the husband's brother, who are now deceased.

Plaintiffs had 32 50-foot reels of such developed film which they wanted spliced together into four reels for convenience of viewing. Plaintiff wife visited defendant Bartell's camera department, with which she had dealt as a customer for at least 10 years. She was told that such service could be performed.

The films were put in the order which plaintiffs desired [and] delivered to the manager of Bartell. The manager placed a film processing packet on the bag and gave plaintiff wife a receipt which contained this language: "We assume no responsibility beyond retail cost of film unless otherwise agreed to in writing." There was no discussion about the language on the receipt. Rather, plaintiff wife told the manager, "Don't lose these. They are my life."

Bartell sent the film package to defendant GAF Corporation, which intended to send them to another processing lab for splicing. Plaintiffs assumed that Bartell did this service and were unaware of the involvement of two other firms.

The bag of films arrived at the processing lab of GAF. [I]t is undisputed that the film was in the GAF lab at the end of one day and gone the next morning. The manager immediately searched the garbage disposal dumpster which already had been emptied. The best guess is that the plaintiffs' film went from GAF's lab to the garbage dumpster to a truck to a barge to an up-Sound landfill where it may yet repose.

We recognized in *McCurdy* that (1) personal property which is destroyed may have a market value, in which case that market value is the measure of damages; (2) if destroyed property has no market value but can be replaced or reproduced, then the measure is the cost of replacement or reproduction; (3) if the destroyed property has no market value and cannot be replaced or reproduced, then the value to the owner is to be the proper measure of damages. However, we have held that in the third situation, damages are not recoverable for the sentimental value which the owner places on the property. *Herberg v. Swartz*, 578 P.2d 17 (Wash.1978).

The defendants argue that plaintiffs' property comes within the second rule of *McCurdy*, *i.e.*, the film could be replaced and that their liability is limited to the cost of replacement film. Their position is not well taken. Defendants' proposal would award the plaintiffs the cost of acquiring film without pictures imposed thereon. That is not what plaintiffs lost. Plaintiffs lost not merely film able to capture images by exposure but rather film upon which was recorded a multitude of frames depicting many significant events in their lives. Awarding plaintiffs the funds to purchase 32 rolls of blank film is hardly a replacement of the 32 rolls of images which they had recorded over the years.

The law, in those circumstances, decrees that the measure of damages is to be determined by the value to the owner, often referred to as the intrinsic value of the property. Restatement of Torts 911 (1939). Necessarily the measure of damages in these circumstances is the most imprecise of the three categories. Yet difficulty of assessment is not cause to deny damages to a plaintiff whose property has no market value and cannot be replaced or reproduced. *Jacqueline's Washington, Inc. v. Mercantile Stores Co.*, 498 P.2d 870 (Wash.1972); Restatement of Torts 912 (1939).

The fact that damages are difficult to ascertain and measure does not diminish the loss to the person whose property has been destroyed. Indeed, the very statement of the rule suggests the opposite. If one's destroyed property has a market value, presumably its equivalent is available on the market and the owner can acquire that equivalent property. However, if the owner cannot acquire the property in the market or by replacement or reproduction, then he simply cannot be made whole.

The problem is to establish the value to the owner. Market and replacement values are relatively ascertainable by appropriate proof. Recognizing that value to the owner encompasses a subjective element, the rule has been established that compensation for sentimental or fanciful values will not be allowed. That restriction was placed upon the jury in this case by the court's damages instruction.

What is sentimental value? The broad dictionary definition is that sentimental refers to being "governed by feeling, sensibility, or emotional idealism . . . " Obviously that is not the exclusion contemplated by the statement that sentimental value is not to be compensated. If it were, no one would recover for the wrongful death of a spouse or a child. Rather, the type of sentiment which is not compensable is that which relates to "indulging in feeling to an unwarranted extent" or being "affectedly or mawkishly emotional . . . "

Under these rules, the court's damages instruction[1] was correct. In essence it allowed recovery for the actual or intrinsic value to the plaintiffs but denied recovery for any unusual sentimental value of the film to the plaintiffs or a fanciful price which plaintiffs, for their own special reasons, might place thereon.

It was proper to reject defendants' proposed damages instruction since it was an erroneous statement of the law. It would have allowed "the amount of money which will reasonably and fairly compensate the plaintiffs for such damages as you find were proximately caused by the negligence of the defendants. If you find for the plaintiffs, your verdict should include the cost to replace or reproduce the lost or destroyed property."

The proposed instruction did not limit recovery to replacement cost only, which was defendants' theory of the case, nor did it deny recovery for sentimental value alone. Consequently, it was too broad. In fact, it was a more liberal damages instruction than the one given. It is not error to refuse an instruction which is not a correct statement of the law.

[Discussion of the validity of the clause limiting damages is omitted.]

NOTES AND QUESTIONS

1. *Options.* Can plaintiff choose the preferred approach to measuring loss? Or does this case establish a hierarchy for damage awards: first, consider market value; if that fails, consider cost to replace (or repair, if the property has not been destroyed); and only if both of those approaches fail, resort to the subjective value of the item to the owner, disregarding undue sentiment? Is such a rigid hierarchy required? Is it consistent with the way *Terra–Products, supra* at 588, suggested the measure be chosen? Might there be cases where the alternatives to market value make sense even if market value could be determined?

---

[1] Instruction No. 11: "It is the duty of the court to instruct you as to the measure of damages. You must determine the amount of money which will reasonably and fairly compensate plaintiff for such damages as you find were proximately caused by the negligence of any one or all of the defendants.

"In reaching your verdict you should consider the following elements: the value of the film to the plaintiff, the actual or intrinsic value of the film including cost of film and processing such film and such other considerations as will fairly and justly compensate plaintiffs for any loss sustained had the damage in question not been sustained.

"The law does not permit recovery for the sentimental value of the film to the plaintiff or a fanciful price which plaintiff might for special reasons place thereon.

"The burden of proving damages rests with the plaintiff and it is for you to determine whether any particular element has been proved by a preponderance of the evidence. Your award must be based upon evidence and not upon speculation, guess or conjecture. The law had not furnished us with any fixed standards by which to measure value to plaintiff or actual or intrinsic values of lost property to its owner. With reference to these matters, you must be governed by your own judgment, by the evidence in the case and by these instructions."

2. *Personal Possessions.* In *Wall v. Platt*, 169 Mass. 398, 48 N.E. 270 (1897), a railroad caused a fire that destroyed the plaintiff's home and possessions. Most of the possessions—clothing, furniture, china, etc.—were used. Used clothing and furniture can be obtained at thrift stores, flea markets, and estate sales. Should the recovery be limited to the cost of obtaining clothing and furniture of a similar age and quality in that market? Plaintiff could use the smaller award to buy new furniture and clothing, but could not replace everything. Yet full cost to replace all the goods with new merchandise puts the plaintiff in a better position than she would have occupied if the fire had not occurred. Can any alternative satisfy both parties' concerns for justice?

3. *Replacement.* What if the films were not irreplaceable? A wedding photographer might lose the film shot at the wedding. But in some cases the guests could be reassembled for new photographs. Would the cost of replacement be the proper remedy under *Mieske*'s hierarchy? *See Wilson v. Sooter Studios Ltd.*, 33 B.C.L.R.(2d) 241 [42 B.L.R. 89, [1989] 3 W.W.R.166, 55 D.L.R.(4th) 303] (British Columbia Ct. App. 1988) (allowing $1000 for breach of contract to take wedding pictures—more than $399 contract price, but less than $7,000 to restage wedding). The photographs would not have as much sentimental value as the originals, but they come closer than no photographs at all. Is that a reason to reject this measure or to augment it with an additional amount to cover the difference in value? Is the difference the kind of unwarranted or mawkish sentiment that should be denied under the third approach?

4. *Exception or Rule?* Both the Restatement (Second) of Torts and the Restatement (Second) of Contracts suggest value to the plaintiff is the preferred measure, if it can be determined. Isn't that subjective value?

> The phrase "value to the owner" denotes the existence of factors apart from those entering into exchange value that cause the article to be more desirable to the owner than to others. Some things may have no exchange value but may be valuable to the owner; other things may have a comparatively small exchange value but have a special and greater value to the owner. The absence or inadequacy of the exchange value may result from the fact that others could not or would not use the thing for any purpose, or would employ it only in a less useful manner. Thus a personal record or manuscript, an artificial eye or a dog trained to obey only one master, will have substantially no value to others than the owner. The same is true of articles that give enjoyment to the user but have no substantial value to others, such as family portraits. Second-hand clothing and furniture have an exchange value, but frequently the value is far less than its use value to the owner. In these cases it would be unjust to limit the damages for destroying or harming the articles to the exchange value.

RESTATEMENT (SECOND) TORTS § 911(1), cmt. 3; RESTATEMENT (SECOND) OF CONTRACTS § 348 (If . . . the loss in value to the injured party is not proved with sufficient certainty, he may recover damages based on (a) the diminution in the market price of the property caused by the breach, or (b) the reasonable cost of completing performance or of remedying the defects if that cost is not clearly disproportionate to the probable loss in value to him).

Is there a reason to prefer subjective value? What danger does subjective value present? Having read *Mieske*, are you satisfied that the danger can be minimized by other doctrines or by careful application of this one?

PROBLEMS

1. *Wedding Photos.* Jennifer negligently started a fire that destroyed photos of the wedding between Angelina Jolie and Brad Pitt. While the couple had no intention of releasing these photos to the press, a tabloid had made a standing offer of $100,000 for anyone who could provide one or more genuine pictures of the wedding. The cost to replace the photos from negatives held by the photographer would be about $2,000. How much should the couple recover? What if reproducing the pictures required restaging the wedding, which would cost $75,000?

2. *Companion Animals.* Arsenio negligently started a fire that destroyed Mr. & Mrs. Love's darling dog, Asta. They would not have sold Asta at any price. But dogs of that breed could be purchased as puppies for $600. (It would take 2 years of food and training to teach the puppy to do all the things Asta did—fetch slippers, play Frisbee, etc.) Dogs of that breed, age and training were generally unavailable on the market, though they sometimes could be found for about $60 at the local pound or humane society. How much should the Loves recover for the loss of Asta? What if Asta was a mutt, so that even puppies of that mix were generally free?

LANDERS V. MUNICIPALITY OF ANCHORAGE

915 P.2d 614 (Alaska 1996).

RABINOWITZ, JUSTICE.

Anchorage police officers [with a warrant] searched Landers' residence and seized a large quantity of marijuana plants, equipment used in drug production, and other personal property. Landers was ultimately convicted of misconduct involving a controlled substance.

During the pendency of the criminal litigation, the Municipality of Anchorage Police Department stored Landers' personal property and eventually disposed of it without notice to Landers. The items seized and disposed of included photographs and videotapes. Landers alleged that the photos were personal family pictures, pictures of girlfriends, and wedding photographs, and that the videotapes were recordings by Landers of events from his life.

Landers subsequently filed a complaint seeking damages for the items of personal property seized and disposed of by the Municipality.

Landers based his request for relief on theories of inadequate bailment, trespass, and conversion, and requested injunctive relief. The Municipality filed a motion *in limine* to exclude at trial any evidence of Landers' sentimental or emotional attachment to any items of personal property disposed of by the municipality. [T]he superior court granted the motion *in limine* on the ground that sentimental or emotional attachment "is so highly subjective as to amount to speculation." . . .

The court instructed the jury that if it finds "that the defendant negligently retained or disposed of an item of plaintiff's property [it] must determine . . . how much money will fairly compensate the plaintiff for that item of loss." [T]he court instructed the jury that the proper measure of damages for Landers' unreturned personal property is its fair market value at the time of seizure. Fair market value was defined as "the amount a fully informed seller would receive from a fully informed buyer in a normal, open market sale." The court further instructed the jury that it "may not award damages for plaintiff's sentimental[,] emotional, or fanciful value of any property including photographs and videotapes."

The jury awarded Landers $1.00 in nominal damages for the loss of miscellaneous photographs and $25.00 in damages for the loss of five videotapes. Since the jury's total award of $771.00 was substantially less than the Municipality's prior offer of judgment, Landers was ordered to pay costs and attorney's fees. Landers now appeals. . . .

The question of whether the superior court erred in excluding evidence of sentimental and emotional value depends upon the appropriate standard for measuring damages for loss of items of personal property such as family photographs and family or personal videotapes. There appear to be three different standards currently employed by courts for measuring damages for loss of personal property. The first standard is the fair market value of the property at the time of loss. *See State v. Stanley,* 506 P.2d 1284, 1292 (Alaska 1973).[5]

[T]he second standard for measuring damages for the conversion of a chattel or destruction of an interest in a thing is the value of the property to the owner. This standard applies where the destroyed or lost property has no real market value or where the value of the property to the owner is greater than the market value. Restatement (Second) of Torts § 911, comment e states that "[t]he phrase 'value to the owner' denotes the existence of factors apart from those entering into exchange value that

---

[5] The superior court applied this standard in the present case. Moreover, in *Richardson v. Fairbanks North Star Borough,* 705 P.2d 454 (Alaska 1985), this court limited the damage award for loss of a pet dog to the dog's market value at the time of death. [W]e stated:

> The superior court correctly held that the Richardsons' subjective estimation of Wizzard's value as a pet was not a valid basis for compensation. Since dogs have legal status as items of personal property, courts generally limit the damage award in cases in which a dog has been wrongfully killed to the animal's market value at the time of death.

cause the article to be more desirable to the owner than to others." Section 911, comment e includes family photographs among those articles which "give enjoyment to the user but have no substantial value to others. [I]t would be unjust to limit the damages for destroying or harming [these] articles to the exchange value."

The value to the owner is the value based upon actual monetary loss resulting from the owner being deprived of the property. A number of courts have held, and the Restatement (Second) of Torts takes the position, that this does not include "any sentimental or fanciful value." Rather, value to the owner may be based on such things as the cost of replacement, original cost, and cost to reproduce. To this effect, Restatement (Second) of Torts § 911, comment e states that if the subject matter cannot be replaced, "as in the case of a destroyed or lost family portrait, the owner will be compensated for its special value to him, as evidenced by the original cost, and the quality and condition at the time of loss." In applying such a standard to the present case, damages for the loss of the photographs would include the cost of purchasing and developing the film, while damages for the loss of the videotapes would include the cost of purchasing the blank videotapes.

The third standard applies where the property has its primary value in sentiment. In this situation the proper measure of damages is value to the owner including sentimental and emotional value.[12] This standard has been adopted by a minority of jurisdictions. In fact, only one case in which a court adopted this standard to measure damages for loss of family photographs was cited to us. In *Bond v. A.H. Belo Corp.,* 602 S.W.2d 105, 106 (Tex.App.1980), a newspaper reporter lost Bond's photographs, newspaper clippings and birth certificates which she had accumulated over time and which could not be replaced. The court held that sentimental value could be considered in calculating damages.[13] Similarly, in *Campins v. Capels,* 461 N.E.2d 712 (Ind.App.1984), the court held that sentimental value could be considered in determining the value

---

[12] However, sentimental value does not mean "mawkishly emotional or unreasonable attachments to personal property." *Campins,* 461 N.E.2d at 721. A court should not allow a substantial recovery for loss of property when the specific owner has an atypical sentimental connection with the item involved. Rather, sentimental value refers to the feelings normally generated by an item of personal property. Thus, a jury could not base a damages award on a claimant's testimony that certain photographs were "priceless."

[13] [T]he court stated:

> It is a matter of common knowledge that [personal items] generally have no market value which would adequately compensate their owner for their loss or destruction. Such property is not susceptible of supply and reproduction in kind, and their greater value is in sentiment and not in the market place. In such cases the most fundamental rule of damages that every wrongful injury or loss to persons or property should be adequately and reasonably compensated requires the allowance of damages in compensation for the reasonable special value of such articles to their owner taking into consideration the feelings of the owner for such property. . . . Where such special value is greater than the market value, it becomes the only criterion for the assessment of damages.

of rings which Capels had received over the years as awards for auto racing.

In *Richardson,* we considered a claim for mental and emotional suffering arising out of the destruction of a pet dog. We held that such recovery is limited to situations in which the trial judge makes a threshold determination that the severity of the emotional distress and the conduct of the offending party warrant a claim of intentional infliction of emotional distress.[14] Likewise, in *Murray v. Feight,* 741 P.2d 1148 (Alaska 1987), we upheld a jury's award of damages for mental and emotional distress arising out of the interference with personal property. However, we held that recovery for emotional distress resulting from interference with chattels should be included within the general recovery for intentional infliction of emotional distress. Thus, in both cases we required the plaintiffs to make out a claim for intentional infliction of emotional distress in order to recover damages for emotional suffering arising out of the destruction of personal property.[15]

Based on our prior decisions and the Restatement (Second) of Torts § 911, and in the absence of a claim for intentional infliction of emotional distress or another intentional tort, we conclude that the appropriate measure of damages applicable in the instant case is that found in § 911 of the Restatement (Second) of Torts, namely, the value of the items to the owner. We thus decline to adopt the minority view which allows damages for loss of items of personal property to be based on sentimental and emotional value. This holding is in accordance with our prior case law and the Restatement (Second) of Torts, and ensures that such damages will not be based on considerations which are difficult to measure.

Based on the foregoing, this case should be remanded to the superior court for a new trial on the issue of damages for the lost photographs and videotapes.

---

[14] [Landers] explicitly states that he did not make any claim for intentional infliction of emotional distress. Landers further observed that since the Municipality is not subject to punitive damages, he did not attempt to show recklessness or intent on the part of the Municipality. Landers further argues that, "Since punitive damages are not allowed against municipalities, a valuation method that assesses the owner's emotional or sentimental value of items not likely to have market value is appropriate."

[15] If Landers had introduced evidence that the Municipality had committed an intentional trespass or conversion he might possibly have recovered enhanced damages. The Restatement (Second) of Torts § 905(b) takes the position that damages for emotional distress resulting from the conversion of chattels should be recoverable. To this effect, comment d to § 905 states as follows:

> One who has a cause of action for a tort may be entitled to recover as an element of damages for that form of mental distress known as humiliation, that is, a feeling of degradation or inferiority or a feeling that other people will regard him with aversion or dislike. *This state of mind may result from . . . the deliberate trespass to land or destruction or dispossession of chattels.*

(Emphasis added.)

NOTES AND PROBLEMS

1. *Comparing Rules. Landers* cites earlier Washington cases on which *Mieske* relied, but not *Mieske*. Is *Mieske* inconsistent with *Landers*? Do they apply a different rule? How do they differ?

2. *Value or Distress? Landers* injects a discussion of emotional distress. Is this an additional element of damages, to be added to the value of the property? Or is distress an alternative to value, to be awarded instead of the value of the property? Should distress be limited to intentional torts? If parents cannot recover distress they suffer when their child is injured outside their presence, how can pet owners recover for their distress when their pet is injured outside their presence? Is there a difference between the cases that can justify these results? While one court considered companionship (and services as a watchdog) as a component of value to the owner, *Brousseau v. Rosenthal*, 110 Misc.2d 1054, 443 N.Y.S.2d 285 (N.Y. Civ. 1980) (awarding $550), distress claims have been limited to intentional infliction of emotional distress. But see *Scheele v. Dustin*, 998 A.2d 697 (Vt. 2010) (denying distress for intentional shooting of dog in owners' presence).

3. *Measuring Intrinsic Value.* The court suggests that subjective value should be measured by the cost plaintiff incurred to obtain the property. Alaska applied this approach in a case involving the shooting of a dog. *Mitchell v. Heinrichs*, 27 P.3d 309 (Alaska 2001). As a minimum, this makes sense. Plaintiff probably valued the property more than the cost to obtain and to maintain it, though some irrational decisions will arise. Is investment also the maximum or would the *Landers* court allow plaintiff to prove he valued the photos more than the cost to obtain them? Is the approach theoretically justified? Does it match any of the valuation techniques suggested in *O'Brien Bros.*, *supra* at 595?

PROBLEMS

1. *Value to the Owner.* How much would Mieske recover if value to the owner was based on the cost to obtain the property? Is this the approach proposed by defendant: the value of unexposed film? Or would other costs be included?

2. *Value of Companion Animals.* As Cameron Client watched helplessly, Natty Neighbor's large terrier grabbed Client's Chihuahua by the neck and shook it until the dog died. Client seeks recovery for Neighbor's negligence.

a. What questions will you ask to ascertain the value of the companion animal?

b. Is this an appropriate case for distress? *McDougall v. Lamm*, 48 A.3d 312 (N.J. 2012).

3. *Natural Resources.* Robin Recluse owned a cabin and 100 acres on a secluded mountain, using them as a weekend wilderness retreat. Lesley Lumber removed trees from the land and sold them. What damages may

Robin recover against Lesley for damage to the property? Would it matter that the market value of the land diminished by a relatively small amount? *See* Restatement (Second) of Torts § 929 comment b (1977). Would it matter if Robin did not use the cabin for recreation, but instead planned to fell the trees for lumber at a later time? Would the same apply to an urban garden adjacent to the owner's home destroyed by machinery that accidentally trespassed on the owner's land while engaged in a construction project next door?

This issue sometimes arises when the government must determine whether to restore wilderness or natural resources that have been damaged or to collect restoration costs from polluters under laws such as the Comprehensive Environmental Response, Compensation and Liability Act of 1960, 42 U.S.C. § 9601 *et seq.* (CERCLA). Efforts to excuse restoration when the cost would exceed the use value of the resources (lumber, not growing trees; seal pelts, not living seals) were rejected as giving inadequate weight to Congress's preference for restoration. *State of Ohio v. United States Department of the Interior*, 880 F.2d 432 (D.C. Cir. 1989).

2. PAIN, SUFFERING, DISTRESS, AND LOSS OF JOY

SEFFERT V. LOS ANGELES TRANSIT LINES

56 Cal.2d 498, 364 P.2d 337, 15 Cal.Rptr. 161 (1961).

JUSTICE PETERS.

Defendants appeal from a judgment for plaintiff for $187,903.75 entered on a jury verdict. Their motion for a new trial for errors of law and excessiveness of damages was denied.

At the trial plaintiff contended that she was properly entering defendants' bus when the doors closed suddenly catching her right hand and left foot. The bus started, dragged her some distance, and then threw her to the pavement. Defendants contended that the injury resulted from plaintiff's own negligence, that she was late for work and either ran into the side of the bus after the doors had closed or ran after the bus and attempted to enter after the doors had nearly closed.

The evidence supports plaintiff's version of the facts. Several eyewitnesses testified that plaintiff started to board the bus while it was standing with the doors wide open. Defendants do not challenge the sufficiency of the evidence. They do contend, however, [the] verdict is excessive. [There] is no merit to this contention.

The evidence most favorable to the plaintiff shows that prior to the accident plaintiff was in good health, and had suffered no prior serious injuries. She was single, and had been self-supporting for 20 of her 42 years. The accident happened on October 11, 1957. The trial took place in

July and August of 1959. The record is uncontradicted that her injuries were serious, painful, disabling and permanent.

The major injuries were to plaintiff's left foot. The main arteries and nerves leading to that foot, and the posterior tibial vessels and nerve of that foot, were completely severed at the ankle. The main blood vessel which supplies blood to that foot had to be tied off, with the result that there is a permanent stoppage of the main blood source. The heel and shin bones were fractured. There were deep lacerations and an avulsion[3] which involved the skin and soft tissue of the entire foot.

These injuries were extremely painful. They have resulted in a permanently raised left heel, which is two inches above the floor level, caused by the contraction of the ankle joint capsule. Plaintiff is crippled and will suffer pain for life.[4] Although this pain could, perhaps, be alleviated by an operative fusion of the ankle, the doctors considered and rejected this procedure because the area has been deprived of its normal blood supply. The foot is not only permanently deformed but has a persistent open ulcer on the heel, there being a continuous drainage from the entire area. Medical care of this foot and ankle is to be reasonably expected for the remainder of plaintiff's life.

Since the accident, and because of it, plaintiff has undergone nine operations and has spent eight months in various hospitals and rehabilitation centers. These operations involved painful skin grafting and other painful procedures. One involved the surgical removal of gangrenous skin leaving painful raw and open flesh exposed from the heel to the toe. Another involved a left lumbar sympathectomy in which plaintiff's abdomen was entered to sever the nerves affecting the remaining blood vessels of the left leg in order to force those blood vessels to remain open at all times to the maximum extent. Still another operation involved a cross leg flap graft of skin and tissue from plaintiff's thigh which required that her left foot be brought up to her right thigh and held at this painful angle, motionless, and in a cast for a month until the flap of skin and fat, partially removed from her thigh, but still nourished there by a skin connection, could be grafted to the bottom of her foot, and until the host site could develop enough blood vessels to support it. Several future operations of this nature may be necessary. One result of this operation was to leave a defective area of the thigh where the normal fat is missing and the muscles exposed, and the local nerves are missing. This condition is permanent and disfiguring.

Another operation called a debridement was required. This involved removal of many small muscles of the foot, much of the fat beneath the

---

[3] Defined in WEBSTER'S NEW INTERNATIONAL DICTIONARY (2d ed.) as a "tearing asunder; forcible separation."

[4] Her life expectancy was 34.9 years from the time of trial.

skin, cleaning the end of the severed nerve, and tying off the severed vein and artery.

The ulcer on the heel is probably permanent, and there is the constant and real danger that osteomyelitis may develop if the infection extends into the bone. If this happens the heel bone would have to be removed surgically and perhaps the entire foot amputated.

Although plaintiff has gone back to work, she testified that she has difficulty standing, walking or even sitting, and must lie down frequently; that the leg is still very painful; that she can, even on her best days, walk not over three blocks and that very slowly; that her back hurts from walking; that she is tired and weak; that her sleep is disturbed; that she has frequent spasms in which the leg shakes uncontrollably; that she feels depressed and unhappy, and suffers humiliation and embarrassment.

Plaintiff claims that there is evidence that her total pecuniary loss, past and future, amounts to $53,903.75. This was the figure used by plaintiff's counsel in his argument to the jury, in which he also claimed $134,000 for pain and suffering, past and future. Since the verdict was exactly the total of these two estimates, it is reasonable to assume that the jury accepted the amount proposed by counsel for each item.

The summary of plaintiff as to pecuniary loss, past and future, is as follows:

Doctor and Hospital Bills	$10,330.50	
Drugs and other medical expenses stipulated to in the amount of	2,273.25	
Loss of earnings from time of accident to time of trial	5,500.00	$18,103.75
Future Medical Expenses		
$2,000 per year for next 10 years	20,000.00	
$200 per year for the 24 years thereafter	4,800.00	
Drugs for 34 years	1,000.00	25,800.00
		43,903.75
Possible future loss of earnings	10,000.00	
Total Pecuniary Loss		53,903.75

There is substantial evidence to support these estimates. The amounts for past doctor and hospital bills, for the cost of drugs, and for a past loss of earnings, were either stipulated to, evidence was offered on, or is a simple matter of calculation. These items totaled $18,103.75. While the amount of $25,800 estimated as the cost of future medical expense, for loss of future earnings and for the future cost of drugs, may seem high, there was substantial evidence that future medical expense is certain to be high. There is also substantial evidence that plaintiff's future earning capacity may be substantially impaired by reason of the injury. The amounts estimated for those various items are not out of line, and find support in the evidence.

This leaves the amount of $134,000 presumably allowed for the nonpecuniary items of damage, including pain and suffering, past and future. It is this allowance that defendants seriously attack as being excessive as a matter of law.

It must be remembered that the jury fixed these damages, and that the trial judge denied a motion for new trial, one ground of which was excessiveness of the award. These determinations are entitled to great weight. The amount of damages is a fact question, first committed to the discretion of the jury and next to the discretion of the trial judge on a motion for new trial. They see and hear the witnesses and frequently, as in this case, see the injury and the impairment that has resulted therefrom. As a result, all presumptions are in favor of the decision of the trial court. The power of the appellate court differs materially from that of the trial court in passing on this question. An appellate court can interfere on the ground that the judgment is excessive only on the ground that the verdict is so large that, at first blush, it shocks the conscience and suggests passion, prejudice or corruption on the part of the jury. The proper rule was stated in *Holmes v. Southern Cal. Edison Co.*, 78 Cal.App.2d 43, 51 [177 P.2d 32], as follows: "The powers and duties of a trial judge in ruling on a motion for new trial and of an appellate court on an appeal from a judgment are very different when the question of an excessive award of damages arises. The trial judge sits as a thirteenth juror with the power to weigh the evidence and judge the credibility of the witnesses. If he believes the damages awarded by the jury to be excessive and the question is presented it becomes his duty to reduce them. When the question is raised his denial of a motion for new trial is an indication that he approves the amount of the award. An appellate court has no such powers. It cannot weigh the evidence and pass on the credibility of the witnesses as a juror does. To hold an award excessive it must be so large as to indicate passion or prejudice on the part of the jurors." . . .

There are no fixed or absolute standards by which an appellate court can measure in monetary terms the extent of the damages suffered by a plaintiff as a result of the wrongful act of the defendant. The duty of an appellate court is to uphold the jury and trial judge whenever possible. The amount to be awarded is "a matter on which there legitimately may be a wide difference of opinion." In considering the contention that the damages are excessive the appellate court must determine every conflict in the evidence in respondent's favor, and must give him the benefit of every inference reasonably to be drawn from the record.

While the appellate court should consider the amounts awarded in prior cases for similar injuries, obviously, each case must be decided on its own facts and circumstances. Such examination demonstrates that such awards vary greatly. Injuries are seldom identical and the amount of pain and suffering involved in similar physical injuries varies widely. These factors must be considered. Basically, the question that should be decided by the appellate courts is whether or not the verdict is so out of line with reason that it shocks the conscience and necessarily implies that the verdict must have been the result of passion and prejudice.

In the instant case, the nonpecuniary items of damage include allowances for pain and suffering, past and future, humiliation as a result of being disfigured and being permanently crippled, and constant anxiety and fear that the leg will have to be amputated. While the amount of the award is high, and may be more than we would have awarded were we the trier of the facts, considering the nature of the injury, the great pain and suffering, past and future, and the other items of damage, we cannot say, as a matter of law, that it is so high that it shocks the conscience and gives rise to the presumption that it was the result of passion or prejudice on the part of the jurors.

Defendants next complain that it was prejudicial error for plaintiff's counsel to argue to the jury that damages for pain and suffering could be fixed by means of a mathematical formula predicated upon a per diem allowance for this item of damages. The propriety of such an argument seems never to have been passed upon in this state. In other jurisdictions there is a sharp divergence of opinion on the subject. It is not necessary to pass on the propriety of such argument in the instant case because, when plaintiff's counsel made the argument in question, defendants' counsel did not object, assign it as misconduct or ask that the jury be admonished to disregard it. Moreover, in his argument to the jury, the defendants' counsel also adopted a mathematical formula type of argument. This being so, even if such argument were error (a point we do not pass upon), the point must be deemed to have been waived, and cannot be raised, properly, on appeal.

The judgment appealed from is affirmed.

TRAYNOR, J. I dissent.

Although I agree that there was no prejudicial error on the issue of liability, it is my opinion that the award of $134,000 for pain and suffering is so excessive as to indicate that it was prompted by passion, prejudice, whim, or caprice.[1]

[1] The award of $53,903.75 for pecuniary loss, past and future, is also suspect. The amount awarded for future medical expenses is $12,196.25 greater than the medical expenses incurred

Before the accident plaintiff was employed as a file clerk at a salary of $375 a month. At the time of the trial she had returned to her job at the same salary and her foot had healed sufficiently for her to walk. At the time of the accident she was 42 years old with a life expectancy of 34.9 years.

During closing argument plaintiff's counsel summarized the evidence relevant to past and possible future damages and proposed a specific amount for each item. His total of $187,903.75 was the exact amount awarded by the jury.

His proposed amounts were as follows:

[Total Pecuniary Loss, as above, amounted to		$ 53,903.75]
Pain and Suffering:		
From time of accident to time of trial (660 days) at $100 a day	$ 66,000.00	
For the remainder of her life (34 years) at $2,000 a year	68,000.00	134,000.00
Total proposed by counsel		187,903.75

The jury and the trial court have broad discretion in determining the damages in a personal injury case. A reviewing court, however, has responsibilities not only to the litigants in an action but to future litigants and must reverse or remit when a jury awards either inadequate or excessive damages.

The crucial question in this case, therefore, is whether the award of $134,000 for pain and suffering is so excessive it must have resulted from passion, prejudice, whim or caprice. "To say that a verdict has been influenced by passion or prejudice is but another way of saying that the verdict exceeds any amount justified by the evidence."

There has been forceful criticism of the rationale for awarding damages for pain and suffering in negligence cases. (Morris, *Liability for Pain and Suffering*, 59 COLUMB. L. REV. 476; Plant, *Damages for Pain and Suffering*, 19 OHIO L.J. 200; Jaffe, *Damages for Personal Injury: The Impact of Insurance*, 18 LAW AND CONTEMPORARY PROBLEMS 219; Zelermyer, *Damages for Pain and Suffering*, 6 SYRACUSE L. REV. 27.) Such damages originated under primitive law as a means of punishing

from the time of the accident to the time of trial, a period of nearly two years. The amount awarded for future loss of earnings is $4,500 greater than plaintiff's past loss of earnings. Yet the evidence indicates that plaintiff's medical care has been largely completed and that the future loss of earnings will not exceed the earnings lost by the prolonged stays in the hospital and the rehabilitation center.

wrongdoers and assuaging the feelings of those who had been wronged. They become increasingly anomalous as emphasis shifts in a mechanized society from ad hoc punishment to orderly distribution of losses through insurance and the price of goods or of transportation. Ultimately such losses are borne by a public free of fault as part of the price for the benefits of mechanization.

Nonetheless, this state has long recognized pain and suffering as elements of damages in negligence cases; any change in this regard must await reexamination of the problem by the Legislature. Meanwhile, awards for pain and suffering serve to ease plaintiffs' discomfort and to pay for attorney fees for which plaintiffs are not otherwise compensated.

It would hardly be possible ever to compensate a person fully for pain and suffering. " 'No rational being would change places with the injured man for an amount of gold that would fill the room of the court, yet no lawyer would contend that such is the legal measure of damages.' " "Translating pain and anguish into dollars can, at best, be only an arbitrary allowance, and not a process of measurement, and consequently the judge can, in his instructions give the jury no standard to go by; he can only tell them to allow such amount as in their discretion they may consider reasonable. [The] chief reliance for reaching reasonable results in attempting to value suffering in terms of money must be the restraint and common sense of the [jury]." (MCCORMICK, DAMAGES, § 88, pp. 318–319.) Such restraint and common sense were lacking here.

A review of reported cases involving serious injuries and large pecuniary losses reveals that ordinarily the part of the verdict attributable to pain and suffering does not exceed the part attributable to pecuniary losses. The award in this case of $134,000 for pain and suffering exceeds not only the pecuniary losses but any such award heretofore sustained in this state even in cases involving injuries more serious by far than those suffered by plaintiff. Although excessive damages is "an issue which is primarily factual and is not therefore a matter which can be decided upon the basis of awards made in other cases," awards for similar injuries may be considered as one factor to be weighed in determining whether the damages awarded are excessive.

The excessive award in this case was undoubtedly the result of the improper argument of plaintiff's counsel to the jury. Though no evidence was introduced, though none could possibly be introduced on the monetary value of plaintiff's suffering, counsel urged the jury to award $100 a day for pain and suffering from the time of the accident to the time of trial and $2,000 a year for pain and suffering for the remainder of plaintiff's life.

The propriety of counsel's proposing a specific sum for each day or month of suffering has recently been considered by courts of several jurisdictions. The reason usually advanced for not allowing such argument is that since there is no way of translating pain and suffering into monetary terms, counsel's proposal of a particular sum for each day of suffering represents an opinion and a conclusion on matters not disclosed by the evidence, and tends to mislead the jury and result in excessive awards. The reason usually advanced for allowing "per diem argument for pain and suffering" is that it affords the jury as good an arbitrary measure as any for that which cannot be measured.

Counsel may argue all legitimate inferences from the evidence, but he may not employ arguments that tend primarily to mislead the jury. A specified sum for pain and suffering for any particular period is bound to be conjectural. Positing such a sum for a small period of time and then multiplying that sum by the number of days, minutes or seconds in plaintiff's life expectancy multiplies the hazards of conjecture. Counsel could arrive at any amount he wished by adjusting either the period of time to be taken as a measure or the amount surmised for the pain for that period.

"The absurdity of a mathematical formula is demonstrated by applying it to its logical conclusion. If a day may be used as a unit of time in measuring pain and suffering, there is no logical reason why an hour or a minute or a second could not be used, or perhaps even a heart-beat since we live from heart-beat to heart-beat. If one cent were used for each second of pain this would amount to $3.60 per hour, to $86.40 per twenty-four hour day, and to $31,536 per year. The absurdity of such a result must be apparent, yet a penny a second for pain and suffering might not sound unreasonable. [The] use of the formula was prejudicial error."

The misleading effect of the per diem argument was not cured by the use of a similar argument by defense counsel. Truth is not served by a clash of sophistic arguments. Had defendant objected to the improper argument of plaintiff's counsel this error would be a sufficient ground for reversal whether or not the award was excessive as a matter of law. Defendant's failure to object, however, did not preclude its appeal on the ground that the award was excessive as a matter of law or preclude this court's reversing on that ground and ruling on the impropriety of counsel's argument to guide the court on the retrial.

I would reverse the judgment and remand the cause for a new trial on the issue of damages.

SHARMAN V. EVANS

High Court of Australia, 1977.
138 C.L.R. 563.

GIBBS and STEPHEN JJ.

The defendant, Dennis Sharman, appeals against the dismissal, by a majority of the New South Wales Court of Appeal, of his appeal from a verdict for $300,547.50 in favour of the plaintiff, June Marilyn Evans.

Miss Evans, then aged twenty, was injured in a motor car accident in December 1971. She suffered very serious injuries including brain stem damage; she was unconscious for almost a month and is now a quadriplegic. This condition, disastrous enough in itself, is in her case aggravated by trauma-caused epilepsy, by unusually severe impairment to her respiratory function as a consequence of the brain injury and by an almost total loss of the ability to speak because of the injury to the larynx. She is fully aware of her plight.

By the time of the trial, in November 1973, Miss Evans had undergone a great number of operations and had endured much pain; her condition had become stabilized and her disabilities could then be summarized, in the reasons for judgment of the learned trial judge (Sheppard J.) in the following terms:

1. She suffers from quadriplegia with the problems to which I have already referred. She has more movement in her right arm than her left but the movement is nevertheless restricted and she cannot make anything like full use of her right hand. She is able to eat, paint and operate a typewriter as well as point to the card to which I have referred but she cannot do up buttons, brush her teeth, or her hair or use a pen. She can be sat in a wheel chair but if she is not propped up she will collapse to one side. She is able to operate, with the use of her right hand, the mechanism of an electric chair but, according to Dr. Griffiths, she is not a good driver. She has no hope, as do some quadriplegics, of ever driving a motor vehicle however it may be adapted.

2. She has the inability to speak which I have mentioned.

3. She is an epileptic but her epilepsy is controlled, for the time being, by drugs.

4. She has lost some intellectual capacity but is still intelligent, capable of reading and painting, and is well aware of her predicament.

5. She has continuing pain in her right shoulder which is relieved by the taking of analgesics.

Before the accident the prospects for Miss Evans' future were bright; she was a healthy, out-going and intelligent girl who was trained for and was experienced in secretarial work; by taking two jobs in her home State of Western Australia she had saved enough money to undertake a two-year full-time course as a resident student at the Commonwealth Bible College in Brisbane. At the time of the accident, she had just completed her first year there, coming dux of her year. She had an understanding with a young man, a fellow student, that they would marry in due course. After the accident their engagement was announced and but for her ultimate decision that she could not permit him to take as his wife a quadriplegic she would by the time of the trial have been married to him; he has a good position and a secure future in the Department of Civil Aviation. Had she resumed her secretarial work after finishing her two-year college course she could have earned at least $70 per week net.

In these circumstances the learned trial judge, in a most carefully reasoned judgment, assessed general damages at $275,000, the agreed special damages of some $25,500 making a total of just over $300,000.

Three consequences of her injuries account in large measure for the size of the award of general damages; her need for intensive nursing and medical attention in the future, her total loss of earning capacity and the gross impairment of the future enjoyment and amenities of her life. She has, in addition, experienced particularly severe pain and suffering and her life expectancy has been substantially reduced.

The learned trial judge did not essay any exact quantification of damages for every item of detriment suffered by the plaintiff. He arrived at a range of from $150,000 to $175,000 for the future cost of her nursing and medical care and at a sum of $6,000 for the shortened life expectancy of the plaintiff. He explained with clarity and in detail his approach to the assessment of damages for each other item but concluded that they did not lend themselves to any precise individual quantification. In arriving at the total of $275,000 for general damages his Honour expressed his keen awareness of the need to guard against overlap in undertaking that process of separate consideration of components of the award which he had felt obliged to engage upon.

[A] variety of difficulties, both of principle and of fact, surround the assessment of damages in this case. They stem from at least three distinct sources: the great increase in the cost of future nursing care should the plaintiff be cared for at home rather than in hospital; a variety of problems involved in assessing compensation for the plaintiff's loss of future earning capacity and, finally, the doubts as to the plaintiff's present life expectancy.

That the learned trial judge should have engaged in a close scrutiny of each head of detriment was, we think, inevitable; that in doing so he should seek to evaluate that detriment in money terms was a necessary consequence of the fact that it is only by recourse to those terms that the plaintiff can be compensated for the wrong done to her. Criticism was directed both to this separate examination of the conventional heads of damage and also to the ascertainment of a sum appropriate as a starting point for compensation under a particular head of damages, followed by a process of discounting or deduction from it. We regard this criticism as misconceived; so long as courts are careful to avoid the risk, inherent in such a procedure, of compensating twice over for the one detriment there seems no better way of applying processes of reasoning and the realistic and methodical evaluation of probabilities to the task of assessing compensation. In cases of any complexity any other approach is open to serious objection, especially in times of rapid inflation. Moreover where the assessment of damages is undertaken by a judge sitting without a jury it is, we think, most desirable that the process of assessment should be described in the reasons for judgment. [It] is only by the setting out in a judgment of the main components of an award of damages, or at least of the approach taken to each component, that the parties may obtain a proper insight into the process of assessment and an adequate opportunity of seeking the correction of error on appeal. In the particular circumstances of this case Sheppard J. found himself unable to assign anything like precise money sums to the different heads of damages; he did however very clearly explain his approach to each head of damages, a course which has lightened the task of appellate courts.

It is appropriate to examine the various heads of damage which presented themselves for assessment so as to appreciate and deal with the various criticisms raised by the appellant. First are those costs which the plaintiff will be obliged to incur in consequence of her injuries, principally although not exclusively, the cost of nursing and medical care. It is clear that she will require such care for the rest of her life. It can be provided either in a hospital in Perth devoted to the care of persons incapacitated as she is or, at very much greater cost, in her own home. The plaintiff would much prefer the latter but the question is whether the defendant should be required to make compensation upon this much more expensive basis. The learned trial judge's award of damages contemplated that the plaintiff, while spending the greater part of her life in hospital, would spend some part of it being cared for at home.

Where the plaintiff is to be cared for in the future will not only directly affect the extent of nursing and medical expenses which are to be compensated for; it will also bear upon the extent of her loss of the amenities and enjoyment of life, a lifetime substantially spent in hospital will greatly aggravate that loss. In our view the medical evidence in this case does not justify the conclusion that the defendant should be required to compensate for future nursing and medical expenses on any basis other than that the plaintiff's future will be one substantially spent in hospital.

The appropriate criterion must be that such expenses as the plaintiff may reasonably incur should be recoverable from the defendant; as Barwick C.J. put it in *Arthur Robinson (Grafton) Pty. Ltd. v. Carter* (1968) 122 CLR 649, at p 661 "The question here is not what are the ideal requirements but what are the reasonable requirements of the respondent." The touchstone of reasonableness in the case of the cost of providing nursing and medical care for the plaintiff in the future is, no doubt, cost matched against health benefits to the plaintiff. If cost is very great and benefits to health slight or speculative the cost-involving treatment will clearly be unreasonable, the more so if there is available an alternative and relatively inexpensive mode of treatment, affording equal or only slightly lesser benefits. When the factors are more evenly balanced no intuitive answer presents itself and the real difficulty of attempting to weigh against each other two incomparables, financial cost against relative health benefits to the plaintiff, becomes manifest. The present case is however one which does to our minds allow of a definite answer; it is a case of alternatives in which the difference in relative costs is great whereas the benefit to the plaintiff of the more expensive alternative is entirely one of amenity, in no way involving physical or mental well-being. This may be demonstrated from the evidence.

Assuming, for convenience of comparison, a life expectancy of twenty years, the future expenses of the plaintiff if confined to hospital would be of the order of a present value, computed on six per cent tables, of $108,500, inclusive of nursing, medical and physiotherapy services and cost of special beds etc. The provision to her of like services at her mother's home over that period would amount to a present value of about $390,000, to which would have to be added a weekly cost for medicaments etc. of about $23 per week and a capital cost of some $11,750 for suitable alterations to her mother's home; moreover this is exclusive of the cost of food and of the cost of providing another home should her mother die during the period and the present home cease to be available to the plaintiff. The benefit to the plaintiff of being cared for at home rather than in hospital is not any benefit to her health but rather to her future enjoyment of life which would be enhanced by a home atmosphere; her life would not thereby be prolonged nor would her physical condition be at all improved; indeed she would be somewhat more at risk physically at home than in hospital. There is no evidence suggesting any likely psychiatric benefits, probable though these might appear to the layman.

In these circumstances the future cost of reasonable nursing and medical attention must, we think, be assessed on the basis of a lifetime substantially spent in hospital.

There is another item of future expense which must enter into the assessment process. Because we conclude that the defendant should not be required to compensate the plaintiff on any basis other than that of a lifetime in hospital it follows that the plaintiff's loss of the enjoyment and amenities of life will be the greater. She must be regarded as wholly deprived of the everyday pleasures of living in the environment of her own home. Instead she will be exposed to a lifetime of institutional life. Not only must this be reflected in the damages to be awarded under the conventional head of pain, suffering and the loss of enjoyment and amenities of life. In the present case it is also appropriate to reflect rather more positively one particular aspect of this situation of permanent hospitalization. The effect of the latter upon the plaintiff can clearly be somewhat mitigated if she is able to vary the monotony of the hospital ward by occasional day visits to her home and by other outings, possibly even by occasional weekends away from hospital. The medical evidence discloses that these would be possible provided that constant nursing attention was provided. Applying again the criterion of reasonableness but now weighing the expense of such attention against the clear benefits in amenity and enjoyment of life that such breaks in a lifetime in hospital would provide we are in no doubt that the plaintiff is entitled to compensation for the cost of such outings. That their cost will be high is apparent from the data as to nursing costs already referred to, to which must be added transportation either by ambulance or by chauffeur-driven car.

We turn next to the question of compensation for lost earning capacity and in particular to an examination of the deductions which should be made in assessing that compensation. In doing so we leave aside, for the present, the question of compensation for loss of earning capacity during the years by which the plaintiff's life expectancy has been shortened, the "lost years."

Both principle and authority establish that where, as here, there is included in the award of damages for future nursing and medical care the plaintiff's entire cost of future board and lodging, there will be overcompensation if damages for loss of earning capacity are awarded in full without regard for the fact that the plaintiff is already to receive as compensation the cost of her future board and lodging, a cost which but for her injuries she would otherwise have to meet out of future earnings. If the true concept be that it is lost earning capacity to the extent to which it is likely to be exercised in the future, rather than loss of future earnings, that is to be compensated it may seem inelegant to speak of deducting from damages for that lost capacity an amount for some saving in outgoings. It would better accord with principle if the savings in board and lodging could be isolated from, and excluded from the damages to be awarded in respect of, hospital expenses. However so long as the true nature of the adjustment is understood no harm is done by making an appropriate deduction from the damages for lost earning capacity. What is to be avoided is double compensation and, as is apparent from what was said by their Lordships in *Shearman v. Folland* (1950) 2 KB 43, it is not a question of estimating the plaintiff's likely future costs for board and lodging and treating them as an outgoing which the consequences of the defendant's tortious act have now spared her from making; that is a notion which is as distasteful as it is misconceived. Rather is it a matter of her already having been compensated for future board and lodging as a component of hospital expenses, so that to disregard this and award the full sum for lost earning capacity, part of which would be used to provide the very item of board and lodging already compensated for, would be to award compensation twice over. Accordingly some no doubt fairly arbitrary proportion of the present value of future hospital expenses regarded as attributable to board and lodging must be taken and deducted from the present value of lost earning capacity; it will be quite irrelevant how expensively or how frugally the plaintiff might in fact have lived had she not been injured.

[Where,] as here, a plaintiff suffers a total loss of earning capacity he will not normally continue to incur all of the outgoings necessary for the realization of that capacity which would have been incurred had his capacity been unaffected; items such as the cost of clothing suitable to his particular employment and of transportation to and from work provide examples, no doubt there are others. Compensation for loss of earning capacity is paid only because it is or may be productive of financial loss and to compensate for total loss of earning capacity without making allowance for the cessation of these outgoings is to compensate for a gross loss when it is only the net loss that is in fact suffered.

On the other hand there are other types of saved expenditure upon which a defendant cannot rely in diminution of damages. It is now well established that no reduction is to be made, when awarding damages for loss of earning capacity, for the cost of maintaining oneself and one's dependents unless an element of double compensation would otherwise intrude, as in the case of hospitalization as a non-fee paying patient or where the cost of future hospital expenses is also awarded and necessarily includes, as in the present case, the patient's board and lodging. . . .

The present plaintiff is now denied many of the opportunities for pleasure-giving expenditure, as distinct from what may be regarded as expenditure on maintenance, which our society affords. Are the savings in expenditure, thus involuntarily thrust upon her by reason of the state to which her injuries have reduced her, to have the effect of reducing the damages awarded for her loss of earning capacity? We think not. They may be left out of reckoning, they neither produce double compensation nor compensate for gross rather than net loss. Indeed to treat them as items going to reduce damages is unjustifiably to assume that because pre-accident avenues of expenditure are now foreclosed to a plaintiff the necessary consequence is a corresponding non-expenditure.

We leave aside the case of the plaintiff who by the nature of his injuries is made wholly incapable of experiencing pleasure. . . .

The present plaintiff still possesses powers of enjoyment through the use of her senses; her sight, her hearing and her taste are unaffected and in place of sport, entertainment, cosmetics and clothes she may find pleasure in recorded music, in a movie projector and the hire of films, in days spent on drives in a chauffeured car, perhaps in special foods. She can thus experience pleasure and ward off melancholia by such distractions as may be to her taste and within her means. Many of her former modes of enjoyment are closed to her but some new ones remain to be explored and from which she will be capable of deriving pleasure. It follows that, still disregarding "lost years," it will be appropriate in any assessment of the plaintiff's damages for lost earning capacity to reduce those damages only in respect of the cost of board and lodging actually provided for in the award of damages for future hospital expenses and in respect of those "saved" outgoings associated with the exercise of earning capacity, that is, fares and the like.

As to "lost years," the plaintiff is to be compensated in respect of lost earning capacity during those years by which her life expectancy has been shortened, at least to the extent that they are years when she would otherwise have been earning income. But, unlike the thirty years of her actual post-accident life expectancy, no outgoings whatever will be involved in respect of that period since it is assumed that the plaintiff will then be dead. What adjustments are, then, to be made on that account in assessing damages for loss of earning capacity in respect of those lost years? This is not a question giving rise to considerations of double compensation; the only element involving any possibility of double compensation, the component of board and lodging contained in the award of future hospital expenses, will have ceased to operate by the time that the "lost years" are reached. It is rather a question of confining an award of damages to no more than compensation, ensuring that the plaintiff is merely compensated for loss and is not positively enriched, at the defendant's expense, by the damages awarded.

It is well established in Australia that there should be taken into account in reduction of damages for the lost earning capacity of "lost years" at least the amount that the plaintiff would have expended on his own maintenance during those lost years. . . .

In these circumstances it would, we think, be wrong to treat *Skelton v. Collins* as any authority for the proposition that only surplus income, in effect savings, are to be taken into account in assessing economic loss in the "lost years." [As] Jolowicz observed in a note in the Cambridge Law Journal (1960), at p. 163, "a dead man has no personal expenses," hence there should be a deduction of "the plaintiff's personal living expenses." . . .

There remains one future aspect of the assessment of damages for loss of earning capacity. Loss must depend upon the likelihood that there would have been a future exercise of that earning capacity, but what of a female plaintiff likely to marry and who may cease to exercise her earning capacity on, or at some time after, marriage? Despite recent changes in patterns of employment of married women this remains a not unusual situation, the woman in effect exchanging the exercise of her earning capacity for such financial security as her marriage may provide. The measure of the one of course bears no necessary relationship to the other and the whole situation must be full of critical uncertainties such as whether the plaintiff marries, the extent if any of her employment after marriage, the success of that marriage and the extent to which it in fact provides her with economic security. Perhaps the only relatively certain factor will be her pre-injury possession of earning capacity and this in itself may be sufficient reason, absent any clear evidence pointing in a contrary direction, for the adoption of the expedient course of simply disregarding the prospect of marriage as a relevant factor in the assessment of such a plaintiff's future economic loss; this course at least recognizes the plaintiff's retention of capacity, which would have been available to her for exercise, in case of need, despite her marriage.

The last two heads of damages which call for particular mention are those conventionally described as pain, suffering and loss of the enjoyment and amenities of life and damages for shortening of life expectancy. As to the latter it bears no relationship to lost earning capacity during "lost years" but is rather the loss of a measure of prospective happiness; it is not compensation for "the mental distress due to the realization of the loss." That forms instead a part of the general damages for pain and suffering. In the present case a figure "of the order of" $6,000 was allowed for this item. If it be correct that compensation under this head is not to take into account the anguish of mind which any appreciation of the loss may cause, that being compensated for under another head, then Windeyer J.'s suggested maximum figure of $6,000, which reflected this very factor, may be thought to have been excessive at the time and to depart from the general standard of the "conventional sum" which the courts have quite arbitrarily fixed upon ever since *Benham v. Gambling*, [1941] A.C. 157. The amount awarded may properly take into account a fall in the value of money but is to be no more than a quite conventional sum, very moderate in amount. In our view, despite the fall in the value of money, $6,000 departs from previous notions of what is appropriate under this curious and unsatisfactory head of damages. We would have thought that the sum of $2,000 is about the amount now appropriate as the conventional award under this head.

It remains only to say something about damages for loss of the enjoyment and amenities of life. It is in this field that there exists the need to recall what has often been said about fairness, moderation and the undesirability of striving to provide an injured plaintiff with "perfect" compensation. The warning against attempting perfectly to compensate means, we think, in the case of pecuniary loss, no more than the need to make allowance for contingencies, for the vicissitudes of life, compensating for probable rather than for merely speculative detriments. But when a non-pecuniary detriment is in question the injunction against "perfect" compensation means rather more. It cannot refer to the exclusion of all question of punishment of the wrongdoer; the word "compensation" standing on its own would be sufficient to do this; rather is it designed to remind that the maiming of a plaintiff and its consequences cannot wholly be made good by an award of damages and that the recognition of this fact is to be no occasion for any instinctive response that no amount is too large to atone for the plaintiff's suffering. Such a response will be unfair to the defendant and may be of little advantage to the plaintiff; many consequences of injury are not capable of remedy by the receipt of damages, particularly those of the most personal character—the loss of the opportunity of a fulfilling marriage, of parenthood, of sexual satisfaction, of the realization of ambitions. It is very much at these detriments that the warning against any attempt at "perfect" compensation must be aimed. The authorities also require, as does good sense, that to the extent that damages awarded under other heads produce freedom from economic uncertainty and the availability of funds for pleasurable activities, the less will be the loss to be compensated under this head. This will be of particular relevance when a considerable sum is assessed for lost earning capacity.

Having made these general observations concerning the award of damages in a case such as the present it remains only to look more specifically at the damages in fact awarded. . . .

[The court reduced the award by $30,000 to $270,547.50, two of five justices dissenting.]

PROBLEMS

1. Should pain and suffering be compensated at all? Justice Traynor's dissent in *Seffert* notes academic debate on this point. Should the law go back to the drawing board here?

a. Does the general rule on remedies help us resolve the question? Will a remedy that excludes recovery for pain and suffering leave the plaintiff in the position she would have occupied if the wrong had not been committed? Will a remedy that includes recovery for pain and suffering meet that goal? Which comes closer? Does that depend on the ability of juries to make appropriate awards? How can we tell whether the awards are appropriate? Should the law define the position but for the wrong as the monetary position but for the wrong, thus eliminating the intractable problem of evaluating nonmonetary injuries?

b. Justice Traynor argues that awards for pain and suffering serve less purpose when the goal is "orderly distribution of losses through insurance and the price of goods or of transportation." Is that because pain and suffering are losses that should not be distributed? Or is the concern that goods and services would cost too much if the price included the pain and suffering caused by their production and distribution? Does that assume that awards for pain and suffering inevitably will be very large? If you could buy insurance against pain and suffering (say, as part of your health insurance policy), how large a premium would you pay? Would that make more sense than relying on liability insurance, which must include not only the value of the pain and suffering, but also the cost of litigation to determine liability? Should pain policies be offered? Why aren't they offered today? If private insurers will not offer pain policies, should the government fill this gap with a program similar to unemployment insurance or social security disability benefits?

c. Justice Traynor suggests that pain and suffering originated as punitive sanctions against wrongdoers. That history is questionable; at least one scholar has suggested that punitive damages originated as compensation for distress and indignity at a time when courts refused to compensate for nonmonetary losses. Dorsey D. Ellis, Jr., *Fairness and Efficiency in the Law of Punitive Damages*, 56 S. CAL. L. REV. 1 (1982). Assume, however, that Traynor is correct. Does the argument prove too much? Is there any difference between punitive damages and compensation for pain that would justify treating them differently? Must we eliminate both punitive damages and pain and suffering in order to achieve the ends he seeks? Would it suffice to exclude punitive damages from liability insurance coverage, so the penalty fell on the wrongdoer, not the insurer?

d. What about deterrence? On one theory, damages should equal the amount of harm so that the wrongdoer has the right incentive to prevent harm, when that will cost less than the harm. The flip side is that when prevention will cost more than the harm prevented, the prevention is inefficient and should not be incurred. If one's goal is to deter optimally, should pain and suffering be included in the recovery? Does the question turn on whether they can be assessed accurately?

2. If pain and suffering should be compensated, is there any way to assess pain appropriately?

a. According to some theorists, a damage award should make the plaintiff indifferent between two states: having both the damage award and the injury; or having neither the damage award nor the injury. Was $134,000 enough to make Ms. Seffert indifferent between having the injury and not having it? Did that amount make her better off than if the injury had not occurred? Will any amount of money hit Ms. Evans' indifference curve? Is the case exceptional?

b. Is the focus on the plaintiffs inappropriate? What about market transactions? Can we look to the market and see how much people charge for the infliction of pain? Is the black market (snuff films, prostitution, etc.) the only place to find such transactions?

c. Can we approximate the price of pain by looking at how much people charge to undertake a risk of pain? Some occupations are more dangerous than others (soldiers, police, firemen), some locations more dangerous than others (high crime areas). The difference in salaries required to get people to work in high risk occupations or areas gives us the price people charge for an X% increase in risk of painful injuries. Can we multiply this figure to determine the implicit price for a 100% risk of injury? Even if not completely accurate, might this give us an approximation that would avoid the grossest excesses of either eliminating pain and suffering or tolerating any outrageous figure a jury decides to award?

d. Could offsetting joys be used as a measure of pain? Money cannot eliminate pain, but can buy pleasures. If fine wine and gourmet food are the only pleasures left Ms. Evans, might an award large enough to provide her those pleasures compensate for the loss of other pleasures (marriage, parenthood, athletics, and any other joyful activity she no longer can pursue) and the physical pain? Would that at least offer juries a framework for decision—one bounded by market measures, rather than completely subjective—that might make an award practical?

e. Is pain completely unmeasurable, at least in terms of money? Are the suggestions above pointless because the awards are inherently speculative and uncontrollable?

3. Do per diem arguments help or hurt? If pain cannot be measured in any plausible way, does thinking about pain by the day (or the hour) change anything? If pain can be measured in a plausible way, does thinking about pain by the day (or the hour) change anything? Is the only point of breaking the time period down into smaller units to trick juries into awarding larger amounts than they ever would have considered? Is that because jurors never would have realized how appropriate the larger amount was? Or would the jurors' innate good sense have avoided an inappropriately large amount, if not beguiled by the per diem argument?

4. Consider the cases. Ms. Evans received about $50,000 to $80,000 (Australian) for pain and suffering; Ms. Seffert received about $134,000 (US). Does that seem right? Is the difference that the damage to Ms. Evans' nerve passages that produced quadriplegia also reduced the amount of pain she felt? Only one shoulder produced persistent pain, whereas Ms. Seffert suffered considerably throughout the surgeries. Is that too narrow an interpretation of pain? Ms. Evans lost considerable opportunity for joy: a life expectancy shortened by about 20 years, a drastically reduced ability to enjoy the years she would live. Should pain and suffering include those losses? Does it? Is pain and suffering limited to the mental distress associated with the lost opportunities? Or is the phrase broad enough to include absence of pleasure?

5. Does the *Sharman* court handle the lost life expectancy appropriately? Ms. Evans lost perhaps 30 years of life, during which she might have experienced joy. Whatever we do with lost income for that period,

how can the court say that $6,000 is too much, that only $2,000 is needed to compensate for the joy lost in those years? What is the virtue of awarding an "arbitrary" or "conventional" sum, of "quite modest amount"? Why is it error to award more?

6. The court in *Sharman* refers to general and special damages. Those words invoke a confusing array of ideas; you probably should never use them. But you may need to understand them as others use them.

In tort cases, special usually refers to out-of-pocket losses, such as medical expenses and lost wages. These losses can be proven relatively easily by looking at medical bills or pay stubs (from before the injury). General damages refers to damages not measurable in market terms: distress, pain, suffering, loss of joy, etc. These are more speculative in amount. This is not exactly how parties in *Sharman* used the terms. They agreed that special damages totaled $25,547.50. But some of the general damages discussed in the opinion (future lost wages and future medical care) would be called special damages by some attorneys. The court treats future pecuniary losses—which must be projected, without receipts for actual expenses—as general damages, presumably because they have not been reduced to a sum certain at the time of trial.

In contract cases, the terminology is almost reversed. General damages refers to market measures, such as the difference between the market price (or cover price) and contract price of performance. These losses usually occur, they flow naturally from the breach. (Note the similarity to the first prong of the test for foreseeability under *Hadley v. Baxendale*, 9 Ex. 341, 156 Eng. Rep. 145 (1854).) Special damages include losses peculiar to the plaintiff, the kind that might not occur in every case. Lost profits and other consequential damages are classified as special. General damages are easily proven by reference to market values and might be reduced to a sum certain before trial; special damages require more speculation about future events and thus defy easy proof.

Another term commonly used by courts is "incidental damages." Incidental damages are expenses incurred in the process of mitigation. For example, where a defendant breached a contract to deliver goods to plaintiff, the costs that plaintiff incurs in finding replacement goods are generally recoverable as incidental damages. *See Mitsui O.S.K. Lines, Ltd. v. Consolidated Rail Corp.*, 743 A.2d 362 (N.J. Super. A.D. 2000).

Not much is gained by distinguishing general and special damages. More specific labels, such as lost profits or pain and suffering, seem more accurate and less prone to misinterpretation. Sometimes the law makes distinctions important, such pleading rules requiring detailed information about special damages but allowing general damages to be pled with a vague statement. Similarly, a contract may make the difference important by disclaiming special damages but not general damages. In practice, lawyers tend to refer to consequential damages rather than special damages in clauses limiting remedies, to avoid the confusion noted here.

7. Concern for pain and suffering stems largely from the impression that tort damages are out of control. While headlines focus on the most spectacular cases, there is considerable debate about the scope of the problem, including some suggestions that damage awards are not so far out of control as many believe. *See, e.g.*, Deborah R. Hensler, *Trends in Tort Litigation: Findings from the Institute for Civil Justice's Research*, 48 Ohio St. L.J. 479 (1987). In an effort to control the largest awards, some states have limited the amount of nonpecuniary losses a plaintiff may recover, at least in some tort actions. *See, e.g.*, CAL. CIVIL CODE § 3333.2 ($250,000 cap on noneconomic damages in medical malpractice actions); Colo. Rev. Stat. § 24–10–114(1) (limiting damages against public entities to $150,000 per person, $600,000 per occurrence). Some courts have rejected limits on state constitutional grounds, while others have upheld them. *Compare, e.g., Lakin v. Senco Products, Inc.*, 329 Or. 62, 987 P.2d 463 (1999) (rejecting cap on nonpecuniary damages) *with Evans v. Alaska*, 56 P.3d 1046 (Alaska 2002) (upholding caps on nonpecuniary and punitive damages, inter alia). These provisions bring the average verdict down, thus improving the solvency of insurers. They achieve that goal at the expense of the people who suffer the worst injuries. David Baldus, John C. MacQueen, & George Woodworth, *Improving Judicial Oversight of Jury Damages Assessments: A Proposal for the Comparative Additur/Remittitur Review of Awards for nonpecuniary Harms and Punitive Damages*, 80 IOWA L. REV. 1109 (1995). Is this compromise more satisfactory than the other ideas discussed? How well does it achieve the goals the legal system sets?

8. *Casey's Inhaler*. Casey's discomfort does not rise to the level of either Ms. Seffert's or Ms. Evans.' Cases involving modest pain will arise more frequently, but will attract far less attention from the media (and, perhaps, from the trial bar). Would rejecting pain in these be justifiable? Is modest pain easier to assess? Would Casey's judgment be inadequate without pain?

WAINWRIGHT V. FONTENOT

774 So.2d 70 (La. 2000).

KIMBALL, J.

At issue in this delictual action is whether a factfinder errs as a matter of law when it declines to award general damages after finding defendant at fault for plaintiff's injuries and awarding special damages for plaintiff's medical expenses. Following a jury trial in the Fourteenth Judicial District Court for the Parish of Calcasieu, the jury completed a Jury Verdict Form in which it found that the conduct of defendant was the legal cause of injuries sustained by plaintiffs' minor child. The jury awarded plaintiff $1,500.00 in medical expenses but no general damages. On appeal, the third circuit concluded that the jury had committed legal error in awarding medical expenses but declining to award general damages for injuries that exhibited objective symptoms. The court then increased the medical expenses award to $7,372.00 and awarded general damages of $40,000.00. We granted writs and, finding that there is no inconsistency in the awards made by the jury in this case, now reverse.

FACTS

In July 1995, there was a late-night grease fire in the kitchen of the Wainwright home. Bert John Wainwright ("Bert"), the father of John Scott Wainwright ("John Scott"), was burned while putting out the fire. Soon thereafter, John Scott began to exhibit signs of stress. When John Scott's anxiety did not subside, Bert and John Scott's mother, Jenna Cay Wainwright ("Jenna"), sought counseling for John Scott with Dr. Charles Monlezun, a clinical social worker.

Dr. Monlezun first saw John Scott on February 7, 1996, and diagnosed him with post-traumatic stress disorder. Following several visits with John Scott, Dr. Monlezun referred John Scott to Dr. John Bambanek, a board-certified child psychiatrist. On March 7, 2000, Dr. Bambanek prescribed Prozac for John Scott. Dr. Bambanek ordered five milligrams of Prozac once daily, which he testified in his video-taped trial deposition was about one-quarter the normal adult dose of twenty milligrams. The Wainwrights filled Dr. Bamabanek's prescription at a pharmacy operated by Walgreen Louisiana Company, Inc. ("Walgreen").

Walgreen does not dispute that, on March 7, 1996, pharmacist Romona Fontenot ("Fontenot") incorrectly filled the prescription by placing on the label instructions for one dose of twenty milligrams per day rather than the five milligrams per day prescribed by Dr. Bambanek. On the morning of March 9, 1996 Bert gave John Scott his first twenty milligram dose of Prozac. The Wainwrights have argued throughout that, almost immediately thereafter, John Scott's emotional state worsened and that he became increasingly combative and aggressive.

Bert gave John Scott a second twenty milligram dose on the morning of March 10, 1996. Again, the Wainwrights argue, John Scott became irrational and violent, threatening his mother with a fireplace poker and indicating that he would do harm to himself. That same day, Jenna called the Walgreen pharmacy and spoke to the pharmacy manager, Sharon Courrege ("Courrege"). Jenna asked Courrege to confirm that the Wainwrights were giving John Scott the correct dosage by checking Dr. Bambanek's original prescription. Courrege admitted at trial that she did not check the original prescription, but told Jenna that she had done so and that twenty milligrams was the dosage prescribed by Dr. Bambanek.

The following day, March 11, 1996, the Wainwrights gave John Scott a third twenty milligram dose of Prozac. The Wainwrights maintain that John Scott again became combative and violent, ultimately requiring Bert to physically restrain him. That afternoon, the Wainwrights consulted Dr. Monlezun about John Scott's erratic behavior over the weekend. Dr. Monlezun in turn called Dr. Bambanek, who confirmed that he had prescribed only five milligrams of Prozac, not the twenty milligrams indicated on the label printed by Fontenot. The Wainwrights then took John Scott to the Children's Clinic in Lake Charles. John Scott was admitted for observation and testing and released the afternoon of March 12, 1996.

On February 6, 1997, Bert and Jenna Wainwright filed suit, individually and on behalf of John Scott, naming as defendants Fontenot, Walgreen and Kemper National Insurance Company, Walgreen's liability insurer. Plaintiffs sought general damages as well as damages for medical expenses, past and future counseling expenses, and loss of consortium for both Bert and Jenna, all of which they urged stemmed from Walgreen's negligence in filling the prescription and John Scott's subsequent overdose. They also urged that John Scott's academic performance had suffered as a result of the overdose.

The case was tried to a jury in the Fourteenth Judicial District Court for the Parish of Calcasieu. In its answers to a Jury Verdict Form, the jury found that Walgreen's conduct was the legal cause of the injuries to John Scott, assessing 99% of the fault to Walgreen and 1% to Bert. The jury awarded plaintiffs $1,500.00 in medical expenses, but declined to award general damages for John Scott or loss of consortium damages to Bert and Jenna. The jury also declined to make any award for future counseling or tutorial expenses.[4]

---

[4] Pertinent to our discussion here are the following interrogatories on the Jury Verdict Form and the jury's responses:

1. Was there any fault on the part of Walgreen Louisiana Company, Inc., which was the legal cause of the injuries to the plaintiffs' son, John Scott Wainwright?

Yes (X) No ( )

If you answered "No" to any of the preceding questions, do not answer any more questions. Sign and date this form and return it to the courtroom. If your answer is "Yes," proceed to Question Number Two.

[Questions Two and Three asked the jury to decide whether any fault was attributable to Bert Wainwright, and, if so, to allocate fault. The jury assessed 99% of the fault to Walgreen and 1% to Bert.]

4. Without consideration for the percentages listed above, what total amounts in dollars and cents will compensate plaintiffs' son, John Scott Wainwright, for his damages?

[Questions Five and Six asked the jury whether Bert and/or Jenna were entitled to damages for loss of consortium. The jury made no award to either of them.]

Pain and suffering	$(0)
Mental anguish	$(0)
Loss of enjoyment of life	$(0)
Medical expenses	$1500.00
Future counseling expenses	$(0)
Future tutorial expenses	$(0)

Plaintiffs timely appealed to the third circuit, urging that the jury erred in awarding inadequate medical expenses, in assigning fault to Bert, and in failing to award general damages, future counseling and tutorial expenses, and loss of consortium damages. In a published opinion, the third circuit panel amended the trial court judgment, increasing the medical expenses award from $1,500.00 to $7,372.00. The court of appeal also awarded general damages for John Scott's injuries, finding that it was legal error for the jury to award medical expenses while declining to award general damages for injuries that presented objective symptoms.

In assessing quantum, the court of appeal reasoned that "when the trier of fact fails to award damages, the abuse of discretion standard does not apply. Rather, an appellate court reviews the quantum issue *de novo*." The majority of the three-judge panel concluded that, based on the trial testimony as to the negative effect of the overdose on John Scott, a general damages award of $40,000.00 was warranted.

One judge concurred in part and dissented in part. He agreed with the majority that the jury had erred in refusing to grant general damages in this case, but dissented as to the increased medical expenses award and the amount of the majority's general damages award. In his view, plaintiffs were entitled to "a general damage award of no more than $2,500 for this regrettable but minor episode."

LAW AND DISCUSSION

The fundamental principle of tort liability in Louisiana is that "[e]very act whatever of man that causes damage to another obliges him by whose fault it happened to repair it." La. Civ.Code art. 2315. Thus, in a negligence action under article 2315, the plaintiff bears the burden of proving fault, causation and damages. "One injured through the fault of another is entitled to full indemnification for damages caused thereby." "[A] defendant takes his victim as he finds him and is responsible for all natural and probable consequences of his tortious conduct."

The term "damages" refers to "pecuniary compensation, recompense, or satisfaction for an injury sustained." The most common type of damages in the delictual context is compensatory damages, which encompasses those damages "designed to place the plaintiff in the position in which he would have been if the tort had not been committed."

Compensatory damages are further divided into the broad categories of special damages and general damages. "Special damages are those which either must be specially pled or have a 'ready market value,' *i.e.*, the amount of the damages supposedly can be determined with relative certainty." Included under the heading of special damages are the plaintiff's medical expenses incurred as a result of the tort. On the other hand, "[g]eneral damages are those which are inherently speculative in nature and cannot be fixed with mathematical certainty. These include pain and suffering[.]"

The assessment of "quantum," or the appropriate amount of damages, by a trial judge or jury is a determination of fact, one entitled to great deference on review. As such, "the role of an appellate court in reviewing general damages is not to decide what it considers to be an appropriate award, but rather to review the exercise of discretion by the trier of fact." Moreover, before a Court of Appeal can disturb an award made by a [factfinder,] the record must clearly reveal that the trier of fact abused its discretion in making its award. Only after making the finding that the record supports that the lower court abused its much discretion can the appellate court disturb the award, and then only to the extent of lowering it (or raising it) to the highest (or lowest) point which is reasonably within the discretion afforded that court.

There is no question that the abuse of discretion standard of review applies when an appellate court examines a factfinder's award of general damages. We are here, however, faced with the somewhat anomalous situation in which a jury has determined that the defendant is both legally at fault for the plaintiff's injuries and liable to him for his medical expenses incurred, yet has declined to make any award at all for general damages, *i.e.,* pain and suffering. Such a verdict has not heretofore been addressed by this court.

The Wainwrights, relying on numerous decisions from the courts of appeal, assert that there is a well-defined rule in Louisiana that it is legal error to award special damages without general damages, and that the jury thus committed legal error in this case. The Wainwrights are correct in their assertion that some of the courts of appeal of this state have held it was legal error for the jury to award special damages without awarding general damage. A close reading of the lower court decisions addressing this issue, however, reveals that what the Wainwrights and the court below assert is a rule is actually no rule at all. Rather, what the courts of appeal have done in cases such as this one is correct jury verdicts that were illogical and inconsistent. That is, the courts of appeal, while purporting to apply a bright line rule, have actually recognized that a jury verdict awarding medical expenses but simultaneously denying damages for pain and suffering will most often be inconsistent in light of the record. The courts have acknowledged, however, that under certain circumstances the evidence of record supports both an award of medical expenses and a concurrent denial of general damages. Effectively, then, the ultimate question has been whether the factfinder made inconsistent awards and thus abused its discretion.

For example, in *Robinson v. General Motors Corp.,* 328 So.2d 751 (La.App. 4 Cir.1976), one passenger in an automobile accident suffered a broken nose and bruised chest, another a bruised leg and ribs, and the third had a visible bump on the head. In a special verdict, the jury awarded plaintiffs the exact amount of their medical expenses and awarded one passenger a day's lost wages, but made no award of general damages. The court found that the jury's denial of general damages was erroneous: "If a jury deems missing work or incurring certain medical expenses unjustified, it may disallow those items, but it may not refuse general damages to plaintiffs with objective injuries." Similarly, in *Bienvenu v. State Farm Mut. Auto. Ins. Co.,* 545 So.2d 581 (La.App. 5 Cir.1989), the jury found defendant 45% at fault for causing plaintiff's injuries, and awarded sums for property damage, lost wages and medical expenses related to a severe cervical and lumbosacral sprain. However, the jury made no award of general damages. The fifth circuit recognized the jury's great discretion in determining damages, but concluded that "it is error of law for the jury to award special damages without awarding an amount for general damages as well." In *Charles v. Cecil Chatman Plumbing and Heating Co.,* 96–299 (La.App. 3 Cir. 10/23/96), 686 So.2d 43, the court reviewed a jury verdict awarding plaintiff past medical expenses but no general damages for pain and suffering. While causation and the extent of plaintiff's injuries were contested, several doctors testified as to the physical effects of the collision on the plaintiff. The court observed that, "[w]hile the jury has wide discretion in assessing the defendant's conceded damages, it is a clear error of law to award special damages for a personal injury and yet, at the same time, refuse to award general damages for *injuries that present objective symptoms.*"

In contrast to the cases discussed above, the third circuit in *Coleman v. U.S. Fire Ins. Co.,* 571 So.2d 213 (La. App. 3 Cir.1990), found there was no error in the jury's award of medical expenses but denial of general damages. There, plaintiff was injured in an automobile collision. While defendant's vehicle was stopped behind plaintiff's at a traffic signal, defendant allowed his vehicle to roll forward, striking plaintiff's rear bumper. The accident resulted in no damage to either vehicle, but plaintiff went to the hospital, where she was examined and released. Following a trial on the merits, the jury awarded plaintiff $300.00 in special damages for medical expenses, but made no award for general damages. The panel of the third circuit concluded that the jury could have found that, while plaintiff sustained no injuries, she was justified in going to the hospital for an examination following the accident. The court thus concluded that there was no inconsistency in the jury's award of medical expenses for the hospital visit and denial of an award for pain and suffering. Similarly, in *Olivier v. Sears Roebuck & Co.,* 499 So.2d 1058 (La. App. 3 Cir.1986), the third circuit again affirmed a jury's award of medical expenses for an examination and denial of general damages where there was serious question as to whether the plaintiff had sustained any injury in the accident. The court observed that "[t]he jury could have reasonably found that, although Mrs. Olivier did not receive any injuries in the accident, she was justified in getting a check-up."

While at first glance these two lines of cases appear to be contradictory, close scrutiny of the court's rationale in each of the cases cited reveals that the particular facts of each case are ultimately determinative. There is no question that the rationale of the *Robinson* line of cases relied upon by the court below has been employed by the courts of appeal in many instances. And we do not dispute that, as a general proposition, a jury verdict such as the one currently before us may be illogical or inconsistent. However, as demonstrated by the *Coleman* and *Olivier* cases, a jury, in the exercise of its discretion as factfinder, can reasonably reach the conclusion that a plaintiff has proven his entitlement to recovery of certain medical costs, yet failed to prove that he endured compensable pain and suffering as a result of defendant's fault. It may often be the case that such a verdict may not withstand review under the abuse of discretion standard. However, it would be inconsistent with the great deference afforded the factfinder by this court and our jurisprudence to state that, as a matter of law, such a verdict must always be erroneous. Rather, a reviewing court faced with a verdict such as the one before us must ask whether the jury's determination that plaintiff is entitled to certain medical expenses but not to general damages is so inconsistent as to constitute an abuse of discretion. Only after the reviewing court determines that the factfinder has abused its much discretion can that court conduct a *de novo* review of the record.

The doctrine supports the proposition that there is no bright line rule at work here. In 1 DAMAGES IN TORT ACTIONS § 4.04[4][a] (Matthew Bender 2000), the authors note that "a few jurisdictions—most notably Louisiana—allow their appellate courts to correct an erroneous 'zero' verdict where an award for pain and suffering would be warranted, and could be evaluated, by the evidence of record." (footnotes omitted) Maraist & Galligan, *supra* § 7–2, also note that "[o]ne way the factfinder may abuse its discretion is by awarding special damages without awarding general damages." (footnote omitted) The writers have noted that a reviewing court's reversal of the jury's finding must be based on the facts in the record.

Additionally, our survey of the approaches used by our sister states further buttresses the conclusion that a verdict awarding medical expenses yet denying general damages is not *per se* invalid. While the courts of many states have acknowledged that such a verdict can be erroneous, they generally have rejected the factfinder's determination as to damages only where the failure to award general damages is factually inconsistent with a reasonable reading of the record, giving due deference to the jury's findings of fact. *See, e.g., Moody v. RPM Pizza, Inc.,* 659 So.2d 877 (Miss.1995); *Robertson v. Stanley,* 285 N.C. 561, 206 S.E.2d 190 (1974); *Laughlin v. Lamkin,* 979 S.W.2d 121 (Ky.Ct.App.1998) *Prescott v. Kroger,* 877 S.W.2d 373 (Tex.Ct.App.1994).

Numerous other courts have declined to overturn such "zero" awards, relying on the reasonableness of the jury's conclusions as to the evidence. As the Supreme Court of Pennsylvania observed in *Catalano v. Bujak,* 537 Pa. 155, 161, 642 A.2d 448, 451 (1994):

> In this case, the jury apparently did not believe that pain and suffering, for example, or missed work, resulted from the injury which [defendant] caused. It did believe that medical and incidental expenses were incurred as a result of the injury, and it awarded damages for those claims. The jury made its determinations, and it is not for this court, absent evidence of unfairness, mistake, partiality, prejudice, corruption, exorbitance, excessiveness, or a result that is offensive to the conscience and judgment of the court, to disturb them.

See also, e.g., Fisher v. Davis, 601 N.W.2d 54 (Iowa 1999); *Nesseth v. Omlid,* 574 N.W.2d 848 (N.D.1998); *Catalano, supra; Gould v. Mans,* 82 S.D. 574, 152 N.W.2d 92 (1967); *Dunbar v. Thompson,* 79 Hawai'i 306, 901 P.2d 1285 (Ct.App.1995); *Bullard v. B.P. Alaska, Inc.,* 650 P.2d 402 (Alaska 1982); *Een v. Rice,* 637 So.2d 331, 333 (Fla.App.1994).

"In a suit for damages, it is the plaintiff's burden to prove the damage he suffered as a result of defendant's fault[.]" *Brannan v. Wyeth Laboratories, Inc.,* 526 So.2d 1101 (La.1988). The onus was thus on the Wainwrights to affirmatively establish, by a preponderance of the evidence, that John Scott was entitled to general damages for pain and suffering. Here, we find no abuse of discretion in the jury's failure to award general damages. Simply put, there was ample evidence from which the jury could conclude that John Scott's brief overdose and hospitalization resulted in no compensable pain and suffering.

First, the medical testimony adduced at trial indicated that, while Dr. Bambanek intended that John Scott receive only a five milligram dose of Prozac, the higher twenty milligram dose he received was not inappropriate for a child of his age. The medical testimony further established that Prozac does not reach an effective dosage level, or "steady state" in a patient's bloodstream, until well after three days of exposure. A reasonable juror might have concluded from this evidence that John Scott could not have begun to exhibit Prozac-related symptoms within hours of his first dose, as his parents claimed he did.

The only evidence offered as to John Scott's erratic behavior over that weekend was the uncorroborated testimony of his parents. Furthermore, there was testimony that John Scott had exhibited similar violent and manic tendencies in the months following the fire in the family home. The jury could have chosen not to believe the testimony of Bert and Jenna, or could have concluded that John Scott's behavior during the weekend of the overdose was actually no worse than it had been prior to the overdose. As we have often observed, we are reluctant to disturb such credibility determinations by the finder of fact.

Finally, the hospital records indicated that John Scott was alert, attentive and calm on his arrival and throughout his stay at Lake Charles Memorial Hospital. John Scott was discharged after one night of observation. The jury could have reasonably concluded that placing John Scott in the hospital was a reasonable precaution for prudent parents to take after finding out that their son had received a twenty milligram dose of Prozac instead of a five milligram dose. Since Walgreen admitted its liability for the overdose, the jury would have been justified in awarding the Wainwrights medical expenses incurred in insuring that John Scott had suffered no adverse effects from the medication. Such a finding by the jury is consistent with the determinations made by the factfinders in *Coleman* and *Olivier, supra.*

Moreover, as the jury concluded that John Scott was entitled to no general damages, it could similarly have concluded that many of John Scott's medical expenses were unrelated to the Prozac incident. The jury's original award of $1,500.00 in medical expenses is consistent with its finding that the only adverse effect on John Scott from the Prozac incident was his one-night stay in the hospital. We cannot say that, based on the record evidence, the jury was wrong to conclude that such a limited award was warranted in this case. We thus reinstate the jury's original award of $1,500.00 in medical expenses.

Our ruling here does not mean that we would reach the same conclusions as the jury were we charged with the factfinding function. However, it is not for us to substitute our findings for the jury's in light of the existence of permissibly conflicting views of the evidence in this case. Our review of the record indicates the award of $1,500.00 for medical expenses is not inconsistent with its denial of general damages, and we therefore conclude the jury committed no abuse of discretion.

DECREE

For the reasons cited herein, the opinion of the court of appeal in this matter is reversed, and the judgment of the trial court is reinstated.

REVERSED. JUDGMENT OF TRIAL COURT REINSTATED.

LEMMON, J., subscribes to the opinion and assigns additional reasons.

JOHNSON, J., dissents and assigns reasons. LEMMON, J., Subscribes to the Opinion and Assigns Additional Reasons.

When a tortfeasor causes an occurrence which subjects the tort victim to the reasonable possibility of serious injury, the tortfeasor is liable for the reasonable expenses incurred by the tort victim in consulting appropriate medical personnel and in insuring that adverse effects of the occurrence will be prevented or minimized. This liability for medical consultation or treatment ensues from the tort even if the tort victim is fortunate enough that serious injury does not actually result.[2]

In the present case, the jury recognized the tortfeasor's responsibility for consultation and treatment immediately following the tort, but (to the benefit of the tortfeasor) limited that responsibility (essentially to the brief hospitalization) because of the factual finding that no long-term serious injury resulted from the tort. That mixed factual-legal determination by the jury (that the tort victim is entitled to reasonable medical expenses for immediate medical consultation and treatment, but not for the further treatment or for general damages) is entitled to great deference.

JOHNSON, J., dissenting.

It would be illogical in this case to find defendant, Walgreen's, at fault for dispensing Prozac to this patient in a dosage four times the strength prescribed, award him medical expenses, but find no injury to justify a damage award for pain and suffering.

In my view, the record supports an award for general damages, and I would affirm the award of $40,000.00 in general damages and medical expenses in the amount of $7,372.00.

NOTES AND QUESTIONS

1. The strength of the default rule enunciated in *Wainwright* varies among jurisdictions. In some jurisdictions, a tort jury award of pecuniary damages without damages for pain and suffering requires reversal *per se*. *See, e.g.*, *Cowan v. Flannery*, 461 N.W.2d 155 (Iowa 1990). In others, courts

[2] This responsibility of a tortfeasor for the consequences of his or her conduct is the very theory of liability for medical monitoring, as this court unanimously held (and as almost every other jurisdiction in the United States has held) in *Bourgeois v. A.P. Green Indus., Inc.*, 97–3188 (La.7/8/98), 716 So.2d 355.

are even more hesitant than the court in *Wainwright* to interfere with the jury's award.

2. In *Wainwright*, the court was aware of the jury's assessment of damages as a result of the jury's answers to special interrogatories. Where no such interrogatories were given, it is within the court's power to question the jury after the verdict. And where the jury's award equals the plaintiff's alleged pecuniary expenses to the penny, courts sometimes infer that the jury has failed to award damages for pain and suffering.

3. *Additur and Remittitur.* In *Wainwright*, the appellate court itself increased the jury's award. In most states, a court may either increase or decrease a jury's damages award—the former is referred to as "additur," the latter "remittitur." Although still maintained by the states, additur is not allowed in federal court after being declared unconstitutional in 1935. *Dimick v. Schiedt*, 293 U.S. 474 (1935). In many states, a court may only grant a motion for additur or remittitur if "the court finds that the jury was influenced by bias, prejudice, or passion, or . . . if the damages were contrary to the overwhelming weight of credible evidence." *Rodgers v. Pascagoula Pub. Sch. Dist.*, 611 So.2d 942 (Miss.1992). However, the plaintiff is typically given the option of a new trial in lieu of remittitur, thus protecting the right to a jury trial. *See, e.g., Bisbal–Ramos v. City of Mayaguez*, 467 F.3d 16, 26 (1st Cir. 2006). In some states, a court may only grant such a motion with the consent of both parties, the option being retrial. *See, e.g., Riddle v. Golden Isles Broadcasting, LLC*, 666 S.E.2d 75 (Ga. App. 2008).

4. *Unconscious Pain and Suffering.* Courts commonly allow awards for medical expenses without pain and suffering where the plaintiff was unconscious or comatose during the period of injury. Indeed, most courts forbid the assessment of pain and suffering damages where the plaintiff did not consciously endure suffering. *See, e.g., Casas v. Paradez*, 267 S.W.3d 170 (Tex. App. 2008). Is such a rule just? Does it fall in line with the potential goal of the law to deter accidents? In fact, might it create perverse incentives?—If you are going to injure someone, do it quickly and make sure that you render the person unconscious!

PROBLEM

1. Bernie was killed by a drunk driver. Although he died at the scene of the accident, the evidence showed that he lay bleeding in his car for approximately fifteen minutes before he lost consciousness and died. In the suit brought by Bernie's estate against the drunk driver, the jury returned a verdict for the plaintiff in an amount that equaled the plaintiff's alleged funeral expenses, but no more. Should the judge grant the plaintiff's motion for additur?

2. *Casey's Inhaler.* If the jury awarded Casey compensation for the value of the misfilled prescription, but not lost income or pain and suffering, should a court grant a new trial on damages or adjust the award upward? What if the jury also included lost income, but not pain and suffering?

McDOUGALD V. GARBER

73 N.Y.2d 246, 536 N.E.2d 372, 538 N.Y.S.2d 937 (1989).

WACHTLER, CHIEF JUDGE.

This appeal raises fundamental questions about the nature and role of nonpecuniary damages in personal injury litigation. By nonpecuniary damages, we mean those damages awarded to compensate an injured person for the physical and emotional consequences of the injury, such as pain and suffering and the loss of the ability to engage in certain activities. Pecuniary damages, on the other hand, compensate the victim for the economic consequences of the injury, such as medical expenses, lost earnings and the cost of custodial care. . . .

I.

On September 7, 1978, plaintiff Emma McDougald, then 31 years old, underwent a Caesarean section and tubal ligation at New York Infirmary. Defendant Garber performed the surgery; defendants Armengol and Kulkarni provided anesthesia. During the surgery, Mrs. McDougald suffered oxygen deprivation which resulted in severe brain damage and left her in a permanent comatose condition. This action was brought by Mrs. McDougald and her husband, suing derivatively, alleging that the injuries were caused by the defendants' acts of malpractice.

A jury found all defendants liable and awarded Emma McDougald a total of $9,650,102 in damages, including $1,000,000 for conscious pain and suffering and a separate award of $3,500,000 for loss of the pleasures and pursuits of life. The balance of the damages awarded to her were for pecuniary damages—lost earnings and the cost of custodial and nursing care. Her husband was awarded $1,500,000 on his derivative claim for the loss of his wife's services. On defendants' post-trial motions, the Trial Judge reduced the total award to Emma McDougald to $4,796,728 by striking the entire award for future nursing care ($2,353,374) and by reducing the separate awards for conscious pain and suffering and loss of the pleasures and pursuits of life to a single award of $2,000,000. Her husband's award was left intact. On cross appeals, the Appellate Division affirmed and later granted defendants leave to appeal to this court.

[What] remains in dispute, primarily, is the award to Emma McDougald for nonpecuniary damages. At trial, defendants sought to show that Mrs. McDougald's injuries were so severe that she was incapable of either experiencing pain or appreciating her condition. Plaintiffs, on the other hand, introduced proof that Mrs. McDougald responded to certain stimuli to a sufficient extent to indicate that she was aware of her circumstances. Thus, the extent of Mrs. McDougald's cognitive abilities, if any, was sharply disputed.

[The] court's charge to the jury on these points was as follows:

> If you conclude that Emma McDougald is so neurologically impaired that she is totally incapable of experiencing any unpleasant or painful sensation, then, obviously, she cannot be awarded damages for conscious [pain].
>
> [Suffering] relates primarily to the emotional reaction of the injured person to the injury. . . . If Emma McDougald is totally unaware of her condition or totally incapable of any emotional reaction, then you cannot award her damages for suffering. If, however, you conclude that [she] is capable of an emotional response at some level, then damages for pain and suffering should be [awarded].
>
> Damages for the loss of the pleasures and pursuits of life, however, require no awareness of the loss on the part of the injured person. [Loss] of the enjoyment of life may, of course, accompany the physical sensation and emotional responses that we refer to as pain and suffering, and in most cases it does. It is possible, however, for an injured person to lose the enjoyment of life without experiencing any conscious pain and suffering. Damages for this item of injury relate not to what Emma McDougald is aware of, but rather to what she has lost. What her life was prior to her injury and what it has been since September 7, 1978 and what it will be for as long as she lives.

We conclude that the court erred, both in instructing the jury that Mrs. McDougald's awareness was irrelevant to their consideration of damages for loss of enjoyment of life and in directing the jury to consider that aspect of damages separately from pain and suffering.

We begin with the familiar proposition that an award of damages to a person injured by the negligence of another is to compensate the victim, not to punish the wrongdoer. The goal is to restore the injured party, to the extent possible, to the position that would have been occupied had the wrong not occurred. To be sure, placing the burden of compensation on the negligent party also serves as a deterrent, but purely punitive damages—that is, those which have no compensatory purpose—are prohibited unless the harmful conduct is intentional, malicious, outrageous, or otherwise aggravated beyond mere negligence.

Damages for nonpecuniary losses are, of course, among those that can be awarded as compensation to the victim. This aspect of damages, however, stands on less certain ground than does an award for pecuniary damages. An economic loss can be compensated in kind by an economic gain; but recovery for noneconomic losses such as pain and suffering and loss of enjoyment of life rests on "the legal fiction that money damages can compensate for a victim's injury" (*Howard v. Lecher*, 42 N.Y.2d 109, 111). We accept this fiction, knowing that although money will neither ease the pain nor restore the victim's abilities, this device is as close as the law can come in its effort to right the wrong. We have no hope of evaluating what has been lost, but a monetary award may provide a measure of solace for the condition created.

Our willingness to indulge this fiction comes to an end, however, when it ceases to serve the compensatory goals of tort recovery. When that limit is met, further indulgence can only result in assessing damages that are punitive. The question posed by this case, then, is whether an award of damages for loss of enjoyment of life to a person whose injuries preclude any awareness of the loss serves a compensatory purpose. We conclude that it does not.

Simply put, an award of money damages in such circumstances has no meaning or utility to the injured person. An award for the loss of enjoyment of life "cannot provide [such a victim] with any consolation or ease any burden resting on him. . . . He cannot spend it upon necessities or pleasures. He cannot experience the pleasure of giving it away."

We recognize that, as the trial court noted, requiring some cognitive awareness as a prerequisite to recovery for loss of enjoyment of life will result in some cases "in the paradoxical situation that the greater the degree of brain injury inflicted by a negligent defendant, the smaller the award the plaintiff can recover in general damages." The force of this argument, however—the temptation to achieve a balance between injury and damages—has nothing to do with meaningful compensation for the victim. Instead, the temptation is rooted in a desire to punish the defendant in proportion to the harm inflicted. However relevant such retributive symmetry may be in the criminal law, it has no place in the law of civil damages, at least in the absence of culpability beyond mere negligence.

Accordingly, we conclude that cognitive awareness is a prerequisite to recovery for loss of enjoyment of life. We do not go so far, however, as to require the fact finder to sort out varying degrees of cognition and determine at what level a particular deprivation can be fully appreciated. With respect to pain and suffering, the trial court charged simply that there must be "some level of awareness" in order for plaintiff to recover. We think that this is an appropriate standard for all aspects of nonpecuniary loss. No doubt the standard ignores analytically relevant levels of cognition, but we resist the desire for analytical purity in favor of simplicity. A more complex instruction might give the appearance of greater precision but, given the limits of our understanding of the human mind, it would in reality lead only to greater speculation.

We turn next to the question whether loss of enjoyment of life should be considered a category of damages separate from pain and suffering. There is no dispute here that the fact finder may, in assessing nonpecuniary damages, consider the effect of the injuries on the plaintiff's capacity to lead a normal life. Traditionally, in this State and elsewhere, this aspect of suffering has not been treated as a separate category of damages; instead, the plaintiff's inability to enjoy life to its fullest has been considered one type of suffering to be factored into a general award for nonpecuniary damages, commonly known as pain and suffering.

Recently, however, there has been an attempt to segregate the suffering associated with physical pain from the mental anguish that stems from the inability to engage in certain activities, and to have juries provide a separate award for each. Some courts have resisted the effort, primarily on the ground that duplicative and therefore excessive awards would result. Other courts have allowed separate awards, noting that the types of suffering involved are analytically distinguishable. Still other courts have questioned the propriety of the practice but held that, in the particular case, separate awards did not constitute reversible error.

[We] do not dispute that distinctions can be found or created between the concepts of pain and suffering and loss of enjoyment of life. If the term "suffering" is limited to the emotional response to the sensation of pain, then the emotional response caused by the limitation of life's activities may be considered qualitatively different. But suffering need not be so limited—it can easily encompass the frustration and anguish caused by the inability to participate in activities that once brought pleasure. Traditionally, by treating loss of enjoyment of life as a permissible factor in assessing pain and suffering, courts have given the term this broad meaning.

If we are to depart from this traditional approach and approve a separate award for loss of enjoyment of life, it must be on the basis that such an approach will yield a more accurate evaluation of the compensation due to the plaintiff. We have no doubt that, in general, the total award for nonpecuniary damages would increase if we adopted the rule. That separate awards are advocated by plaintiffs and resisted by defendants is sufficient evidence that larger awards are at stake here. But a larger award does not by itself indicate that the goal of compensation has been better served.

The advocates of separate awards contend that because pain and suffering and loss of enjoyment of life can be distinguished, they must be treated separately if the plaintiff is to be compensated fully for each distinct injury suffered. We disagree. Such an analytical approach may have its place when the subject is pecuniary damages, which can be calculated with some precision. But the estimation of nonpecuniary damages is not amenable to such analytical precision and may, in fact, suffer from its application. Translating human suffering into dollars and cents involves no mathematical formula; it rests, as we have said, on a legal fiction. The figure that emerges is unavoidably distorted by the translation. Application of this murky process to the component parts of nonpecuniary injuries (however analytically distinguishable they may be) cannot make it more accurate. If anything, the distortion will be amplified by repetition.

Thus, we are not persuaded that any salutary purpose would be served by having the jury make separate awards for pain and suffering and loss of enjoyment of life. We are confident, furthermore, that the trial advocate's art is a sufficient guarantee that none of the plaintiff's losses will be ignored by the jury.

The errors in the instructions given to the jury require a new trial on the issue of nonpecuniary damages to be awarded to plaintiff Emma McDougald. Accordingly, the order of the Appellate Division should be modified by granting a new trial on the issue of nonpecuniary damages of plaintiff Emma McDougald, and as so modified, affirmed.

TITONE, J. (dissenting). The majority's holding represents a compromise position that neither comports with the fundamental principles of tort compensation nor furnishes a satisfactory, logically consistent framework for compensating nonpecuniary loss. Because I conclude that loss of enjoyment of life is an objective damage item, conceptually distinct from conscious pain and suffering, I can find no fault with the trial court's instruction authorizing separate awards and permitting an award for "loss of enjoyment of life" even in the absence of any awareness of that loss on the part of the injured plaintiff. Accordingly, I dissent.

[The] capacity to enjoy life—by watching one's children grow, participating in recreational activities, and drinking in the many other pleasures that life has to offer—is unquestionably an attribute of an ordinary healthy individual. The loss of that capacity as a result of another's negligent act is at least as serious an impairment as the permanent destruction of a physical function, which has always been treated as a compensable item under traditional tort principles. Indeed, I can imagine no physical loss that is more central to the quality of a tort victim's continuing life than the destruction of the capacity to enjoy that life to the fullest.

Unquestionably, recovery of a damage item such as "pain and suffering" requires a showing of some degree of cognitive capacity. Such a requirement exists for the simple reason that pain and suffering are wholly subjective concepts and cannot exist separate and apart from the human consciousness that experiences them. In contrast, the destruction of an individual's capacity to enjoy life as a result of a crippling injury is an objective fact that does not differ in principle from the permanent loss of an eye or limb. As in the case of a lost limb, an essential characteristic of a healthy human life has been wrongfully taken, and, consequently, the injured party is entitled to a monetary award as a substitute, if, as the majority asserts, the goal of tort compensation is "to restore the injured party, to the extent possible, to the position that would have been occupied had the wrong not occurred."

Significantly, this equation does not suggest a need to establish the injured's awareness of the loss. The victim's ability to comprehend the degree to which his or her life has been impaired is irrelevant, since, unlike "conscious pain and suffering," the impairment exists independent of the victim's ability to apprehend it. Indeed, the majority reaches the conclusion that a degree of awareness must be shown only after injecting a new element into the equation. Under the majority's formulation, the victim must be aware of the loss because, in addition to being compensatory, the award must have "meaning or utility to the injured person." This additional requirement, however, has no real foundation in law or logic. "Meaning" and "utility" are subjective value judgments that have no place in the law of tort recovery, where the primary goal is to find ways of quantifying, to the extent possible, the worth of various forms of human tragedy.

Moreover, the compensatory nature of a monetary award for loss of enjoyment of life is not altered or rendered punitive by the fact that the unaware injured plaintiff cannot experience the pleasure of having it. The fundamental distinction between punitive and compensatory damages is that the former exceed the amount necessary to replace what the plaintiff lost. As the Court of Appeals for the Second Circuit has observed, "[the] fact that the compensation [for loss of enjoyment of life] may inure as a practical matter to third parties in a given case does not transform the nature of the damages." (*Rufino v. United States*, 829 F.2d 354, 362).

[In] the final analysis, the rule that the majority has chosen is an arbitrary one, in that it denies or allows recovery on the basis of a criterion that is not truly related to its stated goal. In my view, it is fundamentally unsound, as well as grossly unfair, to deny recovery to those who are completely without cognitive capacity while permitting it for those with a mere spark of awareness, regardless of the latter's ability to appreciate either the loss sustained or the benefits of the monetary award offered in compensation. In both instances, the injured plaintiff is in essentially the same position, and an award that is punitive as to one is equally punitive as to the other. Of course, since I do not subscribe to the majority's conclusion that an award to an unaware plaintiff is punitive, I would have no difficulty permitting recovery to both classes of plaintiffs.

Having concluded that the injured plaintiff's awareness should not be a necessary precondition to recovery for loss of enjoyment of life, I also have no difficulty going on to conclude that loss of enjoyment of life is a distinct damage item which is recoverable separate and apart from the award for conscious pain and suffering. The majority has rejected separate recovery, in part because it apparently perceives some overlap between the two damage categories and in part because it believes that the goal of enhancing the precision of jury awards for nonpecuniary loss would not be advanced. However, the overlap the majority perceives exists only if one assumes, as the majority evidently has, that the "loss of enjoyment" category of damages is designed to compensate only for "the emotional response caused by the limitation of life's activities" and "the frustration and anguish caused by the inability to participate in activities that once brought pleasure" (emphasis added), both of which are highly subjective concepts.

In fact, while "pain and suffering compensates the victim for the physical and mental discomfort caused by the injury; [loss] of enjoyment of life compensates the victim for the limitations on the person's life created by the injury," a distinctly objective loss. In other words, while the victim's "emotional response" and "frustration and anguish" are elements of the award for pain and suffering, the "limitation of life's activities" and the "inability to participate in activities" that the majority identifies are recoverable under the "loss of enjoyment of life" rubric. Thus, there is no real overlap, and no real basis for concern about potentially duplicative awards where, as here, there is a properly instructed jury.

Finally, given the clear distinction between the two categories of nonpecuniary damages, I cannot help but assume that permitting separate awards for conscious pain and suffering and loss of enjoyment of life would contribute to accuracy and precision in thought in the jury's deliberations on the issue of damages. [In] light of the concrete benefit to be gained by compelling the jury to differentiate between the specific objective and subjective elements of the plaintiff's nonpecuniary loss, I find unpersuasive the majority's reliance on vague concerns about potential distortion owing to the inherently difficult task of computing the value of intangible loss. My belief in the jury system, and in the collective wisdom of the deliberating jury, leads me to conclude that we may safely leave that task in the jurors' hands.

For all of these reasons, I approve of the approach that the trial court adopted in its charge to the jury. Accordingly, I would affirm the order below affirming the judgment.

NOTES AND PROBLEMS

1. This case may reveal how theories drive the results of real cases. The court pursues one rationale for tort damages: compensation. Would other rationales produce the same result? Would economists pursuing deterrence take a different approach? How would courts devoted to cost-spreading decide the case?

2. Does the court appreciate the relationship between loss of joy and suffering? It says that loss of joy is a species of suffering. Suffering "can easily

encompass the frustration and anguish caused by the inability to participate in activities that once brought pleasure."

a. How would that work in *Sharman v. Evans*? Is Ms. Evans in anguish over her inability to participate in activities that once brought her pleasure? Or is she adjusting to her new condition, making the best of a bad situation? If she does accept her disabilities and move on with her life, does that lack of anguish show she has not lost any joy?

b. Consider Sean, a young, vigorous athlete who likes nothing better than good competition. After an accident leaves Sean a quadriplegic, these activities are foreclosed. Sean's faith teaches one to accept what life offers. So rather than dwell on the loss, Sean develops new interests and enjoys life as well as possible. At deposition, Sean testifies tennis, cycling, etc., were a lot more fun than the new activities, but shows no anguish over their loss. Will pain and suffering, as understood by the *McDougald* court, compensate Sean for the losses suffered? Is this example unrealistic because Sean's lawyer will coach Sean to show anguish over the inability to play tennis? Is that better for Sean? Is that ethical for the lawyer?

c. Does the court leave an opening for Sean? Can the lawyer argue that the loss of joy is really pecuniary, unlike pain and suffering?

d. *Casey's Inhaler*. Casey not only lost the capacity to work, but also the capacity to ski and play basketball. While it is easier to measure lost income, is losing the ability to work logically different from losing the ability to play? What about the ability to play with the children and help with their care? This might be a benefit to Casey, but a loss to the children or Casey's spouse, compensated in their claim for loss of consortium. But if Casey enjoys these activities, is that loss recoverable? As with Sean, does it depend on whether Casey agonizes over the loss rather than taking it in stride? Can Casey credibly claim to agonize over these losses that are relatively modest (when compared to Sean's losses, at least)?

e. Would any of these arguments help the plaintiff in McDougald? Does her inability to experience substitute joys bar compensation for lost joy the same way her inability to experience pain bars her from recovering for pain and suffering? Does her inability to spend wages bar her recovery of lost wages (or earning capacity)? How persuasive is the court's distinction between pecuniary and nonpecuniary losses? Does it relate to the compensatory goals of tort damages?

3. The principal case muses about the basis for awarding nonpecuniary damages. The rationale for nonpecuniary damages has not

always been apparent to the courts. Lord Halsbury L.C. in *The Mediana* [1900] A.C. 113, 116–117 (H.L.) said:

> Nobody can suggest that you can by any arithmetical calculation establish what is the exact amount of money which would represent such a thing as the pain and suffering which a person has undergone by reason of an accident. In truth, I think it would be very arguable to say that a person would be entitled to no damages for such things. What manly mind cares about pain and suffering that is past? But nevertheless the law recognizes that as a topic upon which damages may be given.

Almost a century after the Lord Chancellor uttered his words, the justification of nonpecuniary damages has again been called in question. The arguments turn on the foundation of tort liability. The first category views liability as mimicking the bargain that the parties would have reached in the absence of transaction costs. Here the plaintiff would have bargained for insurance to cover pecuniary losses. Nonpecuniary losses introduce moral hazards that cause insurance coverage to be infeasible. Alan Schwartz, *Proposals for Products Liability Reform: A Theoretical Synthesis*, 97 YALE L.J. 353, 362–67 (1988). But Professors Croley and Hanson, *The Nonpecuniary Costs of Accidents: Pain and Suffering in Tort Law*, 108 HARV. L. REV. 1785 (1995), argue that consumers may demand insurance of this kind and tort law is a superior institution to provide it. The second, and politically polar, category is founded on the notion that the pool of funds to compensate injuries is limited and more coverage, albeit less generous, could be obtained by restricting damages to economic loss alone: J. O'Connell & R. Simon, PAYMENT FOR PAIN AND SUFFERING: WHO WANTS WHAT, WHEN AND WHY? (1972). Yet others from diverse theoretical viewpoints argue that non-economic damages should be recoverable as representing a real loss, the failure to measure in damages would under-deter tortfeasors, or as a loss which is not rectifiable in money terms but should be compensable redressing the disrespect of the plaintiff's rights wrought by the defendant's wrong.

4. The assessment of pain has been subjected to some medical study but the law has employed very loose standards. Ellen Smith Pryor, *Compensation and the Ineradicable Problems of Pain*, 59 GEO. WASH. L. REV. 239 (1991). Is the stoic to be awarded less?

Pain and suffering may have two sources. Most common is physical pain caused by the injury. Plaintiff also may be able to recover for mental anguish caused by physical injuries, *e.g.*, impotency and loss of desire for sexual intercourse, *Sullivan v. City and County of San Francisco*, 95 Cal.App.2d 745, 214 P.2d 82 (1950), scars and other disfigurements, *Gray v. Washington Water Power Co.*, 30 Wash. 665, 71 P. 206 (1903).

This said, measurement is a mysterious one for the jury. R. Perry Sentell, Jr., *The Georgia Jury and Negligence: The View from the Trenches*, 28 GA. L. REV. 1, 98 (1993). A suggestion by the colorful Melvin Belli is to apply a per diem measure, *i.e.*, to divide the duration of the pain and suffering into time units (days) and to ascribe a value to each unit. *But see Combined Ins. Co. of Am. v. Sinclair*, 584 P.2d 1034, 1050 (Wyo.1978) (criticizing the per diem approach).

5. Loss of enjoyment of life is a much debated aspect of nonpecuniary loss. The first issue is whether it is recognized as a separate element of damages. If so, the question is whether it requires, with pain and suffering, the victim's conscious appreciation of loss. This depends upon the conceptualization of the element. It may be seen as a loss of capacity in which case the issue is one of reduction and does not require a conscious appreciation of loss. The loss of capacity has led some courts to accept hedonic damages (derived from the Greek "hedonikos" meaning pleasure or pleasurable). The damages measure the value of a human being's life divorced from earnings and financial rewards. The courts that accept hedonic damages are divided on whether expert evidence is admissible on the valuation.

KISHMARTON V. WILLIAM BAILEY CONSTRUCTION, INC.

93 Ohio St.3d 226, 754 N.E.2d 785 (2001).

PFEIFER, J.

On July 24, 1991, appellees Donald and Mary Kishmarton entered into a contract with appellant William Bailey Construction, Inc. ("Bailey") for the construction of a residential home to be located in North Royalton, Ohio. The Kishmartons agreed to pay $213,000 (with change orders, $219,000) to Bailey and Bailey agreed to build the house in a "workmanlike manner."

The Kishmartons moved into the house in May 1992. The following winter, the Kishmartons became concerned about water leaking through the ceiling and down the walls. One source of the leaks was the roof vents, which had been installed by Bailey. The vents allowed snow to enter the attic during storms. Another source of the water leaks was ice backup, a condition that occurs when water freezes on the roof area and upon melting leaks into a house. Attempting to fix the problems, Bailey replaced a portion of the gutter near the garage. This and all subsequent attempts to remedy the problem failed, and the leaks continued unabated for several years.

The Kishmartons sued, alleging that Bailey (1) breached its implied warranty and duty to provide workmanlike construction service by building the home in a negligent manner, (2) breached the terms of the express warranty in the construction contract to perform the work in a workmanlike manner, and (3) was negligent in building and constructing the home. After trial and after being instructed as to breach of contract and breach of implied duty to construct in a workmanlike manner, the jury awarded $24,000 damages to the Kishmartons, consisting of $5,000 for the reasonable restoration of the property and $19,000 for loss of enjoyment of the residence, annoyance, and discomfort. The court of appeals upheld the $19,000 award for loss of enjoyment. However, it found the award of $5,000 for restoration to be against the manifest weight of the evidence and reduced that portion of the award to $3,725.

The court of appeals, finding its judgment to be in conflict with the judgments in three other appellate districts, also certified two questions to this court:

(1) Where the vendee and builder-vendor enter into an agreement for the future construction of a residence, does the vendee's claim for breach of an implied duty to construct the house in a workmanlike manner arise *ex contractu* or *ex delicto*?

(2) Regardless of whether the claim is in contract or tort, in such a case, can the plaintiff recover emotional distress damages for loss of enjoyment, annoyance or discomfort?

This court [accepted] jurisdiction. . . .

In *Velotta v. Leo Petronzio Landscaping, Inc.* (1982), 69 Ohio St.2d 376, 23 O.O.3d 346, 433 N.E.2d 147, we held that "[a]n action by a vendee against the builder-vendor of a *completed residence* for damages proximately caused by failure to construct in a workmanlike manner using ordinary care—*a duty imposed by law*—is an action in tort. . . ." (Emphasis *sic.*) We specifically did not address the nature of an action by a vendee against the builder-vendor for breach of a contract to build a residence in the future. Today, we close the loop by [holding] that such actions arise *ex contractu.*

Doing so does little more than acknowledge the obvious. In *Velotta,* the consideration for the purchase price was the structure, a finished product. In this case, "the consideration is the services . . . [to] be performed by the contractor." The contract governs the warranty of good workmanship; therefore, the warranty of good workmanship arises from the contract. . . . Accordingly, we hold that where the vendee and builder-vendor enter into an agreement for the future construction of a residence, the vendee's claim for breach of an implied duty to construct the house in a workmanlike manner arises *ex contractu*. . . .

We now turn to the second certified question to address the issue of whether emotional distress damages may be recovered in this type of contract action. "As [Bailey] has pointed out at length, there appears to be *no case in Ohio,* reported or unreported, in which a builder-vendor has been found liable for damages in the form of loss of enjoyment, annoyance and discomfort by a new home purchaser." (Emphasis *sic.*) While acknowledging the truth of the statement, we recognize that the current status of the law on this issue places Ohio at odds with the Restatement of the Law of Contracts and, more importantly, runs contrary to our state Constitution.

Section 16, Article I of the Ohio Constitution states that "every person, for an injury done him . . . shall have remedy by due course of law." Emotional distress injuries are injuries for which our Constitution guarantees a right to a remedy. Further, it is reasonable to allow emotional distress damages because some contract breaches cause them. To continue to disallow emotional distress damages unfairly exposes innocent persons to harm that a wrongdoer has no incentive to avoid or mitigate. As one commentator put it, "the breaching party to a contract intentionally assumed must bear the full burden of the harm caused, and there should be no exception for emotional distress damages. . . ." Whaley, *Paying for the Agony: The Recovery of Emotional Distress Damages in Contract Actions* (1992), SUFFOLK U.L. REV. 935, 948.

With regard to a breach-of-contract action, Section 353 of the Restatement states: "Recovery for emotional disturbance will be excluded unless the breach also caused bodily harm or the contract or the breach is of such a kind that serious emotional disturbance was a particularly likely result." 3 Restatement of the Law 2d, Contracts (1981) 149, Section 353. Comment *a* to this section explains: "Damages for emotional disturbance are not ordinarily allowed. Even if they are foreseeable, they are often particularly difficult to establish and to measure."

Today we join the minority of courts that allow emotional distress damages in contract cases involving transactions between vendees and builder-vendors by answering the second certified question in the affirmative, consistent with Section 353 of the Restatement of the Law 2d, Contracts. See McGowan, *Property's Portrait of a Lady* (2001), MINN. L. REV. 1037, 1106–1108.

We are confident that allowing emotional distress damages in breach-of-contract actions involving vendees and builder-vendors will not open the floodgates. Section 353 significantly, and we believe rightly, limits the circumstances in which emotional distress damages may be granted. Though proof of emotional distress damages in these cases will be difficult, we are convinced that wronged parties are constitutionally entitled to an opportunity to recover for emotional distress damages. Accordingly, we adopt Section 353 of the Restatement of Law 2d, Contracts (1981) and declare that when vendee's claim for breach of an implied duty to construct a house in a workmanlike manner is successful, recovery for emotional distress damages will be excluded unless the breach also caused bodily harm or the contract or the breach is of such a kind that serious emotional distress was a particularly likely result.

Nevertheless, we hold that the award of $19,000 for loss of enjoyment of the residence, annoyance, and discomfort was improper. Given the instructions the jury received, the award sounds in tort and must be reversed. Furthermore, given the record before us, we conclude that it is not possible for the Kishmartons to establish damages pursuant to Section 353. Accordingly, we affirm the award of $3,725 for restoration of the property, but reverse the award of $19,000 for loss of enjoyment.

Judgment affirmed in part and reversed in part.

MOYER, C.J., and LUNDBERG STRATTION, J., concur.

COOK J., concurs in syllabus and judgment.

DOUGLAS, RESNICK and FRANCIS E. SWEENEY, SR., JJ., dissent and would affirm the court of appeals in all respects.

NOTES AND QUESTIONS

1. Do you agree that plaintiffs could not establish that serious emotional distress was particularly likely to arise from this kind of contract or this kind of breach? How would you either justify or respond to the court's application of this rule?

2. The court notes but rejects concern for opening the floodgates. Any breach of contract might cause distress. Discharged employees often suffer distress, worrying about how to provide for their families or seething under the perceived injustice of their discharge. Even business executives may suffer distress, worrying about the fate of the company or their own advancement within it. Does the court's rationale explain why these claims for distress should be denied? Does the court's rule achieve that result? Which words in the RESTATEMENT (SECOND) OF CONTRACTS § 353 give the court room to reject claims like those of the Kishmartons?

3. Courts historically show considerable restraint in considering claims for distress in contract actions. Breach of promise of marriage was one exception, though largely precluded by statute today. Another rose from breaches by funeral parlors. When coffins fell open on the way from the church to the hearse, plaintiffs suffered little economic loss. But serious distress seemed particularly likely in this situation. More recently, courts have allowed distress (or something like it) when breaches of contract have ruined vacations. *See Fuller v. Healy Transp. Ltd.*, 22 O.R. (2d) 118, 92 D.L.R. (3d) 277 (Co. Ct. 1978); *Jarvis v. Swan Tours Ltd.*, 1 All E.R. 71 (1973). Is a botched home less distressing than a botched vacation?

4. Some jurisdictions allow distress when a breach of contract is willful and wanton, provided distress was foreseeable at the time of contract formation and proven with reasonable certainty. *See, e.g., Giampapa v. American Family Mut. Ins. Co.*, 64 P.3d 230 (Colo.2003) (en banc) (rejecting the "particularly likely" test of the second Restatement of Contracts). Willful and wanton can include a large number of breaches. Many efficient breaches may be "intentional, and without legal justification or excuse," *Id.* at 244, potentially producing liability for distress damages. If a manufacturer canceled a product line, thus breaching without justification contracts to sell that product, should distress be included? What if a landowner canceled a

construction project without excuse? Is some additional requirement needed to prevent this rule from reaching too many breaches of contract? Does one already exist?

5. The existence of a contract claim does not affect the availability of distress for a tort arising from the same transaction. Thus, if distress is available for fraud under tort law, the fact that the fraud induced a contract that defendant breached does not negate the fraud. In a similar vein, where breach of contract produces physical injuries—common in breach of warranty claims, but possible in many contract settings—pain and suffering is generally available, regardless of whether a separate tort could be proven.

6. Limitations on distress in contract puts pressure on lawyers to plead cases in tort. The Kishmartons tried and failed. The reasons for treating some breaches of contract as torts are not always clear. Ohio had ruled that the breach of an implied warranty of workmanlike construction in the sale of an existing home was a duty created by law and thus arose in tort. Should the Kishmartons have omitted any mention of workmanlike construction from the contract, so that they could rely on an implied warranty imposed by law instead? Isn't an implied warranty still a term of the contract, even when supplied by the court as a gap-filler?

These distinctions can affect results significantly. For instance, when an insurer refuses to pay amounts owed under a policy, a breach of contract is clear. But in order to allow recovery for distress, some courts find a way to call the breach a tort, usually by finding a breach of the implied obligation of good faith and fair dealing. *See, e.g., Nichols v. State Farm Mut. Auto Ins. Co.*, 279 S.C. 336, 306 S.E.2d 616 (1983). Allowing distress claims in contract actions can produce the same recovery. *See, e.g., Giampapa v. American Family Mut. Ins. Co.*, 64 P.3d 230 (Colo. 2003) (en banc). But the threshold test may differ: breach of good faith in *Nichols* vs. willful and wanton breach in *Giampapa*. Similarly, while emotional distress is commonly available for the tort of retaliatory discharge, it commonly is denied for breach of employment contracts, even breaches of the obligation of good faith. *See, e.g., Foley v. Interactive Data Corp.*, 47 Cal.3d 654, 254 Cal.Rptr. 211, 765 P.2d 373 (1988). Thus, many practitioners now plead intentional infliction of emotional distress in employment discharge cases, seeking leverage justifying distress recoveries.

PROBLEM: CASEY'S INHALER

Casey might bring a tort claim for negligence or a contract claim for delivering nonconforming goods. Would emotional distress be appropriate for the contract claim? If Casey's relief comes in a malpractice action against the attorney for failing to file the claim, is distress an appropriate element of recovery? What distress would be included?

3. INDIGNITY AND INTANGIBLE LOSSES

Pain and suffering does not describe all nonpecuniary losses. Some emotional losses arise despite the absence of any physical injury and sometimes despite the absence of any pecuniary loss. The law has long allowed compensation for this kind of loss, but has struggled with both the boundaries of these losses and the means by which they can be measured. As you read the following cases, consider the questions asked about pain and suffering: (1) is compensation appropriate at all?; (2) what precise interest is it meant to measure?; and (3)if compensation is appropriate, how can it be measured?

PROBLEM: SCHOOL DESEGREGATION

Recall the basic facts of Brown v. Board of Education, in which African-American students sued a Kansas school district for violation of their constitutional rights in maintaining a racially segregated school system. Recall that the proper vehicle for such an action is 42 U.S.C. § 1983, which imposes on state government actors a form of tort liability for the deprivation of "rights, privileges, or immunities secured" by the Constitution. If you had been the plaintiffs in this case, what type of remedy(ies) would you have sought? What forms of damages? How might one measure the compensatory damages required by the harm caused by segregated schools? Should the plaintiffs be able to recover attorney's fees? Consider these questions again after having read the following cases.

JOAN W. V. CITY OF CHICAGO

771 F.2d 1020 (7th Cir.1985).

SWYGERT, SENIOR CIRCUIT JUDGE.

This is an appeal from a judgment against the City of Chicago in a Section 1983 suit, brought by a person identified for purposes of the suit as "Joan W." At the close of a trial in which liability was conceded, the jury awarded $112,000 in compensatory damages. . . . The City urges that we grant a new trial or, alternatively, a remittitur of damages.

Joan, a physician in her mid-thirties practicing in Chicago, was arrested for a traffic violation on January 28, 1978. Pursuant to a City policy that was subsequently declared unconstitutional by this court, five female police department employees ("the matrons"), strip searched her.

During the search, Joan was forced to remove her clothing and to expose the vaginal and anal areas of her body. The matrons threatened her when she initially refused to comply, used vulgar language, and laughed at her. Joan testified that the incident caused her emotional distress that manifested itself in reduced socializing, poor work performance, paranoia, suicidal feelings, depression, and an inability to disrobe in any place other than a closet. She introduced evidence tending to show that she was peculiarly sensitive to the kind of physical violation she had endured because she was a private person who even during high school gym classes could not completely disrobe in front of others and was conscious of her physical disabilities caused by her chronic arthritis.

The City conceded liability but introduced evidence tending to show that Joan suffered no sexual dysfunction or significant decline in work effectiveness as a result of the incident.

The City's first assignment of error is the alleged prejudicial remarks made by Joan's counsel during closing argument. In rebutting the City's theory that Joan's emotional injuries were insignificant because she had not told various people about the incident, counsel asked, "Would you tell them if they asked you if that had happened to you?" The City did not object to this statement. After the City finished its closing argument, Joan's counsel again addressed the issue of Joan's reticence about the incident by asking the jury, "How would you feel?" The City objected. The judge overruled the objection, and counsel again asked the jury, "How would you feel if you had been taken into a cell and over your repeated protestations you had been forced to undress and do the things that Joan did?"

An appeal to the jury to imagine itself in the plaintiff's position is impermissible because it encourages the jury to depart from its neutral role. This so-called "Golden Rule" argument has been universally condemned by the courts. Joan nevertheless urges three reasons for affirming. First, Joan contends that any objections to the Golden Rule argument were waived by lack of contemporaneous objection. The City did, however, object to the second Golden Rule argument, and this court has recognized that reiterative objections are unnecessary to preserve an objection for appeal.

Second, Joan urges that the Golden Rule argument is not objectionable when it refers only to the assessment of credibility. There is no reason for such a distinction because the jury's departure from its neutral role is equally inappropriate regardless of the issue at stake.

Third, Joan appears to contend that its Golden Rule argument was somehow invited by the City's contention that Joan really did not feel all that badly about the incident. Although otherwise impermissible remarks may be sustained as invited by opposing counsel's prior impermissible remarks in closing argument, there was nothing impermissible about the City's contention. Accordingly, Joan's counsel did not have license under the "invited response" doctrine to retaliate with impermissible remarks of her own.

Nevertheless, counsel's Golden Rule argument should not be held reversible error. Although the remarks were clearly improper, the relevant inquiry is not whether they were improper but whether the district court's response, or lack of response, to the remarks was a prejudicial abuse of discretion. "Naturally, in reviewing questions concerning remarks alleged to have misled the jury, we give great weight to the district judge's judgment." Given the context of the prejudicial remarks and the district judge's assessment of the jury's reaction to them, we hold that the Golden Rule argument was not reversible error.

Although the judge did overrule the City's objection to the Golden Rule argument and did not give a limiting instruction, we have noted that any prejudice can often be cured simply by a general instruction that properly informs the jury on the law of damages. In the case at bar, the judge gave the jury extensive guidance on how to assess damages and warned:

> In deciding the facts of this case you must not be swayed by bias or prejudice or favor as to any party. Our system of law does not permit jurors to be governed by prejudice or sympathy or public opinion. Both the parties and the public expect that you will carefully and impartially consider all of the evidence in the case, follow the law as stated by the Court, and reach a just verdict regardless of the consequences.

Moreover, in denying the City's motion for a mistrial, the judge carefully assessed the prejudicial effect of the Golden Rule argument. She noted that counsel was not unduly emotional in making the argument, and she did not believe that the heavy damages assessed against the City were attributable to the argument. Viewed in totality, and giving great deference to the superior vantage point of the trial judge in assessing the context and effect of the Golden Rule argument, the argument was not so egregious that the judge abused her discretion in refusing to cure the error by ordering a new trial.

The City next contends that the damages award was so excessive as to require either a reversal for a new trial or a remittitur. Whether a damage award is excessive is a recurring problem and has been an issue in several recent cases in this Circuit. With those cases in mind, we discuss the test that is required and then its application to the instant case.

The test is severe. Trial judges may vacate a jury verdict for excessiveness only if it is "monstrously excessive" or if there is "no rational connection between the evidence on damages and the verdict," and appellate review is governed by the extremely limited abuse of discretion standard. Recently, this court added an additional element to the equation where the case under review is but one of a series of similar cases that establish a trend in damage awards: comparability. *Levka v. City of Chicago*, 748 F.2d 421, 425 (7th Cir. 1984) ("One factor we must consider in determining whether to set aside an award is whether the award is out of line compared to other awards in similar cases.").

At least ten strip search suits have been filed against the City in the Northern District of Illinois and tried before a jury. In those cases, the jury returned the following damage awards: $3,300, $15,000, $15,000, $25,000, $25,000, $30,000, $45,000, $50,000 (reduced as excessive to $25,000) [*Levka*], $60,000, and $112,000 in the case at bar.

The manner of the searches depicted in those cases that were reviewed or discussed on appeal, were quite similar, although some searches were more aggravated than others. For example, Mary T. alleged that the matron felt her breasts and threatened that if she did not comply with the search, male officers would be called in to assist [$45,000]. Stella S. was subjected to offensive touching and probing of her orifices by a police officer [$15,000], and Susan B. was forced to squat five times despite her recent hysterectomy [$15,000]. Hinda Hoffman testified that two male police officers were within view when she was strip searched, and a group of prostitutes jeered at her as the search was conducted [$60,000]. Mary Beth G. also testified that she was being viewed by male police personnel during her search [$25,000].

Joan's search was not different in kind from these aggravated searches, which had resulted in damage awards ranging from $15,000 to $60,000. She was required to undress, lift each breast, bend over and spread her buttocks and vagina. Indeed, unlike some of the other litigants, Joan was not touched during the search, nor was she searched within the view of anyone other than female detention personnel. None of the plaintiffs in the strip search cases brought to us on appeal have alleged any physical impairment as a result of the searches nor did Joan W. allege such impairment. They did, however, as did Joan W., allege resulting psychic trauma and emotional distress. This court in Mary Beth G. described some of the trauma endured by four plaintiffs: "*inter alia,* instances of shock, panic, depression, shame, rage, humiliation, and nightmares, with lasting effects on each woman's life." Additionally we observed that "each woman still thinks about the strip search, and each woman's attitudes and relationships with others has been colored by the experiences."

In *Levka*, we also described the emotional trauma claimed by Maria Levka, as a result of her strip search:

> [P]laintiff testified that in the weeks following the strip search she continued to be frightened and became afraid to go out alone at night. She testified that if she tried to go out alone, she would return home and fall apart. According to plaintiff, her fears became so pronounced that she consulted a psychiatrist one month after the search. [P]laintiff claims that she continues to be afraid and that even now she will not go out alone at night. In fact, she testified that she no longer sees movies or attends parties, the ballet, or the theatre.

In sum, the plaintiff there claimed that she "suffered continuous and deep emotional trauma as the result of her strip search."

The emotional distress and trauma claimed by Joan W. was not qualitatively more severe than that claimed by the four plaintiffs in *Mary Beth G.* or by Maria Levka. In other words, when the evidence of the injuries suffered by these other women is compared to that claimed by Joan, there is no difference in kind among them. Joan testified that she never sought psychiatric assistance or other counseling following her postarrest experience. Although she alleged that her social contacts diminished, there is little evidence of this fact in the record. Subsequent to the strip search, Joan became the chief resident at the hospital where she was employed and is now successfully practicing medicine.

In conclusion, we are of the view that considering the totality of the evidence and comparing this case to the other similar cases brought against the City, the jury award of $112,000 for damages is flagrantly extravagant and out of line with the other strip search cases. However reprehensible the City's conduct, the jury does not have discretion to award what are essentially punitive damages where no punitive damages are pled or permitted. Nor should we presume extensive compensatory damages as a matter of law. "Damages are awarded in § 1983 actions to compensate individuals for injuries resulting from the deprivation of their constitutional rights," and "where the award is not rationally proportionate to awards assessed in similar cases for injuries that are no different in kind from those suffered by the plaintiff, then the award is excessive."

On the other hand, we do not believe that the evidence of injury is so slight as to justify an entry of remittitur to the $25,000 base figure established in *Levka*. There are aggravating circumstances in the case at bar that were absent in *Levka*—particularly the taunting of Joan—and although these circumstances are not different in kind from those in the other aggravated cases, a jury could rationally find some differences in degree given the evidence of Joan's peculiar sensitivities to this kind of abuse. We believe the jury could rationally award damages to Joan above the record $60,000 figure awarded Hoffman. Accordingly, we hold the damages excessive only to the extent they exceed $75,000.

The district court's order is reversed, the judgment is vacated, and the cause is remanded to the district court with directions to hold a new trial unless plaintiff accepts the entry of a remittitur reducing the award to $75,000.

NOTES AND QUESTIONS

1. Golden Rule arguments also arise in connection with pain and suffering. "If you lost the use of your legs, how much would you think was fair compensation for that injury?" Could this be countered by the defense asking:

"If you had deprived someone of the use of his legs, how much would you think was fair compensation for that injury?"?

Is anything left of the rule after *Joan W*? Won't courts always give accurate instructions on damages? Will that eliminate the prejudicial effect? Is this like striking the evidence, where an instruction to ignore the response is the best we can do? Is the relation between the damage instruction and the improper closing argument self-evident? Are you convinced the jury understood that plaintiff's counsel's suggestion was an inappropriate way to think about the case? How can the court hold the error was harmless and still conclude the jury awarded excessive damages? Is it harmless only after the remittitur?

2. Is it sensible to limit damages by the awards in other similar cases? How would you attack (or defend) that approach?

3. If we are trying to compensate each plaintiff for her injury, what factors should the court consider in deciding whether this case deserves a larger or smaller award? What did the court consider? Can those factors be explained? How would you argue against those factors? What would you substitute?

4. Did the court apply the factors effectively? Did the more deserving plaintiff get more money? Joan maintains a successful practice and seems to be functioning pretty well, though she undresses in a closet. Maria Levka doesn't go out alone at night. That's not just a social cost; she was a booking agent for musical acts, requiring her to visit nightclubs to see prospective clients perform. Does Joan really deserve three times as much as Maria? There was conflicting evidence concerning whether the strip search caused the decline in Maria's business. Does that explain how the appellate court determined her losses were less than Joan's? Should that matter?

5. Can dignity ever be quantified with any confidence? Should courts simply stop making awards for intangible harms that have no ascertainable effect? Or would that leave defendants free to cause unascertainable harm? Has the court here substituted presumed damages (of $15,000 or $25,000) with an opportunity to collect more if a greater harm is demonstrated?

MEMPHIS COMMUNITY SCHOOL DISTRICT V. STACHURA

477 U.S. 299, 106 S. Ct. 2537, 91 L. Ed. 2d 249 (1986).

JUSTICE POWELL delivered the opinion of the Court.

I

Respondent Edward Stachura is a tenured teacher in the Memphis, Michigan, public schools. [R]espondent taught seventh-grade life science, using a textbook that had been approved by the School Board. The textbook included a chapter on human reproduction. During the 1978–1979 school year, respondent spent six weeks on this chapter. As part of their instruction, students were shown pictures of respondent's wife during her pregnancy. Respondent also showed the students two films concerning human growth and sexuality. These films were provided by the County Health Department, and the Principal of respondent's school had approved their use. Both films had been shown in past school years without incident.

After the showing of the pictures and the films, a number of parents complained to school officials about respondent's teaching methods. These complaints, which appear to have been based largely on inaccurate rumors about the allegedly sexually explicit nature of the pictures and films, were discussed at an open School Board meeting held on April 23, 1979. Following the advice of the School Superintendent, respondent did not attend the meeting, during which a number of parents expressed the view that respondent should not be allowed to teach in the Memphis school system. The day after the meeting, respondent was suspended with pay. The School Board later confirmed the suspension, and notified respondent that an "administration evaluation" of his teaching methods was underway. No such evaluation was ever made. Respondent was reinstated the next fall, after filing this lawsuit.

Respondent sued the School District, the Board of Education [and] various [individuals]. The complaint alleged that respondent's suspension deprived him of both liberty and property without due process of law and violated his First Amendment right to academic freedom.

At the close of trial on these claims, the District Court instructed the jury that on finding liability it should award a sufficient amount to compensate respondent for the injury caused by petitioners' unlawful actions:

> You should consider in this regard any lost earnings; loss of earning capacity; out-of-pocket expenses; and any mental anguish or emotional distress that you find the Plaintiff to have suffered as a result of conduct by the Defendants depriving him of his civil rights.

In addition to this instruction on the standard elements of compensatory damages, the court explained that punitive damages could be awarded, and described the standards governing punitive awards. Finally, at respondent's request and over petitioners' objection, the court charged that damages also could be awarded based on the value or importance of the constitutional rights that were violated:

> If you find that the Plaintiff has been deprived of a Constitutional right, you may award damages to compensate him for the deprivation. Damages for this type of injury are more difficult to measure than damages for a physical injury or injury to one's property. There are no medical bills or other expenses by which you can judge how much compensation is appropriate. In

> one sense, no monetary value we place upon Constitutional rights can measure their importance in our society or compensate a citizen adequately for their deprivation. However, just because these rights are not capable of precise evaluation does not mean that an appropriate monetary amount should not be awarded.
>
> The precise value you place upon any Constitutional right which you find was denied to Plaintiff is within your discretion. You may wish to consider the importance of the right in our system of government, the role which this right has played in the history of our republic, [and] the significance of the right in the context of the activities which the Plaintiff was engaged in at the time of the violation of the right.

The jury found petitioners liable, and awarded a total of $275,000 in compensatory damages and $46,000 in punitive damages. The District Court entered judgment notwithstanding the verdict as to one of the defendants, reducing the total award to $266,750 in compensatory damages and $36,000 in punitive damages.

In an opinion devoted primarily to liability issues, the Court of Appeals for the Sixth Circuit affirmed, holding that respondent's suspension had violated both procedural due process and the First Amendment. Responding to petitioners' contention that the District Court improperly authorized damages based solely on the value of constitutional rights, the court noted only that "there was ample proof of actual injury to plaintiff Stachura both in his effective discharge . . . and by the damage to his reputation and to his professional career as a teacher. Contrary to the situation in Carey v. Piphus, 435 U.S. 247 (1978), there was proof from which the jury could have found, as it did, actual and important damages."

We granted certiorari limited to the question whether the Court of Appeals erred in affirming the damages award in the light of the District Court's instructions that authorized not only compensatory and punitive damages, but also damages for the deprivation of "any constitutional right." We reverse, and remand for a new trial limited to the issue of compensatory damages.

II

Petitioners challenge the jury instructions authorizing damages for violation of constitutional rights on the ground that those instructions permitted the jury to award damages based on its own unguided estimation of the value of such rights. Respondent disagrees with this characterization of the jury instructions, contending that the compensatory damages instructions taken as a whole focused solely on respondent's injury and not on the abstract value of the rights he asserted.

We believe petitioners more accurately characterize the instructions. The damages instructions were divided into three distinct segments: (i) compensatory damages for harm to respondent, (ii) punitive damages, and (iii) additional "compensat[ory]" damages for violations of constitutional rights. No sensible juror could read the third of these segments to modify the first. On the contrary, the damages instructions plainly authorized—in addition to punitive damages—two distinct types of "compensatory" damages: one based on respondent's actual injury according to ordinary tort law standards, and another based on the "value" of certain rights. We therefore consider whether the latter category of damages was properly before the jury.

We have repeatedly noted that 42 U.S.C. § 1983 creates " 'a species of tort liability' in favor of persons who are deprived of 'rights, privileges, or immunities secured' to them by the Constitution." Accordingly, when § 1983 plaintiffs seek damages for violations of constitutional rights, the level of damages is ordinarily determined according to principles derived from the common law of torts.

Punitive damages aside, damages in tort cases are designed to provide "*compensation* for the injury caused to plaintiff by defendant's breach of duty." To that end, compensatory damages may include not only out-of-pocket loss and other monetary harms, but also such injuries as "impairment of reputation . . . , personal humiliation, and mental anguish and suffering." Deterrence is also an important purpose of this system, but it operates through the mechanism of damages that are *compensatory*—damages grounded in determinations of plaintiffs' actual losses.

Carey v. Piphus represents a straightforward application of these principles. *Carey* involved a suit by a high school student suspended for smoking marijuana; the student claimed that he was denied procedural due process because he was suspended without an opportunity to respond to the charges against him. The Court of Appeals for the Seventh Circuit held that even if the suspension was justified, the student could recover substantial compensatory damages simply because of the insufficient procedures used to suspend him from school. We reversed, and held that the student could recover compensatory damages only if he proved actual injury caused by the denial of his constitutional rights. We noted: "Rights, constitutional and otherwise, do not exist in a vacuum. Their purpose is to protect persons from injuries to particular interests. . . ." Where no injury was present, no "compensatory" damages could be awarded.

The instructions at issue here cannot be squared with *Carey,* or with the principles of tort damages on which *Carey* and § 1983 are grounded. The jurors in this case were told that, in determining how much was necessary to "compensate [respondent] for the deprivation" of his constitutional rights, they should place a money value on the "rights" themselves by considering such factors as the particular right's "importance . . . in our system of government," its role in American history, and its "significance . . . in the context of the activities" in which respondent was engaged. These factors focus, not on compensation for provable injury, but on the jury's subjective perception of the importance of constitutional rights as an abstract matter. *Carey* establishes that such an approach is impermissible. The constitutional right transgressed in *Carey*—the right to due process of law—is central to our system of ordered liberty. We nevertheless held that *no* compensatory damages could be awarded for violation of that right absent proof of actual injury. *Carey* thus makes clear that the abstract value of a constitutional right may not form the basis for § 1983 damages.[11]

Respondent nevertheless argues that *Carey* does not control here, because in this case a *substantive* constitutional right—respondent's First Amendment right to academic freedom infringed. The argument misperceives our analysis in *Carey*. That case does not establish a two-tiered system of constitutional rights, with substantive rights afforded greater protection than "mere" procedural safeguards. We did acknowledge in *Carey* that "the elements and prerequisites for recovery of damages" might vary depending on the interests protected by the constitutional right at issue. But we emphasized that, whatever the constitutional basis for § 1983 liability, such damages must always be designed "to *compensate injuries* caused by the [constitutional] deprivation." That conclusion simply leaves no room for non-compensatory damages measured by the jury's perception of the abstract "importance" of a constitutional right.

Nor do we find such damages necessary to vindicate the constitutional rights that § 1983 protects. Section 1983 presupposes that damages that compensate for actual harm ordinarily suffice to deter constitutional violations. Moreover, damages based on the "value" of constitutional rights are an unwieldy tool for ensuring compliance with the Constitution. History and tradition do not afford any sound guidance concerning the precise value that juries should place on constitutional

[11] We did approve an award of nominal damages for the deprivation of due process in *Carey*. Our discussion of that issue makes clear that nominal damages, and not damages based on some undefinable "value" of infringed rights, are the appropriate means of "vindicating" rights whose deprivation has not caused actual, provable injury:

> Common-law courts traditionally have vindicated deprivations of certain "absolute" rights that are not shown to have caused actual injury through the award of a nominal sum of money. By making the deprivation of such rights actionable for nominal damages without proof of actual injury, the law recognizes the importance to organized society that those rights be scrupulously observed; but at the same time, it remains true to the principle that substantial damages should be awarded only to compensate actual injury or, in the case of exemplary or punitive damages, to deter or punish malicious deprivations of rights.

protections. Accordingly, were such damages available, juries would be free to award arbitrary amounts without any evidentiary basis, or to use their unbounded discretion to punish unpopular defendants. Such damages would be too uncertain to be of any great value to plaintiffs, and would inject caprice into determinations of damages in § 1983 cases. We therefore hold that damages based on the abstract "value" or "importance" of constitutional rights are not a permissible element of compensatory damages in such cases.

Respondent further argues that the challenged instructions authorized a form of "presumed" damages—a remedy that is both compensatory in nature and traditionally part of the range of tort law remedies. Alternatively, respondent argues that the erroneous instructions were at worst harmless error.

Neither argument has merit. Presumed damages are a *substitute* for ordinary compensatory damages, not a *supplement* for an award that fully compensates the alleged injury. When a plaintiff seeks compensation for an injury that is likely to have occurred but difficult to establish, some form of presumed damages may possibly be appropriate. In those circumstances, presumed damages may roughly approximate the harm that the plaintiff suffered and thereby compensate for harms that may be impossible to measure. As we earlier explained, the instructions at issue in this case did not serve this purpose, but instead called on the jury to measure damages based on a subjective evaluation of the importance of particular constitutional values. Since such damages are wholly divorced from any compensatory purpose, they cannot be justified as presumed damages.[14] Moreover, no rough substitute for compensatory damages was

[14] For the same reason, Nixon v. Herndon, 273 U.S. 536 (1927), and similar cases do not support the challenged instructions. In *Nixon,* the Court held that a plaintiff who was illegally prevented from voting in a state primary election suffered compensable injury. This holding did not rest on the "value" of the right to vote as an abstract matter; rather, the Court recognized that the plaintiff had suffered a particular injury—his inability to vote in a particular election—that might be compensated through substantial money damages.

Nixon followed a long line of cases, going back to 1703, authorizing substantial money damages as compensation for persons deprived of their right to vote in particular elections. Although these decisions sometimes speak of damages for the value of the right to vote, their analysis shows that they involve nothing more than an award of presumed damages for a nonmonetary harm that cannot easily be quantified:

> In the eyes of the law th[e] right [to vote] is so valuable that damages are presumed from the wrongful deprivation of it without evidence of actual loss of money, property, or any other valuable thing, and the amount of the damages is a question peculiarly appropriate for the determination of the jury, because each member of the jury has personal knowledge of the value of the right.

See also *Ashby v. White* ("As in an action for slanderous words, though a man does not lose a penny by reason of the speaking [of] them, yet he shall have an action"). The "value of the right" in the context of these decisions is the money value of the particular loss that the plaintiff suffered—a loss of which "each member of the jury has personal knowledge." It is *not* the value of the right to vote as a general, abstract matter, based on its role in our history or system of government. Thus, whatever the wisdom of these decisions in the context of the changing scope of compensatory damages over the course of this century, they do not support awards of noncompensatory damages such as those authorized in this case.

required in this case, since the jury was fully authorized to compensate respondent for both monetary and nonmonetary harms caused by petitioners' conduct.

Nor can we find that the erroneous instructions were harmless. When damages instructions are faulty and the verdict does not reveal the means by which the jury calculated damages, "[the] error in the charge is difficult, if not impossible, to correct without retrial, in light of the jury's general verdict." The jury was authorized to award three categories of damages: (i) compensatory damages for injury to respondent, (ii) punitive damages, and (iii) damages based on the jury's perception of the "importance" of two provisions of the Constitution. The submission of the third of these categories was error. Although the verdict specified an amount for punitive damages, it did not specify how much of the remaining damages was designed to compensate respondent for his injury and how much reflected the jury's estimation of the value of the constitutional rights that were infringed. The effect of the erroneous instruction is therefore unknowable, although probably significant: the jury awarded respondent a very substantial amount of damages, none of which could have derived from any monetary loss.[15] It is likely, although not certain, that a major part of these damages was intended to "compensate" respondent for the abstract "value" of his due process and First Amendment rights. For these reasons, the case must be remanded for a new trial on compensatory damages.

The judgment of the Court of Appeals is reversed, and the case is remanded for further proceedings consistent with this opinion.

JUSTICE MARSHALL, with whom JUSTICES BRENNAN, BLACKMUN, and STEVENS join, concurring in the judgment.

I agree with the Court that this case must be remanded for a new trial on damages. Certain portions of the Court's opinion, however, can be read to suggest that damages in § 1983 cases are necessarily limited to "out-of-pocket loss," "other monetary harms," and "such injuries as 'impairment of reputation . . . , personal humiliation, and mental anguish and suffering.'" I do not understand the Court so to hold, and I write separately to emphasize that the violation of a constitutional right, in proper cases, may itself constitute a compensable injury.

Following *Carey,* the Courts of Appeals have recognized that invasions of constitutional rights sometimes cause injuries that cannot be redressed by a wooden application of common-law damages rules. In *Hobson v. Wilson*, 737 F.2d 1, 57–63 (1984), *cert. denied*, 470 U.S. 1084 (1985), which the Court cites, plaintiffs claimed that defendant Federal Bureau of Investigation agents had invaded their First Amendment rights to assemble for peaceable political protest, to associate with others

[15] Throughout his suspension, respondent continued to receive his teacher's salary.

to engage in political expression, and to speak on public issues free of unreasonable government interference. The District Court found that the defendants had succeeded in diverting plaintiffs from, and impeding them in, their protest activities. The Court of Appeals for the District of Columbia Circuit held that injury to a First Amendment-protected interest could itself constitute compensable injury wholly apart from any "emotional distress, humiliation and personal indignity, emotional pain, embarrassment, fear, anxiety and anguish" suffered by plaintiffs. The court warned, however, that that injury could be compensated with substantial damages only to the extent that it was "reasonably quantifiable"; damages should not be based on "the so-called inherent value of the rights violated."

I believe that the *Hobson* court correctly stated the law. When a plaintiff is deprived, for example, of the opportunity to engage in a demonstration to express his political views, "[i]t is facile to suggest that no damage is done." Loss of such an opportunity constitutes loss of First Amendment rights " 'in their most pristine and classic form.' " There is no reason why such an injury should not be compensable in damages. At the same time, however, the award must be proportional to the actual loss sustained.

The instructions given the jury in this case were improper because they did not require the jury to focus on the loss actually sustained by respondent. Rather, they invited the jury to base its award on speculation about "the importance of the right in our system of government" and "the role which this right has played in the history of our republic," guided only by the admonition that "[i]n one sense, no monetary value we place on Constitutional rights can measure their importance in our society or compensate a citizen adequately for their deprivation." These instructions invited the jury to speculate on matters wholly detached from the real injury occasioned respondent by the deprivation of the right. Further, the instructions might have led the jury to grant respondent damages based on the "abstract value" of the right to procedural due process—a course directly barred by our decision in *Carey.*

The Court therefore properly remands for a new trial on damages. I do not understand the Court, however, to hold that deprivations of constitutional rights can never themselves constitute compensable injuries. Such a rule would be inconsistent with the logic of *Carey,* and would defeat the purpose of § 1983 by denying compensation for genuine injuries caused by the deprivation of constitutional rights.

NOTES AND PROBLEMS

1. Carey, described in *Stachura*, presents an interesting twist. Plaintiffs were suspended from school without a hearing. The court determined that, had they been given a hearing, they would have been

suspended anyway. Thus, the loss caused by the deprivation of rights was not the loss of time in school, but simply the loss of the hearing. Evidence of distress did not differentiate distress suffered because the hearing was denied from distress suffered as a result of the suspension. As a result, no loss seemed to result from the lack of a hearing. The court awarded nominal damages (plus attorneys fees). Is that enough to deter violations of constitutional rights? Does it compensate the plaintiffs for the loss they suffered?

2. In *Stachura*, the loss was both procedural and substantive. Not only was plaintiff deprived of a hearing, but the court assumes the plaintiff could not have been suspended, even with pay, had a hearing been held. Stachura, then, could claim compensation for any loss suffered during the time spent away from work. What might that include? He was paid. Is that just a vacation—a gain rather than a loss? Are the other losses attributable to the suspension? Or were they caused by the public outcry, which existed independent of the suspension?

3. Contract damages can be divided into market damages and consequential damages. Both are compensatory. Market damages compensate for the loss of the thing promised; consequential damages compensate for the loss of the way you would have used the thing (usually to earn profits). Can that dichotomy help us find a better way to think about the damages in this case? How would it apply?

4. Does the court give up on presumed damages too easily? The court states that presumed damages are a substitute for compensatory damages in cases where actual loss is hard to measure. That means the trial court should choose between compensatory and presumed damages. On remand (or in future cases), should plaintiffs ask for presumed damages instead of compensation? Would the court accept that approach? Is Marshall's concurrence in the judgment an accurate assessment of what the court held? Or did he really write a dissent?

5. Is the objection to the type of loss or the way the jury was instructed to measure it? The Court objects to valuing the right "as an abstract matter," in relation to our system of government. Should the jury be instructed instead to measure the importance of the right to the plaintiff, in the context of his activities and his life? That would represent compensation for a loss to him. Properly crafted, would the instruction fall within the right to vote cases discussed in footnote 14?

6. How does this relate to the discussion of subjective value? Is the Court's preference for value to the plaintiff based on concern that abstract value might overstate the loss to the plaintiff? (That would make no sense for property; if the market would pay $100 for a thing, then even if plaintiff values it less than $100, she could sell it for $100 on the market. But since constitutional rights are not easily sold, objective value could exceed subjective value.) Or is the Court concerned that distress fully compensates the plaintiff for the loss to him of these rights? Is that what the court did in

Landers, *supra* at 629, meant when it held that sentimental value should be covered by distress at the loss of the thing, not in the value of the thing?

On the other hand, is the Court really concerned about the lack of an objective market value? Without "any sound guidance concerning precise values," juries might have "unbounded discretion" and "award arbitrary amounts without any evidentiary basis." A market for rights would provide an evidentiary basis and constrain discretion. Can any market transaction offer insight into these values?

7. *Nominal Damages*. Even if presumed damages are unavailable in a particular claim, nominal damages (an award in the amount of $1, or similar) are always recoverable in actions for violation of a constitutional right. Nominal damages are also available in actions for breach of contract, in the absence of sufficient proof of general damages. *See, e.g.*, *Cowan v. Flannery*, 461 N.W.2d 155 (Iowa 1990). Nominal damages are not available in suits for negligence, although they are recoverable in actions alleging intentional torts, trespass to real property, and certain other torts. One might reasonably question how any but the very wealthy could afford to hire an attorney in a suit claiming nominal damages. The answer is three-fold. First, plaintiffs almost always seek nominal damages in the alternative, in case other measures of injury do not succeed. Second, actions seeking nominal damages sometimes also provide for an award of attorneys' fees. Third, and most importantly, in most states an award of nominal damages may provide the basis for punitive damages.

4. WRONGFUL DEATH

At common law, tort actions were unavailable (or, if already begun, were terminated) upon the death either of the victim or the alleged tortfeasor. Nor were a tort decedent's surviving relatives able to sue for the damages suffered by them as a result of the decedent's death. Each of these prohibitions has since been revoked by statutes passed in all fifty states and Congress, statutes referred to as "wrongful death acts" and "survival acts."

Wrongful death legislation authorizes suits by a decedent's surviving relatives for injuries suffered by them as a result of the decedent's death. Recoverable damages vary by statute. Some wrongful death acts limit recovery to the survivors' pecuniary losses, most commonly consisting of the decedent's lost wages and the value of any services provided by the decedent. Others also provide for the recovery of loss of consortium, loss of society and companionship, or emotional distress. Wrongful death acts also vary by whom they authorize to bring suit. Most jurisdictions allow suit by surviving spouses and minor children; however, states differ as to how close a relation must be in order to have standing to sue.

Survival acts provide a cause of action to the decedent's estate for pre-death injuries suffered by the decedent. In other words, survival acts allow the decedent's pre-death tort claims to "survive" his or her death.

Significantly, damages recoverable in a survival claim do not encompass the death itself—only damages that the decedent would have been able to recover had he or she lived. Although the types of recoverable damages vary by statute, damages might include pre-death lost wages, medical expenses, funeral expenses, pain and suffering, and loss of enjoyment of life.

Some of the variations among jurisdictions and their underlying justifications are explored in the following cases.

DELONG V. COUNTY OF ERIE

89 A.D.2d 376, 455 N.Y.S.2d 887 (1982),
aff'd, 60 N.Y.2d 296, 457 N.E.2d 717, 469 N.Y.S.2d 611 (1983).

[The decedent had been killed by an intruder. Decedent had called 911. The Dispatcher handled the call negligently precluding the timely arrival of the police. The court held that the defendant city had assumed a special duty of care and was liable for the decedent's death. The question of damages was also taken on appeal. The court found that: (1) the award of $200,000 for conscious pain and suffering of the decedent for the last twelve minutes of the life was not excessive; (2) expert testimony concerning value of services performed by a housewife was properly admitted; (3) the award of $600,000 for wrongful death of the decedent was not excessive.

On the first issue—damages for the pain and suffering in the survival action—the court per Hancock, J. said: [T]he period during which Amalia DeLong, could have suffered from her wounds was brief (from approximately 9:30, when she completed her call, to shortly after 9:42, when she collapsed on the sidewalk), we cannot find the verdict of $200,000 for conscious pain and suffering "so disproportionate to the injur[ies] as to not be within reasonable bounds." The jury could properly have considered in its award the terror Amalia DeLong must have experienced during her ultimate struggle to save herself and her child from a murderous assailant. The court properly and without exception charged the jury that it should consider Amalia DeLong's fear and apprehension in their assessment of the damages.

On the remaining damages and evidentiary issue the court split.]

DENMAN, JUSTICE.

The jury's award of $600,000 on the wrongful death cause of action is not excessive and was not the result of an error at trial. The standard by which damages in a wrongful death action are measured is established by section 5–4.3 of the Estates, Powers and Trusts Law which provides that the amount of recovery is "to be fair and just compensation for the pecuniary injuries resulting from the decedent's death to the persons for whose benefit the action is brought." Despite the fact that the standard for recovery is couched in terms of pecuniary loss, recovery is not limited to compensation for loss of money or property. It has long been recognized that pecuniary advantage results as well from parental nurture and care, from physical, moral and intellectual training, and that the loss of those benefits may be considered within the calculation of "pecuniary injury" (*Tilley v. Hudson River RR Co.*, 24 N.Y. 471). In determining what is just compensation for the pecuniary injury sustained by the decedent's beneficiaries, the courts have considered myriad factors, including the decedent's age, relationship to the person seeking recovery, earning capacity and life expectancy. As we recently noted, "[s]ince there is little probability that the facts in any two wrongful death cases will be alike, and, in arriving at a proper award, an infinite variety of human characteristics and family situations affect the numerous factors which must be examined, each case must be viewed on its own merits with respect to the damages recoverable" (*Franchell v. Sims*, 73 A.D.2d 1, 6, 424 N.Y.S.2d 959).

Amalia DeLong was 28 years old at the time of her death; her husband was also 28. Her three children were eight, six and one years of age. Decedent was a housewife and was not employed outside of the home, but testimony at trial indicated that she participated actively in raising her children. In addition to doing the cooking cleaning, housekeeping and bookkeeping for the family, she also made most of the children's clothes. Over the objection of defendants, plaintiff was permitted to introduce the expert testimony of a professor of economics who calculated that the replacement cost of the services performed by a housewife to a family statistically similar to that of the decedent was $527,659. In determining that the admission of this testimony was error and may have contributed to the size of the verdict, the dissenters rely on the rule of *Zaninovich v. American Airlines*, 26 A.D.2d 155, 271 N.Y.S.2d 866 [1966], in which the court held that expert testimony was inadmissible to establish the cost of providing substitute services for those of a decedent housewife. The court reasoned that "[t]hese are matters within the common ken, and subject to so many variables and choices that no objective standards can be supplied by an expert, if one there be" (*Zaninovich v. American Airlines, supra*, 159, 271 N.Y.S.2d 866). The rule of *Zaninovich* was based on the general evidentiary proposition that expert opinion is not admissible regarding matters within the general knowledge and expertise of the jury. Implicit in the *Zaninovich* rule is the assumption that reliable expert testimony is not available and that the subject matter does not lend itself to scientific measurement. That view seems incongruous in today's technological society and overlooks a wide range of experts and significant data in the various social sciences and in economics. If at one time evaluation of such services resisted precise measurement, that is certainly no longer true and the belief that a jury somehow knows how to make such computations is unrealistic. Even assuming that a jury is familiar with the multiplicity of services which the modern housewife performs for the her family, the economic value of such services cannot be said to be a matter within the common ken. Indeed, the fact that many may take the value of such services for granted is itself a compelling reason for affording a jury a rational standard by which to evaluate those services lest they be undervalued and survivors inadequately compensated. Here a qualified economist testified on the basis of statistical data. He estimated the time spent by an average housewife in the circumstances of decedent on various household tasks, including food preparation, house maintenance, clothing maintenance, family care, and other miscellaneous services, and then estimated the cost of purchasing such services in the employment market. That testimony was relevant to the issues of damages, was within the expertise of the witness whose qualifications were not disputed and was based on extensive economic and sociological data beyond the experience of the average juror.

The Federal courts and courts in a majority of our sister states have long permitted expert testimony in these circumstances, recognizing that although a layman may have a general idea of the type of services performed by a housewife, expert opinion is necessary in order to place a realistic value on those services. Indeed, the courts of this state have not consistently excluded such proof. As early as 1895 in an action to recover the value of housekeeping services, the Court of Appeals noted the difficulty confronting a plaintiff in attempting to establish a value for the variety of duties embraced in the term "housekeeper" and approved the admission of testimony from a person engaged in the business of hiring housekeepers (*Edgecomb v. Buckhout*, 146 N.Y. 332, 40 N.E. 991). As the District court for the Southern District of New York noted over two decades ago when it rejected the argument that such evaluation was not within the realm of permissible expert testimony,

> Popular knowledge and common sense may be and indeed are valuable. But they are not the sole recourse. The fact that parents from time immemorial have taken care of their children does not establish that the views of a professional home economist may not be sounder than those of untrained laymen in determining the cost of those elements that go into the home in order to provide the children with so-called "substitute mother" care. As knowledge becomes more professionalized, specialists will more frequently be called upon as expert witnesses. This is a judicial by-product of an age of pervasive technology and expanding social science.

Recognizing that we espoused the rule of *Zaninovich* in *Ashdown v. Kluckhohn*, 62 A.D.2d 1137, 404 N.Y.S.2d 461, we now reject that view, concluding that it prevents relevant proof of the economic value of a decedent housewife's services, thus incurring the risk of inadequately compensating a decedent's family for the very real costs expended in replacing her services.

Accordingly, the judgment should be affirmed in its entirety.

HANCOCK, JUSTICE, dissenting.

With respect to the verdict of $600,000 for "the pecuniary injuries resulting from the decedent's death to the persons for whose benefit the action is brought," we must differ with our colleagues. In light of other awards for the death of a housewife and mother, we find it excessive (*compare Juiditta v. Bethlehem Steel Corp.*, 75 A.D.2d 126, 428 N.Y.S.2d 535 [1980], upholding an award of $100,000 exclusive of lost wages where decedent had four children; *Simmons v. Kinney Nat. Serv.*, 53 A.D.2d 846, 385 N.Y.S.2d 788 [1976], *aff'd.* 43 N.Y.2d 659, 400 N.Y.S.2d 816, 371 N.E.2d 534, reducing an award of $325,000 for the death of a 30 year old housewife and mother of three children, ten, nine and five years of age, to an award of $250,000; *Rodriguez v. Columbus Hosp.*, 38 A.D.2d 517, 326 N.Y.S.2d 439 [1971], finding excessive an award of $100,000 for the death of a 49 year old housewife who left a husband and three children, ages twelve, ten and eight [and three other cases]).

[A]n error at trial may have contributed to the size of the verdict. [Under] the rule established in *Zaninovich*, it is error to allow expert proof as to the cost of providing a substitute for a housewife's services because "[t]hese are matters within the common ken, and subject to so many variables and choices that no objective standard can be supplied by an expert."

For these reasons, we believe that the award of $600,000 for the wrongful death of Amalia DeLong should be reversed and a new trial granted as to damages.

PROBLEMS

1. Do the remedies here bear any relationship to the general rule of damages? Are we putting the victim in the position the victim would have occupied if the wrong had not been committed? Who is the victim? What would it take to put the victim in the rightful position?

2. The expert apparently broke down the tasks an average housewife performed and quoted the hourly rate required to hire a substitute. Is the problem that the expert did not address the services that Amalia actually performed or how much time she actually spent on them? The "many variables and choices" that differ among families make this average housewife figure a bit tenuous. The majority relies on these differences to explain away the less generous cases the dissent raises. Shouldn't it also acknowledge them in discussing the dissent's concern about the expert testimony?

3. Are the losses here real? If the widower hired substitute caregivers, their cost would be entirely appropriate. But for the wrong, he would not have incurred these costs. In many cases, the surviving spouse contributes more services than before, perhaps with the help of relatives, rather than hiring additional help. Is the market rate still the best measure of loss? Is there a viable alternative? What if the widower neither hires substitutes nor performs the services personally. Is there any loss? Is there any loss to the plaintiff?

4. The expert's figure comes to about $20,500 a year (assuming 50 years at 3% discount rate, spread evenly). [These assumptions are unrealistic: services would be greater in the early years, less when children left, and perhaps less still in old age, as others must assist with the work; raises to keep up with inflation would need to be included; 3% was too low for the period, though more accurate in the 1990s. These errors may not balance out, but the number gives us a starting point for comparison.] In 1982, high priced firms paid starting attorneys about $45,000; government attorneys started at about $32,000. Teachers, who dealt with even more children for even more hours (and then their own at home), started at less than $20,000. Would these numbers (or similar salaries for other occupations) help the jury put things in perspective? Or would they just muddy the waters? Would it at least be pertinent how much a full-time, live-in nanny would earn?

5. The expert testified to the cost of hiring others to provide services formerly provided by the decedent. Did the expert also testify to the savings the family now experiences. Two do not really live as cheaply as one (or five as cheaply as four). Only the net loss should be awarded, right?

6. The surviving spouse might remarry. If he does, should that offset part of the loss? What about benefits from a life insurance policy? How seriously should we take the usual rule for remedies in this setting? (You may wish to return to these questions after we study the benefits rule and avoidable consequences doctrine.)

GREEN V. BITTNER

85 N.J. 1, 424 A.2d 210 (1980).

WILENTZ, C. J.

In the spring of her senior year at high school, Donna Green was killed in an automobile accident. She was a young woman of average intelligence and cheerful disposition; hard-working and conscientious both at home and at school; level-headed and dependable. As her counsel aptly stated in summation, she was "everybody's daughter," not just meaning normal, but what everybody would want a daughter to be.

This action was brought for her wrongful death under N.J.S.A. 2A:31–1 et seq. Liability having been established at a separate trial, the jury in these proceedings were to "give such damages as they shall deem fair and just with reference to the pecuniary injuries resulting from such death [to] the persons entitled to any intestate personal property of the decedent." N.J.S.A. 2A:31–5. The jury apparently found that Donna's survivors, her parents and brothers and sisters, had suffered no pecuniary loss for they awarded no damages whatsoever. In effect her life was adjudicated worthless to others, in a pecuniary sense.

We reverse. Under the circumstances presented to us, such a verdict is a miscarriage of justice. We remand for a new trial in accordance with this opinion on the issue of damages. We hold that when parents sue for the wrongful death of their child, damages should not be limited to the well-known elements of pecuniary loss such as the loss of the value of the child's anticipated help with household chores, or the loss of anticipated direct financial contributions by the child after he or she becomes a wage earner. We hold that in addition, the jury should be allowed, under appropriate circumstances, to award damages for the parents' loss of their child's companionship as they grow older, when it may be most needed and valuable, as well as the advice and guidance that often accompanies it. As noted later, these other losses will be confined to their pecuniary value, excluding emotional loss. Given this expansion of permissible recovery, a verdict finding no damages for the death of a child should ordinarily be set aside by the trial court and a new trial ordered. To sustain such a verdict "would result in a return to the outmoded doctrine that a child is a liability—not an asset." *Bohrman v. Pennsylvania Railroad Co.*, 23 N.J.Super. 399, 409 (App.Div.1952).

We intend, by so holding, to give juries in wrongful death cases involving children the same ability to do justice to their parents, within the limits of existing legislation, as they now have under our cases when children lose a parent. By thus expanding the permissible scope of recovery, we also hope to reduce the pressure on juries to award damages for the parents' emotional suffering, unquestionably the most substantial element of damages in these cases, but legally impermissible.

Donna was one of six children in a warm and close family. She was a good student, did her share of household tasks, including baby-sitting and keeping the younger children busy so that her mother was free to do other things. She worked after school, as well as on weekends and in the summer, and had done so since she was 14. She helped provide for her own material needs and was saving for her forthcoming graduation festivities. She had definite plans to enter college and ultimately to embark on a business career. Although others described her as fun-loving, ebullient and popular, her mother, who concurred, nevertheless characterized her as level-headed. She was always there when she was needed; she always came through. She was a good-hearted, devoted and dependable daughter. At the close of the evidence the trial court charged the jury that their verdict, in accordance with N.J.S.A. 2A:31–5, was to reflect only past, present and future pecuniary losses to the survivors, including any direct financial contributions that Donna might have made, but was not to compensate for grief and sentimental losses. In addition, the trial judge stated, "the term financial loss also includes the reasonable value of benefits which would have been received by a survivor in the nature of services or assistance or guidance if the decedent had continued to live." He qualified this statement by explaining that the jury should "consider the benefits which Donna bestowed upon the survivors in the form of service or assistance; [and] the guidance and training afforded by Donna to such survivor infants and the probabilities of whether and how long Donna would continue to have made such contribution to the welfare of other minor children who are now the survivors." As to the parents' losses, the judge stated: "You [the jury] should consider the services that Donna had performed about the household in the past, such as baby-sitting, cleaning and other types of home chores. In evaluating this claim, you may also consider the likelihood of any additional chores [which] Donna would have undertaken had she grown older about the house." The jury was further instructed to deduct from the value thus determined the costs of feeding, clothing and educating Donna until her majority. This would have included the $4,000 her father was planning to spend for her college tuition.

After deliberating for approximately an hour and a half, the jury returned a verdict of no damages. Plaintiffs' motion for a new trial on damages was denied. The trial judge concluded that "it would be reasonable for this jury to come to [the] conclusion that the value of her services to baby-sit or to dry dishes was far exceeded by the cost to the family of feeding, clothing and educating her. The jury in this particular case followed literally the language of the statute and came to the conclusion that they reached." The judge noted that it is unusual for a jury to come in with a verdict of no recovery, and he expressed sympathy with the parents and their shock when they learned of no award for their daughter's death. He concluded, however, that a clear and convincing miscarriage of justice had not occurred. The Appellate Division affirmed this denial in an unreported opinion.

In fairness to the trial court, its instructions to the jury were substantially in accord with present case law. Furthermore, the charge was objected to in only one respect which the court remedied. Under those instructions, the trial judge was clearly correct when, in ruling on the motion for a new trial, he noted that a jury could very well have concluded that the further cost to the family of maintaining Donna might equal or exceed the pecuniary value of those items of loss which the law, as understood by all concerned, allowed the jury to consider. The charge, as is usual in such cases, focused almost exclusively on the value of household chores that Donna might have performed in the future. While there was some reference to the possibility that she might also have rendered "assistance or guidance," subsequent qualification of this phrase must have led the jury to believe that, at least insofar as the parents were concerned, it referred to the same kind of services Donna had performed in the past, namely, household chores. The entire instruction was practically devoid of any suggestion of a different kind of assistance that a parent or sibling might have received from the decedent in the future. There was no reference, for instance, to the pecuniary value of companionship and advice that Donna might perhaps have given her parents as she and they grew older, the caretaking role that she might have fulfilled towards them over time, whether in the sense of actual physical care and companionship in the event of illness or old age, or services and chores performed simply out of a continuing sense of family obligation. As noted above, such a charge was not compelled by prior holdings, nor was it requested by counsel. The evidence, however, could have supported such a charge, and previous cases did not preclude it.

The development of existing case law elsewhere suggests allowance of such damages as "pecuniary injuries" under wrongful death statutes. This development has probably been influenced by the inconsistent treatment in wrongful death cases between a parent's death and a child's death. In the case of a parent's death, in addition to the usual losses clearly having a monetary value, the law allows damages to be awarded to the surviving children for the loss of guidance and counsel which they might otherwise have received from the parent. The cases do not suggest that the calculation of such damages must cease after the child reaches majority. They are based on an ongoing relationship which exists in fact, regardless of any lack of legal duty on the part of the parent to render such guidance and despite the difficulty of placing a dollar value on it. Such damages are regularly allowed despite the total lack of proof of such dollar value and of the probability that such guidance and counsel would in fact have been rendered. For instance, the law has allowed damages for the loss of a mother's training and nurture, and a father's guidance and advice. It has done the same when the loss was that of a grandparent's solicitous care, and even an adult brother's helpful services to a dependent sister. In the case of a child's death, however, those services to be given a dollar value are almost invariably limited to household chores—as distinguished from cases where special circumstances suggest the probability of future financial contributions by the child to his parent, *e.g.*, where a child has exhibited extraordinary talents suggesting substantial earning [capacity]. *Cf. Gluckauf v. Pine Lake Beach Club, Inc.*, 78 N.J. Super. 8 (App.Div.1963) (15 year old decedent had near-genius I.Q. and special aptitude for science); *Kopko v. New York Live Poultry Trucking Co.*, 3 N.J. Misc. 498, *aff'd*, 102 N.J.L. 440 (Err. & App. 1926) (12 year old violinist had great talent). Some cases allow the jury to consider the possibility of post-majority direct financial help even from what appears to be an average child, given his earnings during minority and the family's special circumstances. Our cases, however, have not recognized that parents whose child is killed may lose as well the future pecuniary benefit of that child's guidance and counsel much as the child would have lost theirs had either of them been killed. Nor have they acknowledged the pecuniary value to the parents of the anticipated companionship of the child when the parents are infirm or aged.

As suggested above, other states, sometimes similarly bound by legislation, sometimes by decisional law, have relaxed the strict pecuniary approach to damages for a child's death where its potential for harsh results is substantial. One of the most noteworthy of these efforts has occurred in Michigan. In *Wycko v. Gnodtke*, 361 Mich. 331, 105 N.W.2d 118 (1960), the Michigan Supreme Court rejected a strict pecuniary loss rule that its courts had engrafted onto a statute that had allowed recovery for losses of a pecuniary nature. The Michigan court pointed out that the era of child labor, and hence the fixation with earnings and services, was over. Rejecting "the bloodless bookkeeping imposed upon our juries by the savage exploitations of the last century," the court held that the worth of a child's life should henceforth be calculated according to his function as part of an ongoing family unit. When *Wycko* was overruled, [the] Michigan Legislature responded by incorporating into its Wrongful Death Act a provision that damages may also include recovery for loss of society and companionship, thus affirming the result in *Wycko*. Mich. Stat. Ann. § 27A.2922. In Minnesota, which has a strict pecuniary loss statute, the Minnesota Supreme Court reached the same result by interpreting the loss of a child's advice, comfort, assistance and protection as a pecuniary loss. *Fussner v. Andert*, 261 Minn. 347, 113 N.W.2d 355 (1961). [Similar] results have occurred in [Nebraska, Washington,] California, Montana, Pennsylvania, South Dakota and the Virgin Islands. . . .

The fact that parents are usually legally entitled to the services of their children until majority seems to have led us in New Jersey to the implicit conclusion that that is the limit of the parents' loss (other than prospective financial contributions). But continuing family relationships—uninterrupted by the death of a family member—encompass more than the exchange of physical chores around the house at various times during the family's history, and even more than direct financial contributions. Perhaps as significant is the apparent absence in infant death cases of the kind of expert testimony that might have helped courts to perceive a greater extent of loss than previously recognized. In any event, we see no reason why the same factual approach used in adult death cases should not be taken when it is a child who has been killed. There is nothing in the statute to distinguish one case from the other: "pecuniary injuries" suffered by the surviving next of kin is the standard for all wrongful death cases. As this Court has said in an infant death case, "the pecuniary injury designated by the statute is nothing more than a deprivation of a reasonable expectation of a pecuniary advantage which would have resulted by a continuance of the life of the deceased," *Cooper v. Shore Electric Co.*, 63 N.J.L. 558, 567 (E. & A. 1899).

What services, what activities, could a daughter or son reasonably have been expected to engage in but for their death and to what extent do any of them have monetary value? Just as the law recognizes that a child may continue performing services after age 18, and that monetary contributions may also be received by the parents thereafter when the child becomes productive, it should similarly recognize that the child may, as many do, provide valuable companionship and care as the parents get older. As noted above, our courts have not hesitated to recognize the need of children for physical help and care. Parents facing age or deteriorating health have the same need, and it is usually their children who satisfy that need. Indeed the loss of companionship and advice which a parent suffers when a child is killed will sometimes be as great as the loss of counsel and guidance which a child suffers when a parent is the victim.

Companionship and advice in this context must be limited strictly to their pecuniary element. The command of the statute is too clear to allow compensation, directly or indirectly, for emotional loss. Companionship, lost by death, to be compensable must be that which would have provided services substantially equivalent to those provided by the "companions" often hired today by the aged or infirm, or substantially equivalent to services provided by nurses or practical nurses. And its value must be confined to what the marketplace would pay a stranger with similar qualifications for performing such services. No pecuniary value may be attributed to the emotional pleasure that a parent gets when it is his or her child doing the caretaking rather than a stranger, although such pleasure will often he the primary value of the child's service, indeed, in reality, its most beneficial aspect. This loss of added emotional satisfaction that would have been derived from the child's companionship is fundamentally similar to the emotional suffering occasioned by the death. Both are emotional rather than "pecuniary injuries," one expressed in terms of actual emotional loss, the other in terms of lost prospective emotional satisfaction. In another sense, the loss of the prospective emotional satisfaction of the companionship of a child when one is older is but one example of the innumerable similar prospective losses occasioned by the child's death—all of which, plus much more, is included in the emotional suffering caused by the death.

Given this jurisdiction's vastly expanded scope both of tort liability and of recoverable damages—including emotional loss, for instance, when a parent actually witnesses a child's death—we know of no public policy which would prohibit awarding damages that fully compensate for the loss of emotional pleasure in this situation, or indeed for the emotional suffering caused by the death. We recognize that our prohibition against such damages deprives the surviving parent of compensation for the real loss. That prohibition is not a matter of our choice, rather it is fundamental to the legislation.

The loss of guidance, advice and counsel is similarly to be confined to its pecuniary element. It is not the loss simply of the exchange of views, no matter how perceptive, when child and parent are together; it is certainly not the loss of the pleasure which accompanies such an exchange. Rather it is the loss of that kind of guidance, advice and counsel which all of us need from time to time in particular situations, for specific purposes, perhaps as an aid in making a business decision, or a decision affecting our lives generally, or even advice and guidance needed to relieve us from unremitting depression. It must be the kind of advice, guidance or counsel that could be purchased from a business adviser, a therapist, or a trained counselor, for instance. That some of us obtain the same benefit without charge from spouses, friends or children does not strip it of pecuniary value.

Having defined the companionship and advice, loss of which is compensable in an action for the wrongful death of a child, we next address some of the concerns arising from this expansion of recovery in these cases.

Absent special circumstances, it could be claimed that the mere parent-child relationship does not show that it is more probable than not that such services would have been rendered had the child lived. Who knows what the child's circumstances would be, or whether the parent would indeed become old or infirm and require such companionship, or need such advice at any time? Given the speculative quality of the inferences, it might further be questioned whether one could realistically attach an estimated pecuniary value to such services. Our answer is, even assuming no special circumstances are proven, that the nature of these cases has led our courts to allow damages even though the inferences, and the estimate of damages, are based on uncertainties. When a parent dies and loss of advice, guidance and counsel is allowed to the surviving children, and when an infant child dies and loss of prospective services is allowed to the parents, the proof that suffices is the parent-child relationship and what we assume the jury can conclude from that relationship alone. Damages are allowed without any showing that the parent had actually been rendering valuable advice, or was likely to do so, or that the child—even if only five months old—was likely to render services around the house. Even in this case the charge of the judge would have allowed the jury to find loss of prospective financial contributions, although there was nothing in the record suggesting that Donna would have made such. [W]e are not about to deny this pecuniary element of prospective companionship and advice from a child because it may be somewhat more conjectural. Our tradition in these cases is to the contrary. Given a normal parent-child relationship, a jury could very well find it is sufficiently probable, had the child lived, that at some point he or she would have rendered the kind of companionship services mentioned herein and, although perhaps even somewhat more conjectural, the kind of advice, guidance and counsel we have described. It will be up to the jury to decide what services would have been rendered, and what their value is, subject to no more or no less control, direction, and guidance from the court than occurs in other wrongful death cases. There need be no showing that companionship and advice will probably be purchased by the parent because of the child's death; it is sufficient that the deceased would have rendered them.

Obviously the use of an expert in these cases could be most helpful, along with such detailed information concerning family circumstances as counsel can provide. . . .

Ascertaining the present value of the prospective services presents no particular problem simply because they will be rendered in the distant future. The same mathematics which allow discounting the value of prospective services to be rendered in two years can be applied to those which may be rendered in twenty.

We do not regard our holding concerning the compensability of loss of companionship as an expansion of recovery in these cases except in the sense that prior cases have not explicitly recognized this element of damage. The loss is within the statutory limit of "pecuniary injuries" and its allowance does not overrule prior cases. . . .

Extension of the scope of recovery in cases involving a child's death should reduce the adverse effect the present restrictive rules probably have on juries. Verdicts in these cases sometimes result from the jury's desire to award the parents something for their emotional suffering (not permitted by law) in view of the severely restricted permissible items of recovery. A compassionate jury, wanting to give the parents something substantial for their emotional loss but being told, in effect, that the measure of recovery is the value of the household chores that might have been performed less the future cost to the parents of maintaining the child, is inclined to set an unrealistically high value on those household chores. A more conscientious jury will add up the numbers and come in with zero. By allowing the jury realistically to measure these additional elements of the losses which may be suffered by parents when a child is killed, we believe that they will be more likely to return verdicts based upon the judge's charge, rather than, as now, to find a way to do some kind of justice despite the judge's charge. Our expectation is that verdicts will more nearly reflect the actual pecuniary losses suffered.

One further consideration suggests that this extension of recovery is warranted. Parents live longer today; the proportion of people age 65 and over in our population continues to grow. And their children retire earlier, become independent sooner, and free of the obligation to support the grandchildren sooner. We suspect that there are many more children aged 45 to 55 who are faced with their parents' need for care and guidance than there were in the past, and who are able to render such care and guidance along with whatever help they may from time to time give to their emancipated children. Nursing homes are not the only vehicle for this assistance. The parents' need is real, and when a middle-aged son or daughter is not there because of a wrongful death, a prospective pecuniary advantage of the aged or infirm parent has been lost. Another factor is of similar significance: while the death rate of the older part of our population continues to decrease, that of the younger has started to increase.

For the reasons set forth above, the decision of the Appellate Division is reversed and the matter is remanded for a new trial as to damages only.

NOTES AND QUESTIONS

1. The court in the principal case included a useful note that gave a profile of the law elsewhere. The note, subject to more recent changes indicated, reads as follows:

> As early as 1964, in *Graf v. Taggert*, 43 N.J. 303, 308–309 n. 1 (1964), this Court pointed to the growing number of jurisdictions which had abandoned the pecuniary loss rule altogether or interpreted pecuniary loss to cover such items as loss of society or companionship. This trend has continued. At present, twelve [now twenty-seven] states have enacted statutes allowing recovery for mental anguish or loss of comfort and companionship: Alaska (comfort and companionship); Arkansas (comfort and companionship, anguish); Florida (comfort and companionship, anguish); Hawaii (comfort and companionship); Kansas (comfort and companionship, anguish); Maryland (comfort and companionship, anguish); Michigan (comfort and companionship); Mississippi (comfort and companionship); Nevada (comfort and companionship); West Virginia (comfort and companionship, interpreted to cover anguish as well); Wisconsin (comfort and companionship); Wyoming (comfort and companionship). Virginia (mental anguish, companionship, comfort, guidance, kindly offices and advice); North Dakota (mental anguish, loss of society and companionship); Ohio (mental anguish, loss of society and companionship); Maine (mental distress, loss of comfort, society, and companionship); Oklahoma (mental anguish, loss of companionship); Oregon (mental suffering, loss of care, comfort, companionship, and society); Missouri (loss of companionship, comfort, instruction, guidance, counsel, training, support, services, and consortium); Wisconsin (loss of society and companionship, mental anguish); Illinois (Loss of companionship and mental

anguish); Rhode Island (loss of companionship for loss of parent by an unemancipated minor or loss of unemancipated child by parent); Delaware (mental anguish); Wyoming (loss of probable future companionship, society, and comfort); Kentucky (loss of affection and companionship for wrongful death of a minor child); Massachusetts (companionship and comfort); North Carolina (society, companionship, comfort, guidance, kindly offices and advice). *See* S. SPEISER, RECOVERY FOR WRONGFUL DEATH 2d § 3:47 n.98 at 317, § 3.53 at 336 (1975).

As noted above, [in] many other jurisdictions, courts unfettered by legislation have taken the initiative in allowing recovery for traditionally non-pecuniary losses. These jurisdictions include Arizona, Idaho, New York, Indiana, Louisiana, Puerto Rico, South Carolina, Texas, Utah, Vermont, Virginia and Washington. *See S. Speiser, supra*, § 3:49 nn.89–95 at 313–16. Even several jurisdictions bound by strict pecuniary loss rules have nevertheless allowed recovery for the "pecuniary value" of such items as comfort and companionship, or advice and counsel. Among these jurisdictions are California, Michigan, Minnesota, Montana, Pennsylvania, South Dakota and the Virgin Islands. *See Speiser, supra*, § 3:49 at 318–22. Those jurisdictions that have not yet abandoned a strict pecuniary loss rule are being urged by commentators to do so.

2. In *Siciliano v. Capitol City Shows*, 124 N.H. 719, 475 A.2d 19 (1984), the majority refused, under its interpretation of the New Hampshire legislation, to allow recovery for the loss of companionship and society of a child. In this case plaintiff claimed damages for the death of a minor daughter in an accident on an amusement ride.

Douglas J., dissenting, noted that the economic conceptualization of the relationship between parent and child was anachronistic. Modern law and society protected the deeper relationship as fundamental to society. No reasons stood in the way of awarding damages for the loss. Another daughter had suffered cerebral injury in the same accident. Damages could include the loss of her society, and Douglas J. opined that the same type of loss should be encompassed in the claim for wrongful death. Is this argument based on disparate treatment convincing?

3. Is the damage award on remand likely to be any larger than the original award? We may assume that the new jury will find some valuable advice that Donna might have offered over the years. Yet much of it will be well in the future. Reduced to present value, the loss will still be quite small, perhaps still less than the cost of her support for the coming years. In addition, if the court may take judicial notice that Donna might support her parents without a legal obligation to do so, should it also recognize that parents often support their children well after they reach majority. Should those expenses, too, be calculated into the savings?

PROBLEMS

1. Were you persuaded that the jury could assume such services merely from the parent-child relationship? Do courts really make that assumption when parents die? In the following situations, should the court allow the jury to include lost services in the recovery merely because the parties were related? In each case, assume the defendant negligently caused Terry's death.

a. Terry's children, Chris (7) and Sean (9), have not seen Terry since their parents were divorced 5 years ago. Does your answer depend on their ages? How?

b. Terry worked two jobs, seeing the children (Chris & Sean) no more than one hour a day, during which time Terry often watched television and drank beer without saying a word to the children.

c. Terry's child Chris (6 months) continues to nurse (not Terry's department) and has not required much supervision of education yet, but Terry dotes on the child.

d. Terry ran away from home at age 15 and has not seen the parents for 6 (or 16 or 26) years.

e. Terry (17) officially lives at home, but spends as little time there as possible. When home, Terry stays in a bedroom with headphones, never speaking to the parents, except perhaps to make hurtful comments and leave again.

f. Terry (17) joined a local gang at 12 and spends time on the street rather than at home. The only time the parents see Terry is to post bail.

g. Terry (17) suffers from paranoid schizophrenia. Terry lives at home because Terry lacks the ability to live without assistance and the parents do not want Terry to be institutionalized. The parents are frightened of Terry and dare not contradict anything Terry says or offer any suggestions for what Terry should do.

h. Terry (age 3) has not performed many chores yet, but seems like an angel to the parents.

2. Perhaps note 3 suggests a different direction. Is the real problem that the courts limit recovery to pecuniary losses, excluding grief, distress, and emotional benefits children provide? Some, perhaps most, juries make substantial awards despite instructions limiting recovery to pecuniary losses. Is the real problem that this jury actually followed the instructions? If so, might a redesign of the wrongful death statutes be a more productive avenue than a modest interpretation that retains their central flaw? Or is the limit to pecuniary losses not a flaw?

MURPHY V. MARTIN OIL CO.

56 Ill.2d 423, 308 N.E.2d 583 (1974).

WARD, JUSTICE

The plaintiff, Charryl Murphy, as administratrix of her late husband, Jack Raymond Murphy, and individually, and as next friend of Debbie Ann Murphy, Jack Kenneth Murphy and Carrie Lynn Murphy, their children, filed a complaint [against] the defendants, Martin Oil Company and James Hocker. Count I of the complaint claimed damages for wrongful death under the Illinois Wrongful Death Act and count II sought damages for conscious pain and suffering, loss of wages and property damage. The circuit court allowed the defendants' motion to strike the second count of the complaint on the ground that it failed to state a cause of [action]. The cause was remanded with directions to reinstate as much of count II as related to loss of wages and property damage. We granted the plaintiff's petition for leave to appeal.

The first count set out the factual background for the complaint. It alleged that on June 11, 1968, the defendants owned and operated a gasoline station in Oak Lawn, Cook County, and that on that date the plaintiff's decedent, Jack Raymond Murphy, while having his truck filled with gasoline, was injured through the defendants' negligence in a fire on the defendants' premises. Nine days later he died from the injuries. Damages for wrongful death were claimed under the Illinois Wrongful Death Act. (Ill. Rev. Stat. 1971, ch. 70, pars. 1 and 2.) The language of section 1 of the statute is: "Whenever the death of a person shall be caused by wrongful act, neglect or default, and the act, neglect or default is such as would, if death had not ensued, have entitled the party injured to maintain an action and recover damages in respect thereof, then and in every such case the person who or company or corporation which would have been liable if death had not ensued, shall be liable to an action for damages, notwithstanding the death of the person injured, and although the death shall have been caused under such circumstances as amount in law to felony."

The second count of the complaint asked for damages for the decedent's physical and mental suffering, for loss of wages for the nine-day period following his injury and for the loss of his clothing worn at the time of injury. These damages were claimed under the common law and under our survival statute, which provides that certain rights of action survive the death of the person with the right of action. (Ill. Rev. Stat. 1971, ch. 3, par. 339.) The statute states:

"In addition to the actions which survive by the common law, the following also survive: actions of replevin, actions to recover damages for an injury to the person (except slander and libel), actions to recover damages for an injury to real or personal property or for the detention or conversion of personal property, actions against officers for misfeasance, malfeasance, or nonfeasance of themselves or their deputies, actions for fraud or deceit, and actions provided in Section 14 of Article VI of 'An Act relating to alcoholic liquors', approved January 31, 1934, as amended." On this appeal we shall consider: (1) whether the plaintiff can recover for the loss of wages which her decedent would have earned during the interval between his injury and death; (2) whether the plaintiff can recover for the destruction of the decedent's personal property (clothing) at the time of the injury; (3) whether the plaintiff can recover damages for conscious pain and suffering of the decedent from the time of his injuries to the time of death.

This State in 1853 enacted the Wrongful Death Act and in 1872 enacted the so-called Survival Act (now section 339 of the Probate Act). This court first had occasion to consider the statutes in combination in 1882 in *Holton v. Daly*, 106 Ill. 131. The court declared that the effect of the Wrongful Death Act was that a cause of action for personal injuries, which would have abated under the common law upon the death of the injured party from those injuries, would continue on behalf of the spouse or the next of kin and would be "enlarged to embrace the injury resulting from the death." In other words, it was held that the Wrongful Death Act provided the exclusive remedy available when death came as a result of given tortious conduct. In considering the Survival Act the court stated that it was intended to allow for the survival of a cause of action only when the injured party died from a cause other than that which caused the injuries which created the cause of action. Thus, the court said, an action for personal injury would not survive death if death resulted from the tortious conduct which caused the injury.

This construction of the two statutes persisted for over 70 years. Damages, therefore, under the Wrongful Death Act were limited to pecuniary losses, as from loss of support, to the surviving spouse and next of kin as a result of the death. Under the survival statute damages recoverable in a personal injury action, as for conscious pain and suffering, loss of earnings, medical expenses and physical disability, could be had only if death resulted from a cause other than the one which gave rise to the personal injury action.

This court was asked in 1941 to depart from its decision in *Holton v. Daly* and to permit, in addition to a wrongful death action, an action for personal injuries to be brought, though the injuries had resulted in the death of the injured person. This court acknowledged that there had been other jurisdictions which held contrary to *Holton v. Daly* and permitted the bringing of both actions, but the court said that any change in the rule in *Holton* must come from the legislature. This court noted the absence of legislative action and permitted a widow to recover for funeral and medical expenses in an action which was independent of and in addition to an action brought by her for damages under the Wrongful Death Act. It was said:

> Viewing the situation realistically, this liability of the surviving spouse for such expenses constitutes very real damages. Since that liability results from defendant's tortious conduct, it is only legally sound, and in accordance with basic negligence principles, that the burden of such damages should fall, not on the innocent victim, but upon the tortfeasor.
>
> [The] estate or the spouse, either or both as the circumstances indicate, are entitled to recover for pecuniary losses suffered by either or both which are not recoverable under the Wrongful Death act, and all cases holding the contrary are overruled.

20 Ill. 2d 301, 310–311.

Later, in *Graul v. Adrian* (1965), 32 Ill. 2d 345, this court approved an action brought for medical and funeral expenses of a child, which had been concurrently brought with an action brought under the Wrongful Death Act.

While the specific ground of decision in Graul was the family-expense section of the Husband and Wife Act, and though some have contended that *Saunders v. Schultz* was based on the liability of the widow there under the Husband and Wife Act, it has become obvious that the Wrongful Death Act is no longer regarded as the exclusive remedy available when the injuries cause death. Too, it is clear that the abatement of actions is not favored.

This disapproval of abatement was expressed in *McDaniel v. Bullard* (1966), 34 Ill. 2d 487, where the parents and sister of an infant, Yvonne McDaniel, had been killed in an automobile collision. An action was begun on behalf of Yvonne under the Wrongful Death Act and shortly after the filing of the action Yvonne died from causes which were unrelated to the collision. This court rejected the defendant's contention that the pending action under the Wrongful Death Act was abated or extinguished upon Yvonne's death. In holding that an action under the Wrongful Death Act survived under the terms of the Survival Act upon the death of the victim's next of kin, this court said: "Today damages from most torts are recognized as compensatory rather than punitive, and there is no reason why an estate that has been injured or depleted by the wrong of another should not be compensated whether the injured party is living or not. The rule of abatement has its roots in archaic conceptions of remedy which have long since lost their validity. The reason having ceased the rule is out of place and ought not to be perpetuated." We concluded that under the Survival Act the action for wrongful death did not abate but might be maintained for the benefit of Yvonne's estate.

This disfavoring of abatement and enlarging of survival statutes has been general. In PROSSER, HANDBOOK OF THE LAW OF TORTS (4th ed. 1971), at page 901, it is said: "[T]he modern trend is definitely toward the view that tort causes of action and liabilities are as fairly a part of the estate of either plaintiff or defendant as contract debts, and that the question is rather one of why a fortuitous event such as death should extinguish a valid action. Accordingly, survival statutes gradually are being extended; and it may be expected that ultimately all tort actions will survive to the same extent as those founded on contract." Prosser observes that where there have been wrongful death and survival statutes the usual holding has been that actions may be concurrently maintained under those statutes. The usual method of dealing with the two causes of action, he notes, is to allocate conscious pain and suffering, expenses and loss of earnings of the decedent up to the date of death to the survival statute, and to allocate the loss of benefits of the survivors to the action for wrongful death.

As the cited comments of Prosser indicate, the majority of jurisdictions which have considered the question allow an action for personal injuries in addition to an action under the wrongful death statute, though death is attributable to the injuries. Recovery for conscious pain and suffering is permitted in most of these jurisdictions. Too, recovery is allowed under the Federal Employer's Liability Act for a decedent's conscious pain and suffering provided it was not substantially contemporaneous with his death.

We consider that those decisions which allow an action for fatal injuries as well as for wrongful death are to be preferred to this court's holding in *Holton v. Daly* that the Wrongful Death Act was the only remedy available when injury resulted in death. The holding in Holton was not compelled, we judge, by the language or the nature of the statutes examined. The statutes were conceptually separable and different. The one related to an action arising upon wrongful death; the other related to a right of action for personal injury arising during the life of the injured person.

The remedy available under *Holton* will often be grievously incomplete. There may be a substantial loss of earnings, medical expenses, prolonged pain and suffering, as well as property damage sustained, before an injured person may succumb to his injuries. To say that there can be recovery only for his wrongful death is to provide an obviously inadequate justice. Too, the result in such a case is that the wrongdoer will have to answer for only a portion of the damages he caused. Incongruously, if the injury caused is so severe that death results, the wrongdoer's liability for the damages before death will be extinguished. It is obvious that in order to have a full liability and a full recovery there must be an action allowed for damages up to the time of death, as well as thereafter. Considering "It is more important that the court should be right upon later and more elaborate consideration of the cases than consistent with previous declarations," we declare *Holton* and the cases which have followed it overruled. . . .

For the reasons given, the judgment of the appellate court is affirmed insofar as it held that an action may be maintained by the plaintiff for loss of property and loss of wages during the interval between injury and death, and that judgment is reversed insofar as it held that the plaintiff cannot maintain an action for her decedent's pain and suffering.

Affirmed in part; reversed in part.

NOTES AND QUESTIONS

1. Does this decision eliminate the need for wrongful death statutes? If the decedent's right to sue for the tort that caused the death survives, then couldn't that action include all the damages now included in the wrongful death recovery? If so, is this a better solution than the wrongful death statute? Would it address some of the problems encountered in the first two cases?

2. When survival and wrongful death legislation coexist, some difficulties can arise concerning overlapping recovery. While survival statutes inure to the benefit of the estate (and through it the heirs), wrongful death statutes often name specific dependents as the proper plaintiffs. Where the dependents are not the heirs, it makes a difference which action recovers the lost wages. Under the Uniform Law Commissioners' Survival and Death Act, the damages recoverable "in behalf of a decedent for an injury causing his death are limited to those that occurred to him before his death, plus reasonable burial expenses paid and payable from his estate." § 2. Thus, the heirs' portion is limited to the pre-death period, while dependents recover for the remainder of the decedent's life expectancy. Without such a provision, the statutes risk double liability: the estate may claim lost wages for life; the dependents may claim lost support for life; but that support would have been paid by the decedent out of his wages. This result is avoided where the heirs and dependants are identical since the damages under the survival action are a benefit flowing from the decedent's death and deductible as a such from the damages under the wrongful death action. The judicial resolution is usually to deduct from the survival action damages for the lost years, the cost of self-maintenance and the cost of maintenance of dependants, leaving a paltry rump of an award. The deduction of self-maintenance is principled since by definition dead men have no living expenses. The deduction of the maintenance of dependants is pragmatic; it avoids double recovery, but at the expense of the heirs. The result favors one set of claimants over another where the legislation appears to give each a full claim to recovery. The problem lies with the language of the statutes and is more neatly taken care of by the legislature. The issue is discussed in *Pickett v. British Rail*

Engineering Ltd., [1980] A.C. 1361 (H.L) and *Skelton v. Collins*, 115 C.L.R. 94 (1966) (High Court of Australia).

3. The previous note discusses the potential for overlapping recovery in survival and wrongful death suits. In one respect, however, the damages recoverable in the two actions leave a significant gap. Neither survival nor wrongful death claims allow recovery of the nonpecuniary value of the decedent's life *to the decedent.* Consider that were one to shoot and kill at point blank range a person with no surviving spouse or children, the law would provide for no tort liability at all. *But see Broughel v. Southern New England Tel. Co.*, 45 A. 435 (Conn.1900) (allowing nominal damages in case of instantaneous death). Should it? If the law allows recovery for "loss of enjoyment of life" in some circumstances, why should it not allow a decedent's estate to recover a decedent's lost enjoyment of life? Is it sensible that the most valuable thing a tortfeasor can take from a victim is his or her life, and yet that injury is not compensable? For discussion, see Jonathan James, *Comment, Denial of Recovery to Nonresident Beneficiaries Under Washington's Wrongful Death and Survival Statutes: Is It Really Cheaper to Kill a Man than to Maim Him?*, 29 Seattle U. L. Rev. 663 (2006).

4. On the other hand, if the tort victim is deceased, why should the law provide for tort recovery at all? Do survival suits serve the goal of compensation when the victim is no longer around to be compensated? Might survival suits serve some other purpose?

5. *Pre-Death Fright.* In jurisdictions that provide for recovery of pre-death pain and suffering, many allow damages for the fright of experiencing one's impending demise. *See, e.g., Shu–Tao Lin v. McDonnell Douglas Corp.*, 742 F.2d 45 (2d Cir. 1984) (upholding damages award for pre-impact fright for airline passenger who likely witnessed "the left engine and a portion of the wing break away at the beginning of the flight, which lasted some thirty seconds between takeoff and crash."); *Beynon v. Montgomery Cablevision Limited Partnership*, 718 A.2d 1161 (Md. 1998) (upholding award for auto accident victim's pre-death fright, evidenced by 71.5 feet of skid marks left by decedent's vehicle).

6. Two issues concerning taxes have vexed courts: (1) whether damages for lost earnings should be based on pre- or post-tax earnings, and (2) whether the jury ought to be instructed about the tax treatment given to damages awards. These questions can affect any personal injury, but often have been addressed in wrongful death cases.

Most courts have held that pre-tax (or gross) earnings should be the basis for calculation and that juries should not be instructed as to the tax treatment accorded to damage awards. Is that consistent with the way remedies for wrongful death are calculated? Is the result different when plaintiff is still alive?

Under § 104(a)(2) of the Internal Revenue Code, the amount of compensatory or punitive damages received on account of personal injuries may be excluded from gross income. In other words, plaintiffs don't pay tax on the jury award. (Note, however that legislation was introduced into the 104th Congress to amend § 104(a) to exclude punitive damages and emotional distress damages.) The United States Supreme Court in *Norfolk & Western Railway Co. v. Liepelt*, 444 U.S. 490, 100 S. Ct. 755, 62 L. Ed. 2d 689 (1980), held that the jury may be given an instruction that the award was exempt from federal tax. But the majority of state courts have found the impact of taxes should not be accounted for or subject to jury instruction. While acknowledging the respectable authority of some cases, the New York Court of Appeals in *Johnson v. Manhattan & Bronx Surface Transit Operating Auth.*, 71 N.Y.2d 198, 524 N.Y.S.2d 415, 519 N.E.2d 326 (1988), concluded "that such a rule would inject an unacceptably speculative and distracting feature into the jury's consideration of damages, and thus we reject it as a matter of statutory construction, practical policy and sound jurisprudence." *Id.* at 524 N.Y.S.2d 415, 418, 519 N.E.2d at 328–29.

Does the same logic apply to consideration of the taxability of the income from the lump sum award of damages?

Courts have been called on to interpret the meaning of § 104(a)(2)'s exclusion of damages received "on account of personal injuries or sickness." In *Commissioner of Internal Revenue v. Schleier*, 515 U.S. 323, 115 S. Ct. 2159, 132 L. Ed. 2d 294 (1995), the court found that amounts received in settlement of an Age Discrimination in Employment Act claim were not excludable. *See also United States v. Burke* 504 U.S. 229, 112 S. Ct. 1867, 119 L. Ed. 2d 34 (1992) (backpay from Title VII sex discrimination claim not excludable). Regarding the excludability of punitive damages, the courts are split. In *O'Gilvie v. United States*, 66 F.3d 1550 (10th Cir.1995), the court found that punitive damages awarded in a product liability action for wrongful death were not excludable. The court found that the question was a close one—"good reasoning each way." *Id.* at 1560.

5. LOSS OF CONSORTIUM

Like wrongful death, this section deals with victims once-removed from the tort. The victim's spouse may enjoy a claim for losses suffered when the defendant injured the victim. Also like wrongful death, the types of losses involved are not easily measured by market transactions.

WHITTLESEY V. MILLER

572 S.W.2d 665 (Tex.1978).

MCGEE, JUSTICE.

The question presented by this appeal is whether one spouse has an independent action for loss of consortium as a result of physical injuries caused to the other spouse by the negligence of a third party. The vehicle Stewart Miller was driving was involved in a collision with a vehicle driven by David Whittlesey in June 1974. In March 1976, Miller and Whittlesey entered into a settlement agreement whereby Miller released

Whittlesey from liability in connection with the accident for consideration of $9,650. In June 1976, Ann Miller, Stewart's wife, sued Whittlesey for damages, alleging that Whittlesey's negligence had caused personal injury to her husband, thereby depriving her of her husband's consortium. Whittlesey was granted a summary judgment on the basis that a Texas wife could not recover for loss of consortium for the alleged negligent injury to her husband. The court of civil appeals reversed and remanded. We affirm the judgment of the court of civil appeals.

The marital relationship is the primary familial interest recognized by the courts. The remedy for the negligent or intentional impairment of this relationship is a tort action for loss of consortium. Consortium has been the subject of many different definitions by the courts, but it can generally be defined to include the mutual right of the husband and wife to that affection, solace, comfort, companionship, society, assistance, and sexual relations necessary to a successful marriage. This definition primarily consists of the emotional or intangible elements of the marital relationship. In Texas, it does not include the "services" rendered by a spouse to the marriage.[2] These elements have been referred to as a conceptualistic unity, and the action accrues upon the substantial impairment of them.

The loss of consortium can arise from either the intentional or negligent conduct of a third party toward the marital relationship. The intentional impairment of consortium can result in actions for either alienation of affections or criminal conversation. Both actions have been recognized by prior Texas decisions.

The husband's right to recover for the negligent impairment of consortium has existed at common law, although there are no decisions by this court expressly holding this. It has only been within the past 25 years, however, that the wife's cause of action in the United States has been recognized. The general acceptance of this action is reflected in the Restatement (Second) of Torts § 693 (1977), which now states:

> (1) One who by reason of his tortious conduct is liable to one spouse for illness or other bodily harm is subject to liability to the other spouse for the resulting loss of the society and services of the first spouse, including impairment of capacity for sexual [intercourse].

Comment a to the above characterizes the spouse who suffered the bodily harm as a result of the tortious conduct as the "impaired spouse"; the

[2] The term "services" is generally taken to include the performance by a spouse of household and domestic duties. In Texas, it is a concept that is entirely separate and distinct from that of consortium. In our community property system the husband and wife are equal; as such, a spouse's services counterbalance the other spouse's duty to support the community with earnings. Furthermore, the services of the spouse performing such are thus recoverable as a damage to the community.

spouse who brings the independent consortium action is characterized as the "deprived spouse." We find these designations to be pertinent and will use them in the balance of this opinion to assist in simplifying the discussion.

The present action for negligent impairment of consortium contemplates a single tortious act which injures both spouses by virtue of their relationship to each other. While the impaired spouse sustains direct physical injuries, the deprived spouse sustains damage to emotional interests stemming from their relationship. In the respective causes of action, the impaired spouse would have the exclusive right to recover for the normal damages associated with such an injury: bodily injuries, medical expenses, pain and suffering, loss of earnings, et cetera. The deprived spouse would have the right to bring an action for the loss of consortium and seek recovery on the basis of harm to the intangible or sentimental elements. Finally, while the deprived spouse's suit for loss of consortium is considered to be derivative of the impaired spouse's negligence action to the extent that the tortfeasor's liability to the impaired spouse must be established, the consortium action is, nevertheless, independent and apart from that of the impaired spouse's negligence action.

It has been argued that the deprived spouse's loss of consortium is an injury that is too indirect to be compensated because the elements involved are too intangible or conjectural to be measured in pecuniary terms by a jury. We do not agree, for to do so would mean that a jury would also be incompetent to award damages for pain and suffering. The character of harm to the intangible or sentimental elements is not illusory. The loss of companionship, emotional support, love, felicity, and sexual relations are real, direct, and personal losses. It is recognized that these terms concern subjective states which present some difficulty in translating the loss into a dollar amount. The loss, however, is a real one requiring compensation, and "the issue generally must be resolved by the 'impartial conscience and judgment of jurors who may be expected to act reasonably, intelligently and in harmony with the evidence.' " *Rodriguez v. Bethlehem Steel Corp.*, 115 Cal. Rptr. at 777, 525 P.2d at 681.

[The] law is not static; and the courts, whenever reason and equity demand, have been the primary instruments for changing the common law through a continual re-evaluation of common law concepts in light of current conditions. Providing either spouse with a cause of action for loss of consortium would allow us to keep pace with modern society by recognizing that the emotional interests of the marriage relationship are as worthy of protection from negligent invasion as are other legally protected interests.

Therefore, we hold that either spouse has a cause of action for loss of consortium that might arise as a result of an injury caused to the other spouse by a third party tortfeasor's negligence. This holding not only aligns Texas with the majority of jurisdictions recognizing the action for either spouse, but it also corrects a paradox in the law of this state in that heretofore the marital relationship has been protected from only intentional [invasions].

Whittlesey argues that there is a possibility of a double recovery if the cause of action is allowed. To allow the deprived spouse to recover for damages arising from an injury to the impaired spouse after the impaired spouse has been compensated would mean the community could recover twice for the same injury. This is not so. First, as we have previously indicated in this opinion, there is no duplication of recovery. Each spouse recovers for losses peculiar to the injury sustained by each of them. On the one hand, the impaired spouse recovers for those distinct damages arising out of the direct physical injuries. On the other hand, the recovery for the loss of consortium by the deprived spouse is predicated on separate and equally distinct damages to the emotional interests involved. Furthermore, it cannot be said that the character of the deprived spouse's recovery for loss of consortium is community property. It is clear that a recovery for personal injuries in Texas, other than that for loss of earning capacity, is the separate property of that spouse.

Accordingly, we affirm the judgment of the court of civil appeals.

NOTES AND QUESTIONS

1. What is included in consortium? The court lists "affection, solace, comfort, companionship, society, assistance, and sexual relations necessary to a successful marriage." Short of unconsciousness, does an impaired spouse provide any less affection, solace, comfort, companionship, or society to the deprived spouse? While an unconscious spouse might be unable to provide affection, solace, comfort, companionship, and society, would a conscious spouse be less supportive merely because injured?

2. Should services be included? How do services differ from assistance, which is on the court's list? Do household tasks such as supervising children, overseeing their intellectual and moral training, cooking, cleaning, etc., constitute assistance or services? If the impaired spouse participated in these tasks, but the deprived spouse now must take over these functions (perhaps temporarily), shouldn't the award include some amount for the deprived spouse's lost time or the increased difficulty of these tasks? Did the court's analysis persuade you? What other arguments might justify excluding services?

3. Is there a trap here? Did plaintiffs take two bites at the apple: settle the impaired spouse's claim, then come back for more under the guise of the deprived spouse's claim? Should joinder be compelled? Would that solve the problem? Should the court treat the tort and the consortium claim as a single claim, perhaps to be brought by a single entity (the community, the family)?

BELCHER V. GOINS

184 W.Va. 395, 400 S.E.2d 830 (1990).

MCHUGH, JUSTICE.

Phyllis Belcher, mother of the plaintiff, Stephanie L. Belcher, was injured when the car she was driving was negligently struck head-on by a car driven by the defendant, Sherry L. Goins. Phyllis Belcher's claim against the defendant has been settled and dismissed with prejudice.

At the time of the collision the plaintiff was over eighteen years of age but resided in her mother's home with her mother. The plaintiff was not in or near her mother's car at the time of the collision.

As a count in her amended complaint, the plaintiff sought recovery from the defendant for "loss of love, companionship, and consortium of and from her mother," for mental anguish and for nursing and household services provided by the plaintiff to her mother after her mother was injured.

The defendant moved to dismiss for failure to state a claim upon which relief may be granted. The trial court [denied] such motion [but,] upon the joint application of the parties, certified the following five questions, each answered in the affirmative by the trial court:

(1) Does a child have a claim for loss of consortium against a tort-feasor occasioned because of injuries to a parent?

(2) Does a child have a claim for mental anguish against a tort-feasor for negligent injuries suffered by a parent?

(3) Does a child have a claim against a tort-feasor for nursing, domestic, or household services provided by the child to a parent as a result of injuries suffered by a parent?

(4) Are the following elements included and encompassed within the broad definition of loss of consortium: mental anguish suffered by a family member as a result of an injury to another family member, loss of love, companionship, society of and from an injured family member, and provision for nursing, household or domestic services provided by a family member to another injured family member?

(5) Does a child, regardless of age, have a claim for loss of consortium against a tort-feasor as a result of injuries inflicted upon a parent[,] provided the child resides in the same household with the injured parent?

Because most of these questions are overlapping or closely related, we have combined all but the third question for purposes of our discussion. The third question will be discussed separately. Limiting our holding to a minor child, and to a handicapped child who is dependent upon the injured parent, we answer each of the first four questions in the affirmative, except for the third question and the corresponding part of the fourth question relating to nursing, domestic or household services. We answer the fifth question in the negative.

II

Traditionally, at common law "consortium" was defined as consisting of the alliterative trio of (1) services, (2) society and (3) sexual relations, and the husband was entitled to recover damages from a tortfeasor when one or more of these elements of the relationship with his wife were lost or impaired due to an injury to her. . . .

Similarly, "parental consortium" refers to the relationship between parent and child and is the right of the child to the intangible benefits of the companionship, comfort, guidance, affection and aid of the parent. As a leading text writer has stated, it is useful to refer to the parent-child relationship, as well as the husband-wife relationship, as constituting consortium; the important aspects of the parent-child relationship, apart from the parent's duty of pecuniary support, are the intangibles which follow from living together as a family, including the affection, society, companionship, the mutual learning and the moral support given and received. 1 H. CLARK, THE LAW OF DOMESTIC RELATIONS IN THE UNITED STATES, § 12.1, at 651 (2d ed. 1987).

The legislature of this state has recognized the validity of a claim by family members, including minor children, for damages for loss of consortium, including mental anguish, in cases involving the wrongful death of a family member [often referred to as solatium]. The wrongful death statute allows distribution of net damages, including non-economic damages, to those persons named in the decedent's will, or, if there be no will, to those persons who would be the decedent's heirs or next of kin under the laws of descent and distribution. Net damages distributable to these family members "[include] damages for the following: (A) Sorrow, mental anguish, and solace which may include society, companionship, comfort, guidance, kindly offices and advice of the decedent; [and] (B) compensation for reasonably expected loss [of] (ii) services, protection, care and assistance provided by the decedent[.]" W. Va. Code, 55–7–6(c)(1)(A) & (B)(ii) [1989].

There is a split of authorities as to whether a minor child has a legally cognizable claim for loss or impairment of parental consortium, against a tortfeasor who negligently injures, but does not kill, the minor child's parent. Adhering to the early common-law rule, most state courts have refused to recognize such a claim. Of the approximately thirty-four states in which state appellate courts have decided the issue, about twenty-five states have refused to recognize a minor child's claim for loss or impairment of parental consortium in a nonfatal injury case. The Restatement (Second) of Torts § 707A (1976) states the majority view:

"One who by reason of his [or her] tortious conduct is liable to a parent for illness or other bodily harm is not liable to a minor child for resulting loss of parental support and care." This Restatement position pre-dated all of the minority-view cases. The initial rationale for this rule was that, for purposes of tortious interference with domestic relations, a child was viewed as being analogous to a servant of the father without any legal right to the care and assistance of the father as master. 3 W. BLACKSTONE, COMMENTARIES *142–43.

Two of the more prominent, modern reasons for the majority rule are (1) judicial inertia, that is, as with wrongful death consortium claims, courts should defer to the legislature for recognition of a claim for loss or impairment of parental consortium resulting from nonfatal physical injury to the parent; and, alternatively, (2) judicial policy or "line drawing," that is, although they need not defer to the legislature, courts should refuse to recognize such a claim because it involves a type of tort claim, specifically, one for indirect, emotional injury, which traditionally has been disfavored at common law due to the potentially broad scope or reach of the duty. Stated another way, should the tortfeasor inflicting nonfatal physical injury be liable also for consortium impairment claims of siblings, grandchildren or others who could demonstrate emotional injuries similar to those of minor children?

However, even those courts refusing to recognize a claim for loss or impairment of parental consortium in nonfatal injury cases do recognize the reality and the seriousness of the injury sustained by the minor child. For example, the Supreme Court of Kansas acknowledged this point in *Hoffman v. Dautel*, 189 Kan. 165, 368 P.2d 57 (1962):

> It is common knowledge that a parent who suffers serious physical or mental injury is unable to give his [or her] minor children the parental care, training, love and companionship in the same degree as he [or she] might have but for the injury. Hence, it is difficult for the court, on the basis of natural justice, to reach the conclusion that this type of action will not lie. Human tendencies and sympathies suggest otherwise. Normal home life for a child consists of complex incidences in which the sums constitute a nurturing environment. When the vitally important parent-child relationship is impaired and the child loses the love, guidance and close companionship of a parent, the child is deprived of something that is indeed valuable and precious. No one could seriously contend otherwise.

Id. at 168–69, 368 P.2d at 59.

Dean Roscoe Pound, the eminent jurisprudential scholar, as early as the year 1916, lamented the early common-law rule denying a claim for loss or impairment of parental consortium in cases involving nonfatal physical injury to the parent. Pound, *Individual Interests in the Domestic*

Relations, 14 MICH. L. REV. 177, 185–86 (1916). Since 1980, nine state courts of last resort have recognized such a claim. These courts analogize a parental consortium claim in a nonfatal injury case to a parental consortium claim in a wrongful death case and to a spousal consortium claim in a wrongful death case or in a nonfatal injury case; in these analogous situations recovery of non-pecuniary damages is allowed, and, therefore, the claim in question should also be allowed. These courts also emphasize that the concept of a claim for spousal consortium was judicially created and that courts have the inherent power, and should exercise that power, to evolve the common law by recognizing new claims under changed societal conditions, in this context, the modern view that minor children have many of the same rights as adults, rather than being mere chattels. Furthermore, these courts recognizing the parental consortium claim respond to the fear of an ever-widening circle of liability by limiting the scope of the tortfeasor's duty to the immediate or nuclear family of the physically injured plaintiff, and then only so far as the parent/minor child (or parent/minor or handicapped child) relationship, in addition to the husband-wife relationship. Of course, the legislature subsequently may agree completely or disagree completely with the judicial recognition of a new claim; or the legislature subsequently may delineate somewhat different contours to the new claim.

Several reasons typically have been offered to deny recognition of a parental consortium claim in a nonfatal injury case: (1) the weight of precedent refuses to recognize such a claim; (2) courts should defer to the legislature in this area; (3) double recovery; (4) multiplicity of actions; (5) difficulty of assessing the amount of damages; (6) increased liability insurance costs; (7) adverse effect on family relations; and (8) exposure to potentially unlimited liability. Virtually all of the courts recognizing a parental consortium claim in a nonfatal injury case address these matters. This Court believes each of these reasons are unpersuasive. We address each of these points in order.

First, this Court is more concerned with the persuasiveness of precedent than with the weight of precedent. While thirteen of the twenty-two state courts of last resort which have decided this issue since 1980 have denied a claim for parental consortium in a nonfatal injury case, we are not bound by the mere weight of judicial precedent but rather by the rule which embodies the more persuasive reasoning. [This] Court concludes that the analysis of those decisions which have recognized a parental consortium claim in a nonfatal injury case is more persuasive than the analysis of those decisions which have rejected that claim.

Second, with respect to deferral to the legislature, in addition to observing that the analogous claim for spousal consortium was judicially created, we echo the sentiments of the Vermont court in *Hay*:

> The argument that this Court should prohibit the present claim for parental consortium from going to a jury because the issue is more appropriate for legislative resolution is wholly unpersuasive; such an argument ignores our responsibility to face a difficult legal question and accept judicial responsibility for a needed change in the common law. This Court has often met changing times and new social demands by expanding outmoded common law concepts.
>
> [When] confronted with these difficult and complex issues, this Court did not shirk its duty and retreat into the safe haven of deference to the legislature. [One] of the principal purposes of the [common] law of torts is to compensate people for injuries they sustain as a result of the negligent conduct of others. Virtually all of the other courts recognizing the claim at issue also expressly refused to defer to the legislature for substantially the same reasons.

Related to deferral to the legislature are two subsidiary arguments: lack of legal entitlement to parental consortium and the distinction between spousal and parental consortium. As to the former, we, like almost all of the courts recognizing the claim in question, believe the legislature has implicitly recognized legal entitlement to parental consortium in nonfatal injury cases by explicitly recognizing entitlement to parental consortium in wrongful death cases. "With a parent's death, the loss of consortium is permanent. With a parent's serious injury, the loss of consortium may be either temporary or permanent depending on the nature and extent of the [parent's] injury. We trust the factfinder to sort that out according to the evidence." *Nulle v. Gillette–Campbell County Joint Powers Fire Board*, 797 P.2d 1171, 1175 (Wyo.1990). Stated succinctly, "we think it entirely appropriate to protect the [minor] child's reasonable expectation of parental society when the parent suffers negligent[, serious] injury rather than death."

Another basis for recognizing legal entitlement to parental consortium is the similarity of such consortium to spousal consortium, which is already judicially recognized. While the element of sexual relations is present in spousal, but not in parental, consortium, we are not persuaded that this single distinction is significant enough to deny the minor child's claim. "Sexual relations are but one element of the spouse's consortium action. The other elements—love, companionship, affection, society, comfort, services and solace—are similar in both relationships and in each are deserving of protection." *Berger v. Weber*, 411 Mich. 1, 14, 303 N.W.2d 424, 426 (1981).

We also reject the third major reason for denying a claim of parental consortium in a nonfatal injury case, specifically, double recovery. The argument is that, as a practical matter, juries already award damages for loss or impairment of parental consortium in a nonfatal injury case as an undisclosed part of the parent's recovery of non-economic damages. This argument, however, actually is support for open recognition of the minor child's action. The double recovery problem is easily eliminated by limiting the injured parent's recovery in this area to the loss or impairment of the parent's pecuniary ability to support the child; similarly, the child's cause of action would be limited to the loss of the parent's society, companionship and the like. Rather than having juries make blind calculations of the minor child's loss in determining an award to the parent, the minor child's loss would be argued openly in court and the jury would be instructed to consider the minor child's loss separately. Special verdicts should also be used.

Moreover, this same argument as to double recovery would apply also to spousal consortium (the physically injured spouse's award might include an undisclosed amount for the other spouse's consortium loss or impairment). As in a parental consortium case, in a spousal consortium case the jury should be instructed as to the distinctive types of damages of the parties. We will assume that juries follow the court's instructions, including these instructions.

The fourth major reason for denying a parental consortium claim in a nonfatal injury case, namely, multiplicity of actions, is likewise unsound as a reason for totally denying such a claim. Virtually all of the courts recognizing this type of claim address this argument by requiring joinder of the minor children's parental consortium claims with the injured parent's claim, unless that is not feasible. We adopt this approach, too.

[Fifth,] we find unpersuasive the argument that the claim at issue should not be recognized because of the difficulty in assessing the amount of damages. A factfinder's calculation of damages for a minor child's loss of parental consortium is not any more difficult than the calculation necessary for indeterminate damages in other actions, such as for spousal consortium in a nonfatal injury case, spousal or parental consortium in a wrongful death case or for pain and suffering in a nonfatal injury case. As an adjunct to this argument, it has been contended that monetary compensation will not enable the minor child to regain what was lost (the society, companionship and the like) when the parent was seriously injured. This Court agrees with the following response to that contention:

> Although a monetary award may be a poor substitute for the loss of a parent's society and companionship, it is the only workable way that our legal system has found to ease the injured party's tragic loss. We recognize this as a shortcoming of our society, yet we believe that allowing such an award is clearly preferable to completely denying recovery.

Theama, 117 Wis.2d at 523, 344 N.W.2d at 520.

Another reason advanced for denying recognition of a parental consortium claim in a nonfatal injury case is that recognition of such a claim would increase the liability insurance costs to society. We are unswayed by this assertion and concur with these comments:

> [P]roperly, the provision and cost of such [liability] insurance varies with potential liability under the law, not the law with the cost of insurance. [No] doubt there are genuine wrongs that courts are ill suited to set right, and others that do not merit the social costs of litigation. But if these costs are to be the reason for denying an otherwise meritorious cause of action, that is one judgment to be made by legislatures rather than by courts.

Norwest v. Presbyterian Intercommunity Hospital, 293 Or. 543, 552, 652 P.2d 318, 323 (1982) (refusing to recognize a parental consortium claim in a nonfatal injury case because such a claim involves indirect, emotional injury, which is normally not protected against at common law).

A seventh reason offered for opposing recognition of the claim in question is that each of the minor children likely would attempt to magnify the quality of his or her relationship with the parent vis-a-vis the other minor children in order to enhance his or her own damage award. The same situation is present, however, in wrongful death actions.

Finally, there is the fear of exposure to liability to a potentially unlimited number of people who could claim and prove a loss or impairment of consortium because of the close relationship with the physically injured person. This fear is unfounded:

> In an era of ever-increasing caseloads in both the trial and appellate courts of this state, and where our society is being increasingly criticized for its propensity for litigation, the recognition of a new cause of action is not a step which we take lightly. However, it is the rights of the new class of plaintiffs, and the desire to see justice made available within our legal system, which are of paramount importance.

Hay, 145 Vt. at 539–40, 496 A.2d at 943. The "new class of plaintiffs" which we recognize here is limited to minor children, as well as physically or mentally handicapped children of any age who are dependent upon the injured parent physically, emotionally and financially. Because of the crucial role of the parent in these vitally important relationships, damages are almost certain to be inflicted when a tortfeasor interferes with these relationships by seriously injuring the parent physically.

We note that two state courts of last resort, namely, those in Arizona and Washington, have allowed recovery of parental consortium damages by any adult child, as well as by a minor child, in a case involving nonfatal injury to the parent. There is some logic to that approach, in that adult children, too, may suffer a real loss when the parent-child relationship is disturbed by the tortious infliction of physical injuries upon the parent. We note also that the West Virginia wrongful death statute allows recovery of parental consortium damages by adult, as well as by minor, children. Nevertheless, due to the very broad impact of extending this new common-law claim to all adult children, this Court at this time declines to follow the Arizona and Washington opinions in this regard.

In summary, this Court concludes that each of the above reasons offered for not recognizing a parental consortium claim in a nonfatal injury case is without merit. We particularly believe that the procedural concerns (double recovery, multiplicity of actions, etc.) should not bar recognition of this claim, for "if existing procedures make it difficult to consolidate different claims for trial or to avoid overlapping recoveries for the same loss, the obvious answer is not to deny that there is a claim but to reform the procedures. Shortfalls in procedural reform do not justify shortchanging otherwise valid claims." *Norwest*, 293 Or. at 552–53, 652 P.2d at 323. We have outlined above the procedures to be utilized in this new type of action. . . .

Based upon all of the above, we state our holdings. First, "parental consortium" refers to the intangible benefits to a minor child arising from his or her relationship with such child's natural or adoptive parent. It includes society, companionship, comfort, guidance, kindly offices and advice of such parent and the protection, care and assistance provided by the parent. Consistent with the wrongful death statute, parental consortium also includes sorrow and mental anguish concerning the impairment of the relationship.

Second, any minor child, or a physically or mentally handicapped child of any age who is dependent upon his or her natural or adoptive parent physically, emotionally and financially, may maintain a cause of action for loss or impairment of parental consortium, against a third person who seriously injures such child's parent, thereby severely damaging the parent-child relationship.

Third, in determining the amount of damages to award the minor or handicapped child, the relevant factors include, but are not limited to, such child's age, the nature of the child's relationship with the parent, the child's emotional and physical characteristics and whether other consortium-giving relationships are available to such child.

Fourth, a claim for parental consortium ordinarily must be joined with the injured parent's action against the alleged tortfeasor.

Fifth, when there is a parental consortium claim, the nonfatally injured parent is entitled to claim recovery for the loss or impairment of the parent's pecuniary ability to support the minor or handicapped child, while the minor or handicapped child is entitled to claim recovery for loss or impairment of those non-pecuniary elements constituting parental consortium.

Sixth, because a minor or handicapped child's claim for loss or impairment of parental consortium and the parent's claim for physical injuries are based upon the same conduct of the alleged tortfeasor, and because the child's claim is secondary to the parent's primary claim, any percentage of comparative contributory negligence attributable to the parent will reduce the amount of the child's recovery of parental consortium damages.

Seventh, [the] principles of this opinion are fully retroactive, even to the very limited number of cases which are otherwise subject to this opinion and in which the parent's action for physical injuries has already been settled or finally adjudicated. . . .

[We] wish to point out that a minor or handicapped child's claim for loss or impairment of parental consortium is different from a claim for negligent infliction of emotional distress. Negligent infliction of emotional distress usually requires that the plaintiff witness a physical injury to a closely related person, suffer mental anguish that manifests itself as a physical injury and the plaintiff must be within the zone of danger so as to be subject to an unreasonable risk of bodily harm created by the defendant. In contrast, a minor or handicapped child's claim for loss or impairment of parental consortium does not require that such child be within the zone of danger. Consortium claims are sui generis.

The third certified question, *see supra* section I., raises the issue of whether parental consortium includes the value of nursing, domestic or household services provided by a child to the injured parent. We hold that this item is not an element of parental consortium.

The courts recognizing a parental consortium claim in a nonfatal injury case do not include as an element of such consortium the value of these or any other services provided by a child to the injured parent. Instead, the injured parent would be entitled to claim recovery of the value of such services provided by a child or by anyone else providing such services with or without charge. Thus, "parental consortium" does not include the value of nursing, domestic or household services provided by a minor or handicapped child to the injured parent.

The plaintiff here was not a minor or handicapped child at the time the cause of action accrued. Accordingly, having answered the certified questions, we remand this case with directions for the trial court to enter judgment for the defendant on this claim.

Certified questions answered; case remanded with directions.

NOTES

1. The decisions referred to in the principal case from Arizona and Washington respectively are: *Villareal v. State Department of Transportation*, 160 Ariz. 474, 774 P.2d 213 (1989) (minor and adult children; parent's physical injuries must be so serious and permanently disabling as to destroy or nearly destroy parent-child relationship); *Ueland v. Pengo Hydra–Pull Corp.*, 103 Wash.2d 131, 691 P.2d 190 (1984) (en banc) (expressly not limited to minor children because jury would fix appropriate damages for adult children).

2. Consortium cases are to be distinguished from actions for intentional or negligent infliction of emotional distress. The consortium action is interference with a familial relationship and stands as an exception to the rule that a plaintiff must show that the wrong invaded that plaintiff's person or property interests. The latter actions, for negligent infliction of emotional distress, are traditional, depending upon the defendant's invasion of the plaintiff's psychic tranquility. Students will recall that the courts have limited recourse to these causes of action. *See Clohessy v. Bachelor*, 237 Conn. 31, 675 A.2d 852 (1996) (finding that mother and brother of deceased may have an action for emotional distress suffered when witnessing the death).

3. The court in the principal case included a helpful footnote that sums up state law on the subject. With amendments to bring it up to date the footnote reads:

> The following are opinions of state appellate courts recognizing a common-law claim for loss or impairment of parental consortium in a nonfatal injury case: *Hibpshman v. Prudhoe Bay Supply, Inc.*, 734 P.2d 991 (Alaska 1987) (minor children; "tortiously inflicted" injuries upon parent, even when parent is not so severely injured as to be in a vegetative state); *Villareal v. State Department of Transportation*, 160 Ariz. 474, 774 P.2d 213 (1989) (minor and adult children; parent's physical injuries must be so serious and permanently disabling as to destroy or nearly destroy parent-child relationship); [*Giuliani v. Guiler*, 951 S.W.2d 318 (Ky.1997);] *Ferriter v. Daniel O'Connell's Sons, Inc.*, 381 Mass. 507, 508–17, 413 N.E.2d 690, 691–96 (1980) (first state court of last resort to recognize such a claim; minor children; parent "seriously" injured) [superseded by MASS. GEN. LAWS ch. 152, § 24 (Workers' Compensation)]; *Morgan v. Lalumiere*, 22 Mass. App. Ct. 262, 269–70, 493 N.E.2d 206, 211 (*Ferriter* extended to physically or mentally handicapped adult child residing with injured parent and who was dependent upon parent physically, emotionally and financially), *review denied* 398 Mass. 1103, 497 N.E.2d 1096 (1986); *Berger v. Weber*, 411 Mich. 1, 303 N.W.2d 424 (1981) (only minor children, apparently; expressly not limited to instances of "severely" injured parents), *affirming as modified* 82 Mich. App. 199, 267 N.W.2d 124 (1978) (first state appellate court to recognize such a claim); [*Keele v. St. Vincent Hospital and Health Care Center*, 258 Mont. 158, 852

P.2d 574 (1993); *Gallimore v. Children's Hosp. Med. Ctr.*, 67 Ohio St.3d 244, 617 N.E.2d 1052 (1993); *Williams v. Hook*, 804 P.2d 1131 (Okla.1990); *Reagan v. Vaughn,* 804 S.W.2d 463, 467 (Tex.1990)]; *Hay v. Medical Center Hospital*, 145 Vt. 533, 496 A.2d 939 (1985) (minor children; permanently comatose parent); *Ueland v. Pengo Hydra–Pull Corp.*, 103 Wash.2d 131, 691 P.2d 190 (1984) (en banc) (expressly not limited to minor children because jury would fix appropriate damages for adult children; "tortiously injured" parent); *Theama v. City of Kenosha*, 117 Wis.2d 508, 344 N.W.2d 513 (1984) (expressly limited to minor children; negligently injured parent); *Nulle v. Gillette–Campbell County Joint Powers Fire Board*, 797 P.2d 1171 (Wyo.1990) (minor children; "tortiously inflicted" injuries upon parent); *Craft v. Hermes Consolidated, Inc.*, 797 P.2d 559 (Wyo.1990) (following *Nulle*).

Minor children or, in some instances, minor and adult children are entitled under statutes in some states to recover for lost or impaired parental consortium in cases involving nonfatal injuries suffered by the parent. *See, e.g.*, Fla. Stat. Ann. § 768.0415 (West 1988) (changing result reached by Supreme Court of Florida in *Zorzos v. Rosen*, 467 So.2d 305 (Fla.1985)); see also the dramshop statute involved in *Gail v. Clark,* 410 N.W.2d 662 (Iowa 1987), mentioned above at the outset of section II.A. of this opinion, and the wrongful death/wrongful injury statute involved in the Iowa case of *Audubon–Exira Ready Mix, Inc. v. Illinois Central Gulf R.R.*, 335 N.W.2d 148 (1983).

Most of the commentators strongly favor recognition of a parental consortium claim in a nonfatal injury case. *See, e.g.*, 1 H. Clark, The Law of Domestic Relations in the United States § 12.6, at 689–92 (2d ed. 1987); Prosser and Keeton on the Law of Torts § 125, at 935–36 (W. Keeton gen. ed. 5th ed. 1984); Love, *Tortious Interference with the Parent–Child Relationship: Loss of an Injured Person's Society and Companionship*, 51 Ind. L.J. 590 (1976); Petrilli, *A Child's Right to Collect for Parental Consortium Where Parent Is Seriously Injured*, 26 J. Fam. L. 317 (1988); *see also* Bainbridge, *Loss of Consortium Between Parent and Child*, 71 A.B.A.J. 46 (Oct. 1985).

But recently some courts have rejected the cause of action. *Mendillo v. Board of Educ.*, 246 Conn. 456, 717 A.2d 1177 (1998); *Karagiannakos v. Gruber*, 274 Ill.App.3d 155, 210 Ill.Dec. 737, 653 N.E.2d 932 (1995), *appeal denied*, 164 Ill.2d 565, 660 N.E.2d 1271, 214 Ill.Dec. 322 (1995); *Barton–Malow Co. v. Wilburn*, 556 N.E.2d 324 (Ind.1990); *Klaus v. Fox*, 259 Kan. 522, 912 P.2d 703 (1996); *Gaver v. Harrant*, 316 Md. 17, 557 A.2d 210 (Ct.App.1989); *Thompson v. Love*, 661 So.2d 1131 (Miss.1995); *Guenther by Guenther v. Stollberg*, 242 Neb. 415, 495 N.W.2d 286 (1993); *Harrington v. Brooks Drugs, Inc.*, 148 N.H. 101, 808 A.2d 532 (2002); *De Angelis v. Lutheran Med. Ctr.*, 58 N.Y.2d 1053, 1055, 462 N.Y.S.2d 626, 627, 449 N.E.2d 406, 407 (1983); *Taylor v. Beard*, 104 S.W.3d 507 (Tenn.2003).

PROBLEMS

1. *Casey's Inhaler.* Does Casey's spouse have a claim for consortium based on Casey's reduced ability to help around the house? Do Casey's children have a claim for consortium based on Casey's reduced ability to play with and counsel them? Does either question depend on whether Casey is the wife/mother or husband/father?

2. *Teenage Consortium.* On his way to school, Sonny was hit by a car and injured. He was unconscious in the hospital for two weeks. When he regained consciousness, he was unable to leave his bed (at home) for another two months. In addition to Sonny's negligence claim, Sonny's parents sued the driver for loss of consortium. Sonny was an average teenager, who could be cajoled into mowing the lawn and occasionally loading the dishwasher, but provided few other services around the house. Sonny devoted most of his time to an MP-3 player, surfing the web, playing video games, watching TV, and homework (in about that order). He spent relatively little time conversing with his parents, except when his homework proved too frustrating. What arguments can you raise for or against the parents' claim for lost consortium? *See Gallimore v. Children's Hosp. Med. Ctr.*, 67 Ohio St.3d 244, 617 N.E.2d 1052 (1993).

C. LIMITATIONS ON RECOVERY

1. CAUSATION, FORESEEABILITY, AND CERTAINTY

In your first year studies, you may have learned that causation is an element of liability in negligence cases. Plaintiff must show both cause in fact (but for causation) and proximate or legal cause (that the injury is not so remote from the negligent act that liability is cut off). In some cases, legal cause may turn on whether an injury is reasonably foreseeable to the defendant. Foreseeability also may contribute to decisions regarding whether defendant had a duty to the plaintiff.

Causation also plays a role as a limitation on recovery, even in cases where liability does not require causation. The general rule for damages embodies an implicit requirement of causation. Any loss that would have resulted even if the defendant had not committed the wrong cannot be recovered. Rather, that loss is part of the position the plaintiff would have occupied even if the wrong had not occurred.

This general rule forces the law to consider counterfactual situations, situations that would have existed if facts (events) had occurred differently (specifically, if defendant had not committed the wrong). That task is inherently speculative. In easy cases, factfinders may be relatively certain of what would have happened: if defendant had not run the red light, plaintiff would not have been hit by the car and, thus, would not have suffered any injuries. The argument that plaintiff would have suffered the same or similar injuries anyway (say, by being hit by a different car) rarely is plausible. But as injuries become more remote, as the chain of causation lengthens, determination of just what would have occurred if the defendant had not committed the wrong becomes harder.

This section deals with several doctrines that limit plaintiff's recovery for losses that are somewhat remote from the wrongdoing. All of these doctrines reflect a central concern that the wrong may not really be responsible for the loss, that the plaintiff might have suffered the loss (or part of it) even if the defendant had acted legally. Sometimes that concern involves a direct assessment of causation. Sometimes concerns for causation are expressed through other doctrines. Certainty, for instance, asks how sure we are that the plaintiff would have been better off if the wrong had not occurred.

MCKENNON V. NASHVILLE BANNER PUBLISHING COMPANY

513 U.S. 352, 115 S.Ct. 879, 130 L.Ed.2d 852 (1995).

JUSTICE KENNEDY delivered the opinion of the Court.

[For] some 30 years, petitioner Christine McKennon worked for respondent Nashville Banner Publishing Company. She was discharged, the Banner claimed, as part of a work force reduction plan necessitated by cost considerations. McKennon, who was 62 years old when she lost her job, thought another reason explained her dismissal: her age. She filed suit [alleging] that her discharge violated the Age Discrimination in Employment Act of 1967 (ADEA or Act), 29 U.S.C. § 621 *et seq.* (1988 ed. and Supp. V). The ADEA makes it unlawful for any employer:

> to discharge any individual or otherwise discriminate against any individual with respect to his compensation, terms, conditions, or privileges of employment, because of such individual's age.

29 U.S.C. § 623(a)(1). McKennon sought a variety of legal and equitable remedies available under the ADEA, including backpay.

In preparation of the case, the Banner took McKennon's deposition. She testified that, during her final year of employment, she had copied several confidential documents bearing upon the company's financial condition. She had access to these records as secretary to the Banner's comptroller. McKennon took the copies home and showed them to her husband. Her motivation, she averred, was an apprehension she was about to be fired because of her age. When she became concerned about her job, she removed and copied the documents for "insurance" and "protection." A few days after these deposition disclosures, the Banner sent McKennon a letter declaring that removal and copying of the records was in violation of her job responsibilities and advising her (again) that she was terminated. The Banner's letter also recited that had it known of McKennon's misconduct it would have discharged her at once for that reason.

For purposes of summary judgment, the Banner conceded its discrimination against McKennon. The District Court granted summary judgment for the Banner, holding that McKennon's misconduct was grounds for her termination and that neither backpay nor any other remedy was available to her under the ADEA. The United States Court of Appeals for the Sixth Circuit affirmed on the same rationale. We granted certiorari to resolve conflicting views among the Courts of Appeals on the question whether all relief must be denied when an employee has been discharged in violation of the ADEA and the employer later discovers some wrongful conduct that would have led to discharge if it had been discovered earlier. We now reverse.

II

We shall assume, as summary judgment procedures require us to assume, that the sole reason for McKennon's initial discharge was her age, a discharge violative of the ADEA. Our further premise is that the misconduct revealed by the deposition was so grave that McKennon's immediate discharge would have followed its disclosure in any event. The District Court and the Court of Appeals found no basis for contesting that proposition, and for purposes of our review we need not question it here. We do question the legal conclusion reached by those courts that after-acquired evidence of wrongdoing which would have resulted in discharge bars employees from any relief under the ADEA. That ruling is incorrect.

The Court of Appeals considered McKennon's misconduct, in effect, to be supervening grounds for termination. That may be so, but it does not follow that the misconduct renders it "'irrelevant whether or not [McKennon] was discriminated against.'" We conclude that a violation of the ADEA cannot be so altogether disregarded.

The ADEA, enacted in 1967 as part of an ongoing congressional effort to eradicate discrimination in the workplace, reflects a societal condemnation of invidious bias in employment decisions. The ADEA is but part of a wider statutory scheme to protect employees in the workplace nationwide. See Title VII of the Civil Rights Act of 1964, 42 U.S.C. § 2000e *et seq.* (1988 ed. and Supp. V); the Americans with Disabilities Act of 1990, 42 U.S.C. § 12101 *et seq.* (1988 ed., Supp. V); the National Labor Relations Act, 29 U.S.C. § 158(a); the Equal Pay Act of 1963, 29 U.S.C. § 206(d). The ADEA incorporates some features of both Title VII and the Fair Labor Standards Act of 1938, which has led us to describe it as "something of a hybrid." The substantive, antidiscrimination provisions of the ADEA are modeled upon the prohibitions of Title VII. Its remedial provisions incorporate by reference the provisions of the Fair Labor Standards Act of 1938. 29 U.S.C. § 626(b). When confronted with a violation of the ADEA, a district court is authorized to afford relief by means of reinstatement, backpay, injunctive relief, declaratory judgment, and attorney's fees. In the case of a willful violation of the Act, the ADEA authorizes an award of liquidated damages equal to the backpay award. 29 U.S.C. § 626(b). The Act also gives federal courts the discretion to "grant such legal or equitable relief as may be appropriate to effectuate the purposes of [the Act]."

The ADEA and Title VII share common substantive features and also a common purpose: "the elimination of discrimination in the workplace." Congress designed the remedial measures in these statutes to serve as a "spur or catalyst" to cause employers "to self-examine and to self-evaluate their employment practices and to endeavor to eliminate, so far as possible, the last vestiges" of discrimination. Deterrence is one object of these statutes. Compensation for injuries caused by the prohibited discrimination is another. The ADEA, in keeping with these purposes, [grants] an injured employee a right of action to obtain the authorized relief. The private litigant who seeks redress for his or her injuries vindicates both the deterrence and the compensation objectives of the ADEA. It would not accord with this scheme if after-acquired evidence of wrongdoing that would have resulted in termination operates, in every instance, to bar all relief for an earlier violation of the Act.

The objectives of the ADEA are furthered when even a single employee establishes that an employer has discriminated against him or her. The disclosure through litigation of incidents or practices that violate national policies respecting nondiscrimination in the work force is itself important, for the occurrence of violations may disclose patterns of noncompliance resulting from a misappreciation of the Act's operation or entrenched resistance to its commands, either of which can be of industry-wide significance. The efficacy of its enforcement mechanisms becomes one measure of the success of the Act.

The Court of Appeals in this case relied upon two of its earlier decisions, *Johnson v. Honeywell Information Systems, Inc.,* 955 F.2d 409 (CA6 1992); *Milligan–Jensen v. Michigan Technological Univ.,* 975 F.2d 302 (CA6 1992), and the opinion of the Court of Appeals for the Tenth Circuit in *Summers v. State Farm Mutual Automobile Ins. Co.,* 864 F.2d 700 (1988). Consulting those authorities, it declared that it had "firmly endorsed the principle that after-acquired evidence is a complete bar to any recovery by the former employee where the employer can show it would have fired the employee on the basis of the evidence." *Summers,* in turn, relied upon our decision in *Mt. Healthy City Bd. of Ed. v. Doyle,* 429 U.S. 274 (1977), but that decision is inapplicable here.

In *Mt. Healthy* we addressed a mixed-motives case, in which two motives were said to be operative in the employer's decision to fire an employee. One was lawful, the other (an alleged constitutional violation) unlawful. We held that if the lawful reason alone would have sufficed to justify the firing, the employee could not prevail in a suit against the employer. The case was controlled by the difficulty, and what we thought was the lack of necessity, of disentangling the proper motive from the improper one where both played a part in the termination and the former motive would suffice to sustain the employer's action.

That is not the problem confronted here. [T]he case comes to us on the express assumption that an unlawful motive was the sole basis for the firing. McKennon's misconduct was not discovered until after she had been fired. The employer could not have been motivated by knowledge it did not have and it cannot now claim that the employee was fired for the nondiscriminatory reason. Mixed motive cases are inapposite here, except to the important extent they underscore the necessity of determining the employer's motives in ordering the discharge, an essential element in determining whether the employer violated the federal antidiscrimination law. As has been observed, "proving that the same decision would have been justified . . . is not the same as proving that the same decision would have been made."

Our inquiry is not at an end, however, for even though the employer has violated the Act, we must consider how the after-acquired evidence of the employee's wrongdoing bears on the specific remedy to be ordered. Equity's maxim that a suitor who engaged in his own reprehensible conduct in the course of the transaction at issue must be denied equitable relief because of unclean hands, a rule which in conventional formulation operated *in limine* to bar the suitor from invoking the aid of the equity court, has not been applied where Congress authorizes broad equitable relief to serve important national policies. We have rejected the unclean hands defense "where a private suit serves important public purposes." *Life Mufflers, Inc. v. International Parts Corp.*, 392 U.S. 134, 138 (1968) (Sherman and Clayton Antitrust Acts). That does not mean, however, the employee's own misconduct is irrelevant to all the remedies otherwise available under the statute. The statute controlling this case provides that "the court shall have jurisdiction to grant such legal or equitable relief as may be appropriate to effectuate the purposes of this chapter, including without limitation judgments compelling employment, reinstatement or promotion, or enforcing the liability for [amounts owing to a person as a result of a violation of this chapter]." 29 U.S.C. § 626(b). In giving effect to the ADEA, we must recognize the duality between the legitimate interests of the employer and the important claims of the employee who invokes the national employment policy mandated by the Act. The employee's wrongdoing must be taken into account, we conclude, lest the employer's legitimate concerns be ignored. The ADEA, like Title VII, is not a general regulation of the workplace but a law which prohibits discrimination. The statute does not constrain employers from exercising significant other prerogatives and discretions in the course of the hiring, promoting, and discharging of their employees. In determining appropriate remedial action, the employee's wrongdoing becomes relevant not to punish the employee, or out of concern "for the relative moral worth of the parties," but to take due account of the lawful prerogatives of the employer in the usual course of its business and the corresponding equities that it has arising from the employee's wrongdoing.

The proper boundaries of remedial relief in the general class of cases where, after termination, it is discovered that the employee has engaged in wrongdoing must be addressed by the judicial system in the ordinary course of further decisions, for the factual permutations and the equitable considerations they raise will vary from case to case. We do conclude that here, and as a general rule in cases of this type, neither reinstatement nor front pay is an appropriate remedy. It would be both inequitable and pointless to order the reinstatement of someone the employer would have terminated, and will terminate, in any event and upon lawful grounds.

The proper measure of backpay presents a more difficult problem. Resolution of this question must give proper recognition to the fact that an ADEA violation has occurred which must be deterred and compensated without undue infringement upon the employer's rights and prerogatives. The object of compensation is to restore the employee to the position he or she would have been in absent the discrimination, but that principle is difficult to apply with precision where there is after-acquired evidence of wrongdoing that would have led to termination on legitimate grounds had the employer known about it. Once an employer learns about employee wrongdoing that would lead to a legitimate discharge, we cannot require the employer to ignore the information, even if it is acquired during the course of discovery in a suit against the employer and even if the information might have gone undiscovered absent the suit. The beginning point in the trial court's formulation of a remedy should be calculation of backpay from the date of the unlawful discharge to the date the new information was discovered. In determining the appropriate order for relief, the court can consider taking into further account extraordinary equitable circumstances that affect the legitimate interests of either party. An absolute rule barring any recovery of backpay, however, would undermine the ADEA's objective of forcing employers to consider and examine their motivations, and of penalizing them for employment decisions that spring from age discrimination.

Where an employer seeks to rely upon after-acquired evidence of wrongdoing, it must first establish that the wrongdoing was of such severity that the employee in fact would have been terminated on those grounds alone if the employer had known of it at the time of the discharge. The concern that employers might as a routine matter undertake extensive discovery into an employee's background or performance on the job to resist claims under the Act is not an insubstantial one, but we think the authority of the courts to award attorney's fees, mandated under the statute, and to invoke the appropriate provisions of the Federal Rules of Civil Procedure will deter most abuses.

The judgment is reversed, and the case is remanded to the Court of Appeals for the Sixth Circuit for further proceedings consistent with this opinion.

QUESTION

Where would plaintiff have been if the defendant had not discriminated against her? Would she have been fired anyway? When? Or would she have worked there indefinitely, her misconduct undetected? Can the court on remand possibly answer that question? Is it the right question anyway? Would any other question produce a better calculation of damages?

PROBLEMS

1. *Mixed Motive.* Suppose defendant discovered Ms. McKennon's breach of confidentiality before it fired her. Would that mean she could recover nothing? What if defendant considered firing her for the wrong reasons, but fortuitously discovered this legitimate reason before acting?

2. *Reason for Discharge.* Does your answer to the first problem depend on the severity of plaintiff's misconduct? Consider these variations:

a. McKennon drives recklessly on duty, potentially giving rise to tort liability for the employer.

b. McKennon harasses other employees illegally, potentially giving rise to liability for the company, but not physical injuries to others.

c. McKennon embezzled funds from the employer.

d. McKennon did a poor job and the employer found someone better.

e. McKennon was competent, but the employer found someone better.

3. *Reason for Discovery.* Does your answer to the first problem depend on why the employer discovered the legitimate reason? Suppose it was scrutinizing McKennon's conduct because it felt she was too old and wanted to discharge her for that reason?

4. *Negligent Appraisal.* Landis Ohner sought real estate financing from Big Bank for a parcel of property. Ohner hired Hap Praiser to appraise the property for the transaction. Hap negligently appraised the property, concluding it was worth $10 million when in fact it was worth only $500,000. Big Bank, in reliance on the appraisal, lent Ohner $8 million, secured by a nonrecourse mortgage on the real estate. When Ohner failed to make the payments, Bank foreclosed on the property and sold it at auction. Due to a decline in the real estate market, the property brought only $300,000. In an action against Hap Praiser, how much can Big Bank recover? Would your answer be different if Bank hired Hap?

5. *Casey's Inhaler*. Was Casey's loss caused by the pharmacist's negligence, the underlying condition, or other factors? Would Casey have had perfect attendance that winter but for the misfilled prescription?

In your first year studies, you may have learned that foreseeability limits recovery in contract cases. The doctrine usually applies to consequential damages, particularly those where the plaintiff's harm results from unusual factors, the kind that the defendant would not ordinarily expect. For instance, an egg producer may expect a buyer to resell them, but may not anticipate that the eggs will be used in medical research. Unlike resale profits, losses to medical research might not be foreseeable.

"Damages are not recoverable for loss that the party in breach did not have reason to foresee as a probable result of the breach when the contract was made." RESTATEMENT (SECOND) OF CONTRACTS § 351(1). Several features are critical:

(1) The breach need not be foreseeable; the loss must be foreseeable *if* a breach occurs;

(2) The loss need not be foreseen, only foreseeable (objectively, by a reasonable person);

(3) Foreseeability is assessed at contract formation, not at the time of breach;

(4) The loss must seem probable, not merely possible.

In many cases, defendant should foresee the losses because they are likely to occur in the natural course of events. A manufacturer selling to a wholesaler should foresee that breach might preclude the buyer from reselling the goods to another. Alternatively, losses may become foreseeable because the party informs the other of the prospect of losses. This will be vital when the losses might occur in an unusual way, through factors a defendant would not ordinarily expect.

In your first year studies, you may have learned that "Damages are not recoverable for loss beyond an amount that the evidence permits to be established with reasonable certainty." RESTATEMENT (SECOND) OF CONTRACTS § 352; *see also* RESTATEMENT (SECOND) OF TORTS § 912 (requiring "as much certainty as the nature of the tort and the circumstances permit"). The rule does not require absolute precision, only reasonable certainty.

Certainty often arises when plaintiff seeks recovery for the failure of a project that might have failed anyway. For example, a person planning to open a new restaurant or to build a new golf course might go bankrupt within a year or become wildly successful. When defendant's wrong precludes the project from going forward, it is difficult to predict whether the wrong prevented gains or saved the plaintiff from additional losses. The certainty doctrine allows the court to limit a jury's ability to speculate (guess) how much plaintiff might have gained.

Because both doctrines tend to arise in relation to consequential damages, cases often discuss both doctrines.

SCHONFELD V. HILLIARD

218 F.3d 164 (2d Cir.2000).

[The Hilliards, owners of small midwestern cable companies, formed International News Network (INN). They hired Schonfeld, former president of CNN, and gave him one-third of INN. In March 1994, the British Broadcasting Corporation (BBC) granted INN the exclusive right to carry BBC news broadcasts on American cable television, provided INN obtained at least 500,000 subscribers. INN intended to create a subsidiary to operate the BBC cable station. In June, however, INN agreed to sell the rights to Cox Cable Communications for $1.7 million ($700,000 at closing; $100,000/year for ten years thereafter) plus 5% equity in Cox's proposed BBC channels. When Cox missed a deadline, the Hilliards refused to extend the deadline and canceled the deal—apparently deciding it would be more profitable to market BBC newscasts themselves rather than sell the rights to Cox.

Revised FCC rules led INN to accelerate their plans. In December 1994, INN and BBC entered new contracts replacing the March agreement. The Interim and December agreements required INN (among other things) to pay BBC $20 million in installments, beginning January 3, 1995. In order to persuade Schonfeld and BBC to give up the March agreement and accept the December agreement, the Hilliards orally promised that they personally would provide the additional funds INN needed under the agreement. It appeared this promise was fraudulent. The Hilliards tried to raise the money from another investor—one it knew BBC would not accept. When that effort failed, INN defaulted on its payments to BBC. Rather than sue for breach, BBC agreed to rescind the agreements (leaving it free to sell the rights to others, such as Cox).

Schonfeld sued the Hilliards on his own behalf and on behalf of INN (a shareholder derivative action). He alleged breach of contract, breach of fiduciary duty, and fraud. Relying on *Kenford Co. v. County of Erie,* 67 N.Y.2d 257, 261, 493 N.E.2d 234, 235, 502 N.Y.S.2d 131, 132 (1986) ("*Kenford I*"), the trial court found lost profits uncertain and granted summary judgment for defendant on all claims except fraud. The court limited damages on the fraud claim to $15,000 under the out-of-pocket rule.]

MCLAUGHLIN, CIRCUIT JUDGE:

The damages requested by Schonfeld fall under three distinct categories: (1) lost profits that INN would have received had the Channel been successfully launched; or (2) in the alternative, the market value of the lost supply agreements ("lost asset" damages); and (3) punitive damages (solely in connection with his fraud and breach of fiduciary duty claims). . . .

To establish lost profit damages, Schonfeld relied on: (1) INN's Business Plan; (2) the revenues projected by Cox in connection with its own proposed BBC news channel; (3) the BBC's, the Hilliards' and Schonfeld's "belief" that the proposed operating entity would be profitable; and (4) the reports and deposition testimony of two damage experts—Donald Curtis and William Grimes.

Donald Curtis, a certified public accountant at Deloitte & Touche LLP, testified that damages from lost profits were between $112 to $269 million. Curtis based these figures on the revenue and expense projections contained in the INN Business Plan. William Grimes, a cable industry executive, testified to the assured success of the Channel by comparing it to other cable channels such as CNN and The Learning Channel. The defendants moved to preclude the testimony of these experts for failure to meet the scientific reliability standards set forth in *Daubert v. Merrell Dow Pharm.*, 509 U.S. 579 (1993), and its progeny.

With respect to lost asset damages, Schonfeld relied entirely on the purchase price contained in the Cox Agreement to establish the market value of the March and December Supply Agreements. Calculating a present value for the portion of the purchase offer that comprised a 5% equity interest in the Cox channels, and adding this amount to the cash portion of the offer, Curtis concluded that the total purchase price agreed to in the Cox Agreement was $17.13 million. . . .

Plaintiff, Schonfeld, now appeals, arguing that the district court erred by: (1) excluding the expert testimony offered to support his claim for lost asset damages; (2) dismissing all claims (other than fraud) for failure to establish the existence of, or entitlement to, the damages sought; and (3) limiting his recovery under the fraud claim to $15,000.

For the reasons set forth below, we affirm in part, reverse in part, vacate and remand.

Discussion

We review a district court's grant of summary judgment *de novo,* drawing all inferences and resolving all ambiguities in favor of the non-movant. Summary judgment is proper only if the admissible evidence establishes that "there is no genuine issue as to any material fact and that the moving party is entitled to a judgment as a matter of law."

I. Lost Profits

Schonfeld argues that the district court erred by dismissing his damage claims for lost profits. We agree with the district court.

In an action for breach of contract, a plaintiff is entitled to recover lost profits only if he can establish both the existence and amount of such damages with reasonable certainty. "[T]he damages may not be merely speculative, possible or imaginary." Although lost profits need not be proven with "mathematical precision," they must be "capable of measurement based upon known reliable factors without undue speculation." *Ashland Mgt. Inc. v. Janien,* 82 N.Y.2d 395, 403, 624 N.E.2d 1007, 1010, 604 N.Y.S.2d 912, 915 (1993). Therefore, evidence of lost profits from a new business venture receives greater scrutiny because there is no track record upon which to base an estimate. Projections of future profits based upon "a multitude of assumptions" that require "speculation and conjecture" and few known factors do not provide the requisite certainty.

The plaintiff faces an additional hurdle: he must prove that lost profit damages were within the contemplation of the parties when the contract was made. "The party breaching the contract is liable for those risks foreseen or which should have been foreseen at the time the contract was made." Where the contract is silent on the subject, the court must take a "common sense" approach, and determine what the parties intended by considering "the nature, purpose and particular circumstances of the contract known by the parties . . . as well as what liability the defendant fairly may be supposed to have assumed consciously." *Kenford Co. v. County of Erie,* 73 N.Y.2d 312, 319, 537 N.E.2d 176, 179, 540 N.Y.S.2d 1, 4 (1989) ("*Kenford II*").

The district court found Schonfeld's lost profit claims "highly analogous" to those raised in *Kenford I.* We do too. In *Kenford I,* Erie County had entered into a contract with the Kenford Company, Inc. and Dome Stadium, Inc. ("DSI") for the construction and operation of a domed stadium. In exchange for the donation of the land, the contract provided that the County would begin construction within 12 months of the contract date and that, upon its completion, the County would enter into a 20-year management agreement with DSI. DSI sued the County for breach of contract when construction was not timely commenced, seeking lost profits that it would have received under the management agreement. The Court of Appeals held that DSI could not recover lost profits because their existence could not be proven with sufficient certainty.

Here, the district court concluded that the Channel was a new entertainment venture similar to the proposed stadium in *Kenford I.* The operating entity's profits, the court noted, "were purely hypothetical, stemming from the sale of untested programming to a hypothetical subscriber base, sold to advertisers at a hypothetical price and supported by hypothetical investors and carriers." After reviewing the seemingly endless list of assumptions upon which Schonfeld's expert relied in determining lost profits, the court held that Schonfeld could establish neither the existence nor the amount of lost profits with reasonable certainty. The court also concluded that lost profits were not within the contemplation of the parties. We fully agree with the district court's analysis.

A. *The Channel's Status as a "New Business"*

To evade the *Kenford I* analysis, Schonfeld argues that the district court should not have characterized the Channel as a "new business." He emphasizes that he and the Hilliard brothers were experienced cable channel operators and BBC news programming has been distributed around the world for many years. Accordingly, he claims that the Channel is more analogous to the introduction in *Ashland* of a new but tested investment strategy by an existing financial management corporation with an extensive customer base. This argument is unpersuasive.

It is undisputed that the Channel's operating entity never saw the light of day. Had the entity been created, it would have introduced first an existing product, BBC international news programming, and then a *new product,* the "Americanized" version, into a *new market,* the United States. In addition, the Channel had no established customer base. The Hilliards had only 66,000 subscribers and Russ Hilliard testified that they were having trouble finding the 500,000 subscribers necessary to preclude the BBC from terminating the March Supply Agreement. Finally, the Hilliards, Schonfeld and the BBC had never jointly operated a cable channel, so there is no historic record of operations from which lost profits could be projected. Therefore, the district court correctly determined that the Channel would have been a new business.

B. *Reasonable Certainty of Lost Profits*

Schonfeld contends that the existence of lost profits was sufficiently established by the evidence that Cox, Schonfeld, the Hilliards and the BBC all *believed* that profits from the Channel were reasonably certain. However, "[t]he entrepreneur's 'cheerful prognostications' are not enough." 1 *Dobbs Law of Remedies* § 3.4. Further, Cox's profit projections for the international news channel were based on Cox's *own* existing cable operations. INN and the non-existent operating entity had no such established operations. Indeed, Schonfeld's expert, Curtis, admitted that if Cox's projected costs replaced those in INN's Business Plan, the Channel would be doomed as "a lost venture."

In addition, the district court properly held that Curtis's projections based on INN's Business Plan are legally insufficient. These projections presume that: (1) an operating entity would have been formed and operated for 20 years; (2) an estimated $44 million in pre-launch financing would have been raised; (3) the hypothetical subscriber levels would have been reached; (4) carriage agreements would have been entered; (5) advertisers would have been found at the assumed rates; (6) all projected expenses would have proved correct; (7) marketing costs would have remained constant and expenditures would have been sufficient to attract and maintain subscriber interest; and (8) the type and amount of equity interest held by each investor, including INN, would have been determined in the manner alleged by Schonfeld. Curtis was unaware that some cable owners are paid to carry a channel and admitted that, if the Channel's operating entity had to pay for carriage, it would not survive.

Subject as they are to the changing whims and artistic tastes of the general public, claims for profits lost in unsuccessful entertainment ventures have received a chilly reception in the New York courts. *See* Melvin Simensky, *Determining Damages for Breach of Entertainment Agreements,* 8 Ent. and Sports Law. 1, 12–13 (1990). Curtis believes he adjusted his profit figures to take such factors into account by providing for a 25% variance on the projected cash flows of the operating entity. In his deposition, he stated that he chose the 25% variance based on his experience with the cable industry. However, Curtis failed to establish that this variance would adequately account for any inaccuracies in the revenue and expense assumptions discussed above as well as any changes in consumer demand for British-style news reporting.

Indeed, Curtis failed to account for the effects of *any* general market risks on the Channel's probability of success. These risks include: (1) the entry of competitors; (2) technological developments; (3) regulatory changes; or (4) general market movements. As the district court correctly noted, "[f]ailure to control for adverse market conditions allows the false inference that plaintiff's venture was an assured success." Therefore, the court properly held that Schonfeld failed to establish a foundation for the existence of lost profits.[1]

In addition, Grimes's testimony regarding likely profits based on his comparisons to existing cable channels was properly rejected. It rested on a foundation of sand. Schonfeld failed to establish the high degree of correlation between INN or the non-existent operating entity and the proffered firms (in terms of, *inter alia,* investors, management and cost structures) upon which the probative quality of this evidence depends.

Schonfeld contends that the district court ignored the "wrongdoer rule" which Schonfeld believes required that the burden of uncertainty as to the amount of damages be shifted to the Hilliards. The "wrongdoer

---

[1] For this reason, the district court did not, and we need not, reach the issue of whether Curtis's expert testimony should be excluded under *Daubert* and its progeny.

rule," however, is not that broad. It provides that, "*when the existence of damage is certain,* and the only uncertainty is as to its amount, . . . the burden of uncertainty as to the amount of damage is upon the wrongdoer." The rule does not apply here for the simple reason that the *existence* of lost profit damages cannot be established with the requisite certainty.

C. *The Contemplation of the Parties*

Finally, Schonfeld maintains that he adduced sufficient evidence to establish that liability for lost profits was within the parties' contemplation at the time the Hilliards promised to fund the Interim Agreement. He contends that this case is similar to *Travellers Int'l, A.G. v. Trans World Airlines, Inc.,* 41 F.3d 1570 (2d Cir.1994) where we upheld an award of lost profits when TWA breached its duty of good faith and fair dealing under a joint venture agreement with Travellers to market Travellers' getaway packages. We disagree.

In *Travellers,* the plaintiff was seeking to recover profits that would have been realized under the very contract that the defendant was accused of breaching. Further, we noted that TWA had "near exclusive control" over the marketing of the getaway packages and, therefore, the profitability of the business. Thus, when it renewed its contract with Travellers, it "fairly may be supposed to have assumed consciously that lost profits damages would be an appropriate remedy" or at least "to have warranted Travellers reasonably to suppose that TWA had assumed such liability."

Our case is distinguishable in several respects. Schonfeld is not seeking profits that would have accrued under the alleged oral agreement to fund, or even under the Interim Agreement. Rather, Schonfeld wants to recover lost profits that INN or a non-existent operating entity might have received from the operation of the Channel. Further, the profitability of the Channel was highly uncertain when the Hilliards promised to fund the Interim Agreement. Nor did they exercise "near exclusive control" over the profitability of the venture. In light of "the nature, purpose and particular circumstances of the contract known by the parties," by orally promising to provide up to $20 million to fund the Interim Agreement, the Hilliards cannot "be supposed to have assumed" liability for approximately $269 million in lost profits that might have been garnered in the future by a non-existent operating entity.

For all the foregoing reasons, we affirm the district court's grant of summary judgment dismissing all claims insofar as they seek damages for lost profits.

II. Lost Asset Damages

A. *Distinction between Damages for the Market Value of a Lost Income-Producing Asset and Lost Profits That Could Have Been Derived Therefrom*

Schonfeld faults the district court for: (1) failing to distinguish his claims for the market value of the lost supply agreements from his request for lost profits; and (2) dismissing his lost asset claims. Schonfeld is correct.

In an action for breach of contract, a plaintiff may seek two distinct categories of damages: (1) "general" or "market" damages; and (2) "special" or "consequential" damages. A plaintiff is seeking general damages when he tries to recover "the value of the very performance promised." General damages are sometimes called "market" damages because, when the promised performance is the delivery of goods, such damages are measured by the difference between the contract price and the market value of the goods at the time of the breach.

"Special" or "consequential" damages, on the other hand, seek to compensate a plaintiff for additional losses (other than the value of the promised performance) that are incurred as a result of the defendant's breach. The type of consequential damages most often sought is lost operating profits of a business. However, lost profits are not the only kind of consequential damages. A defendant's breach of contract may also cause a plaintiff to lose an asset that was in its possession prior to the breach. In some instances, the asset lost is an *income-producing* asset, the fair market value of which may be based, in whole or in part, on a buyer's projections of what income he could derive from the asset in the future. Damages seeking to recover the market value for a lost income-producing asset have sometimes been referred to as "hybrid" damages.

Although lost profits and "hybrid" lost asset damages are both consequential, rather than general, in nature, courts have universally recognized that they are separate and distinct categories of damages.

When the defendant's conduct results in the loss of an income-producing asset with an ascertainable market value, the most accurate and immediate measure of damages is the market value of the asset at the time of breach—not the lost profits that the asset could have produced in the future. *See* 1 *Dobbs Law of Remedies* at § 3.3(7) (Market value damages are "based on future profits as estimated by potential buyers who form the 'market'" and "reflect the buyer's discount for the fact that the profits would be postponed and . . . uncertain.").

Applying these principles to Schonfeld's claims, it is clear that he is seeking two separate and distinct categories of consequential damages: (1) lost profits; and (2) "hybrid" damages for the market value of a lost income-producing asset. As we have already noted, Schonfeld cannot recover the consequential damages he seeks for lost profits. However, this holding in no way impairs his ability to establish his claim for "hybrid" damages seeking the market value of the lost supply agreements.

Relying on *Kenford I,* the district court held that Schonfeld's lost asset claims were indistinguishable from DSI's claims for profits that it could have earned under the stadium management contract. The court's reliance on *Kenford I,* however, was misplaced. In *Kenford I,* DSI never sought to recover damages for the market value of the management agreement—damages that in that instance would have been general damages because the very performance promised was the execution of the agreement. For whatever reason, the only damages sought by DSI were consequential damages for lost profits. Thus, *Kenford I* does not stand as a bar to Schonfeld's seeking to recover the market value of the supply agreements.

We therefore turn to the proof necessary to recover "hybrid" consequential damages measured by the market value of a lost income-producing asset.

B. *Proof Requirements for "Hybrid" Consequential Damages*

Some of the confusion in this area is traceable to the law of evidence. The same kind of market-value proof is sometimes required to prove general damages as to prove "hybrid" damages for the loss of an income-producing asset. But the two remain analytically distinct. Like lost profits, "hybrid" damages are one step removed from the naked performance promised by the defendant; and their existence and extent depend on the individual circumstances of the plaintiff. Therefore, as with all consequential damages, a plaintiff must prove that liability for the loss of the asset was within the contemplation of the parties at the time the contract was made, and the asset's value should be proven with reasonable certainty.

The market value of an income-producing asset is inherently less speculative than lost profits because it is determined at a single point in time. It represents what a buyer is willing to pay for *the chance* to earn the speculative profits. Therefore, it is appropriate to apply these proof requirements more leniently than is the case with proof of lost profits.

Although not expressly stated by Russ Hilliard at the time the oral promise to fund the Interim Agreement was made, the Hilliards' liability for the loss of both the Interim and December Supply Agreements was clearly within the contemplation of all the parties. Indeed, Schonfeld introduced Russ Hilliard's own testimony acknowledging that the BBC would not have agreed to enter into the Interim and December Supply Agreements had the Hilliards not promised to fund the Interim Agreement. Thus, the only remaining issues with respect to Schonfeld's claims for lost asset damages are whether he can establish both their existence and their amount with reasonable certainty.

Schonfeld correctly argues that the district court erred in holding that: (1) he failed to establish that the March and December Supply Agreements were valuable, "recoverable" assets; and (2) even if they were, he could not establish their market values with reasonable certainty.

a. *"Recoverable" Assets*

The goal of awarding damages for the market value of a lost asset is "to make sure the defendant's tort or contract breach does not leave the plaintiff with assets or net worth less than that to which she is entitled." Therefore, so long as the lost asset has a determinable market value, a plaintiff may seek to recover that value whether the asset is "tangible or intangible property or almost any kind of contract right." A supply contract, for instance, is a form of intangible property that has an ascertainable value.

It is undisputed that the March and December Supply Agreements, wherein the BBC granted INN a 20-year exclusive programming license, were INN's most valuable assets.[2] Indeed, Russ Hilliard and Bruce Dickenson of Daniels testified that, other than the cash in its bank account, the supply agreements were the *only* valuable assets that INN possessed. Russ Hilliard also conceded that: (1) Schonfeld and the BBC would not have agreed to abandon the March Supply Agreement and enter into the Interim and December Supply Agreements had the Hilliards not promised to fund the Interim Agreement; and (2) INN lost the December Supply Agreement, in part, as a result of the Hilliards' failure to fund. We conclude that Schonfeld has established the existence of lost asset damages with the requisite certainty.

b. *Competent Evidence of Market Value*

When a defendant's breach of contract deprives a plaintiff of an asset, the courts look to compensate the plaintiff for the "market value" of the asset "in contradistinction to any peculiar value the object in question may have had to the owner." Although it is easier to determine an asset's market value when it is actively traded on a standardized exchange or commodities market, an asset does not lose its value simply because no such market exists. Admittedly, in such instances, "the determination of a market value involves something of a fiction."

In determining the market value of unique or intangible assets, New York courts have embraced the hypothetical market standard enunciated by the Supreme Court in *United States v. Cartwright,* 411 U.S. 546, 551

[2] Properly parsed, Schonfeld seeks to recover the market value of the lost December Supply Agreement in connection with his breach of contract, promissory estoppel, breach of fiduciary duty and corporate waste and mismanagement claims. He seeks to recover the market value of the March Supply Agreement in connection with his fraud claim.

(1973): "The fair market value is the price at which the property would change hands between a willing buyer and a willing seller, neither being under any compulsion to buy or to sell and both having reasonable knowledge of relevant facts." If no prior sales history is available, experts may give their opinion of the asset's value; and evidence of sales of comparable assets may be introduced. If he is sufficiently qualified, even an asset's owner may testify as to its market value.

If, fortunately, the asset at issue has a sales history, then despite the lack of a traditional market, it is easier for the court to determine the asset's market value as of the time it was lost. Indeed, it is well-established that a recent sale price for the subject asset, negotiated by parties at arm's length, is the "best evidence" of its market value. Once a plaintiff has produced such evidence, the burden is on the defendant to demonstrate "special circumstances which would negate [the relevance] of a prior arm's-length purchase price."

Although the "sale price rule" is usually seen only in the context of completed transactions, the price at which a party offered to sell the subject property in an unsuccessful transaction nevertheless may be introduced as a party admission when offered against that party. Furthermore, if the sale price offered as evidence against the defendant by the plaintiff is contained in a contract that was negotiated by the parties at arm's length, it remains admissible even though the transaction contemplated by the contract was never completed if: (1) the performance promised is not yet due under the contract and the parties still intend to perform; or (2) the transaction contemplated under the contract would have occurred but for the defendant's actions or the interference of a third-party. . . .

[W]e hold that the district court improperly excluded Curtis's expert testimony with regard to the market value of the supply agreements. We also conclude that the Cox Agreement is competent evidence of the market values of the March and December Supply Agreements. Indeed, using the Cox Agreement as a benchmark, Schonfeld will likely be able to establish their market values with reasonable certainty on remand.

First, it is undisputed that the Cox Agreement was negotiated at arm's length and that Cox is a well-informed leader in the cable television industry. Further, the Cox Agreement established a price at which Cox agreed to buy and, more importantly, INN agreed to sell INN's programming rights under the March Supply Agreement. Therefore, Schonfeld offered what we consider "the best evidence" of the market value of the March Supply Agreement.

It is true that the sale anticipated by the Cox Agreement never occurred and was "subject to the BBC not voicing objections," the approval of Cox's board of directors, and the receipt of a non-binding letter of its intent to invest from TCI Cable. However, Schonfeld introduced evidence that the conditions could have been met, and the deal could have gone through, had the Hilliards agreed to grant an extension of time to work out the few remaining issues. Therefore, the district court should have "placed considerable weight" on the Cox Agreement as evidence of the value of the March Supply Agreement.

Even if the deal with Cox would not have gone through, the Cox Agreement clearly establishes the price at which the Hilliards were willing to sell their rights under the March Supply Agreement. Therefore, under the rules of evidence, the price set forth in the Cox Agreement is admissible against the Hilliards as a party admission.

The Hilliards argue that the purchase price contained in the Cox Agreement should be disregarded as "unique to Cox" because Cox had an established cable network and a pre-existing relationship with the BBC. They contend that the supply agreements would not have the same value to any other purchaser because of their complexity and the substantial limitations and obligations, both financial and promotional, contained therein. This argument is unpersuasive and contrary to New York law. *Plaza Hotel Assocs. v. Wellington Assocs.*, 37 N.Y.2d 273, 333 N.E.2d 346, 372 N.Y.S.2d 35 (1975).

Cox's resources and business position are not determinative of whether the Cox Agreement is competent evidence of the market value of the supply agreements. Any offer is *by definition* unique to the purchaser because the value of an asset to the purchaser depends on the purchaser's needs, resources and circumstances. The value placed on an asset by a purchaser, however, does not become evidence of the asset's market value unless it is also the price at which a reasonably informed seller is willing to sell the asset. Here, Cox "was obviously aware of the conditions and restriction found [in the March Supply Agreement], but nonetheless it agreed upon a price that it thought reasonable under the circumstances." Further, it was a price at which INN was willing to sell its rights.

Finally, the Hilliards argue that, even if the Cox Agreement is competent evidence of the market value of the March Supply Agreement, it is not admissible to establish the market value of the December Supply Agreement because of material differences in the terms. However, evidence of sale prices negotiated at arm's length for the purchase of "comparable" property is admissible as evidence of the market value of the property at issue.

c. *The Value Established by the Cox Agreement*

The only remaining issue is whether the market values for the March and December Supply Agreements can be established with reasonable certainty using the Cox Agreement as a benchmark. The agreement provided that the total purchase price would be paid as follows: (1) $700,000 cash upon the signing of the definitive agreements required by the Cox Agreement; (2) $1 million (in annual installments $100,000) paid over ten years; and (3) a 5% equity interest in Cox's two BBC channels.

The district court held that, "[a]lthough the offer proposed an up-front payment, most of INN's compensation was contingent on the revenue generated by the two proposed channels in the tenth year of operations" and such revenue forecasts are "insufficient to prove damages with reasonable certainty." Ultimately, the district court "excluded as irrelevant and speculative" all expert testimony proffered in support of Schonfeld's claims for lost asset damages and dismissed all claims insofar as they sought to recover such damages. In so holding, the district court applied an improper "all or nothing" approach with respect to the Cox Agreement, *i.e.,* if the *entire* purchase price established by the Cox Agreement cannot be determined with reasonable certainty, then Schonfeld cannot establish the market value of the supply agreements.

However, if he can successfully establish the Hilliards' liability, Schonfeld is entitled, as a matter of law, to recover market value damages *to the extent* that they can be proven with reasonable certainty. Further, pursuant to the "wrongdoer rule," where, as here, "the existence of damage is certain, and the only uncertainty is as to its amount, . . . the burden of uncertainty as to the amount of damage is upon the wrongdoer." Therefore, the burden of uncertainty here is upon the Hilliards.

In light of the Cox Agreement, a reasonable jury could find that INN's programming rights were worth at least $700,000 plus the present value of $1 million paid over ten years, for a total of approximately $1.39 million.[3] In addition, the Cox Agreement provides sufficient information to calculate a dollar value for the 5% equity portion of the purchase price. Cox retained the right to buy out INN's 5% interest in the tenth year of operations at a price of 20% of the tenth-year gross revenues of both channels. Incorporated into the Cox Agreement by reference are revenue projections for the news channel made by Cox that were previously forwarded to INN.[4] Therefore, on remand, Schonfeld ought to be able to establish, with reasonable certainty, the total amount that Cox was willing to pay and INN was willing to accept for the March Supply Agreement on June 2, 1994.

Using the purchase price contained in the Cox Agreement as a benchmark, Schonfeld may introduce expert testimony on remand as to the market values of the March and December Supply Agreements as of the dates on which they were caused to be abandoned or lost. The

[3] Curtis calculated the present value of $1 million paid over ten years to be $687,000.

[4] The district court acknowledged that certain aspects of the Cox projections "arguably render them more certain than the INN forecast." For instance, "Cox has a record of expenses, an established management and a ready distribution system for new programming" and revenues only had to be projected ten (rather than twenty) years into the future.

Hilliards, of course, may introduce evidence with respect to the *weight* to be accorded the Cox Agreement and may offer independent evidence with respect to the market values of the March and December Supply Agreements. . . .

In addition, to the extent that Schonfeld seeks to recover the market value of the March Supply Agreement in connection with his fraud claim, that claim was improperly limited to $15,000. "Under New York law, the measure of damages for fraud is governed by the 'out-of-pocket' rule which permits recovery for a plaintiff's reliance interest," including damages incurred by "passing up other business opportunities." Therefore, Schonfeld may seek to recover the market value of the March Supply Agreement which INN abandoned in reliance on the Hilliards' promises. . . .

IV. Defendants' Additional Arguments on Appeal

The Hilliards argue that we should nevertheless affirm the district court's grant of summary judgment because the oral promise to fund is unenforceable. The bases for this contention are twofold: (1) the alleged promise was so indefinite that there could not have been a "meeting of the minds;" and (2) the promise is not in writing as is necessary to modify the Shareholders' Agreement and is also required by the New York Statute of Frauds.

Both of these grounds were briefed by the parties below, but the district court elected not to address them. Although we are empowered to affirm a district court's decision on a theory not considered below, it is our distinctly preferred practice to remand such issues for consideration by the district court in the first instance. This is particularly appropriate when, as here, such theories have been briefed and argued only cursorily in this Court. We therefore remand to allow the district court to consider these arguments in the first instance.

NOTES AND QUESTIONS

1. *Preponderance vs. Certainty.* What does the certainty doctrine add to the rule requiring a plaintiff to prove her claim by a preponderance of evidence? Does it require more evidence? Or does it change the decisionmaker from the jury to the judge? In the cases on pain and indignity, and even those on property damage, the judges said they gave great deference to jury determinations. If so, is the rule likely to have much impact?

2. *Existence or Amount.* The court says it requires certainty both as to the existence of the loss and the amount of the loss. Did it apply the rule that way? Is the amount of the lost asset value reasonably certain? It still requires some estimation.

3. *Wrongdoer Exception.* The court mentions the wrongdoer rule. This exception to the certainty requirement applies "where the defendant by his

own wrong has prevented a more precise computation." *Bigelow v. RKO Radio Pictures, Inc.*, 327 U.S. 251, 66 S.Ct. 574, 90 L.Ed. 652 (1946). In *Bigelow*, defendants had conspired to prevent plaintiff's theater from obtaining movies until after favored theaters had already shown them. Plaintiff showed (i) its actual profits for the period of the conspiracy, (ii) its actual profits in the period immediately before the conspiracy precluded it from obtaining newer films (about $125,000 more than (i)), and (iii) the profits earned during the period of the conspiracy by similar theaters that did show newer films (the beneficiaries of the conspiracy) (about $116,000 more than (i)). Was this enough to establish that plaintiff had incurred a loss? Was this enough to estimate the amount of the loss with reasonable certainty? Or was it necessary to invoke the exception holding that the defendant's conduct had precluded proof with reasonable certainty? Will the exception swallow the rule? Every breach of contract makes it hard for plaintiff to show how much profit it would have made if defendant had performed. If the Hilliards had performed, Schonfeld could show the amount of profit from the deal. Why did the court reject the wrongdoer rule here?

The effect of the wrongdoer rule is to eliminate the requirement that the amount of loss be proven with reasonable certainty, while retaining the requirement that the existence of losses be proven with reasonable certainty. Sometimes courts simply state the certainty rule in that way. *See Giampapa v. American Family Mut. Ins. Co.*, 64 P.3d 230, 244 (Colo.2003) (en banc).

4. *Nominal or Presumed Damages*. The requirement that a loss exist—or, as termed in antitrust and some tort cases, fact of damage (as opposed to amount of damage)—does not apply universally. In contract cases, a plaintiff who has shown a breach but no loss usually is entitled to nominal damages. If fact of damage need not be shown at all to recover nominal damages, does it make sense to require fact of damage to be shown with reasonable certainty before allowing the jury to award lost profits?

Some common law torts presume damages once the elements of the tort are established. An example, now riddled with constitutional law inroads, is defamation. Other torts, however, apply a "no harm, no foul" rule, requiring the plaintiff to establish damage as an element of liability. The prime example is the action in negligence, where damage is the gist of the action. Fraud is another example.

5. *Expert Opinion*. As *Schonfeld* illustrates, courts do not give credence to every estimate an expert offers. If it did, very few applications of the certainty doctrine would remain. It might block recovery only when an expert failed to make any estimate of the amount of loss or even to offer an example of monetary loss caused by the breach. *See ESPN, Inc. v. Office of the Commissioner of Baseball*, 76 F.Supp.2d 416 (S.D.N.Y. 1999). While courts give more credence to economic projections than they once did, those projections are scrutinized for credibility. Why did the court reject the estimated profits in *Schonfeld*? Could you spot those kinds of flaws and argue them effectively on your own? Or will you need to hire an expert to help you

through the numbers in every case? Will all your clients be able to afford that?

6. *Proving Asset Value.* Schonfeld was fortunate that the Cox offer evinced the value of the license. Without that offer, could the lost asset value be proven with sufficient certainty? Would capitalization of earnings be allowed? If not, would plaintiff be limited to nominal damages?

7. *Reliance Alternative.* When courts cannot calculate lost profits with reasonable certainty, they sometimes allow recovery of the reliance interest instead of the expectation interest. RESTATEMENT (SECOND) OF CONTRACTS § 347. Reliance seeks to put the plaintiff in the position it would have occupied if the promise had never been made, rather than the position she would have occupied if the promise had been performed (the expectation interest). Would the reliance interest have been of any benefit to the plaintiff here? What would the reliance interest include? Is it any more certain than expectation?

Sometimes reliance is as close as the court can come to expectation: that is, it will compensate the plaintiff for any expenses incurred so far, but not for any profits that might have been generated if the promise had been performed (in effect, assuming plaintiff would have broken even on the venture, with no profit but no loss). *See* Michael B. Kelly, *The Phantom Reliance Interest in Contract Damages*, 1992 WIS. L. REV. 1755. Would that remedy be appropriate here if the Cox offer did not exist? What would it include? Are there any dangers to this approach?

8. *Defining Foreseeability.* Did the court apply the foreseeability test properly? Were lost profits unforeseeable—even to an investor in the project that was supposed to produce the profits? Compare the court's statement of foreseeability to that in the second Restatement. Are there any differences that might explain the court's application of foreseeability to the case?

Schonfeld relies heavily on two prior decisions. *Kenford Co. v. County of Erie*, 67 N.Y.2d 257, 493 N.E.2d 234, 502 N.Y.S.2d 131 (1986) (Kenford I) and *Kenford Co. v. County of Erie*, 73 N.Y.2d 312, 537 N.E.2d 176, 540 N.Y.S.2d 1 (1989) (Kenford II). Kenford donated land to Erie County (Buffalo) in exchange for promises to build a domed stadium on the land and to hire Kenford to manage the stadium. Kenford also stood to profit when its other land surrounding the stadium appreciated. When the County abandoned the project, Kenford sought damages for breach. After summary judgment on liability, the case focused on damages. *Kenford I* rejected lost profits on the management contract based on certainty and foreseeability. *Kenford II* rejected lost appreciation of the surrounding land, but did not rely on uncertainty. The court's foreseeability analysis (similar to that in *Kenford I*) is excerpted here:

> In the case before us, it is beyond dispute that at the time the contract was executed, all parties thereto harbored an expectation and anticipation that the proposed domed stadium facility would bring about an economic boom in the County and would result in

> increased land values and increased property taxes. . . . We cannot conclude, however, that this hope or expectation of increased property values and taxes necessarily or logically leads to the conclusion that the parties contemplated that the County would assume liability for Kenford's loss of anticipated appreciation in the value of its peripheral lands if the stadium were not built. . . .
>
> . . .
>
> Undoubtedly, Kenford purchased the peripheral lands in question with the hope of benefiting from the expected appreciation in the value of those lands once the stadium was completed and became operational. In doing so, Kenford voluntarily and knowingly assumed the risk that, if the stadium were not built, its expectations of financial gain would be unrealized. There is no indication that either Kenford or the County reasonably contemplated at the time of the contract that this risk was assumed, either wholly or partially, by the County. To hold otherwise would lead to the irrational conclusion that the County, in addition to promising to build the domed stadium, provided a guarantee that if for any reason the stadium were not built, Kenford would still receive all the hoped for financial benefits from the peripheral lands it anticipated to receive upon the completion of the stadium.

73 N.Y.2d at 319–21, 537 N.E.2d at 179–80, 540 N.Y.S.2d at 3–5.

If the parties anticipated that property values (including land owned by Kenford) would increase when the stadium was built, didn't each have reason to know that Kenford probably would lose that appreciation as a result of the breach? What more does foreseeability require?

9. *Foreseeability Per Se.* Can the contract itself establish foreseeability? In *Spectrum Sciences and Software vs. United States*, 98 Fed. Cl. 8 (2011), the court's analysis of foreseeability refers only to multiple terms that forbid sharing plaintiff's proprietary information. Does the prohibition itself establish that the loss was foreseeable?

Exercise: Based on the facts of *Schonfeld*, draft a clause that would satisfy the foreseeability requirement. Exchange papers with a classmate. Comment on your classmate's clause, including whether it will satisfy the foreseeability test, how it might be drafted more effectively, and whether you would advise your client to agree to a contract that contained this term. (Request any modifications that might make it acceptable). [Variation: use problem 6 below instead of *Schonfeld* for the factual background.]

10. *Tacit Agreement?* The foreseeability test was created by *Hadley v. Baxendale*, 9 Ex. 341, 156 Eng. Rep. 154 (1854) (mill was shut down pending replacement of a shaft; carrier misdirected the shaft, delaying replacement; no damages for lost profits because not foreseeable). Oliver Wendell Holmes criticized it as too generous. *Globe Refining Co. v. Landa Cotton Oil Co.*, 190 U.S. 540, 23 S.Ct. 754, 47 L.Ed. 1171 (1903). He argued that foreseeability of loss was insufficient; liability exists only if the defendant tacitly agreed to

pay damages of that sort. The test was expressly rejected by the Uniform Commercial Code (§ 2–715 comment 2) and the Restatement (Second) of Contracts (§ 351 comment a). A minority of states continue to apply it. Has New York joined that minority?

11. *Purpose.* Is there any point to requiring foreseeability? If the loss was caused by the breach and is proven with reasonable certainty, why does it matter whether the loss was foreseeable? Whom is the law protecting? From what? The problems below may probe the rule.

Your answer may depend on another twist in the rule. What, exactly, must be foreseeable in order to recover: the amount of the loss, the type of the loss, or something else? If defendant knows that a breach will cause plaintiff to lose profits, does it matter that defendant may not know how much profit plaintiff will lose? *See Evra Corp. v. Swiss Bank Corp.*, 673 F.2d 951 (7th Cir. 1982).

The Uniform Commercial Code allows recovery of consequential damages for "any loss resulting from general or particular requirements and needs of which the seller at the time of contracting had reason to know and which could not reasonably be prevented by cover or otherwise." UCC § 2–715(2)(a). For now, set aside the last phrase, which embodies the avoidable consequences doctrine. Does this language deny recovery when defendant could not foresee the amount of plaintiff's loss, the type of loss, or something else? Does "general or particular requirements or needs" mean anything more than the performance specified by the contract? Won't defendant always have reason to know what goods the plaintiff needs and when she needs them? Does the contract specify when plaintiff wants them, not when she needs them? Will losses ever flow naturally from the breach in this setting? Even if defendant knows plaintiff is a wholesaler, who intends to resell (say, at a normal profit), would she have reason to know that plaintiff *needs* the goods, as opposed to wants them? Or does "needs" refer to the reason plaintiff needs the performance, such as how it will use the performance?

12. *Circumvention.* Consider lost-asset value. The asset here has value because it might produce profits later. That is true for many assets—apartment buildings, shopping malls, bonds (and remember barges?). To calculate the value of such assets, appraisers often estimate the profits the assets will yield over time and discount them to present value (capitalization of earnings, discussed *supra* at 597). Does "lost asset value" circumvent the foreseeability rule (and the certainty rule)? Or do foreseeability and certainty continue to apply? Do they have any force in the context of asset value? If not, is that a problem? Is foreseeability so important that we should reject efforts to evaluate assets merely to preserve the rule?

PROBLEMS

1. *Turning Real Estates.* Seller promised Buyer a parcel of real estate in exchange for $1 million. Seller breached. Buyer had arranged to resell the parcel for $1.5 million. Naturally, buyer had not mentioned this resale to

Seller. Can Buyer recover the lost profit on resale from Seller? Would you advise Buyer to tell Seller about the proposed resale? When should Buyer have revealed it?

2. *Foreseeability and Avoidability.* Lender promised Borrower a mortgage on certain real estate at an advantageous interest rate. Lender breached. Borrower was unable to find a substitute loan in time to close the deal. Lender admits that it could foresee that Borrower might need to pay a higher interest rate to find a substitute mortgage, but states that it had no reason to know that Borrower would be unable to find a substitute in the time available. On these facts, what can Borrower recover from Lender? What if Borrower did find a substitute loan, but at an interest rate much higher than Lender had reason to foresee at the time of the original agreement?

3. *Reselling Goods.* Manufacturer agreed to supply Wholesaler with all of its requirements for aspirin at a fixed price per case. Manufacturer breached. Wholesaler never told Manufacturer that it intended to resell the goods, but Manufacturer knew that Wholesaler was a wholesaler. Can Wholesaler recover profits it would have earned by reselling the goods? Does it matter whether Manufacturer had reason to know how much Wholesaler would mark up the goods?

4. *Foreseeability of Cover Price.* Wholesaler promised Restaurateur all of its requirements for tomatoes at a fixed price per bushel. Wholesaler breached. Restaurateur covered with substitute tomatoes, but an unanticipated shortage in the market required Restaurateur to pay far more than either party reasonably could have anticipated when the contract was formed. Can Restaurateur recover the additional cost of tomatoes from Wholesaler? Is that because the damages are foreseeable or because they don't need to be foreseeable?

5. *Casey's Inhaler.* Was Casey's unemployment foreseeable by the pharmacy at the time the prescription was filled? Would that matter to the tort claim? Should the damages for tort and contract differ in this respect? What if recovery is in tort against an attorney, who negligently failed to file the contract claim? What about negligent failure to file the tort claim? Even if the unemployment was foreseeable, was the amount of loss foreseeable? What arguments might the pharmacy raise? How might Casey's counsel respond?

6. *Fire Damage.* Fire destroyed plaintiff's hydroponic tomato operation because defendant utility had cut power to the business without notice. Without power, the electric water pumps would not operate, impeding efforts by employees and firefighters to control the blaze. (Lack of water also would harm the hydroponic crop directly, but the fire occurred before lack of water injured the crop.) Defendant knew that plaintiff operated a hydroponic farm. Defendant did not know that plaintiff lacked any backup generators or other means to draw water when electricity was shut off. Failure to give notice of

the shutdown breached a contract. What losses can plaintiff recover in a contract claim?

a. *Exercise*: Draft a notice to the utility on behalf of plaintiff that would provide the defendant sufficient notice of the potential losses. When should notice be provided? How would you advise your client to proceed after you draft the notice?

b. *Tort*. If shutting off the power and failing to restore it promptly at the request of firefighters constituted negligence, what losses can plaintiff recover?

7. *Nuclear Waste*. The U.S. government breached a contract to dispose of plaintiff's spent nuclear fuel. In order to deal with the waste, plaintiff spent $3 million dollars lobbying the state legislature to obtain permission to store the spent fuel temporarily at the reactor site. The state also demanded that plaintiff contribute $6 million to a clean energy development fund as a condition of receiving permission. Plaintiff also spent $600,000 to conduct a flood study and build a barrier to conceal the storage facility from view, as required by the state legislature. Should plaintiff recover any of these expenses for breach of contract? Does it matter that, at the time the contract was made, the original owner had an exception that would have allowed it to store the spent fuel on site without additional permission, but the exception did not apply to plaintiff, a successor in interest?

LOUISIANA EX REL. GUSTE V. M/V TESTBANK

752 F.2d 1019 (5th Cir.1985),
cert. denied, 477 U.S. 903, 106 S.Ct. 3271, 91 L.Ed.2d 562 (1986).

PATRICK E. HIGGINBOTHAM, CIRCUIT JUDGE:

We are asked to abandon physical damage to a proprietary interest as a prerequisite to recovery for economic loss in cases of unintentional maritime tort. We decline the invitation.[1]

I

In the early evening of July 22, 1980, the M/V SEA DANIEL, an inbound bulk carrier, and the M/V TESTBANK, an outbound container ship, collided at approximately mile forty-one of the Mississippi River Gulf outlet. At impact, a white haze enveloped the ships until carried away by prevailing winds, and containers aboard TESTBANK were damaged and lost overboard. The white haze proved to be hydrobromic acid and the contents of the containers which went overboard proved to be approximately twelve tons of pentachlorophenol, PCP,[*] assertedly the largest such spill in United States history. The United States Coast Guard closed the outlet to navigation until August 10, 1980 and all fishing, shrimping, and related activity was temporarily suspended in the outlet and four hundred square miles of surrounding marsh and waterways.

Forty-one lawsuits were filed and consolidated before the same judge in the Eastern District of Louisiana. These suits presented claims of shipping interests, marina and boat rental operators, wholesale and retail seafood enterprises not actually engaged in fishing, seafood restaurants, tackle and bait shops, and recreational fishermen. They proffered an assortment of liability theories, including maritime tort, private actions pursuant to various sections of the Rivers & Harbors Appropriation Act of 1899, and rights of action under Louisiana law. . . .

Defendants moved for summary judgment as to all claims for economic loss unaccompanied by physical damage to property. The district court granted the requested summary judgment as to all such claims except those asserted by commercial oystermen, shrimpers, crabbers and fishermen who had been making a commercial use of the embargoed waters. The district court found these commercial fishing

---

1 We do not address intentional tort or ultrahazardous activity, such as blasting.

* [In his dissent, Judge Wisdom included the following footnote:] Pentachlorophenol (PCP) is toxic to both human and marine life in even moderate quantities. PCP contains dioxin, which has been tentatively linked to cancer in humans and other mammals. This PCP is not phencyclidine [(phenylcyolohexyl) piperidine], or "angel dust," which is also designated by the initials PCP.

interests deserving of a special protection akin to that enjoyed by seamen.[2]

On appeal a panel of this court affirmed, concluding that claims for economic loss unaccompanied by physical damage to a proprietary interest were not recoverable in maritime tort. 728 F.2d 748 (5th Cir.1984). The panel, as did the district court, pointed to the doctrine of *Robins Dry Dock & Repair Co. v. Flint,* 275 U.S. 303 (1927). [We] then took the case en banc. . . .

Plaintiffs urge that the requirement of physical injury to a proprietary interest is arbitrary, unfair, and illogical, as it denies recovery for foreseeable injury caused by negligent acts. At its bottom the argument is that questions of remoteness ought to be left to the trier of fact. Ultimately the question becomes who ought to decide—judge or jury—and whether there will be a rule beyond the jacket of a given case. The plaintiffs contend that the "problem" need not be separately addressed, but instead should be handled by "traditional" principles of tort law. Putting the problem of which doctrine is the traditional one aside, their rhetorical questions are flawed in several respects.

Those who would delete the requirement of physical damage have no rule or principle to substitute. Their approach fails to recognize limits upon the adjudicating ability of courts. We do not mean just the ability to supply a judgment; prerequisite to this adjudicatory function are preexisting rules, whether the creature of courts or legislatures. Courts can decide cases without preexisting normative guidance but the result becomes less judicial and more the product of a managerial, legislative or negotiated function.

Review of the foreseeable consequences of the collision of the SEA DANIEL and TESTBANK demonstrates the wave upon wave of successive economic consequences and the managerial role plaintiffs would have us assume. The vessel delayed in St. Louis may be unable to fulfill its obligation to haul from Memphis, to the injury of the shipper, to the injury of the buyers, to the injury of their customers. Plaintiffs concede, as do all who attack the requirement of physical damage, that a line would need to be drawn—somewhere on the other side, each plaintiff would say in turn, of its recovery. Plaintiffs advocate not only that the lines be drawn elsewhere but also that they be drawn on an ad hoc and discrete basis. The result would be that no determinable measure of the limit of foreseeability would precede the decision on liability. We are told that when the claim is too remote, or too tenuous, recovery will be denied.

---

[2] Stated more generally, the summary judgment denied the claims asserted by shipping interests suffering losses from delays or rerouting, marina and boat operators, wholesale and retail seafood enterprises not actually engaged in [fishing] the area, seafood restaurants, tackle and bait shops, and recreational [fishermen]. The rights of commercial fishermen who survived summary judgment are not before us.

Presumably then, as among all plaintiffs suffering foreseeable economic loss, recovery will turn on a judge or jury's decision. There will be no rationale for the differing results save the "judgment" of the trier of fact. Concededly, it can "decide" all the claims presented, and with comparative if not absolute ease. The point is not that such a process cannot be administered but rather that its judgments would be much less the products of a determinable rule of law. In this important sense, the resulting decisions would be judicial products only in their draw upon judicial resources.

The bright line rule of damage to a proprietary interest, as most, has the virtue of predictability with the vice of creating results in cases at its edge that are said to be "unjust" or "unfair." Plaintiffs point to seemingly perverse results, where claims the rule allows and those it disallows are juxtaposed—such as vessels striking a dock, causing minor but recoverable damage, then lurching athwart a channel causing great but unrecoverable economic loss. The answer is that when lines are drawn sufficiently sharp in their definitional edges to be reasonable and predictable, such differing results are the inevitable result—indeed, decisions are the desired product. But there is more. The line drawing sought by plaintiffs is no less arbitrary because the line drawing appears only in the outcome—as one claimant is found too remote and another is allowed to recover. The true difference is that plaintiffs' approach would mask the results. The present rule would be more candid, and in addition, by making results more predictable, serves a normative function. It operates as a rule of law and allows a court to adjudicate rather than manage.

That the rule is identifiable and will predict outcomes in advance of the ultimate decision about recovery enables it to play additional roles. Here we agree with plaintiffs that economic analysis, even at the rudimentary level of jurists, is helpful both in the identification of such roles and the essaying of how the roles play. Thus it is suggested that placing all the consequence of its error on the maritime industry will enhance its incentive for safety. While correct, as far as such analysis goes, such *in terrorem* benefits have an optimal level. Presumably, when the cost of an unsafe condition exceeds its utility there is an incentive to change. As the costs of an accident become increasing multiples of its utility, however, there is a point at which greater accident costs lose meaning, and the incentive curve flattens. When the accident costs are added in large but unknowable amounts the value of the exercise is diminished.

With a disaster inflicting large and reverberating injuries through the economy, as here, we believe the more important economic inquiry is that of relative cost of administration, and in maritime matters administration quickly involves insurance. Those economic losses not recoverable under the present rule for lack of physical damage to a proprietary interest are the subject of first party or loss insurance. The rule change would work a shift to the more costly liability system of third party insurance. For the same reasons that courts have imposed limits on the concept of foreseeability, liability insurance might not be readily obtainable for the types of losses asserted here. As Professor James has noted, "[s]erious practical problems face insurers in handling insurance against potentially wide, open-ended liability. From an insurer's point of view it is not practical to cover, without limit, a liability that may reach catastrophic proportions, or to fix a reasonable premium on a risk that does not lend itself to actuarial measurement." By contrast, first party insurance is feasible for many of the economic losses claimed here. Each businessman who might be affected by a disruption of river traffic or by a halt in fishing activities can protect against that eventuality at a relatively low cost since his own potential losses are finite and readily discernible. Thus, to the extent that economic analysis informs our decision here, we think that it favors retention of the present rule. . . .

In conclusion, having reexamined the history and central purpose of the doctrine of *Robins Dry Dock* as developed in this circuit, we remain committed to its teaching. Denying recovery for pure economic losses is a pragmatic limitation on the doctrine of foreseeability, a limitation we find to be both workable and useful. Nor do we find persuasive plaintiffs' arguments that their economic losses are recoverable under a public nuisance theory, as damages for violation of federal statutes, or under state law.

Accordingly, the decision of the district court granting summary judgment to defendants on all claims for economic losses unaccompanied by physical damage to property is AFFIRMED.

GEE, CIRCUIT JUDGE, with whom CLARK, CHIEF JUDGE, joins, concurring:

[T]he overarching issue in the appeal . . . is, *who* should deal with questions of such magnitude as the rule for which the dissent contends would, again and again, draw before the courts? An oil spill damages hundreds, perhaps thousands, of miles of coastal area. A cloud of noxious industrial gas leaks out, kills thousands, and injures thousands more. A commonly-used building material is discovered, years after the fact, to possess unforeseen lethal qualities affecting thousands who have worked with it. The long-term effects of inhaling coal dust are found to be disabling to a significant proportion of veteran miners. None of these illustrations is fanciful; each has arisen in recent times and presented itself for resolution to our body politic. Congress has dealt effectively with Black Lung; it has signally failed to deal with the ravages of asbestosis [and] a swelling wave of individual asbestosis claims, to be resolved on a case by case basis, pushes slowly through our court system, threatening to inundate it and to consume in punitive damage awards to early claimants the relatively meager assets available to compensate the general class affected, many of whom have not yet suffered the onset of symptoms. [T]he dispute-resolution systems of courts are poorly equipped to manage disasters of such magnitude and that we should be wary of adopting rules of decision which, as would that contended for by the dissent, encourage the drawing of their broader aspects before us. . . .

The limited resources available to compensate asbestosis victims are only a particular illustration of the intrusion of this factor. The more general problem arises whenever individual courts contemporaneously grant sweeping awards against the same entity, perhaps a governmental one, in unconnected causes. However just each particular award may be, the cumulative effect—produced by individual proceedings to which questions of fiscal limitations and necessary trade-offs are foreign and irrelevant—may be irrational. It follows that we should decline to adopt rules of decision which set ourselves such tasks, tasks that are of their nature beyond our competence to deal with justly. . . .

JERRE S. WILLIAMS, CIRCUIT JUDGE, concurring specially:

My brother Higginbotham in his opinion for the Court correctly points out that the issue of liability to the commercial fishermen who were financially injured because of this ship collision and resultant spillage is not before us and is an undecided issue in this Circuit. I have considerable doubt that commercial fishermen can establish a proprietary interest in the right to fish in their fishing waters. Certainly the common legal synonym for "proprietary interest" is "ownership," as legal lexicons attest.

It would be preferable, in my view, to have the rule include a clear recognition that the rights of commercial fishermen were more accurately defined by the Court in *Union Oil Co. v. Oppen,* 501 F.2d 558 (9th Cir.1974). The Court agreed that ordinarily there is no recovery for economic losses unaccompanied by physical damage. It found, however, that commercial fishermen were foreseeable plaintiffs whose interests the oil company had a duty to protect when conducting its operations which resulted in the spillage. The commercial fishermen properly recover because their livelihood comes from a "resource" of the water which was polluted. Yet, physical property owned by them was not damaged and it is doubtful that a proprietary interest could have been shown.

WISDOM, CIRCUIT JUDGE, with whom ALVIN B. RUBIN, POLITZ, TATE, and JOHNSON, CIRCUIT JUDGES, join, dissenting.

Robins is the Tar Baby of tort law in this circuit. And the brier-patch is far away. This Court's application of *Robins* is out of step with contemporary tort doctrine, works substantial injustice on innocent victims, and is unsupported by the considerations that justified the Supreme Court's 1927 decision.

Robins was a tort case grounded on a contract. Whatever the justification for the original holding, this Court's requirement of physical injury as a condition to recovery is an unwarranted step backwards in torts jurisprudence. The resulting bar for claims of economic loss unaccompanied by any physical damage conflicts with conventional tort principles of foreseeability and proximate cause. I would analyze the plaintiffs' claims under these principles. Although this approach requires a case-by-case analysis, it comports with the fundamental idea of fairness that innocent plaintiffs should receive compensation and negligent defendants should bear the cost of their tortious acts. Such a result is worth the additional costs of adjudicating these claims, and this rule of liability appears to be more economically efficient. Finally, this result would relieve courts of the necessity of manufacturing exceptions totally inconsistent with the expanded *Robins* rule of requiring physical injury as a prerequisite to recovery. . . .

II. The Inapplicability of *Robins Dry Dock* to This Case

Whatever the pragmatic justification for the original holding in *Robins,* the majority has extended the case beyond the warrant of clear necessity in requiring *a physical injury* for a recovery of economic loss in cases such as the one before the court. *Robins* prevented plaintiffs who were neither proximately nor foreseeably injured by a tortious act or product from recovering solely by claiming a contract with the injured party. The wisdom of this rule is apparent. This rule, however, has been expanded now to bar recovery by plaintiffs who would be allowed to recover if judged under conventional principles of foreseeability and proximate cause.

Because the centerpiece of this litigation has been *Robins,* the holding of this cited case merits scrutiny. A ship's time charterer was required under contract to turn the vessel over to a dry dock for maintenance. The charterer owed no rent during the time the ship was under repair. The drydocker, who had contracted with the owner of the ship for the work, negligently damaged the ship's propeller. During the additional delay caused by repairs to the propeller, the charterer lost expected profits from the use of the ship. The charterer sued the shipyard for these economic losses. The Supreme Court denied relief, holding that the shipyard's damage to the propeller wronged only the owner of the ship. The Court further held that the charterer had lost merely the benefit of his contract for hire and had suffered no legally cognizable claim:

> [The plaintiff's] loss arose only through [its] contract with the owners—and while intentionally to bring about a breach of contract may give rise to a cause of action, no authority need be

> cited to show that, as a general rule, at least, a tort to the person or property of one man does not make the tort-feasor liable to another merely because the injured person was under a contract with that other, unknown to the doer of the wrong. The law does not spread its protection so far.

275 U.S. at 308–09, 48 S. Ct. at 135, 72 L. Ed. at 292 (citations omitted).

Robins held only that if a defendant's negligence injures party *A,* and the plaintiff suffers loss of expected income or profits because it had a contract with *A,* then the plaintiff has no cause of action based on the defendant's negligence.

It is a long step from *Robins* to a rule that requires *physical damage* as a prerequisite to recovery in maritime tort. The majority believes that the plaintiff's lack of any contractual connection with an injured party, taken with the *Robins* rule, forecloses liability: "If a plaintiff connected to the damaged chattels by contract cannot recover, others more remotely situated are foreclosed *a fortiori.*" This conclusion follows readily from the reasoning that if uninjured contracting parties are barred from recovery, and if contracting parties have a closer legal relationship than non-contracting parties, then a party who is not physically injured and who does not have a contractual relation to the damage is surely barred.

This argument would be sound in instances where the plaintiff suffered no loss *but for a contract* with the injured party. We would measure a plaintiff's connection to the tortfeasor by the only line connecting them, the contract, and disallow the claim under *Robins.* In the instant case, however, some of the plaintiffs suffered damages whether or not they had a contractual connection with a party physically injured by the tortfeasor. These plaintiffs do not need to rely on a contract to link them to the tort: The collision proximately caused their losses, and those losses were foreseeable. These plaintiffs are therefore freed from the *Robins* rule concerning the recovery of those who suffer economic loss because of an injury to a party with whom they have contracted.

Because *Robins* provides an overly restrictive bar on recovery, courts have over the years developed a number of exceptions. The traditional exceptions allow recovery for certain husband-wife claims, recovery for negligent interference with contract when the interference results from a tangible injury to the contractor's person or property, and recovery for persons employed on fishing boats to recover for lost income when the employment contract is disrupted by a third party's negligent injury to the ship or equipment.

Many opinions go beyond these traditional exceptions, both in the Fifth Circuit and in other courts. In both the Second and the Fourth Circuits courts have recently limited the applicability of the *Robins* rule in maritime torts. In the Fourth Circuit, District Judge Merhige refused to dismiss claims for economic losses suffered by commercial fishermen, local boat, and tackle and bait shop owners, but did dismiss claims by the plaintiffs who purchased and marketed seafood from commercial fishermen. Those losses, although foreseeable, were too indirect. *Pruitt v. Allied Chemical Corp.,* 523 F.Supp. 975 (E.D. Va.1981).

Finally, the ramparts have been breached in the Ninth Circuit. Although the majority says that *Union Oil Co. v. Oppen,* 9 Cir.1974, 501 F.2d 558, is "not contrary" to our Court's affirmation of the *Robins* rule, a close reading of *Oppen* indicates that this is incorrect. In *Oppen,* a mishap in 1969 at an offshore oil drilling platform introduced hundreds of thousands of gallons of oil into the ocean off the coast of Santa Barbara, California. Although a strict application of the extensions of *Robins* would have barred all recovery, the Ninth Circuit allowed fishermen to recover for the loss of their livelihood. After acknowledging the "widely recognized principle" that a plaintiff could not recover for the negligently induced loss of "a prospective pecuniary advantage," the Court noted the many exceptions to this rule, "in which defendants engaged in certain professions, businesses, or trades have been held liable for economic losses resulting from the negligent performance of tasks within the course of their callings." The Court regarded the real question to be whether Union owed a duty to the fishermen. This in turn depended on whether Union could foresee a risk of harm to fishermen:

> [W]e can not escape the conclusion that under California law the presence of a duty on the part of the defendants in this case would turn *substantially on foreseeability. That being the crucial determinant,* the question must be asked whether the defendants could reasonably have foreseen that negligently conducted drilling operations might diminish aquatic life and thus injure the business of commercial fishermen. We believe the answer is yes.

Id. at 569 (emphasis added).

The inapplicability of *Robins* to plaintiffs who have been proximately and foreseeably injured by the collision illustrates the fundamental weakness of founding a rule of recovery in tort upon *Robins*. Conventional tort principles do not apply in *Robins* because the connection between the plaintiff and the tort was a contract, not a tortious act or a defective product. In cases where the parties have suffered losses only because they are parts of a chain of contracting parties, only one of whom was physically injured, *Robins* provides a bright-line rule to limit claims. Whatever the justification for this rule in its original context, however, we should not extend it to instances where the parties are not linked merely in a contractual chain. Instead, we should allow recovery in instances where each of the parties alleges a loss that occurred outside this contractual chain, where each injured party, isolated from another injured party, can assert an injury that is cognizable when judged by our usual rules of proximate cause and foreseeability. There is only one justification for the requirement of physical injury: If *Robins* establishes a policy of restricting the type of plaintiff who can recover for a defendant's negligence, physical property damage furnishes an easily discernible boundary between recovery and nonrecovery.

Rather than limiting recovery under an automatic application of a physical damage requirement, I would analyze the plaintiffs' claims under the conventional tort principles of negligence, foreseeability, and proximate causation. I would confine *Robins* to the "factual contours" of that case: A plaintiff's claim may be barred only if the claim is derived solely through contract with an injured party. The majority's primary criticism of this approach to a determination of liability is that it is potentially open ended. Yet, there are well-established tort principles to limit liability for a widely-suffered harm. Under the contemporary law of public nuisance, courts compensate "particularly" damaged plaintiffs for harms suffered from a wide-ranging tort, but deny recovery to more generally damaged parties. Those parties who are foreseeably and proximately injured by an oil spill or closure of a navigable river, for example, and who can also prove damages that are beyond the general economic dislocation that attends such disasters should recover whether or not they had contractual dealings with others who were also damaged by the tortious act. The limitation imposed by "particular" damages, together with refined notions of proximate cause and forseeability, provides a workable scheme of liability that is in step with the rest of tort law, compensates innocent plaintiffs, and imposes the costs of harm on those who caused it.

IV. Advantages of the Alternate Rule of Recovery

The advantages of this alternate rule of recovery are that it compensates damaged plaintiffs, imposes the cost of damages upon those who have caused the harm, is consistent with economic principles of modern tort law, and frees courts from the necessity of creating a piecemeal quilt of exceptions to avoid the harsh effects of the *Robins* rule.

A. Extrinsic Notions of Fairness and Case-by-Case Adjudication

If tort law fails to compensate plaintiffs or to impose the cost of damages on those who caused the harm, it should be under a warrant clear of necessity. When a rule of law, once extended, leads to inequitable results and creates principles of recovery that are at odds with the great weight of tort jurisprudence, then that rule of law merits scrutiny. A strict application of the extension denies recovery to many plaintiffs who should be awarded damages.[37] Conventional tort principles of

[37] A "fishermen's exception" blunts some of the sharpest aspects of this harshness, but it is theoretically difficult to justify that recovery while denying the claims of others similarly situated.

foreseeability, proximate causation, and "particular" damages would avoid such unfairness.

It is true that application of foreseeability and proximate causation would necessitate case-by-case adjudication. But I have a more optimistic assessment of courts' ability to undertake such adjudication than the majority. Certainly such an inquiry would be no different from our daily task of weighing such claims in other tort cases.[38]

B. The Economic Arguments

The economic arguments regarding allocation of loss that purportedly favor the *Robins* rule of nonliability are not as clear to me as they appear to be to the majority. It is true that denial of recovery may effectively spread the loss over the victims. It is not certain, however, that victims are generally better insurors against the risk of loss caused by tortious acts having widespread consequences. Although the victims do possess greater knowledge of their circumstances and their potential damages, we do not know whether insurance against these types of losses is readily available to the businesses that may be affected. We do know that insurance against this kind of loss is already available for shippers. Imposition of liability upon the shippers helps ensure that the potential tortfeasor faces incentives to take the proper care. The majority's point is well taken that the incentives to avoid accidents do not increase once potential losses pass a certain measure of enormity. But in truth we have no idea what this measure is: Absent hard data, I would rather err on the side of receiving little additional benefit from imposing additional quanta of liability than err by adhering to *Robins'* inequitable rule and bar victims' recovery on the mistaken belief that a "marginal incentive curve" was flat, or nearly so. If a loss must be borne, it is no worse if a "merely" negligent defendant bears the loss than an innocent plaintiff absorb the damages.

---

[38] The majority criticizes foreseeability because it necessitates a case-by-case determination of liability. But this criticism of "foreseeability" as the criterion for judgment applies with equal force to well-established tort law for physical injury. The unquestioned concepts of foreseeability and proximate cause as established in *Palsgraf* and its progeny are open to the same condemnation that the majority makes of a rule of liability that would abandon *Robins:*

> The result would be that no determinable measure of the limit of foreseeability would precede the decision on liability. We are told that where a claim is too remote, or too tenuous, recovery will be denied. Presumably then, as among all plaintiffs suffering foreseeable economic loss, recovery will turn on a judge['s] or jury's decision. . . . The point is not that such a process cannot be administered but rather than its judgments would be much less the product of a determinable rule of law.

The majority opinion favors a bright line rule, as opposed to a case-by-case determination of liability, because it enables courts to "adjudicate" rather than to "manage". A bright line rule such as the one the majority proposes, however, requires no adjudication whatsoever. Judges need merely to preside over a self-executing system of limited liability where recovery is predicated upon an easily determined physical injury. The application of such a rule, rather than a case-by-case determination, seems more "management" than adjudication.

V. Conclusion

The *Robins* approach restricts liability more severely than the policies behind limitations on liability require and imposes the cost of the accident on the victim, who is usually not in a superior position to obtain insurance to cover this loss. I would apply a rule of recovery based on conventional tort principles of proximate cause and foreseeability and limit eligibility only by the requirement that a claimant prove "particular" damages.

NOTES AND PROBLEMS

1. *Other Limitations.* The majority opinion does not rest on foreseeability, apparently assuming that plaintiffs could establish foreseeability here. Did the majority give up too soon? Would this case satisfy the foreseeability test studied in *Schonfeld*? How would you apply that test? Should a different foreseeability test apply? What test? What results would it produce?

2. *Too Generous?* The concurring opinions raise the question of whether commercial fisherfolk qualify under the rule. Fisherfolk typically do not own the waters they fish, though some oysterers might lease oyster beds. (Are the oysterers' leaseholds different from the ship charter in *Robins*?) Could fishers establish the required proprietary interest to maintain a tort action? Or will they lose when their case comes up on appeal? Did the denial of summary judgment for defendant establish that plaintiffs did have a proprietary interest or merely allow them to prove it? Even if proven, foreseeability would remain an issue for these plaintiffs. *Pruitt* and *Union Oil* extended recovery to fisherfolk, but both courts acknowledged that they were making exceptions to the requirement of physical injury in order to permit recovery. *Pruitt* went further, extending the exception to marinas that supply sport fishermen, largely as a substitute for recreational fishermen, whose identity would be difficult to ascertain and whose damages would be difficult to assess.

3. *Endless Liability.* Where would liability cut off under the dissent's approach? That will depend on the evidence in each case. Can you predict whether the evidence in this case would allow recovery for the various classes that brought suit: shipping interests, marina and boat rental operators, wholesale and retail seafood enterprises not actually engaged in fishing, seafood restaurants, tackle and bait shops, and recreational fishermen? What about customers of shippers, whose expected merchandise arrived three weeks late? What about valets parking cars at seafood restaurants?

4. *Overrule* Robins*?* Is the dissent's approach faithful to *Robins*? Is the loss to the charterer in *Robins* any less foreseeable than the loss to the seafood restaurants or shipping firms in *Testbank*? If so, would traditional

tort principles allow recovery there, independent of the contract? Would *Robins* retain any vitality under this approach?

5. *Efficiency*. From an economic perspective, where should the loss fall? Does the majority or the dissent have the better arguments here? Do theories of corrective justice offer a different approach?

6. *Casey's Inhaler*. Casey's physical symptoms were caused by the underlying medical condition, not the inhaler. Could the pharmacy argue that tort should not apply because the loss was economic, forcing Casey to rely on the contract action? (Also consider that question in the next case, involving a misfilled prescription for contraceptives.) Would it matter if Casey's condition did not deteriorate—if the condition and its effect on work, leisure and household chores remained the same after the prescription as it had been for the preceding three years? What about the malpractice claims: the attorney's negligence did not cause the physical symptoms, just the loss of money that might have compensated for them.

7. *Exceptions*. Would physical injury be required in all torts? What about loss of consortium claims? While the victim suffered physical injury, the spouse did not. Is there any reason to allow recovery to the spouse but deny it to the fisherfolk's customers? Aren't the losses here even more tangible than the losses suffered by the deprived spouse? What about fraud or libel? Does legal malpractice cause physical injuries? Does tortious interference with contract? These torts obviously are excepted from the requirement of physical injury. What other exceptions might be appropriate? Would any of them cover this case?

2. AVOIDABLE CONSEQUENCES AND RELATED DOCTRINES

In your first year studies, you may have learned that a plaintiff "is not entitled to recover damages for any harm that he could have avoided by the use of reasonable effort or expenditure after the commission of the" wrong. RESTATEMENT (SECOND) OF TORTS § 918. If reducing the loss would require "undue risk, burden or humiliation," plaintiff may recover the losses despite failing to avoid them. RESTATEMENT (SECOND) OF CONTRACTS § 350. The avoidable consequences doctrine, sometimes called mitigation of damage, leaves plaintiff uncompensated if she should have avoided the damages in the first place. The rule emerges from an even more basic concept: plaintiff cannot recover for losses that she did avoid. This more basic concept, sometimes called the benefits rule, often hides in the definition of damage recoveries rather than acting as a limitation on the amounts recovered. The basic damage principle—putting plaintiff in the position she would have occupied if the wrong had not occurred—implicitly rejects awarding amounts for losses plaintiff did not suffer. To do so would put plaintiff in a better position than she would have occupied but for the wrong.

a. Benefits Rule

We saw a simple example of the benefits rule in *Basiliko, supra* at 576. Plaintiff was awarded the market value of the land promised, offset by the amount he would have had to pay if the transaction had been completed. If no breach had occurred, plaintiff would not have kept the purchase price and obtained the land. He would hold one or the other. The benefit of the breach (keeping the price) was offset against the harm of the breach (not obtaining the land). In some cases, benefits may offset the breach entirely, as where the price kept equals or exceeds the market value of the promised performance. These results are built into the basic damage formulas of contracts.

In tort, the benefits are not always so obvious, in part because they may not be benefits that the plaintiff sought. Of course, Basiliko did not seek to keep the contract price, either, but the benefit was unmistakable.

TROPPI V. SCARF

31 Mich. App. 240, 187 N.W.2d 511 (1971).

LEVIN, PRESIDING JUDGE.

In this case we consider the civil liability of a pharmacist who negligently supplied the wrong drug to a married woman who had ordered an oral contraceptive and, as a consequence, became pregnant and delivered a normal, healthy child.

I.

A summary judgment was entered dismissing the complaint of the plaintiffs, John and Dorothy Troppi, on the ground that it does not state a claim upon which relief can be granted. In our appraisal of the correctness of the trial judge's ruling we accept as true plaintiffs' factual allegations.

In August 1964, plaintiffs were the parents of seven children, ranging from six to sixteen years of age. John Troppi was 43 years old, his wife 37.

While pregnant with an eighth child, Mrs. Troppi suffered a miscarriage. She and her husband consulted with their physician and decided to limit the size of their family. The physician prescribed an oral contraceptive, Norinyl, as the most desirable means of insuring that Mrs. Troppi would bear no more children. He telephoned the prescription to defendant, Frank H. Scarf, a licensed pharmacist. Instead of filling the prescription, Scarf negligently supplied Mrs. Troppi with a drug called Nardil, a mild tranquilizer.

Believing that the pills she had purchased were contraceptives, Mrs. Troppi took them on a daily basis. In December 1964, Mrs. Troppi became pregnant. She delivered a well-born son on August 12, 1965.

Plaintiffs' complaint alleges four separate items of damage: (1) Mrs. Troppi's lost wages; (2) medical and hospital expenses; (3) the pain and anxiety of pregnancy and childbirth; and (4) the economic costs of rearing the eighth child.

In dismissing the complaint the judge declared that whatever damage plaintiffs suffered was more than offset by the benefit to them of having a healthy child.

II.

Contraception, conjugal relations, and childbirth are highly charged subjects. It is all the more important, then, to emphasize that resolution of the case before us requires no intrusion into the domain of moral philosophy. At issue here is simply the extent to which defendant is civilly liable for the consequences of his negligence. In reversing and remanding for trial, we go no further than to apply settled common-law principles.

We begin by noting that the fundamental conditions of tort liability are present here. The defendant's conduct constituted a clear breach of duty. A pharmacist is held to a very high standard of care in filling prescriptions. When he negligently supplies a drug other than the drug requested, he is liable for resulting harm to the purchaser. . . .

We assume, for the purpose of appraising the correctness of the ruling dismissing the complaint, that the defendant's negligence was a cause in fact of Mrs. Troppi's pregnancy. The possibility that she might become pregnant was certainly a foreseeable consequence of the defendant's failure to fill a prescription for birth control pills; we therefore, could not say that it was not a proximate cause of the birth of the child.

Setting aside, for the moment, the subtleties of the damage question, it is at least clear that the plaintiffs have expended significant sums of money as a direct and proximate result of the defendant's negligence. The medical and hospital expenses of Mrs. Troppi's confinement and her loss of wages arose from the defendant's failure to fill the prescription properly. Pain and suffering, like that accompanying childbirth, have long been recognized as compensable injuries.

This review of the elements of tort liability points up the extraordinary nature of the trial court's holding that the plaintiffs were entitled to no recovery as a matter of law. We have here a negligent, wrongful act by the defendant, which act directly and proximately caused injury to the plaintiffs.

What we must decide is whether there is justification here for a departure from generally applicable, well-established principles of law. . . .

IV.

. . . We conclude that there is no valid reason why the trier of fact should not be free to assess damages as it would in any other negligence case.

[For the court's discussion of public policy limitations on damages, see the next section.]

Overriding Benefit. It is arguable that the birth of a healthy child confers so substantial a benefit as to outweigh the expenses of his birth and support. In the great majority of cases, this is no doubt true, else, presumably, people would not choose to multiply so freely. But can we say, as a matter of law, that a healthy child always confers such an overriding benefit?

The so-called 'benefit rule' is pertinent. The Restatement declares:

> Where the defendant's tortious conduct has caused harm to the plaintiff or to his property and in so doing has conferred upon the plaintiff a special benefit to the interest which was harmed, the value of the benefit conferred is considered in mitigation of damages, where this is equitable.

Restatement, Torts, § 920.

Thus, if the defendant's tortious conduct conferred a benefit to the same interest which was harmed by his conduct, the dollar value of the benefit is to be subtracted from the dollar value of the injury in arriving at the amount of damages properly awardable.

Since pregnancy and its attendant anxiety, incapacity, pain and suffering are inextricably related to child bearing, we do not think it would be sound to attempt to separate those segments of damage from the economic costs of an unplanned child in applying the "same interest" rule. Accordingly, the benefits of the unplanned child may be weighed against all the elements of claimed damage.

The trial court evidently believed . . . that application of the benefits rule prevents any recovery for the expenses of rearing an unwanted child. This is unsound. Such a rule would be equivalent to declaring that in every case, as a matter of law, the services and companionship of a child have a dollar equivalent greater than the economic costs of his support, to say nothing of the inhibitions, the restrictions, and the pain and suffering caused by pregnancy and the obligation to rear the child.

There is a growing recognition that the financial "services" which parents can expect from their offspring are largely illusory. As to companionship, cases decided when "loss of companionship" was a compensable item of damage for the wrongful death of a child reveal no tendency on the part of juries to value companionship so highly as to outweigh expenses in every foreseeable case.

Our discussion should not be construed as an expression of doubt as to the efficacy of the benefits rule in cases like the one before us. On the contrary, we believe that rule to be essential to the rational disposition of this case and the others that are sure to follow. The benefits rule allows flexibility in the case-by-case adjudication of the enormously varied claims which the widespread use of oral contraceptives portends.

What must be appreciated is the diversity of purposes and circumstances of the women who use oral contraceptives. Unmarried women who seek the pleasures of sexual intercourse without the perils of unwed motherhood, married women who wish to delay slightly the start of a family in order to retain the career flexibility which many young couples treasure, married women for whom the birth of another child would pose a threat to their own health or the financial security of their families, all are likely users of oral contraceptives. Yet it is clear that in each case the consequences arising from negligent interference with their use will vary widely. A rational legal system must award damages that correspond with these differing injuries. The benefits rule will serve to accomplish this objective.

Consider, for example, the case of the unwed college student who becomes pregnant due to a pharmacist's failure to fill properly her prescription for oral contraceptives. Is it not likely that she has suffered far greater damage than the young newlywed who, although her pregnancy arose from the same sort of negligence, had planned the use of contraceptives only temporarily, say, while she and her husband took an extended honeymoon trip? Without the benefits rule, both plaintiffs would be entitled to recover substantially the same damages.

Application of the benefits rule permits a trier of fact to find that the birth of a child has materially benefitted the newly wed couple, notwithstanding the inconvenience of an interrupted honeymoon, and to reduce the net damage award accordingly. Presumably a trier of fact would find that the "family interests" of the unmarried coed has been enhanced very little.

The essential point, of course, is that the trier must have the power to evaluate the benefit according to all the circumstances of the case presented. Family size, family income, age of the parents, and marital status are some, but not all, the factors which the trier must consider in determining the extent to which the birth of a particular child represents a benefit to his parents. That the benefits so conferred and calculated will vary widely from case to case is inevitable.

[The court's discussion of avoidable consequences and uncertainty is omitted.]

Reversed and remanded for trial.

NOTES AND QUESTIONS

1. *Other Limitations.* The court rejected defendant's argument that plaintiffs should have minimized their losses by putting the child up for adoption (or aborting the fetus—a felony at the time, but legal today). After you read the cases on avoidable consequences, consider how you would argue for or against this result. The court also rejected the certainty challenge. How would you argue that issue?

2. *Contract or Tort.* Why isn't this a UCC case? The seller delivered the wrong goods. Foreseeable consequential damages include the birth. Why bother proving negligence? More importantly, would this avoid the benefits rule, which is not included in the UCC or the Restatement (Second) of Contracts? Should it?

3. *Same Interest.* Do the limitations on benefits included in the Restatement make any sense? Does it matter whether the benefit is to the pecuniary or nonpecuniary interests of the plaintiffs? Some numbers might help illustrate the problem. Suppose the pecuniary harms (cost of childrearing, health care during pregnancy, lost wages) total $300,000, the nonpecuniary harms (pain during childbirth, distress over giving less attention to older siblings) $200,000, the pecuniary benefits (the child's services) $0, and the nonpecuniary benefits (the child's companionship) $400,000. How much should plaintiff recover? Should the benefit to the nonpecuniary interest offset the entire award? Or should they offset only the nonpecuniary losses? Suppose there were pecuniary benefits, too—say, the pregnancy produced octuplets. Pecuniary costs would be larger (say, $600,000). What if publicity produced a book contract or reality TV show that earned $600,000. Should the plaintiffs recover nothing? If the book contract netted $500,000, should they recover the remaining $100,000? Even though they already net $100,000 better than if no breach had occurred (because nonpecuniary benefits exceed nonpecuniary costs, offsetting the loss on pecuniary costs)?

Perhaps the interests are not properly identified. Should we distinguish, instead, the plaintiffs' interests as parents from their interests as individuals. Professor Capron argues that as parents, they incurred childrearing costs and the joys of companionship. But expenses during pregnancy and the mother's pain in childbirth affect the plaintiffs as individuals, not as parents. Alexander Morgan Capron, *Tort Liability in Genetic Counselling*, 79 COLUM. L. REV. 618, 638–39 n. 91 (1979); *but see* RESTATEMENT SECOND OF TORTS § 920 comment. b, illustrations 4–6 (1979) (distinguishing pecuniary from nonpecuniary interests).

4. *Unwanted Benefits.* The Restatement also expresses concern with allowing defendants to "force a benefit upon [plaintiff] against his will."

RESTATEMENT (SECOND) OF TORTS § 920 COMMENT F. (1979). Does that suggest the entire benefit should be ignored in *Troppi*? Plaintiff sought to avoid—indeed, paid defendant to help prevent—precisely the benefit defendant now claims credit for providing. Does that mean the benefit should not be included in the calculation? Or is that merely evidence that the calculation must produce a net harm, since the value to plaintiffs of the child must be less than the value to plaintiffs of no child?

5. *Motivation*. Does it matter why plaintiffs wanted to avoid the benefit? In an omitted section, *Troppi* distinguished a case in which plaintiff had a vasectomy to avoid endangering his wife's health. *Christensen v. Thornby*, 192 Minn. 123, 255 N.W. 620 (1934).

> The plaintiff husband in *Christensen* made no claim that the child itself or the economic consequences of its birth were unwanted. The operation was directed at the threat to his wife's health. Since her health remained unimpaired, no damage was suffered. That the husband could not have foreseen that his wife would emerge unscathed and his anxiety was therefore quite justified was a factor the court did not discuss.

Is the point that plaintiffs had a net benefit? Had there been a loss—had the wife suffered some injury—would it be appropriate to offset the benefits? How should plaintiff's anxiety affect the analysis?

6. *Evolving Doctrine*. Michigan repudiated *Troppi* in *Rouse v. Wesley,* 196 Mich. App. 624, 494 N.W.2d 7 (1992), joining a majority of jurisdictions that deny recovery for the cost of raising a healthy child. *Rouse* did not prevent recovery of other costs associated with the negligence, including medical costs and pain during pregnancy. Does that ruling make any sense under the benefits rule?

7. *Collateral Benefits*. Plaintiffs often receive benefits that they would not receive but for the breach. Wrongful death plaintiffs may be the beneficiaries of an insurance policy. A tort victim may receive compensation under a health or disability insurance policy. The next section addresses these benefits.

PROBLEMS

1. *Intentional Wrongs that Benefit Plaintiffs*. Bill and Gloria want a child, but Gloria suffers from a medical condition that makes it dangerous for her to become pregnant and have a child. Bill hired Sean, a surgeon, to perform a vasectomy to prevent Gloria from facing that risk. Sean intentionally botched the vasectomy, hoping that Gloria would conceive and avoid the complications, thus producing a net benefit for the family. Gloria did conceive, gave birth, and suffered no adverse health consequences. Bill and Gloria admit to you (their lawyer) that, given the outcome, they feel better off than if the vasectomy had been successful. They are outraged, however, that Sean would make that decision for them. What recovery, if any, may they receive? How will the benefits rule apply?

2. *Intentional Wrongs that Harm and Benefit Plaintiffs.* In problem 1, suppose Gloria's condition was aggravated by the pregnancy. The cost to deal with the complications was $20,000, which also caused $100,000 of distress. Still, Bill and Gloria tell you (their attorney) that the child's value is immense and cannot be measured in money. How would you calculate their recovery, given the benefits rule?

3. *Negligent Sterilization.* In problem 2, would the calculation be any different if Sean had been negligent rather than intentionally botching the vasectomy?

4. *Genetic Counseling.* Rob and Virginia want to have children. They consult Leslie, a doctor specializing in genetic testing, to determine whether either of them carries the Tay–Sachs gene. The gene is recessive. If both parents carry it, there is a 25% chance that the child will suffer from the disease. Leslie, after performing the usual tests, tells them that neither one carries the gene. In fact, they both carry the gene, but Leslie negligently mixed their samples with those of another couple.

a. If Rob and Virginia have a child that does not exhibit Tay–Sachs, what recovery might they receive?

b. If Rob and Virginia have a child that does exhibit Tay–Sachs, what recovery might they receive?

c. Might the other couple, erroneously informed that they did risk Tay–Sachs, have any recovery?

5. *Defamation and Notoriety.* Al, a security guard, finds a bomb in a major shopping mall. He reports the bomb to authorities, who remove and disarm it without incident. Later, authorities falsely state that Al planted the bomb. Al loses his job and cannot find another. But upon his exoneration, Al writes a book about the experiences. Assuming that Al can make out a case for libel, will damages for lost wages be offset by the earnings on the book? Should the court award distress caused by the libel? Should that be offset by any notoriety Al now receives (Jay Leno, David Letterman, the Colbert Report, The Daily Show, etc.)?

6. *Unwanted Notoriety.* Chandra is a religious ascetic recluse. Based on Chandra's reputation as a wise and holy person, pilgrims seek Chandra out and ask advice. Misunderstanding some of Chandra's advice, a local newspaper published stories that Chandra was a dangerous terrorist. As a result, a few local vigilantes tried to drive Chandra out of the area and threatened to kill Chandra. Chandra sues for libel. Can any damages be offset by arguments that Chandra's notoriety may increase the number of pilgrims seeking advice? What if the notoriety produces an offer of $1 million if Chandra will write a book? Does it matter whether Chandra accepts or rejects the offer?

7. *Casey's Inhaler.* Casey's condition limited contributions to household chores. Is that a benefit that should be offset against recovery? That time became leisure time, didn't it? So did some of the time Casey would

have spent at work. Some (but not much) time was spent looking for other work, but the rest was Casey's to spend on other activities (though not strenuous activities). Should lost income be offset by the value of additional leisure time gained?

b. Collateral Source (Exception to the Benefits) Rule

Not all benefits of breach are subtracted from the recovery. Some benefits are treated as appropriately belonging to the plaintiff. The collateral source rule draws the line between benefits that the defendant provided (by committing the tort) and benefits that were provided by others. Defendants are the but-for cause of all the benefits addressed here; benefits plaintiffs would have received regardless of the tort are not subtracted under the benefits rule. Thus, defendants cannot claim a credit for all the benefits plaintiffs receive—even if this might produce compensation that exceeds plaintiffs' actual losses.

SUNNYLAND FARMS V. CENTRAL NEW MEXICO ELECTRIC COOPERATIVE

301 P.3d 387 (N. Mex. 2013).

CHAVEZ, J. This case comes before us because of a fire that destroyed a hydroponic tomato facility belonging to a new business, Sunnyland Farms, Inc. (Sunnyland). The day before the fire, Sunnyland's electricity had been shut off by its local utility, the Central New Mexico Electrical Cooperative (CNMEC), for nonpayment. Sunnyland's water pumps were powered by electricity, and without power, Sunnyland's facility had no water. Sunnyland sued CNMEC, alleging both that CNMEC had wrongfully suspended service, and if its electrical service had been in place, firefighters and Sunnyland employees would have been able to stop the fire from consuming the facility.

After a bench trial, the trial court found CNMEC liable for negligence and breach of contract. The trial court awarded damages, including lost profits, of over $21 million in contract and tort, but reduced the tort damages by 80% for Sunnyland's comparative fault. It also awarded $100,000 in punitive damages. The . . . Court of Appeals[:] (1) reversed the contract judgment, (2) vacated the punitive damages, (3) held that the lost profit damages were not supported by sufficient evidence, (4) affirmed the trial court's offset of damages based on CNMEC's purchase of a subrogation lien, and (5) affirmed the trial court's rulings on pre- and post-judgment interest. . . .

D. THE TRIAL COURT'S OFFSET OF DAMAGES WAS CONTRARY TO NEW MEXICO'S PUBLIC POLICY

Sunnyland Farms was insured by West American Insurance Co., which paid it approximately $3.2 million. West American and its parent company, Ohio Casualty Insurance Co., were plaintiffs in this action against CNMEC. However, CNMEC settled with them prior to the start of trial. Under the terms of the settlement, CNMEC paid West American $1.3 million and acquired its subrogation lien against Sunnyland. After CNMEC was found liable, it moved to offset the damages against it based on its purchase of West American's subrogation interest. The trial court granted the motion and offset CNMEC's liability by the full subrogation lien of just over $3.2 million. The Court of Appeals upheld this setoff. . . .

"[S]ubrogation is an equitable remedy." Ordinarily, we review a trial court's exercise of its equitable powers for abuse of discretion. . . . In this case, [however,] the question is whether the law permitted the trial court to award an offset to the defendant, CNMEC. . . .

This question implicates a number of policy considerations, including New Mexico's policy against allowing "double recovery" for plaintiffs. In general, plaintiffs may not collect more than the damages awarded to them, or, put another way, they may not receive compensation twice for the same injury.

However, the collateral source rule is an exception to the rule against double recovery. The classic statement of the collateral source rule is that "[c]ompensation received from a collateral source does not operate to reduce damages recoverable from a wrongdoer." In other words, if a plaintiff is compensated for his or her injuries by any source unaffiliated with the defendant, the defendant must *still* pay damages, even if this means that the plaintiff recovers twice.

There are several justifications for the collateral source rule. If the plaintiff can recover his or her full damages from the defendant, the plaintiff has the means to reimburse the collateral source. This allows the ultimate burden of compensating the plaintiff to fall on the defendant, rather than on blameless but generous parties. "The right of redress for wrong is fundamental. Charity cannot be made a substitute for such right, nor can benevolence be made a set-off against the acts of a tort-feasor." Additionally, knowing that they have some likelihood of being reimbursed may make third parties more likely to help victims during the time before they are able to collect from the defendant.

If the third party or collateral source does *not* seek compensation, its contribution could benefit either the defendant, by reducing the damages that the defendant must pay, or the plaintiff, by allowing the plaintiff to recover twice. In New Mexico, the collateral source rule dictates that the contribution of a collateral source must operate to benefit the plaintiff rather than the defendant. " 'Whether [the collateral contribution] is a gift or the product of a contract of employment or of insurance, the purposes of the parties to it are obviously better served and the interests of society are likely to be better served if the injured person is benefitted than if the wrongdoer is benefitted.' " Lastly, a plaintiff's "double recovery" is likely to be more egregious in theory than in practice; in reality, plaintiffs rarely receive their full damages, since they must pay attorney fees out of their damages. Allocating the collateral contribution to their benefit, rather than to the benefit of the defendant, makes it more likely that the plaintiff will be fully compensated.

In the present case, part of the question is whether a collateral source, *i.e.* Sunnyland's insurer, remains "collateral" to the defendant after settling with it and transfering its subrogation rights to it. If CNMEC's settlement payment to West American transforms the insurance payments into a non-collateral contribution, then CNMEC can offset the damages it must pay to Sunnyland by the amount of the insurance payments. We note that in general, New Mexico has a policy of encouraging settlements, which would suggest that we should allow such an offset. CNMEC accurately observes that several other states permit offsets where a defendant has settled with the plaintiff's insurer. Sunnyland counters that allowing this offset would undermine New Mexico's collateral source rule and allow an insurer to subrogate against its own insured, contrary to *State ex rel. Regents of N.M. State Univ. v. Siplast, Inc.,* 117 N.M. 738, 741–42, 877 P.2d 38, 41–42 (1994).

We disagree with Sunnyland that allowing the offset would violate the rule stated in *Siplast.* In *Siplast,* we were concerned that allowing an insurer to subrogate against its own insured would increase litigation and create conflicts of interest. Neither of those considerations would be implicated by allowing defendants to step into the shoes of insurers and assume their right of subrogation.

However, we have one concern here that was not at issue in *Siplast:* subrogation is not truly a right, but an equitable remedy. "Subrogation, whether created by contract or by operation of law, is an equitable remedy and equitable principles control its application. "The remedy is for the benefit of one secondarily liable who has paid the debt of another and to whom *in equity and good conscience* should be assigned the rights and remedies of the original creditor." The question is whether the principles of equity permit a defendant to assert a right of subrogation that it acquires from the plaintiff's insurer.

We hold that they do not. We recognize that "[t]he person asserting the right to subrogation must be without fault." While there was no malice proven on the part of the defendant in this case, CNMEC does not contest the trial court's findings that it was negligent and breached its contract with Sunnyland. We have stated that "the right [of subrogation] flows from principles of justice and equity." When the party exercising the right is an innocent third party who compensated the plaintiff, justice and equity dictate that the party should have the right to recover from the plaintiff, regardless of whether the compensation originated in generosity or contractual obligation. A defendant is not similarly situated to such a party. A defendant who has been found liable is ordinarily expected to pay the plaintiff's full damages, and requiring him or her to do so does not offend principles of justice or equity. It does not matter that the defendant has attempted to step into the shoes of the collateral source by contract. Equity concerns itself with the substance of a matter, not with its form.

Our holding does not prevent a defendant from settling with the plaintiff's insurance company, but it does mean that the defendant will not be able to exercise any subrogation lien that it acquires as part of that settlement. The defendant should settle with the plaintiff's insurers with the full knowledge that neither the insurers' previous payments to the plaintiff, nor the defendant's payments to the insurers at the time of settlement, will offset the damages that the defendant must pay to the plaintiff. This holding also does not limit the right of insurers to sell or transfer their subrogation liens, so long as they do not transfer the liens to the defendant.

NOTES AND QUESTIONS

1. *Double Recovery.* If plaintiff recovers the full loss from the defendant, but does not repay those who helped foot the bills (*e.g.*, insurer, relatives, or charities), damages provide plaintiff a net gain rather than merely compensating for losses. That seems inconsistent with the fundamental rule: to put plaintiff in the position she would have occupied but for the wrong. Subrogation rights will eliminate excess recovery in some cases, but not all. Insurers (and other payors) may not include subrogation clauses in their policies, may waive rights they have, or may overlook the opportunity to assert them.

2. *Abolish Subrogation?* Courts could avoid excess recovery by abolishing both the collateral source rule and subrogation. Plaintiff then recovers only the losses that she incurred, with no obligation to repay those who subsidized plaintiff before recovery. Might that be preferable? First-party insurance (health, life, disability, no-fault auto) is generally cheaper and faster than third-party insurance (the tortfeasor's liability policy or deep pocket), which requires lengthy and expensive litigation to administer. What reasons did the court offer for permitting overcompensation? Were they persuasive?

New York offers one example of how the collateral source rule might be reshaped.

> (c) Actions for personal injury, injury to property or wrongful death. In any action brought to recover damages for personal injury, injury to property or wrongful death, where the plaintiff seeks to recover for the cost of medical care, dental care, custodial care or rehabilitation services, loss of earnings or other economic loss, evidence shall be admissible for consideration by the court to establish that any such past or future cost or expense was or will,

with reasonable certainty, be replaced or indemnified, in whole or in part, from any collateral source such as insurance (except for life insurance), social security (except those benefits provided under title XVIII of the social security act), workers' compensation or employee benefit programs (except such collateral sources entitled by law to liens against any recovery of the plaintiff). If the court finds that any such cost or expense was or will, with reasonable certainty, be replaced or indemnified from any collateral source, it shall reduce the amount of the award by such finding, minus an amount equal to the premiums paid by the plaintiff for such benefits for the two-year period immediately preceding the accrual of such action and minus an amount equal to the projected future cost to the plaintiff of maintaining such benefits. In order to find that any future cost or expense will, with reasonable certainty, be replaced or indemnified by the collateral source, the court must find that the plaintiff is legally entitled to the continued receipt of such collateral source, pursuant to a contract or otherwise enforceable agreement, subject only to the continued payment of a premium and such other financial obligations as may be required by such agreement.

(d) Voluntary charitable contributions excluded as a collateral source of payment. Voluntary charitable contributions received by an injured party shall not be considered to be a collateral source of payment that is admissible in evidence to reduce the amount of any award, judgment or settlement.

N.Y. Civil Practice Laws Revised § 4545(c), (d). Sections (a) and (b) include similar provisions covering malpractice claims and claims against public employers.

Is this approach better? Will it avoid excessive recovery? Will it undermine the other goals of damage judgments? What other purposes might it serve?

3. *Remedying Undercompensation.* Occasionally advocates justify rules that exceed compensation by pointing to other rules that undercomepensate: foreseeability, certainty, and attorneys' fees all can reduce the compensation plaintiff actually recovers. Is double compensation of *some* medical expenses (those reimbursed) in *some* cases (those without subrogation) the best way to deal with contingent attorneys' fees eating into the plaintiffs' compensatory awards? It will be pure coincidence if the contingent fee equals the reimbursed medical expenses. How far would this argument go? Will every policy that awards plaintiffs more than they lost be justifiable because it will help pay for the attorneys? Is anything left of the compensation rule?

4. *Justifying the Rule.* Are there better reasons to retain the collateral source rule? Consider two possibilities:

a. "The 'collateral benefit' rule of tort law rests on the belief that the wrongdoer should be made to pay—the better to deter like conduct—whether or not the victim has providently supplied another source of compensation." *Carter v. Berger,* 777 F.2d 1173, 1175 (7th Cir.1985).

b. Are the collateral sources also victims of the tort? Should they have claims much as spouses have claims for loss of consortium? Does it matter whether the insurers actually suffer the loss? Premiums pass the loss on to others—the whole point of insurance. *See Blue Cross and Blue Shield of New Jersey v. Philip Morris, Inc.*, 138 F.Supp.2d 357 (E.D.N.Y. 2001). Traditionally, the law precludes plaintiffs from assigning or splitting personal injury claims (but not contract claims). Does the collateral source rule, combined with subrogation, circumvent that prohibition? Should it? Should the prohibition itself be reconsidered? For an interesting proposal of this sort, see Thomas A. Smith, *A Capital Markets Approach to Mass Tort Bankruptcy*, 104 YALE L.J. 367 (1994).

5. *Free Care.* Often victims receive care from members of their family. These services would otherwise be rendered by professionals. The prevailing rule is that plaintiffs may recover the reasonable value of services from the defendant. The services are provided with a donative intent and the wrongdoer should not benefit from the provision of gratuitous services. *Selleck v. Janesville*, 104 Wis. 570, 80 N.W. 944 (1899). What if the services are provided by a third party? For example, in *Plank v. Summers*, 203 Md. 552, 102 A.2d 262 (1954), plaintiffs were injured in an automobile accident for which Summers, a private citizen, was liable. All plaintiffs were enlisted in the United States Navy and received free medical care for their accident injuries. The Maryland Court of Appeals held that the plaintiffs could recover for the free medical services. The issue also arises in suits against the United States, where the United States provided medical care to the plaintiffs. *United States v. Brooks*, 176 F.2d 482 (4th Cir.1949), found that the benefits should be set off against the damages. Does the rule apply? Is the United States a collateral course in these cases? Disability payments, pensions, and social security are distinguishable; victims contribute to these funds, as they do to an insurance policy. *United States v. Price*, 288 F.2d 448 (4th Cir.1961). The application of *Brooks* to future medical care has been controversial since it would oblige the victim to seek care from the governmental agency, rather than a private provider. But the prospect of "double recovery" in *Burke v. United States,* 605 F.Supp. 981 (D.Md.1985), a United States Torts Claims Act case, sufficed to persuade the court to take account of the benefit plaintiff would receive for future medical care. The Court reasoned that plaintiff had not contributed to the fund which supplied her with future medical benefits. (She was the spouse of a retired serviceman.) Is it true that military health benefits are properly classified as "non-contributory"? Are there other arguments for treating public benefits as not collateral benefits?

Contract cases can provide similar examples. Are unemployment benefits offset against the recovery of lost wages? Plaintiff could not have received both wages and benefits. Unemployment insurance is funded from taxes on employers, not employees directly. Should this matter? Is the employee better off not working if she can recover more in the lawsuit than she would have earned by working?

6. *Reform*. During the past twenty years, the collateral source rule has come under attack by advocates of the tort reform movement. Six states have abrogated the rule altogether. Thirty-three states have enacted statutes modifying the doctrine in some respect. Eleven states—Arkansas, Louisiana, Mississippi, New Mexico, North Carolina, South Carolina, Texas, Vermont, Virginia, West Virginia, and Wyoming—have kept the rule unmodified. *See* Adam G. Todd, *An Enduring Oddity: The Collateral Source Rule in the Face of Tort Reform, the Affordable Care Act, and Increased Subrogation*, 43 MCGEORGE L. REV. 965 (2012). From the reformers' point of view, abrogation of the collateral source rule holds the promise of simplifying and reforming the tort process for the better. For criticism of the rule, *see* American Law Institute Reporters' Study, "Enterprise Responsibility for Personal Injury," Vol. II pp. 161–182 (1991) (recommending abolition of the collateral benefits rule except for life insurance).

Reforms of the collateral source rule are not always welcomed by the courts. For example, Kansas attempted reforms three times (1976, 1986, and 1992). Each attempt was struck down as constitutionally infirm. The 1992 reform allowed evidence of collateral source benefits where the claimant demands damages in excess of $150,000. The Kansas Supreme Court in *Thompson v. KFB Insurance Company*, 252 Kan. 1010, 850 P.2d 773 (1993), held that this provision unreasonably discriminated in favor of those demanding $150,000 or less and unduly burdened those seeking judgments in excess of $150,000. As such the legislation violated the equal protection clause of the United States Constitution and § 1 of the Bill of Rights of the Kansas Constitution.

PROBLEMS

1. *Unemployment Insurance*. Company illegally fired Worker. While seeking substitute employment, Worker collected unemployment insurance for five weeks. During that period, Worker's wages would have totaled $15,000. Unemployment compensation totaled $3,000. After five weeks, Worker found a job that paid $2,900 a week—$100 a week less than Company paid. After 10 weeks, Worker got a raise to $3,000 a week. How much may Worker recover? *Compare Monroe v. Oakland Unified School Dist.*, 114 Cal.App.3d 804, 170 Cal.Rptr. 867 (1981) *with Dehnart v. Waukesha Brewing Co.*, 21 Wis.2d 583, 124 N.W.2d 664 (1963). Does it matter whether the discharge is a tort or a breach of contract? Whether the breach of contract is innocent—say, the employer closes for lack of business?

2. *Casey's Inhaler*. Does it matter if the defendant was not the employer? Should Casey's unemployment compensation be treated differently? Does that depend on whether the state finances unemployment compensation by a tax on employers?

3. *Altered Retirement.* Driver negligently injured Pedestrian. Pedestrian's injuries proved disabling, forcing Pedestrian to take a medical retirement five years earlier than she intended. Over her life expectancy, Pedestrian will collect $850,000 in medical retirement benefits. But for the injury, Pedestrian would have collected $900,000 in regular retirement benefits. In addition, Pedestrian would have worked five more years before retiring. How much may Pedestrian recover? *See Rotolo Chevrolet v. Superior Court*, 105 Cal.App.4th 242, 129 Cal.Rptr.2d 283 (2003).

4. *Underinsured Motorist.* Driver negligently injured Cyclist, causing $300,000 in injuries. State Health Organization paid $50,000 to Cyclist to cover medical costs. Driver carried $100,000 in liability insurance. The insurer paid Cyclist $80,000 and State Health Organization $20,000. State Health Organization then waived any further claim to subrogation. Cyclist then claimed $200,000 from his automobile insurance policy's coverage for underinsured motorists. How much should Cyclist recover on this claim? *See Heritage Mutual Ins. Co. v. Graser*, 254 Wis.2d 851, 647 N.W.2d 385 (App.2002).

5. *Billed vs. Collected.* Defendant's vehicle negligently hit plaintiff, causing extensive medical care. The hospital charges totaled $400,000. Plaintiff was indigent, covered by Medicaid. Medicaid paid $100,000, full compensation for the services under the schedule of payments Medicaid allowed. How much can plaintiff recover against the defendant? Would the answer differ if a private health insurer had negotiated an arrangement with the hospital (say, a PPO agreement) obtaining discounted fees for people it insured). *Scott v. Garfield*, 454 Mass. 790, 912 N.E.2d 1000 (Mass. 2009); *Howell v. Hamilton Meats & Provisions*, 52 Cal. 4th 541, 129 Cal.Rptr.3d 325, 257 P.3d 1130 (2011).

6. *Apportioning Recovery.* Sunnyland lost more than $21 million, but was awarded only $4.2 million because it bore 80% of the fault. The insurer paid $3.2 million. If the insurer sought compensation from the award, how much should it receive?

7. *Apportioning Injuries.* Plaintiff suffered personal injuries that produced medical costs of $1 million, lost wages of $100,000, and significant pain. Health insurance covered $900,000 of the medical costs. Disability insurance paid $60,000 of the lost wages. Defendant paid $800,000 to settle the suit. How much should each insurer receive? If the settlement agreement specified an amount attributable to pain and suffering, should that affect the apportionment?

c. The Avoidable Consequences Doctrine

The avoidable consequences doctrine requires courts to treat losses that should have been avoided as if they had been avoided. That is, when a plaintiff, by reasonable conduct, could have reduced the size of the loss, the court refuses to compel defendant to pay for those avoidable losses. Thus, when Luten Bridge Company kept building the bridge even after

Rockingham County repudiated the contract, the additional expenses incurred—those that could have been avoided by halting construction—were subtracted from the contract price in calculating damages. *Rockingham County v. Luten Bridge Co.*, 35 F.2d 301 (4th Cir.1929). Luten Bridge did not avoid those costs, but it could have avoided them by acting reasonably (stopping). In effect, Luten Bridge's unreasonable persistence, not Rockingham County's breach, became the proximate cause of that portion of the loss.

You may have studied the flip side: plaintiff can recover for any expenses reasonably incurred in an effort to avoid the loss. Incidental damages under the UCC are an example. When Neri failed to pay for the boat, the court awarded Retail Marine the cost of storing and insuring it until sold to someone else (in addition to other damages caused by the breach). *Neri v. Retail Marine Corp.*, 30 N.Y.2d 393, 334 N.Y.S.2d 165, 285 N.E.2d 311 (1972). These expenses were reasonable to minimize the risk that the boat would lose value on resale. Medical expenses in tort are another example: treating an injury is reasonable in order to minimize the harm, so the cost of treatment is recoverable. These recoveries often are adequately explained by the normal damage rule—putting plaintiff in the position she would have occupied if the wrong had not occurred—without regard to the avoidable consequences doctrine.

Life, however, can spin a lot of variations on these themes, requiring some careful application. These cases are some examples.

S. J. GROVES & SONS CO. V. WARNER CO.

576 F.2d 524 (3rd Cir.1978).

WEIS, CIRCUIT JUDGE.

[T]he Pennsylvania Department of Transportation undertook the erection of the Girard Point Bridge in Southwest Philadelphia and selected American Bridge Company as the prime contractor. Plaintiff-appellant Groves was awarded a subcontract for the placement of the bridge's concrete decks and parapets and contracted with the defendant Warner for the delivery of ready-mixed concrete for use at the Girard Point site. . . . Warner fail[ed] to deliver adequate supplies at scheduled times. The case was tried to the court[, which] entered judgment in favor of the plaintiff in the amount of $35,401.28. Dissatisfied with the denial of a large part of its claimed damages, Groves appealed. . . .

Groves expected to pour concrete for the decks of the bridge in the mornings and then to use some of the crew to construct parapets in the afternoons. This general plan was frustrated by Warner's frequent failures to make deliveries in compliance with Groves' instructions. As a result, deck pours originally scheduled for the mornings often extended into the afternoons and evenings and created overtime labor expense.

Concerned with its lagging progress, Groves considered securing other sources of concrete as early as 1971 but found no real alternatives. It was too expensive to build its own batching plant at the site and the only other source of ready-mixed concrete in the area was the Trap Rock Company. Trap Rock, however, was not certified to do state work in 1971 and its price was higher than Warner's. Moreover, the production facilities at Trap Rock were limited, as was the number of trucks it had available. Meanwhile, Warner continued to assure Groves that deliveries would improve.

Despite its promises, Warner's performance continued to be erratic and on June 21, 1972, the Pennsylvania Department of Transportation ordered all construction at Girard Point halted until the quality of Warner's service could be discussed at a conference. A meeting took place the next day. Based on Warner's renewed assurances of improved performance, state officials allowed work to resume on June 26, 1972. From that date until July 20, 1972, Warner's delivery service improved significantly, although it still did not consistently meet Groves' instructions. In the months following and until completion in October of 1972, Warner's performance continued to be uneven and unpredictable.

. . . On July 11, 1972, Trap Rock was certified by the state and the next day agreed to accept the same price as Warner. Groves, nevertheless, decided to continue with Warner as its sole supplier.

The district judge found that Warner had acted in bad faith by deliberately overcommitting its ability to manufacture and deliver enough concrete, providing an inadequate number of trucks to service Groves' project, and following a policy of providing delivery at only 75 percent of the ordered rate. On that basis, the court stripped Warner of the protection offered by the no-claim-for-delay clause in its contract and awarded damages. In the court's view, on June 15, 1972 Groves had no reasonable expectation that Warner's performance would improve to "totally satisfactory levels" and by July 11, 1972, "there were no practical impediments to employing Trap Rock as a supplemental supplier." The court therefore concluded that "as of July 12, 1972, Groves had an obligation to utilize Trap Rock as a supplemental supplier . . . in order to mitigate any possible 'delay damages' resulting from Warner's service." Accordingly, the court did not award Groves all the delay damages it sought, allowing only $12,534 for [losses incurred] before, but not after, July 12, 1972. . . .

The district court determined that since the contract was essentially one for the sale of a product with an additional requirement of proper and timely delivery, the Uniform Commercial Code should govern. The court described the transaction between Groves and Warner as an installment contract, an agreement to deliver goods in "separate lots to be separately accepted." Where there is non-conformity with respect to one or more installments which substantially impairs the value of the whole contract, there is a breach of the whole. UCC § 2–612(3). In the district court's view, such a breach occurred as of July 12, 1972 and should have been apparent to Groves. The district court reasoned that in order to recover consequential damages for defective performance after that date, Groves had to prove that it had complied with the obligation to "cover" or otherwise mitigate damages incurred after Warner's breach in July, 1972. Since Trap Rock was available in July, 1972 as a source of ready-mixed concrete, the district court held that Groves was under "a duty to attempt to prevent the consequential damages . . . by obtaining the supplemental supplier" and that Groves' failure to do so barred it, as a matter of law, from receiving such compensation. In this ruling the trial court erred.

The requirement of cover or mitigation of damages is not an absolute, unyielding one, but is subject to the circumstances. Comment 2 to § 2–712 says:

> (t)he test of proper cover is whether at the time and place the buyer acted in good faith and in a reasonable manner, and it is immaterial that hindsight may later prove that the method of cover used was not the cheapest or most effective.

Essentially the cover rules are an expression of the general duty to mitigate damages and usually the same principles apply.[5] The burden of proving that losses could have been avoided by reasonable effort and expense must be borne by the party who has broken the contract. . . .

In July, 1972, Groves found itself confronted with a breach by Warner and the consequent necessity to choose among a number of alternative courses of action. In the circumstances, Groves could have:

1. Declared the contract breached, stopped work, and held Warner liable for all damages. This was not a realistic alternative.
2. Set up its own cement batching plant at the job site. Time and expense made this impractical.
3. Accepted Warner's assurances that it would perform satisfactorily in the future, see § 2–609(1). The court, however, found that it would have been unreasonable to have any faith in continued assurances from Warner.
4. Substituted Trap Rock for Warner for the remainder of the contract. The court made no finding on the reasonableness of this choice but it appears questionable whether Trap Rock had the resources to meet all of Groves' requirements.

[5] It has been said that there is not a "duty" on the part of a plaintiff to mitigate damages but rather the principle is that he is entitled to only those damages which he could not avoid by reasonable effort. The "duty" to mitigate cannot be enforced and it is only when recovery is sought that the defense may be invoked. The test for plaintiff's efforts is reasonableness.

5. Engaged Trap Rock as a supplemental supplier; or
6. Continued dealing with Warner in the belief that though its performance would not be satisfactory, consequential damages might be less than if the other alternatives were adopted.

Of the six alternatives, Groves was seemingly faced with three practical ones all subject to drawbacks. Groves had to: allow Warner to continue in the hope of averting even greater losses; substitute Trap Rock for all of Warner's work a choice made doubtful by Trap Rock's ability to handle the project; or, lastly, use Trap Rock as a supplemental supplier.

The last choice the option chosen by the district court was subject to several difficulties which the court did not discuss. Even if Trap Rock supplied part of the contract with perfect scheduling, there would be no guarantee that Warner would do so. The element of erratic deliveries by Warner would not necessarily be cured, nor would the problems with the quality of concrete it delivered to the site. The presence of two independent suppliers acting separately might indeed pose problems more severe than those which existed before. Moreover, Trap Rock received some of its raw material from Warner and Groves suspected that Warner might not have been too cooperative if part of the Girard Bridge contract were taken away by Trap Rock.

Confronted with these alternatives, Groves chose to stay with Warner, a decision with which the district court did not agree. The court's preference may very well have been the best; that, however, is not the test.

> Where a choice has been required between two reasonable courses, the person whose wrong forced the choice can not complain that one rather than the other was chosen. The rule of mitigation of damages may not be invoked by a contract breaker as a basis for hypercritical examination of the conduct of the injured party, or merely for the purpose of showing that the injured person might have taken steps which seemed wiser or would have been more advantageous to the defaulter.

There are situations in which continuing with the performance of an unsatisfactory contractor will avoid losses which might be experienced by engaging others to complete the project. In such a setting, mitigation is best served by continuing existing arrangements. As the troubled Prince of Denmark once observed we " . . . rather bear those ills we have, Than fly to others that we know not of. . . ."

There is another unusual feature in this case. Engaging Trap Rock as an additional source of supply was a course of action open to Warner as well as Groves. Indeed, on other commercial work Warner had used Trap Rock as a supplemental supplier. Warner could have augmented its deliveries to Groves by securing extra trucks and concrete from Trap Rock as needed. Such an arrangement by Warner would have had the distinct advantage of having one subcontractor directly answerable to Groves for proper delivery, timing and quality.

Where both the plaintiff and the defendant have had equal opportunity to reduce the damages by the same act and it is equally reasonable to expect the defendant to minimize damages, the defendant is in no position to contend that the plaintiff failed to mitigate. Nor will the award be reduced on account of damages the defendant could have avoided as easily as the plaintiff. The duty to mitigate damages is not applicable where the party whose duty it is primarily to perform a contract has equal opportunity for performance and equal knowledge of the consequences of nonperformance.

Here, where the alternative the court imposed upon Groves was available to Warner as well, Warner may not assert Groves' lack of mitigation in failing to do precisely that which Warner chose not to do. Particularly is this so in light of the finding that Warner breached the contract in bad faith.

Thus, either upon the ground that Groves should not be faulted for choosing one of several reasonable alternatives or upon the basis that Warner was bound to procure an additional supplier, we hold that the district court erred in imposing on Groves as a matter of law a duty to engage Trap Rock. Accordingly, we vacate that portion of the court's judgment which allowed damages for delay only until July 12, 1972. We remand for assessment of damages from that point to completion of the contract on the same basis as that used for the pre-July 12 delay damages. In all other respects, the judgment of the district court will be affirmed.

NOTES AND PROBLEMS

1. *Comparative Reasonableness.* Often, a plaintiff may have more than one reasonable alternative for minimizing the loss. Is there any room for a court to determine which move would have been more reasonable? Or does *Groves* permit recovery for losses as long as the plaintiff did not make an unreasonable choice? Do you blame the trial court for believing it was unreasonable to expect Warner to meet deadlines after two years of experience? Is this 20–20 hindsight? Did the appellate court differ because it viewed the problem from Groves' position at the time? Or did the trial court lack an appreciation of the business difficulties its preferred course would involve?

2. *Mitigation by Defendant?* Consider the alternative holding: that Warner had an equal opportunity to minimize the loss by hiring Trap Rock, so Groves didn't need to take that step. Won't this often be true? If cover is possible, can't defendant always find substitute goods for the plaintiff? What

remains of UCC § 2–715's limitation to losses "which could not reasonably be prevented by cover or otherwise"? Is this holding more an estoppel: defendant, having failed to take the action, cannot object that plaintiff failed to do it? Or is it just evidence of reasonableness: if it was unreasonable not to do something, why didn't you do it (or tell plaintiff to do it) at the time instead of waiting until litigation to raise the issue? Might this, too, avoid 20–20 hindsight? *See* Michael B. Kelly, *Defendant's Responsibility To Minimize Plaintiff's Loss: A Curious Exception to the Avoidable Consequences Doctrine*, 47 S. CAR. L. REV. 391 (1996).

3. *Late Delivery*. Plaintiff hired defendant to deliver time sensitive advertising brochures by Dec. 16. The documents arrived late, but instead of waiting to unload later that day, the driver took the semi-trailer to a holding lot, where it remained until Dec. 27. For about $500, either party could have sent a driver to get the trailer and complete delivery. Plaintiff kept asking defendant to deliver; defendant kept saying it would try. Plaintiff lost $80,000 for brochures that became worthless. How much can plaintiff recover? See *R.R. Donnelly & Sons v. Vanguard Transportation Systems*, 641 F. Supp. 2d 707 (N.D. Ill. 2009).

PARKER V. TWENTIETH CENTURY–FOX FILM CORP.

3 Cal.3d 176, 474 P.2d 689, 89 Cal.Rptr. 737 (1970).

BURKE, J.

Plaintiff [Shirley Maclaine] is well known as an actress. . . . Under the contract, . . . plaintiff was to play the female lead in defendant's contemplated production of a motion picture entitled "Bloomer Girl." The contract provided that defendant would pay plaintiff a minimum "guaranteed compensation" of $53,571.42 per week for 14 weeks commencing May 23, 1966, for a total of $750,000. [D]efendant decided not to produce the picture and by a letter dated April 4, 1966, it notified plaintiff of that decision. . . .

By the same letter and with the professed purpose "to avoid any damage to you," defendant instead offered to employ plaintiff as the leading actress in another film tentatively entitled "Big Country, Big Man" (hereinafter, "Big Country"). The compensation offered was identical, as were 31 of the 34 numbered provisions or articles of the original contract.[1] Unlike "Bloomer Girl," however, which was to have been a musical production, "Big Country" was a dramatic "western type" movie. "Bloomer Girl" was to have been filmed in California; "Big Country" was to be produced in Australia. Also, certain terms in the

---

1 Among the identical provisions was the following found in the last paragraph of Article 2 of the original contract: "We [defendant] shall not be obligated to utilize your [plaintiff's] services in or in connection with the Photoplay hereunder, our sole obligation . . . being to pay you the guaranteed compensation herein provided for."

proffered contract varied from those of the original.[2] Plaintiff was given one week within which to accept; she did not and the offer lapsed. Plaintiff then commenced this action seeking recovery of the agreed guaranteed compensation.

[Defendant denies] that any money is due to plaintiff [and] pleads as an affirmative defense [plaintiff's] allegedly deliberate failure to mitigate damages, asserting that she unreasonably refused to accept its offer of the leading role in "Big Country."

Plaintiff moved for summary judgment, the motion was granted, and summary judgment for $750,000 plus interest was entered in plaintiff's favor. . . .

The general rule is that the measure of recovery by a wrongfully discharged employee is the amount of salary agreed upon for the period of service, less the amount which the employer affirmatively proves the employee has earned or with reasonable effort might have earned from other employment. However, before projected earnings from other employment opportunities not sought or accepted by the discharged employee can be applied in mitigation, the employer must show that the other employment was comparable, or substantially similar, to that of which the employee has been deprived; the employee's rejection of or failure to seek other available employment of a different or inferior kind may not be resorted to in order to mitigate damages.

In the present case defendant has raised no issue of *reasonableness of efforts* by plaintiffs to obtain other employment; the sole issue is whether plaintiff's refusal of defendant's substitute offer of "Big Country" may be used in mitigation. Nor, if the "Big Country" offer was of employment different or inferior when compared with the original "Bloomer Girl" employment, is there an issue as to whether or not plaintiff acted reasonably in refusing the substitute offer. Despite defendant's arguments to the contrary, no case cited or which our research has discovered holds or suggests that reasonableness is an element of a wrongfully discharged employee's option to reject, or fail to seek, different

---

[2] Article 29 of the original contract specified that plaintiff approved the director already chosen for "Bloomer Girl" and that in case he failed to act as director plaintiff was to have approval rights of any substitute director. Article 31 provided that plaintiff was to have the right of approval of the "Bloomer Girl" dance director, and Article 32 gave her the right of approval of the screenplay.

Defendant's letter . . . eliminated or impaired each of those rights. . . . "Article 31 . . . will not be included . . . as it is not a musical and it thus will not need a dance director. [I]n Articles 29 and 32, you were given certain director and screenplay approvals and you had preapproved certain matters. Since there simply is insufficient time to negotiate with you regarding your choice of director and regarding the screenplay and since you already expressed an interest in performing the role in 'BIG COUNTRY, BIG MAN,' we must exclude from our offer . . . any approval rights . . . ; however, we shall consult with you respecting the director . . . and . . . with respect to the screenplay and any revisions or changes therein. . . ."

or inferior employment lest the possible earnings therefrom be charged against him in mitigation of damages.[5]

Applying the foregoing rules to the record in the present case, . . . it is clear that the trial court correctly ruled that plaintiff's failure to accept defendant's tendered substitute employment could not be applied in mitigation of damages because the offer of the "Big Country" lead was of employment both different and inferior, and that no factual dispute was presented on that issue. The mere circumstance that "Bloomer Girl" was to be a musical review calling upon plaintiff's talents as a dancer as well as an actress, and was to be produced in the City of Los Angeles, whereas "Big Country" was a straight dramatic role in a "Western Type" story taking place in an opal mine in Australia, demonstrates the difference in kind between the two employments; the female lead as a dramatic actress in a western style motion picture can by no stretch of imagination be considered the equivalent of or substantially similar to the lead in a song-and-dance production.

---

[5] Instead, in each case the reasonableness referred to was that of the *efforts* of the employee to obtain other employment that was not different or inferior; his right to reject the latter was declared as an unqualified rule of law. Thus, *Gonzales v. Internat. Assn. of Machinists, supra.*, 213 Cal.App.2d 817, 823–824, holds that the trial court correctly instructed the jury that plaintiff union member, a machinist, was required to make "such *efforts* as the average [member of his union] desiring employment would make at that particular time and place" (italics added); but, further, that the court *properly rejected* defendant's *offer of proof of* the *availability of other kinds of employment* at the same or higher pay than plaintiff usually received and all outside the jurisdiction of his union, as plaintiff could not be required to accept different employment or a nonunion job.

In *Harris v. Nat. Union etc. Cooks, Stewards, supra.*, 116 Cal.App.2d 759, 761, the issues were stated to be, inter alia, whether comparable employment was open to each plaintiff employee, and if so whether each plaintiff made a *reasonable effort* to secure such employment. It was held that the trial court *properly sustained an objection to an offer to prove a custom of accepting a job in a lower rank* when work in the higher rank was not available, as "The duty of mitigation of damages . . . does not require the plaintiff 'to seek or to accept other employment of a different or inferior kind.' "

See also: *Lewis v. Protective Security Life Ins. Co.* (1962) 208 Cal.App.2d 582, 584 [25 Cal.Rptr. 213]: "*honest effort* to find similar employment. . . ." (Italics added.)

de la [sic] Falaise v. Gaumont–British Picture Corp., 39 Cal.App.2d 461, 469: "reasonable effort."

Erler v. Five Points Motors, Inc. (1967) 249 Cal.App.2d 560, 562 [57 Cal.Rptr. 516]: Damages may be mitigated "by a showing that the employee, by the exercise of *reasonable diligence and effort*, could have procured comparable employment. . . ." (Italics added.)

Savitz v. Gallaccio (1955) 179 Pa.Super. 589 [118 A.2d 282, 286]; Atholwood Dev. Co. v. Houston (1941) 179 Md. 441 [19 A.2d 706, 708]; Harcourt & Co. v. Heller (1933) 250 Ky. 321 [62 S.W.2d 1056]; Alaska Airlines, Inc. v. Stephenson (1954) 217 F.2d 295, 299 [15 Alaska 272]; United Protective Workers v. Ford Motor Co. (7th Cir.1955) 223 F.2d 49, 52 [48 A.L.R.2d 1285]; Chisholm v. Preferred Bankers' Life Assur. Co. (1897) 112 Mich. 50 [70 N.W. 415]; each of which held that the *reasonableness of the* employee's *efforts*, or his excuses for failure, to find other similar employment was properly submitted to the jury as a question of fact. NB: *Chisholm* additionally *approved* a jury *instruction* that a *substitute offer* of the employer to work for a lesser compensation was *not to be considered in mitigation*, as the employee was not required to accept it.

Williams v. National Organization, Masters (1956) 384 Pa. 413 [120 A.2d 896, 901 [13]]: "Even assuming that plaintiff . . . could have obtained employment in ports other than . . . where he resided, *legally* he was not compelled to do so in order to mitigate his damages." (Italics added.)

Additionally, the substitute "Big Country" offer proposed to eliminate or impair the director and screenplay approvals accorded to plaintiff under the original "Bloomer Girl" contract and thus constituted an offer of inferior employment. No expertise or judicial notice is required in order to hold that the deprivation or infringement of an employee's rights held under an original employment contract converts the available "other employment" relied upon by the employer to mitigate damages, into inferior employment which the employee need not seek or accept. . . .

The judgment is affirmed.

SULLIVAN, ACTING C. J.

The basic question in this case is whether or not plaintiff acted reasonably in rejecting defendant's offer of alternate employment. The answer depends upon whether that offer (starring in "Big Country, Big Man") was an offer of work that was substantially similar to her former employment (starring in "Bloomer Girl") or of work that was of a different or inferior kind. To my mind this is a factual issue, which the trial court should not have determined on a motion for summary judgment. . . .

The familiar rule requiring a plaintiff in a tort or contract action to mitigate damages embodies notions of fairness and socially responsible behavior which are fundamental to our jurisprudence. Most broadly stated, it precludes the recovery of damages which, through the exercise of due diligence, could have been avoided. Thus, in essence, it is a rule requiring reasonable conduct in commercial affairs. This general principle governs the obligations of an employee after his employer has wrongfully repudiated or terminated the employment contract. Rather than permitting the employee simply to remain idle during the balance of the contract period, the law requires him to make a reasonable effort to secure other employment.[1] He is not obliged, however, to seek or accept any and all types of work which may be available. Only work which is in the same field and which is of the same quality need be accepted.[2]

Over the years the courts have employed various phrases to define the type of employment which the employee, upon his wrongful discharge, is under an obligation to accept. Thus in California alone it has been held that he must accept employment which is "substantially similar,"

[1] The issue is generally discussed in terms of a duty on the part of the employee to minimize loss. The practice is long-established and there is little reason to change despite Judge Cardozo's observation of its subtle inaccuracy. "The servant is free to accept employment or reject it according to his uncensored pleasure. What is meant by the supposed duty is merely this, that if he unreasonably reject, he will not be heard to say that the loss of wages from then on shall be deemed the jural consequence of the earlier discharge. He has broken the chain of causation, and loss resulting to him thereafter is suffered through his own act."

[2] This qualification of the rule seems to reflect the simple and humane attitude that it is too severe to demand of a person that he attempt to find and perform work for which he has no training or experience. Many of the older cases hold that one need not accept work in an inferior rank or position nor work which is more menial or arduous. This suggests that the rule may have had its origin in the bourgeois fear of resubmergence in lower economic classes.

"comparable employment," employment "in the same general line of the first employment," "equivalent to his prior position," "employment in a similar capacity," employment which is "not . . . of a different or inferior kind. . . ."

For reasons which are unexplained, the majority cite several of these cases yet select from among the various judicial formulations which they contain one particular phrase, "Not of a different or inferior kind," with which to analyze this case. I have discovered no historical or theoretical reason to adopt this phrase, which is simply a negative restatement of the affirmative standards set out in the above cases, as the exclusive standard. Indeed, its emergence is an example of the dubious phenomenon of the law responding not to rational judicial choice or changing social conditions, but to unrecognized changes in the language of opinions or legal treatises.[4] However, the phrase is a serviceable one and my concern is not with its use as the standard but rather with what I consider its distortion.

The relevant language excuses acceptance only of employment which is of a *different kind.* It has never been the law that the mere existence of *differences between two jobs in the same field* is sufficient, as a matter of law, to excuse an employee wrongfully discharged from one from accepting the other in order to mitigate damages. Such an approach would effectively eliminate any obligation of an employee to attempt to minimize damage arising from a wrongful discharge. The only alternative job offer an employee would be required to accept would be an offer of his former job by his former employer.

Although the majority appear to hold that there was a difference "in kind" between the employment offered plaintiff in "Bloomer Girl" and that offered in "Big Country," an examination of the opinion makes crystal clear that the majority merely point out differences between the two *films* (an obvious circumstance) and then apodically assert that these constitute a difference in the *kind of employment.* The entire rationale of the majority boils down to this; that the "*mere circumstances*" that "Bloomer Girl" was to be a musical review while "Big Country" was a straight drama "demonstrates the difference in kind" since a female lead in a western is not "the equivalent of or substantially similar to" a lead in a musical. This is merely attempting to prove the proposition by repeating it. It shows that the vehicles for the display of the star's talents

[4] The earliest California case which the majority cite, *de la [sic] Falaise*, states "The 'other employment' which the discharged employee is bound to seek is employment of a character substantially similar to that of which he has been deprived; he need not enter upon service of a different or inferior kind. . . ." *de la [sic] Falaise* cites, in turn, . . . 18 R.C.L. (Ruling Case law) 529. That digest, however, states only that the "discharged employee . . . need not enter upon service of a *more menial kind.*" (Italics added.) It was in this form that the rule entered California law explicitly, *Gregg v. McDonald* (1925) 73 Cal. App. 748, 757 [239 P. 373], quoting the text verbatim. . . .

are different but it does not prove that her employment as a star in such vehicles is of necessity different *in kind* and either inferior or superior.

I believe that the approach taken by the majority (a superficial listing of differences with no attempt to assess their significance) may subvert a valuable legal doctrine.[5] The inquiry in cases such as this should not be whether differences between the two jobs exist (there will always be differences) but whether the differences which are present are substantial enough to constitute differences in the *kind* of employment or, alternatively, whether they render the substitute work employment of an *inferior kind.*

It seems to me that *this* inquiry involves, in the instant case at least, factual determinations which are improper on a motion for summary judgment. Resolving whether or not one job is substantially similar to another or whether, on the other hand, it is of a different or inferior kind, will often (as here) require a critical appraisal of the similarities and differences between them in light of the importance of these differences to the employee. This necessitates a weighing of the evidence, and it is precisely this undertaking which is forbidden on summary judgment. . . .

It is not intuitively obvious, to me at least, that the leading female role in a dramatic motion picture is a radically different endeavor from the leading female role in a musical comedy film. Nor is it plain to me that the rather qualified rights of director and screenplay approval contained in the first contract are highly significant matters either in the entertainment industry in general or to this plaintiff in particular. Certainly, none of the declarations introduced by plaintiff in support of her motion shed any light on these issues. Nor do they attempt to explain why she declined the offer of starring in "Big Country, Big Man." Nevertheless, the trial court granted the motion, declaring that these approval rights were "critical" and that their elimination altered "the essential nature of the employment." . . .

PROBLEMS

1. *Discharged Factory Worker.* Let's start with some of the doctrinal implications, some of which are buried in footnote 5 of the court's opinion. These are easier to see in a more ordinary job. Consider, therefore, Gladis, an assembly-line worker for Ford earning $800 a week ($20/hour for 40 hours). She is wrongfully discharged on January 1. Her contract would expire July 1, 26 weeks (or $20,800) later. (Does it matter whether the discharge is a breach

[5] The values of the doctrine of mitigation of damages in this context are that it minimizes the unnecessary personal and social (e.g., nonproductive use of labor, litigation) costs of contractual failure. If a wrongfully discharged employee can, through his own action and without suffering financial or psychological loss in the process, reduce the damages accruing from the breach of contract, the most sensible policy is to require him to do so. I fear the majority opinion will encourage precisely opposite conduct.

of contract term for 1 year of employment, a tort, or a discrimination claim?) How much can she recover if:

a. Gladis already had another job offer at $800 a week and started without missing a day of work?

b. She never looks for work, but no jobs in her field are available in her town?

c. After 6 weeks of diligent searching, she takes a job in her field for $600 a week and keeps it through July 1? Does it matter whether the job is in another city? Does it matter if the job was outside her field?

d. After 6 weeks of diligent searching, she found a job outside her field for $600 a week, but turned it down and failed to find another job in her field despite diligent effort?

e. After 6 weeks of diligent searching, she found a similar job in her field (same title, same duties, same prestige, same opportunities for advancement, etc.), but was offered only $600 a week. She turned it down and failed to find another job in her field despite diligent effort?

f. After 6 weeks of diligent searching, she found a similar job in her field in a nearby town for $800 a week but turned it down and failed to find another job in her field despite diligent effort?

g. After 6 weeks of diligent searching, she takes work in her field for $1000 per week and keeps it through July 1 (20 weeks)?

h. After 6 weeks of diligent searching, she takes work in her field for $800 per week, but is laid off five weeks later and, despite diligent efforts, cannot find additional work? What if the new job paid $1000 a week?

2. *Discharged Teacher*. How would the doctrine apply in closer cases? Consider Anna: she is credentialed to teach a math and social studies in secondary schools. For two years she has been teaching algebra in a suburban public high school. In October of her third year, she was discharged in breach of contract. (She is not tenured, so only the rest of this year need be considered.) Which of the following positions should be subtracted from her pay if she refused them?

a. A position with defendant teaching history? What about geometry?

b. A position with a private high school in the same town teaching history? Geometry? What about algebra?

c. Would the answer to b. change if the private high school were religious? Does the religion matter?

d. A position with a junior high school teaching history? Geometry? Algebra? Does it matter whether the junior high is run by defendant, is private, or is religious?

e. Does the quality of the schools make a difference? The age of the facilities? The socio-economic composition of the student body?

f. A position with a company that offers tutoring services? Does the subject matter?

g. Suppose defendant shows that Anna could have made significant amounts as a private tutor?

3. *Relocation.* In problem 2, what if the job required her to move? For any position that was sufficiently similar, how would location make a difference? Would you still subtract the income she could have earned if she turned down a position:

a. In an adjacent suburb, 15 minutes away?

b. Downtown, 40 minutes away?

c. A remote suburb, 40 minutes away?

d. If she was discharged from a rural school, where the nearest other school (public or private) was 40 minutes away, would your answer be different?

e. A city 60 miles away, in the same state? In a different state (say, Chicago to Milwaukee)?

4. *Show Business.* Do these doctrinal responses apply with equal force to *Parker*? How much could Maclaine recover if:

a. She took the role in *Big Country, Big Man* on the terms offered in the case? *Cf.* Two Mules for Sister Sara (1970) (Clint Eastwood, Shirley Maclaine).

b. Another studio offered her a role indistinguishable from the role in *Bloomer Girl* (a musical comedy, same theme, filmed in Los Angeles, with approval-rights on the choreographer, script, and director), but at a salary of $500,000 and she took the role?

c. On the facts in b., what if turned down the role?

d. What if another studio offered her a role in *Big Country, Big Man* for $750,000 and she turned it down? Would it matter if the offer included approval rights on the script and director? If the offer was for $850,000 instead of $750,000? Would it matter if the film were to be shot in Los Angeles instead of Australia?

5. *Mitigating with Defendant.* When defendant offers a new transaction that would reduce the plaintiff's loss, should the court consider the reasonableness of that decision? Or should courts hold rejection reasonable as a matter of rule? Did *Parker* answer that question?

Consider another case. Defendant delivered free fill dirt to plaintiff, but delivered more than was authorized. Defendant offered to remove the excess for about $10,000 (half the going rate), but plaintiff refused. Eventually, plaintiff suffered losses significantly exceeding $22,000. Removal by defendant would have avoided both the cost of paying another to remove the dirt and any consequential losses suffered because the dirt was there (*e.g.*, construction delays). Should damages be limited to $10,000? Does it matter whether the excess was a breach of contract or a trespass? See *DeRosier v. Utility Systems of America*, 780 N.W.2d 1 (Minn. App. 2010).

6. *Breaching Employees.* When the shoe is on the other foot, does avoidable consequences still apply?

a. What if Gladis quit in breach of contract? Can Ford recover lost profits from her? Can Ford recover anything?

b. What if Maclaine quit in breach of contract, causing Twentieth Century Fox to cancel the Bloomer Girl project. Could the studio recover their projected profits on the film from her? Can the studio recover anything? *See Anglia Television Ltd. v. Reed*, 3 All E.R. 690 (C.A. 1971).

7. *Construction.* Landis Ohner hired Connor Construction (Connor) to build an apartment complex for $2 million. Six months into the project, Ohner cancelled the project and discharged Connor. Which, if any, of the following amounts can Connor recover as damages for breach of contract:

a. Materials purchased for the project but not yet incorporated into the building?

b. Wages for employees hired for the project, but idled by the cessation of work?

c. Amounts due on equipment rented for the project, even though the rental period extends beyond the discharge date?

d. Overhead—the portion of the costs of the central office included in the bid on this project, even for periods after the project was cancelled?

e. Profits Connor could have made by bidding on another job that would fill the time Ohner's project would have required? Does it matter whether Connor actually gets such a job? Does it matter whether Connor actually profits on it? What if Connor's substitute job produced losses? Should those losses be added to the recovery?

NOTES AND QUESTIONS

1. *Collateral Source.* Why aren't subsequent jobs collateral benefits? The new employer may be entirely independent of the breaching employer. The employee invests in the new job the way one invests in an insurance policy. Should wages from other employment not be subtracted at all?

2. *No Efforts.* Why didn't the studio raise Maclaine's failure to seek any other role? If she made no effort to seek other employment, what else (if anything) would the studio need to prove in order to reduce the damage award? How much effort would it take to show an adequate search? See *Orzel v. City of Wauwatosa*, 697 F.2d 743, 756–57 (7th Cir.1983) (age discrimination plaintiff who, over two years, took one part time job, applied for one full time job, and put his name on file with state job service devoted "reasonable diligence in attempting to find alternative employment"). Can a court rely on necessity to force employees to seek work, making it unnecessary to evaluate adequacy of efforts?

3. Is *Parker* a case where doctrine escapes the policies it implements? Consider three policies:

a. *Avoiding Waste.* By building a bridge where the road had been cancelled, Luten Bridge Co. wasted materials and labor. By sitting idle instead of making a movie, Shirley Maclaine wasted her talents. Each may spend (or waste) their resources as they wish, but not at defendant's expense. Should the law encourage them to minimize waste by denying recovery.

b. *Proximate Cause.* While defendant's breach is a but-for cause of the injury, so is plaintiff's failure to make reasonable efforts to find a substitute job. When plaintiff acts unreasonably, perhaps her conduct is the proximate cause, cutting off defendant's liability.

c. *Just Compensation.* To put plaintiff in the position she would have occupied if the wrong had not occurred, we need to pay her the salary, minus any cost avoided because of the breach. Maclaine avoided the cost of having to work for 14 weeks. Being paid to do nothing is not the same as being paid to work. She is better off now than she would have been if the contract had been performed. Would working on *Big Country, Big Man* also miss the mark? See Michael B. Kelly, *Living Without the Avoidable Consequences Doctrine in Contract Remedies*, 33 San Diego L. Rev. 175 (1996). Which comes closer to the position she would have occupied but for the wrong?

4. Your answers to the problems may turn on a fundamental distinction between rules and standards. The limitations identified by the court in footnote 5 and the problems may be factors to take into account in determining reasonableness or may be rules to be applied regardless of what is reasonable in a given case. How do you think the court in *Parker* considered them? Did the dissent agree?

COLLINS ENTERTAINMENT CORPORATION V. COATS AND COATS RENTAL AMUSEMENT

368 S.C. 410, 629 S.E.2d 635 (2006).

JUSTICE WALLER:

. . . In 1996, Collins Entertainment Corporation (Collins) contracted to lease video poker machines to two bingo hall operations known as Ponderosa Bingo and Shipwatch Bingo. The six-year lease required that any purchaser of the premises assume the lease. In 1997, American Bingo and Gaming Corporation (American) purchased the assets of the bingo parlors. American failed to assume the lease and removed Collins' machines from the premises. Collins brought this action against American alleging unfair trade practices, civil conspiracy, and intentional interference with contract. The matter was referred to a master in equity for trial. The master found American liable for intentional interference with contract and awarded Collins actual damages of $157,449.66 and punitive damages of $1,569,013.00. The Court of Appeals affirmed.

[Collins placed 19 of the 20 machines removed from Shipwatch and Ponderosa into other premises. Thus, it received rent for these machines despite the breach. The damage award did not subtract the rent received from the recovery because Collins was a lost volume seller.]

Comment f to Section 347 of the Restatement (Second) of Contracts states, in part, "if the injured party could and would have entered into the subsequent contract, even if the contract had not been broken, and could have had the benefit of both, he can be said to have lost volume and the subsequent transaction is not a substitute for the broken contract." This theory of damages has come to be known as the "lost volume seller" doctrine. A lost volume seller is one whose willingness and ability to supply is, as a practical matter, unlimited in comparison to the demand for the product. Thus, "[t]he lost volume seller theory allows [for the] recovery of lost profits despite resale of the services that were the subject of the terminated contract if the seller . . . can prove that he would have entered into both transactions but for the breach." *Gianetti v. Norwalk Hosp.,* 266 Conn. 544, 833 A.2d 891 (2003). *See also Comeq, Inc. v. Mitternight Boiler Works,* 456 So. 2d 264, 268–69 (Ala. 1984) (the reason for the rule is based on the idea that the lost volume seller would have received two profits, not just one, if the buyer had not breached, so that a recovery of both profits is necessary to put the seller in as good a position as if there had been no breach). Although the lost volume seller theory is commonly understood to apply to contracts involving the sale of goods, it applies with equal force to contracts involving the performance of personal services. Whether a seller is a lost volume seller is a question of fact. . . .

American asserts adoption of the lost volume seller doctrine eliminates a seller's duty to mitigate damages. It contends we should adopt the position advanced by the Pennsylvania Supreme Court in *Northeastern Vending Company v. PDO, Inc.,* 414 Pa. Super. 200, 606 A.2d 936 (1992), in which the court declined to adopt the lost volume seller doctrine stating, summarily, that it would erode the duty to mitigate damages.[4] We decline to adopt the Pennsylvania approach because we do not find the doctrine erodes the duty to mitigate damages. On the contrary, the doctrine realizes that in certain situations, even where a buyer **does** mitigate, if the seller would have made the second sale in any event, then the lost volume measure of damages places him in the same position he would have been had the buyer not repudiated. As the Court in *R.E. Davis Chemical v. Diasonics Inc.,* 826 F.2d 678, 683, n. 3 (7th Cir.1987), stated, "by definition, a lost volume seller cannot mitigate damages through resale. Resale does not reduce a lost volume seller's damages because the breach has still resulted in its losing one sale and a corresponding profit." . . .

Further, we find the legislature's adoption of S.C. CODE ANN. § 36–2A–528(2) is consistent with adoption of the lost volume seller doctrine. Section 36–2A–528(2) (dealing with leased goods) tracks the language of S.C. CODE ANN. § 36–2–708(2) (seller's damages for sales) . . . , upon which the lost volume seller doctrine is premised. . . . By adoption of S.C. CODE ANN. § 36–2A–528(2), we find the Legislature has tacitly approved of the lost volume seller doctrine.

American next asserts there is insufficient evidence in the record to demonstrate that Collins is a lost volume seller. We disagree. There is no one set test to determine whether one is a lost volume seller. According to one commentator:

> Professor Harris has developed three main requirements that a lost volume seller must meet: (1) the person who bought the resold entity would have been solicited by the plaintiff had there been no breach or resale; (2) the solicitation would have been successful; and (3) the plaintiff could have performed that additional contract. Most American courts and commentators have adopted these requirements.

Saidov, *The Methods for Limiting Damages Under the Vienna Convention on Contracts for the International Sale of Goods,* 14 Pace Int'l L. Rev. 307 (Fall 2002), *citing* Jerald B. Holisky, *Finding the Lost Volume Seller: Two Independent Sales Deserve Two Profits under Illinois Law,* 22 J. Marshall L. Rev. 363, 375 (1988).

---

[4] It appears Pennsylvania is the only jurisdiction which rejects the concept of the lost volume seller.

Here, there is testimony in the record which indicates that Collins had surplus machines on hand and that, had another location been available, it could and would have supplied those locations with video machines. Further, Collins did place 19 of the 20 machines which were removed from Shipwatch and Ponderosa into other premises. As found by the Master, it is patent that Collins had excess inventory with which to supply and rotate machines through all of its customers.

American argues there has been no showing by Collins that the specific type of machines removed from the Shipwatch and Ponderosa were available at its warehouses, such that it has failed in its burden to demonstrate it had . . . excess capacity. We disagree. Initially, although American argued there was insufficient evidence of excess capacity below, it made no argument with respect to the specific types of machines at issue. Accordingly, as this specific argument was not raised below, it is not preserved. In any event, Collins presented testimony from its assistant comptroller for accounting that, although there were ten machines in each location (*i.e.*, the Shipwatch and Ponderosa), a total of 48 machines rotated through the locations. Livingston also testified that "we had machines in the warehouse that could have easily replaced these 48 at the 130 locations." Livingston's testimony is sufficient to establish that Collins had more supply capacity of these machines than it had demand. Moreover, the lease agreement between Collins and Coats and Coats Rental gives Collins the right to furnish "all video game terminals and all coin operated music and amusement machines, to include a special multi-player Black Jack/Poker unit." We find no requirement (other than one multi-player poker unit) that Collins place any particular machines on the premises, such that Collins was free to have utilized any of its machines at the Ponderosa and Shipwatch. Accordingly, Collins was not required to demonstrate excess capacity as to a specific type of machine.

Contrary to the arguments raised by American, we find adoption of the lost volume seller doctrine does not eliminate a seller's duty to mitigate his damages. The doctrine simply recognizes that, in situations in which the seller has excess capacity and would, in any event, have made both sales, the lost volume measure of damages is to place the seller in the same position he would have been had the buyer not repudiated. Further, there is sufficient evidence to demonstrate that Collins was, in fact, a lost volume seller in this case. Accordingly, the opinion of the Court of Appeals utilizing the lost volume seller doctrine is affirmed.[8]

MOORE, J., concurs.

---

[8] The dissent contends adoption of the lost volume seller doctrine is inappropriate, claiming the doctrine does not apply to tort claims. However, American never argued below that the doctrine did not apply to Collins' claim for tortious interference with contract. . . .

JUSTICE PLEICONES, concurring:

I concur in the majority's express adoption of the lost-volume-seller doctrine and in the result. A lost-volume seller, or lessor, cannot mitigate his damages, so there is no duty to try. Evidence in the record supports the finding that Collins is a lost-volume lessor. I write separately because my analysis differs from the majority's on some issues.

As noted in the dissent: "The nexus between the two causes of action [breach of contract and tortious interference with contract] is the breach of the contract, for . . . breach of the contract is an element of both causes of action. This is the element from which the injured party's actual damages flow on both the contract and tort claims." *Collins Music Co. v. Smith,* 332 S.C. 145, 147, 503 S.E.2d 481, 481 (Ct. App. 1998). . . . The nature of the claim, whether contract or tort, does not affect the method of determining the damages flowing from the plaintiff's loss of contract expectations, and the lost-volume-seller doctrine merely provides one such method. There is no reason that the doctrine cannot apply in a tortious-interference case.

With respect to the dissent's conclusion that Collins has received a double recovery, I agree, but the writ of certiorari that we granted did not encompass the issue.

CHIEF JUSTICE TOAL dissenting: . . .

Because the lost volume seller doctrine applies in breach-of-contract cases only, and because the present case involves a tort, the court of appeals, in my view, erred in adopting and applying the doctrine.

Moreover, in my view, the court of appeals erred in affirming the trial court's calculation of damages. A plaintiff may not recover twice for the same injury. . . .

In the present case, Collins was awarded actual damages for the breach-of-contract claim in the amount of $232,628.00, plus $66,255.00 in pre-judgment interest. Collins was also awarded $157,449.66[3] in actual damages for the tortious-interference claim, plus $1,569,013.00 in punitive damages.

In my view, Collins should not have received two separate actual damages awards for a single breach of contract. By awarding damages under both the breach-of-contract and tortious-interference claims, the trial court improperly awarded Collins the lost benefits of the contract twice. Because the evidence regarding damages was the direct and

3 Like the award for breach of contract, the award for tortious interference was calculated by taking Collins' average revenue experience prior to the breach, multiplied by the number of weeks remaining in the contract [as provided in the liquidated damage clause]. The difference in this award, though, is that license fees and other operating expenses were deducted from the final amount.

natural consequence of a single breach, Collins was not entitled to the full amount of actual damages under both causes of action.

[I]]n the present case, Collins settled its claim for breach of contract against Coats. In addition, Collins sought damages against American Bingo for tortious interference of contract. As a result, any recovery from American Bingo would have to be set off against any recovery from Coats. *See* Restatement 2d Torts § 774(2) (stating that payments made by the third person in settlement of the claim must be credited against the liability for causing the breach and go to reducing the damages for the tort). Accordingly, I write to prevent a *third* recovery on the part of Collins.

BURNETT, J., concurs.

NOTES AND PROBLEMS

1. *Double Recovery.* None of the justices endorses allowing Collins to recover for the lost rental value in both the contract suit against Coats and the action for interference with contract against American Bingo. The loss caused by a breach of contract often is identical to the loss caused by one who induced the breach of contract. Recovering twice puts the plaintiff in a better position that it would have occupied if the wrong had not occurred. Faced with a procedural impediment to correcting this problem, should the court have adopted a different rule regarding lost volume sellers?

2. *Moonlighting.* Carmen worked the day shift at a factory. After being discharged, Carmen took a job driving a cab on the night shift. The hours did not overlap; if not discharged, Carmen could have worked both jobs simultaneously. If Carmen's discharge was illegal, should earnings driving a cab be subtracted from recovery against the former employer? Does it matter whether the discharge breached a contract, a tort duty, or a statute? What facts might affect your analysis?

SAWYER V. COMERCI

264 Va. 68, 563 S.E.2d 748 (Va. 2002).

JUSTICE HASSELL, SR.

Plaintiff, Norma J. Sawyer, administrator of the estate of Norman Lee Plogger, filed a motion for judgment against Cathy Comerci, D.O. . . . .

[Mr. Plogger] went to the Stonewall Jackson Hospital emergency room . . . because he experienced continuous pain on the right side of his abdomen.

Dr. Comerci, the emergency room physician "on call" that night, evaluated Mr. Plogger, ordered certain laboratory tests, and performed an examination upon him. . . . Mr. Plogger had seen his family physician a few days earlier, and his physician informed Mr. Plogger that he had a viral illness. . . . Even though Mr. Plogger had experienced abdominal pains for several months . . . he had not mentioned this pain to his physician, Dr. Thomas Hamilton.

Dr. Comerci concluded that Mr. Plogger should be admitted to the hospital as a patient because he had blood in his stool and his white blood count was elevated. The elevation in Mr. Plogger's white blood count led Dr. Comerci to believe that either "an inflammatory process or infection" was occurring in his body.

Dr. Comerci felt that a surgeon should evaluate Mr. Plogger, and she made a telephone call to Dr. Robert Irons, the hospital's "on call" surgeon, seeking such evaluation. . . .

Dr. Comerci believed that Mr. Plogger needed surgical intervention to resolve the bleeding. Dr. Irons told Dr. Comerci that he did not believe that Mr. Plogger had "an acute surgical abdomen" and recommended that Dr. Comerci refer Mr. Plogger to Dr. Hamilton. Dr. Comerci placed a telephone call to Dr. Hamilton.

[T]he emergency room nurses approached Dr. Comerci and informed her that Mr. and Mrs. Plogger were about to leave the hospital again. . . .

[W]hen Mr. and Mrs. Plogger began to leave the second time, [Dr. Comerci] asked them to wait. Dr. Comerci stated: " . . . I talked with Dr. Hamilton and I told him that I had a problem, that I had a man that I felt needed to be admitted, and I told him why, but that the man didn't want to be admitted; apparently his wife had an appointment the next day in Roanoke; they wanted to get out of there . . . [Dr. Hamilton] said, I guess if he doesn't want to stay, I will just see him tomorrow. I said, I don't think you'll see him tomorrow, they're going to be in Roanoke. And he said, [f]ine, have him call the office tomorrow and I'll see him Monday."

Approximately 10:15 that night, Mr. and Mrs. Plogger left the hospital's emergency room. They had been in the emergency room since about 7:30 p.m. Dr. Comerci testified that Mrs. Plogger "had said all along, [Mr. Plogger] can't stay; I have an appointment in the morning; we have to go to Roanoke."

When Mr. Plogger was discharged from the hospital's emergency room at 10:15 p.m., Dr. Comerci tried to persuade him to remain. However, he refused to do so. Dr. Comerci recorded a statement on Mr. Plogger's progress notes after he had left the emergency room that stated, among other things: "Patient and especially the patient's wife are difficult to talk with and despite repeated explanation do not seem to understand the possibility of the seriousness of his condition; however, agree to follow up with Dr. Hamilton on Friday."

Generally, a patient who leaves a hospital against the advice of the physician is asked to sign a document, described as an "against medical advice form." Dr. Comerci did not think that this form was available in the emergency room at that time. Consequently, Mr. Plogger did not sign this form.

Mr. Plogger returned to the hospital's emergency room three days later on April 5, 1997 with complaints of a sore throat. Dr. Comerci evaluated his abdomen, examined his throat, and diagnosed his throat condition as either oral candidiasis or oral thrush, conditions unrelated to his abdominal complaints.

Even though the discharge instructions that Mr. Plogger received during his emergency room visit on April 2, 1997 directed him to meet with Dr. Hamilton on April 4, Mr. Plogger did not do so. When Dr. Comerci treated Mr. Plogger at the emergency room on April 5, she " 'reiterated [that] he absolutely needed to follow up with his doctor on Monday [April 7] regarding [his] abdomen, and to come back if it was worse at all." Dr. Comerci "was still concerned" about Mr. Plogger's abdominal condition. According to Dr. Hamilton, Mr. Plogger failed to make an appointment to see him on April 4, 1997. Dr. Hamilton stated that "there is no record that [Mr. Plogger] made an appointment for any of those days after the 2nd of April."

On Monday morning, April 7, Mr. Plogger returned to the emergency room by ambulance. He was acutely short of breath, his skin was very pale, his lips were blue, and he was sweating. He was admitted to the hospital, where he died the following day.

The plaintiff presented evidence at trial that Dr. Comerci failed to comply with the applicable standard of care imposed upon a reasonably prudent emergency room physician when she treated Mr. Plogger on April 2, 5, and 7, 1997, and that her acts and omissions were proximate causes of his death. Dr. Comerci presented expert witness testimony that she complied with the standard of care and that Mr. Plogger's death was not caused by any act or omission by her.

[The court held that Dr. Comerci was not entitled to a jury instruction on contributory negligence because] she failed to establish a *prima facie* case that Mr. Plogger was guilty of contributory negligence.

The circuit court gave the following instruction to the jury, over the plaintiff's objection:

> A patient who claims that he has been negligently treated by a physician has a duty to use ordinary care to avoid loss or minimize or lessen the resulting damage.
>
> If the jury believes that Norman Plogger failed to use ordinary care to follow the instructions of Dr. Comerci to make an

appointment with and see his family physician, his estate may not recover for any portion of the harm which, by such care, could have been avoided.

The plaintiff contends that there was insufficient evidence to support this instruction and, therefore, the circuit court erred by granting it. Responding, the defendant argues that there was evidence to support the instruction. We agree with the defendant.

We have held that a plaintiff has a duty to mitigate his damages. In the context of a medical negligence claim, we have stated that "a patient's neglect of his health following his physician's negligent treatment may be a reason for reducing damages, but does not bar all recovery." *Lawrence [v. Wirth]*, 226 Va. [408,] 412, 309 S.E.2d [315,] 317 [(1983)]. Generally, whether a plaintiff acted reasonably to minimize his damage is a question for the jury. . . .

We hold that there is sufficient evidence in this record that would permit the jury to find as a matter of fact that Mr. Plogger failed to mitigate his damages. For example, Dr. Donald G. Gregg, who testified on behalf of the plaintiff as an expert witness, stated that Mr. Plogger should have been admitted to the hospital, "[a]nd one of the ways to do that was to go see his family doctor as instructed and be evaluated" and that had he done so, "he would have survived." As we have already stated, when Mr. Plogger was discharged from the emergency room on April 2, 1997, he received instructions that directed him to make an appointment with his family physician. However, that physician, Dr. Hamilton, testified that Mr. Plogger failed to make any appointment to see him for treatment.

[The court held that the trial court erroneously prevented plaintiff from cross-examining defendant's expert about having testified for Dr. Comerci in an earlier case, an issue that went to credibility.]

We will reverse the judgment of the circuit court and remand this case for a new trial consistent with the views expressed in this opinion.

NOTES AND QUESTIONS

1. *On Remand.* The jury reached a verdict for Dr. Comerci. *Sawyer v. Comerci*, 2003 WL 25443355 (Trial Order) (Va. Cir. Ct. July 11, 2003) (NO. CL98000073–00). One cannot tell whether the jury decided that Dr. Comerci had met the standard of care or whether it decided Mr. Plogger had failed to act reasonably to minimize the loss.

2. *Refusing Surgery.* A recommendation to see the family doctor poses little cost or risk for the plaintiff. A recommendation to undergo surgery involves more hardship for the plaintiff. In *Verrett v. McDonough Marine Service*, 705 F.2d 1437 (5th Cir. 1983), the court reduced the award for future pain and suffering because plaintiff refused a laminectomy that would have prevented the pain. While many cases recite the avoidable consequences

doctrine, most find that refusing the surgery was reasonable based on the cost, the risk, and the prospect for success. Some suggest that it is reasonable to refuse surgery based on even a small risk of injury or death. Every surgery involving a general anesthetic carries a small risk of death. Does that make it reasonable to refuse surgery regardless of the benefits and other costs?

3. *Reasonable to the Plaintiff?* In *Small v. Combustion Engineering*, 209 Mont. 387, 681 P.2d 1081 (1984), plaintiff refused low-risk knee surgery with a 92% chance of success, a decision the court found objectively unreasonable. But Small suffered from manic-depressive disorder, which "conscripts his mind with the possibility of failure, reinjury, and pain. From this perspective, the claimant's refusal to submit to knee surgery is not unreasonable." 681 P.2d at 1084. The court affirmed an award of permanent disability.

To what extent does this convert the reasonable person standard into a subjective, good-faith test? Once we take into account all of the factors that distort plaintiff's reason, won't any decision made in good faith be reasonable from the plaintiff's perspective? Can we stop part-way down this slippery slope? Can we consider gender, religion, and mental disability, but stop short of poor education, statistical fallacies, or lack of imagination?

4. *Religious Reasons.* What if a plaintiff refuses objectively reasonable medical treatment for religious reasons? Is the avoidable consequences doctrine a rule generally and neutrally applicable? *See Employment Division v. Smith*, 494 U.S. 872, 110 S. Ct. 1595, 108 L. Ed. 2d 876 (1990). If so, the cost of accommodating the plaintiff's beliefs must fall on her. Does applying the avoidable consequences doctrine inherently involve finding that the religious beliefs (as applied to this treatment) are unreasonable? Would a jury instruction asking what a "reasonable Jehovah's Witness" would do avoid that inquiry? Is that any worse than considering a reasonable person with manic-depressive disorder? Might an instruction favoring one religion violate the establishment clause? See *Williams v. Bright*, 230 A.D.2d 548, 658 N.Y.S.2d 910 (1997), *rev'g* 167 Misc.2d 312, 632 N.Y.S.2d 760 (1995). Can the court simply ignore the religious issue? Consider this analysis:

> No one suggests that the State, or, for that matter, anyone else, has the right to interfere with that religious belief. But the real issue here is whether the consequences of that belief must be fully paid for here on earth by someone other than the injured believer.

Id. at 552, 658 N.Y.S.2d 910, 632 N.Y.S.2d 913.

5. *Lack of Precautions.* In *S.C. Johnson & Son v. Morris*, 779 N.W.2d 19 (Wis. App. 2010), defendant bribed plaintiff's employees to submit inflated invoices to plaintiff. Defendant sought to reduce damages by the amount plaintiff could have avoided by supervising its employees more closely, thus discovering the scheme earlier or perhaps preventing it from occurring at all. If proven, should damages be reduced by the amount plaintiff could have avoided by acting reasonably? *See* RESTATEMENT SECOND OF TORTS § 918(2).

6. *Precautions before Breach.* Occasionally a plaintiff can minimize the loss by taking precautions before the breach occurs. Drivers can wear seatbelts, cyclists can wear helmets. If failure to take these precautions is unreasonable, how should that unreasonableness be addressed? Given seat belt laws, failure to buckle up might be negligent *per se*—though some statutes expressly reject that outcome.

The avoidable consequences doctrine arguably applies only to conduct "after the commission of the tort." RESTATEMENT (SECOND) OF TORTS § 918. Nonetheless, some courts have reduced recovery for damages that a seat belt would have prevented under this doctrine. *See, e.g., Spier v. Barker*, 35 N.Y.2d 444, 323 N.E.2d 164, 363 N.Y.S.2d 916 (1974). That court believed it carved out a limited exception because pretort precautions will not be possible in many cases. Is that so?

The benefits of exercise are increasingly recognized. Could a defendant (say, a doctor whose prescription led to heart problems) argue that plaintiff would have suffered less severe injuries had she exercised more often? Might exercise allow a pedestrian to avoid an injury altogether, say by getting out of harm's way more quickly? Is exercise an unreasonable precaution?

The difficulty can arise in contract cases. Even before a breach, the plaintiff can minimize its exposure by not relying too heavily on performance. Consider a variant of *Groves*: if Groves suspected, even before a breach, that Warner would not perform adequately, Groves could arrange for Trap Rock to stand by with supplemental supplies. That would minimize the loss. But should Groves receive less compensation if it fails to do so? If the arrangements with Trap Rock involve costs—Trap Rock is unlikely to stand by without a fee—should Warner pay Groves those costs? Who pays the cost of those precautions if Warner does not breach? Is a seat belt rule plausible only because buckling up has virtually no costs? Would everyone agree that buckling up is costless?

One state, by statute, reduces pain and suffering that a seat belt would have prevented but does not reduce medical costs or lost wages, even if a seat belt might have reduced those damages. COLO. REV. STAT. § 42–4–237(7). Is that a suitable compromise?

7. *Comparative Negligence?* Should comparative negligence take account of the failure to wear a seat belt? What if the plaintiff's fault in failing to wear a seat belt adds to plaintiff's fault in operating or maintaining the vehicle to produce a net fault greater than the defendant's fault? Some states deny recovery in those circumstances. Should plaintiff's fault in failing to wear a seat belt be considered in reducing damages that the seat belt would not have avoided? Courts have implemented a multiple step approach to segregate the portion of the fault attributable to the seat belt from diminishing recovery inappropriately. *See, e.g., Waterson v. General Motors Corp.*, 111 N.J. 238, 272–73, 544 A.2d 357, 375 (N.J. 1988).

Contract law handles precautions before breach under rules governing repudiation and reasonable grounds for insecurity. Unequivocal repudiation is treated as a breach, even if performance is not yet due. UCC § 2–610; RESTATEMENT (SECOND) OF CONTRACTS § 250. By changing the time the breach occurs, the avoidable consequences doctrine kicks in earlier. Fear that the other party might breach allows plaintiff to demand adequate assurances of performance. UCC § 2–609; RESTATEMENT (SECOND) OF CONTRACTS § 251. Failure to provide assurance is a repudiation. This didn't help Groves much; Warner continually gave assurances but failed to live up to them. Nor will it help if the plaintiff does not demand assurances. Changing the timing of the breach does not require the plaintiff to treat the breach as total—that is, to cancel the contract and look for a substitute. The trial court in *Groves* basically ruled it was unreasonable for Groves not to pursue these options more aggressively. While disagreeing on the facts, the appellate court did not reject the reasonableness inquiry.

PROBLEMS

1. *Casey's Inhaler.* Dr. Park discovered the pharmacy's error a year after it occurred. If Casey had spoken with Dr. Park sooner—say, when the symptoms got worse instead of better—the mistake might have been discovered more quickly (as it was in *Fontenot v. Wainwright*). What portion of Casey's loss should be denied on the ground that Casey could have prevented it by reasonable action? Should the analysis involve comparative negligence or avoidable consequences?

2. *Seat Belts.* Donna Driver and Tommy Turner collided at an intersection. Turner made a left turn in front of Driver, failing to yield the right of way as required by law. Driver, however, was traveling faster than the legal limit at the time. Driver's speed contributed to the accident, which might not have occurred at all if she had not been speeding. Assume that a jury could conclude that she was 25% negligent. In addition, Driver was not wearing her seatbelt. Driver sued Turner for her injuries. Driver's losses include $20,000 for medical care, $30,000 in lost earnings, and $150,000 for pain and suffering. If Driver had been wearing her seatbelt, experts agreed that her injuries would have been relatively minor, probably requiring no more than an overnight stay in the hospital for observation and a few days off work, perhaps totaling $5,000 in pecuniary losses and only 10% of the total pain and suffering ($15,000). How much should Driver recover? Specifically, if Turner's insurance company offers $15,000, should you advise your client to accept it or to litigate the case? Does it matter whether you treat the seat belt defense under the avoidable consequences doctrine or as comparative negligence?

3. PUBLIC POLICY

In your first year studies you may have understood that public policy is used in two ways.: (1) as a reason to urge a court to interpret a doctrine favorably or create an exception to the doctrine; and (2) as a contract doctrine making some contracts or terms void because they violate public policy. The doctrine discussed here is similar to the latter.

It allows a party to argue that, despite liability for a wrong, a particular remedy should not be granted because it would violate public policy. Sometimes the policy relates to the wrong itself; the remedy is inconsistent with the purpose of the rule creating liability. More commonly, the issue involves a different, conflicting policy.

TROPPI V. SCARF

31 Mich.App. 240, 187 N.W.2d 511 (1971).

[The facts of the case are presented above starting on page 769].

Public Policy. The trial court found that "to allow damages such as claimed here would be in contravention of public policy." A judicial declaration of preemptive public policy should express the manifest will of the people. Not only does contraception not violate the public policy of the State of Michigan, the legislature has recently enacted two separate statutes designed to foster the use of contraceptives. Family planning services may be supplied to medically indigent women by the State, upon request; the availability of such services is to be made known to prospective recipients of public health services. . . .

Where the State's advocacy of family planning is so vigorous as to include payments for contraceptives as part of the welfare program, public policy cannot be said to disfavor contraception. The notion that public policy may favor contraception for the poor, yet disapprove of it for the more affluent, is unworthy of serious discussion.

Contraceptives are used to prevent the birth of healthy children. To say that for reasons of public policy contraceptive failure can result in no damage as a matter of law ignores the fact that tens of millions of persons use contraceptives daily to avoid the very result which the defendant would have us say is always a benefit, never a detriment. Those tens of millions of persons, by their conduct, express the sense of the community. . . .

In theory at least, the imposition of civil liability encourages potential tortfeasors to exercise more care in the performance of their duties, and, hence, to avoid liability-producing negligent acts. Applying this theory to the case before us, public policy favors a tort scheme which encourages pharmacists to exercise great care in filling prescriptions. To absolve defendant of all liability here would be to remove one deterrent against the negligent dispensing of drugs. Given the great numbers of women who currently use oral contraceptives, such absolution cannot be defended on public policy grounds.

TAYLOR V. KURAPATI

236 Mich.App. 315, 600 N.W.2d 670 (1999).

WHITBECK, J.

Plaintiffs Brandy and Brian Taylor [appeal] the trial court's order granting summary disposition in favor of defendants Surender Kurapati, M.D., and Annapolis Hospital with respect to their wrongful birth and negligent infliction of emotional distress claims.

[During Mrs. Taylor's pregnancy, Dr. Kurapati, an agent of Annapolis and a specialist in radiology, interpreted her ultrasound test.] Kurapati concluded [that] there were no visible abnormalities with the fetus. . . . Shelby Taylor was born on April 19, 1994, with "gross anatomical deformities including missing right shoulder, fusion of left elbow, missing digits on left hand, missing femur on left leg and short femur on right." A study at the University of Michigan Hospital suggested that Shelby Taylor had femur-fibula-ulna syndrome. [T]he Taylors alleged that [Kurapati's negligent] failure to reveal the disabilities deprived the Taylors of their right to make a reproductive decision regarding the pregnancy. In addition to their claim of medical malpractice, the Taylors also alleged that, because of defendants' negligence, they suffered emotional distress at witnessing the birth of their child. [The trial court granted defendants' motions for summary disposition of plaintiffs' claims.]

[The court took up the issue of whether to overturn cases recognizing actions for wrongful birth. In the process, it recounted precedent recognizing recovery for births caused by another's negligence, including *Troppi v. Scarf.*] However, in *Rinard v. Biczak,* 441 N.W.2d 441 (Mich. App. 1989), this Court reached a far different conclusion. *Rinard* involved a suit by the plaintiffs against the defendant physician in which the plaintiffs alleged medical malpractice for the defendant's failure to diagnose Mrs. Rinard's pregnancy. At trial, the plaintiffs testified that Mrs. Rinard probably would have sought to terminate the pregnancy had the defendant properly diagnosed that pregnancy. The jury awarded the plaintiffs damages for the cost of raising their healthy child. The *Rinard* panel reversed, holding that neither natural nor adoptive parents can recover the costs of "raising a normal, healthy child because those costs are outweighed by the benefits of that child's life."

> In a proper hierarchy of values, the benefit of life should not be outweighed by the expense of supporting it. A court " 'has no business declaring that among the living are people who never should have been born.' "
>
> Another reason for not allowing the recovery of child-rearing costs as an element of damages is that, to maximize their recovery under the benefits rule, parents must demonstrate that

> they did not want their child and that the child is of minimal value to them. Michigan should not allow " 'the unseemly spectacle of parents disparaging the "value" of their children or the degree of their affection for them in open court.' " A related concern is for the child who may learn that his parents did not want him to exist and sued to have the person who made his existence possible provide for his support. . . .

This Court resolved, at least partially, this conflict in *Rouse* [*v. Wesley,* 494 N.W.2d 7 (Mich.App.1992)]. [T]he plaintiffs sued over an unsuccessful tubal ligation performed on Mrs. Rouse. [Mrs.] Rouse thereafter conceived [and] delivered a sixth, and healthy, child. While the trial court permitted the plaintiffs to maintain the action for medical costs and pain and suffering, it granted the defendants summary disposition with respect to the plaintiffs' claim for damages for the cost of raising the child to the age of majority, following the decision in *Rinard.* The *Rouse* panel held that in the context of a wrongful conception action, a plaintiff may not recover the customary cost of raising and educating the child. In reaching this narrow decision, the *Rouse* panel articulated a broader concept and one that we consider to be of surpassing importance:

> [We] recognize that the cost of raising a child to majority is significant and may, in certain circumstances, impose a hardship upon the child's parents. *We further recognize, however, that all human life is presumptively valuable. Simply stated, a child should not be considered a "harm" to its parents so as to allow recovery for the customary cost of raising the child.* Our Supreme Court has held in the context of wrongful death actions that the benefits of the services of a minor child to the child's parents are at least as great as the cost of raising the child to majority. *Similarly, in the context of a wrongful pregnancy action, we hold as a matter of law that the value of the life of a child will always outweigh the customary cost of raising that child to majority. The benefits rule is therefore inapplicable in a wrongful pregnancy action.*

We recognize that the *Rouse* decision did *not* rule out a wrongful conception action for medical costs and pain and suffering. We further recognize that *Rouse* dealt with an unwanted, *but healthy,* child while wrongful birth actions deal with unwanted, *and disabled,* children. We do *not* concede, however, that an intermediate appellate court of this state should implicitly endorse the view that the life of a disabled child is worth less than the life of a healthy child. If *all* life is presumptively valuable, how can we say that what we really mean is that all lives *except for the lives of the disabled* are presumptively valuable? If we say that the benefits rule is inapplicable to the lives of *healthy* children, how can we then continue, at least implicitly, to apply that rule to the lives of *disabled* children? If we conclude that in a proper hierarchy of values, the expense of supporting life should not outweigh the benefit of that life, how can we say that what we really mean is that such expense should not outweigh the benefit of lives of healthy children, *but can outweigh the benefit of lives of disabled children?* If we say that a court "has no business declaring that among the living are people who never should have been born," how can we continue to say—and here virtually explicitly through the device of compensating the parents for the expenses of that "wrongful birth"—that courts *can* go about the business of declaring that living, *but disabled,* children should never have been born? To say the least, this Court's language in its partial repudiation of the wrongful conception doctrine in *Rouse* raises the most troubling of questions about the continued viability of the wrongful birth tort in Michigan.[35]

This Court has partially repudiated the birth-related tort of wrongful conception and totally rejected the birth-related tort of wrongful life. Both of these causes of action are closely analogous to the birth-related tort of wrongful birth. Nevertheless, this Court, without any action by the Legislature or the Michigan Supreme Court, has continued to recognize the tort of wrongful birth. The resulting jurisprudence defies all logic. Below, we explore the origins of the wrongful birth tort in Michigan and respond to various arguments for its continuation.

C. Wrongful Birth: A Misshapen Jurisprudence

(3) The Slippery Slope of the Benefits Rule

At its intellectual core, the wrongful birth tort this Court created in *Eisbrenner* relies on the benefits rule this Court adopted in *Troppi.* To say the very least, continued reliance on this rule has some far-reaching, and profoundly disturbing, consequences. This rule invites the jury in wrongful birth cases to weigh the costs to the parents of a disabled child of bearing and raising that child against the benefits to the parents of the life of that child. This rule thus asks the jury to quantify the unquantifiable with respect to the benefits side of the equation. Further, to posit a specific question: how does a jury measure the benefits to the parents of the *whole life* of the disabled child, when the potential of that child is unknown at the time of suit? How, for example, would a hypothetical Grecian jury, operating under Michigan jurisprudence, measure the benefits to the parents of the *whole life* of Homer, the blind singer of songs who created the *Iliad* and the *Odyssey?* Absent the ability to foretell the future and to quantify the value of the spoken and then the written word, how, exactly, would the jury do that?

---

[35] While consideration of some of the rationale of "wrongful conception" cases is analytically crucial to our decision, the case at hand involves a claim for "wrongful birth," not wrongful conception. Thus, we do not address the issue whether wrongful conception claims, as distinct from wrongful birth claims and as limited by *Rouse* [remain] tenable.

Further, the use of the benefits rule in wrongful birth cases can slide ever so quickly into applied eugenics. The very phrase "wrongful birth" suggests that the birth of the disabled child was wrong and should have been prevented. If one accepts the premise that the birth of one "defective" child should have been prevented, then it is but a short step to accepting the premise that the births of classes of "defective" children should be similarly prevented, not just for the benefit of the parents but also for the benefit of society as a whole through the protection of the "public welfare." This is the operating principle of eugenics[, which] "espouses the reproduction of the 'fit' over the 'unfit' (positive eugenics) and discourages the birth of the 'unfit' (negative eugenics)."[45] . . .

Finally, we should not forget the influence that the Third Reich's experiments with sterilization had on the American eugenics movement. . . .

To our ears, at the close of the twentieth century, this talk of the "unfit" and of "defectives" has a decidedly jarring ring; we are, after all, above such lethal nonsense. But are we? We know now that we all have at least five recessive genes but, according to Bowman, when scientists map the human genome, they will unveil many more potentially harmful genes in each of us. Will we then see the tort of wrongful birth extended to physicians who neglect or misinterpret genetic evidence and thereby fail to extend the option of a eugenic abortion to the unsuspecting parents of a genetically "unfit" and "defective" child? Our current acceptance of the wrongful birth tort would require the answer to this question in Michigan to be: yes.

We further note that it is but another short half step from the concept of preventing the birth of an "unfit" or "defective" child to proposing, for the benefit of the child's overburdened parents and of the society as a whole, that the existence of the child should not be allowed to continue. Again, this sounds preposterous, but is it? . . .

If the elderly have a duty to die—indeed, to be starved to death—then why not the disabled child? After all, if that child never should have been born, then that child has no real right to go on living, thereby imposing the costs of the child's continued existence on the parents and society. This, we conclude, is the logical end of the slippery slope inherent in the application of the benefits rule through the wrongful birth tort.

(4) Conclusion

We conclude that this intermediate appellate court should not continue to recognize the wrongful birth tort without the slightest hint of approval from the Michigan Supreme Court or our Legislature. At least five states have taken legislative action to prohibit "wrongful birth" suits while one state has taken legislative action to permit such suits. If society

[45] See Bowman, *The Road to Eugenics,* 3 U. Chic. L. Sch. Roundtable 491 (1996).

is to recognize such a tort, it should do so through the action of a majority of the legislature, whose role it is to set social policy. We therefore reconsider our pre-1990 decisions establishing the wrongful birth tort and hold that, as a matter of law, it has no continued place in our jurisprudence. [Discussion of the statute of limitations and negligent infliction of emotional distress omitted.]

DOCTOROFF, P.J. (*concurring in part and dissenting in part*).

I concur with the majority's conclusion that plaintiffs' wrongful birth claim is barred by the statute of limitations and with the majority's resolution of plaintiffs' negligent infliction of emotional distress claim. However, I dissent from the majority opinion with respect to its purported abolition of the wrongful birth tort where this Court's recognition of that tort was not challenged by the parties or decided by the trial court.

First, the majority's attempt to abolish the wrongful birth tort [is] merely dictum with no precedential value. . . . Moreover, the majority's conclusion that the wrongful birth tort should be abolished was made without the aid of briefing or argument by the parties.

NOTES AND QUESTIONS

1. *Divided Authorities. Troppi* may look easy, but it was not universal. One court rejected plaintiff's contract claim because public policy could not tolerate treating a healthy (fifth) child as a loss. *Shaheen v. Knight*, 11 Pa.Dist. & Co.R.2d 41 (Pa.1957) ("to allow damages for the normal birth of a normal child is foreign to the universal public sentiment of the people"). The High Court of Australia recently collected precedent from around the globe (in more than 600 footnotes), ultimately affirming an award for costs of raising a healthy child. *Cattanach v. Melchior*, 199 A.L.R. 131 (2003) (2003 WL 21653096).

2. *Genetic Counseling*. Other contexts can make the policy issues even closer. To avoid a child with serious genetic defects, some parents choose to abort after an ultrasound or other test reveals the defect. A failure to perform the test carefully can preclude the opportunity to make that choice. In a state that decrees life begins at conception, would public policy preclude recovery for damages that could have been avoided only by abortion? Does the constitutional right precluding a state from criminally punishing an abortion include a constitutional right precluding a state from applying the public policy doctrine to state law tort damages? Does the constitution preclude the state from having a public policy or simply from embodying it by prohibiting abortion?

3. *Liability Issue?* On one view, *Taylor* rejects liability rather than a remedy. It purports to reject a cause of action for wrongful birth, wrongful life, or wrongful conception. But these actions are not distinct grounds for liability; they are defined by the injury (the birth), not the wrong. Most cases are medical malpractice, though *Troppi* involves pharmaceutical negligence

(or breach of a sales contract). The court did not reject these causes of action, just damages related to the birth. Thus, in *Barnes v. Vettraino*, 2003 WL 1558229 (No. 235357) (Mich. App. Mar 25, 2003), the court awarded damages associated with a delayed but successful abortion. The dissent noted the incentive this creates: doctors can avoid liability by never revealing a diagnosed genetic condition. The majority hoped professional ethics would prevent such conduct.

Does the policy announced in *Taylor* apply to intentional misconduct that produces a child? Suppose a doctor withholds information about a birth defect, knowing that the parents would abort if accurately informed. Will the resulting birth support a damage claim? By statute, Michigan recognized claims resulting from gross negligence or intentional misconduct. MICH. COMP. L. § 600.2971. But gross negligence that occurred before the effective date of the statute remained irremediable. *Wilson v. Mercy Hosp.*, 2003 WL 245823 (No. 234562) (Mich. App. Feb. 4, 2003). Would that apply to intentional wrongs, too? What if the statute had not been adopted?

4. *Identifying the Policy. Taylor* did not rest on a policy against abortion. Can the court's policy be stated succinctly? When stated, is it still apparent that this is the policy of the state? Is the policy here based on equal protection? Or is the court simply unwilling to associate itself with a position it finds unseemly? Is unwillingness to "soil the judicial ermine" sufficient basis for public policy?

5. *Interpretive Technique.* Sometimes the doctrine prevents statutes from being misapplied. Consider *Brunswick Corp. v. Pueblo Bowl–O–Mat*, 429 U.S. 477, 97 S.Ct. 690, 50 L.Ed.2d 701 (1977). Brunswick sold equipment to bowling alleys. When buyers defaulted on the payments, Brunswick would buy the bowling alley and operate it in order to collect some of the money owed. In this way, Brunswick acquired more bowling alleys than any other business. The owner of a local bowling alley sued Brunswick for antitrust violations, alleging as damages that if Brunswick had not bought a local competitor, it would have gone out of business and, thus, plaintiff would have obtained more revenue by picking up a share of those customers. The trial court held that Brunswick's conduct tended to create a monopoly, in violation of the antitrust laws. On appeal, the Supreme Court held that plaintiff's damages were not recoverable. The statute was designed to protect competition, but plaintiff's damages stemmed from too much competition (Brunswick keeping a bowling alley open instead of letting it close). That kind of loss was not what the statute sought to protect.

6. *Competing Policies.* The doctrine also comes into play when both parties are wrongdoers. For instance, suppose an employer reports employees who are not legally in the country to the INS because the employees tried to organize a union. Discrimination against employees based on union activity violates the National Labor Relations Act. If the employees sue, are they entitled to reinstatement and back pay? How can they be entitled to jobs that it was illegal for them to have in the first place? Does one public policy

preclude relief that another public policy requires? *See Sure–Tan, Inc. v. NLRB*, 467 U.S. 883, 104 S.Ct. 2803, 81 L.Ed.2d 732 (1984).

7. *Balancing Interests*. On one view, *Troppi* is a case of competing policies. The court considers not only the public policy against contraception (which it rejects), but also the public policy favoring tort recoveries to deter wrongdoing. Should *Shaheen* (which accepted the policy against treating healthy children as a net loss) have balanced that policy against the policy favoring contract recoveries to deter breaches? Are some policies too important to balance? Consider the following approach:

> A promise or other term of an agreement is unenforceable on grounds of public policy if legislation provides that it is unenforceable or the interest in its enforcement is clearly outweighed in the circumstances by a public policy against the enforcement of such terms.

RESTATEMENT (SECOND) OF CONTRACTS § 178(1) (1981). The first provision leaves room for the legislature to draw the balance itself; the second addresses legislative silence. Could a court balance policies favoring union activity with policies disfavoring illegal immigration? How?

D. AGREED REMEDIES

1. LIQUIDATED DAMAGES

In your first year studies, you may have learned that penalty clauses are void because they violate public policy. Liquidated damage clauses, however, are enforceable. The difference depends on the substance of the provision. A clause providing a reasonable estimate of the loss is a liquidated damages clause. A clause providing an unreasonably large recovery is a penalty. A liquidated damages provision can serve many useful functions. Agreement in advance can minimize costly efforts to prove damages at a trial or arbitration. In addition, the clause can reduce uncertainty as to the amount of damages, either by limiting damages that might be too large or providing damages that might be difficult to prove with certainty. Liquidated damages also may promote settlement, especially if liability is relatively clear. As a general matter, then, courts should allow the parties to fix the amount of damages in advance.

RIDGLEY V. TOPA THRIFT AND LOAN ASSOCIATION

17 Cal.4th 970, 953 P.2d 484, 73 Cal.Rptr.2d 378 (1998).

WERDEGAR, J.

Defendant loaned plaintiffs $2.3 million for two years, secured by real property plaintiffs had improved and intended to sell. Plaintiffs sold the property before the loan matured and, on defendant's demand, repaid the loan principal, together with a prepayment fee of about $113,000, equal to six months' interest. Under the parties' loan agreement, plaintiffs owed defendant a prepayment fee at the time of sale only if plaintiffs had been more than 15 days late with any scheduled interest payment or had defaulted on any other contractual obligation to defendant; the fee was imposed here because plaintiffs had been late with an interest payment.

Plaintiffs sued to recover the prepayment charge they had paid. The question presented is whether such a prepayment charge, conditioned on late interest payments, constitutes an unenforceable liquidation of damages or penalty for late payment of interest (Civ. Code, § 1671, subd. (b)) or an enforceable provision for alternative performance, that is, a surcharge compensating defendant for prepayment of the principal. We conclude the trial court correctly understood the prepayment provision here to be a penalty for delinquency in meeting the contractual interest payments and thus correctly held the penalty to be unenforceable, because it bore no relationship to the potential damages defendant would incur from a late interest payment. We therefore reverse the judgment of the Court of Appeal, which reversed the trial court's judgment for plaintiffs.

Factual and Procedural Background

Plaintiff Robert M. Ridgley is an architect and property developer. In 1990, as part of Robert's business, he purchased a parcel in Encino (the Property) in order to build a luxury custom home for speculation and sale. As of late 1990, the construction was almost complete and the home was on the market for sale. The construction loan was coming due and Robert was looking for a bridge loan, *i.e.*, a short-term loan between the construction loan and the buyer's permanent loan.

After negotiation, the parties agreed on the terms of a loan in the amount of $2.3 million. Repayment of the principal was due December 21, 1992. Interest payments, at a variable rate of interest, were due monthly on the 21st day of the month. The Note, in its preprinted text, contained provision for a prepayment charge, as follows:

> Borrower may at any time prepay the outstanding principal balance of this Note in whole or in part; provided, however, Borrower will pay to Lender a prepayment charge of six (6) months' interest at the rate in effect at the time of prepayment on the amount prepaid. Such a prepayment charge will be made whether such prepayments are made voluntarily, involuntarily or upon acceleration of this Note. No such prepayment charge will be made on prepayments made five (5) or more years after the date of this Note.

During negotiations, Robert objected to the five-year prepayment charge provision. In response, Topa inserted a typewritten addendum stating:

> Provided All Scheduled Payments Have Been Received Not More Than 15 Days After Their Scheduled Due Date, and Further Provided That There Have Been No Other Defaults Under the Terms of This Note or Any Other Now Existing or Future Obligation of Borrower to Topa, Then No Prepayment Charge Will Be Assessed If This Loan Is Paid in Full After June 21, 1991.

[Interest was paid on time through January 1, 1992, in part because Topa agreed to accept interest payments on the first instead of the twenty-first of each month. No further payment was made until March 12, 1992.] By February, the Property was in escrow and scheduled to close in April.

Topa made a payment demand to the escrow officer for $2,365,502, which included a prepayment charge of $113,046, as well as a demand fee and a late charge purportedly for the March payment, these charges and fees together totaling $114,622. Plaintiffs objected to these assessments. Topa agreed to and did release the deed of trust on the Property and maintained the $114,622 balance as a lien on plaintiffs' house. Plaintiffs ultimately paid off this balance, plus accrued interest, when they refinanced their house.

Plaintiffs sued Topa [to recover the prepayment charges.] The causes of action were tried to the court, which ruled "that the prepayment clause as written by [Topa] was in fact a late charge and a penalty in the nature of an unenforceable forfeiture. Judgment therefore is awarded to [plaintiffs] and against [Topa] in the sum of $114,622.42" plus interest paid, prejudgment interest, costs and attorney's fees.

Topa appealed from the judgment for plaintiffs, who also appealed, challenging the adequacy of the attorney's fee award. The Court of Appeal reversed the judgment, concluding the prepayment charge was "not made invalid by conditioning a waiver upon a lack of default. Accordingly, we hold that as the penalty was triggered by the prepayment, it was a valid prepayment provision and was not an invalid late charge or forfeiture." We granted plaintiffs' petition for review. We reverse and remand for consideration of plaintiffs' appeal.

Discussion

The central question is whether the provision contained in the parties' typewritten addendum should be viewed as a charge for prepayment of the loan principal (the position taken by Topa and the Court of Appeal majority) or as a penalty for delinquency in a monthly interest payment (the position taken by plaintiffs, the trial court and the dissenting Court of Appeal justice). We briefly review the law regarding both late payment penalties and charges for prepayment of principal.

Civil Code section 3275, unchanged since 1872, provides: "Whenever, by the terms of an obligation, a party thereto incurs a forfeiture, or a loss in the nature of a forfeiture, by reason of his failure to comply with its provisions, he may be relieved therefrom, upon making full compensation to the other party, except in the case of a grossly negligent, willful, or fraudulent breach of duty." The breaching party may raise section 3275 as an equitable defense to enforcement of the contractual provision or as grounds for relief in an action for restitution of the property forfeited.

California law has also long recognized that a provision for liquidation of damages for contractual breach—for example, a preset late payment penalty—can under some circumstances be designed as, and operate as, a contractual forfeiture. To prevent such operation, our laws place limits on liquidated damages clauses. Under the 1872 Civil Code, a provision by which damages for a breach of contract were determined in anticipation of breach was enforceable only if determining actual damages was impracticable or extremely difficult. 1872 Civ. Code, §§ 1670, 1671. As amended in 1977, the code continues to apply that strict standard to liquidated damages clauses in certain contracts (consumer goods and services, and leases of residential real property (§ 1671(c), (d))), but somewhat liberalizes the rule as to other contracts: "[A] provision in a contract liquidating the damages for breach of the contract is valid unless the party seeking to invalidate the provision establishes that the provision was unreasonable under the circumstances existing at the time the contract was made." § 1671 (b).

A liquidated damages clause will generally be considered unreasonable, and hence unenforceable under section 1671(b), if it bears no reasonable relationship to the range of actual damages that the parties could have anticipated would flow from a breach. The amount set as liquidated damages "must represent the result of a reasonable endeavor by the parties to estimate a fair average compensation for any loss that may be sustained." In the absence of such relationship, a contractual clause purporting to predetermine damages "must be construed as a penalty." In short, "[a]n amount disproportionate to the anticipated damages is termed a 'penalty.' A contractual provision imposing a 'penalty' is ineffective, and the wronged party can collect only the actual damages sustained."

In contrast to late payment fees, contractual charges for *prepayment* of the loan principal are generally considered valid provisions for alternative performance, rather than penalties or liquidated damages for breach. Payment before maturity is not a breach of the contract, but simply an alternative mode of performance on the borrower's part; the prepayment charge is not a penalty imposed for default, but an agreed form of compensation to the lender for interest lost through prepayment, additional tax liability or other disadvantage.

If fairly characterized simply as a prepayment charge, then, the clause at issue here was valid.[3] If viewed as a charge for late payment of interest, however, the clause has to meet the reasonableness standard of section 1671, and must be deemed unreasonable, and unenforceable as a penalty, under *Garrett*.[4] The complication presented by this case is that the charge here was contingent on *both* events, prepayment of principal *and* late payment of an interest installment (or other default). It can be described, therefore, as both a prepayment charge and a late payment penalty.

We have consistently ignored form and sought out the substance of arrangements which purport to legitimate penalties and forfeitures. Looking to the substance rather than the form of the disputed provision, we agree with the superior court and the Court of Appeal dissenter that it was invalid because it was intended to, and did, operate as a penalty for late payment. However one describes its form, the intent and effect of the disputed provision here was that any late payment or other default by plaintiffs would result in a severe penalty—the inability to sell the Property without payment of a sizable preset charge. The circumstances of this transaction rendered the forfeited opportunity to sell without penalty before maturity of the loan particularly significant to plaintiffs, who had improved the Property with the intent of selling it and had obtained the Topa loan merely to "bridge" the period until sale. To Topa, moreover, the value of the disputed provision was clearly to be found in its operation as a penalty for late payment rather than as compensation for prepayment. After plaintiffs made six months of interest payments (after June 21, 1991, that is), Topa would impose the prepayment charge *only* if during the period of the loan plaintiffs had made a late payment or were otherwise in contractual default. That contractual stipulation shows that, from Topa's viewpoint, the purpose of the threatened charge, after June 21, 1991, was to coerce timely payment of interest, not to compensate Topa for interest payments lost through prepayment of principal.

As the dissenting justice below explained,

---

[3] In the present case, of course, plaintiffs' prepayment was not at their own option; instead, it resulted from Topa's demand for accelerated payment on sale. The prepayment charge provision, however, expressly applied to acceleration, and plaintiffs do not challenge its validity on that basis, but because it was triggered by a late interest payment.

[4] Topa proffers no plausible argument that a charge of six months' interest on the principal represents "the result of a reasonable endeavor by the parties to estimate a fair average compensation for any loss that may be sustained" for late payment of an interest installment. The contract, moreover, expressly provides for a reasonable late payment fee equal to 10 percent of the payment.

> In effect, by limiting its unconditional recovery of prepayment interest to the first six months, Topa was saying it would recover enough in interest payments during that period to compensate fully for lost future interest payments as well as the administrative costs of negotiating this loan and then replacing it with a new loan from another borrower for whatever term remained on this loan. But to ensure the Ridgleys would not be late on any of their interest payments (or default on any other terms of the contract), Topa held over their heads the threat of a $113,000 prepayment penalty which could be collected only "in the event of [such] default."
>
> [Topa does not explain] the logical relationship between a borrower's late payment of one of the monthly interest charges and the rationale for allowing lenders to collect prepayment penalties. [I]t is difficult to comprehend how Topa suffered a greater loss at the time the Ridgleys paid off this loan because they had been late with one payment (or even had it been two or three or more) than they would have had the Ridgleys been current with every payment during the period the loan remained in effect. To put it another way, the amount of Topa's lost future interest payments and extra administrative expenses is determined by *when* the Ridgleys paid off the loan and not by whether they were or were not late with some interest payments during the period the loan was in effect. Accordingly, it is more than apparent this prepayment penalty is being imposed as a penalty for the Ridgleys' default in being tardy with one or more monthly interest payments and not to compensate Topa for its lost future interest payments or extra administrative expenses attendant to relending this money.

That would not be fatal, of course, if the amount of the preset charge constituted a reasonable attempt to estimate potential losses from late payment. "A liquidated damages provision is not invalid merely because it is intended to encourage a party to perform, so long as it represents a reasonable attempt to anticipate the losses to be suffered." *Weber, Lipshie & Co. v. Christian* (1997) 52 Cal.App.4th 645, 656 60 Cal.Rptr.2d 677]. But, as mentioned earlier, the charge of six months' interest on the entire principal, imposed for any late payment or other default, cannot be defended as a reasonable attempt to anticipate damages from default.

Topa describes the disputed provision as a "conditional waiver of the prepayment charge" and contends that "[i]f this Court recognizes the right of Topa to the payment of a charge upon prepayment of the loan, then it must also recognize that Topa could waive that right upon conditions bargained for in the context of the commercial transaction at issue." We disagree. That the prepayment fee might have been imposed without condition does not imply it may validly be imposed on the condition of plaintiffs' late payment of interest. A forfeiture or unreasonable penalty, imposed only upon the other party's default, is unenforceable even though the same money, property or other consideration might have validly been bargained for as a form of contractual performance. A contrary conclusion would allow unreasonable late charges and other penalties to escape legal scrutiny through simple rephrasing as a conditional waiver. Under Topa's "conditional waiver" theory, virtually any penalty or forfeiture could be enforced if characterized as a waiver. To accept that theory would be to "condone a result which, although directly prohibited by the Legislature, may nevertheless be indirectly accomplished through the imagination of inventive minds." We will not do so.

Because Topa's demand for a prepayment fee of $113,046 was based on an unenforceable penalty provision, the superior court correctly found for plaintiffs. The judgment of the Court of Appeal is reversed.

The matter is transferred to the Court of Appeal for consideration of plaintiffs' appeal.

MOSK, J.

I dissent. In this commercial transaction, involving a "bridge loan" in connection with the building for sale of a luxury "spec" home, the loan document included a clause to the following effect: If borrowers prepaid the loan within six months, there would be a prepayment charge of six months' interest. After that time, "provided all scheduled payments have been received not more than 15 days after their scheduled due date" and there were no other defaults, no prepayment charge would be assessed. The majority now conclude that although lender had a right to impose a prepayment charge in a commercial transaction of this kind, the fee here was a disguised penalty for late payment.

I disagree. The prepayment clause was a negotiated agreement between sophisticated commercial parties. The original loan agreement included a straight prepayment requirement. For an additional consideration, the lender agreed to modify the loan agreement to waive the prepayment charge after six months, on the condition that borrowers made timely payments and avoided default. The condition was not met. Borrowers were late on several payments. The late payments did not trigger a penalty; indeed, lender waived late fees and even agreed to a new payment schedule. Borrowers, however, failed to meet the condition that they had negotiated for avoiding a prepayment charge. They could have continued to make payments through the life of the loan. They chose instead to prepay. Even with the prepayment charge they incurred a significant savings—in the amount of approximately two months of scheduled payments.

Nor do I agree that regarding the provision at issue here as a conditional waiver of the prepayment charge would encourage hypothetical devious lenders to achieve a result prohibited by the Legislature. Rather, the result of the majority's holding will be to limit the ability of commercial borrowers to negotiate to avoid the expense of prepayment charges.

RED SAGE LIMITED PARTNERSHIP V. DESPA DEUTSCHE SPARKASSEN IMMOBILIEN–ANLAGE–GASELLSCHAFT MBH

254 F.3d 1120 (D.C.Cir.2001).

TATEL, CIRCUIT JUDGE:

A Washington, D.C. restaurant sought a declaration that its landlord breached an exclusive use covenant by renting space in the same building to a specialty cake shop. The restaurant claimed that under its lease, the breach entitled it to a 50 percent rent abatement. The district court granted summary judgment for the landlord, finding that under the circumstances of this case, a 50 percent rent abatement would constitute an unenforceable penalty. Because we conclude that the rent abatement, negotiated by sophisticated parties, was not an unreasonable estimate of the damages likely to result from a breach of the exclusive covenant, and because the landlord's additional arguments for summary judgment fail, we reverse and remand for further proceedings.

I

Red Sage Limited Partnership operates an "internationally known . . . fine dining" restaurant in the Westory building, a Washington D.C. office building. In the same building, Red Sage operates several private dining rooms used for catering and special events, a casual Tex–Mex restaurant, and the Red Sage Market, a take-out facility that sells sandwiches, salads, snacks, cold drinks, tea, coffee, and desserts, including a variety of whole cakes available by special order.

Red Sage first leased space in the Westory building in September of 1990. At that time, the building was owned by 607 14th Street Associates Limited Partnership. Insofar as the original landlord, through his wife, had an ownership interest in Red Sage, the original lease was not negotiated at arm's length. The lease provided that "[t]enant shall use and occupy the Leased Premises solely as a bar and/or a restaurant." The lease also included the following exclusive covenant and penalty clause:

34. *Exclusive Covenant*

(a) To the extent permitted by law, Landlord covenants that during the Term it shall not permit any other tenant within the Building to operate a bar, restaurant or food service establishment of any kind (a "Competing Use").

The provisions of this Section 34 shall be enforceable only so long as Tenant is operating a bar and/or a restaurant in the Leased Premises.

* * *

(e) In the event that a Competing Use is operated in the Building at any time during the Term and Landlord has violated its covenants under this Section 34, then (i) one half (½) of the Base Rent payable hereunder shall be abated during the period that the Competing Use is operated in the Building, and (ii) Tenant may terminate this Lease if the operation of the Competing Use continues for a period of six (6) months after written notice thereof by Tenant to Landlord. . . . The provisions of this subsection (e) shall not limit . . . any other remedies which Tenant may have against Landlord for violating its obligations under this Section.

[I]n 1996, 14th Street Associates and Red Sage executed an Amended and Restated Lease. The amended lease contained the same exclusive covenant and penalty clause as the original lease, but included a revised tenant use provision [to include] "any and all activities incidental or related thereto, including, but not limited to, operating a retail general store primarily selling t-shirts, sweatshirts, souvenirs, spices, baked goods, foods and other items related to Tenant's bar and restaurant." The new lease also set base rent at "six and one-half percent . . . of [Red Sage's] Gross Revenues, but in no event less than Four Hundred Thousand Dollars." The parties do not dispute that this lease was executed at arm's length.

In 1997, in preparation for the sale of the Westory Building to DespaEuropa—Red Sage's current landlord and appellee in this case—14th Street Associates and Red Sage again amended the lease. This amendment left intact the tenant use, base rent, exclusive covenant, and penalty clause provisions in the amended lease, stating that "[a]ll terms and provisions of the Lease which are not amended hereby are hereby ratified and confirmed in all respects." Red Sage asserts that Despa was "actively involved" in negotiating the 1997 amendment, since "reformulation of the Red Sage Lease was a precondition to the purchase of the Westory Building by Despa." Despa asserts that it "was not involved in any way in the negotiations for or the drafting of the Red Sage Lease, but rather inherited it as a second or third generation owner of the building." It is undisputed, however, that a Despa representative signed the 1997 amendment, endorsing it "Accepted and Agreed."

Later that year, Despa purchased the Westory building and, the following year, leased space in the building to a specialty store known as

Cakes & Company, triggering the dispute. Cakes' original lease permitted it to operate a "bakery/café" selling "specialty cakes, baked goods, coffee, non-alcoholic beverages and associated paper goods," but Despa later amended the lease, deleting the reference to operating a "café" and permitting Cakes to sell food items only for consumption off the premises. The parties agree that Cakes primarily sold whole cakes—prepared elsewhere and decorated on-site—for weddings and special occasions. It also sold tea, coffee, single slices of cake, and some of the same prepackaged drinks sold by Red Sage Market. Cakes had no menu, wait staff, or customer tables or chairs. In Cakes' first four months of operation, its gross sales were almost $95,000, its gross profits around $50,000, and its net income about $11,000.

Learning of the lease to Cakes, Red Sage wrote to Despa, asserting that the landlord was violating the exclusive covenant in Red Sage's lease and requesting a 50 percent rent abatement. Despa replied: "The exclusive right you currently enjoy in your lease . . . pertains to a competing 'food service operation.' Cakes & Company could not infringe upon the highly stylized and critically acclaimed Red Sage."

Red Sage then sued Despa in the Superior Court for the District of Columbia, seeking a declaration that Despa "has breached and continues to breach section 34 of the Lease, [and] that as a result of this breach Red Sage is entitled to an abatement of one-half of the Base rent. . . ." Despa removed the case to federal court. . . .

Despa [moved] for summary judgment on the ground that the rent abatement provision in Red Sage's lease constituted an unenforceable penalty. [T]he district court granted Despa's motion, finding that since "a rent abatement of $200,000 . . . would indeed impose an improper penalty," Despa was entitled to judgment as a matter of law.

At some point following the grant of summary judgment, Cakes closed its shop in the Westory building and terminated its lease with Despa. The dispute in this case thus concerns the value of the abatement for the period during which Cakes operated. "We review a grant of summary judgment de novo, applying the same standard as the district court. Summary judgment is appropriate when there is no genuine issue as to any material fact and the moving party is entitled to judgment as a matter of law."

II

We begin with a threshold issue: Red Sage urges us to treat the rent abatement provision not as a liquidated damages clause, but rather as a contractual provision adjusting rent in response to changed conditions. Noting that parties to a lease sometimes agree in advance that rent will change upon the occurrence of future conditions, Red Sage argues that the rent abatement provision here reflects the parties' understanding that "the premises leased by Red Sage" would be "less valuable to Red Sage if there exist[ed] [another] bar, restaurant, or food service establishment in the [b]uilding." Acting on this understanding, the parties "provided for a partial abatement of base rent in the event a Competing Use is operated in the building." "[N]ot knowing the precise nature of the . . . food service establishment which might some day be located in the Building," they "predetermined" that a competing use would diminish the "value of Red Sage's premises" by "one half of the Base Rent." The abatement provision, Red Sage argues, is "no different than provisions in leases for increased rental in the event of a holdover tenancy, which are routinely enforced even if the increased rental is three, four or even five times the normal rental rate."

This argument requires little discussion. Under D.C. law, "the written language of a contract governs the parties' rights unless it is not susceptible of clear meaning." Here, we think it clear from the language of the contract that the rent abatement provision was a liquidated damages clause, not a rent adjustment. To begin with, the clause states both that "[r]ent . . . shall be abated" if the landlord "*violate*[*s*]" the exclusive covenant and that the rent abatement "shall not limit . . . any other *remedies* which Tenant may have against Landlord for violating its obligations under this Section" (emphasis added). This language strongly suggests that the rent abatement is a "remed[y]" for a "viola[tion]" of the lease, rather than a mere adjustment for changed circumstances. Reinforcing this conclusion, the provision allows Red Sage not only to abate its rent if the exclusive lease covenant is violated, but also to "terminate [its] lease if the operation of the Competing Use continues for a period of six . . . months after written notice thereof by Tenant to Landlord." The possibility of termination is in some tension with the notion of a rent adjustment, since it contemplates not an ongoing landlord-tenant relationship under different terms, but an end to the relationship altogether. Finally, Red Sage's analogy to tenant holdover cases actually undermines its argument: while Red Sage does cite one case from another jurisdiction treating a double rent provision for holdover tenants as a simple rent adjustment, the District of Columbia case it cites treats a similar provision as a liquidated damages clause.

We thus turn to Red Sage's main argument: that, assuming the rent abatement provision is a liquidated damages clause, it is valid and enforceable. In reaching a contrary conclusion, the district court invoked the principle that "[i]f there is doubt as to whether the parties intended to provide for legitimate liquidated damages, courts routinely construe liquidated damages provisions as penalties" and thus decline to enforce them "to prevent forfeitures." In applying this principle, the court neither developed an evidentiary record of nor relied on extrinsic evidence regarding the parties' intent. Instead, the court found "considerable doubt" about the parties' intentions regarding the rent abatement clause for two other reasons. First, "[t]he absence of arms length negotiation undercuts the ordinary presumption that the language on which the contracting parties have agreed accurately reflects their intent." Second, since "Red Sage Market . . . did not exist when the lease was written," even if the rent abatement clause represented a "reasonable effort" by the parties to estimate damages from breach of the exclusive covenant, that estimate "obviously related to . . . competition from a substantial 'food service establishment,' and not from a small operation that would not compete with Red Sage's principal business of operating a restaurant." Thus finding that the parties had not clearly intended to provide for liquidated damages in a case like this, the court construed the rent abatement as a penalty and refused to enforce it.

[N]oting that summary judgment is inappropriate "if extrinsic evidence supports more than one reasonable interpretation of [a] contract," Red Sage points out that it submitted an affidavit from the drafter of the original lease stating that the rent abatement provision was intended to estimate damages from breach of the exclusive covenant. The same affidavit, while acknowledging that Red Sage Market did not exist at the time, made clear that *none* of Red Sage's businesses was operating at that time, and that *all* aspects of its operation, including the Market, were contemplated by the parties.

We need not resolve this aspect of Red Sage's challenge to the district court's decision, however, because both the district court's reasoning and Red Sage's responses concern the original 1990 lease negotiated between 14th Street Associates and Red Sage, and as we read the record, Red Sage's dispute with Despa concerns the 1997 amended lease. Unlike the 1990 lease, the later lease was negotiated at arms length, and Red Sage Market was operating in 1997. We therefore consider for the first time whether the rent abatement provision in the 1997 amended lease was a penalty clause, focusing in the first instance on its plain language.

In *Davy v. Crawford*, 147 F.2d 574 (D.C.Cir.1945), this court set out standards for deciding whether a liquidated damages provision is an unenforceable penalty under District of Columbia law. Because of its importance to this case, we quote the relevant passage in full:

> [T]he parties to a contract may agree in advance to a sum certain which shall be forfeited as liquidated damages for breach of the contract without reference to the actual damages found at the time of the breach. But if such an agreement is for a penalty it is void. In order to determine whether or not the provision should be construed as a penalty the contract must be construed as a whole as of the date of its execution. If under the circumstances and expectations of the parties existing at the time of execution it appears that the provision is a reasonable protection against uncertain future litigation the provision will be enforced even

> though no actual damages were proved as of the date of the breach. If, on the other hand, it appears that the stipulation is designed to make the default of the party against whom it runs more profitable to the other party than performance would be, it will be void as a penalty. Thus, damages stipulated in advance should not be more than those which at the time of the execution of the contract can be reasonably expected from its future breach, and agreements to pay fixed sums plainly without reasonable relation to any probable damage which may follow a breach will not be enforced.

Davy, 147 F.2d at 575 (citations omitted). The D.C. Code governing leases, enacted many years after *Davy*, sets forth essentially the same standard: "Damages payable by either party for default . . . may be liquidated in the lease agreement, but only at an amount or by a formula that is reasonable in light of the then anticipated harm caused by the default." D.C. Code Ann. § 28:2A–504(a).

Applying these standards, we think the rent abatement provision in the 1997 amended lease is valid as a matter of law. To begin with, as Red Sage claims, at the time the lease was signed, the parties could reasonably have believed the damages resulting from a breach of the exclusive covenant would be difficult to ascertain, rendering future litigation "uncertain." Disagreeing with this conclusion, Despa suggests that damages to Red Sage's restaurant business from a competing food service establishment would have been easy to calculate by analyzing overhead and table turnover to derive the value of lost sales. As Red Sage points out, however, even if it could demonstrate a decline in sales, "isolat[ing] the new competitor as the sole reason for the decline" would be "almost impossible," making damages difficult to prove. Moreover, "[l]ost sales do not represent the only damages potentially arising from competition . . . damages may take the form of lost opportunities whereby the new competitor, instead of having an impact on existing sales, affects the restaurant's ability to increase sales." Damages might also include a variety of intangible losses such as lost goodwill, which would likewise be difficult to calculate and prove.

We also cannot say that the abatement is "plainly without reasonable relation to any probable damage which may follow a breach." Despa disagrees, arguing that it would have been unreasonable to think the damages resulting from Cakes' competition with Red Sage Market—which the lease describes as an "incidental use" and which produces only a small portion of Red Sage's total income—would amount to 50 percent of its rent for *all* its operations, especially in view of the fact that the same measure of damages would apply to competition from a large-scale operation such as another bar and restaurant. The question before us, however, is not whether a 50 percent rent abatement would have been a reasonable estimate of anticipated damages from a competitor on the scale of Cakes. We read the exclusive covenant as intending to ensure that Red Sage will be the only "bar, restaurant[,] or food service establishment of any kind" in the Westory building: as Red Sage put it in its motion for summary judgment, the purpose of the covenant was to "prevent[ ] another destination restaurant from opening in the Westory Building" and "to prevent[ ] the location of another food service business in the Westory Building to service the office tenants." The rent abatement provision sets damages for a breach of this covenant, and such a breach could involve a wide variety of competing uses giving rise to a wide range of possible damages. The question we must ask is thus whether a 50 percent reduction in base rent was reasonable as a single formula intended to estimate damages from a wide variety of possible competing uses.

Although it is true, as Red Sage itself acknowledges, that the parties might well have anticipated that damages from a competitor like Cakes would probably be less than 50 percent of base rent ($200,000 in this case), the parties might also have anticipated that damages from a competing restaurant would be considerably greater than this amount. (Though its net income was not especially high, Red Sage's annual gross income in a recent year was around $6.5 million.) Accordingly, as a single formula designed to capture the expected value of damages from breach of the exclusive covenant, we cannot say that half of base rent was unreasonable as a matter of law.

Nor do we think the rent abatement provision "appears . . . designed to make the default of the party against whom it runs more profitable to the other party than performance would be." Although in this case the rent abatement clause might well result in Red Sage receiving more than it actually lost as a result of Cakes' competition, the clause might significantly underestimate Red Sage's damages in other circumstances, such as if the landlord were to rent space to another upscale, full-service restaurant. In other words, the provision does not guarantee Red Sage a windfall in case of a breach. *Cf. Raffel v. Medallion Kitchens of Minn.*, 139 F.3d 1142, 1144–46 (7th Cir.1998) (invalidating as a penalty a lease provision requiring tenant to pay a "windfall" equivalent to seven months' rent if rent was more than thirty days late).

Despa's strongest argument is that the very use of a single formula to capture such a wide range of damages renders the clause unenforceable. Because the rent abatement provision "applies to a variety of types of defaults, each of which could have vastly differing degrees of damages associated with them," Despa urges us to declare it "null and void, under the reasoning that there could not have been a good faith attempt to pre-estimate possible damages, since the real and obvious possibility existed that the damages provided for would turn out to be excessive." In support of this claim, Despa relies on *Davy*, which involved a lease for a house. Under the lease, the tenant had an option to purchase at the end of a fixed rental period. The lease required a "down payment," which it described as "compensation for the option to purchase and also liquidated damages for failure to exercise it." But the lease also provided that the down payment (together with any accumulated equity in the house) would be forfeited for breach of "any covenant" in the lease, including such things as promises to pay gas, electric, and water bills on time. The court found that the forfeiture provision was an unenforceable penalty in part because the damages applicable to a major breach—failure to exercise the option to purchase—would also have applied to a "minor and insubstantial default" on the part of the breaching party. According to Despa, the same is true here: under Red Sage's interpretation of the lease, the 50 percent abatement applies whether the "competing use" is a small-scale operation like Cakes that competes incidentally with Red Sage, or a full-scale restaurant competing directly with Red Sage's principal businesses.

This case, however, differs from *Davy* in at least four significant ways. First, the provision at issue in *Davy* called for forfeiture of a fixed sum regardless of the nature of the breach. The rent abatement provision at issue here, in contrast, does not set damages as a single sum: because the provision applies only as long as a competing use is present, damages will vary with the duration of the competing use. Second, the provision at issue in *Davy* appears to have been one-sided: the down payment would have been forfeited for failure to exercise the option, or for a variety of smaller breaches, but never, it seems to us, in a situation that would have disadvantaged the landlord. Here, because the rent abatement clause could just as easily have under- as over-estimated actual damages, the provision appears not to have been intended to penalize Despa. Third—and closely related—the court in *Davy* found the lease as a whole, including both the liquidated damages provision and other parts of the contract, to have an "unconscionable and overreaching character" that heavily favored the landlord at the expense of the tenant. Here, neither party claims that the lease as a whole is unconscionable and overreaching. Finally, and perhaps most important, the agreement in *Davy* appears to have involved a corporate landlord and a private individual. The rent abatement provision in Red Sage's lease, in contrast, was negotiated by sophisticated parties, and District of Columbia courts, as well as Maryland courts, to which District of Columbia courts often look for guidance, are generally reluctant to disturb terms agreed upon by such parties.

All liquidated damages clauses, if implemented in situations where damages are difficult to estimate, will generally end up either over- or under-estimating actual damages. And while the range of possible damages in this case is quite wide, the parties may have had good reason for wanting a broad exclusive use covenant: for example, they may have wished to ensure expansive protection for Red Sage's food service operations. The parties may also have had good reason for wanting a single formula for calculating damages from a breach of the exclusive covenant: they may have worried that specifying different levels of damages to cover different levels of breach could have enmeshed them in time-consuming and expensive disagreements over which damages applied to a particular breach. We do not know exactly why the parties agreed to this particular clause, nor is it our role to discern their precise intentions. Because the provision is neither obviously one-sided nor obviously intended to impose a penalty that would coerce performance, because the actual estimate is not clearly unreasonable in relation to the range of possible damages, and because both parties are sophisticated businesses, we find that as a liquidated damages clause covering operations of the scale of Cakes and larger, the rent abatement provision in Red Sage's lease is enforceable as a matter of law.

* * *

In sum, we find that as a matter of law, the rent abatement provision would constitute neither an unenforceable penalty nor an unreasonable restraint of trade as applied to Cakes. Because we agree with the district court that the phrase "food service establishment of any kind" cannot be definitively construed as a matter of law, we remand to the district court to determine whether, in light of the contract's language, the parties' intent, and the nature of Cakes' operation, Despa's lease to Cakes entitles Red Sage to a rent abatement.

NOTES AND QUESTIONS

1. *Penalties.* Courts agree that a liquidated damages provision is enforceable, but that a penalty provision violates public policy and therefore is void. The parties cannot waive the public policy against penalties. The nature of the public interest has been questioned by academics, including academics on the bench. *See Lake River Corp. v. Carborundum Co.*, 769 F.2d 1284 (7th Cir.1985) (Posner, J.); Charles Goetz & Robert Scott, *Liquidated Damages, Penalties and the Just Compensation Principle: Some Notes on an Enforcement Model and a Theory of Efficient Breach*, 77 COLUM. L. REV. 554 (1977). Some penalties seem benign, even intuitive, such as library fines on overdue materials. Courts and legislatures have become more liberal in their acceptance of remedies specified in a contract. What public policy compels courts to refuse to enforce penalties even if both parties agree that they want a penalty? Do the cases here illustrate that concern? Should the policy be abandoned, limited, or approached in a different way?

2. *Identifying Penalties.* How do courts differentiate a penalty provision from a liquidated damages provision? The California court is typical

in rejecting the label applied by the parties. Substance, not form, governs. But what substance? Several approaches have been tried.

a. *Restatement of Contracts § 339 (1932).* Neither court mentions the old two part test: damages may be fixed in the contract if they are both difficult to prove and the amount provided is reasonable in relation to the actual loss. But some courts continue to state the provision this way, sometimes even in the face of statutory provisions that specify a different formulation.

b. *UCC Sales.* The Uniform Commercial Code adopts a variation on this test: "Damages for breach by either party may be liquidated in the agreement, but only at an amount that is reasonable in light of the anticipated or actual harm caused by the breach, the difficulties of proof of loss, and the inconvenience or nonfeasibility of otherwise obtaining an adequate remedy. A term fixing unreasonably large liquidated damages is void as a penalty." UCC § 2–718; *see also* Restatement (Second) of Contracts § 356. How does this differ from the two part test above? Does it make liquidated damage clauses harder or easier to defend?

c. *UCC Leases.* The court in *Red Sage* quoted a different UCC provision, one relating to leases of goods (not realty): "Damages payable by either party for default . . . may be liquidated in the lease agreement but only at an amount or by a formula that is reasonable in light of the then anticipated harm caused by the default. . . ." UCC § 2A–504(1). The notes imply that the provision governing goods may not provide parties enough leeway to provide for remedies in the lease, whereas this provision allows "greater flexibility." Does it? Does it make liquidated damage clauses harder or easier to defend? It does delete the last sentence of § 2–718. Will that affect the outcome of cases?

d. *Intent.* Some courts focus on the parties' intent when drafting the provision. The trial court in *Red Sage* not only relied on intent, but also presumed bad intent: "[i]f there is doubt as to whether the parties intended to provide for legitimate liquidated damages, courts routinely construe liquidated damages provisions as penalties." Intent tests can produce a very strict test. For example, confronted with a clause that seems fair under the circumstances of the actual breach, courts sometimes call it a penalty if it also would have applied to a less harmful breach. Because it would have acted as a penalty in that (hypothetical) case, it must have been intended as a penalty. How would you answer that argument if the UCC applied? Recourse to hypothetical breaches is less common today, but courts continue to discuss intent.

e. *California Law for Businesses.* By statute, California offers another approach: except in consumer transactions, "a provision in a contract liquidating the damages for breach of the contract is valid unless the party seeking to invalidate the provision establishes that the provision was unreasonable under the circumstances existing at the time the contract was made." CAL. CIV. CODE § 1671(b). In allocating the burden of proof to the party challenging the clause, the statute follows the majority approach. Is this clause better than the other provisions identified here?

f. *California Law for Consumers* For consumer transactions, "a provision in a contract liquidating damages for the breach of the contract is void except that the parties to such a contract may agree therein upon an amount which shall be presumed to be the amount of damage sustained by a breach thereof, when, from the nature of the case, it would be impracticable or extremely difficulty to fix the actual damage. CAL. CIV. CODE § 1671(d). Does this return to the old Restatement of Contracts? Is there any reason to include a liquidated damage provision if it will be governed by this rule?

g. *Unconscionability*. Utah recently decided that liquidated damage provisions did not require a separate test. Rather, the test for unconscionability applied here as it does for any other contract provision. *Commercial Real Estate Investment v. Comcast of Utah II*, 285 P.3d 1193 (Utah 2012). Will that test be easier to apply? Will it provide more predictability to parties wondering whether their liquidation clause will be enforceable? Does the approach have other advantages?

3. *Rightful Position Test?* Both courts mention a more general standard: liquidated damages should not make the party better off than if the contract had been performed. That standard has some appeal. It reflects our general principle that damages should put the plaintiff in the position she would have occupied if the wrong had not occurred, not a better position. Can that standard be applied directly? If it is, will the clauses retain any value? In *Red Sage*, enforcing the clause seems likely to make the plaintiff better off than if defendant had performed (by excluding Cakes initially). Is the case wrongly decided?

4. *Alternative Performance*. In both cases, the plaintiffs try to describe their clauses as something other than liquidated damage provisions: alternative rent or prepayment fees. Contracts may specify alternative ways in which a party may perform, often as a way of adjusting performance to new conditions. As long as the conditions are not breach, the alternative does not resemble a penalty. Are these just ways to hide a breach? Consider the following problems.

PROBLEMS

1. *Bonus*. Landis Ohner agreed to pay Jennie Contractor $10 million to build a strip mall on land owned by Ohner. The contract required completion by October 21. The contract provided that Contractor would receive a bonus of $100,000 per day for each day completion was early, up to a maximum of

$2 million. Is this a liquidated damages clause? Can Contractor argue that she should receive $12 million even if the job is finished on October 21?

2. *Late Fee.* Landis Ohner agreed to pay Jennie Contractor $12 million to build a strip mall on land owned by Ohner. The contract required completion by October 1 and included a liquidated damage provision calling for damages of $100,000 per day for each day completion was delayed, to a maximum of $2 million. Is this a liquidated damages clause? Is the substance any different from the clause in the preceding problem?

3. *Negotiations.* Suppose that Ohner offered Contractor the contract in problem 2, but during negotiations the parties changed the term, finally signing the contract in problem 1. Is this a liquidated damages clause?

4. *Implications.* Does this shed any light on the dispute between the majority and the dissent in *Ridgely*? Should the law reach out to invalidate (or at least demand justification for) any clause that can achieve the same results as a penalty? Even when the clause comes into play without a breach? Or does it suggest that commercial parties can achieve desired effects by many means, making it pointless to ban some while tolerating others?

5. *Alternative Performance.* Is a cell phone carrier's early termination fee an alternative performance or an amount payable because of breach? Is this any different from a take-or-pay clause in contracts involving oil and gas? *Compare Minnick v. Clearwire U.S.*, 275 P.3d 1127 (Wash. 2012) *with In re Cellphone Termination Fee Cases*, 122 Cal. Rptr. 3d 726 (Cal. App. 2011).

2. LIMITATIONS ON DAMAGES

Just as parties may agree to include damages that the courts ordinarily might not allow, parties may agree to exclude recovery for things that the law ordinarily might allow. Consequential damages are commonly excluded by various means. Sometimes parties agree to limit recovery to a particular formula, such as repair or replacement. In other cases parties may explicitly exclude consequential losses. In other cases, parties may use both terms. As with liquidated damages, the law generally will enforce the parties' desires concerning the remedy, subject to reservations that apply to any agreement between the parties.

PIERCE V. CATALINA YACHTS, INC.

2 P.3d 618 (Alaska 2000).

BRYNER, JUSTICE.

After finding that Catalina Yachts, a sailboat manufacturer, breached its limited warranty to repair a defect in a boat that it sold to Jim and Karen Pierce, a jury awarded the Pierces monetary damages for the reasonable cost of repair. Before submitting the case to the jury, the trial court dismissed the Pierces' claim for consequential damages, finding it barred by an express provision in the warranty. On appeal, the

Pierces contend that they were entitled to consequential damages despite this provision. We agree, holding that because Catalina acted in bad faith when it breached the warranty, the company cannot conscionably enforce the warranty's provision barring consequential damages. Accordingly, we remand for a trial to determine consequential damages.

II. Facts and Proceedings

In June 1992 Jim and Karen Pierce purchased a forty-two-foot sailboat newly built by Catalina Yachts. Catalina gave the Pierces a limited warranty, promising to repair or pay for repair of any below-waterline blisters that might appear in the gel coat—a smooth outer layer of resin on the boat's hull.[1] The warranty expressly disclaimed Catalina's responsibility for consequential damages.

In June 1994 the Pierces hauled the boat out of the water to perform maintenance and discovered gel-coat blisters on its hull and rudder. They promptly notified Catalina of the problem and submitted a repair estimate of $10,645, which included the cost of removing and replacing the gel coat below the waterline. Catalina refused to accept this estimate, insisting that the hull only needed minor patching. Six months later, after their repeated efforts failed to convince Catalina that the gel coat needed to be replaced, the Pierces sued the company, claiming tort and contract damages. They later amended their complaint to allege a separate claim for unfair trade practices.

Before trial, the superior court ruled that the limited warranty's provision barring consequential damages was not unconscionable. Based on this ruling, the court later precluded the Pierces from submitting their consequential damages claim to the jury, restricting the Pierces' recovery on their claim of breach of contract to their cost of repair, as specified in the limited warranty. The jury awarded the Pierces $12,445 as the reasonable cost of repair, specifically finding that the Pierces had given Catalina timely notice of the blister problem, that Catalina breached its gel-coat warranty, that it acted in bad faith in failing to honor its warranty obligations, and that the Pierces could not have avoided any of their losses.

The Pierces appeal, contending that the trial court erred in striking their claim for consequential damages, in excluding evidence supporting their unfair trade practices claim, and in calculating the attorney's fee award. Catalina cross-appeals, also contesting the attorney's fee order.

---

[1] This limited warranty provided, in relevant part: "Catalina will repair or, at its option, pay for 100% of the labor and material costs necessary to repair any below-the-waterline gel coat blisters that occur within the first year after the boat is placed in the water."

III. Discussion

A. *The Pierces Are Entitled to Consequential Damages*

The Pierces' consequential damages argument requires us to consider a question of first impression concerning how a warranty provision that creates a limited remedy interacts with another provision that excludes consequential damages: if the limited remedy fails, should the exclusion of consequential damages survive?

Alaska's commercial code addresses these issues in AS 45.02.719.[3] The first paragraph of this provision, subsection .719(a), authorizes limited warranties, allowing parties entering into commercial transactions to "limit or alter the measure of damages recoverable under [chapter 7 of the U.C.C.], as by limiting the buyer's remedies to . . . repair and replacement of nonconforming goods or parts" and to agree that the limited remedy is "exclusive, in which case it is the sole remedy." But when a limited remedy fails, the second paragraph of AS 45.02.719, subsection .719(b), nullifies the warranty's limitation, restoring the buyer's right to rely on any authorized remedy: "If circumstances cause an exclusive or limited remedy to fail of its essential purpose, remedy may be had as provided in the code."

Courts construing U.C.C. subsection 719(b) agree that a limited warranty to repair "fails of its essential purpose," "when the seller is either unwilling or unable to conform the goods to the contract."

The policy behind the failure of essential purpose rule is to insure that the buyer has "at least minimum adequate remedies." Typically, a limited repair/replacement remedy fails of its essential purpose where (1) the "[s]eller is unsuccessful in repairing or replacing the defective part, regardless of good or bad faith; or (2) [t]here is unreasonable delay in repairing or replacing defective components.

Here, by specifically finding that the Pierces' boat experienced gel-coat blisters, that the Pierces gave Catalina timely notice of the problem,

---

[3] AS 45.02.719 mirrors U.C.C. § 2–719, providing:

(a) Subject to (b) and (c) of this section and AS 45.02.718 on liquidation and limitation of damages,

(1) the agreement may provide for remedies in addition to or in substitution for those provided in this chapter and may limit or alter the measure of damages recoverable under this chapter, as by limiting the buyer's remedies to return of the goods and repayment of the price or to repair and replacement of nonconforming goods or parts; and

(2) resort to a remedy as provided is optional unless the remedy is expressly agreed to be exclusive, in which case it is the sole remedy.

(b) If circumstances cause an exclusive or limited remedy to fail of its essential purpose, remedy may be had as provided in the code.

(c) Consequential damages may be limited or excluded unless the limitation or exclusion is unconscionable. Limitation of consequential damages for injury to the person in the case of consumer goods is prima facie unconscionable, but limitation of damages where the loss is commercial is not.

that Catalina thereafter breached its obligations under the limited gel-coat warranty, and that the Pierces could not have avoided their damages, the jury effectively determined that the gel-coat warranty had failed of its essential purpose. Under subsection .719(b), then, the Pierces seemingly can pursue any remedy available under the commercial code, including consequential damages.

But the Pierces' right to consequential damages under subsection .719(b) is not as certain as it seems. The last paragraph of AS 45.02.719, subsection .719(c), separately provides that consequential damages may be limited or excluded "unless the limitation or exclusion is unconscionable." By validating consequential damages exclusions subject only to unconscionability, subsection .719(c) casts doubt upon subsection .719(b)'s implied promise that, when a limited remedy fails, the buyer may claim consequential damages because they are a "remedy . . . provided in the code."

The commercial code does not directly resolve this tension between subsections .719(b) and .719(c).[11] When, as here, a limited repair remedy fails, and a separate provision of the warranty bars consequential damages, the code fails to say whether a court should apply subsection .719(b) by restoring the buyer's right to seek consequential damages, or whether it should instead apply subsection .719(c) by enforcing the bar against consequential damages "unless . . . unconscionable."[12]

Courts addressing this dilemma in other jurisdictions have come to differing conclusions. Some have found the two subsections to be dependent, ruling that when a warranty fails, subsection .719(b)'s command to restore all available remedies trumps subsection .719(c)'s approval of a specific clause that bars consequential damages, regardless of whether that clause might itself be unconscionable. Other courts have applied a case-by-case analysis. But the majority of jurisdictions view these subsections to be independent, ruling that when a warranty fails, a separate provision barring consequential damages will survive under subsection .719(c) as long as the bar itself is not unconscionable.

We believe that the majority approach best serves the Uniform Commercial Code's underlying purposes "to simplify, clarify and modernize the law governing commercial transactions; to permit the continued expansion of commercial practices through custom, usage and agreement of the parties; [and] to make uniform the law among the various jurisdictions." Moreover, this approach balances the purposes of subsections .719(b) and (c) by allowing parties latitude to contract around

[11] *See S.M. Wilson & Co.*, 587 F.2d at 1375 ("The failure of the limited repair warranty to achieve its essential purpose makes available . . . the remedies 'as may be had as provided in this code.' This does not mean, however, that the bar to recovery of consequential damages should be eliminated.").

[12] This ambiguity has been the subject of extensive comment. *See, e.g.*, Hagen, *supra* note 7 (citing numerous articles proposing clarification).

consequential damages, while protecting buyers from unconscionable results. We therefore adopt the independent approach as the most sensible rule in light of precedent, reason, and policy.

Courts applying this approach recognize that contractual provisions limiting remedies and excluding consequential damages shift the risk of a limited remedy's failure from the seller to the buyer; they examine the totality of the circumstances at issue—including those surrounding the limited remedy's failure—to determine whether there is anything "in the formation of the contract or the circumstances resulting in failure of performance that makes it unconscionable to enforce the parties' allocation of risk."

In determining whether an exclusion is unconscionable, courts examine the circumstances existing when the contract was signed, asking whether "there was . . . reason to conclude that the parties could not competently agree upon the allocation of risk." Courts are more likely to find unconscionability when a consumer is involved, when there is a disparity in bargaining power, and when the consequential damages clause is on a pre-printed form; conversely, they are unlikely to find unconscionability when "such a limitation is freely negotiated between sophisticated parties, which will most likely occur in a commercial setting."

In addition to inquiring into the circumstances at the time of the sale, courts examine the case "[f]rom the perspective of later events," inquiring whether "it appears that the type of damage claimed . . . came within the realm of expectable losses." The reason for the limited warranty's failure affects this analysis:

> Whether the preclusion of consequential damages should be effective in this case depends upon the circumstances involved. The repair remedy's failure of essential purpose, while a discrete question, is not completely irrelevant to the issue of the conscionability of enforcing the consequential damages exclusion. The latter term is "merely an allocation of unknown or undeterminable risks." Recognizing this, *the question . . . narrows to the unconscionability of the buyer retaining the risk of consequential damages upon the failure of the essential purpose of the exclusive repair remedy.*

And in examining why a limited remedy failed of its essential purpose, courts consider it significant if the seller acted unreasonably or in bad faith.

In the present case, the nature of the Pierces' warranty and the circumstances surrounding Catalina's breach weigh heavily against enforcing the consequential damages bar. The contract at issue was a consumer sale, not a commercial transaction between sophisticated businesses with equivalent bargaining power. Catalina unilaterally drafted the damages bar and evidently included it in a preprinted standard limited warranty. Moreover, the jury's sizable award for the reasonable cost of repairing the boat's gel coat establishes that Catalina's breach deprived the Pierces of a substantial benefit of their bargain. Though some gel-coat blistering might have been foreseeable, a defect of this magnitude does not fit neatly "within the realm of expectable losses."

But the decisive factor in this case is the nature of Catalina's breach, which caused the limited remedy to fail of its essential purpose. The jury specifically found that Catalina acted in bad faith in failing to honor its warranty. This finding virtually establishes a "circumstance[] resulting in failure of performance that makes it unconscionable to enforce the parties' allocation of risk."[28] Because the jury found that Catalina consciously deprived the Pierces of their rights under the warranty, the company cannot conscionably demand to enforce its own warranty rights against the Pierces.

Moreover, in light of Catalina's bad faith, allowing the company to enforce the consequential damages bar would conflict with the commercial code's imperative that "[e]very contract or duty in the code imposes an obligation of good faith in its performance or enforcement." Finally, because it is self-evident that the Pierces did not bargain to assume the risk of a bad faith breach by Catalina, enforcing the bar against consequential damages would thwart AS 45.02.719's basic goal of implementing the parties' agreement.

For these reasons, we hold the superior court erred in ruling that it would be conscionable to enforce the warranty's bar against consequential damages and in declining to allow the Pierces to present their consequential damages claim to the jury.[31] We further hold that this error requires us to remand the case for a trial to determine the extent of these damages.

---

[28] In holding that the jury's finding of bad faith establishes unconscionability, we do not suggest that unconscionability is ordinarily a question of fact; we merely recognize bad faith and breach to be predicate facts that will ordinarily preclude an ultimate finding of conscionability. We agree with Catalina that unconscionability under AS 45.02.719(c) ultimately presents an issue of law for the court, rather than one of fact for the jury. But as we have pointed out, under the independent analysis articulated in *Chatlos,* the legal issue of unconscionability hinges on the totality of the circumstances, including the circumstances surrounding a limited remedy's failure. Because questions concerning breach of a warranty and the parties' good faith involve issues of fact, when disputed evidence requires the trial court to submit these factual issues to the jury, the court's decision on the ultimate question of unconscionability should ordinarily await the jury's factual determinations.

[31] We need not decide whether the trial court correctly decided that Catalina's inclusion of the consequential damages waiver in its standard limited warranty was not, in itself, unconscionable. Since the Pierces do not challenge this finding, we assume for purposes of this decision that the waiver, standing alone, was conscionable. We hold only that, given Catalina's bad faith breach of the limited warranty, *enforcement* of the waiver would be unconscionable.

CHILDREN'S SURGICAL FOUNDATION V. NATIONAL DATA CORP.

121 F. Supp. 2d 1221 (N.D. Ill. 2000).

ALESIA, DISTRICT JUDGE.

[Plaintiff] Children's Surgical Foundation, Incorporated ("plaintiff") has brought a breach of contract action against defendant National Data Corporation ("defendant"). In its complaint, plaintiff alleges that it entered into a contract with defendant whereby defendant would provide a variety of services for plaintiff, including billing and data processing. Plaintiff claims that defendant breached that agreement in several respects, including failing to properly code claims, to post payments, and to timely bill patients or payors. Further, plaintiff claims that, because of those breaches, it has suffered damages in excess of $6 million which it now seeks to collect from defendant. In response, defendant has filed a motion for partial dismissal, arguing that plaintiff cannot state a claim for the amount of damages it alleges in its complaint.

In its motion, defendant asks the court to dismiss all portions of plaintiff's complaint that seek damages in excess of the limitation clause contained in the contract. Specifically, defendant contends that the contract entered into between plaintiff and defendant contained a damage-limitation clause which states:

> 9. *Limitation of Liability.* In the event of any error or omission in the performance of services hereunder, Company [Defendant] may, at its election, reperform the work at no additional cost to Client [Surgical]. Notwithstanding the foregoing, it is expressly understood and agreed that the Company's liability for any loss or damage arising from any cause whatsoever shall be limited to the total amount billed or billable to Client for Company's services in the billing period in which the services that gave rise to the loss or damage were performed. The liability hereunder is established as liquidated damages and as a limitation of liability and not as a penalty. . . .

[D]efendant argues that this clause limits the amount of damages plaintiff can recover for any breach. Thus, defendant contends that plaintiff's exclusive remedy is for the amount of money it paid to defendant for defendant's services during the months in question—not the amount of money lost in plaintiff's receivables. In response, plaintiff argues that this limitation clause is unconscionable. Further, plaintiff argues that enforcement of that clause violates defendant's implied covenant of good faith and fair dealing.

II. Discussion . . .

B. Unconscionability

[T]he express terms of the contract provide for specific, limited remedies . . . In response, plaintiff claims that the paragraph of the contract to which defendant refers is unconscionable.

First, there are no allegations in plaintiff's complaint that any part of the contract is unconscionable. In fact, plaintiff's complaint provides no notice of the theory of unconscionability, nor are any facts alleged which—even if taken as true—would support such a theory. The contract, therefore, is valid in its entirety and the plaintiff is bound by the express terms of that agreement. Thus, under the contract's damage-limitation clause, plaintiff is limited to the amount of damages provided for in paragraph 9. Accordingly, the court grants defendant's motion for partial dismissal and dismisses those portions of plaintiff's complaint that seek damages in excess of the limitation clause expressed in paragraph 9 of the contract.

However, under Federal Rule of Civil Procedure 15(c), the court could allow plaintiff the opportunity to amend the complaint to include the allegations of unconscionability as a defense. Therefore, the court will address the merits of plaintiff's claim that the limitation provision was unconscionable.

In a commercial setting, the terms of a contract—and its allocation of risks among the parties—are generally accepted by the courts. Further, Texas law allows contracting parties to limit their liability in damages to a specified amount. Courts will only invalidate a contract when it is so unfair and one-sided that it violates all notions of fair play and justice and is unconscionable. However, while unconscionability prevents oppression and unfair surprise, it is not used to disturb the allocation of risks because of superior bargaining power.

To determine whether a contract is unconscionable, the court must look at the circumstances surrounding the agreement, the alternatives which were available to the parties at the time the contract was entered into, the bargaining ability of the parties, and whether the contract is illegal or against public policy. However, mere inequality of bargaining power is not a sufficient reason to hold a contract unenforceable.

In general, the courts have enumerated several factors to consider in deciding whether a contract is unconscionable: (1) the entire atmosphere in which the agreement was made; (2) the alternatives, if any, available to the parties at the time the contract was made; (3) the "nonbargaining" ability of one party; (4) whether the contract was illegal or against public policy; and (5) whether the contract was oppressive or unreasonable.

More specifically, the Texas courts have developed a two-part test to determine whether a contract is unconscionable. First, the court must address the procedural aspect of the contract, meaning how did the parties arrive at the terms in controversy. Second, the court must look at the substantive aspect of the contract, meaning are there legitimate, commercial reasons justifying the terms of the contract. The first question, dealing with procedural unconscionability, is concerned with assent and focuses on the facts surrounding the bargaining process. The second question, dealing with substantive unconscionability, is concerned with the fairness of the resulting agreement. Under Texas law, the party asserting unconscionability bears the burden of proving both the substantive and procedural unconscionability of the contract.

1. Procedural Unconscionability

A contract may be procedurally unconscionable if the plaintiff presents evidence of the seller's overreaching or sharp practices combined with the buyer's ignorance or inexperience. The commercial context of a contract is important in determining procedural unconscionability. For example, in *Lindemann,* the court considered the unconscionability of a damages limitation clause contained in a sales agreement for the purchase of an herbicide. In that case, the plaintiffs were "experienced and sophisticated" farmers who were familiar with the herbicide at issue in the litigation. In finding that the plaintiffs failed to prove procedural unconscionability, the court found that (1) the *Lindemann* plaintiffs knew or should have known of the contractual limitation of damages and (2) an arm's-length relationship is presumed in a UCC, commercial transaction. Likewise, in this case, plaintiff is a sophisticated hospital, comprised of equally sophisticated doctors and business people, with experience in billing patients and payors. As such, plaintiff should have known of the risks involved in the untimely billing of certain patients/payors. Further, although the contract at issue is not a sales agreement necessarily covered by the UCC, this was a commercial transaction and, accordingly, an arm's-length relationship exists between the parties.

Plaintiff, however, argues that the contract is unconscionable because the agreement was wholly one-sided. In support of this argument, plaintiff contends that defendant had total control over the plaintiff's accounts, receivables, and collection data and because the contract gave defendant power of attorney for plaintiff. The court finds these arguments unpersuasive. The defendant was hired by the plaintiff to provide a billing service for plaintiff so it is not surprising that defendant had control over plaintiff's accounts, receivables and collection data—this information, provided by the plaintiff in the first place, was necessary for defendant to perform its duties.

Further, this was a commercial contract with sophisticated, commercial entities on either side. Plaintiff claims that it was not represented by an attorney and, therefore, it was unable to understand the risk it was taking in signing the contract. However, in both its complaint and its response brief, plaintiff clearly states that many of the bills had to be submitted within a specific time frame in order for the amount due to be collectable. Thus, plaintiff was aware of the fact that if certain claims were not filed within a certain time frame, then that amount would be unrecoverable. As a sophisticated entity with equally sophisticated representatives, plaintiff should have been able to understand the risk involved in untimely billing. The court finds that any claim of ignorance would be unconvincing. Plaintiff knew or should have known of the risk involved, regardless of the presence of an attorney, and should have considered that risk before signing a contract that contained such a damage-limitation clause as the one in the present agreement.

Further, there does not seem to be any real disparity in bargaining power. Plaintiff was a business looking for a company to handle its billing—it did not have to enter into the contract with defendant but could have continued to do their own billing or hired another firm to do so. In fact, plaintiff states that defendant was one of a few firms who handle such services. Although plaintiff claims that defendant had the technology which plaintiff needed, plaintiff could have declined defendant's services if the contract was unsatisfactory to plaintiff and gone with another company. Also, plaintiff does not state that it was not aware of the limited-liability clause. In fact, that clause was in bold-face language. Thus, the damage-limitation clause would not have been a surprise. Finally, while plaintiff says that it did not negotiate the terms of the contract, plaintiff never states that it attempted to negotiate but was prevented from doing so by defendant or that defendant offered a "take-it-leave-it" contract. Thus, in looking at the totality of circumstances surrounding the contract's formation, the court finds that the agreement—including the limitation of liability clause—is not procedurally unconscionable. Therefore, plaintiff's damages amount is governed by the contract.

2. *Substantive Unconscionability*

A contract may be substantively unconscionable if the terms are one-sided or oppressive. Texas courts have stated that substantive unconscionability results when "no man in his senses and not under a delusion would enter into and . . . no honest and fair person would accept" a contract on such terms. In determining whether a contract is substantively unconscionable, the court looks at the fairness of resulting agreement.

Defendant argues that the clause is a valid limitation of liability in damages, which is recognized under Texas law. The court agrees. The parties in this case assumed certain risks and the contract detailed those risks (for example, paragraph 9 clearly states that the liability was limited even in instances of omission). Plaintiff could have opted to find another means of billing if it did not want to assume such a risk. Thus, while the contract may not be favorable for plaintiff, it is a fair agreement which provides a minimum adequate remedy for plaintiff. That clause is not invalid and plaintiff is still entitled to that amount. Thus, plaintiff cannot show that paragraph 9 of the contract is substantively unconscionable. Plaintiff's claim for damages is limited to the relief provided in paragraph 9 of the contract.

Plaintiff cannot show that the contract, and the damage-limitation clause contained in that contract, is either procedurally or substantively unconscionable. Accordingly, the court grants defendant's motion for partial dismissal and plaintiff's damages claim is limited to the amount specified in paragraph 9 of the contract.

C. Implied Covenant of Good Faith and Fair Dealing

In response to defendant's motion to dismiss, plaintiff also argues that enforcement of the liability-limiting clause would result in a breach of defendant's implied covenant of good faith and fair dealing because the clause deprives plaintiff from the benefit of its bargain. Defendant replies that Texas law does not recognize this implied warranty and, even if it did, the implied covenant does not apply because the express, unambiguous terms of the contract are controlling.

Some Texas courts have held that it is "well established under Texas law that 'accompanying every contract is a common law duty to perform with care, skill, reasonable expedience and faithfulness the thing agreed to be done. . . .' " However, more recently, Texas courts have held that there is no implied covenant of good faith and fair dealing for all contracts, but that covenant is reserved for those situations where there is a "special relationship"—such as that of a fiduciary relationship—between the parties. *See Crim Truck & Tractor Co. v. Navistar Int'l Trans. Corp.,* 823 S.W.2d 591, 595, n. 5 (Tex.1992) (citing *English v. Fischer,* 660 S.W.2d 521, 522 (Tex.1983)).

Plaintiff argues that, if enforced, that paragraph would breach this implied duty. The court disagrees. First, in the present case, the contract at issue is commercial in nature and, therefore, lacking in any "special" relationship between plaintiff and defendant. The court, therefore, doubts that any such implied covenant exists between the two parties under Texas law. Second, the enforcement of this clause limits the amount of damages plaintiff could receive, it does not relieve defendant of any implied duty to perform with "care and skill." Thus, the enforcement of such a clause would not breach this limited covenant. Further, at issue in the present dispute is the express clause contained in paragraph 9 of the contract. The court will not allow an implied duty—that may or may not even exist—to control over the express terms of the contract. Thus, the limited remedies provided for in the damage-limitation clause in paragraph 9 of the contract are exclusive and enforceable. Accordingly, the court grants the defendant's partial motion for dismissal.

NOTES AND QUESTIONS

1. *Limitations and Exclusions.* The *Pierce* court, like others, recognizes two provisions in the contract: one limits the remedy to repair of the defect, the other excludes consequential damages. Either one precludes recovery of consequential damages: one by replacing them with a different measure, the other by simply disclaiming them. Different statutory provisions govern the effectiveness of these two clauses. The substitute remedy (repairs) is effective unless it fails of its essential purpose. The disclaimer of consequential damages is effective unless it is unconscionable. Does this two track system make sense? Why invoke a stricter standard for disclaimers of consequential damages than for other limitations? Is one type of limitation harsher than the other? Is one fairer?

2. *Essential Purpose.* What is the essential purpose of a clause limiting remedies? Is it to provide plaintiff with minimally adequate remedies, as suggested in *Pierce*? Or is it to reduce defendant's liability? How can a clause fail that purpose? Does the court react to that failure or cause it?

3. *Reconciling Cases.* The approach taken in *Children's Surgical* is heavily influenced by the UCC, even though the code does not govern the case. Do the two cases differ because the facts differ or because the courts take a different approach to the law? Are any differences justified by the difference between goods and services? Could either case be better reasoned?

4. *Unconscionability.* Any contract term may be stricken for unconscionability. UCC § 2–302. Each case mentions aspects of § 2–302 in discussing § 2–719. But under § 2–302, unconscionability is evaluated at the time of contract formation—before any bad faith by Catalina Yachts. Considering the nature or effect of the breach implies unconscionability means something different under § 2–719. *Razor v. Hyundai Motor America,* 854 N.E.2d 607, 621 (Ill. 2006).

Does unconscionability require both substantive and procedural unconscionability under § 2–719, as it probably does under § 2–302? If so, will excluding consequential damages ever be unreasonably favorable to one party or oppressive to the other without a physical injury? Exclusion is specifically authorized by the UCC, suggesting no generalized policy against these provisions. Unless the effects of the breach can be considered, will any clause be so outrageous that it cannot be tolerated?

5. *Reading Closely.* The disclaimer in *Children's Surgical* does not expressly disclaim consequential damages (in the quoted passage, at least). Did the court apply the wrong test to this provision?

6. *Liquidation or Limitation.* The term in *Children's Surgical* raises another possibility: it purports to liquidate damages as well as limit them. Could the clause be struck down as an unreasonable liquidated damages

clause? Is the price of the services provided a reasonable effort to estimate the loss to the plaintiff? Is it a penalty? There is something odd about saying a clause awarding plaintiffs money penalizes them, even if it does not give plaintiffs as much as they would like.

A plaintiff may argue that an inadequate liquidation clause is optional rather than exclusive. If so, plaintiff may choose to seek the liquidated amount or the actual damages, at her election. The clause in *Children's Surgical* does not state whether it is exclusive or optional. How should a court decide? Do you think the drafter intended the clause to be optional? Do the UCC provisions quoted in these cases offer any guidance? *See Northern Illinois Gas Co. v. Energy Cooperative*, 122 Ill.App.3d 940, 78 Ill.Dec. 215, 461 N.E.2d 1049 (1984). Proposed revisions clarify that § 2–719 (which contains the provision regarding optional remedies) does not apply to liquidated damages. Does that mean liquidated damages are always exclusive? Might it merely mean that the determination must be made on a case by case basis, without regard to the presumption supplied by § 2–719?

PROBLEMS

1. *Faulty Alarm.* Plaintiff's liquor store lost $100,000 in a robbery because the alarm system provided by defendant failed to operate. Defendant's contract provided it was "not liable for losses which may occur in cases of malfunction or nonfunction of any system . . . even if due to [defendant's] negligence or failure of performance." It went on to limit liability to $10,000, the amount of the annual service charge. Should the clauses be enforceable? Would your answer be different if the alarm protected plaintiff's residence rather than a business? Does the type of loss matter?

2. *Disastrous Exclusions.* In *Children's Surgical*, suppose that a glitch in defendant's software prevented all of plaintiff's bills from being sent out for six months, depriving plaintiff of all claims for services rendered during that period. Would the magnitude of the loss to plaintiff change the outcome of the case?

3. *Intentional Breach.* If defendant knew about the bug shortly after the contract was signed, but did not disclose it, would *Children's Surgical* prevail? Alternatively, if an employee with a grievance against plaintiff planted the bug and skillfully concealed it for six months, would anything in the court's opinion allow a different result? Can plaintiff find a more effective remedy?

4. *Casey's Inhaler.* When filling the prescription at Green Wall, Casey signed a form that acknowledged he had been counseled about the prescription. The form included a term limiting damages for misfilled prescriptions to a refund of the contract price. If Casey's claim is in contract, is that provision enforceable? Is the limitation enforceable in tort? If it is enforceable, how much can Casey recover?

E. PUNITIVE DAMAGES

Punitive or exemplary damages are not really damages. Like restitution, they are monetary recoveries but are not designed to offset the loss the defendant caused the plaintiff. Rather, they serve different purposes. Those purposes are mixed and have changed over time. Originally courts used language of punishment to justify augmenting damages where antiquated doctrines otherwise would have prevented full compensation. As these doctrines have been eliminated or relaxed, punitive damages have been explained as an effort to achieve deterrence where compensatory damages might fall short of providing an adequate incentive for future precautions. Others suggest that punitive damages serve to measure harm to parties and social interests beyond the plaintiff. Catherine M. Sharkey, *Punitive Damages As Societal Damages*, 113 YALE L. J. 347 (2003). These rationales sever punitive damages from the constraints on recovery inherent in the normal damage rule (plaintiff's actual loss). Free of the compensatory reference and fueled by the rhetoric of punitive damages, juries were able and, in some cases, willing to award large sums. The political lens was turned to the large awards as tort reform took center stage. Instability is the hallmark of this branch of the law.

This section seeks to address three questions that practitioners confront: (1) What must be proven in order to justify an award of punitive damages? (2) How should punitive damages be calculated? and (3) What limits apply to the amount of punitive damages?

KOLSTAD V. AMERICAN DENTAL ASSOCIATION

527 U.S. 526, 119 S.Ct. 2118, 144 L.Ed.2d 494 (1999).

JUSTICE O'CONNOR delivered the opinion of the Court.

Under the terms of the Civil Rights Act of 1991 (1991 Act), punitive damages are available in claims under Title VII of the Civil Rights Act of 1964 (Title VII) and the Americans with Disabilities Act of 1990 (ADA). Punitive damages are limited, however, to cases in which the employer has engaged in intentional discrimination and has done so "with malice or with reckless indifference to the federally protected rights of an aggrieved individual." 42 U.S.C. § 1981a(b)(1). We here consider the circumstances under which punitive damages may be awarded in an action under Title VII.

I

In September 1992, Jack O'Donnell announced that he would be retiring as the Director of Legislation and Legislative Policy and Director of the Council on Government Affairs and Federal Dental Services for respondent, American Dental Association (respondent or Association).

Petitioner, Carole Kolstad, was employed with O'Donnell in respondent's Washington, D.C., office, where she was serving as respondent's Director of Federal Agency Relations. When she learned of O'Donnell's retirement, she expressed an interest in filling his position. Also interested in replacing O'Donnell was Tom Spangler, another employee in respondent's Washington office. At this time, Spangler was serving as the Association's Legislative Counsel, a position that involved him in respondent's legislative lobbying efforts. Both petitioner and Spangler had worked directly with O'Donnell, and both had received "distinguished" performance ratings by the acting head of the Washington office, Leonard Wheat.

Both petitioner and Spangler formally applied for O'Donnell's position, and Wheat requested that Dr. William Allen, then serving as respondent's Executive Director in the Association's Chicago office, make the ultimate promotion decision. After interviewing both petitioner and Spangler, Wheat recommended that Allen select Spangler for O'Donnell's post. Allen notified petitioner in December 1992 that he had, in fact, selected Spangler to serve as O'Donnell's replacement. Petitioner's challenge to this employment decision forms the basis of the instant action.

After first exhausting her avenues for relief before the Equal Employment Opportunity Commission, petitioner filed suit against the Association in Federal District Court, alleging that respondent's decision to promote Spangler was an act of employment discrimination proscribed under Title VII. In petitioner's view, the entire selection process was a sham. Counsel for petitioner urged the jury to conclude that Allen's stated reasons for selecting Spangler were pretext for gender discrimination, and that Spangler had been chosen for the position before the formal selection process began. Among the evidence offered in support of this view, there was testimony to the effect that Allen modified the description of O'Donnell's post to track aspects of the job description used to hire Spangler. In petitioner's view, this "preselection" procedure suggested an intent by the Association to discriminate on the basis of sex. Petitioner also introduced testimony at trial that Wheat told sexually offensive jokes and that he had referred to certain prominent professional women in derogatory terms. Moreover, Wheat allegedly refused to meet with petitioner for several weeks regarding her interest in O'Donnell's position. Petitioner testified, in fact, that she had historically experienced difficulty gaining access to meet with Wheat. Allen, for his part, testified that he conducted informal meetings regarding O'Donnell's position with both petitioner and Spangler, although petitioner stated that Allen did not discuss the position with her.

The District Court denied petitioner's request for a jury instruction on punitive damages. The jury concluded that respondent had discriminated against petitioner on the basis of sex and awarded her backpay totaling $52,718. Although the District Court subsequently denied respondent's motion for judgment as a matter of law on the issue of liability, the court made clear that it had not been persuaded that respondent had selected Spangler over petitioner on the basis of sex, and the court denied petitioner's requests for reinstatement and for attorney's fees.

In a split decision, a panel of the Court of Appeals for the District of Columbia reversed the District Court's decision denying petitioner's request for an instruction on punitive damages. The Court of Appeals subsequently agreed to rehear the case en banc, limited to the punitive damages question. In a divided opinion, the court affirmed the decision of the District Court. Based on the 1991 Act's structure and legislative history, the court determined, specifically, that a defendant must be shown to have engaged in some "egregious" misconduct before the jury is permitted to consider a request for punitive damages.

We granted certiorari to resolve a conflict among the Federal Courts of Appeals concerning the circumstances under which a jury may consider a request for punitive damages under § 1981a(b)(1).

II

Prior to 1991, only equitable relief, primarily backpay, was available to prevailing Title VII plaintiffs; the statute provided no authority for an award of punitive or compensatory damages. With the passage of the 1991 Act, Congress provided for additional remedies, including punitive damages, for certain classes of Title VII and ADA violations. The 1991 Act limits compensatory and punitive damages awards, however, to cases of "intentional discrimination"—that is, cases that do not rely on the "disparate impact" theory of discrimination. Section 1981a(b)(1) further qualifies the availability of punitive awards:

> A complaining party may recover punitive damages under this section against a respondent (other than a government, government agency or political subdivision) if the complaining party demonstrates that the respondent engaged in a discriminatory practice or discriminatory practices *with malice or with reckless indifference to the federally protected rights of an aggrieved individual.*

Congress plainly sought to impose two standards of liability—one for establishing a right to compensatory damages and another, higher standard that a plaintiff must satisfy to qualify for a punitive award.

The Court of Appeals sought to give life to this two-tiered structure by limiting punitive awards to cases involving intentional discrimination of an "egregious" nature. We credit the en banc majority's effort to effectuate congressional intent, but, in the end, we reject its conclusion that eligibility for punitive damages can only be described in terms of an employer's "egregious" misconduct. The terms "malice" and "reckless" ultimately focus on the actor's state of mind. While egregious misconduct is evidence of the requisite mental state, § 1981a does not limit plaintiffs to this form of evidence, and the section does not require a showing of egregious or outrageous discrimination independent of the employer's state of mind.

Moreover, § 1981a's focus on the employer's state of mind gives some effect to Congress' apparent intent to narrow the class of cases for which punitive awards are available to a subset of those involving intentional discrimination. The employer must act with "malice or with reckless indifference *to the [plaintiff's] federally protected rights.*" § 1981a(b)(1) (emphasis added). The terms "malice" or "reckless indifference" pertain to the employer's knowledge that it may be acting in violation of federal law, not its awareness that it is engaging in discrimination.

We gain an understanding of the meaning of the terms "malice" and "reckless indifference," as used in § 1981a, from this Court's decision in *Smith v. Wade*, 461 U.S. 30 (1983). Congress looked to the Court's decision in *Smith* in adopting this language in § 1981a. Employing language similar to what later appeared in § 1981a, the Court concluded in *Smith* that "a jury may be permitted to assess punitive damages in an action under § 1983 when the defendant's conduct is shown to be motivated by evil motive or intent, or when it involves reckless or callous indifference to the federally protected rights of others." While the *Smith* Court determined that it was unnecessary to show actual malice to qualify for a punitive award, its intent standard, at a minimum, required recklessness in its subjective form. The Court referred to a "subjective consciousness" of a risk of injury or illegality and a " 'criminal indifference to civil obligations.' " Applying this standard in the context of § 1981a, an employer must at least discriminate in the face of a perceived risk that its actions will violate federal law to be liable in punitive damages.

There will be circumstances where intentional discrimination does not give rise to punitive damages liability under this standard. In some instances, the employer may simply be unaware of the relevant federal prohibition. There will be cases, moreover, in which the employer discriminates with the distinct belief that its discrimination is lawful. The underlying theory of discrimination may be novel or otherwise poorly recognized, or an employer may reasonably believe that its discrimination satisfies a bona fide occupational qualification defense or other statutory exception to liability. In *Hazen Paper Co. v. Biggins,* 507 U.S. 604, 616 (1993), we thus observed that, in light of statutory defenses and other exceptions permitting age-based decisionmaking, an employer may knowingly rely on age to make employment decisions without recklessly violating the Age Discrimination in Employment Act of 1967 (ADEA).

Accordingly, we determined that limiting liquidated damages under the ADEA to cases where the employer "knew or showed reckless disregard for the matter of whether its conduct was prohibited by the statute," without an additional showing of outrageous conduct, was sufficient to give effect to the ADEA's two-tiered liability scheme.

Respondent urged that the common law tradition surrounding punitive awards includes an "egregious misconduct" requirement. We assume that Congress, in legislating on punitive awards, imported common law principles governing this form of relief. Most often, however, eligibility for punitive awards is characterized in terms of a defendant's motive or intent. Indeed, "[t]he justification of exemplary damages lies in the evil intent of the defendant." Accordingly, "a positive element of conscious wrongdoing is always required."

Egregious misconduct is often associated with the award of punitive damages, but the reprehensible character of the conduct is not generally considered apart from the requisite state of mind. Conduct warranting punitive awards has been characterized as "egregious," for example, *because* of the defendant's mental state. See Restatement (Second) of Torts § 908(2) (1979) ("Punitive damages may be awarded for conduct that is outrageous, because of the defendant's evil motive or his reckless indifference to the rights of others"). Respondent, in fact, appears to endorse this characterization. That conduct committed with the specified mental state may be characterized as egregious, however, is not to say that employers must engage in conduct with some independent, "egregious" quality before being subject to a punitive award.

To be sure, egregious or outrageous acts may serve as evidence supporting an inference of the requisite "evil motive." "The allowance of exemplary damages depends upon the bad motive of the wrong-doer *as exhibited by his acts*." "[W]here there is no evidence that gives rise to an inference of actual malice or conduct sufficiently outrageous to be deemed equivalent to actual malice, the trial court need not, and indeed should not, submit the issue of punitive damages to the jury." Likewise, under § 1981a(b)(1), pointing to evidence of an employer's egregious behavior would provide one means of satisfying the plaintiff's burden to "demonstrat[e]" that the employer acted with the requisite "malice or . . . reckless indifference." Again, however, respondent has not shown that the terms "reckless indifference" and "malice," in the punitive damages context, have taken on a consistent definition including an independent, "egregiousness" requirement.

The inquiry does not end with a showing of the requisite "malice or . . . reckless indifference" on the part of certain individuals, however. The plaintiff must impute liability for punitive damages to respondent. The en banc dissent recognized that agency principles place limits on vicarious liability for punitive damages. Likewise, the Solicitor General as *amicus* acknowledged during argument that common law limitations on a principal's liability in punitive awards for the acts of its agents apply in the Title VII context.

While we decline to engage in any definitive application of the agency standards to the facts of this case, it is important that we address the proper legal standards for imputing liability to an employer in the punitive damages context. This issue is intimately bound up with the preceding discussion on the evidentiary showing necessary to qualify for a punitive award.

The common law has long recognized that agency principles limit vicarious liability for punitive awards. Observing the limits on liability that these principles impose is especially important when interpreting the 1991 Act. In promulgating the Act, Congress conspicuously left intact the "limits of employer liability" established in *Meritor Savings Bank, FSB v. Vinson,* 477 U.S. 57, 72 (1986).

Although jurisdictions disagree over whether and how to limit vicarious liability for punitive damages, our interpretation of Title VII is informed by "the general common law of agency, rather than . . . the law of any particular State." The common law as codified in the Restatement (Second) of Agency (1957), provides a useful starting point for defining this general common law. The Restatement of Agency places strict limits on the extent to which an agent's misconduct may be imputed to the principal for purposes of awarding punitive damages:

> Punitive damages can properly be awarded against a master or other principal because of an act by an agent if, but only if:
>
> > (a) the principal authorized the doing and the manner of the act, or
> >
> > (b) the agent was unfit and the principal was reckless in employing him, or
> >
> > (c) the agent was employed in a managerial capacity and was acting in the scope of employment, or
> >
> > (d) the principal or a managerial agent of the principal ratified or approved the act.

Restatement (Second) of Agency, § 217 C; see also Restatement (Second) of Torts § 909 (same).

"Unfortunately, no good definition of what constitutes a 'managerial capacity' has been found," and determining whether an employee meets this description requires a fact-intensive inquiry. "In making this determination, the court should review the type of authority that the employer has given to the employee, the amount of discretion that the employee has in what is done and how it is accomplished." Suffice it to say here that the examples provided in the Restatement of Torts suggest that an employee must be "important," but perhaps need not be the employer's "top management, officers, or directors," to be acting "in a managerial capacity."

Additional questions arise from the meaning of the "scope of employment" requirement. The Restatement of Agency provides that even intentional torts are within the scope of an agent's employment if the conduct is "the kind [the employee] is employed to perform," "occurs substantially within the authorized time and space limits," and "is actuated, at least in part, by a purpose to serve the" employer. Restatement (Second) of Agency, § 228(1). According to the Restatement, so long as these rules are satisfied, an employee may be said to act within the scope of employment even if the employee engages in acts "specifically forbidden" by the employer and uses "forbidden means of accomplishing results." On this view, even an employer who makes every effort to comply with Title VII would be held liable for the discriminatory acts of agents acting in a "managerial capacity."

Holding employers liable for punitive damages when they engage in good faith efforts to comply with Title VII, however, is in some tension with the very principles underlying common law limitations on vicarious liability for punitive damages—that it is "improper ordinarily to award punitive damages against one who himself is personally innocent and therefore liable only vicariously." Restatement (Second) of Torts, § 909, Comment *b*. Where an employer has undertaken such good faith efforts at Title VII compliance, it "demonstrat[es] that it never acted in reckless disregard of federally protected rights."

Applying the Restatement of Agency's "scope of employment" rule in the Title VII punitive damages context, moreover, would reduce the incentive for employers to implement antidiscrimination programs. In fact, such a rule would likely exacerbate concerns among employers that § 1981a's "malice" and "reckless indifference" standard penalizes those employers who educate themselves and their employees on Title VII's prohibitions. Dissuading employers from implementing programs or policies to prevent discrimination in the workplace is directly contrary to the purposes underlying Title VII. The statute's "primary objective" is "a prophylactic one," it aims, chiefly, "not to provide redress but to avoid harm." The purposes underlying Title VII are advanced where employers are encouraged to adopt antidiscrimination policies and to educate their personnel on Title VII's prohibitions.

In light of the perverse incentives that the Restatement's "scope of employment" rules create, we are compelled to modify these principles to avoid undermining the objectives underlying Title VII. Recognizing Title VII as an effort to promote prevention as well as remediation, and observing the very principles underlying the Restatements' strict limits on vicarious liability for punitive damages, we agree that, in the punitive damages context, an employer may not be vicariously liable for the discriminatory employment decisions of managerial agents where these decisions are contrary to the employer's "good-faith efforts to comply with Title VII." As the dissent recognized, "[g]iving punitive damages protection to employers who make good-faith efforts to prevent discrimination in the workplace accomplishes" Title VII's objective of "motivat[ing] employers to detect and deter Title VII violations."

We leave for remand the question whether petitioner can identify facts sufficient to support an inference that the requisite mental state can be imputed to respondent. [I]t remains to be seen whether petitioner can make a sufficient showing that Allen acted with malice or reckless indifference to petitioner's Title VII rights. Even if it could be established that Wheat effectively selected O'Donnell's replacement, moreover, several questions would remain, *e.g.,* whether Wheat was serving in a "managerial capacity" and whether he behaved with malice or reckless indifference to petitioner's rights. It may also be necessary to determine whether the Association had been making good faith efforts to enforce an antidiscrimination policy. We leave these issues for resolution on remand.

For the foregoing reasons, the judgment of the Court of Appeals is vacated, and the case is remanded for proceedings consistent with this opinion.

NOTES AND QUESTIONS

1. Every court employs some language to distinguish between conduct that is merely wrongful and conduct that is so wrongful that it justifies punitive damages. California, for example, requires "oppression, fraud, or malice, express or implied." CAL. CIV. CODE § 3294. Do verbal formulations of the threshold provide much guidance? Could you apply them to your clients' case and predict whether punitive damages would be upheld? Is the test in *Kolstad* any different? Is it any better?

2. Express malice refers to a purpose to cause harm. Purpose can be hard to prove when a defendant denies it. Evidence that the harmful effects were a likely result suggests that the defendant intended them, but defendant may claim ignorance of those effects, no matter how likely. Even if implausible, that claim may be hard to rebut. Implied malice loosens the burden of proof. Rather than requiring juries to conclude defendant is lying, courts may treat reckless disregard of likely harms as the equivalent of purpose, in effect inferring malice. In other cases, however, implied malice may slide into gross negligence, extending punitive damages to cases with no real malice at all. *See Darcars Motors of Silver Spring v. Borzym*, 150 Md.App. 18, 818 A.2d 1159 (2003). Recently, some courts have tried to limit the use of punitive damages to true cases of malice. *See, e.g., Linthicum v. Nationwide Life Ins. Co.*, 150 Ariz. 326, 723 P.2d 675 (1986) (requiring an "evil mind," not merely "gross negligence or reckless disregard of the circumstances").

3. Should punitive damages be awarded in all cases that meet the threshold or in only some of them? For example, every fraud case will meet the California threshold. Should punitive damages be denied in some fraud cases because the fraud was not sufficiently severe? One court took the opposite approach to intentional infliction of emotional distress: "Since the outrageous quality of the defendant's conduct forms the basis of the action, the rendition of compensatory damages will be sufficiently punitive." *Knierim v. Izzo*, 22 Ill.2d 73, 174 N.E.2d 157 (1961). Is that rule any less coherent than asking a jury (which hears only one case) to decide whether it is especially egregious?

PROBLEMS

1. Does the purpose of punitive damages help determine the proper standard for awarding them? The stated purpose is to deter misconduct. Of course, all wrongdoing, not just intentional or reckless wrongdoing, should be deterred—and compensatory damages also deter wrongdoing. Punitive damages would be apt only when the deterrence of compensatory damages seems inadequate. Does an intent or recklessness test identify the cases where compensation is unlikely to deter? Consider the following variations on *Kolstad.*

a. Wheat and Allen honestly (but incorrectly) believed that Spangler was the better choice for the job. Would compensatory damages adequately deter or are punitive damages required? Or is this a case where there should be no liability at all?

b. Wheat and Allen, after careful investigation, honestly but incorrectly believe that they legally can consider gender in deciding whom to promote. Would compensatory damages adequately deter or are punitive damages required?

c. Wheat and Allen realize their decision to hire Spangler is discriminatory, but anticipate that Kolstad might not sue, hoping to get the next promotion instead. Would compensatory damages adequately deter or are punitive damages required? Would it matter if they knew she would sue, but thought the difficulties of proof might keep her from recovering much money?

d. Wheat and Allen know they will lose a discrimination case but don't care. The benefit to them of working with a man is worth any reasonable price a jury might assess as compensatory damages. Would compensatory damages adequately deter or are punitive damages required? Is this case likely to get to a jury?

2. Are the cases less instructive because the harms are entirely pecuniary? What if the alleged wrong were a battery that caused physical injury, but:

a. Defendant believed plaintiff had consented to the touching.

b. Defendant believed the conduct was legal without consent (say, by necessity or defense of others).

c. Defendant believed plaintiff would not sue.

d. Defendant didn't care; the joy of the battery was worth the likely compensatory damages.

MORE NOTES AND QUESTIONS

1. The last problem is the clearest justification for punitive damages. An economist might argue for efficient tort—refusing to discourage harms when the benefit to defendant exceeds the harm to the plaintiff—if the benefit involved something useful to society. But where the benefit is perverse glee derived from harming another, few would support taking that benefit into account. Punitive damages help to remove the incentive to commit such torts. If we could measure the perverse glee directly, we could try to confiscate it via restitution. Punitive damages may be more practical. Does a malice standard limit punitive damages to these cases? Should it?

2. What about the possibility that a party will not sue? Once the party does sue, won't compensatory damages adequately deter? If not, should the likelihood of suit factor into the legitimacy of punitive damages? People with real physical injuries seem more likely to sue than people with merely economic harm. Should we assess greater punitive damages for economic torts than for personal injury cases? Torts that are likely to evade detection might be underdeterred. Should stealthy wrongs (embezzlement, legal malpractice, breach of fiduciary duty) be punished, but not obvious wrongs (personal injuries from defective products, battery)? Does a threshold test based on intent have anything to do with this distinction? Might negligence claims also go unfiled, thus producing too little deterrence? Will other legal mechanisms, such as class action suits, counteract the possibility of unfiled suits, thus achieving optimal deterrence without increasing the award in some individual suits? If unfiled claims justify punitive damages, should punitive damages be denied in class action suits, where compensation to the class covers claims that otherwise might have gone unfiled? *See Eisen v. Carlisle & Jacquelin*, 479 F.2d 1005 (2d Cir. 1973), *vacated and remanded*, 417 U.S. 156, 94 S.Ct. 2140, 40 L.Ed.2d 732 (1974) (*infra* at 999).

3. Punitive damages against a corporation pose some difficulty. Many states simply apply respondeat superior. Others follow an approach similar to *Kolstad*, requiring some indication that responsible management officials were involved in or aware of the misconduct and either condoned it or failed to act strongly enough to prevent it. Which approach is better? Does it vary by context? Employees often face harassment or discrimination at the hands of relatively low-level supervisors. Is management responsible for every jerk that works hard enough to earn a promotion into a position of petty power? What will punitive damages deter in this setting? What about an employee who drives recklessly in the course of employment? Can management, even low level supervisors, keep tabs of every driver they send out? Is deterrence

really what is at stake? Would a retribution theory justify punitive damages against the corporation?

4. Could management be ordered to prevent the misconduct of subordinates? Recall *Rizzo v. Goode*, 423 U.S. 362, 96 S.Ct. 598, 46 L.Ed.2d 561 (1976) where the Court rejected an injunction against city officials ordering them to enact a program to prevent police abuses because the officials had committed no wrong. Can that be squared with punitive damages against corporate officials if they do not prevent abuses by their subordinates, even if the officials have committed no wrong?

5. The deterrent value of punitive damages diminishes if insurance covers them. But the ability to collect punitive damages diminishes if insurance does not cover them. In some states, public policy precludes insuring punitive damages. *See, e.g., Soto v. State Farm Ins. Co.*, 83 N.Y.2d 718, 613 N.Y.S.2d 352, 635 N.E.2d 1222 (1994). Others, noting that punitive damages apply to some cases of unintentional misconduct (such as gross negligence), allow liability insurers to pay them. *See, e.g., Harrell v. Travelers Indemnity Co.*, 279 Or. 199, 567 P.2d 1013 (1977); *American Home Assurance Co. v. Safway Steel Prods. Co.*, 743 S.W.2d 693 (1987). Does this call for even larger punitive damages, so the sting remains even after translated into increased premiums? That will make liability insurance even harder to afford, especially for smaller businesses and individuals. Are punitive damages inappropriate in these contexts, since they are imposed on parties (insurers and their other insureds) with no wrongful mental state and little ability to prevent future wrongs?

PROBLEMS

1. Driver injured Pedestrian while driving recklessly. Pedestrian offered to settle the claim for $100,000 (the limits of Driver's insurance policy), but Insurer (in bad faith) refused to settle the claim. At trial, Pedestrian recovered compensatory damages of $500,000 and punitive damages of $200,000 against Driver. When Driver sues Insurer for bad faith refusal to settle, the additional $400,000 in compensatory damages is recoverable. Are the punitive damages recoverable? Does it matter whether the state's public policy rejects coverage of punitive damages? *PPG Industries v. Transamerica Ins. Co.*, 20 Cal.4th 310, 84 Cal.Rptr.2d 455, 975 P.2d 652 (1999).

2. Plaintiff sued Defendant for a malicious tort. Attorney negligently allowed the dismissal of Plaintiff's claim for punitive damages. Plaintiff recovered full compensatory damages at trial. In an action against Attorney for malpractice, can Plaintiff recover the punitive damages that would have been awarded if the Attorney had exercised due care? Does it matter whether the state's public policy rejects coverage of punitive damages? *See Ferguson v. Lieff, Cabraser, Heimann & Bernstein, LLP*, 30 Cal.4th 1037, 135 Cal.Rptr.2d 46, 69 P.3d 965 (2003).

GRIFF, INC. V. CURRY BEAN CO., INC.

138 Idaho 315, 63 P.3d 441 (2003).

KIDWELL, JUSTICE.

Griff, Inc. (Griff) filed suit against Curry Bean Company, Inc. (Curry) for breach of contract. A jury awarded Griff compensatory and punitive damages totaling $538,621.20. The district court awarded attorney fees to Griff, including fees expended attempting to collect on the judgment. Curry timely filed this appeal.

Griff grew pinto beans and pink beans near Twin Falls. Curry operated a bonded agricultural warehouse. Griff had an ongoing relationship with Curry whereby Griff deposited its beans with Curry. Then, Curry would mill and market the beans. Upon sale of the beans to a third party, Curry would pay Griff the price received for the beans minus a three-dollar milling and marketing charge per cut weight (cwt. [100 pounds]).

In 1996, Griff delivered 39,271.09 cwt. of beans to Curry. Curry eventually sold all of the beans to third parties. A dispute arose regarding whether the beans were sold in 1996 or 1997 and whether they were marketed by Curry to third parties or purchased by Curry to cover a "short position." The dispute created uncertainty about the price that Curry owed Griff for the beans—beans were significantly less expensive in 1997 than in 1996. Griff contended that the beans were sold upon delivery to Curry, rather than a third party, in 1996, so that Curry could cover its short position. Pursuant to Griff's contention, the price of the beans was established upon delivery in 1996. Curry, on the other hand, argued that it sold Griff's beans on the same terms that it had always sold them—the price for the beans was not established until Curry sold the beans to a third party. Curry contended that this occurred in 1997.

Griff filed suit against Curry, alleging breach of contract. Subsequently, the district court allowed Griff to amend its complaint to include a prayer for punitive damages. . . .

At trial, the jury found that Curry purchased Griff's beans in three lots, one in May 1996 at $28.00 per cwt., and two in June 1997 at $27.50 per cwt. Curry appeals the jury's findings regarding timing and price of the contracts. . . . Curry moved for judgment notwithstanding the verdict and for a new trial. [T]he district court denied both motions. . . .

"Punitive damages are not favored in law and should be awarded in only the most unusual and compelling circumstances." Idaho Code § 6–1604 states that a party seeking punitive damages must prove "oppressive, fraudulent, wanton, malicious or outrageous conduct by the party against whom the claim for punitive damages is asserted."

The evidence at trial supported the conclusion that Hull [Curry's agent] intended to defraud Griff during negotiations and that Hull altered business records in anticipation of litigation. Richard [Griff] testified that in spring 1996, Hull told him that Curry could sell as many beans to end users as Griff could deliver. Hull admitted at trial that Curry was in a short position during the spring of 1996. One may infer that Hull omitted the fact that the beans Curry wanted to purchase were not for market, rather, they were intended to cover Curry's short position.

The DPR [Curry's Daily Position Register] originally reflected that Curry counted Griff's beans as Curry's own "company owned beans" in May and June 1996. Marti Hill, a bookkeeper for Curry, testified that Hull told her to alter the DPR in 1998 to show that Curry purchased Griff's beans in 1997 rather than 1996. Hill made other changes, but could not remember if she "was advised or did it on [her] own." Notably, the market price of beans was significantly lower in May and June 1997 than in May and June 1996. From this evidence, one may infer that Hull instructed Hill to falsify records to reflect purchases by Curry at times when the price of beans was lower than it was in May and June 1996.

Accepting all the evidence adverse to Curry as true, and drawing all inferences in favor of Griff, the jury could find that Hull's conduct, on behalf of Curry, was fraudulent. Therefore, substantial, competent evidence supports the jury's punitive damage award.

Curry's argument that the punitive damage award cannot stand because the trial record lacks evidence that Hull was an officer or director is without merit. To recover punitive damages against a corporation, one must show that an officer or director participated in, or ratified, the conduct underlying the punitive damage award. [The] complaint alleges that Hull was an "agent, shareholder, officer and director of Curry." Curry's answer "[admits] the allegations. . . .

Curry argues that the punitive damage award is excessive and should be vacated because it constituted 48.65% of Curry's value as of 1999, and that the disproportionality shows the award was intended as punishment rather than as a deterrent. Griff, however, contends that the punitive damage award levied against Curry is not disproportional. It may appear disproportional, but only because Curry transferred assets to third parties to reduce its net worth. Therefore, Griff argues, the punitive damage award should stand.

To determine whether a punitive damage award is excessive, this Court must ascertain "whether the punitive damage award appears to have been given under the influence of passion or prejudice." "Proportionality is a factor to be considered in evaluating whether a punitive award is excessive." However, this Court also must consider "the prospective deterrent effect of such an award upon persons situated similarly to the defendant, the motives actuating the defendant's conduct, the degree of calculation involved in the defendant's conduct, and the extent of the defendant's disregard of the rights of others."

Bonded warehousemen hold positions of trust and confidence. They store valuable commodities and they facilitate agribusiness, an important aspect of Idaho's economy, and it is important that bonded warehousemen remain trustworthy. The punitive damage award of $93,497.82 does constitute a significant portion of Curry's 1999 assets. The award is not disproportionate to the compensatory damages awarded. In light of the overall circumstances of this case, including Curry's dishonest conduct and its status as a bonded warehouse, the award is appropriate to serve the purpose of deterring future similar conduct by Curry and other bonded warehouses. Therefore, we affirm the punitive damage award.

NOTES AND QUESTIONS

1. *Griff* awarded punitive damages in a case based on breach of contract. Courts often allow such damages when the breach also constitutes a tort for which punitive damages would be allowed. The finding that defendant defrauded plaintiff apparently sufficed here. Is this really the kind of case where punitive damages are appropriate? One substantial business tried to pay another substantial business less than it owed. That's business. Does the spoliation of evidence alter the nature of the wrong? Can it justify punitive damages even though neither pled nor proven?

2. Financial torts are a common source of punitive damages. Tortious interference with contract is one way to elevate a contract loss into punitive damages. To limit this technique, courts have held that a party to a contract cannot be held liable for interfering with it, only for breaching it. Breach of fiduciary duty is a staple of business litigation, especially as shareholder derivative actions and suits among partners. Consider *Time Warner Entertainment Co. v. Six Flags Over Georgia, L.L.C.*, 254 Ga. App. 598, 563 S.E.2d 178 (2002), *cert. denied*, 538 U.S. 977, 123 S.Ct. 1783, 155 L.Ed.2d 665 (2003). Time Warner owned five Six Flags parks, but was the general partner in two others, including the one at issue. Time Warner's partnership would expire, leaving the limited partner (Six Flags Over Georgia, LLC or SFOG) complete ownership of the theme park. As the expiration neared, Time Warner invested less in improvements. In the short run, improvements would benefit both partners: Time Warner received 70% of the income from the park, SFOG the other 30%. Before long, however, SFOG would be the sole owner, capturing all the benefits of any investment by Time Warner—unless the partnership were renewed. Negotiations to renew the partnership were uncertain. Thus, to avoid a windfall to SFOG, Time Warner postponed investments. Looking after its own self-interest constituted a breach of fiduciary duty to its partner. The jury returned a verdict in favor of plaintiff for $197,296,000 in compensatory damages and $257,000,000 in punitive damages. Is this the kind of case where punitive damages are important? In fiduciary cases, the remedy of tracing and disgorgement of profits will confiscate any benefit defendant obtains, even if that exceeds plaintiffs

losses. Is that an adequate deterrent, making punitive damages superfluous? On the other hand, if the law will exceed compensation via restitution, is there any reason not to exceed compensation via punitive damages in this context?

3. Methods for calculating the amount of punitive damages require attention. *Griff* is typical in listing factors to be considered by a jury in assessing punitive damages. Again, the list varies from state to state, often including express mention of the defendant's wealth. Are these factors adequate guidance for a jury? Can they be applied with any consistency?

4. The purpose of punitive damages might offer a better starting point for calculations. If the purpose is to deter, then the amount should be based on what is needed to deter.

> The award's appropriate severity, therefore, is measured not by any reference to a need or entitlement on the part of the plaintiff, but by its efficacy to deter a defendant from repeating such malicious acts and to deter others from committing similar malicious acts in the future. The total focus is on the defendant and the defendant's conduct.

Darcars Motors of Silver Spring v. Borzym, 150 Md.App. 18, 818 A.2d 1159, 1186–87 (2003). Do the factors help juries arrive at the amount needed to deter? Or do they inject other considerations?

5. Courts often expressly rely on the deterrence purpose when limiting punitive damages. For example, in *Liggett Group v. Engle*, 853 So.2d 434 (Fla.App. 2003) (class action against tobacco companies), the court reversed punitive damages of $145 billion. Defendants had a combined net worth of only $8.3 billion. The award would destroy them, not deter them. Might the same be said for Curry. The jury here awarded nearly half of Curry's net worth as punishment for one dishonest business deal. Is that commensurate with deterrence? Or should punitive damages serve retribution, without regard to deterrence and rehabilitation? If so, do they cross the line into criminal sanctions? Even if a retributive theory was plausible, would it justify punitive damages against a corporation? Will the retribution fall on the wrongdoer or on less culpable shareholders?

6. If punitive damages are intended to deter, the question becomes how much deterrence is appropriate. In *Time Warner*, the compensatory damages exceeded $197 million. That alone would deter a lot of misconduct. Would compensatory damages provide too little deterrent? Might punitive damages provide too much deterrent? On what do the answers to these questions depend?

7. Consider the Ford Pinto. As a result of a combination of design features, the Pinto was slightly more susceptible than most cars to catch fire when struck from behind. Ford became aware of the problem and could have remedied the defect for about $9 per car. That would have cost about $125 million (estimates varied). It also would have pushed the price over $2,000 per car, a target Ford was under tremendous pressure to meet. (The Pinto

was promoted as America's answer to the VW Beetle and small, inexpensive Japanese cars that were beginning to erode the American market.) Instead, Ford marketed the car with the defect and did not recall the cars until 1978. In *Grimshaw v. Ford Motor Co.*, 119 Cal.App.3d 757, 174 Cal.Rptr. 348 (1981), the jury awarded $125 million in punitive damages, approximately the amount Ford saved by not correcting the design. The court reduced the punitive award to $3.5 million. Compensatory damages slightly exceeded $3 million: $2.5 million to one victim, $560,000 to the survivors of another. Would compensatory damages be a sufficient deterrent? Would punitive damages overdeter?

The case is famous for a document that was never admitted into evidence and that has been distorted in many reports: a memorandum in which Ford allegedly weighed the savings against the expected costs. *See* Gary Schwartz, *The Myth of the Ford Pinto Case*, 43 RUTGERS L. REV. 1013 (1991). The document calculated the benefits at $49.5 million by valuing, among other things, 180 deaths at $200,000 each and 180 serious burns at $67,000 each. The document did not relate to the Pinto, but to all cars by all manufacturers affected by a proposed new regulation by the National Highway and Traffic Safety Administration. But what if it had been a calculation of the costs and benefits of the Pinto? Would it justify punishment? Or should it justify a defense verdict on the ground that the alternative design was not cost effective? *See Barker v. Lull Engineering Co.*, 20 Cal.3d 413, 143 Cal.Rptr. 225, 573 P.2d 443 (1978).

8. *Nominal damages as basis for punitives*. An award of punitive damages must "attach" to some underlying compensatory award. *See, e.g.*, *Rivera v. City of New York*, 40 A.D.3d 334 (N.Y. 2007). The question has arisen whether nominal damages provide sufficient basis for punitives. Most jurisdictions have held that nominal damages may support punitive damages. *See, e.g.*, *Jacque v. Steenberg Homes, Inc.*, 563 N.W.2d 154 (Wis. 1997) (allowing punitive damages award in suit for trespass to land in which plaintiff received only nominal compensatory damages). A minority of jurisdictions have held the contrary. *See, e.g.*, *Gevedon v. Gevedon*, 853 N.E.2d 718 (Ohio App. 2006) ("We previously have recognized that 'actual compensatory damages rather than nominal damages are necessary to support an award of punitive damages.' " (citation omitted)).

PROBLEMS

1. If the calculation had used a more realistic value for life, would punitive damages still be appropriate? Is the miscalculation an error in judgment rather than malicious? Does it matter how big the error gap is? Consider these variations:

a. Suppose that accurate predictions suggested that the harm from the design would be limited to 5 deaths. If Ford valued those deaths at $10 million each (far more than the likely damages), they might leave the design unchanged: spending $125 million to save $50 million seems unjustified. Should punitive damages be awarded? How big would the savings have to be before 5 deaths could be justified?

b. Every automaker knows, to a certainty, that selling cars in America produces over 40,000 deaths a year (worldwide over 1 million). Suppose that a truly crash-proof car could be produced but only by increasing the cost of each car sold by $100,000 (for all that armor plating). Are the savings—$100,000 times the number of cars sold—worth the lives lost because our cars are not crash-proof? Or should automakers that refuse to make these armored behemoths face huge punitive damages to remove the savings and then some?

c. Don't most people make exactly this kind of cost benefit analysis? If it is never acceptable to put a price on the risk of death, why did only 53% of Pinto owners respond to the recall? They could have reduced the risk of death for the cost of a day of cab rides.

2. Approximately 27 people died in Pintos up to 1978. Should every Pinto plaintiff receive $3.5 million? $125 million? $4.63 million ($125 million/27)? Should the allocation of punitive damages include burn victims who survived? In what ratio? Should there be any concern for excessive punitive damages overdeterring?

Compare the concern here to double jeopardy. Punitive damages, like criminal penalties, seek to deter. Constitutionally, we forbid double punishment in criminal settings. Can we prevent double punishment when using punitive damages? Should we?

3. Criminal sanctions offer an alternative to punitive damages in some cases. The Pinto defects violated statutory provisions. Congress had specified the sanction for those violations at $1,000 per vehicle, up to a maximum of $800,000. Should courts assess larger penalties because Congress imposed such small ones? Or has Congress spoken for the public, making the cost benefit analysis for the courts? (The comparable California statute for selling a car that did not comply to federal safety standards was $50 for the first offense, $100 for a second.)

Enormous punitive damages awards in a small number of cases have generated considerable pressure to bring punitive damages under control. The remittitur in *Grimshaw* reflects the concern. Nonetheless, the United States Supreme Court has entered the fray. The next case traces the efforts to impose a constitutional limit on punitive damages.

STATE FARM MUTUAL AUTOMOBILE INSURANCE COMPANY v. CAMPBELL

538 U.S. 408, 123 S.Ct. 1513, 155 L.Ed.2d 585 (2003).

[Campbell negligently caused a traffic accident that killed Ospital and permanently disabled Slusher. Campbell's denial of fault, though initial plausible, soon became obviously untenable. Yet Campbell's insurer, State Farm, refused offers to settle the claims for the policy limit of $50,000 ($25,000 per claimant). Despite the likelihood of a judgment beyond policy limits, State Farm assured the Campbells that their assets were safe and that they did not need separate counsel. A jury held Campbell liable for $185,849 in damages. State Farm refused to cover the excess liability. Slusher and Ospital released Campbell in exchange for 90% of the proceeds of Campbell's bad faith action against State Farm.

After Campbell lost on appeal, State Farm paid the entire $185,849 judgment. The Campbells nonetheless filed a claim for bad faith, fraud, and intentional infliction of emotional distress. At a bifurcated trial, a jury held State Farm's decision not to settle was unreasonable. At the damage trial before a different jury, State Farm argued that it made an honest mistake that did not warrant punitive damages. The Campbells introduced evidence of a national scheme to meet corporate fiscal goals by capping payouts on claims company wide. The trial court admitted extensive expert testimony regarding fraudulent practices by State Farm in its nation-wide operations. The jury awarded the Campbells $2.6 million in compensatory damages and $145 million in punitive damages, which the trial court reduced to $1 million and $25 million respectively. The Utah Supreme Court reinstated the $145 million punitive damages award.]

JUSTICE KENNEDY delivered the opinion of the Court.

[I]n our judicial system compensatory and punitive damages, although usually awarded at the same time by the same decisionmaker, serve different purposes. Compensatory damages "are intended to redress the concrete loss that the plaintiff has suffered by reason of the defendant's wrongful conduct." By contrast, punitive damages serve a broader function; they are aimed at deterrence and retribution.

While States possess discretion over the imposition of punitive damages, [t]he Due Process Clause of the Fourteenth Amendment prohibits the imposition of grossly excessive or arbitrary punishments on a tortfeasor. "[E]lementary notions of fairness enshrined in our constitutional jurisprudence dictate that a person receive fair notice not only of the conduct that will subject him to punishment, but also of the severity of the penalty that a State may impose." To the extent an award is grossly excessive, it furthers no legitimate purpose and constitutes an arbitrary deprivation of property.

Although these awards serve the same purposes as criminal penalties, defendants subjected to punitive damages in civil cases have not been accorded the protections applicable in a criminal proceeding. This increases our concerns over the imprecise manner in which punitive damages systems are administered. "[Jury] instructions typically leave the jury with wide discretion in choosing amounts, and the presentation of evidence of a defendant's net worth creates the potential that juries will use their verdicts to express biases against big businesses, particularly those without strong local presences." [Vague] instructions, or those that merely inform the jury to avoid "passion or prejudice," do little to aid the decisionmaker [to] assign appropriate weight to evidence that is relevant [as opposed to] tangential or only inflammatory.

In light of these concerns, in [*BMW of North America, Inc. v.*] *Gore*[, 517 U.S. 559 (1996)], we instructed courts reviewing punitive damages to consider three guideposts: (1) the degree of reprehensibility of the defendant's misconduct; (2) the disparity between the actual or potential harm suffered by the plaintiff and the punitive damages award; and (3) the difference between the punitive damages awarded by the jury and the civil penalties authorized or imposed in comparable cases. We [later] mandated appellate courts to conduct *de novo* review of a trial court's application of them to the jury's award. Exacting appellate review ensures that an award of punitive damages is based upon an " 'application of law, rather than a decisionmaker's caprice.' " *Cooper Industries, Inc. v. Leatherman Tool Group, Inc.*, 532 U.S. 424, 436 (2001).

Under the[se] principles [i]t was error to reinstate the jury's $145 million punitive damages award. We address each guidepost of *Gore* in some detail.

A

"[T]he most important indicium of the reasonableness of a punitive damages award is the degree of reprehensibility of the defendant's conduct." We have instructed courts to determine the reprehensibility of a defendant by considering whether: the harm caused was physical as opposed to economic; the tortious conduct evinced an indifference to or a reckless disregard of the health or safety of others; the target of the conduct had financial vulnerability; the conduct involved repeated actions or was an isolated incident; and the harm was the result of intentional malice, trickery, or deceit, or mere accident. The existence of any one of these factors weighing in favor of a plaintiff may not be sufficient to sustain a punitive damages award; and the absence of all of them renders any award suspect. It should be presumed a plaintiff has been made whole for his injuries by compensatory damages, so punitive damages should only be awarded if the defendant's culpability, after having paid compensatory damages, is so reprehensible as to warrant the imposition of further sanctions to achieve punishment or deterrence.

[State] Farm's handling of the claims against the Campbells merits no praise. [E]mployees altered the company's records to make Campbell appear less culpable. State Farm disregarded the overwhelming likelihood of liability and the near-certain probability that, by taking the case to trial, a judgment in excess of the policy limits would be awarded. State Farm amplified the harm by at first assuring the Campbells their assets would be safe from any verdict and by later telling them, postjudgment, to put a for-sale sign on their house. While we do not suggest there was error in awarding punitive damages based upon State Farm's conduct toward the Campbells, a more modest punishment for this reprehensible conduct could have satisfied the State's legitimate objectives, and the Utah courts should have gone no further.

This case, instead, was used as a platform to expose, and punish, the perceived deficiencies of State Farm's operations throughout the country. [State] Farm [was] condemned for its nationwide policies rather than for the conduct direct toward the Campbells. . . .

The Campbells contend that State Farm has only itself to blame for the reliance upon dissimilar and out-of-state conduct evidence. The record does not support this contention. From their opening statements onward the Campbells framed this case as a chance to rebuke State Farm for its nationwide activities. ("[T]his is a very important case. . . . [I]t transcends the Campbell file. It involves a nationwide practice. And you, here, are going to be evaluating and assessing, and hopefully requiring State Farm to stand accountable for what it's doing across the country, which is the purpose of punitive damages"). [In] opposing State Farm's motion to exclude such evidence under *Gore,* the Campbells' counsel convinced the trial court that there was no limitation on the scope of evidence that could be considered under our precedents.

A State cannot punish a defendant for conduct that may have been lawful where it occurred. Nor, as a general rule, does a State have a legitimate concern in imposing punitive damages to punish a defendant for unlawful acts committed outside of the State's jurisdiction. Any proper adjudication of conduct that occurred outside Utah to other persons would require their inclusion, and, to those parties, the Utah courts, in the usual case, would need to apply the laws of their relevant jurisdiction.

Here, the Campbells do not dispute that much of the out-of-state conduct was lawful where it occurred. They argue, however, that such evidence was not the primary basis for the punitive damages award and was relevant to the extent it demonstrated, in a general sense, State Farm's motive against its insured. This argument misses the mark. Lawful out-of-state conduct may be probative when it demonstrates the deliberateness and culpability of the defendant's action in the State where it is tortious, but that conduct must have a nexus to the specific harm suffered by the plaintiff. A jury must be instructed, furthermore, that it may not use evidence of out-of-state conduct to punish a defendant for action that was lawful in the jurisdiction where it occurred. . . .

For a more fundamental reason, however, the Utah courts erred in relying upon this and other evidence: The courts awarded punitive damages to punish and deter conduct that bore no relation to the Campbells' harm. A defendant's dissimilar acts, independent from the acts upon which liability was premised, may not serve as the basis for punitive damages. A defendant should be punished for the conduct that harmed the plaintiff, not for being an unsavory individual or business. Due process does not permit courts, in the calculation of punitive damages, to adjudicate the merits of other parties' hypothetical claims against a defendant under the guise of the reprehensibility analysis, but we have no doubt the Utah Supreme Court did that here. ("Even if the harm to the Campbells can be appropriately characterized as minimal, the trial court's assessment of the situation is on target: 'The harm is minor to the individual but massive in the aggregate' "). Punishment on these bases creates the possibility of multiple punitive damages awards for the same conduct; for in the usual case nonparties are not bound by the judgment some other plaintiff obtains

The same reasons lead us to conclude the Utah Supreme Court's decision cannot be justified on the grounds that State Farm was a recidivist. Although "[a] recidivist may be punished more severely than a first offender," in the context of civil actions courts must ensure the conduct in question replicates the prior transgressions.

The Campbells have identified scant evidence of repeated misconduct of the sort that injured them. Nor does our review of the Utah courts' decisions convince us that State Farm was only punished for its actions toward the Campbells. Although evidence of other acts need not be identical to have relevance in the calculation of punitive damages, the Utah court erred here because evidence pertaining to claims that had nothing to do with a third-party lawsuit was introduced at length. Other evidence concerning reprehensibility was even more tangential. For example, the Utah Supreme Court criticized State Farm's investigation into the personal life of one of its employees and, in a broader approach, the manner in which State Farm's policies corrupted its employees. The Campbells attempt to justify the courts' reliance upon this unrelated testimony on the theory that each dollar of profit made by underpaying a third-party claimant is the same as a dollar made by underpaying a first-party one. For the reasons already stated, this argument is unconvincing. The reprehensibility guidepost does not permit courts to expand the scope of the case so that a defendant may be punished for any malfeasance, which in this case extended for a 20-year period. In this case, because the Campbells have shown no conduct by State Farm similar to that which harmed them, the conduct that harmed them is the only conduct relevant to the reprehensibility analysis.

B

[W]e have been reluctant to identify concrete constitutional limits on the ratio between harm, or potential harm, to the plaintiff and the punitive damages award. We decline again to impose a bright-line ratio which a punitive damages award cannot exceed. Our jurisprudence and the principles it has now established demonstrate, however, that, in practice, few awards exceeding a single-digit ratio between punitive and compensatory damages, to a significant degree, will satisfy due process. In *Haslip,* in upholding a punitive damages award, we concluded that an award of more than four times the amount of compensatory damages might be close to the line of constitutional impropriety. [We have] referenced a long legislative history, dating back over 700 years [providing] for sanctions of double, treble, or quadruple damages to deter and punish. While these ratios are not binding, they are instructive. They demonstrate what should be obvious: Single-digit multipliers are more likely to comport with due process, while still achieving the State's goals of deterrence and retribution, than awards with ratios in range of 500 to 1, or, in this case, of 145 to 1.

Nonetheless, because there are no rigid benchmarks that a punitive damages award may not surpass, ratios greater than those we have previously upheld may comport with due process where "a particularly egregious act has resulted in only a small amount of economic damages." *Gore* (positing that a higher ratio *might* be necessary where "the injury is hard to detect or the monetary value of noneconomic harm might have been difficult to determine"). The converse is also true, however. When compensatory damages are substantial, then a lesser ratio, perhaps only equal to compensatory damages, can reach the outermost limit of the due process guarantee. The precise award in any case, of course, must be based upon the facts and circumstances of the defendant's conduct and the harm to the plaintiff.

In sum, courts must ensure that the measure of punishment is both reasonable and proportionate to the amount of harm to the plaintiff and to the general damages recovered. In the context of this case, we have no doubt that there is a presumption against an award that has a 145–to–1 ratio. The compensatory award in this case was substantial; the Campbells were awarded $1 million for a year and a half of emotional distress. This was complete compensation. The harm arose from a transaction in the economic realm, not from some physical assault or trauma; there were no physical injuries; and State Farm paid the excess verdict before the complaint was filed, so the Campbells suffered only minor economic injuries for the 18-month period in which State Farm refused to resolve the claim against them. The compensatory damages for the injury suffered here, moreover, likely were based on a component which was duplicated in the punitive award. Much of the distress was caused by the outrage and humiliation the Campbells suffered at the actions of their insurer; and it is a major role of punitive damages to condemn such conduct. Compensatory damages, however, already contain this punitive element. See Restatement (Second) of Torts § 908, Comment *c,* p. 466 (1977) ("In many cases in which compensatory damages include an amount for emotional distress, such as humiliation or indignation aroused by the defendant's act, there is no clear line of demarcation between punishment and compensation and a verdict for a specified amount frequently includes elements of both").

The Utah Supreme Court sought to justify the massive award by pointing to State Farm's purported failure to report a prior $100 million punitive damages award in Texas to its corporate headquarters; the fact that State Farm's policies have affected numerous Utah consumers; the fact that State Farm will only be punished in one out of every 50,000 cases as a matter of statistical probability; and State Farm's enormous wealth. . . . The Texas award [should] have been analyzed in the context of the reprehensibility guidepost only. The failure of the company to report the Texas award is out-of-state conduct that [might] have had some bearing on the degree of reprehensibility, [but] was dissimilar, and of such marginal relevance that it should have been accorded little or no weight. The award was rendered in a first-party lawsuit; no judgment was entered in the case; and it was later settled for a fraction of the verdict. With respect to the Utah Supreme Court's second justification, the Campbells' inability to direct us to testimony demonstrating harm to the people of Utah (other than those directly involved in this case) indicates that the adverse effect on the State's general population was in fact minor.

The remaining premises for the Utah Supreme Court's decision bear no relation to the award's reasonableness or proportionality to the harm. [T]he argument that State Farm will be punished in only the rare case, coupled with reference to its assets (which, of course, are what other insured parties in Utah and other States must rely upon for payment of claims) had little to do with the actual harm sustained by the Campbells. The wealth of a defendant cannot justify an otherwise unconstitutional punitive damages award. *Gore,* 517 U.S., at 585 ("The fact that BMW is a large corporation rather than an impecunious individual does not diminish its entitlement to fair notice of the demands that the several States impose on the conduct of its business"); see also *id.,* at 591 (BREYER, J., concurring) ("[Wealth] provides an open-ended basis for inflating awards when the defendant is wealthy. . . . That does not make its use unlawful or inappropriate; it simply means that this factor cannot make up for the failure of other factors, such as 'reprehensibility,' to constrain significantly an award that purports to punish a defendant's conduct"). The principles set forth in *Gore* must be implemented with care, to ensure both reasonableness and proportionality.

C

The third guidepost in *Gore* is the disparity between the punitive damages award and the "civil penalties authorized or imposed in comparable cases." We note that, in the past, we have also looked to criminal penalties that could be imposed. The existence of a criminal penalty does have bearing on the seriousness with which a State views the wrongful action. When used to determine the dollar amount of the award, however, the criminal penalty has less utility. Great care must be taken to avoid use of the civil process to assess criminal penalties that can be imposed only after the heightened protections of a criminal trial have been observed, including, of course, its higher standards of proof. Punitive damages are not a substitute for the criminal process, and the remote possibility of a criminal sanction does not automatically sustain a punitive damages award.

Here, we need not dwell long on this guidepost. The most relevant civil sanction under Utah state law for the wrong done to the Campbells appears to be a $10,000 fine for an act of fraud, an amount dwarfed by the $145 million punitive damages award. The Supreme Court of Utah speculated about the loss of State Farm's business license, the disgorgement of profits, and possible imprisonment, but here again its references were to the broad fraudulent scheme drawn from evidence of out-of-state and dissimilar conduct. This analysis was insufficient to justify the award.

IV

An application of the *Gore* guideposts to the facts of this case, especially in light of the substantial compensatory damages awarded (a portion of which contained a punitive element), likely would justify a punitive damages award at or near the amount of compensatory damages. The punitive award of $145 million, therefore, was neither reasonable nor proportionate to the wrong committed, and it was an irrational and arbitrary deprivation of the property of the defendant. The proper calculation of punitive damages under the principles we have discussed should be resolved, in the first instance, by the Utah courts.

The judgment of the Utah Supreme Court is reversed, and the case is remanded for proceedings not inconsistent with this opinion.

[JUSTICE SCALIA and JUSTICE THOMAS each wrote dissenting opinions, briefly stating that the Constitution did not constrain the States' discretion over punitive damages.]

JUSTICE GINSBURG, dissenting.

Not long ago, this Court was hesitant to impose a federal check on state-court judgments awarding punitive damages. In *Browning–Ferris Industries of Vt., Inc. v. Kelco Disposal, Inc.,* 492 U.S. 257 (1989), the Court held that neither the Excessive Fines Clause of the Eighth Amendment nor federal common law circumscribed awards of punitive damages in civil cases between private parties. Two years later, in *Pacific Mut. Life Ins. Co. v. Haslip,* 499 U.S. 1 (1991), the Court observed that "unlimited jury [or judicial] discretion . . . in the fixing of punitive damages may invite extreme results that jar one's constitutional sensibilities"; the Due Process Clause, the Court suggested, would attend to those sensibilities and guard against unreasonable awards. Nevertheless, the Court upheld a punitive damages award in *Haslip* "more than 4 times the amount of compensatory damages, [more] than 200 times [the plaintiff's] out-of-pocket expenses," and "much in excess of the fine that could be imposed." And in *TXO Production Corp. v. Alliance Resources Corp.,* 509 U.S. 443 (1993), the Court affirmed a state-court award "526 times greater than the actual damages awarded by the jury."[1]

It was not until 1996, in *Gore,* that the Court, for the first time, invalidated a state-court punitive damages assessment as unreasonably large. If our activity in this domain is now "well-established," it takes place on ground not long held.

[U]nlike federal habeas corpus review of state-court convictions, the Court "work[s] at this business [of checking state courts] alone," unaided by the participation of federal district courts and courts of appeals. It was once recognized that "the laws of the particular State must suffice [to superintend punitive damages awards] until judges or legislators authorized to do so initiate system-wide change." I would adhere to that traditional view.

I

The large size of the award upheld by the Utah Supreme Court in this case indicates why damage-capping legislation may be altogether fitting and proper. Neither the amount of the award nor the trial record, however, justifies this Court's substitution of its judgment for that of Utah's competent decisionmakers. In this regard, I count it significant that, on the key criterion "reprehensibility," there is a good deal more to the story than the Court's abbreviated account tells.

Ample evidence allowed the jury to find that State Farm's treatment of the Campbells typified its "Performance, Planning and Review" (PP & R) program [with] "the explicit objective of using the claims-adjustment process as a profit center." "[T]he PP & R program . . . has functioned, and continues to function, as an unlawful scheme . . . to deny benefits owed consumers by paying out less than fair value in order to meet preset, arbitrary payout targets designed to enhance corporate profits." That policy, the trial court observed, was encompassing in scope; it "applied equally to the handling of both third-party and first-party claims."

[Justice Ginsburg then recited a number of examples of State Farm's misconduct, emphasizing conduct involving Utah and the Campbells. For example, State Farm claims adjusters would support optimistic projections of liability by inserting false statements about claimants in

[1] By switching the focus from the ratio of punitive to compensatory damages to the potential loss to the plaintiffs had the defendant succeeded in its illicit scheme, the Court could describe the relevant ratio in *TXO* as 10 to 1.

the file. In the Campbell case, a manager ordered an adjuster to write in the file that Todd Ospital (who was killed in the accident) was speeding because he was on his way to see a "pregnant girlfriend." In truth, "[t]here was no "pregnant girlfriend."]

Regarding liability for verdicts in excess of policy limits, the trial court referred to a State Farm document titled the "Excess Liability Handbook" [which] instructed adjusters to pad files with "self-serving" documents, and to leave critical items out of files, for example, evaluations of the insured's exposure. Divisional superintendent Bill Brown [ordered] adjuster Summers to change the portions of his report indicating that Mr. Campbell was likely at fault and that the settlement cost was correspondingly high. . . . State Farm's policy [was] "deliberately crafted" to prey on consumers who would be unlikely to defend themselves: "the weakest of the herd"—"the elderly, the poor, and other consumers who are least knowledgeable about their rights and thus most vulnerable to trickery or deceit, or who have little money and hence have no real alternative but to accept an inadequate offer to settle a claim at much less than fair value." The Campbells themselves [appeared] economically vulnerable and emotionally fragile. [Mr.] Campbell had residuary effects from a stroke and Parkinson's disease.

To further insulate itself from liability, trial evidence indicated, State Farm made "systematic" efforts to destroy internal company documents that might reveal its scheme, efforts that directly affected the Campbells. . . .

State Farm's "wrongful profit and evasion schemes," the trial court underscored, were directly relevant to the Campbells' case.

> [H]igh-level manager Bill Brown was under heavy pressure from the PP & R scheme to control indemnity payouts during the time period in question. In particular, when Brown declined to pay the excess verdict against Curtis Campbell, or even post a bond, he had a special need to keep his year-end numbers down, since the State Farm incentive scheme meant that keeping those numbers down was important to helping Brown get a much-desired transfer to Colorado. . . .

State Farm's "policies and practices," the trial evidence thus bore out, were "responsible for the injuries suffered by the Campbells," and the means used to implement those policies could be found "callous, clandestine, fraudulent, and dishonest." The Utah Supreme Court, relying on the trial court's record-based recitations, understandably characterized State Farm's behavior as "egregious and malicious."

II

The Court dismisses the evidence describing and documenting State Farm's PP & R policy and practices as essentially irrelevant, bearing "no relation to the Campbells' harm." . . . Once one recognizes that the Campbells did show "conduct by State Farm similar to that which harmed them," it becomes impossible to shrink the reprehensibility analysis to this sole case, or to maintain, at odds with the determination of the trial court, that "the adverse effect on the State's general population was in fact minor."

Evidence of out-of-state conduct, the Court acknowledges, may be "probative [even if the conduct is lawful in the state where it occurred] when it demonstrates the deliberateness and culpability of the defendant's action in the State where it is tortious . . . " The evidence was admissible, the trial court ruled: (1) to document State Farm's "reprehensible" PP & R program; and (2) to "rebut [State Farm's] assertion that [its] actions toward the Campbells were inadvertent errors or mistakes in judgment." Viewed in this light, there surely was "a nexus" between much of the "other acts" evidence and "the specific harm suffered by [the Campbells]."

III

When the Court first ventured to override state-court punitive damages awards, it did so moderately. The Court recalled that "[i]n our federal system, States necessarily have considerable flexibility in determining the level of punitive damages that they will allow in different classes of cases and in any particular case." Today's decision exhibits no such respect and restraint. No longer content to accord state-court judgments "a strong presumption of validity," the Court announces that "few awards exceeding a single-digit ratio between punitive and compensatory damages, to a significant degree, will satisfy due process."[2] Moreover, the Court adds, when compensatory damages are substantial, doubling those damages "can reach the outermost limit of the due process guarantee." In a legislative scheme or a state high court's design to cap punitive damages, the handiwork in setting single-digit and 1–to–1 benchmarks could hardly be questioned; in a judicial decree imposed on the States by this Court under the banner of substantive due process, the numerical controls [seem] to me boldly out of order.

I remain of the view that this Court has no warrant to reform state law governing awards of punitive damages. Even if I were prepared to accept the flexible guides prescribed in *Gore,* I would not join the Court's swift conversion of those guides into instructions that begin to resemble marching orders. For the reasons stated, I would leave the judgment of the Utah Supreme Court undisturbed.

---

[2] *TXO Production Corp. v. Alliance Resources Corp.,* 509 U.S. 443, 462, n. 8 (1993), noted that "[u]nder well-settled law," a defendant's "wrongdoing in other parts of the country" and its "impressive net worth" are factors "typically considered in assessing punitive damages." It remains to be seen whether, or the extent to which, today's decision will unsettle that law.

NOTES AND QUESTIONS

1. On remand, the Utah Supreme Court held that the insurer's conduct warranted punitive damages of $9,018,780.75, nine times the compensatory damages for emotional distress. *Campbell v. State Farm Mut. Auto. Ins. Co.*, 98 P.3d 409 (Utah 2004).

2. Does this decision supplant state law on when and how to assess punitive damages? Most states use similar factors already. Are they compelled to use these and no others? These questions have particular bite regarding evidence of defendant's wealth. Press reports suggested the decision precluded plaintiffs from introducing such evidence in the future. Do you agree? *See Eden Electrical Ltd v. Amana Co.*, 258 F.Supp.2d 958 (N.D.Iowa 2003).

3. Before *Campbell*, courts already struggled with the requirement in *Cooper Industries* that courts use de novo review. *Time Warner* concluded that de novo review was required only for challenges under the constitution, not under state law. *See Time Warner Entertainment Co. v. Six Flags Over Georgia, L.L.C.*, 254 Ga. App. 598, 563 S.E.2d 178 (2002), *cert. denied*, 538 U.S. 977, 123 S.Ct. 1783, 155 L.Ed.2d 665 (2003). It also concluded that defendant had preserved its claim that the punitive damages violated Georgia law but had waived the claim under the U.S. Constitution.

4. Is *Campbell* likely to produce many different decisions in punitive damage cases? Is any court that would have affirmed an award under state law likely to reject it under *Campbell*? Professor Ted Eisenberg led an empirical study on punitive damages and found "a strong and statistically significant relationship between compensatory and punitive damages," specifically that about 80% of all punitive damage awards fell within a compensatory-to-punitives multiple of 8.117. Theodore Eisenberg et al., *The Predictability of Punitive Damages*, 26 J. LEGAL STUD. 623 (1997).

5. Some states limit the amount of punitive damages that the plaintiff may keep. From a deterrence standpoint, it doesn't matter who receives the punitive award as long as defendant pays it. Once fully compensated for the loss, the plaintiff has no vested claim to the punitive award. By statute or judicial decision, some states now direct a portion of punitive awards into the coffers of the state or into a program for the benefit of the public or tort victims generally. *See* Iowa Code § 668A.1(2) (60%); Fla. Stat. § 768,73(2) (75%); *Dardinger v. Anthem Blue Cross & Blue Shield*, 98 Ohio St.3d 77, 781 N.E.2d 121 (2002) (amount discretionary with court; of $30 million, plaintiff received $10 million plus litigation costs and fees). These provisions often reduce the state's share in order to cover plaintiff's attorneys' fees and other costs of suit. Some courts, however, have rejected legislative confiscation of punitive damages. *See Kirk v. Denver Pub. Co.*, 818 P.2d 262 (Colo. 1991) (takings clause).

6. If the state receives the punitive damage award, isn't it really a fine? If so, aren't criminal procedures required to impose it? Does it matter

whether the state receives the money or simply directs that it be given to a particular charity or fund?

7. The use of punitive damages to cover attorneys' fees is understandable. As long as the American rule persists, damages are inherently undercompensatory. But why should attorneys' fees come out of the portion reserved to the state? Should plaintiffs' share be limited to the amount of attorneys' fees and other litigation costs? That would complete compensation without creating a potential windfall to encourage excessive litigation.

8. Should the Campbell single-digit guideline apply where a plaintiff's punitive damages accompany an award of nominal damages? Courts have generally rejected such a limitation. *See, e.g., Mendez v. County of San Bernardino*, 540 F.3d 1109 (9th Cir. 2008) (upholding $5,000 punitive damages award in conjunction with $1.00 in nominal damages in civil rights claim); *JCB, Inc. v. Union Planters Bank, NA*, 539 F.3d 862 (8th Cir. 2008) (ordering punitive damages award of $108,750 alongside nominal damages of $1.00 in trespass action).

MATHIAS V. ACCOR ECONOMY LODGING, INC.

347 F.3d 672 (7th Cir. 2003).

POSNER, CIRCUIT JUDGE.

The plaintiffs brought this diversity suit governed by Illinois law against . . . the "Motel 6" chain of hotels and motels. One of these hotels (now a "Red Roof Inn," though still owned by the defendant) is in downtown Chicago. The plaintiffs, a brother and sister, were guests there and were bitten by bedbugs, which are making a comeback in the U.S. as a consequence of more conservative use of pesticides. The plaintiffs claim that in allowing guests to be attacked by bedbugs in a motel that charges upwards of $100 a day for a room and would not like to be mistaken for a flophouse, the defendant was guilty of "willful and wanton conduct" and thus under Illinois law is liable for punitive as well as compensatory damages. The jury agreed and awarded each plaintiff $186,000 in punitive damages though only $5,000 in compensatory damages. The defendant appeals, complaining primarily about the punitive-damages award. . . .

The defendant argues that at worst it is guilty of simple negligence, and if this is right the plaintiffs were not entitled by Illinois law to any award of punitive damages. It also complains that the award was excessive—indeed that any award in excess of $20,000 to each plaintiff would deprive the defendant of its property without due process of law. The first complaint has no possible merit, as the evidence of gross negligence, indeed of recklessness in the strong sense of an unjustifiable failure to avoid a *known* risk, was amply shown. In 1998, EcoLab, the extermination service that the motel used, discovered bedbugs in several rooms in the motel and recommended that it be hired to spray every room, for which it would charge the motel only $500; the motel refused. The next year, bedbugs were again discovered in a room but EcoLab was asked to spray just that room. The motel tried to negotiate "a building sweep [by EcoLab] free of charge," but, not surprisingly, the negotiation failed. By the spring of 2000, the motel's manager "started noticing that there were refunds being given by my desk clerks and reports coming back from the guests that there were ticks in the rooms and bugs in the rooms that were biting." She looked in some of the rooms and discovered bedbugs. The defendant asks us to disregard her testimony as that of a disgruntled ex-employee, but of course her credibility was for the jury, not the defendant, to determine.

Further incidents of guests being bitten by insects and demanding and receiving refunds led the manager to recommend to her superior in the company that the motel be closed while every room was sprayed, but this was refused. This superior, a district manager, was a management-level employee of the defendant, and his knowledge of the risk and failure to take effective steps either to eliminate it or to warn the motel's guests are imputed to his employer for purposes of determining whether the employer should be liable for punitive damages. The employer's liability for compensatory damages is of course automatic on the basis of the principle of respondeat superior, since the district manager was acting within the scope of his employment.

The infestation continued and began to reach farcical proportions, as when a guest, after complaining of having been bitten repeatedly by insects while asleep in his room in the hotel was moved to another room only to discover insects there; and within 18 minutes of being moved to a third room he discovered insects in that room as well and had to be moved still again. (Odd that at that point he didn't flee the motel.) By July, the motel's management was acknowledging to EcoLab that there was a "major problem with bed bugs" and that all that was being done about it was "chasing them from room to room." Desk clerks were instructed to call the "bedbugs" "ticks," apparently on the theory that customers would be less alarmed, though in fact ticks are more dangerous than bedbugs. . . . Rooms that the motel had placed on "Do not rent, bugs in room" status nevertheless were rented.

It was in November that the plaintiffs checked into the motel. They were given Room 504, even though the motel had classified the room as "DO NOT RENT UNTIL TREATED," and it had not been treated. Indeed, that night 190 of the hotel's 191 rooms were occupied, even though a number of them had been placed on the same don't-rent status as Room 504. . . .

Although bedbug bites are not as serious as the bites of some other insects, they are painful and unsightly. Motel 6 could not have rented any rooms at the prices it charged had it informed guests that the risk of being bitten by bedbugs was appreciable. Its failure either to warn guests or to take effective measures to eliminate the bedbugs amounted to fraud and probably to battery as well.... There was, in short, sufficient evidence of "willful and wanton conduct" within the meaning that the Illinois courts assign to the term to permit an award of punitive damages in this case.

But in what amount? In arguing that $20,000 was the maximum amount of punitive damages that a jury could constitutionally have awarded each plaintiff, the defendant points to the U.S. Supreme Court's recent statement that "few awards [of punitive damages] exceeding a single-digit ratio between punitive and compensatory damages, to a significant degree, will satisfy due process." *State Farm Mutual Automobile Ins. Co. v. Campbell,* 538 U.S. 408, 123 S.Ct. 1513, 1524 (2003). The Court went on to suggest that "four times the amount of compensatory damages might be close to the line of constitutional impropriety." Hence the defendant's proposed ceiling in this case of $20,000, four times the compensatory damages awarded to each plaintiff. The ratio of punitive to compensatory damages determined by the jury was, in contrast, 37.2 to 1.

The Supreme Court did not, however, lay down a 4–to–1 or single-digit-ratio rule—it said merely that "there is a presumption against an award that has a 145–to–1 ratio"—and it would be unreasonable to do so. We must consider why punitive damages are awarded and why the Court has decided that due process requires that such awards be limited. The second question is easier to answer than the first. The term "punitive damages" implies punishment, and a standard principle of penal theory is that "the punishment should fit the crime" in the sense of being proportional to the wrongfulness of the defendant's action, though the principle is modified when the probability of detection is very low (a familiar example is the heavy fines for littering) or the crime is potentially lucrative (as in the case of trafficking in illegal drugs). Hence, with these qualifications, which in fact will figure in our analysis of this case, punitive damages should be proportional to the wrongfulness of the defendant's actions.

Another penal precept is that a defendant should have reasonable notice of the sanction for unlawful acts, so that he can make a rational determination of how to act; and so there have to be reasonably clear standards for determining the amount of punitive damages for particular wrongs.

And a third precept, the core of the Aristotelian notion of corrective justice, and more broadly of the principle of the rule of law, is that sanctions should be based on the wrong done rather than on the status of the defendant; a person is punished for what he does, not for who he is, even if the who is a huge corporation.

What follows from these principles, however, is that punitive damages should be admeasured by standards or rules rather than in a completely ad hoc manner, and this does not tell us what the maximum ratio of punitive to compensatory damages should be in a particular case. To determine that, we have to consider why punitive damages are awarded in the first place.

England's common law courts first confirmed their authority to award punitive damages in the eighteenth century, see Dorsey D. Ellis, Jr., "Fairness and Efficiency in the Law of Punitive Damages," 56 S. CAL. L. REV. 1, 12–20 (1982), at a time when the institutional structure of criminal law enforcement was primitive and it made sense to leave certain minor crimes to be dealt with by the civil law. And still today one function of punitive-damages awards is to relieve the pressures on an overloaded system of criminal justice by providing a civil alternative to criminal prosecution of minor crimes. An example is deliberately spitting in a person's face, a criminal assault but because minor readily deterrable by the levying of what amounts to a civil fine through a suit for damages for the tort of battery. Compensatory damages would not do the trick in such a case, and this for three reasons: because they are difficult to determine in the case of acts that inflict largely dignatory harms; because in the spitting case they would be too slight to give the victim an incentive to sue, and he might decide instead to respond with violence—and an age-old purpose of the law of torts is to provide a substitute for violent retaliation against wrongful injury—and because to limit the plaintiff to compensatory damages would enable the defendant to commit the offensive act with impunity provided that he was willing to pay, and again there would be a danger that his act would incite a breach of the peace by his victim.

When punitive damages are sought for billion-dollar oil spills and other huge economic injuries, the considerations that we have just canvassed fade. As the Court emphasized in *Campbell,* the fact that the plaintiffs in that case had been awarded very substantial compensatory damages—$1 million for a dispute over insurance coverage—greatly reduced the need for giving them a huge award of punitive damages ($145 million) as well in order to provide an effective remedy. Our case is closer to the spitting case. The defendant's behavior was outrageous but the compensable harm done was slight and at the same time difficult to quantify because a large element of it was emotional. And the defendant may well have profited from its misconduct because by concealing the infestation it was able to keep renting rooms. Refunds were frequent but may have cost less than the cost of closing the hotel for a thorough fumigation. The hotel's attempt to pass off the bedbugs as ticks, which some guests might ignorantly have thought less unhealthful, may have postponed the instituting of litigation to rectify the hotel's misconduct. The award of punitive damages in this case thus serves the additional purpose of limiting the defendant's ability to profit from its fraud by escaping detection and (private) prosecution. If a tortfeasor is "caught" only half the time he commits torts, then when he is caught he should be punished twice as heavily in order to make up for the times he gets away.

Finally, if the total stakes in the case were capped at $50,000 (2 × [$5,000 + $20,000]), the plaintiffs might well have had difficulty financing this lawsuit. It is here that the defendant's aggregate net worth of $1.6 billion becomes relevant. A defendant's wealth is not a sufficient basis for awarding punitive damages. *State Farm Mutual Automobile Ins. Co. v. Campbell, supra,* 123 S.Ct. at 1525. That would be discriminatory and would violate the rule of law [by] making punishment depend on status rather than conduct. Where wealth in the sense of resources enters is in enabling the defendant to mount an extremely aggressive defense against suits such as this and by doing so to make litigating against it very costly, which in turn may make it difficult for the plaintiffs to find a lawyer willing to handle their case, involving as it does only modest stakes, for the usual 33–40 percent contingent fee.

In other words, the defendant is investing in developing a reputation intended to deter plaintiffs. It is difficult otherwise to explain the great stubborness [sic] with which it has defended this case, making a host of frivolous evidentiary arguments despite the very modest stakes even when the punitive damages awarded by the jury are included.

[W]e note that "net worth" is not the correct measure of a corporation's resources. It is an accounting artifact that reflects the allocation of ownership between equity and debt claimants. A firm financed largely by equity investors has a large "net worth" (= the value of the equity claims), while the identical firm financed largely by debt may have only a small net worth because accountants treat debt as a liability.

All things considered, we cannot say that the award of punitive damages was excessive, albeit the precise number chosen by the jury was arbitrary. It is probably not a coincidence that $5,000 + $186,000 = $191,000/191 = $1,000: *i.e.*, $1,000 per room in the hotel. But as there are no punitive-damages guidelines, corresponding to the federal and state sentencing guidelines, it is inevitable that the specific amount of punitive damages awarded whether by a judge or by a jury will be arbitrary. [The] judicial function is to police a range, not a point.

[I]t would have been helpful had the parties presented evidence concerning the regulatory or criminal penalties to which the defendant exposed itself by deliberately exposing its customers to a substantial risk of being bitten by bedbugs. That is an inquiry recommended by the

Supreme Court. But we do not think its omission invalidates the award. We can take judicial notice that deliberate exposure of hotel guests to the health risks created by insect infestations exposes the hotel's owner to sanctions under Illinois and Chicago law that in the aggregate are comparable in severity to that of the punitive damage award in this case.

[This case involves] a misdemeanor, punishable by up to a year's imprisonment or a fine of $2,500, or both. 720 ILCS 5/12–5(b); 730 ILCS 5/5–8–3(a)(1), 5/5–9–1(a)(2). Of course a corporation cannot be sent to prison, and $2,500 is obviously much less than the $186,000 awarded to each plaintiff in this case as punitive damages. But this is just the beginning. Other guests of the hotel were endangered besides these two plaintiffs. And, what is much more important, a Chicago hotel that permits unsanitary conditions to exist is subject to revocation of its license, without which it cannot operate. We are sure that the defendant would prefer to pay the punitive damages assessed in this case than to lose its license.

AFFIRMED.

NOTES AND QUESTIONS

1. The court suggests that punitive damages are needed to provide a civil venue for enforcement of minor crimes. Does this observation have implications for the way in which courts award punitive damages? Do you agree that compensatory sanctions will not adequately deter torts that cause little physical injury? Do the concerns that led to the creation of punitive damages in the 18th Century still apply today?

2. Did the court follow *State Farm* or rebel against it? Could you reframe the arguments to be more persuasive or to produce a different result?

3. The court talks of both punishment and deterrence. Does it treat these as two separate purposes for punitive damages or as parts of a single purpose? Does the purpose help resolve the case? Or is this discussion mere surplusage?

4. In its final paragraph, the court states that "Other guests of the hotel were endangered besides these two plaintiffs." Does consideration of this factor square with the Supreme Court's language in State Farm? The Supreme Court addressed this question in the following case.

PHILIP MORRIS USA V. WILLIAMS

549 U.S. 346, 127 S.Ct. 1057, 166 L.Ed.2d 940 (2007).

BREYER, J., delivered the opinion of the Court, in which ROBERTS, C.J., and KENNEDY, SOUTER, and ALITO, JJ., joined. STEVENS, J., and THOMAS, J., filed dissenting opinions. GINSBURG, J., filed a dissenting opinion, in which SCALIA and THOMAS, JJ., joined.

JUSTICE BREYER delivered the opinion of the Court.

The question we address today concerns a large state-court punitive damages award. We are asked whether the Constitution's Due Process Clause permits a jury to base that award in part upon its desire to *punish* the defendant for harming persons who are not before the court (*e.g.,* victims whom the parties do not represent). We hold that such an award would amount to a taking of "property" from the defendant without due process.

I

This lawsuit arises out of the death of Jesse Williams, a heavy cigarette smoker. Respondent, Williams' widow, represents his estate in this state lawsuit for negligence and deceit against Philip Morris, the manufacturer of Marlboro, the brand that Williams favored. A jury found that Williams' death was caused by smoking; that Williams smoked in significant part because he thought it was safe to do so; and that Philip Morris knowingly and falsely led him to believe that this was so. The jury ultimately found that Philip Morris was negligent (as was Williams) and that Philip Morris had engaged in deceit. In respect to deceit, the claim at issue here, it awarded compensatory damages of about $821,000 (about $21,000 economic and $800,000 noneconomic) along with $79.5 million in punitive damages.

The trial judge subsequently found the $79.5 million punitive damages award "excessive" and reduced it to $32 million. Both sides appealed. The Oregon Court of Appeals rejected Philip Morris' arguments and restored the $79.5 million jury award. Subsequently, Philip Morris sought review in the Oregon Supreme Court (which denied review) and then here. We remanded the case in light of *State Farm Mut. Automobile Ins. Co. v. Campbell.* The Oregon Court of Appeals adhered to its original views. And Philip Morris sought, and this time obtained, review in the Oregon Supreme Court.

Philip Morris then made two arguments relevant here. First, it said that the trial court should have accepted, but did not accept, a proposed "punitive damages" instruction that specified the jury could not seek to punish Philip Morris for injury to other persons not before the court. In particular, Philip Morris pointed out that the plaintiff's attorney had told the jury to "think about how many other Jesse Williams in the last 40 years in the State of Oregon there have been. . . . In Oregon, how many people do we see outside, driving home . . . smoking cigarettes? . . . [C]igarettes . . . are going to kill ten [of every hundred]. [And] the market share of Marlboros [*i.e.,* Philip Morris] is one-third [*i.e.,* one of every three killed]." In light of this argument, Philip Morris asked the trial court to tell the jury that "you may consider the extent of harm suffered by others in determining what [the] reasonable relationship is" between any punitive award and "the harm caused to Jesse Williams" by Philip Morris' misconduct, "[but] you are not to punish the defendant for the impact of its alleged misconduct on other persons, who may bring lawsuits of their own in which other juries can resolve their claims. . . ." The judge rejected this proposal and instead told the jury that "[p]unitive damages are awarded against a defendant to punish misconduct and to deter misconduct," and "are not intended to compensate the plaintiff or anyone else for damages caused by the defendant's conduct." In Philip Morris' view, the result was a significant likelihood that a portion of the $79.5 million award represented punishment for its having harmed others, a punishment that the Due Process Clause would here forbid.

Second, Philip Morris pointed to the roughly 100–to–1 ratio the $79.5 million punitive damages award bears to $821,000 in compensatory damages. Philip Morris noted that this Court in *BMW* emphasized the constitutional need for punitive damages awards to reflect (1) the "reprehensibility" of the defendant's conduct, (2) a "reasonable relationship" to the harm the plaintiff (or related victim) suffered, and (3) the presence (or absence) of "sanctions," *e.g.*, criminal penalties, that state law provided for comparable conduct. And in *State Farm,* this Court said that the longstanding historical practice of setting punitive damages at two, three, or four times the size of compensatory damages, while "not binding," is "instructive," and that "[s]ingle-digit multipliers are more likely to comport with due process." Philip Morris claimed that, in light of this case law, the punitive award was "grossly excessive."

The Oregon Supreme Court rejected these and other Philip Morris arguments. In particular, it rejected Philip Morris' claim that the Constitution prohibits a state jury "from using punitive damages to punish a defendant for harm to nonparties." And in light of Philip Morris' reprehensible conduct, it found that the $79.5 million award was not "grossly excessive."

Philip Morris then sought certiorari. It asked us to consider, among other things, (1) its claim that Oregon had unconstitutionally permitted it to be punished for harming nonparty victims; and (2) whether Oregon had in effect disregarded "the constitutional requirement that punitive damages be reasonably related to the plaintiff's harm." We granted certiorari limited to these two questions.

For reasons we shall set forth, we consider only the first of these questions. We vacate the Oregon Supreme Court's judgment, and we remand the case for further proceedings.

* * *

III

In our view, the Constitution's Due Process Clause forbids a State to use a punitive damages award to punish a defendant for injury that it inflicts upon nonparties or those whom they directly represent, *i.e.,* injury that it inflicts upon those who are, essentially, strangers to the litigation. For one thing, the Due Process Clause prohibits a State from punishing an individual without first providing that individual with "an opportunity to present every available defense." Yet a defendant threatened with punishment for injuring a nonparty victim has no opportunity to defend against the charge, by showing, for example in a case such as this, that the other victim was not entitled to damages because he or she knew that smoking was dangerous or did not rely upon the defendant's statements to the contrary.

For another, to permit punishment for injuring a nonparty victim would add a near standardless dimension to the punitive damages equation. How many such victims are there? How seriously were they injured? Under what circumstances did injury occur? The trial will not likely answer such questions as to nonparty victims. The jury will be left to speculate. And the fundamental due process concerns to which our punitive damages cases refer—risks of arbitrariness, uncertainty and lack of notice—will be magnified.

Finally, we can find no authority supporting the use of punitive damages awards for the purpose of punishing a defendant for harming others. We have said that it may be appropriate to consider the reasonableness of a punitive damages award in light of the *potential* harm the defendant's conduct could have caused. But we have made clear that the potential harm at issue was harm potentially caused *the plaintiff*. We did use the term "error-free" (in *BMW*) to describe a lower court punitive damages calculation that likely included harm to others in the equation. But context makes clear that the term "error-free" in the *BMW* footnote referred to errors relevant to the case at hand. Although elsewhere in *BMW* we noted that there was no suggestion that the plaintiff "or any other BMW purchaser was threatened with any additional potential harm" by the defendant's conduct, we did not purport to decide the question of harm to others. Rather, the opinion appears to have left the question open.

Respondent argues that she is free to show harm to other victims because it is relevant to a different part of the punitive damages constitutional equation, namely, reprehensibility. That is to say, harm to others shows more reprehensible conduct. Philip Morris, in turn, does not deny that a plaintiff may show harm to others in order to demonstrate reprehensibility. Nor do we. Evidence of actual harm to nonparties can help to show that the conduct that harmed the plaintiff also posed a substantial risk of harm to the general public, and so was particularly reprehensible-although counsel may argue in a particular case that conduct resulting in no harm to others nonetheless posed a grave risk to the public, or the converse. Yet for the reasons given above, a jury may not go further than this and use a punitive damages verdict to punish a defendant directly on account of harms it is alleged to have visited on nonparties.

Given the risks of unfairness that we have mentioned, it is constitutionally important for a court to provide assurance that the jury will ask the right question, not the wrong one. And given the risks of arbitrariness, the concern for adequate notice, and the risk that punitive damages awards can, in practice, impose one State's (or one jury's) policies (*e.g.,* banning cigarettes) upon other States—all of which accompany awards that, today, may be many times the size of such awards in the 18th and 19th centuries, it is particularly important that States avoid procedure that unnecessarily deprives juries of proper legal guidance. We therefore conclude that the Due Process Clause requires States to provide assurance that juries are not asking the wrong question, *i.e.,* seeking, not simply to determine reprehensibility, but also to punish for harm caused strangers.

IV

Respondent suggests as well that the Oregon Supreme Court, in essence, agreed with us, that it did not authorize punitive damages awards based upon punishment for harm caused to nonparties. We concede that one might read some portions of the Oregon Supreme Court's opinion as focusing only upon reprehensibility. But the Oregon court's opinion elsewhere makes clear that that court held more than these few phrases might suggest.

The instruction that Philip Morris said the trial court should have given distinguishes between using harm to others as part of the "reasonable relationship" equation (which it would allow) and using it directly as a basis for punishment. The instruction asked the trial court to tell the jury that "you *may* consider the extent of harm suffered by others *in determining what [the] reasonable relationship is*" between Philip Morris' punishable misconduct and harm caused to Jesse Williams, "*[but] you are not to punish the defendant for the impact of its alleged misconduct on other persons, who may bring lawsuits of their own* in which other juries can resolve their claims. . . ." And as the Oregon Supreme Court explicitly recognized, Philip Morris argued that the Constitution "prohibits the state, acting through a civil jury, from using punitive damages to punish a defendant for harm to nonparties."

The court rejected that claim. In doing so, it pointed out (1) that this Court in *State Farm* had held only that a jury could not base its award upon "dissimilar" acts of a defendant. It added (2) that "[i]f a jury cannot punish for the conduct, then it is difficult to see why it may consider it at all." And it stated (3) that "[i]t is unclear to us how a jury could 'consider' harm to others, yet withhold that consideration from the punishment calculus."

The Oregon court's first statement is correct. We did not previously hold explicitly that a jury may not punish for the harm caused others. But we do so hold now. We do not agree with the Oregon court's second statement. We have explained why we believe the Due Process Clause prohibits a State's inflicting punishment for harm caused strangers to the litigation. At the same time we recognize that conduct that risks harm to many is likely more reprehensible than conduct that risks harm to only a few. And a jury consequently may take this fact into account in determining reprehensibility. Cf., *e.g., Witte v. United States,* 515 U.S. 389, 400, 115 S.Ct. 2199, 132 L.Ed.2d 351 (1995) (recidivism statutes taking into account a criminal defendant's other misconduct do not impose an " 'additional penalty for the earlier crimes,' but instead . . . 'a stiffened penalty for the latest crime, which is considered to be an aggravated offense because a repetitive one' " (quoting *Gryger v. Burke,* 334 U.S. 728, 732, 68 S.Ct. 1256, 92 L.Ed. 1683 (1948))).

The Oregon court's third statement raises a practical problem. How can we know whether a jury, in taking account of harm caused others under the rubric of reprehensibility, also seeks to *punish* the defendant for having caused injury to others? Our answer is that state courts cannot authorize procedures that create an unreasonable and unnecessary risk of any such confusion occurring. In particular, we believe that where the risk of that misunderstanding is a significant one—because, for instance, of the sort of evidence that was introduced at trial or the kinds of argument the plaintiff made to the jury—a court, upon request, must protect against that risk. Although the States have some flexibility to determine what *kind* of procedures they will implement, federal constitutional law obligates them to provide *some* form of protection in appropriate cases.

V

As the preceding discussion makes clear, we believe that the Oregon Supreme Court applied the wrong constitutional standard when considering Philip Morris' appeal. We remand this case so that the Oregon Supreme Court can apply the standard we have set forth. Because the application of this standard may lead to the need for a new trial, or a change in the level of the punitive damages award, we shall not consider whether the award is constitutionally "grossly excessive." We vacate the Oregon Supreme Court's judgment and remand the case for further proceedings not inconsistent with this opinion.

It is so ordered.

JUSTICE STEVENS, dissenting.

* * *

Of greater importance to me, however, is the Court's imposition of a novel limit on the State's power to impose punishment in civil litigation. Unlike the Court, I see no reason why an interest in punishing a wrongdoer "for harming persons who are not before the court," should not be taken into consideration when assessing the appropriate sanction for reprehensible conduct.

Whereas compensatory damages are measured by the harm the defendant has caused the plaintiff, punitive damages are a sanction for the public harm the defendant's conduct has caused or threatened. There is little difference between the justification for a criminal sanction, such as a fine or a term of imprisonment, and an award of punitive damages. In our early history either type of sanction might have been imposed in litigation prosecuted by a private citizen. And while in neither context would the sanction typically include a pecuniary award measured by the harm that the conduct had caused to any third parties, in both contexts the harm to third parties would surely be a relevant factor to consider in evaluating the reprehensibility of the defendant's wrongdoing. We have never held otherwise.

In the case before us, evidence attesting to the possible harm the defendant's extensive deceitful conduct caused other Oregonians was properly presented to the jury. No evidence was offered to establish an appropriate measure of damages to compensate such third parties for their injuries, and no one argued that the punitive damages award would serve any such purpose. To award compensatory damages to remedy such third-party harm might well constitute a taking of property from the defendant without due process. But a punitive damages award, instead of serving a compensatory purpose, serves the entirely different purposes of retribution and deterrence that underlie every criminal sanction. This justification for punitive damages has even greater salience when, as in this case, see Ore.Rev.Stat. § 31.735(1) (2003), the award is payable in whole or in part to the State rather than to the private litigant.

While apparently recognizing the novelty of its holding, the majority relies on a distinction between taking third-party harm into account in order to assess the reprehensibility of the defendant's conduct—which is permitted-from doing so in order to punish the defendant "directly"—which is forbidden. This nuance eludes me. When a jury increases a punitive damages award because injuries to third parties enhanced the reprehensibility of the defendant's conduct, the jury is by definition punishing the defendant—directly—for third-party harm.[2] A murderer

[2] It is no answer to refer, as the majority does, to recidivism statutes. In that context, we have distinguished between taking prior crimes into account as an aggravating factor in penalizing the conduct before the court versus doing so to punish for the earlier crimes. But if enhancing a penalty for a present crime because of prior conduct that has already been punished is permissible, it is certainly proper to enhance a penalty because the conduct before the court, which has never been punished, injured multiple victims.

who kills his victim by throwing a bomb that injures dozens of bystanders should be punished more severely than one who harms no one other than his intended victim. Similarly, there is no reason why the measure of the appropriate punishment for engaging in a campaign of deceit in distributing a poisonous and addictive substance to thousands of cigarette smokers statewide should not include consideration of the harm to those "bystanders" as well as the harm to the individual plaintiff. The Court endorses a contrary conclusion without providing us with any reasoned justification.

* * *

Essentially for the reasons stated in the opinion of the Supreme Court of Oregon, I would affirm its judgment.

* * *

NOTES AND QUESTIONS

1. What about Judge Posner's point (in *Mathias*) that punitive damages awards should consider the likelihood that the defendant will be caught and sued by other similar plaintiffs? Is such consideration valid after *Philip Morris*? (Consider these questions again after reading *Exxon*, *infra* at 889.)

2. As one reason the Court offers for prohibiting consideration of the defendant's malfeasance against nonparties, the Court states the following: "[A] defendant threatened with punishment for injuring a nonparty victim has no opportunity to defend against the charge, by showing, for example in a case such as this, that the other victim was not entitled to damages because he or she knew that smoking was dangerous or did not rely upon the defendant's statements to the contrary." Does the fact that the nonparty was not in fact injured (but might have been) by defendant's deceit make the defendant's conduct any less reprehensible? On the other hand, the law only recognizes as complete a wrong that results in injury. Does the Court contradict itself in later stating that: "We have said that it may be appropriate to consider the reasonableness of a punitive damages award in light of the *potential* harm the defendant's conduct could have caused. But we have made clear that the potential harm at issue was harm potentially caused *the plaintiff*."? For discussion of this general jurisprudential quandry, albeit not specifically in the context of punitive damages, see John C.P. Goldberg & Benjamin C. Zipursky, *Tort Law and Moral Luck*, 92 CORNELL L. REV. 1123 (2007).

3. Are you convinced of the jury's ability to separate consideration of harm to nonparties in the manner the Court suggests?

4. Although much of the discussion in this section has involved the federal constitutional boundaries of punitive damages, states also impose a variety of statutory and common-law limitations. The following case, decided

under federal maritime common-law, discusses these standards and their underlying justifications.

EXXON SHIPPING COMPANY V. BAKER

554 U.S. 471, 128 S.Ct. 2605, 171 L.Ed.2d 570 (2008).

SOUTER, J., delivered the opinion of the Court, in which ROBERTS, C.J., and SCALIA, KENNEDY, and THOMAS, JJ., joined, and in which STEVENS, GINSBURG, and BREYER, JJ., joined, as to Parts I, II, and III. SCALIA, J., filed a concurring opinion, in which THOMAS, J., joined. STEVENS, J., GINSBURG, J., and BREYER, J., filed opinions concurring in part and dissenting in part. ALITO, J., took no part in the consideration or decision of the case.

JUSTICE SOUTER delivered the opinion of the Court.

* * *

I

On March 24, 1989, the supertanker *Exxon Valdez* grounded on Bligh Reef off the Alaskan coast, fracturing its hull and spilling millions of gallons of crude oil into Prince William Sound. The owner, petitioner Exxon Shipping Co. (now SeaRiver Maritime, Inc.), and its owner, petitioner Exxon Mobil Corp. (collectively, Exxon), have settled state and federal claims for environmental damage, with payments exceeding $1 billion, and this action by respondent Baker and others, including commercial fishermen and native Alaskans, was brought for economic losses to individuals dependent on Prince William Sound for their livelihoods.

A

The tanker was over 900 feet long and was used by Exxon to carry crude oil from the end of the Trans–Alaska Pipeline in Valdez, Alaska, to the lower 48 States. On the night of the spill it was carrying 53 million gallons of crude oil, or over a million barrels. Its captain was one Joseph Hazelwood, who had completed a 28-day alcohol treatment program while employed by Exxon, as his superiors knew, but dropped out of a prescribed follow-up program and stopped going to Alcoholics Anonymous meetings. According to the District Court, "[t]here was evidence presented to the jury that after Hazelwood was released from [residential treatment], he drank in bars, parking lots, apartments, airports, airplanes, restaurants, hotels, at various ports, and aboard Exxon tankers." The jury also heard contested testimony that Hazelwood drank with Exxon officials and that members of the Exxon management knew of his relapse. Although Exxon had a clear policy prohibiting employees from serving onboard within four hours of consuming alcohol, Exxon presented no evidence that it monitored Hazelwood after his return to duty or considered giving him a shoreside assignment. Witnesses testified that before the *Valdez* left port on the night of the disaster, Hazelwood downed at least five double vodkas in the waterfront bars of Valdez, an intake of about 15 ounces of 80-proof alcohol, enough "that a non-alcoholic would have passed out."

The ship sailed at 9:12 p.m. on March 23, 1989, guided by a state-licensed pilot for the first leg out, through the Valdez Narrows. At 11:20 p.m., Hazelwood took active control and, owing to poor conditions in the outbound shipping lane, radioed the Coast Guard for permission to move east across the inbound lane to a less icy path. Under the conditions, this was a standard move, which the last outbound tanker had also taken, and the Coast Guard cleared the *Valdez* to cross the inbound lane. The tanker accordingly steered east toward clearer waters, but the move put it in the path of an underwater reef off Bligh Island, thus requiring a turn back west into the shipping lane around Busby Light, north of the reef.

Two minutes before the required turn, however, Hazelwood left the bridge and went down to his cabin in order, he said, to do paperwork. This decision was inexplicable. There was expert testimony that, even if their presence is not strictly necessary, captains simply do not quit the bridge during maneuvers like this, and no paperwork could have justified it. And in fact the evidence was that Hazelwood's presence was required, both because there should have been two officers on the bridge at all times and his departure left only one, and because he was the only person on the entire ship licensed to navigate this part of Prince William Sound. To make matters worse, before going below Hazelwood put the tanker on autopilot, speeding it up, making the turn trickier, and any mistake harder to correct.

As Hazelwood left, he instructed the remaining officer, third mate Joseph Cousins, to move the tanker back into the shipping lane once it came abeam of Busby Light. Cousins, unlicensed to navigate in those waters, was left alone with helmsman Robert Kagan, a nonofficer. For reasons that remain a mystery, they failed to make the turn at Busby Light, and a later emergency maneuver attempted by Cousins came too late. The tanker ran aground on Bligh Reef, tearing the hull open and spilling 11 million gallons of crude oil into Prince William Sound.

After Hazelwood returned to the bridge and reported the grounding to the Coast Guard, he tried but failed to rock the *Valdez* off the reef, a maneuver which could have spilled more oil and caused the ship to founder. The Coast Guard's nearly immediate response included a blood test of Hazelwood (the validity of which Exxon disputes) showing a blood-alcohol level of .061 eleven hours after the spill. Experts testified that to have this much alcohol in his bloodstream so long after the accident, Hazelwood at the time of the spill must have had a blood-alcohol level of around .241, three times the legal limit for driving in most States.

* * *

IV

*** Exxon raises an issue of first impression about punitive damages in maritime law, which falls within a federal court's jurisdiction to decide in the manner of a common law court, subject to the authority of Congress to legislate otherwise if it disagrees with the judicial result. In addition to its resistance to derivative liability for punitive damages and its preemption claim already disposed of, Exxon challenges the size of the remaining $2.5 billion punitive damages award. Other than its preemption argument, it does not offer a legal ground for concluding that maritime law should never award punitive damages, or that none should be awarded in this case, but it does argue that this award exceeds the bounds justified by the punitive damages goal of deterring reckless (or worse) behavior and the consequently heightened threat of harm. The claim goes to our understanding of the place of punishment in modern civil law and reasonable standards of process in administering punitive law, subjects that call for starting with a brief account of the history behind today's punitive damages.

A

The modern Anglo-American doctrine of punitive damages dates back at least to 1763, when a pair of decisions by the Court of Common Pleas recognized the availability of damages "for more than the injury received." *Wilkes v. Wood,* Lofft 1, 18, 98 Eng. Rep. 489, 498 (1763) (Lord Chief Justice Pratt). In *Wilkes v. Wood*, one of the foundations of the Fourth Amendment, exemplary damages awarded against the Secretary of State, responsible for an unlawful search of John Wilkes's papers, were a spectacular £4,000. And in *Huckle v. Money,* 2 Wils. 205, 206–207, 95 Eng. Rep. 768, 768–769 (K.B.1763), the same judge who is recorded in *Wilkes* gave an opinion upholding a jury's award of £300 (against a government officer again) although "if the jury had been confined by their oath to consider the mere personal injury only, perhaps [£20] damages would have been thought damages sufficient."

Awarding damages beyond the compensatory was not, however, a wholly novel idea even then, legal codes from ancient times through the Middle Ages having called for multiple damages for certain especially harmful acts. See, *e.g.,* Code of Hammurabi § 8 (R. Harper ed.1904) (tenfold penalty for stealing the goat of a freed man); Statute of Gloucester, 1278, 6 Edw. I, ch. 5, 1 Stat. at Large 66 (treble damages for waste). But punitive damages were a common law innovation untethered to strict numerical multipliers, and the doctrine promptly crossed the Atlantic to become widely accepted in American courts by the middle of the 19th century.

B

Early common law cases offered various rationales for punitive-damages awards, which were then generally dubbed "exemplary," implying that these verdicts were justified as punishment for extraordinary wrongdoing, as in Wilkes's case. Sometimes, though, the extraordinary element emphasized was the damages award itself, the punishment being "for example's sake," "to deter from any such proceeding for the future."

A third historical justification, which showed up in some of the early cases, has been noted by recent commentators, and that was the need "to compensate for intangible injuries, compensation which was not otherwise available under the narrow conception of compensatory damages prevalent at the time." But see Sebok, What Did Punitive Damages Do? 78 Chi.–Kent L.Rev. 163, 204 (2003) (arguing that "punitive damages have never served the compensatory function attributed to them by the Court in *Cooper*"). As the century progressed, and "the types of compensatory damages available to plaintiffs . . . broadened," the consequence was that American courts tended to speak of punitive damages as separate and distinct from compensatory damages.

Regardless of the alternative rationales over the years, the consensus today is that punitives are aimed not at compensation but principally at retribution and deterring harmful conduct. This consensus informs the doctrine in most modern American jurisdictions, where juries are customarily instructed on twin goals of punitive awards. The prevailing rule in American courts also limits punitive damages to cases of * * * "enormity," where a defendant's conduct is "outrageous," owing to "gross negligence," "willful, wanton, and reckless indifference for the rights of others," or behavior even more deplorable.[10]

Under the umbrellas of punishment and its aim of deterrence, degrees of relative blameworthiness are apparent. Reckless conduct is not intentional or malicious, nor is it necessarily callous toward the risk of harming others, as opposed to unheedful of it. Action taken or omitted in order to augment profit represents an enhanced degree of punishable culpability, as of course does willful or malicious action, taken with a purpose to injure. Cf. Alaska Stat. § 09.17.020(g) (2006) (higher statutory limit applies where conduct was motivated by financial gain and its adverse consequences were known to the defendant); Ark.Code Ann. § 16–55–208(b) (2005) (statutory limit does not apply where the defendant intentionally pursued a course of conduct for the purpose of causing injury or damage).

[10] These standards are from the torts context; different standards apply to other causes of action.

Regardless of culpability, however, heavier punitive awards have been thought to be justifiable when wrongdoing is hard to detect (increasing chances of getting away with it) or when the value of injury and the corresponding compensatory award are small (providing low incentives to sue). And, with a broadly analogous object, some regulatory schemes provide by statute for multiple recovery in order to induce private litigation to supplement official enforcement that might fall short if unaided.

C

State regulation of punitive damages varies. A few States award them rarely, or not at all. Nebraska bars punitive damages entirely, on state constitutional grounds. Four others permit punitive damages only when authorized by statute: Louisiana, Massachusetts, and Washington as a matter of common law, and New Hampshire by statute codifying common law tradition. Michigan courts recognize only exemplary damages supportable as compensatory, rather than truly punitive, while Connecticut courts have limited what they call punitive recovery to the "expenses of bringing the legal action, including attorney's fees, less taxable costs."

As for procedure, in most American jurisdictions the amount of the punitive award is generally determined by a jury in the first instance, and that "determination is then reviewed by trial and appellate courts to ensure that it is reasonable." Many States have gone further by imposing statutory limits on punitive awards, in the form of absolute monetary caps, see, *e.g.*, Va.Code Ann. § 8.01–38.1 (Lexis 2007) ($350,000 cap), a maximum ratio of punitive to compensatory damages, see, *e.g.*, Ohio Rev.Code Ann. § 2315.21(D)(2)(a) (Lexis 2001) (2:1 ratio in most tort cases), or, frequently, some combination of the two, see, *e.g.*, Alaska Stat. § 09.17.020(f) (2006) (greater of 3:1 ratio or $500,000 in most actions). The States that rely on a multiplier have adopted a variety of ratios, ranging from 5:1 to 1:1.[12]

Despite these limitations, punitive damages overall are higher and more frequent in the United States than they are anywhere else. In England and Wales, punitive, or exemplary, damages are available only for oppressive, arbitrary, or unconstitutional action by government servants; injuries designed by the defendant to yield a larger profit than

---

[12] See, *e.g.*, Mo.Rev.Stat. Ann. § 510.265(1) (Vernon Supp.2008) (greater of 5:1 or $500,000 in most cases); Ala.Code §§ 6–11–21(a), (d) (2005) (greater of 3:1 or $1.5 million in most personal injury suits, and 3:1 or $500,000 in most other actions); N.D. Cent.Code Ann. § 32–03.2–11(4) (Supp.2007) (greater of 2:1 or $250,000); Colo.Rev.Stat. Ann. § 13–21–102(1)(a) (2007) (1:1).

Oklahoma has a graduated scheme, with the limit on the punitive award turning on the nature of the defendant's conduct. See Okla. Stat., Tit. 23, § 9.1(B) (West 2001) (greater of 1:1 or $100,000 in cases involving "reckless disregard"); § 9.1(C) (greater of 2:1, $500,000, or the financial benefit derived by the defendant, in cases of intentional and malicious conduct); § 9.1(D) (no limit where the conduct is intentional, malicious, and life threatening).

the likely cost of compensatory damages; and conduct for which punitive damages are expressly authorized by statute. Even in the circumstances where punitive damages are allowed, they are subject to strict, judicially imposed guidelines. The Court of Appeal in *Thompson v. Commissioner of Police of Metropolis,* [1998] Q.B. 498, 518, said that a ratio of more than three times the amount of compensatory damages will rarely be appropriate; awards of less than £5,000 are likely unnecessary; awards of £ 25,000 should be exceptional; and £50,000 should be considered the top.

For further contrast with American practice, Canada and Australia allow exemplary damages for outrageous conduct, but awards are considered extraordinary and rarely issue. Noncompensatory damages are not part of the civil-code tradition and thus unavailable in such countries as France, Germany, Austria, and Switzerland. And some legal systems not only decline to recognize punitive damages themselves but refuse to enforce foreign punitive judgments as contrary to public policy.

D

American punitive damages have been the target of audible criticism in recent decades, but the most recent studies tend to undercut much of it. A survey of the literature reveals that discretion to award punitive damages has not mass-produced runaway awards, and although some studies show the dollar amounts of punitive-damages awards growing over time, even in real terms,[13] by most accounts the median ratio of punitive to compensatory awards has remained less than 1:1.[14] Nor do the data substantiate a marked increase in the percentage of cases with

---

[13] See, *e.g.,* RAND Institute for Civil Justice, D. Hensler & E. Moller, Trends in Punitive Damages, table 2 (Mar.1995) (finding an increase in median awards between the early 1980s and the early 1990s in San Francisco and Cook Counties); Moller, Pace, & Carroll, Punitive Damages in Financial Injury Jury Verdicts, 28 J. Legal Studies 283, 307 (1999) (hereinafter Financial Injury Jury Verdicts) (studying jury verdicts in "Financial Injury" cases in six States and Cook County, Illinois, and finding a marked increase in the median award between the late 1980s and the early 1990s); M. Peterson, S. Sarma, & M. Shanley, Punitive Damages: Empirical Findings 15 (RAND Institute for Civil Justice 1987) (hereinafter Punitive Damages: Empirical Findings) (finding that the median punitive award increased nearly 4 times in San Francisco County between the early 1960s and the early 1980s, and 43 times in Cook County over the same period). But see T. Eisenberg et al., Juries, Judges, and Punitive Damages: Empirical Analyses Using the Civil Justice Survey of State Courts 1992, 1996, and 2001 Data, 3 J. of Empirical Legal Studies 263, 278 (2006) (hereinafter Juries, Judges, and Punitive Damages) (analyzing Bureau of Justice Statistics data from 1992, 1996, and 2001, and concluding that "[n]o statistically significant variation exists in the inflation-adjusted punitive award level over the three time periods"); Dept. of Justice, Bureau of Justice Statistics, T. Cohen, Punitive Damage Awards in Large Counties, 2001, p. 8 (Mar.2005) (hereinafter Cohen) (compiling data from the Nation's 75 most populous counties and finding that the median punitive damage award in civil jury trials decreased between 1992 and 2001).

[14] See, *e.g.,* Juries, Judges, and Punitive Damages 269 (reporting median ratios of 0.62:1 in jury trials and 0.66:1 in bench trials using the Bureau of Justice Statistics data from 1992, 1996, and 2001); Vidmar & Rose, Punitive Damages by Juries in Florida, 38 Harv. J. Legis. 487, 492 (2001) (studying civil cases in Florida state courts between 1989 and 1998 and finding a median ratio of 0.67:1). But see Financial Injury Jury Verdicts 307 (finding a median ratio of 1.4:1 in "financial injury" cases in the late 1980s and early 1990s).

punitive awards over the past several decades.[15] The figures thus show an overall restraint and suggest that in many instances a high ratio of punitive to compensatory damages is substantially greater than necessary to punish or deter.

The real problem, it seems, is the stark unpredictability of punitive awards. Courts of law are concerned with fairness as consistency, and evidence that the median ratio of punitive to compensatory awards falls within a reasonable zone, or that punitive awards are infrequent, fails to tell us whether the spread between high and low individual awards is acceptable. The available data suggest it is not. A recent comprehensive study of punitive damages awarded by juries in state civil trials found a median ratio of punitive to compensatory awards of just 0.62:1, but a mean ratio of 2.90:1 and a standard deviation of 13.81. Even to those of us unsophisticated in statistics, the thrust of these figures is clear: the spread is great, and the outlier cases subject defendants to punitive damages that dwarf the corresponding compensatories. The distribution of awards is narrower, but still remarkable, among punitive damages assessed by judges: the median ratio is 0.66:1, the mean ratio is 1.60:1, and the standard deviation is 4.54. Other studies of some of the same data show that fully 14% of punitive awards in 2001 were greater than four times the compensatory damages, with 18% of punitives in the 1990s more than trebling the compensatory damages. And a study of "financial injury" cases using a different data set found that 34% of the punitive awards were greater than three times the corresponding compensatory damages.

Starting with the premise of a punitive-damages regime, these ranges of variation might be acceptable or even desirable if they resulted from judges' and juries' refining their judgments to reach a generally

---

[15] See, *e.g.,* Cohen 8 (compiling data from the Nation's 75 most populous counties, and finding that in jury trials where the plaintiff prevailed, the percentage of cases involving punitive awards was 6.1% in 1992 and 5.6% in 2001); Financial Injury Jury Verdicts 307 (finding a statistically significant decrease in the percentage of verdicts in "financial injury" cases that include a punitive damage award, from 15.8% in the early 1980s to 12.7% in the early 1990s). But see Punitive Damages: Empirical Findings 9 (finding an increase in the percentage of civil trials resulting in punitive damage awards in San Francisco and Cook Counties between 1960 and 1984).

One might posit that ill effects of punitive damages are clearest not in actual awards but in the shadow that the punitive regime casts on settlement negotiations and other litigation decisions. See, *e.g.,* Financial Injury Jury Verdicts 287; Polinsky, Are Punitive Damages Really Insignificant, Predictable, and Rational? 26 J. Legal Studies 663, 664–671 (1997). But here again the data have not established a clear correlation. See, *e.g.,* Eaton, Mustard, & Talarico, The Effects of Seeking Punitive Damages on the Processing of Tort Claims, 34 J. Legal Studies 343, 357, 353–354, 365 (2005) (studying data from six Georgia counties and concluding that "the decision to seek punitive damages has no statistically significant impact" on "whether a case that was disposed was done so by trial or by some other procedure, including settlement," or "whether a case that was disposed by means other than a trial was more likely to have been settled"); Kritzer & Zemans, The Shadow of Punitives, 1998 Wis. L.Rev. 157, 160 (1998) (noting the theory that punitive damages cast a large shadow over settlement negotiations, but finding that "with perhaps one exception, what little systematic evidence we could find does not support the notion" (emphasis deleted)).

accepted optimal level of penalty and deterrence in cases involving a wide range of circumstances, while producing fairly consistent results in cases with similar facts. But anecdotal evidence suggests that nothing of that sort is going on. One of our own leading cases on punitive damages, with a $4 million verdict by an Alabama jury, noted that a second Alabama case with strikingly similar facts produced "a comparable amount of compensatory damages" but "no punitive damages at all." As the Supreme Court of Alabama candidly explained, "the disparity between the two jury verdicts . . . [w]as a reflection of the inherent uncertainty of the trial process." *BMW of North America, Inc. v. Gore,* 646 So.2d 619, 626 (1994) *(per curiam).* We are aware of no scholarly work pointing to consistency across punitive awards in cases involving similar claims and circumstances.

E

The Court's response to outlier punitive damages awards has thus far been confined by claims at the constitutional level, and our cases have announced due process standards that every award must pass. Although "we have consistently rejected the notion that the constitutional line is marked by a simple mathematical formula," we have determined that "few awards exceeding a single-digit ratio between punitive and compensatory damages, to a significant degree, will satisfy due process"; "[w]hen compensatory damages are substantial, then a lesser ratio, perhaps only equal to compensatory damages, can reach the outermost limit of the due process guarantee."

Today's enquiry differs from due process review because the case arises under federal maritime jurisdiction, and we are reviewing a jury award for conformity with maritime law, rather than the outer limit allowed by due process; we are examining the verdict in the exercise of federal maritime common law authority, which precedes and should obviate any application of the constitutional standard. Our due process cases, on the contrary, have all involved awards subject in the first instance to state law. * * *

Our review of punitive damages today, then, considers not their intersection with the Constitution, but the desirability of regulating them as a common law remedy for which responsibility lies with this Court as a source of judge-made law in the absence of statute. Whatever may be the constitutional significance of the unpredictability of high punitive awards, this feature of happenstance is in tension with the function of the awards as punitive, just because of the implication of unfairness that an eccentrically high punitive verdict carries in a system whose commonly held notion of law rests on a sense of fairness in dealing with one another. Thus, a penalty should be reasonably predictable in its severity, so that even Justice Holmes's "bad man" can look ahead with some ability to know what the stakes are in choosing one course of action or another. See

The Path of the Law, 10 Harv. L.Rev. 457, 459 (1897). And when the bad man's counterparts turn up from time to time, the penalty scheme they face ought to threaten them with a fair probability of suffering in like degree when they wreak like damage. The common sense of justice would surely bar penalties that reasonable people would think excessive for the harm caused in the circumstances.

F

1

With that aim ourselves, we have three basic approaches to consider, one verbal and two quantitative. As mentioned before, a number of state courts have settled on criteria for judicial review of punitive-damages awards that go well beyond traditional "shock the conscience" or "passion and prejudice" tests. Maryland, for example, has set forth a nonexclusive list of nine review factors under state common law that include "degree of heinousness," "the deterrence value of [the award]," and "[w]hether [the punitive award] bears a reasonable relationship to the compensatory damages awarded." Alabama has seven general criteria, such as "actual or likely harm [from the defendant's conduct]," "degree of reprehensibility," and "[i]f the wrongful conduct was profitable to the defendant."

These judicial review criteria are brought to bear after juries render verdicts under instructions offering, at best, guidance no more specific for reaching an appropriate penalty. In Maryland, for example, which allows punitive damages for intentional torts and conduct characterized by "actual malice," juries may be instructed that

"An award for punitive damages should be:

"(1) In an amount that will deter the defendant and others from similar conduct.

"(2) Proportionate to the wrongfulness of the defendant's conduct and the defendant's ability to pay.

"(3) But not designed to bankrupt or financially destroy a defendant."

In Alabama, juries are instructed to fix an amount after considering "the character and degree of the wrong as shown by the evidence in the case, and the necessity of preventing similar wrongs."

These examples leave us skeptical that verbal formulations, superimposed on general jury instructions, are the best insurance against unpredictable outliers. Instructions can go just so far in promoting systemic consistency when awards are not tied to specifically proven items of damage (the cost of medical treatment, say), and although judges in the States that take this approach may well produce just results by dint of valiant effort, our experience with attempts to produce consistency in the analogous business of criminal sentencing leaves us doubtful that anything but a quantified approach will work. A glance at the experience there will explain our skepticism.

The points of similarity are obvious. "[P]unitive damages advance the interests of punishment and deterrence, which are also among the interests advanced by the criminal law."

It is instructive, then, that in the last quarter century federal sentencing rejected an "indeterminate" system, with relatively unguided discretion to sentence within a wide range, under which "similarly situated offenders were sentenced [to], and did actually serve, widely disparate sentences." Instead it became a system of detailed guidelines tied to exactly quantified sentencing results, under the authority of the Sentencing Reform Act of 1984, 18 U.S.C. § 3551 *et seq.* (2000 ed. and Supp. V).

The importance of this for us is that in the old federal sentencing system of general standards the cohort of even the most seasoned judicial penalty-givers defied consistency. Judges and defendants alike were "[l]eft at large, wandering in deserts of uncharted discretion," which is very much the position of those imposing punitive damages today, be they judges or juries, except that they lack even a statutory maximum; their only restraint beyond a core sense of fairness is the due process limit. This federal criminal law development, with its many state parallels, strongly suggests that as long "as there are no punitive-damages guidelines, corresponding to the federal and state sentencing guidelines, it is inevitable that the specific amount of punitive damages awarded whether by a judge or by a jury will be arbitrary."

2

This is why our better judgment is that eliminating unpredictable outlying punitive awards by more rigorous standards than the constitutional limit will probably have to take the form adopted in those States that have looked to the criminal-law pattern of quantified limits. One option would be to follow the States that set a hard dollar cap on punitive damages, a course that arguably would come closest to the criminal law, rather like setting a maximum term of years. The trouble is, though, that there is no "standard" tort or contract injury, making it difficult to settle upon a particular dollar figure as appropriate across the board. And of course a judicial selection of a dollar cap would carry a serious drawback; a legislature can pick a figure, index it for inflation, and revisit its provision whenever there seems to be a need for further tinkering, but a court cannot say when an issue will show up on the docket again.

The more promising alternative is to leave the effects of inflation to the jury or judge who assesses the value of actual loss, by pegging punitive to compensatory damages using a ratio or maximum multiple. As the earlier canvass of state experience showed, this is the model many States have adopted and Congress has passed analogous legislation from time to time, as for example in providing treble damages in antitrust, racketeering, patent, and trademark actions. And of course the potential relevance of the ratio between compensatory and punitive damages is indisputable, being a central feature in our due process analysis.

Still, some will murmur that this smacks too much of policy and too little of principle. But the answer rests on the fact that we are acting here in the position of a common law court of last review, faced with a perceived defect in a common law remedy. Traditionally, courts have accepted primary responsibility for reviewing punitive damages and thus for their evolution, and if, in the absence of legislation, judicially derived standards leave the door open to outlier punitive-damages awards, it is hard to see how the judiciary can wash its hands of a problem it created, simply by calling quantified standards legislative.

History certainly is no support for the notion that judges cannot use numbers. The 21-year period in the rule against perpetuities was a judicial innovation, and so were exact limitations periods for civil actions, sometimes borrowing from statutes, but often without any statutory account to draw on. And of course, adopting an admiralty-law ratio is no less judicial than picking one as an outer limit of constitutionality for punitive awards.

Although the legal landscape is well populated with examples of ratios and multipliers expressing policies of retribution and deterrence, most of them suffer from features that stand in the way of borrowing them as paradigms of reasonable limitations suited for application to this case. While a slim majority of the States with a ratio have adopted 3:1, others see fit to apply a lower one, see, *e.g.,* Colo.Rev.Stat. Ann. § 13–21–102(1)(a) (2007) (1:1); Ohio Rev.Code Ann. § 2315.21(D)(2)(a) (Lexis 2005) (2:1), and a few have gone higher, see, *e.g.,* Mo. Ann. Stat. § 510.265(1) (Supp.2008) (5:1). Judgments may differ about the weight to be given to the slight majority of 3:1 States, but one feature of the 3:1 schemes dissuades us from selecting it here. With a few statutory exceptions, generally for intentional infliction of physical injury or other harm, the States with 3:1 ratios apply them across the board (as do other States using different fixed multipliers). That is, the upper limit is not directed to cases like this one, where the tortious action was worse than negligent but less than malicious, exposing the tortfeasor to certain regulatory sanctions and inevitable damage actions; the 3:1 ratio in these States also applies to awards in quite different cases involving some of the most egregious conduct, including malicious behavior and dangerous activity carried on for the purpose of increasing a tortfeasor's financial gain. We confront, instead, a case of reckless action, profitless to the tortfeasor, resulting in substantial recovery for substantial injury. Thus, a legislative judgment that 3:1 is a reasonable limit overall is not a judgment that 3:1 is a reasonable limit in this particular type of case.

* * *

3

There is better evidence of an accepted limit of reasonable civil penalty, however, in several studies mentioned before, showing the median ratio of punitive to compensatory verdicts, reflecting what juries and judges have considered reasonable across many hundreds of punitive awards. We think it is fair to assume that the greater share of the verdicts studied in these comprehensive collections reflect reasonable judgments about the economic penalties appropriate in their particular cases.

These studies cover cases of the most as well as the least blameworthy conduct triggering punitive liability, from malice and avarice, down to recklessness, and even gross negligence in some jurisdictions. The data put the median ratio for the entire gamut of circumstances at less than 1:1, meaning that the compensatory award exceeds the punitive award in most cases. In a well-functioning system, we would expect that awards at the median or lower would roughly express jurors' sense of reasonable penalties in cases with no earmarks of exceptional blameworthiness within the punishable spectrum (cases like this one, without intentional or malicious conduct, and without behavior driven primarily by desire for gain, for example) and cases (again like this one) without the modest economic harm or odds of detection that have opened the door to higher awards. It also seems fair to suppose that most of the unpredictable outlier cases that call the fairness of the system into question are above the median; in theory a factfinder's deliberation could go awry to produce a very low ratio, but we have no basis to assume that such a case would be more than a sport, and the cases with serious constitutional issues coming to us have naturally been on the high side. On these assumptions, a median ratio of punitive to compensatory damages of about 0.65:1 probably marks the line near which cases like this one largely should be grouped. Accordingly, given the need to protect against the possibility (and the disruptive cost to the legal system) of awards that are unpredictable and unnecessary, either for deterrence or for measured retribution, we consider that a 1:1 ratio, which is above the median award, is a fair upper limit in such maritime cases.

* * *

V

Applying this standard to the present case, we take for granted the District Court's calculation of the total relevant compensatory damages at

$507.5 million. A punitive-to-compensatory ratio of 1:1 thus yields maximum punitive damages in that amount.

We therefore vacate the judgment and remand the case for the Court of Appeals to remit the punitive damages award accordingly.

* * *

JUSTICE STEVENS, concurring in part and dissenting in part.

While I join Parts I, II, and III of the Court's opinion, I believe that Congress, rather than this Court, should make the empirical judgments expressed in Part IV.

* * *

The Court concedes that although "American punitive damages have been the target of audible criticism in recent decades," "most recent studies tend to undercut much of [that criticism]." It further acknowledges that "[a] survey of the literature reveals that discretion to award punitive damages has not mass-produced runaway awards." The Court concludes that the real problem is large *outlier* awards, and the data seem to bear this out. But the Court never explains why abuse-of-discretion review is not the precise antidote to the unfairness inherent in such excessive awards.

Until Congress orders us to impose a rigid formula to govern the award of punitive damages in maritime cases, I would employ our familiar abuse-of-discretion standard: "If no constitutional issue is raised, the role of the appellate court, at least in the federal system, is merely to review the trial court's 'determination under an abuse-of-discretion standard.'"

* * *

JUSTICE GINSBURG, concurring in part and dissenting in part.

I join Parts I, II, and III of the Court's opinion, and dissent from Parts IV and V.

* * *

[A]ssuming a problem in need of solution, the Court's lawmaking prompts many questions. The 1:1 ratio is good for this case, the Court believes, because Exxon's conduct ranked on the low end of the blameworthiness scale: Exxon was not seeking "to augment profit," nor did it act "with a purpose to injure." What ratio will the Court set for defendants who acted maliciously or in pursuit of financial gain? Should the magnitude of the risk increase the ratio and, if so, by how much? Horrendous as the spill from the *Valdez* was, millions of gallons more might have spilled as a result of Captain Hazelwood's attempt to rock the boat off the reef. Cf. *TXO Production Corp. v. Alliance Resources Corp.*, 509 U.S. 443, 460–462, 113 S.Ct. 2711, 125 L.Ed.2d 366 (1993) (plurality opinion) (using potential loss to plaintiff as a guide in determining whether jury verdict was excessive). In the end, is the Court holding only that 1:1 is the maritime-law ceiling, or is it also signaling that any ratio higher than 1:1 will be held to exceed "the constitutional outer limit"? On next opportunity, will the Court rule, definitively, that 1:1 is the ceiling due process requires in all of the States, and for all federal claims?

Heightening my reservations about the 1:1 solution is JUSTICE STEVENS' comment on the venturesome character of the Court's decision. In the States, he observes, fixed ratios and caps have been adopted by legislatures; this Court has not identified "[any] state *court* that has imposed a precise ratio" in lieu of looking to the legislature as the appropriate source of a numerical damage limitation.

* * *

For the reasons stated, I agree with JUSTICE STEVENS that the new law made by the Court should have been left to Congress. I would therefore affirm the judgment of the Court of Appeals.

JUSTICE BREYER, concurring in part and dissenting in part.

I join Parts I, II, and III of the Court's opinion. But I disagree with its conclusion in Parts IV and V that the punitive damages award in this case must be reduced.

* * *

F. ATTORNEYS' FEES

In your first year studies, you may have learned the American Rule on attorneys fees: each party pays its own attorney. This broke from the British system, which generally awarded fees to the prevailing party. Exceptions, however, are rife.

1. By contract, parties may agree to fee-shifting arrangements—much as they can agree to include uncertain damages via a liquidated damages clause. These clauses are fairly common in adhesion contracts, such as bank loan documents and residential leases. At least one state treats them as reciprocal, even if as written they allow fees only to one party. *See* CAL. CIV. CODE § 1717.

2. In family law cases, especially divorces, courts commonly order one spouse to pay the other's attorney.

3. Fees incurred in collateral litigation are recoverable as consequential damages. For instance, a seller of land often gives the buyer a warranty of title. If a third party asserts a successful claim, the cost of defending that suit are damages caused by the breach of warranty.

Buyer may collect fees incurred defending against the third party claim, but not fees incurred suing seller for the breach of warranty.

4. Litigation misconduct may produce fee awards in two ways. Most obvious is contempt of court. Courts may assess fees against parties who violate court orders, shifting the cost of further court proceedings to the party who made them necessary. Similarly, parties who bring frivolous claims, defenses, or motions may be required to pay their opponents' fees in responding to them. *See, e.g.,* FED. R. CIV. P. 11. In some cases, fees may be assessed against the offending lawyer instead of (or in addition to) the party.

5. Statutory exceptions have increased dramatically over the last 50 years. Both state and federal statutes covering a broad array of misconduct make special provision for recovery of attorneys' fees.

6. At least one nonexception deserves note: the common fund rule. An attorney whose work for one client produces a fund that benefits others may have a restitution claim to compensation from the fund. This does not involve shifting the attorneys' fee to the opposing party; she pays the fund and no more. Rather, it provides a mechanism for attorneys to collect fees from persons with whom they have no direct attorney-client relationship. Class actions and shareholder derivative suits are examples of the common fund rule at work.

The frontiers of these exceptions produce battles, either seeking to create new exceptions or to expand the interpretation of existing ones. The Court rejected the private attorney general exception in *Alyeska Pipeline Service Co. v. Wilderness Society*, 421 U.S. 240, 95 S.Ct. 1612, 44 L.Ed.2d 141 (1975). The Court recognized a fee claim for creating a common benefit, though not a monetary common fund, in *Hall v. Cole*, 412 U.S. 1, 93 S.Ct. 1943, 36 L.Ed.2d 702 (1973). Consider one recent foray into the scope of exceptions allowing fee shifting.

BUCKHANNON BOARD AND CARE HOME, INC. V. WEST VIRGINIA DEPARTMENT OF HEALTH AND HUMAN RESOURCES

532 U.S. 598, 121 S.Ct. 1835, 149 L.Ed.2d 855 (2001).

CHIEF JUSTICE REHNQUIST delivered the opinion of the Court.

Numerous federal statutes allow courts to award attorney's fees and costs to the "prevailing party." The question presented here is whether this term includes a party that has failed to secure a judgment on the merits or a court-ordered consent decree, but has nonetheless achieved the desired result because the lawsuit brought about a voluntary change in the defendant's conduct. We hold that it does not.

Buckhannon Board and Care Home, Inc., which operates care homes that provide assisted living to their residents, failed an inspection by the West Virginia Office of the State Fire Marshal because some of the residents were incapable of "self-preservation" as defined under state law. On October 28, 1997, after receiving cease and desist orders requiring the closure of its residential care facilities within 30 days, Buckhannon, on behalf of itself and other similarly situated homes and residents (hereinafter petitioners), brought suit in the United States District Court for the Northern District of West Virginia against the State of West Virginia, two of its agencies, and 18 individuals (hereinafter respondents), seeking declaratory and injunctive relief[1] that the "self-preservation" requirement violated the Fair Housing Amendments Act of 1988 (FHAA) and the Americans with Disabilities Act of 1990 (ADA).

Respondents agreed to stay enforcement of the cease and desist orders pending resolution of the case and the parties began discovery. In 1998, the West Virginia Legislature enacted two bills eliminating the "self-preservation" requirement and respondents moved to dismiss the case as moot. The District Court granted the motion, finding that the 1998 legislation had eliminated the allegedly offensive provisions and that there was no indication that the West Virginia Legislature would repeal the amendments.[2]

Petitioners requested attorney's fees as the "prevailing party" under the FHAA, 42 U.S.C. § 3613(c)(2) ("[T]he court, in its discretion, may allow the prevailing party . . . a reasonable attorney's fee and costs"), and ADA, 42 U.S.C. § 12205 ("[T]he court . . . , in its discretion, may allow the prevailing party . . . a reasonable attorney's fee, including litigation expenses, and costs"). Petitioners argued that they were entitled to attorney's fees under the "catalyst theory," which posits that a plaintiff is a "prevailing party" if it achieves the desired result because the lawsuit brought about a voluntary change in the defendant's conduct. Although most Courts of Appeals recognize the "catalyst theory," the Court of Appeals for the Fourth Circuit rejected it in S–1 and S–2 v. State Bd. of Ed. of N. C., 21 F.3d 49, 51 (C.A.4 1994) (en banc) ("A person may not be a 'prevailing party' . . . except by virtue of having obtained an enforceable judgment, consent decree, or settlement giving some of the legal relief sought"). The District Court accordingly denied the motion and, for the same reason, the Court of Appeals affirmed.

---

1 The original complaint also sought money damages, but petitioners relinquished this claim on January 2, 1998.

2 The District Court sanctioned respondents under Federal Rule of Civil Procedure 11 for failing to timely provide notice of the legislative amendment. [In their Rule 11 motion, plaintiffs requested fees and costs totaling $62,459 to cover the expense of litigating after defendants became aware, but did not disclose, that elimination of the rule was likely. In the alternative, plaintiffs sought $3,252 to offset fees and expenses incurred in litigating the Rule 11 motion. The District Court, stating that "the primary purpose of Rule 11 is to deter and not to compensate," awarded the smaller sum. Dissent footnote 2.]

In the United States, parties are ordinarily required to bear their own attorney's fees—the prevailing party is not entitled to collect from the loser. See Alyeska Pipeline Service Co. v. Wilderness Society, 421 U.S. 240, 247 (1975). Under this "American Rule," we follow "a general practice of not awarding fees to a prevailing party absent explicit statutory authority." Congress, however, has authorized the award of attorney's fees to the "prevailing party" in numerous statutes in addition to those at issue here, such as the Civil Rights Act of 1964, the Voting Rights Act Amendments of 1975, and the Civil Rights Attorney's Fees Awards Act of 1976.

In designating those parties eligible for an award of litigation costs, Congress employed the term "prevailing party," a legal term of art. Black's Law Dictionary 1145 (7th ed.1999) defines "prevailing party" as "[a] party in whose favor a judgment is rendered, regardless of the amount of damages awarded. In certain cases, the court will award attorney's fees to the prevailing party.—Also termed *successful party*." This view that a "prevailing party" is one who has been awarded some relief by the court can be distilled from our prior cases.[5]

In Hanrahan v. Hampton, 446 U.S. 754 (1980) *(per curiam),* we reviewed the legislative history of § 1988 and found that "Congress intended to permit the interim award of counsel fees only when a party has prevailed on the merits of at least some of his claims." Our "[r]espect for ordinary language requires that a plaintiff receive at least some relief on the merits of his claim before he can be said to prevail." We have held that even an award of nominal damages suffices under this test.

In addition to judgments on the merits, we have held that settlement agreements enforced through a consent decree may serve as the basis for an award of attorney's fees. Although a consent decree does not always include an admission of liability by the defendant, it nonetheless is a court-ordered "chang[e] [in] the legal relationship between [the plaintiff] and the defendant."[7] These decisions, taken together, establish that enforceable judgments on the merits and court-ordered consent decrees

---

[5] We have never had occasion to decide whether the term "prevailing party" allows an award of fees under the "catalyst theory" described above. Dicta in Hewitt v. Helms alluded to the possibility of attorney's fees where "voluntary action by the defendant . . . affords the plaintiff all or some of the relief . . . sought," but we expressly reserved the question. And though the Court of Appeals for the Fourth Circuit relied upon our decision in Farrar v. Hobby in rejecting the "catalyst theory," Farrar "involved no catalytic effect." Thus, there is language in our cases supporting both petitioners and respondents, and last Term we observed that it was an open question here.

[7] We have subsequently characterized the Maher opinion as also allowing for an award of attorney's fees for private settlements. But this dicta ignores that Maher only "held that fees *may* be assessed . . . after a case has been settled by the entry of a consent decree." Private settlements do not entail the judicial approval and oversight involved in consent decrees. And federal jurisdiction to enforce a private contractual settlement will often be lacking unless the terms of the agreement are incorporated into the order of dismissal.

create the "material alteration of the legal relationship of the parties" necessary to permit an award of attorney's fees.

We think, however, the "catalyst theory" falls on the other side of the line from these examples. It allows an award where there is no judicially sanctioned change in the legal relationship of the parties. Even under a limited form of the "catalyst theory," a plaintiff could recover attorney's fees if it established that the "complaint had sufficient merit to withstand a motion to dismiss for lack of jurisdiction or failure to state a claim on which relief may be granted." This is not the type of legal merit that our prior decisions, based upon plain language and congressional intent, have found necessary. . . . A defendant's voluntary change in conduct, although perhaps accomplishing what the plaintiff sought to achieve by the lawsuit, lacks the necessary judicial *imprimatur* on the change. Our precedents thus counsel against holding that the term "prevailing party" authorizes an award of attorney's fees *without* a corresponding alteration in the legal relationship of the parties.

The dissenters chide us for upsetting "long-prevailing *Circuit* precedent." But, as Justice Scalia points out in his concurrence, several Courts of Appeals have relied upon dicta in our prior cases in approving the "catalyst theory." Now that the issue is squarely presented, it behooves us to reconcile the plain language of the statutes with our prior *holdings*. We have only awarded attorney's fees where the plaintiff has received a judgment on the merits or obtained a court-ordered consent decree—we have not awarded attorney's fees where the plaintiff has secured the reversal of a directed verdict or acquired a judicial pronouncement that the defendant has violated the Constitution unaccompanied by "*judicial* relief." Never have we awarded attorney's fees for a nonjudicial "alteration of actual circumstances." While urging an expansion of our precedents on this front, the dissenters would simultaneously abrogate the "merit" requirement of our prior cases and award attorney's fees where the plaintiff's claim "was at least colorable" and "not . . . groundless." We cannot agree that the term "prevailing party" authorizes federal courts to award attorney's fees to a plaintiff who, by simply filing a nonfrivolous but nonetheless potentially meritless lawsuit (it will never be determined), has reached the "sought-after destination" without obtaining any judicial relief.[8]

---

8 Although the dissenters seek support from Mansfield, C. & L.M. R. Co. v. Swan, 111 U.S. 379 (1884), that case involved costs, not attorney's fees. "[B]y the long established practice and universally recognized rule of the common law . . . the prevailing party is entitled to recover a judgment for costs," but "the rule 'has long been that attorney's fees are not ordinarily recoverable.' " Courts generally, and this Court in particular, then and now, have a presumptive rule for costs which the Court in its discretion may vary. In Mansfield, the defendants had successfully removed the case to federal court, successfully opposed the plaintiffs' motion to remand the case to state court, lost on the merits of the case, and then reversed course and successfully argued in this Court that the lower federal court had no jurisdiction. The Court awarded costs to the plaintiffs, even though they had lost and the defendants won on the jurisdictional issue, which was the only question this Court decided. In no ordinary sense of the

Petitioners nonetheless argue that the legislative history of the Civil Rights Attorney's Fees Awards Act supports a broad reading of "prevailing party" which includes the "catalyst theory." We doubt that legislative history could overcome what we think is the rather clear meaning of "prevailing party"—the term actually used in the statute. Since we resorted to such history in Garland, Maher, and Hanrahan, however, we do likewise here.

The House Report to § 1988 states that "[t]he phrase 'prevailing party' is not intended to be limited to the victor only after entry of a final judgment following a full trial on the merits," while the Senate Report explains that "parties may be considered to have prevailed when they vindicate rights through a consent judgment or without formally obtaining relief." Petitioners argue that these Reports and their reference to a 1970 decision from the Court of Appeals for the Eighth Circuit indicate Congress' intent to adopt the "catalyst theory."[9] We think the legislative history cited by petitioners is at best ambiguous as to the availability of the "catalyst theory" for awarding attorney's fees. Particularly in view of the "American Rule" that attorney's fees will not be awarded absent "explicit statutory authority," such legislative history is clearly insufficient to alter the accepted meaning of the statutory term.

Petitioners finally assert that the "catalyst theory" is necessary to prevent defendants from unilaterally mooting an action before judgment in an effort to avoid an award of attorney's fees. They also claim that the rejection of the "catalyst theory" will deter plaintiffs with meritorious but expensive cases from bringing suit. We are skeptical of these assertions, which are entirely speculative and unsupported by any empirical evidence (*e.g.,* whether the number of suits brought in the Fourth Circuit has declined, in relation to other Circuits, since the decision in *S–1 and S–2*).

Petitioners discount the disincentive that the "catalyst theory" may have upon a defendant's decision to voluntarily change its conduct, conduct that may not be illegal. "The defendants' potential liability for

---

word can the plaintiffs have been said to be the prevailing party here—they lost and their opponents won on the only litigated issue—so the Court's use of the term must be regarded as a figurative rather than a literal one, justifying the departure from the presumptive rule allowing costs to the prevailing party because of the obvious equities favoring the plaintiffs. The Court employed its discretion to recognize that the plaintiffs had been the victims of the defendants' legally successful whipsawing tactics.

[9] Although the Court of Appeals in Parham awarded attorney's fees to the plaintiff because his "lawsuit acted as a catalyst which prompted the [defendant] to take action . . . seeking compliance with the requirements of Title VII," it did so only after finding that the defendant had acted unlawfully. Thus, consistent with our holding in Farrar, Parham stands for the proposition that an enforceable judgment permits an award of attorney's fees. And like the consent decree in Maher v. Gagne, the Court of Appeals in Parham ordered the District Court to "retain jurisdiction over the matter for a reasonable period of time to insure the continued implementation of the appellee's policy of equal employment opportunities." Clearly Parham does not support a theory of fee-shifting untethered to a material alteration in the legal relationship of the parties as defined by our precedents.

fees in this kind of litigation can be as significant as, and sometimes even more significant than, their potential liability on the merits," and the possibility of being assessed attorney's fees may well deter a defendant from altering its conduct.

And petitioners' fear of mischievous defendants only materializes in claims for equitable relief, for so long as the plaintiff has a cause of action for damages, a defendant's change in conduct will not moot the case.[10] Even then, it is not clear how often courts will find a case mooted: "It is well settled that a defendant's voluntary cessation of a challenged practice does not deprive a federal court of its power to determine the legality of the practice" unless it is "absolutely clear that the allegedly wrongful behavior could not reasonably be expected to recur." If a case is not found to be moot, and the plaintiff later procures an enforceable judgment, the court may of course award attorney's fees. Given this possibility, a defendant has a strong incentive to enter a settlement agreement, where it can negotiate attorney's fees and costs.

We have also stated that "[a] request for attorney's fees should not result in a second major litigation" and have accordingly avoided an interpretation of the fee-shifting statutes that would have "spawn[ed] a second litigation of significant dimension." Among other things, a "catalyst theory" hearing would require analysis of the defendant's subjective motivations in changing its conduct, an analysis that "will likely depend on a highly factbound inquiry and may turn on reasonable inferences from the nature and timing of the defendant's change in conduct." Although we do not doubt the ability of district courts to perform the nuanced "three thresholds" test required by the "catalyst theory"—whether the claim was colorable rather than groundless; whether the lawsuit was a substantial rather than an insubstantial cause of the defendant's change in conduct; whether the defendant's change in conduct was motivated by the plaintiff's threat of victory rather than threat of expense—it is clearly not a formula for "ready administrability."

Given the clear meaning of "prevailing party" in the fee-shifting statutes, we need not determine which way these various policy arguments cut. In Alyeska, we said that Congress had not "extended any roving authority to the Judiciary to allow counsel fees as costs or otherwise whenever the courts might deem them warranted." To disregard the clear legislative language and the holdings of our prior cases on the basis of such policy arguments would be a similar assumption of a "roving authority." For the reasons stated above, we hold that the "catalyst theory" is not a permissible basis for the award of attorney's fees under the FHAA and ADA.

---

[10] Only States and state officers acting in their official capacity are immune from suits for damages in federal court. Plaintiffs may bring suit for damages against all others, including municipalities and other political subdivisions of a State.

The judgment of the Court of Appeals is *Affirmed.*

JUSTICE SCALIA, with whom JUSTICE THOMAS joins, concurring.

I join the opinion of the Court in its entirety, and write to respond at greater length to the contentions of the dissent.

"Prevailing party" is not some newfangled legal term invented for use in late 20th-century fee-shifting statutes. . . . The term has been found within the United States Statutes at Large since at least 1867. [I]t is no stranger to the law.

At the time 42 U.S.C. § 1988 was enacted, I know of no case, state or federal, in which—either under a statutory invocation of "prevailing party," or under the common-law rule—the "catalyst theory" was enunciated as the basis for awarding costs. Indeed, the dissent cites only one case in which (although the "catalyst theory" was not expressed) costs were awarded for a reason that the catalyst theory would support, but today's holding of the Court would not. . . . And that case is irrelevant to the meaning of "prevailing party," because it was a case *in equity.* While costs were awarded in actions *at law* to the "prevailing party," an equity court could award costs "as the equities of the case might require." The other state or state-law cases the dissent cites as awarding costs despite the absence of a judgment all involve a judicial finding—or its equivalent, an acknowledgement by the defendant—of the merits of plaintiff's case. Moreover, the dissent cites *not a single case* in which this Court—or even any other federal court applying federal law prior to enactment of the fee-shifting statutes at issue here—has regarded as the "prevailing party" a litigant who left the courthouse emptyhanded. If the term means what the dissent contends, that is a remarkable absence of authority. . . .

It is undoubtedly true, as the dissent points out by quoting a nonlegal dictionary, that the word "prevailing" can have other meanings in other contexts: "prevailing winds" are the winds that predominate, and the "prevailing party" in an election is the party that wins the election. But when "prevailing party" is used by courts or legislatures in the context of a lawsuit, it is a term of art. It has traditionally—and to my knowledge, prior to enactment of the first of the statutes at issue here, *invariably*—meant the party that wins the suit or obtains a finding (or an admission) of liability. Not the party that ultimately gets his way because his adversary dies before the suit comes to judgment; not the party that gets his way because circumstances so change that a victory on the legal point for the other side turns out to be a practical victory for him; and not the party that gets his way because the other side ceases (for whatever reason) its offensive conduct. Words that have acquired a specialized meaning in the legal context must be accorded their *legal* meaning. . . .

The dissent distorts the term "prevailing party" beyond its normal meaning for policy reasons, but even those seem to me misguided. They rest upon the presumption that the catalyst theory applies when "*the suit's merit* led the defendant to abandon the fray, to switch rather than fight on, to accord plaintiff sooner rather than later the principal redress sought in the complaint." What the dissent's stretching of the term produces is something more, and something far less reasonable: an award of attorney's fees when the merits of plaintiff's case remain unresolved—when, for all one knows, the defendant only "abandon[ed] the fray" because the cost of litigation—either financial or in terms of public relations—would be too great. In such a case, the plaintiff may have "prevailed" as Webster's defines that term—"gain[ed] victory by virtue of strength or superiority." But I doubt it was greater strength in financial resources, or superiority in media manipulation, rather than *superiority in legal merit,* that Congress intended to reward.

It could be argued, perhaps, that insofar as abstract justice is concerned, there is little to choose between the dissent's outcome and the Court's: If the former sometimes rewards the plaintiff with a phony claim (there is no way of knowing), the latter sometimes denies fees to the plaintiff with a solid case whose adversary slinks away on the eve of judgment. But it seems to me the evil of the former far outweighs the evil of the latter. There is all the difference in the world between a rule that denies the extraordinary boon of attorney's fees to some plaintiffs who are no less "deserving" of them than others who receive them, and a rule that causes the law to be the very instrument of wrong—exacting the payment of attorney's fees to the extortionist. . . .

The dissent's ultimate worry is that today's opinion will "impede access to court for the less well-heeled." But, of course, the catalyst theory also harms the "less well-heeled," putting pressure on them to avoid the risk of massive fees by abandoning a solidly defensible case early in litigation. Since the fee-shifting statutes at issue here allow defendants as well as plaintiffs to receive a fee award, we know that Congress did not intend to *maximize* the quantity of "the enforcement of federal law by private attorneys general." Rather, Congress desired an *appropriate* level of enforcement—which is more likely to be produced by limiting fee awards to plaintiffs who prevail "on the merits," or at least to those who achieve an enforceable "alteration of the legal relationship of the parties," than by permitting the open-ended inquiry approved by the dissent. . . .

The Court today concludes that a party cannot be deemed to have prevailed, for purposes of fee-shifting statutes such as 42 U.S.C. §§ 1988, unless there has been an enforceable "alteration of the legal relationship of the parties." That is the normal meaning of "prevailing party" in litigation, and there is no proper basis for departing from that normal meaning. Congress is free, of course, to revise these provisions—but it is my guess that if it does so it will not create the sort of inequity that the catalyst theory invites, but will require the court to determine that there was at least a substantial likelihood that the party requesting fees would have prevailed.

JUSTICE GINSBURG, with whom JUSTICE STEVENS, JUSTICE SOUTER, and JUSTICE BREYER join, dissenting.

The Court today holds that a plaintiff whose suit prompts the precise relief she seeks does not "prevail," and hence cannot obtain an award of attorney's fees, unless she also secures a court entry memorializing her victory. The entry need not be a judgment on the merits. Nor need there be any finding of wrongdoing. A court-approved settlement will do.

The Court's insistence that there be a document filed in court—a litigated judgment or court-endorsed settlement—upsets long-prevailing Circuit precedent applicable to scores of federal fee-shifting statutes. The decision allows a defendant to escape a statutory obligation to pay a plaintiff's counsel fees, even though the suit's merit led the defendant to abandon the fray, to switch rather than fight on, to accord plaintiff sooner rather than later the principal redress sought in the complaint. Concomitantly, the Court's constricted definition of "prevailing party," and consequent rejection of the "catalyst theory," impede access to court for the less well-heeled, and shrink the incentive Congress created for the enforcement of federal law by private attorneys general.

In my view, the "catalyst rule," as applied by the clear majority of Federal Circuits, is a key component of the fee-shifting statutes Congress adopted to advance enforcement of civil rights. Nothing in history, precedent, or plain English warrants the anemic construction of the term "prevailing party" the Court today imposes. . . .

The Court today detects a "clear meaning" of the term prevailing party that has heretofore eluded the large majority of courts construing those words. "Prevailing party," today's opinion announces, means "one who has been awarded some relief by the court." The Court derives this "clear meaning" principally from Black's Law Dictionary, which defines a "prevailing party," in critical part, as one "in whose favor a judgment is rendered." . . .

As the Courts of Appeals have long recognized, the catalyst rule suitably advances Congress' endeavor to place private actions, in civil rights and other legislatively defined areas, securely within the federal law enforcement arsenal.

The catalyst rule stemmed from modern legislation extending civil rights protections and enforcement measures. The Civil Rights Act of 1964 included provisions for fee awards to "prevailing parties" in Title II (public accommodations), Title VII (employment), but not in Title VI (federal programs). The provisions' central purpose was "to promote vigorous enforcement" of the laws by private plaintiffs; although using the two-way term "prevailing party," Congress did not make fees available to plaintiffs and defendants on equal terms. Christiansburg Garment Co. v. EEOC, 434 U.S. 412, 417, 421 (1978) (under Title VII, prevailing plaintiff qualifies for fee award absent "special circumstances," but prevailing defendant may obtain fee award only if plaintiff's suit is "frivolous, unreasonable, or without foundation").

Once the 1964 Act came into force, courts commenced to award fees regularly under the statutory authorizations, and sometimes without such authorization. In Alyeska, this Court reaffirmed the "American rule" that a court generally may not award attorney's fees without a legislative instruction to do so. To provide the authorization Alyeska required for fee awards under Title VI of the 1964 Civil Rights Act, as well as under Reconstruction Era civil rights legislation and certain other enactments, Congress passed the Civil Rights Attorney's Fees Awards Act of 1976.

As explained in the Reports supporting § 1988, civil rights statutes vindicate public policies "of the highest priority," yet "depend heavily on private enforcement." Persons who bring meritorious civil rights claims, in this light, serve as "private attorneys general." Such suitors, Congress recognized, often "cannot afford legal counsel." They therefore experience "severe hardshi[p]" under the "American Rule." Congress enacted § 1988 to ensure that nonaffluent plaintiffs would have "effective access" to the Nation's courts to enforce civil rights laws. That objective accounts for the fee-shifting provisions before the Court in this case, prescriptions of the FHAA and the ADA modeled on § 1988.

Under the catalyst rule that held sway until today, plaintiffs who obtained the relief they sought through suit on genuine claims ordinarily qualified as "prevailing parties," so that courts had discretion to award them their costs and fees. Persons with limited resources were not impelled to "wage total law" in order to assure that their counsel fees would be paid. They could accept relief, in money or of another kind, voluntarily proffered by a defendant who sought to avoid a recorded decree. And they could rely on a judge then to determine, in her equitable discretion, whether counsel fees were warranted and, if so, in what amount.[10]

Congress appears to have envisioned that very prospect. The Senate Report on the 1976 Civil Rights Attorney's Fees Awards Act states: "[F]or purposes of the award of counsel fees, parties may be considered to have prevailed when they vindicate rights through a consent judgment *or without formally obtaining relief*." In support, the Report cites cases in

[10] Given the protection furnished by the catalyst rule, aggrieved individuals were not left to worry, and wrongdoers were not led to believe, that strategic maneuvers by defendants might succeed in averting a fee award. Apt here is Judge Friendly's observation construing a fee-shifting statute kin to the provisions before us: "Congress clearly did not mean that where a [Freedom of Information Act] suit had gone to trial and developments have made it apparent that the judge was about to rule for the plaintiff, the Government could abort any award of attorney fees by an eleventh hour tender of information."

which parties recovered fees in the absence of any court-conferred relief. The House Report corroborates: "[A]fter a complaint is filed, a defendant might voluntarily cease the unlawful practice. *A court should still award fees* even though it might conclude, as a matter of equity, that *no formal relief,* such as an injunction, is needed." These Reports, Courts of Appeals have observed, are hardly ambiguous.

The Court identifies several "policy arguments" that might warrant rejection of the catalyst rule. A defendant might refrain from altering its conduct, fearing liability for fees as the price of voluntary action. Moreover, rejection of the catalyst rule has limited impact: Desisting from the challenged conduct will not render a case moot where damages are sought, and even when the plaintiff seeks only equitable relief, a defendant's voluntary cessation of a challenged practice does not render the case moot "unless it is 'absolutely clear that the allegedly wrongful behavior could not reasonably be expected to recur.' " Because a mootness dismissal is not easily achieved, the defendant may be impelled to settle, negotiating fees less generous than a court might award. Finally, a catalyst rule would "require analysis of the defendant's subjective motivations," and thus protract the litigation.

The Court declines to look beneath the surface of these arguments, placing its reliance, instead, on a meaning of "prevailing party" that other jurists would scarcely recognize as plain. Had the Court inspected the "policy arguments" listed in its opinion, I doubt it would have found them impressive.

In opposition to the argument that defendants will resist change in order to stave off an award of fees, one could urge that the catalyst rule may lead defendants promptly to comply with the law's requirements: the longer the litigation, the larger the fees. Indeed, one who knows noncompliance will be expensive might be encouraged to conform his conduct to the legal requirements before litigation is threatened.

As to the burden on the court, is it not the norm for the judge to whom the case has been assigned to resolve fee disputes (deciding whether an award is in order, and if it is, the amount due), thereby clearing the case from the calendar? If factfinding becomes necessary under the catalyst rule, is it not the sort that "the district courts, in their factfinding expertise, deal with on a regular basis"? Might not one conclude overall, as Courts of Appeals have suggested, that the catalyst rule "saves judicial resources," by encouraging "plaintiffs to discontinue litigation after receiving through the defendant's acquiescence the remedy initially sought"?

The concurring opinion adds another argument against the catalyst rule: That opinion sees the rule as accommodating the "extortionist" who obtains relief because of "greater strength in financial resources, or superiority in media manipulation, rather than *superiority in legal merit.*"

This concern overlooks both the character of the rule and the judicial superintendence Congress ordered for all fee allowances. The catalyst rule was auxiliary to fee-shifting statutes whose primary purpose is "to promote the vigorous enforcement" of the civil rights laws. To that end, courts deemed the conduct-altering catalyst that counted to be the substance of the case, not merely the plaintiff's atypically superior financial resources, media ties, or political clout. And Congress assigned responsibility for awarding fees not to automatons unable to recognize extortionists, but to judges expected and instructed to exercise "discretion." So viewed, the catalyst rule provided no berth for nuisance suits or "thinly disguised forms of extortion." . . .

The Court states that the term "prevailing party" in fee-shifting statutes has an "accepted meaning." If that is so, the "accepted meaning" is not the one the Court today announces. It is, instead, the meaning accepted by every Court of Appeals to address the catalyst issue before our 1987 decision in Hewitt and disavowed since then only by the Fourth Circuit. A plaintiff prevails, federal judges have overwhelmingly agreed, when a litigated judgment, consent decree, out-of-court settlement, or the defendant's voluntary, postcomplaint payment or change in conduct in fact affords redress for the plaintiff's substantial grievances.

NOTES AND QUESTIONS

1. The case, particularly the dissent, offers considerable background on recently enacted fee-shifting statutes. Our heritage—the British legal system—pursues a completely different approach: they award the prevailing party fees in every case. Why did America depart from that heritage? What is protected by forcing the parties to pay for their own attorneys? Would a background rule allowing winners to recover their fees be better than a series of ad hoc statutes enacting that rule in a few settings?

2. Recent fee-shifting statutes don't really enact a loser-pays system. They allow the prevailing party to recover fees. But prevailing plaintiffs recover their fees as a matter of course, while prevailing defendants recover only if the plaintiff's claim was frivolous. Does that make sense? Consider two explanations:

a. When plaintiff wins, attorneys' fees are an entirely foreseeable element of damages caused by the defendant's illegal conduct. Plaintiffs should recover them as a matter of course. But when defendant wins, her fees are not the result of any misconduct by the plaintiff unless he should not have brought the suit in the first place. That applies to frivolous suits. Because claims brought in good faith are not wrongful, no claim for fees accrues to the defendant.

b. Congress wants to encourage the types of claims covered by fee-shifting statutes. Damages often will be relatively modest, but the

> misconduct, especially by the government, is important to correct. The government is not particularly good at detecting its own misconduct, even if it had enough attorneys and investigators for this purpose. Victims are the people most likely to know about the misconduct, but may not be able to afford to bring the misconduct to light if they must pay their own attorney. The statutes remove this impediment, in effect paying the victims to become the watchdogs of the government. They act for the public good, at least when they prevail. Fees tax the wrongdoers for the enforcement activity made necessary by their misconduct. Defendants, even when they have done nothing wrong, do not need any incentive to pay attorneys to defend themselves. Thus, fee shifting can favor plaintiffs.

Which explanation seems to have motivated Congress? Which motivates the Court? Would one explanation produce a different result in this case? Is that better or worse?

3. Consider Scalia's concern about extortion. Plaintiffs are virtually immune from paying fees—their own or defendants—even if plaintiffs have resources. Contingent contracts keep their own attorney from collecting unless they win; the law precludes recovery by defendant unless the claim is obviously spurious. They have everything to gain and nothing to lose by bringing a lawsuit. They can extract settlements by bringing nuisance suits; as long as they survive a motion to dismiss, discovery may cost more than settlement. Should Congress reduce the relative advantages plaintiffs enjoy in litigation? At least, should the court narrowly construe statutes to avoid exacerbating the imbalance Congress has created? Is the dissent too focused on defendants who are wrongdoers to see the effects of litigation on defendants who are not wrongdoers?

4. The catalyst theory is not entirely dead. In cases under the Freedom of Information Act, Congress amended the law in 2007 to allow recovery if the claimant "substantially prevailed." 5 U.S.C. 552(a)(4)(E). Some states continue to apply the catalyst theory in applying their statutes. *See, e.g., Mason v. City of Hoboken*, 196 N.J. 51, 951 A.2d 1017 (N.J. 2008). In other cases, defendants have not objected to fees despite *Buckhannon*. *Iverson v. Braintree Property Assocs.*, 2008 WL 552652 (Civil Action No. 04cv12079–NG.) (D. Mass. 2008) (suggesting that settlements supported fee awards despite dicta in *Buckhannon*).

BAXTER V. CROWN PETROLEUM PARTNERS

2000 WL 269747 (N.D.Tex. 2000).

SOLIS, J.

Plaintiffs seek an award of attorneys' fees incurred through their counsel for the above captioned underlying case. n September 7, 1999, this Court signed a judgment for Plaintiffs in the principal amount of $121,042.10, plus pre-judgment interest, costs of court, statutory attorneys's fees to be established in amount by later order of this Court, and post judgment interest on all of the sums at 5.224% per annum.

A. Discussion

Defendants do not dispute that Plaintiffs are entitled to reasonable attorneys' fees pursuant to the Court's judgment. Rather, Defendants argue that the number of hours devoted to this case and the rate of compensation are excessive, and that Plaintiffs' attorney failed to exercise proper billing judgment. Defendants further assert that the amount sought by Plaintiffs' attorney is too high relative to the result attained. Defendants maintain that Plaintiffs' attorneys' fees should be awarded in an amount between $20,000–$30,000.

1. Applicable Law

The determination of reasonable attorneys' fees calls for a three-step procedure. First, the trial court must determine the reasonable number of hours expended on the litigation and the reasonable hourly rates for participating attorneys. The reasonable number of hours must then be multiplied by the reasonable hourly rate. The product of this multiplication is the "lodestar," which may be adjusted upward or downward depending upon the circumstances of the case.

In considering whether to adjust the lodestar amount upward or downward, this Court must consider the following twelve factors: (1) the time and labor required for the case; (2) the novelty and difficulty of the issues involved; (3) the skill required to litigate the case; (4) the ability of the attorney to accept other work; (5) the customary fee for similar work in the community; (6) whether the fee is fixed or contingent; (7) time limitations imposed by the client or the circumstances of the case; (8) the amount involved and results obtained; (9) the attorneys' experience, reputation and ability; (10) the "undesirability" of the case; (11) the nature and length of the attorney-client relationship; and (12) awards in similar cases. *Johnson v. Georgia Highway Express, Inc.*, 488 F.2d 714, 717–19 (5th Cir.1974), *overruled on other grounds, Blanchard v. Bergeron*, 489 U.S. 87 (1989). The court will pay "special heed" to the time and labor involved, the customary fee, the amount in controversy and results obtained, and the experience, reputation and ability of counsel.

2. Lodestar Calculation

The first step in the lodestar analysis requires the Court to determine the reasonable number of hours expended by Plaintiffs' attorney on the lawsuit, as well as the reasonable hourly rates for each of those individual attorneys. Plaintiffs offer time records and affidavits to demonstrate that Plaintiffs' attorney, Gary Vodicka, worked a total of 1026.7 hours on this matter. Vodicka reduced these hours by 300 hours to a total of 726.85 hours to deduct for time spent on paralegal and secretarial work and portions for travel time to hearings, depositions and for telephone conferences with the client. Plaintiffs also offer time records for Mr. Pyke of Rader, Campbell, Fisher & Pyke at 116.5 hours. Both these attorneys seek an hourly rate of $175.00 an hour.

3. Defendants' Arguments

Defendants first argue that the attorneys' fee requested by Plaintiffs is not a reasonable one because this was a relatively simple case, save for the actions of Mr. Vodicka himself. Defendants claim that it was Vodicka, and not the Defendants, who caused the parties to incur more in attorneys fees than was necessary by running the overall fees via unreasonable, unwarranted legal actions. Defendants also maintain that this was a simple suit on an account or an action for breach of contract or quantum meruit and therefore the attorneys fees should be considerably less than those requested.

The evidence shows, however, that this was not a simple case. The matter involved multiple parties, seven defendants, four separate actions and multiple issues. The case was aggressively defended by Defendants with the use of two law firms and four lawyers against Mr. Vodicka, a solo practitioner. Mr. Pyke and his law firm were primarily used as co-counsel during the trial.

The evidence shows that Defendants mounted a vigorous defense to this lawsuit. Defendants contested Plaintiff Baxter was hired, that if he was hired he was hired for them, whether he did quality work, whether he did quality for work them [sic], whether his work, if any, should be offset by any equitable defenses, whether adequate records were kept to support the claim, whether the individual partners should be liable and whether Plaintiff committed malpractice. Defendants deposed Plaintiff for three days. They served on him a *34 page letter* setting out specific areas of inquiry for the remainder of Plaintiff's deposition. Defendants designated *some 644 items/subsections of inquiry* for this deposition. Defendants requested approximately 17 hearings with Magistrate Judge Kaplan. They raised a motion to dismiss for lack of personal jurisdiction, which they later dismissed. Defendants denied basic requests for admissions; they sought leave to file a malpractice claim against plaintiff, they raised various defenses against Plaintiff. These defenses included whether Plaintiffs' fees were reasonable, whether the partnerships were liable for them, whether Defendants were personally liable for them, whether Plaintiffs' claims were barred by statute of limitations, whether Plaintiffs' claims should be barred by fiduciary duties, among others.

Indeed, Defendants did not view this case as a mere breach of contract, suit on an account or quantum meruit. They treated it as a complex case deserving a considerable defense. Certainly, the Court does not suggest that Defendants should not have engaged in any of the foregoing; they are entitled to aggressively defend their case, if they so choose. However, they cannot engage in an aggressive defense and then be heard to complain when Plaintiffs' attorneys' fees escalate as a result. A party cannot contest every issue and every claim and then complain that the fees should have been less because plaintiff could have tried the case with less resources and fewer hours. Having kicked the snow loose at the top by a vigorous, aggressive defense, defendants must now bear the consequences of the attorney fee avalanche at the bottom.

(a) *Plaintiffs' Challenged Conduct*

Defendants complain that much of Vodicka's actions for which he seeks attorneys fees compensation were unreasonable and unnecessarily complicated the matter. [The court rejected most of the 20 challenges because the defendants failed to specify why the time spent was unreasonable or excessive. A few points are illustrative.]

4. Defendants state that Vodicka spent an inordinate amount of time drafting a petition for what should have been a simple breach of contract case. First, the Court knows of no authority that dictates how long a petition must be in a breach of contract case nor do Defendants direct the Court to any such authority. Second, excluding the personal jurisdiction issues (which were anticipated by Plaintiffs and indeed raised and subsequently dropped by Defendants), the petition itself was sixteen (16) pages long, which does not seem an unreasonable length. Third, a party must be given latitude to advance reasonable arguments and theories and the Court will not proscribe Plaintiffs from doing so by pre-determining a specific length for a petition. . . .

11. The time spent for document review is unreasonable because Vodicka produced an excessive number of documents for this case. Indeed, Plaintiff has the duty to produce *all responsive* documents, regardless of the number, and any claim by Defendants that Plaintiffs produced too many documents is absurd. . . .

14. The time spent by Vodicka on jury instructions was unreasonable and none of his submitted jury instructions were used at trial. Plaintiffs are obligated to research and submit jury instructions for trial. Plaintiffs cannot predetermine which instructions, if any, will actually be given to the jury. Because legal research is often the most critical component of determining which arguments to raise, the Court declines to reduce or omit these hours simply because the instructions were never submitted to the jury. . . .

19. Vodicka filed an unnecessarily long response to Defendants' Motion for Summary Judgment. Plaintiffs are obligated to research and answer each and every issue raised by Defendants in their motion for summary judgment, regardless of length.

(b) *Contingency Fee Agreement*

Second, Defendants argue that because Plaintiffs' attorney had a contingent fee agreement with his clients, his attorneys' fee may only be the percentage of the judgment agreed to. Although the contingency fee agreement is a factor to consider under the *Johnson* factors, it is not determinative of the reasonableness of the attorneys' fee award. "There is authority for the suggestion that a contingent fee contract should *not* be considered in determining reasonable attorneys fees, except to establish the employment of counsel and the purpose for which counsel were employed." "What a plaintiff may be bound to pay and what an attorney is free to collect under a fee agreement are not necessarily measured by the "reasonable attorney fee" that a *defendant* must pay pursuant to a court order." *Venegas v. Mitchell*, 495 U.S. 82, 89 (1990) (emphasis added). "The fact that [Vodicka] agreed to a one-third contingency fee arrangement with his client does not determine the amount of attorneys fees [Vodicka] may recover. The recovery of attorneys fees is provided for by statute, the amount of which must be found by the trier of fact and must be supported by the evidence."

The U.S. Supreme Court does not allow the trial court to *enhance* the lodestar figure to compensate the attorney for the contingent fee arrangement between plaintiff and attorney where the attorney should have received a higher figure due to the contingent fee agreement. *City of Burlington v. Dague*, 505 U.S. 557, 564 (1992). It seems logical that this Court is likewise disallowed from *reducing* the lodestar figure to be in line with the contingent fee agreement between the attorney and plaintiff. Plaintiffs are entitled to a *reasonable attorneys' fee* pursuant to Texas Civil Practice and Remedies Code Chapter 38. This Court will consider the contingency fee agreement between Plaintiffs and Mr. Vodicka under the *Johnson* factors but will not reduce the fee awarded based on that factor alone. . . .

B. The *Johnson* Factors

(a) The Time and Labor Required for the Case

Plaintiffs' Application sets forth in great detail the time and labor expended on this case. A brief recapitulation of Plaintiffs' labors are as follows: Vodicka sought and obtained pre-judgment writs of garnishment for a portion of Plaintiffs' recovery which assured collection of a great percentage of Plaintiffs' judgment. Vodicka spent considerable time anticipating and preparing for personal jurisdiction motions. He attended approximately 25 hearings, reviewed 30,000 pages of Defendants' documents, responded to summary judgment, had several meetings with opposing counsel for conferencing and joint status reports, prepared experts, defended against Defendants' attempt to file a malpractice counterclaim against his client, attended a three day deposition of his client and attempted to resolve and work on several discovery disputes.

Vodicka also prepared for and won a four-day jury trial and prepared and attended post-trial equitable defense hearings.

Despite the foregoing work, which was considerable, it nevertheless appears to the Court that the total hours billed for this work by Mr. Vodicka is somewhat excessive. The time and labor required for the case (726.85 hours) warrant a reduction, which is more fully discussed below.

(b) The Novelty and Difficulty of the Issues Involved

The case involved partnership issues, which also presented personal jurisdiction issues. Statute of limitation issues also existed as did the prejudgment garnishment of Defendants' assets with accompanying writs seeking the dissolution of the garnishment action. Furthermore, the case involved post verdict suggestions and finding of fact and conclusions of law based on conflict of interest. Several of the aforementioned issues were novel given the situation and were of first impression within the particular circumstances of the case.

(c) The Skill Required to Litigate the Case

It appears to this Court that the level of skill required to litigate this case was high. Vodicka, a solo practitioner, obtained various writs of garnishment and pursued this case against several other lawyers, two of whom are board certified trial lawyers in federal court, two law firms and multiple defendants. The case involved oil and gas law, bankruptcy law, partnership law, agency law and conflicts law, among others. The case also involved partnership aspects with multiple defendants. Pyke and Vodicka also needed and possessed experience with federal civil procedure, Texas law and jury trials to litigate this case.

(d) The Ability of the Attorney to Accept Other Work

The evidence shows that Mr. Vodicka was precluded from expending time on other cases due to the time spent on this case. The evidence further shows that once discovery was placed on a fast track between the Spring of 1988 and mid-September of 1988, Mr. Vodicka did not devote much time to any other legal matter. The evidence shows Mr. Pyke's firm was unaffected by this case.

(e) The Customary Fee for Similar Work in the Community

Mr. Vodicka's and Mr. Pyke's rate is $175.00 per hour. The Court finds that this rate and fee is consistent with, if not lower than, those prevailing for similar services by professionals of reasonable skill, experience and reputation in the community in which this case has been filed and where Mr. Vodicka and Mr. Pyke practice law.

(f) Whether the Fee Is Fixed or Contingent

Mr. Vodicka has an arrangement with his clients for a contingency fee. The Court has considered the contingent fee arrangement in reaching its attorneys' fee award but will not limit this fee to the contingent fee arrangement. The attorneys' fee figure is properly calculated via the lodestar method and to limit the fee to the contingent fee arrangement constitutes a deviation from the lodestar calculation. Mr. Pyke's firm was paid on an hourly basis.

(g) Time Limitations Imposed by the Client or Circumstances

The case imposed time limitations on Mr. Vodicka, especially during the fast track discovery schedule and responding to summary judgment, preparing for trial and a week long trial. Priority work during these periods delayed Mr. Vodicka from his other legal work. Mr. Pyke's firm was employed on relatively short notice.

(h) The Amount Involved and Results Obtained

The case involved approximately $153,000 as damages (including interest). The attorneys' fees sought are for substantially the same amount. Defendants maintain that because the application amount exceeds the principal amount of the judgment, that fact alone is evidence that the attorneys' fees are excessive.

The amount of damages awarded is only one among the many factors to be considered. An attorneys fee award substantially the same amount as the judgment obtained might, at first glance, appear excessive. Several courts, however, have held attorneys fee awards in far greater amounts to be reasonable. For example, the court in *Great Northern American Stationers v. Ball* upheld an attorneys fee award in the amount of $225,008. where the damages were only $90,724.38. Ball, 770 S.W.2d 631, 633 (Tex.App.–Dallas 1989, writ dism'd). Similarly, the court in *Flint & Assoc. v. Intercontinental Pipe & Steel, Inc.*, upheld an attorneys fee award in the amount of $162,000 where the damages recovered were only $24,067.14. 739 S.W.2d 622, 626 (Tex.App.–Dallas 1987, writ denied). "The determination of what is reasonable cannot be made by application of some mechanical formula. Rather, the court must take into consideration the entire nature of the case."

Having preliminarily established that an attorney fee award higher than the judgment amount is permitted by law, this Court must nevertheless consider the relation of the judgment in this particular case to the award sought. It is the Court's opinion that, considering the nature of this particular case, the award sought is indeed high relative to the damages awarded. A reduction is warranted.

(i) The Attorney's Experience, Reputation and Ability

Mr. Vodicka has had experience working for two judges and has been in private practice for a considerable time. He has much practice in federal court and state court litigation. Mr. Pyke similarly has a reputable academic background, much experience and a good reputation in the community.

(j) The Undesirability of the Case

The case was not an undesirable one.

(k) The Nature and Length of the Attorney–Client Relationship

Prior to this case, neither Vodicka nor Pyke had represented Plaintiffs in any matter.

(l) Awards in Similar Cases

This Court finds that the attorneys' fee sought by Mr. Vodicka in this case is somewhat higher when considered in relation to those awarded in other cases with an equal amount of complexity. Therefore, a reduction is warranted. The Court finds the amount sought by Mr. Pyke to be similar to other cases with an equal amount of complexity.

C. Adjustments to the Lodestar Amount

Having considered the foregoing *Johnson* factors, the Court must now determine whether an adjustment is warranted. Although this case was hotly contested and involved difficult and novel issues, it appears to this Court that 726.85 hours spent by Mr. Vodicka is excessive. The Court reaches this conclusion based on the time and labor expended on this case (given the nature of the case), the amount involved and the results obtained and awards in similar cases. Accordingly, the Court finds a reduction of twenty-five percent of Mr. Vodicka's time is warranted.

D. The Lodestar Calculation

Having considered the *Johnson* factors and determined that a twenty-five percent adjustment is warranted, the Court must now arrive at the lodestar amount. The Court finds that a total of 545.13 hours for Mr. Vodicka at a rate of $175.00 an hour is reasonable. Therefore, the lodestar amount for Mr. Vodicka is $95,397.75. The Court agrees with Defendants that Pyke should not recover attorneys' fees for the hours spent reviewing Vodicka's time entries and records. Unfortunately, however, Defendants fail to specify what amount of time Pyke spent reviewing these records and by what amount such hours should be reduced. . . . The Court may estimate the time an attorney spent on compensable issues when the affidavit lacks sufficient detail to precisely determine the attorney's fee. The Court therefore estimates that 10.8 were spent on reviewing Vodicka's time records. Therefore, Pyke's total hours are 116.5, minus 10.8 hours for a total of 105.7 at $175.00 an hour, totaling $18,497.50.

In addition to the attorneys' fees already discussed, Plaintiffs' counsel requests $22,500.00 in fees to cover the anticipated appeal of this matter to the Fifth Circuit. The Court finds that $10,000.00 is a reasonable amount of attorneys' fees in the event of an appeal to the Fifth Circuit. Therefore, Plaintiffs will be entitled to $10,000 in attorneys' fees should they prevail on an appeal taken. . . .

For the reasons set forth above, it is hereby ORDERED that Plaintiffs' counsel Vodicka is awarded $95,397.75 in attorneys fees, $10,339.97 in costs and $10,000 in appellate fees. It is also ORDERED that Plaintiff's counsel Pyke is awarded $18,497.50 in attorneys' fees.

1. *Allocating Fee Awards.* Who gets the $95,397.75 awarded to Vodicka? Most federal statutes allow the *party* to recover a reasonable attorney's fee. But the court's final sentence appears to award these fees to the attorneys, not to the parties. Vodicka's contract allows one third of the recovery. How much must Baxter pay Vodicka?

a. Suppose the award was larger—say $3 million, including punitive damages ($3.1 million with fees). How much should Vodicka recover?

b. Would you negotiate a different fee agreement with clients whose cases arise under fee-shifting statutes? Are there ethical limits on what you can negotiate? Does the attorney's fiduciary duty attach only after retainer, leaving freedom of contract to reign when negotiating fees?

2. *Adjusting Lodestar.* Do the *Johnson* factors help explain the court's decision at all? The lodestar includes the reasonable number of hours and the reasonable hourly fee. Do the additional factors capture anything that isn't already part of the lodestar?

One factor that generated considerable litigation was the contingency enhancement. Hourly rates are paid whether the attorney wins or loses. The fee shifting statute (or the contingent fee contract) pays only if the attorney wins. Would an attorney who risked no pay charge a higher hourly fee than one who was assured payment? Is $175 per hour a fee inflated to account for the risk or is it based on what attorneys charge when their fees are not contingent? If the latter, should Vodicka be entitled to a higher hourly rate? *See City of Burlington v. Dague*, 505 U.S. 557, 112 S.Ct. 2638, 120 L.Ed.2d 449 (1992). *Dague* holds that courts cannot increase the award of fees beyond the lodestar (hours times rate) to take into account the risk that the attorney might have recovered nothing at all. Has risk dropped out of the calculation? How could you persuade a court, faithful to *Dague*, to take risk into account?

3. *Fees Exceeding Recovery.* Does it make sense to allow attorneys to recover more than their clients? The court suggests this could happen, though the facts did not justify that result here. Is it wasteful to spend $147,000 to recover $121,000 (plus interest)? Would a plaintiff spend her own money that way? Should the law allow her to spend defendant's money so unreasonably? Should we apply the avoidable consequences

doctrine to fee awards, denying recovery of any fees that are unreasonable in relation to the recovery? *See City of Riverside v. Rivera*, 477 U.S. 561, 106 S.Ct. 2686, 91 L.Ed.2d 466 (1986) (attorney fees exceeding $245,000 affirmed, even though compensatory and punitive damages totaled $33,350).

a. *Rivera* was a civil rights case. The police broke up plaintiff's party, using teargas and unnecessary force, and arrested several guests without probable cause. The injuries were relatively modest, making large compensatory damages difficult to prove. Apparently, police earn so little that modest punitive damages seemed likely to deter. Is this case more important than the amount of damages would indicate? Is it worth $245,000 to bring this claim, even though the harm done was far less than that?

b. Now reconsider *Baxter*: as nearly as we can tell, he got the shaft from his partners in an oil and gas firm. Is fee shifting less important for cases like *Baxter*? Is proportionality more appropriate here?

4. *Minimal Success*. Should a plaintiff who prevails on a small part of the claim recover fees? In *Farrar v. Hobby*, 506 U.S. 103, 113 S. Ct. 566 (1992), the Court held that a plaintiff who recovers $1 in nominal damages was a prevailing party, but could not recover attorneys' fees because the success was so minor compared the $17 million sought. Should this preclude attorneys' fees in cases like *Carey v. Piphus*, 435 U.S. 247, 254, 98 S.Ct. 1042, 1047, 55 L.Ed.2d 252 (1978), in which plaintiffs established the right of students to due process prior to suspension, but recovered only nominal damages? The majority opinion implied that it might. But Justice O'Connor, one of the five, wrote separately to suggest *Carey* vindicated important rights, making fees appropriate despite the lack of significant damages. She also suggested that an important public purpose might justify a fee award regardless of the size of a monetary award, citing *Rivera*.

Consider *Aponte v. City of Chicago*, 728 F.3d 724 (7th Cir. 2013). Executing a warrant, officers caused considerable damage to personal property in plaintiff's apartment. Plaintiff sued seeking $25,000 in compensatory damages and $100,000 in punitive damages, but recovered only $100 from one officer (of nine) on one count. Should fees be awarded?

5. *Proportional Fees*. Should fee awards be limited to a percentage of the plaintiff's award?. How would that work in *Rivera*? If damages were larger (say, $2.5 million), would a percentage work better than lodestar?

6. *Conditioning Settlement on Fee Waivers*. *Baxter* ended in judgment. Many cases settle. In settlement negotiations, what if the defendant offers your client an ample recovery, provided your client

waives any claim to fees in addition to the settlement? (Is that necessary? Would a settlement that didn't include fees fully protect the defendant after *Buckhannon*?) *See Evans v. Jeff D.*, 475 U.S. 717, 106 S.Ct. 1531, 89 L.Ed.2d 747 (1986).

7. *Drafting a Fee Agreement.* Draft a provision for a retainer agreement governing fees that might be collected as a result of the litigation. Assume a 33% percent contingent fee arrangement in the event fees are not awarded—or draft your own fee provision. Consider your ethical obligations to your client as well as the risks you face. If appropriate, draft a provision governing fees in the event of cancellation or discharge, too.

CHAPTER 8

REMEDIES IN CONTEXT

■ ■ ■

CHAPTER OVERVIEW: You have studied each remedy separately, and you understand the tools available for the work you must do as a lawyer. This chapter offers you the chance to use those tools. Selecting the right tool for the task is not always easy. In carpentry, when you see a nail, you know to grab the hammer. Legal problems may not be so easy to recognize; problems come in many shapes, without labels to help you distinguish the nails from the screws. As an old adage provides, "To a man with a hammer, everything begins to look like a nail." In this chapter, with classmates and a professor to help you work through the possibilities, we will try to help you get ready for the days when you will need to make these judgments on your own.

Each of the following units starts with a problem, a hypothetical case with a little more detail than most problems earlier in the book. They are followed by a case or two, with questions to help you probe the issues raised in the cases. From there, you should be able to advise a client on the risks and rewards of various legal approaches to the problem, selecting the best one for the circumstances.

A. POTENTIAL HARM: MISDIAGNOSIS

Sean, 35, is a public school teacher earning $37,000 a year. Sean lives an active life, including cycling, kayaking, camping, hiking, and other outdoor activities. Living in southern California, Sean can enjoy these activities on weekends throughout the year, though summer vacations from school provide opportunities for prolonged trips. Each year Sean has a checkup with Doctor Grey, Sean's primary care physician at the HMO. Each year, Sean asks Dr. Grey to examine all moles on Sean's body for signs of cancer. Each year, Dr. Grey examines the moles and reports to Sean that none of the moles show any indication of being cancerous. In 2001, however, Dr. Grey overlooked a change in the color and size of one of the moles on Sean's back, where Sean cannot see it. Dr. Grey again reported that none of the moles showed any indication of being cancerous. In fact, however, that mole was not a mole at all, but melanoma, the most virulent form of skin cancer. Had Dr. Grey discovered the melanoma in

2001, Sean would have had a 40% chance of successful treatment. The melanoma was not discovered until 2002, when Sean suffered a hiking accident out of town and was seen by another doctor, who immediately noticed the problem. At that point, the melanoma was active and malignant. Sean's treatment included: (1) surgery; (2) massive radiation treatment; and (3) chemotherapy.

These treatments cost about $250,000, though the HMO covers all but $250 of the costs. The surgery required Sean to be hospitalized for nearly a week and to remain away from work for another two weeks. The radiation treatments made it nearly impossible for Sean to work for three weeks on each of the two occasions when it was required. Because Sean had substantial accumulated sick leave, Sean received full pay for the time away from work. However, Sean now has no sick leave remaining; any additional absences for medical reasons (including colds) will result in loss of pay. In addition, the radiation causes severe nausea and saps nearly all of Sean's energy. The chemotherapy also causes nausea and fatigue, but does not require Sean to miss any work. Sean cannot be outside in the sun unless fully protected against the sun by opaque clothing (sunblock is insufficient). Between the physical effects of treatment and the stricture to remain out of the sun, Sean is unable to pursue any of the outdoor activities Sean previously enjoyed. Despite the treatment, Sean has only a 5% chance of surviving for two more years. Assuming that Dr. Gray's failure to diagnose the melanoma in 2001 was negligent, what recovery may Sean have against Dr. Grey?

Variation: Would your analysis be any different if the condition were a less virulent form of cancer, where the chance of recovery was 75% if discovered in 2001, but was only 25% because it was discovered in 2002?

MATSUYAMA V. BIRNBAUM

890 N.E.2d 819 (Mass. 2008).

MARSHALL, C.J.

We are asked to determine whether Massachusetts law permits recovery for a "loss of chance" in a medical malpractice wrongful death action, where a jury found that the defendant physician's negligence deprived the plaintiff's decedent of a less than even chance of surviving cancer. We answer in the affirmative.[3] As we later explain more fully, the loss of chance doctrine views a person's prospects for surviving a serious medical condition as something of value, even if the possibility of recovery was less than even prior to the physician's tortious conduct. Where a

[3] The loss of chance doctrine is also known as the "lost opportunity" doctrine. See Restatement (Third) of Torts: Liability for Physical Harm § 26 comment n (Proposed Final Draft No. 1, 2005) (Draft Restatement). See generally King, Jr., Causation, Valuation, and Chance in Personal Injury Torts Involving Preexisting Conditions and Future Consequences, Yale L.J. 1353, 1365–1366 (1981) (King I).

physician's negligence reduces or eliminates the patient's prospects for achieving a more favorable medical outcome, the physician has harmed the patient and is liable for damages. Permitting recovery for loss of chance is particularly appropriate in the area of medical negligence. Our decision today is limited to such claims.

The case before us was tried before a jury in the Superior Court. In response to special questions, the jury found the defendant physician [Birnbaum] negligent in misdiagnosing the condition of the decedent over a period of approximately three years. They found as well that the physician's negligence was a "substantial contributing factor" to the decedent's death. They awarded $160,000 to the decedent's estate for the pain and suffering caused by the physician's negligence, and $328,125 to the decedent's widow and son for the decedent's loss of chance. The defendants appealed, asserting, among other things, that loss of chance was not cognizable under the Massachusetts wrongful death statute,[5] or otherwise. We granted their application for direct appellate review.

We conclude that recognizing loss of chance in the limited domain of medical negligence advances the fundamental goals and principles of our tort law. We also conclude that recognizing a cause of action from loss of chance of survival under the wrongful death statute comports with the common law of wrongful death as it has developed in the Commonwealth. The application of the doctrine to the evidence in this case supported the jury's findings as to loss of chance liability. Finally, although we determine that some portions of the jury instructions do not conform in all respects to the guidelines we set out below, they were broadly consistent with our decision today. Accordingly, we affirm.

1. *Background.* * * *

In June, 2000, the plaintiff [decedent Matsuyama's wife] filed suit against Birnbaum and Medical Associates. Her complaint, as amended, alleged wrongful death, breach of contract, and negligence against both defendants. Trial began in the Superior Court in July, 2004. The jury heard testimony from, among others, the plaintiff's expert witness, Dr. Stuart Ira Finkel, a gastroenterologist. Finkel testified that, in his opinion, Birnbaum breached the applicable standard of care in evaluating and treating Matsuyama, resulting in Matsuyama's death. Specifically, Finkel opined that, in light of Matsuyama's complaints, symptoms, and risk factors, including the presence of H. pylori [a bacteria associated with gastric cancer], his Japanese ancestry, his having lived in Japan or Korea for extended periods, his smoking history, and other well-known risk

[5] General Laws c. 229, § 2, provides in relevant part: "A person who . . . by his negligence causes the death of a person . . . shall be liable in damages." General Laws c. 229, § 6, provides: "In any civil action brought under section two . . . damages may be recovered for conscious suffering resulting from the same injury, but any sum so recovered shall be held and disposed of by the executors or administrators as assets of the estate of the deceased."

factors, an internist exercising the expected standard of care would have ordered an upper gastrointestinal series X-ray or an endoscopy, or referred Matsuyama to a specialist for endoscopy, beginning in 1995. The expert also testified that the appearance of Matsuyama's seborrheickeratosis [a skin lesion] in September, 1997, "could have and should have" triggered a suspicion of stomach cancer "right then and there." Finkel told the jury that if Birnbaum had ordered the appropriate testing on Matsuyama in 1995, the cancer "would have been diagnosed" and "treated in a timely fashion when it might still have been curable." As a result of Birnbaum's failure to make a timely diagnosis, Finkel opined, the cancer metastasized to an advanced, inoperable phase, resulting in Matsuyama's premature death.[14]

In the course of his testimony, Finkel offered an extensive discussion of the tumor-lymph nodes-metastasis (TNM) method for classifying gastric cancer into separate "stages," from stage 0 to stage 4, with each higher stage signaling a more advanced cancer and carrying a statistically diminished chance for survival, as measured by the standard gastric cancer metric of five years cancer free after treatment. Patients with stage 0, in which the cancer is confined to the stomach lining, have a better than 90% survival rate, Finkel averred; at stage 1, the survival rate drops to between 60% and 80%; at stage 2, between 30% and 50%; at stage 3, between 10% and 20%; and at stage 4, less than 4%. Finkel opined that, as a result of Birnbaum's breach of the standard of care, Matsuyama lost the opportunity of having gastric cancer "diagnosed and treated in a timely fashion when it might still have been curable."

Dr. Mark Peppercorn, a gastroenterologist, testified as an expert for the defense. He testified that Birnbaum did not deviate from the accepted standard of care over the course of his treatment of Matsuyama; that Matsuyama's type of stomach cancer had "a different biology, a different characteristic from garden variety, if you want to use that poor term, cancer"; and that his type of cancer did not manifest symptoms until it was in an advanced stage. Peppercorn testified that staging of cancers is done by oncologists for treatment, not actuarial, purposes, with the following presumed five-year survival rates: at stage 1, from 60% to 90%; at stage 2, 25% to 40%; at stage 3, up to 10%; and at stage 4, "practically zero; less than [5%], probably."

In addition to the medical expert testimony, the jury heard testimony from the plaintiff's forensic economist, Dr. Dana Hewins. Hewins testified

---

[14] The plaintiff also called two of the physicians who treated Matsuyama for gastric cancer. Dr. Benjamin Smith, who performed the endoscopic evaluation on Matsuyama in May, 1999, testified that the existence of cancer cannot be determined by physical examination alone, and that endoscopy with biopsies was the acknowledged "gold standard" for diagnosing gastric cancer. Dr. Charles Fuchs, Matsuyama's oncologist, testified, among other things, that Matsuyama had several known risk factors for gastric cancer, that endoscopy with a biopsy was the best way to determine the presence of such cancer, and that early stage detection of gastric cancer portends a better chance of survival.

that, using the standard statistical measures and methods in his field, Matsuyama, had he not died when he did, could have been expected to work an additional 17.7 years, during which time Matsuyama's net earnings from his income minus his personal consumption would have been $466,235. Hewins also testified that Matsuyama could have been expected to live an additional 28.32 years (to age seventy-five), during which time the monetary value of his household services would have been $157,225. Thus, had Matsuyama attained his full work life and life expectancies, he would have contributed $623,460 to his household. Hewins did not offer any projections concerning what Matsuyama would have contributed in wages or services to his family had he died later than he did but earlier than his full work life and life expectancies.

After a six-day trial, the case went to the jury. In response to special questions, the jury found Birnbaum negligent in Matsuyama's treatment, but found him not grossly negligent. They also found that Birnbaum's negligence was a "substantial contributing factor" to Matsuyama's death,[20] and awarded Matsuyama's estate $160,000 for pain and suffering caused by the negligence. Then, in response to a special jury question, the jury awarded damages for loss of chance, which they calculated as follows: they awarded $875,000 as "full" wrongful death damages,[21] and found that Matsuyama was suffering from stage 2 adenocarcinoma at the time of Birnbaum's initial negligence and had a 37.5% chance of survival at that time. They awarded the plaintiff "final" loss of chance damages of $328,125 ($875,000 multiplied by .375). Judgment entered against the defendants, jointly and severally, on the negligence-wrongful death count in the amount of $328,125, later amended to $281,310. A separate judgment entered against the defendants, jointly and severally, for damages in the amount of $160,000 on the counts for conscious pain and suffering.

2. *Loss of chance.* Although we address the issue for the first time today, a substantial and growing majority of the States that have considered the question have indorsed the loss of chance doctrine, in one form or another, in medical malpractice actions.[23] We join that majority to

---

[20] The judge instructed the jury that "substantial" "doesn't mean that Mr. Matsuyama's chance of survival was [50%] or greater, only that there was a fair chance of survival or cure had Dr. Birnbaum not been negligent and had he conformed to the applicable standard of care."

[21] This figure was an aggregate amount that included, in the words of the special question, losses for Matsuyama's "expected net income, services, protection, care, assistance, society, companionship, comfort, guidance, counsel and advice."

[23] The highest courts of at least twenty States and the District of Columbia have adopted the loss of chance doctrine. See Thompson v. Sun City Community Hosp., Inc., 141 Ariz. 597, 688 P.2d 605 (1984); Ferrell v. Rosenbaum, 691 A.2d 641 (D.C.1997). One additional State's high court recognized loss of chance, Falcon v. Memorial Hosp., 436 Mich. 443, 462 N.W.2d 44 (1990), but the Legislature subsequently amended its medical malpractice statute to state that a "plaintiff cannot recover for loss of an opportunity to survive or an opportunity to achieve a better result unless the opportunity was greater than 50%." Mich. Comp. Laws Ann. § 600.2912a(2) (West), as amended by 193 Mich. Pub. Acts 78, § 1 (effective April 1, 1994). Ten States' high courts have, in contrast, refused to adopt the loss of chance doctrine. See *Gooding v.*

ensure that the fundamental aims and principles of our tort law remain fully applicable to the modern world of sophisticated medical diagnosis and treatment.

The development of the loss of chance doctrine offers a window into why it is needed. The doctrine originated in dissatisfaction with the prevailing "all or nothing" rule of tort recovery. Under the all or nothing rule, a plaintiff may recover damages only by showing that the defendant's negligence more likely than not caused the ultimate outcome, in this case the patient's death; if the plaintiff meets this burden, the plaintiff then recovers 100% of her damages. Thus, if a patient had a 51% chance of survival, and the negligent misdiagnosis or treatment caused that chance to drop to zero, the estate is awarded *full* wrongful death damages. On the other hand, if a patient had a 49% chance of survival, and the negligent misdiagnosis or treatment caused that chance to drop to zero, the plaintiff receives nothing. So long as the patient's chance of survival before the physician's negligence was less than even, it is logically impossible for her to show that the physician's negligence was the but-for cause of her death, so she can recover nothing.[26] Thus, the all or nothing rule provides a "blanket release from liability for doctors and hospitals any time there was less than a 50 percent chance of survival, regardless of how flagrant the negligence."

As many courts and commentators have noted, the all or nothing rule is inadequate to advance the fundamental aims of tort law. Fundamentally, the all or nothing approach does not serve the basic aim of "fairly allocating the costs and risks of human injuries," The all or nothing rule "fails to deter" medical negligence because it immunizes "whole areas of medical practice from liability." *McMackin v. Johnson County Healthcare Ctr.,* 73 P.3d 1094, 1099 (Wyo.2003), *S.C.,* 88 P.3d 491 (Wyo.2004). It fails to provide the proper incentives to ensure that the care patients receive does not slip below the "standard of care and skill of the average member of the profession practising the specialty." And the all or nothing rule fails to ensure that victims, who incur the real harm of losing their opportunity for a better outcome, are fairly compensated for their loss.

As the Supreme Court of Wyoming recently stated:

University Hosp. Bldg., Inc., 445 So.2d 1015 (Fla.1984); *Manning v. Twin Falls Clinic & Hosp., Inc.,* 122 Idaho 47, 830 P.2d 1185 (1992). Two other States' high courts have held that loss of chance claims are incompatible with their States' wrongful death statutes, but have not decided whether loss of chance claims are otherwise actionable. See *United States v. Cumberbatch,* 647 A.2d 1098, 1102–1104 (Del.1994); *Joshi v. Providence Health Sys. of Or. Corp.,* 342 Or. 152, 149 P.3d 1164 (2006). Other States' high courts have not addressed the issue or have explicitly left the question open. See, e.g., *Holt v. Wagner,* 344 Ark. 691, 43 S.W.3d 128 (2001).

[26] This is because, when a plaintiff loses a less than even chance of survival, it was *less* likely than not that the negligence was a but-for cause of death. See *Alholm v. Wareham,* 371 Mass. 621, 626–627, 358 N.E.2d 788 (1976), quoting *Bigwood v. Boston & N. St. Ry.,* 209 Mass. 345, 348, 95 N.E. 751 (1911).

"First, the loss of an improved chance of survival or improvement in condition, even if the original odds were less than fifty percent, is an opportunity lost due to negligence. Much treatment of diseases is aimed at extending life for brief periods and improving its quality rather than curing the underlying disease. Much of the American health care dollar is spent on such treatments, aimed at improving the odds. In the words of the Delaware Supreme Court, '[i]t is unjust not to remedy such a loss.' Second, immunizing whole areas of medical practice from liability by requiring proof by more than fifty percent that the negligence caused the injury fails to deter negligence conduct. As Judge Posner wrote in *DePass v. United States,* 'A tortfeasor should not get off scot free because instead of killing his victim outright he inflicts an injury that is likely though not certain to shorten the victim's life.' "

Courts adopting the loss of chance doctrine also have noted that, because a defendant's negligence effectively made it impossible to know whether the person would have achieved a more favorable outcome had he received the appropriate standard of care, it is particularly unjust to deny the person recovery for being unable "to demonstrate to an absolute certainty what would have happened in circumstances that the wrongdoer did not allow to come to pass."

Despite general agreement on the utility of the loss of chance doctrine, however, courts adopting it have not approached loss of chance in a uniform way. The unsettled boundaries of the doctrine have left it open to criticisms similar to those that the defendants have leveled here: that the loss of chance doctrine upends the long-standing preponderance of the evidence standard; alters the burden of proof in favor of the plaintiff; undermines the uniformity and predictability central to tort litigation; results in an expansion of liability; and is too complex to administer. While these objections deserve serious consideration, the doctrine of loss of chance, when properly formulated, survives these criticisms.

Addressing the specific arguments advanced by the defendants is useful for delineating the proper shape of the doctrine. The defendants argue that the loss of chance doctrine "lowers the threshold of proof of causation" by diluting the preponderance of the evidence standard that "has been the bedrock of the Massachusetts civil justice system." Some courts have indeed approached the issue of how to recognize loss of chance by carving out an exception to the rule that the plaintiff must prove by a preponderance of the evidence that the defendant "caused" his injuries. We reject this approach. "It is fundamental that the plaintiff bears the burden of establishing causation by a preponderance of the evidence. Therefore, in a case involving loss of chance, as in any other negligence context, a plaintiff must establish by a preponderance of the evidence that the defendant caused his injury.

However, "injury" need not mean a patient's death. Although there are few certainties in medicine or in life, progress in medical science now makes it possible, at least with regard to certain medical conditions, to estimate a patient's probability of survival to a reasonable degree of medical certainty. That probability of survival is part of the patient's condition. When a physician's negligence diminishes or destroys a patient's chance of survival, the patient has suffered real injury. The patient has lost something of great value: a chance to survive, to be cured, or otherwise to achieve a more favorable medical outcome. Thus we recognize loss of chance not as a theory of causation, but as a theory of injury.[29]

Recognizing loss of chance as a theory of injury is consistent with our law of causation, which requires that plaintiffs establish causation by a preponderance of the evidence. In order to prove loss of chance, a plaintiff must prove by a preponderance of the evidence that the physician's negligence caused the plaintiff's likelihood of achieving a more favorable outcome to be diminished. That is, the plaintiff must prove by a preponderance of the evidence that the physician's negligence caused the plaintiff's injury, where the injury consists of the diminished likelihood of achieving a more favorable medical outcome. The loss of chance doctrine, so delineated, makes no amendment or exception to the burdens of proof applicable in all negligence claims.

We reject the defendants' contention that a statistical likelihood of survival is a "mere possibility" and therefore "speculative." The magnitude of a probability is distinct from the degree of confidence with which it can be estimated. A statistical survival rate cannot conclusively determine whether a particular patient will survive a medical condition. But survival rates are not random guesses. They are estimates based on data obtained and analyzed scientifically and accepted by the relevant medical community as part of the repertoire of diagnosis and treatment, as applied to the specific facts of the plaintiff's case. Where credible evidence establishes that the plaintiff's or decedent's probability of survival is 49%, that conclusion is no more speculative than a conclusion, based on similarly credible evidence, that the probability of survival is 51%.

The defendants also point out that "[t]he cause, treatment, cure and survivability related to cancer is tremendously uncertain and complex,"

---

[29] The Draft Restatement points out that "recognizing lost opportunity as harm is preferable to employing a diluted substantial-factor or other factual-causation test, thereby leaving recovery to the unconstrained inclination of any given jury and providing some fortunate plaintiffs with a full measure of damages for their physical harm while denying any recovery to others." Draft Restatement, *supra* at § 26 comment n.

and argue that loss of chance is "rife with practical complexities and problems." Such difficulties are not confined to loss of chance claims. A wide range of medical malpractice cases, as well as numerous other tort actions, are complex and involve actuarial or other probabilistic estimates. Wrongful death claims, for example, often require, as part of the damages calculation, an estimate of how long the decedent might have lived absent the defendant's conduct. The calculation of damages in a claim for lost business opportunities may be similarly complex.[31]

The key is the reliability of the evidence available to the fact finder. In earlier periods, Massachusetts courts grappling with what we would now call loss of chance claims often lacked reliable expert evidence of what the patient's chances of survival or recovery would have been absent the alleged negligence. More recently, as we noted above, at least for certain conditions, medical science has progressed to the point that physicians can gauge a patient's chances of survival to a reasonable degree of medical certainty, and indeed routinely use such statistics as a tool of medicine. Reliable modern techniques of gathering and analyzing medical data have made it possible for fact finders to determine based on expert testimony—rather than speculate based on insufficient evidence—whether a negligent failure to diagnose a disease injured a patient by preventing the disease from being treated at an earlier stage, when prospects were more favorable. The availability of such expert evidence on probabilities of survival makes it appropriate to recognize loss of chance as a form of injury. Through appropriate expert evidence, a plaintiff in a medical malpractice case may be able to sustain her burden of showing that, as a result of defendant's negligence, a decedent suffered a diminished likelihood of achieving a more favorable medical outcome.

We are unmoved by the defendants' argument that "the ramifications of adoption of loss of chance are immense" across "all areas of tort." We emphasize that our decision today is limited to loss of chance in medical malpractice actions. Such cases are particularly well suited to application of the loss of chance doctrine. First, as we noted above, reliable expert evidence establishing loss of chance is more likely to be available in a medical malpractice case than in some other domains of tort law. Second, medical negligence that harms the patient's chances of a more favorable outcome contravenes the expectation at the heart of the doctor-patient relationship that "the physician will take every reasonable measure to obtain an optimal outcome for the patient." Third, it is not uncommon for patients to have a less than even chance of survival or of achieving a better outcome when they present themselves for diagnosis, so the

[31] Determining causation under the "all or nothing" rule involves a similar use of statistical evidence. See *Jorgenson v. Vener,* 616 N.W.2d 366, 371 (S.D.2000) ("[A]lthough the doctrine [of loss of chance] relies on statistical evidence in order to assign a value to the lost chance, such use of mathematical calculations is already necessary under the traditional standards of causation and valuation. As Professor King points out, 'How else . . . do we even know whether we are talking about a better-than-even chance when applying the all-or-nothing rule?' ").

shortcomings of the all or nothing rule are particularly widespread. Finally, failure to recognize loss of chance in medical malpractice actions forces the party who is the least capable of preventing the harm to bear the consequences of the more capable party's negligence.

In sum, whatever difficulties may attend recognizing loss of chance as an item of damages in a medical malpractice action, these difficulties are far outweighed by the strong reasons to adopt the doctrine. We turn now to the defendants' argument that the wrongful death statute does not allow for loss of chance.

3. *Wrongful death statute.* The wrongful death statute imposes liability on anyone who "by his negligence causes the death of a person." The defendants contend that the language of the statute—"causes the death"—precludes loss of chance claims and allows only claims that the defendant was a but-for cause of the decedent's death. This interpretation is not required by the wrongful death statute.

* * * [The court here concludes that the wrongful death statute was meant to incorporate, not supersede, the common law of wrongful death.]

Like all common-law causes of action, our common law of wrongful death evolves to meet changes in the evolving life of the Commonwealth. Although wrongful death did not traditionally encompass loss of chance of survival, we conclude that claims for loss of chance of survival are sufficiently akin to wrongful death claims as to be cognizable under the wrongful death statute, which governs the procedural requisites for such claims.[37] Now that medical science has developed credible methods of quantifying the extent to which the malpractice damaged the patient's prospects for survival, and in light of the strong public policy favoring compensation for victims of medical malpractice and the deterrence of deviations from appropriate standards of care, loss of chance of survival rightly assumes a place in our common law of wrongful death, and we so hold. * * *

---

[37] Other States have considered the question whether their own wrongful death statutes allow for recovery under a loss of chance theory. Many have found, for differing reasons, that they do. See, e.g., *Cahoon v. Cummings,* 734 N.E.2d 535, 539–540 (Ind.2000); *Perez v. Las Vegas Med. Ctr.,* 107 Nev. 1, 805 P.2d 589 (1991); *McKellips v. Saint Francis Hosp., Inc.,* 741 P.2d 467 (Okla.1987).One State's high court has held that loss of chance claims are cognizable under that State's survival statute, which explicitly provides for the survival of "causes of action for death," Mo.Rev.Stat. § 537.020 (1986) *Wollen v. DePaul Health Ctr.,* 828 S.W.2d 681, 686 (Mo.1992). The court's reasoning relies on the idea that the injury involved in a loss of chance of survival case is death, rather than the loss of chance itself. We do not so hold. In any event, in Massachusetts, a loss of chance claim brought under our survival statute, G.L. c. 228, § 1, rather than our wrongful death statute, would not appear to allow recovery for "the reasonably expected net income, services, protection, care, assistance, society, companionship, comfort, guidance, counsel, and advice of the decedent." G.L. c. 229, § 2.

4. *Damages.* Our conclusion that loss of chance is a separate, compensable item of damages in an action for medical malpractice does not fully resolve the issues on appeal. We must consider, among other things, how the loss of the likelihood of a more favorable outcome is to be valued. The first question is *what* is being valued. In this case, the patient's prospects for achieving a more favorable outcome were measured in terms of the patient's likelihood of surviving for a number of years specified by the relevant medical standard: for gastric cancer, the five-year survival rate. There is no single measure that will apply uniformly to all medical malpractice cases. Precisely what yardstick to use to measure the reduction in the decedent's prospects for survival-life expectancy, five-year survival, ten-year survival, and so on—is a question on which the law must inevitably bow to some extent to the shape of the available medical evidence in each particular case.

A second, more challenging issue is how to calculate the monetary value for the lost chance. Courts adopting the loss of chance doctrine have arrived at different methods for calculating such damages. The most widely adopted of these methods of valuation is the "proportional damages" approach. Under the proportional damages approach, loss of chance damages are measured as "the percentage probability by which the defendant's tortious conduct diminished the likelihood of achieving some more favorable outcome." The formula aims to ensure that a defendant is liable in damages only for the monetary value of the *portion* of the decedent's prospects that the defendant's negligence destroyed. In applying the proportional damages method, the court must first measure the monetary value of the patient's full life expectancy and, if relevant, work life expectancy as it would in any wrongful death case. But the defendant must then be held liable only for the portion of that value that the defendant's negligence destroyed.

Deriving the damages for which the physician is liable will require the fact finder to undertake the following calculations:[41]

[41] These calculations will determine the loss of chance damages. We pause to clarify the issue of damages for pain and suffering, of which there are potentially two kinds. First, a jury could find, on appropriate evidence, that a physician's negligence caused pain and suffering quite apart from the loss of chance. Compensatory damages for this type of pain and suffering should be awarded in the same manner as in any malpractice case; they are not part of the proportional damages calculation.

Second, a jury could find, on appropriate evidence, that the ultimate injury—in this case, dying of gastric cancer—involved pain and suffering. This second category of pain and suffering would more likely than not have occurred even absent the physician's negligent conduct. Thus, the physician may only be held liable for this pain and suffering to the extent that his negligent conduct diminished the decedent's likelihood of avoiding this outcome. Thus, this second category of pain and suffering is properly subject to the proportional damages calculation set out here. * * *

(1) The fact finder must first calculate the total amount of damages allowable for the death under the wrongful death statute, or, in the case of medical malpractice not resulting in death, the full amount of damages allowable for the injury. This is the amount to which the decedent would be entitled if the case were *not* a loss of chance case: the full amount of compensation for the decedent's death or injury.

(2) The fact finder must next calculate the patient's chance of survival or cure immediately preceding ("but for") the medical malpractice.

(3) The fact finder must then calculate the chance of survival or cure that the patient had as a result of the medical malpractice.

(4) The fact finder must then subtract the amount derived in step 3 from the amount derived in step 2.

(5) The fact finder must then multiply the amount determined in step 1 by the percentage calculated in step 4 to derive the proportional damages award for loss of chance.

To illustrate, suppose in a wrongful death case that a jury found, based on expert testimony and the facts of the case, that full wrongful death damages would be $600,000 (step 1), that the patient had a 45% chance of survival prior to the medical malpractice (step 2), and that the physician's tortious acts reduced the chances of survival to 15% (step 3). The patient's chances of survival were reduced 30% (*i.e.*, 45% minus 15%) due to the physician's malpractice (step 4), and the patient's loss of chance damages would be $600,000 multiplied by 30%, for a total of $180,000 (step 5).

We are not unmindful of the criticism of the proportional damages approach. However, we are in accord with those courts that have determined that the proportional damages method is the most appropriate way to quantify the value of the loss of chance for a more favorable outcome, because it is an easily applied calculation that fairly ensures that a defendant is not assessed damages for harm that he did not cause.

From our analysis thus far, it should be evident that the value of "the loss of opportunity to allow events to play out in order to see if the plaintiff's condition was in fact amenable to restoration," is a matter beyond the average juror's ken; the evidence will necessarily come from experts. Expert testimony is required to ascertain what measure of a more favorable outcome is medically appropriate (for example, five-year survival as in this case), to determine what statistical rates of survival apply in what circumstances, for example, a 37.5% chance of survival, and to apply these rates to the particular clinical circumstances of the patient.

* * *

Judgment affirmed.

NOTES AND QUESTIONS

1. Loss of chance is not limited to death cases. For example, in *Jorgenson v. Vener*, 616 N.W.2d 366 (S.D. 2000), plaintiff lost a leg that might have been saved if defendant had recognized and treated an infection sooner.

2. What if a defendant's negligence reduced the plaintiff's chance of survival from 30% to 10% (and plaintiff knows this), but after waiting six months, it has now become clear that the plaintiff will live—does plaintiff have a viable cause of action against defendant?

3. What is the difference between asking (1) whether the plaintiff proved more likely than not that as a result of the defendant's negligence the decedent lost a 37.5% chance of survival and (2) whether the plaintiff proved to a 37.5% probability that the decedent died due to the defendant's negligence?

4. What if the plaintiff could prove that the defendant's negligence more likely than not caused a 70% lost chance of survival? Should the plaintiff be limited to a recovery of 70% damages?

5. Many courts limit loss of chance claims to the medical malpractice context. *See* Restatement (Third) of Torts: Liability for Physical Harm § 26 cmt. n (Proposed Final Draft No. 1, 2005).

6. The standard according to which the plaintiff must prove loss of chance varies among jurisdictions. Although this court used the standard of "reasonable degree of medical certainty," did its application of that term match the term's colloquial meaning? In fact, the "medical certainty" standard has met with much criticism for its uncertainty or its severity. *See, e.g., Bara v. Clarksville Memorial Health Systems*, 104 S.W.3d 1 (Tenn. App. 2002) (explaining that all elements of a tort cause of action must be proved by the preponderance of the evidence). Some jurisdictions instead apply a "reasonable certainty" or "reasonable probability standard." *See, e.g., Alberts v. Schultz*, 975 P.2d 1279 (N.J. 1999) (explaining that New Jersey's "reasonable certainty" standard is coterminous with a "preponderance of the evidence" standard).

7. Returning to the burning question of the introductory hypothetical: how should Sean proceed?

B. POTENTIAL HARM: CHEMICAL EXPOSURE

On April 1, a truck carrying toxic chemicals was involved in a multiple-vehicle accident on an interstate highway. The chemicals spilled onto the highway. Winds carried fumes to a nearby shopping mall. About 50 people were exposed to the fumes before the area could be closed down and evacuated. Jan was one of those people. Jan experienced severe headaches, shortness of breath, nausea, and faintness. Jan was taken to the hospital for observation, but was released early on April 3 with no continuing symptoms. Jan, however, is concerned that the chemical involved has been associated with cancer in laboratory animals. Epidemiological studies suggest that humans exposed to a large dose for a short term (as Jan was) have a higher incidence of cancer. Whereas most people have a 5% chance of cancer, Jan now has a 20% chance of cancer. The risks are exacerbated because Jan is a smoker. Jan would have only a 10% chance if Jan immediately and permanently stopped smoking.

Assume the spill was the result of negligence by the company transporting the chemicals. If Jan sues the carrier what remedy or remedies should Jan seek? How likely is Jan to obtain the relief you propose? What alternatives, if any, should Jan consider? Can Jan wait until cancer symptoms develop and then seek compensation for the effects of the disease? Can she sue now and sue again if she develops cancer symptoms?

STERLING V. VELSICOL CHEMICAL CORPORATION

855 F.2d 1188 (6th Cir. 1988).

RALPH B. GUY, JR., CIRCUIT JUDGE, on rehearing.

In August, 1964, the defendant, Velsicol Chemical Corporation (Velsicol), acquired 242 acres of rural land in Hardeman County, Tennessee. The defendant used the site as a landfill for by-products from the production of chlorinated hydrocarbon pesticides at its Memphis, Tennessee, chemical manufacturing facility. Before Velsicol purchased the landfill site and commenced depositing any chemicals into the ground, it neither conducted hydrogeological studies to assess the soil composition underneath the site, the water flow direction, and the location of the local water aquifer, nor drilled a monitoring well to detect and record any ongoing contamination. From October, 1964, to June, 1973, the defendant deposited a total of 300,000 55-gallon steel drums containing ultrahazardous liquid chemical waste and hundreds of fiber board cartons containing ultrahazardous dry chemical waste in the landfill.

Shortly after Velsicol began its disposal operations at the landfill site, local residents and county, state, and federal authorities became concerned about the environmental impact of the defendant's activities. As a result of this concern, the United States Geological Survey (USGS), in 1967, prepared the first of several reports on the potential contamination effects of the chemicals deposited into the landfill up to that time. The 1967 report indicated that chlorinated hydrocarbons had migrated down into the subsoil and had contaminated portions of the surface and subsurface environment adjacent to the disposal site. While the chemicals had not reached the local water aquifer, the USGS concluded that both the local and contiguous ground water were in danger of contamination. Subsequent to publication of the 1967 USGS report, Velsicol expanded the size of the landfill disposal site from twenty to forty acres.

State authorities increasingly became concerned about the defendant's disposal of ultrahazardous chemicals at the site. In 1972, the state filed an administrative action to close the landfill because the chlorinated hydrocarbons buried at the site allegedly were contaminating irreparably the subsurface waters. The state ordered Velsicol to cease disposal of all toxic chemicals by August 21, 1972, and all other chemicals by June 1, 1973.

[In] 1978, forty-two plaintiffs sued Velsicol in the Circuit Court of Hardeman County, Tennessee, on behalf of themselves and all others similarly situated for damages and injunctive relief. The complaint sought $1.5 billion in compensatory damages and $1 billion in punitive damages. The defendant removed the action to the United States District Court for the Western District of Tennessee, alleging diversity of citizenship and the requisite amount in controversy. Shortly after removal, all but fifteen of the original forty-two plaintiffs settled their claims. [The] complaint sought relief for involuntary exposure to certain chemical substances known to cause cancer, affect the central nervous system and permanently damage other organs of the human body, and for loss of value to their real property in the region affected by the chemicals. Additionally, seven individual civil actions involving fourteen plaintiffs were instituted against Velsicol alleging that the defendant negligently disposed of toxic chemical wastes. The district court, on its own motion and over the defendant's objection, certified a Fed. R. Civ. P. 23(b)(3) class action thereby consolidating the separate [lawsuits].

After a bench trial of the five claims, the district court found Velsicol liable to the plaintiffs on legal theories of strict liability, common law negligence, trespass, and nuisance. The court concluded that the defendant's hazardous chemicals, which escaped from its landfill and contaminated plaintiffs' well water, were the proximate cause of the representative plaintiffs' injuries. The district court awarded the five individuals compensatory damages totaling $5,273,492.50 for their respective injuries, plus prejudgment interest dating back to July, 1965, of $8,964,973.25. All damages, except for $48,492.50 to one plaintiff for property damage claims, were awarded for personal injuries. The district court also awarded $7,500,000 in punitive damages to the class as a whole. The court deferred to individual hearings, to be held after trial, the issues of causation and injury of any other persons purporting to be members of the class entitled to share in this award.

On appeal, the defendant argues that the district court lacked subject matter jurisdiction over the class members and impermissibly certified the case as a class action. The defendant further argues the district court erred in finding that the plaintiffs were exposed to its chemicals and that there was a causal connection between their exposure, if any, and their resultant injuries. Accordingly, the defendant asserts the district court improperly awarded compensatory damages to the plaintiffs for their alleged injuries. Defendant also asserts that prejudgment interest on the compensatory award and punitive damages should not have been awarded. We address the defendant's arguments seriatim.

[The Court discussed the issues of subject matter jurisdiction and class action certification.]

Proximate Causation

The main thrust of Velsicol's argument on appeal is that there was insufficient evidence to support a finding of causation between its disposal of toxic chemicals and plaintiffs' injuries. Velsicol further argues that the various types of injuries identified by the district court were based upon impermissibly speculative and conjectural evidence.

[T]he court, as is appropriate in this type of mass tort class action litigation, divided its causation analysis into two parts. It was first established that Velsicol was responsible for the contamination and that the particular contaminants were capable of producing injuries of the types allegedly suffered by the plaintiffs. Up to this point in the proceeding, the five representative plaintiffs were acting primarily in their representative capacity to the class as a whole. This enabled the court to determine a kind of generic causation—whether the combination of the chemical contaminants and the plaintiffs' exposure to them had the capacity to cause the harm alleged. This still left the matter of individual proximate cause to be determined. Although such generic and individual causation may appear to be inextricably intertwined, the procedural device of the class action permitted the court initially to assess the defendant's potential liability for its conduct without regard to the individual components of each plaintiff's injuries. However, from this point forward, it became the responsibility of each individual plaintiff to show that his or her specific injuries or damages were proximately caused by ingestion or otherwise using the contaminated water. We cannot emphasize this point strongly enough because generalized proofs will not suffice to prove individual damages. The main problem on review stems from a failure to differentiate between the general and the particular. This is an understandably easy trap to fall into in mass tort litigation. Although many common issues of fact and law will be capable of resolution on a group basis, individual particularized damages still must be proved on an individual basis.

To the extent that the plaintiffs seek damages for their bodily injuries, they must prove to a "reasonable medical certainty," though they need not use that specific terminology, that their ingestion of the contaminated water caused each of their particular injuries.

While upon review of the record in its entirety we cannot say that the district court abused its discretion in making its determination of the proximate causation between Velsicol's chemical dumping operations, the resultant contamination of the plaintiffs' water supply and the capacity of the contaminated water to cause the harms alleged, we find the district court erred in attributing all of the representative plaintiffs' alleged injuries to drinking or otherwise using the contaminated water. We, therefore, address each category of the district court's damage award.

Compensatory Damages

Velsicol argues that, even assuming proof of a proximate causation, the district court improperly awarded the five representative plaintiffs compensatory damages for their respective injuries and disabilities. [The court described the five representative plaintiffs, their exposure to Velsicol's chemicals, and their respective injuries.]

Based upon these findings, the district court awarded the five representative plaintiffs compensatory damages for the following injuries:

	Sterling	**Wilbanks**	**Ivy**	**Johnson**	**Marness**
Extent of Injury and Disability, Including Increased Risk of Cancer and Disease	$150,000	$150,000	$ 75,000	$150,000	$250,000
Immune System Impairment	75,000	75,000	75,000	150,000	500,000
Post-Traumatic Stress Disorder	50,000	25,000	50,000	250,000	
Fear of Increased Risk of Cancer and Disease	75,000	100,000	50,000	250,000	250,000
Physical Pain Emotional Suffering	125,000	250,000	50,000	125,000	150,000
Impaired Quality of Life	150,000	75,000	50,000	100,000	500,000
Real Property	48,492.50				
Lost Wages Earning Capacity				250,000	500,000
Learning Disorders					150,000
TOTAL	$673,472.50	$675,000	$350,000	$1,275,000	$2,300,000

A. Extent of Injury and Disability

Velsicol asserts there was insufficient medical proof of the causal connection between ingestion of contaminated water and certain injuries. First, we focus upon that portion of the award attributed to the plaintiffs' actual physical injuries and then upon the portion of the award attributed to their increased susceptibility to cancer and other diseases.

1. Presently Ascertainable Injuries

[In] seeking damages for actual physical injuries, a plaintiff must prove to a reasonable medical certainty that his or her injuries were caused by a defendant's acts or omissions. To this extent, an award is not insulated from review merely because the trial court refrains from particularizing the basis of a general injury award. If, for example, a plaintiff fails to establish sufficient causation between a defendant's acts and a specific injury, we may, nonetheless, remand the entire award to exclude that portion of the award, if any, attributed to that specific injury for which proof is [lacking].

2. Increased Risk of Cancer and Other Diseases

Plaintiffs sought to recover damages for the prospect that cancer and other diseases may materialize as a result of their exposure. The district court awarded the five representative plaintiffs damages predicated upon their being at risk for, or susceptible to, future disease.

Where the basis for awarding damages is the potential risk of susceptibility to future disease, the predicted future disease must be medically reasonably certain to follow from the existing present injury. While it is unnecessary that the medical evidence conclusively establish with absolute certainty that the future disease or condition will occur, mere conjecture or even possibility does not justify the court awarding damages for a future disability which may never materialize. Tennessee law requires that the plaintiff prove there is a reasonable medical certainty that the anticipated harm will result in order to recover for a future injury. Therefore, the mere increased risk of a future disease or condition resulting from an initial injury is not compensable. While neither the Tennessee courts, nor this court, has specifically addressed damage awards for increased risk or susceptibility to cancer and kidney and liver diseases, numerous courts have denied recovery where plaintiffs alleged they might suffer from these future diseases or conditions as a result of existing injuries. [In] *Hagerty v. L & L Marine Services, Inc.*, 788 F.2d 315 (5th Cir.), *reconsideration denied*, 797 F.2d 256 (5th Cir.1986) (en banc), a plaintiff who was accidentally drenched with chemicals containing known carcinogens, sued for damages including compensation for the increased risk that he would develop cancer in the future as a result of his exposure. The court concluded that because he did not allege with medical certainty that he would develop cancer in the future, he did not state a claim. The court reasoned that plaintiff's increased risk of cancer was not presently compensable because he could not show that the toxic exposure would more probably than not lead to [cancer].

In the instant case, the district court found an increased risk for susceptibility to cancer and other diseases of only twenty-five to thirty percent. This does not constitute a reasonable medical certainty, but rather a mere possibility or speculation. Indeed, no expert witnesses ever testified during the course of trial that the five representative plaintiffs had even a probability—*i.e.*, more than a fifty percent chance—of developing cancer and kidney or liver disease as a result of their exposure to defendant's chemicals.

For the foregoing reasons, the district court's award of compensatory damages to each of the five representative plaintiffs is remanded for recalculation to exclude that portion of the damage award attributed to increased susceptibility to cancer and other diseases.

B. Fear of Increased Risk of Cancer and Other Diseases

Velsicol next argues that the district court erroneously awarded the five representative plaintiffs compensatory damages or, in the alternative, excessive damages for fear of increased risk of contracting cancer and other diseases. Mental distress, which results from fear that an already existent injury will lead to the future onset of an as yet unrealized disease, constitutes an element of recovery only where such distress is either foreseeable or is a natural consequence of, or reasonably expected to flow from, the present injury. However, damages for mental distress generally are not recoverable where the connection between the anxiety and the existing injury is either too remote or tenuous. While there must be a reasonable connection between the injured plaintiff's mental anguish and the prediction of a future disease, the central focus of a court's inquiry in such a case is not on the underlying odds that the future disease will in fact materialize. To this extent, mental anguish resulting from the chance that an existing injury will lead to the materialization of a future disease may be an element of recovery even though the underlying future prospect for susceptibility to a future disease is not, in and of itself, compensable inasmuch as it is not sufficiently likely to occur. In the context of certain types of injuries and exposures to certain chemicals, cancerphobia has been one basis of claims for mental anguish damages.

In Tennessee, damages for fear arising from an increased risk of disease are recoverable. *Laxton v. Orkin Exterminating Co.*, 639 S.W.2d 431 (Tenn.1982). In *Laxton*, the plaintiffs' water supply was contaminated by the carcinogens chlordane and heptachlor when defendant serviceman sprayed the exterior of plaintiffs' house for termites. The Department of Water Quality Control told plaintiffs to cease using the water for any purpose and to obtain a new water source. As a result of ingesting the contaminated water for over a period of eight months, the plaintiffs worried about their health and the health of their children. The court awarded the plaintiffs $6,000 each for their mental suffering resulting from their reasonable apprehension of the harmful effects to their own and their children's health due to consuming or otherwise using the contaminated water. The *Laxton* court noted that the period of "mental anguish" deserving compensation was confined to the time between the discovery of ingestion of toxic substances and the determination that puts to rest the fear of future injury.

In the instant case, the plaintiffs' fear clearly constitutes a present injury. Each plaintiff produced evidence that they personally suffered from a reasonable fear of contracting cancer or some other disease in the future as a result of ingesting Velsicol's chemicals. Consistent with the extensive line of authority in both Tennessee and other jurisdictions, we cannot say that the district court erred in awarding the five representative plaintiffs damages for their reasonable fear of increased risk of cancer and other diseases.

[The] evidence credited by the court shows that each of the plaintiffs suffered from, and should be compensated for, a reasonable fear of contracting cancer or some other diseases in the future. The only issue is the amount of reasonable compensation. In *Laxton*, the court limited the amounts of recovery to $6,000 for each plaintiff's reasonable fear of future disease from ingesting known carcinogens over an extended period of time. In the instant case, the district court awarded plaintiffs damages ranging from $50,000 to $250,000. We find these awards to be excessive, particularly where plaintiffs failed to prove at trial that they have a significant increased risk of contracting cancer and other diseases. Upon a review of the opinion and the adopted findings of fact, we are unable to find any basis upon which the district court differentiated its damage awards to each plaintiff for his or her fear of increased risk of cancer and other diseases. The *Laxton* court awarded each plaintiff $6,000 for his or her fear of increased susceptibility to cancer from consuming known carcinogens for a duration of eight months. Using *Laxton* as a guidepost, we, accordingly, vacate the district court's award and award each of the five representative plaintiffs damages based upon the duration of their exposure to the contaminated water.

[For] the foregoing reasons, we AFFIRM IN PART, REVERSE IN PART, and REMAND for recalculation of damages.

ADDITIONAL PROBLEMS

1. Is there a difference between increased risk of disease and loss of chance? Is saying plaintiff has a 20% greater chance of getting cancer the same as saying she lost a 20% chance of avoiding cancer? Do we need to convert this into her chance to survive cancer in order to make the situation

analogous? Can we do that until we know how early the cancer is discovered? Are these insurmountable theoretical difficulties or merely practical problems of proof? If the theory is the same, should courts adopt both or neither? (In 1979, Tennessee appeared to have recognized loss of chance, but in 1993 rejected it.)

2. The risks of cancer involved often are very small, though they can be made to sound larger. A 300% increase in the risk may mean plaintiff went from a 3% chance to a 9% chance. Should the court award people 6% of the discounted value of the cost of treatment they might incur in the future if they develop the disease? Or have they really suffered no loss today other than distress?

3. The court allowed recovery for distress but "only where such distress is either foreseeable or is a natural consequence of, or reasonably expected to flow from, the present injury." Is this a *Hadley*-like foreseeability test, requiring near inevitability? Or is this a reasonable person test, designed to deny distress to people who wildly overreact to truly minor exposures? Would other distress damages—such as Joan W. and Stachura—also be limited by foreseeability? Did these cases reject the test or was it so obviously met that it did not merit discussion?

Laxton v. Orkin Exterminating Co., 639 S.W.2d 431 (Tenn. 1982), raised another interesting point: parents could recover for distress over their children's exposure. Is this because the parents were in the zone of danger? Because the parents perceived their children drinking the water (that, at the time, they did not realize was contaminated)? Or is this case simply irreconcilable with cases denying recovery for distress to parents when their children are grievously injured?

NOTES AND QUESTIONS

1. In *Potter v. Firestone Tire & Rubber Co.*, 6 Cal.4th 965, 25 Cal.Rptr.2d 550, 863 P.2d 795 (1993), the California Supreme Court dealt with claims arising from the defendant's dumping of toxic wastes at a landfill. The court concluded that "emotional distress caused by the fear of cancer that is not probable should generally not be compensable in a negligence action." A restructured rule was necessary to avoid "tremendous social cost." In a claim for compensation, not canvassed in the principal case, the court discussed whether plaintiffs could recover the cost of future periodic medical examinations intended to facilitate early detection and treatment of disease caused by exposure to toxic substances, commonly called medical monitoring costs. The court held:

> [T]he cost of medical monitoring is a compensable item of damages where the proofs demonstrate, through reliable medical expert testimony, that the need for future monitoring is a reasonably certain consequence of a plaintiff's toxic exposure and that the recommended monitoring is reasonable. In determining the reasonableness and necessity of monitoring, the following factors

> are relevant: (1) the significance and extent of the plaintiff's exposure to chemicals; (2) the toxicity of the chemicals; (3) the relative increase in the chance of onset of disease in the exposed plaintiff as a result of the exposure, when compared to (a) the plaintiff's chances of developing the disease had he or she not been exposed, and (b) the chances of the members of the public at large of developing the disease; (4) the seriousness of the disease for which the plaintiff is at risk; and (5) the clinical value of early detection and diagnosis. Under this holding, it is for the trier of fact to decide, on the basis of competent medical testimony, whether and to what extent the particular plaintiff's exposure to toxic chemicals in a given situation justifies future periodic medical monitoring.

Id. 25 Cal.Rptr.2d at 579, 863 P.2d at 824–25.

Medical monitoring does not preclude recovery for emotional distress. In *Buckley*, below, the court found recovery for both, the medical monitoring to cover the necessary costs to diagnose properly the warning signs of disease, springing from asbestos exposure, and emotional distress thereby arising.

2. On one view, the juristic basis of recovery for medical monitoring is slender. In *Fried v. Sungard Recovery Services, Inc.*, 925 F.Supp. 372 (E.D.Pa. 1996), plaintiff made a claim for medical monitoring. The issue was whether plaintiff was entitled to a jury trial on the claim. To be so entitled plaintiff had to show that the claim was legal rather than equitable in nature. The court held that the award is one for compensatory damages "like any other medical expenses." Proof must be forthcoming that medical monitoring is reasonable and necessary. The court, however, held that if plaintiff had sought the creation of a fund, the remedy would have been equitable.

On another view, medical monitoring costs are an application of the avoidable consequences doctrine. Plaintiffs are entitled to recover the cost of reasonable efforts to minimize their losses. Plaintiffs exposed to dangerous chemicals often can reduce their losses by discovering the diseases earlier, when they are easier to treat. This approach makes monitoring costs seem quite ordinary—unless the risk involves untreatable illnesses.

3. AIDS has given rise to actions brought by persons who due to another's negligence are put in fear of contracting the disease. Most courts have held that damages for emotional distress caused by such fear are recoverable if and only if plaintiff shows actual exposure to the human immunodeficiency virus (HIV). *Carroll v. Sisters of Saint Francis Health Services*, 868 S.W.2d 585 (Tenn. 1993) (plaintiff had pricked her finger on needle while visiting her sister in hospital); *K.A.C. v. Benson*, 527 N.W.2d 553 (Minn. 1995) (plaintiff brought action against physician who performed gynecological examination at time when physician was HIV-positive and had running sores on arms and hands but was wearing gloves; no showing of actual exposure). *But cf. Marchica v. Long Island R.R. Co.*, 31 F.3d 1197 (2d Cir. 1994), *cert. denied* 513 U.S. 1079, 115 S. Ct. 727, 130 L. Ed. 2d 631

(1995) (plaintiff, a railroad worker, feared he would contract AIDS when he was pricked by a hypodermic needle while cleaning up a station notorious as a haven for drug users; plaintiff suffered a physical impact sufficient to recover even though it was never determined that the virus was present in the needle). On the other hand, in *Metro–North Commuter Railroad Co. v. Buckley*, 521 U.S. 424 (1997), the Court held in a FELA (Federal Employers' Liability Act) case that the plaintiff's exposure to asbestos dust did not qualify as a "physical impact" sufficient to allow recovery for emotional distress.

4. Some courts allow recovery in "false positive" cases, in which a plaintiff has been incorrectly informed that she or he has a deadly illness. For example, in *Chizmar v. Mackie*, 896 P.2d 196 (Alaska 1995), the plaintiff sought recovery for the emotional distress caused when the defendant negligently (and incorrectly) informed her that she was HIV positive. The court allowed recovery and noted that the emotional distress might well last beyond the date at which the plaintiff was informed of the misdiagnosis. Analogous cases involve fear experienced by pregnant women as a result of negligent acts that might have affected the fetus. *See, e.g., Jones v. Howard University, Inc.*, 589 A.2d 419 (D.C. App. 1991) (upholding mother's emotional distress claim where defendant negligently performed an X-ray on her during pregnancy).

CLOSING PROBLEM

In ruling that the plaintiffs could not recover for the increased risk of cancer, did the court postpone the claim or deny it? Presumably, some of the plaintiffs will develop cancer later. When they do, can they sue again to recover damages related to the cancer? Should they recover later?

FAULKNER V. CALEDONIA COUNTY FAIR ASSOCIATION

869 A.2d 103 (Vt. 2004).

SKOGLUND, J.

1. In this personal injury action, plaintiff appeals the Caledonia Superior Court's August 28, 2003 decision granting defendants' motion to dismiss. Plaintiff argues on appeal that this action is sufficiently distinct from the lawsuit she filed, and eventually won, for injuries sustained as a result of the same occurrence giving rise to her current lawsuit. Because we agree with the trial court that the doctrine of claim preclusion bars plaintiff from relitigating the personal injury claims she pressed in her first lawsuit, we affirm.

2. The parties do not contest the relevant facts. In 1991, plaintiff sustained injuries when a large metal panel struck her head while she was on an amusement ride at the Caledonia County Fair run by defendant Caledonia County Fair Association (County Fair). In 1994, plaintiff sued the operator of the ride, defendant Marc's Amusement Co.,

Inc. (Marc's), for damages resulting from her head injuries. In 1995, the U.S. District Court rendered a verdict in her favor for $5,000, and she successfully collected that amount.

3. On November 12, 1999, plaintiff suffered her first grand mal seizure. On April 5, 2000, her treating physician diagnosed her with epilepsy and determined that the 1991 head injury was the proximate cause of the epilepsy. In November 2002, plaintiff sued both defendants, seeking damages for the epilepsy that allegedly resulted from the 1991 injury. Defendants jointly filed a motion to dismiss in May 2003.

4. In the decision currently on appeal, the trial court granted defendants' motion to dismiss on two grounds. First, the court agreed with defendants that plaintiff's epilepsy claim was barred by the doctrine of claim preclusion,[3] because plaintiff's current claim differs from her 1994 claim only in that she currently alleges a more serious injury to her head. Further, the court held that its ruling applied to both defendants (even though plaintiff sued only Marc's in her first action) because they were in privity. Second, the trial court found that plaintiff's claim was time-barred under 12 V.S.A. § 512(4). Plaintiff then filed this appeal.

5. In reviewing a trial court's grant of a motion to dismiss, this Court accepts as true "all factual allegations pleaded in the complaint" and draws "all reasonable inferences from those facts." "[W]hether preclusion applies to a given set of facts is a question of law, which we review de novo."

7. The crux of plaintiff's argument is that the trial court erred in applying claim preclusion because the cause of action in her current lawsuit is distinct from her prior lawsuit. However, as the trial court correctly explained, "plaintiff is pursuing the identical case she pursued in 1994 except that she is alleging that the injury to her head was more serious."

8. Under the doctrine of claim preclusion, a final judgment in previous litigation bars subsequent litigation if the parties, subject matter, and cause(s) of action in both matters are the same or substantially identical. The doctrine applies both to claims that were or should have been litigated in the prior proceeding. Claim preclusion flows from the fundamental precept that a final judgment on the merits " 'puts an end to the cause of action, which cannot again be brought into litigation between the parties upon any ground whatever.' "

---

[3] Although the trial court used the term "res judicata," the terms "res judicata" and "claim preclusion" are often used interchangeably. We use the term "claim preclusion" throughout this opinion because "[t]he concept of res judicata embraces two doctrines, claim preclusion and issue preclusion (or collateral estoppel), that bar, respectively, a subsequent action or the subsequent litigation of a particular issue because of the adjudication of a prior action." Because the question before us is whether the current action is barred by plaintiff's prior lawsuit, this case requires us to consider the doctrine of claim preclusion.

9. The doctrine of claim preclusion advances the efficient and fair administration of justice because it serves "(1) to conserve the resources of courts and litigants by protecting them against piecemeal or repetitive litigation; (2) to prevent vexatious litigation; (3) to promote the finality of judgments and encourage reliance on judicial decisions; and (4) to decrease the chances of inconsistent adjudication." By furthering these objectives, the doctrine ensures "the very object for which civil courts have been established, which is to secure the peace and repose of society by the settlement of matters capable of judicial determination. Its enforcement is essential to the maintenance of social order; for, the aid of judicial tribunals would not be invoked . . . if . . . conclusiveness did not attend the judgments of such tribunals."

10. The policies underlying the doctrine of claim preclusion are so fundamental to our precedent-based legal system that the U.S. Supreme Court has refused to recognize "public policy" and "simple justice" as rationales for avoiding the doctrine's strict application. *Federated Dep't Stores, Inc. v. Moitie,* 452 U.S. 394, 401–02 (1981). As the Supreme Court stated, " '[s]imple justice' is achieved when a complex body of law developed over a period of years is evenhandedly applied." The Court also observed that " '[p]ublic policy dictates that there be an end of litigation; that those who have contested an issue shall be bound by the result of the contest, and that matters once tried shall be considered forever settled as between the parties.' " As a result, claim preclusion generally will not yield to the equities of a particular case: "The doctrine of res judicata serves vital public interests beyond any individual judge's ad hoc determination of the equities in a particular case. There is simply 'no principle of law or equity which sanctions the rejection by a federal court of the salutary principle of *res judicata.*' "

11. With these considerations in mind, we turn to the question of whether plaintiff's current lawsuit articulates a new claim, or attempts to relitigate the claim concluded by her prior lawsuit. In determining whether two causes of action are sufficiently similar for claim preclusion purposes, this Court has focused on whether the same evidence will support both of them. This approach tracks the first Restatement of Judgments, which deemed causes of action the same for claim preclusion purposes "if the evidence needed to sustain the second action would have sustained the first action." Restatement of Judgments § 61 (1942).

12. As the U.S. Supreme Court has noted, however, "[d]efinitions of what constitutes the 'same cause of action' have not remained static over time." Indeed, the trend has been toward a broader approach, embodied in the Restatement (Second) of Judgments, requiring a plaintiff to address in one lawsuit all injuries emanating from "all or any part of the transaction, or series of connected transactions, out of which the action arose." Restatement (Second) of Judgments § 24(1)(1982) [hereinafter

Restatement (Second)]; see also 18 Wright et al., *supra,* § 4407 n. 22 (observing that "[t]oo many states have adopted the Restatement test to provide a complete list" and collecting examples). The Supreme Court, in comparing the first and second Restatements, characterized the second Restatement's transaction-based definition as a "more pragmatic approach."

13. Under the second Restatement, the scope of a "transaction" is determined by "giving weight to such considerations as whether the facts are related in time, space, origin, or motivation, whether they form a convenient trial unit, and whether their treatment as a unit conforms to the parties' expectations or business understanding or usage." In making this assessment, "no single factor is determinative." Additionally, "even when there is not a substantial overlap [between proofs relevant to two actions], the second action may be precluded if it stems from the same transaction." Thus, it follows from this flexible definition that "where one act causes a number of harms to, or invades a number of different interests of the same person, there is still but one transaction."

14. Indeed, the current Restatement's approach precludes a second lawsuit arising out of the same transaction as a prior lawsuit even where the second action will include "evidence or grounds or theories of the case not presented in the first action, [or] remedies or forms of relief not demanded in the first action." Moreover, "[i]t is immaterial that in trying the first action [plaintiff] was not in possession of enough information about the damages, past *or prospective,* or that the damages turned out in fact to be unexpectedly large and in excess of the judgment."

15. Adopting these principles, we conclude that plaintiff's claim for relief in the instant case arises out of the same transaction that gave rise to the prior lawsuit. The facts underlying both cases are inextricably "related in time, space, origin, or motivation," because both actions spring from the same "origin"—the 1991 accident. As a result, there is substantial overlap between the proofs of both claims, with the only difference being evidence concerning the existence and cause of plaintiff's epilepsy. However, this discrepancy does not necessarily militate in favor of finding two distinct transactions, because "even when there is not a substantial overlap [of witnesses and proofs], the second action may be precluded if it stems from the same transaction." Indeed, viewed together, plaintiff's two lawsuits depict one act—the 1991 accident—that caused harm to plaintiff. In such situations, "there is still but one transaction."

16. Finally, viewing the two cases as stemming from the same transaction does not undermine the expectations of the parties. There is nothing in the record to suggest that, at the time of plaintiff's first lawsuit, either party expected anything other than the typical result in a personal injury case—namely, a verdict that would conclude the matter between them. As the Restatement approach recognizes, "even when the

injury caused by an actionable wrong extends into the future and will be felt beyond the date of judgment, the damages awarded by the judgment are nevertheless supposed to embody the money equivalent of the entire injury." Therefore, the fact that "in trying the first action [plaintiff] was not in possession of enough information about the damages, past *or prospective,* or that the damages turned out in fact to be unexpectedly large and in excess of the judgment" is "immaterial" to the claim preclusion analysis. Accordingly, we hold that both actions arise out of the same transaction for claim preclusion purposes, and, as a result, that this action is barred by the judgment in the previous action.[5]

17. This case is distinguishable from the cases upon which plaintiff relies that permitted subsequent actions for late-emerging latent diseases resulting from exposure to asbestos or other workplace chemicals. See, *e.g., Pustejovsky v. Rapid–American Corp.,* 35 S.W.3d 643 (Tex.2000) (holding that plaintiff's suit against several suppliers of asbestos products for asbestos-related cancer twelve years after settling suit against a different asbestos supplier for asbestosis was not precluded by claim preclusion); *Rogers v. Kunja Knitting Mills, U.S.A.,* 336 S.C. 533, 520 S.E.2d 815 (Ct.App.1999) (holding that claim preclusion did not bar plaintiff's second lawsuit for damage to internal organs resulting from workplace exposure to chemicals, despite earlier suit for dermatitis contracted from same exposure). In the asbestos cases, courts permit plaintiffs to file second suits for asbestos-related cancer, after filing asbestosis suits, because cancer is a distinct injury unrelated to asbestosis, and it does not surface until well beyond the limitations period. See *Wilson v. Johns–Manville Sales Corp.,* 684 F.2d 111, 117 n. 33 (D.C.Cir.1982) (Ginsburg, J.) (noting that defendant conceded that asbestos-related cancer is separate and distinct from, and not a complication of, asbestosis). As then Circuit Judge Ruth Bader Ginsburg wrote in *Wilson,* an asbestos case "requires [the court] to focus, not on judgments and their preclusive effects, but on statutes of limitations." By contrast, the instant case involves a traumatic injury the consequences of which turned out to be more severe than they appeared at the time of plaintiff's first lawsuit, not two separate and distinct diseases or injuries. Therefore, the asbestos and similar workplace exposure cases are inapposite.

18. The instant case is best viewed not as a latent disease case, but as a "traumatic event/latent manifestation" case, "in which the plaintiff has sustained both immediate and latent injuries caused by a noticeable,

---

[5] We also note that the Restatement contemplates an exception to the application of claim preclusion when "[t]he court in the first action has expressly reserved the plaintiff's right to maintain the second action." If a party provides the court with "special reasons" for doing so, the court should afford the party "an opportunity to litigate in a second action that part of the claim which he justifiably omitted from the first action." The record here does not reveal that plaintiff requested or the court decided in the first action to reserve plaintiff's right to pursue a second action in the event that her injuries turned out to be more severe.

traumatic occurrence." *Albertson v. T.J. Stevenson & Co.,* 749 F.2d 223, 231 (5th Cir.1984). Several courts have held that in such cases a single cause of action accrues for limitations purposes with the occurrence of the traumatic event. See, *e.g., Stephens v. Dixon,* 449 Mich. 531, 536 N.W.2d 755, 758 (1995) (holding that plaintiff's claim for late-emerging neck disorder accrued when plaintiff sustained injuries in car accident, not when she became aware of the disorder); *Jones v. Trs. of Bethany Coll.,* 177 W.Va. 168, 351 S.E.2d 183, 187 (1986) (holding that claim accrues when plaintiff sustains noticeable injury from a traumatic event, even though there may be a latent injury arising from the same event). Indeed, two courts have confronted late-emerging epilepsy claims stemming from traumatic head injuries and concluded that each plaintiff's claim accrued at the time of the initial injuries, not when the epilepsy emerged. *LeBeau v. Dimig,* 446 N.W.2d 800, 802–03 (Iowa 1989); *Rowe v. John Deere,* 130 N.H. 18, 533 A.2d 375, 377–78 (1987). The instant case fits the "traumatic event/latent manifestation" profile—plaintiff's claim accrued when she suffered the blow to her head in 1991, and it is "immaterial" for claim preclusion purposes that her injuries turned out to be more severe than those for which she sought damages in her 1994 lawsuit.

19. Finally, we reject plaintiff's argument that Article 4 of Chapter I of the Vermont Constitution militates against applying claim preclusion here because doing so would be unfair. While the Restatement recognizes that the policies behind claim preclusion may be overcome "for an extraordinary reason," such exceptions are "not lightly to be found but must be based on a clear and convincing showing of need." As examples, the Restatement offers cases involving the validity of a continuing restraint on liberty, child custody, divorce, or a prior litigation that "failed to yield a coherent disposition." Because plaintiff alleges only that her injuries stemming from the 1991 accident turned out to be more serious than they appeared at the time of the first lawsuit, she has not "clearly and convincingly shown that the policies favoring preclusion . . . are overcome for an extraordinary reason." As explained above, the U.S. Supreme Court has recognized that "the mischief which would follow the establishment of precedent for so disregarding this salutary doctrine against prolonging strife would be greater than the benefit which would result from relieving some case of individual hardship."[6]

---

[6] In this regard, it is also worth noting a distinction between the criteria for application of claim preclusion and those used in the context of the related concept of issue preclusion (or collateral estoppel). "[I]ssue preclusion bars the subsequent relitigation of an issue which was actually litigated and decided in a prior case between the same parties resulting in a final judgment on the merits, where that issue was necessary to the resolution of the action." *Am. Trucking Ass'ns v. Conway,* 152 Vt. 363, 369, 566 A.2d 1323, 1327 (1989). In determining whether to apply issue preclusion, we consider, among other elements, whether applying that doctrine in the later action is fair. *Berlin Convalescent Ctr. v. Stoneman,* 159 Vt. 53, 56–57, 615 A.2d 141, 144 (1992). As set forth above, the claim preclusion inquiry does not involve an assessment of the fairness of applying the doctrine in a subsequent action. Therefore, we reject

20. We are mindful that claim preclusion may cause harsh results in individual cases, but on balance we conclude that applying it here best serves the interests of all litigants and promotes the efficient administration of justice, in light of the powerful policy concerns laid out above. As the U.S. Supreme Court aptly recognized, the "doctrine of *res judicata* is not a mere matter of practice or procedure inherited from a more technical time than ours. It is a rule of fundamental and substantial justice, of public policy and of private peace, which should be cordially regarded and enforced by the courts." Therefore, the trial court correctly dismissed the instant case.

Affirmed.

NOTES AND QUESTIONS

1. Are you convinced by the court's distinction between (1) injury caused at the time of defendant's negligence, but not recognized until after suit (*e.g.*, epilepsy), and (2) injury proximately caused by defendant's negligence, but not coming into existence until after suit (*e.g.*, asbestos-induced cancer)? Even if there is a logical distinction between the two injuries, does the distinction justify recovery for one but not the other? Is the plaintiff in *Faulker* presented with a catch–22—either sue at the time of injury, and be barred from suit for later, more serious injuries; or wait to see if more serious injuries arise and risk running afoul of the statute of limitations (not to mention having to pay for injuries currently sustained)? If you would allow the subsequent claim in *Faulkner*, is there a better way to attend to the rule-of-law concerns that the court identifies?

2. As the court notes, the breadth of claim preclusion adopted in *Faulkner* is not universal. For example, in a nuisance action arising from contamination of water by toxic pollutants leaching into the aquifer from a landfill, the New Jersey Supreme Court stated that:

> [t]he single controversy rule, intended " 'to avoid the delays and wasteful expense of the multiplicity of litigation which results from the splitting of a controversy,' " cannot sensibly be applied to a toxic-tort claim filed when disease is manifested years after the exposure, merely because the same plaintiff sued previously to recover for property damage or other injuries. In such a case, the rule is literally inapplicable since, as noted, the second cause of action does not accrue until the disease is manifested; hence, it could not have been joined with the earlier claims.

Ayers v. Township of Jackson, 525 A.2d 287 (N.J. 1987) (citations omitted). For scholarly discussion of the issue, see Note, *Claim Preclusion in Modern Latent Disease Cases: A Proposal for Allowing Second Suits,* 103 HARV. L. REV. 1989, 1991 (1990).

---

plaintiff's argument that, under Article 4 of Chapter I of the Vermont Constitution, it would be unfair to apply claim preclusion here.

C. LIFE AS INJURY

At 73, Sam was diagnosed with prostate cancer. In order to avoid the possibility of sexual dysfunction, a common side effect of surgery, Sam elected chemotherapy to treat the cancer. During chemotherapy, Sam's immune system was somewhat weaker than usual. Sam contracted pneumonia and was hospitalized. During this stay, Sam signed a no-code order. This document informed the hospital that if Sam went into arrest or faced any other emergency, they were not to use extraordinary means to revive or preserve his life. (In effect, don't bring in the crash cart and the defibrillator; just let me die.) Sam executed this order for several reasons, including concern for the severe burdens (emotional and financial) his loved ones would face if he required long-term hospitalization, his perception that his remaining years might be few (due to the cancer) and not entirely enjoyable (due to the cancer, his age, and other factors known best to Sam). After two days in the hospital, Sam did go into cardiac arrest. The hospital, in violation of the no-code order, resuscitated Sam. At the time—whether concurrent with the arrest or shortly after it—Sam suffered a stroke that deprived him of the use of the left side of his body. Sam sued the hospital for wrongful rescue. The claims sound in tort (medical malpractice, battery) and contract (duty to honor the no-code order). What remedy, if any, may Sam obtain? How is a court likely to resolve these issues?

Litigation of this sort more commonly arises at the other end of life, where children (or parents) allege that a physician's negligence caused the birth of a child who should not have been born. You have read one such case, *Troppi v. Scarf*, *supra* at 769, 810, in which a pharmacist's negligence regarding prescription birth control pills produced a healthy child. Similar cases arise when physicians miss genetic defects or diseases that produce serious health problems for a child. Perhaps these claims offer some analogy that would help you address the problem posed here.

TURPIN V. SORTINI

31 Cal.3d 220, 182 Cal. Rptr. 337, 643 P.2d 954 (1982).

KAUS, J.

The allegations of the complaint disclose the following facts. On September 24, 1976, James and Donna Turpin [brought] their first—and at that time their only—daughter, Hope, to [the] Fresno Community Hospital for evaluation of a possible hearing defect. Hope was examined and tested by Adam J. Sortini, a licensed professional specializing in the diagnosis and treatment of speech and hearing defects. [Sortini] negligently examined, tested and evaluated Hope and incorrectly advised her pediatrician that her hearing was within normal limits when, in reality, she was "stone deaf" as a result of an hereditary ailment. Hope's parents did not learn of her condition until October 15, 1977, when it was diagnosed by other specialists. The nature of the condition is such that there is a "reasonable degree of medical probability" that the hearing defect would be inherited by any offspring of James and Donna. [In] December 1976, before learning of Hope's true condition and relying on defendants' diagnosis, James and Donna conceived a second child, Joy. [H]ad the Turpins known of Hope's hereditary deafness they would not have conceived Joy. Joy was born August 23, 1977, and suffers from the same total deafness as Hope.

On the basis of these facts, James, Donna, Hope and Joy filed a complaint setting forth four causes of action. The second cause of action—the only cause before us on this appeal—was brought on behalf of Joy and seeks (1) general damages for being "deprived of the fundamental right of a child to be born as a whole, functional human being without total deafness" and (2) special damages for the "extraordinary expenses for specialized teaching, training and hearing equipment" which she will incur during her lifetime as a result of her hearing impairment. Defendants demurred [and] the trial court sustained the demurrer without leave to amend. Thereafter, the court entered a judgment dismissing the action as to Joy.

Although this is the first case in which we have faced the question of potential tort liability in a "wrongful life" or "wrongful birth" context,[4] there is no dearth of authority in this area. In recent years, many courts in other jurisdictions have confronted similar claims brought by both parents and children against medical professionals whose negligence had allegedly proximately caused the birth of hereditarily afflicted children. The overwhelming majority of the recent cases have permitted parents to recover at least some elements of damage in such actions. At the same time, the out-of-state authorities have uniformly rejected the children's own claims for general damages. [Courts] have been reluctant to permit the child to complain when, but for the defendant's negligence, he or she would not have been born at all. In this context the recent decisions have either concluded that the child has sustained no "legally cognizable injury" or that appropriate damages are impossible to ascertain.

While our court has not yet spoken on the question, California Court of Appeal decisions have addressed somewhat related claims. [In] *Stills v. Gratton* (1976) 55 Cal. App. 3d 698, both an unmarried mother and her healthy son brought consolidated actions against several doctors who had negligently performed a therapeutic abortion, leading to the unexpected and unwanted birth of the child. With respect to the mother's claim, the *Stills* court followed *Custodio* and permitted the action. . . . With respect

[4] While courts and commentators have not always been consistent in their terminology, "wrongful life" has generally referred to actions brought on behalf of children, and "wrongful birth" to actions brought by parents.

to the son's claim, however, the court determined that no cause of action would lie. Although the child had alleged that "he was born out of wedlock and that 'various reasons' affect him to his detriment," the *Stills* court noted that [the] boy "was and is a healthy, happy youngster who is a joy to his mother" and thus that "[h]is only damages, if any, caused by the respondents' conduct is in being born." Relying on earlier Illinois and New York decisions which had rejected similar wrongful life claims by healthy children of unmarried parents, the *Stills* court denied the son's action, suggesting that "[t]he issue involved is more theological or philosophical than legal."

The most recent Court of Appeal decision in this area is *Curlender v. Bio–Science Laboratories,* 106 Cal. App. 3d 811, an action brought solely on behalf of a child, not her parents. Unlike *Custodio* and *Stills*, in which the defendants' negligence had led to the births of healthy, albeit unplanned, children, in *Curlender* the child-plaintiff was afflicted with Tay–Sachs disease, a fatal illness. [The defendant] was a medical laboratory which allegedly had been negligent in performing blood tests which the child's parents had undergone for the specific purpose of determining if their offspring were likely to suffer from Tay–Sachs disease. [The] court distinguished *Stills* as a case in which the unwanted but healthy child had suffered no "injury," and concluded that the severely afflicted child in the case before it had suffered an injury which could properly be the basis of an action in tort. [The] court held that [a] child may "recover damages for the pain and suffering to be endured during the limited life span available to such a child and any special pecuniary loss resulting from the impaired condition." . . .

[A]lthough the cause of action at issue has attracted a special name—"wrongful life"—[plaintiff's] action is simply one form of the familiar [professional] malpractice action. The gist of plaintiff's claim is that she has suffered harm or damage as a result of defendants' negligent performance of their professional tasks, and that, as a consequence, she is entitled to recover under generally applicable common law tort principles.

In this case, although the Turpins' older daughter Hope, and not Joy, was defendants' immediate patient, it was reasonably foreseeable that Hope's parents and their potential offspring would be directly affected by defendants' negligent failure to discover that Hope suffered from an hereditary ailment and defendants do not contend that they owed no duty of care [to] Joy. Nor do defendants assert that the complaint fails to allege adequately either a breach of their duty of care or that Joy's birth was a proximate result of the breach Instead, defendants' basic position [is] that Joy has suffered no legally cognizable injury or rationally ascertainable damages as a result of their alleged negligence. . . .

With respect to the issue of legally cognizable injury, the parties agree that the difficult question here does not stem from the fact that defendants' allegedly negligent act and plaintiff's asserted injury occurred before plaintiff's birth. [I]f Joy's deafness was caused by negligent treatment of her mother during pregnancy, she would be entitled to recover against the negligent party. Joy's complaint attempts, in effect, to bring her action within the scope of the foregoing line of cases, asserting that as a result of defendants' negligence she was "deprived of the fundamental right of a child to be born as a whole, functional human being without total deafness. . . ."

The basic fallacy of [this] analysis is that it [obscures] a critical difference between wrongful life actions and the ordinary prenatal injury cases noted above. In an ordinary prenatal injury case, if the defendant had not been negligent, the child would have been born healthy; thus, as in a typical personal injury case, the defendant in such a case has interfered with the child's basic right to be free from physical injury caused by the negligence of others. In this case, by contrast, the obvious tragic fact is that plaintiff never had a chance "to be born as a whole, functional human being without total deafness"; if defendants had performed their jobs properly, she would not have been born with hearing intact, but would not have been born at all.

A plaintiff's remedy in tort is compensatory in nature and damages are generally intended not to punish a negligent defendant but to restore an injured person as nearly as possible to the position he or she would have been in had the wrong not been done. (See generally Rest.2d Torts, § 901, com. a.) Because nothing defendants could have done would have given plaintiff an unimpaired life, it appears inconsistent with basic tort principles to view the injury for which defendants are legally responsible solely by reference to plaintiff's present condition without taking into consideration the fact that if defendants had not been negligent she would not have been born at all. (*See* Capron, *Tort Liability in Genetic Counseling* (1979) 79 COLUM. L. REV. 619, 654–657.)

[T]he injury which plaintiff has suffered is that, as a result of defendants' negligence, she has been born with an hereditary ailment rather than not being born at all. Although plaintiff has not phrased her claim for general damages in these terms, most courts and commentators have recognized that the basic claim of "injury" in wrongful life cases is "[i]n essence . . . that [defendants], through their negligence, [have] forced upon [the child] the worse [of two alternatives,] that nonexistence—never being born—would have been preferable to existence in [the] diseased state." Given this view of the relevant injury, [some] courts have concluded that the plaintiff has suffered no legally cognizable injury on the ground that considerations of public policy dictate a conclusion that life—even with the most severe of impairments—is, as a matter of law, always preferable to nonlife. The decisions frequently suggest that a contrary conclusion would "disavow" the sanctity and value of less-than-perfect human life.

Although it is easy to understand and to endorse these decisions' desire to affirm the worth and sanctity of less-than-perfect life, we question whether these considerations alone provide a sound basis for rejecting the child's tort action. To begin with, it is hard to see how an award of damages to a severely handicapped or suffering child would "disavow" the value of life or in any way suggest that the child is not entitled to the full measure of legal and nonlegal rights and privileges accorded to all members of society. Moreover, while our society and our legal system unquestionably place the highest value on all human life, we do not think that it is accurate to suggest that this state's public policy establishes—as a matter of law—that under all circumstances "impaired life" is "preferable" to "nonlife." For example, Health and Safety Code section 7186, enacted in 1976, provides in part: "The Legislature finds that adult persons have the fundamental right to control the decisions relating to the rendering of their own medical care, including the decision to have life-sustaining procedures withheld or withdrawn in instances of a terminal condition. [¶] . . . The Legislature further finds that, in the interest of protecting individual autonomy, such prolongation of life for persons with a terminal condition may cause loss of patient dignity and unnecessary pain and suffering, while providing nothing medically necessary or beneficial to the patient." This statute recognizes that—at least in some situations—public policy supports the right of each individual to make his or her own determination as to the relative value of life and death.

Of course, in the wrongful life context, the unborn child cannot personally make any choice as to the relative value of life or death. At that stage, however, just as in the case of an infant after birth, the law generally accords the parents the right to act to protect the child's interests. As the wrongful birth decisions recognize, when a doctor or other medical care provider negligently fails to diagnose an hereditary problem, parents are deprived of the opportunity to make an informed and meaningful decision whether to conceive and bear a handicapped child. Although in deciding whether or not to bear such a child parents may properly, and undoubtedly do, take into account their own interests, parents also presumptively consider the interests of their future child. Thus, when a defendant negligently fails to diagnose an hereditary ailment, he harms the potential child as well as the parents by depriving the parents of information which may be necessary to determine whether it is in the child's own interest to be born with defects or not to be born at all.[9]

---

[9] On occasion it has been suggested that no wrongful life action may be maintained because it is impossible to determine whether, if the "child-to-be" had been informed of the risks,

In this case, in which the plaintiff's only affliction is deafness, it seems quite unlikely that a jury would ever conclude that life with such a condition is worse than not being born at all. Other wrongful life cases, however, have involved children with much more serious, debilitating and painful conditions, and the academic literature refers to still other, extremely severe hereditary diseases.[10] Considering the short life span of many of these children and their frequently very limited ability to perceive or enjoy the benefits of life, we cannot assert with confidence that in every situation there would be a societal consensus that life is preferable to never having been born at all.

[T]he out-of-state decisions are on sounder grounds in holding that—with respect to the child's claim for pain and suffering or other general damages—recovery should be denied because (1) it is simply impossible to determine in any rational or reasoned fashion whether the plaintiff has in fact suffered an injury in being born impaired rather than not being born, and (2) even if it were possible to overcome the first hurdle, it would be impossible to assess general damages in any fair, nonspeculative manner.

Justice Weintraub of the New Jersey Supreme Court captured the heart of the problem simply and eloquently in his separate opinion in *Gleitman v. Cosgrove* (1967) [227 A.2d 689, 711, 22 A.L.R.3d 1411]: "Ultimately, the infant's complaint is that he would be better off not to have been born. Man, who knows nothing of death or nothingness, cannot possibly know whether that is so. [¶] We must remember that the choice is not being born with health or being born without it . . . Rather the choice is between a worldly existence and none at all. . . . To recognize a right not to be born is to enter an area in which no one can find his way."

[P]laintiff relies on numerous cases which hold that when a defendant has negligently caused a legally cognizable injury, recovery should not totally be denied simply because of the difficulty in ascertaining damages. [A]lthough numerous types of harm—for example, pain and suffering and mental distress—are not readily susceptible to valuation, damages for such items are routinely recoverable in professional malpractice actions, and she argues that if juries are capable

---

he or she would have preferred not to be born. . . . We do not, however, deny recovery to an infant who is injured when a doctor negligently fails to provide treatment [even] though we cannot determine whether the infant would have agreed with the parents' choice of treatment. Similarly, it appears anomalous to deny recovery simply because it was not possible for the "child-to-be" to make a choice. In the preconception or fetal stage, as in childhood, it is parents who nearly always make medical choices to protect their children's interests.

[10] In *Curlender*, for example, where the plaintiff was afflicted with Tay–Sachs disease, the complaint alleged that the child "suffers from 'mental retardation, susceptibility to other diseases, convulsions, sluggishness, apathy, failure to fix objects with her eyes, inability to take an interest in her surroundings, loss of motor reactions, inability to sit up or hold her head up, loss of weight, muscle atrophy, blindness, pseudobulper palsy, inability to feed orally, decerebrate rigidity and gross physical deformity.' It was alleged that Shauna's life expectancy is estimated to be four years. The complaint also contained allegations that plaintiff suffers 'pain, physical and emotional distress, fear, anxiety, despair, loss of enjoyment of life, and frustration. . . .' "

of awarding damages for such nonpecuniary harm, they are equally competent to assess appropriate general damages in a wrongful life case.

[T]here is a profound qualitative difference between the difficulties faced by a jury in assessing general damages in a normal personal injury or wrongful death action, and the task before a jury in assessing general damages in a wrongful life case. In the first place, the problem is not [simply] the fixing of damages for a conceded injury, but the threshold question of determining whether the plaintiff has in fact suffered an injury by being born with an ailment as opposed to not being born at all. As one judge explained: "When a jury considers the claim of a once-healthy plaintiff that a defendant's negligence harmed him[,] the jury's ability to say that the plaintiff has been 'injured' is manifest, for the value of a healthy existence over an impaired existence is within the experience [or] imagination of most people. The value of nonexistence—by its very nature—however, is not."

[T]he practical problems are exacerbated when it comes to the matter of arriving at an appropriate award of damages. [Although] the valuation of pain and suffering or emotional distress in terms of dollars and cents is unquestionably difficult in an ordinary personal injury action, jurors at least have some frame of reference in their own general experience to appreciate what the plaintiff has lost—normal life without pain and suffering. In a wrongful life action, that simply is not the case, for what the plaintiff has "lost" is not life without pain and suffering but rather the unknowable status of never having been born. In this context, a rational, nonspeculative determination of a specific monetary award in accordance with normal tort principles appears to be outside the realm of human competence.

The difficulty [is] also reflected in the application of what is sometimes referred to as the "benefit" doctrine in tort damages. Section 920 of the Restatement Second of Torts—which embodies the general California rule on the subject—provides that "[w]hen the defendant's tortious conduct has caused harm to the plaintiff . . . and in so doing has conferred a special benefit to the interest of the plaintiff that was harmed, the value of the benefit conferred is considered in mitigation of damages, to the extent that this is equitable." Under section 920's benefit doctrine, [general] damages must be offset by the benefits incidentally conferred by the defendant's conduct "to the interest of the plaintiff that was harmed." [T]he harmed interest is the child's general physical, emotional and psychological well-being, and as an incident of defendant's negligence the plaintiff has in fact obtained a physical existence with the capacity both to receive and give love and pleasure as well as to experience pain and suffering. Because of the incalculable nature of both elements of this harm-benefit equation, we believe that a reasoned, nonarbitrary award of general damage is simply not obtainable.

Although we have determined that the trial court properly rejected plaintiff's claim for general damages, we conclude that her claim for the "extraordinary expenses for specialized teaching, training and hearing equipment" that she will incur during her lifetime because of her deafness stands on a different footing. [I]n the corresponding "wrongful birth" actions parents have regularly been permitted to recover the medical expenses incurred on behalf of such a child. [C]ourts have recognized (1) that these are expenses that would not have been incurred "but for" the defendants' negligence and (2) that they are the kind of pecuniary losses which are readily ascertainable and regularly awarded as damages in professional malpractice actions. Although the parents and child cannot, of course, both recover for the same medical expenses, we believe it would be illogical and anomalous to permit only parents, and not the child, to recover for the cost of the child's own medical care. If such a distinction were established, the afflicted child's receipt of necessary medical expenses might well depend on the wholly fortuitous circumstance of whether the parents are available to sue and recover such damages or whether the medical expenses are incurred at a time when the parents remain legally responsible for providing such care.

Realistically, a defendant's negligence in failing to diagnose an hereditary ailment places a significant medical and financial burden on the whole family unit. Unlike the child's claim for general damages, the damage here is both certain and readily measurable. Furthermore, in many instances these expenses will be vital not only to the child's well-being but to his or her very survival. If, as alleged, defendants' negligence was in fact a proximate cause of the child's present and continuing need for such special, extraordinary medical care and training, we believe that it is consistent with the basic liability principles of Civil Code section 1714 to hold defendants liable for the cost of such care, whether the expense is to be borne by the parents or by the child. As Justice Jacobs observed in his dissenting opinion in *Gleitman* v. *Cosgrove*: "While the law cannot remove the heartache or undo the harm, it can afford some reasonable measure of compensation towards alleviating the financial burdens."

Moreover, permitting plaintiff to recover the extraordinary, additional medical expenses that are occasioned by the hereditary ailment is also consistent with the established parameters of the general tort "benefit" doctrine discussed above. [T]he harm for which plaintiff seeks recompense is an economic loss. [Unlike] the claim for general damages, defendants' negligence has conferred no incidental, offsetting benefit to this interest of plaintiff.[14] Accordingly, assessment of these special damages should pose no unusual or insoluble problems.[15]

---

[14] [In] *Schroeder*, the court observed: "We are not conferring a windfall on Mr. and Mrs. Schroeder. Although they may derive pleasure from Thomas, that pleasure will be derived in

In sum, [while] a plaintiff-child in a wrongful life action may not recover general damages for being born impaired as opposed to not being born at all, the child—like his or her parents—may recover special damages for the extraordinary expenses necessary to treat the hereditary ailment.

The judgment is reversed and the case is remanded to the trial court for further proceedings consistent with this opinion.

Richardson J., Broussard, J., [and Newman, J.] concurred.

MOSK, J.

I dissent. An order is internally inconsistent which permits a child to recover special damages for a so-called wrongful life action, but denies all general damages for the very same tort. While the modest compassion of the majority may be commendable, they suggest no principle of law that justifies so neatly circumscribing the nature of damages suffered as a result of a defendant's negligence.

BIRD, C. J., concurred.

NOTES AND QUESTIONS

1. In accord with the principal case the Supreme Judicial Court of Massachusetts held, in *Burke v. Rivo*, 406 Mass. 764, 551 N.E.2d 1 (1990), that in a negligent sterilization cases parents may recover the cost of rearing a normal, healthy but unwanted child if "their reason for seeking sterilization was founded on economic or financial consideration." O'Connor, J., vigorously dissented. The valuation of a child's life "is inconsistent with the dignity that the Commonwealth, including its courts, must accord to every human life, and it should not be permitted." The State's interest in strengthening and encouraging family life for the protection and care of children militates against the damage award.

The majority rule in such cases, however, is to limit damages to medical expenses associated with the sterilization procedure, pregnancy, and subsequent sterilization procedure, and for other injuries associated with the unwanted pregnancy (lost wages, loss of consortium, emotional distress). *See Emerson v. Magendantz*, 689 A.2d 409 (R.I. 1997) (citing thirty states as having adopted the "limited recovery" rule). Some states allow full recovery, as in the principal case, and still others allow full recovery with an offset for the benefits of having a child.

2. Not all courts follow *Turpin* in allowing special childrearing costs. In *Simmerer v. Dabbas*, 733 N.E.2d 1169 (Ohio 2000), for example, the

spite of, rather than because of, his affliction. Mr. and Mrs. Schroeder will receive no compensating pleasure from incurring extraordinary medical expenses on behalf of Thomas. There is no joy in watching a child suffer and die from cystic fibrosis."

[15] Permitting recovery of these extraordinary out-of-pocket expenses whether the cost is to be borne by the parents or the child should also help ensure that the available tort remedies in this area provide a comprehensive and consistent deterrent to negligent conduct.

plaintiff who had undergone a sterilization procedure sued her doctor after she became pregnant and gave birth to a child with a heart defect who died at the age of fifteen months. The court denied the plaintiff any recovery on the grounds that although the defendant's negligence caused the pregnancy, it was not a proximate cause of the birth defect.

3. When negligence precludes the opportunity to have an abortion, courts have held that parents have a good cause of action—wrongful birth. In *Smith v. Cote*, 128 N.H. 231, 513 A.2d 341 (1986), the court held that the parents had a good cause of action and the damages should be limited to extraordinary cost ranging beyond the age of majority. In addition, damages include extraordinary maternal care, susceptible to valuation, in seeking medical help or counseling. But general emotional distress is not compensable.

Fewer courts have held that the child has a good cause of action—wrongful life. The wrongful life action is cut asunder by the necessity of claiming that a defective life is worth less *to the child* than no life at all. Nevertheless, some courts have found that the action should lie and damages be pragmatically set to recover the costs of extraordinary medical care but not pain and suffering and impaired childhood. *Procanik v. Cillo*, 97 N.J. 339, 478 A.2d 755 (1984) (a measure that deters malpractice but is not subject to the "wild swings as a claim for pain and suffering"). *See* Michael B. Kelly, *The Rightful Position in "Wrongful Life" Actions*, 42 HASTINGS L.J. 505 (1991); Philip G. Peters, Jr., *Rethinking Wrongful Life: Bridging the Boundary Between Tort and Family Law*, 67 TUL. L. REV. 397 (1992).

PROBLEMS

1. *A* was advised by Dr. *B* that her baby would be born with a congenital birth defect. She agreed that she should undergo an abortion, since in these extraordinary circumstances she concluded that an abortion was comportable with her religious beliefs. However, Dr. *B* had misdiagnosed the fetus's condition; she did not need to undergo the abortion and *A* in consequence suffered mental anguish and depression from her awareness that she had needlessly committed an act in violation of her deep-seated convictions. Should *A* have a good cause of action and for what harm? Should the wrongfully aborted fetus have a good cause of action? How are the damages to be measured? *See Martinez v. Long Island Jewish Hillside Medical Center*, 70 N.Y.2d 697, 518 N.Y.S.2d 955, 512 N.E.2d 538 (1987).

2. What advice do you have for Sam?

D. THE BREACHING EMPLOYEE

In 1991, Chris took a job as a sales representative with Educom, a company that sells software to public schools. The sales job included not only persuading the client to choose Educom software, but also keeping the customer satisfied after the sale. The salary was $35,000 a year, plus a 5% commission. Chris, a former teacher and computer enthusiast, had no sales experience. As a result, Chris had a rough first year, making only $10,000 on commissions and sometimes failing to meet Educom's goal for the month. During the first year Educom sent Chris to several sales training seminars (at company expense) and assigned other Educom sales personnel to help Chris improve. With this assistance plus experience, Chris soon proved excellent in this position. Commissions for the second year totaled $35,000, almost as much as the $36,000 salary. By the third year, Chris regularly sold more than any other salesperson at Educom, earning an increase to 10% commission. Chris also proved adept at post-sale customer relations. Chris was particularly good at explaining to the programmers what improvements the clients wanted in future releases and making helpful suggestions on ways to implement those improvements.

In 1999, the sales of education software began to drop. It appeared that Educom might need to lay off some employees. Chris, who earned $115,000 in 1999 ($55,000 as salary) feared that higher-paid employees might be among the first to go. To avert this, Chris asked Educom for a 5-year contract (starting January 5, 2000). The contract adjusted base salary each year for the cost of living plus five percent, more than most salary increases over Chris's tenure with the firm, but reduced the commission Chris received to 8%. Chris requested this shift from commissions to base salary, fearing a downturn in sales. Educom agreed, wanting to ensure that its most effective salesperson would remain with the firm, even if times were hard. The contract, like the annual contracts Chris signed through the 1990s, contained the following noncompetition clause:

> Employee agrees that if, for any reason, employee leaves employment with Educom before the expiration of this contract, that employee will not accept any position with a company that sells computer software to elementary or secondary educational institutions (or to entities that own, manage, or control such educational institutions) if that company sells its products in any state of the United States where Educom also markets its products. This clause continues to bind the employee until either (i) the date on which this employment would have terminated if employee had not left employment with Educom or (ii) one year after the date the employee leaves employment with Educom, whichever is later. Nothing in this provision relieves employee of the obligation not to reveal any trade secrets of Educom, an obligation that continues perpetually.

In 2000, the market for education software rebounded, particularly in light of education reforms proposed for schools that do not satisfy certain criteria. As a result Educom did not lay off any employees and Chris continued to make considerable commissions. In 2002, Chris earned

$125,000 ($65,000 as base salary). In December 2002, Testcom, a competitor of Educom, offered Chris a position in their product development and customer service department. Chris would not make sales, but would serve clients once others made sales. Chris also would help program developers improve the product to meet client demands. The salary would be $160,000 per year. Chris accepted the offer and began to work for Testcom on January 5, 2003. At the time, 2 years remained on Chris's contract with Educom.

Educom seeks your advice concerning any remedies they may seek against Chris. Compare the plausible courses of action Educom might pursue and recommend the best approach for it to take in this matter.

AMERICAN BROADCASTING COMPANIES V. WOLF

52 N.Y.2d 394, 420 N.E.2d 363, 438 N.Y.S.2d 482 (1981).

COOKE, CHIEF JUDGE.

[Warner Wolf, a colorful sportscaster, worked for ABC from 1976 to 1980. The employment agreement required Wolf to negotiate in good faith with ABC for the 90-day period from December 6, 1979 through March 4, 1980, when his contract expired. Wolf promised not to talk to any other employer from December 6 through January 19. After March 4, Wolf promised not to accept any other offer until he had given ABC a right of first refusal; he could comply with this provision either by refraining from accepting another offer or by first tendering the offer to ABC and working for ABC if they agreed to meet those terms. The first-refusal period expired on June 3, 1980; on June 4 Wolf could accept any job without obligation to ABC.

Before December, Wolf discussed renewal with ABC, but also met with representatives of CBS. On January 2, 1980, ABC met substantially all of Wolf's demands. Wolf rejected the offer, citing ABC's delay in communicating with him and his desire to explore other options.

On February 1, 1980, Wolf orally agreed to work for WCBS–TV in New York. CBS divided his compensation between two agreements: one for services as an on-the-air sportscaster; one for producing sports specials (services technically outside the first-refusal provision, which applied to on-the-air positions). Wolf signed the production agreement on February 4, 1980. At the same time, CBS agreed in writing, in consideration of $100, to hold open an offer of employment as sportscaster until June 4, 1980, when Wolf became free from ABC's right of first refusal. The next day Wolf resigned from ABC.

ABC sued, alleging that Wolf breached both the good-faith negotiation and first-refusal provisions of his contract with ABC. ABC sought specific enforcement of its right of first refusal and an injunction against Wolf's employment as a sportscaster with CBS. At trial, Supreme

Court found no breach, and went on to note that equitable relief would be inappropriate. A divided Appellate Division, while concluding that Wolf had breached both provisions, affirmed on the ground that equitable intervention was unwarranted.]

Initially, we agree with the Appellate Division that defendant Wolf breached his obligation to negotiate in good faith with ABC. When Wolf signed the production agreement with CBS on February 4, 1980, Wolf was unable to extend his contract with ABC. Given Wolf's existing obligation to CBS, any negotiations he engaged in with ABC, without the consent of CBS, after February 4 were meaningless and could not have been in good faith.

At the same time, there is no basis in the record for the Appellate Division's conclusion that Wolf violated the first-refusal provision by entering into an oral sportscasting contract with CBS on February 4. By its own terms, the right of first refusal did not apply to offers accepted by Wolf prior to the March 5 termination of the ABC employment contract. Wolf could not have breached the right of first refusal by accepting an offer during the term of his employment with ABC.[2] Rather, his conduct violates only the good-faith negotiation clause of the contract. The question is whether this breach entitled ABC to injunctive relief that would bar Wolf from continued employment at CBS.[3] To resolve this issue, it is necessary to trace the principles of specific performance applicable to personal service contracts.

Courts of equity historically have refused to order an individual to perform a contract for personal services. Originally this rule evolved because of the inherent difficulties courts would encounter in supervising the performance of uniquely personal efforts.[4] During the Civil War era,

---

[2] In any event, the carefully tailored written agreement between Wolf and CBS consisted only of an option prior to June 4, 1979. Acceptance of CBS's offer of employment as a sportscaster did not occur until after the expiration of the first-refusal period on June 4, 1979.

[3] In its complaint, ABC originally sought specific enforcement of the right of first refusal. ABC now suggests that Wolf be enjoined from performing services for CBS for a two-year period. Alternatively, ABC requests this court to "turn the clock back to February 1, 1980" by: (1) setting aside Wolf's agreement with CBS and enjoining CBS from enforcing the agreement; (2) ordering Wolf to enter into good-faith negotiations with ABC for at least the period remaining under the negotiation clause when Wolf breached it; (3) ordering Wolf to honor the 90-day first-refusal period should the parties fail to reach agreement; and (4) enjoining CBS from negotiating with Wolf "for a period sufficient to render meaningful the above-described relief."

[4] The New York Court of Chancery in De Rivafinoli v. Corsetti (4 Paige Chs. 264, 270) eloquently articulated the traditional rationale for refusing affirmative enforcement of personal service contracts: "I am not aware that any officer of this court has that perfect knowledge of the Italian language, or possesses that exquisite sensibility in the auricular nerve which is necessary to understand, and to enjoy with a proper zest, the peculiar beauties of the Italian opera, so fascinating to the fashionable world. There might be some difficulty, therefore, even if the defendant was compelled to sing under the direction and in the presence of a master in chancery, in ascertaining whether he performed his engagement according to its spirit and intent. It would also be very difficult for the master to determine what effect coercion might produce upon the defendant's singing, especially in the livelier airs; although the fear of imprisonment would unquestionably deepen his seriousness in the graver parts of the drama. But one thing at least is

there emerged a more compelling reason for not directing the performance of personal services: the Thirteenth Amendment's prohibition of involuntary servitude. It has been strongly suggested that judicial compulsion of services would violate the express command of that amendment. For practical, policy and constitutional reasons, therefore, courts continue to decline to affirmatively enforce employment contracts.

Over the years, however, in certain narrowly tailored situations, the law fashioned other remedies for failure to perform an employment agreement. Thus, where an employee refuses to render services to an employer in violation of an existing contract, and the services are unique or extraordinary, an injunction may issue to prevent the employee from furnishing those services to another person for the duration of the contract (see, e. g., Shubert Theatrical Co. v. Gallagher, 206 App.Div. 514, 201 N.Y.S. 577). Such "negative enforcement" was initially available only when the employee had expressly stipulated not to compete with the employer for the term of the engagement. Later cases permitted injunctive relief where the circumstances justified implication of a negative covenant. In these situations, an injunction is warranted because the employee either expressly or by clear implication agreed not to work elsewhere for the period of his contract. And, since the services must be unique before negative enforcement will be granted, irreparable harm will befall the employer should the employee be permitted to labor for a competitor.

After a personal service contract terminates, the availability of equitable relief against the former employee diminishes appreciably. Since the period of service has expired, it is impossible to decree affirmative or negative specific performance. Only if the employee has expressly agreed not to compete with the employer following the term of the contract, or is threatening to disclose trade secrets or commit another tortious act, is injunctive relief generally available at the behest of the employer. Even where there is an express anticompetitive covenant, however, it will be rigorously examined and specifically enforced only if it satisfies certain established requirements. Indeed, a court normally will not decree specific enforcement of an employee's anticompetitive covenant unless necessary to protect the trade secrets, customer lists or good will of the employer's business, or perhaps when the employer is exposed to special harm because of the unique nature of the employee's services. An otherwise valid covenant will not be enforced if it is unreasonable in time, space or scope or would operate in a harsh or oppressive manner. There is, in short, general judicial disfavor of anticompetitive covenants contained in employment contracts.

certain; his songs will be neither comic, or even semi-serious, while he remains confined in that dismal cage, the debtor's prison of New York."

Underlying the strict approach to enforcement of these covenants is the notion that, once the term of an employment agreement has expired, the general public policy favoring robust and uninhibited competition should not give way merely because a particular employer wishes to insulate himself from competition. Important, too, are the "powerful considerations of public policy which militate against sanctioning the loss of a man's livelihood." At the same time, the employer is entitled to protection from unfair or illegal conduct that causes economic injury. The rules governing enforcement of anticompetitive covenants and the availability of equitable relief after termination of employment are designed to foster these interests of the employer without impairing the employee's ability to earn a living or the general competitive mold of society. . . .

Applying these principles, ABC's request for injunctive relief must fail. There is no existing employment agreement between the parties; the original contract terminated in March, 1980. Thus, the negative enforcement that might be appropriate during the term of employment is unwarranted here. Nor is there an express anticompetitive covenant that defendant Wolf is violating, or any claim of special injury from tortious conduct such as exploitation of trade secrets. In short, ABC seeks to premise equitable relief after termination of the employment upon a simple, albeit serious, breach of a general contract negotiation clause. To grant an injunction in that situation would be to unduly interfere with an individual's livelihood and to inhibit free competition where there is no corresponding injury to the employer other than the loss of a competitive edge. . . .

Equally unavailing is ABC's request that the court create a noncompetitive covenant by implication. Although in a proper case an implied-in-fact covenant not to compete for the term of employment may be found to exist, anticompetitive covenants covering the postemployment period will not be implied. Indeed, even an express covenant will be scrutinized and enforced only in accordance with established principles.

This is not to say that ABC has not been damaged in some fashion or that Wolf should escape responsibility for the breach of his good-faith negotiation obligation.[10] Rather, we merely conclude that ABC is not

[10] It should be noted that the dissenter would ground relief upon the first-refusal clause, a provision of the contract that defendant did not breach. The dissenting opinion fails to specify why the first-refusal clause—or for that matter any other provision of the contract that defendant did not breach—is relevant in determining the availability of equitable relief. And, while the dissent correctly noted the flexibility of equitable remedies, this does not mean that courts of equity totally dispense with governing rules. Our analysis of the relevant principles, guided by important underlying policy considerations, reveals that this case falls well beyond the realm where equitable intervention would be permissible. The dissenting opinion would now create a new agreement for the parties, and apply the first-refusal clause backwards into the period of the ABC employment, under the guise of equitable interpretation. Although the reach of equity may be broad, so far as we are aware equitable principles have never sanctioned the

entitled to equitable relief. Because of the unique circumstances presented, however, this decision is without prejudice to ABC's right to pursue relief in the form of monetary damages, if it be so advised.

Accordingly, the order of the Appellate Division should be affirmed.

NOTES AND ADDITIONAL PROBLEMS

1. Judge Fuchsberg dissented, in part because the majority interpreted the contract so rigidly, following the letter of the agreement, but ignoring the purposes the parties sought to achieve. There is precedent: Portia gave Shylock a rather rigid reading as well. William Shakespeare, The Merchant of Venice. Perhaps the parties should have anticipated the way in which one of them might seek to circumvent the provisions and closed the various loopholes. Today, courts tend to use the obligation of good faith to extend the letter of a contract to cover acts that undermine the purpose of the contract. Does this case imply that employees need not act in good faith?

2. What damages, if any, can ABC collect? How would you prove them?

3. Recall *Washington Capitols Basketball Club, Inc. v. Barry*, 304 F.Supp. 1193 (N.D.Cal.1969), in which the court gave the Capitols negative specific relief (an injunction prohibiting Barry from playing for any other team except the Capitols), but refused to grant affirmative specific performance (requiring Barry to play for the Capitols). Why is the court willing to enter a prohibitory injunction when it is unwilling to enter a mandatory injunction? Should the court also have entered a mandatory injunction?

4. Courts sometimes deploy language of involuntary servitude rather lightly in these situations. Forcing an employee to keep a promise is involuntary servitude only if one ignores the promise, which was voluntarily made. Which expression of the employee's will counts: the contract or the breach? That should be a hard question, though courts often dismiss it. Even without a constitutional gloss, however, the concerns about the court's capacity to supervise enforcement probably justify denying specific performance in most cases.

5. Who is the wrongdoer here: the employee or the new employer? Will gaps in the remedy against one be filled by the remedy against the other? Will the combination reach the rightful position? Will it exceed it? *See* David F. Partlett, *From Victorian Opera to Rock and Rap: Inducement to Breach of Contract in the Music Industry*, 66 TUL. L. REV. 771 (1992).

6. What advice do you have for Chris?

---

creation of a new and different contract between sophisticated parties merely to condemn conduct which was permissible under an actual written agreement.

E. THE DISCHARGED EMPLOYEE

In 2000, Juan Perez began work for ManuCorp, a manufacturer of automobile parts. Juan operated a drill press. Juan's employee evaluation reports were decent; his supervisors noted minor concerns about attendance and attitude, but always recommended the average raise or slightly more. Over the years, his wages rose to $15 an hour, usually increasing about one percent more than the inflation rate. Other workers with similar evaluations worked at ManuCorp until retirement, so Juan was not particularly concerned about these small criticisms. On January 4, 2003, ManuCorp laid off Juan and about 45 other employees. While termed a layoff, the company says that it selected the employees with the worst evaluations for discharge. Juan believes ManuCorp discriminated on the basis of race or national origin; that other employees with the same evaluations or worse were retained. After a week without work, Juan took a part time job at a local automobile parts store in order to feed the family. Juan is a runner, finding parts in stock and taking them where they are needed—sometimes to the sales counter, sometimes delivering them to auto repair shops, sometimes delivering them to peoples' homes. The job pays $8 an hour, plus occasional tips on home deliveries (about $10 a week). Juan searches the newspaper classifieds for jobs in manufacturing. Juan also checks the jobs posted at the local unemployment insurance office. After 12 weeks, no manufacturing jobs in town have opened up. There are very few manufacturing companies in this town, so Juan is not sure if one will ever open up—and if it does, Juan knows 44 other people likely to apply for it.

You have been consulted by Juan. What remedies, if any should you pursue? What advice, if any, would you give Juan for how to proceed?

FORD MOTOR CO. V. EQUAL EMPLOYMENT OPPORTUNITY COMMISSION

458 U.S. 219, 102 S.Ct. 3057, 73 L.Ed.2d 721 (1982).

JUSTICE O'CONNOR delivered the opinion of the Court.

This case presents the question whether an employer charged with discrimination in hiring can toll the continuing accrual of backpay liability under § 706(g) of Title VII, 42 U.S.C. § 2000e–5(g), simply by unconditionally offering the claimant the job previously denied, or whether the employer also must offer seniority retroactive to the date of the alleged discrimination.[1]

---

[1] The dissent asserts that by so "fram[ing] the question presented" we have "simply and completely misstate[d] the issue." [N]either party agrees with the dissent. [P]etitioner summarizes the question presented as "whether back pay due an employment discrimination claimant continues to accrue after the claimant has rejected an unconditional job offer that does not include retroactive seniority or back pay." The respondent sums up the question [as] "[w]hether an employer who unlawfully refused to hire job applicants because they were women

In June and July 1971, Judy Gaddis and Rebecca Starr applied at a Ford Motor Co. (Ford) parts warehouse located in Charlotte, N.C., for jobs as "picker-packers," "picking" ordered parts from storage, and "packing" them for shipment. At the time, no woman had ever worked in that capacity at the Ford warehouse. [Both]women were qualified for the positions: Gaddis and Starr recently had been laid off from equivalent jobs at a nearby General Motors (GM) warehouse . . . Ford, however, filled the three vacant positions with men. . . .

In January 1973, GM recalled Gaddis and Starr to their former positions at its warehouse. The following July, while they were still working at GM, a single vacancy opened up at Ford. Ford offered the job to Gaddis, without seniority retroactive to her 1971 application. Ford's offer, however, did not require Gaddis to abandon or compromise her Title VII claim against Ford. Gaddis did not accept the job, in part because she did not want to be the only woman working at the warehouse, and in part because she did not want to lose the seniority she had earned at GM. Ford then made the same unconditional offer to Starr, who declined for the same reasons. Gaddis and Starr continued to work at the GM warehouse, but in 1974 the warehouse was closed and they were laid off. They then unsuccessfully sought new employment until September 1975, when they entered a Government training program for the unemployed. . . .

In contrast to Gaddis's [and] Starr's difficulties, at least two of the three men hired by Ford in 1971 were still working at the warehouse at the time of the trial in 1977.

In July 1975, the EEOC sued Ford alleging that Ford had violated Title VII of the Civil Rights Act of 1964 by refusing to hire women at the Charlotte warehouse. The Commission sought injunctive relief and backpay for the victims.

After trial, the District Court found that Ford had discriminated against the three women on the basis of their sex and awarded them backpay in an amount equal to "the difference between the amount they would have earned had they been hired in August 1971, and the amounts actually earned or reasonably earnable by them" between that date and the date of the court's order. The District Court rejected Ford's contention that Gaddis and Starr were not entitled to backpay accruing after the dates on which they declined Ford's offer of employment. The United States Court of Appeals for the Fourth Circuit affirmed. . . .

Section 706(g) of the Civil Rights Act of 1964 governs the award of backpay in Title VII cases. In pertinent part, § 706(g) provides:

> If the court finds that the respondent has intentionally engaged in or is intentionally engaging in an unlawful employment

can terminate its liability for back pay by subsequently offering the applicants positions without seniority at a time when they had obtained, and accumulated seniority in, other jobs."

> practice charged in the complaint, the court *may* enjoin the respondent from engaging in such unlawful employment practice, and order such affirmative action as *may* be appropriate, which *may* include, but is not limited to, . . . hiring of employees, *with or without* back pay, . . . or any other equitable relief as the court deems appropriate. . . . Interim earnings or amounts earnable with reasonable diligence by the person or persons discriminated against *shall* operate to reduce the back pay otherwise allowable (emphasis added).

Under § 706(g), then, "backpay is not an automatic or mandatory remedy; [it] is one which the courts 'may' invoke" in the exercise of their sound "discretion [which] is equitable in nature." Nonetheless, while "the power to award backpay is a discretionary power," a "court must exercise this power 'in light of the large objectives of the Act,'" and, in doing so, must be guided by "meaningful standards" enforced by "thorough appellate review."

In this case, Ford and the EEOC offer competing standards to govern backpay liability. Ford argues that if an employer unconditionally offers a claimant the job for which he previously applied, the claimant's rejection of that offer should toll the continuing accrual of backpay liability. The EEOC, on the other hand, defends the lower court's rule, contending that backpay liability should be tolled only by the rejection of an offer that includes seniority retroactive to the date on which the alleged discrimination occurred. Our task is to determine which of these standards better coincides with the "large objectives" of Title VII.

The "primary objective" of Title VII is to bring employment discrimination to an end by "'achiev[ing] equality of employment opportunities and remov[ing] barriers that have operated in the past to favor an identifiable group . . . over other employees.'" "[T]he preferred means for achieving" this goal is through "[c]ooperation and voluntary compliance."

To accomplish this objective, the legal rules fashioned to implement Title VII should be designed, consistent with other Title VII policies, to encourage Title VII defendants promptly to make curative, unconditional job offers to Title VII claimants, thereby bringing defendants into "voluntary compliance" and ending discrimination far more quickly than could litigation proceeding at its often ponderous pace. . . .

The rule tolling the further accrual of backpay liability if the defendant offers the claimant the job originally sought well serves the objective of ending discrimination through voluntary compliance, for it gives an employer a strong incentive to hire the Title VII claimant. While the claimant may be no more attractive than the other job applicants, a job offer to the claimant will free the employer of the threat of liability for further backpay damages. Since paying backpay damages is like paying an extra worker who never came to work, Ford's proposed rule gives the Title VII claimant a decided edge over other competitors for the job he seeks.

The rule adopted by the court below, on the other hand, fails to provide the same incentive, because it makes hiring the Title VII claimant more costly than hiring one of the other applicants for the same job. To give the claimant retroactive seniority before an adjudication of liability, the employer must be willing to pay the additional costs of the fringe benefits that come with the seniority that newly hired workers usually do not receive. More important, the employer must also be prepared to cope with the deterioration in morale, labor unrest, and reduced productivity that may be engendered by inserting the claimant into the seniority ladder over the heads of the incumbents who have earned their places through their work on the job. . . . As a result, the employer will be less, rather than more, likely to hire the claimant.

In sum, the Court of Appeals' rule provides no incentive to employers to hire Title VII claimants. The rule advocated by Ford, by contrast, powerfully motivates employers to put Title VII claimants to work, thus ending ongoing discrimination as promptly as possible.

Title VII's primary goal, of course, *is* to end discrimination; the victims of job discrimination want jobs, not lawsuits. But when unlawful discrimination does occur, Title VII's secondary, fallback purpose is to compensate the victims for their injuries. To this end, § 706(g) aims " 'to make the victims of unlawful discrimination whole' " by restoring them, " 'so far as possible . . . to a position where they would have been were it not for the unlawful discrimination.' " We now turn to consider whether the rule urged by Ford not only better serves the goal of ending discrimination, but also properly compensates injured Title VII claimants.

If Gaddis and Starr had rejected an unconditional offer from Ford before they were recalled to their jobs at GM, tolling Ford's backpay liability from the time of Ford's offer plainly would be consistent with providing Gaddis and Starr full compensation for their injuries. An unemployed or underemployed claimant . . . is subject to the statutory duty to minimize damages set out in § 706(g). This duty, rooted in an ancient principle of law,[15] requires the claimant to use reasonable diligence in finding other suitable employment. Although the . . . claimant need not go into another line of work, accept a demotion, or take a

---

[15] See generally, *e.g.*, C. McCormick, Law of Damages 127–158 (1935): "Where one person has committed [a] legal wrong against another, it is incumbent upon the latter to use such means as are reasonable under the circumstances to avoid or minimize the damages. The person wronged cannot recover for any item of damage which could thus have been avoided." In connection with the remedial provisions of the NLRA, we said: " . . . Since only actual losses should be made good, it seems fair that deductions should be made not only for actual earnings by the worker but also for losses which he willfully incurred."

demeaning position,[16] he forfeits his right to backpay if he refuses a job substantially equivalent to the one he was denied. Consequently, an employer charged with unlawful discrimination often can toll the accrual of backpay liability by unconditionally offering the claimant the job he sought, and thereby providing him with an opportunity to minimize damages.[18]

An employer's unconditional offer of the job originally sought to an unemployed or underemployed claimant, moreover, need not be supplemented by an offer of retroactive seniority to be effective, lest a defendant's offer be irrationally disfavored relative to other employers' offers of substantially similar jobs. The claimant, after all, plainly would be required to minimize his damages by accepting another employer's offer even though it failed to grant the benefits of seniority not yet earned.[19] Of course, if the claimant fulfills the requirement that he minimize damages by accepting the defendant's unconditional offer, he remains entitled to full compensation if he wins his case. A court may grant him backpay accrued prior to the effective date of the offer, retroactive seniority, and compensation for any losses suffered as a result of his lesser seniority before the court's judgment.

Ford's proposed rule also is consistent with the policy of full compensation when the claimant has had the good fortune to find a more attractive job than the defendant's, because the availability of the better job terminates the ongoing ill effects of the defendant's refusal to hire the claimant. For example, if Gaddis and Starr considered their jobs at GM to be so far superior to the jobs originally offered by Ford that, even if Ford had hired them at the outset, they would have left Ford's employ to take the new work, continuing to hold Ford responsible for backpay after Gaddis and Starr lost their GM jobs would be to require, in effect, that Ford insure them against the risks of unemployment in a new and independent undertaking. Such a rule would not merely restore Gaddis and Starr to the " 'position where they would have been were it not for the

---

[16] See, *e.g., NLRB v. Madison Courier, Inc.*, 153 U.S.App.D.C. 232, 245–246, 472 F.2d 1307, 1320–1321 (1972) (employee need not "seek employment which is not consonant with his particular skills, background, and experience" or "which involves conditions that are substantially more onerous than his previous position"). . . .

Some lower courts have indicated, however, that after an extended period of time searching for work without success, a claimant must consider taking a lower-paying position. If the claimant decides to go into a dissimilar line of work, or to accept a demotion, his earnings must be deducted from any eventual backpay award.

[18] The claimant's obligation to minimize damages [does] not require him to settle his claim against the employer, in whole or in part. Thus, an applicant or discharged employee is not required to accept a job offered by the employer on the condition that his claims against the employer be compromised.

[19] For the same reasons, a defendant's job offer is effective to force minimization of damages by an unemployed or underemployed claimant even without a supplemental offer of backpay, since the claimant would be required to accept another employer's offer of a substantially similar job without a large front-end, lump-sum bonus.

unlawful discrimination,'" it would catapult them into a better position than they would have enjoyed in the absence of discrimination.

Likewise, even if Gaddis and Starr considered their GM jobs . . . substantially equivalent to the positions they would have held at Ford . . . ,[24] their rejection of Ford's unconditional offer could be taken to mean that they believed that the lingering ill effects of Ford's prior refusal to hire them had been extinguished by later developments. If, for example, they thought that the Ford and GM jobs were identical in every respect, offering identical pay, identical conditions of employment, and identical risks of layoff, Gaddis and Starr would have been utterly indifferent as to which job they had—Ford's or GM's. Assuming that they could work at only one job at a time, the ongoing economic ill effects caused by Ford's prior refusal to hire them would have ceased. . . .

In both of these situations, the claimant has the power to accept the defendant's offer and abandon the superior or substantially equivalent replacement job. [A]cceptance of the defendant's unconditional offer would preserve fully the ultimately victorious claimant's right to full redress for the effects of discrimination. The claimant who chooses not to follow this path does so, then, not because it provides inadequate compensation, but because the value of the replacement job outweighs the value of the defendant's job supplemented by the prospect of full court-ordered compensation. In other words, the victim of discrimination who finds a better or substantially equivalent job no longer suffers ongoing injury stemming from the unlawful discrimination.

[The] sole question that can be raised regarding whether the rule adequately compensates claimants arises in that narrow category of cases in which the claimant believes his replacement job to be superior to the defendant's job without seniority, but inferior to the defendant's job with the benefits of seniority. In the present case, for example, it is possible that Gaddis and Starr considered their GM jobs more attractive than the jobs offered by Ford, but less satisfactory than the positions they would have held at Ford if Ford had hired them initially. If so, they were confronted with two options. They could have accepted Ford's unconditional offer, preserving their right to full compensation if they prevailed on their Title VII claims, but forfeiting their favorable positions at GM. Alternatively, they could have kept their jobs at GM, retaining the possibility of continued employment there, but, under the operation of the rule advocated here by Ford, losing the right to claim further backpay from Ford after the date of Ford's offer. The court below concluded that

[24] It is possible that they did so value the GM jobs, since they applied at Ford only after being laid off at GM, and since after being recalled to the GM jobs they rejected Ford's offer. The possibility that Gaddis and Starr considered their GM jobs superior to the positions they would have had at Ford had Ford hired them at the outset is not merely a "hypothetical case." We cannot infer that they so valued their GM jobs, however, solely from their rejection of Ford's offer.

under these circumstances Ford's rule would present Gaddis and Starr with an "intolerable choice," depriving them of the opportunity to receive full compensation.

We agree that Gaddis and Starr had to choose between two alternatives. We do not agree, however, that their opportunity to choose deprived them of compensation. After all, they had the option of accepting Ford's unconditional offer and retaining the right to seek full compensation at trial, which would comport fully with Title VII's goal of making discrimination victims whole. Under the rule advocated by Ford, if Gaddis and Starr chose the option of remaining at their GM jobs rather than accept Ford's offer, it was because they thought that the GM jobs, plus their claims to backpay accrued prior to Ford's offer, were *more* valuable to them than the jobs they originally sought from Ford, plus the right to seek full compensation from the court.[26] It is hard to see how Gaddis and Starr could have been deprived of adequate compensation because they chose to venture upon a path that seemed to them more attractive than the Ford job plus the right to seek full compensation in court.

If the choice presented to Gaddis and Starr was difficult, it was only because it required them to assess their likelihood of prevailing at trial. But surely it cannot be contended for this reason alone that they were deprived of their right to adequate compensation. It is a fact of life that litigation is risky and that a plaintiff with a claim to compensation for his losses must consider the possibility that the claim might be lost at trial, either wrongly, because of litigation error, or rightly, because the defendant was innocent. . . .

Therefore, we conclude that, when a claimant rejects the offer of the job he originally sought, as supplemented by a right to full court-ordered compensation, his choice can be taken as establishing that he considers the ongoing injury he has suffered at the hands of the defendant to have

---

[26] Employees value a job for many reasons besides the rate of pay, including, for example, the presence of other workers of the employee's own sex, the availability of recreational facilities at the worksite, staggered work hours, better health benefits, longer vacations, and so forth. What makes one job better than another varies from one employee to another.

Gaddis and Starr presumably rejected Ford's offer because they thought their jobs at GM were worth more to them than full compensation (Ford's offer plus a court award) discounted by the risks of litigation. In essence, the position adopted by the court below and advocated here by the EEOC turns on the fact that we cannot be sure that, had Gaddis and Starr known they were going to win their lawsuit, they still would have rejected Ford's offer. Had they known they were going to win, of course, they would have rejected the Ford job only if they valued the GM jobs more than they valued the combination of Ford's job plus the value of court-ordered compensation *un*discounted by the risks of litigation. To agree with the EEOC is, in effect, to contend that a claimant is not made whole for purposes of Title VII unless he decided to stay at a replacement job that was worth to him more than the sum of (1) the defendant's job, (2) the right to seek full court-ordered compensation, and, in addition, (3) a sum analogous to insurance against the risk of loss at trial. We discern, however, no reason for concluding that Title VII requires the defendant to insure the claimant against the possibility that the defendant might prevail in the lawsuit.

been ended by the availability of better opportunities elsewhere. For this reason, we find that, absent special circumstances,[27] the simple rule that the ongoing accrual of backpay liability is tolled when a Title VII claimant rejects the job he originally sought comports with Title VII's policy of making discrimination victims whole. . . .

Although Title VII remedies depend primarily upon the objectives discussed above, the statute also permits us to consider the rights of "innocent third parties." The lower court's rule places a particularly onerous burden on the innocent employees of an employer charged with discrimination. Under the court's rule, an employer may cap backpay liability only by forcing his incumbent employees to yield seniority to a person who has not proved, and may never prove, unlawful discrimination. As we have acknowledged on numerous occasions, seniority plays a central role in allocating benefits and burdens among employees. In light of the " 'overriding importance' these rights," we should be wary of any rule that encourages job offers that compel innocent workers to sacrifice their seniority to a person who has only claimed, but not yet proved, unlawful discrimination. . . .

We reverse the judgment of the Court of Appeals and remand for proceedings consistent with this opinion.

JUSTICE BLACKMUN, with whom JUSTICES BRENNAN and MARSHALL join, dissenting.

After finding that petitioner Ford Motor Company had discriminated unlawfully against Judy Gaddis and Rebecca Starr because of their sex, the Court of Appeals affirmed the District Court's backpay award to the two women "as a proper exercise of discretion founded on not clearly erroneous factual determinations." The Court today reverses this unremarkable holding with a wide-ranging advisory ruling stretching far beyond the confines of this case. The Court's rule provides employers who have engaged in unlawful hiring practices with a unilateral device to cut off their backpay liability to the victims of their past discrimination.

The Court frames the question presented as "whether an employer charged with discrimination in hiring can toll the continuing accrual of backpay liability [simply] by unconditionally offering the [Title VII] claimant the job previously denied, or whether the employer also must offer seniority retroactive to the date of the alleged discrimination." In my view, the Court simply and completely misstates the issue. The question before us is not which of two inflexible standards should govern accrual of

---

[27] If, for example, the claimant has been forced to move a great distance to find a replacement job, a rejection of the employer's offer might reflect the costs of relocation more than a judgment that the replacement job was superior, all things considered, to the defendant's job. In exceptional circumstances, the trial court, in the exercise of its sound discretion, could give weight to such factors when deciding whether backpay damages accrued after the rejection of an employer's offer should be awarded to the claimant.

backpay liability in *all* Title VII cases, but whether the District Court's award of backpay relief to Gaddis and Starr *in this case* constituted an abuse of discretion. . . .

[I]n Title VII cases, the equitable discretion of district courts should be guided by a heavy presumption in favor of full backpay awards. [Full backpay furthers] two broad purposes underlying Title VII[: providing] "the spur or catalyst which causes employers [to] self-examine and to self-evaluate their employment practices and to endeavor to eliminate, so far as possible, the last vestiges" of discrimination[; and making "persons whole for injuries suffered on account of unlawful employment discrimination." . . .

To determine the backpay remedy to which Gaddis and Starr were entitled, the District Court attached no legal significance to the women's decision to decline beginning employment at Ford nearly two years after they unlawfully had been denied those same jobs and six months after they had begun accumulating seniority elsewhere.[5] [T]he Court of Appeals found no abuse of discretion in the District Court's failure to terminate the backpay awards in July 1973.

The Court's approach authorizes employers to make "cheap offers" to the victims of their past discrimination. Employers may now terminate their backpay liability unilaterally by extending to their discrimination victims offers they cannot reasonably accept. Once an employer has refused to hire a job applicant, and that applicant has mitigated damages by obtaining and accumulating seniority in another job, the employer may offer the applicant the same job that she was denied unlawfully several years earlier. . . . If, as here, the applicant declines the offer to preserve existing job security, the employer has successfully cut off all future backpay liability to that applicant. By insulating a discriminating employer from proper liability for his discriminatory acts, the Court's rule reduces his "incentive to shun practices of dubious legality" and hinders the eradication of discrimination.

The Court's rule also violates Title VII's second objective—making victims of discrimination whole. . . . Had petitioner not discriminated against Gaddis and Starr, both would have begun to work at Ford in August 1971. By July 1973, both would have accumulated nearly two years of seniority. Because of Ford's discrimination, however, each experienced long periods of unemployment and temporary employment before obtaining jobs elsewhere. The District Court therefore determined that only full backpay awards, mitigated by wages earned or reasonably earnable elsewhere, would make Gaddis and Starr whole.

---

[5] The District Court . . . reconstructed a probable employment history at Ford for each woman, calculating what each would have received but for petitioner's unlawful discrimination. Second, the court . . . subtracted from the backpay awards any amounts Gaddis and Starr actually earned or reasonably could have earned after August 1971.

This Court now truncates those awards simply because Gaddis and Starr refused to accept Ford's offers of beginning employment in 1973. Yet even if Gaddis and Starr had accepted those offers, they would not have been made whole. Deprived of two years of seniority, Gaddis and Starr would have enjoyed lesser health, life, and unemployment insurance benefits, lower wages, less eligibility for promotion and transfer, and greater vulnerability to layoffs than persons hired after they were unlawfully refused employment. Even if Gaddis and Starr had continued to litigate the question of their retroactive seniority after accepting Ford's offer, they still would have spent many years at Ford "subordinate to persons who, but for the illegal discrimination, would have been[,] in respect to entitlement to [competitive seniority] benefits[,] [their] inferiors."

The Court claims that its new rule "powerfully motivates employers to put Title VII claimants to work, thus ending ongoing discrimination as promptly as possible." In fact, the discrimination is not ended, because a discrimination victim who accepts a "cheap offer" will be obliged to work at a seniority disadvantage, and therefore will suffer ongoing effects from the employer's discriminatory act. The Court also alleges that its rule promotes "cooperation and voluntary compliance" with Title VII by giving both employers and claimants incentives to make and accept "unconditional" job offers. If the Court's rule furthers this end, however, it does so only by weakening the bargaining position of a claimant vis-a-vis the employer. Discrimination victims will be forced to accept otherwise unacceptable offers, because they will know that rejection of those offers truncates their backpay recovery. . . .

[I] am disturbed by the Court's efforts to justify its rule by relying on situations not presented by this case. For example, the Court partially rests its rule on an "unemployed or underemployed claimant's statutory obligation to minimize damages" by accepting an unconditional job offer without seniority. Because Gaddis and Starr were fully employed when Ford finally offered them jobs, however, neither the District Court nor the Court of Appeals exempted unemployed or underemployed victims of discrimination from accepting offers like Ford's.[12] Similarly, the Court analyzes the hypothetical case of a Title VII claimant who "has had the good fortune to find a more attractive job than the defendant's." But [the] Court finally acknowledges that . . . "[w]e cannot infer" how much Gaddis and Starr "valued their GM jobs . . . solely from their rejection of Ford's offer."

Equally unconvincing is the Court's repeated invocation of, and preoccupation with, "the rights of 'innocent third parties,'" and the

[12] The purpose of § 706(g)'s "mitigation of damages" requirement is to encourage claimants to work while their Title VII claims are being adjudicated. The Court cannot deny that Gaddis and Starr fully mitigated damages by seeking and obtaining other employment while litigating their claims against Ford.

"disruption of the existing seniority system[s]," that would result from adoption of the Court of Appeals' "rule." The Court nowhere demonstrates how *petitioner's* labor relations would have suffered had it extended offers of retroactive seniority to Gaddis and Starr. The details of Ford's collective-bargaining agreement were not litigated [below]. The Court cannot justify reversal in the case at hand by vague reference to classes of claimants and third parties who are not before the Court. To the extent that it seeks to do so, its intricate argument is both irrelevant and advisory.

NOTES AND QUESTIONS

1. There is a litigation lesson here: the party who frames the question has a significant advantage. What would happen if the question presented were "Whether the plaintiffs unreasonably failed to minimize their loss by refusing the jobs offered by Ford?" Was it unreasonable to keep the GM jobs rather than move to Ford with no seniority? If either choice would be reasonable, does the avoidable consequences doctrine offer any justification for denying subsequent losses? Can the result here be squared with *S.J. Groves & Sons v. Warner Co.*, *supra* at 784?

2. Section 706(g) deducts from backpay "[i]nterim earnings or amounts earnable with reasonable diligence." This sounds like the avoidable consequences doctrine. Does this language have a different purpose here, perhaps a purpose related to the antidiscrimination context rather than remedies generally? The court considers the rule as a way to limit the time for which backpay is available. That may not matter in contract cases, where the failure to specify the period of employment makes the contract terminable at will. But in cases of wrongful discharge or discrimination, there is no set period during which the employment would have continued but for the wrong. Should the defendant be a guarantor of lifetime employment in these settings? Is this language how Congress provided a cut-off date? Or did the court address a problem Congress overlooked by reinterpreting language intended for a different end?

3. Is the outcome determined by the judges' perspectives? The majority considers the case from Ford's point of view, seeking what is reasonable from their standpoint. The dissent considers reasonableness from the employees' point of view. Is either one wrong? Should the Supreme Court consider the policy implications as well as the resolution of the case itself?

JONES & LAUGHLIN STEEL CORP. V. PFEIFER

462 U.S. 523, 103 S.Ct. 2541, 76 L.Ed.2d 768 (1983).

JUSTICE STEVENS delivered the opinion of the Court.

Respondent was injured in the course of his employment as a loading helper on a coal barge. As his employer, petitioner was required to compensate him for his injury under § 4 of the Longshoremen's and Harbor Workers' Compensation Act (Act).

Petitioner owns a fleet of barges that it regularly operates on three navigable rivers in the vicinity of Pittsburgh, Pa. Respondent was employed for 19 years to aid in loading and unloading those barges.... On January 13, 1978, while carrying a heavy pump, respondent slipped and fell on snow and ice that petitioner had negligently failed to remove from the gunnels of a barge. His injury made him permanently unable to return to his job with the petitioner, or to perform anything other than light work after July 1, 1979....

The District Court's calculation of damages was predicated on a few undisputed facts. At the time of his injury respondent was earning an annual wage of $26,025. He had a remaining work expectancy of 12½ years. On the date of trial (October 1, 1980), respondent had received compensation payments of $33,079.14. If he had obtained light work and earned the legal minimum hourly wage from July 1, 1979, until his 65th birthday, he would have earned $66,352.

The District Court arrived at its final award by taking 12½ years of earnings at respondent's wage at the time of injury ($325,312.50), subtracting his projected hypothetical earnings at the minimum wage ($66,352) and the compensation payments he had received under § 4 ($33,079.14), and adding $50,000 for pain and suffering. The court did not increase the award to take inflation into account, and it did not discount the award to reflect the present value of the future stream of income. The court instead decided to follow a decision of the Supreme Court of Pennsylvania, which had held "as a matter of law that future inflation shall be presumed equal to future interest rates with these factors offsetting." *Kaczkowski v. Bolubasz*, 491 Pa. 561, 583. Thus, although the District Court did not dispute that respondent could be expected to receive regular cost-of-living wage increases from the date of his injury until his presumed date of retirement, the court refused to include such increases in its calculation, explaining that they would provide respondent "a double consideration for inflation." For comparable reasons, the court disregarded changes in the legal minimum wage in computing the amount of mitigation attributable to respondent's ability to perform light work.

It does not appear that either party offered any expert testimony concerning predicted future rates of inflation, the interest rate that could be appropriately used to discount future earnings to present value, or the possible connection between inflation rates and interest rates. Respondent did, however, offer an estimate of how his own wages would have increased over time, based upon recent increases in the company's hourly wage scale.

The Court of Appeals affirmed. [It] first noted that [federal] law controlled[, then] held that in defining the content of that law, inflation must be taken into account. . . . The court understood, however, that the task of predicting future rates of inflation is quite speculative. It concluded that such speculation could properly be avoided in the manner chosen by the District Court—by adopting Pennsylvania's "total offset method" of computing damages. The Court of Appeals approved of the way the total offset method respects the twin goals of considering future inflation and discounting to present value, while eliminating the need to make any calculations about either, "because the inflation and discount rates are legally presumed to be equal and cancel one another." . . .

The District Court found that respondent was permanently disabled as a result of petitioner's negligence. He therefore was entitled to an award of damages to compensate him for his probable pecuniary loss over the duration of his career, reduced to its present value. It is useful at the outset to review the way in which damages should be measured in a hypothetical inflation-free economy. We shall then consider how price inflation alters the analysis. Finally, we shall decide whether the District Court committed reversible error in this case.

In calculating damages, it is assumed that if the injured party had not been disabled, he would have continued to work, and to receive wages at periodic intervals until retirement, disability, or death. An award for impaired earning capacity is intended to compensate the worker for the diminution in that stream of income. The award could in theory take the form of periodic payments, but in this country it has traditionally taken the form of a lump sum, paid at the conclusion of the litigation. . . .

The lost stream's length cannot be known with certainty; the worker could have been disabled or even killed in a different, non-work-related accident at any time. The probability that he would still be working at a given date is constantly diminishing.[10] Given the complexity of trying to make an exact calculation, litigants frequently follow the relatively simple course of assuming that the worker would have continued to work up until a specific date certain. In this case, for example, both parties agreed that the petitioner would have continued to work until age 65 (12½ more years) if he had not been injured.

Each annual installment[11] in the lost stream comprises several elements. The most significant is, of course, the actual wage. In addition,

---

[10] For examples of calculations that take this diminishing probability into account, and assume that it would fall to zero when the worker reached age 65 *see* Fitzpatrick, *The Personal Economic Loss Occasioned by the Death of Nancy Hollander Feldman: An Introduction to the Standard Valuation Procedure*, 1977 Economic Expert in Litigation, No. 5, pp. 25, 44–46 (Defense Research Institute, Inc.) (hereafter Fitzpatrick); Hanke, *How To Determine Lost Earning Capacity*, 27 PRAC. LAWYER 27, 29–33 (July 15, 1981).

[11] Obviously, another distorting simplification is being made here. Although workers generally receive their wages in weekly or biweekly installments, virtually all calculations of lost

the worker may have enjoyed certain fringe benefits, which should be included in an ideal evaluation of the worker's loss but are frequently excluded for simplicity's sake.[12] On the other hand, the injured worker's lost wages would have been diminished by state and federal income taxes. Since the damages award is tax-free, the relevant stream is ideally of after-tax wages and benefits. *See Norfolk & Western R. Co. v. Liepelt*, 444 U.S. 490 (1980). Moreover, workers often incur unreimbursed costs, such as transportation to work and uniforms, that the injured worker will not incur. These costs should also be deducted in estimating the lost stream.

In this case the parties appear to have agreed to simplify the litigation, and to presume that in each installment all the elements in the stream would offset each other, except for gross wages. However, in attempting to estimate even such a stylized stream of annual installments of gross wages, a trier of fact faces a complex task. The most obvious and most appropriate place to begin is with the worker's annual wage at the time of injury. Yet the "estimate of the loss from lessened earnings capacity in the future need not be based solely upon the wages which the plaintiff was earning at the time of his injury." C. MCCORMICK, DAMAGES § 86, p. 300 (1935). Even in an inflation-free economy—that is to say one in which the prices of consumer goods remain stable—a worker's wages tend to "inflate." This "real" wage inflation reflects a number of factors, some linked to the specific individual and some linked to broader societal forces.[13]

With the passage of time, an individual worker often becomes more valuable to his employer. His personal work experiences increase his hourly contributions to firm profits. To reflect that heightened value, he will often receive "seniority" or "experience" raises, "merit" raises, or even promotions. Although it may be difficult to prove when, and whether, a particular injured worker might have received such wage increases, they may be reliably demonstrated for some workers.

Furthermore, the wages of workers as a class may increase over time. Through more efficient interaction among labor, capital, and technology, industrial productivity may increase, and workers' wages may enjoy a share of that growth. Such productivity increases—reflected in real increases in the gross national product per worker-hour—have been a permanent feature of the national economy since the conclusion of World War II. Moreover, through collective bargaining, workers may be able to

---

earnings, including the one made in this case, pretend that the stream would have flowed in large spurts, taking the form of annual installments.

[12] These might include insurance coverage, pension and retirement plans, profit sharing, and in-kind services.

[13] [I]n speaking of "societal" forces we are primarily concerned with those macroeconomic forces that influence wages in the worker's particular industry. The term will be used to encompass all forces that tend to inflate a worker's wage without regard to the worker's individual characteristics.

negotiate increases in their "share" of revenues, at the cost of reducing shareholders' rate of return on their investments. Either of these forces could affect the lost stream of income in an inflation-free economy. In this case, the plaintiff's proffered evidence on predictable wage growth may have reflected the influence of either or both of these two factors.

To summarize, the first stage in calculating an appropriate award for lost earnings involves an estimate of what the lost stream of income would have been. The stream may be approximated as a series of after-tax payments, one in each year of the worker's expected remaining career. In estimating what those payments would have been in an inflation-free economy, the trier of fact may begin with the worker's annual wage at the time of injury. If sufficient proof is offered, the trier of fact may increase that figure to reflect the appropriate influence of individualized factors (such as foreseeable promotions) and societal factors (such as foreseeable productivity growth within the worker's industry).

Of course, even in an inflation-free economy the award of damages to replace the lost stream of income cannot be computed simply by totaling up the sum of the periodic payments. For the damages award is paid in a lump sum at the conclusion of the litigation, and when it—or even a part of it—is invested, it will earn additional money. It has been settled since our decision in *Chesapeake & Ohio R. Co. v. Kelly*, 241 U.S. 485 (1916), that "in all cases where it is reasonable to suppose that interest may safely be earned upon the amount that is awarded, the ascertained future benefits ought to be discounted in the making up of the award."[20]

The discount rate should be based on the rate of interest that would be earned on "the best and safest investments." Once it is assumed that the injured worker would definitely have worked for a specific term of years, he is entitled to a risk-free stream of future income to replace his lost wages; therefore, the discount rate should not reflect the market's premium for investors who are willing to accept some risk of default. Moreover, since under *Norfolk & Western R. Co. v. Liepelt*, 444 U.S. 490 (1980), the lost stream of income should be estimated in after-tax terms, the discount rate should also represent the after-tax rate of return to the injured worker.

Thus, although the notion of a damages award representing the present value of a lost stream of earnings in an inflation-free economy rests on some fairly sophisticated economic concepts, the two elements that determine its calculation can be stated fairly easily. They are: (1) the amount that the employee would have earned during each year that he could have been expected to work after the injury; and (2) the appropriate discount rate, reflecting the safest available investment. The trier of fact

[20] Although this rule could be seen as a way of ensuring that the lump-sum award accurately represents the pecuniary injury as of the time of trial, it was explained by reference to the duty to mitigate damages.

should apply the discount rate to each of the estimated installments in the lost stream of income, and then add up the discounted installments to determine the total award.[22]

Unfortunately for triers of fact, ours is not an inflation-free economy. Inflation has been a permanent fixture in our economy for many decades, and there can be no doubt that it ideally should affect both stages of the calculation described in the previous section. The difficult problem is how it can do so in the practical context of civil litigation. . . .

The first stage of the calculation required an estimate of the shape of the lost stream of future income. For many workers, including respondent, a contractual "cost-of-living adjustment" automatically increases wages each year by the percentage change during the previous year in the consumer price index calculated by the Bureau of Labor Statistics. Such a contract provides a basis for taking into account an additional societal factor—price inflation—in estimating the worker's lost future earnings.

The second stage of the calculation requires the selection of an appropriate discount rate. Price inflation—or more precisely, anticipated price inflation—certainly affects market rates of return. If a lender knows that his loan is to be repaid a year later with dollars that are less valuable than those he has advanced, he will charge an interest rate that is high enough both to compensate him for the temporary use of the loan proceeds and also to make up for their shrinkage in value.[23]

---

[22] At one time it was thought appropriate to distinguish between compensating a plaintiff "for the loss of time from his work which has actually occurred up to the time of trial" and compensating him "for the time which he will lose in [the] future." C. MCCORMICK, DAMAGES § 86 (1935). This suggested that estimated future earning capacity should be discounted to the date of trial, and a separate calculation should be performed for the estimated loss of earnings between injury and trial. *Id.*, §§ 86, 87. It is both easier and more precise to discount the entire lost stream of earnings back to the date of injury—the moment from which earning capacity was impaired. The plaintiff may then be awarded interest on that discounted sum for the period between injury and judgment, in order to ensure that the award when invested will still be able to replicate the lost stream. *See In re Air Crash Disaster Near Chicago, Illinois, on May 25, 1979*, 644 F.2d 633, 641–646 (C.A.7 1981); 1 SPEISER § 8:6, p. 723.

[23] The effect of price inflation on the discount rate may be less speculative than its effect on the lost stream of future income. The latter effect always requires a prediction of the future, for the existence of a contractual cost-of-living adjustment gives no guidance about how big that adjustment will be in some future year. However, whether the discount rate also turns on predictions of the future depends on how it is assumed that the worker will invest his award.

On the one hand, it might be assumed that at the time of the award the worker will invest in a mixture of safe short-term, medium-term, and long-term bonds, with one scheduled to mature each year of his expected worklife. In that event, by purchasing bonds immediately after judgment, the worker can be ensured whatever future stream of nominal income is predicted. Since all relevant effects of inflation on the market interest rate will have occurred at that time, future changes in the rate of price inflation will have no effect on the stream of income he receives. On the other hand, it might be assumed that the worker will invest exclusively in safe short-term notes, reinvesting them at the new market rate whenever they mature. Future market rates would be quite important to such a worker. Predictions of what they will be would therefore also be relevant to the choice of an appropriate discount rate, in much the same way that they are always relevant to the first stage of the calculation. We perceive no intrinsic reason to prefer one assumption over the other, but most "offset" analyses seem to adopt the latter.

At one time many courts incorporated inflation into only one stage of the calculation of the award for lost earnings. In estimating the lost stream of future earnings, [n]o increase was allowed for price inflation, on the theory that such predictions were unreliably speculative. In discounting the estimated lost stream of future income to present value, however, they applied the market interest rate. The effect of these holdings was to deny the plaintiff the benefit of the impact of inflation on his future earnings, while giving the defendant the benefit of inflation's impact on the interest rate that is used to discount those earnings to present value. Although the plaintiff in such a situation could invest the proceeds of the litigation at an "inflated" rate of interest, the stream of income that he received provided him with only enough dollars to maintain his existing nominal income; it did not provide him with a stream comparable to what his lost wages would have been in an inflationary economy. This inequity was assumed to have been minimal because of the relatively low rates of inflation.

In recent years, of course, inflation rates have not remained low. There is now a consensus among courts that the prior inequity can no longer be tolerated. There is no consensus at all, however, regarding what form an appropriate response should take.

Our sister common-law nations generally continue to adhere to the position that inflation is too speculative to be considered in estimating the lost stream of future earnings; they have sought to counteract the danger of systematically undercompensating plaintiffs by applying a discount rate that is below the current market rate. Nevertheless, they have each chosen different rates, applying slightly different economic theories. In England, Lord Diplock has suggested that it would be appropriate to allow for future inflation "in a rough and ready way" by discounting at a rate of 4¾%[, a rate] roughly equivalent to the rates available "[in] times of stable currency." The Supreme Court of Canada has recommended discounting at a rate of 7%, a rate equal to market rates on long-term investments minus a government expert's prediction of the long-term rate of price inflation. And in Australia, the High Court has adopted a 2% rate, on the theory that it represents a good approximation of the long-term "real interest rate."

In this country, some courts have taken the same "real interest rate" approach as Australia. They have endorsed the economic theory suggesting that market interest rates include two components—an estimate of anticipated inflation, and a desired "real" rate of return on investment—and that the latter component is essentially constant over time. They have concluded that the inflationary increase in the estimated lost stream of future earnings will therefore be perfectly "offset" by all but the "real" component of the market interest rate.[26]

Still other courts have preferred to continue relying on market interest rates. To avoid undercompensation, they have shown at least tentative willingness to permit evidence of what future price inflation will be in estimating the lost stream of future income.

Within the past year, two Federal Courts of Appeals have decided to allow litigants a choice of methods. Sitting en banc, the Court of Appeals for the Fifth Circuit has [held] it acceptable either to exclude evidence of future price inflation and discount by a "real" interest rate, or to attempt to predict the effects of future price inflation on future wages and then discount by the market interest rate. *Culver v. Slater Boat Co.*, 688 F.2d 280, 308–310 (1982). [T]he Seventh Circuit has taken a substantially similar position.

Finally, some courts have applied a number of techniques that have loosely been termed "total offset" methods. What these methods have in common is that they presume that the ideal discount rate—the after-tax market interest rate on a safe investment—is (to a legally tolerable degree of precision) completely offset by certain elements in the ideal computation of the estimated lost stream of future income. They all assume that the effects of future price inflation on wages are part of what offsets the market interest rate. The methods differ, however, in their assumptions regarding which if any other elements in the first stage of the damages calculation contribute to the offset.

[In] *Beaulieu v. Elliott*, 434 P.2d 665 (Alaska 1967), [t]he Supreme Court of Alaska ruled that [no] discount was to be applied. It held that the market interest rate was fully offset by two factors: price inflation and real wage inflation. Significantly, the court did not need to distinguish between the two types of sources of real wage inflation—individual and societal—in order to resolve the case before it. It simply observed:

> It is a matter of common experience that as one progresses in his chosen occupation or profession he is likely to increase his earnings as the years pass by. In nearly any occupation a wage earner can reasonably expect to receive wage increases from time to time. This factor is generally not taken into account

[26] What is meant by the "real interest rate" depends on how one expects the plaintiff to invest the award. If one assumes that the injured worker will immediately invest in bonds having a variety of maturity dates . . . then the relevant "real interest rate" must be the difference between (1) an average of short-term, medium-term, and long-term market interest rates in a given year and (2) the average rate of price inflation in subsequent years (i. e., during the terms of the investments). It appears more common for "real interest rate" approaches to rest on the assumption that the worker will invest in low-risk short-term securities and will reinvest frequently. Under that assumption, the relevant real interest rate is the difference between the short-term market interest rate in a given year and the average rate of price inflation during that same year. . . .

> when loss of future wages is determined, because there is no definite way of determining at the time of trial what wage increases the plaintiff may expect to receive in the years to come. However, this factor may be taken into account to some extent when considered to be an offsetting factor to the result reached when future earnings are not reduced to present value.

Thus, the market interest rate was deemed to be offset by price inflation and all other sources of future wage increases. . . .

The litigants and the amici in this case urge us to select one of the many rules that have been proposed and establish it for all time as the exclusive method in all federal trials for calculating an award for lost earnings in an inflationary economy. We are not persuaded, however, that such an approach is warranted. For our review of the foregoing cases leads us to draw three conclusions. First, by its very nature the calculation of an award for lost earnings must be a rough approximation. Because the lost stream can never be predicted with complete confidence, any lump sum represents only a "rough and ready" effort to put the plaintiff in the position he would have been in had he not been injured. Second, sustained price inflation can make the award substantially less precise. Inflation's current magnitude and unpredictability create a substantial risk that the damages award will prove to have little relation to the lost wages it purports to replace. Third, the question of lost earnings can arise in many different contexts. In some sectors of the economy, it is far easier to assemble evidence of an individual's most likely career path than in others. These conclusions all counsel hesitation. . . .

The Court of Appeals correctly noted that respondent's cause of action "is rooted in federal maritime law." The fact that Pennsylvania has adopted the total offset rule for all negligence cases in that forum is therefore not of controlling importance in this case. . . .

In calculating an award for a longshoreman's lost earnings caused by the negligence of a vessel, the discount rate should be chosen on the basis of the factors that are used to estimate the lost stream of future earnings. If the trier of fact relies on a specific forecast of the future rate of price inflation, and if the estimated lost stream of future earnings is calculated to include price inflation along with individual factors and other societal factors, then the proper discount rate would be the after-tax market interest rate. But since specific forecasts of future price inflation remain too unreliable to be useful in many cases, it will normally be a costly and ultimately unproductive waste of longshoremen's resources to make such forecasts the centerpiece of litigation under § 5(b). As Judge Newman has warned: "The average accident trial should not be converted into a graduate seminar on economic forecasting." For that reason, both plaintiffs and trial courts should be discouraged from pursuing that approach.

On the other hand, if forecasts of future price inflation are not used, it is necessary to choose an appropriate below-market discount rate. As long as inflation continues, one must ask how much should be "offset" against the market rate. Once again, that amount should be chosen on the basis of the same factors that are used to estimate the lost stream of future earnings. If full account is taken of the individual and societal factors (excepting price inflation) that can be expected to have resulted in wage increases, then all that should be set off against the market interest rate is an estimate of future price inflation. This would result in one of the "real interest rate" approaches described above. Although we find the economic evidence distinctly inconclusive regarding an essential premise of those approaches,[30] we do not believe a trial court adopting such an approach in a suit under § 5(b) should be reversed if it adopts a rate between 1 and 3% and explains its choice.

There may be a sound economic argument for even further setoffs. Professor Carlson [contends] that in the long run the societal factors excepting price inflation—largely productivity gains—match (or even slightly exceed) the "real interest rate." Carlson, *Economic Analysis v. Courtroom Controversy*, 62 A.B.A.J. 628 (1976). He thus recommended that the estimated lost stream of future wages be calculated without considering either price inflation or societal productivity gains. All that would be considered would be individual seniority and promotion gains. If this were done, he concluded that the entire market interest rate, including both inflation and the real interest rate, would be more than adequately offset.

Although such an approach has the virtue of simplicity and may even be economically precise, we cannot at this time agree with the Court of Appeals for the Third Circuit that its use is mandatory in the federal courts. Naturally, Congress could require it if it chose to do so. And nothing prevents parties interested in keeping litigation costs under control from stipulating to its use before trial. But we are not prepared to impose it on unwilling litigants, for we have not been given sufficient data to judge how closely the national patterns of wage growth are likely to reflect the patterns within any given industry. . . .

As a result, the judgment below must be set aside. In performing its damages calculation, the trial court applied the theory of *Kaczkowski v. Bolubasz* as a mandatory federal rule of decision, even though the

---

30 The key premise is that the real interest rate is stable over time. It is obviously not perfectly stable, but whether it is even relatively stable is hotly disputed among economists. In his classic work, Irving Fisher argued that the rate is not stable because changes in expectations of inflation (the factor that influences market interest rates) lag behind changes in inflation itself. I. FISHER, THE THEORY OF INTEREST 43 (1930). He noted that the "real rate of interest in the United States from March to April, 1917, fell below minus 70 percent!"

petitioner had insisted that if compensation was to be awarded, it "must be reduced to its present worth." Moreover, this approach seems to have colored the trial court's evaluation of the relevant evidence. At one point, the court noted that respondent had offered a computation of his estimated wages from the date of the accident until his presumed date of retirement, including projected cost-of-living adjustments. It stated: "We do not disagree with these projections, but feel they are inappropriate in view of the holding in *Kaczkowski*." Later in its opinion, however, the court declared: "We do not believe that there was sufficient evidence to establish a basis for estimating increased future productivity for the plaintiff, and therefore we will not inject such a factor in this award."

On remand, the decision on whether to reopen the record should be left to the sound discretion of the trial court. It bears mention that the present record already gives reason to believe a fair award may be more confidently expected in this case than in many. The employment practices in the longshoring industry appear relatively stable and predictable. The parties seem to have had no difficulty in arriving at the period of respondent's future work expectancy, or in predicting the character of the work that he would have been performing during that entire period if he had not been injured. Moreover, the record discloses that respondent's wages were determined by a collective-bargaining agreement that explicitly provided for "cost of living" increases and that recent company history also included a "general" increase and a "job class increment increase." Although the trial court deemed the latter increases irrelevant during its first review because it felt legally compelled to assume they would offset any real interest rate, further study of them on remand will allow the court to determine whether that assumption should be made in this case.

We do not suggest that the trial judge should embark on a search for "delusive exactness." It is perfectly obvious that the most detailed inquiry can at best produce an approximate result. And one cannot ignore the fact that in many instances the award for impaired earning capacity may be overshadowed by a highly impressionistic award for pain and suffering. But we are satisfied that whatever rate the District Court may choose to discount the estimated stream of future earnings, it must make a deliberate choice, rather than assuming that it is bound by a rule of state law.

The judgment of the Court of Appeals is vacated, and the case is remanded for further proceedings consistent with this opinion.

NOTES

1. We introduced present value calculations in Chapter 7. Capitalization of earnings involves reducing future income streams to present value. Whether the income is wages, rents, or profits, the technique is the

same. Technique, however, is the last step in the process. First, the lawyer (or, for wealthy clients, the expert witness) must ascertain the inputs: the remaining years of work, the likely compensation (including fringe benefits, but less job expenses) for those years, and the discount rate. Judgment goes into selecting each of those inputs, so opposing parties (and their experts) may present differing testimony on those points. Justice Stevens offers a particularly cogent analysis of how to select an appropriate interest rate.

2. Parties can agree to periodic payments, even though American courts do not order them. Structured settlements allow defendants to pay over time or to buy annuities that will pay plaintiff over time. For tax reasons, structured settlements may be advantageous to both parties. Plaintiffs, however, must take precautions against subsequent insolvency—by defendant or by the provider of the annuity defendant purchases. Even without insolvency, breach of a settlement agreement is possible. Plaintiff is left with a contract claim, regardless of the nature of the original action.

ADDITIONAL PROBLEMS

1. *Who Calculates Present Value?* Can discounting be left to the trier of fact? A bench trial is no panacea. Law students sometimes say they came to law school instead of business school precisely to avoid numbers. One of them might be your judge. Is a jury any better? Can they be instructed how to perform accurate present value calculations? They could always adopt an expert's opinion in its entirety, with the calculations intact. But if they think one expert exaggerated wages (or inflation) while the other underestimated them, new calculations based on these numbers would be needed. Is this a justification for the offset method? Might jurors, affected personally by inflation, include compensation for it on their own?

2. *Periodic Payment of Damages.* Could courts avoid the problem by ordering periodic payments? It may not help some questions. Plaintiff's work-life expectancy will not get any clearer if she is no longer able to work. But the inflation rate will be known each year and wage increases, at least for employers still in business, would be somewhat easier to ascertain. Periodic payments are the norm for alimony and child support. Are the problems any worse for other types of litigation? Would you advise your client ask a court to award damages stated as an amount per month for a period of time? If offered periodic payments as a settlement, would you advise your client to accept them? What would you discuss with your client offering that advise?

3. Advise Juan Perez what remedies he may expect.

F. THE COAL MINING LEASE

The following case may be a familiar one. It appears in many Contracts casebooks. Yet it presents an interesting set of problems for the practicing lawyer. Reread the case, then consider the problems at the end of the case.

PEEVYHOUSE V. GARLAND COAL & MINING COMPANY

1962 Okla. 267, 382 P.2d 109 (Okla.1962),
cert. denied, 375 U.S. 906, 84 S.Ct. 196, 11 L.Ed.2d 145 (1963).

JACKSON, JUSTICE.

[Briefly] stated, the facts are as follows: plaintiffs owned a farm containing coal deposits, and in November, 1954, leased the premises to defendant for a period of five years for coal mining purposes. A "stripmining" operation was contemplated in which the coal would be taken from pits on the surface of the ground, instead of from underground mine shafts. In addition to the usual covenants found in a coal mining lease, defendant specifically agreed to perform certain restorative and remedial work at the end of the lease period. It is unnecessary to set out the details of the work to be done, other than to say that it would involve the moving of many thousands of cubic yards of dirt, at a cost estimated by expert witnesses at about $29,000.00. However, plaintiffs sued for only $25,000.00.

[The jury] returned a verdict for plaintiffs for $5000.00—only a fraction of the "cost of performance," *but more than the total value of the farm even after the remedial work is done.*

[On] appeal, the issue is sharply drawn. Plaintiffs contend that the true measure of damages in this case is what it will cost plaintiffs to obtain performance of the work that was not done because of defendant's default. Defendant argues that the measure of damages is the cost of performance "limited, however, to the total difference in the market value before and after the work was performed."

It appears that this precise question has not heretofore been presented to this court. In Ardizonne v. Archer, 72 Okl. 70, 178 P. 263, this court held that the measure of damages for breach of a contract to drill an oil well was the reasonable cost of drilling the well, but here a slightly different factual situation exists. The drilling of an oil well will yield valuable geological information, even if no oil or gas is found, and of course if the well is a producer, the value of the premises increases. In the case before us, it is argued by defendant with some force that the performance of the remedial work defendant agreed to do will add at the most only a few hundred dollars to the value of plaintiffs' farm, and that the damages should be limited to that amount because that is all plaintiffs have lost.

Plaintiffs rely on *Groves v. John Wunder Co.*, 286 N.W. 235. In that case, the Minnesota court, in a substantially similar situation, adopted the "cost of performance" rule as opposed to the "value" rule. The result was to authorize a jury to give plaintiff damages in the amount of $60,000, where the real estate concerned would have been worth only $12,160, even if the work contracted for had been done.

It may be observed that *Groves v. John Wunder Co.,* is the only case which has come to our attention in which the cost of performance rule has been followed under circumstances where the cost of performance greatly exceeded the diminution in value resulting from the breach of contract. Incidentally, it appears that this case was decided by a plurality rather than a majority of the members of the court.

Defendant relies principally upon *Sandy Valley & E. R. Co., v. Hughes*, 175 Ky. 320, 194 S.W. 344; *Bigham v. Wabash–Pittsburg Terminal Ry. Co.*, 223 Pa. 106, 72 A. 318; and *Sweeney v. Lewis Const. Co.*, 66 Wash. 490, 119 P. 1108. These were all cases in which, under similar circumstances, the appellate courts followed the "value" rule instead of the "cost of performance" rule. Plaintiff points out that in the earliest of these cases (Bigham) the court cites as authority on the measure of damages an earlier Pennsylvania tort case, and that the other two cases follow the first, with no explanation as to why a measure of damages ordinarily followed in cases sounding in tort should be used in contract cases. Nevertheless, it is of some significance that three out of four appellate courts have followed the diminution in value rule under circumstances where, as here, the cost of performance greatly exceeds the diminution in value.

The explanation may be found in the fact that the situations presented are artificial ones. It is highly unlikely that the ordinary property owner would agree to pay $29,000 (or its equivalent) for the construction of "improvements" upon his property that would increase its value only about ($300) three hundred dollars. The result is that we are called upon to apply principles of law theoretically based upon reason and reality to a situation which is basically unreasonable and unrealistic.

In *Groves v. John Wunder Co.,* in arriving at its conclusions, the Minnesota court apparently considered the contract involved to be analogous to a building and construction contract, and cited authority for the proposition that the cost of performance or completion of the building as contracted is ordinarily the measure of damages in actions for damages for the breach of such a contract.

In an annotation following the Minnesota case beginning at 123 A.L.R. 515, the annotator places the three cases relied on by defendant (Sandy Valley, Bigham and Sweeney) under the classification of cases involving "grading and excavation contracts."

We do not think either analogy is strictly applicable to the case now before us. The primary purpose of the lease contract between plaintiffs and defendant was neither "building and construction" nor "grading and excavation." It was merely to accomplish the economical recovery and marketing of coal from the premises, to the profit of all parties. The special provisions of the lease contract pertaining to remedial work were incidental to the main object involved.

Even in the case of contracts that are unquestionably building and construction contracts, the authorities are not in agreement as to the factors to be considered in determining whether the cost of performance rule or the value rule should be applied. The American Law Institute's RESTATEMENT OF THE LAW, CONTRACTS, Volume 1, Sections 346(1)(a)(i) and (ii) submits the proposition that the cost of performance is the proper measure of damages "if this is possible and does not involve unreasonable economic waste"; and that the diminution in value caused by the breach is the proper measure "if construction and completion in accordance with the contract would involve unreasonable economic waste." (Emphasis supplied.) In an explanatory comment immediately following the text, the Restatement makes it clear that the "economic waste" referred to consists of the destruction of a substantially completed building or other structure. Of course no such destruction is involved in the case now before us.

On the other hand, in McCormick, Damages, Section 168, it is said with regard to building and construction contracts that "[in] cases where the defect is one that can be repaired or cured without undue expense" the cost of performance is the proper measure of damages, but where "[the] defect in material or construction is one that cannot be remedied without an expenditure for reconstruction disproportionate to the end to be attained" (emphasis supplied) the value rule should be followed. The same idea was expressed in *Jacob & Youngs, Inc. v. Kent*, 230 N.Y. 239, 129 N.E. 889, as follows: "The owner is entitled to the money which will permit him to complete, unless the cost of completion is grossly and unfairly out of proportion to the good to be attained. When that is true, the measure is the difference in value."

It thus appears that the prime consideration in the Restatement was "economic waste"; and that the prime consideration in McCormick, Damages, and in *Jacob & Youngs, Inc. v. Kent,* was the relationship between the expense involved and the "end to be attained"—in other words, the "relative economic benefit."

In view of the unrealistic fact situation in the instant case, and certain Oklahoma statutes to be hereinafter noted, we are of the opinion that the "relative economic benefit" is a proper consideration here. This is in accord with the recent case of *Mann v. Clowser*, 190 Va. 887, 59 S.E.2d 78, where, in applying the cost rule, the Virginia court specifically noted that "[the] defects are remediable from a practical standpoint and the costs are not grossly disproportionate to the results to be obtained" (Emphasis supplied).

[We] therefore hold that where, in a coal mining lease, lessee agrees to perform certain remedial work on the premises concerned at the end of the lease period, and thereafter the contract is fully performed by both parties except that the remedial work is not done, the measure of damages in an action by lessor against lessee for damages for breach of contract is ordinarily the reasonable cost of performance of the work; however, where the contract provision breached was merely incidental to the main purpose in view, and where the economic benefit which would result to lessor by full performance of the work is grossly disproportionate to the cost of performance, the damages which lessor may recover are limited to the diminution in value resulting to the premises because of the non-performance.

[Damages lowered to $300; affirmed 4–3]

IRWIN, JUSTICE (dissenting).

[Although] the contract speaks for itself, there were several negotiations between the plaintiffs and defendant before the contract was executed. Defendant admitted in the trial of the action, that plaintiffs insisted that the above provisions be included in the contract and that they would not agree to the coal mining lease unless the above provisions were included.

In consideration for the lease contract, plaintiffs were to receive a certain amount as royalty for the coal produced and marketed and in addition thereto their land was to be restored as provided in the contract.

Defendant received as consideration for the contract, its proportionate share of the coal produced and marketed and in addition thereto, the right to use plaintiffs' land in the furtherance of its mining operations.

The cost for performing the contract in question could have been reasonably approximated when the contract was negotiated and executed and there are no conditions now existing which could not have been reasonably anticipated by the parties. Therefore, defendant had knowledge, when it prevailed upon the plaintiffs to execute the lease, that the cost of performance might be disproportionate to the value or benefits received by plaintiff for the performance.

Defendant has received its benefits under the contract and now urges, in substance, that plaintiffs' measure of damages for its failure to perform should be the economic value of performance to the plaintiffs and not the cost of performance.

[In] my judgment, we should follow the case of *Groves v. John Wunder Company*, 205 Minn. 163, 286 N.W. 235, which defendant agrees "that the fact situation is apparently similar to the one in the case at bar," and where the Supreme Court of Minnesota held: "The owner's or employer's damages for such a breach (*i.e.* breach hypothesized in 2d syllabus) are to be measured, not in respect to the value of the land to be improved, but by the reasonable cost of doing that which the contractor promised to do and which he left undone."

[Therefore,] in my opinion, the plaintiffs were entitled to specific performance of the contract and since defendant has failed to perform, the proper measure of damages should be the cost of performance. Any other measure of damage would be holding for naught the express provisions of the contract; would be taking from the plaintiffs the benefits of the contract and placing those benefits in defendant which has failed to perform its obligations; would be granting benefits to defendant without a resulting obligation; and would be completely rescinding the solemn obligation of the contract for the benefit of the defendant to the detriment of the plaintiffs by making an entirely new contract for the parties.

NOTES AND QUESTIONS

1. The court did not mention the negotiations that preceded the contract. Defendant offered plaintiffs $3,000 in exchange for the right not to reclaim the land. Plaintiffs refused to deal on those terms, agreeing to the lease only if it included a promise to reclaim the land. Judith Maute, Peevyhouse v. Garland Coal Co. *Revisited: The Ballad of Willie and Lucille*, 89 NW. U.L. REV. 1341 (1995).

2. The court makes much of the different types of contracts: construction, grading, oil drilling, coal mining lease. Does it make sense to have different rules for different categories of cases? Should the same factors influence the choice in each category, on a case by case basis? *See* Christopher T. Wonnell, *The Abstract Character of Contract Law*, 22 CONN. L. REV. 437 (1990). How narrowly should we draw the categories? *Groves v. John Wunder Co.*, 205 Minn. 163, 286 N.W. 235 (1939), reached the opposite result in a similar transaction, where gravel was taken instead of coal. Should we have one rule for coal and another for gravel? Is mining the proper category? Is *Groves* just wrong?

ADDITIONAL PROBLEMS

1. *Demand for Relief.* Suppose the Peevyhouses had consulted you before filing suit. What remedy or remedies would you request in the complaint? Or would you advise them not to sue at all? Draft a complaint.

2. *Appeal.* Suppose the decision above was issued by an *intermediate* appellate court. The Peevyhouses consult you about their prospects on appeal to the state Supreme Court. Would you advise them to proceed or to give up? If you would proceed, how would you demonstrate the error in the appellate court decision? Draft a brief making the arguments (but omit citations).

3. *Contract Negotiations.* After *Peevyhouse* is decided, the Irkhomes consult you. The Wreath Coal Co. has approached them seeking to lease a portion of their family farm for purposes of strip mining coal under the land. The coal company has offered $3,000 in lieu of reclaiming the land. The Irkhomes want to ensure that the land will be restored to its original condition, but suspect that reclamation will cost more than $3,000 (probably

$30,000). Draft a counteroffer for them to make that will achieve their goals (if accepted).

G. TRANSIT FARES

Santiago, California, provides public transportation via buses and light rail. Fares vary by mode and length of trip, but average about $1.75 a trip. In addition, Santiago offers residents monthly passes good for unlimited travel on all public transportation for $75 a month. On July 3, Santiago decided to raise fares, effectively immediately: the average trip rose to $2; the monthly passes to $85. Santiago had already sold and distributed monthly passes for July at the $75 rate. In order to collect the fare increase from pass-holders, it refused to honor passes unless pass-holders paid an additional $0.25 per trip.

You represent the pass-holders. Assume that the city's action breaches its contract with your clients. Can you protect their legal rights under the passes?

EISEN V. CARLISLE & JACQUELIN

479 F.2d 1005 (2d Cir.1973),
vacated and remanded, 417 U.S. 156, 94 S.Ct. 2140, 40 L.Ed.2d 732 (1974).

MEDINA, CIRCUIT JUDGE:

[Plaintiff brought a class action alleging that defendants had overcharged commissions on sales of shares in odd-lots—not evenly divisible by 100. The claim arose under the antitrust laws, allowing treble damages. The amount of overcharges, even if trebled, were individually minuscule (perhaps $3.90 per average claimant). The class, even limited to those who traded between May 1, 1962, and June 30, 1966, consisted of about 6 million members from many different countries, with cumulative claims estimated at $120 million. Rule 23 required plaintiff to give notice to all members of the class (or at least the 2.5 million who could be identified). Plaintiff, however, refused to pay for notice or to post a bond to reimburse defendant for the cost of notice if plaintiff lost on the merits. The trial court initially refused to certify the class, but the decision was reversed and remanded for more careful consideration. On remand, the trial court certified the class.]

In our prior opinion we stated unequivocally that actual notice must be given to those whose identity could be ascertained with reasonable effort and that "in this type of case" plaintiff must pay the expense of giving notice to these members of the class. We further stated that if this could not be done there might be no other alternative than the dismissal of the case as a class action. For some reason not clear to us Judge Tyler disregarded these holdings and concluded that he had discretion, even with reference to those members of the class who could be easily identified, to provide for such notice as he thought to be reasonable in the light of the facts of this particular case.

Thus he directed actual notice only to "the approximately 2000 or more class members who had ten or more transactions during the relevant period" and to "5000 other class members selected at random" from the 2,500,000 class members who could easily be identified. With respect to the rest of the 6,000,000 members of the class, Judge Tyler ordered [publications that] we consider to be a totally inadequate compliance with the notice requirements of amended Rule 23. . . . [After] a "brief" preliminary hearing on the merits [of the antitrust claim] Judge Tyler concluded that the defendants must bear 90% of [the notification] expenses.

[Judge Tyler] realized that it was highly improbable that any great number of claims would, for a variety of reasons, ultimately be filed by the 6,000,000 members of the class. No claimant in the 6 years of the progress of the action had shown any interest in Eisen's claim. The average [class] member would be entitled to damages of $3.90. As the costs of administration might run into the millions of dollars, it was not likely that a rush of claimants would eventuate no matter how extensive the publication. As he had surmised in the beginning, and as Chief Judge Lumbard stated in his dissent, the class action was hopelessly unmanageable. So Judge Tyler tried to pull the case out of this morass by resorting to the "fluid recovery," which had been used as a vehicle for carrying out a voluntary settlement in the *Drug Cases*, State of West Virginia v. Chas. Pfizer & Co., 314 F.Supp. 710 (S.D.N.Y.1970).

The concept of this "fluid recovery" is very simple. Having decided that there is no conceivable way in which any substantial number of individual claimants can ever be paid, "the class as a whole" is substituted for the 6,000,000 claimants. Thus the first round of notices becomes relatively unimportant. [Step Two] involves a trial of the case to a judge and jury on the merits—not a preliminary mini-trial this time, but a real full scale trial of the private triple damage antitrust case. In some way the damages to "the class as a whole" will be assessed and the defendants, it seems to be assumed, will promptly pay this huge sum into court. . . . With the money in hand, [we] are to have the real notices soliciting the filing of claims, the processing of these claims, the fixing of counsel fees and the payment of the general expenses of administration. [I]t is quite apparent that some of the original 6,000,000 claimants will receive nothing, because they have never heard of the case or for other reasons have failed to file claims and have them processed, and many other new traders, who had no transactions in the period from mid-1962 to mid-1966, will receive some payments. According to Judge Tyler, at least those members of the original class of 6,000,000 who "have maintained their odd-lot activity, will reap the benefits of any recovery."

As far as we are aware there has never been, nor can there ever be, a reliable or even rational estimate of how many traders, whether speculators or investors, can be said to be expected to continue as such after the lapse of 10 years or so. As it is suspected that relatively few claims will be filed and the damages assessed are supposed to cover the losses of "the class as a whole," there will be a huge residue, similar to the amounts paid to various charities "to advance public health projects" in the *Drug Cases*, and this residue is to be used for the benefit of all odd-lot traders by reducing the odd-lot differential "in an amount determined reasonable by the court until such time as the fund is depleted." We are at a loss to understand how this is to be done, but it is suggested that it "might properly be done under SEC supervision or at least with SEC approval." . . .

[W]e think the three cases cited by Judge Tyler as "respectable precedent" for fluid class recovery are all distinguishable. These three cases are: *Bebchick v. Public Utilities Commission*, 318 F.2d 187 (App.D.C.), *cert. denied*, 373 U.S. 913 (1963); the *Drug Cases*, 314 F.Supp. 710 (S.D.N.Y.), *aff'd* 440 F.2d 1079 (2d Cir.1971); and *Daar v. Yellow Cab Company*, 433 P.2d 732 (Cal.1967).

Judge Wyatt's extraordinary feat of judicial administration in carrying out the terms of the one hundred million dollar settlement in the *Drug Cases* deserves all the praise it has received. But it was a consensual affair made possible by the agreement of the parties and without objection to the assumption by the District Court of jurisdiction to accept and administer the fund. Here we have no fund. There is no settlement. Every issue is contested and litigated. And authority to permit this action to proceed as a class action must be found within the four corners of amended Rule 23, as interpreted in the Reviser's Note. Applying this test we hold Eisen's class action must be dismissed. *Bebchick* was not a class action in any sense of the word. Amended Rule 23 was not involved. In the exercise of its powers of review, the Court of Appeals for the District of Columbia Circuit reversed a judgment of the District Court approving the action of the Public Utilities Commission of the District of Columbia supporting a fare increase by the transit company. In the meantime, the additional cash fares, now found to be illegal, had been collected. There was no way to direct refunds as those who paid these cash fares could not be identified. So, also in the exercise of its powers of review the Court of Appeals directed the amount of these additional cash fares to be set up in the books of the transit company to be used, in the discretion of the regulatory commission "to benefit bus riders as a class in pending or future rate proceedings." We cannot find that this case has any bearing on any of the issues in this amended Rule 23 case. Finally, *Daar* was a case arising under a state class action statute very different in its phraseology from amended Rule 23. The ruling was made on a demurrer to the complaint so the approach to the legal issues was entirely different from the making of a judicial determination, on the basis of proof, of whether or not the requirements of amended Rule 23 had been met. Moreover, the court was evidently of the view that the individuals who had been damaged by the alleged overcharge in taxi fares would ultimately have to prove their separate and individual damages. . . .

When discoursing on the arts or belles-lettres colorful language stimulates the imagination, beguiles one into useful symbolism and opens up the avenues to creative thought. But in the process of rationalizing legal conclusions and arriving at a sound and proper determination of questions of the interpretation of statutes, procedural rules and constitutional limitations, clichés and rhetorical devices generally miss the mark. Something more substantial is necessary to establish a base for the proper decision of difficult and complex questions of law. One reason for this is that the solution is found more often than not by the application of fundamentally simple principles.

Thus statements about "disgorging" sums of money for which a defendant may be liable, or the "prophylactic" effect of making the wrongdoer suffer the pains of retribution and generally about providing a remedy for the ills of mankind, do little to solve specific legal problems. The result of this approach is almost always confusion of thought and irrational, emotional and unsound decisions. In cases involving claims of money damages all litigation presumes a desire on the part of the judicial establishment to make the wrongdoer pay for the wrongs he has committed, but to do this by applying settled or clearly stated principles of law, rather than by some process of divination. Punishment of wrongdoers is provided by law for criminal acts in statutes making it a crime punishable by fine or imprisonment to violate the antitrust laws. In certain civil suits punitive damages may be awarded; and in private antitrust cases the possible recovery of triple the loss actually suffered by a plaintiff is very properly praised as a supplementary deterrent. But none of these considerations justifies disregarding, nullifying or watering down any of the procedural safeguards established by the Constitution, or by congressional mandate, or by the Federal Rules of Civil Procedure, including amended Rule 23. It is a historical fact that procedural safeguards for the benefit of all litigants constitute some of the most important and salutary protections against oppressions, including oppressions by those whose intentions may be above reproach. . . .

From the beginning it has been Judge (then Chief Judge) Lumbard's view that as a class action the case is unmanageable and that it should be dismissed as a class action. It turns out that he was right. As soon as the evidence on the remand disclosed the true extent of the membership of the class and the fact that Eisen would not pay for individual notice to the members of the class who could be identified, and the evidence further disclosed that the class membership was of such diversity and was so dispersed that no notice by publication could be devised by the ingenuity of man that could reasonably be expected to notify more than a relatively small proportion of the class, a ruling should have been made forthwith dismissing the case as a class action. This dismissal could have saved several years of hard work by the judge and the lawyers and wholly unnecessary expense running into large figures. The fact that the cost of obtaining proofs of claim by individual members of the class and processing such claims was such as to make it clear that the amounts payable to individual claimants would be so low as to be negligible also should have been enough of itself to warrant dismissal as a class action. Other cases involving millions of diverse and unidentifiable members of an alleged class had been dismissed as unmanageable or altered in composition. And so even Eisen and his counsel conceded that the class was not manageable unless the "fluid recovery" procedures were adopted. . . .

Where there are millions of dispersed and unidentifiable members of the class notices by publication giving the essential information required by amended Rule 23 are a farce. And, when it comes to the filing and processing of claims, lawyers specializing in class actions have stated that the only effective way to induce any reasonable number of members of the class to file claims is to conduct full-scale campaigns on TV and radio, solicit appearances by advocates of consumers' rights such as Ralph Nader, letters from Congressmen to their constituents, public statements by various state attorneys general "and coverage in various news media, union newsletters and the like," also to persuade the Federal Communications Commission to classify announcements of this character as "public service announcements."

All the difficulties of management are supposed to disappear once the "fluid recovery" procedure is adopted. The claims of the individual members of the class become of little consequence. If the damages to be paid were only the aggregate of the sums found due to individual members of the class, after their claims had been processed, it is fairly obvious that in cases like *Eisen* the expenses of giving the notices required by amended Rule 23 and the general costs of administration of the action would exceed the amount due to the few members of the class who filed claims and the individual members of the class would get nothing.

But if the "class as a whole" is or can be substituted for the individual members of the class as claimants, then the number of claims filed is of no consequence and the amount found to be due will be enormous, affording, we are told, plenty of money to pay all expenses, including counsel fees, and a residue so large as to justify reduction of the oddlot differential for years in the future, for the benefit of all traders, past, present and future, who are to be considered to be members of "the class as a whole."

Even if amended Rule 23 could be read so as to permit any such fantastic procedure, the courts would have to reject it as an unconstitutional violation of the requirement of due process of law. But as it now reads amended Rule 23 contemplates and provides for no such procedure. Nor can amended Rule 23 be construed or interpreted in such fashion as to permit such procedure. We hold the "fluid recovery" concept and practice to be illegal, inadmissible as a solution of the manageability problems of class actions and wholly improper. . . .

[I]f amended Rule 23 furnishes no satisfactory solution in situations where immense numbers of consumers have been mulcted in various ways by illegal charges, it would seem that some means should be provided by law for the redress of these wrongs to the community and to society as a whole. The numerous decisions by courts in these class action cases have at least exposed the lack of adequate remedy under existing laws. From our extensive study of the whole situation in working on this *Eisen* case it would seem that amended Rule 23 provides an excellent and workable procedure in cases where the number of members of the class is not too large. It seems doubtful that further amendments to Rule 23 can be expected to be effective where there are millions of members of the class, without some infringement of constitutional requirements. The problem is really one for solution by the Congress. Numerous administrative agencies protect consumers in various ways. It should, we think, be possible for the Congress to create some public body to do justice in the matter of consumers' claims in such fashion as to afford compensation to the injured consumer. If penalties are to be imposed upon wrongdoers, at least let the Congress decide how the money is to be spent.

Another possibility, suggested by [the American College of Trial Lawyers], is a further amendment to amended Rule 23 [to permit a court to dispense with notice in damage class actions, as already allowed when classes seek injunctive relief]. The procedure involved in applying for prospective injunctive relief is relatively simple and inexpensive, social and economic reforms may be implemented and an end put to illegal practices with far more benefit to the community than that derived from minimal or token payments to individual members of a class. Attorney's fees in such cases should also provide adequate incentive to counsel for the representative or representatives of the class.[28]

---

[28] In his recent book Federal Jurisdiction: A General View, containing his 1972 Columbia University James S. Carpentier Lectures, Chief Judge Friendly makes this comment on class actions pursuant to amended Rule 23, at page 120, omitting footnotes:

> Something seems to have gone radically wrong with a well-intentioned effort. Of course, an injured plaintiff should be compensated, but the federal judicial system is not adapted to affording compensation to classes of hundreds of people with $10 or even

For the reasons stated in this opinion[,] as a class action, the case is dismissed, without prejudice to the continuance of so much of the claim asserted in the complaint as refers to Eisen's alleged individual rights against the defendants.

HAYS, CIRCUIT JUDGE (concurring in the result):

I concur in the result because I am unable to accept the ruling of the district court requiring the defendants to pay 90 per cent of the cost of notice, since, if the defendants should finally prevail, they would not be reimbursed for this expenditure.

[Opinions on denial of rehearing en banc are omitted.]

NOTES

1. The Supreme Court decision vacating *Eisen* reads like an affirmance, rejecting the class action. It deals with issues of notice and costs, not the fluid class recovery points.

2. The notice requirement seems to protect defendants—if you assume that the class representatives would win the suit. If the class loses, those who opt out are better off (or at least no worse off) than those in the class. Notice protects their ability to decide whether to opt in or out. Is that protection of any use in cases like *Eisen*? Even so, might plaintiffs as a whole be better off without a judicially created exception to the notice requirement?

3. Fluid class recovery gives the remedy to people who may not have been victims. In *Eisen*, for example, the persons selling odd-lots after the case ended would receive discounts on their commissions totaling the amount that persons were overcharged during 1962–1966 (or the unclaimed portions of that amount). While some traders who lost would be among those who gained, others who lost may have died or stopped trading, while some who began trading after 1966 would gain. Should such rough justice be allowed? Is there any theoretical (or pragmatic) justification for the court requiring defendant to provide financial benefits to persons whom defendant had not wronged? What if the court awarded class members more than their actual losses (as a way of distributing damages that other class members did not claim)?

4. When defendants settle, these questions are easier. After paying the attorneys and any class members who prove their losses, money may remain. The *Eisen* court offered no objection to judicial distribution of these funds, praising the Judge Wyatt in the *Drug Cases*. Occasional disputes may arise

---

$50 claims. The important thing is to stop the evil conduct. For this an injunction is the appropriate remedy, and an attorney who obtains one should be properly compensated by the defendant, although not in the astronomical terms fixed when there is a multimillion dollar settlement. If it be said that this still leaves the defendant with the fruits of past wrong-doing, consideration might be given to civil fines, payable to the government, sufficiently substantial to discourage engaging in such conduct but not so colossal as to produce recoveries that would ruin innocent stockholders or, what is more likely, produce blackmail settlements. This is a matter that needs urgent attention.

over how to disburse the funds. *See, e.g.*, *Houck ex rel. United States v. Folding Carton Administration Committee*, 881 F.2d 494 (7th Cir. 1989) (rejecting donation of surplus to law schools for antitrust research). Courts have been reluctant to assess damages for the full class, thus entering a judgment that may exceed claims by class members. *See, e.g.*, *Allapattah Services Inc. v. Exxon Corp.*, 333 F.3d 1248 (11th Cir. 2003) (affirming trial court's refusal to assess total amount Exxon overcharged its distributors for fuel as class damages).

5. Some fluid class recoveries have been authorized outside damage actions. Antidiscrimination suits can produce injunctions ordering employers or unions to fill future openings with persons from groups against whom they have discriminated in the past. *See, e.g.*, *Local 28, Sheet Metal Workers v. EEOC*, 478 U.S. 421, 106 S.Ct. 3019, 92 L.Ed.2d 344 (1986) (plurality). The beneficiaries may not be the people denied prior opportunities, but merely share a relevant characteristic with past victims. Race in many ways poses special problems for the courts. Is this an exception to the *Eisen* rule? Or is *Eisen* ripe for reevaluation?

ADDITIONAL PROBLEMS

1. *Carefully Calculated Compensation.* If rough justice—granting the remedy to someone similar to the victim—is good enough, what remains of the general rule, seeking the plaintiff's position if no wrong had occurred? What remains of any doctrine seeking to define the loss with some accuracy? Is any guess good enough? Or is guessing permissible only when there is no practical alternative? Might judges (and lawyers) be too quick to conclude that no alternative was practical if an easy out like guesses were available?

2. *Fees or Class Action?* Antitrust laws allow a prevailing plaintiff to recover attorneys' fees in addition to treble damages. Does that permit Eisen and other members of the class to pursue their claims? Has the defendant made a strategic error here?

3. *Passholders.* Time for the problem: how will you protect the holders of monthly passes?

H. THE VEGETARIANS

JacDonking is a large international chain of fast food restaurants. In 1994, the company decided to deep-fry potatoes in vegetable oil, rather than animal fat, in all of their restaurants. The company was driven by a shift in public appreciation of the health benefits of low cholesterol oils. The company ran an advertising campaign announcing the changed policy nationwide. As a result, a number of vegetarians, including many of the Hindu faith, began eating JacDonking's french fried potatoes. Unknown to these vegetarian customers, JacDonking's potatoes are treated with small amounts of animal fat at the processing plant where they are produced. The animal fat enhances the flavor of the potatoes.

(The use of animal fat in processing the potatoes applies to the American market; JacDonking restaurants in India, where large portions of the population are Hindu, use potatoes that have not been treated with animal fat.) JacDonking did not mention their use of animal fat in processing the potatoes in their 1994 advertising campaign. In 2000, the public learned that JacDonking's potatoes had been treated with animal fat prior to being fried in vegetable oil. As a result, many customers are outraged. Among them is a class of Hindus who feel their souls (atman) have been tainted by the animal products they have unwittingly ingested. Also outraged are nonreligious vegetarians who feel very strongly about not eating any animal tissue. A third group are health-conscious eaters who sought to avoid cholesterol by eating JacDonking's fries.

Assume that the advertising campaign contained a material misrepresentation for which JacDonking may be held liable.

1. What remedies, if any, might each of these groups recover? (If the remedies are identical regardless of the reason for their objections, you need not repeat the analysis for each group.)

2. The ads also may violate laws governing false or misleading advertising or unfair business practices. Consider researching the statutes applicable in your jurisdiction to see if they provide additional or different remedies.

3. If the ads violate regulatory laws, the laws may not provide a private cause of action. If the state unfair trade practice act in your jurisdiction can only be enforced by the state attorney general's office, what if any action might you take in this regard?

I. DEFAMATION

PROBLEM

Consider the following statement of facts from an 1890 case:

> The appellant, an unmarried young lady, about 20 years of age, who sues by her father, as her next friend, alleges that the appellee falsely, maliciously, and with a design to injure her standing in society, and to bring her into public ridicule, shame, and disgrace, and to break off a marriage agreement existing between her and Charles Bean, a person altogether eligible, spoke of her, in the presence and hearing of quite a number of persons, in substance, these slanderous words: "Boys, I have a damned hard tale on Cordie Hardin. I will tell you after dinner. "After dinner he said: "Cordie Hardin went to the store of Chris Pauley to buy some groceries, and while Chris Pauley was waiting on her she let a big fart that was heard all over the house. Two or three young men being present, Chris Pauley

> looked at them and laughed, and they walked out of doors. Chris Pauley having fixed up the groceries, she took them, left the house and got on her horse, and forgot her gloves. She got down, and came back into the store. He supposed she was demoralized by what she had done, the fact being impressed on her mind so strongly. She said when she came back into the store: 'Mr. Pauley, did you see anything of that fart I let in here a while ago?' His reply was 'No, but I smelt it damned strong.' Boys, ain't that a damned hard one on her?" That the utterance of the foregoing words injured her standing in society, and brought her into public ridicule, shame, disgrace, etc., and caused said Bean, he having heard and believing said report, to break off said engagement.

Hardin v. Harshfield, 12 S.W. 779 (Ky. 1890). Assuming that the plaintiff's factual allegations are accurate, has the defendant defamed the plaintiff? If so, what damages would be appropriate? What are the defendant's strongest arguments against recovery?

GIBSON V. PHILIP MORRIS, INC.

685 N.E.2d 638.

JUSTICE HOPKINS delivered the opinion of the court:

Defendants, Philip Morris, Inc. (Philip Morris), Edward Giancola, Beverly Brock, and Charles J. Robinson (collectively defendants), appeal the trial court's judgment and award of both compensatory and punitive damages in favor of plaintiff, Randy Gibson, on his complaint for defamation. Defendants contend that, in this bench trial, plaintiff failed to prove the elements of defamation and that the trial court erred in awarding both compensatory and punitive damages. We affirm for the reasons set forth below.

FACTS

Plaintiff testified that, on January 24, 1983, he was hired by Giancola, a division manager, as a sales representative for Philip Morris. Plaintiff was promoted to division manager in June 1989. As division manager, plaintiff often kept incentive items in his garage for distribution to his sales representatives. In July 1989, plaintiff was demoted for reasons unrelated to this appeal, and Giancola again became plaintiff's immediate supervisor when he resumed plaintiff's former position of division manager. On November 20, 1989, plaintiff was discharged by Giancola for "falsification and selling incentive items." The falsification allegation was based upon plaintiff's alleged failure to report a change in his work schedule on his daily activity report (DAR) on two separate occasions. The allegation of selling incentive items was based upon Brock's, Robinson's, and Jim Lumbattis's written statements to Giancola, wherein they alleged they saw Marlboro belt buckles (a Philip Morris incentive item) offered for sale at a yard sale at plaintiff's home in August 1988. Plaintiff filed a complaint against defendants, claiming wrongful discharge and defamation based upon Brock's and Robinson's written statements.

* * *

The trial court ruled against plaintiff on his wrongful discharge cause of action but ruled for him on his defamation cause of action and awarded plaintiff $15,000 for lost wages, $100,000 for lost benefits at $20,000 per year for five years, $100,000 for personal humiliation, mental anguish, and suffering, and $1,000,000 for punitive damages. It is from this order that defendants appeal.

ANALYSIS

Defendants contend that plaintiff failed to prove his cause of action for defamation in four respects: (1) that Brock's and Robinson's statements were true, not false, or that the innocent construction rule applied, (2) that, if the statements were defamatory, there was no publication of the statements, (3) that the defamatory statements were qualifiedly privileged and were not made with actual malice, and (4) that plaintiff suffered no injury. Defendants also contend that the court erred in awarding compensatory and punitive damages for the defamation.

To prove a claim of defamation, a plaintiff must show that the defendant made a false statement concerning plaintiff, that there was an unprivileged publication of the defamatory statement to a third party by defendant, and that plaintiff was damaged. Statements can be either defamatory *per quod, i.e.,* requiring extrinsic facts to explain the defamatory character of the statements, or defamatory *per se.* Four categories of statements are considered defamatory *per se:* (1) words that impute the commission of a criminal offense, (2) words that impute infection with a loathsome communicable disease, (3) words that impute an inability to perform or want of integrity in the discharge of duties of office or employment, or (4) words that prejudice a party, or impute lack of ability, in his or her trade, profession, or business. Even if a statement is defamatory, it may not be regarded as defamatory *per se* if the statement is *reasonably* capable of an innocent construction. It is a question of law whether a statement is subject to an innocent construction. A court is not required to strain to find an unnatural but possibly innocent meaning to determine that the innocent construction rule applies. In addition to these principles, we are compelled to view all the evidence and the inferences to be drawn therefrom in the light most favorable to the winner, the plaintiff.

Defendants contend that the "gist" of Giancola's report was true or, alternatively, that the statements are subject to an innocent construction in that it was true that plaintiff "offered for sale" the incentive items even if he did not sell them, which is dischargeable conduct under Philip Morris's policies. * * *

* * * [U]nder the circumstances presented here, Brock's and Robinson's statements could have been found false by implication and could have been found to have been written in such a manner as to impute plaintiff with a want of integrity (theft of company property) in the discharge of his employment, the third category of defamation *per se.*

Further, Brock's and Robinson's statements are not subject to the innocent construction rule, application of which would remove the statements from the defamation *per se* category. We cannot see that there is any construction of the statements other than what is actually said, that incentive items were offered for sale at a yard sale at plaintiff's home, which, if true, violates Philip Morris's employment policy. The innocent construction rule does not apply within this context. Thus, the trial court properly found that Brock's and Robinson's statements were defamatory *per se.*

Next, defendants contend that plaintiff's cause of action fails because there was no publication of the statements, other than internally within the corporation. Defendants assert that interoffice reports within a corporation are only the corporation talking to itself and do not constitute publication. In support of their argument, defendants cite to numerous cases in other jurisdictions. None of these cases are binding on this court.

* * * [The court here determined that the statements were not privileged.]

Next, defendants contend that plaintiff failed to prove any injury from the defamation. Defendants argue that plaintiff's loss of employment was not a compensable injury for the defamation because plaintiff would have been rightfully discharged for the falsification of his DARs alone. The supreme court stated in *Bryson* that if a statement falls into one of the actionable *per se* categories, a plaintiff, in order to recover, need not plead or prove actual damage to his reputation, and injury to a plaintiff's reputation is presumed. *Bryson,* 174 Ill.2d at 87. We determined previously that plaintiff's cause of action fell into one of the categories of defamation *per se.* Thus, whether plaintiff could have been discharged for other reasons is irrelevant to whether he proved injury for his defamation cause of action. Injury to plaintiff's reputation is presumed, and the only facts that plaintiff had to prove in his defamation *per se* cause of action were that the statements made against him were false and that the statements were an unprivileged publication. The plaintiff made such proof.

We next consider defendants' arguments regarding damages. Defendants assert that the award of compensatory damages was erroneous because (a) the statements were defamatory *per quod,* which does not allow for the type of damage alleged, *i.e.,* damage to health, mental anguish, and general economic loss, (b) the damages flowed from plaintiff's discharge, which was proper, and not from the defamation, and (c) the damages were based on speculation and did not bear a reasonable relation to any loss suffered by plaintiff. Having already determined earlier in this opinion that plaintiff proved that Brock's and Robinson's statements were defamatory *per se,* we need not discuss defendants' contention that the damages awarded were inappropriate for defamation *per quod.*

Defendants contend that because plaintiff's compensatory damages flowed from his discharge, which the trial court deemed proper, and not from the defamation, there was no causation between the defamation and the discharge, and the court erred in awarding compensatory damages based upon plaintiff's discharge. * * * We disagree with defendants that no damages can be awarded for discharge if there is any reason, other than the defamation, that substantiates the discharge. This would defeat the purpose of allowing an action for defamation. Further, if there were legitimate reasons to discharge plaintiff, why defame his character to discharge him? The process which led to plaintiff's discharge commenced with the defamatory statements, giving credence to the inference that, if the statements had not been given, plaintiff would not have come under scrutiny for possible discharge.

The award of damages for defamation is an unsettled area of law. In Illinois, actual damages need not be pleaded or proved in a defamation *per se* action, as damage is presumed. The Restatement (Second) of Torts, sections 620 to 623 (1977), sets forth the types of damages recoverable in a defamation lawsuit. The Restatement (Second) of Torts states that damages for defamation *per se* include nominal damages, general damages for harm to the plaintiff's reputation, damages for special harm that a plaintiff alleges and proves he has sustained through the conduct of third persons, and damages for mental suffering and resulting bodily harm. Restatement (Second) of Torts, § 620, Scope Note, at 317 (1977). The law on damages for defamation *per se* in Illinois corresponds to the Restatement (Second) of Torts. Presumed damages, in Illinois, are damages for economic loss ("special damages"), damages for mental suffering, personal humiliation, and impairment of personal and professional reputation and standing in the community. Presumed damages are based upon the rationale that it is often extremely difficult, if not impossible, to present evidence to support an award of compensatory damages based upon the actual harm sustained.

Plaintiff's damages for lost wages and lost benefits are "special damages," *i.e.,* pecuniary losses, which are presumed and need not be proved. In addition, the evidence supported the award. Plaintiff proved that his annual salary with Philip Morris at the time of his discharge was $39,500 and that he was unemployed for almost seven months. Plaintiff's records showed that he earned $28,596 in 1990. With regard to plaintiff's lost benefits, the exhibits admitted at trial revealed that plaintiff's benefits with Philip Morris were approximately $20,000 per year. Plaintiff testified that none of his subsequent positions equalled his benefits package at Philip Morris, most notably his pension and profit-sharing plan. The court calculated the lost benefits at $20,000 per year for five years. Defendants offered no evidence to contradict plaintiff's evidence. Thus, this evidence, if believed, supports the trial court's award of $115,000 for pecuniary loss.

The court also awarded plaintiff $100,000 for "personal humiliation, mental anguish and suffering." Again, damages for the elements of personal humiliation, mental anguish, and suffering are presumed damages, not easily quantifiable. At trial, plaintiff testified that he was unable to sleep as a result of his discharge and that he was afraid he would not be able to provide for his family. Plaintiff's wife confirmed these problems and stated that plaintiff sought medical help. A friend of plaintiff's, Jack Stork, testified that plaintiff was devastated and was not the same person after his discharge. This evidence was uncontradicted and supported plaintiff's claim for emotional distress, and the court's award of $100,000 for this element of damages is affirmed.

Lastly, defendants claim that the award of $1,000,000 in punitive damages from defendant Philip Morris violated their substantive and procedural due process rights and that the award was not supported by the evidence. In *Bryson,* our supreme court stated that the issue of the award of punitive damages in the absence of actual malice has not been considered yet as a matter of State law, and the court declined to address this issue as it was not raised or briefed by either party. There is a clear inference that if "actual malice" exists, punitive damages would be appropriate.

* * *

Here, the trial court determined that $1,000,000 in punitive damages was needed to adequately bring this matter to defendant Philip Morris's attention. The trial court observed the demeanor and attitude of plaintiff's coemployees and his supervisors within the Phillip Morris corporate structure. The trial court observed defendants' efforts to exculpate the effects of defendants' conduct toward plaintiff. Defendants failed to investigate Brock's and Robinson's defamatory statements fully and acted with reckless disregard of plaintiff's reputation. The statements were not the result of an investigation but were gratuitous gossip maliciously conjured into a reason for discharge. This evidence supports a determination that defendant Philip Morris's actions constituted "actual malice," and we affirm the trial court's award of punitive damages.

CONCLUSION

For the foregoing reasons, the judgment of the circuit court of Madison County is affirmed.

Affirmed.

NOTES AND QUESTIONS

1. As this court holds, where a plaintiff succeeds in proving defamation *per se*, the jury is permitted to award presumed damages—that is, an amount of damages for harm to the plaintiff's reputation without any evidence of the plaintiff's actual loss in that regard. In addition to presumed damages, the plaintiff may also collect proven pecuniary loss and damages for emotional distress. Dan B. Dobbs, Law of Remedies § 7.3(2) (2d ed. 1993). The law regarding presumed damages varies according to jurisdiction. Many states have passed statutes or created common law proscribing the recovery of presumed damages under certain circumstances—for example, most states prohibit the recovery of presumed damages against a media defendant if the defendant printed a retraction. *Id.*

In an action for defamation *per quod*, a plaintiff must prove pecuniary damages in order to complete the cause of action. If the plaintiff succeeds in doing so, the plaintiff may then also recover presumed damages and damages for emotional distress. *Id.*

2. Some jurisdictions have also recognized categories of *per se* defamation for "imputing unchastity to a woman," *see, e.g.*, Tacket v. Delco Remy Division of General Motors Corp., 937 F.2d 1201 (7th Cir. 1991), and "imputing homosexuality." *See, e.g.*, Matherson v. Marchello, 473 N.Y.S.2d 998 (N.Y. Sup. Ct., App. Div. 1984). Why do you suppose these categories (and the ones listed in *Gibson*) arose? Might the award of presumed damages for these categories hurt the social interests sought to be protected? Might these categories have other counterproductive results?

3. Evidence of the plaintiff's preexisting bad reputation is relevant to the jury's calculation of presumed damages. Similarly, a plaintiff's damages might be mitigated by actions of the defendant to reduce defamatory harm—for example, by publishing a retraction.

And now for the remainder of *Hardin v. Harshfield*:

> In an action to recover special damages for the utterance of words not actionable in themselves it is not necessary that the words of themselves should convey the meaning of an injurious imputation. It is sufficient if the words used were intended to convey such imputation, and did in fact convey it to the minds of the persons who heard them, and had the effect intended. All that is required is that the words used, coupled with the manner,

tone, look, or wink of the person using them, are capable of conveying the meaning intended. For instance, to say of a woman that she was fond of showing her petticoat to men, coupled with such manner, tone, gesture, or wink as to convey to the minds of the speaker's listeners that the woman was lewd or lascivious, and such meaning was so intended, and the listeners did in fact so understand it, such language, if uttered falsely and maliciously, and did degrade the woman in public estimation, would be actionable. To falsely and maliciously say of a physician, lawyer, or shoemaker that he is a quack, jackleg, or cobbler, entitles the person thus spoken of to damages commensurate with the injury that such language has done his profession or trade. The reason is much stronger for protecting defenseless and helpless woman against false and malicious imputations, that tend to humiliate and degrade them in society. Kentucky manhood demands that they should be protected, and the guilty party mulcted in damages commensurate with the humiliation and degradation thus inflicted. The language, taken all together, attributed to the appellee, was capable of making the impression upon the hearers that the appellant was an immodest, indiscreet, coarse, vulgar young woman, which, if so understood and believed, would lower and degrade her in the estimation of good and refined society. If any man had engaged to marry her because of her supposed modesty, discretion, and exemplary conduct, such a report, if believed by him, would doubtless, and should, cause him to break the engagement. It is alleged that the appellee falsely and maliciously used said language for the purpose of humiliating and degrading the appellant, etc., and of breaking off said engagement, and it did have the desired effect; and, as said, the language, taking it all together, was capable of producing such an effect. The person speaking the words and intending them to have an injurious effect, it is enough that such words, taken all together, have, in common sense and reason, some connection with the damage said to have ensued from them; but it is not enough that the unwarrantable caprice of some person has caused a damage to result from them which the speaker did not intend, and had no reason to apprehend. It is said that, the accusation being false, Bean, though believing it, and acting on that belief, wrongfully broke the engagement. If the words had been true, as just intimated, Bean would have been perfectly justified in breaking off the engagement, provided he had made it in consideration of the belief that the appellant was a modest, discreet, and innocent young lady. It turns out, however, that the words, the truth of which he believed and acted on as true, were false and slanderous, and Bean made a mistake in believing them to be true; but appellee spoke them, as is alleged, for the purpose that they should be believed, and produce a damaging effect upon the standing and marital prospects of the appellant; and it does not lie in his mouth to say that Bean should not have believed his slanderous language to be true. He caused the wrongful impression to be made that brought such serious consequences upon the appellant, and is responsible to her for it.

It is also said that there is no allegation that the appellee uttered this language in the presence of Bean, and, if other persons repeated the appellee's language to Bean, which caused him to break off the engagement, the appellee is not responsible, unless he authorized such person to repeat the language. There are two objections to this proposition: *First*. It would allow the appellee to invent and utter a slander in the hearing of persons, and if they spread it far and wide, believing it to be true, the appellee would not be responsible for their utterances thus made. It cannot be true that a person may invent and utter language damaging to another, and say to the other that "the person who acted on these utterances did not get them from me, but from the persons that heard me speak them; therefore I am not liable to you for the injury." It seems to us that the reply that "you were the author of this language, and the persons repeating simply acted as your mouth-piece, and the foundation of the person's action is traceable to you, and you are responsible for it. Besides, *second*, you did not utter this language to these persons in confidence, rather with an injunction not to repeat it, but you uttered it as though they were at perfect liberty to repeat it; and you, by thus uttering it, authorized them to repeat it, and you doubtless intended them to repeat it, so you are responsible for any damage that has ensued from uttering said language." The judgment is reversed, with directions for further proceedings consistent with this opinion.

NOTES AND QUESTIONS

1. Is *Hardin* an action for libel or slander? *Per se* or *per quod*?

2. Do you agree with this court's assessment of whether the defendant's words were defamatory? Do the court's conclusions rest on dated notions of gender and gender relations?

3. Is this a case in which presumed damages for harm to reputation is (or should be) appropriate?

The Louisville Sentinel runs a series of articles alleging corruption in Louisville's Metro Government. In its series, the Sentinel makes repeated and serious allegations accusing Louisville Mayor Rambo H. Royster of corruption and marital infidelity. Specifically, the Sentinel alleged that

Mayor Rambo received large campaign contributions from major road contractors, and repaid them with large governmental contracts. In addition, the Sentinel alleged that Mayor Rambo, a married man with three children, was having an affair with an exotic dancer. You work for a local law firm that Mayor Rambo has approached for advice. What remedies are available to him? How would you advise the Mayor to proceed? As you formulate an answer, consider the following cases.

NEW YORK TIMES CO. V. SULLIVAN

376 U.S. 254, 84 S.Ct. 710, 11 L.Ed.2d 686 (1964).

MR. JUSTICE BRENNAN delivered the opinion of the Court.

We are required in this case to determine [the] extent to which the constitutional protections for speech and press limit a State's power to award damages in a libel action brought by a public official against critics of his official conduct.

Respondent L.B. Sullivan is one [of] three elected Commissioners of the City of Montgomery, Alabama. [His duties involve] supervision of the Police Department, Fire Department, Department of Cemetery and Department of Scales. He brought this civil libel action against [petitioners], who are Negroes and Alabama clergymen, [and] the New York Times Company, a New York corporation which publishes the New York Times, a daily newspaper. [An Alabama jury] awarded him $500,000 [against] all the petitioners, and the Supreme Court of Alabama affirmed.

[Respondent alleges that he was] libeled by statements in a full-page advertisement [in] the New York Times. . . . Entitled "Heed Their Rising Voices," the advertisement began by stating that "As the whole world knows[,] thousands of Southern Negro students are engaged in widespread non-violent demonstrations in positive affirmation of the right to live in human dignity as guaranteed by the U.S. Constitution and the Bill of Rights." It went on to charge that "in their efforts to uphold these guarantees, they are being met by an unprecedented wave of terror by those who would deny and negate that document which the whole world looks upon as setting the pattern for modern [freedom]." Succeeding paragraphs [illustrate] the "wave of terror" by describing certain alleged events. The text concluded with an appeal for funds for three purposes: support of the student movement, "the struggle for the right-to-vote," and the legal defense of Dr. Martin Luther King, Jr., leader of the movement, against a perjury indictment then pending in Montgomery.

The text appeared over the names of 64 persons, many widely known for their activities in public affairs, religion, trade unions, and the performing arts. Below these names, and under a line reading "We in the south who are struggling daily for dignity and freedom warmly endorse this appeal," appeared the names of the four individual petitioners and of

16 other persons, all but two of whom were identified as clergymen in various Southern cities. The advertisement was signed at the bottom of the page by the "Committee to Defend Martin Luther King and the Struggle for Freedom in the South," and the officers of the Committee were listed.

[T]he third [paragraph] and a portion of the sixth were the basis of respondent's claim of libel. They read as follows: Third paragraph: "In Montgomery, Alabama, after students sang 'My Country, 'Tis of Thee' on the State Capitol steps, their leaders were expelled from school, and truckloads of police armed with shotguns and tear-gas ringed the Alabama State College Campus. When the entire student body protested to state authorities by refusing to re-register, their dining hall was padlocked in an attempt to starve them into submission." Sixth paragraph: "Again and again the Southern violators have answered Dr. King's peaceful protests with intimidation and violence. They have bombed his home almost killing his wife and child. They have assaulted his person. They have arrested him seven times—for 'speeding,' 'loitering' and similar 'offenses.' And now they have charged him with 'perjury'—a felony under which they could imprison him for ten [years]."

Although neither of these statements mentions respondent by name, he contended that the word "police" in the third paragraph referred to him as the Montgomery Commissioner who supervised the Police Department, so that he was being accused of "ringing" the campus with police. He further claimed that the paragraph would be read as imputing to the police, and hence to him, the padlocking of the dining hall in order to starve the students into submission. As to the sixth paragraph, he contended that since arrests are ordinarily made by the police, the statement "They have arrested [Dr. King] seven times" would be read as referring to him; he further contended that the "They" who did the arresting would be equated with the "They" who committed the other described acts and with the "Southern violators." Thus, he argued, the paragraph would be read as accusing the Montgomery police, and hence him, of answering Dr. King's protests with "intimidation and violence," bombing his home, assaulting his person, and charging him with perjury. Respondent and six other Montgomery residents testified that they read some or all of the statements as referring to him in his capacity as Commissioner.

It is uncontroverted that some of the statements contained in the two paragraphs were not accurate descriptions of events which occurred in Montgomery. Although Negro students staged a demonstration on the State Capital steps, they sang the National Anthem and not "My Country, 'Tis of Thee." Although nine students were expelled[,] this was not for leading the demonstration at the Capitol, but for demanding service at a lunch counter in the Montgomery County Courthouse on another day. Not the entire student body, but most of it, had protested the expulsion, not by refusing to register, but by boycotting classes on a single day; virtually all the students did register for the ensuing semester. The campus dining hall was not padlocked on any occasion, and the only students who may have been barred from eating there were the few who had neither signed a preregistration application nor requested temporary meal tickets. Although the police were deployed near the campus in large numbers on three occasions, they did [not] "ring" the campus, and they were not called to the campus in connection with the demonstration on the State Capitol steps[.] Dr. King had not been arrested seven times, but only four; and although he claimed to have been assaulted some years earlier in connection with his arrest for loitering outside a courtroom, one of the officers who made the arrest denied that there was such an assault.

On the premise that the charges in the sixth paragraph could be read as referring to him, respondent was allowed to prove that he had not participated in the events described. Although Dr. King's home had in fact been bombed twice when his wife and child were there, both of these occasions antedated respondent's tenure as Commissioner, and the police were not only not implicated in the bombings, but had made every effort to apprehend those who were. Three of Dr. King's four arrests took place before respondent became Commissioner. Although Dr. King had in fact been indicted (he was subsequently acquitted) on two counts of perjury, each of which carried a possible five-year sentence, respondent had nothing to do with procuring the indictment.

Respondent made no effort to prove that he suffered actual pecuniary loss as a result of the alleged libel.[3] One of his witnesses, a former employer, testified that if he had believed the statements, he doubted whether he "would want to be associated with anybody who would be a party to such things that are stated in that ad," and that he would not re-employ respondent if he believed "that he allowed the Police Department to do the things that the paper say he did." But neither this witness nor any [other] testified that [he] actually believed the statements in their supposed reference to respondent.

The cost of the advertisement was approximately $4800, and it was published by the Times upon an order from a New York advertising agency acting for the signatory Committee. The agency submitted the advertisement with a letter [certifying] that the persons whose names appeared on the advertisement had given their [permission]. The manager of the Advertising [Department] testified that he had approved the advertisement [because] he knew nothing to cause him to believe that

[3] Approximately 394 copies of the edition of the Times containing the advertisement were circulated in Alabama. Of these, about 35 copies were distributed in Montgomery County. The total circulation of the Times for that day was approximately 650,000 copies.

anything in it was false, and because it bore the endorsement of "a number of people who are well known and whose reputation" he "had no reason to question." Neither he nor anyone else at the Times made an effort to confirm the accuracy of the advertisement, either by checking it against recent Times news stories [or] by any other means.

[Because] of the importance of the constitutional issues involved, we granted [certiorari]. We reverse the judgment. . . .

II.

Under Alabama law[, o]nce "libel per se" has been established, the defendant has no defense as to stated facts unless he can persuade the jury that they were true in all their particulars. His privilege of "fair comment" for expressions of opinion depends on the truth of the facts upon which the comment is based. Unless he can discharge the burden of proving truth, general damages are presumed, and may be awarded without proof of pecuniary injury. A showing of actual malice is apparently a prerequisite to recovery of punitive damages, [and] defendant may [forestall] a punitive award by a retraction meeting the statutory requirements. Good motives and belief in truth do not negate an inference of malice, but are relevant only in mitigation of punitive damages[.]

The question before us is whether this rule of liability, as applied to an action brought by a public official against critics of his official conduct, abridges the freedom of speech and of the press that is guaranteed by the First and Fourteenth Amendments.

Respondent relies heavily [on] statements of this Court to the effect that the Constitution does not protect libelous publications. Those statements do not foreclose our inquiry here. . . . The general proposition that freedom of expression upon public questions is secured by the First Amendment has long been settled by our decisions. The constitutional [safeguard] "was fashioned to assure unfettered interchange of ideas for the bringing about of political and social changes desired by the people." "The maintenance of the opportunity for free political discussion to the end that government may be responsive to the will of the people and that changes may be obtained by lawful means, an opportunity essential to the security of the Republic, is a fundamental principle of our constitutional system." *Stromberg v. California*, 283 U.S. 359, 369. . . .

Thus we consider this case against the background of a profound national commitment to the principle that debate on public issues should be uninhibited, robust, and wide-open, and that it may well include vehement, caustic, and sometimes unpleasantly sharp attacks on government and public officials. The present advertisement, as an expression of grievance and protest on one of the major public issues of our time, would seem clearly to qualify for the constitutional protection.

The question is whether it forfeits that protection by the falsity of some of its factual statements and by its alleged defamation of respondent.

Authoritative interpretations of the First Amendment guarantees have consistently refused to recognize an exception for any test of truth—whether administered by judges, juries, or administrative officials—and especially one that puts the burden of proving truth on the speaker. The constitutional protection does not turn upon "the truth, popularity, or social utility of the ideas and beliefs which are offered." [E]rroneous statement is inevitable in free debate, and [it] must be protected if the freedoms of expression are to have the "breathing space" that they "need [to] survive," *N.A.A.C.P. v. Button*, 371 U.S. 415, 433. . . .

Injury to official reputation [affords] no more warrant for repressing speech that would otherwise be free than does factual error. Where judicial officers are involved, this Court has held that concern for the dignity and reputation of the courts does not justify the punishment as criminal contempt of criticism of the judge or his decision. This is true even though the utterance contains "half-truths" and "misinformation." Such repression can be justified, if at all, only by a clear and present danger of the obstruction of justice. If judges are to be treated as "men of fortitude, able to thrive in a hardy climate," surely the same must be true of other government officials, such as elected city commissioners. Criticism of their official conduct does not lose its constitutional protection merely because it is effective criticism and hence diminishes their official reputations.

If neither factual error nor defamatory content suffices to remove the constitutional shield from criticism of official conduct, the combination of the two elements is no less inadequate. . . .

What a State may not constitutionally bring about by means of a criminal statute is likewise beyond the reach of its civil law of libel. The fear of damage awards under a rule such as that invoked by the Alabama courts here may be markedly more inhibiting than the fear of prosecution under a criminal statute. [The] judgment awarded in this case—without the need for any proof of actual pecuniary loss—was one thousand times greater than the maximum fine provided by the Alabama criminal [libel] statute, and one hundred times greater than that provided by the Sedition Act. And since there is no double-jeopardy limitation applicable to civil lawsuits, this is not the only judgment that may be awarded against petitioners for the same publication. Whether or not a newspaper can survive a succession of such judgments, the pall of fear and timidity imposed upon those who would give voice to public criticism is an atmosphere in which the First Amendment freedoms cannot survive. Plainly the Alabama law of civil libel is "a form of regulation that creates hazards to protected freedoms markedly greater than those that attend reliance upon the criminal law."

The state rule of law is not saved by its allowance of the defense of truth. [A] rule compelling the critic of official conduct to guarantee the truth of all his factual assertions—and to do so on pain of libel judgments virtually unlimited in amount—leads to a comparable "self-censorship." Allowance of the defense of truth, with the burden of proving it on the defendant, does not mean that only false speech will be deterred. . . . Under such a rule, would-be critics of official conduct may be deterred from voicing their criticism, even though it is believed to be true and even though it is in fact true, because of doubt whether it can be proved in court or fear of the expense of having to do so. They tend to make only statements which "steer far wider of the unlawful zone." The rule thus dampens the vigor and limits the variety of public debate. It is inconsistent with the First and Fourteenth Amendments.

The constitutional guarantees require, we think, a federal rule that prohibits a public official from recovering damages for a defamatory falsehood relating to his official conduct unless he proves that the statement was made with "actual malice"—that is, with knowledge that it was false or with reckless disregard of whether it was false or not. . . .

Such a privilege for criticism of official conduct is appropriately analogous to the protection accorded a public official when he is sued for libel by a private citizen. In *Barr v. Matteo*, 360 U.S. 564, 575, this Court held the utterance of a federal official to be absolutely privileged if made "within the outer perimeter" of his duties. [The] threat of damage suits would otherwise "inhibit the fearless, vigorous, and effective administration of policies of government" and "dampen the ardor of all but the most resolute, or the most irresponsible, in the unflinching discharge of their duties." Analogous considerations support the privilege for the citizen-critic of government. [It] would give public servants an unjustified preference over the public they serve, if critics of official conduct did not have a fair equivalent of the immunity granted to the officials themselves. [We] conclude that such a privilege is required by the First and Fourteenth Amendments.

[While] Alabama law apparently requires proof of actual malice for an award of punitive damages, where general damages are concerned malice is "presumed." Such a presumption is inconsistent with the federal rule. . . .

Since respondent may seek a new trial, [considerations] of effective judicial administration require us to review the evidence in the present record to determine whether it could constitutionally support a judgment for [respondent]. We must "make an independent examination of the whole record," so as to assure ourselves that the judgment does not constitute a forbidden intrusion on the field of free expression.

Applying these standards, we consider that the proof presented to show actual malice lacks the convincing clarity which the constitutional standard demands, and hence [would] not constitutionally sustain the judgment for respondent under the proper rule of law. [Even] assuming that [the individual respondents authorized] the use of their names on the advertisement, there was no evidence [that] they were aware of any erroneous statements or were in any way reckless in that regard. The judgment against them is thus without constitutional support.

As to the Times, we similarly conclude that the facts do not support a finding of actual malice. The statement by the Times' Secretary [that] he thought the advertisement was "substantially correct," affords no [warrant] for the Alabama Supreme Court's conclusion [of bad faith and maliciousness]. The statement does not indicate malice at the time of the publication; even if the advertisement was not "substantially correct" [that] opinion was at least a reasonable one, and there was no evidence to impeach the witness' good faith in holding it. The Times' failure to retract upon respondent's demand [is] likewise not adequate evidence of malice. . . . Whether or not a failure to retract may ever constitute such evidence, there are two reasons why it does not here. First, the letter written by the Times reflected a reasonable doubt on its part as to whether the advertisement could reasonably be taken to refer to respondent at all. Second, it was not a final refusal, since it asked for [an] explanation—a request that respondent chose to ignore. . . .

[T]here is evidence that the Times published the advertisement without checking its accuracy against the news stories in the Times' own files. The mere presence of the stories in the files does not, of course, establish that the Times "knew" the advertisement was false, since the state of mind required for actual malice [involves] the persons [having] responsibility [for] publication of the advertisement. With respect to the failure of those persons to make the check, the record shows that they relied upon their knowledge of the good reputation of many of those whose names were listed as sponsors of the advertisement, and upon the letter from A. Philip Randolph, known to them as a responsible individual, certifying that the use of the names was authorized. There was testimony that the persons handling the advertisement saw nothing in it that would render it unacceptable under the Times' policy of rejecting advertisements containing "attacks of a personal character"; their failure to reject it on this ground was not unreasonable. We think the evidence against the Times supports at most a finding of negligence in failing to discover the misstatements, and is constitutionally insufficient to show the recklessness that is required for a finding of actual malice.

[The] judgment of the Supreme Court of Alabama is reversed and the case is remanded to that court for further proceedings not inconsistent with this opinion.

Reversed and remanded.

MR. JUSTICE BLACK, with whom MR. JUSTICE DOUGLAS joins (concurring).

[T]he Federal Constitution has dealt with this deadly danger to the press in the only way possible without leaving the free press open to destruction—by granting the press an absolute immunity for criticism of the way public officials do their public duty. . . .

MR. JUSTICE GOLDBERG, with whom MR. JUSTICE DOUGLAS joins (concurring in the result).

[In] a democratic society, one who assumes to act for the citizens in an executive, legislative, or judicial capacity must expect that his official acts will be commented upon and criticized. Such criticism cannot, in my opinion, be muzzled or deterred by the courts at the instance of public officials under the label of libel. . . .

NEAR V. STATE OF MINNESOTA

283 U.S. 697, 51 S.Ct. 625, 75 L.Ed. 1357 (1931).

MR. CHIEF JUSTICE HUGHES delivered the opinion of the Court.

[The] county attorney of Hennepin county brought this action to enjoin the publication of what was described as a "malicious, scandalous and defamatory newspaper, magazine or other periodical," known as The Saturday Press, published by the defendants in the city of Minneapolis. The complaint alleged that the defendants, on September 24, 1927, and on eight subsequent dates in October and November, 1927, published and circulated editions of that periodical which were "largely devoted to malicious, scandalous and defamatory articles" [which] charged, in substance, that a Jewish gangster was in control of gambling, bootlegging, and racketeering in Minneapolis, and that law enforcing officers and agencies were not energetically performing their duties. [There] is no question but that the articles made serious accusations against the public officers named and others in connection with the prevalence of crimes and the failure to expose and punish them.

[The trial court issued a TRO] forbidding the defendants to publish, circulate, or have in their possession any editions of the periodical from September 24, 1927, to November 19, 1927, inclusive, and from publishing, circulating or having in their possession, "any future editions of said The Saturday Press" and "any publication, known by any other name whatsoever containing malicious, scandalous and defamatory matter of the kind alleged in plaintiff's complaint herein or otherwise." [Following a hearing, the court issued a permanent injunction.]

[T]he operation and effect of the statute in substance is that public authorities may bring the owner or publisher of a newspaper or periodical before a judge upon a charge of conducting a business of publishing scandalous and defamatory matter—in particular that the matter consists of charges against public officers of official dereliction—and, unless the owner or publisher is able and disposed to bring competent evidence to satisfy the judge that the charges are true and are published with good motives and for justifiable ends, his newspaper or periodical is suppressed and further publication is made punishable as a contempt. This is of the essence of censorship.

The question is whether a statute authorizing such proceedings in restraint of publication is consistent with the conception of the liberty of the press as historically conceived and guaranteed. In determining the extent of the constitutional protection, it has been generally, if not universally, considered that it is the chief purpose of the guaranty to prevent previous restraints upon publication. The struggle in England, directed against the legislative power of the licenser, resulted in renunciation of the censorship of the press. * * *

The objection has also been made that the principle as to immunity from previous restraint is stated too broadly, if every such restraint is deemed to be prohibited. That is undoubtedly true; the protection even as to previous restraint is not absolutely unlimited. But the limitation has been recognized only in exceptional cases. "When a nation is at war many things that might be said in time of peace are such a hindrance to its effort that their utterance will not be endured so long as men fight and that no Court could regard them as protected by any constitutional right." *Schenck v. United States*, 249 U.S. 47, 52. No one would question but that a government might prevent actual obstruction to its recruiting service or the publication of the sailing dates of transports or the number and location of troops. On similar grounds, the primary requirements of decency may be enforced against obscene publications. * * *

[The] fact that for approximately one hundred and fifty years there has been almost an entire absence of attempts to impose previous restraints upon publications relating to the malfeasance of public officers is significant of the deep-seated conviction that such restraints would violate constitutional right. Public officers, whose character and conduct remain open to debate and free discussion in the press, find their remedies for false accusations in actions under libel laws providing for redress and punishment, and not in proceedings to restrain the publication of newspapers and periodicals. * * *

The importance of this immunity has not lessened. While reckless assaults upon public men, and efforts to bring obloquy upon those who are endeavoring faithfully to discharge official duties, exert a baleful influence and deserve the severest condemnation in public opinion, it cannot be said that this abuse is greater, and it is believed to be less, than that which characterized the period in which our institutions took shape. Meanwhile, the administration of government has become more complex, the opportunities for malfeasance and corruption have multiplied, crime has grown to most serious proportions, and the danger of its protection by unfaithful officials and of the impairment of the fundamental security of life and property by criminal alliances and official neglect, emphasizes the primary need of a vigilant and courageous press, especially in great cities. The fact that the liberty of the press may be abused by miscreant purveyors of scandal does not make any the less necessary the immunity of the press from previous restraint in dealing with official misconduct. Subsequent punishment for such abuses as may exist is the appropriate remedy, consistent with constitutional privilege.

[The] statute in question cannot be justified by reason of the fact that the publisher is permitted to show, before injunction issues, that the matter published is true and is published with good motives and for justifiable ends. If such a statute, authorizing suppression and injunction on such a basis, is constitutionally valid, it would be equally permissible for the Legislature to provide that at any time the publisher of any newspaper could be brought before a court, or even an administrative officer [and] required to produce proof of the truth of his publication, or of what he intended to publish and of his motives, or stand enjoined. If this can be done, the Legislature may provide machinery for determining in the complete exercise of its discretion what are justifiable ends and restrain publication accordingly. And it would be but a step to a complete system of censorship. The recognition of authority to impose previous restraint upon publication in order to protect the community against the circulation of charges of misconduct, and especially of official misconduct, necessarily would carry with it the admission of the authority of the censor against which the constitutional barrier was erected. The preliminary freedom, by virtue of the very reason for its existence, does not depend, as this court has said, on proof of truth.

Equally unavailing is the insistence that the statute is designed to prevent the circulation of scandal which tends to disturb the public peace and to provoke assaults and the commission of crime. Charges of reprehensible conduct, and in particular of official malfeasance, unquestionably create a public scandal, but the theory of the constitutional guaranty is that even a more serious public evil would be caused by authority to prevent publication. * * *

For these reasons we hold the statute, so far as it authorized the proceedings in this action under clause (b) of section 1, to be an infringement of the liberty of the press guaranteed by the Fourteenth Amendment. * * *

Judgment reversed.

MR. JUSTICE BUTLER (dissenting).

[The] distribution of scandalous matter is detrimental to public morals and to the general welfare. It tends to disturb the peace of the community. Being defamatory and malicious, it tends to provoke assaults and the commission of crime. It has no concern with the publication of the truth, with good motives and for justifiable ends. [Defendants] stand before us upon the record as being regularly and customarily engaged in a business of conducting a newspaper sending to the public malicious, scandalous, and defamatory printed matter.

[The] Minnesota statute does not operate as a previous restraint on publication within the proper meaning of that phrase. It does not authorize administrative control in advance such as was formerly exercised by the licensers and censors, but prescribes a remedy to be enforced by a suit in equity. In this case there was previous publication made in the course of the business of regularly producing malicious, scandalous, and defamatory periodicals. [The] restraint authorized is only in respect of continuing to do what has been duly adjudged to constitute a nuisance. [There] is nothing in the statute purporting to prohibit publications that have not been adjudged to constitute a nuisance. It is fanciful to suggest similarity between the granting or enforcement of the decree authorized by this statute to prevent further publication of malicious, scandalous, and defamatory articles and the previous restraint upon the press by licensers as referred to by Blackstone and described in the history of the times to which he alludes.

PROBLEMS

1. In light of the *Near* and *N.Y. Times* cases, would you recommend that Mayor Rambo file suit against the Sentinel for the allegedly defamatory allegations? If so, what relief would you seek?

2. If Mayor Rambo wants to sue the Sentinel, would you be willing to take the case on a contingency fee basis or would you demand an hourly rate?

3. Suppose that, after reading the *Near* and *N.Y. Times* decisions and talking to Mayor Rambo and doing some investigation, you have concluded that the Sentinel's allegations are inaccurate. If the Mayor wants to prove that the Sentinel acted with "actual malice," how would he go about doing so? Would you recommend that the Mayor undertake such a course of action? Is it likely to be cheap or expensive?

4. In light of *Near*, *New York Times*, and *Gertz*, what remedies (if any) are available to the plaintiffs like those in *Near*? How do defamed public officials and public figures vindicate their reputations? What happened to the notion that equity will act when a plaintiff's legal remedies are inadequate?

5. Suppose that, in addition to the Mayor, the road contractor also comes to see you. He believes that the Sentinel's argue suggests that he has

offered illegal bribes to public officials and he wants to sue the Sentinel. What remedies might be available to the contractor? In answering this question, please consider the following case (*Kramer*) and notes.

6. *Schmoldt v. Oakley*, 390 P.2d 882 (Okla. 1964), involved the following facts:

> In 1961 plaintiff sold a new Pontiac automobile to Hans Schmoldt, defendant, delivering with it a warranty covering the first 12,000 miles that the car was driven. There was a transmission failure after the car had been driven approximately 30,000 miles which resulted in expense of $561.00 for repair thereof for which sum defendant made claim to plaintiff, exhibiting him a letter which he prepared to send the Pontiac Division of General Motors Corporation, and unless his claim was honored satisfactorily to him, he would make it known generally in the community that he had been ill treated. Upon the rejection of his claim defendant displayed upon his said Pontiac automobile a sign 7 x 2 ½ feet in size which read: "LIKE TO HAVE A REAL LEMON—BUY THIS PONTIAC BY GENERAL MOTORS Ed 3–4607 FOR DETAILS" and then drove and parked his car upon the street and in the vicinity of plaintiff's place of business. Upon the sign, suspended by strings, defendant hung real lemons.
>
> Plaintiff's petition alleged wrongful interference with plaintiff's business, that he was the only manufacturer's franchised Pontiac dealer in the vicinity, and that defendant's conduct was injurious to his business; that defendant's conduct was motivated by an attempt by defendant to get from plaintiff that to which he was not entitled by resort to conduct which utilized threats, intimidation and coercion.

Given holdings like *Near* and *Kramer*, what remedies are available to plaintiff? Would it matter whether defendant's car was really a "lemon?" But how is the term "lemon" defined? Under these facts, can defendant's car be appropriately labeled a "lemon?" Consider the *Kramer* case and notes.

7. Do domestic relations protective orders implicate prior restraints? Some enjoin communication with the ex-spouse, and many enjoin the individual from parking his/her car in the vicinity of the ex-spouse's new residence. If the car contained a sign, advocating on a matter of public interest, would the presence of the sign render the order illegitimate? Or is the original order valid so long it was issued without regard to the speech? Does the prior restraint have the same effect when it precludes speech for non-speech reasons as when it precludes speech for speech reasons? Consider the following case and notes.

KRAMER V. THOMPSON

947 F.2d 666 (3d Cir. 1991).

BECKER, CIRCUIT JUDGE.

These appeals [present the] question under Pennsylvania law of the ability of a judge to enjoin future libels and to compel the retraction of past libels. * * *

[The] parties' relationship began in July 1982, when Thompson retained Kramer to bring a securities fraud claim against Thompson's former broker, Prudential–Bache, Inc. [I]n the fall of 1985, Kramer was contacted by an F.B.I. agent to whom Thompson previously had complained about his investment losses at Prudential–Bache. The agent asked Kramer whether the stocks at issue were completely worthless. Kramer responded that Thompson had purchased the stocks for roughly $120,000 and later had sold them for approximately $15,000. Thus, while informing the agent that Thompson had suffered a very substantial loss, Kramer also informed the agent that technically the stocks were not worthless. When Thompson learned of this conversation, however, he became enraged, and accused Kramer of deliberately dissuading the F.B.I. from investigating the matter. The parties' relationship deteriorated rapidly thereafter and, in October 1985, Thompson discharged Kramer as his counsel.

Seeking to ensure that he ultimately would be compensated for his services, Kramer refused to return the case files to Thompson until the latter agreed to deposit the proceeds of any future judgment or settlement with the court pending resolution of the attorney's fees issue. Thompson would not agree, and Kramer secured an order from the district court which provided that any funds recovered would be placed in escrow, and that the fee dispute would be arbitrated. Kramer then made the case files available to Thompson and his new counsel.

On February 4, 1986, Thompson wrote to the Disciplinary Board of the Pennsylvania Supreme Court (the "Disciplinary Board") alleging that Kramer had failed to represent him effectively in the Prudential–Bache action. At about the same time, Thompson began writing a series of critical and accusatory letters about Kramer to various private attorneys, federal judges, F.B.I. agents, federal and state prosecutors, newspapers, and television stations in the Philadelphia area. With varying degrees of repetition, these letters alleged that Kramer: (1) had "thrown" Thompson's case; (2) had deliberately destroyed certain documents related to the case; (3) had used drugs and was a member of the highly publicized "Yuppie Drug Ring" organized by Philadelphia dentist Lawrence Lavin; (4) was connected to organized crime; and (5) had committed arson on his own car. Kramer demanded a retraction, but Thompson refused.

Kramer thereupon brought a libel action against [Thompson]. [The] court eventually entered a default judgment on the issue of [liability]. [After the judgment was entered], Thompson ceased to write critically about Kramer for approximately two years. In early 1989, however, Thompson became aware of a suit filed by Kramer in federal district court against Mano Arco, a garage that had performed repair work on Kramer's car. Kramer's suit alleged that Mano Arco's negligent workmanship had been responsible for the fire that engulfed his car while it was travelling on the New Jersey Turnpike. Thompson took it upon himself to contact, first by phone and then by letter, the lawyer for Mano Arco. After informing the lawyer of his view that Kramer had committed arson on his own car, Thompson resumed his accusations that Kramer had thrown Thompson's securities fraud case, and that he was involved in the Yuppie Drug Ring and the underworld. Thompson's letter to Mano Arco's attorney purported to [copy] the state Disciplinary Board, the federal judge hearing the case, The Philadelphia Inquirer, the United States Justice Department, and Kramer.

[Kramer then filed the present libel action]. Having determined that Thompson's statements were per se libelous in that they were false and made in reckless disregard of their truth or falsity, the court directed a verdict for Kramer at the close of Kramer's [case]. The court restricted the scope of Thompson's case to evidence relevant to the calculation of compensatory and punitive damages. Heeding the court's suggestion that his only hope for mitigating damages was to demonstrate contrition, Thompson took the witness stand, delivered a grudging and rambling apology, and promised not to publish future defamatory statements. * * *

[The] jury ultimately awarded Kramer $100,000 in compensatory and $38,000 in punitive damages, and the district court entered judgment accordingly on April 10, 1990. The court simultaneously entered a permanent injunction, prohibiting Thompson from making further statements about Kramer of the type adjudged libelous, and ordering him to write letters of retraction to all persons who had received prior libelous communications. * * *

After learning that Thompson had failed to send all the retraction letters required by the court's permanent injunction, Kramer moved to hold Thompson in contempt of court. Although declining to hold Thompson in civil contempt, the district court, inter alia, again ordered him to make the appropriate retractions.

Shortly thereafter, Thompson submitted a petition, which he later amended, seeking leave to appear as amicus curiae in the case of *Matthews v. Freedman*, then pending before this court. *Matthews* involved an appeal by Kramer of sanctions imposed on him by a district court in a matter unrelated to his litigation with Thompson. Thompson's petition contained renewed accusations that Kramer had "thrown" his case, was associated with the Yuppie Drug Ring, and generally was guilty of perjury, forgery, fraud, and extortion. In the petition, Thompson also repudiated the prior retraction letter that the district court had "forced" him to write. Thompson sent copies of his petition to the Disciplinary Board, U.S. Attorney's Office, F.B.I., I.R.S., and lawyers associated with the *Matthews* case.

Kramer filed a second motion to hold Thompson in contempt. This time, the district court declared Thompson in civil contempt of the permanent injunction, and ordered that he be confined and fined $500 per day until he purged himself of contempt by withdrawing all statements and court filings related to the Matthews case. Thompson then drafted, and the court edited and approved, the required letter of withdrawal. The court also ordered Thompson to advise the Clerk of this court [that] he had "admitted under oath in the trial of this matter that he defamed Steven Kramer and promised the jury, before verdict, that he apologized and would not in the future make such statements as were accused as defamatory by plaintiff."

On August 24, 1990, the district court entered an expanded injunction [which] essentially provided Kramer with two forms of equitable relief, in addition to the $138,000 in damages awarded by the jury. First, the court, threatening civil contempt, enjoined Thompson initially from issuing new statements of the type found libelous, and ultimately from contacting anyone with whom Kramer does business. Second, the injunction required Thompson to retract or withdraw various previously issued libelous statements and court filings. * * *

A. Injunction Against Further Defamatory Statements

[Thompson] relies primarily upon *Willing v. Mazzocone*, 482 Pa. 377, 393 A.2d 1155 (1978), which he argues is on all fours with the instant dispute, and which stands for the proposition that the Pennsylvania Constitution does not tolerate an injunction against libelous speech. * * *

In 1968, defendant Helen Willing retained plaintiffs Carl Mazzocone and Charles Quinn, who practiced law together, to represent her in a worker's compensation claim. The two lawyers successfully obtained a settlement for Willing, from which she collected disability benefits for several years. In addition to their fee, Mazzocone and Quinn deducted $150 from the settlement as costs of the case. They claimed, and their records verified, that the money had been paid to one Dr. Robert DeSilverio, a psychiatrist who had been retained to testify on Willing's behalf.

At some point, for an unknown reason (and contrary to all available evidence), Willing came to believe that Mazzocone and Quinn had diverted for their own benefit $25 of the $150 allegedly paid to Dr. DeSilverio. For two days in 1975, Willing marched in protest in an area adjacent to the court buildings at City Hall in Philadelphia where the Court of Common Pleas, before which Mazzocone and Quinn practiced, was located. While marching, Willing wore a "sandwich-board" sign around her neck and on which she had written:

LAW–FIRM OF QUINN–MAZZOCONE Stole money from me—and Sold-me-out-to-the INSURANCE COMPANY

To attract attention while marching, Willing pushed a shopping cart bearing an American flag, continuously rang a cow bell, and blew on a whistle.

Mazzocone and Quinn attempted unsuccessfully to discourage Willing from further public protest. The two then filed a complaint in equity in the Court of Common Pleas of Philadelphia County seeking an injunction against further demonstration. The court found that there was no factual basis for Willing's defamatory protest, but noted that "either by reason of eccentricity or an even more serious mental instability," Willing could not be convinced that she had not been defrauded. The court enjoined Willing from further demonstration or picketing and from "carrying placards which contain defamatory and libelous statements and or uttering, publishing and declaring defamatory statements against [Mazzocone and Quinn]."

On appeal, the Superior Court of Pennsylvania affirmed the [injunction]. [That court] openly rejected the "traditional view that equity does not have the power to enjoin the publication of defamatory matter." The court noted that four reasons traditionally have been offered to justify equity's refusal to enjoin defamation:

> (1) equity will afford protection only to property rights; (2) an injunction would deprive the defendant of his right to a jury trial on the issue of the truth of the publication; (3) the plaintiff has an adequate remedy at law; and (4) an injunction would be unconstitutional as a prior restraint on freedom of expression.

The court then went on to state that "the logic and soundness of these reasons have been severely criticized by numerous commentators," and that "[o]ur own analysis compels us to conclude that blind application of the majority view to the instant case would be antithetical to equity's historic function of maintaining flexibility and accomplishing total justice whenever possible." The court then reviewed each of the four traditional justifications.

First, the court noted that the Pennsylvania Supreme Court had expressly repudiated the maxim that equity will protect property rights but not personal rights. Pennsylvania apparently is now in line with the Restatement and the vast majority of other jurisdictions in this regard.

Second, the Superior Court reasoned that the argument that a defendant has a right to a jury determination as to the truth of a publication "loses all persuasion [in] those situations where the plaintiff has clearly established before a judicial tribunal that the matter sought to be enjoined is both defamatory and false." * * *

Third, the Superior Court challenged the precept that plaintiffs do not need equitable relief because they have an adequate remedy at law for damages. In particular, the Superior Court reasoned that Mazzocone and Quinn did not have an adequate remedy at law because: (1) the value of their professional and personal reputations, and the diminution in that value resulting from Willing's libel, were difficult to prove and measure; (2) given Willing's apparent mental instability, it was reasonable to assume that she would continue to libel the plaintiffs, necessitating a multiplicity of damage actions on their behalf; and (3) Willing was indigent, rendering any action for damages a "pointless gesture" in any event. In light of these factors, the Superior Court concluded that Mazzocone and Quinn did not have an adequate remedy at law.

Fourth, although the Superior Court acknowledged that the argument that an injunction against defamation is an unconstitutional prior restraint on free expression "is by far the most cogent of all the reasons offered in support of the traditional view," it reasoned that not all restrictions on speech constitute prior restraints. [The court adopted a] pragmatic approach [which weighs], on a case-by-case basis, the likelihood that the alleged defamatory statements were true, the magnitude of the harm done to the plaintiff if the speech is not restrained, the adequacy of legal remedies, and, most importantly, whether the public interest will be disserved by suppressing the speech. Under this pragmatic approach, the court concluded, the injunction against Willing should not be considered an unconstitutional prior restraint.

[The court found] no public interest so substantial or significant as to permit defendant's continuing false accusations concerning plaintiff's professional conduct. On the other hand, the injury to plaintiff's reputation can be extensive and irreparable if the defendant is permitted to continue her activities. Under these circumstances, the court below properly granted the injunction.

The Supreme Court of Pennsylvania reversed [on] two grounds. First, invoking Blackstone and referencing the pernicious English Licensing Acts, the Supreme Court noted that the Commonwealth of Pennsylvania long has rejected any prior restraint on the exercise of speech * * *.

Second, the Supreme Court [rejected] the Superior Court's argument that Mazzocone and Quinn did not have an adequate remedy at law because Willing was indigent and unable to satisfy a damages action. In unequivocal terms, the Supreme Court stated that Willing's constitutional rights should not be contingent upon her financial status. * * *

The Supreme Court added that, [i]n deciding whether a remedy is adequate, it is the remedy itself, and not its possible lack of success that is the determining factor. "The fact, if it be so, that this remedy may not be successful in realizing the fruits of recovery at law, on account of the insolvency of the defendants, is not of itself or [sic] ground of equitable inference."

[In] short, *Willing* may be summarized as follows. The Superior Court was presented with a case which, in its view and that of many of the commentators, cried out for reexamining the common-law precept that equity will not enjoin a defamation. The Superior Court, after carefully considering each of the traditional justifications for the precept, found one no longer viable and the remaining three unpersuasive given the certainty that Willing's statements were false, the likelihood that she would continue to issue libelous statements, her inability to satisfy a damages judgment, and the fact that the public had little interest in the speech at issue. The Supreme Court, however, stood firmly behind the traditional bar to equitable relief, holding essentially that Willing's constitutional rights to uncensored speech and trial by jury were paramount even though, as a practical matter, she would be immune to a damages action after the speech were issued.

Given the similarities between *Willing* and the instant dispute, [it] arguably would be appropriate to overturn the district court's injunction against Thompson without further elaboration. We believe, however, [that] there is a material difference between the two cases that makes further analysis unavoidable.

[Thompson] was enjoined from further defamatory speech as an adjunct to Kramer's successful action at law for damages. Because the district court directed a verdict in Kramer's favor on the issue of liability, leaving to the jury only the issue of damages, we recognize that it is not entirely accurate to state that Thompson was afforded a jury determination as to the veracity of his statements. However, since the directed verdict is functionally equivalent to a jury award, at least in theory, Thompson's comments were found to be libelous after a full and fair jury trial.

The existence of a jury trial is a potentially crucial distinction between *Willing* and this case. Two of the three traditional reasons for barring equity from enjoining a defamation, as prescribed by the Pennsylvania Supreme Court in *Willing*, are obviated once a jury has determined that the enjoined statements are indeed libelous. First, it obviously cannot be said that a defendant has been denied the right to a jury determination of the veracity of his statements if a judge issues an injunction against further statements after a jury has determined that the same statements are untrue and libelous. Second, not all injunctions against speech constitute prior restraints. The United States Supreme Court has held repeatedly that an injunction against speech generally will not be considered an unconstitutional prior restraint if it is issued after a jury has determined that the speech is not constitutionally protected. The Pennsylvania cases appear to be in accord. Because libelous speech is not protected by either the United States or the Pennsylvania Constitutions, it follows that, once a jury has determined that a certain statement is libelous, it is not a prior restraint for the court to enjoin the defendant from repeating that statement.

[As a result, this] case appears to be reducible to the following question: Would the Pennsylvania Supreme Court have [been] willing to permit an exception to the rule that equity will not enjoin a defamation in cases where there already has been a jury determination that the defendant's statements were libelous?

[T]he available evidence leads us to the conclusion that the Pennsylvania Supreme Court would overturn the injunction against prospective libel issued by the district court against Thompson. In reaching this conclusion, we are persuaded by five factors.

First, the maxim that equity will not enjoin a libel has enjoyed nearly two centuries of widespread acceptance at common law. The welter of academic and judicial criticism of the last seventy years has, in truth, done little more than chip away at its edges. In any event, as evidenced by the Pennsylvania Supreme Court's unqualified rejection of the Superior Court's "modern" view in *Willing*, Pennsylvania would appear firmly bound to the traditional rule. This may well be due to the extraordinary reverence and solicitude with which the Commonwealth of Pennsylvania has viewed the right of free expression, tracing back to the experiences in England of its founder William Penn and carried forward in the Commonwealth's various Constitutions. [Whatever] the reason, the fact remains that the Supreme Court of Pennsylvania appears entirely comfortable with the common-law [bar].

Second, although an exception to the general rule has been recognized [where] there has been a jury determination of the libelous nature of specific statements, we would do well not to overstate the degree of acceptance that has been accorded to this exception. The fact that three state supreme courts have affirmatively adopted the exception in the last two decades may represent the trickle that presages the collapse of the common-law dam. But, for now, it remains a trickle. And as far as we can tell, the Pennsylvania Supreme Court is more likely to plug the holes in the dam than to contribute to its destruction.

Third, even if we thought that the Pennsylvania Supreme Court might be inclined to adopt the jury determination exception, we doubt that this is the case in which it would do so. The district court in this case took the decidedly unusual step of directing a verdict on the issue of liability against Thompson before he put on a defense, finding that the statements were so patently libelous that no justification or defense could possibly exist. In theory, of course, a directed verdict at law is tantamount to a jury verdict. From the defendant's perspective, however, a directed verdict is indistinguishable from the decree of a court sitting in equity. Given the fear of judicial censorship that has pervaded this area of jurisprudence, and the almost talismanic significance that the case law attaches to the decisions of juries, we think it likely that, even if the Pennsylvania Supreme Court were willing to adopt this exception, it would do so only when there actually has been a jury determination regarding the libelous nature of the defendant's statements.

Fourth, and perhaps most importantly, [the Pennsylvania Supreme Court] continues to place great emphasis on the adequate remedy doctrine as a bar to equitable relief. Indeed, even a jury determination that particular statements are libelous does not address the traditional notion that equity should not intervene where legal remedies (*i.e.*, damages) are adequate, either in practice or even just in theory. * * *

[From] our reading, we must conclude [that the Pennsylvania Supreme Court] would have denied an injunction even on the facts of this case.

[For] the foregoing reasons, we will reverse those portions of the district court's orders that enjoined Thompson from repeating the statements deemed libelous and from communicating with anyone doing business with Kramer.

B. Mandatory Retraction and Withdrawal of Prior Statements and Court Filings

We need not tarry very long over those portions of the district court's orders that sought to force Thompson to write letters of retraction to recipients of prior libelous statements and to withdraw libelous court filings. [We] have not found a single case in which such a remedy has been awarded.

Many states have enacted statutes that provide for the mitigation of compensatory or punitive damages in cases where a libel defendant, typically a newspaper, voluntarily retracts prior to trial. No statutes to our knowledge, however, compel retraction. The reasons for the reluctance of state legislatures and courts to provide for mandatory retraction are apparent enough. [N]one of the statutes provide for a compulsory [retraction]; they all leave it up to the defamer as to whether he will retract, even after formal demand from the defamed person. Retraction is a defense, not an award in the plaintiff's favor. Compulsory retraction has obvious defects. The sincerity of a compelled retraction may be doubted, and by reason of that fact it may fall short of achieving real vindication for the defamed person. Third persons may feel that the defamer is merely saying what the law requires him to say without changing his true opinion.

[Also, c]ommentators have raised a serious question [whether] compelled retraction could withstand first amendment scrutiny. [I]t may very well be a serious invasion of liberty of the press to compel a newspaper to publish as true what the editor believes to be false. And that is what a retraction is, if the editor persists in thinking his supposed libel correct.

[In] *Miami Herald [Publishing Co. v. Tornillo*, 418 U.S. 241 (1974)], the Supreme Court was called upon to assess the constitutionality of a Florida statute that provided a so-called "right of reply" to political candidates whose personal or official records were assailed by the media. Under the statute, newspapers were required to print, free of cost to the candidate, and subject to punishment if they refused, any reply that a candidate wished to make to the newspapers' charges. The Court declared the statute unconstitutional stating: [T]he Court has expressed sensitivity as to whether a retraction or requirement constituted the compulsion exerted by government on a newspaper to print that which it would not otherwise print. The clear implication has been that no such compulsion to publish that which " 'reason' tells them should not be published" is unconstitutional. A responsible press is an undoubtedly desirable goal, but press responsibility is not mandated by the Constitution and like many other virtues cannot be legislated.

A "right of reply" differs from a mandatory retraction in that the former merely requires the defamer to provide space for a reply, whereas the latter requires the defamer to mouth or pen the words the plaintiff would have him say. As such, the unconstitutionality of compelled retraction would seem to follow a fortiori from the Court's declaration that Florida's "right of reply" statute is unconstitutional. * * *

Coughlin [*v. Westinghouse Broadcasting and Cable, Inc.*], 689 F.Supp. 483 (E.D.Pa.1988), held "that a carefully crafted retraction statute could well be constitutional." Judge Pollak denied the plaintiff's claim, however, concluding that even if mandatory retraction would survive constitutional scrutiny, such a cause of action properly should originate with the Pennsylvania legislature, not the courts. We agree.

In sum, we find no support for the various retractions and withdrawals forced upon Thompson by the district court. Consequently, those orders of the district court compelling such retractions and withdrawals, and the associated contempt citations, must be reversed.

NOTES

1. *Public Figures.* In *Curtis Publishing Co. v. Butts*, 388 U.S. 130, 87 S.Ct. 1975, 18 L.Ed.2d 1094 (1967), the Court extended *New York Times* protections to defamatory statements made regarding public figures. The Saturday Evening Post alleged that the University of Georgia's Athletic Director had conspired to fix a football game. The jury returned a verdict for $60,000 in general damages and $3,000,000 in punitive damages. In the companion case of *Associated Press v. Walker*, 388 U.S. 130, 87 S.Ct. 1975, 18 L.Ed.2d 1094 (1967), an Associated Press article claimed that Walker, a private citizen who had been in the United States Army, had taken command of a violent crowd and had personally led a charge against federal marshals. A verdict of $500,000 compensatory damages and $300,000 punitive damages was returned. The Court treated both Butts and Walker as public figures and held that the *New York Times* actual malice standard applied to both of them:

> [T]he public interest in the circulation of the materials here involved, and the publisher's interest in circulating them, is not less than that involved in *New York Times*. [B]oth Butts and Walker commanded a substantial amount of independent public interest at the time of the publications; both, in our opinion, would have been labeled "public figures" under ordinary tort rules. Butts may have attained that status by position alone and Walker by his purposeful activity amounting to a thrusting of his personality into the "vortex" of an important public controversy, but both commanded sufficient continuing public interest and had sufficient access to the means of counterargument to be able "to expose through discussion the falsehood and fallacies" of the defamatory statements.
>
> These similarities and differences between libel actions involving persons who are public officials and libel actions involving those circumstanced as were Butts and Walker, viewed in light of the principles of liability which are of general applicability in our society, lead us to the conclusion that libel actions of the present kind cannot be left entirely to state libel laws, unlimited by any overriding constitutional safeguard, but that the rigorous federal requirements of *New York Times* are not the only appropriate accommodation of the conflicting interests at stake. We consider and would hold that a "public figure" who is not a public official may also recover damages for a defamatory falsehood whose substance makes substantial danger to reputation apparent, on a showing of highly unreasonable conduct constituting an extreme departure from the standards of investigation and reporting ordinarily adhered to by responsible publishers.

Mr. Chief Justice Warren concurred:

> [A]lthough they are not subject to the restraints of the political process, "public figures," like "public officials," often play an influential role in ordering society. And surely as a class these

> "public figures" have as ready access as "public officials" to mass media of communication, both to influence policy and to counter criticism of their views and activities. Our citizenry has a legitimate and substantial interest in the conduct of such persons, and freedom of the press to engage in uninhibited debate about their involvement in public issues and events is as crucial as it is in the case of "public officials." The fact that they are not amenable to the restraints of the political process only underscores the legitimate and substantial nature of the interest, since it means that public opinion may be the only instrument by which society can attempt to influence their conduct.

2. *Private Individuals. Gertz v. Robert Welch, Inc.*, 418 U.S. 323, 94 S.Ct. 2997, 41 L.Ed.2d 789 (1974), limited *New York Times* and *Butts* as applied to private individuals. In *Gertz,* the American Opinion, a monthly magazine which includes views from the John Birch Society, suggested, inter alia, that petitioner was directly involved in the "frame-up" of a police officer. The Court concluded that the *New York Times* "actual malice" standard did not apply:

> The *New York Times* standard [administers] an extremely powerful antidote to the inducement to media self-censorship of the common-law rule of strict liability for libel and slander. And it exacts a correspondingly high price from the victims of defamatory falsehood. [W]e conclude that the state interest in compensating injury to the reputation of private individuals requires that a different rule should obtain with respect to them.
>
> [W]e have no difficulty in distinguishing among defamation plaintiffs. The first remedy of any victim of defamation is self-help—using available opportunities to contradict the lie or correct the error and thereby to minimize its adverse impact on reputation. Public officials and public figures usually enjoy significantly greater access to the channels of effective communication and hence have a more realistic opportunity to counteract false statements then private individuals normally enjoy. Private individuals are therefore more vulnerable to injury, and the state interest in protecting them is correspondingly greater.
>
> [An] individual who decides to seek governmental office must accept certain necessary consequences of that involvement in public affairs. He runs the risk of closer public scrutiny than might otherwise be the case. And society's interest in the officers of government is not strictly limited to the formal discharge of official duties. * * *
>
> [No] such assumption is justified with respect to a private individual. He has not accepted public office or assumed an "influential role in ordering society." He has relinquished no part of his interest in the protection of his own good name, and

> consequently he has a more compelling call on the courts for redress of injury inflicted by defamatory falsehood. Thus, private individuals are not only more vulnerable to injury than public officials and public figures; they are also more deserving of recovery.
>
> [We] hold that, so long as they do not impose liability without fault, the States may define for themselves the appropriate standard of liability for a publisher or broadcaster of defamatory falsehood injurious to a private individual. This approach provides a more equitable boundary between the competing concerns involved here. It recognizes the strength of the legitimate state interest in compensating private individuals for wrongful injury to reputation, yet shields the press and broadcast media from the rigors of strict liability for defamation. * * *
>
> [The] strong and legitimate state interest in compensating private individuals for injury to reputation [extends] no further than compensation for actual injury. [T]he States may not permit recovery of presumed or punitive damages, at least when liability is not based on a showing of knowledge of falsity or reckless disregard for the truth.
>
> The common law of defamation [allows] recovery of purportedly compensatory damages without evidence of actual loss. Under the traditional rules pertaining to actions for libel, the existence of injury is presumed from the fact of publication. [T]he doctrine of presumed damages invites juries to punish unpopular opinion rather than to compensate individuals for injury sustained by the publication of a false fact. [T]he States have no substantial interest in securing for plaintiffs such as this petitioner gratuitous awards of money damages far in excess of any actual injury.
>
> [A]ctual injury is not limited to out-of-pocket loss. Indeed, the more customary types of actual harm inflicted by defamatory falsehood include impairment of reputation and standing in the community, personal humiliation, and mental anguish and suffering. Of course, juries must be limited by appropriate instructions, and all awards must be supported by competent evidence concerning the injury, although there need be no evidence which assigns an actual dollar value to the injury.

3. *Time, Inc. v. Firestone*, 424 U.S. 448, 96 S.Ct. 958, 47 L.Ed.2d 154 (1976), involved an allegedly defamatory article published by Time Magazine. Time reported on a wealthy socialite's divorce and made allegations about her sexual conduct. The Court concluded that she should be treated as a private individual:

> Petitioner contends that because the Firestone divorce was characterized by the Florida Supreme Court as a "cause celebre," it must have been a public controversy and respondent must be considered a public figure. But in so doing petitioner seeks to equate

> "public controversy" with all controversies of interest to the public. Were we to accept this reasoning, we would reinstate the doctrine advanced in the plurality opinion in *Rosenbloom v. Metromedia, Inc.*, 403 U.S. 29 (1971), which concluded that the New York Times privilege should be extended to falsehoods defamatory of private persons whenever the statements concern matters of general or public interest. In *Gertz,* however, the Court repudiated this position, stating that "extension of the New York Times test proposed by the Rosenbloom plurality would abridge (a) legitimate state interest to a degree that we find unacceptable."
>
> Dissolution of a marriage through judicial proceedings is not the sort of "public controversy" referred to in *Gertz,* even though the marital difficulties of extremely wealthy individuals may be of interest to some portion of the reading public. Nor did respondent freely choose to publicize issues as to the propriety of her married life. She was compelled to go to court by the State in order to obtain legal release from the bonds of matrimony. We have said that in such an instance "[r]esort to the judicial process [is] no more voluntary in a realistic sense than that of the defendant called upon to defend his interests in court." *Boddie v. Connecticut,* 401 U.S. 371, 376–377 (1971). Her actions, both in instituting the litigation and in its conduct, were quite different from those of General Walker in *Curtis Publishing Co., supra.* She assumed no "special prominence in the resolution of public questions." We hold respondent was not a "public figure" for the purpose of determining the constitutional protection afforded petitioner's report of the factual and legal basis for her divorce.

4. In *Dun & Bradstreet, Inc. v. Greenmoss Builders*, 472 U.S. 749, 105 S.Ct. 2939, 86 L.Ed.2d 593 (1985), the Court gave the states greater leeway to impose liability in cases involving private individuals enmeshed in cases that do not "involve matters of public concern." *Dun* involved a credit reporting agency that provided a false credit report. Since the case did not involve a matter of public interest, the Court concluded that presumed and punitive damages could be imposed even without a showing of "actual malice."

PROBLEM

Could either Mayor Rambo or the contractor sue the Sentinel for intentional infliction of emotional distress? Consider the following notes.

NOTES

The Court has applied the *New York Times* "actual malice" standard to suits for emotional distress. In *Hustler Magazine v. Falwell*, 485 U.S. 46, 108 S.Ct. 876, 99 L.Ed.2d 41 (1988), the facts were as follows:

> Petitioner Hustler Magazine, Inc., is a magazine of nationwide circulation. Respondent Jerry Falwell, a nationally known minister who has been active as a commentator on politics and public [affairs].
>
> The inside front cover of the November 1983 issue of Hustler Magazine featured a "parody" of an advertisement for Campari Liqueur that contained the name and picture of respondent and was entitled "Jerry Falwell talks about his first time." This parody was modeled after actual Campari ads that included interviews with various celebrities about their "first times." Although it was apparent by the end of each interview that this meant the first time they sampled Campari, the ads clearly played on the sexual double entendre of the general subject of "first times." Copying the form and layout of these Campari ads, Hustler's editors chose respondent as the featured celebrity and drafted an alleged "interview" with him in which he states that his "first time" was during a drunken incestuous rendezvous with his mother in an outhouse. The Hustler parody portrays respondent and his mother as drunk and immoral, and suggests that respondent is a hypocrite who preaches only when he is drunk. In small print at the bottom of the page, the ad contains the disclaimer, "ad parody—not to be taken seriously." The magazine's table of contents also lists the ad as "Fiction; Ad and Personality Parody."
>
> [Respondent sued claiming] that publication of the ad parody in Hustler entitled him to recover damages for libel, invasion of privacy, and intentional infliction of emotional distress.

The Court held that Hustler's publication of the ad was constitutionally privileged:

> The sort of robust political debate encouraged by the First Amendment is bound to produce speech that is critical of those who hold public office or those public figures who are "intimately involved in the resolution of important public questions or, by reason of their fame, shape events in areas of concern to society at large." *Associated Press v. Walker*, decided with *Curtis Publishing Co. v. Butts*, 388 U.S. 130, 164 (1967) (Warren, C.J., concurring in result). [Such] criticism, inevitably, will not always be reasoned or moderate; public figures as well as public officials will be subject to "vehement, caustic, and sometimes unpleasantly sharp attacks," *New York Times, supra*, 376 U.S., at 270. * * *
>
> [Since] *New York Times Co. v. Sullivan*, 376 U.S. 254 (1964), we have consistently ruled that a public figure may hold a speaker liable for the damage to reputation caused by publication of a defamatory falsehood, but only if the statement was made "with knowledge that it was false or with reckless disregard of whether it was false or not." * * *

Respondent argues, however, that a different standard should apply in this case because here the State seeks to prevent not reputational damage, but the severe emotional distress suffered by the person who is the subject of an offensive publication. In respondent's view, and in the view of the Court of Appeals, so long as the utterance was intended to inflict emotional distress, was outrageous, and did in fact inflict serious emotional distress, it is of no constitutional import whether the statement was a fact or an opinion, or whether it was true or false. It is the intent to cause injury that is the gravamen of the tort, and the State's interest in preventing emotional harm simply outweighs whatever interest a speaker may have in speech of this type.

Generally speaking the law does not regard the intent to inflict emotional distress as one which should receive much solicitude, and it is quite understandable that most if not all jurisdictions have chosen to make it civilly culpable where the conduct in question is sufficiently "outrageous." But in the world of debate about public affairs, many things done with motives that are less than admirable are protected by the First Amendment. [W]hile such a bad motive may be deemed controlling for purposes of tort liability in other areas of the law, we think the First Amendment prohibits such a result in the area of public debate about public figures.

Were we to hold otherwise, there can be little doubt that political cartoonists and satirists would be subjected to damages awards without any showing that their work falsely defamed its subject. [The] appeal of the political cartoon or caricature is often based on exploitation of unfortunate physical traits or politically embarrassing events—an exploitation often calculated to injure the feelings of the subject of the portrayal. The art of the cartoonist is often not reasoned or evenhanded, but slashing and one-sided. One cartoonist expressed the nature of the art in these words: "The political cartoon is a weapon of attack, of scorn and ridicule and satire; it is least effective when it tries to pat some politician on the back. It is usually as welcome as a bee sting and is always controversial in some quarters." Long, *The Political Cartoon: Journalism's Strongest Weapon*, THE QUILL 56, 57 (Nov. 1962). * * *

[Respondent] contends, however, that the caricature in question here was so "outrageous" as to distinguish it from more traditional political cartoons. There is no doubt that the caricature of respondent and his mother published in Hustler is at best a distant cousin of the political cartoons described above, and a rather poor relation at that. If it were possible by laying down a principled standard to separate the one from the other, public discourse would probably suffer little or no harm. But we doubt that there is any such standard, and we are quite sure that the pejorative description "outrageous" does not supply one. "Outrageousness" in the area of political and social discourse has an inherent subjectiveness about it which would allow a jury to impose liability on the basis of the jurors' tastes or views, or perhaps on the basis of their dislike of a particular expression. * * *

We conclude that public figures and public officials may not recover for the tort of intentional infliction of emotional distress by reason of publications such as the one here at issue without showing in addition that the publication contains a false statement of fact which was made with "actual malice," *i.e.*, with knowledge that the statement was false or with reckless disregard as to whether or not it was true. This is not merely a "blind application" of the *New York Times* standard, it reflects our considered judgment that such a standard is necessary to give adequate "breathing space" to the freedoms protected by the First Amendment.

Here it is clear that respondent Falwell is a "public figure" for purposes of First Amendment law.[5] The jury found against respondent on his libel claim when it decided that the Hustler ad parody could not "reasonably be understood as describing actual facts about [respondent] or actual events in which [he] participated." The Court of Appeals interpreted the jury's finding to be that the ad parody "was not reasonably believable," and in accordance with our custom we accept this finding. Respondent is thus relegated to his claim for damages awarded by the jury for the intentional infliction of emotional distress by "outrageous" conduct. But for reasons heretofore stated this claim cannot, consistently with the First Amendment, form a basis for the award of damages when the conduct in question is the publication of a caricature such as the ad parody involved here. * * *

PROBLEM

Is there an alternative to defamation litigation? The Uniform Correction or Clarification of Defamation Act encourages defamation plaintiffs to request, and defamation defendants to give, corrections or clarifications. § 3 provides that: "A person may maintain an action for defamation only if [the] person has made a timely and adequate request for correction or clarification from the [defendant]." The goal of the Act is to provide "a strong incentive for an early request and a significant penalty for failure to make one." The Act requires the person challenging a statement's truth to state why it is false, and provide the information necessary to evaluate the claim. If the correction or clarification is made, the defamation plaintiff can recover only "provable economic loss." "In limiting recovery of damages to provable economic loss as mitigated by the correction or clarification, the Act anticipates that any loss

---

[5] Neither party disputes this conclusion. Respondent is the host of a nationally syndicated television show and was the founder and president of a political organization formerly known as the Moral Majority. He is also the founder of Liberty University in Lynchburg, Virginia, and is the author of several books and publications.

caused by the publication can be significantly reduced by publication of the correction or clarification. The burden of proving mitigation of economic loss, however, rests with the publisher." Is this approach preferable?

J. PRIVACY

Speech that invades privacy presents special problems for the courts. In their landmark article *The Right to Privacy*, 4 HARVARD L. REV. 193 (1890), Justice Brandeis & Samuel Warren forcefully articulated the need to protect privacy:

> [The] intense intellectual and emotional life, and the heightening of sensations which came with the advance of civilization, made it clear to men that only a part of the pain, pleasure, and profit of life lay in physical things. Thoughts, emotions, and sensations demanded legal recognition. . . .
>
> Recent inventions and business methods call attention to the next step which must be taken for the protection of the person, and for securing to the individual what Judge Cooley calls the right "to be let alone." Instantaneous photographs, and newspapers enterprise have invaded the sacred precincts of private and domestic life; and numerous mechanical devices threaten to make good the prediction that "what is whispered in the closet shall be proclaimed from the house-tops." For years there has been a feeling that the law must afford some remedy for the unauthorized circulation of portraits of private persons and the evil of the invasion of privacy by the newspapers, long keenly felt, has been but recently discussed by an able writer. * * *
>
> Of the desirability—indeed of the necessity—of some such protection, there can, it is believed, be no doubt. The press is overstepping in every direction the obvious bounds of propriety and of decency. Gossip is no longer the resource of the idle and of the vicious, but has become a trade, which is pursued with industry as well as effrontery. To satisfy a prurient taste the details of sexual relations are spread broadcast in the columns of the daily papers. To occupy the indolent, column upon column is filled with idle gossip, which can only be procured by intrusion upon the domestic circle. The intensity and complexity of life, attendant upon advancing civilization, have rendered necessary some retreat from the world, and man, under the refining influence of culture, has become more sensitive to publicity, so that solitude and privacy have become more essential to the individual; but modern enterprise and invention have, through invasions upon his privacy, subjected him to mental pain and distress, far greater than could be inflicted by mere bodily injury.

> Nor is the harm wrought by such invasions confined to the suffering of those who may be made the subjects of journalistic or other enterprise. In this, as in other branches of commerce, the supply creates the demand. Each crop of unseemly gossip, thus harvested, becomes the seed of more, and, in direct proportion to its circulation, results in a lowering of social standards and of morality. Even gossip apparently harmless, when widely and persistently circulated, is potent for evil. It both belittles and perverts. It belittles by inverting the relative importance of things, thus dwarfing the thoughts and aspirations of a people. When personal gossip attains the dignity of print, and crowd the space available for matters of real interest to the community, what wonder that the ignorant and thoughtless mistake its relative importance. Easy of comprehension, appealing to that weak side of human nature which is never wholly cast down by the misfortunes and frailties of our neighbors, no one can be surprised that it usurps the place of interest in brains capable of other things. Triviality destroys at once robustness of thought and delicacy of feeling. No enthusiasm can flourish, no generous impulse can survive under its blighting influence. * * *

PROBLEM

May a magazine appropriate someone's name and likeness for purposes of satire? Consider the facts in *Dworkin v. Hustler Magazine, Inc.*, 867 F.2d 1188 (9th Cir.1989):

> Andrea Dworkin is a prominent and outspoken feminist author and activist. She is a vocal advocate for the prohibition of pornography, and was one of the principal drafters of the ordinance against pornography enacted by the city of Indianapolis and struck down as unconstitutional. *See American Booksellers Ass'n, Inc. v. Hudnut*, 771 F.2d 323 (7th Cir.1985), *aff'd mem.*, 475 U.S. 1001 (1986). By her own admission, she is a public figure in this case. Hustler Magazine is a pornographic periodical. Much of its content consists of what we have recently described as "disgusting and distasteful abuse." *See Ault v. Hustler Magazine, Inc.*, 860 F.2d 877, 884 (9th Cir.1988). It is frequently named as a defendant in lawsuits such as this.
>
> Predictably, Dworkin's beliefs and Hustler's editorial viewpoint are inimical to one another, and each party regards the other with hostility. In February, March, and December of 1984, Hustler published features mentioning Dworkin's name in a derogatory fashion. These features (the "Features") are the basis for the claims asserted in this case.

> The February Feature is a cartoon, which, as described in the plaintiffs' complaint, "depicts two women engaged in a lesbian act of oral sex with the caption, 'You remind me so much of Andrea Dworkin, Edna. It's a dog-eat-dog world.' " The March Feature is a ten page pictorial consisting of photographs of women engaged in, among other things, acts of lesbianism or masturbation. Some of the photographs depict obviously staged scenes that include posed violence and phony blood. One photograph, supposedly of a Jewish male, has a caption stating: "While I'm teaching this little shiksa the joys of Yiddish, the Andrea Dworkin Fan Club begins some really serious suck-'n'-squat. Ready to give up the holy wafers for matzoh, yet, guys?" The December Feature was included in the "Porn from the Past" section of the magazine. It shows a man performing oral sex on an obese woman while he masturbates. A portion of the caption states: "We don't believe it for a minute, but one of our editors swears that this woman in the throes of ecstasy is the mother of radical feminist Andrea Dworkin."

Relying on *Falwell v. Hustler Magazine*, the Ninth Circuit affirmed the trial court's dismissal of most of the causes of action and its granting of summary judgment on the remainder. The court explicitly rejected Dworkin's claim that First Amendment protections only apply to "high-minded" discourse. Could Dworkin have recovered from Hustler on a "right of publicity" theory? What arguments can be made on her behalf? How might Hustler Magazine respond?

EASTWOOD V. SUPERIOR COURT

149 Cal.App.3d 409, 198 Cal.Rptr. 342 (1983).

THOMPSON, ASSOCIATE JUSTICE.

[The] Enquirer publishes a weekly newspaper known as the "National Enquirer" which enjoys wide circulation and is read by a great number of people. In its April 13, 1982 edition of the National Enquirer, the Enquirer published a 600-word article about Eastwood's romantic involvement with two other celebrities, singer Tanya Tucker and actress Sondra Locke. On the cover of this edition appeared the pictures of Eastwood and Tucker above the caption "Clint Eastwood in Love Triangle with Tanya Tucker."

The article is headlined "Clint Eastwood in Love Triangle" and appears on page 48 of this edition. Eastwood alleges the article is false and in this regard alleges: "(a) The offending article falsely states that Eastwood 'loves' Tucker and that Tucker means a lot to him." (b) The offending article falsely states that Eastwood was, in late February, 1982, swept off his feet and immediately smitten by Tucker; that Tucker makes his head spin; that Tucker used her charms to get what she wanted from Eastwood; and that Eastwood now daydreams about their supposedly enchanted evenings together. "(c) The offending article falsely states that Eastwood and Tucker, in late February, 1982, shared 10 fun-filled romantic evenings together; were constantly, during that period, in each other's arms; publicly 'cuddled' and publicly gazed romantically at one another; and publicly kissed and hugged. (d) The offending article falsely states that Eastwood is locked in a romantic triangle involving Tucker and Sondra Locke ('Locke'); is torn between Locke and Tucker; can't decide between Locke and Tucker; is involved in a romantic tug-of-war involving Locke and Tucker; that Locke and Tucker are dueling over him; that Tucker is battling Locke for his affections; and that when he is with Locke, Tucker is constantly on his mind. (e) The offending article falsely states that, in or about late February of 1982, there were serious problems in Eastwood's relationship with Locke; that he and Locke at that time had a huge argument over marriage; that he and Locke had a nasty fight; and that Locke stormed out of his presence. (f) The offending article falsely states that after his supposed romantic interlude with Tucker, Locke camped at his doorstep and, while on hands and knees, begged Eastwood to 'keep her', vowing that she wouldn't pressure him into marriage; but that Eastwood acted oblivious to her pleas."

Eastwood further asserts that Enquirer "published the offending article maliciously, willfully and wrongfully, with the intent to injure and disgrace Eastwood, either knowing that the statements therein contained were false or with reckless disregard of [their] falsity." Enquirer used Eastwood's name and photograph without his consent or permission. As a consequence thereof, Eastwood alleges that he has suffered mental anguish and emotional distress and seeks both compensatory and punitive damages.

[Eastwood also] alleges that the Enquirer made a telecast advertisement in which it featured Eastwood's name and photograph and mentioned prominently the subject article. [Eastwood] alleges that the telecast advertisements as well as the cover of the April 13 publication were calculated to promote the sales of the Enquirer. Eastwood asserts that the unauthorized use of his name and photograph has damaged him in his right to control the commercial exploitation of his name, photograph and likeness, in addition to injuring his feelings and privacy. Eastwood seeks damages under both the common law and Civil Code section 3344.

[Enquirer] demurred to the second cause of action for invasion of privacy through appropriation of name, photograph and likeness on the basis it failed to state a cause of action on two grounds: (1) Eastwood's name and photograph were not used to imply an endorsement of the Enquirer; and (2) Eastwood's name and photograph were used in connection with a news account. [The trial court sustained the demurrer and this petition followed.]

[California] has long recognized a common law right of privacy which provides protection against four distinct categories of invasion. These four distinct torts identified by Dean Prosser and grouped under the privacy rubric are: (1) intrusion upon the plaintiff's seclusion or solitude, or into his private affairs; (2) public disclosure of embarrassing private facts about the plaintiff; (3) publicity which places the plaintiff in a false light in the public eye; and (4) appropriation, for the defendant's advantage, of the plaintiff's name or likeness.

Moreover, the fourth category of invasion of privacy, namely, appropriation, "has been complemented legislatively by Civil Code section 3344, adopted in 1971."

Civil Code section 3344, subdivision (a), provides in pertinent part as follows: "Any person who knowingly uses another's name, photograph, or likeness, in any manner, for purposes of advertising products, merchandise, goods, or services, or for purposes of solicitation of purchases of products [without] such person's prior consent [shall] be liable for any damages sustained by the person [injured] as a result thereof."

[A] common law cause of action for appropriation of name or likeness may be pleaded by alleging (1) the defendant's use of the plaintiff's identity; (2) the appropriation of plaintiff's name or likeness to defendant's advantage, commercially or otherwise; (3) lack of consent; and (4) resulting injury.

In addition, to plead the statutory remedy provided in Civil Code section 3344, there must also be an allegation of a knowing use of the plaintiff's name, photograph or likeness for purposes of advertising or solicitation of purchases. Furthermore, recent judicial construction of section 3344 has imposed an additional requirement. A "direct" connection must be alleged between the use and the commercial purpose.

[Here,] Eastwood has alleged that the Enquirer employed his name, photograph and likeness on the front page of the subject publication and in related telecast advertisements, without his prior consent, for the purpose of promoting the sales of the Enquirer. Therefore, Eastwood states an actionable claim in his second cause of action under either the common law or section 3344, or both, if two conditions are satisfied: (1) Enquirer's use of Eastwood's name, photograph and likeness constitutes an appropriation for commercial purposes, and (2) Enquirer's conduct constitutes an impermissible infringement of Eastwood's right of publicity.

[Enquirer] argues that the failure of Eastwood to allege the appearance of an "endorsement" of the Enquirer is fatal to stating a cause of action for commercial appropriation.

[T]he appearance of an "endorsement" is not the sine qua non of a claim for commercial appropriation. Thus, in *Stilson v. Reader's Digest Assn., Inc.* (1972) 28 Cal.App.3d 270, 104 Cal.Rptr. 581, the allegedly wrongful use involved a magazine's inclusion of individuals' names in letters soliciting participation in a sweepstake designed to promote subscription. The letters stated that the recipient and other named individuals had been chosen to receive "lucky numbers." No statement or implication that these individuals had consented to promote the magazine was made or implied. Assessing the legal significance of this promotional endeavor, the court stated that "[t]he unauthorized use of one's name for commercial exploitation is actionable."

[*Lugosi v. Universal Pictures*] recognized that the right of publicity includes not only the power to control the exploitation of one's personality through licensing agreements, but also the right to obtain relief, both injunctive and/or for damages, when a third party appropriates one's name and likeness for commercial purposes without permission. (25 Cal.3d at p. 819, 160 Cal.Rptr. 323, 603 P.2d 425.)

[A]part from its inconsistency with the common law, Enquirer's suggested limitation of the scope of actionable commercial appropriation is at odds with the clear language of Civil Code section 3344. The statute imposes liability on a person "who knowingly uses another's name, photograph, or likeness, in any [manner]." [We] therefore find that Enquirer's argument is without merit.

Turning to whether the Enquirer has commercially exploited Eastwood's name, photograph or likeness, we note that one of the primary purposes of advertising is to motivate a decision to purchase a particular product or service.

The first step toward selling a product or service is to attract the consumers' attention. Because of a celebrity's audience appeal, people respond almost automatically to a celebrity's name or picture. Here, the Enquirer used Eastwood's personality and fame on the cover of the subject publication and in related telecast advertisements. To the extent their use attracted the readers' attention, the Enquirer gained a commercial advantage. Furthermore, the Enquirer used Eastwood's personality in the context of an alleged news account, entitled "Clint Eastwood in Love Triangle with Tanya Tucker" to generate maximum curiosity and the necessary motivation to purchase the newspaper.

Moreover, the use of Eastwood's personality in the context of a news account, allegedly false but presented as true, provided the Enquirer with a ready-made "scoop"—a commercial advantage over its competitors which it would otherwise not have.

Absent a constitutional or statutory proscription, we find that Eastwood can show that such use is a subterfuge or cover-up for commercial exploitation.

We therefore conclude that Eastwood has sufficiently alleged that the Enquirer has commercially exploited his name, photograph, and likeness under both the common law and section 3344, subdivision (a).

Enquirer argues that Eastwood's second cause of action fails to state an actionable claim under California law because the use of his name and photograph in the telecast advertisements, the cover page, and the story is expressly exempted from liability as a news account under the provisions of Civil Code section 3344, subdivision (d).

[I]mplicit in this issue are major constitutional [questions]. Publication of matters in the public interest, which rests on the right of the public to know, and the freedom of the press to tell it, cannot ordinarily be actionable.

[Freedom] of the press is constitutionally guaranteed, and the publication of daily news is an acceptable and necessary function in the life of the community. The scope of the privilege extends to almost all reporting of recent events even though it involves the publication of a purely private person's name or likeness.

Moreover, "there is a public interest which attaches to people who, by their accomplishments, mode of living, professional standing or calling, create a legitimate and widespread attention to their activities. Certainly, the accomplishments and way of life of those who have achieved a marked reputation or notoriety by appearing before the public such as actors [may] legitimately be mentioned and discussed in [print]." (*Carlisle v. Fawcett Publications, Inc., supra*, 201 Cal.App.2d at p. 746, 20 Cal.Rptr. 405.) Thus, a celebrity has relinquished " 'a part of his right of privacy to the extent that the public has a legitimate interest in his doings, affairs or character.' "

Yet absolute protection of the press in the case at bench requires a total sacrifice of the competing interest of Eastwood in controlling the commercial exploitation of his personality. Often considerable money, time and energy are needed to develop the ability in a person's name or likeness to attract attention and evoke a desired response in a particular consumer market. Thus, a proper accommodation between these competing concerns must be defined, since "the rights guaranteed by the First Amendment do not require total abrogation of the right to privacy," and in the case at bench, the right of publicity.

Ordinarily, only two branches of the law of privacy, namely, public disclosure and false light, create tension with the First Amendment, because of their intrusion on the dissemination of information to the public. Normally, in a commercial appropriation case involving the right of publicity, the only question is who gets to do the publishing, since the celebrity is primarily concerned with whether he gets the commercial benefit of such publication.

All fiction is false in the literal sense that it is imagined rather than actual. However, works of fiction are constitutionally protected in the same manner as topical new stories.

[Eastwood] asserts that the alleged news account is entirely false, and is a cover-up or subterfuge for commercial appropriation of his name and likeness * * *.

We have no doubt that the subject of the Enquirer article—the purported romantic involvements of Eastwood with other celebrities—is a matter of public concern, which would generally preclude the imposition of liability. However, Eastwood argues that the article, and thereby the related advertisements, are not entitled to either constitutional protection or exemption from liability as a news account because the article is a calculated falsehood.

[Enquirer] contends [that] it is the manifest character of the article which is determinative as to whether it is news under section 3344, subdivision (d). Enquirer argues that the statute, by its terms, refers only to generic categories; it does not distinguish between news accounts that are true or false. Thus, whether an article is a news account does not turn on the truth or falsity of its content. We disagree.

The spacious interest in an unfettered press is not without limitation. This privilege is subject to the qualification that it shall not be so exercised as to abuse the rights of individuals. Hence, in defamation cases, the concern is with defamatory lies masquerading as truth. Similarly, in privacy cases, the concern is with nondefamatory lies masquerading as truth. Accordingly, we do not believe that the Legislature intended to provide an exemption from liability for a knowing or reckless falsehood under the canopy of "news." We therefore hold that Civil Code section 3344, subdivision (d), as it pertains to news, does not provide an exemption for a knowing or reckless falsehood.

Moreover, wherever the line in a particular situation is to be drawn between news accounts that are protected and those that are not, we are quite sure that the First Amendment does not immunize Enquirer when the entire article is allegedly false.

Finally, Enquirer contends that falsity is the predicate, not for commercial appropriation, but for false light claims. We disagree.

As noted earlier, all fiction is literally false, but enjoys constitutional protection.

However, the deliberate fictionalization of Eastwood's personality constitutes commercial exploitation, and becomes actionable when it is presented to the reader as if true with the requisite scienter.

Here, Eastwood failed to incorporate from his first cause of action that the article was published with knowledge or in reckless disregard of its falsity. Accordingly, we find that such failure renders the second cause of action insufficient to make the Enquirer's expressive conduct actionable under the common law or Civil Code section 3344, subdivision (a).

[Let] a peremptory writ of mandamus issue requiring the respondent court to set aside its order sustaining the demurrer to Eastwood's second cause of action without leave to amend, and to grant Eastwood leave to amend his second cause of action.

PROBLEM

Given the court's conclusions regarding the content of the article, would it have been appropriate to grant injunctive relief (assuming that there was sufficient likelihood that the paper was planning to print more such articles)? Would an injunction have been permissible given the prohibition against prior restraints?

NOTES

1. *Ali v. Playgirl, Inc.*, 447 F.Supp. 723 (S.D.N.Y.1978), involved a suit by Muhammad Ali, former heavyweight boxing champion of the world, against Playgirl, Inc. for unauthorized printing, publication and distribution of a portrait of a nude person referred to simply as "mystery man" in the February, 1978, issue of Playgirl Magazine (Playgirl). The court concluded that Playgirl had appropriated Ali's likeness:

> [Even] a cursory inspection of the picture which is the subject of this action strongly suggests that the facial characteristics of the black male portrayed are those of Muhammad Ali. The cheekbones, broad nose and wideset brown eyes, together with the distinctive smile and close cropped black hair are recognizable as the features of the plaintiff, one of the most widely known athletes of our time. In addition, the figure depicted is seated on a stool in the corner of a boxing ring with both hands taped and outstretched resting on the ropes on either side. Although the picture is captioned "Mystery Man," the identification of the individual as Ali is further implied by an accompanying verse which refers to the figure as "the Greatest." This court may take judicial notice that plaintiff Ali has regularly claimed that appellation for himself and that his efforts to identify himself in the public mind as "the Greatest" have been so successful that he is regularly identified as such in the news media.

> It is also clear that the picture has been used for the "purpose of trade" within the meaning of § 51. [T]here is [no] informational or newsworthy dimension to defendants' unauthorized use of Ali's likeness. * * *
>
> Finally, defendants concede that Ali did not consent to the inclusion of his likeness in the February, 1978 Playgirl Magazine. * * *
>
> The foregoing discussion [establishes] the likelihood that plaintiff will prevail on his claim that his right of publicity has been violated by the publication of the offensive portrait. * * *
>
> The distinctive aspect of the common law right of publicity is that it recognizes the commercial value of the picture or representation of a prominent person or performer, and protects his proprietary interest in the profitability of his public reputation or "persona." [This] common law publicity right is analogous to a commercial entity's right to profit from the "goodwill" it has built up in its name, and the interest which underlies protecting the right of publicity " 'is the straightforward one of preventing unjust enrichment by the theft of good will.' " Kalven, *Privacy in Tort Law: Were Warren and Brandeis Wrong?*, 31 LAW AND CONTEMPORARY PROBLEMS, 326, 331 (1966), quoted in *Zacchini, supra*, 433 U.S. at 576.
>
> Accordingly, this right of publicity is usually asserted only if the plaintiff has "achieved in some degree a celebrated status." [D]efendants' unauthorized publication of the portrait of Ali amounted to a wrongful appropriation of the market value of plaintiff's likeness.

2. *Zacchini v. Scripps–Howard Broadcasting Co.*, 433 U.S. 562, 97 S.Ct. 2849, 53 L.Ed.2d 965 (1977), involved an entertainer who performed a "human cannonball" act in which he was shot from a cannon into a net some 200 yards away. The entertainer performed his act in a fair ground surrounded by grandstands. A reporter filmed the act and showed it on the news. The entertainer sued for damages claiming that the station unlawfully appropriated his property. The news station claimed that it was immune from suit under the First Amendment. The Supreme Court disagreed:

> The broadcast of a film of petitioner's entire act poses a substantial threat to the economic value of that performance. [T]his act is the product of petitioner's own talents and energy, the end result of much time, effort, and expense. Much of its economic value lies in the "right of exclusive control over the publicity given to his performance"; if the public can see the act free on television, it will be less willing to pay to see it at the fair. The effect of a public broadcast of the performance is similar to preventing petitioner from charging an admission fee. "The rationale for [protecting the right of publicity] is the straightforward one of preventing unjust enrichment by the theft of good will. No social purpose is served by having the defendant get free some aspect of the plaintiff that would

have market value and for which he would normally pay." Kalven, *Privacy in Tort Law Were Warren and Brandeis Wrong?*, 31 Law & Contemp. Prob. 326, 331 (1966). Moreover, the broadcast of petitioner's entire performance, unlike the unauthorized use of another's name for purposes of trade or the incidental use of a name or picture by the press, goes to the heart of petitioner's ability to earn a living as an entertainer. Thus, in this case, Ohio has recognized what may be the strongest case for a "right of publicity" involving, not the appropriation of an entertainer's reputation to enhance the attractiveness of a commercial product, but the appropriation of the very activity by which the entertainer acquired his reputation in the first place.

[There] is no doubt that entertainment, as well as news, enjoys First Amendment protection. It is also true that entertainment itself can be important news. *Time, Inc. v. Hill.* But it is important to note that neither the public nor respondent will be deprived of the benefit of petitioner's performance as long as his commercial stake in his act is appropriately recognized. Petitioner does not seek to enjoin the broadcast of his performance; he simply wants to be paid for it. Nor do we think that a state-law damages remedy against respondent would represent a species of liability without fault contrary to the letter or spirit of *Gertz v. Robert Welch, Inc.*, 418 U.S. 323 (1974). Respondent knew that petitioner objected to televising his act, but nevertheless displayed the entire film.

MR. JUSTICE POWELL dissented:

Although the Court would draw no distinction, I do not view respondent's action as comparable to unauthorized commercial broadcasts of sporting events, theatrical performances, and the like where the broadcaster keeps the profits. There is no suggestion here that respondent made any such use of the film. Instead, it simply reported on what petitioner concedes to be a newsworthy event, in a way hardly surprising for a television station by means of film coverage. The report was part of an ordinary daily news program, consuming a total of 15 seconds. It is a routine example of the press' fulfilling the informing function so vital to our system.

The Court's holding that the station's ordinary news report may give rise to substantial liability has disturbing implications, for the decision could lead to a degree of media self-censorship. Hereafter, whenever a television news editor is unsure whether certain film footage received from a camera crew might be held to portray an "entire act," he may decline coverage even of clearly newsworthy events or confine the broadcast to watered-down verbal reporting, perhaps with an occasional still picture. The public is then the loser. This is hardly the kind of news reportage that the First Amendment is meant to foster.

3. *Legislative Protections for Privacy.* In *The Florida Star v. B.J.F.*, 491 U.S. 524, 109 S.Ct. 2603, 105 L.Ed.2d 443 (1989), The Florida Star was found civilly liable for publishing the name of a rape victim in violation of state law. The Star obtained the name from a publicly released police report. The Court overturned the judgment:

> In our view, this case is appropriately analyzed with reference to such a limited First Amendment principle. It is the one, in fact, which we articulated in *Daily Mail* in our synthesis of prior cases involving attempts to punish truthful publication: "[I]f a newspaper lawfully obtains truthful information about a matter of public significance then state officials may not constitutionally punish publication of the information, absent a need to further a state interest of the highest order." 443 U.S., at 103. According the press the ample protection provided by that principle is supported by at least three separate considerations, in addition to, of course, the overarching " 'public interest, secured by the Constitution, in the dissemination of truth.' " *Cox Broadcasting, supra*, 420 U.S., at 491 *quoting Garrison, supra*, 379 U.S., at 73.

4. *The N.Y. Times "Actual Malice" Standard and Privacy Cases.* In *Time, Inc. v. Hill*, 385 U.S. 374, 87 S.Ct. 534, 17 L.Ed.2d 456 (1967), the Supreme Court applied the "actual malice" standard to a "false light" case. However, since *Gertz* was decided in 1974, it is unclear whether *Hill* is still good law. The Restatement takes no position on this issue. *See* Restatement (Second) of Torts § 652. The California Supreme Court has applied constitutional restrictions on defamation claims to false light claims, when privacy invading language is also arguably defamatory. *Fellows v. National Enquirer, Inc.*, 42 Cal.3d 234, 228 Cal.Rptr. 215, 721 P.2d 97 (1986). Otherwise, wouldn't false light claims be an easy way to circumvent the constitutional restrictions on libel actions?

ADDITIONAL PROBLEMS

1. In a similar case, Cardtoons, L.C. ("Cardtoons") produced parody trading cards featuring caricatures of major league baseball players. The majority of the cards contained caricatures of active major league baseball players on the front and humorous commentary about their careers on the back. Also included were other cards, all of which parodied professional baseball players. After the Major League Baseball Players Association (MLBPA) demanded that Cardtoons stop producing the cards, Cardtoons sought a declaratory judgment that its parody trading cards did not infringe the MLBPA's publicity rights. Should the MLBPA be able to enjoin Cardtoons from producing the cards?

2. *Does the action for right of publicity allow someone to prevent another from exhibiting his/her own face?* Consider *Onassis v. Christian Dior–New York, Inc.*, 122 Misc.2d 603, 472 N.Y.S.2d 254 (1984), which involved the following facts:

[J.] Walter Thompson's Lansdowne Division, in conjunction with noted photographer Richard Avedon, hit upon the idea of running a series of ads featuring a trio known as the Diors (one female and two males), who were characterized by an article in Newsweek Magazine as idle rich, suggestively decadent, and aggressively chic. Indeed, it was suggested that this menage a trois, putatively inspired by the characters portrayed by Noel Coward, Alfred Lunt and Lynn Fontanne in Coward's 1933 play "Design for Living," would become the most notorious personae in advertising since Brooke Shields refused to let anything come between her and her Calvins (for the uninitiated, blue jeans advertised under designer Calvin Klein's label). To emphasize the impression of the unconventional, the copy for one ad had read, "When the Diors got away from it all, they brought with them nothing except 'The Decline of the West' and one toothbrush." Evidently, to stir comment, the relationship portrayed in the ad campaign was meant to be ambiguous, "to specify nothing but suggest everything." The 16 sequential ads would depict this steadfast trio in varying situations leading to the marriage of two (but not the exclusion of the third), birth of a baby, and their ascent to Heaven (subject to resurrection on demand).

Thus, the Diors, and by association their products, would be perceived as chic, sophisticated, elite, unconventional, quirky, audacious, elegant, and unorthodox. The advertisement for the wedding, which is the one challenged here, is headed "Christian Dior: Sportswear for Women and Clothing for Men." Portrayed in the ad are the happy Dior trio attended by their ostensible intimates, all ecstatically beaming—Gene Shalit, the T.V. personality, model Shari Belafonte, actress Ruth Gordon, and Barbara Reynolds, a secretary who bears a remarkable resemblance to plaintiff Jacqueline Onassis. The copy, in keeping with the desired attitude of good taste and unconventionality, reads: "The wedding of the Diors was everything a wedding should be: no tears, no rice, no in-laws, no smarmy toasts, for once no Mendelssohn. Just a legendary private affair." Of course, what stamps it as "legendary" is the presence of this eclectic group, a frothy mix, the most legendary of which would clearly be Jacqueline Kennedy Onassis, shown discreetly behind Gordon and Shalit, obviously delighted to be in attendance at this "event."

That the person behind Gordon and Shalit bore a striking resemblance to the plaintiff was no mere happenstance. Defendants knew there was little or no likelihood that Mrs. Onassis would ever consent to be depicted in this kind of advertising campaign for Dior. She has [never] permitted her name or picture to be used in connection with the promotion of commercial products. Her name has been used sparingly only in connection with certain public services, civic, art and educational projects which she has

> supported. Accordingly, Lansdowne and Avedon, once the content of the picture and the make-up of the wedding party having been determined, contacted defendant Ron Smith Celebrity Look-Alikes to provide someone who could pass for Jacqueline Kennedy Onassis. That agency, which specializes in locating and providing persons who bear a close resemblance to well-known personalities on request (and for a fee), came up with defendant Barbara Reynolds, regularly an appointments secretary to a congressman, who, with appropriate coiffure and appointments looks remarkably like Mrs. Onassis, and has made this resemblance an adjunct to her career.
>
> The ad was run in September and October of 1983 in several upscale publications including Esquire, Harper's Bazaar, The New Yorker, and the New York Times Magazine. It received widespread circulation, and apparently was the subject of considerable comment, as was the entire series. Dior reportedly committed 2.5 million dollars to the campaign, and boasted that as a result, sales went through the roof.

If Ms. Onassis were still alive and sought injunctive relief, should she be granted such relief on the theory that Dior used (and plans to use) her likeness in violation of her right of privacy? If so, how should the order be framed? May the court prohibit Reynolds from making ads for Dior given her likeness to Ms. Onassis? May it prohibit her from exhibiting her face?

3. Suppose a business appropriates a "phrase" associated with a famous entertainer? In *Carson v. Here's Johnny Portable Toilets, Inc.*, 698 F.2d 831 (6th Cir.1983):

> [Appellant,] John W. Carson (Carson), is the host and star of "The Tonight Show," a well-known television program broadcast five nights a week by the National Broadcasting Company. Carson also appears as an entertainer in night clubs and theaters around the country. From the time he began hosting "The Tonight Show" in 1962, he has been introduced on the show each night with the phrase "Here's Johnny." This method of introduction was first used for Carson in 1957 when he hosted a daily television program for the American Broadcasting Company. The phrase "Here's Johnny" is generally associated with Carson by a substantial segment of the television viewing public. In 1967, Carson first authorized use of this phrase by an outside business venture, permitting it to be used by a chain of restaurants called "Here's Johnny Restaurants." [Since then, he has authorized its use in other businesses]
>
> Appellee, Here's Johnny Portable Toilets, Inc., is a Michigan corporation engaged in the business of renting and selling "Here's Johnny" portable toilets. Appellee's founder was aware at the time he formed the corporation that "Here's Johnny" was the introductory slogan for Carson on "The Tonight Show." He indicated

> that he coupled the phrase with a second one, "The World's Foremost Commodian," to make "a good play on a phrase."

Should the tort of commercial appropriation be available when defendant has appropriated only the phrase "Here's Johnny?" Is it permissible for Carson to use the right of publicity to appropriate a phrase thereby removing that phrase from free usage?

4. Finally, consider *White v. Samsung Electronics America, Inc.*, 971 F.2d 1395 (9th Cir.1992), which involved game show hostess Vanna White of the show "Wheel of Fortune." The court described this show as "one of the most popular game shows in television history. An estimated forty million people watch the program daily." The court noted that Vanna White had capitalized on her fame by marketing her identity to various advertisers. The facts were as follows:

> [Deutsch] prepared [a] series of advertisements [for Samsung]. The series ran in at least half a dozen publications with widespread, and in some cases national, circulation. Each of the advertisements in the series followed the same theme. Each depicted a current item from popular culture and a Samsung electronic product. Each was set in the twenty-first century and conveyed the message that the Samsung product would still be in use by that time. By hypothesizing outrageous future outcomes for the cultural items, the ads created humorous effects. For example, one lampooned current popular notions of an unhealthy diet by depicting a raw steak with the caption: "Revealed to be health food. 2010 A.D." Another depicted irreverent "news"-show host Morton Downey Jr. in front of an American flag with the caption: "Presidential candidate. 2008 A.D."
>
> The advertisement which prompted the current dispute was for Samsung video-cassette recorders (VCRs). The ad depicted a robot, dressed in a wig, gown, and jewelry which Deutsch consciously selected to resemble White's hair and dress. The robot was posed next to a game board which is instantly recognizable as the Wheel of Fortune game show set, in a stance for which White is famous. The caption of the ad read: "Longest-running game show. 2012 A.D." Defendants referred to the ad as the "Vanna White" ad. Unlike the other celebrities used in the campaign, White neither consented to the ads nor was she paid.

Has White's "right of publicity" been violated by public display of the robot? Should this case be handled the same as the *Dworkin* case referred to in problem #1?

5. Consider *Nader v. General Motors Corp.*, 25 N.Y.2d 560, 307 N.Y.S.2d 647, 255 N.E.2d 765 (App. 1970), which involved the following facts:

> The plaintiff, an author and lecturer on automotive safety, has, for some years, been an articulate and severe critic of General Motors' products from the standpoint of safety and design. According to the

> complaint—which, for present purposes, we must assume to be true—the appellant, having learned of the imminent publication of the plaintiff's book "Unsafe at any Speed," decided to conduct a campaign of intimidation against him in order to "suppress plaintiff's criticism of and prevent his disclosure of information about its products." To that end, the appellant authorized and directed the other defendants to engage in a series of activities which, the plaintiff claims in his first two causes of action, violated his right to privacy.
>
> Specifically, the plaintiff alleges that the appellant's agents (1) conducted a series of interviews with acquaintances of the plaintiff, "questioning them about, and casting aspersions upon [his] political, [social,] racial and religious [views]; his integrity; his sexual proclivities and inclinations; and his personal habits"; (2) kept him under surveillance in public places for an unreasonable length of time; (3) caused him to be accosted by girls for the purpose of entrapping him into illicit relationships; (4) made threatening, harassing and obnoxious telephone calls to him; (5) tapped his telephone and eavesdropped, by means of mechanical and electronic equipment, on his private conversations with others; and (6) conducted a "continuing" and harassing investigation of him.

Do these allegations constitute the tort of "invasion of privacy?" If so, what remedy should be imposed? If an injunction is issued, how should it be framed? In answering this problem, consider the following case.

GALELLA V. ONASSIS

353 F.Supp. 196 (S.D.N.Y. 1972).

COOPER, DISTRICT JUDGE.

[Plaintiff, a free-lance photographer, sued defendant Onassis and her Secret Service agents for false arrest, malicious prosecution and interference with his business. Defendant counterclaimed seeking compensatory and punitive damages of $1.5 million and injunctive relief, based on claimed violations of her common law, statutory and constitutional rights of privacy and intentional infliction of emotional distress, assault, harassment and malicious prosecution. * * *

[Galella] described himself as "the world's only American paparazzi." [The] record establishes at least these differences between the behavior of other photographers and reporters and the attack of the paparazzi:

1. Assaults and batteries. Galella's physical movements were always unnerving and often frightening. Many witnesses testified to his "jumping," "lunging," "leaping," "rushing out," "snaking in and out," "dashing at me," "touching," "bumping," "scuffling," "blocking," "thrusting" his camera and circling (sometimes with assistants) in close orbit about defendant and her children. [The] constance of this Galella

practice, applied by him with such unrestrained and relentless vigor, borders on the cruel.

At times the threat of physical harm was heightened, as it appeared that the propeller of his boat might cut defendant's legs or that his wash might capsize John's boat or that John would fall from his bicycle or his horse. At other times there were deliberate or predictable contacts or physical consequences—the "flicking" of his camera strap, "pushing," "brushing," after-images of endless flashbulbs, John falling to his knees at night or Caroline falling off her water skis.

2. Offensive mouthings. Unlike other members of the press, Galella "grunts," "yells," makes "strange sounds," "laughs" and calls to defendant: "How do you like me?"; "The Marines have landed!"; "Ha Ha," "Snuggle up to Santa"; "Glad to see me back, aren't you, Jackie?" And to Caroline: "I am not making you nervous, am I, honey?" (he was making her cry); "How do you like the great paparazzi being back again!"

3. Bogus events. Galella forces his subjects into ersatz happenings. He hired a costumed Santa to try to force himself close to defendant so as to create an unreal situation. This false, forced, attempted pose echoes the startled expression which Galella seeks to arouse by his assaults and taunts. News is real; Galella promotes the phony.

4. Self-aggrandizement. Professing anonymity, Galella actually abjured it. His strength was endless in his quest for the limelight. Galella made a career not only of photographing Mrs. Onassis but of being known as one who has done so. The record before this Court shows that he has persistently arranged to have himself photographed with Mrs. Onassis. He has posed for photographs to be published in nationwide and worldwide magazines disclosing the "disguises" he dons to photograph Mrs. Onassis. He boasts openly of the intimate knowledge he has of her every move. He revels in the attention that comes to him as a result of the extreme measures only he is willing to practice.

5. Seeking a "PAYOFF." No self-respecting reporter will suppress his story for a price. Not so Galella, who offered to cease his activities for money or a job.

6. Incessant surveillance. Reporters diligently track their stories down, but when the story is over, they go away. They do not, like Galella, camp for years at their subject's door and dog their every step. The result of Galella's surveillance is that Mrs. Onassis may not enter or leave her home without Galella's knowledge and is faced with the constant threat that he will follow her hour after hour wherever she goes.

7. "Secret Agent" tactics. Outside of movieland, reporters do not normally hide behind restaurant coat racks, sneak into beauty parlors, don "disguises," hide in bushes and theatre boxes, intrude into school buildings and, when ejected, enlist the aid of schoolchildren, bribe

doormen and romance maids. The chases that figure in the trial record here would not be performed by a news reporter when there is no news afoot.

[Galella] profited by being the only American paparazzi. He had the field to himself; no one else was willing to harass, torment and victimize a subject. He alone was unchecked by inner prohibitions. He alone believes in his right to harass defendant. At trial, when we asked plaintiff's counsel whether a public figure must submit to harassment, there was no response.

Galella's objective? To establish himself as the peerless photographer who could capture the comings and goings and doings of Mrs. Onassis and her children, and by frightening them, to obtain unusual photographs which bring him handsome returns—financial and otherwise. He made it a world venture. His renown would take him into other fields, other subjects. Personal publicity was the touchstone. The instant suit, we have found, was a publicity stunt coupled with an anticipated settlement—the former objective was achieved; the latter failed.

Galella's persistent paparazzi attack brought this testimony from defendant: "It caused me anguish. It caused me fear for my safety, for the safety of my children. At times it caused me terror, distress, no peace, no peace of mind, fear for what was going to happen to them and to me when we would encounter him again; also being under surveyance [sic], imprisoned in your house, all that deportment over all this time was—caused an enormous strain and unhappiness, and all of that on me, for myself and for my children."

[Mrs. Onassis'] severe emotional distress is evident and reasonable. [Mrs.] Onassis and her children are people who have a very special fear of startling movements, violent activity, crowds and other hostile behavior. It is clear that the assassinations of the first husband of Mrs. Onassis and of her brother-in-law (Senator Robert F. Kennedy) are matters of common knowledge to virtually every citizen. These matters were certainly known to Galella, who "specializes" in the affairs of Mrs. Onassis and who chronicled her brother-in-law's funeral. These events make Mrs. Onassis and her children particularly susceptible to Galella's erratic behavior and make his acts all the more outrageous and utterly devoid of any sensitivity whatever for his subjects.

The trial record abounds with the extraordinary lengths to which defendant went to avoid contact with him. She cancelled plans, went out the back way of her residence as well as the side door at restaurants (he admitted once she left through the restaurant kitchen door) and tried to avoid him at other places she patronized (even at that, she seldom succeeded), checked to see if he were about the building, tried to hire cars with different license plates (which he promptly noted).

[Galella] asserts that the First Amendment is a complete defense to the counterclaim and intervenor complaint. We reject this contention; it is unsupported by legal authority.

The proposition that the First Amendment gives the press wide liberty to engage in any sort of conduct, no matter how offensive, in gathering news has been flatly rejected.

[Defendant] is a public figure. Nevertheless, the First Amendment does not immunize all conduct designed to gather information about or photographs of a public figure. There is no general constitutional right to assault, harass, or unceasingly shadow or distress public figures.

[Clearly,] the First Amendment protects freedom of expression with respect to public affairs—matters relevant to the self-government of the nation. It extends to "all issues about which information is needed or appropriate to enable members of the society to cope with the exigencies of their period." Doubtless, Mrs. Onassis is a public figure, whose life has included events of great public concern. But it cannot be said that information about her comings and goings, her tastes in ballet, the food that she eats, and other minutiae which are the sole product of Galella's three years of pursuit, bear significantly upon public questions or otherwise "enable the members of society to cope with the exigencies of their period." It merely satisfies curiosity.

[It] might be argued that the Court should not place itself in the position of drawing lines and of weighing the value of various communications so as to deny to some of them, under certain circumstances, the protection of the First Amendment. But that is what courts are for. [We] see no constitutional violence done by permitting defendant to prevent intrusion on her life which serves no useful purpose.

[P]laintiff's persistent threatening of Mrs. Onassis' person by jumping from concealed locations, following her at close distances at high speeds and otherwise carrying out the paparazzi attack, constitutes civil assault. On those occasions when there has been an offensive contact—flicking with a camera strap, bumping, brushing—the further tort of battery was committed by Galella.

[Plaintiff's] endless snooping [also] constitutes tortious invasion of privacy.

[Plaintiff's] surveillance [of defendant is continuous] to the point where he is notified of her every movement. He waits outside her residence at all hours. He follows her about irrespective of what she is doing: trailing her up and down the streets of New York, chasing her out of the city to neighboring places and foreign countries when she leaves for recreation or vacation, haunting her at restaurants (recording what she eats), theatres, the opera and other places of entertainment, and pursuing her when she goes shopping, getting close to her at the counter and inquiring of personnel as to her clothing purchases. His surveillance is so overwhelmingly pervasive that he has said he has not married because he has been unable to "get a girl who would be willing to go looking for Mrs. Onassis at odd hours."

He studies her habits, the operations of her household and the procedures of the Secret Service in guarding her children. He has kept her under such close observation for so long a period of time that he has commented at considerable length on her personality, her shopping tastes and habits, and her preferences for entertainment. With evident satisfaction, he referred, while testifying, to his "usual habitual observation." He has intruded into her children's schools, hidden in bushes and behind coat racks in restaurants, sneaked into beauty salons, bribed doormen, hatcheck girls, chauffeurs, fishermen in Greece, hairdressers and schoolboys, and romanced employees. In short, Galella has insinuated himself into the very fabric of Mrs. Onassis' life and the challenge to this Court is to fashion the tool to get him out.

[As] we see it, Galella's conduct falls within the formulation of the right of privacy as expressed in this opinion. The surveillance, close-shadowing and monitoring were clearly "overzealous" and therefore actionable. Moreover, Galella's corruption of doormen, romancing of the personal maid, deceptive intrusions into children's schools, and return visits to restaurants and stores to inquire about purchases were all exclusively for the "purpose of gathering information of a private and confidential nature."

[As] Dean Prosser has pointed out, "The law of privacy comprises four distinct kinds of invasion of four different interests of the plaintiff, which are tied together by the common name, but otherwise have almost nothing in [common]": (i) commercial appropriation of one's name or likeness, (ii) intrusion, (iii) public disclosure of private facts and (iv) publicity which places the plaintiff in a false light in the public eye. W. PROSSER, LAW OF TORTS § 117 at 804–12 (4th ed. 1971). * * *

[F]reedom from extensive shadowing and observation has come to be protected in most other jurisdictions.

[Plaintiff also committed the tort of infliction of mental distress.] [T]he totality of plaintiff's conduct was extreme, intentional and outrageous, and the emotional distress experienced by defendant and her children was severe and reasonably so. The record demonstrates there is substantial basis for their reactions and concerns; they were indeed harassed, threatened and denied privacy by plaintiff's offensive conduct. * * *

[Finally,] the Constitution itself creates a right of privacy. [The] essence of the privacy interest includes a general "right to be left alone," and to define one's circle of intimacy; to shield intimate and personal characteristics and activities from public gaze; to have moments of freedom from the unremitted assault of the world and unfettered will of others in order to achieve some measure of tranquillity for contemplation or other purposes, without which life loses its sweetness. The rationale extends to protect against unreasonably intrusive behavior which attempts or succeeds in gathering information, and includes, but is not limited to, such disparate abuses of privacy as the unreasonable seeking, gathering, storing, sharing and disseminating of information by humans and machines.

It has been cogently suggested that the right to privacy proscribes dehumanizing conduct which assaults "liberty, personality and self-respect." Fried, *Privacy*, 77 Yale L.J. 475, 485 (1968).

The claim that this constitutional right runs only against "state action" overlooks the fact that the act of a court—even the entry of a judgment denying relief—is state action within the meaning of the Fourteenth Amendment. Hence, the denial of relief in this case—relief essential to vindicate a basic human and constitutional right—would itself violate the Constitution.

[D]efendant's "right to be left alone" is exactly what plaintiff relentlessly invaded as the trial record here overwhelmingly demonstrates.

[Injunctive] relief appears appropriate either as implicit in the statute or on common law principles of equity. * * *

Permanent injunctive relief is available where there is no adequate remedy at law, where the balance of the equities favor the moving party, and where success on the merits (probability of success for a preliminary injunction) have been demonstrated. As we have already dealt with the merits, we confine the present analysis to the first two points.

No adequate remedy at law. We conclude there is no adequate remedy at law because of: the recurrent nature of plaintiff's invasions of defendant's rights; the need for a multiplicity of damage actions to assert defendant's rights; the imminent threat of continued emotional and physical trauma; and the difficulty of evaluating the injuries in this case in monetary terms.

[The] record demonstrates that Galella's surveillance and harassment of Mrs. Onassis has already gone on for a number of years and will continue, by his own account, for "another four or five years." Hence, Mrs. Onassis' legal remedies are inadequate on this ground alone.

Balance of the equities. The equities clearly balance in favor of defendant, particularly in view of our order which is addressed to protecting Galella's ability to continue his livelihood and our expressed willingness throughout the trial to receive evidence showing that the distances heretofore provided were unduly burdensome. Galella's attitude toward his subjects as well as to the orders of this Court are not impressive landmarks on his journey to establishing a balance of the equities in his favor.

One cannot violate another's rights, thereby reaping an ill-gotten profit, and then resist injunctive relief on the ground that it will prevent him from making similar future profits. In the face of such a situation, the Chancellor does not smile.

The injunction contemplated does not "put Galella out of business" as he has claimed—it merely moderates the way he can conduct himself in the pursuit of that "business."

We regarded the portion of the proposed order which would have completely prevented Galella from photographing Mrs. Onassis or her children to be clearly overbroad, struck it, and will not include it in a final order. Galella's occupation is lawful and the objective of the order is to modify his conduct, not to prevent his photography.

For practical reasons, the injunction cannot be couched in terms of prohibitions upon Galella's leaping, blocking, taunting, grunting, hiding and the like. Nor have abstract concepts—harassing, endangering—proved workable. No effective relief seems possible without the fixing of proscribed distances.

We must moreover make certain plaintiff keeps sufficiently far enough away to avoid problems as to compliance with the injunction and injurious disobedience. Disputes concerning his compliance may be frequent, thereby necessitating repeated application to the Court. Hence, the restraint must be clear, simple and effective so that Galella's substantial compliance cannot seriously be disputed unless a violation occurs.

Of major importance in determining the scope of the relief to be afforded here is the attitude which Galella has demonstrated toward the process of this Court in the past. Galella blatantly violated our restraining orders of October 8 and December 2, 1971. He did so deliberately and in full knowledge of the fact of his violation. His deliberate disobedience to the subpoena and his attempts to obstruct [justice], together with the perjury that infected his testimony, do not warrant mere token relief.

In light of Galella's repeated misbehavior, it is clear that only a strong restraint—an injunction which will clearly protect Mrs. Onassis' rights and leave no room for quibbling about compliance and no room for evasion or circumvention—is appropriate in this case.

[Necessarily] the fixing of proscribed distances will occasionally place plaintiff at a disadvantage compared with photographers whose behavior is more civil. But as the Seventh Circuit observed in granting a trade secret injunction: "[B]y its inequitable conduct, appellant has precluded itself from enjoying the rights of the general public to the patent [disclosure]." *Shellmar Products Co. v. Allen–Qualley Co.*, 87 F.2d 104, 108 (7th Cir.1936), *cert. denied*, 301 U.S. 695 (1937).

As for the actual distance to be proscribed, we must bear in mind that plaintiff never moved to modify the distances heretofore imposed by our restraining order, even after the Court had clearly and explicitly invited him to do so if he could prove it was too harsh.

NOTE

Injunctions to stop harassment are exceedingly difficult to draft. The problem is that harassment can take so many forms and can be so difficult to define. Moreover, the order must provide effective protection to plaintiff without unduly or unconstitutionally restricting defendant's freedom. In *Galella v. Onassis*, the court's original injunction prohibited Galella from approaching within 100 yards of Mrs. Onassis' home; 75 yards from the children; 50 yards from Mrs. Onassis; "from performing surveillance" of Mrs. Onassis or her children; and "from commercially appropriating [Mrs. Onassis'] photograph for advertising or trade purposes." The Second Circuit modified the order, finding it broader than necessary. *See Galella v. Onassis*, 487 F.2d 986 (2d Cir.1973). Galella was cited for contempt again about 10 years later. *Galella v. Onassis*, 533 F.Supp. 1076 (S.D.N.Y.1982). Today, many jurisdictions have enacted "anti-stalking," "bubble zone," "peeping Tom," and other kinds of civil and criminal legislation to prevent harassment.

K. LEAFLETING

PROBLEM

Randall Johnson wants to deliver religious pamphlets door-to-door in the City of Glenview Hills, Kentucky. A local ordinance prohibits all solicitations and all distribution of pamphlets or literature within the city limits except by mail. Johnson has come to you for legal advice. He is extremely upset because today, when he was distributing religious literature door-to-door in Glenview Hills, the police ordered him to desist and leave. Johnson, fearing for the souls of the unsaved who have not received his literature, wants to return immediately. What remedies are available to him?

ORGANIZATION FOR A BETTER AUSTIN V. KEEFE

402 U.S. 415, 91 S.Ct. 1575, 29 L.Ed.2d 1 (1971).

MR. CHIEF JUSTICE BURGER delivered the opinion of the Court.

We granted the writ in this case to consider the claim that an order of the Circuit Court of Cook County, Illinois, enjoining petitioners from distributing leaflets anywhere in the town of Westchester, Illinois, violates petitioners' rights under the Federal Constitution.

Petitioner Organization for a Better Austin (OBA) is a racially integrated community organization in the Austin neighborhood of Chicago. Respondent is a real estate broker whose office and business activities are in the Austin neighborhood. He resides in Westchester, Illinois, a suburb of Chicago some seven miles from the Austin area.

OBA is an organization whose stated purpose is to "stabilize" the racial ratio in the Austin area. For a number of years the boundary of the Negro segregated area of Chicago has moved progressively west to Austin. OBA, in its efforts to "stabilize" the area—so it describes its program—has opposed and protested various real estate tactics and activities generally known as "blockbusting" or "panic peddling."

It was the contention of OBA that respondent had been one of those who engaged in such tactics, specifically that he aroused the fears of the local white residents that Negroes were coming into the area and then, exploiting the reactions and emotions so aroused, was able to secure listings and sell homes to Negroes. OBA alleged that since 1961 respondent had from time to time actively promoted sales in this manner by means of flyers, phone calls, and personal visits to residents of the area in which his office is located, without regard to whether the persons solicited had expressed any desire to sell their homes. As the "boundary" marking the furthest westward advance of Negroes moved into the Austin area, respondent is alleged to have moved his office along with it.

Community meetings were arranged with respondent to try to persuade him to change his real estate practices. Several other real estate agents were prevailed on to sign an agreement whereby they would not solicit property, by phone, flyer, or visit, in the Austin community. Respondent who has consistently denied that he is engaging in "panic peddling" or "blockbusting" refused to sign, contending that it was his right under Illinois law to solicit real estate business as he saw fit.

Thereafter, during September and October of 1967, members of petitioner organization distributed leaflets in Westchester describing respondent's activities. There was no evidence of picketing in Westchester. The challenged publications, now enjoined, were critical of respondent's real estate practices in the Austin neighborhood; one of the leaflets set out the business card respondent used to solicit listings, quoted him as saying "I only sell to Negroes," cited a Chicago Daily News article describing his real estate activities and accused him of being a "panic peddler." Another leaflet, of the same general order, stated that: "When he signs the agreement, we stop coming to Westchester." Two of the leaflets requested recipients to call respondent at his home phone number and urge him to sign the "no solicitation" agreement. On several days leaflets were given to persons in a Westchester shopping center. On two other occasions leaflets were passed out to some parishioners on their way to or from respondent's church in Westchester. Leaflets were also left at the doors of his neighbors. The trial court found that petitioners' "distribution of leaflets was on all occasions conducted in a peaceful and orderly manner, did not cause any disruption of pedestrian or vehicular traffic, and did not precipitate any fights, disturbances or other breaches of the peace." One of the officers of OBA testified at trial that he hoped that respondent would be induced to sign the no-solicitation agreement by letting "his neighbors know what he was doing to us."

Respondent sought an injunction in the Circuit Court of Cook County, Illinois, on December 20, 1967. After an adversary hearing the trial court entered a temporary injunction enjoining petitioners "from passing out pamphlets, leaflets or literature of any kind, and from picketing, anywhere in the City of Westchester, Illinois."

On appeal to the Appellate Court of Illinois, First District, that court affirmed. It sustained the finding of fact that petitioners' activities in Westchester had invaded respondent's right of privacy, had caused irreparable harm, and were without adequate remedy at law. The Appellate Court appears to have viewed the alleged activities as coercive and intimidating, rather than informative and therefore as not entitled to First Amendment protection. The Appellate Court rested its holding on its belief that the public policy of the State of Illinois strongly favored protection of the privacy of home and family from encroachment of the nature of petitioners' activities.

It is elementary, of course, that in a case of this kind the courts do not concern themselves with the truth or validity of the publication. Under *Near v. Minnesota*, 283 U.S. 697 (1931), the injunction, so far as it imposes prior restraint on speech and publication, constitutes an impermissible restraint on First Amendment rights. Here, as in that case, the injunction operates, not to redress alleged private wrongs, but to suppress, on the basis of previous publications, distribution of literature "of any kind" in a city of 18,000.

This Court has often recognized that the activity of peaceful pamphleteering is a form of communication protected by the First Amendment. In sustaining the injunction, however, the Appellate Court was apparently of the view that petitioners' purpose in distributing their literature was not to inform the public, but to "force" respondent to sign a no-solicitation agreement. The claim that the expressions were intended to exercise a coercive impact on respondent does not remove them from the reach of the First Amendment. Petitioners plainly intended to influence respondent's conduct by their activities; this is not fundamentally different from the function of a newspaper. Petitioners were engaged openly and vigorously in making the public aware of respondent's real estate practices. Those practices were offensive to them, as the views and practices of petitioners are no doubt offensive to others. But so long as the means are peaceful, the communication need not meet standards of acceptability.

Any prior restraint on expression comes to this Court with a "heavy presumption" against its constitutional validity. Respondent thus carries a heavy burden of showing justification for the imposition of such a restraint. He has not met that burden. No prior decisions support the claim that the interest of an individual in being free from public criticism of his business practices in pamphlets or leaflets warrants use of the injunctive power of a court. Designating the conduct as an invasion of privacy, the apparent basis for the injunction here, is not sufficient to support an injunction against peaceful distribution of informational literature of the nature revealed by this record. [R]espondent is not attempting to stop the flow of information into his own household, but to the public. Accordingly, the injunction issued by the Illinois court must be vacated.

Reversed.

L. OBSCENITY

PROBLEM

A local ordinance requires that all pictures be submitted to the local "movie review board" prior to exhibition. Exhibition is only allowed if a license is granted. A client has come to you for advice. The client wants to exhibit a film that he believes is not obscene, but does not want to submit the film to the movie review board. Must the client do so? If the client wants a judicial remedy, what remedy might you seek?

FREEDMAN V. STATE OF MARYLAND

380 U.S. 51, 85 S.Ct. 734, 13 L.Ed.2d 649 (1965).

MR. JUSTICE BRENNAN delivered the opinion of the Court.

Appellant sought to challenge the constitutionality of the Maryland motion picture censorship statute, Md. Ann. Code, 1957, Art. 66A, and exhibited the film "Revenge at Daybreak" at his Baltimore theatre without first submitting the picture to the State Board of Censors as required by § 2 thereof. The State concedes that the picture does not violate the statutory standards and would have received a license if properly submitted, but the appellant was convicted of a § 2 violation despite his contention that the statute in its entirety unconstitutionally impaired freedom of expression. * * *

In *Times Film Corp. v. City of Chicago*, 365 U.S. 43, we considered and upheld a requirement of submission of motion pictures in advance of exhibition. The Court of Appeals held, on the authority of that decision, that "the Maryland censorship law must be held to be not void on its face as violative of the freedoms protected against State action by the First and Fourteenth Amendments." This reliance on *Times Film* was misplaced. The only question tendered for decision in that case was "whether a prior restraint was necessarily unconstitutional under all circumstances." The exhibitor's argument that the requirement of submission without more amounted to a constitutionally prohibited prior restraint was interpreted by the Court in *Times Film* as a contention that the "constitutional protection includes complete and absolute freedom to exhibit, at least once, any and every kind of motion picture [even] if this film contains the basest type of pornography, or incitement to riot or to forceful overthrow of orderly [government]." The Court held that, on this "narrow" question, the argument stated the principle against prior restraints too broadly; citing a number of our decisions, the Court quoted the statement from *Near v. State of Minnesota*, 283 U.S. 697, 716, that "[t]he protection even as to previous restraint is not absolutely unlimited." In rejecting the proffered proposition in *Times Film* the Court emphasized, however, that "[i]t is that question alone which we decide," and it would therefore be inaccurate to say that *Times Film* upheld the specific features of the Chicago censorship ordinance.

Unlike the petitioner in *Times Film*, appellant does not argue that § 2 is unconstitutional simply because it may prevent even the first showing of a film whose exhibiting may legitimately be the subject of an obscenity prosecution. [A]ccepting the rule in *Times Film*, he argues that § 2 constitutes an invalid prior restraint because, in the context of the remainder of the statute, it presents a danger of unduly suppressing protected expression. He focuses particularly on the procedure for an initial decision by the censorship board, which, without any judicial participation, effectively bars exhibition of any disapproved film, unless and until the exhibitor undertakes a time-consuming appeal to the Maryland courts and succeeds in having the Board's decision reversed. Under the statute, the exhibitor is required to submit the film to the Board for examination, but no time limit is imposed for completion of Board action, § 17. If the film is disapproved, or any elimination ordered, § 19 provides that "The person submitting such film or view for examination will receive immediate notice of such elimination or disapproval, and if appealed from, such film or view will be promptly reexamined, in the presence of such person, by two or more members of the Board, and the same finally approved or disapproved promptly after such re-examination, with the right of appeal from the decision of the Board to the Baltimore City Court of Baltimore City. There shall be a further right of appeal from the decision of the Baltimore City Court to the Court of Appeals of Maryland, subject generally to the time and manner provided for taking appeal to the Court of Appeals."

Thus there is no statutory provision for judicial participation in the procedure which bars a film, nor even assurance of prompt judicial review. Risk of delay is built into the Maryland procedure, as is borne out by experience; in the only reported case indicating the length of time required to complete an appeal, the initial judicial determination has taken four months and final vindication of the film on appellate review, six months. * * *

Although the Court has said that motion pictures are not "necessarily subject to the precise rules governing any other particular method of expression," it is as true here as of other forms of expression that "[a]ny system of prior restraints of expression comes to this Court bearing a heavy presumption against its constitutional validity." *Bantam Books, Inc. v. Sullivan, supra*, 372 U.S. at 70. "[U]nder the Fourteenth Amendment, a State is not free to adopt whatever procedures it pleases for dealing with obscenity [without] regard to the possible consequences for constitutionally protected speech." *Marcus v. Search Warrant*, 367 U.S. 717, 731. The administration of a censorship system for motion pictures presents peculiar dangers to constitutionally protected speech. Unlike a prosecution for obscenity, a censorship proceeding puts the initial burden on the exhibitor or distributor. Because the censor's business is to censor, there inheres the danger that he may well be less responsive than a court—part of an independent branch of government—to the constitutionally protected interests in free expression. And if it is made unduly onerous, by reason of delay or otherwise, to seek judicial review, the censor's determination may in practice be final.

Applying the settled rule of our cases, we hold that a noncriminal process which requires the prior submission of a film to a censor avoids constitutional infirmity only if it takes place under procedural safeguards designed to obviate the dangers of a censorship system. First, the burden of proving that the film is unprotected expression must rest on the censor. As we said in *Speiser v. Randall*, 357 U.S. 513, 526, "Where the transcendent value of speech is involved, due process certainly requires [that] the State bear the burden of persuasion to show that the appellants engaged in criminal speech." Second, while the State may require advance submission of all films, in order to proceed effectively to bar all showings of unprotected films, the requirement cannot be administered in a manner which would lend an effect of finality to the censor's determination whether a film constitutes protected expression. The teaching of our cases is that, because only a judicial determination in an adversary proceeding ensures the necessary sensitivity to freedom of expression, only a procedure requiring a judicial determination suffices to impose a valid final restraint. To this end, the exhibitor must be assured, by statute or authoritative judicial construction, that the censor will, within a specified brief period, either issue a license or go to court to restrain showing the film. Any restraint imposed in advance of a final judicial determination on the merits must similarly be limited to preservation of the status quo for the shortest fixed period compatible with sound judicial resolution. Moreover, we are well aware that, even after expiration of a temporary restraint, an administrative refusal to license, signifying the censor's view that the film is unprotected, may have a discouraging effect on the exhibitor. Therefore, the procedure must also assure a prompt final judicial decision, to minimize the deterrent effect of an interim and possibly erroneous denial of a license.

Without these safeguards, it may prove too burdensome to seek review of the censor's determination. Particularly in the case of motion pictures, it may take very little to deter exhibition in a given locality. The exhibitor's stake in any one picture may be insufficient to warrant a protracted and onerous course of litigation. The distributor, on the other hand, may be equally unwilling to accept the burdens and delays of litigation in a particular area when, without such difficulties, he can freely exhibit his film in most of the rest of the country; for we are told that only four States and a handful of municipalities have active censorship laws.

It is readily apparent that the Maryland procedural scheme does not satisfy these criteria. First, once the censor disapproves the film, the exhibitor must assume the burden of instituting judicial proceedings and of persuading the courts that the film is protected expression. Second, once the Board has acted against a film, exhibition is prohibited pending judicial review, however protracted. Under the statute, appellant could have been convicted if he had shown the film after unsuccessfully seeking a license, even though no court had ever ruled on the obscenity of the film. Third, it is abundantly clear that the Maryland statute provides no assurance of prompt judicial determination. We hold, therefore, that appellant's conviction must be reversed. The Maryland scheme fails to provide adequate safeguards against undue inhibition of protected expression, and this renders the § 2 requirement of prior submission of films to the Board an invalid previous restraint.

How or whether Maryland is to incorporate the required procedural safeguards in the statutory scheme is, of course, for the State to decide. But a model is not lacking: In *Kingsley Books, Inc. v. Brown*, 354 U.S. 436, we upheld a New York injunctive procedure designed to prevent the sale of obscene books. That procedure postpones any restraint against sale until a judicial determination of obscenity following notice and an adversary hearing. The statute provides for a hearing one day after joinder of issue; the judge must hand down his decision within two days after termination of the hearing. The New York procedure operates without prior submission to a censor, but the chilling effect of a censorship order, even one which requires judicial action for its enforcement, suggests all the more reason for expeditious determination of the question whether a particular film is constitutionally protected.

The requirement of prior submission to a censor sustained in *Times Film* is consistent with our recognition that films differ from other forms of expression. Similarly, we think that the nature of the motion picture industry may suggest different time limits for a judicial determination. It is common knowledge that films are scheduled well before actual exhibition, and the requirement of advance submission in § 2 recognizes this. One possible scheme would be to allow the exhibitor or distributor to submit his film early enough to ensure an orderly final disposition of the case before the scheduled exhibition date—far enough in advance so that the exhibitor could safely advertise the opening on a normal basis. Failing such a scheme or sufficiently early submission under such a scheme, the statute would have to require adjudication considerably more prompt than has been the case under the Maryland statute. Otherwise, litigation might be unduly expensive and protracted, or the victorious exhibitor might find the most propitious opportunity for exhibition past. We do not mean to lay down rigid time limits or procedures, but to suggest considerations in drafting legislation to accord with local exhibition practices, and in doing so to avoid the potentially chilling effect of the Maryland statute on protected expression.

Reversed.

MR. JUSTICE DOUGLAS, whom MR. JUSTICE BLACK joins, concurring.

[M]ovies are entitled to the same degree and kind of protection under the First Amendment as other forms of expression. [I] do not believe any form of censorship—no matter how speedy or prolonged it may be—is permissible. As I see it, a pictorial presentation occupies as preferred a position as any other form of expression. If censors are banned from the publishing business, from the pulpit, from the public platform—as they are—they should be banned from the theatre. [Any] authority to obtain a temporary injunction gives the State "the paralyzing power of a censor." The regime of *Kingsley Books* "substitutes punishment by contempt for punishment by jury trial." I would put an end to all forms and types of censorship and give full literal meaning to the command of the First Amendment.

NOTES

Vance v. Universal Amusement Co., Inc., 445 U.S. 308, 100 S.Ct. 1156, 63 L.Ed.2d 413 (1980), involved a Texas statute allowing the state to abate "nuisances" defined to include "the commercial manufacturing, commercial distribution, or commercial exhibition of obscene material." The state was authorized to obtain judgments "abating said nuisance and enjoining the defendants from maintaining the same, and ordering that said house be closed for one year [unless certain conditions are met]." The Court struck down the law:

> [When] coupled with the Texas Rules of Civil Procedure, [the statute] authorizes prior restraints of indefinite duration on the exhibition of motion pictures that have not been finally adjudicated to be obscene. Presumably, an exhibitor would be required to obey such an order pending review of its merits and would be subject to contempt proceedings even if the film is ultimately found to be nonobscene. Such prior restraints would be more onerous and more objectionable than the threat of criminal sanctions after a film has been exhibited, since nonobscenity would be a defense to any criminal prosecution.
>
> Nor does the fact that the temporary prior restraint is entered by a state trial judge rather than an administrative censor sufficiently distinguish this case from *Freedman v. Maryland.* [That] a state trial judge might be thought more likely than an administrative censor to determine accurately that a work is obscene does not change the unconstitutional character of the restraint if erroneously entered.
>
> [T]he absence of any special safeguards governing the entry and review of orders restraining the exhibition of named or unnamed motion pictures, without regard to the context in which they are displayed, precludes the enforcement of these nuisance statutes against motion picture exhibitors.

Mr. Justice White dissented:

> [The] Art. 4667(a) injunction does, in a sense, "restrain" future speech by declaring punishable future exhibitions of obscene motion pictures. But in this weak sense of the term criminal obscenity statutes would also be considered "prior restraints." Prior restraints are distinct from, and more dangerous to free speech than, criminal statutes because, through caprice, mistake, or purpose, the censor may forbid speech which is constitutionally protected, and because the speaker may be punished for disobeying the censor even though his speech was protected. Those dangers are entirely absent here. An injunction against the showing of unnamed obscene motion pictures does not and cannot bar the exhibitor from showing protected material, nor can the exhibitor be punished, through contempt proceedings, for showing such material. The Art. 4667(a) injunction, in short, does not impose a traditional prior restraint. On the contrary, it seems to me functionally indistinguishable from a criminal obscenity statute. Since an appropriately worded criminal statute is constitutionally valid, I believe that Art. 4667(a) is valid also. * * *

M. ADMISSION CASES

Admission cases, in which an individual seeks admission to a club or association, present comparable concerns. Consider the following.

PROBLEMS

1. Gus Who applied for membership in the Seneca Gardens Country Club (Seneca), a private club located in the City of Seneca Gardens. Seneca, which has a total of 112 members, does not allow the public to use its facilities except at the invitation of a club member. Membership in the club is difficult to obtain. The club does not advertise, and does not accept unsolicited applications for membership. An applicant must be sponsored by an existing club member, and unanimously approved by Seneca's Board of Directors.

Mr. Who wants to join the club for two reasons: all of his friends belong and he hopes to make business contacts (Who sells insurance). Who's application for membership is denied. Under club rules, any member is entitled to veto an applicant. Two members, who didn't like Who, "blackballed" him.

Mr. Who believes that he was "maliciously" denied admission. Mr. Who sues seeking damages and an order compelling the club to admit him. Is a court likely to order Seneca to admit Who to membership? In *Falcone*, the Court suggests that "golf clubs" and "fraternal organizations" enjoy "freedom from legal restraint." Does a country club also enjoy that freedom? Why shouldn't a court review the club's justifications for denying Mr. Who admission? If the court finds that the club acted arbitrarily and capriciously, why shouldn't the court order the club to admit Mr. Who to membership or award him damages?

2. After *Roberts*, would a different result obtain if Mr. Who was turned down because of his race (Mr. Who is black) or religion in violation of a local ordinance prohibiting social clubs from discriminating on such grounds?

FALCONE V. MIDDLESEX COUNTY MEDICAL SOCIETY

34 N.J. 582, 170 A.2d 791 (1961).

The opinion of the court was delivered by JACOBS, J.

[After] pre-medical study, Dr. Falcone enrolled in the Philadelphia College of Osteopathy. While there he received a full medical course and in 1946 was awarded the degree of Doctor of Osteopathy (D.O.). Thereafter he served a one-year internship and a three-year residency at the Detroit Osteopathic Hospital. He presented his credentials to the New Jersey State Board of Medical Examiners, passed the prescribed medical examination, and in 1950 received a certificate from the State Board which set forth that Italo John Falcone, D.O. had passed examination and "is hereby licensed to practice Medicine and Surgery in the State of New

Jersey." The Philadelphia School is an accredited school of osteopathy and, after a personal inspection, was approved as in good standing by the New Jersey State Board of Medical Examiners; although the Philadelphia School affords a full traditional medical course as well as osteopathic teaching, it has not been recognized as an approved medical college by the American Medical Association (A.M.A.). In November 1951, after seven months' attendance, plus credit for his work at the Philadelphia School, Dr. Falcone graduated from the College of Medicine of the University of Milan with the degree of Doctor of Medicine and Surgery (M.D.). The College of Medicine of the University of Milan was then and still is recognized as an approved medical college by the American Medical Association. Following his graduation from Milan, Dr. Falcone completed a sixteen months' internship at St. Peter's General Hospital in New Brunswick and thereafter he had a short residency in surgery at the Jersey City Medical Center. The St. Peter's internship had the approval of the American Medical Association; the residency at the Jersey City Medical Center had no such approval and was terminated by Dr. Falcone when he became aware of that fact.

In 1953 Dr. Falcone was admitted as an associate member of the Middlesex County Medical Society. The by-laws of the Society provide that a physician may not be an associate member for more than two years. In 1956 the Society declined to admit Dr. Falcone as an active member, assigning as its reason that he had been "licensed to practice as a Doctor of Osteopathy and, not as a Doctor of Medicine." This reason was unsound since Dr. Falcone's license unrestrictedly authorized him to practice medicine and surgery although it did refer to him as the holder of the degree of D.O. Nothing in the Society's written by-laws purports to preclude membership by a licensed physician who holds an M.D. from an A.M.A. approved medical school (as does Dr. Falcone) but the record does indicate that the Society's committee on medical ethics applies an unwritten membership requirement of four years of study at a medical college approved by the A.M.A. This requirement, if effective, would preclude membership by Dr. Falcone since the A.M.A. has not approved the Philadelphia School and Dr. Falcone's actual attendance at the A.M.A. approved school at Milan was not of the prescribed duration; and it would preclude his membership despite the uncontroverted evidence that he is a duly licensed and duly registered New Jersey physician who meets all of the qualifications prescribed in the written by-laws; that he has consistently practiced surgery and obstetrics and has never practiced osteopathy; that he is regarded by medical colleagues who are members of the Society, as a qualified physician and surgeon; and that he has not engaged in any conduct which would raise any question as to his professional ethics and competency.

The Society's declaration of his ineligibility and its refusal to admit him to membership have had seriously adverse economic and professional effects on Dr. Falcone. He was a member of the medical staffs of the Middlesex General Hospital and St. Peter's General Hospital in New Brunswick but was dropped because they, like other hospitals in the area, require that their staff physicians be members of the County Medical Society. It seems entirely evident that Dr. Falcone cannot successfully continue his practice of surgery and obstetrics or properly serve his surgical and obstetric patients without the use of local hospital facilities; he testified that in order to earn a livelihood it is necessary "to belong to the local society" for "otherwise, you cannot use the hospitals." The virtual monopoly which the Society possesses in fact over the use of local hospital facilities results from the well known interrelationship between the County Society, the State Medical Society, the American Medical Association and the Joint Commission on Accreditation of Hospitals. Over thirty years ago Professor Chafee, in his discussion of nonprofit associations, pointed to the distinction between the customary social and fraternal organizations on the one hand and trade unions and professional societies on the other hand; he noted that whereas exclusion or expulsion from a social or fraternal organization may result in little more than hurt feelings, exclusion or expulsion from a trade union or a professional society may result, as here, in deprivation of the invaluable opportunity "to earn a livelihood." 43 Harv.L.Rev., at p. 1022. In a more recent discussion addressed specially to medical societies, the editors of the Yale Law Journal, after pointing out that exclusion or expulsion from a local medical society results, as a practical matter, in the deprivation of hospital facilities, descriptively noted that "non-membership amounts to a partial revocation of licensure to practice medicine." 63 Yale L.J. at p. 953.

After the County Society refused to admit him to full membership, Dr. Falcone appealed to the State Medical [Society]. [The] County Society's position in the Law Division, repeated in this court, is that it is a voluntary organization which is at liberty to prescribe its own rules and that Dr. Falcone has "no judicially enforceable right of admission to membership." In the Law Division, Judge Vogel determined that, in the light of its virtual monopolistic control of the practice of medicine in the area, the County Society must be dealt with as involuntary in nature and subject to judicial scrutiny; he expressly found that the County Society's requirement of four years' study in a medical college approved by the A.M.A., as applied to Dr. Falcone, "contravenes the public policy of the State" and entered judgment directing that it admit him to full membership.

[Courts] have been understandably reluctant to interfere with the internal affairs of membership associations and their reluctance has ordinarily promoted the health of society. Nevertheless, in particular situations, where the considerations of policy and justice were sufficiently compelling, judicial scrutiny and relief were not found wanting; for the most part these situations involved improper expulsions from preexisting membership which called forth judicial directions for reinstatement or other suitable relief. In granting relief courts have, on various occasions, discussed specific legal theories resting on protection of the member's property interests, his contractual rights, and his advantageous relationships with the association; on other occasions they have, without discussion of specific legal theories, set aside the expulsion as being unreasonable, contrary to natural justice or violative of public policy. *See* Cox, *'The Role of Law in Preserving Union Democracy,'* 72 HARV.L.REV. 609, 613 (1959). * * *

In *Trautwein v. Harbourt*, 40 N.J.Super. 247, 123 A.2d 30 (App.Div.1956), the court recently dealt with an action for damages by plaintiffs who alleged that they were maliciously denied admission to membership in the Order of the Eastern Star, a fraternal organization of New Jersey. In rejecting the plaintiffs' claim for relief the court differentiated the expulsion cases and distinguished exclusion cases involving organizations "membership in which is an economic necessity" or "those which are repositories of civic, civil or political rights."

We are here in nowise concerned with a social or fraternal organization such as the Order of the Eastern Star. We are here concerned with [an] organization, membership in which may here [be] viewed as "an economic necessity"; in dealing with such an organization, the court must be particularly alert to the need for truly protecting the public welfare and advancing the interests of justice by reasonably safeguarding the individual's opportunity for earning a livelihood while not impairing the proper standards and objectives of the organization.

[When] courts originally declined to scrutinize admission practices of membership associations they were dealing with social clubs, religious organizations and fraternal associations. Here the policies against judicial intervention were strong and there were no significant countervailing policies. When the courts were later called upon to deal with trade and professional associations exercising virtually monopolistic control, different factors were involved. The intimate personal relationships which pervaded the social, religious and fraternal organizations were hardly in evidence and the individual's opportunity of earning a livelihood and serving society in his chosen trade or profession appeared as the controlling policy consideration. Here there have been persuasive indications [that] in a case presenting sufficiently compelling factual and policy considerations, judicial relief will be available to compel admission to membership; we are entirely satisfied [that] Dr. Falcone has presented such a case.

[T]he County Medical Society is not a private voluntary membership association with which the public had little or no concern. It is an association with which the public is highly concerned and which engages in activities vitally affecting the health and welfare of the people. [It] is a component part of the State Medical Society which was granted a charter by the Legislature in 1864. The Legislature has granted authority to the State Society to confer the degree of Doctor of Medicine although the record suggests that the State Society has never availed itself of this authority; and the Legislature has provided that certain appointments to the State Board of Medical Examiners shall be made from a list furnished to the Governor by the State Society. Through its interrelationships, the County Medical Society possesses, in fact, a virtual monopoly over the use of local hospital facilities. As a result it has power, by excluding Dr. Falcone from membership, to preclude him from successfully continuing in his practice of obstetrics and surgery and to restrict patients who wish to engage him as an obstetrician or surgeon in their freedom of choice of physicians. Public policy strongly dictates that this power should not be unbridled but should be viewed judicially as a fiduciary power to be exercised in reasonable and lawful manner for the advancement of the interests of the medical profession and the public generally; the evidence firmly displays that here it was not so exercised and that Dr. Falcone was fairly and justly entitled to the relief awarded to him in the Law Division.

The doctrinal controversy between the American Medical Association and the American Osteopathic Association need not detain us since the record establishes that Dr. Falcone received a full medical course along with the degree of D.O. at the Philadelphia School, received the degree of M.D. from the College of Medicine of the University of Milan (an A.M.A. accredited medical school), received an unrestricted license to practice medicine and surgery from the New Jersey State Board of Medical Examiners after passing the prescribed examination, completed internships at the Detroit Osteopathic Hospital and St. Peter's General Hospital (the latter being approved by the A.M.A.), consistently practiced surgery and obstetrics but not osteopathy, is regarded by his medical colleagues as a qualified physician and surgeon, and has not engaged in any conduct which would raise any question as to his ethics and competency as a member of the medical profession. In the light of all of the foregoing, the effort of the County Society to apply its unwritten requirement of four years' attendance at an A.M.A. approved medical college so as to exclude Dr. Falcone from membership, must be viewed as patently arbitrary and unreasonable and beyond the pale of the law. When the County Society engages in action which is designed to advance medical science or elevate professional standards, it should and will be sympathetically supported. When, however, as here, its action has no relation to the advancement of medical science or the elevation of professional standards but runs strongly counter to the public policy of our State and the true interests of justice, it should and will be stricken down. The judgment entered in the Law Division is in all respects:

Affirmed.

BLATT V. UNIVERSITY OF SOUTHERN CALIFORNIA

5 Cal.App.3d 935, 85 Cal.Rptr. 601 (1970).

SCHWEITZER, ASSOCIATE JUSTICE.

[The Order of the Coif ("Coif") recognizes scholastic achievement by law students. Members are elected from law students in the top 10 percent of their law school classes at accredited schools. Plaintiff claims that officials of the University of Southern California chapter represented to him that, if he were in the top 10 percent of his graduating class, he would be elected to Coif membership. Plaintiff ranked fourth in a graduating class of 135.]

Plaintiff alleges that in June 1967 the committee elected seven or eight members to the Order who ranked below him in scholastic achievement; that plaintiff was not elected because "membership was restricted to students who, being eligible for the school's Law Review, accepted the invitation to work on the Law Review and completed their assignments successfully"; that said reason "was unreasonable, arbitrary and contrary to the representations" mentioned above, and was not applicable to plaintiff because it was a policy adopted after said representations were made to plaintiff; that prior to the adoption of the policy plaintiff served on the Law Review and submitted articles for publication therein; that after the adoption of the policy, plaintiff was not advised that it applied to him but was advised that the policy was applicable only to day students who thereafter became eligible for Law Review work; that plaintiff relied upon this advice and information and did not thereafter apply for or accept a Law Review assignment, although he did thereafter submit articles for publication in the Law Review, none of which, however, were published; and that other students who did not complete Law Review work and were in a similar position to plaintiff were elected to the Order.

The complaint concludes by alleging that plaintiff is qualified and entitled to membership in the Order, that defendants breached their promises and representations, and that he was denied membership therein by arbitrary and discriminatory action based upon erroneous and invalid reasons. The complaint seeks a declaration of the rights and duties of the parties, a determination that plaintiff is entitled to election to membership in the Order, and an order directing defendants to admit plaintiff to membership.

Plaintiff argues that organizations whose membership offers the member educational, professional or financial advantage cannot arbitrarily and discriminatorily deny admission to one who has met and complied with all the stated and represented requirements of membership. He admits that the courts in the past have refused to interfere with professional and honorary societies to compel one's admission but calls our attention to recent cases where courts have interfered to compel admission to membership in voluntary associations that have some effect upon the applicant's professional or economic success, or where the association has a professional or economic interest. He attributes this change in judicial attitude primarily to the recognition by the courts of the increasing effect that private and voluntary organizations have on the individual's ability and access to the economic marketplace and his opportunities to earn a living or practice his trade or profession.

[Plaintiff] alleges that "[e]lection to the Order of the Coif elevates the esteem, standing and position of the law student elected in the eyes of the school faculty, fellow students, judges, the legal profession and the public at large; and greatly enhances his employment possibilities and economic position after graduation and admittance to the Bar." He contends that his allegation that nonelection will adversely affect his professional and economic interests is sufficient to bring him within the purview of the cited cases, that this is a question of fact, not of law, and therefore he should be permitted to offer evidence in support of this allegation. In effect he argues that the courts may compel admission to membership in voluntary organizations in any situation where membership may enhance or affect one's professional or economic interests. Such is not the law. The cited cases do not support this contention; they are expressly limited in application to situations affecting the right to work in a chosen occupation or specialized field thereof. We have been unable to find any authority that supports plaintiff's contention.

To adopt plaintiff's contention would subject to judicial review the membership selection activity and policies of Every voluntary organization because it is difficult to conceive of any organization that does not in some respect involve or affect professional or economic interests of its members. It would also subject to judicial review procedures used in selecting persons for advanced and honorary degrees, and for selection of members for such honorary societies as Phi Beta Kappa, each of which presumably have some resultant professional or economic benefit. We know of no compelling factual or policy consideration for holding that judicial relief should be made available to compel admission to membership in every voluntary organization, especially in honorary organizations where outstanding scholars or leaders of a profession are best qualified to evaluate the record of those being considered for membership.

Membership in the Order does not give a member the right to practice the profession of law. It does not signify qualification for any specialized field of practice. It has no direct bearing on the number or type of clients that the attorney-member might have or on the income he will make in his professional practice. It does not affect his basic right to earn a living. We hold that in the absence of allegations of sufficient facts of arbitrary or discriminatory action, membership in the Order is an honor best determined by those in the academic field without judicial interference. Plaintiff's allegations of arbitrary or discriminatory action on the part of the election committee are insufficient to state a cause of action. No justiciable issue has been presented.

Plaintiff [also] contends that his complaint states a cause of action for breach of contract; that the necessary elements of a contract are present; that there was an offer, representations by defendant individuals that if he ranked in the top 10 per cent of his class, he would be eligible for election to membership in the Order; and that there was his acceptance, he "worked very hard" to and did achieve grades which placed him in the top 10 per cent of his class. Plaintiff recognizes that the offer spoke in terms of eligibility for election and not that he would be elected, but states that there were only two requisites for election as to persons in the top 10 per cent: first, "activities that contribute directly to legal education such as legal research and writing," and second, whether he was of fit character. He argues that since the complaint alleged, and the demurrer admitted that he was rejected for neither of these grounds, the court, in determining the sufficiency of the complaint, must accept as true his allegations that he complied with all the subjective and objective requirements for admittance.

Plaintiff seeks to establish a unilateral contract, one in which a promise is given in exchange for an act, forbearance or a thing. There was no benefit flowing to defendants as a result of plaintiff's hard work or his class ranking. Any benefit that accrued inured to plaintiff. Consequently there was no consideration for any alleged promise or representations of defendants. Therefore, if any contract existed, it was because of the doctrine of promissory estoppel, a substitute for consideration. * * *

Plaintiff argues that the alleged promise in this case is similar to cases where a promisor was estopped from denying the promised payment of a bonus, pension or reward. * * *

An impassioned argument of detriment and change of position by plaintiff has been submitted. He points out that he might well have decided to take an easier path through law school and graduate with an average scholastic record instead of attaining excellence; that he had this initial choice; that after the individual defendants "enticed" him by their promises, he took the tougher road; that his extra effort for scholastic achievement was in reliance upon and motivated by the representations of the promised award. He compares election to the Order to a prize offered for certain achievements, stating that election is not a mere gratuity granted without achievement, but is the promised award for inspired achievement.

The bonus pension and reward cases relied on by plaintiff are not applicable here since in each case the promisee suffered actual detriment in foregoing an act, in refusing other employment or in expending definite and substantial effort or money in reliance on a promise. [I]n this case the alleged promises or representations were such that it cannot be said that they induced "action [of] a Definite and substantial character on the part of the promisee." (REST. CONTRACTS, § 90.)

[E]ven if it be assumed that the doctrine of promissory estoppel were applicable, we note that plaintiff has not pleaded a breach of contract. There is no allegation that it was promised that he would in fact be admitted to membership if he graduated in the top 10 per cent of his class. The allegation is that he "would be eligible for election" if he attained such position. The complaint alleges that his name was on the eligible list and did receive consideration by the election committee under the general standards set forth in the Order's constitution. This is all that the individual defendants promised. The facts pleaded do not support the alleged conclusion that there was a breach of contract.

Judgment affirmed.

NOTES

Roberts v. United States Jaycees, 468 U.S. 609, 104 S.Ct. 3244, 82 L.Ed.2d 462 (1984), involved the Junior Chamber of Commerce, an organization dedicated to:

> [such] educational and charitable purposes as will promote and foster the growth and development of young men's civic organizations in the United States, designed to inculcate in the individual membership of such organization a spirit of genuine Americanism and civic interest, and as a supplementary education institution to provide them with opportunity for personal development and achievement and an avenue for intelligent participation by young men in the affairs of their community, state and nation, and to develop true friendship and understanding among young men of all nations.

The Jaycees had historically discriminated by admitting women only to "associate membership." When the Minneapolis and St. Paul chapters began admitting women as regular members, the national organization threatened to revoke their charters. In response, the chapters filed charges with the Minnesota Department of Human Rights alleging a violation of the Minnesota Human Rights Act which applied to "a business, accommodation, refreshment, entertainment, recreation, or transportation facility of any kind, whether licensed or not, whose goods, services, facilities, privileges, advantages or accommodations are extended, offered, sold, or otherwise made available to the public."

When the state department found probable cause and ordered an evidentiary hearing, the national organization sought declaratory and injunctive relief preventing enforcement of the Act. The suit claimed violations of the male members' constitutional rights of free speech and association. The Supreme Court rejected the challenge:

> Our decisions have referred to constitutionally protected "freedom of association" in two distinct senses. In one line of decisions, the Court has concluded that choices to enter into and maintain certain intimate human relationships must be secured against undue intrusion by the State because of the role of such relationships in safeguarding the individual freedom that is central to our constitutional scheme. In this respect, freedom of association receives protection as a fundamental element of personal liberty. In another set of decisions, the Court has recognized a right to associate for the purpose of engaging in those activities protected by the First Amendment—speech, assembly, petition for the redress of grievances, and the exercise of religion. The Constitution guarantees freedom of association of this kind as an indispensable means of preserving other individual liberties.
>
> The intrinsic and instrumental features of constitutionally protected association may, of course, coincide. In particular, when the State interferes with individuals' selection of those with whom they wish to join in a common endeavor, freedom of association in both of its forms may be implicated. The Jaycees contend that this is such a case. Still, the nature and degree of constitutional protection afforded freedom of association may vary depending on the extent to which one or the other aspect of the constitutionally protected liberty is at stake in a given case. * * *
>
> The Court has long recognized that, because the Bill of Rights is designed to secure individual liberty, it must afford the formation and preservation of certain kinds of highly personal relationships a substantial measure of sanctuary from unjustified interference by the State. [The] personal affiliations that exemplify these considerations, and that therefore suggest some relevant limitations on the relationships that might be entitled to this sort of constitutional protection, are those that attend the creation and sustenance of a family—marriage, childbirth, the raising and education of children, and cohabitation with one's relatives. Family relationships, by their nature, involve deep attachments and commitments to the necessarily few other individuals with whom one shares not only a special community of thoughts, experiences, and beliefs but also distinctively personal aspects of one's life. Among other things, therefore, they are distinguished by such attributes as relative smallness, a high degree of selectivity in decisions to begin and maintain the affiliation, and seclusion from others in critical aspects of the relationship. As a general matter,

only relationships with these sorts of qualities are likely to reflect the considerations that have led to an understanding of freedom of association as an intrinsic element of personal liberty. Conversely, an association lacking these qualities—such as a large business enterprise—seems remote from the concerns giving rise to this constitutional protection. Accordingly, the Constitution undoubtedly imposes constraints on the State's power to control the selection of one's spouse that would not apply to regulations affecting the choice of one's fellow employees.

Between these poles, of course, lies a broad range of human relationships that may make greater or lesser claims to constitutional protection from particular incursions by the State. Determining the limits of state authority over an individual's freedom to enter into a particular association therefore unavoidably entails a careful assessment of where that relationship's objective characteristics locate it on a spectrum from the most intimate to the most attenuated of personal attachments. We need not mark the potentially significant points on this terrain with any precision. We note only that factors that may be relevant include size, purpose, policies, selectivity, congeniality, and other characteristics that in a particular case may be pertinent. In this case, however, several features of the Jaycees clearly place the organization outside of the category of relationships worthy of this kind of constitutional protection.

The undisputed facts reveal that the local chapters of the Jaycees are large and basically unselective groups. At the time of the state administrative hearing, the Minneapolis chapter had approximately 430 members, while the St. Paul chapter had about 400. Apart from age and sex, neither the national organization nor the local chapters employ any criteria for judging applicants for membership, and new members are routinely recruited and admitted with no inquiry into their backgrounds. In fact, a local officer testified that he could recall no instance in which an applicant had been denied membership on any basis other than age or sex. Furthermore, despite their inability to vote, hold office, or receive certain awards, women affiliated with the Jaycees attend various meetings, participate in selected projects, and engage in many of the organization's social functions. Indeed, numerous non-members of both genders regularly participate in a substantial portion of activities central to the decision of many members to associate with one another, including many of the organization's various community programs, awards ceremonies, and recruitment meetings.

In short, the local chapters of the Jaycees are neither small nor selective. Moreover, much of the activity central to the formation and maintenance of the association involves the participation of strangers to that relationship. Accordingly, we conclude that the Jaycees chapters lack the distinctive characteristics that might afford constitutional protection to the decision of its members to exclude women. We turn therefore to consider the extent to which application of the Minnesota statute to compel the Jaycees to accept women infringes the group's freedom of expressive association.

An individual's freedom to speak, to worship, and to petition the government for the redress of grievances could not be vigorously protected from interference by the State unless a correlative freedom to engage in group effort toward those ends were not also guaranteed. [W]e have long understood as implicit in the right to engage in activities protected by the First Amendment a corresponding right to associate with others in pursuit of a wide variety of political, social, economic, educational, religious, and cultural ends. In view of the various protected activities in which the Jaycees engages, that right is plainly implicated in this case.

Government actions that may unconstitutionally infringe upon this freedom can take a number of forms. Among other things, government may seek to impose penalties or withhold benefits from individuals because of their membership in a disfavored group; it may attempt to require disclosure of the fact of membership in a group seeking anonymity, and it may try to interfere with the internal organization or affairs of the group. By requiring the Jaycees to admit women as full voting members, the Minnesota Act works an infringement of the last type. There can be no clearer example of an intrusion into the internal structure or affairs of an association than a regulation that forces the group to accept members it does not desire. Such a regulation may impair the ability of the original members to express only those views that brought them together. Freedom of association therefore plainly presupposes a freedom not to associate.

The right to associate for expressive purposes is not, however, absolute. Infringements on that right may be justified by regulations adopted to serve compelling state interests, unrelated to the suppression of ideas, that cannot be achieved through means significantly less restrictive of associational freedoms. We are persuaded that Minnesota's compelling interest in eradicating discrimination against its female citizens justifies the impact that application of the statute to the Jaycees may have on the male members' associational freedoms.

On its face, the Minnesota Act does not aim at the suppression of speech, does not distinguish between prohibited and permitted activity on the basis of viewpoint, and does not license enforcement authorities to administer the statute on the basis of such constitutionally impermissible criteria. Nor does the Jaycees contend that the Act has been applied in this case for the purpose of hampering the organization's ability to express its views. Instead, as the Minnesota Supreme Court explained, the Act reflects the State's strong historical commitment to eliminating discrimination and assuring its citizens equal access to publicly available goods and services. That goal, which is unrelated to the suppression of expression, plainly serves compelling state interests of the highest order.

[By] prohibiting gender discrimination in places of public accommodation, the Minnesota Act protects the State's citizenry from a number of serious social and personal harms. [T]his Court has frequently noted that discrimination based on archaic and overbroad assumptions about the relative needs and capacities of the sexes forces individuals to labor under stereotypical notions that often bear no relationship to their actual abilities. It thereby both deprives persons of their individual dignity and denies society the benefits of wide participation in political, economic, and cultural life. * * *

[A] State enjoys broad authority to create rights of public access on behalf of its citizens. Like many States and municipalities, Minnesota has adopted a functional definition of public accommodations that reaches various forms of public, quasi-commercial conduct. [I]n explaining its conclusion that the Jaycees local chapters are "place[s] of public accommodations" within the meaning of the Act, the Minnesota court noted the various commercial programs and benefits offered to members and stated that "[l]eadership skills are 'goods,' [and] business contacts and employment promotions are 'privileges' and ['advantages']." Assuring women equal access to such goods, privileges, and advantages clearly furthers compelling state interests.

[The] Jaycees has failed to demonstrate that the Act imposes any serious burdens on the male members' freedom of expressive association. [Over] the years, the national and local levels of the organization have taken public positions on a number of diverse issues, and members of the Jaycees regularly engage in a variety of civic, charitable, lobbying, fundraising, and other activities worthy of constitutional protection under the First Amendment. There is, however, no basis in the record for concluding that admission of women as full voting members will impede the organization's ability to engage in these protected activities or to disseminate its preferred views. The Act requires no change in the Jaycees' creed of promoting the interests of young men, and it imposes no restrictions on the organization's ability to exclude individuals with ideologies or philosophies different from those of its existing members. Moreover, the Jaycees already invites women to share the group's views and philosophy and to participate in much of its training and community activities. Accordingly, any claim that admission of

> women as full voting members will impair a symbolic message conveyed by the very fact that women are not permitted to vote is attenuated at best.
>
> [It is] arguable that [the] admission of women as voting members will change the message communicated by the group's speech because of the gender-based assumptions of the audience. Neither supposition, however, is supported by the record. [In] the absence of a showing far more substantial than that attempted by the Jaycees, we decline to indulge in the sexual stereotyping that underlies appellee's contention that, by allowing women to vote, application of the Minnesota Act will change the content or impact of the organization's speech.

EXERCISES

1. Windy Hills University (Windy U.), a state university, has one of the best law schools in the country. However, Windy U. is located in a state with a history of de jure segregation and has a tragic history of discrimination against minorities. In recent years, Windy U. has been trying to overcome its history, but the University's success rate has been low. Recently, Ben Johnson was denied admission to Windy U.

Johnson has come to you for advice. Johnson believes that he was discriminated against on the basis of race (Johnson is black). Johnson shows you documents indicating that Windy U. has a relatively low numbers of blacks and Hispanics on its faculty (only 1 faculty member is black, and none are Hispanic) and student body (1% of the student body is black or Hispanic in a state with 20% blacks and Hispanics). In addition, Johnson tells you that he overheard the Chair of the Admissions Committee speaking to another Committee member. Both made disparaging remarks about blacks and Hispanics.

After reviewing various papers provided by Johnson and talking to Windy U. officials, you learn that Windy U. admits law students based on a composite index which includes an applicant's undergraduate grade point average and score on the Law School Admissions Test (LSAT). Johnson's composite score was 6.6. Windy U. automatically admitted all applicants with a composite score of 6.9 or higher. Applicants with lower scores were "discretionary admits." Windy U. admitted 60% of all students with a 6.7 composite, 50% of all students with a 6.6 composite, and 30% of all students with a 6.5 composite. Only 6 minority students were admitted to the class of 180. No black student with a composite score of 6.5 or 6.6 was admitted.

Suppose that you were inclined to take Johnson's suit against Windy U. What remedies might you seek on his behalf? What obstacles might you anticipate?

2. Recently, several rejected applicants to the University of Texas (UT) School of Law sued claiming reverse discrimination (the rejected applicants, who were white, claim that UT gave illegal preferences to black and Mexican-

American applicants). The Fifth Circuit Court of Appeals ultimately concluded that the school had illegally discriminated. What remedies should be available to the rejected applicants? The same remedies available to Johnson in the prior exercise? What obstacles do you anticipate in the UT case? *See Hopwood v. State of Texas*, 78 F.3d 932 (5th Cir. 1996).

N. EXPULSION

Are "expulsion" cases treated differently than "admission" cases? Consider the following.

PROBLEMS

1. *Are different remedies available in an expulsion case than in an admission case?* The Peninsula Golf and Country Club ("Peninsula Club" or "Club"), is a nonprofit, private, social and recreational club. The Club has a golf course, tennis courts, a restaurant and bar. These facilities are for members. Others may enter only as the guests of members. Membership is available only to those who are unanimously accepted by the Club's Board of Directors.

In 1970, Eugene and Mary Ann Klein, husband and wife, obtained a regular family membership in the Club. The Kleins paid their initiation fee and monthly dues with community property funds, and both used the facilities and attended its social events. In 1981, the Kleins were divorced. The divorce decree awarded the family membership at Peninsula Club to Mary Ann. Shortly thereafter, the Club revoked Mary Ann's membership and tendered her a refund check for the initiation fee. The Club did so based on section 7.5 of its bylaws which stated that a regular family membership could be held only in the name of an adult male.

Suppose that you are an attorney, and Mary Ann has come to you for advice. Would you advise her to sue the club? What remedies can she hope to receive? Would you expect a court to respond differently to an expulsion case than to an admission case? *See Warfield v. Peninsula Golf and Country Club*, 214 Cal.App.3d 646, 262 Cal.Rptr. 890 (1989).

2. Would you advise Mary Ann differently if you knew that the Club leased its facilities to outsiders a few times a year, and that state law prohibits sexual discrimination by a "business establishment"? The law provides in pertinent part: "All persons within the jurisdiction of this state are free and equal, and no matter what their sex, race, color, religion, ancestry, national origin, or blindness or other physical disability are entitled to the full and equal accommodations, advantages, facilities, privileges, or services in all business establishments of every kind whatsoever."

BOARD OF CURATORS OF THE UNIVERSITY OF MISSOURI v. HOROWITZ

435 U.S. 78, 98 S.Ct. 948, 55 L.Ed.2d 124 (1978).

MR. JUSTICE REHNQUIST delivered the opinion of the Court.

Respondent, a student at the University of Missouri–Kansas City Medical School, was dismissed by petitioner officials of the school during her final year of study for failure to meet academic standards. Respondent sued [alleging] that petitioners had not accorded her procedural due process prior to her dismissal. [We] granted certiorari to consider what procedures must be accorded to a student at a state educational institution whose dismissal may constitute a deprivation of "liberty" or "property" within the meaning of the Fourteenth Amendment. * * *

I

Respondent was admitted with advanced standing to the Medical School in the fall of 1971. During the final years of a student's education at the school, the student is required to pursue in "rotational units" academic and clinical studies pertaining to various medical disciplines such as obstetrics-gynecology, pediatrics, and surgery. Each student's academic performance at the school is evaluated on a periodic basis by the Council on Evaluation, a body composed of both faculty and students, which can recommend various actions including probation and dismissal. The recommendations of the Council are reviewed by the Coordinating Committee, a body composed solely of faculty members, and must ultimately be approved by the Dean. Students are not typically allowed to appear before either the Council or the Coordinating Committee on the occasion of their review of the student's academic performance.

In the spring of respondent's first year of study, several faculty members expressed dissatisfaction with her clinical performance during a pediatrics rotation. The faculty members noted that respondent's "performance was below that of her peers in all clinical patient-oriented settings," that she was erratic in her attendance at clinical sessions, and that she lacked a critical concern for personal hygiene. Upon the recommendation of the Council on Evaluation, respondent was advanced to her second and final year on a probationary basis.

Faculty dissatisfaction with respondent's clinical performance continued during the following year. For example, respondent's docent, or faculty adviser, rated her clinical skills as "unsatisfactory." In the middle of the year, the Council again reviewed respondent's academic progress and concluded that respondent should not be considered for graduation in June of that year; [the] Council recommended that, absent "radical improvement," respondent be dropped from the school.

Respondent was permitted to take a set of oral and practical examinations as an "appeal" of the decision not to permit her to graduate. Pursuant to this "appeal," respondent spent a substantial portion of time with seven practicing physicians in the area who enjoyed a good reputation among their peers. The physicians were asked to recommend whether respondent should be allowed to graduate on schedule and, if not, whether she should be dropped immediately or allowed to remain on probation. Only two of the doctors recommended that respondent be graduated on schedule. Of the other five, two recommended that she be immediately dropped from the school. The remaining three recommended that she not be allowed to graduate in June and be continued on probation pending further reports on her clinical progress. Upon receipt of these recommendations, the Council on Evaluation reaffirmed its prior position.

The Council met again in mid-May to consider whether respondent should be allowed to remain in school beyond June of that year. Noting that the report on respondent's recent surgery rotation rated her performance as "low-satisfactory," the Council unanimously recommended that "barring receipt of any reports that Miss Horowitz has improved radically, [she] not be allowed to re-enroll in [the] School of Medicine." The Council delayed making its recommendation official until receiving reports on other rotations; when a report on respondent's emergency rotation also turned out to be negative, the Council unanimously reaffirmed its recommendation that respondent be dropped from the school. The Coordinating Committee and the Dean approved the recommendation and notified respondent, who appealed the decision in writing to the University's Provost for Health Sciences. The Provost sustained the school's actions after reviewing the record compiled during the earlier proceedings.

To be entitled to the procedural protections of the Fourteenth Amendment, respondent must in a case such as this demonstrate that her dismissal from the school deprived her of either a "liberty" or a "property" interest. Respondent has never alleged that she was deprived of a property interest. Because property interests are creatures of state law, respondent would have been required to show at trial that her seat at the Medical School was a "property" interest recognized by Missouri state law. Instead, respondent argued that her dismissal deprived her of "liberty" by substantially impairing her opportunities to continue her medical education or to return to employment in a medically related field.

[We] have recently had an opportunity to elaborate upon the circumstances under which an employment termination might infringe a protected liberty interest. In *Bishop v. Wood*, 426 U.S. 341 (1976), we upheld the dismissal of a policeman without a hearing; we rejected the theory that the mere fact of dismissal, absent some publicizing of the reasons for the action, could amount to a stigma infringing one's liberty: "In *Board of Regents v. Roth*, 408 U.S. 564, we recognized that the nonretention of an untenured college teacher might make him somewhat less attractive to other employers, but nevertheless concluded that it would stretch the concept too far "to suggest that a person is deprived of 'liberty' when he simply is not rehired in one position but remains as free as before to seek another." This same conclusion applies to the discharge of a public employee whose position is terminable at the will of the employer when there is no public disclosure of the reasons for the discharge. * * *

We need not decide, however, whether respondent's dismissal deprived her of a liberty interest in pursuing a medical career. Nor need we decide whether respondent's dismissal infringed any other interest constitutionally protected against deprivation without procedural due process. Assuming the existence of a liberty or property interest, respondent has been awarded at least as much due process as the Fourteenth Amendment requires. The school fully informed respondent of the faculty's dissatisfaction with her clinical progress and the danger that this posed to timely graduation and continued enrollment. The ultimate decision to dismiss respondent was careful and deliberate. These procedures were sufficient under the Due Process Clause of the Fourteenth Amendment. We agree with the District Court that respondent "was afforded full procedural due process by the [school]. In fact, the Court is of the opinion, and so finds, that the school went beyond [constitutionally required] procedural due process by affording [respondent] the opportunity to be examined by seven independent physicians in order to be absolutely certain that their grading of the [respondent] in her medical skills was correct."

In *Goss v. Lopez*, 419 U.S. 565 (1975), we held that due process requires, in connection with the suspension of a student from public school for disciplinary reasons, "that the student be given oral or written notice of the charges against him and, if he denies them, an explanation of the evidence the authorities have and an opportunity to present his side of the story." The Court of Appeals apparently read *Goss* as requiring some type of formal hearing at which respondent could defend her academic ability and performance. All that *Goss* required was an "informal give-and-take" between the student and the administrative body dismissing him that would, at least, give the student "the opportunity to characterize his conduct and put it in what he deems the proper context." But we have frequently emphasized that "[t]he very nature of due process negates any concept of inflexible procedures universally applicable to every imaginable situation." The need for flexibility is well illustrated by the significant difference between the failure of a student to meet academic standards and the violation by a student of valid rules of conduct. This difference calls for far less stringent procedural requirements in the case of an academic dismissal.

Since the issue first arose 50 years ago, state and lower federal courts have recognized that there are distinct differences between decisions to suspend or dismiss a student for disciplinary purposes and similar actions taken for academic reasons which may call for hearings in connection with the former but not the latter. [Reason,] clearly supports the perception of these decisions. A school is an academic institution, not a courtroom or administrative hearing room. In *Goss*, this Court felt that suspensions of students for disciplinary reasons have a sufficient resemblance to traditional judicial and administrative factfinding to call for a "hearing" before the relevant school authority. While recognizing that school authorities must be afforded the necessary tools to maintain discipline, the Court concluded: "[I]t would be a strange disciplinary system in an educational institution if no communication was sought by the disciplinarian with the student in an effort to inform him of his dereliction and to let him tell his side of the story in order to make sure that an injustice is not [done]."

"[R]equiring effective notice and informal hearing permitting the student to give his version of the events will provide a meaningful hedge against erroneous action. At least the disciplinarian will be alerted to the existence of disputes about facts and arguments about cause and effect." Even in the context of a school disciplinary proceeding, however, the Court stopped short of requiring a formal hearing since "further formalizing the suspension process and escalating its formality and adversary nature may not only make it too costly as a regular disciplinary tool but also destroy its effectiveness as a part of the teaching process."

Academic evaluations of a student, in contrast to disciplinary determinations, bear little resemblance to the judicial and administrative fact-finding proceedings to which we have traditionally attached a full-hearing requirement. In *Goss*, the school's decision to suspend the students rested on factual conclusions that the individual students had participated in demonstrations that had disrupted classes, attacked a police officer, or caused physical damage to school property. The requirement of a hearing, where the student could present his side of the factual issue, could under such circumstances "provide a meaningful hedge against erroneous action." The decision to dismiss respondent, by comparison, rested on the academic judgment of school officials that she did not have the necessary clinical ability to perform adequately as a medical doctor and was making insufficient progress toward that goal. Such a judgment is by its nature more subjective and evaluative than the typical factual questions presented in the average disciplinary decision. Like the decision of an individual professor as to the proper grade for a student in his course, the determination whether to dismiss a student for academic reasons requires an expert evaluation of cumulative information and is not readily adapted to the procedural tools of judicial or administrative decisionmaking.

Under such circumstances, we decline to ignore the historic judgment of educators and thereby formalize the academic dismissal process by requiring a hearing. The educational process is not by nature adversary; instead it centers around a continuing relationship between faculty and students, "one in which the teacher must occupy many roles—educator, adviser, friend, and, at times, parent-substitute." *Goss v. Lopez*, 419 U.S., at 594 (Powell, J., dissenting). This is especially true as one advances through the varying regimes of the educational system, and the instruction becomes both more individualized and more specialized. In *Goss*, this Court concluded that the value of some form of hearing in a disciplinary context outweighs any resulting harm to the academic environment. Influencing this conclusion was clearly the belief that disciplinary proceedings, in which the teacher must decide whether to punish a student for disruptive or insubordinate behavior, may automatically bring an adversary flavor to the normal student-teacher relationship. The same conclusion does not follow in the academic context. We decline to further enlarge the judicial presence in the academic community and thereby risk deterioration of many beneficial aspects of the faculty-student relationship. We recognize, as did the Massachusetts Supreme Judicial Court over 60 years ago, that a hearing may be "useless or harmful in finding out the truth as to scholarship."

"Judicial interposition in the operation of the public school system of the Nation raises problems requiring care and restraint. * * *

[W]e agree with the District Court that no showing of arbitrariness or capriciousness has been made in this case. Courts are particularly ill-equipped to evaluate academic performance. The factors discussed in Part II with respect to procedural due process speak a fortiori here and warn against any such judicial intrusion into academic decisionmaking.

The judgment of the Court of Appeals is therefore

Reversed.

MR. JUSTICE MARSHALL, concurring in part and dissenting in part.

[R]esolution of this case under our traditional approach does not turn on whether the dismissal of respondent is characterized as one for "academic" or "disciplinary" reasons. In my view, the effort to apply such labels does little to advance the due process inquiry, as is indicated by examination of the facts of this case.

[A] talismanic reliance on labels should not be a substitute for sensitive consideration of the procedures required by due process. When the facts disputed are of a type susceptible of determination by third parties, as the allegations about respondent plainly were, there is no more reason to deny all procedural protection to one who will suffer a serious loss than there was in *Goss v. Lopez*, and indeed there may be good reason to provide even more protection. A court's characterization of the reasons for a student's dismissal adds nothing to the effort to find procedures that are fair to the student and the school, and that promote the elusive goal of determining the truth in a manner consistent with both individual dignity and society's limited resources. * * *

TEDESCHI V. WAGNER COLLEGE

49 N.Y.2d 652, 404 N.E.2d 1302, 427 N.Y.S.2d 760 (App. 1980).

MEYER, JUDGE.

[Plaintiff] Nancy Jean Tedeschi was admitted to Wagner College, a private institution, in September, 1976. She was a part-time student taking courses in mathematics, Latin and psychology. Her performance during the fall semester presented both academic and social problems, however. Dr. Thompson, her Latin professor, testified that she did not participate in class, did not know the required material and only once of the several times called upon was able to answer correctly even a simple question about Latin grammar. Her conduct during class was also disruptive in that three or four times during each period she would pick up her handbag and leave the room, returning after two to five minutes.

On the evening of December 20, 1976 Ms. Tedeschi sat for her Latin examination, but at the end of it dramatically tore up her blue book and did not hand it in. In response to her question, Dr. Thompson advised her that without an examination score her grade for the course would be an F. Beginning at 4 a.m. the next morning and continuing until late in the evening of December 22, Dr. Thompson was subjected to a barrage of telephone calls in which Ms. Tedeschi repeatedly threatened to commit suicide, or to "fix" Dr. Thompson, and at one point appeared in a distraught condition at the front door of his home. Only when the police were summoned and advised plaintiff of the possible criminal consequences did the calls cease.

On January 10, 1977 through his secretary, Dr. Wendel, the academic dean, contacted plaintiff and her mother by telephone to arrange a meeting with them for the purpose of discussing plaintiff's academic situation, in view of her incomplete grades in two courses. Plaintiff, however, refused to meet stating that there was no problem. There followed, nevertheless, another series of harassing calls by plaintiff to Dr. Thompson. Later that evening in a telephone conversation between Dr. Thompson and Nancy's mother, Mrs. Tedeschi refused to discuss the matter with college officials and insisted that any problem should be presented to her in a formal letter from the college. The next day plaintiff was orally advised by Dr. Wendel that she was suspended by the college because of her bad character and the repeated disruption of her Latin class. Thereafter she met with the academic dean, the dean of students and an assistant to the president, who testified that during the interviews plaintiff's conduct was irrational and discussion fruitless. By letter dated January 13, 1977 plaintiff was advised by the dean of students, Dr. Guttu, that after consultation with Dr. Wendel and other members of the faculty and the administration, she was "withdrawn from classes for the 1977 spring semester" but could, if she wished, reapply in the fall. Shortly thereafter plaintiff's tuition for the spring semester was refunded. Plaintiff's mother testified that she called the school several times to arrange a hearing, but without success.

Plaintiff then began this action alleging that she had not been granted a hearing or afforded an opportunity to defend herself and that she had been arbitrarily frustrated in completing her education. She asked for an order reinstating her and for damages. The trial court found [no] constitutional violation [and] the Appellate Division [affirmed]. The majority [noted] the college guideline quoted below but held that plaintiff had rebuffed several attempts by the college to arrange a [conference].

The guideline referred to is part of a publication distributed by the office of the dean of students entitled 1976–1977 Guidelines of Wagner College. The portion pertinent to this appeal reads:

> Whenever it shall appear that any student is not making satisfactory progress in his studies, and that his scholastic standing does not meet the requirements specified by the Committee on Academic Standards he shall be discharged from the College. If for any other cause a student is deemed to be an unfit member of the College, the Dean of Students may notify parents or guardians in order that they may have an opportunity to withdraw the student.
>
> A student may be suspended or expelled from the College by the Dean of Students or the Dean of Academic Affairs. If he is suspended or expelled for any cause other than failure in his academic work, and has not had recourse to a hearing before an established College Court, he shall have the right to be heard by the Student–Faculty Hearing Board which shall present its findings to the president of the college for final determination.

The differentiation between suspension or expulsion for academic unfitness and suspension or expulsion for causes other than academic failure drawn in that guideline reflects the dichotomy in decisional law drawn along similar lines.

Suspension or expulsion for causes unrelated to academic achievement [involve] determinations quite closely akin to the day-to-day work of the judiciary. Recognizing the present day importance of higher education to many, if not most, employment opportunities, the courts have, therefore, looked more closely at the actions of educational institutions in such matters.

The legal theory upon which review should be predicated in such cases is, however, not entirely clear. Plaintiff argues [that] the student-private college relationship is contractual and that it is an implied term of the contract that rules such as the Wagner College Guidelines will be adhered to by the college.

Contract theory is not wholly satisfactory, however, because the essentially fictional nature of the contract results in its generally being assumed rather than proved, because of the difficulty of its application, and because it forecloses inquiry into, and a balancing of, the countervailing interests of the student on the one hand and the institution on the other. An added problem is that when urged in academic achievement as distinct from nonacademic matters the contract tends to be limited to the implied in law condition of good faith, *i.e.*, not to act arbitrarily to the ultimate confusion of the rules applicable in the two situations.

An alternate basis for review of nonacademic disputes between students and private colleges, the application of the principles of the law of associations, is supported by case law in some other States. [The] law of associations accords judicial relief to an association member suspended or expelled without adherence to its rules. * * *

The parallel between associations and universities is, of course, not exact since students do not participate in the governance of a university with the same voice as generally do members in the functioning of an association. The situation is further confused by the facts that at least in part the association law under discussion is stated in terms of contract and that in several cases the obligation to follow its own rules has been applied to a private university without reference to contract law.

[Whether] by analogy to the law of associations, on the basis of a supposed contract between university and student, or simply as a matter of essential fairness in the somewhat one-sided relationship between the institution and the individual, [when] a university has adopted a rule or guideline establishing the procedure to be followed in relation to suspension or expulsion that procedure must be substantially observed.

[The] guideline permits either the dean of students or the dean of academic affairs to expel or suspend a student. The withdrawal letter forwarded on January 13, 1977 by the dean of students was, therefore, in conformance with its provisions. But the guideline does not stop there. It requires a further hearing by the Student–Faculty Hearing Board and review of that board's findings by the president of the college in any case in which suspension is for a cause other than academic failure and the student has not had a hearing before an established college court.

Dr. Guttu testified that the college court normally dealt with civil disorders or complaints by one student against another, but that cannot avail the college for it is undisputed that no court or board of any kind ever considered Nancy's case. As to the cause for Nancy's suspension, the Appellate Division found that it was based on her irrational and disruptive conduct. It, thus, apparently tacitly overruled the Trial Judge's reference to academic standing as a cause, but even if it did not, the further proceedings required by the guideline would still be mandated. This is because a suspension for both academic and other causes is necessarily, at least in part, a suspension for a cause other than academic failure. That is not to say that the board would have the right, not given it by the guideline, to review Nancy's scholastic standing as a ground for suspension, but simply to require that she have what the guideline accords her: review of the cause other than academic failure that it involved.

The college argues that Nancy's informal meetings with the two deans and the president's assistant was sufficient compliance with the guideline. Though those meetings may have been sensitive and fair, [it] constituted no acceptable substitute for a hearing board composed of both students and faculty. The college also suggests that the refusal of Mrs. Tedeschi to meet with its officials constituted a waiver of Nancy's hearing rights, but the guideline itself refutes that, since the purpose of such a meeting is simply to give the parent the possibility of avoiding embarrassment by withdrawing the student. * * *

Under the guideline plaintiff was properly suspended but was entitled to review of her suspension by the hearing board and the president. So much of the complaint as sought money damages and the right to a due process hearing based on claimed "state action" was properly dismissed, but she was entitled to judgment directing review by that body and that official as the guidelines require.

[What] the guideline contemplates, and what this opinion holds that it requires is review, by the Student–Faculty Hearing Board and by the president, of the nonacademic cause for Ms. Tedeschi's suspension. The apparent purpose of that review is the different viewpoint that may be taken by a hearing board composed of faculty and students than will be taken by a dean, whether the dean of students or the dean of admissions. No reason, other than the possible burden on the college in holding such a hearing, is suggested by the dissent for denying her that right.

[T]he order [is] reversed, with costs, and the case remitted to Supreme [Court] with directions to enter judgment reinstating plaintiff as a student for the September, 1980 term of the college, unless prior to the opening of that term she has been accorded a hearing by the Student–Faculty Hearing Board.

GABRIELLI, JUDGE (dissenting).

[Since a] hearing could be nothing more than a painful exercise in futility given the peculiar circumstances in this case, I am compelled to dissent.

[The] statements of the school authorities, taken together, paint a portrait of a distraught, emotionally disturbed young woman who seemed incapable of controlling her own feelings of aggression and was equally incapable of fulfilling her responsibilities as a student in an institution of higher learning. Ms. Tedeschi habitually disrupted her Latin class throughout her first semester at the college and, indeed, failed to complete two of the three courses in which she was enrolled. The rapid deterioration of her emotional state culminated in a series of harassing telephone calls and suicide threats which, understandably, alarmed the authorities at the school. Under the circumstances, it cannot be said that the college officials reacted in an arbitrary or unfair manner. To the contrary, in attempting to bring Ms. Tedeschi and her mother in for an informal interview to discuss the student's academic and emotional difficulties, the school officials obviously were hoping to reach a solution which would spare this unfortunate young woman further unnecessary embarrassment. That this is so is reflected in the college's final letter to Ms. Tedeschi, which stated that she was being asked to withdraw from classes, but indicated that she was free to apply for readmission if and when she straightened out her emotional difficulties. I cannot imagine a fairer resolution of the immediate problem, particularly in view of Ms. Tedeschi's continued inability to discuss the concerns of the school officials in a calm and rational manner.

[What] possible constructive purpose would be served by such a hearing we are not told. [T]here was never any reason to believe that the student had an alternate version of the facts to present to a neutral hearing body. To the contrary, the evidence accepted by the trial court demonstrates that Ms. Tedeschi and her mother had repeatedly rebuffed efforts by the school authorities to elicit their side of the story. * * *

O. COVENANTS NOT TO COMPETE

Lumley v. Wagner, [1852] 42 Eng.Rep. 687, is, perhaps, the most famous personal services case. Joanna Wagner agreed to sing at Benjamin Lumley's Her Majesty's Theatre for a period of three months, and simultaneously agreed not to sing for anyone else during that period. ("Mademoiselle Wagner engages herself not to use her talents at any other theatre, nor in any concert or reunion, public or private, without the written authorization of Mr. Lumley.") During the contract period,

Frederick Gye, lessee of the Royal Italian Opera, Covent Garden, hired Wagner to sing at his theatre for more money. Gye acted with "full knowledge" of the agreement. The injunctions were granted, and defendants moved to discharge them before the Lord Chancellor. The court refused the motion thereby continuing the injunction:

> [The] present is a mixed case, consisting not of two correlative acts to be done—one by the Plaintiff, and the other by the Defendants, which state of facts may have and in some cases has introduced a very important difference—but of an act to be done by J. Wagner alone, to which is superadded a negative stipulation on her part to abstain from the commission of any act which will break in upon her affirmative covenant; the one being ancillary to, concurrent and operating together with, the other. The agreement to sing for the Plaintiff during three months at his theatre, and during that time not to sing for anybody else, is not a correlative contract, it is in effect one contract; and though beyond all doubts this Court could not interfere to enforce the specific performance of the whole of this contract, yet in all sound construction, and according to the true spirit of the agreement, the engagement to perform for three months at one theatre must necessarily exclude the right to perform at the same time at another theatre. It was clearly intended that J. Wagner was to exert her vocal abilities to the utmost to aid the theatre to which she agreed to attach herself. I am of opinion that if she had attempted, even in the absence of any negative stipulation, to perform at another theatre, she would have broken the spirit and true meaning of the contract as much as she would not do with reference to the contract into which she has actually entered.
>
> [It] was objected that the operation of the injunction in the present case was mischievous, excluding the Defendant J. Wagner from performing at any other theatre while this Court had no power to compel her to perform at Her Majesty's Theatre. It is true that I have not the means of compelling her to sing, but she has no cause of complaint if I compel her to abstain from the commission of an act which she has bound herself not to do, and thus possibly cause her to fulfil her engagement. [T]hough, in continuing the injunction, I disclaim doing indirectly what I cannot do directly.

NOTES

1. *Express Covenants.* In *Lumley v. Wagner*, the contract contained an express agreement by Wagner not to compete against Lumley (a/k/a "negative covenant"), and the court indicated that it would have "implied" such an

agreement had one not been expressly included in the contract. However, some courts are reluctant to imply a negative covenant. *See Pingley v. Brunson*, 272 S.C. 421, 252 S.E.2d 560 (1979) ("As a rule, the court does not award injunction in the absence of an express negative covenant in the contract").

2. *Sale of a Business*. Courts also enforce covenants not to compete against former employees and the former owners of businesses, but they usually impose several limitations. As the court explained in *Hamer Holding Group, Inc. v. Elmore*, 202 Ill.App.3d 994, 560 N.E.2d 907, 148 Ill.Dec. 310 (1990):

> It is well settled that a party seeking to preserve the status quo indefinitely by means of a permanent injunction must show that it possesses a clear protectable interest for which there is no adequate remedy at law and that irreparable injury would result if the relief is not granted. The burden of proof is heavier for obtaining permanent, as compared to preliminary, injunctive relief. Unless there exist special circumstances warranting protection, a business entity has no protectable interest in its clientele. In the case of covenants not to compete, special circumstances may exist on two separate planes, distinguishable by the type of agreement in which the covenant is anchored. If the covenant is ancillary to the sale of a business by the covenantor to the covenantee, then all the covenantee must show is that the restriction is reasonable as to time, geographical area and scope of prohibited business activity. If, however, the covenant is ancillary only to an employment agreement, the covenantee must show additional special circumstances, such as a near-permanent relationship with his employer's customers and that but for his association with the employer, the former employee would not have had contact with the customers, or the existence of customer lists, trade secrets or other confidential information. Illinois courts have historically distinguished between the two types of covenants, based on the unique interest which each seeks to protect. Whereas a covenant ancillary to an employment contract shields the employer from the possibility of losing his clientele to an employee who appropriates proprietary customer information for his own benefit, and also shields him from the possibility of losing customers with whom he enjoys a near-permanent relationship; a covenant ancillary to the sale of a business ensures the buyer that the former owner will not walk away from the sale with the company's customers and goodwill, leaving the buyer with an acquisition that turns out to be only chimerical.

PROBLEMS

1. *Uniqueness.* Ordinarily, a negative covenant will not be enforced except against a "unique" employee. But what constitutes uniqueness? Defendants, who were under contract to play football for the Winnipeg Rugby Football Club, Ltd. (Winnipeg) through the close of the 1955 season, agreed to play for the Cleveland Browns during the same period. Winnipeg sought preliminary injunctive relief preventing defendants from playing for Cleveland. The testimony revealed that defendants were "good" football players, but "not specially skilled" by National Football League standards. However, the Winnipeg club particularly needed players of their ability level. Under the circumstances, is injunctive relief appropriate? How should a court determine whether a player is "unique"—from the plaintiff's perspective or a "market" perspective? Is it really possible for the "plaintiff's perspective" to differ from the "market perspective?" *See Winnipeg Rugby Football Club v. Freeman*, 140 F.Supp. 365 (N.D.Ohio 1955); *Central New York Basketball, Inc. v. Barnett*, 181 N.E.2d 506 (Ohio Com.Pl.1961).

2. In the heavyweight boxing division, plaintiff Machen was the top ranked challenger to Floyd Patterson, heavyweight champion of the world. Defendant Johnansson was the European champion, but was ranked only 8th in the world. In exchange for plaintiff's agreement to fight defendant, defendant agreed to give plaintiff a "return fight" should he win. Plaintiff wanted that clause because, by fighting defendant, plaintiff was giving defendant the chance to improve his world ranking at plaintiff's expense. Should defendant succeed, plaintiff wanted the chance to redeem himself. Defendant agreed not to fight anyone else before the return fight.

Defendant knocked plaintiff out in the first round. Because of the knockout, defendant was offered the chance to fight Floyd Patterson for the heavyweight championship six weeks later. Defendant accepted the offer spurning plaintiff's demands for a "return fight."

Plaintiff sues defendant for breach of contract. Is plaintiff entitled to injunctive relief? If so, how should the relief be framed? *See Machen v. Johansson*, 174 F.Supp. 522 (S.D.N.Y., 1959).

3. A nephew wished to engage in an acting career which his family viewed as demeaning. In consideration for the nephew's promise not to perform within 100 miles of the family's area of residence, the uncle gave the nephew a large sum of money. If the nephew decides to perform in a nearby town (25 miles away), can the uncle obtain specific performance of the agreement?

P. REINSTATEMENT VIA INJUNCTION

Washington Capitols Basketball Club, Inc. v. Barry states the general rule: that an agreement to perform a personal services contract will not be specifically enforced in favor of the employer. Should the rule be different when the employer breaches the contract?

1. *Reinstatement for discrimination.* One situation in which the courts will order an employer to reinstate an employee is when the employee has been discharged in violation of civil rights laws. In *Brown v. Trustees of Boston University*, 891 F.2d 337 (1st Cir., 1989), an assistant professor was refused tenure on the basis of her sex. The court ordered the university to reinstate her with tenure:

> [Courts] have quite rarely awarded tenure as a remedy for unlawful discrimination, and those that have, have done so under circumstances distinguishable from those here. The University argues that tenure is a significantly more intrusive remedy than remedies ordinarily awarded in Title VII cases, such as reinstatement or seniority, because a judicial tenure award mandates a lifetime relationship between the University and the professor. The University further contends that due to the intrusiveness of tenure awards and the First Amendment interest in academic freedom, a court should not award tenure unless there is no dispute as to a professor's qualifications. Thus, the University concludes, the district court should not have awarded tenure to Brown, because there existed a dispute as to her qualifications.
>
> We agree that courts should be "extremely wary of intruding into the world of university tenure decisions." However, once a university has been found to have impermissibly discriminated in making a tenure decision, as here, the University's prerogative to make tenure decisions must be subordinated to the goals embodied in Title VII. The Supreme Court has ruled that the remedial provision of Title VII, 42 U.S.C. § 2000e–5 (1982),[22] requires courts to fashion the most complete relief possible for victims of discriminatory employment decisions. Once Title VII liability has been imposed, a court should deny "make whole" relief "only for reasons which, if applied generally, would not frustrate the central statutory purposes of eradicating discrimination throughout the economy and making persons whole for injuries suffered through past discrimination."
>
> We see no reason to deny Brown such "make whole" relief here. We disagree with the University's characterization of the tenure award as an infringement on its First Amendment right to determine for itself who may teach. In often-quoted language,

---

[22] The statute provides: If the court finds that the respondent has intentionally engaged in [an] unlawful employment [practice], the court may . . . order such affirmative action as may be appropriate, which may include, but is not limited to, reinstatement or hiring of employees, with or without back [pay], or any other equitable relief as the court deems [appropriate]. No order of the court shall require the admission or reinstatement of an individual [if] such individual [was] refused advancement [for] any reason other than discrimination on account of race, color, religion, sex or national [origin]. 42 U.S.C. s 2000e–5(g).

> Justice Frankfurter defined academic freedom as " 'an atmosphere in which there prevail the four essential freedoms of a university—to determine for itself on academic grounds who may teach, what may be taught, how it shall be taught, and who may be admitted to study.' " *Sweezy v. New Hampshire*, 354 U.S. 234, 263 (1957) (Frankfurter, J., concurring in result). Academic freedom does not include the freedom to discriminate against tenure candidates on the basis of sex or other impermissible grounds. Our decisions in this area have formulated a university's prerogatives similarly. While we have been and remain hesitant to interfere with universities' independent judgment in choosing their faculty, we have said that we will respect universities' judgment only "so long as they do not discriminate." Kumar, 774 F.2d at 12, (Campbell, C.J., concurring).
>
> The University also argues that the special needs of academic institutions counsel imposition of less restrictive alternative remedies. However, the University suggests none. Some amici suggest that Brown be reinstated for a three year probationary period, or be subjected to a non-discriminatory tenure decision. Aside from the impracticality of the latter, well over eight years after the original decision, these suggestions fall far short of remedies which will make Brown whole. According to the jury's verdict, she was offered the three year extension because of discrimination. The jury found that, "but for" sex discrimination, Brown would immediately have been granted tenure. Awarding her tenure is the only way to provide her the most complete relief possible. * * *

2. *Reinstatement for Violation of Constitutional Rights.* Reinstatement might also be ordered when an employee is discharged in violation of her right to free speech. In *Endress v. Brookdale Community College*, 144 N.J.Super. 109, 364 A.2d 1080 (1976), Endress was fired for expressing concern about the College's contracting procedures in the school newspaper. Finding a violation of her First Amendment right to free speech, the court ordered the College to rehire her with tenure (absent the dismissal, plaintiff's contract would have been renewed three days later, and she would have automatically received tenure):

> The college contends that as the employment contract was one which called for the rendering of personal services by plaintiff, specific performance could not be adjudged. It is settled law, of course, as the trial judge here readily acknowledged, that personal service contracts are generally not specifically enforceable affirmatively.

> But we held in *Katz v. Gloucester Cty. College Bd. of Trustees*,125 N.J.Super. 248, 250, 310 A.2d 490 (App.Div.1973), that it was no longer open to question that a public agency may neither dismiss from employment nor withhold renewal of a contract from a nontenured public employee for a reason or reasons founded upon the exercise of a constitutionally protected right. Although not clearly articulated below by the trial judge on the dismissal and reinstatement issue, it is thoroughly clear from a reading of the entire opinion that he was of the view, with support in the record, that plaintiff's employment was terminated improperly because of her exercise of First Amendment rights of free speech and press. In such case, the remedy of specific performance is appropriate. In *American Ass'n of Univ. Prof. v. Bloomfield College*, 136 N.J.Super. 442. [A] lack of precedent, or more novelty, is no obstacle to equitable relief which may be appropriate in a particular fact complex. In view of the uncertainty in measuring damages because of the indefinite duration of the contract and the importance of the status of plaintiffs in the milieu of the college teaching profession, it is evident that the remedy of damages at law would not be complete or adequate.

PROBLEMS

1. Suppose that the Washington Capitols refuse to allow Rick Barry to play for their team (believing that Barry's style of play does not fit their game plan). Barry sues the Capitols seeking to force them to put him on their team. Should Barry be able to obtain either affirmative specific performance or negative specific performance against the Capitols? Are the same considerations, which prompt courts to withhold relief on behalf of the employer, present when the employee seeks specific performance? If you were asked to represent the Capitols, how would you argue that injunctive relief is inappropriate? How might Barry respond to these arguments?

2. On March 22, 1982, Actress Vanessa Redgrave agreed to narrate six performances of Stravinsky's "Oedipus Rex" for the Boston Symphony Orchestra (BSO). The performances were scheduled for April, 1982. Because of Ms. Redgrave's outspoken position on Israel and the Palestine Liberation Organization, anonymous callers threatened the BSO with "severe adverse consequences" if it went ahead with the performances. The BSO cancelled the concerts. Ms. Redgrave claims that the cancellation has adversely affected her ability to obtain employment and seeks an order requiring the BSO to go ahead with the concert series. Should the injunction be granted? What arguments might the BSO raise in opposition to the request for injunctive relief? How might Ms. Redgrave respond to those arguments? Can Ms. Redgrave obtain negative specific performance?

3. In 1994, the NAACP's Board of Directors voted to remove Benjamin Chavis as its Executive Director. The Board alleged that Mr. Chavis kept secret an agreement to pay $322,400 in Association funds to settle a sex discrimination and sexual harassment suit by a former employee. Mr. Chavis sued the Board claiming that it did not follow proper procedures in dismissing him (*i.e.*, he wasn't given notice of the charges, or an opportunity to prepare his defense and call witnesses on his behalf). Mr. Chavis sought reinstatement pending the completion of proper procedures. The Board argued against reinstatement claiming that there was antipathy between Mr. Chavis and the Board, that would make it difficult for them to work together, and that reinstatement would undermine the confidence of contributors to the organization, thereby diminishing contributions. Is a court likely to order the Board to reinstate Mr. Chavis?

4. In a case like *Brown v. Trustees of Boston University*, after the court found the University guilty of discrimination, would it have been appropriate for the court to enter an injunction prohibiting Boston University from discriminating "on the basis of sex with respect to the appointment, promotion and tenure of faculty members, and in particular with respect to the promotion, salary or other benefits to which the plaintiff may become entitled?"

5. Suppose that Stinky Dog, a famous rock singer, agrees to cut an album for BCA Records. The record is to be cut within two years. In exchange, BCA agrees to provide Stinky with $1 million as well as to buy him a house on the California coast near Los Angeles. The land and house are worth $2.3 million. BCA agrees to provide Stinky with the land now, and the $1 million after the record is cut. After the contract is signed, BCA refuses to buy the land for Stinky. What remedies are available to Stinky?

EXERCISES

1. Ms. Abigail Wagner, a famous opera singer, agrees to sing at the Windsor Theater in New York for a period of three months. The contract provides that Ms. Wagner will "not use her talents at any other theater . . . without the written authorization of Mr. Lumley (the owner and manager of the Windsor)." In exchange for Ms. Wagner's agreement, the Windsor agrees to pay Ms. Wagner $2,500. a week during the pendency of the contract. Mr. Wagner was expected to perform 3 nights per week.

After working at the Windsor for three weeks, the City Opera of New York offers Ms. Wagner a one year contract at $500,000. for the year. Under the terms of this contract, Ms. Wagner does not have to perform as often. Moreover, the City Opera offer includes television and radio exposure. The City Opera is broadcast nationally on Saturday afternoons, and City wants to use Ms. Wagner as a "featured performer" one Saturday a month. Ms. Wagner likes the City contract because it allows her to "save her voice." The City offer has one catch: Ms. Wagner is required to begin immediately.

Ms. Wagner takes a short time (about two seconds) to reflect on the City offer, and decides to accept. Wagner gives notice to Lumley that she is "terminating" her contract effective immediately. Lumley is beside himself. Lumley had planned his performances and his advertising around the Wagner contract, and he had even increased ticket prices (from $25. to $50.) because she was so good. With Wagner's departure, he is without his "star" performer. Lumley feels sure that he will be facing irate patrons demanding refunds.

Lumley calls around to various talent agencies in a desperate attempt to find a substitute for Wagner, but to no avail. The only singers that are available have far less talent, and far less drawing ability. In desperation, Lumley decides to close down the theater for a month, provide refunds to patrons, and try to develop a new show around a new star. As it turns out, Lumley was closed for 6 weeks and had to reopen with a lesser "star" at normal prices. Lumley had to pay a talent agency $5,000. to find this "lesser star." In addition, Lumley had to arrange for new sets and costumes, and had to train a new supporting case—at an additional cost of $75,00. Once the Windsor reopened, the new opera played to a half-empty theater (the theater holds 2,000 people) for the next six weeks rather than the sell-out crowds that had been expected.

At the time Wagner left, Lumley was in the process of signing-up a new star to begin performing at the end of Wagner's contract. When Wagner left and the theater closed, prospective performers became very jittery about the Windsor. Most performers felt that the Windsor, sitting empty, had a cloud over its future, and didn't want to sign with a theater that had such an unenviable reputation. Investors were reluctant to pump money into the Windsor.

Wagner's career, by contrast to the Windsor's future, was definitively on the upswing. After three performances at City, and the exposure that came from those performances, Wagner was offered a five year recording contract at a salary of $1 million per year.

Draft a memorandum, not to exceed ten pages, analyzing the causes of action and potential remedies that might be available to Lumley.

2. Suppose that Wagner does not receive an offer from City, and does not breach her contract with Lumley. Instead, Lumley fires her. Wagner was particularly upset about the firing because she really liked the operas that the Windsor was performing. Moreover, she hoped that her performances would bring her great attention and acclaim, and would lead to a "really big break." In fact, Wagner hoped to land a contract with the City Opera of New York and eventually to obtain a recording contract.

After her termination, Wagner tried to get other work, but was unable to do so. Other opera houses, knowing that she had been fired by Lumley, were worried that she might be a troublemaker. Wagner ended up without income (other than unemployment benefits of $342. per week). In addition, she had to do without life insurance, health insurance, social security and pension benefits (all of which were being provided by Windsor). Unfortunately, Wagner was too well off to qualify for Medicaid, and was forced to purchase her own health insurance at a cost of $400. per month.

Prepare a memorandum, not to exceed 10 pages, analyzing the causes of action and remedies that might be available to Wagner.

Q. THERE'S A REMEDY FOR THAT

You have been consulted by Sean, general counsel for BSS, a telecommunications company. BSS has concerns about an advertising campaign run buy Horizon, a competitor. Sean relates the following facts.

BSS provides mobile (cellular) telephone service. In addition, it sells phones and accessories. The most popular cell phone—the ePhone, produced by Pomegranate, Inc.—works only on BSS's network. The popularity of the ePhone has produced a huge increase in customers for BSS since its introduction three years ago. Horizon, in an effort to win customers away from BSS, has embarked on an advertising campaign that places two U.S. maps side by side. One shows BSS's coverage area for its 3G (third generation) cell phone network in red. This map has huge areas of white space, showing no coverage. The other shows Horizon's coverage area for its 3G network in blue. The map shows relatively little white space. Both maps are accurate representations of the companies' respective 3G networks and are labeled as such. BSS believes that the maps mislead the public. Some prospective customers believe that BSS offers no cell phone coverage in the white areas, a false impression. In television ads, the maps are on screen only briefly, making it difficult for consumers to see that the label refers only to 3G networks. In print ads, people have time to notice the labels, but may overlook them. BSS believes that the ads violate laws regulating truth in advertising and unfair business practices. It would like to sue to enjoin the ads and, if possible, collect damages for business lost as a result of the ads.

The amount of business lost is difficult to ascertain. BSS sales of the ePhone increased by an average of 2% per month before the Horizon ads began to appear. Since the Horizon ads began to appear, BSS sales of the ePhone have increased by only 1% per month. Sales of other smartphones phones that use the 3G network had been relatively steady, but began to decline by 2% per month after the Horizon ads appeared. The losses affect not only profit on the phones (which is minimal), but also sales and profits on service plans including data packages (which use the 3G network). New 2-year data plans were increasing by about 1% per month before the Horizon ad, but now are decreasing by about 1% per month. Finally, sales of regular BSS phones and service plans have declined slightly since the ads began. In each case, sales before the ads began were already slightly depressed by the economy. Sales since the ads began are even worse than the already reduced sales immediately before the ads.

BSS does not know Horizon's sales data for this quarter, but suspects that their sales have increased (for smartphones and regular phones). Data on the size of the increase may be available when quarterly reports are made to shareholders in January 2010.

PROBLEMS

1. What remedy (or combination of remedies) would you advise your client to seek?

2. If you seek an injunction, what would you ask the court to enjoin? Do you expect to get that injunction, once Horizon objects to its language? What is the broadest injunction you realistically expect? What is the narrowest injunction you realistically anticipate?

3. If you seek an injunction, would you seek a TRO? Would you give notice to the other party or seek *ex parte* relief?

4. If Horizon asked you to represent them at the TRO hearing, what would you do? You have two hours to prepare. What facts do you need? What are the most important issues to develop?

5. BSS asks whether a preliminary injunction is likely. How would you respond?

6. What public policies might be implicated by this injunction? Are there constitutional issues at stake? How would you raise (or resist) constitutional arguments?

7. If you get an injunction, will you still request monetary relief? What monetary relief would you request? What problems do you anticipate in establishing your entitlement to the relief? What evidence will help you establish your entitlement? (For Horizon, what evidence would help you defeat monetary demands?)

CHAPTER 9

INTEGRATED PROBLEMS AND EXERCISES

■ ■ ■

CHAPTER OVERVIEW: This final chapter will give you the opportunity to work through various problems and exercises that are not categorized by area of law (*e.g.*, contracts, torts, etc.). In other words, the problems are designed to allow you to cut across subject matter areas and simply examine "problems." This is much the way that actual lawyers handle issues. It is rare for a client to come to a lawyer with a detailed assessment of the case (*e.g.*, I have a restitution case in which we need to seek an equitable lien). More commonly, clients relate a mass of facts to lawyers (some of them relevant, some of them irrelevant), and the lawyer is expected to work through those facts and make sense of them. You will have the chance to engage in a similar exercise in this chapter.

A. PROBLEMS

The Rock Concert

Plaintiff's apartment building adjoins defendant's shopping center, Plaza Antigua. During the past two years, defendant has held 6 rock music events to promote business at the center. The concerts have attracted between 4,000 and 7,000 people.

Plaintiff has a number of complaints about the concerts: defendant's property is not large enough to accommodate crowds of 4,000 people; concertgoers use plaintiff's property damaging the grass and leaving a huge amount of trash behind; some of the concerts have been very loud; and the concerts continue well past midnight on weeknights.

Plaintiff's tenants have complained bitterly. Plaza Antigua has announced a full concert schedule for the summer, and the tenants fear that the concerts will involve noise, large crowds, and lots of trash. Some tenants have given notice of their intent to move.

Assume that you have just been hired to represent plaintiff. What can you hope to achieve on plaintiff's behalf, and what is the best way to achieve it? Is negotiation preferable to litigation? Is there a compromise solution that might satisfy all parties? What are the downsides to litigation? *See McQuade v. Tucson Tiller Apartments, Ltd.*, 25 Ariz.App. 312, 543 P.2d 150 (1975).

Court-Required Counseling

A family court adopts a rule requiring the parents of minor children to obtain counseling before a divorce will be granted. The court believes that the rule will make parents more sensitive to the needs of their children in a divorce situation, and may result in some reconciliations.

The counseling must be done with a court-approved counseling agency. Because the area where the court sits is predominately Catholic, the only approved counseling service, Catholic Social Services, happens to be run by the local Catholic diocese. Its course is entitled "Parents Are for Good," and purports to offer a "secular curriculum." However, prior participants in the course have complained that the course has religious content.

Suppose that a non-Catholic couple with minor children wants to obtain a divorce, but is unwilling to be counseled by a Catholic agency. If the court refuses to grant the divorce absent the counselling, what remedies are available to the couple? How would you proceed?

The Water Sprinkler

Women's Medical Center (WMC) is an obstetrics and gynecological clinic that offers abortion services. The clinic can be entered from the west side via a private walkway, or by a public sidewalk which parallels 46th Street. Anti-abortion demonstrators often picket the clinic, but are restricted to the public sidewalk area.

An automatic sprinkler system waters the lawn between 7:15 am and 8:30 am from April to October. Four separate cycles operate at intervals, each watering a separate portion of the lawn for 10 to 15 minutes. When a given cycle is in use, the sidewalk bordering that section of the lawn being watered gets wet. Anyone and anything on the sidewalk bordering the section being sprinkled also get wet.

Ron Johnson prays and demonstrates against abortion outside the clinic. He pickets, hands out literature, and gives advice regarding abortion alternatives to any clinic patient who is willing to listen. Johnson usually goes to the clinic between 7:15 a.m. and 8:30 a.m.—the time when women visit the clinic for abortion procedures, and when he has the best chance to dissuade women from having abortions.

Johnson complains that spray from the water sprinklers, which at times is 5 feet high, inhibits him from standing on the public sidewalk in front of the clinic. He and his literature get wet and he is forced into the street to stay dry, thereby endangering his safety and making it more difficult to speak to women entering the clinic.

Suppose that you have been hired to represent Johnson. What remedies are available to Johnson? What steps would you take on Johnson's behalf, and in what order? *See Hartford v. Womens Services, P.C.*, 239 Neb. 540, 477 N.W.2d 161 (1991).

The Suicidal Patient

In 1992, Brenda Young suffered a seizure which left her badly paralyzed. Brenda needs total care: feeding, bathing, and diapering. At night, she is tied to her bed so that she can't push herself over the padded bedrails. Most of the time, Brenda screams and thrashes, sometimes uttering words like "water" or "bury me."

After the seizure, Brenda executed a power of attorney authorizing her mother to end all medical treatment if she became incapacitated. However, following a second seizure, the hospital put Brenda on a ventilator and inserted intravenous feeding tubes into her body. In this way, the hospital maintained Brenda's life through a two month coma, despite her mother's objection that Brenda did not want life support.

Brenda eventually came out of the coma and regained her faculties. However, she has made it clear that she wants to die. Brenda has refused food, but the hospital force-feeds her through tubes.

Brenda has hired you to evaluate her legal options. Can she prevent the hospital and her doctors for treating and feeding her against her wishes? If so, what remedies are available to her? If Brenda truly wants to die, how would you advise her to proceed?

The False Positive

Two years ago, Vernelle Wax was diagnosed with the AIDS virus. Earlier, Ms. Wax had received a blood transfusion. Then, while she was undergoing an examination for a thyroid problem, she received the AIDS diagnosis. Doctors informed Ms. Wax that it was unclear how long she would live.

The diagnosis had severe repercussions for Ms. Wax. When she left the doctor's office, she drove at a "high rate of speed" to her mother's home where she burst in screaming, crying and hollering. She then broke the news to her three teenage sons whose father had died several years earlier.

During the next two years, while Ms. Wax lived with the "knowledge" of her AIDS diagnosis, she suffered depression, anger and despair. She panicked at the onset of a mild cold. In addition, she frequently laid awake at night worrying about her sons: "Who's going to take care of them? Why am I going to die? Why did it happen to me? I never bothered anybody." In desperation, she left her sons with her mother and began to make preparations for death.

In order to fight the AIDS virus, Wax's doctor put her on didanosine (a/k/a ddl). The drug caused her to suffer fatigue and vomiting.

Two years later, when Wax joined a hospice AIDS support group, she was urged to undergo a second AIDS test. The test revealed that Wax did not have the AIDS virus.

What causes of action and remedies might be available to Wax against her doctors, the clinic for which they work, and the laboratory that performed the first blood test? How would the remedies be measured?

Self-Incrimination & Parallel Proceedings

Kentucky's Natural Resources and Environmental Protection Cabinet (Cabinet), which has responsibility for enforcing State and Federal environmental laws, brings a civil action against Louisville Dog Chow, Inc. (Louisville, Inc.) for environmental violations. In particular, the Cabinet contends that Louisville Inc. discharged waste water without a permit as required by federal and state law. The Cabinet seeks an order prohibiting further discharges without a permit, as well as restitutionary damages (designed to clean up any adverse environmental effects) of $10,000.

While the civil proceeding is pending, the Environmental Cabinet's Environmental Crimes Task Force (Task Force) begins investigating Louisville Inc. for criminal violations pertaining to the discharge. If violations are found, the Task Force has the power to bring charges against both the company and any employees who participated in the violation.

Suppose that you represent Louisville, Inc. in the civil proceeding. You fear that it will be difficult to defend Louisville, Inc. in that proceeding. All employees with knowledge of the alleged violation are reluctant to testify for fear that they will incriminate themselves. You're not sure whether you can present a viable case without their testimony.

Under the circumstances, how should your defense proceed? Can you represent both the corporation and the knowledgeable employees? What remedies are available to Louisville, Inc.? *See Hale v. Henkel*, 201 U.S. 43, 26 S.Ct. 370, 50 L.Ed. 652 (1906); *Wilson v. United States*, 221 U.S. 361, 31 S.Ct. 538, 55 L.Ed. 771 (1911); *United States v. Kordel*, 397 U.S. 1, 90 S.Ct. 763, 25 L.Ed.2d 1 (1970); *United States v. LaSalle National Bank*, 437 U.S. 298, 98 S.Ct. 2357, 57 L.Ed.2d 221 (1978); *Securities and Exchange Commission v. Dresser Industries, Inc.*, 628 F.2d 1368, 202 U.S.App.D.C. 345 (D.C.Cir.1980).

The Terminated Distributor

Sappenfield Distributors (Sappenfield) distributes liquor in Indiana. When two of Sappenfield's major suppliers terminated their contracts, Sappenfield was faced with a difficult choice: sell its distributorship at the best possible price or continue operating on a smaller scale.

Sappenfield decided to sell, and began negotiating with another Indiana distributor regarding the terms. At this time, Carberry Imports, Inc. (Carberry) was Sappenfield's only remaining supplier. Knowing that negotiations were ongoing for Sappenfield's sale, Carberry promised that Sappenfield could continue to act as Carberry's distributor for Northern Indiana. Based on this representation, Sappenfield turned down the negotiated selling price it was offered. One week later, Carberry withdrew its account from Sappenfield. Realizing it could no longer continue to operate, Sappenfield went back to the negotiating table, this time settling for an amount $550,000 below the first offer.

Can Sappenfield recover the price differential from Carberry? How might Sappenfield frame its cause of action? How might Carberry defend? *See D & G Stout, Inc. v. Bacardi Imports, Inc.*, 923 F.2d 566 (7th Cir.1991).

The Vanishing Park

In 1959, defendant Patton purchased real property on Whidbey Island. A portion of this acreage was waterfront property. Later that same year, Patton called the local newspaper and announced that a portion of the property would be dedicated as a public park for the people of Island County. The newspaper published a story to that effect.

In 1961, Patton platted a portion of the property and called it "Patton's Hideaway No. 1." Additional land was platted in 1962 and called "Patton's Hideaway No. 2." The recorded plat for Patton's Hideaway No. 2 contained the word "park" in an area outside of the platted lots. Additional land was platted in 1969 as Patton's Hideaway No. 3. Patton told the plaintiffs from time to time that the "park" land would be reserved as a park for the benefit of property owners in Patton's Hideaway No. 1, 2 and 3, and that a clubhouse and lavatories would be built. None of this was ever done.

In 1966, Patton platted "Patton's Beachwood Manor." It is this portion of Patton's property that the plaintiffs, as owners of property in Patton's Hideaway No. 1, allege was dedicated for use as a park. The Beachwood Manor plat was approved by the Board of County Commissioners in February of 1966 and recorded in March of 1966. There was a hearing on the proposed plat and the land was posted, as required by then existing law. In the process of platting, roads were cut, lots were staked and fire hydrants and water mains were placed in the property.

Plaintiffs have approached you for advice and representation. They want to force the developer to hold lots 1, 2 and 3 of the Beachwood Manor as a public park. How would you advise plaintiffs? Can plaintiffs force the developer to dedicate this land as a park? How? On what theory? What defenses might the developer interpose? *See Knudsen v. Patton*, 26 Wash.App. 134, 611 P.2d 1354 (1980).

Enjoining the Docudrama

In one month, the National Broadcasting Company (NBC) plans to air a "docudrama" entitled "Billionaire Boys Club." The docudrama portrays Joe Bobson's planning and committing a murder, and suggests a possible motive for the murder. In addition, the docudrama shows Bobson's involvement with a social group referred to as the "Billionaire Boys Club," and portrays "Bobson's personality, activities, and business affairs in ways that further connect him to this murder."

Bobson has already been convicted of murdering one person, and is about to stand trial for the murder depicted in the docudrama. Bobson believes that the film will severely prejudice his right to a fair trial in the second case. In addition, since Bobson's conviction in the first case is on appeal, Bobson worries that the airing of the docudrama will prejudice his right to a fair trial in that case should it be retried.

What remedies might be available to Bobson? If you were asked to represent him, what strategy would you use? As you consider this case, please read *Sheppard v. Maxwell*, 384 U.S. 333, 6 Ohio Misc. 231, 86 S.Ct. 1507, 16 L.Ed.2d 600 (1966); *Nebraska Press Association v. Stuart*, 427 U.S. 539, 96 S.Ct. 2791, 49 L.Ed.2d 683 (1976); *Hunt v. National Broadcasting Co., Inc.*, 872 F.2d 289 (9th Cir.1989).

The Pig Factory

Over the last five years, Hogget Farm has been transformed from a traditional Iowa farm to a highly mechanized pig factory. Hogget is owned and operated by Amon Goeth just outside of Cedar Rapids, Iowa. The farm/factory is state-of-the-art with an enormous air-conditioned aluminum barn that houses 20,000 hogs in stainless steel pens. The hogs are fed by a rotating conveyor belt. Since the pigs cannot move, their waste falls through grates and is mechanically collected and stored in large pits outside the building.

Iowa Housing, Inc. (Iowa Housing) began to develop subdivisions near Cedar Rapids during the 1980s. Five hundred lots were sold to residents. Iowa Housing has another two hundred lots, about half of which have been sold over the last two years while Hogget Farm has been in full production. Iowa Housing has had trouble selling the last of its lots because of the stench and flies that are attracted to Hogget's operation.

Iowa Housing has contracted with Pastoral Realtors to sell the remaining lots. One of these was sold to Mr. and Mrs. Elderly, who had come from California to live in the bucolic Iowa countryside where they would be closer to their beloved covered bridges. They were shown the land one winter day by Barry Briney, who works with Pastoral Realtors. The Elderlys asked Barry Briney whether this was a quiet spot (since Mrs. Elderly had a disorder that magnified the sounds of machinery and traffic). Barry Briney said: "Rest assured this is the quietest spot in the quietest state." With that, the Elderlys purchased a lot that looked down upon what they thought was a pleasing pond which at the time was frozen. They referred to a survey prepared by Chart & Co. some eighteen months earlier for Iowa Housing that described the area as a natural pond. The survey was supplied by Barry to the Elderlys. The Elderlys imagined that their grandchildren could skate on the pond in winter and play there in the summer. Unfortunately, the pond was an artificial pit containing the pigs' waste.

Animal rights activists are concerned about the inhumane conditions existing in pig farms/factories and have formed an organization, "Save Babe," which targets large pig factories for perpetrating cruelties upon pigs. Large numbers of "Babe Savers," as they called themselves, descended upon Cedar Rapids from out-of-state, causing traffic jams and disturbing the tranquil life of residents. They brought their pet pigs and paraded outside the farm, disrupting the delivery and dispatch of pigs for slaughter. Trained in Arkansas, they would run into the assembled pigs with "soueee" cries, stampeding them. The organizers of "Save Babe" also printed flyers in Arkansas, which they mailed to Iowa for distribution. The flyers stated the following: "The Hoggett Farm is a massive Nazi concentration camp for pigs." A photograph of a pathetic pig, which was said to come from the Hogget Farm, was displayed on the flyer. The featured pig was a pathetic specimen with festering sores and was obviously diseased. The caption to the photograph read: "Compliments of Herr Goeth, Commandant."

Amon Goeth was of German extraction and was offended by the references to the Nazis. He insisted that the treatment of pigs was humane.

A "Babe Saver" went undercover, took a job in the factory, and secretly filmed the processes and purloined the formula for the feed provided to the pigs. This film and information was given to Fox, who aired a program that was entitled "Hog Hell."

The program contained extensive footage of the operations and revealed the composition of the feed. It showed Amon Goeth carrying a rifle in a scene redolent of the sadistic commandant in *Schindler's List* shooting prisoners. In fact, the film had been taken when Amon Goeth was hunting for quail in the Iowa countryside and then spliced to make it appear that he was stalking pigs as they were herded to market.

The program also alleged that the pig effluent from the plant was seeping into the groundwater and poisoning domestic supplies. Fox received a very favorable response to the program and intends to repeat it.

The film taken in the factory reveals the processing system that had been developed at great cost by Goeth at Hogget Farm and which had been kept secret from the rest of the pig industry.

Advise the following of their causes of action and possible remedies:

1. the Elderlys;

2. the Cedar Rapids residents and Iowa Housing;

3. Amon Goeth in his action against "Save Babe" or against Fox.

It also transpires that Jewish organizations are upset about the tenor of the "Save Babe" campaign. Briefly advise the organizations.

Prison Conditions

Felons Joe Ponzi and Daniel Storm were arrested after their latest run-in with ace child mischief-maker, Macaulay Dalkins. The presiding judge sentenced Joe and Daniel to twenty years at the New York State maximum security prison complex in Cockroach, N.Y.

Cockroach Motel, as the inmates like to refer to it, was built in 1970. At the time it was the most modern penal facility in New York. It has 1200 cells, built for single occupancy, a gymnasium (without the climbing ropes), workshop, library, hospital ward, commissary, and a barbershop.

Upon check-in at the "motel," Joe and Daniel (who had reserved single rooms in advance), were shocked to find that due to overbooking the two would be sharing a cell. It turns out that the prison is filled to 140% of its capacity of 1200 inmates. When the prison was built in 1970 the planners did not foresee the dramatic rise in crime, and the accompanying increase in prison population.

As often happens when two felons end up in close confines Joe and Daniel began to quarrel. On one evening in particular, Joe and Daniel got into a violent discussion on the best way to seek revenge on Macaulay. Joe, in disgust, beat Daniel over the head with a wash basin. Daniel fell to the floor with a nasty gash to his forehead. Unfortunately for Daniel, the infirmary at the prison had become a victim of budget cuts. During the night hours when all the "guests" are supposed to be tucked into their beds, the prison has no doctors or nurses on call. Luckily for Daniel his head had been toughened due to his frequent run-ins with Macaulay so he suffered only a minor concussion.

To make matters worse for our two felons, the food served in the cafeteria left much to be desired. Kitchen staff have told Joe and Daniel that they often see insects flying around the food prep area, and it is not uncommon for milk to be left unrefrigerated for hours at a time.

The next day Joe and Daniel had had enough. After two days in prison they could tell things were not going to work out, so like all good Americans they want to file suit against the prison. Unfortunately, the two have contacted you about representation. Can they sue the prison? If so, on what theory? What remedies are they likely to obtain? *See Farmer v. Brennan*, 511 U.S. 825, 114 S.Ct. 1970, 128 L.Ed.2d 811 (1994); *Alabama v. Pugh*, 438 U.S. 781, 98 S.Ct. 3057, 57 L.Ed.2d 1114 (1978); *Hutto v. Finney*, 437 U.S. 678, 98 S.Ct. 2565, 57 L.Ed.2d 522 (1978).

The Dissolving Athletic Conference

The Metro Conference, an athletic association, had seven members (the University of Louisville, Tulane University, the University of North Carolina—Charlotte, the University of South Florida, the University of Southern Mississippi, Virginia Commonwealth University, and Virginia Tech University). In 1995, five of the schools developed a plan which would have ejected Virginia Tech and Virginia Commonwealth from the conference. Following the ejection, the conference planned to add a number of new members (the University of Houston, the University of Cincinnati, the University of Memphis, DePaul University, Marquette University, St. Louis University, and the University of Alabama—Birmingham).

For purposes of this problem, you can assume that Conference members share all revenue from television appearances by member schools, as well as all revenues from National Collegiate Athletic Association basketball tournament appearances. These revenues amount to approximately $1 million per school per year.

Suppose that you represent Virginia Tech and Virginia Commonwealth, and that they want advice about how to proceed. How would you advise them? Who might they sue, and on what theory? Is preliminary relief available to them?

The Tobacco Suits

A number of states have brought class action suits against tobacco companies for the cost of treating Medicaid patients for diseases caused by smoking. The suits assume that nicotine is addictive, and that smoking leads to diseases such as emphysema, lung cancer, etc. Assuming that the states prevail, how would their damages be measured?

The Paralegal

John Merrell, a paralegal at a Louisville law firm that represents tobacco companies, was assigned to work on sensitive documents in damage suits against the companies. At one point, John removed a number of the most sensitive documents from the firm and turned them over to individuals suing the tobacco companies. The documents purportedly show that tobacco companies have known for thirty years that tobacco is addictive. Plaintiffs believe that the documents will help them show that tobacco companies consciously attempted to "hook" their customers on cigarettes. Tobacco plaintiffs regard this information as particularly useful because it helps them overcome the typical defense raised in tobacco cases: that the smoker knew about the harms of tobacco, but smoked nonetheless. If the companies intentionally tried to addict smokers to their products, then plaintiffs have a better chance of holding the companies responsible for the deaths and suffering that result from tobacco-related illnesses.

The tobacco companies have come to you for legal advice. They fear that the documents are damaging to their interests, and complain that the documents were turned over to the law firms in the expectation that they would be kept confidential under both the attorney-client and work product privileges.

What remedies are available to the companies? What are the advantages and disadvantages of the various options? What arguments do you anticipate that the plaintiffs (in the tobacco litigation) will raise against you? How will you respond to those arguments?

The Photo

Cynthia Cheatham designs clothing and frequently displays her scantily clad derriere at gatherings of motorcycle enthusiasts. Cheatham claims that her special arrangement of curvaceous flesh and scanty clothing is closely associated with her. She refers to the arrangement as her "trade dress" which she defines to include "denim shorts with the seat cut out, fishnet stockings, belt chain and belt bearing the logo of Harley–Davidson motorcycles." Louisville Courier–Journal A–9 (April 19, 1994).

An Ohio T-shirt manufacturer took a picture of Cheatham's backside at a biker festival. The photo, taken without Cheatham's knowledge or consent, was sold to two magazines. In addition, it was plastered on the front of T-shirts and sold at motorcycle rallies.

Cheatham wants to sue the photographer, the magazines and the T-shirt manufacturer. What causes of action and remedies might be available to her? How would you advise her to proceed?

The "SLAPP" Suit

The Wolf Pen Branch Preservation Association (Association) was formed to preserve the rural beauty and tranquility of the Wolf Pen Branch area. When Burnett Properties, Inc. announced its intention to build the "Wolf Pen Woods" subdivision (which would cover 50 acres), the Association strongly urged the County Planning Commission to deny approval citing various "problems with the development." Burnett Properties, incensed by the delay of its project, sued the Association and its members in federal court claiming "misrepresentation" "fraud" "racketeering" and "conspiracy to harm" the development. Burnett has obtained a preliminary injunction prohibiting further misrepresentations.

If you represent the Association, what do you do now?

B. EXERCISES

The Stolen Bull

You are a new associate at the largest law firm in Jackson Hole, Wyoming. Mr. John West is a prosperous cattle rancher who owns a 500 acre cattle ranch near Jackson Hole. Mr. West has been in business for approximately 20 years. He is the firm's largest client.

This morning, Mr. West dropped by the firm. Mr. West was very agitated because his prize bull, Burt IV, was stolen from his field about three weeks ago. West learned about the theft from his neighbor and friend, Pete Johnson. Johnson told West the following facts;

> I was working in my own field when I saw a dark blue Ford pickup truck drive up to West's property. The man backed the truck over the fence knocking it down, and then pulled the truck up to a loading chute. The man then led Burt, who was alone in the field, to the chute, loaded him in the truck, and drove off. I got a good look at the man. I thought I recognized him as Mark Downing, another local farmer.

Johnson, who was stunned by the series of events, took no action. Immediately thereafter, Johnson called West and told him what had happened. West immediately phoned the police who promised to "look into the matter." So far, the police have done nothing.

Mr. West wants information about his legal rights. In anticipation of a second meeting with Mr. West, the firm's senior partner (Bob Cronkite) has asked you to analyze the case. Cronkite reminds you that a lawyer's choice of a cause of action can have remedial consequences, and asks you to think about the various theories on which West might sue Downing (or others).

Research the case and prepare a memorandum delineating the causes of action open to Mr. West, as well as the range of possible defendants. The memo should not exceed 20 pages. Once you do, evaluate the theories. Explain what Mr. West can hope to gain under each theory as well as the benefits and risks of each course of action.

As you prepare your memo, you may have questions about the facts. If your professor designates someone to serve as Mr. West, you may interview that person to develop the facts. If not, your memo should suggest how factual variances affect your choice of a cause of action and your remedial options.

Geraldine & the Birdwatchers

Geraldine Green was an officer in the State Environmental Department. In common with other departmental officers, Geraldine signed an agreement not to disclose information that she learned in her capacity as an officer except in the course of authorized official business.

Geraldine was also President of the Birdville Birdwatchers Society ("the Society"). A faction in the Society led by Woody Wood had been attempting to force the Society to take strong political environmental positions on the preservation of forests surrounding Birdville. Geraldine had been resisting the pressure, arguing that the Birdwatchers Society should not take overt political stances. She decided that the faction should be purged from the Society.

Without consulting her Society members and against its bylaws, Geraldine approached a journalist friend, Renee Rapporter, with information. In exchange for Renee's promise not to disclose her identity, Geraldine agreed to provide "inside information" to Renee. Over drinks, Geraldine told Renee that she had first met Woody in her student days at Berkeley in the 1960s. "We all have our peccadilloes," she said. "I even attended a meeting of the Symbionese Liberation Army;* wow, was that scary!" She went on, "Well, Woody was a math major, and guess who his instructor was?" "None other than Ted Kaczynski. They struck up quite a friendship . . . you know, talked about Kant and the horrors of modern technological society and all of that stuff." She added: "I think they may have kept in touch for awhile."

After another glass of Pinot Noir, she added: "I want you to know, from information that I have access to at the Department, that any preservation of the forest as a habitat for the birds is futile. Birdville Chemicals has poisoned all the water in the forest. It's not in any official report, that's all whitewash. Guess who made a big political contribution to the election of Senator Smith, and guess who has the power to appoint

* The radical group that, among other things, kidnapped Patty Hearst, the heiress to the Hearst newspaper empire.

the higher-ups in the Department? That's heavy-duty secret, no attribution or it's my skin."

Renee consulted her editor at the Birdville Truth about the story. They felt that the story needed to be attributed and further researched. Renee found that Woody had worked with defense firms after graduation from Berkeley and that those defense firms were engaged in research on high explosives. Inquiries about poisoned water in the forest drew a blank from the department.

Without further ado, the following story appeared in the Birdville Truth:

Birdville, Dead Forests, and the Unabomber

> In what is an unlikely concatenation of events, our Birdwatchers Society has been taken over by radical elements with a sympathy for the tactics of the Unabomber. We were told by a source in the Society and in the Department of the Environment that Woody Wood was a comrade in arms with Ted Kaczynski in the radical politics of Berkeley in the 1960s. Mr. Wood is a bomb-making expert and kept in very close touch with Kaczynski during his decades in the Montana wilderness. Our source, herself tragically touched by an association with the infamous Symbionese Liberation Army, warns this reporter against the "catastrophes of radical environmentalism." We were told: "This is the very mad fringe that will ruin the Birdwatchers Club."
>
> But there is more to tell, our source says: "Birdville Chemicals has conspired with Senator Smith to poison the waters of our beautiful forests. This is plain vanilla political graft."

Subsequent to the publication of the story, the following events occurred:

1. The Society's membership, incensed that Geraldine had publicly revealed the Society's internal affairs, expelled her from membership. Because of the expulsion, Geraldine was no longer able to enjoy the companionship of her former friends in the Society on field trips, and she was shunned by the Society's members.

2. The Department of the Environment fired Geraldine the next day, on the grounds that her disclosure of information was contrary to the non-disclosure agreement she had signed on engaging in employment;

3. Geraldine applied for a job in a local college. The college, in compliance with usual routine, asked for a letter of reference from the Department of the Environment, her former employer. The letter stated in part:

> Geraldine was a dedicated officer of this Department for five years, but she cannot be trusted. She has a fundamentally mendacious nature.

Naturally, Geraldine did not get the job. Furthermore, she is unable to find employment anywhere in the state.

Geraldine has come to you for advice. Please advise of any causes of action that may be available to her. Your advice should be set forth in a memo not to exceed twenty pages. In the memo, you should evaluate the causes of action in terms of the likelihood of success and the desirability (and downside) of available remedial options.

Breach of Confidentiality

[On] October 28, 1982, the Louisville Tribune published a story which stated that a candidate (Tom Jackson) for the Kentucky Supreme Court (in Kentucky, judges are elected) had been convicted of shoplifting in another state. The Tribune identified its source, Ben Johnson, despite the fact that the Tribune's reporter had promised Johnson confidentiality and anonymity in exchange for the information about Jackson.

Johnson sued the Tribune for breach of contract and misrepresentation. The Tribune defended on the basis that the "public's right to know," as guaranteed by the First Amendment, overrides the Tribune's promises. The case was tried to a jury which found in favor of Johnson and awarded damages in the sum of $250,000.

The case is now on appeal. Your professor will assign you to one of two groups. If you are assigned to group #1, write the appeal on behalf of the Tribune. If you are assigned to group #2, write the reply brief for Johnson. Follow the rules of court of the federal circuit in your area, the Rules of Court at the end of Chapter 4.

Commercial Exploitation?

In August 1985, Tammy Dee Acker was murdered during a robbery at the home of her elderly father. She was stabbed eleven times, and with such ferocity that the knife passed entirely through her body. The assailants stole $1.9 million in cash from Acker's elderly father, Dr. Roscoe. In addition, they choked Dr. Acker with an electrical cord and left him for dead.

In 1993, Harper Collins Publishers, Inc. of New York published 30,600 hardcover copies of a book ("A Dark and Bloody Ground") about the murder. On the cover of the book was a blood splattered picture of Tammy. The picture, which contained a simulated bloodstain, had been entered at the robbers' murder trial (without the simulated bloodstain). 28,000 copies of the book have been distributed to bookstores. Harper Collins still has possession of 3,800 volumes of the book.

The family of Tammy Acker wants to stop Harper Collins from publishing the book. They claim that the book, particularly the blood-splattered cover, constitutes blatant commercialization of the murder. They have come to you for advice.

Your instructor will assign you to one of two groups. If you are assigned to group #1, you will represent the Acker family. Prepare the documents necessary to obtain a temporary restraining order against Harper Collins prohibiting distribution of the book. If you are assigned to group #2, draft the responsive brief on behalf of Harper Collins. Both groups should comply with the Rules of Court set forth at the end of Chapter 4.

Gender Equity

The Beechwood High School Tigers, located in Fort Mitchell, Kentucky, have won four straight Class A state football championships. The school memorialized its teams with an "Avenue of Champions."

Recently, a group of parents petitioned the school for a soccer team. The parents wanted the team so that their daughters could play. The school's principal refused the petition. The parents appealed the refusal to the School's Management Council (composed of the School's football coach, the director of the band, the teacher who oversees the color guard, and two parents whose children happen to play football) which upheld the principal.

The Council justified its decision on three grounds. First, the Council felt that the school already offered a range of sports for girls. Second, the Council felt that there wasn't much interest in girls' soccer. A recent survey indicated that girls were more interested in participating in track than in soccer. However, the school didn't start a track team either. Third, the principal and the Council feared that, since Beechwood is a small school, it wouldn't be able to sustain a soccer program. If girls' soccer is added, students might demand a boys' team and the pool of boys talent will be diffused among the football and soccer teams.

The parents believe that the Council's decision violates Title IX which obligates schools to provide equal athletic opportunities to both boys and girls. The parents feel that the School puts so much money and effort into boys' football that it is forced to neglects girls' sports.

The Council believes that it is in compliance with Title IX. The Council notes that 54% of all boys and 53% of all girls at the school participate in at least one sport. The school offers six sports for boys and an equal number for girls. In the fall, boys can play football or golf and girls can play volleyball or golf. The soccer parents respond that the principal's statistics are misleading. The school counts golf as a co-ed sport because it is open to girls, but no girl has ever participated in that sport. In addition, the schools' statistics include both varsity and junior varsity athletics. When only varsity athletics are considered, boys participate at a two to one rate compared to girls. The principal claims that the varsity differential results from the fact that older girls lose interest in sports.

Draft a memorandum analyzing the rights and remedies available to the soccer parents. Evaluate their chances of forcing the school to found a girls' soccer team.

Reverse Discrimination?

In November 1995, California voters enacted the following amendment to the state Constitution:

> The state shall not discriminate against, or grant preferential treatment to, any individual or group on the basis of race, sex, color, ethnicity, or national origin in the operation of public employment, public education, or public contracting.

The amendment was self-executing: individuals aggrieved could sue the state for violation of the provision even if the legislature failed to enact any legislation implementing the provision in more detail. Assume that remedies for violation of the provision will seek to place the plaintiff in the position she would have occupied if the wrong had not occurred, subject to limiting doctrines generally applicable in the common law.

In December 1995, Jessica Gudunov applied for a position as an actuary with the San Diego office of the California Department of Insurance. Ms. Gudunov received the second-highest score on the required civil service examination. Bess O'Vall, another applicant, received the highest score. Based only on these scores, the Department of Insurance decided to hire Ms. O'Vall instead of Ms. Gudunov. The starting salary for the job was $36,000 per year. Ms. Gudunov has made efforts to find work with private insurance companies (the primary employers of actuaries). So far, she has been unable to find work as an actuary in San Diego or the surrounding communities. She has not sought work outside of San Diego County or outside of the insurance industry.

In January 1996, Ms. Gudunov sued the Department of Insurance for violation of the constitutional amendment quoted above. She contended that Ms. O'Vall learned of the job by reading an ad the Department of Insurance placed in a magazine called *Modern African-American*. The readership of the magazine consists almost entirely of African-Americans. Ms. Gudunov claimed that, by placing an ad in that magazine, the state granted a preference based on race, by providing more opportunity for African-Americans, as a group, to hear about and apply for the position than people of other ethnic backgrounds. The Department of Insurance posted the job at the worksite and advertised in local newspapers, as required by state law. The only additional advertising done by the Department was the ad in *Modern African-American*. Ms. O'Vall admits that she would not have learned of the job if it had not been advertised in *Modern African-American*. Based on affidavits establishing these facts, the trial court granted summary judgment for Ms. Gudunov on the issue of liability.

Prepare a memorandum analyzing Ms. Gudunov's potential remedies—with particular attention to any arguments the state may raise to minimize or eliminate these remedies. Consider any responses Ms. Gudunov's counsel might make to your arguments and how you could reply to them. To the extent possible, evaluate the likely outcome of each issue you raise.

Key Personnel

In January 1995, the University of South Dakota College of Law (USD) needed to hire a new professor. It made an offer to Leslie, an experienced lawyer with exceptionally good credentials. Leslie accepted the offer on February 1. On March 15, Leslie received an offer to teach law at Harvard. Leslie decided to accept the offer even though it meant breaching the contract with USD. Because Leslie notified USD of the decision after March 15, USD was unable to locate any other qualified professor (regular, visiting, or adjunct) to cover the courses Leslie would have taught. (Not everyone wants to live in South Dakota.) Assume USD will have no difficulty proving liability for breach of contract.

a. Can USD demonstrate that it will suffer an irreparable injury? How would you support your conclusion?

b. Could USD obtain injunctive relief ordering Leslie to teach there for the 1996–1997 school year? How would you support your conclusion?

c. Could USD obtain any other equitable relief? How would you support your conclusion. Use only the space provided below?

d. Could USD recover damages for breach of contract against Leslie? How you would support your conclusion?

e. If available, how would damages be calculated?

Marital Discord

Kelly, an heiress, recently discovered her husband, Sam, was involved with another woman. The affair was open and flagrant, causing Kelly considerable embarrassment. Upon discovering the affair, Kelly took an axe to AccuVin, a wine storage facility where Sam stored their collection of fine wines, and smashed the entire collection. Sam has sued her for dissipation of community assets. (Assume the destruction violates a spouse's fiduciary duty to preserve community property.) AccuVin has sued for the cost to clean up glass and wine from the facility following the rampage. CalCasCo, an insurance company, seeks recovery of $1 million it paid to Chris, who owned the locker immediately below Sam's, for damage caused when wine flooded that locker.

Kelly admits the conduct and shows no signs of repentance. She also has no inclination to settle with Sam. She seeks your advice concerning whether she can defeat the lawsuits and, if not, how much she will owe. No divorce action is pending; neither Kelly nor Sam has expressed any intention to file for divorce. Sam signed a prenuptial agreement that, if enforceable, would limit him to a car, some clothing, and $2,000 per month for life—a pittance compared to his current lifestyle. Kelly seems satisfied by her vengeance—and says she can obtain more satisfaction by remaining married to Sam than by divorcing him. Each complaint is a civil suit for damage to property. (The actions were filed separately; they may or may not be consolidated for trial.) Any amount recovered by Sam must be paid from Kelly's separate property and becomes Sam's separate property.

Kelly kept records of Sam's wine purchases. (The couple agreed to spend only $15,000 per year on wine, a limit Kelly closely monitored.) Her records indicate that the portion of the collection in the locker when she destroyed it cost about $90,000 to acquire over the last seven years. She recalls conversations in which Sam estimated the current value of the wine, based on auction reports in wine magazines. The most recent estimate—on April 15, 1999—placed the value at $250,000. Auction prices, however, involve full case lots. Most of Sam's wine were partial cases—either because they did not buy full cases or because they consumed some of the bottles. A few of the most recent purchases, which have appreciated the least, were still full cases. Full cases are more appealing to investors, who bid at auctions. Smaller groups of bottles might draw about 80% of the per bottle price of full cases, but that is hard to confirm since partial cases rarely are sold at auction. Sam did not hold the collection for investment, but for consumption. The couple drank wine often and sometimes gave a bottle as a gift. They never sold any of it. Sam's complaint alleges the value of the wine was $600,000. When asked about this, Sam said that he had purchased additional wine without telling Kelly and stored it in the locker. The complaint also requests $1 million for emotional distress, $3 million for loss of enjoyment of the wine, and $10 million in punitive damages.

AccuVin's complaint demands $50,000 in damages. AccuVin hired a service to clean the facility following the rampage, at a cost of $5,000. In addition, AccuVin had to close its facility to all customers to protect them from the broken glass strewn all over the building by Kelly's destructiveness. They remained closed for two days, including a Saturday, when many customers come to remove wine from their lockers.

The inconvenience may give rise to several claims against AccuVin by its customers. In addition, AccuVin anticipates that some customers may move their business to other storage facilities in light of the inconvenience.

CalCasCo paid $1 million to Chris, its insured, for depreciation of Chris's wine collection. Chris owns a particularly valuable collection of wine, including many very old bottles, dating back to the 19th century. The total value of his collection is about $20 million. Chris has carefully preserved these bottles as an investment. Kelly's rampage flooded the locker. (The lockers consist of steel grating, which allows air to circulate and cool the wine, but also allows liquid to flow freely when bottles break.) The wine and bottles are intact, but the labels were damaged severely. The labels on some older bottles virtually disintegrated, making it impossible (in some cases) to identify the year or producer. Without the labels, investors are unlikely to pay market value for the wines. Other wines have stains that damaged the labels. Investors may believe the damage reflects careless storage, again reducing the value of the wine. Chris filed a claim with CalCasCo, which insured his wine collection. The claim sought $1.8 million in damage, but Chris settled with the insurer, accepting $1 million as full payment. CalCasCo now seeks compensation from Kelly.

Evaluate Kelly's position. Advise her concerning any arguments she may raise to reduce or negate the claims. Offer your best estimate of how much each plaintiff may collect. California law applies. California is a no-fault state, refusing to take misconduct by a spouse into account in divorce actions, even for purposes of dividing community property or setting spousal support. In addition, California enacted the following provision governing actions for destruction of community property:

> 1101(g): Remedies for breach of the fiduciary duty by one spouse . . . shall include, but not be limited to, an award to the other spouse of . . . an amount equal to 50 percent of any asset . . . [destroyed] in breach of the fiduciary duty plus attorney's fees and court costs. However, in no event shall interest be assessed on the managing spouse [*i.e.*, defendant].

La Vendetta

The facts of the preceding question are unchanged—except that Sam has filed motions seeking a temporary restraining order (TRO) and a preliminary injunction ordering Kelly not to damage, to destroy, or to sell any other community assets. In an affidavit attached to the motion for a TRO, Sam avers that Kelly said "If you really like that 1964 Mercedes convertible, you should drop the lawsuit." Kelly denies making the remark, but says (to you, confidentially, with a gleam in her eye) that she wishes she had thought of it. Sam also avers that only twelve 1964

Mercedes convertibles remain in original condition (*i.e.*, original parts, not imitation parts, which reduce the value of classic cars) anywhere in the world, only three in North America. The most recent sale of one of these cars occurred in 1992, for a price of $1.5 million. Sam avers that the car is priceless, in that he would not sell it for any amount of money.

Kelly expresses concern that this injunction might impede her management of the family assets—a role she typically has performed throughout their marriage. By statute, each spouse is entitled to equal control of the assets. Sam typically has allowed Kelly to manage community investments. Each spouse buys and consumes regularly without consulting the other.

The hearing on the TRO will occur in four hours. The hearing on the motion for a preliminary injunction probably will occur within 2 weeks. Advise Kelly on how to prevent entry of each order. What will you do to prepare for the TRO hearing? What arguments will you raise to avoid an injunction or to protect your client in the event that an injunction is issued? What will you do to prepare for the preliminary injunction hearing? What arguments will you raise to avoid an injunction or to protect your client in the event that an injunction is issued? What other advice would you offer your client to protect her interests.

Concluding Problem: Bad Hips

Legtech manufactures prosthetic knees and hips. These devices, when surgically implanted, typically last about 15 years before requiring replacement. Many factors contribute to the early failure of the devices, including the skill of the surgeon, the weight of the patient, the patient's compliance with post-implantation instructions, and (occasionally) the defects in the device itself. Because the causes are very difficult to determine, Legtech does not offer a warranty on its prosthetics, but sells them as is. Hospitals buy the devices, then charge patients for them when they are implanted. Typically, insurers (including Medicare, for older patients) cover the cost of the devices and the surgery to implant them. The devices themselves cost about $15,000, the surgery to implant them about $40,000, and the post-surgical care about $10,000.

In 2009, Legtech noticed an increase the number of their devices that failed prematurely, some as early as one year after initial implantation. An internal investigation revealed that a one of their machines was not working properly. The machine tested the strength of a critical component of the prosthetics, rejecting parts that were not up to standards. The failure of this machine allowed an unknown number of substandard parts to pass inspection, being used in Legtech's products. Legtech and Mach Corp. (the manufacturer of the machine) cooperated to solve this problem in August 2010. After that, no defective parts were used in Legtech devices.

Legtech had an inventory of 2,000 devices manufactured before the problem was discovered (worth about $30 million). The vast majority of these devices met the quality control standards. Legtech predicted that between 2% and 8% of them contained parts that did not meet the quality control standards and, therefore, might fail in fewer than 15 years. The only way to test the part would be to disassemble the devices, which could not be done without destroying the devices—effectively wasting the entire inventory. In addition, devices already sold faced the same risk of premature failure. Recalling the devices already sold to hospitals but not yet used would increase the loss. The number of unused devices is unknown, but probably is between 1,000 and 5,000 devices. Rather than destroy a huge number of perfectly good devices, Legtech did not disclose the difficulty, did not recall the devices already sold, and continued to sell their inventory.

People who receive a defective device face the cost of a second surgery. Before replacement, they face reduced mobility and discomfort as the first device fails. The surgery and recovery also require time and involve discomfort. Any surgical procedure involves some minor risk of death, related to anesthesia. In addition, any hospital stay risks complications, such as infections.

1. Do Hospitals, who buy the devices from Legtech, have any claims against Legtech? What remedy might they seek? How could Legtech minimize its liability?

2. Do patients who receive Legtech prosthetics have any claims against Legtech? What remedy might they seek? How could Legtech minimize its liability?

3. If Legtech can establish that Mach Corp. is liable for the failure of the testing machine, what remedies might it seek from Mach Corp.? How could Mach Corp. minimize its liability?

INDEX

References are to Pages